The Timberclads
in the Civil War

ALSO BY MYRON J. SMITH, JR.
AND FROM McFARLAND

*The Fight for the Yazoo, August 1862–July 1864:
Swamps, Forts and Fleets on Vicksburg's Northern Flank* (2012)

The CSS Arkansas: *A Confederate Ironclad on Western Waters* (2011)

The USS Carondelet: *A Civil War Ironclad on Western Waters* (2010)

*Le Roy Fitch: The Civil War Career
of a Union River Gunboat Commander* (2007)

The Baseball Bibliography, 2d ed. (four volumes, 2006)

The Timberclads in the Civil War

The *Lexington*, *Conestoga* and *Tyler* on the Western Waters

MYRON J. SMITH, JR.

Foreword by B. Franklin Cooling

McFarland & Company, Inc., Publishers
Jefferson, North Carolina, and London

The present work is a reprint of the illustrated case bound edition of The Timberclads in the Civil War: The Lexington, Conestoga and Tyler on the Western Waters, *first published in 2008 by McFarland.*

LIBRARY OF CONGRESS CATALOGUING-IN-PUBLICATION DATA

Smith, Myron J.
The timberclads in the Civil War : the Lexington, Conestoga and Tyler on the western waters / Myron J. Smith, Jr. ; foreword by B. Franklin Cooling.
p.   cm.
Includes bibliographical references and index.

ISBN 978-0-7864-7721-0
softcover: acid free paper ∞

1. Mississippi River Valley — History — Civil War, 1861–1865 — Riverine operations. 2. United States. Navy — History — Civil War, 1861–1865. 3. Warships — Mississippi River Valley — History — 19th century. 4. Warships — United States — History — 19th century. 5. Lexington (Steamer : 1861–1865) 6. Conestoga (Steamer) 7. Tyler (Steamer) 8. United States — History — Civil War, 1861–1865 — Riverine operations. I. Title.
E470.8.S64   2013   973.7'5 — dc22   2008029599

BRITISH LIBRARY CATALOGUING DATA ARE AVAILABLE

© 2008 Myron J. Smith, Jr.. All rights reserved

No part of this book may be reproduced or transmitted in any form or by any means, electronic or mechanical, including photocopying or recording, or by any information storage and retrieval system, without permission in writing from the publisher.

Front cover: Timberclad gunboats fitting out at Cincinnati for government service on the Mississippi, 1861

Manufactured in the United States of America

*McFarland & Company, Inc., Publishers
Box 611, Jefferson, North Carolina 28640
www.mcfarlandpub.com*

For Fred

Table of Contents

Foreword by B. Franklin Cooling	1
Preface	5
List of Abbreviations	9

1. Rivers and Rebellion, January–April 1861	11
2. Commander Rodgers Goes West, April–June 1861	40
3. From Cincinnati into the War Zone, June–August 1861	68
4. New Men, Hotter War, September 1–October 9, 1861	96
5. Columbus-Belmont, October 10–November 9, 1861	129
6. Skirmishing and Fleet Building, November–December 1861	166
7. Fort Henry: Preparations and Battle, January–February 1862	189
8. To Florence and Fort Donelson, February 1862	225
9. Tennessee River–Columbus–Island No. 10, February–March 1862	253
10. Tennessee River: Shiloh, March–April 1862	281
11. White River and the C.S.S. *Arkansas*, June–July 1862	317
12. An Anniversary, POW Convoys, and the Death of a Timberclad Hero, July–December 1862	361
13. 1863: Arkansas Post to Helena	389
14. Peripheral Streams and Red River, 1863–1864	424
15. Cavalry Versus Timberclads, June 1864	465

Epilogue: Winding Down, July 1864–August 1865	478
Chapter Notes	483
Bibliography	519
Index	537

Foreword
by B. Franklin Cooling

As I stated in a 1996 essay on the Civil War on inland waters, Americans of that era could relate to the first stanza of Francis Miles Finch's poignant 1867 tribute, "The Blue and Gray": "by the flow of the inland river, whence the fleets of iron have fled." Those rivers were the interstate highways of the time. Heartland America rested its economic and social fabric in large part upon them, for railroads were in their infancy and highways hardly the ribbons of concrete and asphalt we know today. The federal government in particular had supported navigation improvements and, with war's onset, named its principal field armies for those streams, not for the states or land areas as did the Confederacy. Regrettably, the history of the naval war has never been as popular as that of the great and bloody confrontations on land. Naval strategy was mostly subsumed by army strategy. Fascination with the great land battles and leaders and the shifting sands of land campaigning persists to this day, a circumstance not likely to change with the approaching sesquicentennial of the Civil War in 2011. Possibly such fascination exists because one can walk the actual ground where the carnage and sacrifice of Shiloh, Antietam, Fredericksburg, Chickamauga, Atlanta or Franklin, to name but a few, took place. Certainly this enables each generation to grapple anew with the meaning of over 600,000 deaths, nearly as many maimings and untold numbers of psychological cripples from the uniformed participants, as well as an estimated 50,000 civilians killed during the war.[1]

All statistics for that period are problematic, but one thing remains certain. Study of the Civil War constantly transitions in breadth and depth and the once subordinated theater of operations, the west, has undergone a renaissance. That is where the navy fits in. It is true that small un-navigable rivers and creeks such as the Green, Barren, Harpeth, Duck, Elk and others in the upper heartland all figured in the land campaigns. Yet, it was the navigable rivers that formed the basis for the inland naval story. As both a complement to the land campaigns and a unique chapter in the country's maritime history as a whole, the riverine warfare offers new perspectives to breadth and depth of our understanding the American *Iliad*. A case can be made that is was in the west that the Civil War was won and lost — in fact, due to the rivers. On those rivers were built the careers and experiences of some of the era's most famous naval professionals as well as those of citizen sailors, just as land generals and soldier volunteers manned the citizen armies.[2]

The naval war itself enjoyed a trifold focus—high-seas raiding, coastal and amphibious operations and—the greatest story of the lot—the war on western rivers. Here was fought ship against ship, ship against shore batteries, sailors against regulars and irregulars in butternut and gray. Hearts of oak (as well as iron plate) were tested against not only the enemy but also against the vagaries of the waterways, the ever-changing channels of mighty rivers like the Mississippi, and the whims of army leaders and comrades. This is not to say there was more glamour than in chasing the *Alabama* and *Shenandoah* raiders or watching Farragut damn the torpedoes in Manila Bay. But on the brown water wavelets of the Mississippi and her numerous tributaries could be found "the peoples war" so aptly captured in President Abraham Lincoln's phrase. For, if anything, the brown-water sailors of the riverine war struggled like their army comrades with a hostile, combatant populace, disease, boredom, and death in the shadows from marksmen known as bushwhackers.

Then, too, it was here that blending of old (wooden) and new (iron plated) stream-driven warship technology was hammered out by Union gunboats. It was also here that shipboard ordinance dueled with similar guns of shore batteries as rifled and smoothbore armament tested the resilience and blood of crews and officers alike. But, most importantly, on the western waters, the United States Navy participated in what today we style stabilization and occupation and reconstruction efforts that cut across civil-military as well as army-navy relationships. Winning the hearts and minds of the populace, or not, as the case may be, was fully as important from 1861 to 1865 as in twentieth and twenty-first century conflicts. Once the din of battle subsided, the less appealing yet absolutely vital tasks of restoration and policing of river commerce, enforcing trade regulations, conducting reconnaissance patrols, convoying troop and supply transports and suppressing guerrilla infestations occupied the Western Flotilla. Of course, the navy, like the army, helped runaway slaves by ersatz emancipation and enlisted them to the ranks, for the sea service was color-blind. In fact, "showing the flag" often took precedence in humdrum operations on those enigmatic backwash streams in the war zone. Such became the role of the Western, later Mississippi, Squadron and its various divisional subordinates.[3]

Army-navy cooperation (today styled joint operations) stood uppermost. The Union navy's gunboats provided the phalanx of Union military victory in the west. And, in the vanguard stood three unsung, even anachronistic, craft euphemistically styled "timberclads," in juxtaposition to the more advanced ironclads in warship parlance. Instead of iron-plated protection, the *Lexington*, *Tyler*, and *Conestoga* enjoyed 5-inch wood protective bulwarks around the decks. Essentially, they were converted riverboats—the first of many, nay, the majority, of naval vessels on inland rivers. Ironically, they were first acquired and served under army auspices as part of the Quartermaster Department's combat and service support role. Formulation of the river flotilla under Commander John Rodgers and naval constructor Samuel M. Pook witnessed the typical American response to wartime urgency—a stopgap measure of procurement and conversion of civilian riverboats prior to construction of new and better craft for combat. Thus, like weaponry procured at the start of war generally, the gunboats *Lexington*, *Tyler* and *Conestoga* were obsolete before they even got underway, yet they were representative of the hasty mustering and mobilization of men and materiel from available resources. Even their conversion by Cincinnati's Marine Railway and Drydock Company reflected development of a wartime emergency shore support base the replicated America's way of war—reliance on a "militia system" for manpower and materiel from the private or civilian sector.

Hardly sophisticated in naval design, the paddle-wheel propulsion of the gunboats, quite primitive even by contemporary standards (river snags and shoals ruled out the common submarine screw propeller), even their basic engines were identical to those of a quarter century before. The timberclads nonetheless provided stopgap firepower once combat began in earnest in the fall of 1861. The trio became more famous in the winter, supporting operations against Forts Henry and Donelson, capture of the Confederate bastion at Columbus, Kentucky, on the Mississippi, while *Lexington* and *Tyler* helped take Island Number 10 to ward off Union disaster at Shiloh. By this time, however, the three ranked only in the second echelon of the navy's river flotilla as the first ironclads came on line. Nonetheless, the timberclads proved the value of shallow draught, bantam mosquito boats at war when they made raids all the way to Muscle Shoals, Alabama, on the Tennessee River soon after Fort Henry's fall on February 6, 1862, thus illustrating chinks in the Confederacy's western defenses that federal land inertia failed to exploit at the time. Later, on the Mississippi tributaries feeding from Arkansas and Louisiana as well as on that Great River, the timberclads contributed to the history of the army's Western Gunboat Flotilla as it transitioned to the navy's Mississippi Squadron.[4]

In a sense, the timberclad trio aptly fit the image of Mark Twain's Victorian houses on barges—merchant craft—conscripted for war. Their distinctive tall smokestacks (euphemistically styled "chimleys" by some observant Confederate youths) and twin paddle-wheel houses and pilothouses only partially camouflaged in the makeover silhouettes, they served and fought alongside more glamorous and heavier gunned and constructed ironclads. The *Conestoga* was lost during the war, as was her comrade ironclad *Cairo*, although the latter to an enemy mine, while *Conestoga* succumbed more ingloriously to collision with a former Confederate gunboat, the *General Price*, then flying the Stars and Stripes. Yet, as naval historian Don Caney suggests, "Their contribution to the war effort was far from insignificant, particularly in the backwaters and bayous of the Mississippi River system." He quoted President Abraham Lincoln's post–Vicksburg tribute to the navy: "Nor must Uncle Sam's web feed be forgotten. At all the watery margins they have been present," as "wherever the ground was a little damp they have made their tracks." Canney observed that the chief executive most assuredly had the timberclads in mind.[5]

Historian Myron Smith has rescued the *Lexington*, *Tyler*, and *Conestoga* contribution to this effort from the dustbin of history: the nooks and crannies of official and private documents long forgotten. Anyone perusing the official records of both the army and the navy in the Civil War will recognize that contribution, just as they will praise the rescue mission provided by the author and his book.

B. Franklin Cooling is a professor of history in the Industrial College of the Armed Forces at the National Defense University, Washington, D.C.

Preface

DURING THE EARLY MONTHS OF 1861, political and economic forces on both sides of the Mason-Dixon Line stumbled through the darkness of hatred, mistrust, and slow communications and hastened toward a conflict that would consume the United States. In the period between January and May, there was hope in some quarters that this increasing drift would somehow bypass citizens in the Mississippi Valley. After all, people from many walks of life and of various persuasions from the northwest to the Deep South depended upon commerce with one another for their existence.

Sadly, restraint was not shown. Both sides worked to create military establishments and to curtail economic intercourse. By July, battles and skirmishes in different locales demonstrated that the conflict would not be short. In the north, plans were made to crush the Rebellion in a great strategy known popularly as the Anaconda. The South would be attacked by ground forces while naval forces would squeeze it from all sides. As this approach gradually unfolded, the bulk of the fighting was concentrated in two major theaters, the east (of the Appalachians) and the west.

Throughout the remainder of 1861 the fighting was largely concentrated in the border states, including western Virginia, Missouri, and Kentucky. Federal troops under Maj. Gen. George B. McClellan cleared Confederate forces from what is now West Virginia, helping keep that territory in the Union. Extraordinary efforts by soldiers and civilians kept Missouri, even after Maj. Gen. John C. Frémont succeeded McClellan, who went east. Governor Beriah Magoffin attempted to hold Kentucky neutral but without success. In early September, Maj. Gen. Leonidas Polk occupied Columbus, leading Brig. Gen. Ulysses S. Grant to take Paducah.

Less than a month after Fort Sumter fell in April, Cmdr. John Rodgers, USN, was sent west by the Navy Department to advise McClellan on nautical matters involved with the establishment of a Western Flotilla. This army organization would grow up around three hastily converted passenger steamers purchased in June.

Because they were made of wood and protected by oak timber thick enough to stop a rifle bullet, the gunboat trio became known as the "timberclads." All three were distinguishable at a distance by their extraordinarily tall smokestacks, called "chimneys."

After completing a much-delayed voyage to the military base at Cairo, Illinois, in early August, the *Lexington, Conestoga,* and *Tyler* represented all of the U.S. nautical power available on the inland rivers of the Midwest.[1] Working under army orders, their naval commanders labored in support of the land forces to snuff out a rebellion grown out of hand by the fall.

Although Rodgers also oversaw the launching of an ironclad construction program under St. Louis engineer James B. Eads, his Western Flotilla was soon turned over to a more senior naval officer, Capt. Andrew Hull Foote. He was joined by a number of colorful naval officers like Roger Stembel, Henry Walke, James W. Shirk, and William Gwin.

As more vessels and men arrived in early winter, demands upon the unit grew. Foote, injured in the spring of 1862, was succeeded in turn by Capt. Charles H. Davis, both men holding the rank of flag officer. In October 1862, the organization was turned over to the U.S. Navy and took the name of Mississippi Squadron. The timberclads participated in every major western theater action bordering anywhere near the great rivers during that first year of conflict. Paducah, Columbus, Belmont, Fort Henry, Fort Donelson, Shiloh, Island No. 10, and White River spring immediately to mind. Initially, the timberclads served as front-line vessels, providing bombardment and support for Grant at Belmont. As the ironclads came on line, the timberclads assumed secondary armed reconnaissance, patrol, convoy escort, and gunfire support roles.

To accommodate army support requirements on the tributaries of the Mississippi, the Western Flotilla and its successor organization required many more boats than the three wooden gunboats or the seven Eads ironclads. New ironclad vessels came on line but these, like the timberclads, were too heavy to operate in the rivers at certain low-level stages of the year. As the naval support demand increased, a new kind of small, lightly protected, and shallow draft warship was devised. Known as the "tinclad," more than 50 of these joined the western fleet beginning in the fall of 1862.

Despite the addition of the tinclads and a number of other powerful vessels, such as the *Choctaw* and the river monitor *Osage*, the big guns of the timberclads ensured that employment for them could be found in the two years of war remaining. Even as their physical condition, hull and power plant aged, their ability to on occasion make a difference was manifest to all who rode aboard these vessels or viewed their black profiles.

Even as the *Lexington* and *Conestoga* were being refreshed following their work on the White River in June 1862, the third member of the trio, *Tyler,* was called upon, with two other flotilla units, to face the wrath of the mighty Confederate armorclad *Arkansas*. Thereafter, the boats, occasionally together but usually as single vessel components of miscellaneous task groups, participated in a number of memorable campaigns or army support operations.

Conestoga, the smallest and fastest of the three, was constantly in motion upon the Mississippi. Just prior to her accidental loss in a collision on March 8, 1864, she was part of an antiguerrilla sweep into the reaches of the Black and Ouachita rivers of Louisiana.

Lexington worked in the Yazoo River campaign of November–December 1862 before her transfer to the Cumberland and Tennessee rivers in the spring of 1863. A favorite of her commanders, the Pennsylvania-built side-wheeler remained on those streams until May, participating in, among other activities, the February Battle of Dover and the April burning of Palmyra and support of the Streight "Mule brigade" incursion into north Alabama. During March–May 1864, the *Lexington* participated in expeditions up the Black and Ouachita rivers. She was the only timberclad to accompany the Red River Expedition, in which she added to her laurels with defensive bombardments at Blair's Landing and as the first vessel over Colonel Bailey's famous dam. In June, she helped to repel an attack on White River Station, Arkansas.

The *Tyler* was the largest of the timberclads and, after her fight with the *Arkansas,* was also involved in support of army operations on the Yazoo River. On July 4, 1863, she added significant luster to her already sparkling laurels with a memorable role in the defense of Helena, Arkansas. *Tyler* spent most of the remainder of the war in the Arkansas area, guarding convoys and protecting army units from Confederate attack. Her most memorable fight during this time and, indeed, the last major combat by any of the timberclads, occurred on June 24, 1864. On that date, she, together with two tinclads, prevented the Rebel blockade of the White River in a firefight with the troopers of Brig. Gen. Joseph O. "Joe" Shelby at Clarendon.

Both the *Lexington* and the *Tyler* were guard ships in the areas between Natchez and the mouth of the Red River for the remainder of the Civil War. They were withdrawn from service in May 1865 and sold for the identical price of $6,000 in a giant government auction at Mound City, Illinois, on August 17 of that year.

This work covers in detail the role of the timberclads in the western theater during the first two years of their existence. Semi-routine station-keeping and escort duties, with an occasional firefight, marked their existence in mid–1863 to mid–1864 and we review all of the major incidents in that year. As the Rebellion in the west subsided through April 1865, the two survivors were pretty much "used up" and seldom moved. Their activities in that final period, as well as their deactivation, are considered in the epilogue.

Forty years ago, when hair still rode atop my head, I was drawn to the story of the western gunboats in connection with my postgraduate work. I was in a different stage of my career, living in an eastern locale where much of the expertise on the topic then congregated. Conversations and correspondence with the late distinguished historians Bruce Catton and Edward E. Geoghegan opened my eyes to the unheralded contribution of the Pook ironclads, in particular the *Carondelet*. A wonderful chat with the then–Washington, D.C., based park historian Edwin C. Bearss provided an enthusiastic boost to my journeys through the non-electronic National Archives and Library of Congress. Frank Cooling, then at the Army War College and Historical Research Center at Carlisle Barracks, threw open the vast resources of his institution for a look at boats which, in 1861–1862, belonged to the military. It was there that I first gained some insights into the role of the timberclads on the western waters.

In the years since my initial work on the *Carondelet* was finished and a Civil War bibliography was published, I drifted away from the Civil War scene. Other activities, both professional and literary, claimed my time and energy. Still, during those years, I squirreled away information on various aspects of the western gunboat navy, hoping to write one day about it or some of its vessels or people — if no one beat me to them.

So it was that a couple of years ago, in returning to this interest to pen a biography of the noted tinclad commander Lt. Col. Le Roy Fitch, I was amazed at the paucity of work in this area. I would have thought graduate students, if not others, would have been all over it. True, there were a number of campaign histories penned during the intervening years on the Civil War western theater. A number of these mention naval support (including Belmont, Vicksburg, and Shiloh), a couple of biographies of men like Porter and Foote, one new work on Ellet's marine brigade, two or three overall Civil War naval histories, and a number of periodical articles.

Still, the same published information that was available on the timberclads that that I saw at the end of the sixties and beginning of the 1970s was largely what was available to me in 2007. In those years, there were two notable exceptions: the publication by John Y. Simon of Grant's papers and Jay Slagle's biography of Seth Phelps. Gary Joiner's new *Mr. Lincoln's Brown Water Navy: The Mississippi Squadron*[2] appeared just as this manuscript was being sent to the publisher. It is the latest in a line of footnoted brown-water naval history surveys dating back to John D. Milligan, heavy on Mississippi River action and light on the secondary tributaries, with the exception of Joiner's Red River specialty.

Perhaps even more astonishing to me was the lack of new biographical information on the men who commanded the timberclads, all of whom played major roles in the western war and three of whom became postwar admirals. Other than the coverage of Phelps and Fitch, who briefly skippered the *Lexington*, this dearth is stunning. A host of individuals are worthy of profile. Dissertations, books, or articles could examine the contributions of Henry Walke, Rodger Stemble, William Gwin, James W. Shirk, James M. Pritchett, Thomas O. Selfridge, Jr., and George M. Bache, just to mention the commissioned officers. There were many volunteer officers who also served with distinction aboard the timberclads and whose names are sprinkled throughout our text. Admiral John Rodgers, who birthed the vessels, deserves a new examination, as does Admiral Charles H. Davis and the squadron's administrative and logistical genius, Fleet Captain Alexander M. Pennock, who applied what was best about the "old boats" to the tinclad concept.

After their first few months of service, as newer units joined the Western Flotilla, the *Conestoga, Lexington,* and *Tyler* were increasingly known as "the old boats" or "the wooden boats." When David Dixon Porter arrived at Cairo, Illinois, in October 1862 to take over the new Mississippi Squadron, he saw them at anchor. According to his delightful if not always factual *Incidents and Anecdotes*, the bushy-bearded commander was moved to offer a line of poetry in their honor:

> See the old warriors out in the stream,
> Open in many a wood-end and seam![3]

Perhaps unappreciated at the time Porter's ditty was composed, the three "old gunboats" still had plenty of fight left in them and work to do. Their exploits both before and after 1862 have not been chronicled in depth and that is a deficiency *The Timberclads in the Civil War* hopes to remedy.

Personnel at a number of libraries and archives helpfully provided insight and information during the research and writing stages of this outing. Among them were the kind folks manning the libraries and collections of the U.S. Navy Department, Library of Congress, National Archives, University of Tennessee, University of Arkansas, East Tennessee State University, Kentucky Historical Society, U.S. Army Historical Center, Missouri Historical Society, Tennessee State Library and Archives, West Virginia Department of Archives and History, Illinois State Library, Chicago Historical Society, The Ohio State University, Nashville Public Library, Greeneville–Greene County Public Library, and Tusculum College.

I would like to tip my hat in thanks to Frank Cooling for his kind foreword. Tennessee state historian Walter T. Durham and West Virginia state archivist Fred Armstrong provided encouragement, as did *North and South* magazine editor Keith Poulter. Finally, to all who have offered their friendship and support, both of this work and of past efforts, I extend my warmest acknowledgments.

Myron J. Smith, Jr.
Chuckey, Tennessee

List of Abbreviations

Army

Army Rank
Pvt.	Private
Cpl.	Corporal
Sgt.	Sergeant
Lt.	Lieutenant
Capt.	Captain
Maj.	Major
Gen.	General
Lt. Gen.	Lieutenant General
Maj. Gen.	Major General
Brig. Gen.	Brigadier General
Col.	Colonel
Lt. Col.	Lieutenant Colonel

Navy

Navy Rank
Acting Rear Adm.	Acting Rear Admiral
Rear Adm.	Rear Admiral
Cdr.	Commodore
Capt.	Captain
Cmdr.	Commander
Lt. Cmdr.	Lieutenant Commander
Lt.	Lieutenant

CHAPTER 1

Rivers and Rebellion, January–April 1861

RECENTLY PAROLED BY SOUTHERNERS after a failed attempt to destroy the dry dock at Norfolk's Gosport Navy Yard, Cmdr. John Rodgers II was on special duty in Washington, D.C., in May 1861 when Secretary of the Navy Gideon Welles ordered him to Cincinnati, Ohio. There he was to assist the U.S. Army in the development of a riverine force. When ready, it would help execute a blockade of the Mississippi River and its larger tributaries then being established at Cairo, Illinois.

The son of Cdr. John Rodgers (1772–1838) of War of 1812 fame and brother-in-law of the army's brand new quartermaster general, Montgomery C. Meigs, the clean-shaven and balding 49-year-old Maryland-born Rodgers was a large man "who considered himself fit when his weight was below 200 pounds." A dedicated professional with a reputation for generosity toward his subordinates, Rodgers was originally appointed as a midshipman 33 years earlier. An accomplished and dutiful seaman known as "the scientific sailor," Rodgers had won fame as second commander of the North Pacific Exploring Expedition (1854–1856) and was familiar with ocean steam navigation. While availability, nautical knowledge, family connections, and command experience were all decided plusses in his new appointment, a major negative was one he shared with almost every other federal naval officer: he "knew virtually nothing of riverine warfare."[1]

To understand the possible use of gunboats on the great rivers of the Mississippi Valley during the American Civil War, one must first and foremost realize the importance of the mid–19th century geography and commerce of that watery system and its impact upon logistical requirements. As Charles Boynton wrote in 1867, "It was clear that the whole seaboard might be regained, even to Florida, and yet the rebellion remain as dangerous as ever, if the rebels could hold the Mississippi River and the valley up to or near the Ohio."

While traveling west, Cmdr. Rodgers probably took every opportunity to familiarize himself with the many supply chain aspects of the war about to be faced by Northern military forces operating in the region. Additionally, he undoubtedly carefully examined the few available guidebooks and reports on those streams and their peculiarities while listening closely to comments from his trip companion, engineer James B. Eads. As the two rode on,

Tyler and *Lexington* at Shiloh, April 1862 (Library of Congress).

they could sample local newspaper coverage to supplement press reports already seen on the outbreak of the war. Many editors projected important roles in the growing conflict for the great rivers in the center of the nation.

As Adam I. Kane points out in his recent study, there was, through most of the first half of the 19th century, two primary means of transportation in the west — roads and rivers.[2] To these were added railroads in the decade or so before the Civil War, with competition between the two transport modes joined by 1861. Steamboat historian Louis C. Hunterhas opined that "before the outbreak of the Civil War the end of the steamboat era was clearly foreshadowed." Others have argued that this was not the case and that steamer tonnage actually continued to grow.

Commander Rodgers and Captain Eads arrived in Cincinnati early on May 19. We do not know exactly how they made their way to the "Queen City," but the journey was undoubtedly made partially, if not totally, by train. After all, it was possible to reach Cincinnati from Pittsburgh (the Pennsylvania city did not add an "h" until 1882, but we will use it here anyway) in just 15 hours and from Marietta in several hours less. In the interest of speed, is likely that Rodgers and Eads traveled to western Ohio by rail, over tracks owned by the Baltimore and Ohio Railroad and its affiliates. If so, the trip initially took the men from Washington, D.C., to Baltimore and then on to Cumberland, Maryland, and Grafton, Virginia. From the latter point, they probably took the Northwestern Virginia Railroad spur on to Parkersburg, Virginia, on the Ohio River. Parkersburg is about 20 miles south of Marietta, Ohio, and could have been reached by stagecoach or river packet. There Eads and Rodgers would have boarded a direct Marietta and Cincinnati Railroad train west to the Queen City.[3]

Travel by land in the South and Midwestern states was at that time usually arduous and sometimes quite expensive, particularly for the shipment of goods. Prior to and during the Civil War, it was more economical to transport goods by river than road or rail.[4] Indeed, that remains the case for certain material even today. There was during the conflict, however, a direct relationship between the available transport modes, especially for the Union, and the conduct of successful military operations. Without full control of all lines of communication, the U.S. Army would not be able to "operate in anything but the most static of fashions."[5]

The three modes of transport — road, rail, and water — were available to the opposing forces in 1861–1865. First and most common among these was the six horse- or mule-drawn wagon, each of which could carry up to one ton of goods. Using one formula, the supply of a 100,000 man army, with its attached cavalry and artillery, ten days out from its supply base "would be computed at 10,975 wagons utilizing 68,850 draft animals." Additionally, wagons were often broken down and forage for the animals had to be transported in the same vehicles, thereby cutting down on space available for supplies. Obviously, something better was required or required in combination.

Railroad trains, abundant in the area north of the Mason-Dixon Line, offered significant bulk delivery advantages over wagons and were, wrote Alan Aronson, the "optimal" method of supply delivery. They could haul large amounts of supply over land which frequently corresponded to an army's advance route and could do so in a timely fashion. They made it much easier to open or expand large supply depots, such as the one established in 1864 at Johnsonville, Tennessee, on the Tennessee River.

On the other hand, railways everywhere were vulnerable to natural obstructions and weather. Many were single-track lines that could accommodate only so many trains daily. Additionally, creeks and gullies had to be bridged, viaducts maintained, track laid and repaired, tunnels cut, and rock slides cleared. Added to these worries were Confederate marauders, mostly mounted, who began their assaults, in Missouri for example, about the time of Fort Sumter. The Rebels came to fear Union attacks as well, whether from gunboat landing parties against bridges or armies like Sherman's against whole line stretches. "Ripping up railroad tracks and bringing down bridges," Lawrence M. Smith wrote recently, "became prime military missions during the Civil War."

Still, every flatcar could transport at least two wagons (and other such gear as could be fitted aboard). Mathematicians calculated that, with efficient rolling stock available properly loaded, "a single railroad could accumulate provisions for an army of 300,000 to 400,000 for four to five days within a 24-hr. period."

Water transport was the most efficient way for the warring North and South to move supplies in large quantities. This was particularly true in the Western theater, where roads and railroads were both fewer and highly exposed to military action or the whims of nature. Indeed, in that region, steamboats were "the first man-made apparatus to radically interrupt the Arcadian wilderness, collapse vast distance, and discharge the artifacts of distant cultures into remote places." They "galvanized and connected" outpost cities from New Orleans to St. Louis and Cincinnati and thus "reshaped much of America, economically and structurally."

The majority of the steamers, whether strictly cargo or packets (cargo and passengers operating to a schedule), were owned in the north and removed from southern rivers at the outbreak of the conflict. Consequently, the Confederacy had many fewer available bottoms to fill and a huge logistical disadvantage. Still, those that were available to the Rebels were used as efficiently as possible as long as possible, even if their life spans before capture or destruction were relatively short.

Wherever available, steamboats could provide significant lift. One Ohio River steamboat, it was estimated, could carry 500 tons of cargo, which translated into sufficient rations and forage for a 40,000 man army and 18,000 animals. Two hundred and fifty wagons or 125 rail flatcars would be needed to haul the same amount. For the fiscal year ending July 30,

1863, Capt. Charles Parsons presented a comparison on the use of the rivers and railroads in handling subsistence, ordnance, medical, and quartermaster stores: by railroad, 193,023 troops and 153,102,100 pounds of goods; by river, 135,989 troops and 337,912,363 pounds of goods.

Without water access, other less efficient transport modes had to be employed, but whenever possible, rivers were preferred. As Maj. Gen. William T. Sherman put it, "I am never easy with a railroad which takes a whole army to guard, every foot of rail being essential to the whole; whereas they can't stop the Tennessee [he was writing about that stream in the source for this quote] and each boat can make its own game." Wagon trains and railway trains could be captured, destroyed, or delayed by roving soldiers; steamships were seldom stopped save by nature or fairly heavy field or naval cannon.[6]

When taken together with the Missouri River (which is slightly longer than the Mississippi but outside of our story), the Mississippi is the largest water artery in the United States. From the headwaters of the former, the two streams flow a combined distance of 3,872 miles. Taken alone from its source in Lake Itasca in northwest Minnesota, the Mississippi flows 2,480 miles south to the Gulf of Mexico. Only the watersheds of the Amazon River and the Congo River exceed the size of her drainage basin, which covers over 1.2 million square miles, including all or parts of 31 states, some of which were not yet in the Union in 1861.

The river's name was taken originally from the Ojibwa (Chippewa) tribe word *Misi-ziibi* or the Algonquin term *Missi Sepe*, which translated poetically as "father of waters." In his 1842 *American Notes*, English novelist and visitor Charles Dickens was more blunt: "But what words shall describe the Mississippi, great father of rivers, who (praise be to heaven) has no children like him! An enormous ditch ... running liquid mud."

The Mississippi River, known as early as 1814 as the "Nile of North America," is divided into three geographical parts: the Headwaters, the Upper Mississippi River, and the Lower Mississippi River. The Headwaters is the reach from the source (Lake Itasca) downstream to St. Anthony Falls in Minneapolis, Minnesota, whereas the Upper Mississippi River extends from St. Anthony Falls downstream to the mouth of the Ohio River at the 37th parallel of north latitude, where it splashes the tip of Illinois and divides Kentucky on the east from Missouri on the west. The islands of the Upper Mississippi River are numbered consecutively from the source down to the junction of the Ohio River; in 1814, there were 68, mostly small islands.

Below the Mississippi-Ohio junction, the giant stream is known as the Lower Mississippi and meanders southward 1,097 miles to Head-of-Passes in the Gulf of Mexico, on the same meridian as Cairo, Egypt. It was the great trunk route for steamboat traffic; the Upper Mississippi and all of the tributaries were secondary.

This stern-wheeler, photographed on the Mississippi River near Memphis in 1906, is almost identical in profile to those of her type plying the Western Rivers in the 1860s. Note the huge cloud of smoke escaping her tall chimneys (Library of Congress).

The valley through which the river flows is known as the Mississippi Alluvial Plain, comprising floodplains and low terraces that are almost level to slightly sloping and which are joined by a number of southerly flowing tributaries. From Cairo, at the tip of Illinois, the Mississippi passed through a long alluvial stretch forming the eastern or western borders of six states.

This great basin reaches out to an average width of some 75 miles and there are few natural barriers to impede the Mississippi's flow. Relief along her banks is generally slight, and floods remain common. The banks on the western or right side of the stream are not high. There are, however, numerous heights, hills or bluffs, on the left, or eastern, edge and these provided the most inhabitable sites.

Mississippi River Packet. Photographed near Memphis in 1906, this side-wheel Mississippi packet is identical in many ways to those earlier sisters that plied the great river in the 1860s. Note her rudder arrangement aft and her staging planks forward (Library of Congress).

Almost every settlement at lower points along the river was then protected by built-up embankments or dikes, known as levees. Many are so guarded still today. Indeed, the lower river's natural floodplain has been reduced about 90 percent in area by levee construction, which began in 1727. The Lower Mississippi River valley contains about 2,700 kilometers of levees along both sides of the river.

Bottomland hardwood forests cover some areas (though not as many as in the early part of the 19th century) and swamps are not uncommon. A large amount of hardwood was burned for fuel and employed for other purposes a century ago (including the construction of steamboats). Cottonwoods and willows were among the most common trees viewed from the water. Today much of the floodplain supports agriculture.

Although the Illinois-Louisiana portion of the Mississippi was not provided with locks and dams over the last century akin to the Upper stretch, it has been extensively channeled to help regulate its width and depth, the lack of which was a serious 19th century problem. At the time of the Civil War, however, the course of the twisting lower silt-laden river was so devious few realized that, as the crow flew north to south, the Ohio was only 480 miles from the Gulf of Mexico.

The short segment of the Upper Mississippi River extending from the mouth of the Missouri River (near St. Louis, Missouri) to the mouth of the Ohio is often termed the Middle Mississippi River. For purposes of this narrative, we are not concerned with the Upper Mississippi above St. Louis.[7]

The Union army's aging general in chief, Winfield Scott, and its quartermaster general, Montgomery C. Meigs, were among those who were convinced fairly early on in the spring of 1861 that an armed conflict between north and south was about to happen. Wishing to be prepared, they dispatched chief engineer Brevet Brig. Gen. Joseph G. Totten to the west to inventory logistical challenges and possibilities, with particular attention to be given to river transportation.

During his travels, the sprightly 73-year-old Totten talked to river people, gathering all sorts of local information on transportation and carefully recording his figures. Among these was a table provided by veteran steamboat outfitter and captain J.S. Neal of Madison, Indiana, enumerating all of the important landing places for steamers from Cairo to New Orleans. We have chosen the Neal list, with its mileage chart and attendant remarks, as the basis for our review of the principal towns and points of the Lower Mississippi.

Neal's list is supplemented by the views of other 19th century rivermen and visitors, including Mark Twain, Navy paymaster Edward J. Huling, *New York Herald* correspondent Henry Thompson, and the noted British journalist William H. Russell.[8]

In addition to New Orleans and Cairo, the Middle and Lower Mississippi host along their tree lined or marshy banks a number of communities important in this account.

Aside from the metropolis of St. Louis, its suburb of Carondelet further down was an important Middle Mississippi River boat building site during the Civil War. Downstream on the Missouri side were Cape Girardeau (noted for its rocky bluffs and valuable rock quarries) and Commerce, an enclave of Union sympathizers. As Flag Officer Andrew Hull Foote and others would learn in November and December 1861, the shoals and other obstructions of this part of the river would greatly impede the transfer of warships.

At the mouth of the Ohio, 215 miles below St. Louis by water, was boot-shaped Cairo (locally pronounced *Kay-ro* or *Care-o*), which we will elaborate upon further elsewhere, and the beginning of the Lower Mississippi. Suffice it to say here that, because the Mississippi current was so swift and its lowland banks were very swampy, the Ohio River side of the town saw most of the commercial development.

In September 1863, *New York Herald* newsman Henry Thompson, in a piece entitled "The Old Route," observed that the lighter or darker color of the Mississippi was often determined by the soil content in the rising of the various rivers flowing into it. For example, the Ohio gave a yellower or clear hue, while the Red offered a reddish cast.

The journalist told his readers that a great struggle appeared to occur at the confluence of the Ohio and Mississippi, as the "immense body of clear water of the former" rushed with great force into the turbid latter. Indeed, "for some two or three miles below Cairo, there appear to be two channels," he wrote. "The clear water of the Ohio took the eastern side and the muddy Mississippi the western." Later, the water in the eastern channel became progressively more yellow and dark as it became one with the "Father of Waters."

The islands in the Lower Mississippi below Cairo were recorded in order beginning with Island No. 1, five miles downstream close to the left shore. Island No. 10, which has since disappeared, was a two-mile-long strip of land located in a great horseshoe river bend just above New Madrid.

The usually brownish river current was very swift (three to five miles per hour and sometimes faster during rising or flooding). Interestingly, little thought was given to using the turbid water for drinking and culinary purposes. One observer, a gunboat paymaster, later recalled that "though at first the appearance of it is rather forbidding, a person soon comes to like it, and it is drunk with a relish." He forgot to add that, to make it more palatable, the water was often held in jars overnight, allowing the sediment to settle.

Journalist Thompson added that "I have seen a tumbler of Mississippi water, after standing a short time, become clear as crystal to within an inch of the bottom, but that inch is formed of fine particles we in the North call mud." He went on to add that "Many prefer drinking this water to any other in the country; spring water not excepted."

Settled by Abram Bird in 1798, strategic Bird's Point, on fairly high ground, juts out at a point southeast across the Mississippi from Cairo. Norfolk (across from Island No. 1), Belmont (2,000 feet across the river opposite Columbus, Kentucky), and New Madrid are Missouri locations prominent to our story.

Norfolk Landing is no longer recognized as any kind of town, but remains on the maps of Mississippi County, three miles down the Missouri shore from Bird's Point. In Civil War days, it was an old left bank steamboat stop just across from the Kentucky ruins of Fort Jefferson, a federal outpost established in 1780.

A mile long, Island No. 1 lay close to the left shore two miles farther on; it has since merged into Kentucky. Islands 2–4 were grouped almost together about eight miles farther down and hugged the left bank as well.

Belmont, Missouri, was also pretty much just a place for steamers to land. Two or three houses were situated here on low, weedy, treed farmland. Roads led down the river 48 miles to New Madrid and inland about 12 to the town of Charleston.

A curve in the river above Belmont, also in Mississippi County, is known as Lucas Bend and was named for Missouri's territorial governor, J.B.C. Lucas. New Madrid, the town in the county of that name, is the next "show me" location of importance, being situated in the river curve holding Island No. 10, seventy miles below Cairo. Surrounded by marshland, the low-lying village remains famous for its December 1811 destruction by earthquakes along the New Madrid Fault.

Heading south on the Kentucky bank, the initial town of major importance was Columbus, 18 miles, or about two hours steaming time, below Cairo. With approximately 2,000 residents, it lay directly along the waterway in wooded lowlands. "From the river, it has a very clean and beautiful appearance," opined the *Herald*'s Thompson.

On April 22, 1861, a week after the bombardment of Fort Sumter, the Mobile & Ohio Railroad completed a spur to the growing commercial center, linking it to Paducah and Mobile. Its wharf was not, however, greatly developed, consisting, as one English journalist put it, of "wooden piles in the bank which afforded a resting place for the gangplank." Throughout its history, the 4,000 acres or so of the town were often flooded. After a particularly bad flood in 1927, the community's 40 buildings were taken down, loaded on trucks, and relocated and reassembled higher up on drier ground. Today, a large portion of the original village location is submerged.

A great embankment, known as Iron Bluff, ran into the river behind Columbus. The 250-foot-high spur north of the town, against which the river washed for a distance of about two miles, was known as the Iron Bluffs, while the five-mile stretch below the community and a mile above the head of six-mile-long Wolf Island was called the Chalk Bluffs. The names of these ridges were based on earth color and composition.

Atop these commanding summits, which gradually declined inland for five or six miles, one could see some 20 miles upriver and down. The Mississippi at the base of the bluffs took a short rapid southwestern turn, becoming deep and narrow. Incidentally, Wolf Island was also known as Island No. 5 because it was the fifth one found south of the confluence of the Ohio and Mississippi rivers. Even though it lay close to the Missouri bank, it was actually owned by the State of Kentucky.

The county seat of Fulton County, the town of Hickman, once known as Mills Point, is 12 miles beyond and sits a mile above Island No. 6. It was noted for its tobacco trade in prewar days. People landing there found a village with four churches, one bank, and a newspaper office. They could proceed along the east riverbank to the heights behind Columbus. Some 14 miles below New Madrid, on the Tennessee bank, lay the "straggling hamlet" of Tiptonville. It was essentially a steamboat landing from whence goods arriving from the interior, via a bridge over Reelfoot Lake, were shipped.

As the great Mississippi meandered southward, with bluffs on one side and unremarkable scenery upon the other, its pea-soup colored water threw up for the unwary the occasional tree trunk or sandbar. Travelers like journalist Russell also spied "masses of leaves, decaying vegetation, stumps of trees, forming small floating islands, or giant cotton-tree, pines, and balks of timber whirling down the current." Many a gunboatman would observe the same phenomenon in the years ahead.

The first of four Chickasaw bluffs, also known as the Cane Hills, rose in the Volunteer State, some 80 miles below Island No 10 and an equal distance above Memphis. It was home to the cotton-trading center of Fulton, in Lauderdale County, at its foot and Fort Pillow, at its head, atop a promontory between the Mississippi and the Hatchie rivers. The main shipping channel ran within musket-shot of the river bank.

Twelve miles below Fort Pillow, just below the mouth of the Hatchie and opposite Island No. 40, was the town of Randolph, in Tipton County. The second Chickasaw bluff rises gradually from the Mississippi, forming a ridge behind the town. The third Chickasaw bluff, like the others named for the Native American tribe, rose at Old River, near Island No. 36.

Memphis, a strategically important Tennessee city of 25,000 inhabitants in Shelby County, was situated atop the fourth and lowest of the Chickasaw bluffs. There were no suitable locations for fortification in the town's immediate vicinity. While passing upriver in June 1861, the English war correspondent William H. Russell was taken to visit a tarpaulin-covered cotton bale parapet erected close to the edge of the bank, which rose to almost perpendicular heights 60–150 feet above the waters of the Mississippi. There a six-gun battery was mounted.

The next important town below Memphis was Helena, Arkansas, built on one of the few high banks on the right side of the stream at a point about halfway between Memphis and Vicksburg. "With its buildings and sawmills," remarked one Northern observer, "[it] resembles Greenpoint, Brooklyn." High hills rose immediately to the community's rear; they could be "seen for miles and miles along the Mississippi."

Approximately 380 miles south of Cairo on the west bank, near the location of Island No. 72, lies the mouth of the White River. About 10 miles downstream was Napoleon, situated a few hundred yards south of the mouth of the Arkansas River. Cyprus Bend was a short distance below the town. Paymaster Huling reported that both Helena and Napoleon had terrible wartime reputations as hellholes plagued with "gamblers, thieves, murderers, and people of those classes."

A small, presumably less-evil point that would also enter military annals was Gaines' Landing, 40 miles beyond. Prior to the war, Texas-bound settlers were debarked at this point and it came to have two stores and several houses.

Over on the left side of the river in Mississippi is a string of noteworthy communities, some large and small mostly built atop bluffs, which would be recorded in military reports. Included in the number was Skipwith's Landing, 52 miles below Gaines where the U.S. Navy would station coal barges.

The Yazoo River enters below Island No. 103, approximately nine miles above the curve adjacent to the Walnut Hills and north of Vicksburg, the noted Yazoo delta community. The important prewar landing of Milliken's Bend would gain prominence. Paw Paw Island, at the foot of the curve, rose some 40 to 50 feet higher than the river.

Vicksburg achieved everlasting fame as the elevated fortress city of the Mississippi. It is 90 miles down from Memphis, while the village of Warrenton, which had a prewar population of about 300, is 10 miles farther. Grand Gulf, another strongpoint with a prewar population of 300, was 30 miles below Vicksburg at the mouth of the Big Black River. Rodney is 20 miles beyond Grand Gulf and Natchez is 35. With 15,000–20,000 inhabitants, the latter town was built on the east bank's highest ground.

The mouth of the Red River appeared on the opposite bank about 11 or so miles below Natchez in a great bend along the Louisiana shore about 175 miles south of Vicksburg and some 765 miles south of Cairo. From Baton Rouge to New Orleans, wrote Mark Twain in the 1870s, "the great sugar-plantations border both sides of the river all the way." Island No. 126, the final island of the Lower Mississippi, was approximately 45 miles south of Baton Rouge.[9]

A significant number of major and minor watersheds are tributaries to the Mississippi and these include several that became familiar waters for gunboats and military steamers during the course of the 1861–1865 conflict. Those rivers of the Lower Mississippi flowed south (often in a roundabout manner) and included such natural highways as the White, Arkansas, Yazoo, and Red. Likewise, the huge Ohio River also flows south, but its two major southern tributaries, the Tennessee and the Cumberland, move north. That we might better understand the physical restraints under which certain operations were conducted, these seven rivers are here described, beginning with those exiting directly off the Lower Mississippi.

The first major tributary to enter the Lower Mississippi south of the Ohio River is the White River, a 722-mile confluence that flows swiftly south from the Boston Mountains in northwest Arkansas. After looping north toward Branson, Missouri, the White then streams to the southeast through Arkansas, exiting into the Mississippi near the head of Island No. 72, about 380 miles south of Cairo. Its mouth is opposite Montgomery Point, Mississippi. Steamboatmen of the day noted that, in the upper part of its course, the river flowed between hills and high bluffs, while its lower course wound through a huge alluvial bottom.

The Civil War era river was narrow and crooked but navigable about 400 miles up from its mouth, past St. Charles to Batesville and, at times of low water, was often employed as a substitute for the Arkansas River. The color of the river water is light gray, giving the stream its name. Compared to the dark hue of the Mississippi, the White looked almost clear to some observers.

About 10 miles north of the White's mouth was a stream known as the "Cut-off" that provided a connection with the Arkansas River. This passage was sufficiently wide and deep to accommodate most of the steamers plying the two streams, though it was prone to occasionally throwing up a snag. The water levels, higher or lower, between the two rivers flowed back and forth between the two, depending upon each other's stage; if the water level of the Mississippi were higher than either, it flowed first up the White then through the Cut-off and into the Arkansas.[10]

The mouth of the Arkansas River was about 10 miles down the Mississippi River beyond that of the White River. The fifth longest river in the United States and the second largest tributary of the Mississippi-Missouri system, this 1,450-mile-long waterway rises in Colorado. Flowing east through Kansas and Oklahoma, it enters Arkansas at Fort Smith and continues 600 miles southeast past Little Rock to exit into the Mississippi at Napoleon.

Long since taken over by the forces of nature, the Post of Arkansas was located about 50 miles from the river's mouth. Smaller steamboats were able, often with great difficulty, to navigate much of the stream, though most prewar boats worked the Napoleon–Little Rock–Fort Smith route, connecting with larger steamers at Napoleon.

Rivermen supposedly informed *New York Herald* writer Finley Anderson in 1863 that they expected the Father of Waters to sweep away Napoleon. "To all lovers of decency and good morals," the scribe suggested, "this is a consummation devoutly to be wished."

As the lower channel of the Arkansas was at the time very winding and prone to snags and sandbars, steamboats often chose to avoid as much of it as possible. Instead, they would enter the Arkansas via the Cut-off from the White River, returning to the Mississippi by the same route.[11]

After the Ohio, the Yazoo is the second longest tributary to flow into the Mississippi River from the east. Confined within the borders of the state of Mississippi, the 188-mile-long stream is formed by the confluence of the Tallahatchie River and the Yalobusha River at Greenwood.

Lined with natural levees, the Yazoo parallels the Mississippi for miles before finally joining it at a point below Island No. 103, approximately nine miles above the curve adjacent to the Walnut Hills and north of Vicksburg. This waterway and the ones entering it were home to great swaths of underbrush and wildlife and could be very difficult to navigate.

In July 1862 when the Confederate armorclad *Arkansas* dashed down the stream to Vicksburg, the *New York Herald*'s Henry Knox told his readers something about the Yazoo. Though narrow and sluggish, he said, it was very deep in places, often "showing no bottom to a line of 50 feet in length." The water had a slightly brackish taste and was very dark, contrasting with the lighter yellow of the Mississippi. The point of junction between the two was visible for a considerable distance. Knox went on to say that the banks of the river were generally high "and the bluffs afford excellent positions for planting batteries and stopping navigation." There were few settlements, "an occasional cotton plantation being al that can be seen."[12]

The most southerly Mississippi tributary to appear in our account is the Red, sometimes known as the Red River of Louisiana. It owes its inclusion in our list primarily to the great Banks-Porter expedition of 1864 in which the timberclad *Lexington* was the oldest naval unit present. The 1,360-mile-long Red rises near Amarillo in northern Texas, in the northern part of the Staked Plains, or Llano Estacado, and flows east by south in Texas, between Texas and Oklahoma, and to Fulton, in southwestern Arkansas; it there turns southeast and continues in a general southeasterly direction through Louisiana past Shreveport to the banks of the Mississippi, where it discharges partly into the Mississippi above Baton Rouge. The stream's mouth was in a great bend along the Louisiana shore about 175 miles south of Vicksburg and some 765 miles south of Cairo.

Reviewing the Red River expedition some years later, Admiral Mahan also commented upon the difficulties of the stream in the area between Alexandria and Shreveport, where the Navy ran into trouble:

> The river, which gets its name from the color of its water, flows through a fertile and populous country, the banks in many places being high, following in a very crooked channel a general southeasterly direction. In this portion of its course it has a width of seven hundred to eight hundred feet, and at low water a depth of four feet. The slope from Shreveport to Alexandria at high water is a little over a hundred feet, but immediately above the latter place there are two small rapids, called the Falls of Alexandria, which interrupt navigation when the water is low. The annual rise begins in the early winter, and from December to June the river is in fair boating condition for its usual traffic; but water enough for the gunboats and transports to pass the Falls could not be expected before the spring rise in March. The river, however, can never be confidently trusted.[13]

The Ohio River begins at the confluence of the Allegheny and Monongahela rivers at the Point in downtown Pittsburgh and flows 981 miles to join the Mississippi at Cairo. It flows through or along the borders of six states, and its watershed encompasses 14 states. The Ohio carries the largest volume of water of any upper tributary of the Mississippi. In fact, it typically carries a much greater volume of water than the Upper Mississippi itself.

From Pittsburgh, the Ohio flows to the northwest through western Pennsylvania before making an abrupt, almost 180 degree, turn to the south-southwest at the state line with West Virginia (Virginia until 1863), where it then forms the border between that state and Ohio. The stream then follows a roughly southwestern and then western course between Ohio, Indiana, Illinois, and Kentucky until it joins the Mississippi from the east at Cairo. At its mouth, the Ohio is wider than the Mississippi itself.

In the 1860s, at low water during the summer when rainfall was slight, the Ohio had an average depth of 30 inches over the bars, most of which were sandy and not dangerous. At Cincinnati, the pool stage was about 10 feet, two to five feet less than at other times of the year. At the beginning of the 21st century, the pool stage through most of the year is around 28 feet. During the Civil War, historian David M. Smith has said, the Ohio was "significantly shallower and, as importantly, not as wide as it is today."

Interestingly, the original Virginia charter went not to the middle of the Ohio River, but to its far shore, so the entire river was included. Wherever the river serves as a boundary between states—Kentucky and Virginia (now West Virginia) on the south and Ohio, Indiana, Illinois and Kentucky, also on the south, the river essentially belongs to the two states on the south that were later divided from Virginia. Due to its role as a natural geographic dividing line between North and South, the Ohio River was earlier seen as the watery stripe dividing free states and slave states. In addition to Pittsburgh and Cairo, the Ohio River has a number of historic communities along its banks. Those in Virginia (now West Virginia) include, in alphabetical order, Huntington, New Martinsville, Paden City, Parkersburg, Weirton, and Wheeling.

Also to the south, in Kentucky, we have Ashland, Brandenburg, Caseyville, Concordia, Covington, Henderson, Lewisport, Louisville, Newport, Owensboro, and Paducah at the mouth of the Tennessee River (with a population of 4,000 in 1863), Smithland at the mouth of the Cumberland River, Stephensport, and Union Town, exactly 400 miles west of Cincinnati. The key city of Louisville, 369 miles from the mouth of the Ohio and 150 miles west of Cincinnati, was founded at the only major natural navigational barrier on the river which concerns us, the Falls of the Ohio.

These falls were a series of rapids where the river flowed over hard, fossil-rich limestone beds. The first Ohio River locks were built here before the Civil War to circumnavigate the falls; the Louisville and Portland Canal was 2.5 miles long and 50 feet wide, and its lock could pass a boat through that was 180 feet long and 49.7 feet wide. In 1860, 1,520 steamboats and 1,299 other craft transited the canal. The Cumberland Bar, near Smithland, marked the mouth of the Cumberland River. Mound City is eight miles above the Ohio's confluence with the Mississippi and seven miles from Cairo. Both of these Illinois communities served during the war as home ports to important northern naval facilities.

To the north in Ohio, the riverbank towns include Belpre; the "Queen City" of Cincinnati, the largest city in the Midwest; Gallipolis; Ironton; Marietta; Pomeroy; and Steubenville. In Indiana, Amsterdam (now New Amsterdam), Cannelton (with many coal mines), Clarksville, Derby Landing (now Derby), Enterprise, Evansville (350 miles west of Cincinnati with a direct rail line to Indianapolis), Fredonia, Grandview, Jeffersonville (terminus of the Jeffersonville and Indianapolis Railroad) and Leavenworth.

Continuing on with our list of leading Hoosier Ohio River communities, there was Madison (100 miles west of Cincinnati and 50 miles east of Louisville and terminus for the Madison and Indianapolis Railroad), Mauckport, Mount Vernon, New Albany, Rockport (also noted for its coal production), Rome, Tell City, and Troy.

Ohio River towns in Illinois are Brookport, Elizabethtown, Golconda, Metropolis (with a population of 400 in 1863), Mound City — home of the naval base — and Shawneetown. The distance from Cincinnati to Cairo by steamer in 1861 was 550.7 miles.[14]

The Tennessee River is the largest tributary of the Ohio River. It is approximately 650 mi (1,046 km) long, covers 41,000 square miles, and drains portions of 60 Tennessee counties and seven states. It is formed at the confluence of the Holston and French Broad rivers on the east side of Knoxville. From Knoxville, it flows southwest toward Chattanooga before crossing into Alabama. The Flint and Elk rivers enter at the great bend of the river as it loops through north Alabama, eventually forming a small part of the state's border with Mississippi, before returning to the Volunteer State.

Flowing north again through the Western Tennessee Valley, the Duck River (fed by the Buffalo River) enters the Tennessee south of New Johnsonville (the original Johnsonville was lost to the TVA dams of the 1930s), while the Big Sandy River joins not far from Paris Landing. The final part of the Tennessee's run is in Kentucky, where it flows into the Ohio River at Paducah, some 12 miles west of the mouth of the Cumberland River.

Of the three rivers above the Lower Mississippi discussed here, the Tennessee saw the least use by antebellum steamboat companies. Two huge natural obstructions gave those who employed the river considerable pause and halted others from considering the prospect. The first was a huge 30-mile-long gorge cut through Walden's Ridge at Chattanooga. Second, in North Alabama, the Foot of Big Muscle, the Muscle Shoals, began a half mile beyond Florence. This was a series of obstructions almost 40 miles long. It was made up of shifting gravel bars, rapids, snags, rock reefs, and a narrow channel which often fatally wounded boats. Of the Foot, or head of navigation, it was noted in 1863 that "only four foot at the highest stages of water [was] ever known."

During the war, Union gunboats were forced to guard the Tennessee river, above and below Muscle Shoals, because the great river could be readily crossed by Confederates in many spots.

The Duck River Sucks, 134 miles from the mouth of the river, were considered very dangerous due to the extremely crooked channel and the strong current over its rocks. At low water, these shoals were considered by the U.S. Navy to be "one of the most favorable places for locating a battery on the river." This and the other named natural obstacles played such a significant role in Northern river naval strategy that, when Rear Adm. Porter divided the rivers under his command up into districts in 1863, he created two districts to cover the Tennessee, one above Muscle Shoals and one below.

The Tennessee River as far as the Muscle Shoals at Florence, Alabama, has a number of historic communities along its banks, though not as many large towns as are found along the huge Ohio. Those in Kentucky, with 1863 populations as provided by Lt. Col. Fitch include Paducah, located on the west bank near the Ohio confluence and 50 miles from Cairo (population 4000), Birmingham (population 200), Aurora, and Callowaytown (disappeared by 1870). It was approximately 90 miles from Paducah to the state line. In the 1860s, the Tennessee River averaged about 1,420 feet in width. The wooded banks were mostly flat and overflowed at high water. High hills were situated about 1 or 2 miles back of the banks.

Crawford, a correspondent for the *Wisconsin State Journal*, has left a detailed travelogue of a trip he made up the Tennessee in May 1862 to visit the battlefield at Shiloh. His information-laden account offered readers then and now a visual picture of the sights experienced daily by the gunboatmen steaming upon those waters. "The whole scenery along the Tennessee River is magnificent," he wrote, "grand and lovely." Heavy forests of timber skirted the banks, "sycamore, maple, hickory, and cypress." From Paducah to the state line and beyond, "The trees on either shore hang full of the mistletoe, an evergreen parasite, which contrasted strangely enough with the different hues of the various kinds of trees on which it fastens itself."

The land beyond the river was "generally high, sometimes, and for miles, it is rocky, the ledges rising out of the water and extending up some eight to 20 feet." Inland, the land extended back and "not unfrequently [sic] rising higher are covered with timber." In many places, it "seems as if the bank is but a high ridge, dividing the river from vast swamps, which are nevertheless covered with magnificent trees."

Perhaps the greatest surprise experienced by the Union sailors and soldiers passing upstream, even in the months after Shiloh, was "the almost entire want of the evidence of civilization along the broad and noble river." In the whole distance from Paducah to Fort Henry, "there were not ten farms." Occasionally, Crawford wrote home, a log hut or two would appear in small clearings, "but they are many miles apart."

Locations of interest in Tennessee include Pine Bluff, Buffalo Landing, Paris Landing, New Portland, Reynoldsburg, Fowler's Landing, Perryville and East Perryville (population 30), Marvin's Bluffs, Brownsport, Cedar Creek, Decatur, and Carrollville.

Fort Henry, which first brought large numbers of Federals to the river, was located two miles over the Kentucky border on the eastern bank. Danville, site of a noted railroad bridge, was 115 miles from Paducah, while the east bank town of Clifton (population 300) was 75 miles further up. Clifton, according to Crawford, was a "neat-looking village" situated "on a high and uneven bank." The defunct town of Carrollton was a mile below.

Additional towns included Point Pleasant, Cerro Gordo, Coffee's Landing, and Savannah (population 500), the latter 33 miles above Clifton. "A very old town," it had "but one street and that runs east from the river." Pittsburgh Landing (233 miles above Paducah and site of the famous 1862 battle) was the next important point, though hardly known before the fight. Big Bend Landing was above. Eastport was the major Mississippi community on the river in the 1860s. Alabama towns include Chickasaw, Waterloo, Tuscumbia, and Florence (population of 1,000).[15]

The 687-mile-long Cumberland River begins in Letcher County in eastern Kentucky on the Cumberland Plateau and flows southeast before crossing into northern Tennessee; it then curves back up into western Kentucky, running parallel with the Tennessee River. At one point prior to the TVA era, the two streams came to within about a mile of one another at a narrow neck of land which was known on the Cumberland as Kelly's Landing. Upriver from Dover, the Cumberland veered away from her sister and headed east toward Nashville.

The Cumberland drains an 18,000 square mile watershed and runs north into the Ohio River at Smithland, Kentucky. The Lower Cumberland, which winds through highland valleys and ridges, runs 192 miles from Smithland to Nashville and has an average width of 600 to 700 feet. Burnside, 358 river miles above Nashville, was the head of low-water navigation on the Upper Cumberland. The Cumberland Valley between Burnside and Carthage, Tennessee, is about a mile to a mile and a half wide, with the river varying in width from 550 to 600 feet. At the time of the Civil War, the riverbanks were "generally very thickly wooded with heavy hills overlooking the banks." When the Cumberland began to fall, "the water recedes so fast that there is great danger to being caught," wrote Lt. Cmdr. Fitch in 1863. The stream frequently rose and fell "with such rapidity that a difference of from eight to twelve feet in 24 hours" was "of no uncommon occurrence."

At Carthage, the valley and the river widen south into the Central Basin, and the river eventually reenters the Highland Rim about 14 miles below Nashville. Steamboat navigation on the Upper Cumberland was confined to the higher water periods from December through May. In the 1860s, the river averaged about 600 feet wide "inside the trees" lining its banks.

At least 10 major shoals obstructed the Lower Cumberland, with the most challenging being the 4.3-mile-long obstacle formed of gravel bars and rocky ledges and collectively known as the Harpeth Shoals. In the early 1860s, boats had "great difficulty" getting above Harpeth Shoals, about 160 miles from the mouth and 35 miles from Nashville. At low water, the Cumberland River was not navigable for boats drawing over 15 inches, that being the average depth on Harpeth Shoals. Indeed, many Nashville-bound craft from Louisville and the north never made it that far, being halted by shoals at Eddyville, just upstream from Smithland.

The Upper Cumberland between Carthage and Burnside was impeded at low water by 16 shoals and bars. At almost any time, the river became very narrow in making the turns and frequently boats got "very much broken up," Fitch reported in 1863. "In making the trip to Carthage," he continued," boats frequently are compelled to lower their smokestacks and then suffer much from having their upper works much broken up by the branches of trees." In the summer, naval coverage of the Cumberland was all but impossible. Fitch observed that the stream was "so low during the summer and the bars so frequent and close as to prevent an effectual patrol, even had we all the boats for it alone."

Among the towns and cities on the Cumberland River in Tennessee and Kentucky between Carthage and Smithland which may be mentioned in our narrative are the following: in Tennessee, Ashland City (near the head of Harpeth Shoals, some 33 miles below Nashville), Betseytown (at the foot of Harpeth Shoals), Carthage, Clarksville (a major port due to Harpeth Shoals, which blocked access to Nashville below at low water), Cumberland City, Dover (near Fort Donelson), Gallatin, Gratton, Lebanon, Nashville, Palmyra, Rome, and Watkins.

River communities in Kentucky included Canton (where Cumberland River conflict began on October 18, 1861, in a skirmish between Col. Nathan B. Forrest and the U.S.S. *Conestoga*), Rockcastle, Eddyville (site of a large Union supply depot), Eureka, Iuka, Kuttawa, Pickneyville, Smithland, which was something of a boomtown during the conflict, and Woodville.

Lt. Cmdr. Fitch gave Porter, his superior, few notes as to his impressions of these towns, the most important of which were Nashville ("The Star of the Cumberland"), Clarksville (today, the state's fifth largest town), and Smithland ("the first town on the bluff," located a mile upstream from the mouth of the Cumberland). He did, however, note, in a March 17, 1863, review of the river itself that "Palmyra, between Donelson and Clarksville, and Beatstown [Betsy Town] Landing, at Harpeth Shoals, are the most noted guerrilla haunts. I have burned and destroyed all the stores or houses near the shoals frequented by guerrillas."[16]

Before proceeding further, it may be best to digress and review the seasons of navigation on the western waters. These would have been among the most important lessons absorbed by Cmdr. John Rodgers either on his way to Cincinnati in May 1861 or upon his arrival. They would certainly be brought home to him as he tried to get his three timberclads to Cairo during July and early August.

From the beginning of the steamboat period in the 1820s to its end in the 20th century, all riverboat activities were governed first and foremost by the moisture or lack thereof in the various seasons. These seasons were different in different parts of the Mississippi River system, depending upon geographical location. It was generally recognized that river depth increased as one moved from a stream's headwaters to its mouth or from tributary to main river.

Rains, snow, floods, and drought determined the river depths and thus the size of vessel which could operate in any given stream at any given time. In the words of famed steamboat historian Louis Hunter, "Each part of the river system rose and fell almost continuously according to a variety of controlling conditions, many of which were not shared by other parts at the same time." In practice, the maxim became that the smaller the river or the lower the stream, the lighter the boat draft required.

Usually beginning in the early spring, melting snow and ice plus rain swelled streams. These ran into the smaller rivers, like the Nolichuckey in Tennessee, which, in turn, ran into the intermediate tributaries like the Tennessee River, and then eventually raised the levels of such trunk rivers as the Mississippi and the Ohio.

This annual "spring rise" marked the opening of the steamboat navigation season, the duration of which was different for every river, depending upon its ecology and physical characteristics, particularly shoals. The steaming period on the larger rivers depended not only on this one rise, but also on various rises or "freshs," which were, in turn, determined by the weather. The rise in the spring of 1861 was unusually high "as the snows on the Great Plains had been deep during the past Winter."

Generally, the hotter summer months saw a drop in the river stages, particularly in the upper half of the Mississippi Valley; water levels could fall so far as to greatly restrict navigation or prohibit it entirely. In the Ohio, Cumberland, and Tennessee rivers, and even in the White River in Arkansas, the low water period usually began sometime in June and ended about the last of September. Even though, for example, the Lower Ohio was "very high" at the end of April 1861, it would be quite reduced by July.

Severe summer thunderstorms could result in a "fresh," which might, at least briefly, allow intensification of previously restricted gunboat activities. Skilled rivermen aboard both naval and civilian steamers could tell a river's stage, rising or falling, by using a lead or even by watching driftwood.

When Brig. Gen. Totten stopped at Madison, Indiana, during the spring of 1861 to listen to the Neal brothers discuss river matters, they were quite specific regarding drafts of water in the Ohio:

> Four feet draft with some certainty after middle of October; five feet draft 1st of November; six feet draft with great certainty after 15th of November. This, in ordinary seasons, a very dry summer and dry early autumn, will give less water in October, but the middle of November will very surely give from five to six feet draft.

Totten also took the opportunity to visit with his cousin, Edward D. Mansfield, of Morrow, Ohio, on the hills of the Little Miami, near Cincinnati. Mansfield, a well-known newspaperman, writer, and former college professor, was also asked to assemble information.

Speaking of the river drafts, Mansfield relied on his own travels up and down the Ohio and the Mississippi to inform the general that "the lower Ohio will probably have as much as five feet of water till the middle of July, the lowest water being generally in September and October.... In the Mississippi River, there is more water so that from Cairo down there will be little or no difficulty." The most dangerous places at low water, from Mansfield's own observations, were between Cairo and Memphis.

Other physical aspects of the Western rivers not appreciated by those unfamiliar with them included such concepts as crooked channels; those watery paths were not straight, but tended to weave across the different expanses, often revealing themselves by depth or color. In a September 17, 1862, report to Navy Assistant Secretary Gustavus V. Fox, Flag Officer Charles H. Davis sought to convey some sense of this phenomenon to the uninitiated: "There are no fixed channels in these great rivers, as there are in the sounds, estuaries, and harbors of the Atlantic; quite otherwise; the channels are always changing, not only from year to year, but from season to season, during the period of rise and fall particularly."

Oftentimes, little hills, plateaus, bars, or even islands appeared in the rivers. At one point, it was noted that some 98 islands could be seen in the Ohio River. Additionally, boulders, unmarked sunken boats, and thick foliage could pose dangers. Trees often grew right down to the banks, and, largely due to erosion, just as often fell in; as "snags," they could hit and even sink steamboats. Rapids, particularly the Falls of the Ohio at Louisville and Muscle Shoals, on the Tennessee about 250 miles above its mouth, were the most dangerous navigational obstructions, though swift currents were always to be avoided.

The fall rise, which was more unpredictable as to its beginning or end than that in the spring, could often be counted upon to provide good steaming into December. Commonly, the main rivers in our Western theater of operations did not freeze in wintertime and, as would be demonstrated in the Fort Henry and Fort Donelson campaigns, riverine warfare activities could be continued. Conventional wharves were few; boats could and did tie up along or push into banks as required.[17]

To say that the political situation was tense in the wake of the election of Illinois native Abraham Lincoln to the White House on November 6, 1860, would be a huge understatement. On December 3, the second session of the 36th U.S. Congress had assembled in the nation's capital. President James Buchanan's constitutionally required state of the union message of that date recognized that the slave states had certain grievances and deprecated the possible dissolution of the Union, but simultaneously announced that the Federal government was impotent to prevent it.

In the days that followed Buchanan's speech and the opening of Congress' last prewar session, newspapers from cities big and small would intensify their reporting of the uncertainty-filled public discourse. Many sectional leaders from the South threatened secession, while significant blocks of northern citizens would either seek compromise to avert the Union's dissolution or demand that the government stand fast and impose its laws in the south.

On December 18, Sen. John J. Crittenden offered a compromise, rejected by Lincoln and his followers, that would have recognized even further the "rights" of the slaveholders. Allies of the president in Congress were strongly committed to compromise, both on political grounds and because of the perceived impact the crisis was having upon the national economy.

With land travel primitive, uncertain, and time-consuming, the people of America's central section during the first six decades of the 19th century were dependent upon water transportation on the Mississippi River and its 50 navigable tributaries. Despite differing geographic features, the great rivers of the area helped to create a regional unity from differing political interests, fostering networks of rural market exchanges between various communities in the south and larger, more urban centers of the north.

During the 1850s, the growing Northern railway system had siphoned off much of the upper midwest grain previously exported to the seaboard via New Orleans. Now, it was increasingly shipped by railroad and canal to the Great Lakes and on to the east via the Erie Canal.

The export traffic of the Mississippi Valley was by 1861, as Kenneth M. Stamp has noted, chiefly intra–Mississippi Valley, with the South a huge midwestern market. Thus commerce came to have a significant impact on both regional and national outlooks.

Steamboats on the "Father of Waters" and such streams as the Ohio, Cumberland, Tennessee, White, Red, Missouri, Wabash, and Kanawha moved both people and goods and provided the backbone of the Western region's commerce. As New Orleans lost its import in the intra-valley trade, Cincinnati became, in the words of E. Merton Coulter, "the chief distributing center for the Ohio valley and in an increasing degree for the whole Cotton South."

A dozen or more steamboats arrived at the Queen City every day, almost equally split between those plying the rivers up and down. Regular steamer lines, home-ported at Cincinnati, dispatched their vessels daily for Madison, Louisville, Evansville, and on to Nashville or to St. Louis, Cairo, Memphis, the Arkansas River, and New Orleans. Flatboats transported such bulk cargoes as salt.

Even with the coming of the railroad, among the possibilities most feared by those at the northern end of the river system as the secession movement unfolded in 1860–1861 was the creation of a hostile, southern, indeed, foreign, power that could choke off trade. As the soon-to-be-called Confederates became increasingly aggressive and civil war threatened, opinion and concern in the upper Midwest crystallized behind the slogan "Free Navigation of the Mississippi."

Many northerners began to consider the extreme measures that might be necessary to protect their vital water arteries to the south and to the world in the event compromise failed. While it was true that commerce with the eastern seaboard had grown, citizens of the upper midwest also recognized that much of their prosperity was still tied to the Cotton South.

Midwestern legislators participated in the ferocious legislative debates which surrounded the Crittenden Compromise and the several other proposals designed to find some middle ground between the extremists. As trade with the South began to dwindle during this time of uncertain political conditions, merchants, shippers, farmers, and others, especially in Ohio, Indiana, and Illinois, supported work by state legislatures and Congress to find national compromise. Though not realized that day, the work of the peace advocates was, in fact, really doomed on December 20 when South Carolina enacted an ordinance of secession.

In rapid succession, between January 9 and February 1, 1861, Mississippi, Florida, Alabama, Georgia, Louisiana, and Texas seceded from the United States. With former president John Tyler as chair, a peace conference was held at Washington, D.C., behind closed doors starting on February 4. Delegates from the North, Midwest, and South attended, but could reach no Union-saving compromise. On February 8, the seceded states met in convention at Montgomery and established the provisional government of the Confederate States of America. The new entity began to discuss or exercise the various prerogatives of national government, including those affecting mid-continent river commerce.

In a dramatic call for "Freedom of the Mississippi," editors of the *New York Times* noted on February 21 that it was one thing for merchants and importers of the Midwest to pay U.S. customs duties on goods sent to other countries through the port of New Orleans. If, however, these proceeds were taken by Louisiana for its own use or on behalf of the whole Confederacy, such action would clearly be seen as a tax on the foreign commerce of the Mississippi Valley and a clear interference with the free navigation of the Father of Waters.

The editors of the New York paper did not believe that the states interested in unobstructed navigation would submit very long to being so illegally "plundered for the benefit of a movement they abhor." Unhappy consequences would surely follow, it predicted, if Rebel customs agents persisted in the "mad attempt" to "make the industry and trade of the great West pay tribute" to the "so-called Southern Confederacy."

In February, there was a political stalemate, with midwestern farmers and eastern capitalists both seeking compromise. This changed as March headed to an April crisis. Historian Stamp summed up the situation thus: "Most Westerners preferred to maintain their rights on the Mississippi by preserving the Union. An secessionists generally promised that they would never disrupt river commerce." Capitalists and Yankee businessmen also "carefully measured the consequences of disunion and the collapse of central authority" and decided that both were "intolerable."

While internal trade concerns surfaced in the weeks after Christmas 1860, a more dangerous game was also being played between Washington and the departing Southern states: the seizure of Federal forts and arsenals. Arsenals and fortifications were taken over in South Carolina, Georgia, Florida, Louisiana, Arkansas, and Texas. On January 9, gunners at Charleston had fired on the unarmed *Star of the West,* preventing it from reinforcing Fort Sumter.

The administration of President Buchanan continued to demonstrate its impotence and confusion as the collective national wait for Lincoln's new regime raced along. The U.S. Congress, despite the election of many new Republican members, failed to fill the chief executive's void by refusing to come down strongly for either compromise or enforcement. In the end, the weak congressional effort to prevent an armed split proved unsuccessful and its supporters were largely branded appeasers.

In his March 4, 1861, inaugural address, Abraham Lincoln, the tall former Illinois lawyer-politician, rejected compromise with the South. The reaction from southern newspapers was acerbic. The *Charleston Mercury* screamed that "the Ourang-Outang at the White House" had sounded "the tocsin of battle" while the Richmond *Dispatch* in still-loyal Virginia concluded that the speech "inaugurates civil war."[18]

In the weeks after Lincoln and his team came to power, chaos and confusion reigned everywhere. At least four southern states teetered on the brink of secession, an equal number of border states were shaky, and the new Confederacy worked to bolster its position as quickly as possible. Beginning from scratch, it "was criticized and may have seem indifferent to forwarding the men and tools of war" to key areas as might have been expected. Still, "It should be remembered," Cumberland River historian Byrd Douglas wrote in 1961, "that the Confederacy was an infant republic." Each southern state was initially responsible for its own protection and customs collections, as all of the seceding states were clinging "to the traditional doctrine of 'States Rights'" — which had many faults requiring time and patience to overcome.[19]

The Rebel states, meanwhile, increased their demand for northern goods and raw materials throughout the year's first quarter and were largely able to fulfill their needs. Requests for manufactured items were less frequently honored now and credit relations declined, but other traffic mushroomed. The upper midwest's desire for free river navigation and a slowness in Washington to curtail north-south commerce along watery avenues meant all kinds of war material and supplies for the Confederate "independent army" were bought and sent from river communities such as St. Louis, Cairo, Louisville, and Cincinnati.

Goods for locations in Georgia, Alabama, Mississippi, and South Carolina via Nashville and Memphis, as well as Vicksburg, Baton Rouge, and New Orleans, were carried by bottoms largely owned in the North. The packet trade for passengers and mixed cargo also rose. At the same time, vast amounts of cotton, flaxseed, peanuts, raisins, and other produce, as well as whiskey, brandy, and furniture, came north from Louisiana, Alabama, Georgia, and Mississippi via Tennessee and Kentucky. Newspapers along the rivers detailed the trade and here we note several examples:

On February 7, a South Carolina army major purchased thousands of bushels of corn, 4,000 casks of bacon, and 47,000 barrels of pork at Cincinnati. On the 24th, a steamer passed the Queen City transporting 100 tons of metal to Vicksburg, where it would be turned into cannon balls. Two days later, Jefferson Davis, the new president of the Confederacy, sent an order through the river town requesting "the finest dapple-gray horses that could be found in Ohio." On February 28, a Confederate army commissary general, with a line of credit of $500,000 from New Orleans banks, visited St. Louis to purchase supplies for 20,000 soldiers. At the beginning of March, a chartered St. Louis boat took a full cargo of corn, flour, lard, and bacon south, filling his order.

Though taken years later, this circa 1906 scene of commerce at the Memphis landing would be similar to that threatened by the onset of war in 1861 (Library of Congress).

New Albany, Indiana, a major Ohio River port across from Louisville, permitted transport south of Hoosier and some Buckeye produce and goods; boats from that town could hardly handle all of the Dixie requests. From 10 to 20 boats tied up at the Cairo wharf daily in the weeks after Christmas, while steamers from Cincinnati took passengers and cargo up the Tennessee River all the way to Florence, Alabama. On March 13, the *Cincinnati Daily Enquirer* reported that 18 steamboats "were loading at the wharf of this city to leave within a few days on the downstream trade." It should also be noted that the railroads of the region also worked overtime supplying Confederate needs.

For their part, Southern merchants and growers forwarded vast numbers of cotton bales to the markets of the north. From Nashville, Memphis, and several Mississippi River towns, steamers took their cargoes to St. Louis and to Ohio River towns, including Louisville and Cincinnati. The quantities were huge. For the week ending on March 7, a total of 19,455 bales were shipped out of Memphis alone, including 6,166 to the Ohio River, 1,240 to St. Louis, and 2,700 to New Orleans for foreign destinations. Other cargoes sent up included molasses, sugar, coffee, and empty barrels. During the first quarter, over 1,000 tons of produce was shipped weekly from Cairo to Memphis.[20]

It would take more than political difficulties, no matter how rough, to halt the inland trade. The Confederacy did not directly implement commercial policies to disrupt it. Indeed, the new government consciously encouraged Southern and other shippers to send their Midwest-bound foreign imports via New Orleans rather than New York. It also passed free-trade laws that favored Midwestern grain and provisions. The free list included gunpowder, lead, arms, bacon, pork, hams, lard, beef, flour, wheat, corn and corn meal, oats, rye, barley, and other agricultural products and livestock.

Thus it was that when the *Star of the West* was fired upon by South Carolinian cannoneers over on the East Coast, no reduction in Cincinnati to New Orleans trade occurred. As late as April 5, three cannon from Baltimore were allowed to pass through Cincinnati en route to Jackson even though they were clearly marked "for the Southern Confederacy."

There were, however, incidents on the Mississippi which threatened disruption of "free navigation" for Midwesterners and which brought howls of protest. On January 9, as reported in the *Cincinnati Daily Enquirer* six days later, Mississippi governor John J. Pettis, reacting to intelligence received from Louisiana, ordered action taken to stop two steamers, the *Marengo* and the *Silver Wave*, believed to be bringing ordnance downriver to reinforce Federal installations.

Walking down to the state arsenal in Jackson, the Democrat executive ordered the Quitman battery to move over to positions on the landing at Vicksburg and in the Walnut Hills, there to "prevent any hostile expedition from the Northern States descending the river." All vessels ascending the river were to stop and submit to inspection by specially appointed officers. If a hailed vessel did not stop, the gunners were to fire a blank first and employ live ammunition thereafter.

By the time the Jackson cannoneers joined with other units already at Vicksburg, rumors about the *Silver Wave* expedition had mushroomed. Not only was the steamer, which was expected on the evening of the 12th, carrying cannon, it also had aboard 500 hooligans—"Wideawakes"—who would come ashore and pillage the town.

The *Silver Wave* did not materialize as expected, but the volunteer defenders were not to be disappointed. The following evening, as the men stood ready and waiting at their 6-pounders, another steamboat rounded De Soto Point in the dark and headed toward the town landing.

Betrayed by sparks from her chimneys and the chugging sound made by her engines, the regularly scheduled Cincinnati–New Orleans packet *A.O. Tyler* was targeted for the first blank round. Captain John Collier, part owner of the craft, did not know what to make of the firing and so continued on.

Another shot, this one live, was fired across the bow of the *A.O. Tyler* and splashed into the muddy Mississippi beyond. As the artillerymen prepared to shoot again, the *City of Louisiana*, whose identity was known, steamed between the defenders and Collier's boat, bringing an order to cease fire. Collier was hailed and ordered to bring his craft in. At the dock, he was advised of the "Wideawake" scare and ordered to take his boat upstream to a point below Fort Hill where it could be inspected — even though both he and the *Tyler* were well known. By and by the *Silver Wave* did appear. She, too, was searched and when no contraband of war or ruffians were found, both steamers were permitted to depart. Cmdr. Rodgers would later purchase the *A.O. Tyler* at Cincinnati and have it converted into the gunboat *Tyler*. Seven months to the day later, on August 13, the *Tyler* would, according to several writers, fire the first hostile naval shots heard on the Western waters. Seventy-one years later, historian Charles Henry Ambler would refer to the January incident as "possibly the first shot of the Civil War."

As might be expected, the ratcheting up of what had so far been a war of regional words was not well greeted in shipping circles. The *Memphis Evening Argus* on January 17 remarked how "Cincinnati steamboat men have been thrown into a fever." Northern editors protested the Pettis blockade. The *Cincinnati Daily Commercial* referred to this "foretaste of southern independence" by labeling the gunfire as "piracy and murder." The *Evening Argus* noted how the "abolition journals of Cincinnati howl over it and are greatly incensed. We would like to see them help themselves." The editor of the *Evansville Daily Journal* was blunt: "Not the slightest interruption of the navigation of the Mississippi will be allowed by the people of the Northwest."

These actions occasioned a renewal of Northern demands for "free navigation of the Mississippi" and led to dozens of protesting and threatening editorials in Yankee newspapers, including many friendly to the new Confederacy. Simultaneously, legislators in state assemblies in the Upper Midwest blasted the "indignities." A number of Chicago packers refused to ship their products to New Orleans and insurance rates were raised on all goods going South.

The guns still frowned from Vicksburg on January 24, the day the *Louisville Daily Journal* reported its receipt of telegraphic dispatches indicating that a battery of sixteen 32-pounders had been planted "upon the Memphis bluff to bring boats to there as they are brought to at Vicksburg." Calmer heads prevailed, however, and the river press along the Ohio was able to shape public sentiment toward peace, keeping it in line with economic interests.

Referring to "King Cotton," the editor of the *Cincinnati Daily Commercial* wrote on January 25 that "His Royal Highness" would continue seeking available markets that could supply him with pork, whiskey, and flour and that he would "not sink steamboats carrying these cargoes." The *New York Herald* on January 28 reasoned that the batteries "were temporary affairs, built to prevent the reinforcement of the forts at points below Vicksburg, more especially those at New Orleans."[21]

By March, the new Confederate government had introduced its revenue system and its rules for use of that portion of the Mississippi over which it claimed sovereignty. The free trade aspects noted above were included; however, there was also introduced "a complicated system of appraisement, inspection, surveying [and] bonding." Whether duties, fees, and imposts would be levied next was the great question facing midwesterners.

Isolationist fears, occasionally expressed earlier, resurfaced, as the winter waned, to be replaced with real worry over war's possibilities. Words which Indiana governor-elect Oliver Morton had expressed the previous November seemed equally true now, even as farmers prepared for planting and rivermen looked to the rise. "We would," he had written, "be shut up in the interior of a continent, surrounded by independent, perhaps hostile nations, through whose territories we could obtain egress to the seaboard only upon such terms as might be agreed to by treaty."

Years later, Evansville historian Milford M. Miller remarked that "Each steamboat from the lower Ohio and Mississippi rivers brought news of the action and feeling of the South and local indignation arose progressively with each steamboat arrival."

President Lincoln notified South Carolina on April 6 that he was sending a peaceful relief expedition to Fort Sumter in Charleston harbor. This was unacceptable to the state, which called for the post's surrender on April 11. When Maj. Robert Anderson refused, shore batteries opened on him next day, compelling his surrender 34 hours later. The bombardment was intense but bloodless; nevertheless, it marked the formal opening of the War Between the States.

The first authenticated dispatch reporting the Sumter bombardment reached Cincinnati, St. Louis, Indianapolis, Chicago, and other Midwestern communities on the evening of April 12. Copies of it were posted in windows and on public bulletin boards. Telegraphic reports kept citizens updated. A Queen City resident remembered that "a spirit of vengeance for the insult of the flag seemed to take possession of the entire population. All thoughts of trade and money-getting were swept completely from the minds of the people." Whether that sentiment was completely true or not, the bloodshed would begin within days of the April 15 White House call for 75,000 volunteers from the state militias to put down the rebellion.[22]

When war triumphed over compromise and reason, a majority in the upper Midwest joined with eastern businessmen and others in a determination to preserve the Union. Southern independence would, in the end, not be recognized and markets would not be allowed to peacefully escape national control. There was, however, a period of confusion and indecision, hurried organization and incidents that occurred in late spring and early summer before the Union and Confederate governments could fully organize themselves for the internecine struggle that was coming.

Fearing the loss of the border states of Kentucky and Missouri and the growing disaffection of the "Little Egypt" area of southern Illinois, the Lincoln administration initially demonstrated its own case of "the slows" (a term later applied to Maj. Gen. George B. McClellan) in the matter of north-south river trade. Uncertain additionally as to its jurisdiction vis-à-vis the states over control of inland river traffic and with President Lincoln playing "for bigger stakes" by not interfering with border state trade, it initially left response and initiative to local officials.

These leaders, particularly Governors Richard Yates of Illinois, Oliver Morton of Indiana, and William Dennison of Ohio, were quite concerned not only with smuggling but also with the idea that the mouth of the Mississippi would be obstructed. They were not at all pleased that the National government had pushed them into the forefront. It was they who would take the premier coercive actions in the West, actions that could be disavowed.

There was no doubt that, in terms of international law, trade with the South after Fort Sumter could have been justly interdicted, but it would be July 13 before Congress authorized President Lincoln to officially end all commerce with the Confederacy and a month after that before the chief executive actually declared that "all commercial intercourse" with the seceded states must stop. Keeping neutral Kentucky and uncertain Missouri in the Union was far more important to Lincoln than trade or several unhappy Midwestern governors.

Southern actions were reported at every Ohio River town as northbound boats arrived. For example, on April 15, happy Southern sympathizers in Uniontown, Kentucky, fired cannon at the riverbank in celebration of the Confederate "victory." The guns distressed many who heard them, including several near Shawneetown, Illinois, 12 miles away.

"With eager ears those at the wharf," as historian Milford put it, "learned of each new incident, rumor, or actual event, a few of which were even reported by the press. Among these was a 30-day grace period granted by the Confederate government "to all Northern owned steamboats within Southern ports to close their business and depart." Mobs, militia and armed ruffians at towns and along the banks harassed steamers from North and South.

A mob at Memphis ordered the captain of the *Mason Gem* to lower the "Stars and Stripes." Rather than comply, the boat headed to its Evansville home port ahead of schedule. En route to New Orleans, the steamer *Westmoreland* was taken by Southern soldiers at Napoleon, Arkansas, on April 25. She escaped when her engineers and captain, biding the right moment, put on full steam, broke their lines, and sped away downstream at full speed. One passenger was killed when the gray-clads opened fire and when the boat reached Cairo, the holes in her looked "as if made by grape-shot fired from a cannon."

Next day, the packet *Mars*, en route to Cincinnati from New Orleans, was seized when she put into Helena, Arkansas. Her cargo consisted of turpentine, resin, and sugar. The hijackers were heard to say that her Ohio owners could "have the boat when they take her and not until then."

Authorities at Memphis halted the steamer *Fanny Bullitt* on April 29 and threatened to arrest her captain, Julius A. "Gus" Lemcke. He was accused of hauling a pair of 32-pounder cannon, shot and shell to Cairo for Yankee troops moving into the key Illinois community, a charge which, if true, would have led to the confiscation of his boat. Upon inspection, his cargo was found to consist of rosin, sugar, and turpentine and the *Fanny Bullitt* was released.[23]

Although lying north of the Ohio River, Cincinnati in 1861 was perceived as a Southern city in terms of trade and culture. The Fort Sumter bombardment, as noted, had a significant psychological impact on its citizens. "From the tenor of the dispatches," editorialized the *Cincinnati Daily Commercial* on April 15, "we should not be surprised to hear that supplies for the South were cut off in all directions. The war fever like the river is booming high." Within a short period, patriotic Cincinnatians were refusing to make shipments to the South and specifically to Kentucky.

Within days, there followed "a miniature civil war between Louisville on one side and her neighboring river cities on the north. As Union sympathizers sought to shut down Southern access to Northern goods, "Louisville became the busiest city in the Ohio valley." Attracted by the chance of huge profits, some enterprising people sought to get their product to this town, which, as the northern terminus of the Louisville and Nashville Railroad, now offered a blockade-free artery into Dixie.

Cincinnati threatened to use force to keep local products from reaching Kentucky, while consideration was also given to blocking the mouth of the Wabash river. "Till this species of neutral rascality is at an end," citizens of Jeffersonville and New Albany were warned by the *Cincinnati Daily Commercial* not to send across the river "one dime's worth of any supplies—not even a pound of butter or a dozen eggs."

On April 18, a mob of Louisville Confederate sympathizers took over a horse battery of two 6-pounders. The fieldpieces were rushed down to a river bend below the city to halt a steamer reported to be en route from St. Louis to Pittsburg with arms for Pennsylvanians. When it was determined that the cargo was, in fact, consigned to Kentucky militiamen, the cannon were meekly returned. Next day, provisions for Nashville were seized by Cincinnati officials, along with a large shipment of powder and 30 boxes of guns destined for Tennessee and Arkansas via Louisville.

Although Governor Dennison promised a Louisville delegation that he would not interfere with cross-river trade, he could not prevent strong Union sympathizers from acting on their own. A number of merchants in the Queen City declared in a formal resolution that they would not trade with any state which had not professed loyalty to Washington, whether neutral or not. Others organized a home guard to suppress contraband trade. With no legal authority, they nevertheless took it upon themselves to search depots, watch steamers, and order all suspicious bales or boxes returned to the warehouse.

Buckeye fears deepened in the weeks following Sumter and her conciliatory view of Kentucky's self-proclaimed neutrality evaporated. On April 21, Governor Dennison ordered telegraph operators not to transmit armament requests for any parties except the State of Ohio or the Federal government. A week later, he required railroads and express companies to inspect for, apprehend, and stop all contraband headed south. The legislature also set up an inspection system to examine all freight entering or leaving Ohio. At Cincinnati, home guardsmen instituted inspections of Covington- and Newport-bound ferryboat passengers, but these and other searches could not stop the easy and illicit Kentucky trade.[24]

Anti-contraband, anti-rebellion sentiment along the Indiana riverbank was, in some places, as hot as it was in Ohio, but in other locales it was less hostile. When local captain J.B. Archer put his steamer *Commercial* into the Evansville wharf from "down the river" on

Son of War of 1812 hero Commodore John Rodgers, Cmdr. John Rodgers II (1812–1882) was the architect of the Army's 1861 Western Flotilla and the man who purchased the steamers brought into service as the timberclads *Lexington*, *Conestoga*, and *Tyler*. An intrepid explorer, he also oversaw the initial construction of the Eads ironclads, while finding time to serve as captain of the *Tyler* on several missions. Having run afoul of Maj. Gen. John C. Frémont, Rodgers was succeeded by Flag Officer Andrew H. Foote in September. Rodgers later served as captain of several monitors off the East Coast. He was commissioned a rear admiral in 1869 (Naval Historical Center).

April 19, he refused to lower his new Confederate flag. A well-regarded member of the town's citizenry, he was nevertheless ordered to end the insult or leave. He soon departed to New Albany, where that city's wharfmaster gave him 10 minutes to comply. Archer cast off immediately rather than comply.

About the same time, other steamers were reported en route from Louisville with Kentucky volunteers for the Southern army. One of these, the *Autocrat*, was fingered by informers, but when she put into Evansville she was deserted save for her crew. Upon departing, she paddled over to Owensboro, where she took on men for the Rebel cause.

Another boat, the *Peytona*, was carrying secessionist troops. Rather than approach Evansville, where freight and passengers awaited her, she hugged the Kentucky shore and put in at Henderson. There she was met by sympathizers who fired off a cannon and muskets, made speeches, and escorted the recruits to the Kentucky town's famous Hancock House for feasting and additional oratory. Supporters boasted they would have "invaded" Evansville if people from that town had made an effort to stop the *Peytona*. Although Governor Morton asked President Lincoln on May 4 to halt the easy and growing contraband traffic with Kentucky, no formal answer was received. The state legislature set up a committee to decide what state trade regulations were required, but no immediate decisions were taken.[25]

Of the three Yankee states bordering the Ohio, Illinois was the least concerned with Kentucky trade. Rather, she sought to regulate trade along her river frontiers, acting directly against it with a blockade at Cairo. The decision by the Springfield government to act was not taken without some risk. Southern Illinois, as historian Drew E. VandeCreek has noted, was a hotbed of secessionist sentiment. The *Cairo City Gazette* declared that "the sympathies of our people are mainly with the South." A public outdoor meeting in Pope County echoed the South's right to secede, and a rally in Williamson County sought to split "Little Egypt" from Illinois and join the Confederacy.

On April 16, Illinois Governor Richard Yates was convinced that something had to be done to secure Cairo, at the southern tip of his state. That day he had heard from the co-owner of the *Chicago Daily Tribune*, Dr. Charles H. Ray, who pointed out the geography of the location and called it the most important military position in the entire west. Not only did the town command the commerce of the great Ohio and Mississippi rivers that passed alongside it, but also those streams were, in fact, fortifications protecting loyal Illinois from the South.

Ray was not the only one who thought highly of Cairo's location. Its importance seemed to be common knowledge all along the rivers and with the U.S. War Department. On April 18, Secretary of War Simon Cameron asked that Illinois take over strategic Cairo just as soon as a force could be raised to do so. So universal was sentiment concerning the value of the town's location that Confederate Col. M.C. Galloway, stationed at Memphis, quickly learned of the Cameron wire. He in turn messaged Confederate war secretary Leroy P. Walker that "It was telegraphed from Washington to Cairo [Springfield] to-day that Cairo will be made base of operations on the Mississippi River and several Southern ports will be blockaded."

Next day, Richard Yates became the first northwest governor to take direct military action against Southern interests, action recommended by others but occasioned by his receipt of the Cameron telegram. The state leader turned right around the same day and ordered that a militia expedition be immediately dispatched south from Chicago and surrounding communities to the town via the Illinois Central Railroad.

With four six-pounder cannon, 44 horses, and 595 untried troops entrained in 26 cars behind two locomotives, this expeditionary force was under the command of Gen. Richard Kellogg Swift, assisted by Capt. John Pope, U.S.A. These first Union regiments activated in the Civil War western theater reached the tip of the state on April 22. They remained quartered in their rail cars overnight, cars that were parked on the railway tracks just inside the earthen Ohio River levee.

Swift learned from the mayor of the town that threats had been received to blow up the tall levees or the long flights of wooden steps that led down from them at street intersections to the level part of the town. The mayor also reported that a group of 80 deputized loyalists, the Cairo Guard, were patrolling and no incidents had occurred. Early on the 23rd the troops detrained and set up their positions along the riverbank at the confluence of the Mississippi and the Ohio. Many camped in a brickyard and the fairgrounds.

Fiercely determined, the expedition was poorly armed, having only such shotguns and rifles that could be obtained in Chicago area stores or from relatives or homes prior to departure. There was no shot, shell or canister for the cannon, but these would be "provided with slugs hurriedly made" locally. In Springfield, Governor Yates speedily convened the Illinois General Assembly in special session to take care of another missing detail: legal authorization for the volunteers' movement.

James B. Eads (1820–1887), a Mississippi River entrepreneur, was among the first to recommend a concrete plan of action to the Federal government for gunboat warfare along the western rivers. His plan, which envisioned the use of armored vessels (including some of his own) converted from steamboats was presented to the Navy Department and resulted in the dispatch of Cmdr. John Rodgers to Cincinnati (*Battles and Leaders*).

Copies of a proclamation from Yates were handed out to citizens and posted indicating that the bluecoats had arrived through "no distrust of their loyalty to the Government, but under orders from the War Department at Washington, to repel expected invasion from the States." About the same time, a fieldpiece from the Chicago Light Artillery and soldiers from the Chicago Zouaves were detailed aboard the large steam tugboat *Swallow*, which thus became the first of several extemporaneous "gunboats" the Northern army manned exclusive of the U.S. Navy on western rivers during the war.

The decision to garrison Cairo turned out to be one of the more important decisions made by any state government in the early days of the Civil War. "In the hands of the Union," wrote historian Coulter 45 years after the takeover, "Cairo, the most southern point in northern territory, was a dagger pointing at the heart of the confederacy." Still, the town's local economy was paralyzed as commerce downstream to New Orleans dried up. Within weeks, the triweekly Cairo–New Orleans service would be suspended.

Within a few days of arrival, three camps had been established by the Illinois volunteers: one at the point where a distillery was torn down to accommodate an artillery battery; one three miles from town on the Mississippi levee where another battery was erected; and the third on the Ohio levee at a sawmill below the mouth of the Little Cache River. The largest of these, at the boot sole of the peninsula, was called Camp Defiance. Gen. Swift was succeeded in command of the garrison on April 24 upon the arrival from Springfield of Col. Benjamin M. Prentiss and seven newly raised volunteer companies.

As might be anticipated, the exuberant South was not immediately impressed with the several thousand men camped out in a town whose reputation for decorum left much to be desired. Upon learning of these Cairo invaders, the editor of the *Charleston Courier* wrote on April 30 that "fully three hundred are supposed to be negroes, and the remainder have been picked up from the gutters of Chicago and among the Dutch [German immigrants]." If an attack were properly conducted, the South Carolina paper continued, "a force of one thousand firm-hearted Southern men would drive them from the place."[26]

The Yankee soldiers and artillerymen at Cairo wasted no time in exercising their control over commerce headed north into the Ohio River from the Mississippi or continuing south on the "Father of Waters." Among their inaugural missions was the suppression of the Galena lead traffic and the contraband trade in dry goods conducted by Louisville, St. Louis, and Cincinnati with the rebellious cities on the Lower Mississippi. The *Cairo City Weekly Gazette* summarized the blockade for its readers on April 26: "No provisions headed for the South can pass through Cairo. All steamers leaving Cairo for insurrectionary ports will be examined. Any arms, munitions of war, or other supplies will be taken off."

Boats passed Cairo daily carrying on this "Southern trade." On April 25, Col. Prentiss' cannoneers fired a shot across the bow of the steamboat *Baltic,* forcing her to land and submit to an examination of her cargo. A more serious incident was about to occur involving reportedly illegal goods that were about to be shipped from St. Louis to Nashville.

Governor Yates received intelligence on April 24 that a pair of steamboats were about to depart St. Louis transporting contraband arms and ammunition. The vigilant state commander-in-chief immediately wired Col. Prentiss asking that they be halted. The suspect steamers *C.E. Hillman* and *John D. Perry* duly appeared out on the Mississippi about eight miles above Cairo on the morning of April 26. Alerted by Prentiss, the patrolling *Swallow* approached and hailed the deeply laden *Hillman,* demanding she stop. Her progress labored, the craft failed to respond, requiring that the faster militarized craft come alongside. Capt. Smith of the Chicago Zouaves went aboard to make inquiry and order the boat to Cairo for inspection. The captain of the Cumberland-bound steamer, protesting that the Illinois officer (whose commission came from Governor Yates and not the U.S. government) had no right to stop him, instead tied up at the Bird's Point wharf boat, refusing to take his boat across to Cairo for interrogation. When the *Swallow* indicated she would be fired upon if she did not move, the *Hillman*'s crew took their baggage and abandoned ship.

After the *Hillman*'s men deserted, the *Swallow* put aboard sufficient men to move her over to the Illinois shore. At the same time but with far less fanfare, the *Perry*, en route from St. Louis to Memphis, was also brought to for review. When no contraband was found, she was released.

When the manifest and cargo of the *C.E. Hillman* were checked, however, that steamboat was found to be transporting 100 tons of lead (3,500 pigs) consigned to the State of Tennessee, which was still 10 days away from its formal secession, along with a thousand kegs of powder, crates of revolvers, and cavalry accoutrements. All of these shipments, along with the steamer, were seized. Captain Henry T. Dexter of the Cairo to Evansville mail steamer

Charley Bowen later provided an eyewitness account of the incident to the editor of the Evansville newspaper.

The reaction in Nashville was predictable. The Tennessee General Assembly vigorously protested that Illinois was "making war upon the commerce of non-seceding states," closing up avenues of trade and causing the people to suffer "all the privations of a blockade." Tennessee governor Isham G. Harris wired War Secretary Walker on the day of the seizure, apprising the Confederate government at Montgomery of the development. On April 27, the *Nashville Union* wondered if "the Governor of Illinois intends to send us in bullets the hundred tons of lead which he has piratically obtained from the *Hillman*."

Two days later, Governor Harris wrote a scathing letter to President Lincoln protesting the seizure and the interruption of free trade and demanding to know if Washington approved the Illinois action. He simultaneously took possession of $5,000 cash and $75,000 worth of Tennessee bonds held by the U.S. Customs Collector at Nashville, property which would be held "in trust" until the National government restored the *Hillman* and the state's property.

Although Secretary Cameron approved of the seizure, the *Hillman*, minus its contraband cargo, was released to its owners on April 29. The same day, another steamer, the *Julius H. Smith*, slipped by Cairo and made it to Paducah with a Confederacy-bound cargo of 450 Colt rifles. Still, from this time on, every effort was made to interdict all further shipments to posts under insurrectionary control.[27]

Although no general commercial policy was announced by the Federal government at the outset of the conflict, there were rules against contraband. Indeed, as early as April 19, President Lincoln had established a blockade against the ports of those states in rebellion. The problem at this point in the insurrection's uncertain history was that a number of Southern and border states were still loyal or officially loyal and not subject to Federal blockade. Whatever action could be taken from Washington had to be carefully cloaked by revenue and internal security requirements. As long as Kentucky claimed "neutrality" and the National government hesitated, "the Confederacy profited very substantially."

On May 2, about two weeks after the fall of Fort Sumter, Treasury Secretary Salmon P. Chase began the slow Federal strangulation of the contraband trade along the big rivers. That day he issued a circular to U.S. Customs surveyors, collectors, and other officers ordering them to examine the manifests of steamboats, flatboats, and railroad cars they believed headed south and to seize all "arms munitions of war, provisions, or other supplies." Under this and subsequent writs, almost everything became contraband down to and including "all books of military instruction."

Initially, the instructions received by different agents conflicted. Local customs officers were at first left to determine just which areas were held by insurrectionists and what, in fact, was contraband. It was still, and would remain, impossible to prevent goods from reaching the Confederacy via Kentucky, but officials in both cities and states on the northern banks of the Ohio River were determined to try.

Adding to the confusion were orders received from Lt. Gen. Scott by the Illinois troops at Cairo, also on May 2. The commanding general was concerned that the detention of cargoes headed to Kentucky from states along the Ohio was seen as "irritating to Kentucky." Such interdiction was to be halted. When Maj. Gen. McClellan at Cincinnati heard of this on May 7, he fired off a memo questioning Scott's restriction and asking if he had discretion to stop shipments known to be headed to the Southern army. The next day, McClellan was reassured that Secretary Cameron had actually decided on May 2 "that provisions must be stopped at Cairo."

Meanwhile, Secretary Chase's orders did not reach the customs agents and wharfmasters of all of the Ohio River communities for another week. When they were received at Evansville, historian Milford later reported, the policy was "naturally taken very seriously." In fact, "with this edict, the wharf assumed a martial air." On the day it arrived, the *Glendale* passed up the river, her calliope playing "Yankee Doodle" as loudly as possible. It seemed that "enthusiasm for the Northern cause was raised another degree or so."[28]

CHAPTER 2

Commander Rodgers Goes West, April–June 1861

IN MAY 1861, ABOUT A MONTH after the fall of Fort Sumter, U.S. Navy Commander John Rodgers was detailed West in a move so little noticed at the time that it was not recorded in those Northern newspapers, such as the *Philadelphia Enquirer* and *New York Herald*, which regularly reported military and naval postings. Rodgers, a well-connected and knowledgeable officer, was to "consult the interests of the government and the western country in preparing a protection to the commerce of the river." It was he who would bear "the burden of the difficult construction and organization of the navy's stepchild, the river fleet."

As Rodgers traveled to Cincinnati, in the company of noted engineer James B. Eads, he undoubtedly took opportunities en route to beef up his slight knowledge of the Mississippi Valley, its rivers, people, and commerce. It is likely that he learned of, or refreshed his knowledge of, the various local events involving trade and regional intercourse and incidents outlined in the previous chapter. He probably knew or sensed from conversations held before his departure from Washington, D.C., that some midwesterners and others were no longer talking much about the river trade. These folks now looked at the great waterways "in terms of military strategy"—highways over which to move the soldiers who would snuff out the rebellion by carrying the fight south.[1]

When news of Fort Sumter's surrender on April 13 and Lincoln's call-up were received in St. Louis, Missouri, two members of the president's cabinet, the new attorney general, Edward Bates, and the new postmaster general, Montgomery Blair, had already been in discussions with the chief executive, himself a westerner from Illinois, concerning the movements on the Mississippi River. They knew that the "Father of Waters" was the key to success in the middle of the country. "Hold the stream and you hold all," as Fletcher Pratt put it years later. According to historian Gibson, Bates was "probably the first person to propose to Lincoln" a Cairo blockade. This concept was easily agreed upon, but how could it be accomplished?

"At this point, Bates and Montgomery exchanged glances," Pratt writes. "The latter nodded and both Missourians together began to speak of James B. Eads, the St. Louis apple boy who had made himself an engineer and a millionaire...." Both of the Missourians had known the entrepreneur. "Though not large in stature," according to John D. Milligan, "he combined vast amounts of confidence and ambition with genuine engineering talents." On his own, Eads had written his friend Bates regarding his concerns over the "Father of Waters." Later made famous by his construction of the steel St. Louis arch bridge, the 40 year old called for aggressive action to defeat the Rebels and suggested he had a plan for "vigorous action" that might prove helpful in wresting the Lower Mississippi away from the South.

Bates also believed that the Mississippi should be guarded at Cairo and a naval force created to serve on that stream. Eads' letter provided the former congressman with the first realistic plan that he could present to the president and he determined to do so as soon as possible. In his April 17 acknowledgment of the riverman's message, Bates advised Eads that he had already been in contact with Lincoln and his cabinet regarding the substance of his message and that his presence would soon be required in the nation's capital, as "it will be necessary to have the aid of the most thorough knowledge of our Western rivers and the use of steam on them...."

Capt. Eads received Bates' summons on April 24 and immediately entrained for Washington, D.C., where he arrived several days later, "gaunt and plausible, with a headful of ideas and a trunkful of drawings." After detraining and acquiring his baggage, Eads made his way to the Justice Department where he and Bates conferred on the engineer's ideas: the Mississippi and its tributaries would be blockaded and then retrieved using, among other resources, a flotilla of gunboats converted from three owned by his Missouri Wrecking Company.

On April 29, Eads was taken by Acting General Bates before President Lincoln and the cabinet to explain his ideas for creating a river navy to aid in a campaign to first blockade and then to recover the river valley. The proposed crusade would be based on an amphibious force operating from the low-lying town of Cairo, where the Ohio River flowed into the Mississippi and where those two streams physically separated pro–Union Illinois from the border states of Kentucky and Missouri. Most of the cabinet thought these ideas were workable, except Secretary of War Simon Cameron, a Pennsylvanian who, according to Boynton "...seemed to think that the idea of Judge Bates in regard to gunboats for the rivers was useless or impracticable, and manifested no interest whatever in the plan."[2]

James Eads, who also delivered his ideas in writing the same day at the request of an appreciative Navy Secretary Welles, also received a positive read on them from Commodore Hiram Paulding, then at the Washington Navy Yard. Paulding examined the engineer's plan and quizzed him in person on several points before quickly "reporting in favor of its adoption." There was, however, no immediate word from the government on whether or not it would press for implementation. War Secretary Cameron continued to appear "wholly indifferent." Other opinions and concepts emerged in the days ahead that would radically change that Keystone attitude.[3]

Eads and Bates were not the only ones considering plans to militarily end the Southern insurgency. On April 18, Ohio governor William Dennison and others sought the counsel of George B. McClellan, who was then residing in Cincinnati as president of the Ohio and Mississippi Railroad, quite possibly the same Cincinnati–St. Louis line over which both Eads and Rodgers made part of their trips east and west. McClellan, a well-regarded former U.S. Army engineer captain was then at the height of his organizational and administrative genius. About the same time, McClellan, who was seeking a military role for himself in the spreading conflict, sent a report of his own to Dennison on the defense of the Queen City, which he emphasized was "the most important strategical point in the valley of the Ohio."[4]

On the strength of this report and recommendations from prominent Buckeyes, Dennison, with Washington's approval, appointed McClellan to head Ohio's militia on April 23. The railway expert immediately wrote to Lt. Gen. Winfield Scott asking the general-in-chief to confirm his opinion that his duty lay in the protection of Cincinnati and the Ohio River line, as well as the assumption of a nonaggressive stance toward still-loyal but confused Kentucky and Virginia.

Because the telegraph wires to Washington were down, McClellan sent his report by messenger. As he waited for a response that would take a week to arrive, the new Brig. Gen. of volunteers immediately set to work bringing order out of the chaos that was then rampant in Ohio military circles. Setting up a new camp at Cincinnati that he named for the governor, the man who would one day be known as "The Little Napoleon" dashed off orders left and right for all manner of goods and personnel changes or organizational improvements, readily agreed to by state officials who deferred to his decisions and stayed out of the way.

On April 27, "Little Mac," another nickname by which McClellan was known, sent another progress report to Scott, even though he had yet to receive a reply to his first report. A portion of the narrative was a grand strategic recipe "intended to relieve the pressure upon Washington, & tending to bring the war to a speedy close." For starters, key points along the Ohio had to be garrisoned, especially Cairo and Cincinnati. Then victory could be achieved in one of two ways. Send an army through western Virginia and down the Kanawha valley to Richmond or send a two pronged attack, one pincher via Nashville and the other via South Carolina and Georgia, that would encircle the Rebels. This plan, sent upstairs to the national leadership during the chaotic first weeks of the Rebellion, has been called "the first recorded attempt at an overall strategy for prosecuting the war." It beat Eads' suggestions onto paper by two days and Scott's by a week.[5]

On May 3, Union army chief Lt. Gen. Scott replied to McClellan describing his own strategy for crushing the rebellion. The elderly leader, who was largely immobile and was believed out of touch by some, had been a military commander since the War of 1812. He knew war and he knew that any fight with the South would be long and difficult. When President Lincoln had called for Union volunteers back in April, Scott warned him that if the South were invaded at any point any time soon, "I will guarantee that at the end of the year you will be further from a settlement than you are now." His unheeded warning would hauntingly return at Bull Run creek in July.

But now it was springtime and Scott had the opportunity to refine and offer his strategic concept in some detail. At the heart of his victory formula, according to most historians, lay the idea of strangling the South along the Mississippi and its tributaries, using inland river highways to mount and support amphibious assaults to crush the strong points of the divided parts, eventually reopening the mighty stream to United States commerce. The elderly general based his strategy on a powerful U.S. Navy coastal blockade and called for a decisive "movement down the Mississippi to the ocean, with a cordon of posts at proper points ... the object being to clear out and keep open this great line of communication...." Scott's New Orleans push from Cairo would be "spearheaded by a specially built fleet of gunboats." The whole scheme when fully implemented would encircle the eastern Confederacy and crush it. He hinted that McClellan would have charge of any enterprise undertaken under the plan as commander of a new military Department of the Ohio that would be announced within days.

This was the famous Western river-based "Anaconda Plan." It was often ridiculed and would not be fast or simple to apply, but, in the end it was, with modifications, followed as the basis of the Union's war-fighting master strategy. The concept had the advantage of being easy for everyone, from private to president, to understand and get behind. "From this time on," wrote T. Harry Williams, "the occupation of the line of the great river became an integral part of his [Lincoln's] strategic thinking." The Confederacy, for its part, devised no real countermeasures to the Union formula and such preparations as could be made to resist the scheme would, in the end, prove useless.[6]

While Generals Scott and McClellan were exchanging ideas, the midwestern interdiction campaign continued from Cairo. Cannon fire was heard again on May 3 when a warning shot skipped ahead of the steamer *Sir William Wallace*, en route downstream from St. Louis. After coming to the dock for inspection, she was released. Later, the *Alonzo Child* was also brought to for examination. Numerous craft passed down the river, deeply laden, but not all were inspected. A grace period, due to expire at the end of the month, was in place and those vessels transporting grain and cattle were allowed to steam down. It was suspected that some of the vessels allowed to pass actually had contraband aboard. Meanwhile, as "Zouave," the *New York Times* correspondent at the tip of Illinois reported on May 5, numerous steamers were heading up the Ohio, loaded with refugees who had fled the South leaving all of their possessions behind.[7]

James B. Eads remained in Washington as May swept on and wondered what was happening with his proposal. The Cabinet now had access to the plans of Scott, McClellan, and Eads, to say nothing of those from a large number of other Northern celebrities, from politicos to newspaper owners. Along the Ohio River, according to historian Ambler, many supported the concept that a fleet of gunboats could not only aid in river defense, but also serve "as an indispensable auxiliary in the aggressive warfare which was to be waged."

A few citizens had concerns that plunging fire from Rebel shore batteries, such as those at Memphis or Vicksburg, could destroy them. The editor of the *Cincinnati Daily Commercial* was not one of these. He insisted in his May 8 issue that protected gunboats could defy shore gunners and could, in any event, be "indispensable as convoys." Additionally, they would give local rivermen choosing to serve aboard a chance to "try their prowess, nothing being too hazardous for them."

Secretary of War Simon Cameron, convinced that an inland river effort was not a marine enterprise, now refused to recognize any U.S. Navy jurisdiction over an inland stream. Pointing out that the outfitting of any western river gunboats was Army business—sort of "a floating artillery wing," he prepared to ask Lincoln and his colleagues to support his turnabout contention.

Secretary Welles, coming off his subordinates' badly mismanaged loss of the Gosport Navy Yard, was preoccupied with the "immense problems of the Atlantic and Gulf blockade." The great-bearded former Connecticut newspaperman was probably not disappointed when, at the next cabinet meeting following the Eads presentation, the secretary of war suddenly "claimed jurisdiction over the whole movement." Cameron's powerful associates agreed with his position that any western naval force should really come under the purview of the army. If President Lincoln and the others had required an inland river flotilla plan from Welles, it would have required him to undertake the time-consuming prospect of developing a comprehensive amphibious warfare scheme, as historian Chamberlain put it, "capable alike for assault of fortified positions or to meet attack from such naval combinations as the South might organize."

Hubbub reigned in the capital city and in every department of the government over the next several weeks, while many of the best and brightest military and naval officers quit the Federal service to join those of their respective states. The Navy Department had many more pressing concerns than building a few craft out in the middle of the country. So it was that in the confusion, excitement, and inter-service rivalries which marked the Federal buildup, the Eads plan was amalgamated into one sponsored, financed, and controlled by the War Department.

On May 6, the Confederate congress passed an act recognizing a state of war with the federal government and authorized the issuance of Letters of Marques allowing private vessels to capture U.S. merchantmen. Maryland remained unsettled following the Baltimore riots of April 19 and troops coming to the Federal capital still had to be brought down Chesapeake Bay from the mouth of the Susquehanna to a railhead at Annapolis, Maryland. On May 9, the U.S. Naval Academy was transferred out of Annapolis to Newport, RI, to keep it out of Confederate hands. During these troubled days, apparently, no one remembered to officially notify Capt. Eads concerning the cabinet's decision on his proposal.

The U.S. War Department officially established the Department of the Ohio on May 10 covering the states of Ohio, Indiana, and Illinois. Maj. Gen. McClellan, at Cincinnati, received command. Meanwhile, Maryland was controlled by bayonet and guerrilla warfare and internal civil war was now rampant in Missouri. There were fatal riots in St. Louis over the actions of army man Capt. Nathaniel Lyon, an arch-opponent of South-leaning Democratic governor Claiborne F. Jackson. Under the direction of the postmaster general's brother, Francis P. Blair, Jr., the red-bearded Lyon temporarily halted a Confederate buildup by taking over a militia camp on the edge of the city.

Efforts at conciliation failed along the Ohio and Mississippi that day. Fortunately for the North, soldiers were rapidly working on the fortifications and artillery positions facing the Mississippi River side of Cairo. The reporter in town for the *Chicago Daily Tribune* noted on May 19 that batteries had been erected on the Ohio and Mississippi levees for a distance of three miles on each river. Fourteen brass 6-pounders and a 12-pounder howitzer were distributed over the area.

At Louisville two days later, the steamers *Masonic Gem* and *Pocahontas* prepared to depart for Bowling Green, Kentucky, up the Green River. Parts of their cargoes were marked for Richmond and Nashville and were reported by Northern spies as contraband. When word of these shipments reached Evansville, four companies of the 11th Indiana Regiment went aboard the chartered *W.V. Gillum* and headed off on an interception course for the mouth of the Green River. The Evansville expedition was quickly aborted when word arrived that the boats had not cast off from Louisville after all.[8]

On May 14, the day after the U.S. Army occupied Baltimore, Navy Secretary Welles sent Eads' April 29 proposal over to the War Department where, in light of the recent cabinet decision, "the subject more properly belongs." He also, and belatedly, wrote the engineer, explaining that he had done so. Having undoubtedly already learned the fate of his plan from Bates or maybe unofficially from Welles himself, Eads prepared for his return to St. Louis.

The first problem facing Secretary Cameron and his generals in implementing the Eads-Scott "Anaconda" strategy was one of materiel. There were no regular Union gunboats on the rivers and Western military officers, quite capable, as we have seen, of putting fieldpieces on commercial boats, had no idea exactly what was involved. Turning back to the navy for technical help, Cameron received Welles' promise to speedily make consultants available.

Also on May 14, Cameron wired newly promoted Maj. Gen. McClellan, ordering him to confer with Eads and any navy men sent west. The War Department, the secretary noted, liked Eads ideas, but wanted their man in the field to have an opinion. Once "Little Mac" had heard them out and signed on, he could then place orders for preparation of the boats everyone believed necessary. It likewise appears probable, notes historian Gibson, that, at the time of these interservice interchanges, Lt. Gen. Scott dispatched Brig. Gen. Joseph G. Totten to the Midwest to review the river transportation infrastructure.

When McClellan received the war secretary's directive, sent on the same day as his Maj. Gen. promotion, the busy Buckeye was completing Ohio's mobilization, turning the mob of men, organizational turmoil, and equipage chaos handed him by Governor Dennison into something approaching an actual army. He was even enjoying himself, announcing to a staff officer that this project was really more fun "than running railroads and adding up columns of dollars and cents."

McClellan, who would one day incur Lincoln's disgust for having what the President called "the slows," was not only a general but also a businessman who, in fact, knew that he was methodical. At a time when fast-buck men were everywhere besieging the government with schemes to quickly deliver everything from horses to uniforms and victuals, he made a deliberate effort to know a project fully, no matter how small, before authorizing it. He feared the loss of time that failure could bring "far more than the loss of money."

During his days with the railroad, the general learned something about rivers and steamboats, far less than Eads, of course, but probably more than any of the as yet unknown navy people who were coming to help. Turning steamers into gunboats, on the other hand, required some expert thought and for this McClellan initially turned to one of the more knowledgeable rivermen in town, "Commodore" William J. Kountz.

Born in Wellsville, Ohio, in 1817, Kountz worked his way up, first with keelboats and then with steamers, becoming a steamboat pilot in 1845. In the following years, he captained and owned numerous craft and built a reputation as an expert on river transport. Along the way he also became known for his quarrelsomeness, obstinacy, and meddling. By 1860, Kountz, now a resident of Allegheny, Pennsylvania, operated a fleet of eight boats, including the well-known packets *City of Memphis* and *Crystal Palace*. According to historian Dave Dawley, Kountz would continue to actively accumulate steamers into the 1880s.

McClellan and Kountz were friends and business associates as well as water-rail competitors before the war. In 1858, while with the Illinois Central, McClellan and St. Louis rivermen and businessmen established the St. Louis and New Orleans Packet Company, which began operations with 10 steamers in 1860. Days after his appointment as Department of the Ohio commander, the former railroad president turned to Kountz for advice and assistance in matters related to river transportation and also, in accordance with his own thinking and that of Lt. Gen. Scott, the process for turning riverboats into warships. McClellan soon appointed Kountz his superintendent of river transportation. It is clear that neither the soldier nor the civilian commodore had any preconceived ideas about just how much military shipping or naval force was going to be required or exactly how it should be organized. It is equally apparent that they were having conversations on the subject before Eads or his U.S. Navy associate arrived.[9]

On May 16, Cmdr. Rodgers, on duty at the U.S. Navy Hydrographic Office, received anticipated active-service orders. He was probably not consulted prior to their receipt and may have been surprised to learn that he was to report to Maj. Gen. McClellan at Cincinnati "in regard to the expediency of establishing a naval armament on the Mississippi and Ohio Rivers." The new Department of the Ohio commander, who earlier in the month had evidenced an interest in safeguarding the region in his correspondence with Lt. Gen. Scott, was to be consulted not only out of courtesy to his command position, but also because, as the chief War Department deputy in the region, he would have charge of building, under authority of the quartermaster general, any waterborne force.

Accommodating Cameron two days earlier, Secretary Welles had cut orders to send the most knowledgeable available sailor in town out West to serve as nautical advisor to the soldiers. At War Department urging, he would accompany Eads home, stopping first at Cincin-

On the Ohio. A stern-wheeler heads towards Cincinnati from Cairo on the Ohio River. This scene would likely resemble the scene viewed by Cmdr. John Rodgers as he traveled east following his first visit to the tip of Illinois (Library of Congress).

nati to confer with Maj. Gen. McClellan and going on to Cairo to inspect for possible acquisition one of the largest boats in which the engineer had an interest.

Secretary Welles may have taken the time to brief Rodgers on his mission's restrictions before his departure and emphasized that the Polar explorer's assignment came with very limited authority. Although the commander would fall under army orders and funding, he would be allowed to requisition his own department only for sailors and naval ordnance. Conversely, he could make all the recommendations to the War Department that Cameron and his generals would hear. Whatever problems arose under this anomalous permit, Rodgers was expected to work out with McClellan or local military officers, municipal officials, businessmen, and rivermen. A couple of junior U.S. Navy officers would be detailed later to help him assist the military, but, in the end, western river gunboats were army business, not that of Welles, and they were not to cost or unduly concern the Navy Department.[10]

As he entrained with Eads for Cincinnati, Rodgers may have reflected upon his own time in command of the congressionally authorized North Pacific Exploring and Surveying Expedition. Originally second in command of that enterprise when it set sail aboard the U.S.S. *Vincennes* in June 1853, Lt. Rodgers was forced to take it over in July 1854. After having charted many islands, the expedition's original chief, Cmdr. Cadwalader Ringgold, was taken seriously ill when the sloop of war arrived off the coast of China and, by order of Cdr. Matthew Calbraith Perry, was invalided home.

Often out of sight of land, away from U.S. jurisdiction, and definitely unable to report to Washington, Rodgers relied upon his own initiative and good judgment to successfully complete the North Sea mission, returning to New York on July 18, 1856. The necessities of "acting out the exigencies of the hour" encountered in these years of independent command taught the famous commodore's son the ability to operate without undue oversight or, in his opinion, the obligation to pen constant progress reports for his superiors. It became his practice to labor in public silence, whether while compiling the survey results in the years before the war or while addressing the Mississippi gunboat requirement of 1861. Rodgers may, in the words of Johnson, his biographer, "have disliked the prospect" of serving under any army general, especially one 14 years younger. He may now also have believed that he was entrusted to find a largely unsupported success from a midwestern challenge every bit as mysterious to the eastern naval establishment as the Bering Sea. Welles' unusual charge was, in the words of naval historian Ivan Musicant, "an inefficient way of running a war. Its consequences were felt soon enough, and the arrangement would not last."

Used to issuing orders or receiving them, Rodgers "had a reputation as an officer who was not wont to be deterred by obstacles in the performance of his duties." He saw small need to "report little obstructions only to suggest means of overcoming them." The explorer's honest, no nonsense, and usually blunt approach to problem solving, though admirable to some people in those days of its absence, would turn out, unfortunately for him, not to be politic.

Within days of his Cincinnati arrival, Cmdr. Rodgers learned that the duty of a western army advisor was not the same as captaining a ship from its quarterdeck. The obstructions to be faced in Cincinnati or St. Louis were not physical, like doldrums or icebergs, but human: greed and graft, cronyism and political favoritism, unusual boat building and construction requirements, strange acquisition procedures, an often-unwieldy military structure, overworked, imperious, or uncertain army commanders, egotistical rivermen, lack of supply, unfit sailors— and that was before a single Confederate was seen. Secretary Welles and the Navy Department were "burdened with nearer and more important duties." Neither would be pleased when the straight-shooting sailor steamed full-speed ahead into all of the aforementioned shoals and, in less than a calendar quarter, forced a leadership change.[11]

Out at Cairo where gunboats would eventually drop anchor, Col. Prentiss was determined to make a test case of the Illinois blockade and to try out in its enforcement the cannon recently placed along the town's levees. On the afternoon of April 18, the transport *Fred Lorenz* steamed around the point, her Stars and Stripes waving bravely in the breeze. As she made to turn up the Ohio, a cannonball brought her to the dock, where she was detained.

Upon inspection, it was found that the cargo of the St. Louis–based steamer consisted of provisions manifested for Paducah and Louisville. A telegraph was sent off to Washington asking what should be done with her: whether she should be permitted to proceed or forced to return back up the Mississippi. Prentiss received his answer early on May 19. The *Fred Lorenz* was turned back to St. Louis with her cargo, deemed "contraband," untouched. "The blockade," cheered the *Tribune* man, "was complete."

The unhappy end of Rogers' Mississippi River saga was in the future. Now the uncertain prospect of helping to establish a western naval armament lay before him. On April 19, he and Capt. Eads detrained at Cincinnati, where they were met and escorted to McClellan's headquarters. There the ocean sailor and the considerably younger and much shorter theater commander cautiously began what would become something of an affinity. For his part, the Buckeye general was very happy to have "an officer of Rodgers' standing and ability" assigned to his command. The commander found McClellan agreeable and, in his case at least, not interested in gunboat micromanagement.

Quite possibly with Eads present and maybe Cdr. Kountz, Rodgers and McClellan discussed what should initially be done on this matter of "interior nonintercourse." It was quickly determined that Rodgers would travel out to Illinois and Missouri to learn firsthand what exactly Eads was proposing for the defense of Cairo.

During his journey, the naval commander was to stop not only at the confluence of the Ohio and the Mississippi, but also at St. Louis and Mound City as well. At those places he was to "obtain all possible information as to the construction of gunboats, floating batteries, etc." McClellan formally directed Rodgers to visit with Eads at St. Louis and to look over the vessels of his Missouri Wrecking Company mentioned in his April communication with Secretary Welles. If they were acceptable and could be converted into warships, "Little Mac" specifically directed Rodgers to "please close the purchase on such terms as you think the interests of the Government require." If Eads' boats wouldn't do, the sailor was to find others that could be turned into gunboats and let the general "know at once the terms on which they can be had."

Although Cmdr. Rodgers had not originally been charged by Secretary Welles with planning anything beyond gunboat ordnance, he was now given to believe by his orders from Maj. Gen. McClellan that he had the authority to act. One historian, Robert C. Suhr, has written that the general, Engineer Eads, and Cmdr. Rodgers "met to discuss the situation on the western rivers." Eads' emphasis on a river blockade, expressed since April, was reviewed. It was after this conference, in which it was decided that "the Union needed three gunboats at Cairo," that "Rodgers took it upon himself to create a flotilla."

Taking his leave, Rodgers informed his superiors of McClellan's travel orders, though perhaps not his purchasing authority. Next morning, as Rodgers and Eads boarded the Ohio and Mississippi Railroad's direct train for St. Louis, Secretary Welles sent an order to Naval Constructor Samuel M. Pook at the Washington Navy Yard requiring that he head out to Cairo and meet Rodgers. There he would undertake such special duty as the commander might desire based upon the designer's not inconsiderable shipbuilding expertise.[12]

It is uncertain whether or not Cmdr. Rodgers and Capt. Eads spent any time in St. Louis reviewing the city's riverfront facilities or riverboats before entraining for Cairo. Though he may have been rudimentarily briefed by Eads on the rail trip to or from Cincinnati, it is also uncertain if the navy man fully realized what a snag boat was or whether Eads was proposing to convert one he partially owned into a true gunboat or a floating battery as noted in his April letter to Secretary Welles or McClellan's travel orders.

Just what exactly James Eads had in mind was not exactly clear because of the term "floating battery." A floating battery was, in fact, the name of a specific kind of unpropelled, heavily armored and armed vessel — essentially a gun platform — made popular during the Crimean War. Backed by Emperor Napoleon III, the French navy employed three such craft in the Allied October 17, 1855, assault on Kinburn. Indeed, 13 years earlier, in 1842, New Jersey engineer Robert L. Stevens had persuaded the U.S. government to grant him $250,000 and two years to build an American craft, the "Stevens Battery." By 1861, the enterprise was still not completed, though it had already consumed $586,717.84. Even as Rodgers made his way to Cairo, there were those calling for the completion of Steven's project and it now fell to him to see whether or not his distinguished Missouri Wrecking Company host was speaking of a similar idea for the western rivers

Shortly after detraining at the Illinois Central rail head above Fort Defiance, Cmdr. Rodgers was given a brief tour of Cairo by Mr. Eads as the men made their way to its hostelry, the St. Charles Hotel. Wearing his uniform, Rodgers was noticed by numerous journalists, but no interviews were given. "The presence in town of Capt. John Rodgers, U.S. Navy, on a mission that is secret as yet," noted the correspondent of the *Chicago Daily Tribune* on May 22, "is reported as having something to do with [a] fleet of gunboats."

William H. Russell, who would visit the town about one month later, saw what Rodgers undoubtedly would have noticed had he come to town by steamboat. "With the exception of the large hotel, which rises far above the levee of the river," the British journalist recorded, "the public edifices are represented by a church and spire, and the rest of the town by a line of shanties and small houses, the rooms and upper stories of which are just visible above the embankment." It is likely, as the two men crossed the bottom of this bowl, that Rodgers' host once more emphasized the importance of the town as a base of inland naval operations. The ocean seaman, whom we believe was visiting the town for the first time, may have been intrigued by the riverman's description of the place as a delta.

Cairo, Eads had written back in April, had "a broad three-mile-long levee front on the Ohio River that was raised about 14 feet above the natural level of the city." The town's steamboat landing was located here just up from that stream's confluence with the Mississippi. A levee of the same height and almost the same length as on the Ohio extended on the Mississippi River side of the town. This one was set back 100 to 1,000 yards from the river's edge to keep it safe from the natural caving of the riverbank.

From this levee, across from the Ohio River, a levee extends of the same height, by which the town is protected from the backwater. Seepage was mostly controlled by the city's steam pumps; however, sufficient water came through to cause muddy streets in the town at all times. The cross-channel banks of the Ohio were within cannon shot of Cairo; however, those on the Missouri shore across the Mississippi were nearly two miles away on the other side of a large sandbar.

The U.S. Army began the demolition of the Illinois Central Railroad track for a hundred yards along the Ohio levee on the Wednesday of Rodgers' visit. The brewery had also been expeditiously removed. Three heavy cannon had arrived that morning for mounting. These would augment the brass 6-pounders that had been in place for several weeks.

Just as he had explained the lay of this vital geography to Washington officials, so too did Eads reinforce its strategic importance, one easy enough for Rodgers to visualize. In a nutshell, batteries at Cairo, afloat and ashore, could "control the passage of vessels bound up or down the Mississippi and Ohio rivers." Eads believed he owned just the vessels to effectively convert into "floating batteries" and doubtless relished the opportunity to show the largest one to Cmdr. Rodgers.[13]

Observing the river traffic passing on two sides of the town and the scurrying Federal soldiers, Rodgers and Eads found their way at any early moment to the banks of the Ohio. All was in readiness for an inspection of the Eads craft originally offered to the government in the engineer's April 29 letter to Secretary Welles.

Cmdr. Rodgers was invited by Capt. Eads to board the giant catamaran snag boat *Submarine No. 7*. At the recommendation of Acting General Bates, who thought she could be useful in the Union war effort, the large vessel was moved here from St. Louis at the beginning of the month. Also prepared for the arrival of the naval officer were drawings and preliminary plans already drawn showing ways she could possibly be converted into a lightly armored naval craft.

One of three boats the Missouri Wrecking Company could make available, the *Submarine No. 7*, powered by a pair of independent engines, was the largest. Designed "for raising sunken steamboats" and clearing river obstructions, she had a pair of hulls, each with seven watertight compartments. The word "submarine" in her name was meant to imply the nature of her business, underwater salvage and obstruction removal.

Capt. Eads pointed to his sketches showing how he thought she could be protected with cotton bales—"like archers of the Hundred Years' War," Fletcher Pratt later quipped—and armed with 32-pounder cannon. Once that was accomplished, it was fully expected that she would draw only four feet of water—one foot less than the minimum depth of the Mississippi between Cairo and Memphis.

Rodgers was probably quite relieved that Eads was not proposing a true floating battery but a powered gunboat. Still, he was not impressed with the catamaran, even after her owner had shown off the machinery that gave her power to raise and cut off snags—the sunken trees which endangered streamers during flood time—between her twin hulls. The naval officer found the catamaran "old and rotten" and, in the words of historian Bearss, "vetoed Eads' plan to turn the big salvage boat into a cotton-clad gunboat."

After the Maryland-born officer balked at the *Submarine No. 7*, Capt. Eads went at him from another direction. The Missouri River, he pointed out, was serviced by a number of strong, fast steamboats. Perhaps some of these could be purchased and converted into gunboats at St. Louis. This would at least avoid any problems with getting them to Cairo from other boatbuilding locations up the Ohio River. This proposal was also rejected.

Taking his leave of Eads and Cairo, Cmdr. Rodgers embarked for Cincinnati, scheduling a brief stop at Mound City as Maj. Gen. McClellan had requested. In refusing the engineer's ideas, Rodgers, perhaps unknowingly, alienated not only Eads, but also his powerful patron, Acting General Bates. Still, at least one student, Robert J. Rombauer, has generously

"Gun-Boats Fitting Out at Cincinnati, Ohio, for Government Service on the Mississippi" was the original caption for this July 13, 1861, *Harper's Weekly* illustration. The scene depicts the conversion of the Ohio River steamers purchased by Cmdr. John Rodgers into the timberclads *Lexington*, *Conestoga*, and *Tyler*. Two of the boats are drawn here, though exactly which two is unknown (Naval Historical Center).

credited Bates, Eads, and Rodgers together with laying "the plans for the Mosquito fleet and the gunboats."[14]

Wishing to learn as much as possible about the great rivers as fast as possible, Cmdr. Rodgers' Cincinnati return trip was made aboard an Ohio River packet, one of the regularly scheduled mail boats. Wearing his impressive U.S. Navy uniform with its three broad gold sleeve stripes, it would have been fairly easy for Rodgers to engage his boat's captain and pilot(s) in conversations. Already familiar with the workings of side-wheelers and screw steamers used on the oceans or eastern rivers, he now heard more about the peculiarities of midwestern streamers that made them different.

Mound City is eight miles above the Ohio's confluence with the Mississippi and seven miles from Cairo. When he stopped by a few weeks later, newsman William Russell found the place "a mere heap of earth, like a ruined brick kiln, which rises to some height and is covered with fine white oaks, beneath which are a few log hugs and hovels, giving the place its proud name." Earlier at this spot, the Maryland seaman listened to the various rivermen encountered while taking the time to visit several river-associated companies. As a result, Cmdr. Rodgers' knowledge of regional steamboat commerce, rivers, and navigational challenges, as well as growing political uncertainty, was further enhanced even over what he may have learned from James Eads. He may also have come to appreciate, far more than he could from the oceans, that, as Mark Twain put it, "the face of the water, in time, became a wonderful book."

While the naval officer was en route back to the Queen City, new war-like actions were occurring in the area from which he had just departed. On the evening of May 22, an armed party aboard the steamer *Iatan* boarded the *J.C. Swon* 30 miles below St. Louis. Charging her captain with transporting contraband from Baton Rouge, the *Iatanites* towed her into port and turned her over to customs. The next morning, Federal troops erected a battery at Bissel's Point, seven miles above St. Louis, to help check steamboats approaching St. Louis from the Missouri River.

Realizing that "time is very precious," Cmdr. Rodgers was back at Cincinnati by May 24, wondering what had happened to Constructor Pook. According to an observer, the city was different now from the one the commander might have visited two months earlier. "The sudden change from the avocations of peace to those of war made the city seem as another place and the people another people," wrote Henry Lowe. "Under the excitement of a great overpowering emotion of patriotism, " he continued, "all classes mingled with a surprising degree of friendliness and good feeling."[15]

It is perhaps ironic that in those days of national confusion Lt. Gen. Scott was also, as noted, attempting to obtain a picture of Midwest river conditions. At almost the same time that Cmdr. Rodgers was visiting St. Louis, Cairo, and Mound City, Brig. Gen. Totten was traveling up and down the Ohio River putting together a dossier. In the process of visiting with many more people than Rodgers, Totten, with help from his cousin, the newspaperman Edward Mansfield, assembled valuable intelligence for U.S. military leadership — intelligence, that, we may add, never made it down to Cmdr. Rodgers' operational level, save what he learned independently.

The information provided to Scott by Totten had currency not because it had up to then been unknown, but because it was written down in a report, with several informational addenda, that brought together insights from many quarters. The same data was reported, often in little paragraphs, in the river sections of individual local western newspapers, but there was no way to quickly analyze these widely scattered narratives. It is probable that Rodgers, Eads, Kountz, McClellan, and others understood the economics of what was happening around them and such knowledge may help to explain why Rodgers rejected Eads' vessel in favor of another approach.

Totten and Mansfield confirmed that most of the many small operators who had run their steamers on the New Orleans trade had now brought their boats permanently north. "For two generations persons have told of thrilling experiences on 'the last boat through,'" wrote Charles Ambler in 1932, "of which there seems to have been more than one in each direction." Except for local packets, the Mississippi River below Cairo was closed to commercial navigation for the first time in 60 years. The same suspension also occurred on the Ohio and its tributaries.

The blockade had a devastating impact on river trade as business dried up and insurance companies refused to assume risks. Some daring rivermen tried to operate flying two flags as needed in a ruse de guerre, but this didn't last long. Most just tied up their boats "and settled down to watch the outcome" of the growing struggle. As Louis Hunter has noted, the great streams were "plunged into a depression from which there was little relief until the second year of the war." By the end of May, the St. Louis levee, usually bustling and exciting, was quiet. A local reporter told his readers that it was "quiet as a graveyard; steamboatmen feared a total suspension of business; and grass, it was prophesied, would soon be growing on the wharf."

The Union now blocked the mouth of both the Mississippi and the Ohio while the Confederacy guarded the center of the former and many of its other tributaries. Still, many realized that free trade over these streams remained essential; one side or the other had to have sufficient power to force the other to open them to advantage. For the North, thought future Admiral David Dixon Porter, opening rather than closing the Father of Waters was the only way to break the "backbone of the rebellion."

When June started, the number of unemployed steamboats on the Upper Mississippi and Ohio rivers presented a buyer's market. Totten found that there were 150 idle boats at St. Louis and another 250 on the Ohio River. At Cincinnati alone, Edward Mansfield noted that 53 vessels of 300 tons or more were in port by June 4, with that number further up within the week. Another 40–50 more were free at Pittsburgh, Wheeling, and other towns. At least 2,000 boat hands were unemployed.

If the U.S. military wanted to move a lot of soldiers in connection with the midwestern portion of the Anaconda Plan, sufficient charterable bottoms were available to lift 120,000. It was Mansfield's opinion that, if the Quartermaster Department employed sufficient "tact and caution in contracting," it could probably obtain their use from the boatmen and shippers for much less than the full prewar value. Unsaid was what Cmdr. Rodgers also figured out: he did not need to convert Capt. Eads' flag boat at a dear price when other more suitable craft were economically available closer to the Queen City seat of war.

McClellan and his relative not only inventoried available steamboat bottoms, but also identified the availability of freight and coal barges. Boat building yards were located at Pittsburgh, Wheeling, Cincinnati, Madison and New Albany, Indiana, and Mound City, with all but the last capable of building engines.

Totten understood that his superior, Scott, was interested in having gunboats constructed on the western waters. The 73 year old had learned that they could be perfectly fitted at any of the five towns mentioned and that, if the government pressed the matter, they could be ready in three months. Totten, who personally knew nothing about gunboat construction or conversion, did not complete his memorandum until he returned to Washington, because he wanted yet another opinion.

To bolster his report's value, the Army's top engineer first went over to the navy's Bureau of Construction, Equipment and Repair. There he presented his findings and requirements to its chief, John Lenthall, a veteran bureaucrat whose knowledge of ship and boat concepts was widely respected. Lenthall went over to his files and brought out a draught for a gunboat. Making a few modifications, he handed the plans to Totten. Himself a blue-water design specialist who "felt slight optimism that armed vessels adequate to fresh-water conditions in the West could be devised," Lenthall, nevertheless, suggested that these might form the basis for a craft "well adapted to operations on the Ohio and Mississippi rivers." As the two men shook hands concluding their interview, Lenthall agreed to send along his gunboat plans within hours, complete with written explanations. The designer probably also told Totten that Samuel M. Pook, his subordinate and also a top naval constructor, had just gone to Cincinnati and that Cmdr. Rodgers was there to oversee ordnance matters.

The army's head engineer, perhaps after consultation with Quartermaster General Meigs, completed his Scott report on June 3. Attaching Lenthall's drawings and explanations, Totten recommended that the navy authorize an officer of the rank of commander and two lieutenants be sent to the Ohio River with the authority to let gunboat contracts and oversee construction. He further suggested that they have full authority, after consulting with local boat and engine builders as well as Constructor Pook, to make modifications to the Lenthall drawings. The brigadier thought 10 boats could be had for $200,000, but he questioned the idea of advertising for bids for fear that "exposing designs" might be injurious and unnecessary.[16]

With McClellan's backing, the technical advice of Naval Constructor Pook (who arrived in town shortly after the commander's letter concerning his whereabouts), and local assistance from Commodore Kountz acting as steamboat broker, Rodgers went steamer hunting. He needed to find three good-quality and not overly expensive Ohio River packets that could be altered to meet the challenge of assembling a little fleet. Then he had to get them down to Cairo before low water made their passage impossible.

Rodgers' exercise of independent command in the Arctic now caused him problems, because his current midwestern assignment had very specific parameters and was not autonomous. Indeed, the shoals he faced were not so much technical — though outfitting the boats would be formidable — as political. Not only did he fail to report his activities to the Navy Department, but when he claimed to have the authority to fit out gunboats, he also managed to alienate powerful and well-connected interests. Several important ears chose to hear him say — or others say that he had said — that he had assumed outfitting authority on his own hook. For someone who had already frosted both inventor Eads and Attorney General Bates, this could not be good.

Jay Slagle, biographer of one of Cmdr. Rodgers' first western river subordinates, Seth Ledyard Phelps, has noted that Rodgers managed to shift to himself from McClellan the angst of some businessmen uncertain over lucrative contracts. Although a certain number of these gentlemen made their unhappy views known to the navy's civilian leadership, we have in the ORN volumes easy access to the printed letter of one of the more important, Pittsburgh congressman James K. Moorhead (1806–1884), late president of the Monongahela Navigation Canal.

Moorhead was informed several days before that Cmdr. Rodgers was in the west "for the purpose of arranging about placing cannon on steamboats." On May 27, the congressman was "astonished to find that he claims to have charge of the entire movements on the water" and was at "Cincinnati buying and arranging for steamboats." He was expected to visit Pittsburgh shortly.

Moorhead, like Cameron, was blunt in his belief that "the Navy Department ... has no jurisdiction on the Ohio and Mississippi rivers" and expressed outrage that Rodgers' action gave "to the Navy a jurisdiction that I think clearly belongs to the Army, and I am proud to be able to add that the public have much the greater confidence in the latter."

It was understood by Moorehead and others that Maj. Gen. McClellan, the Western Theater commander — "a very competent man" — had made arrangements "to secure the best skill amongst our river men for the purpose of purchasing boats." The "skilled" person the politician had in mind when complaining to Washington was fellow Pittsburgher Cdr. Kountz, his informant in this matter. The riverman was unhappy because he was notified earlier by McClellan that his services were required and that he was about to receive "an order to purchase and prepare boats." He did not know at the time of his complaint that, in the end, Rodgers would actually utilize his services to do just that.

In writing to Secretary Welles, the Pennsylvania political leader was not complimentary to Rodgers, going so far as to presume he had engineered his own Midwestern mission "as I could hear of no person having made such a recommendation." "An old sea captain, however well he may understand the sea and seagoing vessels, can, of course," wrote Moorehead, "know nothing of rivers and river steamboats."

Putting aside his vexation over Rodgers' qualifications or the geographical jurisdiction of his parent service, Moorehead appealed directly to Welles' economic sense. Letting the commander purchase boats was a "great mistake" which, if not corrected, would "cost the Government some hundreds of thousands of dollars and may jeopardize or greatly injure the efficiency" of any riverine force.

The same day Moorhead wrote to Welles, the navy secretary received a similar letter from Minnesota congressman Cyrus Aldrich (1808–1871), chairman of the Committee on Indian Affairs. Although not published in the official records, it too condemned arrangements reportedly being made by seagoing webfeet for building or purchasing boats on the Mississippi River.

It is very doubtful whether the Maryland sailor had asked to go to Cincinnati, but he might have agreed with Congressman Moorhead's assessment of his initial river knowledge. For his part, Welles, as he would soon demonstrate, was disturbed by Moorhead's letter (and similar missives received). Still, this dispute was, when compared to the great business of establishing the Atlantic blockade, something of a sideshow in a backwater. The busy secretary acknowledged the concerns of Moorhead and other critics but chose not to offer comment to the commander until he had heard directly from him.

Cmdr. Rodgers — believing from personal interaction that he had McClellan's permission to buy boats — was, if acquainted with it, supposedly oblivious to the political opposition to his acquisition work. Had he, a full commander (equivalent in rank to an army Lt. Col.), not once again, as in the Arctic, been tasked with a duty and responsibility far from what some might call "civilization?" He was certain from his discussions with McClellan, Eads, and others that the army needed to get up a gunboat fleet as quickly as possible. Despite the unique nature of its locale, the mission and objectives of such a flotilla would not be very different from those of more conventional fleets, then or now.

In fact, the navy regular was not unaware of concerns by politicians and local river interests. He was aware from direct conversations that Kountz was, indeed, far more knowledgeable about river craft than he was and that he had originally been led to believe that he would be picking boats for conversion. Thus Cmdr. Rodgers chose Kountz as his local agent. The two, together with newly arrived Naval Constructor Pook, were not only sanctioned by McClellan to acquire boats, but were also granted direct authority by Capt. J.H. Dickerson, assistant quartermaster of Cincinnati.

Cincinnati, Ohio, was known as the "Queen City" and it was to this Ohio River community that Cmdr. John Rodgers traveled in May 1861 to provide advice to the U.S. Army on nautical matters, specifically cannon. Working with Brig. Gen. George B. McClellan, James B. Eads, and others, the navy man went further and actually acquired three vessels to be converted into gunboats (*Harper's Weekly*, September 27, 1862).

With little local fanfare, Cmdr. Rodgers made his way with Mr. Pook and Cdr. Kountz along the Cincinnati wharf and as far upriver as Pittsburgh hunting convertible steamers. Throughout this time, Rodgers failed to paper his trail with reports to his superior, while others, unaware of his exact understanding with McClellan, Dickerson, or the steamboat captain, blasted his activities.[17]

Quite probably from the time he departed St. Louis through his Cairo visit and his Cincinnati return, Cmdr. Rodgers gave thought to what might be necessary for a naval vessel suitable to the western waters. According to his biographer and his own final inland river report to Secretary Welles, the officer was not favorably impressed with the boats available for conversion: "only river steamers with their high pressure boilers on deck, with all their steam connecting entirely exposed and with three story houses of thick white pine plank erected on their hulls." In the end, Rodgers, relying upon Kountz and Pook, accepted what they believed to be the best, most reasonably priced boats available.

To fully appreciate the kind of craft from among which Cmdr. Rodgers and his associates chose, the three initial units of what would be called the Western Flotilla requires some backgrounding. For us, as for Rodgers and his associates, some familiarity with the river steamers then available is absolutely necessary.

By the 1850s, western river steamboat evolution was essentially complete; the vessel's form, retained into the early 20th century, was that of lightly constructed, float-bottomed craft with multiple decks rising high above their waterlines. Mark Twain remembered a side-wheeled steamboat which appeared at his hometown of Hannibal, Missouri, as being a "handsome sight, too:"

> She is long and sharp and trim and pretty; she has two tall, fancy-topped chimneys, with a gilded device of some kind swung between them; a fanciful pilot-house, all glass and "gingerbread," perched on top of the "texas" deck behind them; the paddle-boxes are gorgeous with a picture or with gilded rays above the boat's name; the boiler-deck, the hurricane-deck, and the texas deck are fenced and ornamented with clean white railings; there is a flag gallantly flying from the jack-staff.

In general, the appearance of these commercial passenger-carrying "packets" changed little from the antebellum days of Mark Twain to that of one visited by George Ward Nichols in 1870:

> From her keel to the roof of the upper cabin she includes forty feet. Above that is the "Texas," as it is called, which is an upper row of cabins where the officers quarters are, and upon the top of which is imposed the pilot-house. The main cabin is plainly but well furnished, with large staterooms on either side. Below it is the main deck, where the big boilers and furnaces and engines are. Below this deck again there is a deep, spacious hold, where a thousand or fifteen hundred tons of freight may be stowed away.... Perhaps the most ornamental and most needful parts of this noble creature, as we see her from the outside, are the two big black smokestacks.

The same detail was earlier provided by a *Philadelphia Inquirer* correspondent who used the pen name "Alex," but who may have been their ace reporter, Henry Bentley. Writing from Quincy, Illinois, on August 29, 1861, "Alex" described the layout of the new 394-ton sidewheeler *Sucker State*. Constructed at McKeesport, Pennsylvania, in 1860 and home-ported at Galena, Illinois, the St. Louis and Keokuk packet was similar in appearance to the *Lexington* but 30 tons heavier. She had undertaken this multi-stop trip on August 27 and, like other western boats, was quite different from the steamers his readers might have "seen in the East."

Built atop of the hold of the boat's spoon-shaped hull was a main deck, where the machinery was placed, which extended the entire length of the craft. Passengers, livestock, and light freight not placed into the hold were carried here. The forward portion of the deck was occupied by the deck hands. In front of the boilers, a staircase led to the saloon deck, or second story, of the steamer. The clerks' office was located toward the front of this deck and behind was a social hall and the main saloon, which extended the balance of the boat's length. Staterooms were built on either side.

Wandering higher, "Alex" found the third story, or hurricane deck, which offered a fine promenade by extending the roof and guards of the boat. Up a flight of steps, one found the Texas deck, where the officers' quarters, staterooms, and mess deck were located. The final stairs led to the fifth story, or pilothouse, located between the two tall chimneys. Therein the pilots worked a large wheel that was connected by a series of ropes and chains to the rudder.

Official terminology for the decks in the colorful layout descriptions of Nicholas and "Alex" were, in fact, slightly different. Borrowing from the detail provided in Adam Kane's excellent *The Western River Steamboat*, let us elaborate. Directly above the cargo hold was the open main deck, which hosted all of the machinery, a blacksmith's shop, deck passenger berths (bunks, actually), heads, and hatches covering stairs into the hold. Most passengers were accommodated in cabins on either side of a deck-long central hallway, often called the saloon, on the boiler, saloon, or upper deck.

This next deck up from the main deck was equally as wide as the one below it and also contained washrooms, a bar and a saloon, a pantry, and a baggage room. The saloon hallway was also the dining and social area. The after part, closed off at night by folding doors, was set aside for ladies and children and was usually equipped with a piano. The clerks,' or business, office was located in the forward part of the saloon hallway. The exterior of the boiler deck was largely surrounded by a covered walkway, also called a gallery or a guard; sometimes, the bar and a barbershop were located on this area.

The largely open roof of the boiler or saloon deck was known as the hurricane deck. The open portion usually had skylights to illuminate the saloon on the boiler deck directly below. Forward and covering about a third of the deck was "a long narrow house" with cabins for officers, clerks, pilots and overflow passengers. It was known as the "Texas." The pilothouse was located atop the Texas and was ringed with windows for the pilots; it was either somewhat centered or built on the forward edge. On civilian boats, ladies and gentlemen in escorted groups were often allowed to visit the pilothouse to enjoy the steamer's best view of the surrounding countryside.

Built from multiple sections of sheet iron, the smokestacks Nichols and "Alex" referenced above were actually known, per Mark Twain, as "chimneys" in everyday parlance. The pair came up through the superstructure from the forward end of the boilers below and were essential, as in the case of a fireplace, to the provision of an air supply or draft that aided in the process of fuel combustion. These chimneys were tall, usually between 75 and 90 feet above water, and were often viewed as an aesthetic necessity.[18]

Two or more engines and three or more boilers per vessel were common. Imprecisely built and easily repaired, the engines powering western riverboats were of the lighter-weight, high-pressure variety rather than the low-pressure condensing engines employed elsewhere. Very fuel inefficient, the horizontally oriented poppet-valve engines, with their relatively small but long horizontal cylindrical fire-tube iron boilers, were located on the main deck, and, indeed, occupied a large part of it. The boilers were, as former Acting Assistant Paymaster E.J. Huling remembered, "provided with places where the sand and sediment from the water can be blown out at short intervals when the boat is running."

The location of the machinery on the main deck over the hold was interestingly described by "Alex" for readers of his "Western Letter" in the August 30, 1861, issue of the *Philadelphia Inquirer*: "Upon the deck, immediately over the hold, was placed the boilers, on iron legs, the furnaces being below the boilers, without any surroundings whatever.... The engines, two in number — one working each wheel — are placed upon heavy timbers upon a crank axle, with which each wheel is provided, no shaft being required."

The engine cylinder was about one foot to 20 inches in diameter with a three- to eight-foot piston stroke. The fuel employed was wood or, when available, anthracite coal. The latter fuel was not provided by the ton or hundredweight, as might be expected. Rather, it was obtained by the bushel or the box. In July 1863, Master's mate Symmes E. Browne of the *Tyler* wrote that 500 boxes of coal—1,000 bushels—was sufficient to power his timberclad from Memphis to Cairo.

Given the manner of construction, with various rough approximations in valve, flue, and head fittings, the engines, particularly when overly stoked to obtain speed or poorly maintained, were dangerous. Hot combustion furnace gases were shoved from the rear of the boilers through the boiler water to the front of the boilers, creating a significant amount of steaming water under very high pressure, usually over 100 pounds per square inch. The *Sultana* disaster of 1865 provides the worst example of vulnerability, but steamboat explosions were common. Although the possibility for more sophisticated engines or valve mechanisms had been possible for over 20 years, their introduction "was successfully resisted by riverboat engineers until well after the Civil War.[19]

The steamboat's power plant provided the energy to turn paddle wheels, which were uncomplicated and fairly easy to repair if damaged. True, the water thrown up with each turn was a waste of fuel, but that was not a significant concern when wood was easily available and did not detract from the restoration advantage. Obstructions, snags, logs, and ice caused much damage which could often be readily fixed by the boat's carpenters.

During the first half of the 19th century, most western river craft were powered by sidewheels of fairly significant diameter and width (30 foot diameter and 12 foot width was common), which were mounted about one third of the length forward from the boat's stern. Each was driven by at least one dedicated engine. These big wheels, located in special housings, were particularly helpful in steering the vessels and at those times, as was very common, when it was necessary to back out into a stream after making a bows-on landing. This was the same arrangement as was employed by steamers on the Hudson River and elsewhere in the east.

It has been recorded that those side-wheel packet boats, which could also haul cargo on their main decks and in a shallow hold, were much longer on the Mississippi River than those on the Ohio, while the latter tended to have their wheels located further aft. This difference occurred because of the need for those plying between Cincinnati and the west to get through the locks of the Louisville and Portland Canal, which had been built around the Falls of the Ohio at Louisville.

In contrast to the side-wheel boats, stern-wheelers had a more difficult time in getting established in the years before the Civil War. They were seen as slower and harder to handle. However, rear propulsion did make significant technical gains and was beginning to win larger acceptance by operators. This trend would continue, particularly in the two decades after Appomattox. Pilots and captains, and, during the war, the U.S. Navy recognized that these rear-wheeled boats, generally smaller in size than the side-wheeled packets, had some major advantages over their two-wheeled rivals.

Stern-wheelers were less prone to hit things in the water or to need to stop to avoid ramming floating objects. The rear-wheel location offered a built-in advantage to those needing to get boats off bars or over shoals. Most importantly, the removal of the propulsion wheels from the sides to the rear meant that builders, on about the same hull tonnage, could do away with the heavy side-wheel houses and provide these types with greater beams, thereby lightening draft. The square-sterned boats each had at least three rudders, which were connected by rods "in a rude sort of way, but very strong." Approximately the same size cargo could be carried by stern-wheelers, but the craft could operate in drier seasons, earning more return. "To obtain lightness of draft in relation to tonnage and cargo capacity became the primary object of steamboat builders from an early date," wrote Louis C. Hunter in 1949, "and remained so throughout the steamboat era. The true western river steamboat was first and last a shallow-water boat."

Another advantage was a certain convenience in the use of the vessels as towboats. Instead of towing barges or other boats astern, connected by long lines (towlines), stern-wheelers could lash their tows forward and push them. This practice allowed for greater control over the tows in crooked channels or swift currents.

When it came to the handling of the two different types when employed as warships, both had advantages. As Gary Matthews wrote in a message on the Civil War Navies Message Board:

> In order for a stern-wheeler to come about in a narrow river, the pilot had to put the boat's bow or stern into the bank and then allow the current to swing the opposite end around, whereas a side-wheeler could simply go ahead on one wheel and back on the other. The independent side wheels could also be used to steer a boat if her rudder or steering ropes were damaged, which was a fairly common occurrence.

Acting Rear Adm. David Dixon Porter, when he came on the scene in the fall of 1862, definitely voiced an opinion in favor of side-wheelers, which did not employ tubular boilers. If given a choice, he would have his boats constructed new with extra-large boilers and large cylinders. He, like those before him, beginning with Cmdr. Rodgers in July 1861, would also pay tribute to the saying that "the smaller the river or the lower the stream, the lower the boat draft required."[20]

At the end of May 1861, there were 60 steamboats, averaging over 300 tons each, on the inspection rolls at Cincinnati, of which 53 lay idled in the port or along the riverbank. "Discarding the small ones," another 40 or 50 were available at Wheeling and Pittsburgh. Rodgers, Pook, and their local agent thus had many of the best Ohio River passenger packets to choose from and could afford to be discerning. As all of the riverboats the men examined were "so different from war vessels in all their appliances," even the best would require "considerable alterations ... to fit them for use." Still, this should not have been too difficult because there were eleven boat- and shipbuilding firms in the headquarters town of the Department of the Ohio. In 1860, these firms had a total product of $265,214 and 232 workers. This was not as large a local industry as in, say, New Albany, Indiana, or Mound City, Illinois, but it was adequate and would prove convenient to Rodgers' purpose.

Once in hand, the conversion of these river steamers into gunboats would be "straightforward and easily accomplished," in the words of historian Cannery, "probably without the use of formal plans." It is not difficult to imagine that, prior to their shopping trip, Rodgers and Pook, and possibly Kountz, reviewed the options available to them for turning steamboats into naval craft. Even after careful review and selection, the Maryland-born officer still did not have a favorable impression of riverboats.

On the other hand, without much variety available to please the saltwater sailor, he decided to go ahead and use the best of "the materials offered." He would make a few alterations and hope that these would prove sufficient. Compared to changes made on later riverboat conversions, Rodgers' modifications were quite basic and far more reminiscent of oceangoing men-o'-war. On the other hand, as historian Milligan has pointed out, "he had no precedents to follow, no freshwater experience from which to conclude."

It was undoubtedly Naval Constructor Pook who suggested that the thin pine deckhouses aboard whatever boats were purchased be cut away and replaced with perpendicular uncovered bulwarks pierced for cannon. These would be similar to what would soon be called casemates. These would be constructed of oak planks dense enough to offer their crews protection against small arms fire. Through the expedient of personal musket testing, Rodgers came to the conclusion that five-inch-thick timber would do the job. Joining the *Tyler* about a year later, Master's mate Symmes Browne proudly wrote that his craft was "built in man-of-war style and looks more like a seagoing vessel than our old boat," the Pook turtle *Mound City*.

"In the four years to come, the rivers of America would be home to a variety of 'clads'—ironclads, cottonclads, and tinclads," *Tyler* profiler Steven Davis has noted, but Rodgers' three wooden-covered ex–passenger boats "were the war's only timberclads." The decks of the new acquisitions, although "above average strength," would have to be reinforced further with timbers and beams. That way they could support the weight of the heavy naval batteries that would be placed upon them.

Perhaps nowhere was the disparity between these river "bandboxes" and oceangoing warships more easily discernable than in the location of their power plants. Without masts and sails, steamboats carried their engines and boilers in very exposed locations on the main deck—an exceptionally easy target. To help remedy this huge concern, Pook recommended to Rodgers that the boilers be dropped into the hold, where they could receive some protection from the coal bunkers, and the various steam pipes lowered as far as possible or rerouted to less exposed locations. Whatever they did, the two men realized that the engines and boilers were still vulnerable to cannon and that those aboard would, as Rodgers later wrote, be required to "take our chances."

After a brief survey, Rodgers and his companions agreed upon three sound side-wheel, high pressure boats. These were the *Conestoga*, *Lexington*, and *A.O. Tyler*, with a combined

Cairo from the Ohio Street and Ohio River side of the tip of Illinois, circa 1864. The town was a jewel of Union river defense from the beginning of the war. Notice the close proximity of the railroad tracks and the wharf boats (*Miller's Photographic History*).

tonnage of 1,167. The three had originally been constructed for approximately $97,000, but, because of depressed times on the river, were sold to the government for $62,000, two thirds of their original value. According to Kountz biographer Theodore Parker, it was the commodore, in his capacity as McClellan's river transportation boss, who actually "purchased the three vessels." He then more or less "turned them over" to Rodgers for rebuilding and refitting.

Once Cdr. Kountz had completed purchase arrangements, Rodgers and Pook came quickly to terms with Daniel Morton of the Marine Railway and Drydock Company to make the alterations the three men had earlier discussed. These improvements were to be finished by June 27 for an additional $41,000, making the final cost of each boat about $34,000. The two Washington-based seamen slipped a penalty clause into the Morton contract imposing "a loss of 10 per cent of the whole contract for every day's delay after that time until delivery." Rodgers and Pook were confident that these stringent terms would assure timely delivery of what they had been politely calling wood clad warships, that were known impolitely as "stinkpots," but which history would come to know as the timberclads.[21]

Looking at the three vessels, in alphabetical order, we find that the *Conestoga* was the smallest of the three vessels and also, at $16,200, the least expensive. Built at Brownsville, Pennsylvania, in 1859, the 279-ton craft was officially sold into War Department hands at Pittsburgh on June 3 (some sources say June 7). Capable of a reported 12 knots, she was the fastest of Rodgers' picks. In appearance, she could be differentiated from the *Lexington* because her chimneys were centered and from the *Tyler* due to differences in her wheel box.

Conestoga's two side wheels were powered by two single-cylinder, high-pressure reciprocating beam steam engines. The diameter of the engine cylinders was 24 inches, while the length of their piston strokes was seven feet. Because she did not survive the conflict and no one thought to take her lines during the fighting, we do not have any physical description (length, beam, etc.) for this boat.[22]

The 362-ton *Lexington*, on the other hand, was the newest of Rodgers' acquisitions, having been built by L.M. Speer at Belle Vernon, Pennsylvania, at the end of 1860. She was able to complete two round-trips between Pittsburgh and New Orleans in early 1861 before she was laid up at Cincinnati. At $25,000, this side-wheeler was the most expensive of the three wooden warships. Still, she became the best known of the woodclad trio, even if she was regarded in some circles as the slowest. The *Lexington* was 177.7 feet long, with a beam of 36.10 feet and a six foot depth of hold. One could easily tell her from the *Conestoga* and *Tyler* because her chimneys were erected in a very forward position.

Lexington's two side wheels were also powered by a pair of single-cylinder, high-pressure reciprocating beam engines, which gained their steam from three boilers. The diameter of the engine cylinders was 20 inches, while the length of their piston strokes was six feet. Despite this water-smashing thrust, she could make only seven knots and, by one knot less than *Tyler*, was the slowest timberclad.[23]

The *A.O. Tyler* had quite a checkered past before Fort Sumter. Not only had she been fired upon at Vicksburg back in January 1861, but a year earlier, on January 17, 1860, she also sank and was salvaged. Built at Cincinnati in 1857, the craft was the oldest of the three acquisitions and, at $21,000, the second most expensive. Aside from her size, it would be interesting to know why Cmdr. Rodgers chose her, given her background. Was it possible that he knew the Vicksburg story and wanted to give the vessel a chance to return compliments?

At 420 tons, the *Tyler*, as she became known, was the heaviest of the timberclads. She was also the largest, measuring 180 feet from stem to stern, with a 45.4 feet beam and a six foot depth of hold. Her appearance was differentiated from the *Conestoga* because of differences in her wheel box and from the *Lexington* because her chimneys were centered. When converted, she would have space for a 67-man complement. This is the only one of the three boats for which we know for sure the designated crew size, although we know that Rodgers hoped for the number in the "united crews" to be "198 souls."

Like the others, the *Tyler* was a side-wheeler powered by a pair of single-cylinder, high-pressure reciprocating beam engines. These received steam from four boilers. The diameter of the engine cylinders was 22 inches and the length of their piston strokes was eight feet. Although she too could churn the river into foam, her machinery allowed her a speed of only eight knots, one more than the *Lexington*. Master's Mate Browne called her a "very slow boat, scarcely faster than the ironclad boats."

Cmdr. Rodgers, while not actually admitting he had purchased any boats, sent a requisition to Washington on June 7 requesting ordnance items sufficient for the three just obtained. The solicitation addressed to Secretary Welles was for sixteen 32-pounders of 57 cwt, 16 gun carriages and attendant gear, as well gunpowder, shot and shell. He also asked for small arms, swords and pistols.[24]

While Rodgers in Ohio was affirming Kountz's signature on the side-wheeler sales contracts, Navy Secretary Gideon Welles, back in Washington, continued to take heat from western river concerns, along with Congressmen Moorhead, Aldrich and others, relative to navy interference in army affairs. The complainants were particularly upset by Rodgers' apparent boat purchases.

In his Cincinnati hotel room on June 8, Rodgers, still unaware of the political problems his acquisition action was causing the Navy Department, wrote his superior a report concerning the purchase of the three steamers for naval service. Starting out with assurances that he had consulted with Maj. Gen. McClellan and Constructor Pook, but leaving out the crucial role of Cdr. Kountz, the former explorer reported on the craft. In noting the *A.O. Tyler*, he respectfully sought permission to change the boat's name to *Taylor*, "a name of better augury than *Tyler*," as former president John Tyler was siding with the Confederacy. Following a review of the purchase costs and his arrangement with Daniel Morton, Rodgers asked permission to buy supplies for the boats on the local economy and to engage the "necessary pilots, engineers, and firemen." Obtaining crews could wait a little while until the vessels were ready to receive them.

The commander's letter reached the Navy Department two or three days later, where it raised a firestorm. Here in the first report received from Rodgers since he was ordered West was written proof that the Congressmen and others were right — he had exceeded his orders. Welles, who did not know of his subordinate's arrangements with the Buckeye general or the steamboat commodore, knew only what his subordinate wrote and what some powerful and unhappy people had told him earlier. Embarrassed, he could only point in exasperation to his man's May orders in which Rodgers was specifically detailed to report to McClellan "and that officer would make the necessary requisitions."

On June 11, the displeased navy secretary fired off an extremely blunt telegram to Rodgers informing him that every single force movement on the Mississippi was to be made under the direction and control of the army and that any boat purchases to support such movements were to be made by the War Department. All the three-striper could do was requisition armament and crew — absolutely nothing else.

The next morning, Cmdr. Rodgers, stung by Welles' rebuke, walked over to McClellan's office and shared the message with the army leader. While it was true that Rodgers had "procured these three vessels and arranged for their conversion without written orders from McClellan," "Little Mac" sat down and wrote out an order formally approving their bills of sale. That afternoon, Rodgers, in one of the great breaches of etiquette in U.S. naval history, sent Welles a telegram equally as biting as the one he had received the day before. Noting that the theater commander had given his OK and hoping that a brief sentence would allay the secretary's concern, the Marylander wrote: "The written approval of a superior officer makes an act of purchase his own." In both his written report of June 8 and this telegram, Rodgers, as he later admitted, failed to tell the whole purchasing story or to protect himself by revealing the roles of Kountz and quartermaster Dickerson. One can only believe that, if he had, the censure would not have been as severe.

It is unknown if the secretary received this wire before taking the time on June 12 to send a letter to Rodgers further explaining the reasons why he was not authorized to encumber the Navy Department for goods or services beyond cannon or sailors. There was, Welles put it diplomatically, "great sensitiveness among the boatmen and others on the Western rivers in relation to the water craft that might be required for the Army."

Members of Congress, the man from Connecticut continued, had been writing and complaining to him about Rodgers' movements and his so-called assumed powers. As is the case today, cabinet officers in Lincoln's time did not enjoy being grilled by Congressmen. All were told, as Rodgers was telegraphed, that the famed Arctic searcher was simply "not authorized by this Department to purchase or build boats or make contracts." He'd be several days yet getting that point across to irate midwestern businessmen and politicians.

Secretary Welles once more defined Rodgers' role as a lone blue-suited sailor among soldier officers wearing coats that decades later would be dyed olive drab. Movement in the West, meaning operations and logistics, were under the purview of the army and not the navy. The two branches of the service were not to be "complicated or embarrassed" by separate action or any attempt at a combined movement on interior rivers. Rodgers was, frankly, subordinate to the commanding local army general and was to cooperate with him in any river crossing or navigational requirement. Of course, with this nebulous status, he was free to aid or advise him as situations warranted.

Although he may not have intended it, Welles had established a doctrine that, in World War II, was called unified command. Naval officers on western waters sailed under army orders for the next 18 months.

Perhaps in need of an editor, his own former job, Secretary Welles summed up his Rodgers' communication with one of the longer sentences in the history of naval communication: "The employment of men and their subsistence, together with the necessary engineers, pilots, firemen, etc., for the army movements, including the steamers, properly belong to the Army; and whatever you may do as regards them or either of them will be under the direction of the general in chief and by requisitions on and at the expense of the War Department."[25]

That Rodgers was not relieved by Secretary Welles at this time, especially after the commander's terse telegram was received, can be attributed to several factors. With many of its commissioned leaders departing to the South, the U.S. Navy needed energetic and loyal officers. Rodgers was very experienced and his Western knowledge was improving daily. The navy secretary may have learned the true circumstances under which the boats were acquired and may have decided to leave the oceangoing seaman in his Cincinnati billet, considering that sufficient punishment for his report omissions.

In reality, there was always time to get rid of Rodgers in the future and besides, right now, Rebel activities in West Virginia and on the Mississippi, as well as the operational start of the Atlantic and Gulf Coast blockades, required significant Navy Department attention. On top of this, a new Midwest nautical requirement was at hand beyond this matter of wooden army gunboats.

Two days before the Welles-Rodgers telegram-letter exchange, Lt. Gen. Scott, who liked Brig. Gen. Totten's report, endorsed the memorandum over to War Secretary Cameron along with a recommendation that the army contract the construction of 16 Lenthall gunboats. On June 11, Cameron sent a copy of the whole Totten report, together with Scott's supporting letter, over to the navy secretary, asking that the sea service detail officers out west to oversee construction of the Lenthall boats, as well as their engines.

Welles noted that warship construction was supervised by civilians and recommended that knowledgeable western men be engaged for the work. He would be happy to have one of his naval constructors go on scene to provide technical advice. He also noted, enclosing copies, his letter to Cmdr. Rodgers of earlier in the day. Rodgers and Pook were on scene, let them be overseers. Pook, in particular, could visit various boatbuilders, show them the Lenthall plans, and review and, if necessary, redraw the designs.[26]

Out in Ohio, acquiring the three boats was only a beginning for Cmdr. Rodgers as they still needed to be altered into warships—something no one on western rivers had ever done before—armed and crewed. Getting them ready would prove far more difficult than their location or the mechanics of their purchase.

Supervised and assisted by the on-scene navy people, Daniel Morton's men labored through most of June to get their charges into serviceable condition. Most of the frills usually associated with steamboat superstructures were cut away, along with the hurricane deck and Texas, and in their place, five-inch-thick oak bulkheads were erected, pierced for cannon on the broadside. This wooden armor gave the three their "timberclad" nicknames. Looking at the bulkheads and the general broadside appearance of the boats, one would be reminded of a clapboard house. The main deck behind the bulwarks was strengthened. The pilothouse on each boat was relocated atop what was once called the saloon deck. It was placed amidships behind the chimneys aboard the *Lexington* and forward, before the chimneys, on the *Tyler* and *Conestoga*.

Due to the confusion inherent in such an original and non-blueprinted project and perhaps because of a bit of greed mixed with incompetence, much of the work on the three boats was done poorly, often with inferior material. In the haste necessary for conversion, green timber was employed. Within a very short time it shrank, opening large seams. By fall, both the main decks and cabins would require complete overhaul. Calking would be needed to an extent necessary to keep the magazines dry and the officers and men protected from the weather.

Maj. Gen. McClellan, who had the authority to see that the work was finished properly, was by this time campaigning in western Virginia and could only lend encouragement. Instead, Rodgers and his colleagues were forced to expend much of their badly needed time and energy in attempting to force their contractor to make necessary alterations and corrections.

The navy-required change orders upset the original 19-day conversion time frame. (No penalties were assessed because the new work and repair work orders were so badly muddled together.) Some of the carpentry and painting was actually not completed before Rodgers sent the three downriver. Much of what was finished had to be redone. Some of the alterations would not be satisfactorily completed until early October, and then by hands other than Morton's.

With the blockade officially, if not effectively, begun at the southern end of the Mississippi River, events at the Midwestern confluence of that stream with the Ohio were also unfolding in early June. Telegraphic and other rumors continued to arrive at Cairo almost daily, as they had since at least late April, announcing that Rebel forces would attack the town. The latest had them led by Confederate Army of Tennessee Maj. Gen. Gideon J. Pillow, "the renowned trench-digger and braggart." Similar threats were believed by local Federal leaders to be facing Bird's Point and Mound City.

Bird's Point was fortified by 1,500 troops brought from St. Louis aboard the steamer *Louisiana*; heavy cannon from Pittsburgh joined several from Indiana in Camp Lyon. Southern sympathizer Col. John Bird was, according to George Driggs, held under arrest at Cairo's St. Charles hotel. The 7th Illinois Regiment, meanwhile, occupied Mound City, preventing any possible Confederate destruction of the important shipbuilding facilities. Many Illinois soldiers were puzzled over what had caused the speedy defense buildup at the former point. "We don't apprehend a shade of a fuss here," 8th Illinois private Charles Wright Wills recorded in his diary, "but the officers are making as much preparation as if a Waterloo No. 2 were coming."

Meanwhile, over a thousand Illinois soldiers busily worked to complete the breastworks at Cairo. About June 10 or 11, a number of large cannon arrived from Pittsburgh and were planted. Before anxious eyes, civil and military alike, "the first 32-pound ball was sent booming down the Mississippi, a warning to all traitors to keep at a respectable distance." As the iron sphere splashed into the muddy brown water, "great satisfaction was expressed throughout the camp."

The roar of the great guns helped to distract soldiers and others from boredom, fever and diarrhea in Camp Defiance, "the cantonment on the mud between the levees of the Ohio and Mississippi." Still, all along those two streams, many more were impacted by a terrible heat wave. At Cairo on June 20, English correspondent William H. Russell noticed that "the thermometer was at 100° soon after breakfast." Night offered some relief, as did the streams for those fortunate enough to be sailing on or swimming in them.

Further up the Ohio River, the uncertain status of Kentucky continued to make contra-

Cannon at Cairo. The Illinois troops of Gov. Richard Yates set up camp at Cairo in late April 1861 and soon had cannon in place with which to challenge the passage of vessels believed to be carrying on unlawful intercourse with the seceded Southern states. The artillery, as drawn here by Alexander Simplot, would, with the assistance of an ersatz gunboat, enforce a blockade until the arrival of the timberclad gunboats during the summer (*Harper's Weekly*, June 29, 1861).

band restrictions difficult to enforce and, sometimes, such enforcement as there was proved suspicious. When the brand new New Albany–built stern-wheel packet *Sam Orr*, en route from Evansville to Pittsburgh, put into Louisville, her entire 1,000 barrel flour cargo was seized by creditors. It was reported in local newspapers that the action was a "traitorous plot" between the creditor and the cargo owner to get the flour to the Confederacy.

Some boats on certain routes were exempt from military inspection. The policy in practice was that traffic, even below Cairo, was permitted to Kentucky river towns just so long as no contraband was transported. Examples included the Evansville–Paducah–Cairo mail steamer *Charley Bowen*; the new side-wheel packet *Eugene* on the Louisville–Evansville–Henderson route; the Evansville–Green River operated side-wheeler *Lou Eaves*, built at Evansville in 1859; and the "Big" *Grey Eagle*, another side-wheeler that plied between Louisville and Evansville.

At least one steamer did catch the attention of customs surveyors and was several times warned about the transport of provisions and supplies to suspected Rebel sources in Kentucky. The side-wheeler *Dunbar*, owned by five Paducah brothers, Dick, Joe, Willie, Whyte, and Gus Fowler, all strong Southern sympathizers, began service on her short Evansville–Paducah route in early 1860. The boat's captain was notified that if he were caught his craft would be seized. As June ended, the surveyor of the Port of Louisville announced that he would grant no permits for any goods to pass to the seceded states.

Providing ordnance and other supplies, as well as crewmen, for the Union's initial western naval assets was every bit as big a problem as their physical conversion. Also in mid–June, Rodgers was asked back to Washington by Maj. Gen. McClellan, Secretary Welles, and Quartermaster General Meigs to report on the progress of his mission and to conclude arrangements for the procurement of cannon. While he was gone, the boats were left in charge of Messers. Pook and Morton, as well as their civilian skippers who had been retained aboard: Capt. Daniel Collier of the *A.O. Tyler*, Capt. John A. Duble of the *Conestoga*, and Capt. Williamson of the *Lexington*, who would later serve as master of the chartered steamer *Emerald*.

Anaconda Plan. A humorous look at the 1861 Union victory plan devised by Lt. Gen. Winfield Scott. Brig. Gen. George B. McClellan, Western Theater Commander, also had a scheme for moving against the South, but the one of greatest interest to naval authorities was a blueprint put forward by St. Louis entrepreneur James B. Eads (Library of Congress).

Rodgers arrived back in the national capital about June 16 and immediately met with Gideon Welles. It is possible that the matter of the boat purchase and the sharp telegram exchange was cleared up at this time. Simultaneously, Rodgers was informed that the Bureau of Ordnance was being ordered to supply him "with such ordnance materials as can be spared for the armament of the boats which the Army may purchase on the Ohio or Mississippi rivers and place under your command." This directive, confirmed next day by a written order from the navy secretary, is the first in which the top administrator of the sea service acknowledged Rodgers' possible operational role. Although he remained subject to army orders while acting in his advisory role, he might also find himself with a supportive combat command.

While in town, Rodgers, Secretary Cameron, and Brig. Gen. Meigs also reviewed the gunboat situation and the commander made out a list for his brother-in-law of the cannon and other related ordnance materials that he thought were needed for the three boats. The requirements for items beyond the great guns themselves were duly written up in a requisition that was passed along to the army ordnance bureau for a quick endorsement.

After this round of visits, the War Department, in the person of Quartermaster General Meigs, indicated its approval of Rodgers' actions with regards to the three boats. It also promised, in light of the forthcoming building program, to hereafter honor his requisitions for whatever was needed to equip the embryonic river fleet. Indeed, Meigs became the unofficial "father" of the Western Flotilla. From this time until its transfer to the U.S. Navy in October 1862, the Quartermaster Department paid for the all inland navy purchases, operations, boat construction and modification — everything except officers and guns. Technically something of a waterborne army division subject to the orders of western theater commanders, Rodgers' outfit was actually a special child of the quartermaster general's organization.

On June 18, Cmdr. Rodgers was ordered by Mr. Welles to take the first train to Erie, PA, and at the naval ordnance depot there select the cannon and ordnance materials deemed expedient. Once the shopping list was confirmed, Rodgers was to enumerate for the Bureau of Ordnance the quantities of materials taken. Next day, in a surprisingly quick turnaround on the paperwork perhaps agreed to at senior levels earlier, Welles received Rodgers' army requisition list from Secretary Cameron. The War Department chief formally asked his marine counterpart to provide not only the cannon, but the associated ordnance materials "inasmuch as they can not be procured from the arsenals of the Army." It was, of course, understood that the military would pay for all of the articles furnished by the navy.[27]

Having received his gun authorization, Cmdr. Rodgers took train forthwith "to Erie, selected them, and returned immediately to Cincinnati," arriving by June 24. The smoothbore cannon to be forwarded as soon as possible included ten 8-inch Dahlgrens and seven 32-pounders, plus carriages. Once mounted, the timberclads would have almost instant military credibility.

When he arrived back in the Queen City, Rodgers found Constructor Pook at work reviewing the Lenthall gunboat plans, word that several lieutenants had been ordered west to help him, and that Maj. Gen. McClellan was in town. Taking advantage of his presence, the commander rushed over to Department of the Ohio headquarters to obtain further specific written authority to outfit the boats and move them to Cairo. "Little Mac," verbally and in writing, told his naval advisor to "use your own judgment in carrying out the ends of the Government. Spare no effort to accomplish the object in view of the least possible delay."

Although he now possessed full authority to outfit his tiny flotilla and big guns were on the way, Cmdr. Rodgers still had to get his craft to Cairo as soon as possible. Once the group arrived, the U.S. Army, supported by his "timberclads," could begin implementing the Scott-Eads plan and the naval-amphibious war on inland waters could proceed. And then, as he walked down to the wharf, the Marylander learned the river was rapidly falling.[28]

CHAPTER 3

From Cincinnati into the War Zone, June–August 1861

BY THE END OF JUNE 1861, Commander John Rodgers II of the U.S. Navy, acting under military authorization, had acquired three civilian steamers at Cincinnati to be outfitted as gunboats. When altered, these craft would support the U.S. Army in the implementation of the Midwestern river portion of the grand war strategy known as the Anaconda Plan. Even while workmen from Daniel Morton's Marine Railway and Dry Dock Company labored to rebuild the former side-wheel packets into something none of them had ever seen, Rodgers learned that the Ohio River was rapidly receding. All of his work would be for naught if the craft were stranded by low water.

It was known that the depth of the Ohio declined during the summer as the heat and lack of rain intensified. This year it seemed to come a bit more quickly than usual and there was no significant "June rise" as Brig. Gen. Joseph G. Totten reported normal in his just finished report on river conditions for Lt. Gen. Winfield Scott. Downstream at the gunboats' Cairo, Illinois, destination, it was so hot that thermometers registered 100° in the shade before noon. The soldiers in the camp undertook no drilling "between 8 A.M. and 7 P.M. on account of the heat."

While the soldiers and citizens on the tip of Illinois awaited the Lincoln gunboats, the armed tugboat *Swallow* remained active attempting to interdict steamers smuggling contraband in the waters around Cairo. On June 20, Maj. Gen. Gideon J. Pillow, commanding the Army of the Tennessee, wrote to Confederate Secretary of War Leroy P. Walker complaining that she was "sweeping the river above my batteries, seizing all the steamboats, completely controlling everything out of reach of my batteries." Could not Walker, Pillow asked, have President Jefferson Davis order the Rebel gunboat *McRae* to Memphis "as promptly as possible" to halt the *Swallow*'s activity.

The former Mexican 830-ton bark *Marquis de la Habana* had been purchased at New Orleans by the Confederate government on March 17, 1861. Outfitted and then armed with one 9-inch smoothbore and six 32-pounders, she was commissioned as *McRae* and placed under the command of Lt. Thomas B. Huger. Engine problems and her rig prevented her immediate transfer upstream and another vessel was sent instead.

Built at Cincinnati in 1849, the tugboat *Yankee* was a large and powerful side-wheeler that spent much of her prewar career assisting oceangoing vessels at the mouth of the Mississippi, as a St. Louis paper later put it, "towing up ships from the Balize." The 297-ton workboat was acquired by the Confederate government at New Orleans on May 9. She was strengthened where possible. (Union sources later stated that "she was plated strongly with railroad iron of the T pattern.") Her armament consisted of two 32-pounders in pivot. Although she was now christened C.S.S. *Jackson*, the gunboat would continue to be known in many circles as the *Yankee*. Lt. Washington Gwathmey, C.S.A., was named captain on June 6 and in early July, with a crew of 75, the *Jackson* paddled up to Columbus, where she reported to Maj. Gen. Pillow. Within a few weeks, other elements of the Confederate river defense fleet, under Commodore George N. Hollins, arrived to join the former tug.

Two officers promised by the U.S. Navy had not yet arrived and Cmdr. Rodgers, in consultation with Maj. Gen. George B. McClellan and Naval Constructor Samuel M. Pook, elected to send the boats downstream unfinished rather than have them marooned at the Queen City until late fall. They would have to go with whatever men could be locally recruited and would be captained, initially, by the civilian skippers who had remained aboard to help after their sale. Capt. S.W. Shirley, president of the Louisville & Cincinnati Mail Boat Line, agreed to act as temporary squadron commander. Provisions for the voyage were acquired locally.

With workmen aboard, the escape of the incomplete gunboats from Cincinnati began at 4:00 P.M. on the afternoon of June 24. Captain Daniel Collier's *A.O. Tyler* cast off from the foot of Main Street headed for Lawrenceburg, Indiana. Her machinery was expected to be in working order by the time she reached her destination, but for now she would be towed by the tugboat *Champion*. The reporter who witnessed the boat's departure noted for his readers that the boat was unarmed and would probably receive her cannon at Cairo.

Capt. Williamson's *Lexington* and the *Conestoga*, under Capt. John A. Duble, with Capt. Shirley embarked, departed next morning. Within a few days, the three made it past Jeffersonville, Indiana, Louisville and Shippensport, Kentucky, as far as the entrance to the Louisville and Portland Canal. Low water caused the *Tyler* to ground and the others were halted. The accident badly upset the trio's delivery schedule.

The St. Louis *Daily Missouri Republican* correspondent at Cairo wrote on June 27 that "The gunboat *A.O. Tyler* is expected from Cincinnati to-day and several others will follow in a few days. They will receive their guns and outfits here." A small notice was published in the *New York Times* on July 3 under the headline "Military and Naval Movements": "The steam gunboats *Conestoga* and *Lexington* arrived at Louisville on the 29th, from 'up the river.' They have armaments which are cargoes in themselves."[1]

The three U.S. Navy subordinate officers, ordered to Cincinnati in the middle of June, arrived as the month closed. All three would play significant roles with the timberclads and are thus worthy of individual profile. The first named was the only one of his rank on the western waters to receive a full-scale published biography prior to Lt. Cmdr. Le Roy Fitch and is the only one with a comprehensive collection of archived papers.

Lt. Seth Ledyard Phelps (1824–1885) was appointed a midshipman from Ohio in 1841 and prior to the Civil War served primarily in the Atlantic, including a stint aboard the sloop-of-war *St. Mary*'s and with the squadron assigned to lay a great cable from the U.S. to the UK. On June 19, the 105th ranking sea service lieutenant received orders from the navy secretary, Gideon Welles, to proceed west and join Cmdr. Rodgers at Cincinnati. The appointment came with some pleasure to both Phelps and Rodgers; the two men were friends because the former was a cousin of Anne Rodgers. From the time he reached the Queen City well into 1864, when he resigned, Phelps was involved in one significant Western Flotilla/Mississippi Squadron role after another, winning acclaim from Rear Admirals Foote, Davis, and Porter. After the Rebellion, the former Buckeye naval commander was involved with steamship companies and in activities surrounding a possible Nicaraguan canal. He also served as ambassador to Peru.

The second officer sent to Cincinnati by Welles was Lt. Roger N. Stembel (1810–1900) who, like Cmdr. Rodgers, was a Marylander, but, like Phelps, had received his midshipman appointment (in 1832) from Ohio. Prior to the war, he, too, had seen his share of service on vessels in the Atlantic and, prior to going west, had served at the Philadelphia naval asylum. He hoped for a blockade command, but, despite his forthcoming July promotion to the rank of Cmdr., it never came. Instead, he headed various shore activities from August 1862 through Appomattox. After the war, he did receive squadron commands prior to his 1872 retirement and promotion, two years later, to the rank of Rear Adm.

Joshua Bishop was the youngest of the new arrivals and the least senior in rank. A native of Missouri, he was commissioned a passed midshipman in 1858, a master in February 1861, and a Lt. two months later. Like Phelps, Bishop was active with the Mississippi naval establishment and attained the rank of Lt. Cmdr. in 1865. He retired with the rank of Cmdr. in 1896. Bishop would be one of the few U.S. Navy officers to have certain details of a court-martial case against him heard by the U.S. Supreme Court. Dismissed from the service after an 1868 finding of drunkenness and neglect of duty, he was restored to duty at his old rank in 1871 by a special act of Congress, his career essentially ruined. His appeal for back pay, made through the courts, failed. It is ironic that Bishop owed his initial appointment as a lieutenant to the dismissal of another officer, Lt. William B. Fitzgerald, who "went South."[2]

After Phelps, Stemble, and Bishop reported to Cmdr. Rodgers at Cincinnati, that ranking officer chose to employ their talents on three different assignments. Stemble and Bishop were to handle recruiting and ordnance matters, while Phelps was sent to Louisville to immediately take charge of pushing the unfinished timberclads through to Cairo.

According to the column "Southern Intelligence via Louisville," which appeared in the *Philadelphia Inquirer* on June 29, the *Tyler* had grounded at the eastern end of the Louisville and Portland Canal. She was gotten afloat on June 28 and, with the *Lexington* and *Conestoga*, passed through. Leaking badly, the *Conestoga* then entered dry dock at Portland, three miles west of Louisville, for additional calking. Portland, southeast of New Albany, Indiana, across the Ohio River, is today a Louisville neighborhood. The unidentified newsman providing this picture opined that "It is doubtful if either of the gunboats [presumably *Lexington* and *Tyler*] can get over the Portland bar, or if so, whether they can get to Cairo, on account of the low state of the river."

From Louisville on June 30, Lt. Phelps hired a small boat to take him to find the gunboats down near Portland, which was referred to in some quarters as "that secession hole." He found the *Lexington* just outside the entrance to the Louisville and Portland Canal, while the *Tyler* and refloated *Conestoga* lay about half a mile away. Once alongside the latter, he boarded through a gunport (there was no gangplank or boarding ladder) and shook hands with Capt. Shirley and Capt. Williamson.

The Louisville and Cincinnati Mail Boat Line president took the naval officer around the woodenclad and his initial impression of it, in her unfinished state, was not enthusiastic. Indeed, once he had the chance to view the other two, he would confide to a friend that all three were "sorry looking craft."

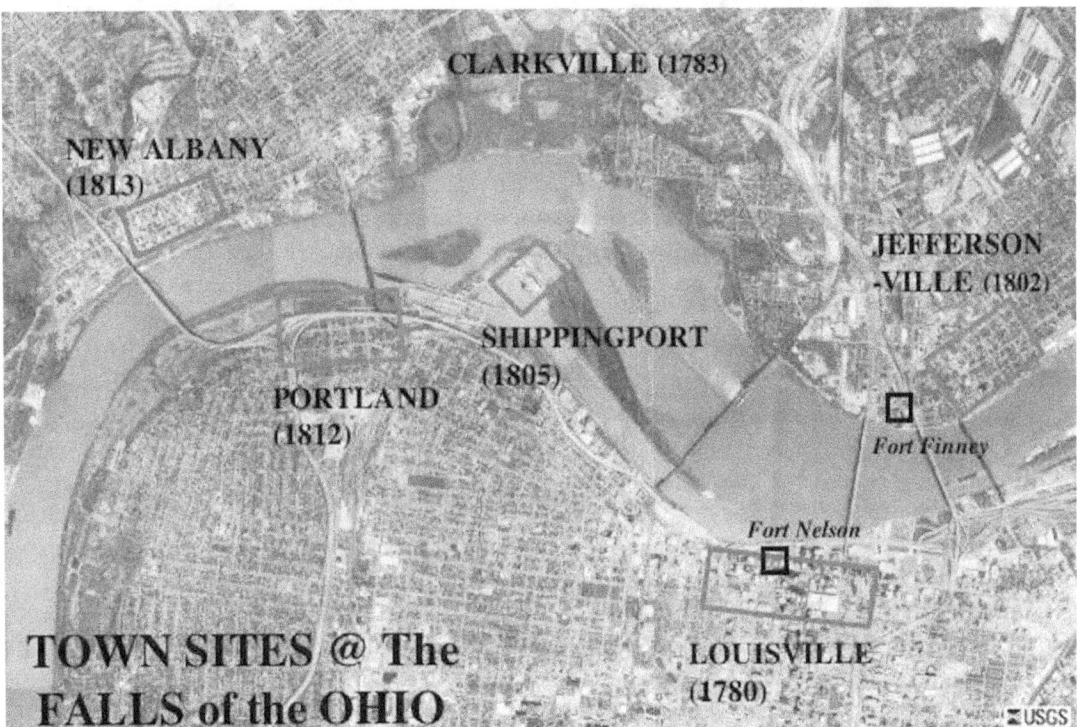

Towns at the Falls of the Ohio. Seen in a modern aerial map, these towns and the long-famous natural obstruction near them played an important part in the early story of the three timberclads. Low water at the Falls of the Ohio prevented *Lexington*, *Conestoga*, and *Tyler* from making an easy passage down the Ohio River to Cairo, Illinois, in the summer of 1861. Even as the vessels were being fitted out, extraordinary measures were taken by Cmdr. Rodgers and Lt. Phelps to both safeguard the boats and enhance their opportunities for passage (U.S. Geological Survey).

The workers pounded away around the touring officers and Phelps learned, while walking with Shirley, that Capt. Lockhart, superintendent of the canal and "an out and out Union man," had, after entreaty from Williamson, advanced the money to pay for calking the *Conestoga*. When they met a little later, Lockhart impressed Phelps. Although he had a coal mine near Cairo and wanted to sell fuel to the gunboats, the gentleman had already spent of his own funds to provide arms to Union sympathizers in Kentucky and had also arranged for local home guard units to keep "a special eye to the safety of the gunboats."

It was thought that it might be possible to dredge the Portland Bar in an effort to cut a two-foot deep channel 300 yards long. Phelps was rowed over to inspect the bar and the prospect was not hopeful, as the current was fast and carried sand from an island above. After dark, a civilian boat grounded on the bar; the current gurgled around it, closing the old channel and opening a brand new one.

After consultation with Capt. Lockhart, Phelps hired three dredge boats, then working on an extension of the Louisville and Portland Canal. They were asked to drop over and dig a path that would allow his craft to pass. At a cost of $210 total per day, the three started cutting about noon on June 30 and were able, after a few hours, to free up the *Conestoga*. She began to move ahead but quickly ran afoul of one of the dredges in the swift current and grounded. Within a short time, a new sandbank rose below the *Conestoga* and *Lexington*.

Dredging resumed on July 1, but no significant progress was made even as the cutting fee rose. Everyone with whom the lieutenant spoke had a different idea as to how or whether a proper channel could be made. Someone suggested that a couple of barges (at $5,000 apiece) be purchased. One could then be tied to each side of a gunboat to provide lift. Such a "camel," if successful, would lower draft and allow passage. This scheme was deemed too expensive and even less practical than the dredges.

Without the digging or lifting options, there was no alternative but to wait for the river to rise. Alteration work would, meanwhile, continue and the vessels, anchored in midstream, would close their gunports and otherwise "button up" every night. Protection would consist of workman tools, hot water hoses, and small arms—when a requested shipment of them arrived from Cincinnati.

Traveling back and forth to Cincinnati over the next several weeks to confer with Cmdr. Rodgers on the progress—or rather, lack of progress—with the three gunboats caused Lt. Phelps to take rooms midway at Louisville's Galt House.

Although Phelps described the problems of moving the gunboats in a lengthy letter to Cmdr. Rodgers on July 2, the Marylander also had other concerns. That same day, Naval Constructor Pook gave Rodgers a draft for two different types of purpose-built ironclad gunboats that he had designed after reviewing the Lenthall drafts and talking to Cincinnati area rivermen. The two men conferred over the designs and reworked them for submission to Quartermaster General Meigs on July 6. At this point, Pook returned to Washington and Rodgers was left to deal exclusively with his timberclads—or so he thought.

Quartermaster General Meigs had the Pook and Lenthall drawings completed, together with engine specifications, by mid-month. Before seeking bids, he sent the package over to Secretary Welles, who asked Engineer in Chief Benjamin Isherwood to review the suggested power plants. Isherwood, who recommended western engines, quickly returned his report to Welles, who forwarded it to the quartermaster general on July 22. Requests for bids were placed in newspapers along the Ohio and Middle Mississippi and on August 5 James B. Eads won the army's contract to build seven ironclad gunboats for delivery within two months at a cost of $89,600.

Although the construction story of the Eads gunboats is really outside the timberclad story, it impacts it in one important way. With Pook gone, Rodgers, by default of his position and location, had to take charge of seeing the ironclad project through. His ability to juggle both construction supervision and operational responsibilities would have a bearing on his future in the West. The two one-time traveling companions would meet again in Missouri in early August, even as Rodgers was attempting to get his wooden warcraft into the fighting.[3]

The three woodenclad boats remained stuck in low water off Louisville for all of July. No one seemed willing or able to give Cmdr. Rodgers or Lt. Phelps an honest or accurate opinion as to when the Ohio would rise. Lt. Phelps was particularly incensed by certain members of the local Pilots Association who fed him false information.

The Cincinnati Pilots Association, one of several similar organizations, was formed before the war to help insure the healthy financial status of its membership. The Rebellion all but guaranteed a high demand for services at rates these pilots hoped would exceed their 1861 monthly salaries of $250. To insure this, despite the current downturn in business, it was conjectured in some quarters that certain pilots were passing false information on river conditions to steamboat owners and government officers in an effort to enhance perceived need for channel-finders. Belying his reputation with some as a "cold fish," Cmdr. Rodgers was able to talk some members into accepting dangerous gunboat berths at $100 less than the going rate—this despite the fact that he was advised that there were some pilots who were not "associationists" but "outside men."

David A. Hiner, afterwards second pilot of the *Lexington*, was believed by Phelps to be feeding him incorrect data. On one occasion in mid–July, Hiner told the lieutenant that the water in the shoals below Louisville was 4.5 feet deep, yet when Phelps himself checked it a few hours later, not 3.5 feet was found. Portland bar depth reports coming from Cincinnati were just as inaccurate or, as Phelps put it, "false and conceived in the hope to further personal interests and those of the pilot association."

At this point, Rodgers and Phelps engaged the river reporter of the *Cincinnati Daily Commercial* to chart the water depth, hoping that this register would be of assistance. When this was accomplished, a seven-year statistical table showed river depth at various points and allowed the commander to predict that he had a five to one chance of a rise sufficient to get the boats to Cairo. Meanwhile, the experts continued to warn Rodgers he could expect that "in November water enough was pretty certain and before that improbable."

Lt. Phelps, meanwhile, occasionally visited the Portland bar himself aboard a flat-bottomed ferryboat, but he often had difficulty in making it to New Albany. At Rodgers request, he also ordered the civilian laborers to continue work on the timberclads without cessation.[4]

Despite the fact that Daniel Morton had promised to have the three boats completed weeks earlier, it took additional time for the work of alteration to be finished. The carpenters, painters, calkers and others did not leave until the third week of July. Phelps, with time on his hands and little water under his craft, angrily reviewed the terrible workmanship. Some of the construction was just wrong or not even finished and he could not understand how "the constructor [Pook]" could have agreed to such poor arrangements" and agreed to the contract. The lieutenant, famous in later years for his extremely bushy sideburns, was confident that Morton would not dispute the navy's catalog of inefficiencies, mistakes, and wrongs and, upon presentation, correct them. "We have a right to insist on it," he cried.

Phelps' list was part of two reports to Rodgers that truly highlight the early war innocence of western boat builders when it came to warship modification. Later on, other Union naval craft built or modified in yards along the western rivers, including some of the tinclads and purpose-built ironclads, like the *Tuscumbia*, one of the worst, also suffered from inadequate workmanship. Others, like the tinclad *Moose*, were regarded as fine vessels. The *Lexington* was the "best done" of the timberclads, but none of the three was "done well." The alterations made aboard the *Conestoga* appeared to be little more than "disgraceful patching."

For starters, when the contractor's people departed the boats, the supply of paint left aboard was exhausted and the work was not finished. The boats were to be painted black on the outside, but the *Lexington* was only half raven-colored. None were painted inside. Hopefully, some paint would be sent down from Cincinnati and those men already shipped or soon to be received would get a taste of what was a traditional sailor job — painting ship.

There was only one ladder to get on deck aboard the *Lexington* and that one was on the forecastle. The *Conestoga* had two ladders, one from a hatch and the second on the forecastle. There was no other way on either boat to get on deck. Additionally, no ladder was provided for access into the after lookout house. The ladders giving entrance up into the pilothouse were "simply perpendicular round ladders (not step ones)." They led to very small holes through which only an "active man" could squeeze. None of the boat davits were put up by the time the last workers returned to Cincinnati.

Lieutenant Phelps had considerable distress over the timberclads' carlines, also called carlings, which were, according to Gershom Bradford, "pieces of fore and aft timbers between deck beams." The one in the middle of the *Conestoga*'s bulwarks, along with two shorter ones, was supported only by temporary posts that were in the way of working the cannon and would have to be taken down. If knocked out without suitable replacement, however, "the pilot-

Timberclads on the Mississippi, summer 1861. This sketch of the *Lexington* (left) and *Conestoga* (right) was drawn for an issue of *Harper's Weekly* by its famed artist, Alexander Simplot. The awe and curiosity inspired by the pair in riverbank residents during their initial months of Civil War service might have been just as he drew it (Naval Historical Center).

house, bell and all, would come down." One of the carlines over the engine was broken in the middle and half of it was missing; the whole needed to be replaced. Additionally, another carline over the engine was not fastened down. Temporary pieces of scantling, or framing, held those carlines under the pilothouse and the one in the cabin.

The decks of the *Lexington* and *Tyler* forward of the boilers offered adequate space for the crews to berth. The boilers of the *Conestoga* were, however, too close to the bow to allow adequate space. Machinery covered the midship deck to the officers' quarters. Perhaps bulwarks could be built on both sides of the top deck between the wheelhouse and pilothouse; topped with a light deck or, at worst, awnings, more crew space could thus be created.

Speaking of cabins, the Buckeye officer was displeased by their arrangement. The contract between the army and Morton called for each warship to have two staterooms and a cabin, two mess rooms with cupboards, and ten staterooms for officers. In actuality, there were two 8 × 10-foot mess rooms, four smaller ones, and eight six-foot square staterooms (with two berths each) aboard the *Conestoga, Lexington,* and *Tyler.* On top of that, the aft gunroom on each boat had to serve as a cabin. The joinery was exceedingly rough. The men who put it in were supposed to be skilled mechanics, but it looked more like the product of "Irish laborers."

Lieutenant Phelps was especially incensed that some cupboards he wanted built aboard the *Conestoga* were missing. Even worse, the captain's head (called a "roundhouse") consisted of nothing more than a narrow, inclined seat connected to an eight-inch zinc pipe leading to the outside at a 45-degree angle. "Nothing less than a regular bowl, with valve, tank, and waterpipe will do in that part of the vessel," he vowed. One assumes the same lavatory errors greeted the commanders of *Tyler* and *Lexington.*

Another structural difficulty concerned the new thwart-ship bars. Designed to replace the beams removed when the boilers were lowered, they had yet to be installed. The same iron ties and bars were left over the boilers. Over on the *Tyler,* a man could not get from the after part of the boat forward "without walking over the boilers." One would have thought that some sort of decking would have been placed over them to form a gangway. The contract called for swinging booms, but none were installed. It might have been possible to install ladders over the side abaft the wheel to ascend to the upper deck and maybe one forward to pass in via a vacant porthole. Cutting a gangplank after the fact would be difficult.[5]

In addition to overseeing the rough conversion of the vessels as efficiently as possible, Cmdr. Rodgers and his three officers had also to see them crewed, supplied and armed. None of these tasks was very easy. Eventually, some supplies were obtained on the local market and forwarded to the gunboats, along with quantities of oil and lead paint.

As July wore on, Cmdr. Rodgers continued, sometimes using his own money and credit, to purchase small numbers of items most sorely required. The project was nerve-wracking to say the least. The Marylander, who failed to share his concerns in official reports at the time, later wrote that July's low water "cost me more anxiety and was more depressing than all the rest. It made it doubtful whether my exertion and my expense were not thrown away; whether, indeed, there was judicious expenditure of money, when it was not apparent that any use could be made of the boats until too late for effective service."

On top of this outfitting worry, Rodgers' learned that his excellent working relationship with Maj. Gen. McClellan was about to end.

When Illinois and Missouri were added to the Department of the Ohio, the powerful Blair family of Missouri became fearful that "Little Mac" would overshadow their man on the scene, Brig. Gen. Nathaniel Lyon. They soon began to lobby President Lincoln to have those two states withdrawn from McClellan's command. The decision was taken by the chief executive upon this political recommendation and the Ohio general learned of it on July 17.

The man chosen to succeed McClellan in a new western command was the noted explorer, and 1856 Republican presidential candidate, John C. Frémont. It was perceived helpful that he also happened to be the son-in-law of the legendary Thomas Hart Benton, mentor of Francis P. Blair, Jr. "The Pathfinder of the West," as he was nicknamed, could not reach St. Louis for about another week. Those days were spent in Washington, D.C., meeting with President Lincoln, Montgomery Blair, Lt. Gen. Scott, and others and in choosing his immediate subordinates, including Brig. Gen. Alexander S. Asboth, an Hungarian freedom fighter who had served under Republican patriot Louis Kossuth.

Also during this time, Frémont received intelligence briefings on what was known of the situation in his new department and undoubtedly heard from the postmaster general or Attorney General Bates about both Eads and Rodgers. Either of those gentlemen could have informed him that their friend, the St. Louis engineer, had a remarkable large snag boat that could be converted into an instrument of war if only Cmdr. Rodgers would approve.

Frémont also met with Quartermaster General Meigs and Assistant Navy Secretary Gustavus Fox to discuss a river thrust and the use of mortar boats to support it. In one audience with the chief executive, he advanced his own plan for action to end Confederate activity in Missouri and, in the words of Allen Nevins, launch "a movement down the Mississippi upon Memphis." Lincoln supposedly gave him a blank check to use his own judgment and do the best he could.

The army's advertisement inviting bids for the construction of ironclad river gunboats was placed in the newspapers of communities along the Ohio and Mississippi in mid–July. At the same time, Francis P. Blair in St. Louis and Postmaster General Montgomery Blair in Washington lobbied Quartermaster General Meigs to make certain that the new craft would be built at or near St. Louis. Not-so-obliquely calling Meigs' attention to his brother-in-law's problems getting the timberclads to Cairo, the correspondents emphasized that constructing the vessels at their location would allow them "to be got out at all seasons of the year, and not high up on the Ohio, where they may [be] tied up and of no use when needed."[6]

While Phelps struggled with the timberclads and the workers aboard them, there remained the problem of obtaining sufficient crews to man them. The Navy Department in Washington was scrambling to fill berths aboard coastal men-o'-war and could spare only a few commissioned officers. Once again, theater commander McClellan came to the procedural rescue of his nautical force. It was he who allowed Cmdr. Rodgers to open local recruiting stations, called "rendezvous" in navy terms, and to ship landsmen. His only requirement was that their number and pay be kept approximately the same as that permitted for members of oceangoing warships of similar class.

Under McClellan's authorization, Cmdr. Stembel and Master Bishop opened recruiting offices in Cincinnati and Louisville. Their efforts met with only limited success due to competition from the army — as well as Southern sympathizers. Additionally, there was a realization on the part of potential enlistees that the ugly oak-covered ex-packets were not protected against cannonballs, and service aboard them could be most hazardous to their futures. This view continued and, several years later, one of the trio's original officers explained to any army acquaintance why local watermen did not want to join the river navy. They believed, he opined, "that the service on Gunboats will be exceedingly dangerous."

There was some suggestion that the gunboat service could be entirely crewed by soldiers, who would train under army, not navy, regulations. Although regular blue-water officers like Stembel shied away, when possible, from inland service, they understood, as Rodgers, Phelps, and others did, that fighting on the brineless streams still required naval organization and discipline, adjusted to the realities of their steamers and the rivers they plied.

Cmdr. Rodgers was encouraged by his subordinates to seek Maj. Gen. McClellan's approval to have naval discipline and communication aboard the vessels of his little squadron, now increasingly known as "the Western Flotilla." Otherwise, the men in charge of the steamers would suffer no end to "annoyances and losses." "The Army is not fit for shipboard," wrote one, "and won't do at all."

By mid–July, the temporary enlistments for a number of the hands taken on at Cincinnati in June to move the boats downstream were coming to an end. Even as these men were discharged and provided government-funded tickets to return home, their places were going — more slowly than desired — to others.

Stembel, Bishop, Rodgers, and Phelps realized that the local "river material is very poor." A number of the original crewmen who wished to remain, including most of the firemen, could not pass the physical once a surgeon was retained to give exams. Almost to a man, the U.S. Navy officers cried for the need of "some few old men-of war men."

This plea for experienced manpower was put on paper and forwarded to Secretary Welles. In his review of the river war, John D. Milligan caught a message from Rodgers to a "Dear Sir," concerning his frustration with the rough and tumble men that did sign on. Perhaps in jest and certainly in frustration with the quality of men he was being asked to accept, the Marylander wrote on June 30 that "I shall read the articles of war every Sunday until they know them, and get a parson at them whenever I can so as to break down their spirit — and let their wives come on board to lecture them on weekdays. With all these helps and hard drill, they will have no time to give trouble."

In an effort to locate a few local men willing to join the Yankee gunboat service, Lt. Phelps opened a little recruiting station right on the locks of the Louisville and Portland Canal. These sat at a point intermediate between the stranded gunboats — grouped together near Shippingport — and Portland. Operating without funds for enlistment handbills or other sea service enticements, the Buckeye officer competed with Confederate sympathizers attempting to encourage the Southern call to arms. Phelps was able to locate a number of Portlanders, including some soldiers, willing to sign shipping articles. Unhappily, the majority failed the required physical — which in those days was relatively simple. One of those who did manage to join was Alfred Phelps, whom his brother appointed paymaster of the *Conestoga*.

If the vessels remained stranded, Phelps expected to move his office over to Portland. In the meantime, to provide a bit more protection, a sergeant of the guard was engaged, a man from New Albany who was able to recruit a company (14 men and a corporal) from his hometown sufficient for the *Conestoga* and her sisters.

Just as the navy men were not impressed with the quality of the potential ratings pool, so too were they disappointed in the boatmen they interviewed for possible officer billets. These people seemed to be sufficiently qualified to operate steamboats and handle questions of freight, but their leadership promise and ability to come under naval discipline appeared sorely lacking.

These judgments were made by Rodgers, Phelps & Co., who were ocean-trained professionals unaccustomed to inland river operations. In the end, their view would not prove altogether accurate. Many steamboat men eventually made excellent volunteer officers and the Union would not have been able to win the river war without them. Although a number of men were engaged to fill subordinate slots, the decision was taken to replace two of the civilian gunboat captains who sought naval appointments; Collier was relieved on July 19 and Williamson on July 21.

Duble was retained as first master of the *Conestoga*. Edward Shaw was appointed first master of the *Tyler* while Jacob S. Hurd became first master of the *Lexington*. Hurd's brother, Jesse Y. Hurd, also a steamboat captain, was the plaintiff in the famous *Hurd v. Rock Island Railroad Company* federal court case of 1856. Having run his *Effie Afton* into a rail bridge, Hurd had sued for damages but lost in the trial during which Abraham Lincoln defended the railroad.

Through dint of their hard work, Rodgers and his officers were able, according to Robert Johnson, to enlist sufficient men to give each boat a half complement. The exact number is unknown, but if the total crew was to run 198 souls that half would be roughly 80–90.[7]

The *New York Times* notice of July 3 was wrong. Neither the *Conestoga* nor the *Lexington* had armaments at this time. Although it is possible that report may have been planted as disinformation, it is probable that it was just a fortunate error.

Providing ordnance and small arms remained a challenge, even after Rodgers made requisitions and visited the Erie naval depot. It certainly appeared all but a crime that the three boats were forced to sit in the middle of the river and rely on fire hoses and sticks — and a few personal pistols — to repel any boarders. Fortunately, no Rebel bands were sufficiently organized in the area during July to attempt to take the craft.

Phelps requested that Rodgers send some small arms down to the boats, but the Marylander had none and no authority to obtain any. He suggested that, while he tried to find some (keeping in mind that Maj. Gen. McClellan had once found rusty smoothbore muskets in the Ohio state armory), his subordinate purchase a few in Louisville.

Any such effort, in the eyes of Lt. Phelps, would display weakness to unfriendly eyes and so he began to look for another way. When arms failed to arrive from Cincinnati in a timely manner, he took the initiative to visit "Fort Joe Holt," the Kentucky loyalist rendezvous near Louisville, and seek assistance from its commander. After a brief conversation, Col. Lovell H. Rousseau of the 3rd Kentucky Infantry (U.S.), ever active in his efforts to aid the Union and keep his state loyal, provided 30 stand of muskets and 500 rounds of cartridges. Ten muskets and cartridges were distributed to each gunboat.[8]

While the navy officers worked to man, arm, and push their boats out, the river rose slightly and continued to increase in depth very gradually, just as the newspaperman's chart had indicated it might. The rise was numbingly slow. Between July 11 and 21, the water rose a scant five inches, even as the height needed remained around four foot. Every day, Lt. Phelps collected the latest information from all available sources and sighed, especially after his own on-site reviews.

On July 21, there was only 30 inches downstream at Scuffletown and, although there was three feet at Flint Island, the channel was very narrow and crooked. Even with the two foot rise which camel barges might provide—an idea since discarded—the water was not deep enough. By July 22, there was a report that the river level near Henderson stood at three feet, with the bars nearby at three to three and a half feet. The depth at Portland bar also improved.

As the sailors anxiously waited, a number of local contractors approached Rodgers and Phelps with schemes to get the gunboats downstream even in the face of low water. Both bluewater officers realized that these were get-rich-quick operators who would probably fail in their efforts even as they milked the public treasury. Indeed, it was suspected that "anyone of these river men is ready to enter into a contract to do it, even if there is not a particle of chance to succeed." Phelps refused all suggestions, fearful that it he let anyone make an attempt his vessels would be scattered "along the bars below here, at out-of-the-way places, and exposed ones."[9]

During his frequently interrupted train trip west from the national capital in late July, Maj. Gen. Frémont gave considerable thought to his plan for warfare upon the western rivers. Visiting with Indiana governor Oliver P. Morton en route, he asked the Hoosier executive to send him some regiments made up entirely of men experienced in steamboating.

The new theater commander crossed the Mississippi to St. Louis on July 25 and immediately got down to business. The man who would be booted out of command in 100 days for inefficiency and corruption got off to a great start. Meeting for lunch with his chief subordinates, he not only took stock of the local military and political situation, but also found the time to concern himself with marine matters.

Brigadier General Asboth had probably informed his chief on the train ride from Washington about the armed naval craft he had witnessed the Austrians employing on the lower Danube River in Europe. Remembering the conversation, Frémont told him to find out what riverboats in the area were immediately available for refitting as gunboats.

At the same time, the "Pathfinder of the West" took it upon himself to invite a veteran St. Louis riverboat skipper, Captain Thomas Maxwell, to be his informal nautical advisor, filling a role similar to that given Cdr. Kountz by Maj. Gen. McClellan. Frémont, however, went further. He authorized Maxwell to organize three companies of a "marine corps" made up of pilots, engineers, mates, firemen, and deckhands.

It is not known for certain when Frémont first met Capt. Eads, but it is apparent that the engineer and the general had a meeting shortly after the new theater commander came into town and quite possibly as early as July 26. In connection with the mission given Brig. Gen. Asboth, Eads undoubtedly made Frémont aware of the availability of *Submarine No. 7* and the circumstances under which its earlier conversion had been rejected. Thereafter, as Nevins reports, "Captain James B. Eads was frequently at headquarters."

On July 27, as the Ohio River rise allowed him to contemplate his departure for Cairo, Cmdr. Rodgers received a brief telegram at Cincinnati from Secretary Welles: "General Frémont is the successor of General McClellan. Report to him."[10]

Meanwhile, Brig. Gen. Gideon J. Pillow's Army of Tennessee had been organizing downstream and fortifications were begun by the Volunteer State at Fort Pillow and Fort Randolph, on the first and second Chickasaw bluffs. After Tennessee joined the Confederacy, Pillow's command was entrusted to Maj. Gen. (and bishop) Leonidas Polk, the North Carolinian in charge of Confederate Department No. 2. Hoping to invade the chaotic region of southern Missouri on behalf of the insurrection, Polk ordered his Tennessee general to capture the river town of New Madrid.

On July 26, a grand expedition under Brig. Gen. Pillow departed Memphis aboard six of the South's remaining Mississippi River packets: *John Simonds, Alonzo Child, W.M. Morrison, New Falls City*, and *E. Howard*, led by the flag boat *Grampus*, under Capt. Marsh Miller. A stop was made at Randolph to add numbers to the regiments already embarked. There was great rejoicing among its local citizens when, on July 28, gray-clad soldiers disembarked from the steamboats onto Missouri soil. It was everywhere expected that these men would take Bird's Point, Cairo or both and if they did not it would only be because they were "not afforded an opportunity."

By the last week of July, the Ohio River had risen sufficiently to allow the *Lexington, Conestoga*, and *Tyler* to start downstream. On July 29, the three sisters got up steam and cleared Portland. They were able to pass over the Portland bar and headed into New Albany. Because low water had caused them to be stranded in Kentucky for so long, the decision was taken to arm them in Indiana before they proceeded further.

While the gunboatmen waited for an additional rise, the small arms dispatched by Master Bishop arrived at the New Albany railroad station. As these were being taken to the boats, preparations were completed to move the great guns that had also caught up with them: ten 8-inch Dahlgrens and seven 32-pounders. Over the next several days, the timberclad crews, supported by 30 new men who had joined from Louisville on July 30, undertook the arduous labor of mounting them.

Four 32-pounders of 42 cwt. were placed aboard the *Conestoga*. Two more 32-pounders of 42 cwt., plus four 8-inch Dahlgren smoothbores of 63 cwt., went aboard the *Lexington*. The *Tyler* received one 32-pounders of 43 cwt. and six 8-inch Dahlgren smoothbores of 63 cwt. The size of these guns was impressive. They, more than the wooden armor, would ensure that the timberclads remained in demand even later in the war when the tinclads— also lightly armored but also lightly gunned — became available.

Cwt. was a British measurement for cannon size. The 32-pounders employed by the Blue and Gray navies came in 27, 32, 42, and 57 cwt. and each hundredweight (cwt.) was equal to 112 pounds. The tubes of the mid-range iron shot guns hauled aboard the *Conestoga* and *Lexington* weighed 4,700 pounds apiece. Their 6.4 inch bores were 92.05 inches long. Using six-pound powder charges, the guns could hurl 32-lb. cannonballs 1,656 yards at 5 degrees elevation in six seconds or a 26-lb. shell 1,710 yards at five degrees elevation in 6.5 seconds.

The iron smoothbore 8-inch Dahlgren cannon available came in 55 or 63 cwt., with the latter size placed aboard *Lexington* and *Tyler*. Their 7,000-pound tubes had 8-inch bores 100.3 inches long. Each required a 9-lb. powder charge to send its 51.5-lb. shell 1,770 yards at 5 degrees of elevation. Time on target was 6.32 seconds. The guns did not come with all of their gear. A grass hawser was made into breechings and gun tackles were jury-rigged from tackle purchased in a general store. Necessary blocks were also procured locally. A small amount of powder and shot was also found and acquired.

Rebels in Paducah, meanwhile, having heard of the gunboats' forthcoming passage, boasted that they would try to take the boats if they came unarmed. The steamers now had guns protruding from their gunports. Fortunately for their crews, the Dixie-leaning Kentuckians did not know that the sailors were as yet untrained in their use.

At the "Secession hole" of Columbus on August 1, local Southern sympathizers seized the steamer *B.F. Cheney*, the packet that ran daily to Cairo, and took her to New Madrid. It was alleged at the time that her captain, and chief owner, had actually turned her over, having withdrawn $8,000 from his bank account the day before his last trip down. Historian J. Thomas Scharf reports that she was actually "running under the orders and signals of Gen. Prentiss" and that, when first taken, her captain and other officers were all arrested and given 20 minutes to get ashore. Whatever the case, the capture of the *Cheney* could be seen as the first Confederate incursion against Kentucky. Upon her departure downstream, the *Cheney*, later valued at $25,000, was cheered by "a large assemblage on the levee." At Hickman, a large Confederate flag was brought aboard and hoisted above the U.S. ensign. This historic sign of victory fluttered over the boat as she made her way to Randolph and Memphis and brought additional huzzahs and cannon salutes.

As August began, the Union military situation in Missouri seemed to be worsening. Maj. Gen. Frémont, with 16,000 soldiers of varying quality, was faced with attacks from irregulars to the south and east as well as those regular Confederate troops in the southwestern part of the state facing Brig. Gen. Lyon. At Cairo, Brig. Gen. Prentiss believed himself outgunned by Polk and Pillow and pleaded with St. Louis for reinforcements. The "Pathfinder" saw the greatest danger at the beleaguered town of Cairo and, while advising other commanders to move out of danger, moved to support Prentiss.

Out at Cairo, the gunboats' destination, the town was overjoyed on August 2 to welcome theater commander Maj. Gen. Frémont, who had put together a secret operation under the nautical command of Capt. Barton Able of the St. Louis–based Atlantic and Mississippi Steamship Company. Barton's armada of steamers, including the *G.W. Graham*, *War Eagle*, *D.A. January*, *Warsaw*, *Jennie Deans*, *Empress*, and *Louisiana*, loaded with some 5,000 reinforcements for Brig. Gen. Prentiss' lightly-garrisoned town, rounded to off Bird's Point. The flag boat of the "Pathfinder of the West," *City of Alton*, chugged to the Cairo wharf. As cannon at Fort Defiance and Fort Prentiss thundered their salute, Frémont and his staff came ashore and received a festive welcome.

They didn't remain in Cairo long. Believing that Brig. Gen. Pillow's New Madrid strike and possible further ambitions were checked, the high command quickly returned to St. Louis. The entire fleet, minus the *Warsaw*, which broke a shaft on her downward trip, arrived back at St. Louis in mid-afternoon on August 4.

On August 5, activities at the Cincinnati recruiting office were placed on hiatus when Master Bishop received orders to transfer out to St. Louis where he would open a rendezvous and enlist 100 sailors. Next day, Bishop lead another detachment of men shipped at the Queen City aboard the steamer *Major Anderson* and saw them delivered to Lt. Phelps at Louisville.

As the civilian steamer continued down towards the canal, Phelps and his recruits went aboard the *Conestoga* and departed for New Albany. There the task group commander released an underage newcomer, William J. Stephens, into the hands of local judge George A. Bicknell. His parents wanted the boy home.

Far away in Washington, D.C., Quartermaster General Meigs and his staff opened the seven ironclad construction bids that had been received. To the great relief of the St. Louis contingent gathered nearby, the low bid was submitted by engineer Eads. He proposed to build between four and 16 boats at a cost of $89,600 a copy and deliver them to Cairo before October 10. If he missed that deadline, he would daily forfeit $100 per boat. Eads was told to come back in two days, at which time he could sign the official contract and discuss details.

A tranquil photograph of the hills of Southern Indiana not far from Cincinnati captured from the deck of an Ohio River steamer in 1943. This view is not unlike that seen from the decks of the three timberclads as they made their way to Cairo in the summer of 1861 (Library of Congress).

On August 6, as if to directly emphasize the need for federal gunboat patrols to protect loyal commerce, the 163-ton side-wheeler *Pocahontas*, built at Cincinnati in 1857, was seized by Rebels in the Tennessee River at the state line. She was en route to Louisville with 60 hogsheads of tobacco, according to the August 7 *Cincinnati Daily Commercial*.[11]

August 7 was a momentous day for both the timberclads and James B. Eads. That morning a check of the Ohio River depth found it was just one foot shallower than the depth of the *Tyler*. Having been long frustrated from making the Cairo run, Lt. Phelps called Masters Hurd and Shaw aboard the *Conestoga* and told them the time to leave had come. After some deliberation, the three men, plus Master Duble, agreed to a straightforward and simple plan. Under full power, the two smaller gunboats would tow the big one over the shoals. Once beyond, assuming none were too damaged to continue, they would make their way downstream, stopping occasionally for coal and making their way past Paducah fully prepared.

Steaming away from the bank out into the river a few hours later, the *Lexington* and *Conestoga* were joined by the *Tyler*. Men aboard the two lighter timberclads threw stout hawsers to sailors at the bow of their big sister. Down below decks, the boilers were brought to full pressure as the coal heavers on all three craft shoveled coal into them as quickly as possible. The water frothed under six paddle wheels and, with clouds of smoke escaping from six chimneys, the combined power of pull-and-push brought the *Tyler* over the obstructing bars.

Back at Louisville, a local newspaperman penned a brief column on what he had witnessed for the next morning's edition: "The gunboats left for Cairo yesterday morning, fully equipped. The three boats have on board sixteen guns, ten of which are 32-pounders and the balance 64-pounders. The boats will run only during the day."

Also that Wednesday, James B. Eads came to the office of Quartermaster General Meigs in Washington and formally signed the contract under which he would construct seven ironclad gunboats for the U.S. Army. At that time, he was also informed that Cmdr. Rodgers, who had assisted Mr. Pook with the design, would oversee their preparation and appoint a construction superintendent and other subordinates as required. Rodgers already knew of this responsibility, one more atop the operational one he was sweating over with the timberclads, and was asked to comment on several technical questions.

The voyage of the timberclads down the Ohio continued without incident on August 8, even as Cmdr. Rodgers in Cincinnati took up his ironclad superintendent duties. The three rounded to off Cannelton, Indiana, 43 miles east of Evansville, late in the day and proceeded to coal. During the process, they were seen by the passing steamer *Linden*, which reported their approach to the editor of the *Evansville Daily Journal*.

Earlier, Cmdr. Rodgers busied himself with the new Eads project. In response to his brother-in-law's communications, the Maryland sailor wrote back, agreeing with him that properly mounted army 42-pounders and navy Dahlgrens would be adequate. He recommended that the battery of each boat be slightly smaller than first imagined to avoid trimming by the stern and suggested casemate armor thickness. In addition to Meigs, Rodgers also wrote Bureau of Ordnance chief Capt. Andrew A. Harwood seeking plans for gun carriages and to Eads himself asking that the boats' armor be made from "only the best charcoal iron." In addition, he named John Litherbury to oversee the Carondelet construction site and ordered him to report to Capt. Eads at St. Louis.

Transactions involving the timberclads and Rodgers continued apace on August 9. They were obscured by the war's big picture, but are important to this story. In the morning, Secretary Welles opened a report from Cmdr. Rodgers, the first received in some time. In it, the Marylander happily reported that the "expected rise" had permitted the gunboats to depart Louisville and that the river depth would now be sufficient to "float them safely to Cairo." Then, in his typical take-charge style, Rodgers went on to inform his superior how he had appointed officers to the boats, basing his arrangements on the naval model. He even listed the salaries he proposed to pay these men. The first masters (Duble, Hurd, and Shaw) each would make $100 a month. Each craft would have a second master ($80), a third master ($60), and two pilots ($150). One hundred dollars per month would be paid to, one each, an assistant surgeon, an acting paymaster, and a chief engineer. The roster would be completed with three assistant engineers ($75), an ($30) armorer, a carpenter ($30) and a striker ($25). The western naval chief was particularly proud of his first masters, all of whom were steamboat captains in civilian life, as well as his success in talking the pilots into accepting salaries $100 per month less than that required by the Pilots' Association. Secretary Welles read the communication and endorsed it for the file: "This whole subject belongs to the War Department."

Maj. Gen. Frémont had never met Cmdr. Rodgers. The "Pathfinder of the West" was, however, well acquainted with members of the Blair family and had seen Capt. Eads in St. Louis before the engineer departed for the ironclad bid opening in Washington. Later this day, Postmaster General Montgomery Blair received a letter from the new Department of the West commander. In it Frémont asked for new levies, new money, and a new western waters naval commander. The key sentences relative to this account read that "It would subserve the public interest if Commander John Rodgers were removed and an officer directed to report to me to have command of the operations on the Mississippi. Show this to President."

Until the day Capt. Andrew Hull Foote showed up as his replacement, Cmdr. Rodgers did not learn from Frémont, the Blairs, Eads, Welles, Assistant Navy Secretary Gustavus Fox, Meigs (who may or may not have known from his brother-in-law Montgomery Blair) or anyone else that his transfer had been requested. Until then, he was allowed to operate his command and provide advice on the construction of the new gunboats, completely unaware that his days in the west were numbered. Lincoln had given Frémont a free hand and, in Rodgers' case, he used it quickly.[12]

Still in the Queen City on the morning of August 10, Cmdr. Rodgers completed a large requisition for the Eads gunboats. Once this postal work was completed, the Marylander boarded a train for Cairo. The *Conestoga*, *Lexington*, and *Tyler*, meanwhile, arrived at Evansville and were welcomed at the wharf by a large crowd. When the local newspaper reported their visit two days later, the *Tyler* was identified as the *A.O. Taylor.*

If the tars aboard the three Yankee woodclads were pleased with their reception, they would have been disheartened to learn then, as they doubtless did shortly thereafter, of the day's military fiasco in Missouri. Coming on the heels of the great Northern defeat at Bull Run Creek, Virginia (First Manassas) on July 31, Brig. Gen. Lyon was defeated (and killed) at Wilson's Creek, southwest of Springfield, by Rebel forces under Brig. Gen. Sterling Price and Ben McCullouch.

Lt. Phelps' gunboats continued down the Ohio on August 11 and worked their way past Paducah without incident. While the *Conestoga* and *Tyler* stopped briefly at Mound City, Cmdr. Stembel's *Lexington* continued on to Cairo, anchoring in front of the city early on the afternoon of August 12. The *Conestoga* and *Tyler* chugged down past Cairo in the still bright early evening and returned, coming to at the wharf on the Ohio River side of the town next to the *Lexington*. The "levee was crowded" with curious civilians and soldiers, reported the local *Cincinnati Daily Gazette* newsman, all wanting to see the "arrival of this long expected fleet."

As Cmdr. Rodgers, "a gallant officer ... the son of Commodore Rodgers," was not expected to reach Cairo before late that night, Lt. Phelps made the Navy's first symbolic welcoming handshake with Federal ground forces, the army's Col. Richard Oglesby of the 8th Illinois. The expanding Federal western army now had a new unit to further its operations where, in the words of historian Milligan, "water furnished the only genuine avenue for communications."

The correspondent, who was probably Joseph McCullagh, who would later serve as volunteer flag secretary for Rear Adm. Andrew H. Foote, gave Queen City readers the first portrait of the timberclads that most had probably yet seen. "They are light draught, remodeled steamers," he wrote, "built into compartments with caulked ceilings and their bulwarks carried up all round with 12-inch timbers." Their armament consisted "of heavy guns, thirty twos and twenty fours." He did not believe the boats would have to wait long to see action, though "the former names of these steamers will probably be exchanged for others more significant, and dating from their new career."[13]

With Brig. Gen. Prentiss now away in command at Ironton, Missouri, Col. Oglesby was very anxious that the strange looking new gunboats assist in the defense of Cairo. As yet, their outfits were unfinished and some renovation was required. Next morning they were permitted to return up the Ohio to Mound City for repairs. It was arranged that in the event of an emergency they could return.

Steaming the eight Ohio River miles early in the morning allowed the *Conestoga* and *Tyler* priority review by the workmen at Hambleton Collier & Company. Lt. Phelps sought to obtain repairs desired back in Louisville, including, for his *Conestoga*, a gangway, pantries, and proper fixtures for his roundhouse.

In the wake of the Wilson's Creek debacle, Maj. Gen. Frémont, on August 14, cast about for fresh troops to reinforce retreating Union soldiers. As no Confederate demonstration was expected against Bird's Point, the theater commander sent new orders that some of the 5,000 reinforcements he had escorted down 10 days earlier be withdrawn. As a result, four regiments were taken aboard steamers the next day and sent to Herculaneum, a port some 30 miles below St. Louis.

To guard the embarkation against any potential mischief, the gunboats *Lexington* and *Conestoga* were ordered back down from Mound City before their repairs could begin. Upon their arrival that evening, Lt Phelps had them anchored in the middle of the stream opposite Cairo, prepared for action. There being insufficient men to man all three boats, the available crews were divided into two parties, one for each of the active vessels. At the same time, a quantity of ammunition was obtained from Fort Defiance and, after it was loaded, Phelps examined the Mississippi for a short distance above and below Bird's Point.

It was during this deployment that the correspondent of the *St. Louis Daily Missouri Democrat* was first able to inspect the craft and talk with rivermen about the ugly black boats. Most of the "old seamen" interviewed had little doubt that they were overpriced and worthless. This damning opinion, shared by many men whom Rodgers and his officers were trying to recruit aboard, was echoed in print:

Major General (later Illinois governor) Richard J. Oglesby (1824–1899) commanded the crucial base at Cairo when the timberclads first arrived. Indeed, it was he who shook hands with Lt. S. Ledyard Phelps in welcoming the vessels to the new war zone (U.S. Army Military History Institute).

> These gun-boats, constructed at an immense expense to the Government, I am sorry to say, have been built on the rotten hulls of old worn out passenger and coal tow-boats, and any man with a pair of good, cowhide, heavy-soled boots could kick out their water sides. There never was a more wanton waste of public money than in their construction. A six-pound ball, well-aimed, would knock their wheels to pieces, and a land battery would, if in range, make them only slaughter pens. There might be some excuse to the War Department, if the boats were entirely new, but there is evidently corruption some where, as the oldest and most rotten hulls have been bought up at the highest prices and varnished over. The cost of repairing them has far exceeded the entire cost of entirely new boats, new hulls, and machinery.[14]

With the troopboats headed upstream toward St. Louis on August 15, the acting task group commander was requested by Col. Oglesby to make a demonstration down the Mississippi toward New Madrid. The purpose, Lt. Phelps was informed, was to gather intelligence, to capture enemy shipping if possible, and to let the Rebels know the Yankee gunboats had arrived. *Conestoga* and *Lexington* cast off during the afternoon and slowly and cautiously made their way south.

The initial wartime cruise of the black-painted timberclads was largely uneventful, according to Northern sources. No enemy was encountered and no batteries fired upon them from either shore. There were no invectives hurled by crowds lined up at any of the towns they passed and no Confederate troop movements spotted along the river. Southern flags were, however, seen flying at Columbus and Hickman.

A pair of steamers "in the service of the Rebels" were chased from James' Bayou, a point below Hickman opposite Island No. 8, but, with an eight-mile head start, they reached the safety of New Madrid before the Buckeye sailor could close. One of the escapees was said to be the recently seized Cairo–Columbus packet *B.F. Cheney*. It is at this point that the story becomes interesting, as the identity of the second steamer is still uncertain. We will, however, hazard a guess. According to the *Memphis Avalanche* of August 16, 1861, the two timberclads pursued one of the vessels not from James' Bayou but from Cairo itself. This second vessel, whose identify has been shrouded, was the *Equality*, a boat thought lost.

The *Equality* was a 90-ton stern-wheeler built at Paducah the previous year and homeported at Evansville, Indiana. Capt. James M. Irwin, late skipper of the steamer *New Uncle Sam*, together with a boarding party, had captured her, lying at the Cairo wharf with steam up. Then, in a bold dash, they put out downstream and made it past the batteries before the soldiers could react. The two Union gunboats were sent in pursuit but were never able to get closer than an hour and a half behind.

The Lytle List notes that the *Equality* was lost in 1861. George Wright reminded this writer in a November 10, 2006, entry on the Civil War Navies Messageboard that the steamer "was snagged and lost on Golconda, Illinois, on May 11, 1861." The *Avalanche* editor reported that the *Equality*, not permanently "lost" but obviously salvaged, underwent a "metamorphosis for war purposes" and became a Confederate transport and ersatz gunboat. We know that she was among the steamers employed to carry Rebel troops to Hickman and Columbus in early September.

In her civilian life, the *Equality* "was not considered of much account." Now she was "understood to have several guns on board, with the necessary ammunition." It is likely that the *Equality*, which was not an official Confederate warship and is listed in no roster, may have fulfilled the same purpose as the U.S. Army gunboat *Swallow*. It is also possible that she was the unnamed gunboat that often, over the next several months, was mentioned in connection with the operations of the C.S.S. *Jackson* (or *Yankee*).

A better candidate than the *Equality*, however, is the *Grampus*, also known as the *Grampus No. 2*, present with the Confederate New Madrid transport fleet back in July. The 252-ton craft, also a stern-wheeler painted black, was constructed at McKeesport, Pennsylvania, in 1856. Owned by Thomas Chester of Pittsburgh, she was engaged as a tugboat, operating up and down the Mississippi and its tributaries from its homeport at Brownsville, Texas. When the war broke out, she was seized by the South and, as the property of a Northerner, confiscated.

The dashing skipper of the *Grampus*, Marsh Miller of Memphis, had fitted a pair of brass 12-pounders aboard and made his vessel into an armed auxiliary and scout boat. Sometime later, the *New York Times* reported that her daring pilot was George Miller of St. Louis. As the *Grampus* would frequently steam upriver on reconnaissance missions, it is quite possible that his vessel, rather than the *Equality*, was the steamer chased this day.

Given the condition of his own boat and the possibility of heavy opposition from "masked batteries," Lt Phelps, as he later noted in his official report, chose not to run in on the Confederate craft. He did, however, unsuccessfully try to draw fire from suspected hidden gun positions. Reconnoitering closely to within two miles of Columbus, the gun crews of the timberclads were exercised from a location in the river bend north of town. After "hovering round" for two hours and sending 18 shells in random directions at intervals of about 10 minutes, Phelps elected to turn back for Cairo. Not a single cannon on the Confederate side responded to the Yankee feint. En route back upstream in the dark, campfires were seen in various locations. The gunboats returned to Cairo just after daylight on August 16 and their commander reported to Oglesby that a force of 8,000–10,000 "State Rebels" were "drilling and waiting for arms from Tennessee."

With concern continuing over the possibility of a Confederate end run on Cairo from the St. Louis region, Col. Oglesby also requested that Cmdr. Stembel and the *Lexington* undertake the first independent gunboat mission on August 16 — in the opposite direction from whence they had just come. With the local army artillery chief Col. Gustave Waagner and his secretary embarked at Col. Oglesby's request, the timberclad departed for "up the river" to observe fortifications being erected at Cape Girardeau.

As the *Lexington* moved upstream, Cmdr. Stembel ordered gunnery practice. After considerable and repeated rehearsal, the new artillerists were permitted to fire two live shots: one a 32-pounder canister shot and the other a 64-pounder shell with a five second fuse.

Puffing her way upstream to within about three miles of Commerce, Missouri, the noisy *Lexington* was hailed by a number of families on the opposite shore from the town. Nosing into the bank, Stembel and Waagner were informed that most of the 500 citizens of the community were fleeing because some 800 Rebels were en route to attack. The timberclad arrived off Commerce about 6:00 P.M. and the men aboard were shocked by the intense excitement among the remaining townspeople. Many of these were gathered on the wharf with their furniture and goods, waiting for some boat to come by and take them aboard.

"Willing to forsake everything for the purpose of getting away for personal safety," families begged Stembel to rescue them. With Waagner's approval, the boat's sailors helped a large number of men, women, and children aboard, together with merchandise and household goods. The *Chicago Daily Tribune* correspondent along on the trip counted "17 women and 43 children at one time gathered in the cabin."

The gunboat returned to Cape Girardeau about 2:00 A.M. on September 17 but, for their safety, did not land her passengers and their possessions until daylight. While they were being offloaded, Col. Waagner and Cmdr. Stembel examined the town's fortifications and, as they returned to the gunboat, received a 13-gun salute. Stembel ordered the *Lexington*'s gunners to fire the same compliment. The *Lexington* started back toward Commerce, touching at Thebes en route. After she came to abreast of Commerce, Stembel and Waagner went ashore with a landing party, only to find the town deserted save for a few diehards. These informed the navy man that the advancing Southerners never made it into the town. Having heard the two shots of the practicing gunners the previous afternoon, they "fled and retreated as far back as Benton, 8 miles from the river."

On Col. Waagner's order, the machinery of a steam flouring mill was removed to prevent it falling into Rebel hands. Additionally, 5,000 bushels of corn were also confiscated. The grain was transferred to the steamer *Memphis* at Cape Girardeau. By 4:00 P.M., the timberclad was back at Bird's Point; she arrived of Cairo three hours later. Two hours after that, she went back up the Mississippi and dropped anchor off Eliza's Point.[15]

While Phelps was downriver and Stembel was up the Mississippi, Cmdr. Rodgers arrived at Cairo from Cincinnati. The Marylander had stopped off at St. Louis on the way to review construction progress on the Eads ironclads. Still unaware of Frémont's request, he looked "forward with some interest to the time when we shall test their efficiency."

Upon seeing the *Lexington* and *Tyler* again, Cmdr. Rodgers probably did not entirely disagree with the *St. Louis Daily Missouri Democrat*'s earlier assessment. A few days later, he wrote to Secretary Welles noting that actually "nothing more had been attempted than to render them bullet-proof." Although this goal was accomplished, many things were not yet right with the craft. For example, there was very little powder for the guns, except that which had been purchased to cover the run by Paducah.

Lack of a quantity of charges might not have been an entirely bad thing at that point because "arrangement for the magazine[s] are far from complete." Until passing-boxes were received, cartridges for the great guns would have to be transferred in men's hats. Additionally, with no magazine screens, there was by necessity an opening to the magazines from the boats' gun decks that were "more exposed in a vessel drawing only 4-½ feet of water to the fire of our own battery than desirable for so inflammatory a material."

The vessels all needed some time in dry dock. The *Tyler*, in particular, was leaking quite badly from having been aground near the Louisville and Portland Canal and also from being dragged over the shoals below New Albany.

Up in St. Louis, Master Bishop continued to attempt, without much success, to ship men at his rendezvous. The detached junior officer thought it might prove beneficial to offer bounties or signing bonuses and wrote to his commander seeking permission to offer them. Rodgers, without the necessary information to make a decision, could only advise that bounties were permissible only if paid for by local military authorities. To aid in recruitment, notices were placarded in newspapers and in prominent locations, not only in St. Louis but also in river communities up and down the Ohio and Mississippi rivers. One of them, spotted at Evansville on August 22, read:

> 100 men wanted for the gunboats—the steamer *Conestoga* will arrive at Evansville on the 25th or thereabouts for enlistment of men for service. Pay, $18 per month. Navy rations together with $100 bounty at the end of the war, with usual land grants. For particulars see handbills. A good chance for seamen.

At Cairo, Rodgers, Phelps, and Stembel organized the available hands on the boats, hoping that either Bishop or Secretary Welles might send some additional bluejackets. The three undertook a rigorous training schedule and, to their pleasure found "the Western river men willing and tractable." Cmdr. Rogers believed these volunteers would "readily make good artillerists" once they learned their duties.[16]

Having relieved Cmdr. Stembel to handle manpower matters ashore, Cmdr. Rodgers, who also wished to take a hand at operational command, agreed to another mission on behalf of Col. Waagner. At daylight on August 18, the gunboat, with the army artillery chief aboard, cruised up to Commerce, where she arrived about 10:00 A.M.

The citizens of Commerce were once more fearful that Rebel troops, reported to number between 800 and a thousand, were descending upon their town. Rodgers and Waagner went ashore and listened to horror stories of destruction, by some Confederates who had already arrived, and learned that most of the community's inhabitants had fled across the river to Santa Fe, Illinois. They promised those remaining to relay their appeals for protection to higher Union authorities upon the *Lexington*'s return to Cairo. Touching at Cairo about 4:00 P.M. to drop off Waagner, the *Lexington* continued on up the Ohio to Mound City. There she transferred a number of men to the *Tyler*, while those remaining aboard were "served clothing."

Following this trip, First Master Hurd sat down with the correspondent of the *Chicago Daily Tribune* to give an interview concerning his gunboat. Quite probably stung by the report in the St. Louis paper days before, Hurd elaborated on his vessel and, in the process, has left us one of the better contemporary descriptions of his timberclad:

> The *Lexington* is 183 feet in length — beam 40 feet, and depth of hold 7 feet. She carries three boilers lowered in the hold, working a pair of 30 feet water wheels. The boat trims at 4 feet, 7 inches water. There are three 4½ feet bulkheads in the hold, the entire length of the boat, and bulkheads running crosswise, forming 35 water tight compartments under the main deck. There are false floors and sidings, equivalent to an inside or double hull, made of three inch oak plan, with fast enings, string pieces, and knee braces; running fore and aft on both sides the extreme length under the main deck. Bulwarks extend clear around the hull, eight feet high from the main deck, and twelve inches through. With the exception of a small space forward for handling lines, the bulwarks are decked entirely over. The quarterdeck extends from the boiler to the aft end of the wheelhouses, and is five feet higher than the boiler deck.

Moving on, Hurd went on to explain much of what may have been obvious to the writer who was with him on the recent Commerce excursion:

> The chimneys are close together, nearly amidships, piercing the boiler deck immediately forward of the quarter deck. The pilothouse stands forward of the chimneys and is bullet-proof. Then there is a look-out on the rear of the quarterdeck, which is also bullet-proof. The bulwarks are pierced for eleven guns, five on either side, and one at the stern. The guns are 32- and 64-pounders.

En route to St. Louis that Sunday afternoon, the steamer *Des Moines* was signaled to the bank about a mile south of Commerce by some men on the Illinois shore. These warned that the Rebels had taken possession of the town and had planted batteries on the hills behind it, firing indiscriminately at targets in the river and across the Mississippi at Santa Fe. Fugitives from the town, meanwhile, fled over to Illinois and also to Cairo. At both points, they told stories of Southerners breaking into and ransacking houses and "offering indignities to such women and children as were left in the place."

The *Tyler* and *Lexington* made a short reconnaissance down the Mississippi early on Monday, August 19. No important discoveries were made, but they did return to report that, in the words of the *Chicago Daily Tribune* correspondent, "the Kentucky and Missouri woods below Norfolk were alive with Rebels."

While the timberclads were down the river, someone found a bottle floating in the Ohio River opposite Mound City. When it was retrieved and opened, it was found to contain a paper directed to Brig. Gen. Pillow providing complete intelligence on the Cairo and Bird's Point defenses.

Back at Cairo later in the morning, Cmdr. Rodgers was dispatched on another mercy mission. The family of a man named Du Peyster needed to be evacuated from the Kentucky shore opposite Norfolk. As the clan was large with many possessions, Col. Oglesby asked the *Lexington* to convoy the steamer *Empress* down to pick them and to await return convoy until the *Tyler* could join them. When the two boats arrived, Mr. Du Peyster indicated that he and his people would not be departing after all. The *Empress* returned to Cairo, leaving the *Lexington* to hold station until the *Tyler* arrived. The two gunboats then steamed up to their usual Ohio River anchorage.

Now that the *Tyler* had returned from Mound City, Rodgers planned to make a reconnaissance trip down toward New Madrid. Definitive news, however, arrived in Cairo in the small hours of August 20 that the Rebel force feared by townspeople had occupied Commerce

Ohio Levee, Cairo, mid–September 1861. The famed artist Alexander Simplot sketched the Ohio River side of the tip of Illinois about the time of the arrival of the three timberclads. The strategic location was taken over earlier in the year and a blockade was established employing field artillery and armed steamers and tugboats (Harper's Weekly, September 17, 1861).

following his earlier departure. At daylight, the *Lexington* and *Tyler* ran alongside of the stone depot and each took aboard twenty-five 32-pound and twenty-five 8-inch empty shells. Armed and determined to dislodge the Confederate invaders of Commerce, the timberclads steamed back up the Mississippi, this time accompanied by the *Empress* and several hundred soldiers.

Arriving off the town about 3:00 P.M., the Maryland officer found it all but deserted. Alerted by scouts of the loud crafts' approach, the Rebels had gathered up some 45 loads of corn from a local mill and made off with that and other merchandise in a 50-wagon train. A few young hotheads remained behind and, from a nearby hill, opened small arms fire on the *Tyler* about 6:00 P.M. "A couple of shells dislodged them and all again became quiet." Rodgers' landing party found a few women and children hiding ashore and took them off to join their families at Santa Fe.

On August 21, the men of the *Lexington* heard firing at the foot of Power's Island and ran down the Mississippi to investigate. All that was seen was a ferryboat lying at the bank. Leaving Rodgers and the *Tyler* at Commerce, Cmdr. Stembel returned to Cairo with the *Empress*. The *Tyler* returned to Cairo briefly on August 22. There Cmdr. Rodgers wrote to Maj. Gen. Frémont advising him of the Commerce excursion and pointing out that Rebel troops could cross into Illinois at that point when the gunboats were not nearby. To prevent that, he recommended that one of his craft cruise generally in the vicinity. He would begin the process himself late next day, remaining for 48 hours.[17]

While Rodgers was away, Cmdr. Stembel found himself involved in a "cutting out" action that would have some impact on the delicate "neutrality" being maintained by Kentucky. Col. Oglesby later referred to the matter as "the affair of the little steamer *W.B. Terry*."

During the weeks when Lt. Phelps was struggling to bring his three timberclads down to Cairo, certain civil steamers continued to maintain mail and civil trade on the Ohio. Although the war brought a depression to the steamboat business, a few shippers and captains were able to operate, providing essential ferry and mail services or under government contract. Offering these services was not without danger. Guerrilla bands and small groups of Confederate soldiers lingered along the Kentucky riverbank waiting to fire upon U.S. flag steamers approaching or departing the landings at Uniontown, Caseyville, Carrsville, Owenboro, and other towns. On June 15, for example, the flag of Capt. W. H. McClurg's *Samuel Orr* was fired upon by a group of Southern sympathizers as she was leaving Owensboro. For protection, a number of steamers were armed. Capt. Henry T. Dexter, famous for the speedy trips of his red-hulled stern-wheeler, particularly on the Evansville–Paducah–Cairo route, mounted a 4-pounder cannon on the forecastle of the *Charley Bowen*.

Kentucky's neutrality still allowed steamers to ply between Northern points, Tennessee, and the Blue Grass river towns, with the rule being "no contraband." These steamers were also a source of intelligence for both sides, bringing upstream or downstream information, rumors, or messages. Sometimes, subterfuge was employed to get goods through from North to South, particularly by Rebel-leaning boat owners or captains. Among the most enterprising of these were the Fowler brothers of Paducah, owners of the *Dunbar*.

Having been warned earlier by federal agents concerning their alleged involvement in contraband trade on the Ohio, *Dunbar* owner Gus Fowler came up with a unique idea to safeguard his vessel. Fowler convinced the captain of the *Samuel Orr* to replace him on the round-trip run from Evansville to Kentucky and on to Pittsburgh. This would permit him to operate up the Tennessee River from Paducah. Another vessel, Capt. Jacob Johnson's small stern-wheel *W.B. Terry*, was, like the *Dunbar*, also believed to be engaged in smuggling operations as she ran her regularly scheduled packet route between Paducah and Florence, Alabama.

Downstream at Cairo, Col. Oglesby received "indisputable proof" from an informant that the *W.B. Terry* was being employed by the Confederate government to ship contraband, even wearing the Confederate flag rather than Old Glory. Other than this testimony, there was no proof, as historian J. Thomas Scharf put it, that the vessel had undertaken any act or conduct "hostile or injurious to the United States." Still, the Cairo post commander decided to investigate. At midnight on August 21–22, Cmdr. Stembel received a hail from a small boat alongside the *Lexington*. Col. Oglesby brought aboard his informant and the news he had reported to army headquarters. When the brief interview concluded, the post commander verbally ordered the gunboat to steam to Paducah and arrest the Rebel.

It took only a few minutes for the *Lexington* to weigh anchor, but many hours were lost in the dark and bad weather before she arrived off the Kentucky town about 7:00 A.M. Once the timberclad had passed the wharf boat of Smedley & Co., where the *W.B. Terry* was tied up, and had inspected a short distance up the Tennessee River, she returned. Cmdr. Stembel's guest now pointed out the *Terry* as the vessel running the illegal trade.

The *Lexington* quickly ran in alongside the steamer, cut her out and made her fast alongside, then speedily rounded off into the river and steamed back to base. Seeing the black gunboat headed toward them, the officers and crew of the *Terry* avoided capture by hastily abandoning ship, taking nothing but the clothes they were wearing. The strike was completed so smoothly and so quickly that it was not resisted by either Rebel military units or local citizens.

The *W.B. Terry* was taken under tow, with a small secessionist flag flying under the national ensign. About 10:00 A.M., the merchantman and her captor hove in sight some five miles above Cairo. At that point, they were spotted by the local correspondent of the *Cincin-

nati Daily Enquirer and several others who watched from the levee as the two come abreast of the Ohio River landings and anchored in the stream.

Cmdr. Stembel turned the *Terry* over to the U.S. Army. Col. Oglesby reviewed her papers, finding proof, he later reported, that she was illegally engaged. Additionally, it was said that 30 Minie rifles and a fieldpiece were found aboard, along with 14 pistol belts, 13 Bowie knives, 100 decks of playing cards— and no freight. The vessel and her equipment were turned over to a local commission appointed by the post commander, who found her value to be approximately $3,000–$5,000.

This "uncalled for outrage," as Scharf later called it, now led to another. Up the Ohio in Kentucky men gathered to plot retaliation. Some saw the *Lexington*'s action as a provocation, a violation of their neutrality; others just wanted to get their craft back by taking another of equal or greater value.

On approach to Paducah from Evansville on the morning of August 23, Capt. McClurg noticed that the *Dunbar* was also coming up the Tennessee into the landing. The *Samuel Orr*'s skipper was not overly concerned; Gus Fowler had promised that no harm would come to his stern-wheeler while she was operating replacement service for him on the Ohio. Disaster struck as she touched the wharf boat.

Waiting for the big steamer was Capt. Johnson of the *W.B. Terry*, Whyte Fowler, Gus's brother, and a number of armed *Terry* officers and local roughnecks. These jumped onto the *Orr*'s lower deck, with Fowler and Johnson racing onto the hurricane deck and drawing their pistols on Capt. McClurg. After that officer surrendered, he was allowed to step onto the wharf boat with Johnson's promise to give back his craft when the *Terry* was returned. In a scuffle down below, the assailants, "or, rather, a drunken mob, armed with old rusty muskets and pistols," fired several shots, wounding two of their own number.

With the *Samuel Orr* in Johnson's hands and with most of her crew still aboard, the Southerners shouted three cheers for Jefferson Davis and took the boat out into the river to make their escape. About a mile above Paducah, the *Orr*'s crew was released but was not permitted to take any clothing or personal effects. Johnson and Fowler took their capture, along with her papers, cargo of groceries, and mail pouches— all valued at $25,000 — on up the Tennessee.

This adventure was taking place as the U.S.S. *Lexington* was standing up the Ohio. Trailing her under convoy was the 206-ton stern-wheeler *Belle Creole* of Cincinnati. In light of the *Terry* capture, her captain was worried about just such an incident as happened with the *Samuel Orr* and had the foresight to ask Col. Oglesby for gunboat protection. Once the five-year-old *Belle Creole* was safely past Paducah, Stembel's craft steamed back to her usual anchorage.

After returning to Paducah early in the afternoon, Capt. McClurg telegraphed news of his loss to military headquarters at Cairo. Just in from the Ohio River, the *Lexington* was ordered to get up steam and go to the rescue. By the time she reached Paducah that night, she was too late to either prevent completion of this Southern retaliation or capture the perpetrators.

News of the twin captures was quickly wired elsewhere and appeared in eastern and midwestern newspapers next day just as Oglesby's formal report reached the headquarters of Maj. Gen. Frémont. As the Cairo commander put it, the Southern retaliation was "more vindictive than sensible" because it destroyed "the last means of illicit trade with the border States north of the Ohio." The colonel could not have known that the timberclad mission would be one of the reasons Maj. Gen. Polk would cite as reason, a few days hence, for the occupation of Columbus.

Gus Fowler and Paducah's Southern sympathizers became very concerned that the Yankee gunboats might take direct retaliation and seize additional vessels from the landing. Before the *Lexington* arrived, the *Dunbar* and another steamer, the *Sam Kirkman* also cleared up the Tennessee. Neither they nor the *Samuel Orr* would ever see the Ohio River again.

Later in the day, the steamer *Emma Duncan*, en route from Cincinnati to St. Louis, put into Evansville. There the Surveyor of the Port found that a large part of her cargo was consigned to Paducah. It was removed and put into storage pending the safe return of the *Samuel Orr*. Eventually it was auctioned.[18]

Meanwhile, there was slow but relentless movement toward the replacement of the Union's Mississippi River naval commander. It took two weeks for the Frémont demand for Rodger's relief to work its way from Montgomery Blair and Abraham Lincoln to Gideon Welles. Ironically, during this time, Frémont himself became embroiled in a storm of criticism and, "in many ways, the Department of the West by mid–August," wrote Allen Nevins, "seemed in dire confusion."

By August 23, Secretary Welles and Assistant Secretary of the Navy Gustavus V. Fox were not only acquainted with the request but had chosen Rodgers' successor. That day a telegram from the latter reached Capt. Andrew Hull Foote, commander of the New York Navy Yard and Secretary Welles' old classmate: "Proceed to Washington, D.C., and report in person at the Department."

Major General John C. Frémont. A famed prewar explorer known as "The Pathfinder" and the first Republican presidential candidate, Maj. Gen. John C. Frémont (1813–1880) commanded the Federal Western Department July–November 1861. Early in his tenure, he demanded the recall and replacement of Cmdr. John Rodgers, first commander of the Western Flotilla. On a more positive note, he did appoint Brig. Gen. Ulysses S. Grant to command Union forces at Cairo, Illinois, and recognized the importance of gunboat control of the Mississippi and Ohio. He was succeeded by Maj. Gen. Henry Halleck (**Battles and Leaders**).

Welles' choice to succeed Cmdr. Rodgers was a "quiet, grey-haired veteran" with an enviable reputation even before this selection. Born in New Haven, Connecticut, the son of a governor and U.S. senator, Foote (1806–1863), promoted to Capt. only in June 1861, became a U.S. Navy midshipman in 1822 and Cmdr. in 1852. Known for his Christian bearing and dedication to the temperance movement, he worked to abolish flogging during the 1840s, was one of the few members of the infamous 1850s retiring board to avoid major condemnation by his colleagues, and personally led an assault force against the barrier forts at Canton, China, in 1856. Later wounded in action at Fort Donelson, he was promoted to the rank of rear admiral, served as chief of the Bureau of Equipment and Recruiting, and was en route to take command of the South Atlantic Blockading Squadron at the time of his death.

Also on August 23, Welles wrote to Cmdr. Rodgers, not about his pending position loss or to mention that his heir apparent had been invited in, but to inform him that his earlier request for Atlantic coast seamen was rejected. It had "been duly considered, but it will be impossible for the Department to grant it." On top of that, the navy was recruiting for the coastal blockade from Great Lakes communities, so Rodgers would have to secure his people from towns along the Ohio and Mississippi.

Over the past month, rumors concerning possible Confederate gunboat arrivals in the Memphis area reached St. Louis and worried the Union commander of the Department of the West. His own operational gunboats were too few in number to be everywhere and Eads' ironclads were still under construction. Maj. Gen. Frémont did not know that, further downstream, both Generals Polk and Pillow regarded their own New Madrid position as untenable. The former thought about falling back on Forts Pillow and Randolph and employing Union City, Tennessee, as the base from which to operate into Missouri. Pillow, on the other hand, favored taking Columbus, in "neutral" Kentucky.

Despite Cmdr. Rodgers' earlier objection, Maj. Gen. Frémont, on August 24, ordered the purchase of James B. Eads' snag boat *Submarine No. 7*. The catamaran was now available at the reduced price of $26,850, though she would require another $40,000 investment for alterations. She was soon transferred from Cairo to the entrepreneur's Carondelet boatyard "with instructions to convert her as speedily as possible into an ironclad gunboat."

In addition and on his own authority, Frémont commanded the construction of 38 mortar boats by builder Theodore Adams, along with necessary tugs to tow them. The conversion of the Wiggins Ferry Company steamer *New Era* into a gunboat was also authorized. Work on these craft would, according to Allen Nevins, be pushed "by torch light all night long." The rough drawings of the mortar boat plans were quickly placed in Eads' hands. Years later, Frémont would look back on these nautical arrangements and conclude that his decision to push ahead with work on craft labeled "useless extravagance" was "historic in the progress of the war."

August concluded with the western gunboats attempting to keep the peace in key locations not far from the confluence of the Mississippi and the Ohio. As the editor of the *St. Louis Daily Missouri Democrat* put it, also on August 24, "The gun-boats are doing all in their power, but they cannot be everywhere at the same time. Since their arrival, except for the *Conestoga*, which is being repaired, they have been in constant active service."

The same might have been said at the time for Cmdr. Rodgers, whom Maj. Gen. Frémont now faulted for spending more time on squadron matters than in overseeing the construction of Eads' ironclads. After he was on the scene for a few days, Rodgers' successor, Capt. Foote, conceded, that much of what he and the Department knew of the western gunboat situation was incorrect. Rodgers had "worked hard and his duties afloat, for want of officers, have prevented his looking out for the building, and to some extent to the equipment, of the steamers on the stocks." Foote continued: "He has overcome many difficulties in getting afloat even three shells of steamers ... [and] deserves great credit for what he has done...."

Historian Milligan later observed that Rodgers' failure to efficiently communicate his operational requirements to the theater commander led directly to the call for his replacement. While this may have had some bearing, these requirements did not commence until after the gunboats arrived at Cairo on August 12 — and Frémont asked for a new man on August 9. From the vantage point of 150 years later, it is hard to avoid the simple conclusion that businessmen supported by political interests in an era of non-instant communications in a widening war combined to cost John Rodgers his command. The sailor, long used to serving as a lone eagle, aided that process with his own reportless command style.

The *Lexington* steamed up to Commerce early on August 24 to relieve the *Tyler*. The Confederates, that day's *Missouri Democrat* reassured its readers, were "careful to keep away from

This sketch of the *Tyler, Lexington,* and *Conestoga* (left to right) appeared in a fall 1861 issue of *Frank Leslie's Illustrated Magazine*. Drawn by the journal's "special artist," it projects the reassuring power of Cmdr. John Rodger's ships as they approached Cairo. Notice the small boatload of onlookers and the giant drifting tree trunks in the water (Naval Historical Center).

that village since the gunboats have been lying there." Commerce was entirely deserted as the *Tyler* prepared to departure the vicinity. As the timberclad neared the Commerce landing for a final observation, she was hailed by a lone man, a resident from half a mile downstream. Arriving aboard via the boat's gig, the visitor informed Cmdr. Rodgers that Confederate officers had come by his home the previous evening to gather information about the gunboats, particularly their deployment schedule. It was their hope to fortify the area once the nautical patrols had ceased.

When the steamer *Diadem* arrived at St. Louis from Pittsburgh on August 26, its captain, Thomas Rogers, reported all was quiet at Paducah. His boat had been hailed a few miles above the town by a delegation of local citizens who assured him that his boat would not be molested if it would land. The Paducahians all expressed regret "at the lawless occurrences of the past few days."

That same day the calm was briefly broken at Commerce. In the evening some six to eight rifle shots were fired at the *Lexington* from different houses in town. Peace was restored, according to the logbook of the *Lexington*, when the sniping was "returned from the boat by one canister and one round shot."

On most days, the mail steamers brought copies of Eastern newspapers to Cincinnati, Louisville, St. Louis and other western communities. The issue of the *New York Herald* for August 27 would be so delivered but Cmdr. Rodgers, occupied as he was aboard the *Tyler*, did not see a copy. If he had, he could not have missed a tiny news capsule buried therein: "Captain Foote was ordered to the command of the United States naval forces on the Western waters—namely, the Mississippi, Missouri, and Ohio rivers."

Various internal Confederate threats within Missouri seemed to wane as August finished. Threats by Rebel field commanders faded amidst confusion, bickering, and even the need for soldiers to return home for the harvest. St. Louis, Cairo, Ironton, Cape Girardeau, and Jefferson City appeared safe for the Union—for the moment. At this point, Maj. Gen.

Frémont decided to go over to the offensive. To this end, the theater commander created a new District of Southeast Missouri on August 28, covering the southern parts of that state and Illinois, and named Brig. Gen. Ulysses S. Grant to command it. The then little-known officer from Ohio was told by Frémont to solidify his position on the Mississippi and chase the Rebels from swampy southeast Missouri. He would also need to acquire a base "for operations against Memphis and Nashville." Consequently, he would "occupy Columbus in Kentucky as soon as possible."

Earlier the same day, the *Lexington* returned to Commerce, relieving the *Tyler*, which returned to Cairo. Cmdr. Stembel patrolled the river between that point and Thebes over the next 24 hours, finally returning to Cairo on the evening of August 29. Next day, at Cape Girardeau, Ulysses Simpson Grant, the war's most famous Northern general, took up his first big command.

Repair work on the *Conestoga* had delayed her recruiting tour up the Ohio. Finally, on August 30, the black-hulled gunboat hove to off Evansville, giving local citizens a chance to see her great guns, and adventuresome youth a chance to sign articles.

Across the country at Washington, D.C., that day, Navy Secretary Welles wrote out two sets of orders. When delivered, he fully expected they would change the direction of what he called "the Western movement," which, in his eyes at least, had finally gained what it had earlier lacked: "the greatest importance."

After discussions between Welles, Fox, and Foote, and most likely several others, the new squadron chief received official instructions to go to St. Louis and take over command of naval operations on the western waters. The veteran officer, who, according to his recent biographer, "must have had serious reservations about accepting the assignment," was to report to and cooperate with Maj. Gen. Frémont and to make all requisitions through him upon the War Department. Anything the army could not supply the navy would — if it did not interfere with coastal blockade requirements. The department would send out additional officers to command the gunboats and handle administrative matters, but recruitment would largely be left to Foote.

The second set of orders was penned to Cmdr. Rodgers, informing him that Capt. Foote was replacing him and requiring that he turn over all squadron papers in his possession. The move was necessary, Welles explained, because the western nautical force was growing and more "officers of judgment and experience" (read: senior to a commander) were wanted. Rodgers was invited to remain as Foote's assistant if he so chose, but otherwise he was free to come back to Washington and seek another command. The secretary sent this communication to Rodgers at St. Louis, but, because he was actively overseeing gunboat operations at Cairo, he did not receive it.

On the last day of the month, the *Lexington* made a lengthy reconnaissance voyage down past Columbus and Hickman. Just downstream of the latter town, she rounded to and returned upriver, firing two shells at suspected Confederate targets while passing a short distance below Columbus about 7:00 P.M.[19]

Chapter 4

New Men, Hotter War, September 1– October 9, 1861

By the first day of September 1861, the small timberclad flotilla under Cmdr. John Rodgers II had already make its presence felt on the Mississippi for short distances above and below Cairo, Illinois. "Each boat," the navy man later wrote with some pride, was valued as much as 5,000 soldiers and no service was "thought too arduous for our zeal or too dangerous for our powers." Still, the operations of *Conestoga*, *Lexington*, and *Tyler* to date were rather small scale flag-showing or town-guardian missions. The former boat even had a chance to undertake a recruiting voyage after coming out of dry dock at the end of August.

That state of affairs was about to change now that Brig. Gen. Ulysses S. Grant, on orders from Maj. Gen. John C. Frémont, had assumed command of Union military operations in the new District of Southeast Missouri. Further south, Confederate leaders Maj. Gen. Leonidas Polk and Brig. Gen. Gideon Pillow were also assessing their options. The western military leadership North and South believed that the time had come for some sort of new action along the "Father of Waters."[1]

It was largely understood by both sides at this time that the major Confederate efforts of July and August to advance deep into southeastern Missouri and maybe capture St. Louis or Cairo were over. Trouble for the Yankees came only from about 1,500 "Swamp Rats" of the Missouri State Guard, under Brig. Gen. M. Jeff Thompson. Both Frémont and Grant hoped he could be quickly contained, if not eliminated, even though his fighters made small war with seeming impunity from the huge bogs that extended from the Arkansas border up toward Cape Girardeau. Still, at least in Frémont's mind, there was great danger from Thompson. The harm his successful pinprick partisan raids were causing would pale if he decided to combine arms with other Confederate field commanders further south or to the west where Maj. Gen. Sterling Price was even then moving toward Lexington on the Missouri River. Any chance of enhanced communications between these Missouri Rebels and those across the river in "neutral" Kentucky had also to be prevented.

Both blue-coated generals now determined to go on the offensive in the southeast and, by so doing, force Polk, Pillow, Thompson, and their associates, real or imagined, onto the defensive. Frémont, in his August 28 orders placing Grant in charge of his new district, ordered that the Missouri side of the Mississippi be patrolled down toward New Madrid. The intelligence gathering programs of both the North and South was now intensified. Information came from a number of sources and it was left to commanders such as Frémont and Grant to weave the reports together into some kind of coherent picture. Among the reports passively available (to greater or lesser degree) to military leaders on both sides were those from sympathizers, prisoners of war (POWs), refugees, and newspapers.

Actively, the North and South sought insights from spies and scouts, interceptions of mail and messages, and land- and water-based patrols. Local Southern generals on the rivers relied on fleet horsemen (cavalry or irregular), because they had more of them than their enemy, along with their irregular forces and few gunboats, The Northern army placed its emphasis on infiltrators, a few cavalrymen, and infantry patrols. The latter in particular would work closely with the gunboats of Rodgers and his successors.

Indeed, the Union naval force would, when not under repair, as it often was in the early days, did more than conduct reconnaissance missions (some of which would now be called "reconnaissance-by-fire") counting cannon. They protected scouting parties, covered amphibious landings, convoyed steamers, and projected Union objectives through constant visits to communities otherwise unguarded from irregular forces and guerrillas.

Three days earlier, Maj. Gen. Frémont ordered Col. Gustave Waagner and a regiment from Cairo, together with the *Lexington* and *Tyler* under Cmdr. Rodgers, to secure the town of Belmont, across from Columbus, Kentucky. There he would destroy any Rebel fortifications and then move on Charleston, Missouri. If the opportunity presented itself, he could move inland against Brig. Gen. Thompson. Once Grant and Waagner had accomplished their goals, the "Pathfinder of the West" expected to occupy Columbus. Events leading to this possibility now rapidly unfolded, but not as he had expected.

On September 1, Maj. Gen. Frémont was informed by Brig. Gen. Grant that Thompson was in retreat toward New Madrid and that another Confederate army, at Greenville, Missouri, was en route south to Arkansas. Meanwhile, Grant, in concert with Brig. Gen. Benjamin M. Prentiss, would move on the "Swamp Rats" from the Cape Girardeau area. Prentiss chose not to take orders from the Buckeye general and refused to cooperate. Consequently, the combined expedition collapsed before it started.

Further south, Col. Waagner's reconnaissance mission, ordered by Maj. Gen. Frémont over a week earlier, was finally ready to depart Cairo. A ruse would initially be employed to mask the movement.

Some miles to the east near Nashville that Sunday, Capt. Jesse Taylor was teaching young Volunteer State recruits to handle cannon at a "camp of artillery instruction." During the day, he received a visit from Lt. Col. Milton A. Haynes of the 1st Regiment Tennessee Artillery. His superior related how the U.S.S. *Lexington* had cut out the *W.B. Terry* late in August and how the *Dunbar* and the *Sam Orr* had fled the Ohio River. The steamboats had taken refuge at Fort Henry, but their captains all feared that the "Lincoln gunboats" would come up the Tennessee and try to capture them. Unhappily, there was no "experienced artillerist" at the bastion and, Tennessee governor Isham G. Harris wanted that deficiency immediately addressed.

Lt. Col. Haynes had no one to send unless Capt. Taylor consented. The young gunner, who was himself convinced "that the first effort of the Federals would be to penetrate our lines by the way of the Tennessee River," agreed to take charge of the fort's artillery. He would arrive on scene in a few days to find six 32-pounders and a 6-pounder iron gun and, shortly thereafter, see his first gunboat, Lt. Phelps' *Conestoga*.

At 5:00 A.M. in the predawn darkness of September 2, the *Tyler*, with both Cmdr. Rodgers and Col. Waagner embarked and steamed up the Mississippi about 20 miles to reconnoiter and noisily suggest to watching eyes that a return to Commerce was imminent. Further south, Cmdr. Stembel repeated the same ploy, taking the *Lexington* down to Norfolk. While the gunboats were acting out their deceptive parts, Col. John McArthur at Bird's Point loaded 600 men of the 12th Illinois Volunteer Infantry aboard the transport *G.W. Graham*. Once Waagner had returned and transferred aboard the steamer, the troopboat, escorted by the *Tyler*, departed "for down the river" at 10:00 A.M. sharp.

At Norfolk, the two Cairo steamers made rendezvous with the *Lexington* and Col. Waagner took a landing party of two companies ashore from the *G.W. Graham*. Finding "nothing

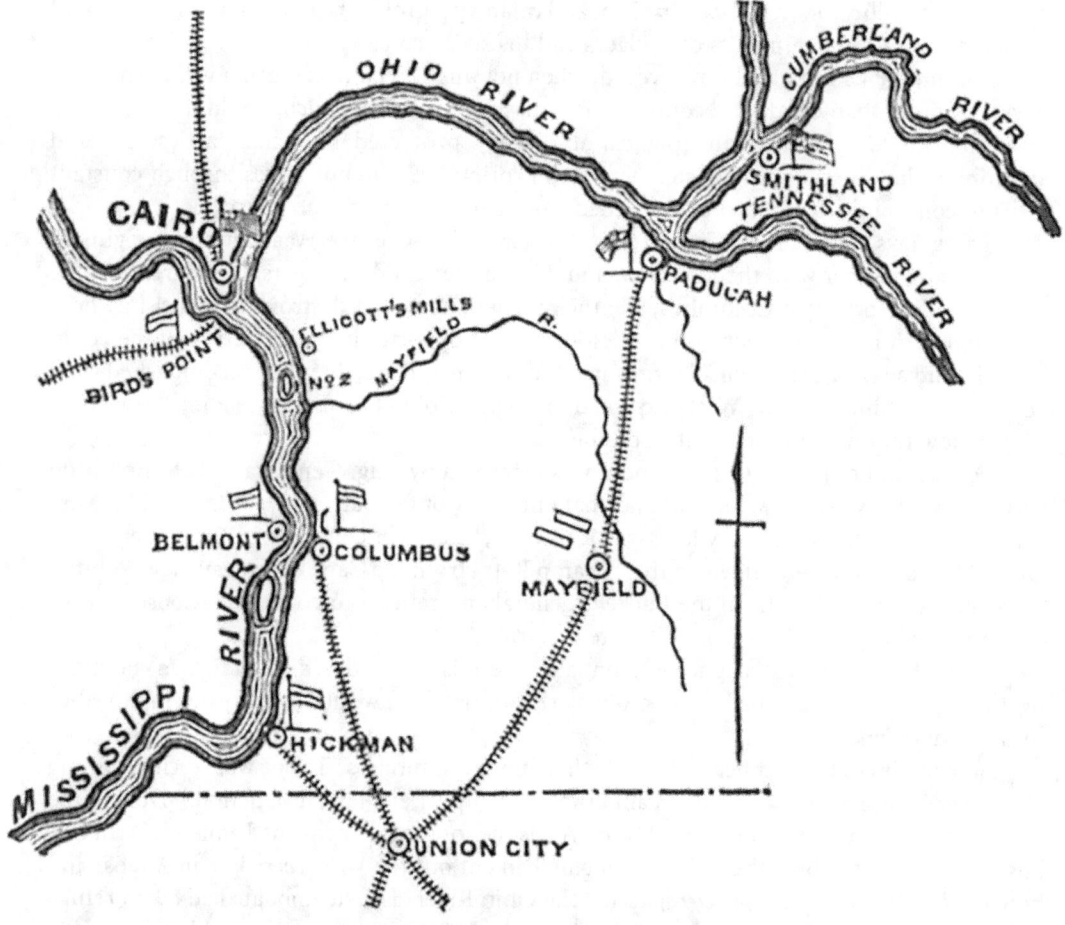

FIELD OF OPERATIONS AGAINST BELMONT.

Cairo-Belmont Area. Although this map was designed to show the run-up to the Battle of Belmont, it serves, for the present purposes, a better use in this chapter. Here can easily be seen the relationships between the towns at the confluence of the Ohio and Mississippi, the Ohio and the Tennessee and the Cumberland, and further down the Mississippi itself (Lossing's *Pictorial Field Book of the Civil War*, **vol. 1).**

of importance," the men reembarked and the three vessels proceeded downstream at noon, arriving at Belmont's steamboat landing an hour or so later. Belmont was not an appropriate name for a three-house settlement on the Missouri shore. Gen. Albert Sidney Johnston's biographer offered a fitting description of the 1861 location a few years later. "It was situated in a dreary, flat 'bottom land,'" he wrote in 1878, "cut up with sloughs, heavily timbered, and approached from the river by two natural terraces or banks."

Three companies went ashore, secured a perimeter, and quickly captured the ferryboat that daily paddled back and forth to Columbus. It would sink next morning. After speaking with a number of local inhabitants, Col. Waagner was able to report that no enemy troops were present between Belmont and Charleston. It was learned that heavy guns were positioned on Island No. 10 and at Union City. Looking across the Mississippi toward the bluffs, he could clearly see a large Confederate flag "flying from the top of a lofty pole in the center of the village." What, he wondered, could he or the Union "do with Columbus? What with Hickman? What with New Madrid?" Waagner did not know that Maj. Gen. Polk was preparing to provide an answer within hours: nothing. He did note that during the night large scale infantry and cavalry movements could be heard directly across the Mississippi on the heights in and near Columbus.

Back at Cairo, correspondent Irving Carson wrote out a long column for the subscribers to the *Chicago Daily Tribune*. After noting the movements of this colonel and that and various regiments, he offered a complaint gleaned from reading a fairly current issue of the *New Orleans Delta*. According to that Southern newspaper, the Rebel gunboat *Grampus* had recently visited Cairo "and defied the whole force concentrated here, gunboats and all." Steamboats being by their nature rather noisy and conspicuous, Carson wondered why no one at the tip of Illinois knew of her salute. Maybe the crew of the boat had a "character of beings bordering on the supernatural" and were able to greet Cairo from 15 to 20 miles away, making it impossible for Carson and other "poor mortals" to discover her. This commentary, the first of several on Capt. Marshall J. "Marsh" Miller's boat that would appear in the pages of the *Tribune* and other Northern newspapers, concluded with a reminder to readers that the *Grampus* had been stolen from northern ownership at Memphis the previous summer.

The water level was falling upstream on the Ohio that day. At Evansville, Lt. Phelps became concerned that if he did not leave right away, he might be stranded. Still, he hated to depart. In four days of recruiting, almost 50 new hands were signed aboard the *Conestoga* and it was anticipated that even more would join could the boat remain. Still, the river dictated movement and it now required him to weigh for Cairo.[2]

At Memphis, Maj. Gen. Polk was worried. A "student" of Kentucky's neutrality, the Confederate general had watched the political situation in that state develop ever since the fall of Fort Sumter. The Cumberland and Tennessee rivers were a natural invasion route into the Volunteer heartland, and daily Kentucky's concessions to the North seemed to increase. Federal taxes were collected and Union military detachments were maintained at Lexington and in Garrard County. In mid–August, the Southerners boycotted state elections, giving the assembly a decidedly Union flavor. Of course, the *Lexington*'s capture of the *W.B. Terry* was viewed as a provocation. If the North ever gained control of the heights at Columbus, it would be impossible to dislodge them.

Still, the "fighting bishop" tried to hold off. Both sides in the conflict realized that the first to violate Kentucky sovereignty by such an overt act as taking a riverfront community would drive the state into the arms of the other. Sensing that his New Madrid position was untenable, Polk wanted to leave that location and fall back to Union City, Tennessee.

Tennessean Pillow believed just the opposite and had said so ever since May. The Iron

Banks at Columbus, he argued, just had to be fortified, their possession a point of "paramount military necessity." If the Confederacy held Columbus, it could "close the door effectively against invasion of Tennessee or descent of the Mississippi." So far, Polk had resisted Pillow's argument that taking the town, whatever the consequences, was militarily the correct move and had ignored the pleas of local citizens who did everything in their power, from hanging out Rebel flags to sending him petitions, to change his mind.

And then Maj. Gen. Polk began receiving reports that Maj. Gen. Frémont was also planning to move on the town. This information came just as Cmdr. Rodgers and Col. Waagner were setting off for Belmont. On September 1, the "fighting bishop" broke down and wrote to Kentucky governor Beriah Magoffin: "I think it of the greatest consequence to the Southern cause in Kentucky or elsewhere that I should be ahead of the enemy in occupying Columbus and Paducah."

Next day, Polk, without informing the Confederate War Department, gave orders for an amphibious advance. He would seize the strategic heights of Columbus before the Federals, thereby, in the words of historian Steven E. Woodworth, "saving Frémont from a serious blunder by making it first himself." Far from committing an error, the uniformed clergyman, like others, believed the little town with its four brick buildings was "a near perfect place to pot batteries." If it were "properly fortified," no Yankee gunboat or steamer would ever pass.

The same day, the steamer *Belle Memphis* departed St. Louis for Cairo. Aboard were Brig. Gen. Grant, his aide-de-camp, Capt. William S. Hillyer, and Master Joshua Bishop.

By September 3, Col. Waagner's "demonstration," at Belmont was well under way. Maj. Gen. Polk at Memphis learned of it in telegrams from Columbus and from messages and petitions from concerned citizens. The Union artilleryman had, meanwhile, received a request from Brig. Gen. Grant that he maintain his position at Belmont and plan to reconnoiter Charleston. The *G. W. Graham* lay at the bank, with *Tyler* and *Lexington* anchored in the river above and below her location.

During the day, Rodgers and Waagner noted that the heavy movements of ground and mounted soldiers continued at Columbus. A number of families were seen departing the town and surrounding farms. In the evening, Union spyglasses confirmed that a brand new secession flag flew over the town. Additionally, the colonel noted, "the people about here are very suspicious."

That evening, Confederate forces on the steamers *John Walsh, W.H.R., Ingomar, Prince, Prince of Wales, William M. Harrison, Equality,* and *Charmer* from New Madrid, escorted by the C.S.S. *Jackson* and the local gunboat *Grampus*, made the short run to Hickman, where they landed and occupied the town.

Between midnight and daylight, Cmdr. Rodgers returned to Cairo to inform Brig. Gen. Grant concerning the sights he and Waagner had observed during the day past. According to the correspondent of the *Chicago Daily Tribune*, among the actions noted was the flight of local residents, most of whom were "convicted by their own conscience of meriting arrest and imprisonment."

On September 4, the same day Brig. Gen. Grant opened his command post at Cairo, 1,500 gray-clad soldiers marched up the east bank and captured Columbus. The local populace was overjoyed and there was no resistance at either place. To ensure there was no opposition from the river, the *Grampus* and *Jackson* anchored below the bluffs. It is unknown if another small ersatz gunboat, the *Jeff Davis*, known to be in the area at the time, was present. According to a September 27 report by the Cairo-based *St. Louis Daily Missouri Republican* reporter that was also carried in the October 3 issue of the *Philadelphia Inquirer*, she was "said to be a stern-wheel boat, formerly a towboat, carrying a few 6-pound guns."

The occupation of the two river towns brought almost as much discord in the South as in the North. Confederate secretary of war Leroy P. Walker ordered Polk to withdraw while Governor Isham G. Harris of Tennessee asked the same. President Jefferson Davis supported the action: "The necessity justified the action." Davis, like Polk, believed, accurately as it turned out, that Frémont and Grant were planning to strike first.

By violating Kentucky's neutrality, the Confederates were seen as aggressors and the Blue Grass State came into the fight on the side of the Union. While Southern generals and politicians debated the action, the press of the North was delighted; "Kentucky Invaded by the Rebels," cheered the *Philadelphia Inquirer* on September 5. That cloudy morning the steamer *Albree* arrived at Cairo from Louisville, reporting that all was quiet along the Ohio, though the river was falling rapidly.[3]

September 4 was also the day of the first gunboat-gunboat combat of the western campaign. Later, on an enhanced scale, the episode would be remembered as the first "'shots in anger' fired at each other in Kentucky by the regular forces of the two nations." The little fight was barely an incident as naval battles go, but it was something of a surprise to the Federals and marked the only time in his four month midwestern tour that Cmdr. Rodgers was in combat against another boat.

That Thursday morning, pursuant to an agreement between Col. Waagner and Rodgers, *Tyler* and *Lexington* undertook a reconnaissance from Belmont downstream toward Hickman. Just before turning into the bend which brought the community into full view, the timberclads discovered a small, black-painted stern-wheeler, "evidently a gunboat." This craft, almost certainly the *Grampus*, beat a hasty retreat, with the two Yankee warboats on her heels.

At Hickman, "dense volumes of smoke were seen up the river and there was great excitement in town," recalled Lt. Col. Frank A. Montgomery, newly arrived with the 1st Mississippi Cavalry. Even as preparations were made to resist a landing of what was perceived as a large enemy force, keen eyes spied first coming into sight "a little stern-wheel boat owned by the Confederates, painted black, with a six-pounder gun on her bow." Montgomery knew this to be the *Grampus*, "commanded by Captain Marsh Miller, an old river pilot whom I had long known."

Miller, Montgomery remembered, was "running for dear life from two huge and, to us, then, formidable looking gun-boats. These were firing occasional shots as they came on, and truly, to new soldiers, as we all were, except General [Benjamin F.] Cheatham, it looked serious." As soon as she arrived opposite the Rebel strongpoint, Miller turned the *Grampus* "in midstream and began firing at the gun-boats," even though all his shots fell far short.

Turning the bend about 11:00 A.M., lookouts with glasses aboard *Lexington* and *Tyler* spotted a much larger Confederate gunboat wearing a huge Rebel flag and lying near the bank about three miles away. Rodgers and Cmdr. Stembel had found the C.S.S. *Jackson*, formerly the tugboat *Yankee*. The timberclads now broke off from the *Grampus* and took the new opponent under fire. According to the excited *St. Louis Daily Missouri Democrat* journalist recording the action, their "balls and shell fell thickly around her." The *Jackson* fired back at the Federal warboats in this opening naval engagement of the western river war, but her shells fell far short.

After three or four shots had been exchanged between *Tyler*, *Lexington*, and the Rebel boat, an 8-inch shell from the *Tyler* was seen to strike the *Jackson*'s wheelhouse. The Confederate steamer's "railroad iron threw it off without any effect."

Moving closer to the town to attack both the *Jackson* and the *Grampus*, a masked battery and four rifled cannon were spied in a ravine near the upper part. A "considerable" Confederate army and a long line of tents extended along the riverfront for more than half a mile.

The alerted Confederate shore batteries now joined in, making the contest very unequal. At this point, the *Tyler* dropped a couple of shells into the Rebel camp, which resulted in a dense cloud of smoke from unknown damage that a Cincinnati reporter believed to be tents and baggage wagons.

An hour later, the Southern gunboats ran alongside the riverbank and made fast. Once *Lexington* and *Tyler* had fired off some 20 shells, they decided to maneuver out in midstream and wait for one of their opponent to cast off. She never did and Cmdr. Rodgers found that the swift current was dragging his craft down toward the Hickman gunners. Unable to cope with both the current and enemy artillery, with very little powder left onboard, few shells, and only half enough gun tackles necessary to work the batteries, the Maryland-born officer decided to break off the fight and retire. The coal supply aboard both timberclads, sufficient for one day's steaming, was running low. Rodgers was impressed by his own crews. He had not originally intended to go "so close as to be very dangerous — as dangerous as it turned out." The volunteer officers and sailors were "remarkably cool under fire," he proudly noted.

The *Lexington* and *Tyler* returned to Cairo, arriving about 6:00 P.M. On the way up they were tailed for a short distance by the *Grampus*, but no additional firing occurred. Having meanwhile stopped long enough to capture eight prisoners and about 40 head of cattle, they passed Columbus. Here they were fired upon, mostly by muskets, but also by at least two large cannon. At the upper part of the town, small arms fire stuck the hulls of the boats and riddled the deck awnings, one going through the *Tyler*'s gig. Two of the last remaining shells were expended in response, along with a quantity of small arms ammunition. At the Chalk Bluffs, they were shot at a second time but were not hit. They also met the *Conestoga*. Having received reports of the cannonade to the south all the way back at Cairo, Brig. Gen. Grant had dispatched her to the rescue. The three returned in company.

Upon his return to Cairo, Cmdr. Rodgers reported the results of the Hickman reconnaissance and engagement in a wire to Secretary Welles. Observations on affairs at Belmont, Hickman, and Columbus were also provided in personal reports to Brig. Gen. Grant and Col. Oglesby. The seaman revealed that Confederate naval presence, with what was believed to be an armorclad, was stronger than anticipated. As a result, the commander advised Grant to withdraw his troops from Belmont. That advice was accepted and the district commander informed Maj. Gen. Frémont of this decision later in the day. The soldiers at Belmont pulled up stakes and marched back to Bird's Point.

Brig. Gen. Grant did not know at this point that Columbus was also being occupied by Pillow's men. He believed there was still time to rush Union troops from Jackson, Missouri, to take possession of the Columbus heights. If that could be accomplished, "New Madrid will fall within five days after."[4]

It became clear to Brig. Gen. Grant that the South had taken over Hickman and Columbus, breaking the fragile neutrality so far maintained by Kentucky. To make certain that the political leadership of that state quickly understood what was occurring, the Buckeye general telegraphed the speaker of the Kentucky House of Representatives informing him of Polk's invasion. Although they now had the prize high above the Mississippi River, the Confederates were clearly the aggressors. Grant's bulletin implied that any Union reaction could only be viewed as necessary response.

On September 5, Charles De Arnaud, one of Maj. Gen. Frémont's staff officers and a scout, brought the Military District of Southeast Missouri commander a warning about Polk's thrust and some significant intelligence. The expatriate Russian was, in fact, a spy who was operating behind Confederate lines when he learned of the Kentucky invasion. His alert confirmed news Grant received from Waagner and Rodgers, and validated his wire to Frankfurt.

What De Arnaud learned specifically altered the Union commander's planning concerning the town of Paducah, at the mouth of the Tennessee River. Though Grant had no other reports on the matter, Frémont's agent claimed to have uncovered evidence that the Confederates were also marching — or were about to start marching — toward the Ohio River and would have control of the port town within the next 24 hours. If that happened, Union positions along that stream would be endangered. De Arnaud argued that Grant should move on the town first and simultaneously wired this belief to Maj. Gen. Frémont. If Northern soldiers took Paducah, they could protect southern Illinois and Ohio River transport, and seize control of the Tennessee River, a dagger pointed into the Confederacy. There was, the spy emphasized, "no time to lose."

Brig. Gen. Grant, who to his credit also saw the strategic possibilities, seized upon the wisdom of De Arnaud's recommendation and put the wheels into motion to reach Paducah before the South did. The rest of the day was taken up readying troops and transport for the move up the Ohio and strengthening nearby defenses. In his recollections, the Cairo-based commander noted that there were plenty of steamers in port, a "good many" available boatmen to man them, coal to fuel them, and the time to assign troops "to go aboard." Telegraph messages were decreased and road traffic was curtailed in an effort to keep Confederates from learning of the preparations.

During the day, with the *Daily Missouri Democrat* reporter still embarked, *Lexington*, *Tyler*, and *Conestoga* coaled and replenished their powder and ordnance supplies. Master Bishop joined the *Tyler* as executive officer. The bluejackets and their officers "were alive with enthusiasm" and expected to go back after the *Jackson* and *Grampus*, hoping to "give the Rebels the best shot in their lockers." Brig. Gen. John A. McClernand, the new Cairo post commander, meanwhile, rushed orders down to the waterfront requiring that Cmdr. Rodgers halt commerce up the Ohio River until further notice. Plans were also put into motion by his soldiers to fortify a spot on the Kentucky shore opposite Cairo and Bird's Point that would be named Fort Holt.

After seeing De Arnaud, Grant twice wired Maj. Gen. Frémont advising that he was no longer thinking in terms of moving on Columbus, but would be heading up the Ohio River instead, leaving about 6:30 P.M. The "Pathfinder" was advised of the unfolding riverfront situation and given the opportunity to prevent a Paducah takeover if he so desired. The second message, sent late in the day, indicated that Grant had concluded his preparations and was ready to move.

Maj. Gen. Frémont, who had coveted the Kentucky town for some time, did not reply in any manner his people at Cairo could understand. Perhaps influenced by a number of foreigners on his staff, the theater commander did telegraph instructions to Grant — in Hungarian. According to Prof. John Simon, it is highly unlikely that this message could, even if received in time, have been translated. "The Pathfinder's" security-conscious wire did authorize Grant to set up Fort Holt and to capture Paducah if he could. Frémont did, however, telegraph President Lincoln — in English — that it looked like the Confederates were moving in force into west Kentucky, capturing Hickman, Columbus, Paducah, and the river shore opposite Cairo. Cmdr. Rodgers had specifically reported danger to Cairo, Frémont added.

Ironically, on the Confederate side, Maj. Gen. Polk, according to his son William, was determined to make his defense along a line from Columbus down to Fort Pillow, via Island No. 10. He originally considered Paducah's capture, but was unable to proceed further after taking Columbus, which he always regarded as "more important than Paducah."

Knowing that the Federals had the means to attack either Columbus or Paducah quickly and without either the necessary number of gunboats or transports to provide support for a waterborne thrust to the mouth of the Tennessee, Polk "felt obliged to forego" that objective. There were no Rebel troops marching on the town as the spy Charles De Arnaud indicated and it would be several days before a regiment or so was sent out to take Mayfield, Kentucky, and guard the Rebel flank.

While all of this excitement was unfolding in the neighborhood of the tip of Illinois, Capt. Foote arrived at St. Louis by train from Washington. He reported to Maj. Gen. Frémont and then boarded an Illinois Central express for the run down to Cairo. Also, deep in the Confederacy, Gen. Albert Sidney Johnston was assigned to take over the entire Western Department as Frémont's opposite number.[5]

Late in the afternoon, Cmdr. Rodgers received new orders from Brig. Gen. Grant. Together with the *Conestoga* under Lt. Phelps, his *Tyler* would convoy a body of Union soldiers up the Ohio under cover of darkness. Cmdr. Stembel's *Lexington* would remain behind to guard Cairo.

Further up the levee, the steamers *Graham*, *Platte Valley*, and *W.B. Terry* took aboard Brig. Gen. Eleazer Paine's 9th Illinois and Col. John McArthur's 12th Illinois, along with a section of Smith's Chicago Artillery under Lt. Charley Willard. When, a little later, Brig. Gen. McClernand wired Maj. Gen. Frémont news of their departure, he called the 1,800–2,000 men embarked "among the most carefully chosen and drilled of the Illinois volunteers."

Although the *St. Louis Daily Missouri Democrat* reporter along on the expedition depicted the 11:30 P.M. departure as a joyous event cheered by "the assembled thousands" onshore, it is rather imagined that there were a few hundred people witnessing what Brig. Gen. Grant hoped was a secure and secret sailing. In any event, the "noble fleet" made for Mound City, with the *Tyler* in the van and the *Conestoga* at the rear.

Grant did not wish to reach Paducah before sunup and was thus not disappointed when the *W.B. Terry*, the ship captured at that port the previous month, broke down as she eased into the bank at Mound City. With the *W.H.B.* available, the troops aboard the *Terry* were shifted to the new charter and held along with the rest of the flotilla for a predawn departure.

Just after midnight, as Cmdr. Rodgers

Lt. General Leonidas Polk (1806–1864) defended the Mississippi River at Columbus, Kentucky, in the fall of 1861, holding the "Gibraltar of the West" for the South until its March 1862 evacuation. He later fought at Shiloh, Perrysville, Stone's River, and Chickamauga before falling to a Federal cannonball during the Atlanta campaign (U.S. Army Military History Institute).

and Grant's Paducah occupation fleet was headed toward Mound City, Capt. Foote arrived at Cairo by rail from St. Louis. There he learned from Brig. Gen. McClernand and Cmdr. Stembel that he was too late to catch Rodgers in port. Rather than wait for the expedition to return, the Washington arrival obtained passage on a steamer and made for Mound City. Near that town early on September 6, Foote encountered the *W.B. Terry*, broken down, "or nearly so," as he later remembered. Proceeding on, he overhauled the *Tyler* and boarded.

The loud hail as the two steamers met brought Cmdr. Rodgers face to face with Foote, a man whom he had met earlier, one of "high reputation." Once the bearded seaman had climbed aboard the timberclad, he explained to the shocked Rodgers why he had come. When leaving St. Louis, Foote did not know of the Paducah expedition and had meant to relieve the Marylander at Cairo. In any event, Foote quickly read his orders and assumed command. Other naval officers more senior to him were en route from the east to beef up the expanded squadron, but Rodgers was invited to continue on, both in command of the *Tyler* for this operation and later as his assistant on the staff of Maj. Gen. Frémont. He "behaved well, officer-like and gentlemanly," Foote later recalled. As soon as possible, the two men made the situation known to Brig. Gen. Grant, who naturally invited both to continue to Paducah.

According to his biographer, Robert E. Johnson, Capt. Foote's arrival was an unpleasant surprise for Rodgers. He had not had a chance to read Secretary Welles' order addressed to him at St. Louis and his brother-in-law, Quartermaster General Meigs, who might have been able to intervene, learned of the Frémont coup too late to help.

Foote hoped that Rodgers would remain. His knowledge of the timberclads, the ironclad building program, the ins and outs of the army supply system and the politics of Frémont's command, and his acquaintance with Grant and other military officers would prove invaluable. As he confided to Assistant Secretary of the Navy Fox, Rodgers did a yeoman job of starting the flotilla and he deserved "great credit for what he has done."

By this time, the Navy Department had issued orders for several other officers to join Capt. Foote in the west. Those of interest included future timberclad captains Cmdr. Henry A. Walke and Lt. William Gwin, James Shirk, Egbert Thompson, and Byron Wilson.

Known as something of a maverick and a great artist, the taciturn Virginian Henry A. Walke (1808–1896) was, arguments to the contrary accepted, one of the most successful and under celebrated of all Civil War naval officers. A midshipman with Captain Foote on the U.S.S. *Natchez* in 1827, Walke served numerous ships and squadrons and was promoted to the rank of commander in 1855. One of many officers involuntarily retired by the infamous Naval Retiring Board set up under congressional legislation of that year, he was eventually returned to duty. Like all "restored officers," he was placed on half pay and throughout the Civil War received only 50 percent of the income his rank would ordinarily provide. In early 1861, while commanding the store ship *Supply* off Pensacola, he elected to remove personnel from the guardian forts and the navy yard rather than allow them to become POWs. His actions, technically violating previous orders, resulted in his court-martial, a "complimentary reprimand," and temporary banishment to the post of light house inspector at Williamsport, New York.

On September 6, Secretary Welles ordered Walke to St. Louis. Later, in command of the famous Pook turtle *Carondelet*, he fought at Forts Henry and Donelson and ran the batteries at Island No. 10. Walke commanded several other vessels during the war, was promoted to captain in 1862 and commodore in 1866. He commanded the Mound City naval station 1868–1870, where he was joined by his former colleague Capt. Egbert Thompson. After becoming a rear admiral in 1870, he retired in 1871, contributing his drawings and memories to books and articles on the conflict. Walke died in New York in early 1896.

Hoosier Lt. William Gwin (1832–1863) was regarded as one of the most promising junior officers in the service. Transferred west from the U.S.S. *Susquehanna*, he would command the flotilla's timberclad division in early 1862, gaining its greatest laurels. Transferred to the flag boat *Benton*, he was wounded in action at Haines Bluff on December 27, 1862, and died a week later.

Born in Pennsylvania, Lt. James W. Shirk (1832–1873) was a midshipman aboard Cdr. Perry's *Mississippi* during the 1850s opening of Japan and was promoted to Lt. in 1856. Constantly at sea prior to his St. Louis assignment, he would later serve as commander of the Tennessee River District, eventually becoming the longest-serving junior officer in the Mississippi Squadron. Commissioned a commander on July 25, 1866, he died on February 10, 1873.

With experience aboard the U.S.S. *Dolphin* and the *Michigan*, Lt.. Egbert Thompson (1822–1881) came to Foote's unit from the Gulf Squadron blockadeer *Powhatan*. After participating in the Battle of Fort Donelson, he followed Cmdr. Walke past the batteries at Island No. 10 in the U.S.S. *Pittsburgh* and participated in the Battle of Memphis. Ironically, he served with Cdr. Walke at the Mound City naval station in 1869–1870. Retired in 1874 with the rank of Capt., he died in January 1881.

Buckeye Lt. Byron Wilson (1837–1893) was named an Acting Midshipman in 1853 and received his present commission in April 1861. He would rise to become a Lt. Cmdr. in 1863 and command the ironclad *Mound City* on the Red River Expedition in 1864. Promoted to Cmdr. in 1872, he reached the rank of Capt. in 1883. He retired in 1893 and died later that year.[6]

In the minutes around 8:00 A.M. on September 6, the Union invasion fleet, under a heavy cloud of chimney smoke, approached Paducah, where a number of secession flags were seen flying. The men aboard *Tyler* and *Conestoga* stood to their guns ready to respond should any Rebel batteries open upon the arriving steamers. The local citizens, according to Grant's *Memoirs*, were already up and anticipating the arrival of a 3,800 man Confederate army reportedly about 16 miles distant. They were surprised to see Yankees instead and there was, consequently, no overt opposition. The U.S. steamers glided in and the troops were unloaded swiftly and without casualties.

The expedition's imbedded St. Louis newsman reported that Col. McArthur's 12th Illinois came ashore at the marine hospital in the lower part of the city, while the latter arrived at the foot of Main Street and marched up it past all the shuttered homes and businesses to the Ohio and New Orleans Railroad depot. There, some $20,000 worth of contraband supplies was found, marked for Memphis, Union City, and New Orleans.

An important piece of the conquest was left to the navy. Cmdr. Rodgers, with a group of *Tyler* marines, immediately sought out the telegraph office. When they were refused admittance, the sailor's guard broke the doors in with musket butts. The signal machine was found disabled, but the premises were secured. Next, Rodgers and company searched the post office, took large numbers of letters and dispatches, and forwarded them over to Brig. Gen. Grant.

After demanding the Rebel banners about town be replaced with U.S. colors, Grant ordered five companies of infantry and several of Lt. Willard's cannon to sally down the railroad for a few miles. No advancing enemy were encountered as far as seven miles south. There a burned railroad bridge and cut telegraph wires were discovered. It was learned during the trek, however, that Brig. Gen. Lloyd Tilghman and his staff, along with a number of Confederate soldiers, had fled the city by rail, taking all of the rolling stock.

While this reconnaissance was taking place, rumors began to spread that forces of Brig. Gen. Pillow were headed toward Paducah, not by rail but down the Tennessee River on steamboats. To check on this possibility, Capt. Foote ordered Lt. Phelps to ascend that stream with the *Conestoga* to watch for movements and to capture any boats she found running in Confederate territory.

The timberclad paddled up the Tennessee some 13 miles, but initially saw no Southern merchantmen. Eventually, a small stern-wheeler did approach, but when she saw the *Conestoga*, she immediately went about and made off. Phelps gave chase and soon ran her ashore. The steamer was the 187-ton, nine-year-old *Jefferson*, bearing a heavy load of tobacco judged to be worth about $8,000. Originally built at McKeesport, Pennsylvania, the vessel was quickly captured and a prize crew returned her to Paducah. She, like other vessels from now on more frequently prized, was seized on the basis of having "given aid and comfort to the Rebels by forwarding provisions and stores to them by the Tennessee and Cumberland rivers."

While the *Conestoga* was away, Brig. Gen. Grant issued a proclamation to the town's citizens offering his protection and placed Brig. Gen. Paine in charge of the occupation. The invasion commander hoped his action would soothe the populace, the majority of whom he believed "would have much preferred the presence of the other army." With his troops safely ashore and unopposed and himself and Capt. Foote embarked, Grant, at noon, ordered two steamboats to put out into the Ohio and begin the four hour run back to Cairo. Back at headquarters by late afternoon, the brigadier began sending reinforcements to Paducah. Foote, with a copy of Grant's citizen proclamation in hand, took the train back to St. Louis to see Maj. Gen. Frémont.

All that Friday and the next day, the *Daily Missouri Democrat* journalist later told his readers that the majority of Paducah's population left the town, voting to insure its safety with its feet. Carriages and wagons, he observed, loaded with families and household goods departed, choking the town's principal street. "A perfect panic seemed to possess them, which no assurance of our officers or troops could allay." The residents were scared that Pillow would come, there would be heavy fighting, and all of the buildings would be "shelled and burned by our gunboats." By Sunday, only about 100 families remained.[7]

Despite the fact that Southern forces were not advancing on the town, Grant's decision to take Paducah was one of the best he made during the entire war. Its capture guaranteed the future southbound invasion route down the Tennessee River to the Union. It also prevented any major Confederate threat to southern Illinois or Northern river transportation from Louisville to Cairo.

When Capt. Foote arrived at Maj. Gen. Frémont's headquarters early on September 7, "The Pathfinder" already had a flattering letter of introduction from Navy Secretary Welles. The general gave his new fleet commander a cordial welcome and pressed him for his view of local naval and military matters, as well as Eads' building and conversion programs.

Having learned something of Cmdr. Rodgers' true worth, Capt. Foote now spoke glowingly of his predecessor's accomplishments. Frémont, never a Rodgers fan, could see the benefit of retaining the nautical explorer on his staff as something of a consultant. As Foote later wrote Welles, Rodgers would be able to give the theater commander the benefit of his wisdom in fitting out the mortar boats and would be available in St. Louis to render essential service by overseeing the different ironclad building and conversion contracts and aiding Foote when he was absent on other business, i.e., fighting the gunboats.

According to the flattering profile of Rodgers which appeared in the August 15, 1863, issue of *Harper's Weekly*, Maj. Gen. Frémont, following his visit with Foote, asked the commander into his office. Expressing great regret that he had earlier asked for his replacement, which could not now be undone, Frémont claimed that the action "arose from error, from false representations of contractors." He urged the naval officer "to accept the place on his staff of executive officer for naval affairs connected with his movements." This position, the illustrated newspaper reported, "was declined."

Acting at Frémont's direction, Capt. Foote, who would next visit the boatbuilders, wrote out an order for mail delivery to Cmdr. Rodgers requiring that he report to St. Louis. He probably knew from their conversation on the *Tyler* that Rodgers did not wish to remain in Missouri as an advisor. At the same time, off Paducah, the Maryland-born officer was even then composing a hurt request to the Navy Department asking for sea duty, as Welles August 30 order permitted. Rodgers' disappointment at not being allowed to remain in charge of the Western Flotilla and by the pending arrival of naval officers senior to himself was palpable: "When the plant thus watered and cultivated gives its first prematurely ripe fruit, the crop is turned over to another with cold words."

The *Conestoga* continued her Tennessee River patrol that morning, September 7. An hour or so into her cruise, the gunboat came upon the 198-ton Louisville-built and home-ported packet *John Gault*, "a fine boat" only four years old. She had over the past several days stopped at various points between Louisville and Smithland, arriving the previous evening at the mouth of the Cumberland. There she was refused permission to land her cargo at the wharf boat.

Early on the seventh, the *John Gault* steamed 25 miles up the Cumberland to Ross's Ferry, where she discharged her consignment to the Nashville packet *J.H. Baldwin*. On the basis of this "trading with the enemy," Phelps claimed her as a prize. The stern-wheeler followed the timberclad back to Paducah and was tied up alongside the *Jefferson* at one of the wharf boats seized by Brig. Gen. Paine the previous day.

The occupation of Paducah entered its second day that Saturday and the town's civilian population continued to depart for the interior. The *Daily Missouri Democrat* reporter witnessed an unhappy incident which added to the confusion. Cmdr. Rodgers, not having as yet departed for St. Louis, had ordered gun drill aboard the *Tyler* that morning and, in the process, an 8-inch shell was accidentally fired into a house on the town levee. The round hit the structure on its line with the pavement and entered the unoccupied lower story, where it exploded. Civilians immediately and naturally believed the timberclad was shelling the town and "the terror of the women and children was duly increased."

Calm was restored, only for panic to resume shortly afterward when Lt. Willard's gunners opened battery practice on the town square, with the rapid and very noisy discharge of 30 rounds. By that time, reinforcements from the 8th Illinois plus the 40th and 41st Illinois and 6th Missouri were arriving from Cairo aboard the steamers *Louisiana*, *Belle Memphis*, and *Empress*, bringing the occupation force to approximately 5,000 soldiers. Additionally, Brig. Gen. Paine was succeeded by Brig. Gen. Charles F. Smith, a taciturn, beloved, and bewhiskered commander who was one of Grant's instructors at West Point.

At Cairo, Brig. Gen. Grant asked Col. Waagner and Cmdr. Stembel to undertake another reconnaissance toward Columbus. With Col. Waagner's troops embarked, the *Lexington* weighed at 5:00 A.M. on Sunday morning and puffed down the Mississippi. About two hours later, as the timberclad was passing Islands No. 3 and No. 4, campfires were seen on the high bluffs a few miles above Columbus on the Kentucky shore. Coming abreast of the foot of Lucas Bend, Cmdr. Stembel's command took fire from two masked Confederate batteries, which luckily overshot. Although Waagner later praised the Rebel artillery work, he also observed their "powder weak and the fuzes entirely too long." The gunboat did not return fire, as the enemy was out of range.

Suspecting that the Confederate gunboats *Jackson* and *Grampus*, and perhaps the *Jeff Davis*, were lying somewhere in Lucas Bend, Waagner asked Stembel to "throw some shell

The Fortifications at Columbus, Kentucky, were not only formidable but were mounted high atop bluffs lining the river. The "Gibraltar of the West" was scouted frequently by the timberclads in the fall of 1861 and her cannon supported Confederate troops during the Battle of Belmont (*Battles and Leaders*).

into the bend." This was quickly done and brought the appearance of the former tugboat and the little black stern-wheeler. Having no desire for an engagement at that time, the *Lexington* rounded to and proceeded back upstream. She was tailed out of range for about three miles by the *Grampus* and was back at Bird's Point by 10:00 A.M.

Ashore, Col. Waagner reported to Brig. Gen. Grant that something like 2,000 graycoats were camped out with six cannon on the Columbus bluffs, while on the Missouri shore opposite, between Belmont and Lucas Bend, another thousand Rebels were established with an unknown number of fieldpieces. Closing his analysis, the artilleryman praised "the cool, calculating and energetic behavior of Captain Stembel, his officers and men." Grant also heard during the day that old scows and steamers were being sunk in the channel near Randolph.

The first major and coordinated Union land-water reconnaissance down the Mississippi since the Confederate capture of Columbus, the Waagner-Stembel mission opened two months of what historian Nathaniel Hughes has called "magnificent rehearsals for the coming strike on Belmont." The Northern infantry gained necessary maneuver experience, while the gunboatmen "learned about the river and the location and limitations of the enemy's heavy guns."

Also on September 8, the *Conestoga* proceeded 12 miles up the Ohio River from Paducah, guarding a small troop convoy. These vessels turned up the Cumberland at Smithland, where that strategic village was also occupied. The timberclad then continued on to make a brief survey of the river road to Nashville. During her Cumberland reconnaissance, Lt. Phelps took a smaller steamer, the 140-ton *Trade Water Belle*. Built at New Albany in 1857, the civilian boat was mistakenly called the *Tradewater Blue* by the newsman reporting her seizure to the citizens of Chicago. After supper, Brig. Gen. Grant wired Maj. Gen. Frémont that spies and refugees had revealed some idea as to the enemy strength at Columbus. Additionally, he noted that there were two Confederate gunboats, one of which came within three miles of Cairo earlier in the day.

For some time, Maj. Gen. Frémont had been developing a grand strategic plan for an offensive in his theater that would clear the enemy from southeast Missouri and allow occupation of the newly occupied Confederate Gibraltar. The blueprint was ready for distribution on September 8 and was duly dispatched to President Lincoln. Its major components included a push by Brig. Gen. Smith from Paducah into the rear of Columbus, the removal (by defeat or expulsion) of gray-clad forces in Missouri. When those initial phases were completed, Smith and Grant would go at Columbus from different directions. Never doubting the fall of the stronghold, Frémont would head to Hickman and take Memphis, bringing a "glorious" triumph for the Union in the west.

Later that night, a scout brought a copy of Maj. Gen. Polk's General Order No. 19 of September 7 for the organization of his Columbus-based troops. A list of Southern steamers tied below the bluffs was also provided, along with a description of the C.S.S. *Jackson*. According to this information, the one-time *Yankee* was "Iron clad and fast." She was also supposedly armed with two cannon, one an 84-pounder and the other a 64-pounder. The Federal rider did not see the *Grampus* or the *Jeff Davis* at Columbus and informed Grant that the *Jackson* was the only boat present.

This scout's report caused Grant, in his follow up telegraph to Maj. Gen. Frémont, to correct his earlier observation that two Rebel gunboats lay at Columbus. It was also learned that Brig. Gen. M. Jeff Thompson was marching toward Norfolk. About 11: 30 P.M., orders were passed to Cmdr. Stembel to proceed down the Mississippi at dawn, keeping abreast of Col. Waagner's troops, who would march on Norfolk along the shore.[8] The civilian exodus from Paduach continued apace on Sunday. Reporters noticed that only one church was open for Sunday services that day, with but "40 hearers."

Having returned to that Kentucky town from Smithland the previous evening, the *Conestoga*, trailed by her three prize steamers, made their way on to Cairo early on September 9. Their arrival made the little Illinois port "quite lively," in the words of the local *Chicago Daily Tribune* reporter, as these were the first captured Confederate boats brought in since the *W.B. Terry* was taken in August.

The captured steamboats and their cargoes were turned over to the local collector of customs, while the officers and crew were detained as POWs. Lt. Phelps also opened his brig to pass along three other prisoners. One had been taken at Paducah and one each on the Tennessee and Cumberland rivers.

While the paperwork involved with the prizes was handled, the *Conestoga* coaled. Simultaneously, Cmdr. Stembel and Col. Waagner reached Norfolk. The soldier received some intelligence that enemy troops were headed his way and passed it along to the timberclad. Capt. Foote, meanwhile, paid a return visit to Paducah, where he conferred with Brig. Gen. Smith and learned that the Tennessee River would soon fall.

As the sun dropped that evening, Brig. Gen. Grant wrote to Lt. Phelps, noting that intelligence suggested the *Lexington* might be attacked. The *Conestoga* was ordered to steam to her assistance as soon as practicable. Casting off, Lt. Phelp's timberclad descended the twinkling starlit water to make rendezvous in the small hours. With watches posted, the two vessels remained in the vicinity of the colonel's camp.

Early on September 10, Col. Waagner's force, led by Col. Oglesby's 8th Illinois and supported by the two timberclads offshore, departed Norfolk for a reconnaissance march along the riverbank down toward Belmont. Sgt. Charles Wright Wills of the 8th noted in his diary how the gunboats kept "a couple of miles ahead of us."

In the lead, the *Lexington* dropped down some distance below the troops, giving her officers a chance to peer down the river with their glasses. No enemy movement was seen. She then returned to a position abreast of Waagner and reported. Next, the *Conestoga* pushed ahead, dropping down toward the head of Island No. 2 to find a reported masked battery. This was approximately the same location where on the previous Sunday two batteries were discovered and the floating Rebel hornets were aroused. Although cannon were not spotted, a body of cavalry was seen along the Missouri bank near the island and the timberclad fired at them with her stern gun.

Upon hearing Phelps' cannon blast, Stembel pushed the *Lexington* downstream. As the two ships approached one another, Confederate cannon, concealed from their view, opened up. One of the Confederate batteries firing on them was mounted and, over the next little while, simply limbered and unlimbered at different locations to engage the boats. "The first we knew of them," Phelps later reported, was "the whiz of their shot which went all over and about us." Upwards of 15 pieces of wheeled artillery were suspected of making all this racket.

Ashore further upstream, Sgt. Wright of the 8th Illinois jotted in his journal that his regiment had marched about five miles "when the gunboats, which were about a mile and one-half ahead of us, opened mouth and thunder! What a rumpus they did keep up." "We could not see them for the thick brush between us and the river, but we thought sure our little fight had come at last."

Keeping pace and maneuvering out of harm's way out on the Mississippi, the bows of the timberclads were kept pointed into the current and their paddle wheels offset the flow. This permitted rather stable gun platforms from which to undertake counter battery fire. Still, over 150 shots were taken by the Rebel cannoneers at the two floating targets and no one would ever be able to say why none hit. "They passed between our chimneys," wrote Phelps, "over our bow & stern, fore and aft, under the counters, etc., but not actually aboard."

Eventually, the horse guns were taken aboard a steamer, which retreated under the protection of the C.S.S. *Jackson* and *Grampus*, newly arrived on the scene. Both vessels flew large Confederate ensigns and both remained well under the batteries on the Columbus bluffs. Although the timberclads took the trio under fire, they were out of range and could not be hit.

There was a lull in the fighting between 1:00 P.M. and 2:00 P.M. The two U.S. gunboats retired upstream a short distance, hoping to induce Southern military units to pursue on land and thereby run into Col. Waagner, who was now at Beckwith's Farm some five miles below Norfolk. The gray-clad soldiers were smarter than that and resisted the lure.

When their ploy was seen to have failed, *Lexington* and *Conestoga* charged back into Lucas Bend, throwing shells at those locations where Stembel had been shot at previously, while also hoping to get a crack at the *Jackson* and *Grampus*. Checking the fall of their shot with glasses, the two gunboat captains later told Brig. Gen. Grant they could see shells exploding in the midst of the Confederate batteries and saw members of the crews carried to the rear, presumably wounded.

Their great paddle wheels splashing, the two timberclads came to a point about two and a half miles from the *Jackson*, where they opened up on her. What happened next is uncertain, except that we know the *Jackson* was hit and damaged. Both Lt. Phelps and Cmdr. Stembel claimed to have made telling shots. The captain of the *Conestoga* later told his superior that his first 8-inch round, launched over a land spit, must have struck the *Jackson* in her side on the ricochet as it touched the water close alongside. Right after that she turned to flee downstream. Over on the *Lexington*, Cmdr. Stembel told a gun crew to charge its piece with a 15-second fuse shell and train the gun on the enemy, using the greatest possible elevation. This could be achieved by removing the wooden quoin, which differed from a wedge, according to Gershom Bradford, by having only one tapered face. After the cannon discharge, the shell was seen to explode in the *Jackson*'s starboard wheelhouse, careening her chimney and causing other damage. Other guns in both boats were fired at the Rebels but no more hits were recorded.

A little over a year later, on January 6, 1863, Acting Rear Admiral David Dixon Porter very carefully wrote out the "Rules for Cutting Fuses in Shrapnel." Using sights, gun captains were to remember that each of its marks represented a second on the fuse. "If you want to fire 1-second fuse," he advised, "fasten the sight at the first mark and point at the object." With good powder, a 1-second fuse would burst at 500 yards, while a 5-second fuse would burst at 1,900 yards. The balls within the shell would be projected some 50 yards beyond.

Regardless of which timberclad caused the most harm during this shoot, both *Jackson* and *Grampus* were seen to retreat back toward Columbus, keeping close under the batteries along the bluffs. The *Lexington* and *Conestoga* continued to engage the local land batteries until approximately 5:00 P.M., at which point the naval captains had succeeded either in silencing their opponents' cannon or in causing their movement.

Returning up toward Norfolk, the wooden warriors were fired upon by Confederate small arms from points all along the bank, with one particularly vicious attack coming from the area around an outhouse. Lt. Phelps ordered his gunners to waste the building and everything around it with canister. It was during this exchange that the boats suffered their only casualty when Quartermaster Nelson Castle was shot in the arm.

While the gunboats were engaged, Col. Oglesby deposited his men "in the front yard of some secesher's deserted house (a fine one)" and took a small party ahead to reconnoiter. Returning none the wiser, Oglesby ordered his men back to Norfolk. The *Conestoga* and *Lexington* put in that landing in early evening. Sgt. Wills remembers that they "reported fighting the *Yankee* and two land batteries, one of which was but three and a half miles below us (and some say but one and a half miles) and had 16 guns. They crippled the dam'd *Yankee*, although the latter carries 84's, while ours hadn't but 64's. Our boats were not touched."[9]

During the day, Brig. Gen. Grant, back at Cairo, received sketchy reports on the fighting. Late in the afternoon, he was able to wire Maj. Gen. Frémont at St. Louis that Waagner's troops from Norfolk had arrived at Beckwith's Farm without finding the enemy. Additionally, the supporting gunboats were engaged "at long shot all day" with two Rebel gunboats. Grant feared the U.S. craft might have gone beyond the masked Confederate batteries.

Frémont in St. Louis shared this wire with Capt. Andrew H. Foote, who had by that time been joined by Cmdr. Walke, Lt. Shirk, plus several other regular officers who would fill administrative slots or ironclad captaincies. Foote, who wanted to avoid any criticism concerning his availability to supervise Eads' construction projects, immediately appointed Walke his task group commander at Cairo.

Walke and Foote, who had known each other since their shared midshipman days when both underwent a religious conversion together, was reminded to report to and cooperate with Ulysses Grant, the local brigadier commanding. Walke, in taking temporary charge of the timberclads, was also told that if the *Tyler* had not yet transferred down to Cairo, he

Left: Flag Officer/Rear Admiral Andrew H. Foote (1806–1863) succeeded Cmdr. John Rodgers in command of the Western Flotilla in September 1861. Foote guided the construction of the Pook turtles and other ironclads that followed the timberclads but always was careful to make certain that his wooden gunboats were carefully employed in the months before the Battles of Fort Henry/Donelson in February 1862. Foote led his unit in the campaigns against Island No. 10, Fort Pillow, and Memphis, but he was forced to depart when wounds received at Donelson made it impossible for him to continue. *Right:* Cmdr. Henry Walke (1808–1896) succeeded Cmdr. John Rodgers in command of the *Tyler* in September 1861. He led the largest timberclad in action against Confederate gunboats near Columbus and in support of Brig. Gen. U.S. Grant's Belmont offensive. In December, he was named captain of the *Carondelet*, which he would make the most famous ironclad on the western rivers. The *Tyler*, under command of Lt. William Gwin, joined with Walke's *Carondelet* in fighting a rearguard action against the advancing Southern armorclad *Arkansas* in July 1862 (both photographs, Library of Congress).

should go up to Paducah and retrieve her, again asking Cmdr. Rodgers to report to Foote at St. Louis post haste. The new operational officer later assessed his friend and commander for an entry in the *Battles and Leaders* series. Called "the Stonewall Jackson of the Navy," Foote "was slow and cautious in arriving at conclusions, but firm and tenacious of purpose." Walke continued: "He was not a man of striking personal appearance, but there was a sailor-like heartiness and frankness about him that made his company very desirable."

In response to Grant's telegraphs, Frémont wired back advising him to make certain that the gunboats moved cautiously, in concert with Waagoner's troops onshore. A more complete wire from Grant well after dark announced the return of the timberclads. Phelps and Stembel had made their way quickly to his headquarters and had reported their Lucas Bend engagements. A total of 16 enemy cannon were said to have fired upon them, but it was also reported that the cannon were all silenced. Large bodies of cavalry were seen on the Missouri side of the Mississippi but no enemy troops were detected over in Kentucky. The *Jackson* was disabled and would have been taken except that she hid under the big gun batteries of Columbus. One man on the *Conestoga* was wounded and the *Lexington*'s machinery was out of order and in need of repair.

While the Cairo nautical task group was occupied with the Confederate gunboats, Maj. Gen. Frémont, at St. Louis, found himself with other worries. Maj. Gen. Price now reappeared in unoccupied Missouri at a little town called Lexington. Unwilling to unleash his Mississippi advance with Price on the loose, Frémont ordered Brig. Gen. Grant to, at least temporarily, forget about the great strategy shared with Lincoln two days earlier and to go over to the defense, checking guerrillas. Frémont knew he could not undertake a two-front offensive and so chose to face the one near Lexington.

When he arrived at Cairo the next morning, Cmdr. Walke found the *Conestoga* the only fully operational gunboat. Meeting Brig. Gen. Grant, with whom he would develop a long and good relationship, the new arrival informed the brigadier and Capt. Foote of that situation. Soon thereafter, his superior wired back orders from St. Louis that he proceed up to Paducah and assume command of the *Tyler*. At the same time, now that the river level was falling, Foote ordered Lt. Phelps to take the *Conestoga* to Paducah, with Walke embarked, to exchange stations with the larger vessel. The *Lexington* had to be repaired and the *Conestoga-Tyler* turnaround could be accomplished in short order.

Brig. Gen. McClernand now requested Brig. Gen. Grant permit the *Conestoga* to convoy a steamer loaded with hay from Smithland to Cairo. Grant replied that he had no gunboat to spare for such a lengthy trip. McClernand also checked in to see whether or not a gunboat was available to protect any supply steamers sent below Norfolk. Meanwhile, his superior heard from a Confederate deserter from Columbus during the day that up to 5,000 reinforcements had been sent across the river to Belmont. It was widely expected, the informant revealed, that attacks would be forthcoming from that point against Bird's Point and Cairo.

Col. Oglesby was sent on a six-mile reconnaissance patrol below Norfolk later on in the day, even though support from the *Conestoga* was not available. Keenly aware of the demand for naval presence, Grant, nevertheless, that afternoon permitted the *Lexington* to make the short voyage over to Mound City for engine repairs. Her return was expected within a day or so.

Capt. Foote, also at St. Louis, waited in vain for over a day for some written detail on the Lucas Bend engagement from his fighting subordinates. He wanted to share the good news in some detail with Secretary Welles and of course the fact that the information, told mostly from an army view, was appearing in local newspapers was not pleasing. That afternoon, he went to Cairo by rail to speak with Cmdr. Stembel and Lt. Phelps and to review with Cmdr. Walke issues confronting their growing naval responsibility on the tip of Illinois. Walke, Stembel and Phelps met him at the depot. Over dinner that night at the St. Charles Hotel, the two timberclad skippers undoubtedly told Foote and Walke of the Lucas Bend engagement in great firsthand detail.

The *Conestoga* duly hove into sight on the Ohio River later on the morning of September 12 and anchored near the *Tyler* and opposite Paducah's marine hospital in a position where her guns could command approaches to the city. Capt. Foote also elected to make the short voyage upstream with Walke to meet and confer both with Rodgers and, next day, with the town's commander, Brig. Gen. Smith.

There is no evidence that Foote and Rodgers met to discuss the latter's future during this Paducah visit except in the letter which the commander wrote that day to Secretary Welles. In it, Rodgers noted that he would be giving up command of the *Tyler* to Cmdr. Walke that afternoon, but that Maj. Gen. Frémont was "quite desirous of having me join his staff, at least temporarily."

One could almost hear Capt. Foote explaining to his predecessor that joining Frémont, the man who had requested his recall, would allow him to continue making some contribution to the growth of the little fleet he had midwifed. Rodgers held no ill will toward Foote, but truly wanted a billet on the East Coast which would give him greater opportunity. Using this message to reiterate his transfer request, the Maryland-born officer consented to stay on until he could "get orders to sea." Following a brief change-of-command ceremony, Lt. Phelps took over the Paducah station.

On the morning of September 13, Capt. Foote, possibly accompanied by Cmdrs. Walke and Rodgers, called upon Brig. Gen. Smith, whom Rodgers had met earlier. The remainder of the day was undoubtedly taken up in conversation and on matters related to Paducah's defense. While his seniors were ashore, Lt. Phelps took the *Conestoga* on a short reconnaissance up the Tennessee.

Further west, Maj. Gen. Price was closing in on Col. James A. Mulligan's 23rd Illinois, the defenders of Lexington. From St. Louis, Maj. Gen. Frémont sent out orders to Brig. Gen. John Pope, Samuel D. Sturgis, and Jefferson C. Davis to sally from their posts at Palmyra, Mexico, and Jefferson City, Missouri, and save Mulligan and his "Irish Brigade." The response would prove ineffective.

Maj. Gen. Frémont now had — putting it kindly — a far less golden reputation than he had enjoyed when first he arrived at St. Louis back in late July. By mid-to-late September and early October, he found himself in a bitter feud with the Blair family, hampered by shortages of supplies, manpower, and funds, plagued by all manner of inefficiencies and corruption in his local command that often cost him what little he had in resources, and an unhappy President Lincoln, who was forced to renounce a local emancipation proclamation published by "The Pathfinder" on August 30. Indeed, the appointment of a strong, though impatient Brig. Gen. Grant and the fortification of Cairo were among the few moves made by Frémont that appeared correct — although not to everyone. And now the political, supply, and military difficulties of his post were crashing down upon him simultaneously.

During the day, the *Chicago Daily Tribune* published further details on the Lucas Bend fight, picked up by its Cairo correspondent the day before from information obtained out of the Rebel citadel at Columbus. The Southerners supposedly admitted that their gunboat *Jackson* was disabled, with 68 dead and many wounded. On the other hand, the Confederates boasted that several hundred "Lincolnites" were killed. That evening, the *Conestoga* returned to Paducah from her patrol too late to allow the temporary station ship *Tyler* to depart. It is unknown whether or not Foote had this *Tribune* report and shared it with Lt. Phelps.

Before dawn on September 14, Cmdr. Walke, with Foote and Rodgers aboard as his guests, took the *Tyler* back to Cairo. From that point, the first and second commanders of the Western Flotilla took the train to St. Louis, where both would now regularly and with some anticipation receive their mail.

It was just about 8:00 A.M. when Walke, as previously ordered, conferred again with Brig. Gen. Grant. The army brigadier pointed out that as a result of the September 11 spy interview his gunboat was needed to reconnoiter the Lucas Bend area, searching for masked batteries and other signs of Confederate activity in or near Belmont. Consequently, the *Tyler*, with several of Grant's staff officers aboard as observers, soon thereafter weighed for Norfolk, where she arrived about lunchtime.

Just after lunch, elements of the 8th and 9th Illinois infantries began a 10-mile march down the river bank "looking for secesh." The black-painted side-wheeler puffed down as nautical escort, out in the river about a mile or so ahead. While the troops were halted for a break, a cloud of dust was observed rising about four miles down on the Missouri shore. "Some of the boys had glasses with them," remembered Sgt. Charles Wright Wills of the 8th, "and made out the cause to be a body of cavalry." The men scrambled into formation and presented a line of battle.

At this point, the *Tyler* steamed in the direction of Lucas Bend. There her captain had his first view of the Columbus, its defenses and the river below them. Here the bluffs were, as he recalled 15 years later, quite formidable, "rising two or three hundred feet above the ordinary surface of the Mississippi, overlooking the course of the river northward and southward about 20 miles." He went on to review — with an error of recollection regarding a floating battery — geography he would come to know intimately, both as a commander and an artist:

> The river at the base of these bluffs takes a short and rapid turn to the southwest, where it becomes very deep and narrow, forming: strong eddies and currents and counter-currents at Columbus. The Confederate batteries are planted upon the spurs of the bluff, one of them about 50 feet above the water, mounting 10 heavy guns, with a large floating battery of 16 guns moored at Columbus landing. Their heaviest rifled guns were planted and pivoted on the summit of the Iron Banks, where they commanded a long range up the river and also to their rear. The enemy's trains of light and heavy artillery (including some Parrot rifle guns) were ample and well organized.

When off Island No. 4, the *Tyler* pumped four shells into suspected Confederate locations on the lower end of the island. She then rounded to and proceeded back up the Mississippi. After a forward meeting with Col. Oglesby, Walke took aboard 100 9th Illinois Infantry soldiers. Then, in response to the colonel's request, the *Tyler* returned to Lucas Bend and fired eight shells into a Confederate camp near Benton.

Ashore, the Federal infantrymen, who saw no action after all, trekked back along the bank at dusk and reached Norfolk about 10:00 P.M., There Wills and his fellow soldiers found that the men embarked aboard the *Tyler* had already been dropped off. The gunboat, after making a stop off Fort Holt where Walke talked to Col. Waagner, returned to Cairo and dropped anchor about 9:00 P.M. After Grant's lieutenants went ashore, Walke wrote out a report to send to Capt. Foote. Among the points covered was the need for repairs to the *Tyler*.

On Sunday morning September 15, the *Tyler* returned to Norfolk and anchored opposite the village. About 5:00 P.M., hands aboard saw a "small stern-wheeler steamer belonging to the rebels" come into sight. The *Tyler* "beat to quarters" even as the *Grampus* fired a single round in her direction. As the saucy Rebel returned downstream, both her captain and Walke knew that the distance between them was too great for a successful chase. The *Tyler* did not get up steam and, in fact, remained in place off Norfolk for the next two days.

The appearance of the *Grampus* disturbed the soldiers who could not tell the difference between her and the *Yankee*, operating as the C.S.S. *Jackson*. Sgt. Charles Wright Wills of the 8th Illinois wrote in his diary that "The *Yankee* came up and shelled the woods where we were the day before. She tried to throw some shells into our camp, but they didn't reach us by a mile and a half. One of our gunboats has to lay here all the time or the *Yankee* would make us skedaddle out of this on double quick."

Capt. Marsh Miller would have known that his little daily scout was causing such a fuss among the bluecoats.

Early the next day at Paducah, Lt. Phelps was the first to send Capt. Foote a written report of the September 10 Lucas Bend engagement. The naval chief immediately shared it with Maj. Gen. Frémont, who passed it on to Secretary Cameron and others in the federal government. Foote himself passed the communiqué on to Secretary Welles.

As soon as Phelps returned aboard, the *Conestoga* cast off from her moorings and, with a reporter aboard from the *St. Louis Daily Republican*, steamed up to Smithland, at the mouth of the Cumberland River 12 miles distant. Here the four-gun warship stopped and sent a marine contingent ashore to impress a pilot to guide their navigation toward Tennessee. As the yawl approached shore, a "nervous half dozen" presumed Southern sympathizers headed off into the bushes. The pilot was not found, as he had gone up river aboard another boat several days earlier. Still, it was noted, the remainder of the town's inhabitants seemed to be Union.

A few minutes after the small boat returned, the *Conestoga* was underway again, "dashing rapidly by the beautiful banks of the little river." The Missouri-based newsman went on to describe the scene along the Cumberland: "Cultivated farms reached down to the water's edge, and orchards laden with fruit stretched along the banks. In other places, rocky bluffs, resembling, although much smaller, those of the Upper Mississippi, gave variety to the scenery."

About 15 miles upstream from the river's mouth, the "Lincoln gunboat" came to the town of Dykesburg, which seemed to be "the dividing point on the river between Secession and Union." Here a crowd gathered along the shore and gave three cheers as the steamer landed. The *Conestoga*'s crew replied, according to the newspaper witness, just as heartily. Ashore, a large U.S. flag was displayed from the roof of a store and Lt. Phelps and several of his officers were warmly greeted. Having come in search of Rebel-leaning vessels transporting contraband, the gunboatmen were advised that the tugboat *Gazelle*, often involved in illicit trade, had passed by the town two days earlier towing "a barge containing $10,000 worth of goods for Secessiondom."

After the gunboat departed Dykesburg and was turning into a bend five miles above, a lookout spotted a small steamer approaching. The crew was beat to quarters, the 32-pounders were manned, and everyone stood to his post. The discovered steamer at first tried to escape but, finding the attempt useless, ran ashore. By the time the *Conestoga*'s boarding party arrived, one man had escaped up the bank with a carpetbag in hand. The only ones left aboard were a young man who managed the engines and the pilot — the same pilot missed at Smithland earlier. Upon examining the craft's papers, it was learned that the boat was, in fact, the *Gazelle*. Most of her crew were off this Sunday and she was engaged in a making a local non-business call.

A bale of domestics found aboard and marked for Nashville, Tenn., was all that Lt. Phelps required to take possession. Several hands, under Third Master Benjamin Sebastian, were detailed aboard the *Gazelle* and once the Stars and Stripes were raised she got underway downstream toward Smithland. The *Conestoga* continued her voyage in the other direction.

Eddyville, with some 1,500 inhabitants in what was observed to be "a beautiful location," came into sight about 2:00 P.M. The town had the opposite reputation from Dykesburg, being strongly pro–Southern. Indeed, residents of the community had reportedly boasted that they had a cannon and threatened "to blow a gun-boat, and especially the *Conestoga*, 'out of the water.'" Whether this was true or not, quarters were again beat and every preparation made to punish any such attempt. As the gunboat glided past the town, great billows of black smoke escaping from her chimneys, a large crowd gathered along the shore. Looking through spyglasses, the men aboard could discern "a remarkably scowling lot of countenances." No overt actions were, however, taken against them.

Vernon K. Stevenson — the president of the Nashville and Chattanooga Railroad, a major in the Confederate army, and a prominent citizen of Tennessee's capital — was honored in 1856 when a new 164-ton, Kingston, Tennessee–built stern-wheeler was named in his honor. The *V.K. Stevenson*, owned by the Hughes concern of Nashville, now plied the Cumberland in support of Rebel iron supply requirements. September 15 was not be a good day for Stevenson's namesake. Knowing that the *V.K. Stevenson* had landed a short time before at Mammoth Furnace, three or four miles upstream, Wiley Sims, a sympathizing fellow steamboat captain, climbed on a mule and set off to warn the transport just after the *Conestoga* passed Eddyville. He would be too late.

About 4:00 P.M., the dark profile of the timberclad approached the Mammoth Furnace wharf, just below a significant stretch of shoals. As she headed in, about 50 individuals comprising the crew of the *V.K. Stevenson* made their escape in various stages of undress by climbing up the nearby bluff. One of the deckhands, ill at the time, later died, as the *Nashville Daily Gazette* put it, "from the exhaustion consequent upon escaping." Incidentally, the Mammoth ironworks were located a short distance behind the bluff and several hundred tons of iron was piled on the shore awaiting shipment.

A boarding party from the *Conestoga* quickly secured the steamer. Sailors inspecting her hold found a cargo comprising 100 tons of pig iron, valued at approximately $30,000, earmarked, according to her papers, for Tennessee. Other hands were surprised to find, in the words of the St. Louis journalist, that "the state rooms were full of bedding, and on a stove some victuals were cooking. A table was covered with bottles of liquors, while some of the beds had just been rid of their occupants."

A towline was passed to the *Stevenson* and, as witnessed by many along the riverbank, she was taken behind the little gunboat the 60 miles downstream to Smithland. After stopping briefly to allow Master Sebastian to bring the *Gazelle* into convoy, the *Conestoga* and her prizes passed from the Cumberland into the Ohio at about 10:00 P.M.

As late as that Monday, September 16, Capt. Foote had yet to receive Cmdr. Stembel's written report of the Lucas Bend engagement and wrote to him chiding him for tardiness. Stembel, of course, had taken his craft to Mound City for machinery repairs. Foote's forwarded message reached him there and, by the same letter, Stembel learned that he was authorized to proceed with cabin, deck and other repairs so long as the *Lexington* could be made available if suddenly required. The delinquent officer hurriedly finished his Lucas Bend report and had it to his superior the next day.

Later in the day, Foote wrote to Cmdr. Walke complaining that he had yet to receive a written report from him on his new Cairo stewardship. The squadron commander was most anxious to be present for any significant downstream expeditions. Walke was downstream in support of Col. Oglesby's continued reconnoitering in the Belmont area. Returning to Cairo late on Monday, the Illinois troop leader informed Brig. Gen. Grant that Belmont was not being reinforced, the garrison continued to number about 3,000 effectives, and there was no sign of any forthcoming offensives.

The damaged C.S.S. *Jackson*, mended enough for the voyage, returned to New Orleans, where she was further repaired and rejoined the makeshift fleet of 62-year-old Cdr. George N. Hollins. Her high-pressure engines making a frightful noise, she would bring up the rear of the line as Hollins' vessels engaged five Federal blockaders at the Head of Passes on the evening of October 12. Although the *Jackson* would survive this encounter unscathed, the former tug would be scuttled following Rear Adm. David G. Farragut's capture of the Crescent City in April 1862.

The *Tyler* remained off Norfolk until Tuesday morning, September 17. As her coal bunker was nearly exhausted, she returned to Cairo that morning to refuel. Shortly after arriving, Cmdr. Walke was told of wild rumors about town that Rebel forces were attacking Northern positions around Fort Jefferson on the Kentucky shore and were on the verge of overrunning them.

As soon as the timberclad was fueled, she cast off from the coal barge and got up steam downstream. Arriving at the reported combat scene anticipating a fight, the gunboatmen found "all quiet and the rumors entirely unfounded." Just to be certain that the peace was maintained, Brig. Gen. Grant ordered that at least one gunboat be stationed off the fort at night. The *Tyler* would hold that station until the *Lexington* could come down from Mound City in a day or two.

A mail boat arrived off Norfolk that evening and two messages were delivered to the *Tyler*'s skipper. One was a telegram in which Walke received his superior's permission to drydock the timberclad, so long as he had at least one wooden gunboat ready to meet the needs of Brig. Gen. Grant. The second was a written order that elaborated on the wire, emphasizing that the gunboat, when under repair, should have her cabins rearranged "as intended by Captain Rodgers before he left the steamer," as well as the placement of a 32-pounder in the stern.

Far upstream that Tuesday, the *Conestoga* had meanwhile arrived at Paducah. There she found that an alarm had been sounded rousing the U.S. Army units onshore against a possible Confederate attack. Lt. Phelps maneuvered his command to a point a little below the principal landing so that, in the event of an assault, his guns could command one of the main entrances to the town. Would any advancing Southerners realize before it was too late that naval cannon "could pour a most destructive fire upon the assailing force"?[10]

On September 19, Capt. Foote was forced to write a difficult memorandum to Maj. Gen. Frémont. Cmdr. Rodgers had informed him that the crews of *Tyler*, *Lexington*, and *Conestoga* had not yet received any pay. In some cases, their families were destitute. The sailor asked Frémont to have Quartermaster General Meigs order the local paymasters to make funds available.

The *Conestoga* became the subject of some army confusion on September 20, the same day Capt. Foote was en route down to Cairo to confer with Grant and to "spend a few days on board the three gunboats in commission." That morning, Brig. Gen. Grant, at Cairo, received a telegram from Maj. Gen. Frémont's headquarters demanding that the *Conestoga* be ordered to St. Louis. As Lt. Phelps was at Paducah and not Cairo, Grant had the request forwarded to Brig. Gen. Smith. Knowing that this would leave his mentor without a gunboat, Grant promised to loan him one of the two at Cairo next day. He would have sent one that day, but one was undergoing repairs and could not be gotten off the stocks and he needed the other.

Brig. Gen. Grant wired St. Louis that the *Conestoga* would depart Kentucky waters the next day, leaving Smith without protection. Later that day, Maj. Gen. Frémont sent two wires to Cairo informing Grant that the Phelps' command was not required after all. This entire exchange between Frémont and Grant, bypassing both Foote and Walke, was one of those conducted in "The Pathfinder's" favorite secret code — the Hungarian language.

That evening, Col. Oglesby at Norfolk received an excited visit from Capt. James Harper of the 7th Iowa. Rebel forces, the caller said, were taking up positions at Puntney Bend on the Kentucky shore. Could this be the start of a Confederate push toward Cairo? Oglesby quickly wrote out a message and sent it to Cmdr. Walke aboard the *Tyler*, anchored offshore from his camp. Acting upon the message, the *Tyler* dropped down to a point where she could view Lucas Bend. Meanwhile, the post commander readied a cavalry company to ride down at daybreak to relieve the gunboat. No enemy movements were spied.

The *Lexington* was nearly finished with her repairs at Mound City by the morning of September 21. About 10:30 A.M., as furnishings were still being shifted, Cmdr. Stembel received telegraphic orders to report to the tip of Illinois as fast as possible. His boat weighed anchor at noon. Just 40 minutes later the timberclad landed at the Graham wharf boat at Cairo. Rushing to flotilla headquarters, Stembel learned that a big downriver reconnaissance was afoot and that the *Lexington*'s cannon were needed.

Brig. Gen. Grant, Stembel learned, had ordered Col. Jacob G. Lauman of the 7th Iowa Infantry to mount a reconnaissance from Elliotts Mills toward the Mississippi at Bends' Landing, on the Kentucky shore above Island No. 2, about 12 miles below Cairo. Col. Oglesby was also instructed to cross over to Fort Jefferson and follow up Lauman's expedition. The *Lexington* and *Tyler* were to provide support and also convoy the troop-laden steamers. The object, according to the diary of Sgt. Charles Wright Wills of the 8th Illinois, was to find and destroy a Confederate battery that scouts warned was being erected on the riverbank.

Shoving off, the two timberclads steamed down to Island No. 1, where they made rendezvous with the troop-laden steamboats *W.H. Brown*, *John Gault*, and *Rob Roy*. These passed down to Norfolk, where they found another troopboat, the *D.A. January*. All in all, the steamboats carried 2,000–2,500 men. Below Island No. 1, the soldiers were landed and marched down the Kentucky beach road, finding that, as Grant later wired Frémont, there were no Confederate outposts closer to Cairo than Columbus. Sgt. Wills put it more forcefully: "We marched down, but of course found no battery."

While the bluecoats were plodding along the shoreline to within about four miles of Columbus, the gunboats took the opportunity to test their big ordnance, hoping to find one or more masked batteries. A total of ten 8-inch shells were fired at possible Rebel locations near the Chalk Bluff. There was, Cmdr. Walke later reported, no response and no hidden guns were discovered. It was observed that, from the gunboats, the enemy encampments near Columbus looked very large. Having gone as far as Lucas Bend, the *Lexington* and *Tyler* rounded to and proceeded back up the river a few miles to find the transports. The expedition completed, the timberclads returned to Cairo.

As darkness fell, a number of Col. Oglesby's cavalry were involved with Rebel riders in a fight that cost the North several horsemen and their steeds. Once they got back to camp, the colonel signaled the passing gunboats for lift, but they did not see him. That night, Oglesby's men were returned to Norfolk by the *D.A. January*.

Capt. Foote arrived at Cairo from St. Louis late that evening. On the morning of September 22, he went over logistical and other matters with Cmdr. Walke before that officer took the *Tyler* to Mound City for repairs. Walke later commented in his memoirs that the *Tyler*, which he always called the *Taylor*, one of "the three pioneers," was incomplete when Rodgers turned her over to him. "Extensive repairs and alterations were required" before she could become fully ready for "her new service."

Late in the afternoon, the flotilla commander had himself rowed out into the Ohio River in order to board the gunboat *Lexington*. After Foote and Cmdr. Stembel inspected ship, bosun's pipes called "all hands on deck." When everyone was assembled, Foote delivered a few brief complimentary remarks. At 4:45 P.M., the commander climbed back over the side and returned to shore — and to a new crisis.[11]

While Capt. Foote was inspecting the *Lexington*, a telegraph arrived at the headquarters of Brig. Gen. Grant from Maj. Gen. Frémont. President Lincoln, the theater commander said, had informed him that Confederate forces had just seized Owensboro, Kentucky, 190 miles up the Ohio River above Paducah and 40 miles above Evansville, Indiana. Knowing that Capt. Foote was in town, Grant was ordered to direct him to have his gunboats "drive the rebels from there and to protect the Ohio River." Frémont did not add Lincoln's rebuke that "perhaps you had better order those in charge of the Ohio River to guard it vigilantly at all points." At the same time he was telegraphing Grant, Maj. Gen. Frémont also sent a message to Capt. Foote advising him of events at Owensboro and indicating that he would receive instructions from Grant to send a "gunboat at once to dislodge them."

Almost instantaneously, Brig. Gen. Grant had written orders passed to Capt. Foote requiring that he take the *Lexington* from Norfolk and the *Conestoga* from Paducah, proceed to Owensboro, and dislodge the Confederates said to have taken possession. He did add "Frémont's instructions are that the Ohio River is to be kept open." Foote immediately notified Cmdr. Walke at Mound City that he should halt his repair work and take the *Tyler* back down to Norfolk. There he was to relieve the *Lexington*. Unfortunately, by the time Walke received Foote's directive, the *Tyler* was already on the ways and was unfit for launching. U.S. forces in the west were down to just two gunboats.

Early on September 23, even before Cmdr. Stembel was ready for departure, Capt. Foote commandeered the steamer *Bee* and proceeded to Paducah. Sometime later, the *Lexington* poured on the coal and also headed up the Ohio River toward Foote's Kentucky destination, arriving at that town in early afternoon. To Foote's great disappointment, the *Conestoga* was not anchored but was up the Cumberland on a reconnaissance mission. While Foote went ashore, the *Bee* was dispatched 15 miles up the Cumberland in a vain search for Lt. Phelps.

After conferring with Brig. Gen. Smith, Capt. Foote sent word to Brig. Gen. Grant that he would be departing upstream shortly, with or without Lt. Phelps. As the Ohio was low and pilots he interviewed were divided on the depth of water required for safe gunboat operations, Foote retained the *Bee* to accompany the *Lexington* and tow her if necessary. He left orders for Phelps, as soon as Phelps returned, to make all possible dispatch up the Ohio to Owensboro. Foote was extremely irritated with Phelps, eventually one of his favorites, and reminded him that his previous standing orders required his captains not only to consult with local army commanders, but also to tell them where they would be cruising and when they might return.

While Capt. Foote made his way up the Ohio, a spy from Columbus found his way to Brig. Gen. Grant's headquarters with a hopeful report. There were now about 2,500 men at Belmont and rumors circulating again for the last week that the landing was being reinforced were wrong.

The *Lexington* and *Bee* continued up the Ohio well after dark. Twice the big gunboat grounded and twice the steamer pulled her off. Finally, at 1:00 A.M. on September 24, Capt. Foote ordered the two boats to anchor until morning. The dash resumed at 8:00 A.M. The *Lexington*, under tow from the *Bee*, passed Shawneetown, Illinois, at 1:30 P.M. and soon thereafter encountered two troopboats, *Stephen Decatur* and *N.W. Thomas*, tied up along the shore. With a two-gun salute from a nearby artillery company, these cast off and followed the gunboat. Just before passing Uniontown around 3:30, Foote had the *Lexington*'s crew beat to quarters. The men stood by their guns until the notorious Southern haunt was passed.

The timberclad and the merchantmen dropped anchor at Evansville about 11:00 P.M. Running ashore, Capt. Foote wired Maj. Gen. Frémont informing him that he was en route to execute his orders. As there were no troops detailed at Evansville to support him, Foote noted that he would take one of the Cincinnati companies he had convoyed up from Shawneetown, its members having volunteered to go along. The river was falling and would soon be too shallow for gunboat operations, but hopefully the Owensboro situation could be dealt with before he was forced back downstream.

Further south at Cairo during the day, Cmdr. Walke had an interview with Brig. Gen.

Grant. The situation with regard to the pay of the gunboatmen was reaching crisis proportion. Walke had learned that his men could not receive their pay unless they claimed it at Cincinnati. Granting the crews leave to visit the Queen City for this purpose would both injure the service and be costly, either to the men or the government, in covering travel fees. Grant immediately wrote to Maj. Gen. Frémont asking his commander to find a way to get sailors paid at Cairo. The question of remuneration would continue to plague the army fleet and caused Capt. Foote to directly write Washington on the matter several times in October.

Cmdr. Henry Walke was commander of the *Tyler* before he was posted to the Pook turtle *Carondelet*. Walke, a Virginia by birth, was a noted artist and this sketch of his first western command appeared in the January 1885 issue of *Century Magazine*.

It is possible that Cmdr. Walke was also briefed on Col. Oglesby's latest reconnaissance toward Belmont. He was able to confirm the Columbus spy's report of inactivity. It is highly unlikely, however, that the naval leadership was fully acquainted with all of the details of the larger Missouri military picture. After Maj. Gen. Price captured Lexington on September 20, Maj. Gen. Frémont determined to salvage what many perceived to be a deteriorating situation by personally campaigning against his foe. To that end, he departed for western Missouri on September 24, leaving orders that Brig. Gens. Smith and Grant work together to contain any mischief from Columbus during his absence. They could attack if some sure opportunity came their way, but right now defense in their salient was required to take precedence over offense.

After a 250 mile run, the *Lexington* finally reached Owensboro on September 25. Two skeleton Kentucky regiments (U.S.A.) were found but, thankfully, no Confederates. Upon landing, Foote encountered no opposition; he enjoyed "free intercourse with the Union people of Owensboro, where the secession feeling is strong." No disrespect was manifested by Southern sympathizers. He met with the town fathers and directed that no Rebel flags were to be flown. Although everything along the river appeared quiet, Cmdr. Stembel was ordered to have as little communication with the shore as practicable.

Even though he found no Rebels to dislodge, Capt. Foote also found he had no Union troops to leave on occupation duty. The Kentuckians departed and the Cincinnati company that had accompanied him on the steamers begged off because it had never actually been mustered into the service in the first place.

Faced with a lack of garrison troops and falling water, Capt. Foote and the Cincinnatians returned to Evansville aboard the *Bee*. There the naval officer wired Maj. Gen. Frémont for a regiment of peacekeeping troops. Governor Oliver P. Morton of Indiana was also urgently petitioned to send 500 men for the same purpose, as was Brig. Gen. Robert Anderson at Louisville. The *Lexington* would patrol the area until the troops arrived or the river fell forcing her to leave. The latter would occur within two days.

Upon returning to Owenboro in the evening, Capt. Foote again conversed with community leaders and reviewed requirements with Cmdr. Stemble. The squadron commander, aboard the *Bee*, returned to Evansville, where he met the *Conestoga* pushing upstream. Lt. Phelps was told to remain a day or two off Owensboro and then return to Cairo. Foote sent reports to Frémont and Secretary Welles. Further south, after dark, alarm bells went off in Union circles as news came in that Confederate forces were crossing the Mississippi River below Norfolk. The alert which followed soon ended. As the *Chicago Times* Cairo reporter put it in a wire home next morning, the report "originated from their gunboat, *Jeff Davis*, landing a mile and a half below Norfolk to wood and reconnoitre."

On September 26, Capt. Foote caught a train from Evansville back to St. Louis, where he could continue his oversight work with the Eads projects. That morning, the *Lexington* conducted a nautical scout up the Ohio toward Hawesville and Cannelton, but encountered nothing suspicious. Later that evening, a skiff from Owensboro came alongside with a communication, possibility concerning reported disturbances at Hawesville, Kentucky.

Work on the *Tyler* continued apace at Mound City. Her bottom was in very bad condition and foul as well. Significant overhaul was required in order to make her safe. Walke, meanwhile, arranged to acquire three 32-pounders at Cairo. These would be mounted aboard as soon as he returned, one in the stern and the others in the forward ports.

While the timberclads were engaged in the Owensboro expedition, Cmdr. John Rodgers II received a reply from Gideon Welles on September 23 acknowledging his 10-day-old request for sea duty. The navy secretary pronounced himself pleased to learn that Maj. Gen. Frémont prized Rodgers' labors and had invited him to remain on his staff. He also informed Rodgers that, when the army originally asked for an officer to go west, the Department had named the Marylander. "Any change made," he wrote, "did not originate here." The cabinet officer promised to get back to him shortly with a new assignment.

Rodgers was not idle while in Frémont's employ. In addition to watching over the Eads projects while Capt. Foote was at Owensboro, the displaced flotilla leader found himself involved with another rebuilding project. In addition to the *Submarine No. 7*, the army theater commander had acquired a center-wheel steamer in late August. This was the Wiggins Ferry Company's 355-ton *New Era*, which was also assigned to the St. Louis engineer's yards for alteration. The Marylander was asked to oversee the effort to make her into a warship.

In the weeks between the time of his succession and his departure East, Rodgers and Eads turned the *New Era* into a fourth timberclad. With a large amount of cargo and vehicle space perfect for heavy ordnance, the craft was 159 feet long with a 47 foot beam. Wooden bulkheads, probably made of oak and, not unlike those on the Cincinnati gunboats, were built 6.5 feet high on the perimeter of the main deck cargo. Openings were provided for nine cannon. The side bulkwarks of the unroofed fore and aft decks rose and angled to join the central saloon deck cabin, while wood also covered the paddle-wheel opening. The original engine, boilers, and single stack were retained.

When she was finished, the *New Era* was ordered into the Missouri River. The water was low and the vessel grounded. Frémont was not pleased and wired Capt. Foote demanding that he come to headquarters to discuss what could be done to get the newest timberclad into action. Next day, the flotilla commander interviewed "The Pathfinder" and then sent a message to Rodgers via Lt. Shirk. It was admitted that given the gunboat's weight and the river depth, there was little chance, even if her guns were removed, to get her operational. Officers at Frémont's headquarters reviewed options for disposing of the boat in the event Rodgers could not get her farther downstream.

Eventually, the center-wheeler was gotten off and returned to St. Louis. There, on October 4, Cmdr. Rodgers was succeeded in command by Cmdr. William D. ("Dirty Bill") Porter. The brother of future Mississippi Squadron commander Rear Adm. David Dixon Porter and, like Walke, a "restored officer," Porter would eventually rebuild the *New Era* into an ironclad christened U.S.S. *Essex*.

His orders to Washington finally received permitted Cmdr. Rodgers to quit St. Louis immediately after Porter took charge of the *New Era*. He had the personal satisfaction of knowing that Frémont's opinion of him had changed by this time and that the vessels that would fight the early battles of the western campaign were all (less two) built or converted under his supervision. As his biographer put it, "Quite possibly, John Rodgers' most important contribution to the eventual Union victory in the Civil War was made during his four months on the Western waters."[12]

The *Conestoga* arrived at Owensboro on the morning of September 27, the same day Maj. Gen. Frémont reached Jefferson City. Shortly after dropping anchor, a messenger came alongside the gunboat from Cannelton in a small skiff and was brought to Lt. Phelps. There were disturbances at Hawesville, the visitor reported. Cmdr. Stemble was apprised of the news, and, in light of possible complaints received the previous evening, ordered Phelps to move upstream and check them out.

When the *Conestoga*'s captain, acting more as a diplomat than a warrior, finished his investigation of rival claims by the citizens of both Cannelton and Hawesville, he found the reasons for the disturbances to be groundless. With the water falling, Phelps was unable to remain and so extracted promises of peaceful coexistence from community leaders in the two towns. The *Conestoga* returned to Owensboro at midnight, allowing the *Lexington* to depart for Cairo. With support from his pilots, Lt. Phelps determined to stay the night and depart on Saturday morning.

With the *Lexington* and *Conestoga* up the Ohio and the *Tyler* in dry dock, the Confederates at Columbus elected to make a reconnaissance upstream with their little gunboat, the *Jeff Davis*. That evening, according to the *St. Louis Daily Missouri Republican* journalist on the scene, the "saucy" ex-towboat steamed to within a mile and a half of the Union camp at Norfolk, Missouri, and put ashore a landing party. While some of the Rebel gunboat's men scouted the vicinity, others spent two or three hours taking on wood. When news of this incursion, the second in two nights, reached the Northern camp, cavalry were dispatched to investigate, but by the time they arrived about 10:00 P.M., "the obnoxious craft" had "turned her head downstream without making any demonstration."

The *Jeff Davis*' sorties occasioned "a slight scare at Norfolk." Although many Union soldiers were billeted at that location, it was unfortified. "A gunboat might have done considerable damage," observed the St. Louis reporter, "by throwing shell into the encampment."

The *Tyler* was launched into the Ohio River from the ways at Mound City on Saturday. Afloat, William L. Hamilton of the Hambleton, Collier Company, with urging from Cmdr. Walke, pushed completion of the alterations and additions originally ordered for all three boats by Cmdr. Rodgers. Among the most serious upgrades required was sufficient calking, which was not finished back in June and July. Consequently, the main deck as well as the cabin had to be reprotected. In reporting this development, Walke informed Capt. Foote that the costs, except for the dockage, would be about the same as the repairs made to the *Lexington* earlier in the month. Hamilton, who was also superintendent of the Eads ironclad construction project at Mound City, did not believe the repairs would take too long.

News of the *Jeff Davis*' sortie and other rumors to his east worried Maj. Gen. Frémont way out in western Missouri. During the afternoon, he wired Brig. Gen. Grant a warning that Confederate forces were evacuating Columbus and headed across the Mississippi to go to the assistance of Maj. Gen. Price's Confederate forces. The Cairo-based brigadier telegraphed back that only the guerrilla's of Jeff Thompson were at Belmont and that everything else in his sector was quiet.

During the night, the Ohio River continued to fall. By Sunday morning, September 29, there was almost three inches too little water for the *Conestoga* to make it over the first bar. Phelps and his crew would spend most of the next four days lightening ship (of everything but her guns) in order to get the timberclad over the bars and on to her next station. The *Lexington* halted at Evansville, Indiana, on the morning of September 29. There Lt. Stemble was asked by the U.S. port surveyor, A.A. Robinson, to keep an eye out for the steamer *Champion No. 2*, owned by D.O. Conn, proprietor of the Curlew Mines in Kentucky. Conn's steamer was engaged in contraband trade and, even worse, in transporting Rebel troops up the Cumberland River to the Tennessee state line.

Later in the afternoon, by coincidence, the timberclad met the suspect steamer at a point some 15 miles below Paducah returning from Cairo where she had delivered coal to U.S. forces. Bringing the merchantman to without firing a shot, Cmdr. Stembel sent a boarding party aboard and took possession without opposition. Mr. Conn was informed that he and his men were prisoners and his boat would be taken back to Illinois and turned over to the Cairo port surveyor, Charles D. Arter. That evening, the *Lexington* and *Champion No. 2* passed Mound City. Cmdr. Walke was signaled that the *Conestoga* remained at Owensboro.

As September ended, the war on the Mississippi Riverfront was quiet. Upon her arrival, the *Lexington* duly turned over the *Champion No. 2* and became the Cairo port guard. She spent the last day of the month loading fifty 32-pounder shells. The *Conestoga* had not arrived and this worried Capt. Foote. In a telegram to Brig. Gen. Grant from St. Louis, he asked whether he should send the *Bee* up to retrieve her, "as she may be aground."

Grant, meanwhile, had traveled up the Ohio to confer with Brig. Gen. Smith. Yet another rumor of Confederate activity out of Columbus had come in, this one from a wounded POW that troops from the citadel were headed toward Paducah. Once again, the report was a false alarm, allowing the district commander to quickly return to Cairo. Incorrectly informed, the *Nashville Banner* reported that a command shakeup had occurred at the mouth of the Tennessee and that Smith was replacing Grant, "the cornstalk chap."

On October 1, the *Conestoga* was still delayed. Foote, noting that he was very busy with the ironclads, offered to go to Cairo and direct any operations required from that point. No movements were seen, but if anything occurred Grant would telegraph an alert. Later in the day, Lt. Phelps dropped anchor off the tip of Illinois and Grant informed Foote, noting that the timberclad should return upstream where her services were much needed. At the same time, Surveyor Arter was informed that Grant's command was taking over the *Champion No. 2* for government use.

Next day, Capt. William S. Hillyer, Brig. Gen. Grant's aide-de-camp, ordered Lt. Phelps to proceed to Paducah. With the *Tyler* still under repairs and the *Conestoga* rerouted, Maj. Gen. Frémont wired Brig. Gen. McClernand that he would send Cmdr. Rodgers and the *New Era* to Cairo until Walke could get back. Stories of possible Confederate movements continued to come in; another was soon disproved concerning Rebel movements from Belmont on Cape Girardeau. Still, by October 4 so far as anyone at Cairo or Paducah could say, Polk and Pillow had no "concerted plan to attack" Paducah, Cairo, or Cape Girardeau.[13]

Once more mending her machinery, the *Lexington* was not available for much of October's premier week. Brig. Gen. Grant, who had received no real information from his spies or scouts, grew concerned over his inability to send a naval force on reconnaissance downstream. During the time he was without gunboat support, yet another alert came in from Frémont's St. Louis headquarters. Gen. Albert Sidney Johnston, according to this latest warning, had assembled a large force at Belmont and, once again, Cape Girardeau was the target. About all he could do was order an infantry unit to march down toward Belmont and send additional scouts.

Meanwhile, further west, Maj. Gen. Frémont, despite significant supply difficulties, was pushing his 30,000-man army on to Tipton. Reinvigorated in the field, "The Pathfinder," was able to show his critics by October's first week that he could still organize, plan, and function far better than they might believe. According to Allen Nevins' history of the war's first year, the march in southwestern Missouri "was the first formidable aggressive movement yet made by a Northern army."

In addition to his Columbus concern, Frémont's lieutenant, Brig. Gen. Grant, had also to worry about the brigade of Brig. Gen. M. Jeff Thompson. Resupplied at New Madrid on October 1, the "Swamp Rats" had started off to attack Cape Girardeau. Unlike Polk or Pillow, Grant had certain information on this raid from informants and civilians and Federal troops were on the trail of the Confederates. After reaching Sikeston on October 4, Thompson, feeling he had insufficient manpower for a strike, retreated west back into the swamps. Cape Girardeau was safe for the moment.

With the *Lexington* available for duty after lunch on October 6, Cmdr. Stembel had only to wait a short time before receiving orders to cruise down as far as Norfolk that evening. At the same time, Grant asked Cmdr. Walke to report with the *Tyler* next morning. Early on October 7, Walke received written orders from Grant to make a cruise down the Mississippi. He and Stembel were to look into rumors of a masked battery that was reported some three miles above Columbus on the Kentucky shore. While the gunboats, once more with members of Grant's staff embarked, chugged out of sight down the river, Capt. Foote got off his train at the Cairo railroad station. He had come down from St. Louis "for the purpose of taking another short cruise," but he arrived too late.

As the two timberclads approached the head of the Iron Bluffs, spyglasses revealed the Rebel steamer *Jeff Davis*. The Southern gunboat kept her distance and Walke could not get his craft close enough to engage. The *Lexington* and *Tyler* continued on until three Confederate artillery emplacements were spied "atop the bluff above the town, in front of the principal camp of the Confederates." At this point, the gunboats opened fire from the river two miles above. Checking his watch, Cmdr. Walke saw it was noon.

The *Lexington* and *Tyler* fired thirty 8-inch shells each and succeeded in drawing counterfire from five Rebel batteries, some of which were seen to be mounting rifled guns. Cmdr. Walke, citing comments by one Charles Cox, a Confederate deserter from Columbus quoted by the *Chicago Journal*, was pleased to learn that an 8-inch shell "passed over the fortifications and fell in an open space of ground behind them." Four of the 100 Southern projectiles the naval officers asserted were fired back at them passed over the two boats. Several came uncomfortably close and one came within 50 feet of the bow of the *Tyler*.

In one example of the kind of exaggeration that persisted throughout the timberclad war, the *Atlantic Democrat* in New Jersey published a report five days later bragging that the brief engagement "lasted an hour." It did, correctly, note that "No damage was done to our boats." Another exaggeration was discounted almost immediately by the reporter from the *St. Louis Daily Republican*. "It is said," he informed his readers next day, "that two balls passed through the smoke stacks of the *Lexington* (a space so narrow that the story is scarcely credible) and that one hot shot crossed her bow."

Not strong enough to stand toe-to-toe with rifled guns, Walke ordered the wooden pair to round to and return to Cairo. The *Tyler* and *Lexington* had accomplished the point of their mission just by drawing fire. Steaming north through the foot of Lucas Bend, the gunboats drew near to Belmont and dropped several shells into the Confederate camp. Rebel cannon returned fire, but no damage was reported by either side. Just above Norfolk, two flatboats were seized and these were towed back to Cairo. Anchoring off the town, Walke and Stembel reported to Grant and Foote on the success of their mission.

Maj. Gen. Leonidas Polk witnessed the attack on the Columbus batteries, several of which he was just mounting on the cliffs. Fire was returned with vigor. Several days later, he wrote a brief review of the combat to Confederate Navy Secretary Stephen R. Mallory, boasting that both gunboats were crippled. "One of them," he reported learning, "sank about 10 miles above this, and the other was so much injured as to be obliged to be relieved of her armament."

War of 1812 veteran Capt. George N. Hollins (1799–1878) commanded the Confederate naval forces on the Mississippi from July 1861 into mid–1862. He led gunboats up the great river to help defend Columbus in the fall of 1861 and several of them fought engagements with the Federal timberclads (Naval Historical Center).

Far away in South Carolina, on October 14, the *Charleston Mercury* published a report from its Nashville correspondent. By this time, the attack of Sunday morning was carried out by "five Lincoln gunboats." Gen. Johnston, who was not present, had, the newspaper suggested, set out to "entice them on" by firing "his small guns whose balls fell short. When they advanced, he opened with his 68's, knocked off one of their wheel houses and chimneys, and swept the deck of one of the boats of her men." This plan was so successful that "the fleet immediately turned tail and steamed up the river."

That night, the *Philadelphia Inquirer* journalist wired his newspaper the latest intelligence, gleaned from one of Brig. Gen. Pillow's deserters who had once lived in northern Illinois. According to news obtained from this POW, Gen. Johnston had 40,000 men at Columbus, had fortified the Mississippi for four miles above the town, and was "expecting an attack from the Federal troops." In short, the Rebels were in defensive mode and were not planning to attack. Next day, the correspondent for the *St. Louis Daily Republican* told his readers that "The details of the engagement yesterday afternoon ... do not present any very exciting feature beyond the expenditure of a large amount of powder and ball by both sides."

Also on October 8, Cairo's top military and naval leadership, along with several newsmen, welcomed the arrival of the *New Era*, accompanied by "a diminutive tug." She was delayed during the night when rammed below St. Louis by the steamer *Hannibal City*. She made slow progress thereafter, even with help from the tug, until safely anchored in the Ohio opposite the town. As one journalist put it, "her strange appearance excited considerable comment. Although the *New Era* had orders for Paducah, Cmdr. Porter's timberclad temporarily brought the Cairo flotilla back to full strength.

That Tuesday also saw the transfer of a giant local wharf boat, the *Graham*, owned by Graham, Halliday & Co., to the levee landing for government storage. Brig. Gen. Grant had entered into a $1,000 per month contract for its use with William Parker Halliday and N.W. Graham. The latter, in fact, was related to a new friend of the brigadier, George Washington "Wash" Graham. Capt. Foote, who applied to the army to share space aboard, would shortly find himself in something of a tussle with Grant over space for naval supplies that would take some weeks to sort out.

On October 9, Capt. Foote got his delayed cruise when he went up to Mound City aboard the *Lexington* to inspect three of the new ironclads under construction at that location. He thereafter returned to St. Louis to oversee the Eads project, and his growing flotilla, from that central location. Cruising off Evansville, Lt. Phelps wrote that the Tennessee and Cumberland rivers were still low, but that the possibilities for enlistment along the Indiana shore of the Ohio were very promising.

Meanwhile, the *St. Louis Daily Democrat* reported that the gunboat *New Era* had just departed for the Missouri River. Drawing three and a half feet of water, this "terrible engine of destruction" was armed with 84-pounder Dahlgrens "under bomb-proof decks" and had a crew of 300, every one of whom was armed with rifles and ready for "deadly conflict." Whether this was a colossal error from a newspaper with a splendid reputation for its gunboat coverage, the case of a journalist writing without witnessing, or a piece of literary deception is unknown. What is known is that the *New Era* was then at Cairo, down the Mississippi south of St. Louis, and not west of the city on the Missouri.

The story is not unlike that told by the correspondent of the *St. Louis Daily Republican* the day before concerning the Rebel gunboat C.S.S. *Jackson*, also known as the *Yankee*. According to the gunboatmen, their Confederate opponent had "certainly departed this life." On the other hand, persons resident in the Cairo-Norfolk area told the scribe that she frequently came up within a short distance of the latter point. It was probable, he concluded, "that she has now gone to Memphis for repairs." In fact, the "*Jackson*" seen near Norfolk was Capt. Marsh Miller's audacious *Grampus*.[14]

Brig. Gen. Joseph D. Webster (1811–1876), both chief of artillery and chief of staff to Brig. Gen. (later Maj. Gen.) Ulysses S. Grant, was intimately acquainted with the timberclads. From the fall of 1861 through the Battle of Shiloh, he was often seen aboard the vessels or coordinating his or Grant's activities with their activities. Webster hastily assembled "Grant's Last Line" at Shiloh on April 6, 1862, and, together with the *Lexington* and *Tyler*, repulsed Confederate charges at the end of the day. Later, he became Chief of Staff to Maj. Gen. William T. Sherman (Library of Congress).

CHAPTER 5

Columbus-Belmont, October 10– November 9, 1861

By the end of the first week of October 1861, the three United States Steam Gunboats *Tyler*, *Lexington*, and *Conestoga* were refreshed after their difficult birth and initial labors. Under the overall direction of Capt. Andrew Hull Foote, they were fully engaged in army support operations, as well as contraband interdiction and other missions undertaken to foster the Union effort in the Upper Mississippi Valley. At the same time, the war had greatly expanded during the past month with Confederate occupation of Columbus, Kentucky, and the Northern seizure of Paducah and Smithland, keys to the great Tennessee and Cumberland rivers.

The western gunboat command, though officered by U.S. Navy personnel, was at this time a creature of the War Department. As such, it was sort of a "floating division" that acted under the orders of appropriate department commanders as well as the brigadiers heading local military districts. At this time, the top billet in the Department of the West, the geographical home to most of the region's fighting at this time, was held by Maj. Gen. John C. Frémont. Among his district lieutenants were Brig. Gen. Ulysses S. Grant at Cairo, Ilinois, and Charles F. Smith at Paducah, Kentucky.

As the war in the West intensified during the fall of 1861, the gunboat flotilla grew as well. By early October, Capt. Foote had four wooden gunboats in commission (the original timberclads, plus the *New Era*). Seven ironclad gunboats were under construction by James B. Eads at Carondelet, Missouri, and Mound City, Illinois, along with 38 mortar boats. Eads' giant snag boat, the *Submarine No. 7*, was also under conversion.

Foote now enjoyed assistance from a total of 12 line officers, nine more than Cmdr. John Rodgers II could rely on in June. His command included floating wharf and receiving vessels at Cairo, with offices for administration and some recruiting at St. Louis, Cincinnati, Chicago, and Cleveland. Dedicated officers such as Cmdr. Roger Perry, Lt. Shirk, and Lt. Joseph Sanford were placed in charge of various shore responsibilities. In the history of the squadron, none was more important or would serve longer than Alexander M. Pennock.

Cmdr. Pennock was, like Cmdr. Walke, a native of Virginia. Both men, like Tennessee's David Farragut, had remained loyal to the Union. After years at sea (1828–1859), Pennock, like Walke, served as a lighthouse inspector in New York State. Plucked back into the mainstream by the Navy Department in September 1861, he was sent west with Flag Officer Foote to help oversee the construction of the Pook Turtles to handle flotilla equipment and became fleet captain that October 20. In January 1862, he took over command of the Cairo naval station. Pennock would hold his post through 1864, gaining during his tenure "a reputation as one of the best wartime executives of the navy." While serving at Cairo, Pennock, who had brought out his wife to be with him, lived in quarters on the receiving ship, where he frequently enjoyed the company of junior officers and visitors at dinner. His friend and colleague Quartermaster George D. Wise would confide to Flag Officer Foote at the end of July 1862 that Pennock "is a good officer for equipment and repairs, and his health is suffering from continued residence in this part of the country."[1]

The *Conestoga* was ordered to Paducah at the beginning of October to provide timberclad presence on the Ohio River and its tributaries. Coming ashore at the Kentucky town, her skipper, Lt. S. Ledyard Phelps, was taken to meet the post commander, Brig. Gen. Smith. His initial impression was probably now very different from that of Col. Lew Wallace of the 11th Indiana Volunteer Infantry, who met the distinguished brigadier about the same time.

"By reputation," Wallace later wrote, Smith "was the best all-around officer in the regular army—a disciplinarian, stern, unsympathetic, and ogre to volunteers, but withal a magnificent soldier of the old school of Winfield Scott." The general was quartered in a Southern-style mansion located in a spacious lot "centered in fruit trees and flowering shrubs." This leader used his borrowed home as both a domicile and an office. He worked out of a well-furnished room, its most prominent piece being a broad table in the middle "littered somewhat with books [and] writing material." It was the kind of table over which large maps could be easily spread. The man to whom Phelps and Wallace reported "was very tall, erect, broad-shouldered, a symmetrical figure in a well-fitted uniform." Wallace, somewhat in awe of the man, remembered that "he held his head high; long white mustaches trailed below his chin shading his lower face."

With the Tennessee River too low for ascent, Smith granted Phelps permission to keep his boat on patrol between Henderson and Hawesville. While so engaged, he was able to take the time to recruit a few new hands along the Indiana shore, especially at Evansville. On October 11, the *Conestoga* returned to Paducah, where she received orders to ascend the Tennessee River and examine a new Confederate position just over the Tennessee state line called Fort Henry.

At the commencement of the Civil War, the economic value of Tennessee and the northern parts of Alabama and Georgia were underappreciated in many Southern circles. Although the value of sectional trade may have been understood, the politics of warfare in that time required that major attention be focused on the two perceived seats of power, Washington, D.C., and Richmond, Virginia. "On to Richmond" was both an all-absorbing battle cry and an approach to securing victory. Confederate military leaders, from Robert E. Lee to Leonidas Polk, Gideon Pillow, and Albert Sidney Johnston, all failed "to grasp fully the importance of the munitions-producing area of Georgia, Tennessee, and Alabama" and failed, consequently, to plan for its defense.

This rebellion's heartland area had much to recommend its protection. The value of the resources available in Tennessee alone are illustrative. Utilizing saltpeter acquired from the caves of East Tennessee, the South's largest gunpowder mills manufactured their deadly powder along the Cumberland River northeast of the state capital. Nashville, the most cosmo-

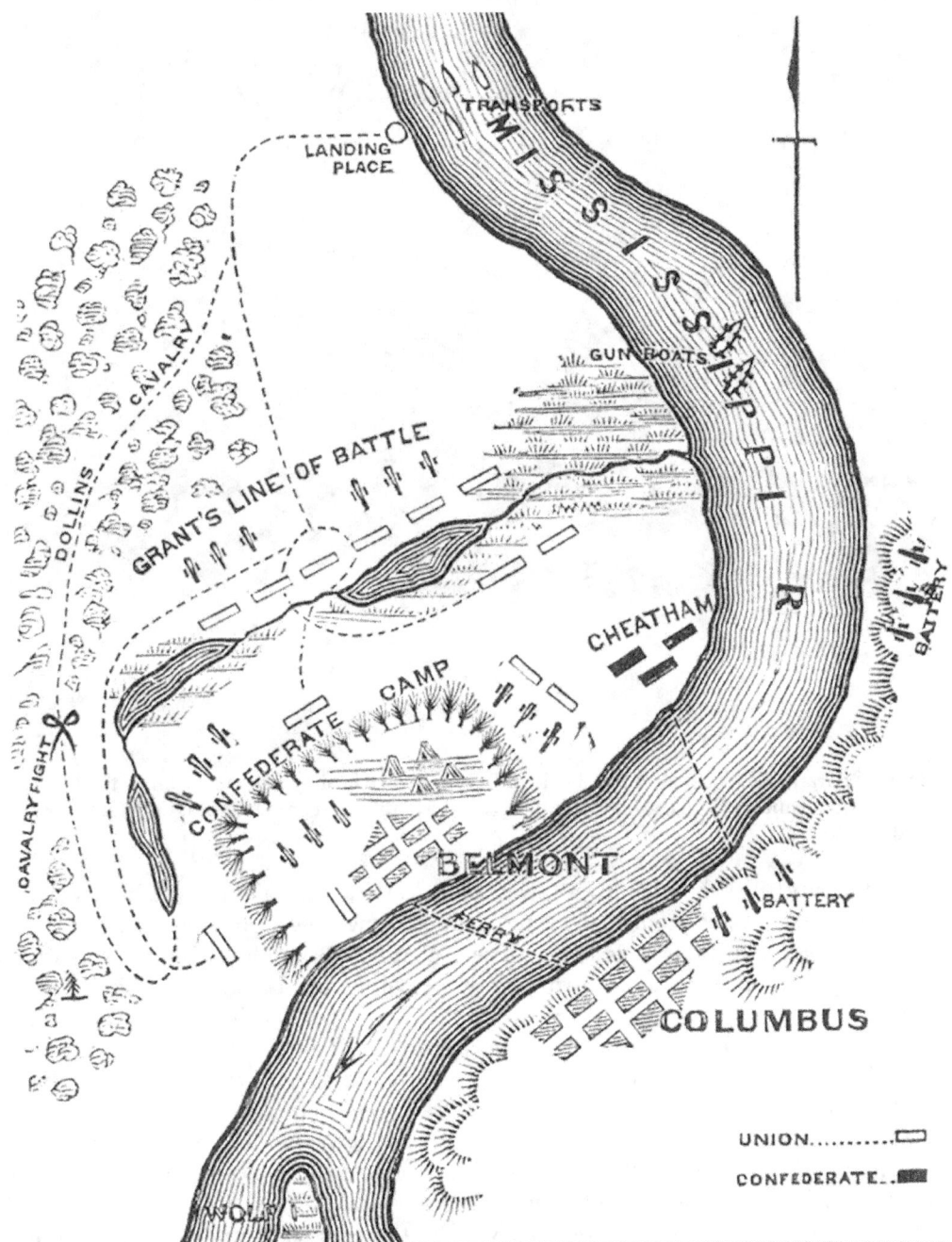

BATTLE OF BELMONT.

The Battle of Belmont was a key early amphibious conflict between Confederate and Union forces on the Mississippi. Federal forces under Brig. Gen. Ulysses S. Grant were transported to their landing beaches on river steamers escorted by the timberclads *Lexington* and *Tyler*. The two gunboats also protected their withdrawal after a day of confused and heavy fighting (Lossing's *Pictorial Field Book of the Civil War*, vol. 1).

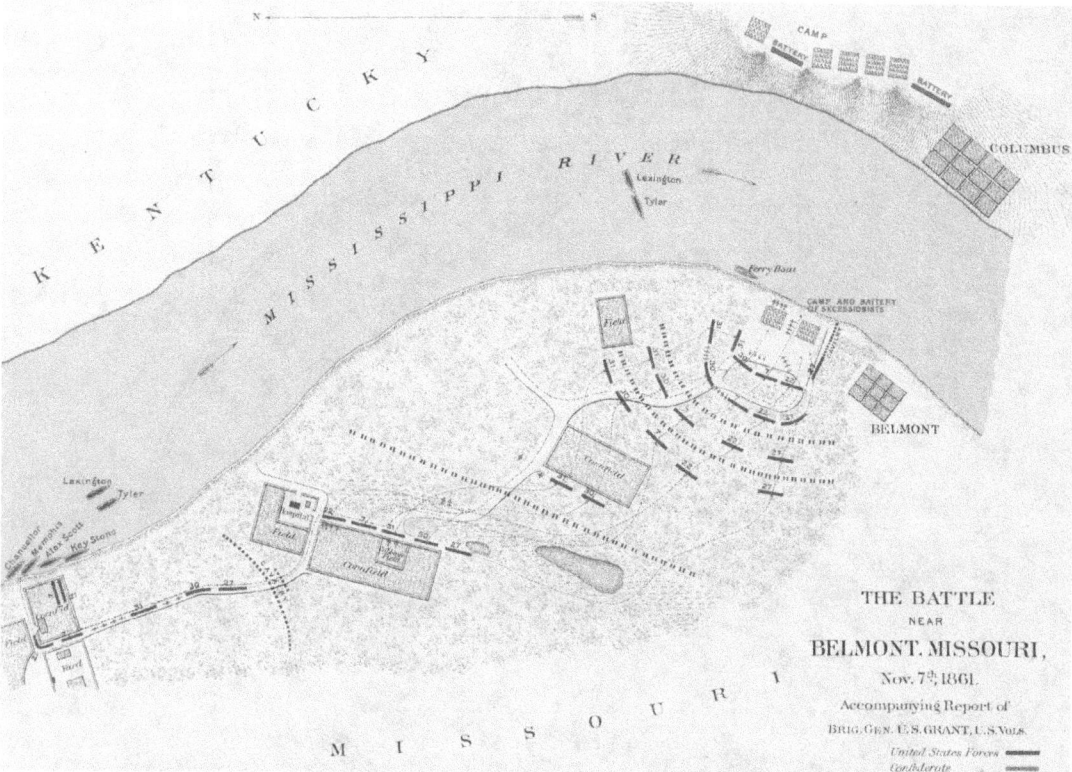

Brig. Gen. Grant's later chart of the Battle of Belmont clearly shows the location of the timberclads *Lexington* and *Tyler* in the Mississippi River adjacent to the combat arena (Official Records–Atlas).

politan U.S. city below the Ohio River (save New Orleans) and a major railroad hub, was also Richmond's greatest war production center. Located along a big loop on the southern bank of the Cumberland River, it is, as succinctly put by Anne J. Bailey, historian of a later campaign, geographically "near the center of a bowl-like valley formed by a string of ridges." City and surrounding Davidson County concerns turned out cannon, small arms, cartridges, saddles, blankets, and all manner of other accouterments. Significantly, 90 percent of all the copper available in the South came from the region surrounding Duckville, Tennessee, and it was the major supplier of available copper percussion caps. In addition to war materiel, the state's foodstuffs were critical to the associated states' success. In this, one Civil War historian has opined that "in the total production of corn, hogs, cattle, mules and horses, the lower Middle Tennessee zone was one of the richest in the *entire Confederacy*."

Failure to protect these assets would have a drastic and tragic impact upon the fortunes of the South if invasion did not come along the Mississippi corridor. Still, as has been suggested by regional historian Byrd Douglas, this development may not have been caused by an overall Southern appreciation for Tennessee's importance. While the Confederacy "was criticized and may have seem indifferent to forwarding the men and tools of war" as might have been expected, "it should be remembered," Douglas wrote in 1961, "that the Confederacy was an infant republic" as yet unable to defend its totality. Each Southern state was initially responsible for its own protection, as all of the seceding states were clinging "to the traditional doctrine of 'States Rights'"—which had many faults requiring time and patient to overcome.

The Scott-Eads plan for the Union's reduction of Confederate positions in the west and an associated great move south along the Mississippi River was not a secret. Indeed, when Tennessee became the last seceded Southern state on June 8, 1861, the outline of the Yankee scheme was widely accepted as strategy on both sides of the Mason-Dixon Line and a guide to the way the western conflict would be fought.

At Nashville, which is located 280 miles northeast of Memphis and 206 miles southwest of Lexington in Kentucky, Governor Isham G. Harris, following the Scott logic, fully expected that his northern border was safe due to Kentucky's neutrality. Not having any particular reason to believe that northern generals would operate outside of the Anaconda Plan, Harris, together with his military advisors Maj. Gen. Polk and Brig. Gen. Pillow, believed that most of the fighting involving Volunteer patriots, more of whom would bear Confederate arms than from any other state save Virginia, would occur along the state's Mississippi River border. Indeed, Brig. Gen. Pillow went so far as to write one concerned citizen that "nothing of military importance [is] to be gained by [the Yankees] ascending [the] Tennessee River." Thus, most available troops of Tennessee's provisional army, including engineers and artillery, were ordered west to help protect a chain of defenses running south from Island No. 10 to Memphis.

Memphis was located 790 miles by the river from New Orleans and 240 from Cairo and, as earlier noted, stood on an elevated bluff on the left bank of the Mississippi River. It had to be kept out the hands of Union troops; not only was it the terminus of the Memphis and Charleston Railroad but it was also " a place of much business activity, being the distributing point for the produce of West Tennessee." Thus it was that only 4,000 soldiers guarded the Cumberland Pass and the vital economic areas of Middle Tennessee at the time James B. Eads was building ironclads near St. Louis and Lt. Phelps' *Conestoga* was preparing to launch the first of several reconnaissance visits.[2]

When Brig. Gen. Pillow's forces, acting on orders from Maj. Gen. Polk, took over Columbus on September 4, 1861, they violated Kentucky's "neutrality" and threw the entire northern border of Tennessee open to invasion. Brig. Gen. Grant, as reviewed in the last chapter, quickly seized the Ohio River community of Paducah, Kentucky, which sat at the mouth of the Tennessee River, and Smithland, lying at the mouth of the Cumberland River. As rivers in the region flow north, the two were, at those points, upstream from Tennessee.

After Gen. Johnston took charge of the Confederate Western Department early in the month, he chose to concentrate his defense on what Brig. Gen. Grant later described as "a line running from the Mississippi River at Columbus to Bowling Green and Mill Springs, Kentucky." It was Governor Harris who sent engineers down the Cumberland and Tennessee rivers to look for places to erect forts.

Work, which progressed only slowly, was begun on two main defensive positions: one named Fort Donelson (after West Point graduate Daniel S. Donelson, Tennessee's attorney general) on the Cumberland River and the other, 12 miles northwest on the Tennessee River, called Fort Henry (in honor of Gustavus A. Henry, the state's senior Confederate senator). Fort Donelson would be mostly abandoned until October. When the *Conestoga* began poking around in the Tennessee River in the fall, Southern leaders were horrified to see that only the unfinished earthworks of Henry offered any protection against the "Linkum gunboats."

The Confederate government took over responsibility for the twin river fortifications and efforts to finish — or at least improve — them were stepped up. The difficulties encountered in rapidly finishing the projects were numerous and almost all involved too few military goods or soldiers and too little time. Cannon shortages, labor shortages, ammunition shortages, and shortages of properly trained troops and gunners were key factors, as was any kind of unified command structure for the two bastions.[3]

Out on the Mississippi River between October 10 and October 12, the *Lexington* and *Tyler* served as escort for the steamer *Aleck Scott*. With an entire regiment aboard and towing a flatboat, the *Scott* (once home to Samuel "Mark Twain" Clemens) was tasked down to a point on the Missouri near Columbus, where a large quantity of corded wood had been discovered. The cordage, intended for Southern purposes, was stacked on property belonging to a man named Hunter.

As the Yankee soldiers stacked the timber, the two gunboats made certain that the *Jeff Davis* did not try to interfere. The Confederate stern-wheeler maneuvered within sight — and out of range — at the foot of Lucas Bend during the entire retrieval operation. Neither side moved to engage and no shots were exchanged. Upon the return of the expedition to Cairo, Cmdr. Walke reported the results to Brig. Gen. Grant and then took the *Tyler* on to Mound City.

Late on October 12, the *Conestoga* chug-a-chugged up the Tennessee River to within a few miles of Fort Henry before dropping anchor for the night. The next morning, the gunboat slowly steamed up to examine the new bastion. Suddenly, rockets shot skyward from shore announcing her approach to those who couldn't already hear her. After she had proceeded a mile, a number of men on the wooded bank opened fire upon her with muskets and rifles. "A shot put an end to further demonstrations of the kind," Lt. Phelps later wrote.

The *Conestoga* came to between two and two and a half miles below Fort Henry, from which vantage point her commander was able to make a deliberate examination by spyglass, over several hours, of the "extensive work." Carefully jotting down notes, Phelps recorded these points: 1) the fortifications were armed with heavy guns, mounted *en barbette*; 2) there was a considerable garrison; 3) it was situated about 1½ miles above the head of Panther Creek Island where the state line left the Tennessee's right bank and crossed the river; 4) there was no channel on the western side of Panther Island; 5) the crooked narrow channel on the island's eastern side continued in that condition until it was within a mile of the fort, where it widened to about 600 feet and gained depth.

On the trip back to Paducah later on the 13th, Phelps recorded the extensive ironworks along the riverbanks. He also heard rumors that the Rebels were converting three steamers into ironclad gunboats at a point five miles above Fort Henry. The rumors were not altogether untrue. There was considerable sentiment in some Confederate quarters for the construction of ironclads to defend the Tennessee River. Indeed, three days hence, Maj. Gen. Polk would inform Rebel Navy Secretary Stephen R. Mallory that such gunboats "were indispensable" to Southern protection. The Columbus commander knew of just such a steamer and it could be purchased for $12,000.

Phelps laid his findings before Brig. Gen. Smith, adding his belief that the garrison held 1,700–1,800 Rebel soldiers. Over the next several days, the post commander learned from other sources that Fort Henry had a garrison of 2,000 and mounted some 20 heavy cannon. He also heard about the ironclad construction program, as well as Confederate plans to attack Paducah in force from several sides, or, as he put it, "the old scheme."

While Walke was conducting services aboard the *Tyler* that Sunday morning, Cmdr. "Dirty Bill" Porter started the *New Era* downstream for a reconnaissance of the Confederate force and batteries on the Iron Banks. While off the Columbus citadel, he took notes and made drawings, also ascertaining that some Southern troops were being thrown across from Kentucky to Missouri. After Porter returned to his Cairo anchorage, he went ashore to confer with Brig. Gen. Grant. He placed his drawings and facts before the brigadier and urged that a joint army and naval force soon attack the enemy troops. He emphasized the importance of having the *New Era* detailed to any such attack, "as she was armed with 9-inch guns." Her presence would "insure a victory — her absence a defeat." Grant would not commit.

About 3:00 P.M. on October 14, lookouts along the shore below Cairo saw the smoke of an ascending steamer over the tops of the trees on the point below the mouth of the Ohio River. Shortly thereafter a large white flag fluttered into view and many spyglasses made out the approaching Confederate gunboat and dispatch vessel *Grampus.* Capt. Marsh Miller brought her slowly up, feeling his way past the guns of Fort Holt and making for the Ohio River. As he steamed slowly beyond Bird's Point, a signal was made requesting parlay. As soon as the little gunboat was spied, Brig. Gen. Grant, Capt. Wash Graham, and several aides and officers boarded the *Aleck Scott* for a rendezvous. The two boats met in the middle of the Ohio River opposite Cairo and were lashed together.

Given permission to come aboard, two Rebel officers gave Grant a communication from Maj. Gen. Polk concerning an exchange of prisoners. Capt. Miller also came across and spent some minutes in conversation with his old friend Wash Graham. The interview between the plainly garbed Grant and the "finely-dressed" gray-clad officers lasted approximately an hour, during which time the *Scott* towed the *Grampus* to the vicinity of Norfolk. Miller and the Scott's captain agreed that, at a signal from the conferees, the boats would part and return to their respective bases.

During this time, the Cairo commandant wrote out a reply for the Columbus commander declining an exchange and asked that, next time they wished to negotiate, the Confederate representatives should come no closer to Cairo than Bird's Point. Prior to leaving, the officers thanked Grant for his courtesy and remarked, according to a reporter present, that "they were obliged for the visit of our gunboats Monday morning, but that no damage was done by our shots."

Returning to base, Brig. Gen. Grant was criticized in some circles for not ordering the *Grampus* detained and sending the Rebel envoys home by land. Miller's steamer had, after all, originally been owned by a Northerner and was confiscated at the outbreak of the war.

The *Conestoga* was refreshed at her temporary Kentucky base and recoaled in time for a second long-range reconnaissance on Monday. From Paducah, he steamed up the Ohio to Smithland and then 60 miles up the Cumberland River to investigate reports that fortifications were under construction upstream. Finding he could ascend no further due to shoals, the gunboatman dropped down to anchor overnight at Eddyville. In what was starting as a long and bloody Tennessee guerrilla war, Union sympathizers in that area were being persecuted by their Dixie-oriented neighbors. Some "Secesh" were even supposedly setting up a battery below the town.

Before leaving for the Ohio, Lt. Phelps took the occasion to visit with community leaders and "found it necessary to use strong language" on them concerning their unneighborliness. If it continued, he warned, the *Conestoga* would return to give them more than a warning. Even as her smoke floated away over the river and the timberclad returned to Paducah that evening, the Southern harassment of Unionists in the Eddyville area resumed. It intensified following the stationing of Capt. M.D. Wilcox's cavalry company at the village of Saratoga Springs, about four miles back of the town.

Brig. Gen. Smith, who had a keen interest in seeing the Rebel construction activities on the banks of the Tennessee for himself, was taken for a short cruise up that river "some miles" the next day. Reaching the obstruction known as the "Chain of Rocks," the bewhiskered brigadier was confident that he could stifle any Rebel gunboats through the simple expedient of sinking at that place "two or three coal barges filled with stone." On October 17, the timberclad ascended the Tennessee some 40 miles to Aurora and seized the steam ferry *Henry* as a prize. She had supposedly been used by the enemy "from time to time."[4]

While the *Conestoga* was visiting the Tennessee and Cumberland rivers, Cmdr. Walke's task group at Cairo was busy keeping an eye on Columbus and the Rebel gunboats known to operate from that citadel. At Columbus, according to Lt. Col. Frank Montgomery of the 1st Mississippi Cavalry, ""the chief excitement of the camp was to gather on the bluff and see the Federal gunboats pursue Captain Marsh Miller as he would return from his daily scout up the river." "There was a long stretch in the river above Columbus without a bend," Montgomery later remembered, and Miller was often gone so long that it was feared that he was sunk or captured. "But presently, his boat would be seen coming under all the steam it could bear, and its whistles screaming as it came, while behind would come the gunboats firing as they came."

Ulysses S. Grant (1822–1885) was deeply involved in the Western Theater from the fall of 1861 through the fall of 1863 before departing east to command all Federal forces. The major general from Ohio worked particularly well with his U.S. Navy colleagues and through the Battle of Shiloh he was keenly aware of the contributions made to his success by the three timberclad gunboats. Indeed, it has been claimed that the *Lexington* and *Tyler* saved his career at both Belmont and Pittsburg Landing (National Archives; photograph by Mathew Brady).

When the *Grampus* finally got under the great guns of Iron Banks, Miller "would stop and turn and pop away with his six pounders." Meanwhile, the Columbus cannon were manned and returned the fire of the gunboats. "No damage was ever done on either side for they never came near enough," Lt. Col. Montgomery recalled. Still, it was "great sport to watch the *Grampus*, which was really handled in a daring manner by Captain Miller, who is still living [ca. 1901], an honored citizen of Memphis."

On October 16, Brig. Gen. Grant was told that a new casemated battery was erected and a new 84-pound rifled cannon brought to the upper end of Columbus. Additionally, a great chain had been delivered which would be thrown across the Mississippi to obstruct navigation. Were these signs that the Rebels were up to some new perfidy?

Grant and Maj. Gen. Frémont received word next day that the "Swamp Rats" of Brig. Gen. M. Jeff Thompson, thought chased away earlier in the month, had returned for another round. This time, the irregular leader moved north towards Fredericktown, occupying the place some 25 miles east of Ironton, on October 17. The undermanned Thompson planned to remain in place only until a stronger Federal force arrived. Again alerted by intelligence, just such a legion, 4,500 men under Col. Joseph Plummer, was en route within hours.

In order to learn if the Columbus Confederates were altering their position, the Cairo commander called in Cmdr.

Walke on the morning of October 18 and verbally ordered him to undertake an urgent downstream reconnaissance. Taking Cmdr. Porter along as a witness, Walke steamed down as far as Lucas Bend. At that point, the *Tyler* fired an 8-inch shell over the Belmont point opposite the Iron Banks. After the discharge, the timberclad rounded to and moved opposite Islands No. 3 and 4, where she pumped one shell into the cornfields of the farm owned by Beckwith and another into those of the plantation owned by Hunter, the man whose wood was recently confiscated. Neither Walke nor Porter could see any change in enemy positions since their last visit.

At this time, Camp Johnston at Belmont was basically an observation post located a little back from the river on 700 acres on a slight eminence in marshy, low ground. It was occupied by the 13th Arkansas Infantry, along with a squadron of cavalry and a battery of artillery. In order that the approaches to the camp might be commanded by the cannon across the river at Columbus, the Rebels felled all of the trees for some distance over about 20 acres along the west bank. The trunks were used to form abatis that might stop any land assault.

When the *Tyler* returned to Cairo, Porter handed Walke an order to proceed up the Ohio River as far as New Caledonia, Illinois, to take possession of the hull of a new steamer being built there. Once in hand, it was to be towed back and turned over to Brig. Gen. Grant. The cannon-wearing towboat duly puffed upstream but found that the hull of "new" steamer was in horrible shape. It was in a sinking condition by the time the *Tyler* dragged it back to Cairo. The calking aboard was so bad that even the sailors detailed to keep her afloat could not prevent her from taking on water. Nevertheless, the job was completed and the craft turned over. Just as civilian steamers such as the *Bee* were ordered from time to time to tow or otherwise assist the gunboats as the war progressed, so too would the gunboats, especially the later tinclads, return the compliment to the civilian merchantmen. The next morning, Brig. Gen. Grant and Cmdr. Walke again conferred. The Buckeye brigadier pronounced himself well pleased with the previous day's nautical scout.[5]

Late that night, miles away, the *Conestoga* was en route up the Cumberland River. Above Eddyville, she met a rise which permitted her to pass the shoals where she was earlier forced to turn back. Nine miles below the Tennessee state line and at about 1:00 A.M. on the morning of October 20, she came across a pair of abandoned flatboats. Boarding parties found them loaded with flour from Canton, Tennessee, and it was speculated that they had been left for pickup by a steamer, which would either haul them to a local market or perhaps supply Rebel troops at Bowling Green, Kentucky. In any event, they were prized and towed back to Paducah. Brig. Gen. Smith ordered the flats sent on to Brig. Gen. Grant at Cairo.

By this time, Capt. Foote, at St. Louis, had received Phelps' reports concerning the possibility that the Confederates were building armorclad warships up the Tennessee River. He even had an opportunity to confer with Cmdr. Porter, whom Maj. Gen. Frémont had ordered to Paducah. After dispatching an itinerary of his anticipated movements for the next two weeks to Navy Secretary Gideon Welles, Foote took the train to Cairo on October 21. The same day, some miles away, Col. Plummer defeated Brig. Gen. Thompson at Fredericktown and forced the Confederates to retreat toward Greenville. The victory was believed by many, including Grant, to have "crushed the Rebellion in South East Missouri."

After a courtesy call on Brig. Gen. Grant, Foote departed for Paducah next morning aboard the *Lexington*. After a brief stop at Mound City to check on Porter and the *New Era*, the flotilla commander reached his Kentucky destination in the evening. Foote arranged with Brig. Gen. Smith at Paducah to send the *Lexington* up the Tennessee on the evening of October 23 to bring back one or two companies of loyal but unarmed Kentucky troops with no transport to the river's mouth. The *Conestoga*, the usual Paducah station boat, was away up the Ohio River and it was unclear as to when she might return.

While Cmdr. Stembel was upstream, Capt. Foote wired Cmdr. Porter, officially ordering him to bring the *New Era* to Paducah as soon as possible. Upon his arrival, he was to report to Brig. Gen. Smith and blockade the Tennessee River to prevent the egress of enemy gunboats reportedly headed toward the Ohio. The *Conestoga*, upon her return, would be sent to guard the new gunboats at Mound City. If Porter really did find himself engaged, Phelps could be telegraphed and would soon steam to his assistance. The colorful Porter wrote back suggesting that Foote and he take *Conestoga*, *Lexington*, and *New Era* up the Tennessee to find the enemy and engage them in battle. Foote wrote back saying that he lacked the authority to undertake any such nautical charge and that they simply "must wait the action of the military."

It seems to the student of Union Civil War western river gunboats that sooner or later almost every kind of adventure befell their captains. At this time, yet another strange episode unfolded, involving a feared secret society and, once again, the enterprising Lt. Phelps.

The Knights of the Golden Circle was a secession-oriented "paramilitary organization modeled after the secret fraternal orders that were so popular in the antebellum United States." Active in the lower Midwest, particularly Illinois and Indiana, this "fifth column" was a real concern to Union authorities from 1861 onward. At one point, members of the group even attempted the assassination of Hoosier governor Oliver P. Morton. Intelligence had reached the *Conestoga* that upwards of 70 K.G.C.'s were about to try to slip across the Ohio from Illinois near Shawneytown to join the Rebel armies in Kentucky. A spy among the disloyal party made rendezvous arrangements with Lt. Phelps before returning to the riverbank to rejoin his order. The gunboat was waiting at the appointed hour, but the K.G.C.'s did not appear. Nothing was ever seen again of the gunboatman's informant.

While Phelps was awaiting his contact and Porter was dreaming of glory, Capt. Foote attempted to recall the *Conestoga*. Telegraphs were sent to many of the ports along the Ohio where the gunboat might call. After the failure of his Shawneetown effort, Phelps had ascended to Evansville, where he found his superior's message at noon on October 23. Once coaled, the smallest of the timberclads made flank speed back to Paducah, arriving at daylight on October 25. There her commander petitioned Capt. Foote on behalf of his crew for needed hammocks, clothing, bags, and especially shoes.

During this period of activity on the Ohio, the situation on the Mississippi near Cairo was very quiet. On October 22, the *Tyler*, at Brig. Gen. Grant's request, escorted the *Belle Memphis* to the Norfolk area. It was undoubtedly during this time frame that the patrolling timberclad pursued a mounted Confederate picket in a chase that was "short but exciting." As Cmdr. Walke recalled in his memoirs, "The faithful horse, with his rider, soon left the tardy gunboat behind." While cavalrymen could always outrun river steamers, they could not always avoid their bite. "A 64-pounder shell overtook them," Walke continued, "and burst so near that nothing more was seen of them after the smoke and dust had cleared off, and the roar of the explosion had subsided."[6]

In the early afternoon of October 25, Lt. Phelps was summoned to the headquarters of Brig. Gen. Smith. There he was joined by Maj. Jesse J. Phillips of the 9th Illinois Volunteer Infantry, who had 300 men of his Companies B, H. and I waiting outside. The U.S. force commander at Paducah had fresh intelligence that a body of cavalry encamped at Saratoga Springs had joined local Southern sympathizers in harassment of the loyal Union people of Eddyville. This was the same town where Phelps had promised retribution for such acts just 10 days earlier. The Rebels had also opened a recruiting station, according to Gen. Johnston's biographer. Smith wanted to do something about the perceived affront and determined the *Conestoga* should be sent back to render chastisement. This time she would be accompanied by soldiers from Phillips' unit. Stealth was essential, otherwise the horsemen would just fade away into the surrounding woods.

Once Smith, Phelps, and Phillips had concluded their half hour meeting, the 300 men boarded the steamer *Lake Erie No. 2* at the wharf about 4:30 P.M. After Lt. Phelps, with Phillips as his guest, was back aboard the *Conestoga*, the signal was given and the two boats cast off for Smithland.

The initial part of the plan called for the black gunboat to put into port and locate guides and pilots for the expedition. It was not anticipated that the troop-laden steamer would land. Smithland was somewhat less than half the distance to Eddyville by land than it was by twisting river and the Confederates had a well-developed alert system. Runners from the mouth of the Cumberland could be far inland well before any steamer moved far upstream. Surprise remained vital to the success of the mission.

Unfortunately, the captain of the *Lake Erie No. 2* either did not know or did not understand the plan. When he got to Smithland, his craft ran directly to the wharf boat rather than standing off. Everyone could see the beaming faces of his gallant blue-clad passengers. Indeed, the troopboat's arrival occasioned local reporter Irving Carson from the *Chicago Daily Tribune*, who used the penname "C," to go aboard and make himself "one of the party."

The unexpected steamer landing occasioned a new strategy between Phelps and Phillips. Originally, it was hoped that a descent near Eddyville could be effected in darkness. This scheme was not abandoned. However, instead of the two boats initially proceeding up the Cumberland together, another tack was adopted. The *Lake Erie No. 2* was sent alone up the Ohio for a few miles. Then, a couple of hours later, the *Conestoga* followed, with a pair of barges in tow. Once the two made rendezvous, the barges were cast off and the gunboat and the steamer rounded to. The latter was herself now taken in tow.

This was the beginning of a ruse to slip by Confederate lookouts. The *Lake Erie No. 2* was entirely darkened, her fires were screened, and her engines were stopped. The noisy *Conestoga*, sparks flying from her chimneys and all lights showing, then boldly dropped back down to Smithland and passed into the Cumberland. In the darkness, no one onshore suspected that the timberclad had a steamer at the end of a line. After passing up to a safe distance above the town, the ruse was ended. The *Lake Erie No. 2* came back to life and the two Union vessels made their best speed up the narrow and crooked river, with the gunboat in the lead.

About 3:00 A.M. on the morning of October 26, the raiders reached New Forge Landing, some 45 miles from Smithland, six miles by land from Eddyville but 15 away by the river and around a bend to boot. Here the three companies were quickly put ashore and, as quietly as possible, they began a seven-mile overland march inland to get up and behind the enemy camp at Saratoga Springs. "The brave boys marched the whole distance in the night without a murmur," noted the embedded Chicago reporter.

While the Northern soldiers slogged their way along a dry stream and over several narrow roads, lanes, and footpaths, the *Conestoga* and the *Lake Erie No. 2* puffed their way up the Cumberland to Eddyville. The troop steamer was left behind a wooded point, while the timberclad anchored off the end of the main street.

While en route to Saratoga Springs, the cautious Union troops paid nocturnal visits to the homes of three or four known Southern sympathizers, taking them prisoner in order that they not sound the alarm. They also supposedly managed to sneak up and disarm the Confederate pickets, again without any disturbance or firearms discharge. Southern accounts maintain that the "pickets had come in for breakfast" and that the camp was attacked "before others had gone out to take their places."

Finally, about 7:00 A.M. having silently reached a point within 600 yards of the main Rebel camp, the 9th Illinois was given the signal to move in, and "then began the fun." When within 200 yards, the Yankees charged upon 75–160 surprised Confederates (numbers vary by account), the Yankees moving so fast that Wilcox was unable to rally his men into a defensive line. The stunned Rebel captain, firing a pair of revolvers at the oncoming midwesterners, went down in a hail of nine minié balls.

After the shooting stopped, seven Confederates, including Wilcox, were found dead, several lay wounded, and the rest had escaped, save 21 POWs and six black slaves. Three bluecoats were wounded. Several horses were killed in the exchange, but 30 others were captured, along with eight mules, two wagons, and a mountain of harness, plus small arms.

A number of Rebels escaped and fled in different directions. Several reached Hopkinsville, where they encountered an informant for the *Louisville Courier*. The Southern reporter was amazed to see that "some of them had their clothes actually riddled with balls, while their persons miraculously escaped injury." The men provided brief details on how the "Lincoln gun-boat from the Ohio, supposed to be the *Conestoga*," made her descent on West Eddyville.

While Phillips and the 9th were sneaking up on Wilcox's camp, Lt. Phelps, at an agreed upon time, threw a cordon of sailors and marines from his timberclad around Eddyville. The bluejackets and leathernecks would, hopefully, prevent any Rebel troops hiding in the town from exiting and any Southern troopers fleeing from Phillips from gaining entrance.

At approximately 10:00 A.M., Capt. Phillips and his men entered the town, bringing in their prisoners (now 24) along with their booty. About the same time, the *Lake Erie No. 2* nosed into the Eddyville bank. The Saratoga Springs strike had actually been more successful than Lt. Phelps expected, forcing him to improvise the lift necessary to get everybody and everything back to Paducah. At first, it was believed that the captured property, horses, and mules, could be towed back aboard the local wharf boat. While beginning the process of cutting its moorings, the craft was found to be leaky and too rotten for towing.

Lt. Phelps next had the seized horses and mules herded aboard the *Lake Erie No. 2* and transferred 100 of the 300 9th Illinois troops to the *Conestoga*. Still, additional capacity was required and so he impressed a flatboat belonging to "a noted secessionist." The remainder of "the plunder," along with the prisoners and slaves (and several guards), now went aboard the flatboat, which would be towed behind the steamer. When all was in readiness for departure, Lt. Phelps, as he had on his last visit, perhaps with Maj. Phillips in company, called available community leaders together to once again warn them as to their loyalties. He assured them that he would hold them, as well as any secessionists living along the banks of the river all the way to the Kentucky-Tennessee line, responsible for any additional depredations committed against local Union people following his departure. Not only would the people be accountable but their property in jeopardy as well.

When the gunboatman was satisfied that his message had been well and truly delivered, the *Conestoga* and *Lake Erie No. 2* departed downriver. They traveled the 62 miles back to Paducah nonstop, arriving at the mouth of the Tennessee River at 8:00 P.M. Checking his watch, Lt. Phelps noted that "we were absent from Paducah 29 hours." At Louisville two days later, the *Courier*'s editor railed: "How long are these murderous, thieving Yankees to be permitted to thus infest our rivers, depredate upon our property, and murder our people?"

Brig. Gen. Smith was very gratified to get a firsthand report of the success from the two officers and pronounced the outing "to have been conducted with good judgment, spirit, and energy." He expected, perhaps wishfully, that it would have an impact on those considering anti–Union activities in the Eddyville region. When Capt. Foote heard of the expedition a few days later, he, too, was pleased and, in a report to Navy Secretary Gideon Welles, commended Phelps, Phillips, and their officers for "their bearing" during the voyage and skirmishing.[7]

While the wooden gunboats of the small Western Flotilla were engaged on the tributaries of the Ohio River or on guard and reconnaissance duty from Mound City to south of Cairo, work on the ironclad gunboats begun by James B. Eads continued at an all-too-leisurely pace. Eads had subcontracted his great project to yards and factories throughout the Midwest. What he had not counted on was the federal government's inability to pay his work estimates at the times specified in the original July arrangement.

While the story surrounding the birth of the ironclad "City Series" gunboats is outside the main thrust of this account, it should be noted that, during the time after September that they were under construction, one of the Cairo-based timberclads was usually tasked with guarding the Mound City yards where three of these "Pook turtles" were abuilding. The Hambledon, Collier and Co. facility was considered far more vulnerable to Confederate raids from Kentucky than Eads' main yards at Carondelet, outside of St. Louis. So it was that through much of October the *Tyler* was at Mound City, the *Lexington* at Cairo, and the *Conestoga* at Paducah. Prior to her departure for the yards, the *New Era* served at either of the two former locations.

Lt. Phelps had the opportunity to make another cruise to the Cumberland river on October 27. This time he was able to capture a large barge, the *Kentucky*, at a point about five miles above Smithland. It belonged to a Memphis company.

Back at Paducah next day, the enterprising junior officer was ordered by Brig. Gen. Smith, in accordance with a wire from Capt. Foote, to return to Mound City and relieve the *New Era* as guard ship for the Eads ironclads. Not everyone who heard or saw Porter's gunboat was impressed. Writing home from Bird's Point the day before, Charles Wright Wills observed as follows: "That gunboat, *New Era*, that the papers blow so much about is of no account as a gunboat.... The men on her have told me that she wouldn't half stand before a land battery that amounted to anything."

Steaming down the Ohio, Lt. Phelps found the *Tyler* as well as the *New Era*, lying off Mound City. The latter was laid up as workers enhanced her battery. Cmdr. Walke ordered the *Conestoga* to continue on down to Cairo, where she arrived late in the evening and dropped anchor next to the *Lexington*. Upon his arrival off the tip of Illinois, Lt. Phelps prepared a report on his latest acquisition for Brig. Gen. Grant. The *Kentucky* was well known among rivermen for its heavy lift capacity on the Ohio and Cumberland rivers. The *Conestoga*'s 1st Master, John Duble, employed her services during his civilian career as a steamboat captain. Then owned by John Lowden, the barge was being employed when it captured to haul stone to Memphis, his hometown, to pave the city wharf.

On October 29, Grant requested that the *Conestoga* tow the barge up to Mound City and have her repaired for use by his command. The same day, Cmdr. Porter and the *New Era* arrived at Paducah. Wednesday morning at Paducah, Cmdr. Porter, possibly grinding his teeth or stroking his famous beard in frustration at the prospect of his having to perform blockade duty, received an unanticipated call to action from Brig. Gen. Smith. The Paducah commander's need would allow the *New Era* to make its only wartime patrol fully rigged as a timberclad.

First thing that morning, Brig. Gen. Smith wired Brig. Gen. Grant that the price to upgrade and calk the *Kentucky* would be somewhere between $350 and $400. Next he met with Cmdr. Porter and asked him to transport up the Cumberland River aboard the *New Era* a man named Hester, who would direct him to a location near Canton, Kentucky, about 20 miles above Eddyville. There they were to pick up a company of loyalist Tennesseans who could find no other safe exit from their part of the country.

Before their conference concluded, Porter took the opportunity to lay before the bewhiskered brigadier the same plans for a Columbus attack that he had given to Grant two weeks earlier. Porter asked Smith to try to persuade the Cairo district chief to make the assault "and to keep the *New Era* for that purpose." Like Grant, Smith would not commit, in this case even to making the suggestion to his opposite. Shortly after Porter's meeting ended, the single-stacked, three-gun ex-ferryboat hoisted anchor and made up the Ohio River. Arriving at Smithland a few hours later, Cmdr. Porter was signaled from shore and asked to put in for a meeting with local U.S. Army officers. The *New Era*'s skipper was informed that a large Confederate force was actively throwing up fortifications up the Cumberland at Ingram's Shoals, a few miles above Eddyville. A company of garrison soldiers were assigned to accompany the timberclad upstream.

Reports on the Ingram's Bar, also known as the Eddy Shoals, obstructions were accurate. Work parties under Lt. Col. Milton A. Haynes, C.S.A., and steamboat captain H.H. Harrison completed the sinking of three 120-foot-long stone-filled coal barges, plus two smaller ones, on Wednesday, October 30. Anticipating that a gunboat might appear to interrupt the detail, it was protected by four fieldpieces, a company of cavalry and two of infantry from Fort Donelson. At Line Island, located three miles below Lineport, itself 15 miles below Dover, two more barges were also sunk, though a small gap was left at the head of the island.

Maj. Jeremy F. Gilmer, chief engineer of the Confederate Western Department, upon reviewing Haynes' activities, pronounced them acceptable. "In all ordinary stages of water," he wrote headquarters, "the obstructions render the river impassable for gunboats and for any other boats at this time." On the other hand, Col. Adolphus Heiman, who had opposed the barge sinkings, prophesized that "This will be a fruitless operation in a river which rises from low water to at least 57 feet and which I myself have often known to rise 10 feet in 24 hours."

In detailing his work for Gen. Albert Sidney Johnston at Bowling Green, Haynes also offered his observations on the political state of affairs along the 45-mile-long stretch of the Cumberland from Eddyville up to Dover. In general, the people were enthusiastic for the South. A few "Lincolnites" were settled here and there and eagerly carried news of Confederate river activities down to Smithland.

While the soldiers were climbing over the stages, the informant Hester approached Cmdr. Porter and told him that he was now convinced that the object of his mission had failed. Could he now please disembark? Quickly concluding that the man was an imposter or perhaps some kind of a provocateur, Porter refused and had him put under guard. Once the bluecoats were aboard, the *New Era* steamed on. Stopping at various points, including Eddyville, the gunboatmen were advised of the troops facing them upstream. All aboard were aware that they could be in combat the next morning.

The *Tyler* had also returned to Cairo on October 30. Early on the morning of October 31, Cmdr. Walke received two requests from Brig. Gen. Grant as part of the same order. Writing from St. Louis, Capt. Foote asked the brigadier to have Walke decide by November 1 which of the three Cincinnati-purchased timberclads should next ascend to Paducah and relieve the *New Era*. More importantly, the *Tyler* was required to make a reconnaissance down the Mississippi as far as possible.

Slipping away, the largest of the original timberclads paddled downstream, proceeding as far as the extreme end of Lucas Bend and below Island No. 4. In keeping with his orders, Cmdr. Walke did not "throw any shell," as no opportunity to "do good execution" presented itself. No enemy troop movements were seen on the Missouri shore and no evident change in the appearance of the countryside there was noticed. There did not appear to be any work going on at any of the locations on the Kentucky shore near Columbus, although checking the shoreline with his spyglass from the *Tyler*, Walke could discern that a number of camp tents seemed to have disappeared from the Iron Banks.

Dropping anchor off Cairo again by 3:00 P.M., Cmdr. Walke informed Brig. Gen. Grant of what he had — or more correctly, had not — found. He also wrote out a report on the day's scout to Capt. Foote. Concluding this message, he noted that he had ordered the *Lexington* to remain at Cairo while the *Conestoga* was sent back to Paducah, she being "best suited for that service."

Further east in the Cumberland River, the *New Era* had pushed up to Ingram's Bar by 6:00 A.M. There Cmdr. Porter found that the stream was almost completely obstructed by the five sunken barges. As the single-chimney timberclad hove to, Cmdr. Porter determined that the men throwing up the blockade had departed in haste upon hearing his approach. Some of their work was unfinished. Just to make certain the enemy was gone, he "fired a good many heavy guns."

Some weeks later, Cmdr. Porter reviewed his cruise for the St. Louis correspondent of the *New York Times*. Porter explained his belief that the retreating obstruction builders had retired to their camp about three miles inland. "Taking his bearing and range, he threw three nine-inch shells into the camp," the journalist told his readers on December 11, "and went on further up the river." W.B. Machen, a Dixie-learning observer traveling in the area, heard about the purposeless cannonade from fleeing nearby residents. He also learned that the *New Era* was "a new boat" that "had the appearance of being much more formidable than those heretofore in the river, mounting much heavier guns." Unable to proceed further, the timberclad "left and went down below Eddyville." Machen, in reporting her visit to Confederate authorities, thought she might have gone out of the river.

The *New Era* did leave after first briefly halting at the site of the previous day's shoot. Landing with a party, Porter looked cautiously about but found only an elderly black man, undoubtedly someone's slave. According to the *Times*, the man told Porter how three "bloo streak" landed nearby followed by "de almightiest bustin's you eber did see!" Satisfied with this story, Porter and his men reboarded the *New Era* and continued to Smithland. There, once again, informant Hester sought to leave the Yankee boat and again Porter refused, requiring that the man return with him to Paducah.

On Friday, November 1, the *Tyler* steamed up to Mound City, while the *Conestoga* moved to relieve Cmdr. Porter and the *New Era*. When she returned to Paducah from the Cumberland, the *New Era* received orders via Brig. Gen. Smith for her return to St. Louis. There the short-time fourth timberclad was scheduled to be converted into the ironclad later christened U.S.S. *Essex*.

Cmdr. Porter was apparently not anxious to miss any forthcoming action and continued to try to get Brig. Gen. Grant to strike in the Columbus area backed by the *New Era*'s three big guns. Arriving at Mound City, he called on Cmdr. Walke "and gave him a copy of my plan." The Virginian undoubtedly thanked him but was in no position to commit or suggest any plan of strategic action.

The *New Era* passed Cairo about 1:00 P.M. and communicated with the port as she departed the Ohio and steamed into the Mississippi. Cairo remained in sight for about five hours that day as the timberclad moved "at low steam against the current at the rate of two miles per hour."

Finally, 15–18 miles upstream in low water, the *New Era* anchored for the night. Porter sent a message to Grant by the passing steamer *Louisiana*, indicating that the *New Era*, if needed for any purpose, could be back at Cairo in an hour and a half. The gunboat was not required, the district commander did not reply, and Porter continued on to St. Louis on Sunday morning.

It might be well now to review Confederate progress on the defenses at Columbus. By the beginning of November, the little Kentucky town had truly become the "Gibraltar of the West." Almost from the time Maj. Gen. Polk had taken over the location atop the tall bluffs back in early September, fortification was undertaken in earnest. By this point, the place was the most heavily armed post in the New World. Three tiers of batteries were constructed on the Iron Banks. The first, 15 feet above the riverbank, was armed with 11-inch howitzers and 10-inch Columbiads. More guns poked out from batteries located midway up the bluffs, while at the top of the cliffs cannon muzzles were visible protruding from a long string of earthen works. Included here was the "Lady Polk," a 128-pounder Whitworth rifle that was the largest cannon in the entire Confederacy. "Where the bluff jets out flush with the river" a mile north of Columbus, a flat shelf was cleared for another battery.

Approximately 140 cannon, under the command of Brig. Gen. John P. McCown, could fire in various directions to protect the Mississippi from Northern incursion. The principal batteries included the Point Coupee (Louisiana) Battery, the Mississippi Battery, the Siege Battery, and the Fort Artillery. Little fortifications were built at intervals along the bluff, "bull pen forts," they were called. With thick sandbag walls and surrounding ditches, each was also fronted by sharpened tree trunks, or abatis. The land defenses of Columbus were manned by 16,507 men on October 31. The positions they held ran for four miles above and below the community and it was these defenses which the gunboats probed whenever they steamed within range.

Extra defenses were being constantly added, including some in the waters offshore. The great chain noted above, with its huge flukes, was nearly ready to deploy, its hundreds of links buoyed by rafts. This measure would be a huge failure, but it did symbolize for the South a rigid determination to defend the great river route. Writing from Memphis on the eve of the Battle of Belmont, an acquaintance of the Columbus commander, Samuel Tate, hoped that efforts to bring up the chain cables from his big Tennessee city would not cease until the entire defense spanned the Mississippi.

In addition to the chain, Maj. Gen. Polk was urged to have Confederate engineers suspend a number of torpedoes, or mines, under the surface of the river offshore from Columbus. His Memphis correspondent Tate wanted as many of these "submarine batteries" put into place as possible. If any were struck by one of the hated "Lincoln gunboats," it should explode and blow it "out of the Mississippi River." Also, according to Mr. Tate, a new Confederate gunboat named the *J.B. Howard* was due at Memphis. It would be armed with six 32-pounders and an 8-inch Columbiad. Once she was outfitted, she would be sent up to Columbus to replace the C.S.S. *Jackson*, long-since departed back down to New Orleans. Though perhaps not correct in this detail, the letter writer was prophetic in his closing sentence: "The month of November will be memorable and bloody."[8]

The beginning of November 1861 was unusually quiet for Capt. Foote and the Western Flotilla. His three active wooden boats were on patrol or guard duty at their designated locations, while work on the *New Era* and the Pook turtles continued apace. The same could not be said for the top U.S. Army general to whom Foote reported. A number of changes were coming, beginning with the retirement of Lt. Gen. Scott on November 1 and his replacement by Maj. Gen. George B. McClellan.

By All Saints Day, Maj. Gen. Frémont and his army were making significant progress in their campaign to come up with Sterling Price and troops from Arkansas, believed just ahead in southwestern Missouri. Lexington had been recaptured, the Osage River was crossed on

Tyler and *Lexington* at Belmont, November 1861. In this drawing by Rear Adm. Henry Walke, the *Tyler* and her sister, the *Lexington*, engage the batteries at Columbus, Kentucky, while Federal forces land above Belmont. The two timberclads were no real match for the big Confederate guns atop the bluffs and steamed back and forth defensively avoiding their shells. In order to create an image appropriate for his *Battles and Leaders* account, the sailor artist was forced to sacrifice perspective. The boats were nowhere near as close to the cliffs as depicted here (*Battles and Leaders*).

an 800-foot pontoon bridge laid in just 36 hours, and the force was regrouped in Springfield. As the week advanced, less than 50 miles separated the two field armies and the Southern commander knew he could not win a pitched battle.

After weeks of adverse comment in the eastern press and faced with the continuing deadly feud with the Blair-Bates alliance, Frémont suspected his days in command were numbered. Following a heated Cabinet meeting, President Lincoln had written out an order on October 24 for the relief of his principal western general. It was forwarded to Brig. Gen. Samuel R. Curtis at St. Louis for delivery. As was often the case with the 16th president's commands, there was a caveat. The message was to be transferred only at an appropriate moment when "The Pathfinder" was not in battle or about to go into one and it was not to be given to him at all if he had won a victory.

On November 2, Capt. Foote wrote from St. Louis with some relief to Navy Secretary Welles, who knew that Frémont was in terminal political difficulty. The cannon, powder, shell, and small arms, as well as almost all of the material stores Foote had so long anticipated for his command, were now finally available. The manpower situation was still difficult, but it was good to know that the department, as promised a little earlier, was sending along 300 drilled sailors. It was hoped that New Englanders, fishermen and landsmen, would follow. "We will soon drill them into efficient gunners," he promised.

Interestingly, the day before, Quartermaster General Montgomery C. Meigs had written to Capt. Foote from Washington, D.C., concerning additional appropriations needed to complete the gunboats and mortar boats then abuilding under Maj. Gen. Frémont's authorization. There were no funds for other than what Meigs and his unit had contracted for earlier, i.e., the Pook turtles. Still, "General Halleck has instructions in regard to the gunboats," Meigs added. Meigs, Welles, Fox, and everyone else of consequence in the federal capital knew that Maj. Gen. Henry ("Old Brains") Halleck was going to succeed both Frémont and Hunter before the month was done.

"The Pathfinder," unaware of his pending dismissal, continued to make plans for battle and to protect his flanks. That Saturday afternoon, Brig. Gen. Grant at Cairo received an order, dated at the departmental headquarters in St. Louis the previous day, requiring that his entire district command be prepared to march, with transport and ammunition, on an hour's notice. His men were to make demonstrations along both sides of the river toward Charleston, Norfolk, and Blandville, the latter a village on the Kentucky side about five miles from Fort Holt.

As Bruce Catton put it, a "demonstation" in the military terminology of the day, was "an ostentatious movement which would look very threatening but which would not lead to anything solid in the way of fighting." Grant's soldiers, then, were to be kept on the march "moving back and forth against these places" without actually attacking.

Just beyond Springfield on the evening of November 2-3, the messenger from Brig. Gen. Samuel R. Curtis, Capt. J. C McKenney (with a pass and dressed as a farmer), gained admittance to Frémont's tent by a ruse and delivered Lincoln's directive. The Department of the West was transferred to Maj. Gen. David Hunter, who, after a tardy arrival, withdrew "The Pathfinder's" army and allowed Maj. Gen. Price to escape from what many believe would have been a crushing defeat. John C. Frémont, who asked for Cmdr. Rodger's removal 15 days after reaching St. Louis, was gone himself 85 days later.[9]

The next day while he awaited his replacement, Maj. Gen. Frémont, technically still in command of his department, sent out new orders, these concerning Brig. Gen. M. Jeff Thompson, who had been spotted on the St. Francis River. Col. William P. Carlin's men from Pilot Knob were sent to chase the "Swamp Rat's" 3,000 guerrillas away from the town of Indian Ford, located below Greenville and west of Bloomfield, about 25 miles or so each way, and back into Arkansas. At Cairo, Brig. Gen. Grant received instructions to send men from both Cape Girardeau and Bird's Point to assist Carlin. News also circulated around the higher echelons of the Western Department that it was, for the moment, basically leaderless: Frémont was out and Hunter had not yet arrived. It was a twilight time when opportunity might be seized.

The Buckeye brigadier reacted by dispatching Col. Richard J. Oglesby from Bird's Point and Col. Joseph Plummer from Cape Girardeau; both were given discretion as to how they would meet their common enemy. Their orders required, however, that they destroy Thompson's outfit, not just push it back. With about 5,000 bluecoats each, they set off on the morning of November 4 after Thompson, who was apparently quite surprised by the size of the pursuit. Oglesby's command steamed first to Commerce and pushed inland from there. Grant himself would "move south" toward Belmont while the garrison of Fort Holt sallied in the direction of Columbus.

Although Maj. Gen. Hunter, Frémont's replacement, had orders not to engage Maj. Gen. Price, he was not to be caught and overwhelmed by him either. Tuesday a telegraph supposedly arrived at Cairo from St. Louis warning that troops from Columbus were being sent to southwestern Missouri via Arkansas' White River. The demonstration previously ordered against the "Gibraltar of the Mississippi" was to be executed immediately.

There remains some doubt as to whether or not this wire ever existed. A correspondent for the *Louisville Daily Journal* later wrote that he saw a letter from army headquarters authorizing Grant to make an attack on Belmont but not on Columbus. Editor John Y. Simon of Grant's *Papers* makes the case that "it [the telegram] is almost surely nonexistent." In any event, this communication would eventually loom large in the mythology of the campaign. Whether or not a real wire or a reinterpretation of orders was the cause of what followed, one thing is certain: the movement would not be little. Ulysses S. Grant, long frustrated with sending small reconnaissance missions to visit Maj. Gen. Polk, was determined on a larger combination and, as some have since suggested, perhaps an actual Belmont attack.

Another piece of possibly unreliable press insight comes from *Belle Memphis* pilot Charles M. Scott, who spoke with a St. Louis correspondent after his boat returned to Cairo from hauling troops to Commerce. According to Scott, a Federal scout named Curry told him that there was one Rebel regiment at Belmont and that two others were under orders to move across the Mississippi next day and hit Oglesby's column in the rear. This was supposedly the intelligence that caused Grant to move against Belmont in an effort to save his subordinate.

Later on November 5, Brig. Gen. Smith at Paducah received a request from Cairo asking that a demonstration be made from the Kentucky port town toward Columbus while Grant's men "menaced" Belmont. Such a joint push could, it was hoped, prevent Columbus from sending reinforcements across the river and perhaps aid Grant's subordinates to complete their missions of eliminating Thompson. It would take Paducah's old soldier less than 24 hours to get four supported infantry regiments and a brigade of some 2,000 men underway toward Milburn and Viola.

At the same time, Col. Oglesby was directed to turn toward New Madrid and link up at Charleston with other soldiers from Bird's Point. By dusk on Wednesday, almost 15,000 Union soldiers in seven columns would be on the march south from Paducah across to Cape Girardeau. For Maj. Gen. Polk at Columbus, the design of these movements was unclear; almost hourly, scouts and citizens brought in fresh reports and rumors. Around 10:00 P.M., Cairo post commander Brig. Gen. McClernand was called to Grant's headquarters and instructed to get his entire brigade readied to board boats the next day. Col. C. Carroll Marsh, at Bird's Point, received his instructions to ready two infantry battalions, plus cavalry and artillery units.

The intelligence apparatus available to the District of Southeast Missouri continued to feed Cairo stories of Confederate plans to rush across the river to aid either Price or Thompson. The latter, incidentally, was not at Indian Ford, but at Bloomfield. Confederate theater commander Albert Sidney Johnston had no plans to succor either of his Missouri colleagues. For over a week, he argued by mail with his Columbus subordinates over his plan to reinforce the army in the areas south of Bowling Green, especially Clarksville on the Cumberland.

Maj. Gen. Polk, for his part, did not believe the press and other intelligence reports that Grant was moving thousands of men just against Thompson. He also knew that there were no plans to reinforce Maj. Gen. Price. Having on the other hand been subjected to weeks of probing reconnaissance raids, there was good reason to suspect an attack might be made upon Columbus. In such an event, every soldier wearing gray would be needed.

Earlier in the day, Gen. Johnston, wearied of argument, had sent definitive orders that an entire division be transferred over to Clarksville from Columbus as soon as possible. The movement was slowed by lack of wagons and the 5,000 men would be unable to leave before November 7.[10]

November 6 was a day of Southern celebration. Jefferson Davis was elected president of the Confederacy. On the same sunny day on the Mississippi, Maj. Gen. Polk resigned. He was not happy with his command, believed his duty of finishing the Columbus fortifications was all but finished, and wanted to return to his clerical duties. It would take some time for his message to reach the Rebel capital.

Up the Ohio at Paducah, Brig. Gen. Smith posted a report on enemy troop strength and conditions in his area to Brig. Gen. Lorenzo Thomas, the U.S. Army adjutant general in Washington, D.C., while also preparing his men to move toward Columbus, he overlooked his notes on the Confederate fortifications being erected on the Cumberland and Tennessee rivers. Two days later, he would send Thomas an addendum. Smith's backup memo found Fort Henry, 71 miles up the Tennessee at the boundary line between Kentucky and the Volunteer State, to be the most important post, with a strong earthworks on the waterside armed with 14 to 16 cannon and garrisoned by about 1,200 soldiers, who "have been under apprehension of attack from here for the past two weeks." Also of great concern to the brigadier were reports that the Confederates "some eight miles above Fort Henry" were endeavoring to convert river steamers into ironclads. Fort Henry was "an obstacle to our gunboats proceeding to look after such work." "The *Conestoga* gunboat, admirably commanded by Lt. Phelps of the Navy, is my only security in this quarter," the aging soldier wrote. "He is constantly moving his vessel up and down the Tennessee and Cumberland." Even now, he was off inspecting the latter.

Determined to head south that evening, Brig. Gen. Grant, down at Cairo, passed orders for troops to assemble and board the largest transports available at the town landing. This process was to be timed for completion so that the night tactics of the Paducah descent could be repeated. Under cover of darkness, the expedition would steam downriver and wait to surprise the enemy at dawn.

About mid-afternoon, the soldiers of McClernand's brigade began climbing the sage planks aboard their troopboats. The 27th Illinois of Col. Napoleon Buford, one of Maj. Gen. Polk's West Point classmates, embarked aboard the *James Montgomery*, as did "C," the *Chicago Daily Tribune* reporter Irving Carson. Congressman-Col. Philip B. Fouke's 30th and Congressman-Col. John A. Logan's 31st Illinois boarded the *Aleck Scott*, the largest steamer at the Cairo levee. That steamer also hosted Brig. Gen. McClernand. The *Rob Roy* and *Chancellor* were tasked to transport all available cavalry while the expedition's wagons were loaded aboard the *Keystone*.

Toward dusk, the five transports steamed across the Mississippi to Bird's Point. There the 22nd Illinois Infantry of Col. Henry Dougherty's second brigade boarded the headquarters boat *Belle Memphis* while Col. Jacob Lauman's 7th Iowa, the only non–Illinois infantry contingent going along, was sent aboard the *James Montgomery*. Additional cavalry and cannon from Capt. Ezra Taylor's Battery A of the 1st Illinois Light Artillery, better known as the Chicago Light Artillery, were distributed among the fleet.

The *St. Louis Daily Missouri Republican* reporter watching the embarkation actually believed Brig. Gen. Grant was taking more transports than was required "in order to make the force appear more formidable than it was." Grant biographer Smith has, on the other hand, called the boats "inadequate" and their loading "hasty."

As the military's men, horses, and items of equipment were being loaded aboard the assault boats, Brig. Gen. Grant sent orders to Cmdr. Walke. The *Tyler* and *Lexington*, maintained in a state of readiness, would join him in undertaking a reconnaissance down the river. They would also providing escort to half a dozen transport steamers. That is all the seamen aboard initially knew about their coming involvement in "the first battle of importance in which our gunboats participated on the Western waters."

The sun was rapidly dropping by the time the bluecoat armada was ready and the U.S.

commanders were aboard their boats. Cloaked by early evening darkness, Brig. Gen. Grant signaled the *Tyler* that the movement could commence. Sliding out into the main channel, Cmdr. Walke took the lead, followed by Cmdr. Stembel's *Lexington*. The second timberclad had, as an observer, a reporter from the *St. Louis Daily Missouri Democrat*.

The *Keystone* was the first civilian boat to get underway behind the gunboats. She was followed by the *Belle Memphis* and *Chancellor*, the *Aleck Scott*, the *James Montgomery*, and the *Rob Roy*. The *Chancellor* quickly got aground, however, halting the entire procession. Pilot Charles Scott of the *Memphis* was directed by Brig. Gen. Grant to drop back and throw a line to the stuck steamer. With her great side wheels thrashing, the headquarters vessel quickly pulled her free, allowing the column to reassemble. Following an exchange of signal whistles, the watery march resumed about 9:00 P.M.

With showers of sparks escaping their chimneys, the U.S. boats paddled south down the Mississippi. Almost all of the men aboard them, including the escort commanders, were ignorant of their ultimate destination. Indeed, most did not even know whether they would continue downstream or turn up into the Ohio River. Bets were taken. After a short wait, the *Tyler* and *Lexington* turned downstream. Wagers were collected by some, while everyone now suspected the target would be Columbus.

After two hours steaming, the armada put into the Kentucky shore near the tip of Island No. 1 at Cook's Bend near Port Jefferson. The point where the boats tied up was eight miles below Cairo and eleven above Columbus. It had been deliberately chosen because Grant wanted his opposite, Maj. Gen. Polk, to assume that Columbus was his target. He also wanted to repeat his Paducah strategy by arriving off the landing site just before daylight.

A guard was posted onshore and watches were set on the steamers. Aboard, some men slept, while most talked, sang, smoked or did some combination of the three. Grant and his immediate staff, according to the recollections of a participant years later, gathered around a table in the former ladies' cabin of the *Belle Memphis* and discussed the upcoming operation under glittering chandeliers. They then slept for a while in chairs around the cabin.

In those early hours after midnight on November 7, the *Tyler* and *Lexington* undertook a reconnaissance downstream. They had not proceeded very far before encountering a dense fog. When added to the clouds on a moonless night, it proved too thick to allow mission completion. The two timberclads rounded to and returned upstream. Toward 2:00 A.M., the expedition commander was awakened. An urgent message had been delivered from Col. W.H.L. Wallace at Charleston, Missouri. According to an informant, Wallace reported, the Confederates had started the day before crossing men from Columbus to Belmont to follow and cut off the column of Col. Oglesby. Brig. Gen. Grant later wrote that this message, the same supposedly heard by Pilot Scott earlier, sparked his decision to attack Belmont rather than make a demonstration.

At about the same hour, orders were issued. The expedition would steam to the rescue of Oglesby beginning promptly at 6:00 A.M. The gunboats would lead, followed by the troopboats. The entire force would go ashore at the lowest spot on the Missouri shore where a landing could be effected safe from the Columbus batteries. The responsibility for choosing the point of debarkation was left entirely to "Captain Walke, commanding naval forces." Walke learned of all this when he returned from his abortive reconnaissance about 3:00 A.M. Prior to that, he was not privy to Grant's campaign design. Ever after, debate would rage as to whether or not such a message was received. Like the earlier controversy on attack versus demonstration, this discussion focuses on the veracity of the brigadier's claim in light of the relatively high Union casualties experienced in the campaign.

Col. Wallace all but said in a letter to his wife that Brig. Gen. Grant's claim was untrue.

As early as 1863, historian John S.C. Abbott reported that "Grant resolved to break up the rebel encampment at Belmont, and thus threaten Columbus." John Simon, editor of the general's papers, was never able to find any written collaboration in a contemporary document or account from him. "He went down the river to look for a fight," Simon has concluded, "though just a little one."

Historian William McFeely flat out states that the decision to attack was made before the fleet departed Cairo. "Grant had set out to fight," he writes, "not demonstrate." If this were not true, Capt. Foote, at St. Louis, whom he had promised to keep apprised, would have been alerted in advance so he could join the expedition and Cmdr. Walke would not have received sailing orders at the last minute. Indeed, as Walke later wrote, he could not tip off Foote because "the general's intentions ... were kept perfectly secret."

On the other hand, the military historian Arthur L. Conger, writing 70 years after the battle, penned an interesting observation not generally visited by naval or Belmont campaign historians, though quoted by Bruce Catton: "Grant's desire to provoke a fight at Belmont may have been at least partly due to indoctrination he was getting from the naval officers at Cairo, a hard-bitten lot who were notoriously anxious to see some real fighting develop." Cmdr. William D. ("Dirty Bill") Porter recommended a strike on October 13, as did Capt. Foote at the end of the month. Pugnacious Henry Walke would gladly have supported either outing.

The journalists for the St. Louis newspapers covering the campaign firmly believed that Grant intended to attack Belmont and then, if possible, Columbus itself. The embedded *Chicago Evening Journal* scribe assessed the occupation of Belmont "desirable as a strategical point." The *Memphis Avalanche* held then — and three days later — that Nationals would take Camp Johnston and then use the Belmont location to strike across the river. Many of the Union soldiers, like Capt. John Seaton of the 22nd Illinois, also believed Columbus the target.

Grant would remain sensitive for the rest of his life to comments that he had acted without orders. After he became Union general in chief in 1864, he had his chief of staff, Brig. Gen. John A. Rawlins, write up a revised report on the battle (backdated to November 17, 1861), which was delivered to the War Department in June 1865 and later inserted in the army *Official Records*. Dying of cancer in 1885, the general came clean that his actions were unsanctioned.[11]

It was calm and clear by 6:00 A.M., according to the *Lexington*'s logbook. Shortly thereafter, the signal was given to cast off from the Kentucky shore and the U.S. amphibious force steamed full ahead down the Mississippi. Approximately an hour later, the two gunboats reached the extreme end of Lucas Bend and rounded to off Hunter's Farm, a short distance above the Iron Bluffs and between three and five miles above Belmont.

The Missouri steamboat landing was on the opposite side of the heavily wooded Belmont Point and out of sight of Columbus. Instead of arriving in the last minutes of predawn darkness, the sun was up as, one by one, five of the troop steamers nosed in to shore. The little *Rob Roy* remained half a mile above. Cmdr. Walke later admitted that, although he did not know it at the time, he had made a faulty landing choice. The picked location was not, in fact, "just without" the "range of their guns."

At 7:30, as the timberclads stood offshore, and the soldiers were landed with their horses, artillery, and equipment from the *Belle Memphis*, *James Montgomery*, *Chancellor*, *Aleck Scott*, and *Keystone*. There was only light opposition from a few Rebel riflemen. In fact, it was so peaceful that expedition medical director Dr. John Brinton witnessed near the *Memphis* a "flock of geese settled in the river not far away." The Yankees climbed up a low but steep bank.

The timberclads *Lexington* and *Tyler* took on the batteries at Columbus on November 7, 1861, to provide covering fire in support of the Federal troops of U.S. Grant then landing at Belmont across the Mississippi River. The action here was later depicted by participant Rear Admiral Henry Walke, 1861 captain of the *Tyler*, in his 1877 memoirs, *Naval Scenes and Reminiscences of the Civil War in the United States* (Naval Historical Center).

Within an hour of debarkation, the infantry was formed into ranks in a clearing in front of a cornfield that stretched back to the edge of a thick timberline. In fact, everywhere the eye could see there were clearings, marshes, and woods. "The early autumnal morning was delightful," thought Dr. Brinton, "the air fresh and invigorating, without being cold." Soon Grant's soldiers, less several companies deployed in a ravine to guard the transports, headed out, determined to circle around and attack Camp Johnston from the side opposite of the Mississippi. ""It was well known what was to be done," wrote the *Tribune*'s man "C." "The whole camp at Belmont was to be taken and destroyed."

Over at Columbus, Maj. Gen. Polk was awakened with the news that a large force of national troops were landing on the Missouri shore. Polk quickly sent his available staff officers to sound the alarm. One went across the river to warn the 13th Arkansas at Belmont's Camp Johnston, another ran to the landing to alert the steamboat captains, while others advised divisional and regimental officers of the danger.

Maj. Gen. Polk was uncertain whether the Belmont landing represented a diversion or the main event. He understood that Federal troops were marching down on him from Paducah and Fort Holt and spies and Yankee newspapers all promoted a direct attack upon his citadel. Until he could make a final determination, he held most of his men on the Kentucky side of the river. He had no "perfect preparations for our reception," as the *Chicago Evening Journal* later told its readers, plans based on full information transmitted to Columbus by "traitors in the camp" at Cairo.

On the other hand, Polk lost no time ordering Brig. Gen. Pillow to reinforce Belmont with the four regiments Johnston had ordered to Clarksville. Within an hour or so, these units would be ferried over to aid Col. James C. Tappan's defense of Camp Johnston. Whistles from the steamers tasked with this transport was clearly heard by Union troops assembling on the

Missouri shore. Mounting up, the city's commander now rode out to check on the bastion's defensive batteries. Along the way, men not otherwise engaged were ordered to assume positions along the perimeter.

Of particular interest to the Confederate commander and his artillery chief, Brig. Gen. McCown, was the Pointe Coupee Battery, made up of Louisianans under Capt. Richard A. Stewart. These men and their Parrot rifles were moved north about two miles to a forward location on the bluff "at the bend of the river." Here they could not only observe enemy gunboat activities but also take the "Lincoln" craft under fire if they ventured within range. As the sun rose, McCown and Stewart could easily see the smoke belching up from the Union steamers. They could not, however, actually see the vessels, as they were hidden by thick timber.

At the Union assembly point, Walter Scates and his fellow gunners of the Chicago Light Artillery could, as later reported by Steven Woodward, "distinctly hear the drums at Columbus beating to arms." While the Federal troops moved off toward Camp Johnston "under marching orders," the timberclads steamed downriver a mile or two past Belmont Point at Grant's request to provide a diversion. Before their departure, all possible measures for defense were taken. To add extra protection, spare deck lines and hawsers were coiled and stacked up to help safeguard the boilers and machinery. The "beat to quarters" was sounded and every jack on both boats manned his battle station.

The *Tyler* and *Lexington* engaged the Confederate batteries on the Iron Banks about 8:30 A.M., throwing "their shot quite lively." By McCown's direct order, Capt. Stewart's Pointe Coupee Battery replied but initially fired short. Joining in, the siege guns of Capt. S.D.H. Hamilton on Stewart's left did little better. Unfortunately for the naval gunners, the Rebel emplacements were so high up that target identification and acquisition was all but impossible. About all that could be ascertained was that clouds of fresh dirt leaped outward upon the burst of shells on the sides of the bluffs. Airbursts over Capt. Stewart's men did no harm.

From the start, the two Union craft stirred up a hornet's nest. Orange tongues of fire now regularly rippled along the "frowning battlements" as Stewart and Hamilton struck back. The noise was deafening. To prevent catastrophe, Walke and Stembel steamed their boats in tight circles, firing away. The Rebel gunners, including those seen by the gunboatmen to be almost directly ahead on a shelf of land (Stewart), were hard pressed to hit these moving targets. Luckily for the sailors, their enemy consistently fired beyond.

Still, the *Daily Missouri Democrat* reporter aboard the *Lexington* observed that Confederate gunners were gaining the range "and their missiles were falling thick and fast around their decks and alongside, splashing and dashing in the water, and cutting fantastic *ricochets* through the air." The newsman later learned from a prisoner that, "at this time, the *Taylor* threw a 32-pdr. shot near General Polk's headquarters."

Occasionally, Confederate shells went way off course and flew almost a half mile upriver, landing even beyond the transports at Hunter's Farm. Cmdr. Walke, peering through his spyglass, was horror-struck to see these shells arching overhead. The enemy cannon had the range to hit Grant's transports, which he now worried were parked too close to the Confederate bastion.

Aboard the *James Montgomery*, where the correspondent Irving Carson was "left in charge," the roar of heavy gunfire bothered everyone's ears. "Many shot fell near us," the *Tribune* writer later told his paper's subscribers, "some short and others beyond, and not a few fearfully near us." Witnesses on all the transports saw shells burst at great heights, while others were "drinking the water." One struck the riverbank within a few feet of the *Montgomery*'s stern.

After only 15 minutes of action, the timberclads broke off their exchange with Columbus and returned upstream to Hunter's Farm. No Columbus bombs had yet landed among the transports, although those aboard were somewhat unnerved by the "horrid music." It was possible for men, both aboard the gunboats in action and the chartered steamers tied up along the shore, to spot the shells fired from Columbus as they passed over and near.

During these opening minutes, Surgeon Brinton saw at least two giant bullets leave Columbus and traced their path all the way over the transports and into the Missouri shore beyond. *New York Herald* newsman DeBenneville Randolph ("D.R.K.") Keim was on the deck of the *Aleck Scott* with her captain, Robert A. Reilly, watching the Columbus batteries through a spyglass. A giant shell, believed an 84-pounder, passed directly over their heads and landed about three quarters of a mile above the huge transport. "Mr. Reeder, the clerk, sent some men for it and they found it buried in the earth over 10 feet," Keim reported.

As the timberclads sped back toward the Union transports, tragedy gripped the Pointe Coupee Battery. One of its several Parrott guns exploded, killing two men and wounding others. The shock of the accident caused the battery to stand down. Hamilton's men continued their bombardment, along with the Whitworth rifle *Lady Polk*. Generals Polk and McCown arrived and observed. Reaching hailing distance, Cmdr. Walke ordered the steamer captains to cast off and move upstream out of range.

Although the sounds of musket fire had been heard all morning, the decibel level of the ground fighting significantly intensified around 10:30 A.M. when the actual battle began, or as Grant later wrote his wife, "The ball may be said to have fairly opened." Within half an hour, the approximately 3,000 Johnny Rebs and 2,800 Yankees were fairly at one another and the "engagement became general."

As Brig. Gen. Grant's forces bore down on the low earthworks surrounding the Confederate post, another naval diversionary sortie was required. The big guns of the Fort Artillery battery at Columbus opened on the Federal positions in the woods beyond Camp Johnston. So too did the bastion's Mississippi Battery under Capt. Melanchthon Smith.

Just after 11:00 A.M., the *Tyler* and *Lexington* charged past Belmont Point ready to reengage Columbus. Even heavier fire was drawn from the upper batteries as the two timberclads resumed their circling maneuvers and, in the words of Brig. Gen. Grant, "exercised the Rebels." During the actual combat following, the *Lexington* alone expended 18 shells and one solid shot. Confederate projectiles again flew all around the gunboats but did no harm. Conversely, the big shells from the timberclads were equally ineffective.

This duel with Stewart and Hamilton allowed the Fort Artillery division to fire at Union troops near Belmont and to provide cover for Rebel transports hauling needed reinforcements and supplies across the river. The fire of the big Columbus guns "was very annoying," the *Chicago Evening Journal* later reported, "the more so as we were not in a position to return it."

Up on the Columbus bluffs, Private Henry Morton Stanley (who would later rescue Livingston in Africa) watched the exchange below. The enemy gunboats, he remembered, "saucily bore down and engaged our batteries.... We novices [in the Dixie Greys, 6th Arkansas] delighted to hear the sound of so many cannon." The naval craft were wildly overmatched against the Columbus batteries. They could only send up "a few shots in return, but they were too harmless to do more than add to the charm of the excitement."

This time the water-land fight lasted 20 minutes before Cmdr. Walke broke off. It was, he later confessed, "too hazardous to have remained long under fire with such frail vessels." The loyal Virginian believed it was his duty at all cost to protect his gunboats, which represented two thirds of the operational Western Flotilla and were really only at Belmont to "protect the land forces in case of a repulse." The destruction of the *Tyler* and *Lexington*, he later wrote, "would have involved the loss of our army and our depot at Cairo, the most important one in the West."

The Confederates watching the timberclads steam away believed they had out-dueled their spunky opponents in this "brisk engagement," just as they had earlier. They were, remembered Lt. Col. Marcus J. Wright of the 154th Senior Tennessee Infantry, "compelled to retire."

Returning to the anchorage above Belmont, the men aboard the *Tyler* and *Lexington* could hear the din of battle ashore. Because the river level was low and the shoreline high, all the Union boats were partially hidden from view to anyone ashore. They were, in fact, "higher than the heads of men standing on the upper decks." Like the men aboard the transport steamers, the gunboatmen had no knowledge of how the fighting was going.

The bluecoat soldiers, despite spirited opposition in a cornfield to the northwest, now pushed Camp Johnston's unseasoned men out of their defenses and back to the riverbank, capturing the post they had briefly occupied two months earlier, along with six fieldpieces. By lunchtime, the equally green Union volunteers had largely accomplished their objectives, and their advance ceased.

The *Chicago Daily Tribune*'s "C" reported next day that Col. Buford "was the first to unfurl the Stars and Stripes in the enemy's camp." The man from the cross-town *Chicago Evening Journal* added that the U.S. flag was raised in the "face of the foe and defiantly usurps the mongrel colors." Instead of consolidating their positions and capturing the Rebels stranded with their backs to the water, Northern commanders allowed discipline to break down. A general picnic of plunder now began.

Out of touch with U.S. Army commanders ashore and with no system for mutual communication, without knowledge of the growing bluecoat success, and with some misgiving, Cmdr. Walke decided that one more run at the Columbus batteries should be attempted, or, as he later put it, "to share in the hottest of the fight." About noon, he signaled Cmdr. Stembel to weigh anchor.

On the bluff at Columbus, Private Stanley and his fellow soldiers were likewise unable to determine what was going on across the river. "A thick haze which settled over the woods" covered their view of the cornfields and other points to such a degree that "we could only guess what was occurring."

Given that the Confederates had consistently overshot the two churning craft earlier in the morning, Cmdr. Walke decided to take them a quarter of a mile closer this time. A brisk fire of shell was opened and there were hopes that this time some damage might be done. The enemy returned fire with vigor and soon it was recorded that their shots were "flying thickly around us." The *Daily Missouri Democrat* reporter aboard the *Lexington* was frank when he later admitted that the gunboatmen did not know whether they had caused any damage or not. As the *Tyler* weaved around the river, a large Rebel shot struck her on the starboard bulwarks and continued obliquely through the spar deck and scantling. It decapitated Seaman Michael Adams and wounded two other men, one seriously, while "bounding across the deck."

The gunboats fired a few more shells and then retreated back toward the transport anchorage. As they departed, they kept firing from their stern guns as long as they were within range. As she departed, the *Tyler* was hit again, in the stern, by a fragment from a heavy shell. Fortunately, the damage was "trifling." Still, readers of the *Memphis Daily Appeal* were told on November 12 that the boat, confused with the *Lexington*," was "sunk from the effects of her injuries." That news was based on intelligence from two exchanged Texan POWs who had reached the Tennessee city from Cairo where "Cairoites" had informed them of the loss.[12]

So far, Maj. Gen. Polk at Columbus had been deterred from sending large scale reinforcements across the river because of reports coming in concerning the columns approaching his town from Fort Holt and Paducah. Now he was also receiving reports that the situation just below him in Missouri had come apart and his Belmont force was all but defeated. Fortunately for Southern arms, he was also apprised that neither Maj. Gen. Smith or the Fort Holt soldiers were close enough to be an immediate threat. This news allowed him to order additional reinforcements to Belmont.

As Cmdr. Walke did not by intention run down past the Columbus batteries, he would not now be in position to halt the Confederate trans-river reinforcement of Pillow's men trapped on the Missouri riverbank. Brig. Gen. Grant did not notice that the gunboats had withdrawn upstream and no one, including Walke, thought to tell him.

Even as the Columbus and timberclad gunners concluded their ammunition trade, the first three of five steamboats, several from as far away as the Yazoo River, began taking gray-clad soldiers over from Kentucky. The Union flank on the Mississippi was unprotected and Southern ferries slipped through. The *Prince*, the *Charm*, and the *Harry W.R. Hill*, better known as the *H.W.R. Hill* or *Hill*, joined later in the day by the *Kentucky* and the *Ingomar*, would make as large a contribution to the battle for the Confederate side as the big side-wheelers from Cairo made for the North.

An entire brigade under Brig. Gen. Benjamin F. Cheatham, together with the 15th Tennessee and 11th Louisiana, were landed by the *Charm*, *Hill*, and *Prince*, in the words of Bruce Catton, "upstream so as to cut the Federals off from their own transports." Maj. Gen. Polk accompanied Cheatham, leaving Brig. Gen. McCown in command at Columbus.

Brig. Gen. Grant arrived at Camp Johnston and found chaos. Bands were playing, men were helping themselves to souvenirs, and officers—even including Maj. Gen. McClernand—were giving victory speeches. The commanding general ordered discipline restored. He even had the Confederate tents burned, hoping to call his Illinois and Iowa troops to order. Nothing seemed to work; the men were out of control and getting them reorganized would take time. On top of this, historian Abbot testified later, "the lurid beacon" caused by the burning tents "brought the guns of Columbus to bear."

At this point, the *Lady Polk* joined other large caliber guns along the Columbus bluffs in firing upon Camp Johnston. The Southern gunners aimed their huge projectiles at the U.S. flag on the pole in its center. The *Memphis Daily Appeal* noted three days later that, additionally, "the famous pivot gun *Lady Davis* was turned loose upon them from this side." She "fired two shots." Fortunately for the Federals, their range was a bit too high. The shot and shell flew over Camp Johnston to explode or lodge in the woods beyond. Both guns later exploded and after the war their remains were trophies at the Mound City Navy Yard.

Surgeon Brinton, who came into camp with Grant, then happened to look across the river and was horrified to see a pair of steamboats crowded with soldiers leaving the levee and heading upstream. They were definitely not the timberclads and the medical man rushed to tell the Buckeye brigadier. Following Brinton's pointing finger, Grant saw the two, "black—or gray—with soldiers from boilder-deck to roof." These were followed by others. At the same time, a scout from the 30th Illinois informed the brigadier that the Confederates huddling on the bank were being reinforced by men from across the river.

With more men becoming aware that, as the *Chicago Evening Journal* reporter put it, "danger was imminent that our retreat would be cut off," Grant ordered his men to fall back to their transports. The soldiers were formed into a column to move quickly back to the Hunter's Farm landing. Out on the water, sailors and soldiers aboard the Confederate steamers could see that Pillow's men had been driven from the camp and that Yankee guns were being set up to oppose their landing.

Union field artillerymen, using their own pieces and several seized from the Rebels, opened up on the Confederate steamers from the parade ground at Camp Johnston doing, as *Tribune* man Carson put it initially, "fearful work." He later admitted that the 6-pounders "were too light to stop them." At least one Rebel transport, Capt. William L. Trask's *Charm*, was forced to change her course under this fire and head for a spot 400 yards away from her original destination. All of the boats kept as close to the shore as they could in order to avoid the U.S. Army cannoneers.

When the *Charm*, *Hill*, and *Prince* came into the beach to drop off reinforcements, they found the landing sites obstructed by Confederate escapees from Camp Johnston. Some of the disorganized men attempted to board and take possession of the *Charm*. As they struggled to get away, they shouted, according to Capt. Trask, "Don't land! We're whipped! Go back!" The fearful were pushed back in the face of the vengeful, while the Yankee cannoneers suffered under shells of the Columbus batteries.

Cmdr. Walke also attempted to interdict the Confederate ferries. With their heavy cannon at extreme elevation, the *Tyler* and *Lexington* fired over the woods on Belmont Point and reportedly dropped their shells in or near the enemy craft. Captured enemy soldiers later supposedly told the naval officer that his guns had damaged the transports as they crossed the river. Perhaps overreaching for credit he should have shared with his colleagues ashore, Walke later claimed that his shoot forced the Rebel steamers "to cross the point almost beyond the reach of our shot and land their troops lower down, which was the very thing we desired to accomplish."

Campaign historian Hughes has high praise for the Yankee military gunners: "The casualties they inflicted and the confusion they created tilted the tables at Belmont." He is less generous toward the naval boss. "The Confederates feared that the gunboats would intervene at any moment while their troops were being ferried across the river," he wrote, "but the gunboats remained tucked out of sight behind the point."

Further contradicting Cmdr. Walke, Hughes points out that Polk's transports disembarked their men "not 'lower down' but higher up, almost on Belmont Point itself." Writing in 1863, historian John Abbott observed that "It is difficult to imagine why the rebels were permitted to cross the broad and rapid Mississippi in force, without opposition, our gunboats being present."

Grant biographer Smith lays the fault at the brigadier's door, insisting that one of the major reasons the North faced defeat at Belmont was "his inability to coordinate his naval support." Brig. Gen. Grant, having observed the Confederate steamers firsthand, could have sent interception orders to Walke, but, in the words of John Y. Simon, there is no indication "that he sent word to the commanders of the two gunboats to shell them." Simon also believes a Union error was the "failure to make the two gunboats an integral part of Grant's battle plan" from the outset.

Chicago Daily Tribune reporter Irving Carson, embedded with the troops, later kindly indicated that "Our gunners made some splendid shots, and the splinters flew quite lively." The *St. Louis Daily Missouri Democrat* newsman aboard the *Lexington* does not mention such a shot. Historian Robert Whitesell goes further, crediting the Columbus batteries with providing the margin of victory. Whether Grant and Walke had coordinated or not and whether Walke had moved closer under the big guns in a suicidal effort to prevent reinforcements reaching Pillow, they would have rained down sufficient fire to sink or discourage the timberclads. "It is quite clear," he wrote in 1963, "that the very accurate supporting fire from the Kentucky batteries not only contributed heavily to the defeat of the Yankee land forces, but they also neutralized the effort of the Yankee naval units."

The Confederates caught on the riverbank were allowed to rally and turned after the retreating nationals. After fresh men of his brigade had disembarked from the *Harry W.R. Hill*, according to a story later related by Mark Twain, Brig. Gen. Cheatham had them "strip their coats off and throw them in a pile, and said, 'Now follow me to h—l or victory.'" Additionally, the Fort Artillery and Mississippi Battery at Columbus opened again on the Federal positions.

Where only minutes before jubilation in victory was paramount, now fear and panic threatened to bring total defeat. By the time some measure of order was restored among the Yankee soldiers, they faced a wall of fresh Confederate infantry separating them from their transport anchorage two miles above. After much screaming, shouting, falling, and dying, the Northern expeditionary force turned and started fighting its way to its boats.

The bluecoats fought their way back toward their transport anchorage "against desperate odds." Wounded soldiers were left with the dead; only two of the six cannon would be carried off. Minie balls and cannon shells of all sizes whizzed everywhere. They were not restricted to either side. On Twain's reconnoiter aboard the *Harry W.R. Hill*, said Mr. Clemens years later, "The balls came booming around. Three cannon-balls went through the chimney; one ball took off the corner of the pilot-house; shells were screaming and bursting all around."

Confusion reigned as frightened Union men ran for their lives or, if lucky enough to have a horse, galloped away. There were some cool heads and steady rifles, but all too often the retreat was pell mell. Grant's biographer, Jean Smith, later noted that the Union army left over 1,000 rifles or muskets on the field.

Col. Napoleon Buford's 27th Illinois struck out on its own to the south and west, eventually heading north along the Bird's Point road toward the site of the morning debarkation. The first Yankee soldiers reaching the transport *James Montgomery* told Acting Mate William Lonergan that, as Bradsby quoted him in Perrin's county history, soldiers from Columbus were "cutting our men to pieces."

Maj. Gen. Polk and his command, trailing the retreating Federals, expected the Northerners to take up a Dunkirk-style defensive perimeter around their landing. The bishop attempted to devise a scheme to envelope and capture as many of his opponents as possible. Even as he planned, the head of his pursuing column was marching within range of the timberclads. It was approaching sundown and the shadows were lengthening.

Col. Preston Smith and his men had just landed in Missouri aboard the packets *Charm* and *Kentucky*. His brigade, comprising the 154th Senior Tennessee Regiment from Memphis and the 1st Mississippi Battalion, with Brig. Gen. Cheatham along, was now turning into a lane off the Hunter's Farm road that led to the steamboat landing. Soon, Smith was able to see the chimneys of three Northern transports.

Of greater concern to the Rebels was a pair of "black monsters" out in midstream. Great plumes of exhaust smoke escaped from both the *Tyler* and *Lexington*. Chasing the retreating Lincolnites, the gray-clad soldiers probably had some idea that they could run into murderous gunboat fire. Still, Smith divided his column into two wings, hoping they could overrun the transports before the gunboat fire stopped them. Later, he recalled that, once his men were in position directly opposite the landing, "I gave the order to charge!"

Meanwhile, even the companies posted to guard the landing site retreated directly onto the *Belle Memphis*, where they were of no use to Brig. Gen. Grant when he arrived to deploy this reserve. Although Grant always maintained this exodus was "no hasty retreat or running away," it was, in fact, just that. When he informed his commander that the Confederates were almost on them, a 22nd Illinois Infantry private was told, as historian Hughes later revealed, "It is no use, the infantry won't come off the boats and the gunboats must cover our retreat."

The *Tyler* and *Lexington* were lying with the transports near the landing beach in the early afternoon. The officer of the deck aboard the latter wrote in the log that the weather was clear and pleasant with a light wind from the southwest. "Heavy firing on the Missouri shore" was tersely recorded. The first Union soldiers appeared about 2:40 P.M. and began a precipitate embarkation in the transports. Surprised at the undisciplined military descent on the boats, Cmdr. Walke inquired as to the state of affairs from Brig. Gen. McClernand, who told him of the rout and retreat. Alerted to the Rebel pursuit, Walke and Stembel prepared to greet the advancing enemy by dropping down below the transports.

"The enemy was coming upon our rear in large force and was so near as to be plainly visible from the deck of the boats," wrote the *Daily Missouri Democrat* reporter aboard the *Lexington*. "As soon as they discovered that we were dropping down," he continued, "they went into the woods." Thus it was that, as the bluecoats scrambled through the cornfield and aboard the troopboats as fast as possible, Confederate forces were just behind them in the woods.

Ashore, McClernand demanded that a couple of Lt. Pat White's field artillery be deployed on the bank. The gunners were able to mount only one. Soon, yelling Southern soldiers began a charge. White and his men got off one blast and then ran their pieces back aboard the *Chancellor*.

Although a number of partial Confederate units joined in the attack, the rush on the landing was mainly conducted by the 154th Senior Tennessee, under Lt. Col. Marcus J. Wright, with Brig. Gen. Cheatham. Observed by Maj. Gen. Polk himself, the Rebels poured what appeared to be a murderous fire into the Union transports. The commanding general later wrote that the enemy "cut his lines and retreated from the shore, many of his soldiers being driven overboard by the rush of those behind them."

The logbook of the *Lexington* did not disagree with the general's claim. Its entry for the day includes the sentence that "At 4 the rebels appeared and began to fire on the boats, when they backed out and retreated up the river." The newsman aboard her later testified that the Southern soldiers "immediately came up to the river bank six or eight deep. When within 100 feet of our transports, they commenced firing on us."

Brig. Gen. Pillow also observed that Southern fire was " so hot and destructive that the troops ... rushed to the opposite side of the boats and had to be forced back by the bayonet to prevent capsizing." This carnage was entirely caused by small arms. Contrary to later Federal reports, the field battery en route to the scene was delayed.

The slaughter of Yankee troops as they fled aboard their boats was overwhelming, claimed the *Memphis Appeal* days later. Bodies were "piled upon the decks to the depth of three or four feet." The decks were "so slippery that men could scarcely stand" and pilots who tried to reach the wheel "were shot down as fast as they approached."

As the Confederate soldiers burst from the cornfield, other small arms fire rang out from spots along the bank and back toward the woods. The Southern soldiers were, however, not actually rushing straight down the bank, but for the most part were dropping to a prone position to avoid return fire. However it was launched, this chorus of popping inspired the deckhands aboard the Yankee transports to run in their staging planks and slip — or cut — their lines as quickly as possible.

Brig. Gen. McClernand made it aboard the *Chancellor*. Brig. Gen. Grant, after a quick scout to the top of the bank, rode his horse aboard the *Belle Memphis* along, as he later recalled, "a single gang-plank" reaching back 12–15 feet from the boat to the shore. He then went to the captain's quarters and lay down on a sofa for a breather. A survivor of his opponent's staff later told the U.S. brigadier that Maj. Gen. Polk had seen Grant's horsemanship and had suggested to riflemen around him that "There is a Yankee. You may try your marksmanship on him if you wish." None did.

In less than regular order, the five U.S. transports backed out into the Mississippi and attempted to maneuver outside of the gunboats' anticipated line of fire and toward the Kentucky side. From their decks, those men lucky enough to have scrambled aboard saw butternut-colored uniforms everywhere onshore. A number of men from the 7th Iowa and 22nd Illinois were trapped on the landing, along with stragglers from other units.

The flag boat *Belle Memphis* experienced the most difficulty getting off. Pilot Scott had to ride his vessel first forward on one wheel and then back on the other to escape a large pilot of driftwood known in the river vocabulary as a "wrack heap." The rocking motion was laborious and frustrating and appeared futile to some.

With their guns elevated to clear the banks, the timberclads had also moved downriver to avoid the transports and improve their firing angle. Now, in addition to firing over the shore, the gunboats had also to contend with the struggling *Belle Memphis* inadvertently slipping into the *Lexington*'s line of fire.

Sensing that the possible loss of a few boards off the flag boat was not a bad exchange under the circumstances, Cmdr. Stembel grabbed his speaking trumpet and hailed the *Memphis Belle*. Several times he told the men lining the decks to throw themselves flat in order to avoid any splinters when the timberclad commenced shooting. Needless to say, the soldiers were scared, appalled — and obedient.

Following Stembel's fair warning, the bow gunners of the *Lexington* and *Tyler* opened on the Confederates as they pushed from the woods into the cornfield separating them from the Union landing. The timberclad gun crews, in an "explosion that shook the heavens," poured grape, canister, and shell with five-second fuses into the gray-clad men wading in the grain. It was "the best music of the day," the *Tribune*'s Carson remembered.

Without field artillerymen in support, the Rebels could not reply with their own thunder and, according to Cmdr. Walke, were silenced "with great slaughter." "The great slaughter," Robert D. Whitesell remarked a century later, "was actually twelve wounded." Still, the "thundering '64's" of the gunboats must have struck awe in the troops of both sides. According to a reporter from the *Ohio State Journal* quoted in Walke's memoirs, "Horses and riders went somersaulting through the air as if hurled by the right hand of a tornado."

Once the *Belle Memphis* worked her way free of her obstruction, "sheered out and went ahead," the gunboats enhanced their blasting symphony with rolling broadsides. Cmdr. Walke later recalled that "We continued our fire with the broadside guns throwing shell on the banks ahead with bow guns to protect the transports and throwing shell from the stern gun upon the enemy's ground so long as we were in reach."

Aboard the *Lexington*, the *Daily Missouri Democrat* reporter jotted down that Rebel fire from shore "was falling thick and fast around us." He remembered the fighting withdrawal as consuming half an hour of "play," during which the *Tyler* threw "some seventy rounds and the *Lexington* between thirty and forty." In this time, the smoke from the battle became so thick and black that the sun could not be seen." That last observation had to be an enthusiastic hyperbole; the smoke was probably very thick all right, but the day was also nearly dark.

Next day, scribe Carson from the *Chicago Daily Tribune* gave the gunboats a mixed review, claiming that they "rendered efficient service in covering our retreat, mowing down the rebels with grape, but at the same time killing some of our own men." There is no documentation suggesting naval fire killed Union soldiers. The *Tribune* story contained several errors, as did the early reporting by all the newspapers, perhaps this one's most grievous error being that "General Johnston was wounded."

Brig. Gen. Grant, hearing the clamor both from his transport's maneuvering and the gunboats, gave up his repose and went forward to watch the battle. The firefight was furious and was later reported most enthusiastically. Postwar naval historian Boynton gleefully noted that Walke and Stembel "poured a perfect storm of death into the rebel masses ... whole ranks mowed down by a broadside." Newsman Keim of the *New York Herald* claimed that the gunboat shelling "made a havoc in them."

Some of the gunboat projectiles found their way into the woods where Col. Buford's 27th Illinois was slogging north. Fortunately there were no injuries. Later, when the firing died down, the separated unit arrived at the river some three miles upstream from Hunter's Farm. It would be alone in the dark — the expeditionary force had already sailed.

The *Memphis Appeal* reported that the Lincolnites knew where the Southern soldiers were "and their range was very accurate." Most of them now fled into the woods or hugged the ground as salvos from the timberclads passed high overhead. Some shells exploded near or among Rebel units half a mile away.

Even though no Southern field artillery was firing back at them, four Union sources plus Boynton later indicated that gunboat shells blasted apart one such piece attempting to block the Union retreat. Next day, reporter Carson informed his *Chicago Daily Tribune* readers that "after all the effects of the enemy, I could not learn that anything larger than musket balls had struck our boats." Still, the power of the naval cannon convinced many enlisted U.S. soldiers, like Private Lindorf Ozburn of the 31st Illinois later quoted by Hughes, that "The gunboats was all that saved us from being shot like hogs."

The gunboats were not the only Yankees returning Rebel fire. Capt. Ezra Taylor and the men of his Chicago Light Artillery were aboard the *Chancellor* with the two fieldpieces earlier rolled aboard off the bank and one operational captured Confederate gun. Turning the transport into a quasi-gunboat, the men fired back at the advancing graycoats with grape and solid shot from these tubes mounted at her bow.

Marksmen fired away with their muskets from the hurricane deck, as did soldiers aboard the huge *Aleck Scott*. In fact, riflemen shot back at the shore from the decks of all five U.S. transports; their pinpricks of orange sparkled far less in the dark than the blasts of the mighty 8-inch and 32-pounders aboard the gunboats.

Given that it was dusk by 5:00 P.M. on this short day, it is hard to imagine what anyone saw. Soldiers and others lining the Columbus bluffs to see the fighting could hear the "battle still raging," but they looked in vain for the visible curtains of fire expected from both sides. In fact, all they could actually see through the dim light and clouds of powder smoke were the muzzle flashes of the timberclad cannon.

The fighting departure conducted in the dusk-to-dark period was nerve-wracking and exciting. The noise was clamorous, all later agreed, and there was a tremendous volume of naval cannon and small arms fire. Shells from the timberclads exploded onshore, ploughing great holes on the riverbanks and sometimes felling trees far inland. The upper decks, pilothouses, windows and chimneys of the troopboats were riddled by Southern musket rounds. Even Brig. Gen. Grant returned to the captain's quarters to find a bullet hole in the sofa he had abandoned to watch the action.

From Columbus, Georgia, a correspondent from the *Macon Daily Telegraph* got off an eight-paragraph report based on private dispatches and eyewitness accounts, all claiming that the day's work "was a bloody battle but a brilliant victory." Losses were believed to be heavy "but less than the enemy's." The Yankees "fled and were hotly pursued to their gunboats. A complete route followed." Returning Southern participants claimed the "woods were filled with the dead and wounded, guns, ammunition, and knapsacks for the distance of seven miles."

Historian John Abbott memorialized for the North the contribution of the gunboats just before sundown on that November day: "As soon as they [the Confederates] approached the river's bank, the gun-boats opened fire. Their terrible missiles, thrown with great rapidity and accurate aim, produced fearful havoc in the rebel ranks. Under the protection of this fire, the embarkation was safely effected."

Capt. Foote told Navy Secretary Welles that the gunboats covering the final retreat "prevented our troops from being almost if not entirely cut to pieces."

Despite this and later claims of "great slaughter," the Belmont evacuation was not only successful but also death- and relatively wound-free. Despite all the shooting, almost nobody was hit. No Federal on the boats or Confederate soldier ashore was killed and, after reviewing the evidence a century plus later, historian Hughes concluded that "The fight probably resulted in a total of 25 wounded from both sides." Exact loss figures were — and are — totaled with every retelling of the battle story. Grant biographer Smith recently sifted through the accounts and tells us that "Casualties were heavy and about equal. Polk lost 642 killed, wounded and captured; Grant, 607. That was roughly 19 percent of the Union troops engaged."

For about half an hour after the Union transports departed up the Mississippi, Confederate troops "hung on the shore, endeavoring to form, and get their guns in position." *Chicago Daily Tribune* reporter Carson recalled that the gunboat cannon were "too much for them." Several times during the first phase of the waterborne retreat, when flashes from the Dahlgrens lit up the scene, "C" believed he saw "a dozen men and horses turn somersaults together."

After the steamers returned to midstream, the *Tyler* and *Lexington* followed in their wake, shooting an occasional shell back toward the enemy soldiers still trying to continue their pursuit along the riverbank. "They seemed actually to court death at the very muzzles of our heavy guns," Carson reflected, "and vast numbers of them sought it not in vain." During the day, the former warship expended 144 charges, three solid shot, 35 grape, and 106 shell.

About six miles up the river, Cmdr. Walke encountered the *Chancellor*, which had dropped out of line and started back downstream, followed by the *Keystone*. Coming within hailing distance, the task group commander was informed by Brig. Gen. McClernand that the 27th Illinois and a cavalry company had been left behind somewhere near Hunter's Farm. Cmdr. Walke was directed to round to and, with the *Lexington*, join him in seeking the men further down the riverbank.

As the gunboats steamed down, the *Chancellor* put into shore and McClernand went ashore personally with a small armed and mounted party to find Col. Buford. The adjutant of the 27th Illinois was soon encountered and led the brigadier to Beckwith's Landing, where the remainder of the regiment was awaiting daylight. About the same time, the *Tyler* and *Lexington* arrived from three or four miles upstream and were duly signaled. With the *Lexington* standing in midstream to provide cover, the *Tyler* nosed into the bank and Cmdr. Walke hurried ashore. There he found McClernand, Buford, the survivors of the 27th, and some 40 Confederate prisoners. The Virginia-born sailor and the Illinois general quickly agreed to have the *Tyler* transport this lost command back to base.

By torchlight in the hour after 6:00 P.M. the soldiers were embarked aboard the largest timberclad and McClernand returned overland to his transport. The *Tyler*'s surgeons tended the wounded, who were made more comfortable by the generosity of crewmen who gave them "their own hammocks and bedding." The POWs were sent to the *Lexington* and, with the embarkation completed, the two steamers departed for "up the river" about 7:00 P.M.

A half hour later, the timberclads came to off the *Chancellor* and the *Keystone*, which had taken on the last of the missing cavalry. Earlier, a fast rider was sent along the shore to alert

The retreat — the Tyler shelling the Rebel troops.

the others that the 27th was found. McClernand's craft cast off just after Walke's arrival and stood upstream. The timberclads got underway again and followed the troopboats up guarding her rear.

As Walke and McClernand were loading Buford's men, Brig. Gen. Grant and the remainder of the transport fleet was en route to Cairo. Out of the fight, the *Rob Roy*, anticipating news, steamed down to greet the bluecoats, and reporters aboard hailed the Ohio general with speaking trumpets. By and by, as the two boats kept company, Grant emerged on deck and, without benefit of a hailing tube, shouted acknowledgment to the scribes on the little boat. Belmont was a great victory, he cried, details later. Grant also hailed the captain of the *Rob Roy* and ordered him to find McClernand and Walke and to have the wounded transferred from the gunboat to the *Roy*. Walke was to remain near Island No. 1 until a local colonel returned from a reconnaissance.

The *Chancellor* and her escort reached Cook's Bend near Island No. 1, where the *Tyler* was dropped off. The *Lexington* and the transport continued on to Cairo, arriving at the wharf boat about 10:40 P.M. It took about an hour to move the soldiers ashore from the gunboat, after which she anchored in midstream. The cavalry reconnaissance holding up Cmdr. Walke was meanwhile completed, allowing the *Tyler* to returned to Cairo, where she dropped her hook near the *Lexington* just after midnight.

The *Belle Memphis* and her consorts reached Cairo an hour earlier than the *Lexington* and came to the levee with the reports from saluting cannon at Fort Holt, Bird's Point, and Fort Prentiss ringing in their ears. Cmdr. Roger Perry was the first to alert naval leadership of the expedition. In a wire to Capt. Foote in St. Louis, Perry announced that Grant's "force of observation" had captured Belmont. Casualties were great, but the gunboats, which had yet to return, had done their duty.

The tip of Illinois was all lit up and people milled everywhere seeking to honor the Northern soldiers for their great triumph. At Columbus and throughout the South, citizens of the Confederacy also believed their arms had scored a victory in the little Belmont scrape on the Missouri shore.[13]

As soon as Brig. Gen. Grant reached his Cairo headquarters, he immediately sent orders to Col. Oglesby countermanding his earlier request that he march on Belmont. With the regiments of the Cairo district commander no longer in the field, the troops of the Illinois colonel would have been badly mauled, if not destroyed, if they had come upon Polk's legions alone. He also sent situation reports to Brig. Gen. Smith and to Maj. Gen. Hunter's St. Louis headquarters. Again, he did not think to write Capt. Foote.

The pending battle between the armies of Maj. Gens. Frémont and Hunter and Price, the supposed cause of Grant's Belmont attack, never happened. In accordance with President Lincoln's orders, the "Pathfinder's" successor did not engage Price. Instead, on November 8, the Union army which John Frémont had so proudly marched southwest from St. Louis the previous month evacuated Springfield and fell back toward the Sedalla-Rolla area. It was 100 miles away before Price even learned it was gone.

Downstream at Columbus, Maj. Gen. Polk wired President Jefferson Davis, claiming

Opposite, top: Hurried reembarkation of Federal troops at Belmont, Missouri, in November 1861. The helter-skelter departure of the transports of Brig. Gen. U.S. Grant was covered by the timberclads. This drawing depicts the scene as seen by its artist, Cmdr. Henry Walke, captain of the *Tyler* (*Battles and Leaders* 1). *Bottom:* The *Tyler* shelling Confederate troops at Belmont. This line engraving from an issue of *Harper's Weekly* depicts the Federal retreat from Belmont on November 7, 1861. Cmdr. Henry Walke's gunboat led a number of transports away from danger, lobbing in shells as she passed (Naval Historical Center).

that Grant's strike had been repulsed and that Confederate arms had won a resounding victory against a Yankee force of over 8,000. The congress at Richmond voted a resolution celebrating "a triumphant victory" against overwhelming odds. The Rebel government was then faced with another crisis closer to home. On November 8, Cdr. Samuel F. DuPont, U.S. Navy, and Brig. Gen. Thomas W. Sherman captured Port Royal, S.C. An active participant in the battle was DuPont's aide, Cmdr. John Rodgers II.

At Memphis, destination for the first Rebel boats with prisoners and wounded, the schools were closed next day and citizens lined the banks waiting for them to arrive. They would be horrified by how many stretchers came onto the landing.

On November 19, the *New York Herald* portrayed Grant's bold move on Belmont as a victory "as clear as ever warriors gained." With one or two exceptions, Northern newspapers concluded, as did the *Cincinnati Daily Gazette* on November 9, that the "undertaking seems to have been creditable to the enterprise of our generals in command of the expedition, and highly honorable to the courage and conduct of the troops." Such claims were reported in other newspapers from Boston to Philadelphia to Pittsburgh and Cleveland — except, initially, for three.

This chorus of good reporting was dampened somewhat by reports in several Midwestern newspapers. The reporters from the St. Louis newspapers who initially believed Columbus the expedition target now considered Belmont a loss. The *St. Louis Daily Missouri Republican* carried the first negative reporting on November 8: "We have met the enemy and they are not ours."

Two days later, the readership of the *St. Louis Daily Missouri Democrat* was struck by its reporter's conclusion: "There is no disguising the fact that we were defeated, and badly, too." "In the disastrous termination of the Cairo expedition to Columbus," claimed the *Chicago Daily Tribune* on November 9, "our troops have suffered a bad defeat." The embedded reporter from the *Chicago Evening Journal* called the enterprise "a disastrous, yet glorious, expedition."

In actuality, Belmont was not really a defeat, but a near-run thing for the inexperienced Union men and commanders. Steven Woodworth has observed that Grant came "about as close to ultimate disaster as it was possible to imagine without actually experiencing utter defeat." There was initial victory against a same-sized Confederate force up until the time the troops celebrated on the parade ground at Camp Johnston. After that, there was the necessity of urgent extraction from a larger force to avoid defeat. "We are at a loss how to characterize the affair," penned the editor of the *Ohio State Journal* for his Columbus readers on November 12. "It was not a success; nor was it a failure."

Although one of the campaign's leading chroniclers, Nathaniel Hughes, later blasted Cmdr. Walke for not taking a more aggressive supporting role and thereby enabling Union arms to possibly win "a stunning victory," Brig. Gen. Grant was generous in his minimal praise of the gunboats. In his official report (the second one cited in the army and navy *Official Records*), the brigadier wrote: "The gunboats *Tyler*, Captain Walke, and *Lexington*, Captain Stembel, convoyed the expedition and rendered most efficient service. Immediately upon our landing they engaged the enemy's batteries on the heights above Columbus, and protected our transports throughout."

Hughes suggests Walke would probably have replied to his criticism "with warmth and logic," and would have pointed out, as earlier noted, that much rode upon the survival of his two boats, and any impetuous gallantry on his part could have been suicidal. He was less generous toward his own superiors, especially Secretary of the Navy Gideon Welles, whom he blamed for not promoting news of the timberclads' participation.

In his memoirs, Rear Adm. Walke, then at his last billet as commander of the Mound

City naval station, reflected on the Belmont campaign at length. Regarding the secretary of the navy, he wrote: "It is very evident that he had no particular friends on board those two gunboats, otherwise we would have had a glowing description of their performance."

Capt. Foote in St. Louis was particularly incensed when he received Cmdr. Perry's telegram. Not only had the brigadier broken his pledge to inform the fleet commander of any movement, but he also did not even let Walke and Stemble know "his intention until he directed them to proceed with his force on the armed reconnaissance toward Belmont." Historian T.K. Kionka sums up Foote's distress: "The fact that the gunboats performed admirably despite his absence made his exclusion the more bitter."

Foote probably muttered to himself that matters might have been different had he been along on the expedition. In no position to publicly comment, he cut orders that Friday for the movement of the steamer *Maria Denning* to Cairo as the flotilla's new advance receiving ship. The vessel would be commanded by Cmdr. Benjamin Dove, another recently arrived "restored" officer.

"It was not much of a battle," opined Bern Anderson in 1962, though John Y. Simon in 1981 thought it "a fairly large battle by the standards of 1861." Still, whatever the overall results of the Belmont campaign may have been—and they are debated to this day—the worth of the Western Flotilla was proved beyond a doubt through its "impressive demonstration of what gunboats could do in support of troops." River war historian John D. Milligan summed up the timberclad contribution to the Battle of Belmont in 1965. "Although the wooden gunboats had proved ineffective against the Columbus batteries," he wrote, "at the landing they had saved Grant's army from what was rapidly deteriorating into a very nasty situation." In addition, the action gave "valuable experience in co-operation to the officers and men of both services."

Belmont marks a highpoint in the story of the timberclad war. While it is true that much work in the area of combined arms liaison remained for Union arms in the west, the expedition had shown what might be accomplished or refined once the Pook turtles were available. This was the first large scale naval support sortie for Cmdr. Rodgers' converted packets and the first of three significant fire support missions they would mount alone during the entire war.

In the weeks after November 7, the timberclad mission steadily changed. Beginning in December, the steamers would provide backup and reconnaissance support for ironclad vessels in many of the larger gunboat expeditions to come. Their armor may have been wooden, but their guns remained larger than those aboard any other river vessels save ironclads. This powerful armament would be vital in the support of Union army aims along the riverbanks beyond the walls of secure fortifications. Timberclad cannon continued to make the craft perfect for other roles. In the years ahead, the trio would serve as station or task group flag boats. They would scout and patrol backwaters and provide firepower in the widening war of convoy protection, counterguerrilla operations, and small amphibious raids.[14]

CHAPTER 6

Skirmishing and Fleet Building, November–December 1861

FROM EARLY NOVEMBER 1861 THROUGH JANUARY 1862, the operations of the federal Western Flotilla were conducted, for the most part, by the three gunboats *Lexington*, *Conestoga*, and *Tyler*. These months, the last in which the timberclad trio would comprise the principal fighting units of the U.S. Army's Mississippi nautical unit, were marked by slow fleet growth hampered by manpower concerns, continued reconnaissance and patrol actions, and the development of a new strategy to overcome the Confederate Mississippi fortress at Columbus, Kentucky.

Rebel leaders within their new citadel spent the winter attempting to strengthen its defenses and, like Capt. Foote, attempting to gain additional manpower. Elsewhere, defensive buildups continued along the Cumberland and Tennessee rivers and near Bowling Green. Commanders were important and not changed on both sides, while limited expeditions and skirmishing passed for fighting operations.

Through blasts of cold weather and warm, coupled with sickness, boredom, and some fatigue, soldiers on both sides were frustrated. Many probably felt much like Southern Pvt. John Hubbard, who found his experience at this time to comprise "dreary nights and weary days with many marches throughout the Purchase but to no end except as training."

Even while *Lexington* and *Tyler* were engaged in the Belmont campaign, the smallest timberclad, *Conestoga*, continued her activities as the station ship at Paducah, Kentucky, at the mouth of the Tennessee River. Indeed, on November 7, Lt. S. Ledyard Phelps and the tars aboard his boat were up the nearby Cumberland River scouting for Rebels and contraband. Passing into Tennessee below Dykesburg, the gunboat was taken under fire all along the stream by "riflemen concealed in the woods."

Bullets and buckshot slammed into the oak bulwarks with particular ferocity as the *Conestoga* passed by Tobacco Port. Continuing on, the timberclad approached the location of a new Confederate fort near the town of Dover. Although he could not learn its armament, he did get its name: Fort Gavock. It would later be known as Fort Donelson. On his way back down, Phelps refused to further tolerate the harassment of hidden snipers as he came above Tobacco Port. The *Conestoga* opened fire with her 32-pounders on a hillside barn. One of the shells exploded quite nearby and "dislodged the fellows," who ran from the structure in several directions.

Stopping at the Tobacco Port landing, the timberclad captain informed the assembled local citizens that such guerrilla tactics were unconscionable and he would not suffer them again. If the steamer came their way again and was shot at, she would stop and burn their town. On top of that, any man, soldier or not, who was captured out of uniform would be treated as a murderer (read: shot). Finally, he used the opportunity to warn Tennesseans that he would take or burn any woodpiles left conveniently lying along the bank "for the use of Rebel vessels."

On November 9, Maj. Gen. George B. McClellan issued orders officially reorganizing his military departments west of the Appalachian mountains. The Department of the Cumberland was discontinued and replaced with the Department of the Ohio. The new entity embraced the states of Ohio, Michigan, Indiana, Kentucky (east of the Cumberland River), and Tennessee. Maj. Gen. Don Carlos Buell was placed in command; he would actually take up the assignment a week later.

Simultaneously, Maj. Gen. Henry Halleck was given command of Maj. Gen. David Hunter's Department of the West, now renamed the Department of the Missouri. It was comprised of Missouri and that part of Kentucky west of the Cumberland. Hunter went to a new Department of Kansas, buttressed between Halleck's domain and the Department of New Mexico, under Col. Edward R. S. Canby.

A few days later, on November 13, Capt. Andrew Hull Foote at St. Louis was promoted to flag officer (the U.S. Navy having no admirals at that time). This rank corresponded to that of major general in the U.S. Army and meant that he was no longer subject to the whims of lesser ranking military officers. Foote probably wished that he had received it a week earlier. Perhaps then Brig. Gen. Ulysses S. Grant would not have left him out of the Belmont scrape.

Downstream at Cairo, Cmdr. Henry Walke received a request from Grant for information on the condition and armament of his gunboats. The expatriate Virginia sailor immediately replied that the *Taylor*, as he always called the *Tyler*, was ready for action. Her armament consisted of "two bow guns and four broadside guns (64 pdrs.) and one stern gun (32 pdr.), with small arms for the crew." The *Lexington*, on the other hand, was having machinery difficulties. Under escort of the *Tyler*, the *Lexington* journeyed next day up to Mound City for repairs. When Brig. Gen. Grant learned that both of his gunboats had gone to Illinois, he wired Cmdr. Walke on the morning of November 15 demanding that the *Tyler* return to Cairo and remain there until Cmdr. Roger Stembel's craft was again service ready.[1]

Ever since the contracts were let to him back in August for the seven ironclad gunboats known as Pook Turtles, St. Louis businessman James B. Eads had worked with first Cmdr. John Rodgers II and then Flag Officer Foote to see the project finished. The engineer had subcontracted much of the undertaking to others along the western rivers and in midwestern communities. Unhappily, government payments lagged and completion of the great effort fell behind schedule. Appropriately named, the *St. Louis*, "the first purpose built iron-plated vessel in either Federal or Confederate navies," was launched at Carondelet, Missouri, on October 12. That day was two days after the contract date for delivery of all seven ironclads to Cairo.

The boat, further glorified as the first ironclad in the Western Hemisphere, was in an

THE GUN-BOAT NEW ERA, JUST BUILT AT ST. LOUIS, MISSOURI.—[SKETCHED BY A CORRESPONDENT.]

The fourth timberclad. Prior to her conversion into the ironclad *Essex*, the single-stack *New Era* served for a short period as the little-known fourth timberclad. Under the command of Cmdr. William Dr. ("Dirty Bill") Porter, she made one cruise up the Tennessee River in the fall of 1861 before undergoing her transformation (Naval Historical Center).

advanced state of construction, yet was so well lowered as, in the words of the *St. Louis Daily Missouri Democrat* reporter covering the event, to float "gracefully upon the water, and nobody hurt, and not even a lady frightened." The same would soon be experienced with the three remaining vessels under construction at Mound City. Veteran rivermen were encouraged to inspect the boat (spies, apparently, be damned). Two days later the newspaper reported that the construction, according to the visitors, was "done in a very substantial and smooth manner." Work on the incomplete craft progressed as they lay moored in the Mississippi off the building ways.

In addition to his warship acquisition challenges, including the Frémont-ordered conversions *Benton* (formerly *Submarine No. 7*) and *Essex* (the fourth timberclad, *New Era*)—to say nothing of 38 mortar boats—Foote was tasked with a variety of other organizational challenges. Chief among these was the need to start a naval base at Cairo, to get his new boats to that town, and to come up with sufficient sailors to man this expanding fleet. Foote, and Rodgers before him, had begged the Navy Department for recruits for months. Barely sufficient jacks were on hand to crew the timberclads. Through October 19, only 100 men had volunteered for the ironclads.[2]

By mid–November, Foote's fortunes improved and worsened, depending upon which challenge he was reviewing at any given time. It was true that he had sufficient officers, but problems with an insufficient number of enlisted personnel persisted. By Maj. Gen. John Frémont's command, a large quantity of flotilla stores and cannon rested in St. Louis depots because there was no room for them at Cairo.

The Mississippi was now beginning to fall and it became imperative to get these items, as well as the Carondelet-built gunboats, downstream. As the level continued to drop, everyone realized, however, that the gunboats themselves might be stranded if an attempt were made to send them down fully loaded with their guns and goods aboard.

The Upper Mississippi was fraught with navigational problems at the best of times. Its 68 consecutively numbered islands were variously spaced from the river's source down to the junction of the Ohio River. In the 200 mile stretch between St. Louis and Cairo, there were 35 such atolls, plus snags, steamboat wrecks, and other obstacles. Sandbars and shifting shores swallowed islands and — more importantly — steamers. While refreshing himself to write *Life on the Mississippi*, Mark Twain was told that "Between St. Louis and Cairo, the steamboat wrecks average one to the mile — two hundred wrecks altogether." It was down this increasingly risky stream that Flag Officer Foote had to send the U.S. ironclads and their auxiliaries if they were to make it to Cairo before spring. As they passed, those crewing them would encounter spectacular outcroppings and colorfully named islands and obstacles.

Among the most dangerous locations encountered was Hat Island, which disappeared around 1869. It was located opposite the mouth of Degognia Creek in Jackson County, Illinois Hat Island was the scene of famed pilot Harold Bixby's "Hat Island Crossing," described in Chapter 7 of *Life on the Mississippi*.

Further down in Jackson County was the community of Grand Tower and across from it was the remarkable 90-foot limestone landmark Tower Rock, or Tower Island. Hugging the Missouri shore, it was saved by President Grant from demolition when the postwar U.S. government set about managing the river. Other scenic rock neighbors included the Devil's Bakeover and the Devil's Table.

Cape Girardeau has been mentioned several times in this text, though the relatively pacific Steersman's Bend below the town has not. Beginning at Thebes and running down to Commerce, Missouri, eight miles below Girardeau and also earlier noted, were a great number of sunken rocks called the Grand Chain. "It was arranged to capture and kill steamboats on bad nights," remembered Twain. "A good many steamboat corpses lie buried there."

Hazards below Commerce included Beaver Dam Rock, near the Missouri shore. Goose Island was later reduced to the size of a steamboat, while behind it was another series of shoals known as the Graveyard. It too claimed many craft but later lost all fright as the river channel changed course. Price's Landing, later also deserted, was located on the Missouri shore a little below Commerce. While Foote and Cmdr. Dove at St. Louis pondered with their pilots the perils of the river, the Quartermaster's Department chartered the *Maria Denning* for Foote. She would be the first to run the watery gauntlet.

Late on November 15, Gustavus Vasa Fox, assistant secretary of the navy, wired Flag Officer Foote that 500 seamen would depart Washington, D.C., for Cairo next day under the command of Lt. Richard Wainwright. They were expected to arrive by train at the tip of Illinois the following Monday. The delighted flag officer in turn telegraphed the news to Cmdr. Roger Perry at Cairo the next morning. Perry was to see Brig. Gen. Grant and make arrangements to house the men pending arrival of the *Maria Denning*.

As soon as the wire was off to Perry, Flag Officer Foote turned his attention to his new receiving ship. Cmdr. Dove was called in and told to assist her owner-captain, a man named Carroll, in getting the *Maria Denning* to Cairo. Carroll and his crew would navigate the boat and protect her from fire, marine obstructions, and so forth while the naval officer and his men would guard the naval cargo. The guns, beds, ordnance stores, and other items kept around St. Louis and needed at Cairo would be loaded aboard over the next couple of days. Indeed, with ordnance alone, her cargo would consist of 82 cannon, 100 shells, 120,000 cannonballs of different sizes, and 400 grape shot.

The *Maria Denning* served as receiving ship at Cairo from November 1861 through April 1862. Racing against the onset of low water and rumors that Confederate guerrillas under Brig. Gen. M. Jeff Thompson planned her destruction, the 870-ton side-wheeler undertook her journey down from St. Louis to the tip of Illinois under escort of the timberclad *Lexington*. Although Thompson was in the vicinity, he did not attack (Naval Historical Center).

Once the *Denning* landed at Cairo, Dove was to inform Brig. Gen. Grant that she was the Western Flotilla's receiving ship. His men were to assist Cmdr. Perry in receiving and securing in proper storage the transported goods. Additionally, Dove was to receive and house the men coming to him from Washington and other sources.

After Dove's interview, Flag Officer Foote next turned his attention to getting down the first ironclad in accordance with the suggestion of Brig. Gen. Meigs. The *St. Louis*, by this time, was nearly finished, although she remained to be armed and otherwise outfitted. Cmdr. John Winslow, yet another "restored" officer sent west, was ordered to take her to Cairo with a skeleton crew from the receiving ship *Emerald*.

Winslow was cautioned that the Pook turtle was still owned by James B. Eads and was, in fact, still in his charge. She would remain his property as workmen strove to finish her downriver. Winslow and 25 seamen were to provide only crew and a guard. Afterwards, using government passes, he and all but two mates were to return to St. Louis by train. In addition to Winslow and his jacks, Foote would ask Brig. Gen. Samuel R. Curtis, St. Louis post commander, to detail an Army lieutenant and 25 soldiers to act as marines.[3]

During the day on November 16, the *Conestoga* lay off Uniontown, Kentucky. She had been ordered there the day before by Paducah district commander Brig. Gen. Charles F. Smith in response to a request from Brig. Gen. William Tecumseh Sherman, who was in command of U.S. forces in eastern and central Kentucky. The fiery red-haired officer, who would become the second-best known Union general after Grant, had heard that a force of Rebels was about to descend upon the place.

Scouts sent out from the gunboat were unable to determine any movement. A man waving a Colt navy revolver rode down to the bank near the gunboat, shouting hurrah for Jefferson Davis and cursing the Yankees. Lt. Phelps sent an armed party in a yawl toward shore to apprehend him, but, before they could reach the rascal, he "took to his horse and raced through the streets of the place for the country."

That evening, Lt. Phelps, satisfied there was no organized and immediate Confederate activity near Uniontown, got underway and steamed down to the mouth of the Cumberland. There his vessel coaled and took provisions aboard. Early on November 17, the *Conestoga* departed Smithland and steamed as far upstream as the new fortifications at Dover would permit. Lt. Phelps was particularly pleased to find no wood facilities for Dixie-leaning steamers running contraband. Even better, no one fired on his boat from the banks or even from the Tobacco Port area where he had experienced so much difficulty earlier.

As the little black gunboat paddled along, the people in homes along its route remained indoors. They did not flee to the woods as they had earlier, "impressed with the belief that we were state prison felons let lose upon them to ravage." At dusk, the *Conestoga* anchored in midstream near the state line with Kentucky. The *Lexington* also returned to Cairo that Sunday, allowing the *Tyler* to return to Mound City and her guardianship of the three Pook turtles then finishing construction at that location.

Next day, following a slight delay for fog, the *Maria Denning* began her hazardous journey to Cairo from St. Louis. Cmdr. Stembel at Cairo received a wire from Flag Officer Foote early in the morning ordering him to proceed to Cape Girardeau and provide convoy for the receiving ship as she steamed from that point down. Stembel was to inform Grant, not ask him, that Foote required him to "go on this duty as the steamer has our guns and valuable ordnance stores on board."

A narrative review of the timberclads' involvement in the transfer of the receiving ship and of the first Pook turtles from Carondelet to Cairo has not previously appeared in print. The *Lexington*'s skipper not only conferred with the brigadier, but also wired the information up to Cmdr. Walke. Once Cmdr. Stembel returned from the telegraph office, his boat stood up the Mississippi. About 1:30 P.M., lookouts saw Rebel cavalry on the Missouri shore below Price's Landing.

Bright and early on Monday morning November 18, the *Conestoga* resumed her descent of the Cumberland River. As she reached the landing at Canton, Kentucky, lookouts determined that most of the people in the town and vicinity had fled. The local decorum was quite different from what it was when the gunboat had ascended. A local citizen, German by birth, hailed Lt. Phelps and reported the reason for the quiet.

Under the command of a determined former Memphis slave owner, a group of 300 cavalrymen from Hopkinsville, who had arrived "after a fatiguing night-march of eight hours," had supposedly taken a fieldpiece about two miles down the river. They had received information that the *Conestoga* was intent upon destroying a Confederate commissary storehouse near the landing. The Rebel leader's name was Nathan Beford Forrest and his horsemen, the Forrest Cavalry, were believed to be feverishly attempting to erect an earthwork from which to engage in "the then novel operation of an attack by cavalry on a gunboat."

Instead of two miles away, the gun, a 4-pounder, was actually masked on the outskirts of Canton, concealed in the brush and timber and behind logs on a wooded point behind a gully that ran nearly parallel with the river. This concealment effectively prevented the gunboatmen from seeing the piece. Most of the dismounted horsemen were also concealed, "while a few were displayed with the hope that a party of marines might thus be inveigled ashore and entrapped."

As Forrest's biographer, Dr. Wyeth, later put it, "The commander of this craft, however, was too clever to be caught in such clumsy fashion." Phelps stopped short, but his boat was still near. From a distance of less than 50 yards, the cannon was fired, getting away just two rounds in Forrest's first battle.

Anticipating trouble, the *Conestoga* was beat to quarters and puffing slowly downstream when attacked. She rounded to and employed her stern gun as it came to bear, but she was unable to get back to the point before Forrest's men had hauled the gun out of sight into the gully. Still, four men stationed under cover 30 yards away now opened fire on the steamer with their Maynard rifles. Sgt. (later Maj.) Thomas B. Sheridan received "the honor of firing the first shot in action by the Forrest Cavalry." With heavy small arms fire also whizzing into the oaken bulwarks from a couple of log houses, Phelps ordered his gunners to spray grape shot and canister into the woods and structures in an effort to clear them out. "The broadsides from the heavy armament of the gunboat," Wyeth later wrote, "made his [Forrest's] position untenable."

Unhappily for the enterprising naval officer, his men could not disperse the Confederates before they were able to limber up their gun and make a clean getaway back to Hopkinsville. On the other hand, the only damage suffered by the gunboat was a large number of holes in the chimneys and the loss of a chimney guy. Sheridan and his three fellow marksmen all missed from close in.

Bedford Forrest was also pleased. His green troops stood their ground and "did not seem to be greatly disturbed by the tremendous noises which the Federal batteries and the screaming missiles were making." This first ever fight between horse soldiers and gunboats went to the U.S. side. It would not be the last such encounter; however. The final battle between U.S gunboats and Forrest's command, at Johnsonville on the Tennessee River in 1864, was not only won by the "Wizard of the Saddle" but was also spectacular.

While en route to Smithland after the Forrest firefight, the *Conestoga* encountered the steamer *Pink Marble* headed upstream toward Tennessee towing a large barge. A boarding party was rowed over to the 71-ton stern-wheeler for the usual contraband inspection. While an officer examined the little boat's papers, the crew found a cargo of machinery destined for the McMinnville cotton factory. Although the sailors anticipated another prize, it was discovered that her documents were in order and had all of the necessary customs stamps. They had to let her go.[4]

Fog again delayed the voyage of the *Maria Denning* on November 19. During daylight (only the bravest — or most foolish — passed at night), the craft steamed by Hat Island. Sure enough, Capt. Carroll's command grounded on a sandbar in 5½ feet of water a little south of the atoll. Two hours were required to set her free.

That morning, the *New York Times* correspondent Franc B. Wilkie, who employed the penname "Galway," visited the Carondelet boatyard to examine the state of gunboat construction. "The greatest activity prevails," he informed his readers, and it was anticipated that the craft would be completed within three weeks. A large American flag was seen to flutter from the top deck of the *Benton*, while further below a temporary sign was nailed bearing the motto "For Memphis and New Orleans."

While all on-scene hands labored to free the *Denning* from her Hat Island trap, Flag Officer Foote, in St. Louis once again, as he had earlier in the month, instructed James B. Eads to move the Carondelet ironclads down to Cairo "on account of the falling of the river and the advanced state of the season." Foote recognized that Eads still controlled the vessels under terms of his contract, but he also understood that their Cairo delivery was very late. He believed the craft were far enough along to make such a journey and promised to provide a guard and any other aid possible so long as it did not interfere with the terms of the contract.

Alerted to some difficulty, Cmdr. Stembel and the *Lexington* elected to steam north of Cape Girardeau, all the way to Tower Island, to meet the *Maria Denning*. At Girardeau, it was learned that Confederate Brig. Gen. M. Jeff Thompson was nearby preparing to cut Dove off somewhere near Price's Landing. The sailor did not know that a large party of "Swamp Rats" had arrived at Price's Landing after a 53-mile ride in less than 10 hours.

Thompson had it in mind to intercept the government-chartered steamer from St. Louis. According to eyewitnesses aboard another boat who spoke with him later in the afternoon, the commanding Swamp Rat knew that the *Maria Denning* would be guarded and that he could probably not capture her. "He wanted to sink her," they remembered, and quoted Thompson saying "'By G-d' she would not get down to Cairo." Men were hidden, so it seemed, behind every paw-paw bush from Price's Landing down to Cairo awaiting their chance.

When opposite Price's Landing, about 4:00 P.M. or 5:00 P.M., a steamer thought to be the *Denning* was hailed by two men from shore garbed in military overcoats. They were taken by the steamer captain for Federal scouts. They had been informed by one O.D. Barrett, lately exchanged as a Camp Jackson soldier, of the steamer's cargo, and met Thompson while en route to Cairo and points south.

As the unsuspecting boat came into the bank to meet the pair, one of them raised his hand and 200 men jumped out of hiding. A hundred soldiers, led by one of the scouts, stormed aboard the vessel only to learn she was Capt. William C. Postal's *Platte Valley* and not the *Maria Denning*. The two who had hailed were the disguised Brig. Gen. Thompson and his adjutant.

Agreeing to free the civilian boat rather than sack and burn her, Thompson nevertheless interviewed the several U.S. officers aboard and took their parole. Additionally, he searched the vessel high and low for Yankee documents. Once the search was concluded, eyewitness federal agent B. F. Livingston later testified, Thompson had "a barrel of common whiskey rolled out for the benefit of the band."

After his business was completed, Thompson and his men departed the *Platte Valley*, which crossed the river to the Illinois side. There one of Agent Livingston's associates procured a horse and sped off toward Cairo. Livingston's messenger rode the 25 miles down to Cairo in two hours. Dashing into army headquarters, he immediately warned that 200–400 Confederates awaited the *Maria Denning*. Brig. Gen. Grant quickly sent word of this development to Cmdr. Walke aboard the *Tyler* and simultaneously ordered a regiment of infantry and an artillery company to board the *Aleck Scott*. Within a short time, the largest timberclad and the biggest Northern troopboat were steaming to the rescue.

As the *Lexington* passed Price's Landing, according to a St. Louis newsman quoted by Frank Moore, Brig. Gen. Thompson and his men lay in wait. They were so close to the gunboat as she passed, Thompson bragged, that his "marksmen could have killed every man on board." Additionally, he had four cannon masked in the brush behind the bank.

Among the cargo being transported to Cairo aboard the chartered *Denning* were several 32-pounders. The *Lexington* and Cmdr. Dove made rendezvous near Tower Island and Cmdr.

Maj. Gen. Charles F. Smith (1897–1862) commanded U.S. troops under Grant from September 1861 to March 1862, at which point he temporarily succeeded him. Invalided by a foot injury, he died from blood poisoning. Smith was very reliant upon the gunboats during this time in command at Paducah and greatly appreciated the work of Lt. S. Ledyard Phelps and the *Conestoga* (*Battles and Leaders*).

Stembel yelled over news of Thompson through a speaking trumpet. Cmdr. Dove now ordered two of the guns removed from storage and mounted on his boat's starboard bow Unhappily, the wind was blowing so hard that it became difficult to handle either the timberclad or the steamer in the turbulent river. Dove and Stembel had hoped to come alongside one another and lash their boats together, then, as they steamed downstream in tandem for a while, seamen could pass ammunition from the *Lexington* to the *Denning*, This did not happen and Dove was forced to rely upon the *Lexington*'s protection exclusively — save a few muskets in the hands of his armed guard.

A little below Cape Girardeau, the *Lexington* and *Maria Denning* were met by the *Tyler* and *Aleck Scott*. This task force had the means of defeating any attack from Thompson. The four vessels maneuvered into convoy formation, with one timberclad in the front and one in the rear, and steamed down to Illinois Point, where they made fast for the night.

Earlier in the day, the *Platte Valley* tied up at Cape Girardeau, where her skipper and his clerk, Tom White, were taken into custody and charged with aiding Thompson's seizure. Capt. Post was, or so the *Chicago Daily Tribune* reported, "well known among steamboat men as a secessionist." It took the steamer captain a week to clear his name and win release.

As soon as the *Maria Denning* and her consorts reached Cairo at 9:00 A.M. on November 20, Cmdr. Dove hurried to the telegraph office to wire Flag Officer Foote's 30 West Fifth Street headquarters in St. Louis: "Arrived safely." The message was sent directly from Brig. Gen. Grant's office with him standing nearby. Unhappily, the recruits expected from the East had not yet arrived.

Fuller details of the episode were telegraphed to Foote by Cmdr. Perry, who also indicated the *Denning*'s cargo, save for the guns and ammunition, was rapidly discharged onto the wharf for movement to other storage. These and other stores and provisions would eventually be transferred to the wharf boat *Graham*. By November 29, wrote a correspondent for the *Chicago Evening Post* quoted in the *New York Times* a week later, there were "21 carloads of ammunition, consisting of round shot, shell, grape and canister" available. "Officers, marines, pilots, engineers, and the whole ship's crews are here," he continued, "ready to take charge as fast as they arrive." Soon, with *Graham*, *Emerald*, and *Maria Denning* available for housing and storage, Foote had a good-sized station.[5]

Brig. Gen. Grant ordered Cmdr. Walke on November 21 to have both *Tyler* and *Lexington* present at Cairo next day. It was anticipated that they might have a role in the transfer of the first two ironclads from St. Louis. Walke simultaneously received a letter from Lt. Phelps congratulating him on his part in the recent Battle of Belmont and lamenting the fact that he could not be present.

Later that Thursday, the eastern bluejackets arrived at the Cairo railroad station and were immediately marched over to and onboard the *Maria Denning*. Already present were several "Western men, principally steamboat hands, with a few Lake sailors." When the newcomers were mustered, Cmdr. Dove found a number missing. These stragglers would come in over the next week.

Just after 8:00 A.M. on November 22, the *Tyler* arrived at Cairo from Mound City and dropped anchor. Orders were sent over to the *Lexington* by small boat for a reconnaissance down the river. With the *Tyler* in the lead, the timberclads stood down the Mississippi. Sometime just before 11:30, the two rounded to at the foot of Island No. 4 and fired four shells at suspected Confederate targets. The little shoot over, the wooden steamers returned to Cairo in reverse order of their departure.

During the day, Maj. Gen. Polk at Columbus was much relieved. Commodore Hollins, the service of whose fleet was requested from the secretary of the navy, had arrived with one of his boats. Which one is not certain, possibly the *General Polk*. "The whole, six in number," the commander noted, "are expected in the next two or three days."

As if to spur both Foote and Eads, Brig. Gen. Grant wired the former that morning informing him that the depth of the Mississippi was just six feet. "Would it not be well," he queried, "to send the gun-boats while it is possible?" As always seems to be the case in wartime, the best laid plans often meet delay.

Also that Friday, Flag Officer Foote telegraphed Cmdr. Stembel to proceed up the Mississippi with the *Lexington* and the *W.H. Brown* to meet the *St. Louis* and the *Pittsburg*, both of which he planned to start down on Saturday morning. The towboat and her gunboat consort could expect to find the Pook turtles near Hat Island. There they were to assist them in getting over the shoals.

Lt. James W. Shirk, aboard the *Emerald*, was now ordered to take 25 hands from his vessel and repair aboard the *Pittsburg* as its temporary skipper. En route to the boat he was to speak with Cmdr. John Winslow of the *St. Louis* and make arrangements with him for the departure of their boats to Cairo. Aboard the *Pittsburg*, all necessary arrangements were completed for departure, including the mounting of a single 12-pounder boat howitzer for defense.

Preparations for getting the ironclads downstream were noticed by the St. Louis newspapers and the problems involved were duly reported. Anticipated cold weather could lower the stages near Hat Island to just over four feet, bottling up the vessels better than any Confederate blockade. On November 23, the concerned *St. Louis Daily Missouri Democrat* warned that "the gun-boats, not quite finished, will not be able to get out of the Mississippi River, unless they are sent away within a few days."

On Sunday evening, Cmdr. Winslow received a message from Flag Officer Foote acknowledging that preparations for getting the *Pittsburg* underway were behind schedule. If it did not appear that she could be gotten ready by noon next day, her temporary captain was to proceed to Cairo in the *St. Louis* without her. Through Herculean efforts, Lt. Shirk was able to have the *Pittsburg* ready for departure by 8:00 A.M. on Monday morning, November 25. The two ironclads, accompanied by the tugboat *Sampson*, departed "for down the river" at that hour,

Downstream at Cairo that day, Brig. Gen. Grant informed Washington that the strength of Columbus had reached a point making it almost impossible to capture by land: 47 regiments of infantry, field artillery, and cavalry, plus 8,000 more soldiers at Camp Beauregard, between Union City and Mayfield.

Further below at Memphis, Lt. John Julius Guthrie, C.S.N., arrived from New Orleans to take command of the floating battery *New Orleans*, which was being towed up to Columbus from the Crescent City. Finding that the converted Pelican Dry dock, originally based at Algiers, Louisiana, had not yet arrived, he sought her out, finally taking command near Columbia, Arkansas.

Fourth Master S. Kellogg of the steamer *Tigress* later sent Cmdr. William D. "Dirty Bill" Porter a description of the *New Orleans* when she lay off Island No. 10. She mounted 10 guns, he claimed: one 9-inch, two or three rifled Parrotts, and the remainder unknown. The first volume of *ORN*, Series II, states that her armament at this time consisted of 20 guns: two 32-pounders, seventeen 8-inch Columbiads, and one 9-inch Columbiad.

She could, Kellogg revealed, be "sunk to water's edge at pleasure; her engine was too weak to enable her to maintain any position in the current." *ORN* says she had two small boilers, with connections for pumping. The vessel was not unlike what Cmdr. John Rodgers II had feared that, the previous spring, James B. Eads wanted to create for him out of the *Submarine No. 7*.

The *St. Louis* and *Pittsburg* duly made rendezvous on November 26 with the *Lexington* and *W.H. Brown* in the vicinity of Hat Island. With the *Brown* moving astern of the ironclads to offer possible assistance, the *Lexington* came alongside of the *Pittsburg* to receive a 9-inch hawser from the latter. As she approached, she stove one of the cutters hoisted on an after davit. Once under way, the quartet had no reported difficulty with shoals in that area and continued steaming slowly south. Proceeding without incident, the three gunboats and their auxiliaries reached Bainbridge, Missouri, on the afternoon of November 27. The small hamlet, no longer inhabited, was located 8–12 miles above Cape Girardeau, near Egypt Mills.

As the gunboats passed in the river offshore, the hawser between the *Lexington* and *Pittsburg* suddenly parted as the latter grounded on a gravel bank. When the ironclad struck abruptly, the *W.H. Brown* behind could not stop and slammed into her stern just inside of the starboard rudder. The impact carried the transport completely through her plank-sheer. With forward movement now ended, Cmdr. Winslow ordered every effort made to free the Pook turtle as soon as possible. Labor as they might, however, jacks from all five vessels were unable to free the *Pittsburg* before dark.

On November 28, Brig. Gen. Grant wrote to Maj. Gen. Henry Halleck at St. Louis, via his assistant adjutant, Capt. John C. Kelton. Confirming that one of the two timberclads stationed at Cairo had gone up the Mississippi on Monday to meet two of the new ironclads, the brigadier indicated that none had arrived. He then went on to launch into a statement of displeasure with the Eads program.

"I have been much dissatisfied with the progress making upon the gunboats being built at Mound City," he wrote, "and have expressed the fear that the detention of those being built at Carondelet would prevent their being brought out this Winter." In light of the traditional December decline in the level of the Mississippi, Grant urged Halleck to order the Carondelet gunboats transferred to Cairo as soon as possible — and as lightly as possible.

No sooner had he completed his message than Grant could hear the whistles of the *St. Louis* heralding her arrival. Earlier that morning, the *St. Louis* had departed Bainbridge for Cairo, accompanied only by the *Sampson*. Arriving near lunchtime, Cmdr. Winslow reported to Grant and wired Flag Officer Foote announcing his safe arrival. He also gave it as his opinion that the *Pittsburg* grounding was caused by "carelessness," but that the *Lexington* and *Brown* would probably get her off during the day.

Hands from the *Lexington* and *Brown* joined the few aboard the *Pittsburg* in working to get the ironclad off. Finally, by 2:30 P.M., they were successful. At this point, the *Brown* maneuvered to take the *Pittsburg* in tow and, while doing so, stove in her remaining cutter. Finally ready, the trio resumed steaming downriver and halted for the night at Burnham's Island, where they took on wood for their boilers.

A few days later, Maj. Gen. Sterling Price would receive a letter from Maj. Gen. Polk written at Columbus that Thursday and sent by one of Price's visiting officers. The message testified that Columbus was now so strengthened that it could be considered "safe from any assault the enemy may make against it." Further, the 1st Division commander had the gunboats of Cdr. Hollins' fleet at his disposal.

The *Pittsburg*, *Lexington*, and *W.H. Brown* got underway at daylight on November 29. At 11:30 A.M. when they reached Cairo, it was snowing heavily. The ironclad's temporary boat howitzer was receipted to Cmdr. Perry, along with all of the other stores and equipment. Reporting to Cmdr. Dove, Lt. Shirk also handed over the *Pittsburgh*'s pennant and ensign. While this change in command was underway, the local *Chicago Post* reporter jotted down his impressions of the new arrivals. They were, he observed, "formidable-looking monsters;

nothing can be seen above the water except iron plate, sloping at an angle of about 45 degrees, to glance any shot that may meet it."

With some trip variation, the remaining ironclad gunboats of the Western Flotilla built or remodeled at Carondelet, together with the receiving ship *Emerald*, were transferred, usually with timberclad assistance, to Cairo. Flag Officer Foote believed that his predecessor, Cmdr. John Rodgers II, would have approved of the work being completed on the *Submarine No. 7*, subsequently known as the *Benton*.

Also at Carondelet about this time, Cmdr. "Dirty Bill" Porter, never one to pass up a PR opportunity, pigeonholed "Egypt," the local *New York Times* reporter. With colorful descriptions, he explained to the newsman how, after having set his uniform aside and donned "felt hat and citizens' clothes," he "industriously applied himself to his task" of converting his timberclad into a formidable ironclad.

Having given up on obtaining an assignment from Brig. Gen. Grant and steamed up to St. Louis at the beginning of the month, the "bulldog" fighting man of the flotilla, as *Times* man "Egypt" styled Porter, set to work with purpose. The reporter, scribbling down the seaman's tale, heard how the son of the famous commodore "completely stripped her of everything but the framework of her hull and entirely remodeled, rebuilt, and planked her, strengthened her with additional timbers and knees, caulked her, put in bulkheads, built strong and ample gun decks, cased her hull with iron plates, in fact, constructed a new vessel, carrying nine heavy guns, and floated her out of her dock in fourteen days."

On the fourteenth day, workers and witnesses informed the reporter, the gunboat captain, "without giving notice," simply "opened the gates of the floating dock, let in the water, and, to the astonishment of the industrious artisans aboard, the craft was in her element." In two weeks, 10 days less than the record Commodore Oliver Hazard Perry set in building his fleet before the Battle of Lake Erie, the timberclad *New Era* was an ironclad, which Porter duly christened with a new name, *Essex*, after his father's renowned vessel.

Carondelet and *Louisville* dropped anchor off the Cairo wharf boat on December 5, while *Benton* and *Essex* arrived sometime later due to grounding and other transit difficulties. Getting them manned and ready would consume much of December and January in an interesting and nerve-wracking administrative history outside the scope of this story. To handle their equipping, Flag Officer Foote named Cmdr. Alexander Pennock permanent fleet captain on November 25.[6]

Fear of Confederate gunboat attacks, both from Columbus and the Tennessee River, occupied the thinking of western naval commanders and others in the weeks before Christmas 1861. There was no serious danger on either count, but that was not known at the time.

On November 28, Brig. Gen. Grant informed Maj. Gen. Halleck that, in addition to the gunboat *Grampus*, Maj. Gen. Polk was expecting a fleet of warboats "from New Orleans under the command of Capt. Hollins." Grant warned that its arrival, given the state of his own fleet, would restore enemy confidence that was "now, from best accounts, much shaken."

Also that Friday, Brig. Gen. Smith at Paducah wired a new rumor to the Cairo district commander. Brig. Gen. Grant was informed that two or three Southern gunboats had supposedly made a "reconnaissance" below Fort Henry. Smith himself admitted "that by reconnaissance, I suppose is really meant they were making a trial trip." Grant was asked if he could send a gunboat for a day or two to join the *Conestoga* in checking out this intelligence. If not, was the request, could he please wire Smith's concern to Foote, which action was taken.

At St. Louis on November 29, the *New York Times* correspondent Wilkie again visited the Carondelet boatyards to check on Eads' progress. There he found work progressing "with tolerable activity." Although two "turtles" had already departed, the others would have to leave for Cairo "ere long" or ice in the river would blockade them until spring.

Early on November 30, the *Conestoga* returned to Paducah from an inspection trip up the Tennessee River ordered in response to the gunboat rumor. Lt. Phelps informed Brig. Gen. Smith that he neither saw nor heard of any Confederate gunboats. Smith telegraphed this information down to Grant but still insisted that he required another gunboat.

The gunboat crewmen were undoubtedly dismayed on their return to see the Given, Fowler & Co. wharf boat sunk. Scuttled by an unknown party, it had about 800 tons of U.S. Army stores and ammunition aboard when it went down. Acclaimed as "a true Southern man" by the *Memphis Avalanche*, the same Gus Fowler who owned the fugitive steamer *Dunbar* was part owner.

After refueling and taking on provisions, the *Conestoga* embarked three companies of infantry with a howitzer aboard the *Lake Erie No. 2* and *New Golden Gate* and set off with them for the Cave-in-the-Rock area. There he would, in Brig. Gen. Smith's words, "look after Rebels at Caseyville."

Brig. Gen. Grant did not have Brig. Gen. Smith's morning message before he wired Flag Officer Foote repeating the Paducah man's contention that two or three Rebel gunboats had made a reconnaissance down the Tennessee River below Fort Henry. He passed along Smith's request for a gunboat, indicating that he had none to spare. The *Lexington* was in the Mississippi, while the *Tyler* guarded the Eads gunboats at Mound City.

At St. Louis, Flag Officer Foote, who in addition to outfitting the ironclads had also to worry over Rebel gunboat threats, was quite concerned with reports about Southern gunboats in the Tennessee River. Were they "larger than ours," he wondered. After lunch, he wired Brig. Gen. Grant at Cairo asking that the *Lexington* and *Tyler* be sent to Paducah. If it were impossible to spare their services, shouldn't U.S. land forces there attempt to block up the river with old barges and so forth as the Rebels further up had tried to do earlier? Phelps and Brig. Gen. Smith were consulted on the matter, Foote indicated, and could advise.

Underreported in all the excitement was another exploit by the indomitable little *Grampus*. During the day, her fearless skipper, Capt. Marsh Miller, took his saucy gunboat near the mouth of a stream not far below Bird's Point. There she landed and, because of "the peculiar color the Captain has had her painted with," she could not be seen "at even a short distance." With several crewmen, Miller stealthily ascended the stream by foot to a spot where a Federal lumber boat was tied up and made prize of it and the 175,000 feet of lumber aboard. They cut it loose and guided it back down to the river, where the *Grampus* took the boat in tow and carried it safely into port at Columbus, where the boards were "put to excellent service." News of this little action appeared in the *Memphis Appeal* and wired from Memphis to Georgia on December 3 and appeared in the *Columbus Daily Enquirer* on December 5. A copy of that issue reached the North and the story appeared in the *New York Times* on December 12.[7]

The Tennessee River was not the only location where what a *New York Times* correspondent on December 3 labeled "the Rebel serpent" was supposedly flexing its gunboat muscle. The Mississippi River south of Cairo, where the Confederate *Grampus* had spied and patrolled for weeks, was another concern — one more real than any further east. The latest worry for Foote, Walke, and the timberclads was a solid fortnight in development.

On November 11, four days after the Battle of Belmont, Maj. Gen. Leonidis Polk, commander of the Confederate 1st Division of the Confederate Western Departmental Columbus, Kentucky, was invited to witness a demonstration of his bastion's most awesome defense. This was the 168-pounder Whitworth rifle christened *Lady Polk*. The giant cannon was the largest in the entire Confederacy and had briefly fired during the recent engagement with Grant's Federals.

When the order to "fire" was given, the *Lady Polk* blew up, along with a nearby powder magazine, killing her gun crew and several officers observing nearby. A number of men were hurt and two were blown into the air and landed on the rocks along the riverbank below. Maj. Gen. Polk, standing directly behind the iron monster, lost his britches and was so badly stunned that he was forced onto sick leave for the next month. With Polk out of action, his command temporarily passed to Brig. Gen. Gideon Pillow. The mercurial Tennessean, whose troops were still under orders for Clarksville, was not content to fill the bishop's seat until he was recovered. No, he still wanted to find a way to take the offensive against Cairo, just as he had attempted to do during the summer.

Two days later, Pillow schemed to obtain Gen. Johnston's permission to move by sending out department-wide daily bulletins and other communications stating that Columbus was under imminent threat of attack from overwhelming U.S. forces. He also wrote to Tennessee governor Harris, Mississippi governor Pettus, and leading Memphis citizens warning that large Northern forces were preparing to attack his "Gibraltar of the West." Anticipating that he would be entirely surrounded in his bluff-top citadel, the Volunteer State's most famous soldier asked Harris to call out all of the militiamen from the western end of the state not already under arms. Further, reports were sent directly to politicians and leaked to the press on the poor state of Columbus' defense. These strongly suggested that any Yankee attack could not be repelled. In addition, Brig. Gen. Pillow sent a message to Cdr. George N. Hollins at New Orleans asking him to bring his fleet up river to the defense of Columbus. Testifying before an investigative committee of the Confederate Congress on September 13, 1862, Cdr. Hollins and Capt. John K. Mitchell revealed the circumstances surrounding the decision to comply with the Columbus request.

Perceiving no immediate threat at New Orleans, Cdr. Hollins believed he "could so something" if he went upstream, particularly since, in his opinion, "there were no [Federal] gunboats of any importance up there." About this same time, Hollins learned of the transfer of the *Maria Denning* from St. Louis to Cairo. He hoped for cooperation from Maj. Gen. Polk upon his arrival. If the Columbus garrison provided assistance, he expected to be able to capture the *Denning*. "To take my three little gunboats on this enterprise without the cooperation asked for," he opined, "would be to throw them away."

The vessels dispatched from New Orleans in November to aid Columbus were the *General Polk*, the *Ivy*, the *McRae*, and the *Jackson*. They were scheduled to be followed in January and February by the *Livingston*, the *Pontchartrain*, the *Maurepas*, and the floating battery *New Orleans*, which latter, in fact, was present before Christmas.

Through the years, there has been some dispute as to whether or not this list is accurate for the months prior to Christmas 1861. Lt. Charles W. Read, executive officer of the *McRae*, later indicated that the group included his ship, plus the ram *Manassas*, the *General Polk*, the *Jackson*, and the *Calhoun*. We choose to believe the list of Cdr. Hollins, whom Scharf calls "the better authority." The *Manassas* attempted the journey, but was damaged, according to the *Savannah Republican*, around December 4, before reaching her destination. After repairing at Memphis, she returned downstream.

We have already described the *McRae* and the *Jackson* (also known as the *Yankee*), the latter having visited the area earlier. The *General Polk* and the *Ivy* are new to our story. Purchased at New Orleans in 1861 for $8,000, the 390-ton side-wheeler *Ed Howard* was rechristened *General Polk* in honor of the Columbus defender. Constructed at New Albany, Indiana, in 1852, the gunboat was 280 feet long, with a beam of 35 feet and an 8-foot depth of hold.

Although details of her power plant are unknown, they were probably standard for her type. The *General Polk* originally carried three 32-pounder naval cannon and was protected by railroad iron cased on her foredeck. Built in 1845 as the *Roger Williams*, the *Ivy* was a 447-ton side-wheeler sold prewar to become *El Paraguay*. On May 16, 1861, she was purchased by Southern interests as the privateer *V.H. Ivy*. She was acquired at New Orleans later in the year for conversion into a gunboat. *Ivy* was 191 feet long, with a 28 foot beam and a nine foot depth of hold. She was powered by one vertical condensing beam engine, with 44-inch diameter cylinders and an 11-inch stroke. Her battery had a gun mounted forward and another aft. On November 12 she carried one each 8-inch smoothbore and a 32-pounder. Her crew totaled 60 officers and men.

While Hollins was paddling upriver, Gen. Johnston, who was taken in by Brig. Gen. Pillow's propaganda, cancelled the transfer of the Tennessean's division. Governor Harris, for his part, called up 30,000 volunteers. These actions caused Pillow to change tactics and now suggest that Columbus would be strong enough to defend herself after all. In fact, it was now time to mount a campaign against Grant's outposts. Almost as soon as Hollins reached Columbus, it is probable that he met with Brig. Gen. Pillow and the two hatched a plan for a demonstration toward Cairo. The commodore from New Orleans would be the first off.[8]

Sunday, December 1, in the Cairo-Columbus area was cold and gloomy, with a stiff breeze and intermittent snow showers. It was the sort of day when anyone would want to stay indoors. Military activity was so slight that newspapermen wrote stories about the comfortable new winter quarters (log cabins) being constructed for the soldiers. For her part, the *Tyler* was on a 16-mile round-trip reconnaissance of the Mississippi.

According to the *Memphis Avalanche* of December 5, Cdr. Hollins' task group departed Columbus between 10 and 11 o'clock A.M. Toward noon, lookouts at Fort Holt spied three unknown steamers ascending the river below Bird's Point and fired a warning signal. Just as its sound was dying away, a puff of smoke could be seen at the bow of the most forward boat. A cannonball was seen to skip along the water like a flat rock before it sank.

Onward the dark shapes came, as Brig. Gen. Grant reported to Maj. Gen. Halleck, to "within about half a mile of range of the nearest point of the camp at Fort Holt." According to Daniel Ambrose of the 7th Illinois, Union witnesses initially received "a little fright."

The Rebel boats were undoubtedly the *General Polk*, *Jackson*, and *Ivy*. Picking up the story in his report, Fort Holt's 7th Illinois officer of the day allowed the trio to close within four and a half miles. Deeming it "imprudent to allow them to progress further," he ordered his batteries to open fire, beginning with the *Lady Grant*, an 8-inch counter to the *Lady Polk* at Columbus. Her shot, fired from the extreme left of the camp, dropped within 200 yards of the lead steamer. The second Confederate gunboat now opened up and, like the first, fired short. Her challenge was met by another 8-inch U.S. cannon from the right side of Fort Holt. In turn, three more Confederate shots came whizzing along to do no damage. At least two Northern bullets overshot their targets.

The *Memphis Avalanche*, in reporting the duel, indicated that Hollins' gunners fired 15 rounds into Camp Holt. During this cannonade, Federal soldiers were seen running for cover, scampering "out of their tents and log huts in great haste." At the same time, lookouts saw a gunboat anchored in the channel about half a mile below Cairo and the *Maria Denning* at the wharf. There was "no response," boasted the newspaper, "either from Cairo, Bird's Point, or Camp Holt." While this exchange was underway, a troop of cavalry and a company from the 28th Illinois were dispatched down the shore to see if they could determine any Rebel intention, either from the river or by land in the rear of the fort. Both parties returned, having uncovered no enemy plans.

As the *New York Times* reporter Franc B. Wilkie told his readers in a December 3 column printed on December 12, the Rebels, after five or six shots, were "Apparently satisfied with this timid demonstration." The three "Dixie tubs" came about and headed back to Columbus, pursued by a Yankee gunboat the newsman believed to be the *Tyler*, but which was, in fact, the *Lexington*. The timberclad followed for seven or eight miles, but could not get close enough to hurl an 8-inch greeting.

Rumors, meanwhile, reached Cairo that Confederate land forces were planning to descend upon Fort Holt. Rapid preparations, including the addition of more cannon, were completed. At Cairo, Cmdr. Dove, the senior naval officer present, sent a message to Cmdr. Walke ordering him to return with the *Tyler*. He also pushed even harder the outfitting of the *St. Louis* and *Pittsburg*. Cannon were rushed aboard the latter that night.

Upon her arrival early that evening, the *Tyler* received orders from Brig. Gen. Grant, through his aide, to steam down with the *Lexington* to Fort Holt. The two timberclads were to remain offshore overnight to protect the Kentucky outpost from an attack by Hollins' gunboats. Walke sent a note to Cmdr. Stembel, via Grant's aide, asking him to follow him down, but the *Lexington* did not move from her anchorage.[9]

When the *Tyler* returned to Cairo on the morning of December 2, a thoroughly miffed Cmdr. Walke conferred with Grant and Flag Officer Foote on Stembel's "disregard to the instruction of the general commanding." They suggested he pass along the order again. When Cmdr. Stembel still did not transfer to Fort Holt, Walke turned the matter over to his superior, asking Foote to give the order. The Flag Officer, sensing that the Rebel gunboat threat was probably contained and needing the *Lexington*'s availability to help his ironclads in the Upper Mississippi, did not immediately act.

The three Confederate gunboats from Columbus again came up in sight of Fort Holt during the afternoon. Once more, they fired several rounds toward Fort Holt, which were returned from the battery there, as well as at Bird's Point. When the firing was heard at Cairo, Brig. Gen. Grant immediately went aboard the transport *W.H. Brown*, which took him over to Bird's Point, from which he hoped to see any gun duel.

Grant did not reach the Missouri shore in order to see any cannonball exchange. Having accomplished their goal, the Rebels went about and made back downstream. After they disappeared around the bend below Bird's Point, a few shells were fired over in that direction from Fort Prentiss at Cairo. The shells, according to Irving Carson of the *Chicago Daily Tribune*, "flew over the Mississippi across Bird's Point and cropped in the river beyond, a distance of over two miles."

At the time of the Rebel appearance, the *Lexington* was lying in the Ohio off Cairo. It took her an hour to get steam up and depart, by which time the Confederate boats had obtained such a good start that they were impossible to catch. Cmdr. Stembel continued down toward Lucas Bend but did not sight Cdr. Hollins' craft. The timberclad returned to her Cairo anchorage before dark.

On December 4, Flag Officer Foote interviewed "a clever observing officer" just back from Columbus under a flag of truce concerning the rumors of an attack on Cairo. The reconnaissance made by Hollins' boats a few days earlier was said by the legal spy to have been for the purpose of mapping Cairo's weak points. From this discussion and other news, the naval leader determined to remain vigilante in the short term, but was "inclined to believe that no offensive move from the enemy will take place."

Maj. Gen. Polk returned to duty on that Wednesday. Brig. Gen. Pillow, still in an offensive mindset in his first visit of the day, petitioned his superior for permission to mount an attack. With Hollins' assistance, he believed he could sink the Yankee timberclads and whatever ironclads were present and capture Fort Holt, Bird's Point, and maybe even Cairo. After hearing out the Tennessean, the bishop refused to allow the plan's execution.

Having argued with Pillow off and on during the fall regarding prospects for an offensive, now that he had returned to duty Maj. Gen. Polk chose to resume defensive planning and operations. His division and brigade officers supported his contention that they were not prepared to move out and that Columbus, if not weak, was not yet quite impregnable. They, too, turned in reports. Theirs concerned Northern strength upriver and led their commander to believe he would be attacked by 50,000 bluecoats any day and hence the need for further strengthening of the citadel. This obsession caused him to refuse all requests to send reinforcements elsewhere, including the Tennessee and Cumberland rivers, and this would play into Maj. Gen. Halleck's hands in January.

Writing from Memphis on December 5, inventor A.L. Saunders informed Maj. Gen. Polk that he had just returned from the railroad station where he had forwarded 19 of his improved submarine batteries to Columbus. Col. William B. Richmond of Polk's staff already had the plans for placement, which Cdr. Hollins would understand. As soon as the remaining 31 mines in the order were built, Saunders would bring them along.

At Cairo that Thursday, the flag officer hoisted his flag aboard the *Lexington*. Cmdr. Stembel's boat would be his flag boat. She would, however, now also assume her place with the *Tyler* off Fort Holt. Civilian steamers under contract would assist the remaining ironclad gunboats coming down from Carondelet. It was now raining heavily and "the Father of Waters" was beginning to rise.

On December 6, the flag officer wired U.S. Army commander McClellan at Washington that his Western Flotilla consisted of 12 gunboats, three of which — the timberclads — were in commission. If Eads turned the ironclads over by the 18th per his promise, Cmdr. Pennock and he would have them ready for active service by the end of the month — assuming of course that the 1,100 men needed to crew them were forthcoming.

A copy of the "Little Mac" memo was also telegraphed to Maj. Gen. Halleck's St. Louis headquarters with the observation that the *St. Louis*, though still technically in Eads' hands, had her armament aboard and could be used for base defense if necessary. Her new commander would be Lt. Leonard Paulding.[10]

On December 7, the Cairo correspondent for the *Cincinnati Daily Commercial* learned that six Rebel gunboats were at Columbus. The newcomer to the group already present (which included the *Grampus*) was the long-awaited *J.B. Howard* from Memphis. The heavily armed gunboat had been promised to Maj. Gen. Polk by Samuel Tate back in late October. Today, we know almost nothing about the *Howard*.

The Queen City newsman went on to confirm that the *Manassas* was repairing at Memphis, having broken her battering ram. Additionally, another gunboat, the *Tuscarora*, caught fire off Helena, Arkansas, on November 23. The *Memphis Avalanche*, in a report probably not read by the journalist, recorded three days later that she was run aground. During the day, the *Conestoga* eased into the *Graham* wharf boat at Cairo. There she received a large quantity of supplies and ammunition before casting off to return up the Ohio to Paducah.

While guarding Fort Holt about 7:00 A.M. on the morning of December 8, lookouts aboard *Lexington* and *Tyler* spotted eight pontoon barges drifting down the river from Cairo. Nervous gunners at the nearby base took them under fire and one was holed by a 32-pounder ball, which went through its side and lodged inboard. The timberclads hoisted anchor and steamed down after the mavericks, halting their descent and bringing them to. Over the next hour or so, the boats of Cmdr. Walke and Stembel each towed four barges back to Cairo where they were left. *Tyler* and *Lexington* then returned to their Fort Holt anchorage, their tars having experienced the most excitement in a week.

During the time of the Confederate gunboat scare at Fort Holt, Brig. Gen. Smith at Paducah had received an urgent request for evacuation from a number of pro–Union families in the Linton, Kentucky, area on the Cumberland River. When the *Conestoga* returned from a two day visit to Cairo, she was sent upstream to find them. Approaching Linton on December 8, the gunboat fired two signal guns by prearrangment. She then moved down toward the lower end of State Line Island, where Phelps expected to spend the night while the refugees came in and assembled. That evening, Lt. Phelps received word that Confederate guerrillas were prowling the nearby woods with the intent of attacking any parties attempting to escape to the gunboat. The enterprising lieutenant then took his gunboat back down to Linton itself, where the loyal Kentuckians were taken onboard.

Harrowing tales of escape were heard by Lt. Phelps and his officers. They also learned that Confederate authorities were intensifying their efforts to fortify the Cumberland River below Dover. In that little town, many virulent diseases were supposedly about and Rebel troops were dying from them. Leaders in Nashville feared visits from the timberclads or the new ironclads, according to the loyalists, and were making every haste to place additional obstructions in the river.

Major General Lew Wallace (1827–1905) was no stranger to the captains of the timberclads. In early 1862, he was a guest aboard the *Conestoga* on one of her nautical reconnaissance missions up the Tennessee River towards Fort Henry. It was his corps that Lt. James Shirk sought to protect early in the action at Shiloh in April (U.S. Army Military History Institute).

Most ominously, the *Conestoga* men heard reports of ironclad gunboats being built on both the Cumberland and the Tennessee. On the former, two were supposedly being built, one each at Clarksville and Nashville. Three gunboats were being constructed on the Tennessee, all represented as being covered not with iron plates, which proved a failure, but with thickly compacted bales of cotton. The most formidable vessel was a 280-foot giant called the *Eastport*.

Dropping anchor off Paducah, Lt. Phelps received orders on the 9th to steam up the Cumberland once more to locate and retrieve additional refugees. Additionally, he was to participate in a unique case of smuggling in reverse. Once her coaling was completed on December 10, the smallest timberclad initially puffed up toward Fort Donelson. Phelps was not able to get close to the new works. As he later explained to his superior, "I have been to the bend where a boat's length would have placed us in sight, but their [artillery] practice has all been precisely at that point."

In addition to gathering intelligence on the growth of the Southern bastion, the gunboat provided cover for Kentucky loyalists, who, to keep them out of the hands of guerrillas, brought small caches of arms to Linton. The *Conestoga* lay to downstream from the citadel on December 11–12.

Unnoticed by anyone on the U.S. side, military or press alike, the Confederate floating battery *New Orleans*, towed by the steamers *Baltic* and *Red Rover*, arrived at Columbus during the day under the command of Lt. John Julius Guthrie, C.S.N.

Early on the 12th, the *Conestoga* lay off Linton taking on a small bounty. Though not huge by usual contraband standards, the ploy did keep 10 muskets and a number of rifles and shotguns out of unfriendly hands. That afternoon, the gunboat returned downriver, making stops along the way in Christian and Trigg counties, Kentucky, to board 60 additional escaping Kentucky loyalists.

There was movement off Fort Holt on that Thursday afternoon as well. Leaving the *Tyler* as guard, the *Lexington* steamed up to Cairo after lunch to pick up Cmdr. Stembel and Flag Officer Foote. Continuing past her forward anchorage, the gunboat was joined by the *Tyler* on a reconnaissance down as far as Cook's Bend, made principally for the flag officer's benefit.

When the timberclads returned to Fort Holt in mid-afternoon, they were met by the new Eads gunboat *St. Louis*. Led by Walke's boat, the three steamers paddled down to Norfolk on a little shakedown cruise for the ironclad. At 4:30, the vessels rounded to and the *St. Louis* fired a couple of practice ("experimental") shots at a target near the Missouri base.

While the *Conestoga* was up the Cumberland, the journalists from the *New York Times* were actively seeking stories to send back to editor Henry J. Raymond. "Egypt" reported on the arrival of the Pook turtles and the ironclads *Benton* and *Essex*. Indeed, he rode down with Cmdr. Porter aboard the latter and was able to take notes firsthand on her many groundings and other adventures prior to her arrival on December 13.

Coming ashore from the *Essex*, "Egypt" found a copy of the latest issue of the *Columbus Confederate News*. Gleaning its pages, he was able to pass on its information that five gunboats now lay below the citadel's guns and that Maj. Gen. Polk was recovering from his injuries. Interestingly enough, Brig. Gen. Grant sent a message to Flag Officer Foote later in the day warning that he expected a Confederate attack to be made upon either Bird's Point or Fort Holt that night or next day. The gunboats should be kept ready, just as he was having four regiments of troops sent aboard transports. The alarm was sounded earlier by reports coming over from the Rebel lines. Picket lines were strengthened and word was sent to St. Louis, where Maj. Gen. Halleck was assured that everyone was prepared and his soldiers "were sleeping on their arms."

Hardly was the ink dry on Grant's message to the navy on that December 13 when, according to "Egypt," three Confederate gunboats, probably the same three which had come up on December 1, made an appearance, loitering below, everyone supposed, "for the purpose of planting submarine batteries." Foote, aboard the *Lexington*, and with the *Tyler*, was in the vicinity and close enough to receive a signal from Fort Holt that the Rebels were out. The two timberclads immediately turned in pursuit, but their enemy was too far away to overhaul. A couple of shots were sent after them, "which hastened their retreat," though, in truth, all that could be seen was "receding smoke beyond Norfolk."

Other than the gunboat sortie, time for the "Condition Red," to borrow a modern alert equivalent, came and passed with no advance by Maj. Gen. Polk — not even a skirmish. Grant's troops stood down or came ashore, while the gunboats returned to their normal routine. Years later, Bruce Catton wondered about Grant: "Did a memory of this fiasco remain with him and lead him, at Shiloh, to relax his guard when he had a Confederate Army in his immediate front?"

Writing from St. Louis during the day, the *New York Times* correspondent "Galway," whose real name was Franc B. Wilkie, tried to offer his readers some perspective on the magnitude of naval preparations at Cairo. "Salaries of the officers reached $60,000 per month," he noted, "while 500,000 bushels of coal have been contracted for and delivered at Cairo." He reported that "clothing to the amount of $40,000 has been contracted for and is on its way hither," while "800 tons of powder have been sent to Cairo."

Next day, "Egypt" took the opportunity to visit Columbus with a flag of truce team sent down by Brig. Gen. Grant to discuss POW issues. While there, he interviewed Cdr. Hollins. "After conversing a half hour with him, fully willing to do justice should he merit it," "Egypt" opined on December 15 in a column sent for publication on the 21st that "I parted with the impression that he is even a greater humbug than the *Manassas*, his pet project." Still, Hollins, who knew Flag Officer Foote in the prewar navy, wanted to pass along his regards. According to Wilkie in the December 31, 1861, issue of the *New York Times*, the Southern sailor was constrained to admit that Foote was 'the right man in the right place.'"

Writing from Paducah, also on December 15 for publication in the same issue as Wilkie, another *New York Times* correspondent, employing the penname "Tennessean," gave his readers detailed early information on both Forts Henry and Donelson. Much less was known about the latter position, he stated. It was believed to "stand on the low grounds near the river." Steps were being taken by the enemy to place fortifications all along the stream, at Clarksville, Harpeth Shoals, and Nashville.

At least 10 steamers plied the Tennessee River between Fort Henry and the Muscle Shoals, he revealed, including one which ran regularly between the fort and a railroad crossing 18 miles above. "A fossilized individual, very much respected once, but now quite fallen and degraded — I mean John Bell," the reporter opined, was hard at work trying to get the Tennessee Legislature to fund gunboat construction on the Cumberland. Nothing had as yet come of the idea.

"Tennessean" concluded his intelligence briefing with a word on new Rebel defenses in the river near Columbus. Submarine batteries (also known as "torpedoes" or mines) were placed in the Mississippi between Polk's bastion and Memphis. Designed to destroy units of the U.S. flotilla, they were anchored in such a way as to be struck by the hull of a passing vessel and exploded on the contact. They were, he learned, arranged so that they could rise or sink with the water level. In great secrecy, successful experiments were supposedly conducted with drifting rafts.[11]

Breaking up the monotony of garrison duty, soldiers at Columbus were able to witness gunnery exercises during December 17–19 by the floating battery *New Orleans*. After beating to quarters at 9:00 A.M. on the first date, Lt. Guthrie exercised his men, but he was not pleased. "The 8-inch, 9-inch and rifled shell proved almost useless," he confided to the deck log, "some exploding within 20 feet of the muzzle." Next day, the cannoneers sent their shell at targets 2,600 yards off. "Nearly the same result as before." Finally, the commander was able to report progress. "Very favorable results" were achieved in practice with hollow shot on December 19.

In a communication to Maj. Gen. Halleck's headquarters on December 18, Brig. Gen. Grant reported the latest intelligence on the Confederate gunboats at Columbus. Coming from both a Federal spy and a deserter from the *Grampus*, it indicated that three of the enemy vessels had returned down the river. It is uncertain whether the information was accurate. It is known, however, that the *Manassas* had long since gone back. Franc Wilkie of the *New York Times* expressed the doubt of many concerning the Rebel fleet at Columbus when he wrote home:

> Most of the New Orleans tugboats draw from 10 to 12 feet, and hence it is an entire impossibility that they could ever get up as far as Columbus— hence the story of the New Orleans fleet having arrived at Columbus is, to say the least, highly improbable. It will not be far from the truth to

put the entire force at Columbus at from 20–35 thousand men — their gunboats at three, and the balance of the fleet at a half dozen tugs and lesser steamers.

"Egypt," the *New York Times* journalist at Cairo, reported on December 19 that the *St. Louis* and *Essex* were ready for action. Machinery changes were, however, being made on the others. Along with other nuggets for his readers, the journalist also reported on the new Columbus river defenses everyone in camp was talking about: the giant cable to be stretched across the Mississippi. It would be held on either side by giant anchors of the kind already referenced elsewhere in this book. Additionally, he gave the number of submarine batteries (mines) in the river as two dozen.

A correspondent from the *St. Louis Daily Missouri Democrat* found naval matters to be "the principal features of attraction in Cairo" on December 22. Activities on land had all "subsided into a very profound and uninterrupted quiet." On the banks and wharves of the Ohio and Mississippi, activity was everywhere. The newsman's colorful description, which also appeared in the December 28 issue of the *New York Times*, allows much credit to the work of Flag Officer Foote and Cmdr. Pennock: "The gunboat fleet is anchored in the stream or flying by the levee; the little tugboats and ship launches manned by gallant man-of-war men, are lying about hither and thither; the sound of the hammer and chisel and saw, and the busy notes of industry arising from all marine quarters, give Cairo just now considerable of the appearance of a navy-yard."

Although physical activity may have been slowed, the administrative workload of Brig. Gen. Grant increased on December 23. On that date, his District of Southeast Missouri was enlarged to include Kentucky east of the Cumberland River and the southern counties of Missouri south of Cape Girardeau. The enlarged command, which now included Brig. Gen. Smith's District of Paducah, was relabeled the District of Cairo.

As Christmas approached, Flag Officer Foote began assigning captains to his new ironclads. Among those slated for new commands were Cmdrs. Walke and Stembel. On Christmas Eve, the former wrote his superior asking if it would be possible for him to transfer over the entire crew of the *Tyler*. Noting that, for the good of the service, breaking up his crew was not acceptable, Foote refused his old comrade. Walke would have to train a new group.

Responding to an order from Foote, Lt. Phelps, long since one of the flag officer's favorites, brought the *Conestoga* to Cairo several days before Christmas. Arriving on Christmas Eve, Phelps, who had his wife and daughter aboard, was honored by a Christmas visit from his commander. While the squadron leader visited, his lieutenant had a chance to slip ashore and purchase some toys to give his youngster when she awakened aboard next morning.

As 1861 came to a close, naval affairs on the Mississippi below Cairo remained, for the most part, quiet. There was one local problem which forced Cmdr. Walke to appeal for help. For some weeks, the soldiers at Fort Holt, which the *Tyler* was guarding, were holding musket practice, during the course of which they occasionally shot in the direction of the timberclad. The bullets came within such close proximity that "the whiz of the ball as it passed could be distinctly heard."

The *Tyler* changed positions three times to avoid any mishaps, but, on the morning of December 29, a minié ball struck one of the gunboat's cannon and glanced into a porthole. Another hit her upper deck. The same life-threatening accidents occurred next day. Three balls narrowly missed the officer of the deck, passing over his head, while a fourth hit the water near where a seaman was washing out his hammock. Cmdr. Walke complained to Flag Officer Foote and also the army about the matter, with a colonel from the latter promising to have the direction of military target practice changed.

This wonderful photograph of the *Tyler* shows the largest of the timberclads tied up to a riverbank. The time and location of the shot is not known, but that does not matter as much as the extraordinary detail visible. Here one can see something of the alterations that turned the *Tyler* into a gunboat, gain perspective of her size from the men on the bank, and note something of shipboard routine in the laundry hung out to dry (Naval Historical Center).

Lt. Phelps and his family were back at Paducah as the year finished. On his just completed round-trip to fleet headquarters, the Conestoga's captain was reminded of a problem that had faced his nation since the war began: contraband trade across the Ohio. Off Paducah on December 30, Phelps wrote to Foote detailing the Ohio River smuggling situation between Evansville and the mouth of the Tennessee. Unscrupulous steamer captains would stop at points along the Kentucky shore to deposit illicit cargoes obtained in both Illinois and Indiana. Sometimes these boats also hauled U.S. government mail.

With the capability to seize steamers at any time, Confederate forces had so far not done so because of the great advantage in goods, information, and communication they had thus far offered. On the other hand, they also promised to burn the boats if the Federals stopped the cross-river mail service, The *Conestoga*'s captain recommended that mail steamers be allowed to land only at fixed points along the north bank of the Ohio. He also reviewed with his superior the general opinion given him by Northern sympathizers along the Kentucky shores. All uniformly agreed that they were protected from violence at the hands of their Dixie-leaning neighbors "only through fear of the gunboats."

Caseyville remained a problem area and Phelps on several occasions warned its civilian leaders of the consequences to the town of violence against loyal people by guerrillas or other Rebel outfits. It was his hope that at Shawneetown, another trouble spot often molested by Confederate riders, a special force of infantry and cavalry provided by Illinois governor Richard Yates and trained by Brig. Gen. Grant would be a big help. When active, this "Shawneetown force" could halt smuggling between Shawneetown and the Cumberland River.

In a quiet moment on New Year's Eve, Flag Officer Foote wrote a private letter to his friend and Washington colleague, Assistant Navy Secretary Fox. In it he reviewed flotilla progress and some of its personnel. Noting that both Cmdrs. Perry and Winslow were sick or hurt and that he expected to lose both men to other posts, he confirmed that Lt. Shirk had also been unwell but had recovered. Shirk, who would suffer several illnesses while in the west, would be ordered to the *Lexington* in the next couple of days and sent to work with Lt. Phelps out of Paducah.

And so it was that 1861 came to an end. In his *Grant Moves South*, the great Civil War historian Bruce Catton summarized the situation as it applied, primarily to the North: "1861 was the year of preparation, the year in which a singular tangle of conflicting strategic plans, personal rivalries, and the slowly emerging imperatives of civil war would presently bring forth new opportunities and new actions." For the inland navy, it was a year of birth, growth, and tentative operations. The infant squadron of Cmdr. Rodgers and Flag Officer Foote would start to mature as 1862 began and would quickly face its first major combat trials.[12]

CHAPTER 7

Fort Henry: Preparations and Battle, January–February 1862

NEW YEAR'S DAY WAS JUST ANOTHER DAY IN THE OFFICE for Flag Officer Andrew H. Foote and his officers. His first order of business was the timberclad *Lexington*. Cmdr. Roger Stembel, who had already been promised an ironclad, was sent an order detaching him from the wooden gunboat and assigning him to the new *Cincinnati*. Next, Lt. James W. Shirk was asked to take over the *Lexington*. Once he had her coaled and provisioned, he was to take her up to Paducah and report to Lt. S. Ledyard Phelps.

Phelps, who probably heard about Shirk's promotion from Foote over Christmas, was offered the next message. In it, he was notified that, as soon as Lt. Shirk arrived at the mouth of the Tennessee, he would be the senior officer of a two-boat task group. Flag Officer Foote, who had taken his subordinate's December 30 message so seriously as to send copies to Maj. Gen. Henry Halleck and Don Carlos Buell and Brig. Gen. Ulysses Grant, now required that Phelps' unit more vigorously guard the Union's extensive interests along the margins of the Ohio, Cumberland, and Tennessee. These assignments completed, the flag officer got off a letter to Navy Secretary Gideon Welles noting Lt. Phelps' new responsibilities. He then turned to the work of his growing naval base, including final preparations to his ironclad flotilla.

Next morning, as Lt. Shirk took command of the *Lexington*, Flag Officer Foote received a request from Brig. Gen. Grant asking that he detail a gunboat to drop down to the head of Island No. 1 to protect the steamer *Rob Roy*. That stern-wheeler was being sent to bring up produce he was purchasing from loyal Kentuckians. Foote passed the message to Cmdr. Walke who executed the wish with his *Tyler*.

At Columbus, Maj. Gen. Leonidas Polk, considering himself under siege, had built up his defense to include 150 cannon and over 21,000 soldiers. This was the largest force anywhere in Gen. Albert Sidney Johnston's entire department. Still, as historian Thomas Connelly tells us, the military bishop's "fear of attack had become almost pathological."

Strategic planning on the Northern side in the west was almost as bad, though somewhat different in practice. Instead of a stubborn commander defending a city, President Abraham Lincoln and Maj. Gen. George B. McClellan found themselves with two generals (Buell and Halleck) who prized their own territories and couldn't agree to attack anywhere. As January began, both of the president's commanders made excuses about why they could not communicate, cooperate, or most importantly, advance somewhere.

On January 3, McClellan, ignorant of Maj. Gen. Polk's fundamental defensive principle, wrote to Maj. Gen. Halleck. It was "of the greatest importance," the U.S. Army's top general spelled out, that reinforcements from Columbus not be sent to aid Confederates near Bowling Green, Kentucky. The reason: Brig. Gen. George H. Thomas had just departed Lebanon, Kentucky, with his 1st Division of the Army of the Ohio headed toward East Tennessee.

To prevent a Rebel transfer, "Little Mac" suggested expeditions and demonstrations, supported by gunboats, up both the Tennessee and Cumberland rivers and against Columbus itself. If the latter place was vulnerable, it "should be taken." Also, whatever kind of mission was sent out, it "should be done speedily, within a few days."

Around 9:30 A.M. on the same day, the ironclad *Essex*, accompanied by the timberclads *Tyler* and *Lexington*, made their own demonstration, proceeding down from Fort Holt to reconnoiter Columbus. As Cmdr. Porter's one-time timberclad came in sight of the Iron Banks, she wore around and lay to. The *Tyler* followed suit as did the *Lexington*. Observations only were conducted by both sides.

About 1:00 P.M., the Yankee warboats started up the river in column ahead: *Essex*, *Tyler*, *Lexington*. As they rounded a bend, a Rebel steamer, called *Mohawk* in the *Tyler*'s logbook, but more likely the *Grampus*, hove in sight standing toward them. The *Tyler* came to on the port side of the *Essex* and the *Lexington* on the *Tyler*'s port quarter. All three in succession wore ship and stood downstream about half a mile before coming to. As the *Grampus* sped away, the *Essex* sent two shells after her without impact; Capt. Marsh Miller had his gunners return one. The day's chase over, the U.S. vessels returned to their advance anchorage.

Sometime between January 3 and 5, the flag officer and Brig. Gen. Grant, no doubt in one of their many discussions, agreed that a reconnaissance south to check on rumors of Confederate submarine batteries was something which should not be put off. It is apparent from the timing of the McClellan letter noted above that this was, at least initially, an independent decision by the Cairo military-naval leadership. As things turned out, it would play well as part of a larger program.

On January 5, Lt. Shirk was summoned back to Cairo from Paducah. He was to tell no one of his return save Lt. Phelps or Brig. Gen. Smith. These new orders were discussed with both his superior and the Cairo district commander before the *Lexington* steamed down the Ohio later in the day.

As was his position for months, Brig. Gen. Smith did not think it prudent, in light of rumored threats against Paducah, to leave the town without a guardboat. Still, he also wanted to have the latest intelligence regarding Fort Henry. Meeting with Phelps after Shirk's departure, the bewhiskered brigadier was convinced by his younger colleague that Confederate Tennessee river gunboats or land forces currently posed no problem.

With Smith's reluctant agreement, the *Conestoga* departed "for up the river" on January 6. The water level in the Tennessee was barely sufficient to float the timberclad, but she managed to ascend as far as the state line. Nothing new was learned about Fort Henry, a work still deemed formidable. Despite many rumors about the bastion, some heard along the way, Lt. Phelps believed that about all there was to know about its batteries and the offshore river obstructions was already known.

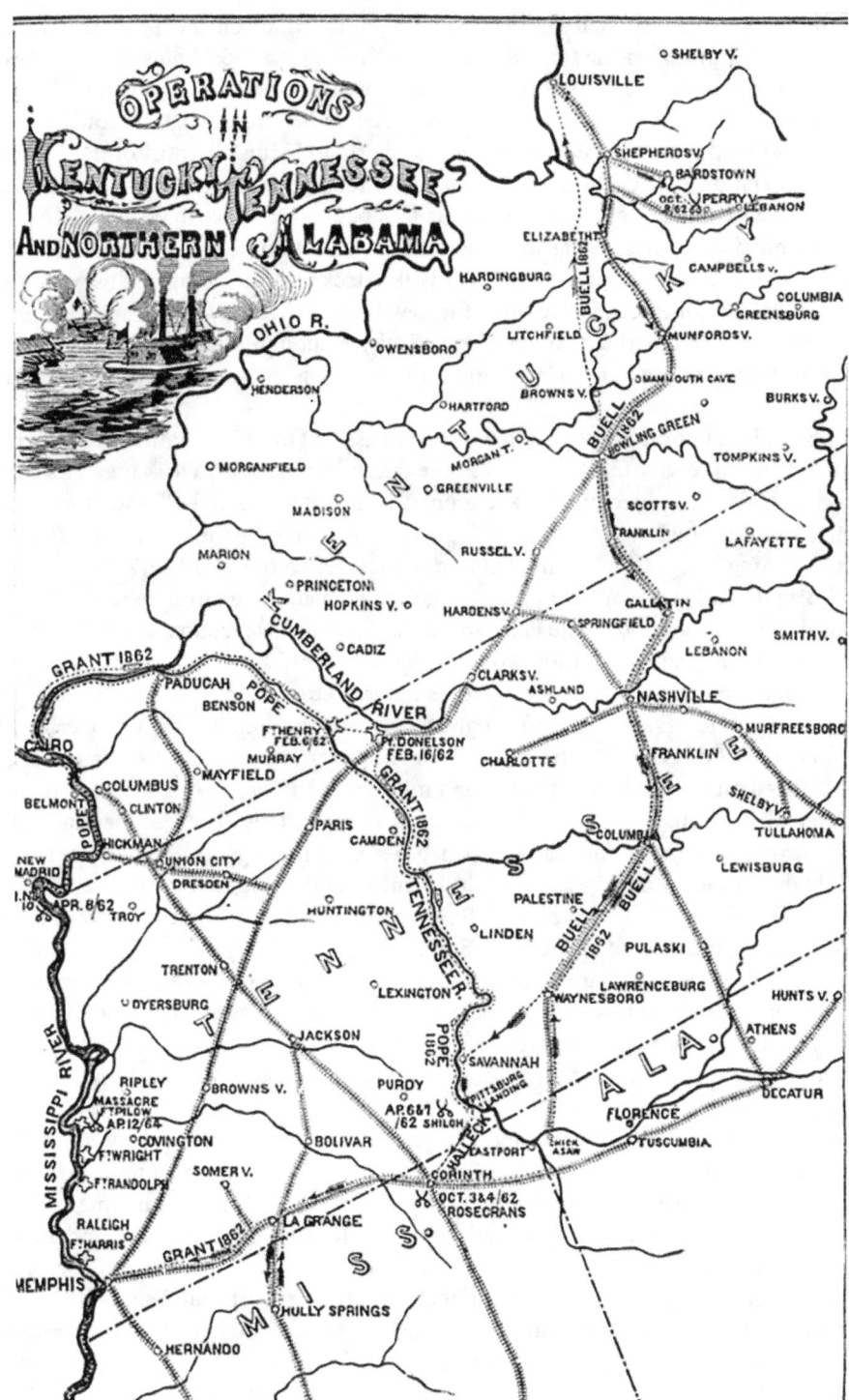

The Tennessee and Cumberland rivers provided a pathway into the heart of the Confederacy for Union gunboats almost from the beginning of the Civil War. Union skippers like Phelps, Gwin, Shirk, and Fitch roamed these rivers hunting guerrillas, guarding convoys, and assisting Federal military forces in operations large and small (Lossing's *Pictorial Field Book of the Civil War*).

While the smallest wooden gunboat battled falling water on the Tennessee River, the *Lexington* reached Cairo. At the same time, Maj. Gen. Halleck at St. Louis sent two messages of interest to our story, the second more so than the first. Lincoln, who had been pressing both Buell and Halleck for action, received word from "Old Brains" that he could spare only 10,000 troops to aid his colleague east of the Cumberland. After all, most of the men he had were either green or busy dealing with military matters in Missouri. After sending this letter off to his commander in chief, Maj. Gen. Halleck penned an order to Grant, asking that his offensive-minded Cairo-based brigadier make a demonstration toward Mayfield, Kentucky.

Such a feint should convince Maj. Gen. Polk attacks were coming against either Camp Beauregard, below Columbus, or possibly the new Rebel fortresses, Henry and Donelson, on the Tennessee and Cumberland Rivers, respectively. Although Grant could "menace" these locations, he was absolutely not to turn his demonstration into an engagement as he had at Belmont.

Although Flag Officer Foote was to be asked to assist, Grant's real mission was to be kept secret even from his own officers. To aid in the deception, he was to leak the news that Fort Donelson was his true objective. "Make a great fuss about moving all your forces toward Nashville," "Old Brains" suggested, "and let it be so reported by the newspapers."

That evening, Brig. Gen. Grant sent a message over to the new Bird's Point post commander, Brig. Gen. Eleazer A. Paine, ordering that a cavalry squadron be readied to depart next morning along the shore while Flag Officer Foote made his reconnaissance. Within a day or so, an even more grand operation would be launched.

Early on the morning of January 7, the *Conestoga* returned to Paducah. Her skipper had hoped to move on to review building progress at Fort Donelson, but the Cumberland River was too low above Eddyville. Lt. Phelps, did learn, however, that tree trunks, chained together, had been placed on the left bank of the river a mile and a half below the Rebel fortress, in the sharp bend where it first became visible to approaching vessels. The Cumberland was only 150 yards wide at this point and the sharpened heads of the logs, facing downstream, were just below the surface. Phelps was also told by informants, not having yet been able to see for himself, that Donelson's right bank battery was on a hill a half mile back from the bank.

While conveying this information to Smith and Foote, Phelps also noted that the forts, especially Donelson, were situated where no great range could be had against them from the river. Additionally, they could only be attacked by gunboats steaming in one narrow and fixed line. There was no space to maneuver in circles as Walke did before Belmont on November 7. On the other hand, if the river rose, some of the disadvantages might disappear due to a higher river stage.

Having no idea why his commander wished Shirk's services, the *Conestoga*'s captain petitioned for her speedy return. With her, he was confident he could watch not only the Cumberland and the Tennessee, but also make trips along the Ohio. With time to loiter at Caseyville, Uniontown, Carrsville and other points, Rebel communication and smuggling routes might be sealed off.

As Lt. Phelps was writing out his Cumberland River report that Tuesday, Flag Officer Foote began his Columbus mine-hunting reconnaissance promptly at 8:00 A.M. His task force comprised the ironclad *Essex*, two tugboats, and the timberclads *Tyler* and *Lexington*. Engineer Corps Col. Joseph D. Webster, from Brig. Gen. Grant's staff, along with some of his lieutenants, joined the fleet commander aboard Walke's timberclad. The Bird's Point cavalry company accompanied the boats along the Missouri shore, with Belmont their destination.

The *Essex* and her wooden consorts weighed anchor about 9:30 A.M. and started downstream, following a small steamer that lookouts had spied off the foot of Island No. 1. The

U.S. craft ran down within range of the Confederate batteries, reaching the vicinity of Island No. 3 about 10:00 A.M. Although the Iron Banks cannon were quickly manned, the U.S. boats were not challenged. Foote, who was not interested in finding masked batteries, withheld his fire as well. The bars, points, and bends of the river were carefully examined. Watching the enemy, the correspondent of the *Memphis Appeal* and nearby officers found it "apparent, however, that the object of the expedition was merely to reconnoiter, if possible, the position of our submarine batteries, infernal machines, etc."

Neither Flag Officer Foote nor anyone else on the U.S. side knew that the floating battery *New Orleans* was present at Columbus and prepared to contest any Yankee naval raid. Her skipper, Lt. John Julius Guthrie, kept a diary and a brief extract from it details the activities of his command this day: "Enemy approaching about 10 o'clock A.M. Mr. Samuel Burnham volunteered his services and was accepted by Captain Guthrie, who placed him in charge of gun No. 3. Beat to quarters. Sunk the dock and prepared for action. About 1 o'clock P.M. the enemy returned toward Cairo. Our men willing and anxious for a fight."

Captured after the fall of Island No. 10, the logbook of Guthrie's command also contains an interesting entry: "Beat to quarters; five gun-boats coming down the river. Did not come within range. Our consort, *Red Rover*, got up steam and got out of danger. The battery, having been sunk, was pumped out."

While the U.S. gunboats sought to confirm rumors of "dangerous obstacles" (read: A.L. Saunders' submarine batteries or mines) or a cross-river chain in the Mississippi, the *Grampus* put out from the Columbus wharf. Lurking out of range near Belmont point, she spied on the Federals as they examined the water "to ascertain the real object of their visit." Only one submarine battery was located during the search. The *Grampus* had become something in the thorn of Union military and naval officers. Among correspondents, she was known as a "species of spouting fish, and this particular one frequently runs up the Mississippi to blow and then runs down again."

Satisfied that there were no other obstructions, "at least until within range of the Rebel batteries," Foote turned on Marsh Miller's boat and ordered her pursuit. Undoubtedly led by the *Lexington* and *Tyler*, the chase was, as usual, fruitless, as the enemy, in the words of *Times* correspondent "Egypt," "whirled and ran away." The Yankees fired several rounds after the *Grampus*, one of which supposedly fell "about 50 feet short." The Confederate gunboat quickly came under the protection of the Columbus batteries, which fired one warning shot at the timberclads.

Once the exercise was completed, Foote's task force returned to Cairo. The flag officer and Webster told "Egypt," who talked to the officers just after they landed, that they were publicly pleased with their outing and "confident of being able to run under the Rebel batteries, if it should require too long a time to shell them out." The cavalry company, possible witnesses to the naval action from the Belmont area, went back to Bird's Point.

The excursion, the noise and jarring of the *Tyler*'s guns, and other strains gave Foote a severe headache. (He had these quite frequently and they occasionally forced him out on sick call.) It was probably left to Col. Webster to report on these marine events to Brig. Gen. Grant.[1] Still suffering from headache, Flag Officer Foote ordered Lt. Shirk back to Paducah on January 8, sending along a note to Lt. Phelps asking him to be certain to cooperate with Brig. Gen. Smith.

While waiting for the *Lexington* to rejoin her, the *Conestoga* was not idle. In the same bad weather that plagued the men around Cairo, the smallest timberclad engaged in a trip up the Ohio River to Caseyville. Her exact mission was to find and protect a detachment of men at Rock Quarry, Kentucky, near Carrsville, who were threatened by Rebel attack.

During the windy, cold and rainy day, marching orders came down from Brig. Gen. Grant's headquarters to his outposts at Bird's Point, Fort Holt, and Paducah, as well as Fort Cairo, once known as Fort Prentiss. As the infantry and cavalry tended to their gear and horses, quartermasters sought transport wagons sturdy enough to travel over winter roads.

Upstream in St. Louis, the *New York Times* correspondent Franc B. Wilkie heard and read the announcement of the long-expected "advance." Believing it would get underway without him, "Galway" hurried to the railroad station, jostled with many others trying to board a southbound express, and secured a seat for Cairo.

On January 9, a recovered Foote met with Brig. Gen. Grant to discuss the "troop expedition planned by General Halleck." Shortly thereafter, he received a written request: The expedition being fitted out would begin deployment that evening when steamers took Brig. Gen. McClernand to Fort Jefferson; several gunboats were requested in order to accompany the force and remain with it, anchoring where they might best offer protection.

After the meeting at Cairo army headquarters, the flag officer wrote out orders sending the *Lexington* and *Conestoga* up the Tennessee. He also took a moment to pen a separate note to Lt. Phelps asking him not to unnecessarily expose his vessels to danger. He hinted at the greater army-navy work that was coming by indicating that he could not join him with heavier boats as soon as he hoped. Demonstrations were sometimes made in war, he opined, when the objective was to avoid serious fighting. Smith, who was privy to Grant's plans, could, he suggested, elaborate.

Phelps did not immediately receive Foote's message. Heavy fog on the Ohio forced him to remain anchored during the early part of the day and he did not reach the vicinity of Carrsville until late in the afternoon. Determining that the workers were in no real danger, the *Conestoga* started back down the Ohio about nightfall.

Foote also penned news of Halleck's reconnaissance in a message to Navy Secretary Gideon Welles. Reviewing his part of the plan, the flag officer revealed that he had ordered the *Lexington* and *Conestoga* up the Tennessee River. He would also send the *Essex* and the *St. Louis* down the Mississippi in convoy of Grant's troopboats and would follow the ironclads aboard the *Tyler* in time to join them when the expedition moved farther down.

The timetable for Grant's initial advance from Cairo could not be met. Rain and cold had conspired to create a blanket of fog. It had yet to lift by noon. If it did not dissipate soon, the steamboats, aboard which troops were assembled, would be unable to depart. "The fog is so dense," the brigadier wired Maj. Gen. Halleck, "that it is impossible to cross the river."

When Franc Wilkie got off the train from St. Louis that morning, he fully expected that the military advance was away. He "broke" for a livery stable to overtake the expedition and when he asked the owner for a horse, he was laughed at. Although the levee was alive and there were tugs and steamboats aplenty in the river and the camps were still crowded with men, there was no advance.

Wilkie went up to Army headquarters and found "a quiet-looking man in a farmer's dress, lazily smoking a meerschaum — and he was the departing general." Grant and his staff were reading and reviewing "the dispatches of a telegraphic reporter for a St. Louis journal." They all appeared to be going nowhere. McClernand's departure was, indeed, put off until morning. Perhaps not accounting for the fog and unhappy that he had rushed down from St. Louis, "Galway" was disappointed. How did dispatches happen to have been published announcing the advance was already underway?

Checking around, "Galway" learned that they were the product of "some government official, handed by him to the agents of the St. Louis and Chicago papers, and, of course, forwarded by them under the supposition that they were reliable." In fact, it was asserted that

Foote's gunboats en route to attack Fort Henry on the Tennessee River. The initial convoy included troopboats as well as naval craft and it halted above Panther Island to offload the soldiers and allow the flag officer to make preparations for his assault. The timberclads are among the vessels depicted here (*Harper's Pictorial History of the Civil War*).

the St. Louis papers were a party to the deception and that Maj. Gen. Halleck himself had originated the canard. Wilkie did not believe the latter assertion. "Old Brains," he assured his readers, was "at once too much of a gentleman and a soldier to perpetrate a huge lie upon the public, even under the pressure of a military or other necessity."

Before lunch, Cmdr. Porter received orders to escort McClernand's transports with his ironclad and the *St. Louis*. Foote promised to come down and join him aboard the *Tyler* in a day or two and the ironclads were not to move until he arrived. The *Times* correspondent "Signal" was aboard the *Essex* and would remain with Porter over the next several days to paint a detailed picture of life aboard his man-o'-war.

In the predawn darkness of January 10, the *Conestoga* returned toward Paducah from her Ohio River sojourn. En route, she found a steamer making a suspicious landing at Hurricane Island, Kentucky, and another backing away from the landing at Ford's Ferry. Sending boarding parties to investigate, Lt. Phelps, to his great disappointment, found that both were licensed to make such landings. There were no prizes on this trip. The *Conestoga* paddled to Paduach late that afternoon and found the *Lexington* anchored off the wharf.

Later Friday morning, Flag Officer Foote informed Cmdr. Porter that Brig. Gen. McClernand's brigade would leave for Fort Jefferson, near Island No. 1, at noon. He was also advised that one or two steamers might proceed as far as Island No. 2 and that one of the ironclads should, in that event, provide escort.

The flag officer still expected to join Porter aboard the *Tyler* on Sunday. Watching from the *Essex*, "Signal" noted that McClernand's troopboats were host to "some 15,000 or 16,000 men, besides horses, baggage wagons, artillery, and all the necessary implements of war."

Under convoy of the *Essex* and *St. Louis*, McClernand's brigade was able to get away during the afternoon. The steamboat armada was fairly long. Several hours after weighing anchor, the troopboats landed eight miles down at the mouth of Mayfield Creek, on the Kentucky shore, where tents were immediately pitched.

Before the expeditionary force from St. Louis could shove off, a steamer blocked the Mississippi River channel north of Cairo when it ran aground. It would be freed the next day. About the same time the transport grounded, Brig. Gen. Grant received a telegram from Maj. Gen. Halleck ordering a delay until he heard more about "movements elsewhere" supposedly being made by Maj. Gen. Buell. Early on January 11, threatening movements were spied near Norfolk, Missouri. Brig. Gen. McClernand sent a massager aboard the *Essex* to warn Cmdr. Porter that three unidentified warships were headed his way on a reconnaissance, together with several other vessels towing a floating battery, possibly the *New Orleans*.

The two ironclads beat to quarters at 10:00 A.M., according to "Signal," and weighed anchor. Under cover of a dense fog, they drifted down with the current to investigate. Within a short time, the troops at Fort Jefferson were able to hear loud cannonading. One of their number, Lt. W.H. Heath, was hustled back up to Cairo by tugboat to inform Brig. Gen. Grant.

As soon as the brigadier heard the news, he sent Col. Webster over to see Flag Officer Foote with a request that he go down in another gunboat, presumably the uncommitted *Tyler*, and take charge of the naval response. The hopeful McClernand expected to hear back that Porter had sunk the Rebels, but in any event, promised to keep Cairo posted.

Moving slowly down the Mississippi in thick fog, Cmdr. Porter saw his enemy at the head of Lucas Bend. More than likely, these were the same three boats seen on December 1: *General Polk*, *Ivy*, and *Jackson*. They positioned across the stream at very long range. Over the next hour, the two U.S. ironclads engaged the faster boats of Cdr. Hollins in a running battle, "brisk on both sides for about 20 minutes, the enemy firing by broadsides." The Rebels disappeared under the guns on the Iron Banks, effectively ending the great fight Porter had desired ever since the time his boat was the timberclad *New Era*. "Signal" would later contend, perhaps correctly, that Cmdr. Porter would have pursued the enemy further, save for Flag Officer Foote's strict standing orders not to engage the Columbus cannon.

Indeed, this watery skirmish was the first major action fought against Confederate fleet units in which the timberclads were not engaged. It marked a passing of the torch, so to speak. From this time on, Cmdr. Rodgers' original three warriors—now more often called the "old wooden gunboats"—were regarded not as the major flotilla elements, but as supporting vessels to an expanding and more heavily armored naval force. Within about a month, their purpose would no longer be to engage enemy forts or warboats. Rather, they would have new or enhanced missions of patrol, the provision of army shore bombardment, guerrillas fighting, and dispatch transport.

While in the vicinity of the Confederate fortress, a pair of suspicious buoys were spotted off the Kentucky shore. Porter, according to "Signal," "fired a musket shot at one of them, the ball striking and sinking it." The gig and cutter were sent to examine the second object and to pull it up. Heaving it back aboard the *Essex*, Porter and his men were convinced that it had marked—he wasn't sure which—either the location of Rebel submarine batteries or the safe channel through the minefield. It was stowed away for later examination ashore.

Foote did not take the *Tyler* downstream. With confidence in Porter to handle matters, he was probably very pleased to hear about a POW interrogation conducted by Brig. Gen. McClernand. According to information from the prisoner, the naval engagement "excited much alarm among the Rebels at Columbus and induced a general belief among them that they were to be immediately attacked by a land force."

An officer aboard the *Essex*, in a letter published in the *New York Times* on January 25, 1862, revealed how his boat, the *St. Louis*, and earlier the timberclads, had visited Columbus regularly for weeks and how after their departures, "the enemy's gunboats came up and fired some blank cartridges at us." The men by now so wanted a crack at Capt. Miller as well as Cdr. Hollins' other craft that Cmdr. Porter sent the latter a challenge attached to a buoy: "Hollins: Why don't you accursed, cowardly rebels bring out your gunboats and fight us. Porter."

Meanwhile, not having heard from Maj. Gen. Buell, an exasperated Maj. Gen. Halleck telegraphed Brig. Gen. Grant authorizing him to "fix your own time for the advance." He would send along reinforcements from St. Louis as soon as he could.

Lt. Phelps and Shirk, aboard the latter's *Lexington*, journeyed up the Tennessee River during the day as far as Seven Mile Island. It was necessary to check the water level because, if the stream were not navigable, it would be impossible to begin the Paducah-based leg of Halleck's grand demonstration. The officers were pleased to find a small rise occurring. After the scout, the *Lexington* returned to Cairo.[2]

With the *Essex* and *St. Louis* back at Cairo for stores and fuel, the *Tyler*, with the *Lexington*, took their place off Fort Holt on January 12. Shortly after 8:00 A.M., U.S. Army officers were rowed out to Cmdr. Walke's vessel and informed him that two enemy gunboats had been sighted lying under the point below. Walke ordered the *Lexington* to proceed to Cairo to report the development to the flag officer, while he went down the river to find the enemy. No sign was seen as far as Norfolk and when the *Tyler* returned to Fort Holt it was time for lunch.

The *Lexington*, with Flag Officer Foote embarked, returned from Cairo shortly after noon. Weighing anchor, the *Tyler* joined her and the two paddled down the river a mile or two below Norfolk. Again, no enemy boats were discovered. The timberclads returned to Fort Holt, but in late afternoon made yet a third reconnaissance down as far as Norfolk—again nothing.

The extra troops from St. Louis did not arrive at Cairo during the day as hoped. Brig. Gen. Grant, however, decided to depart next morning whether they arrived or not. With any luck, the men on his leg of the great demonstration would reach Blandville by January 14. Passing along this information to Brig. Gen. Smith at Paducah, the Ohio brigadier allowed as how his force could meet Smith's and, joined, reach Mayfield by January 16. "This will regulate the time for the departure of your column," Grant suggested.

The three promised infantry regiments were sent down to Cairo from St. Louis aboard steamers on the morning of January 13. The same day, far away in Washington, D.C., President Lincoln sacked War Department Secretary Simon Cameron and replaced him with Edwin M. Stanton, another Buckeye like McClellan, Grant, and Phelps.

Downstream near Fort Jefferson, Cmdr. Porter received an unexpected message. It was from Capt. Miller and read "Sir: The ironclad steamer *Grampus* will meet the *Essex* at any point and time your Honor may appoint and show you that the power is in our hands. An early reply will be agreeable." Miller, every bit as colorful as Porter, did not have an ironclad, but his less heavily armed boat was much faster than the former *New Era*.

It was bitterly cold, with sleet and snow, as Union troops climbed up the steamer stages at Cairo and Bird's Point on January 14. Pushing aside chunks of ice floating in the Mississippi, the troopboats, minus their civilian commodore, who was in jail, churned and sloshed down to Fort Jefferson by dark.

While his troops prepared for their trek in terrible weather late Tuesday afternoon, Maj. Gen. Grant agreed to join Flag Officer Foote aboard the *Tyler*, with *St. Louis* and *Essex* in company, for a short downstream reconnaissance. Meanwhile, according to the *Times'* Franc Wilkie, who was ashore near Fort Jefferson with the troops but who heard — and reported — the story later, the *Grampus* and another boat were dispatched from Columbus "to shell our Union men out."

Upon reaching the river bend about two miles below Island No. 1, the *Grampus* and her consort "modestly came to and honored us with a few shells, which either burst at half way or disappeared in the water." They might have come closer, "Galway" contended, except that Capt. Miller saw the ironclads, "the swarthy couple," lying in the middle of the river and chose to retreat.

The two Federal monsters and the *Tyler* made the obligatory effort to pursue the speedy Rebel boats, rounding to within a mile and a half of Columbus. With a view of forcing a response that would reveal the range of the citadel's guns, the *Essex* and *St. Louis* pumped roundshot at them: "The first two fell short, the next three went hissing savagely through the air, describing a most elegant curve." The second pattern dropped "exactly with the line of fortifications." The Iron Banks batteries returned the compliment with the same vigor but did not score a hit.

"The object of this demonstration," Foote told Secretary Welles, "was in connection with the Army maneuvers." In other words, the previously agreed upon diversion. It also allowed Foote's sailors to check for additional submarine batteries. The flag officer was also convinced, as he let slip to the *Chicago Daily Tribune*, that he could "reduce Columbus but with small loss of life." No torpedoes were found; if any had been planted in large quantities, U.S. officers expected that ice, now floating in the river, would largely destroy them.

A few days later, quoting correspondence from Columbus that had appeared in the *New Orleans Crescent*, the editor of the *Macon Daily Telegraph* told his readers that "great numbers of submarine batteries, or torpedoes, are sunk all over the river, from one shore to the other, or rather buoyed a foot or to beneath the surface." In order to let Confederate craft pass through, a curtain opening was left, but it opened within range of the Iron Banks batteries.

The Georgia editor went on to tell of two interesting incidents with the torpedoes. After Foote's reconnaissance, with the water still cold, "a cake of floating ice struck one of them and the way the ice flew was a caution." On another occasion, "a drift log came along and struck one of the things. The explosion was terrific." The log was thrown high in the air, while the *Grampus* "about a quarter of a mile off, sustained a severe shock."

Standing with Walke and Foote in the pilothouse of the *Tyler*, Brig. Gen. Grant was uncertain whether Porter and Paulding scored any hits on the Columbus batteries. He may not have had his mind fully on this nautical business, as another piece of the water picture, controlled by his own quartermaster department, caused him much embarrassment.

Back on November 16, Cdr. William J. Kountz, who had earlier assisted Cmdr. Rodgers in acquiring the timberclads, was commissioned an assistant quartermaster of volunteers with the rank of Capt. and sent to St. Louis. In mid–December, he was ordered to Cairo to "examine into All River Transportation," its efficiency and expense, by the U. S. government groups reviewing the supposed malfeasance of Maj. Gen. Frémont. Maj. Gen. Halleck, in turn, also appointed him down to serve as master of transportation for the District of Cairo, displacing Capt. George Washington "Wash" Graham.

In only a few short weeks, Kountz managed to make himself one of the most, if not the most, unpopular persons at the tip of Illinois. He was roundly despised by his fellow rivermen, who refused to serve under him — some even left the city to avoid associating with the man. Others in town were displeased with his "wholesale denunciation of everybody connected with the Government here as thieves and cheats."

On January 4, Maj. Gen. Halleck received a petition from 10 of the Cairo district's colonels, including such well known leaders as Richard Oglesby, William H.L. Wallace, John McArthur, John Cook, and Napoleon Buford, plus nine other officers asking that G.W. Graham replace Kountz and that he now have the official army rank of captain and assistant quartermaster. St. Louis entrepreneur Robert Forsyth, who had originally gotten Kountz his appointment by lobbying Maj. Gen. McClellan and Halleck, was the one who passed on the signed document, along with a note saying that he had changed his mind on the riverman and now also endorsed Graham.

A few days later, *St. Louis Daily Missouri Democrat* reporter George W. Beaman at Cairo got wind of another petition being circulated against Kountz. This one, signed by 31 Cairo boatmen and steamer captains boldly stated that, in making the captain's appointment, "a more unpopular man with all classes of boatmen could not have been selected." Copies of this document were sent, according to "G.W.B.," to Brig. Gen. Grant, Francis P. Blair in Washington, D.C., and the newspapers in St. Louis, Louisville, Cincinnati, and Pittsburgh. On January 16, the noted steamer commander Capt. Charles M. Scott also had a letter on the matter published in the *Daily Missouri Democrat*.

The upshot of this displeasure was that Kountz could not fulfill his duty to recruit sufficient crews to man Grant's transports. Additionally, he managed to disobey orders and annoyed the post commander so flagrantly and loudly that he was arrested. Grant now turned back to Capt. Graham, who was able to hire the needed civilian boatmen.[3]

Between them, Brigadier Generals Grant and Smith had about 10,000 bluecoats when their Kentucky adventure started. Grant's prong, led by Brig. Gen. McClernand and Paine, headed off toward Blandsville and Mayfield in what the correspondent from the *New York Herald* called "a cold, drizzling storm." Over the next five days, joined by Grant and his staff, the bluecoats from Cairo and Bird's Point journeyed to within 10–14 miles of Columbus itself. Through execrable weather and over and near roads turned into quagmires they marched and countermarched. A total of 75 miles were covered before Grant quit and returned to their bases.

"The expedition, if it had no other effect," Grant wrote to Halleck on January 20, "served as a fine reconnaissance." Franc B. Wilkie, who made the trek with Brig. Gen. Paine, informed his *New York Times* readers that the whole march was "about as incomprehensible as to its objects and results as anything well can be." There were, "Galway" wrote, "more changes than there are in a dozen cotillions."

It was the leg of this "reconnaissance" carried out by Brig. Gen. Smith from Paducah that holds the greatest interest here. It directly involved Lt. Phelp's two-timberclad task group, when, in the Grant-Foote expedition, the woodclad *Tyler* was essentially just a command ship. Writing from Cairo a few days later, newsman Wilkie would also review this thrust, finding it may have been "the true one." After all, he concluded, the other one, that some wags now called the "Grand Expedition," looked "like an immense humbug."

In something of a foretaste of the quest in Africa years later of then (Dixie Grays) Pvt. Henry Morton Stanley, Wilkie, wondering what had become of Grant's mentor, set off "up the Ohio, as far as Paducah, to obtain, if possible, some information of the missing command of Brig. Gen. Smith." Whether Grant and Smith missed each other (or were ever to meet) "is more than I can tell," the writer revealed. All that was known was "that Brig. Gen. Grant did succeed in retracing his advance from Fort Jefferson and Cairo while Brig. Gen. Smith still wanders among the woody, muddy, perplexing labyrinths of Kentucky."

"Through Graves County into Calloway County far down towards Fort Henry," Brig. Gen. Lew Wallace later recalled, Brig. Gen. Smith led his two brigades on a march "memorable to every man who participated in it." The area into which they pushed "had become an ocean of mud, and there was rain and melting snow, and from the beginning to end no dry place to set a foot could be discovered."

Although most of Smith's men marched overland toward Mayfield in what Wallace called "that Calloway voyage," a few went up the Tennessee aboard the supply boat *V.F. Wilson*. Protected by *Conestoga* and *Lexington*, the steamer, with 500 infantry and artillery under Maj. I.C. Elston aboard, proceeded upriver on January 16. En route, the *Lexington* hit a rock near the point where the Tennessee state line struck the right bank of the river. Shirk was beside himself with rage. He was absolutely convinced that his boat had been deliberately "run upon a rock by a person who represented himself as a Tennessee River pilot." The pilots aboard since at least November were Joseph McCammant and William For, each paid $175 per month, $25 more than either Cmdr. Stembel or Lt. Shirk. Their wages notwithstanding, one of these gentlemen was believed the culprit and was clapped into double irons.

Unable to proceed further because of darkness, the three boats anchored for the night. Following an intercession by Lt. Phelps, and believing his pilot's professions of innocence, Shirk agreed the act was probably not intentional and released his guide. Despite the incident, the man remained with the boat through the great battles and adventures ahead. "Well might a pilot ask himself whether these fussy and dictatorial naval officers would understand the usage of the rivers," asked Donald Davidson 80 years later while reviewing the case, "where the pilot is king in all matters of navigation, or whether, indeed, a deep-sea sailor could begin to comprehend the tricky ways of a great river."

Early the next morning with the aid of the *Conestoga*, the *Lexington* was freed. She did not initially appear much damaged after being worked back into the channel. About this time, Brig. Gen. Smith and parts of his column appeared on the nearby riverbank, having nearly exhausted the week's worth of provisions they were transporting. Great difficulty had been experienced by the soldiers thus far in working wagons through the rain and mud. It took an entire day for one brigade to march three miles.

Finding that it would take the better part of a day to distribute the stores aboard the *V.F. Wilson* to his men, Brig. Gen. Smith decided to scout Fort Henry in person, taking along his chief engineer, Capt. John Rziha. Smith had heard rumors that the place was abandoned, while Phelps learned that a masked Confederate battery comprising two rifled cannon was supposedly located at the foot of Panther Island.

Leaving the *Conestoga* with the *V.F. Wilson*, Smith, Rziha, Phelps, and Shirk proceeded up toward Fort Henry aboard the better-armed *Lexington*, which was now beginning to show signs of a hull leak. "Some distance up they came," "Galway" later learned, "in sight of a point of land whose woody depths looked as if they might hide secession batteries." Pushing slowly ahead to within 800 yards of the location, the timberclad shelled the woods and nearby riverbank. Her fiery shower had a "terrible effect, tearing off huge branches, scarring the grand old trees, digging vast and ugly cavities in the soil, and sending away over hill and valley the echoes" from her Dahlgrens.

Even though the *Lexington* approached abreast the suspect spot, no return fire was drawn. Eventually, a landing was effected. Warming to his observation on the shoot, Wilkie summed up results: "No enemy was discovered, no dead, no wounded, no signs even that a hostile foot had ever trod the sylvan recesses, now so rudely disturbed by National thunderbolts."

Following the unsuccessful search-by-fire, the *Lexington* moved further down to where Fort Henry was seen, alive and bustling. A check of the river showed it 14 feet above where it had been a week earlier. Taking the right-hand channel by Panther Island, the gunboat slowly paddled to within two and a half miles of Fort Henry. Two steamboats, one believed to be the *Dunbar*, were at the fort, but they quickly made away when the timberclad was sighted.

One Confederate shot was drawn in return, falling about a half mile short. Capt. Jesse Taylor later explained why his cannon replied with such apparent under enthusiasm whenever *Conestoga* or *Lexington* favored "the fort with an hour or more of shot and shell." "Their object was to draw our fire and thus obtain the position of our guns," he observed, but "though sorely tempted by the accuracy of their fire," the Rebel cannoneers "deemed it best not to gratify them."

"Having complied with Gen. Smith's wish of feigning an attack at early morn with the whole force in view, " Phelps later reported to Foote, the three boats dropped down to Aurora, where Maj. Elston's men disembarked and set off for Murray, from which they could threaten Paris. The *V.F. Wilson* and her escorts returned to the neighborhood of Fort Henry and anchored about three and a half miles below for the night.

The *Lexington*'s activities caused Brig. Gen. Lloyd Tilghman, in command at Fort Henry, to wire both Gen. Johnston and Maj. Gen. Polk for help, estimating that Elston's force contained about 5,500 men. It would take two days for the Columbus chief to send a cavalry force. Another group of horsemen came from Tennessee governor Isham G. Harris and together they would menace the end of Smith's adventure. Also on January 17, Brig. Gen. Thomas, with his lead elements, reached Logan Cross Roads, Kentucky. Thomas' advance, the cause of the Grant-Smith diversion, was required to make an eight day slog over incredibly bad roads before it arrived at this location about eight miles from Somerset. The Battle of Logan Cross Roads began before dawn on January 18 when Confederate cavalry, in driving rain, attacked Union pickets.

Over on the Tennessee River at 8:00 A.M. that Saturday, the Yankee military boats weighed for Paducah, with the transport carrying wounded men and mail. Brig. Gen. Smith resumed his march overland along the left bank in "easy stages." Having gone only about a half mile up river, the gunboats came across a large barge on the Kentucky side of the state line filled with wood. The timber, originally cut for use in Fort Henry, would provide fuel for the *Lexington* and *Conestoga*, which latter took the barge under tow.

Passing upriver about 10 miles above Fort Henry on their exit, the gunboats were taken under fire from shore. Three men standing on the deck of the *Conestoga* near her chimneys were wounded; Acting Gunner Henry Hunter was struck in the neck. A charge of grapeshot, according to the *Times*' "Tennessean," hastened the Rebel retreat "and then all was still."

Downstream below Cairo late in the afternoon, *New York Times* correspondent Franc B. Wilkie had just arrived at Fort Jefferson to visit the troops when alarms were sounded. The *Grampus* was seen "poking her nose cautiously around the bend below." Troops were immediately sent aboard the steamer *Aleck Scott*, which, together with *St. Louis* and *Essex*, began yet another Federal Miller chase. The *Grampus*, observing the response time of the Yankees, waited until they were underway to turn to and retreat down the river, making, as "Galway" sarcastically noted "magnificent time toward Columbus."

Cmdr. Porter was furious. After a night of reflection, he decided to answer Capt. Miller's challenge of January 13. Bright and early next morning, the bewhiskered captain called his yeoman in and dictated a note he later showed *Times*' reporter "Signal" and Irving Carson of the *Chicago Daily Tribune*:

> To the traitor Marsh Miller, commanding a Rebel Gunboat called the *Grampus:*
> Commander Porter has already thrashed your gunboat fleet; shelled and silenced your Rebel batteries at the Iron Banks; chased your miserable and cowardly self down behind Columbus; but

if you desire to meet the *Essex*, show yourself any morning in Prentys' Bend, and you shall then meet with a traitor's fate — if you have the courage to stand. God and our Country; "Rebels offend both." Porter.

The ship-to-ship engagement did not happen. If the *Essex* were still a timberclad, would such a personal duel have occurred?

Lt. Phelps' two gunboats rounded to off Paducah that afternoon. All of his officers avoided contact with *Times* reporter "Tennessean," who attempted to get an interview. Unable to speak with Phelps or Shirk, he found enough from other sources for three columns in the January 24 issue.

Phelps was undoubtedly pleased, in opening his mail that evening, to find an order from Flag Officer Foote detaching him from the *Conestoga* and sending him to command the new Pook turtle *Cairo*. Stembel already had the *Cincinnati* and it was sent the same day Foote had ordered Cmdr. Walke to take over the *Carondelet*. It appeared as though the flotilla commander was rewarding the good work of his timberclad captains.

In hard fighting over January 18–19, Brig. Gen. Thomas was not only able to blunt the Confederate attack at Logan Cross Road, but also to route the Rebel forces and claim a smashing victory, chasing them to Beech Grove. Led by Maj. Gen. George B. Crittenden, the Southerners were able to escape across the river, but their heavy equipment was taken by the victorious Federals who took over the abandoned camp.

"The weather is very warm," "Galway," at Cairo, told the shivering folks in New York. "the rain falls almost incessantly — heavy fogs rest all over this section." His colleague "Tennessean" provided them with a fuller account from Paducah, one which would prove of even more interest within a few weeks:

> Some days ago, we had a rain, leaving the ground full of water. This was soon scaled up by a hard freeze. On the top of this, we have had snow and sleet covering the ground for an inch or two. Day before yesterday [January 16] a thaw set in, and at night, a rain began to fall, assuming for a while the character of a tremendous thunderstorm. The thunder, lightning and wind soon passed over, but the rain continued almost without interruption for 30 hours, holding up very warm. The rivers are already in good stage and rising rapidly.

By January 24, according to a special dispatch published in the *Chicago Evening Journal*, the Mississippi River at Cairo had risen 25 feet and was still rising.

In the meantime, on January 20, Grant asked Halleck in St. Louis if he might travel to department HQ to present a new plan based on discussions held locally between army and navy men such as himself, McClernand, Foote and Smith. Indeed, Flag Officer Foote urged the visit "for the good of the service." Yes, it was possible that Halleck could reject Grant's thinking. But even if he did, Catton quotes Foote as saying that "his wrath will hardly be so hot as to dry up the Mississippi before you can get back to Cairo."[4]

While the *Conestoga* and *Lexington* were away in support of Brig. Gen. Smith's trek, there was, about this time, a change in command aboard the *Tyler*. Back on January 15, Cmdr. Henry Walke was ordered to take charge of the new Pook turtle *Carondelet*. The following day, Lt. William Gwin read himself aboard the *Tyler* as her second skipper. The largest timberclad remained at Cairo and Fort Holt, ready at Foote's convenience.

Born at Columbus, Indiana, on December 5, 1832, William Gwin was commissioned a midshipman in 1847 and a lieutenant in 1855. At the outbreak of the war, he was assigned to the blockade duty before assuming command of *Commodore Perry* in October 1861. Always remembered for his service at Shiloh and the running battle with the *Arkansas*, Gwin, promoted that July, would command the U.S.S. *Benton* in the December 27, 1862, battle at Haynes

Bluff on the Yazoo River. Mortally wounded there, he died on January 3, 1863. His command of the *Tyler* was central to the timberclad story and his paymaster and friend from that boat, Silas Coleman, idolized him: "Gwin was a man of fine personal appearance, of elegant and winning manners, and courageous to the last degree. He was one of that class of officers who loved a fight, and never knowingly lost an opportunity to engage his vessel."

At Paducah late on January 18, Lt. Shirk sent potentially bad news to Flag Officer Foote at Cairo. After striking the rock while en route up the Tennessee River on January 16, the *Lexington*'s leak steadily worsened and she was now taking on water alarmingly. By the time she returned to the mouth of the river, she was taking, while underway, about an inch and a quarter an hour, considerably more than before the accident.

The timberclad had originally been outfitted with bilge pumps at the time of her purchase the previous spring. They were removed, Shirk subsequently learned, by order of Naval Constructor Pook, who had them replaced with two small hand pumps. These were not keeping the bilge sufficiently clear of water. Her commander asked whether it would be possible for her to be taken into dry dock at Mound City so that her bottom might be calked and the leak stopped.

Upon receipt of Shirk's dispatch via the January 19 morning mail boat, Foote contacted William L. Hamilton, superintendent of the Hambleton and Collier yards at Mound City, asking that he make ready to take the *Lexington* on the ways to stop the leak, to calk the butts, and to repair necessary damages. The flag officer promised Hamilton to order the timberclad down next day and presumed she could make it by dark or the next day, Tuesday.

After contacting Hamilton, Foote replied to Shirk asking him to discuss the matter with Lt. Phelps and instructing the two officers to hold an informal survey of the *Lexington*, together with her carpenters. If they found no increase in the leak, Shirk was to remain at Paducah. If it had worsened, he was to come down immediately, as Hamilton had been asked to haul his boat up the ways Monday evening.

Before Shirk could receive Flag Officer Foote's reply, one more mission intervened. Regular naval officers are, by training, loath to skip any assignment they might possibly fulfill. "Gunboat commanders drove their craft to the limit," opined Tennessee River historian Donaldson, "and would not be put on the ways unless it was absolutely necessary."

On Sunday afternoon, Lt. Phelps passed along a request from Brig. Gen. Smith that the *Lexington* convoy the steamer *V.F. Wilson* to the landing at Aurora where Maj. Elston was dropped off two days earlier. The latter also was towing two barges loaded with five days' provisions and forage. There they could expect to be met. Although she was leaking, Phelps and Shirk believed the timberclad could make the trip, so, after she was coaled, the two steamers departed about 7:00 P.M. *Lexington* and *V.F. Wilson* arrived off Aurora at 3:00 A.M. There was no one there when they dropped anchor.

The two steamers remained off Aurora all day Monday. Foote, who had no idea that the *Lexington* was away, wrote to Lt. Phelps that January 20 to say that, once she was in order and his services could be spared, the flag officer would be pleased to see him at Cairo. The message contained the unhappy news that Phelps would not be getting the new Pook turtle promised earlier. Another more senior officer, the newly arrived Lt. Nathaniel C. Bryant, had to be offered the *Cairo* instead.

Meanwhile, beginning back on January 17, Flag Officer Foote had become involved in a discussion with Maj. Gen. Halleck over possible use of the new mortar boats against the forts on the Tennessee and Cumberland rivers. Foote was not optimistic but wired Lt. Phelps at Paducah for his assessment based on his firsthand knowledge of the bastions.

Just after noon on January 21, a soldier reached the Aurora landing in a dugout with a

Top: The Battle of Fort Henry on February 6, 1862, marked the passing of the timberclads from the front ranks of Union naval forces in the west and their replacement by the Pook turtles. Still, the three "old boats," as they were known six months after their initial appearance, made up a second division that lobbed long-range shots at the Confederate defenses from positions behind the ironclads (Library of Congress). *Bottom:* Bombardment of Fort Henry. Note the timberclads *Conestoga* and *Tyler* on the right (Maclay's *History of the Navy*).

message from Brig. Gen. Smith. His wagon train was some four miles father up the west bank of the river at Crown Point Landing (49 miles from Paducah). As the train was unable to proceed because the recent rains had so swollen the streams tributary to the Tennessee, the two boats needed to transfer up to Smith's location. The *Lexington* and *V.F. Wilson*, with barges, soon arrived and found the brigadier and his command anxious for the latter's cargo.

Upon meeting Brig. Gen. Smith, Shirk was immediately ordered to undertake a reconnaissance up toward Fort Henry. The Paducah commander had heard rumors that it was being evacuated and wanted to ascertain the truth of the matter. As the soldiers unloaded the transport, the timberclad backed out and headed up stream. Shirk had as his passenger the local correspondent from the *New York Herald*.

The *Lexington* paddled up the Tennessee, perhaps more slowly than usual due to her leak, when lookouts shouted out that there was a steamer ahead. Glasses were whipped up and it was quickly determined that the unknown craft was the *Dunbar*, "under steam going up the river and distant about a mile and three-quarters or two miles." Even though his boat was still taking on water, Shirk ordered up full speed.

Back at Aurora later, Shirk heard that Gus Fowler's steamer had scouted up the Tennessee the day before, reaching Birmingham, 35 miles above Paducah. It was claimed that she carried a pair of rifled brass 12-pounders and served not only as a dispatch and supply boat, but also, like the *Grampus*, as an ersatz gunboat. The *Lexington*'s skipper later reported that the *Dunbar* did not look like a gunboat. She had no bulwarks and retained her upper works. She was painted white "and looked like any other river steamboat."

As the black-hued Yankee boat came on, crewmen aboard the Rebel transport saw her bulldog shape and the smoke rising in clouds from her chimneys. The *Lexington*, which had the advantage of first sighting, was close enough to get a 32-pounder shot off as the enemy rounded an island that hid her from view. According to the *Memphis Appeal*, the Rebel pilot "noticed a white streak and ejaculated 'There she is!'" "There she was, sure enough," the newspaper reported. "A volume of smoke issued from the streak—a report followed—nobody hurt."

The alarm was given aboard the *Dunbar* and she sped up river toward Fort Henry. The *Lexington*'s cannonball missed and the Confederate steamer, pouring on the coal, left the timberclad far in her wake, running out of sight even as two shells ineffectively came after her. If, indeed, his boat carried ordnance, Fowler declined returning the compliment of a cannon shot. "Each time the gunboat fired," the Memphis journal continued, "she was necessitated to partially 'round to' and this enabled the *Dunbar* to gain on her." The protection of Fort Henry was distant and "a single shot might disable the unprotected steamer." In some admiration twanged with disappointment, Shirk later admitted that "she is a very fast boat, her speed being equal to one and a half times that of this vessel." The Southern reporter later suggested "the speed of the boats is about equal."

The *Lexington*, according to Southern sources, was able to get off another round. It reportedly passed between the *Dunbar*'s "chimneys, ploughing the river within a few feet of her." Capt. Fowler and his men "urged their boat through the muddy waters, and made preparations for burning her if they saw no other way of preventing her falling a prize to the Federal gunboat." The *Dunbar* was not taken that day; "fortune favored the weak" and she reached the bastion, "beneath whose frowning ramparts her captain felt she was safe."

Having again reduced the power to the great side wheels of his vessel, Lt. Shirk proceeded up to the foot of Panther Island. There about 4:00 P.M. he saw Fort Henry—and the *Dunbar* and an unidentified boat lying under its guns well out of his range. The *Herald* scribe with Shirk noted that the two were upriver steamers "having no other peculiarity than that they each carry two 12-pound rifled guns and are the fastest sailors to be found."

Coming near the picket camp where, several days earlier, masked Confederate batteries were reported, the *Lexington* sent an ineffective shell toward it and another toward the spot where a second Rebel camp may have been. Taking the right-hand channel by Panther Island, the gunboat slowly paddled to within two and a half miles of Fort Henry, where she remained for about half an hour. The gunboat's lookouts were able to see that Fort Henry was alive and bustling. Shirk himself noticed that there were "a large number of men about the fort." A check of the river showed it even higher then it had been just days earlier.

Being alone and unsupported, Lt. Shirk elected not to come within range of the fort's guns; however, according to the timberclad's logbook, he did fire four rounds at the bastion. Having witnessed all that was possible in the failing winter light, the *Lexington* rounded to and stood down to Crown Point. There her skipper reported the results of his reconnaissance to Brig. Gen. Smith. Smith, who had visited Fort Henry aboard the *Conestoga* some time before, wanted to take another look. For some time, he had been convinced that the Tennessee River offered an excellent invasion route into the Rebel confederacy and he wished another view. He would go upstream after breakfast to see for himself.

Meanwhile, far down the river, Lt. Phelps wired Flag Officer Foote that "mortar boats could be used to advantage on the Tennessee and Cumberland Rivers." While he waited for the *Lexington* to return in order to determine for certain whether or not to send her to Mound City, he completed two lengthy treatises on the possible use of mortars against either Fort Henry or Fort Donelson. Then, concerned with the non-return of Lt. Shirk, Phelps weighed anchor from Paducah and steamed up the Tennessee to find him.

New York Times correspondent "Tennessean," who may have watched the *Conestoga*'s departure, laid out for his Eastern readers a bit of the geography of the local rivers and something of their seasonal behavior. "There is at this time," he wrote, "a great freshet running out of the Tennessee and Cumberland Rivers." Both streams were now "at flood tide, throwing out into the Ohio an immense quantity of drift, which covers the face of our river here."

"Tennessean" then waxed upon the golden opportunity the freshet represented. Though a week old when published on January 28, his views were, unknowingly, the same as Smith, Grant, and Foote. "At such a time as this," this writer opined, "our gunboats could ascend the Tennessee to Fort Henry, and after taking that post, which could easily be done, they can ascend to Tuscumbia without interruption." The Cumberland was also a ready avenue for advance, as it had "enough water now in its channel to float any ship in the navy, from Nashville to its mouth."

Taking two of his staff with him, the brigadier boarded the *Lexington* at precisely 9:00 on the morning of January 22 and asked Lt. Shirk to steam upstream to within sight of the earthworks. Among those left behind was a private in Co. A of the Chicago Light Artillery, whose letter written home that day was published in the *Chicago Daily Tribune* a week later. Concluding with the Smith-Shirk visit to Fort Henry, he told his kin that "we all hope he will decide to make an attempt to take it."

After a two hour and 10 minute cruise, the *Lexington* arrived off the foot of Panther Island before moving nearly to the head. She fired two cannonballs and three shells toward Fort Henry, even though Smith and Shirk both knew full well that they were too far off to do much damage. One of the shots fell in the river at the foot of the Confederate works and several shells burst overhead. The same issue of the *Memphis Appeal* that reported the *Dunbar* chase also reported on the *Lexington*'s shoot. "Her firing and its great range awoke the admiration of our boys, who actually cheered her."

A Tennessee soldier from Clarksville was at Fort Henry and witnessed the clash:

Meeting no response, she retired with a white flag flying to the breeze. No damage was done by her shots as they all fell short. However, she again made her appearance with Stars and Stripes flying and opened fire on the Fort. As soon as the first shot was fired by her, the Confederate flag was raised in the Fort ... but as soon as we fired one shot, she responded with a shell (which burst some yards below the Fort) and retired behind the Island.

The one shot fired from Fort Henry was determined to have been from a 32-pounder. It fell about half a mile short of the gunboat.

A little while later, the *Lexington* ascended the starboard side of Panther Island and came to just under two miles from the earthworks. At that point, Shirk was able to draw Rebel fire once more and "returned them one shell, which we did not see strike." Having accomplished his aim, Smith ordered Shirk to stand down the river back to his camp. The *Memphis Appeal* suggested she did more than steam away. "The jar of her own firing disabled her," it claimed. The concussion "knocked her chimneys off, sprung her pilothouse, and, it is supposed, her butts. She is now useless."

While the *Conestoga* was en route up the Tennessee to find the *Lexington*, the editor of the *Florence Gazette* on this date issued something of an ironic balloon of boastfulness that would be punctured in just 18 days. The steamer *Muscle* was—and had been for some time, he noted—transporting contraband cargo between that Alabama community and Eastport, Mississippi. If the Yankees, the journal cried, wanted to know just which illegal goods, they'd have to come and see for themselves.

At the request of the U.S. Army commander, the *Lexington* remained off Crown Point on January 22–23. While Shirk and his men doubtless concerned themselves with the matter of the timberclad's leak, Brig. Gen. Smith wrote out his report for Brig. Gen. Grant. Lt. Phelps arrived at Crown Point aboard the *Conestoga* at dawn on January 23. There he and Lt. Shirk conferred with and took their leave of Brig. Gen. Smith, who, though determined to march out with his men, sent information back for the high command. Written on the back of an envelope and addressed to Capt. John A Rawlins, the message was entrusted to the sailors for forwarding to Cairo. With the *Conestoga* in the lead, the two timberclads departed for Paducah at 8:30 A.M.

And what of Franc B. Wilkie, the *Times* reporter with the penname "Galway?" A few days earlier he came to Paducah from Cairo to find the missing Smith expedition. Coming ashore at the wharf, he found the town "a beautiful little place of some eight thousand inhabitants." The weather was very "agreeable," the sun "was as brilliant and genial as in Springtime," and the streets were "dry and almost dusty." He, like the garrison soldiers, was "mightily pleased" with the location, "for certainly a more pleasant one does not exist."

It is unclear whether or not "Galway" talked to the just-returned naval officers, but whoever he talked to he was certainly not impressed with what he was told concerning the purpose of the Grant-Smith expeditions. "The assertion that the late movement in Kentucky was to effect an extended reconnaissance in the vicinity of Columbus is," he asserted, "sheer nonsense." Just why they went out remained unclear, as did Smith's location.

A new mystery unfolded on the afternoon of January 24 right before the reporter's eyes. Three regiments from Cairo boarded transports for Smithland, Kentucky, and some new objective then unknown. Boarding the mail steamer to that location next morning, Wilkie went off to investigate.

Brig. Gen. Smith and his men moved out that day. When they returned to Paducah on January 25, their lengthy slog had covered only 125 miles. A small Confederate cavalry force had offered some harassment, but, at least initially, according to Thomas Connelly, "With the exception of Tilghman, the Rebel high command considered the move a false alarm."[5]

William Feis, in his study of Grant's secret service, contends that throughout the joint army-navy demonstrations just completed, the Ohio brigadier "remained fixated upon Columbus and had not yet changed his course toward Forts Henry and Donelson."

While considering his talking points with the intellectually formidable Maj. Gen. Halleck on January 21–22, the Ohio brigadier remained determined "to press Halleck for an advance on Columbus." After all, Grant was a man who had shown almost no interest in the Tennessee or Cumberland river fortifications before January. One who, rather, had been fixated on Maj. Gen. Polk's citadel for months, he had personally participated in the recent Columbus demonstration with McClernand rather than go up the Tennessee with Smith.

Just after breakfast on January 23, the day of his trip, Brig. Gen. Grant received the envelope upon which Smith had written his Tennessee River observations. The Cairo district chief was delighted with the review of his West Point mentor. Coupled with news of additional Columbus reinforcements, it caused Grant to consider Fort Henry as a possible objective almost for the first time. Now when he took the train from Cairo to St. Louis to visit the headquarters of the Department of the Missouri commander, he could really bring to the attention of his bookish superior some apparently new strategic thinking.

Based on observations made during his mud slog, the respected Smith opined to Grant that a small force, maybe as few as 3,000, could capture both the high ground across from Fort Henry and the main fortification itself. The roads and ground east of Columbus were rain soaked, making any reinforcement of Brig. Gen. Tilghman almost impossible. In addition, the Tennessee River was rising, giving it sufficient depth not only for Foote's ironclads but also to render inoperable any submarine batteries that had been planted. Finally, Smith argued that "two ironclad gunboats could make short work of Fort Henry."

With more than that number of Pook turtles and a steamboat supply chain, too, Fort Henry appeared to Grant to be a far less dangerous—and possibly just as important—prize as Polk's citadel. With Henry and later with Fort Donelson in hand, Columbus would be turned and rendered militarily useless. And, of course, there would be the added plum of capturing Nashville.

As he approached St. Louis army headquarters, Brig. Gen. Grant believed that his chance to lead an army south was at hand. "But his meeting with Halleck went poorly," Jean Smith, with others, tells us. There has been speculation for years as to what happened. Was Grant tongue-tied? Did his superior think his plan preposterous? Did Halleck already have plans to go after the twin river forts?

According to both Smith and Woodworth, Halleck did not consider Grant's plans preposterous. The "germ of the idea of penetrating the line" from Columbus–Bowling Green via the Tennessee and Cumberland rivers "was as old as the war," wrote Peter Franklin Walker in 1957, "but it was not until January 1862 that Union aims solidified enough for it to be vigorously acted upon." Indeed, the theater commander believed that the Confederate line could not be taken "without an immense siege train and a terrible loss of life." On the other hand, he thought the forts might not be too difficult and could "be turned, paralyzed, and forced to surrender."

Many people, Frank Cooling and others have asserted, claimed to have come up with the idea for a twin rivers campaign: Frémont spy Charles D'Arnaud; John Lellyett from Paducah; Cincinnati army engineer Chyarle Whittlesey; McClellan; Buell; McClernand; a Maryland lady, Anna Ella Carroll, and her friend Charles M. Scott, pilot of the *Belle Memphis* during the Battle of Belmont; Attorney General Bates; Maj. Gen. Halleck; Brig. Gen. William Tecumseh Sherman; and even Grant himself. What caused the failure in the initial conversation between Halleck and Grant was probably the former's prejudice against Grant because he was not "old Army."

Although many claimants to the Union twin rivers strategy were justified in asserting that they had the idea, it was Smith, Foote, and Grant in that order who pushed the timing and the need to act before the Confederacy stepped up its so-far half-hearted river defense efforts, especially at Fort Henry. Later claiming that he was "crestfallen" with his failed visit, Grant no sooner got back to Cairo than he met with Foote. Messages soon buzzed over the wires to St. Louis from both of them asking that Halleck reconsider. They were the bullet, but Halleck would have to decide to pull the trigger.

"Old Brains" was encouraged in his thinking on the Tennessee River approach by other events. These included Lincoln's January 27 General War Order No. 1, which required all of his generals to show some kind of movement on or before February 22.

Interestingly enough, January 27 was also the day when the log jam officially finally broke regarding manpower required for the gunboats. Maj. Gen. Halleck wrote to Brig. Gen. Grant: "Authority is just received from Washington to permit volunteers who desire it to be discharged & recruited by Com. Foote for navy service on the Gun-boats." Even though Grant issued a proclamation to that effect within hours and Halleck reendorsed it on January 29, problems continued. "They are flocking to us," Foote wrote to Assistant Navy Secretary Fox, "but their colonels and captains refused to let them go, and thus far the proclamation is a farce and the gunboats suffer."

During the day, the U.S.S. *Tyler* convoyed transports up the Mississippi River as far as Goose Island before returning to her Cairo anchorage. The river continued to rise slowly and the weather was milder than it had been in some time.

Two days later, Maj. Gen. McClellan telegraphed St. Louis to say that Gen. P.G.T. Beauregard, the Rebel hero of Fort Sumter and First Bull Run, had been ordered west with 15 regiments to assist Gen. Johnston in Kentucky. These developments, along with Foote's promise that he could take the fort with four ironclads, finally persuaded Henry Halleck to act.

In his message to the departmental commander, the flag officer also indicated that "Lt. Comdg. Phelps of the *Conestoga* has been here for a day or two and, in consultation with Genl. Grant, we have come to the conclusion that the Tennessee will soon fall as the Ohio is falling above." It would be best to move soon he advised.

New York Times correspondent Frank B. Wilkie sent a prophetic article to his paper on January 29. "Galway," it will be recalled, had traveled up to Smithland, Kentucky, on January 24, having missed the return of Brig. Gen. Smith's Kentucky adventurers. Located on the east bank of the Cumberland a few hundred yards below its confluence with the Ohio, Smithland was a small place, "but an old one, and contains a population of from 1,200 to 1,600 people." Two forts had been constructed since fall and armed with cannon "sufficient in number and weight to sink, in next to no time, all the rebel gunboats on the Cumberland and Tennessee Rivers." That there were none but the unfinished *Eastport* was not then known.

After interviewing a number of military leaders, "Galway" was able to tell *Times* subscribers that the "nearest points of any importance garrisoned by Rebels are Forts Donelson and Henry ... both distant from her some 60 miles." After describing what was commonly known of the citadels, he went on to predict that "It is more than probable that within the next ten days or fortnight, the occupancy of Fort Henry, and possibly that of the other, will change hands.... I hope in my next to inform you that the Federal flag floats over the ramparts of Fort Henry."

On January 30, twenty-four hours after Wilkie sent off his Smithland piece, Halleck wired Grant: "Make your preparations to take and hold Fort Henry." In his written confirmation of the telegram, he provided his views on how the job should be accomplished, including the use of steamers to transport the troops and supplies up the Tennessee River and how "Flag Officer Foote will protect the transports with his Gun-boats— The *Benton* & perhaps some others should be left for the defense of Cairo." Additionally, he asked that the upstream railroad bridge at Danville be made impassable.

The theater commander also elaborated his new fears. Polk, the object of Grant's pre–January 23 thinking, might try to reinforce Fort Henry from Columbus. Even more critically, Beauregard might show up and tip the balance of regional power to the South. It was just plain urgent "that we cut the lines before he arrives." "Fort Henry," Halleck ordered, "should be taken & held at all hazards."[6]

At the start of 1862, land warfare had not changed much since Caesar's legions invaded Gaul. Due to terrible and often impassable roads and ground for large scale troop movements, armies in December–March generally went into winter quarters, like the log cabins built at Cairo and Columbus. However, because Brig. Gen. Grant needed the high waters of the winter freshets to ascend the twin rivers, the Henry and Donelson campaigns became the only extensive operations of the Civil War deliberately planned and carried through under winter conditions.

To make certain that the situation at Fort Henry had not changed since Shirk and Smith visited, Brig. Gen. Grant ordered one last reconnaissance made of the Confederate bastion. With the *Lexington* since mended at Mound City, the duty fell to the two-boat task group led by Lt. Phelps. As Brig. Gen. Smith was unavailable to accompany him, Lt. Phelps, upon reaching Paducah, called at the home of Brig. Gen. Lew Wallace, whom he had doubtless met during the "Calloway voyage." After explaining that he was going up to see if any new works or guns had been added, Phelps invited the future author of *Ben Hur* to accompany him. Wallace jumped at the opportunity and later called this outing "an experience so altogether novel and full of excitement that in my best thought I class it as one of my choicest memories."

We are fortunate that Wallace decided to go and "see somewhat of sailor life under unusual conditions." Though describing himself as "a landsman of the ultra-lubber variety," he was an excellent narrator, though prone to long 19th century sentences. He has also given us some of the best descriptions of one of the two timberclads making the reconnaissance. Thus we quote him extensively. Although he had seen the *Conestoga* as recently as January 23, Wallace was hard pressed to describe her:

> Indeed, I remember not more of her than that she was flat-bottomed, very broad, and black all over; that her upper deck was in the style of a sea-goer, with bulwarks up to my shoulder; that there was a great gun at her bow, and that the pilot-house and commander's quarters were on the upper deck. I remember, also, the exceeding whiteness of the planking of that deck, the stealthy silence of the ship's going, and the cheerfulness, with which everybody on board went about his duty.

Lew Wallace, like many Army officers, was no stranger to the dinner table:

> ... at meal-times, the table-cloths and napkins did such honor to the laundry, and the tableware was so above suspicion, and the courses brought on were of such wholesome variety and masterly preparation that I could not help rating my host for the advantages of his service compared with ours of the land.

It is clear from this testimony that he did not visit the lower deck at mealtime. Remarking on the high water, the colonel noted that "The river was in good boating condition, and very beautiful despite the touches of winter apparent to the trees."

As the *Lexington* and *Conestoga* cruised up the Tennessee, "Hamlets and farm-houses were frequent; but the people seemed to keep watch against us, and at sight of our smoke in the distance vanished, how and where Heaven knew." Adding a psychological note later historians would comment upon, Wallace noticed how "The gun-boatmen enjoyed the terror they inspired."

That Thursday, "at the coming of night, we invariable dropped anchor in the middle of the stream" to avoid snags, sandbars, and Rebels along the shore. It was an hour and a half shy of sunset when the timberclads halted, but Lt. Phelps promised Wallace on the *Conestoga* that the next morning at 9:00 A.M. "I will give you a look at the fort."

The night was quiet, "its silence more noticeable because of the cessation of the engines and the smothered cough of the escape pipe." All of a sudden, "the baying of a hound was heard. It came from the left shore, and, startled, we looked that way; nor we alone." Every hand aboard stopped to look. It was difficult to see: "At our left, beyond a margin of water 75 or 80 yards in width, and very still and smooth-flowing, the shore was thinly fringed with half-grown willows, fast being denuded of leaves; beyond the willows stretched a cornfield bounded on its farther side by a fence and a woods." The sound of the hounds intensified as an entire pack was heard, perhaps chasing a fox. But this was no four-legged furry creature; it was a black man running for his life, spied jumping over a fence by a gunboat lookout.

Handing his field glasses to Lt. Phelps, the brigadier was appalled when he heard what the officer saw: "They are hunting the man with blood-hounds. He sees the ship and is heading this way." Flushed, Phelps immediately ordered the *Conestoga*'s yawl to row ashore to the rescue. As the "contraband" made for the willows on the bank, riflemen aboard the gunboat, including Phelps and Wallace, shot at the dogs and, in the process, halted the pursuit of three mounted riders. The *Lexington*, anchored some distance away, was not a party to the exchange.

Reaching the riverbank, the fugitive was fortunate enough to climb a willow before the dogs reached him. Presently, the yawl "ran in under him and the sailors landed and drove the hounds off with their oars." The escaped slave, in torn clothes, was brought aboard the "Linkum gunboat" and given medical aid and sanctuary.

The remainder of the night passed peacefully. *Conestoga* and *Lexington* were underway early on January 31. As the two continued upriver, the usual routine of ship was maintained. Brig. Gen. Wallace accompanied Phelps in his rounds of the quarters aboard the former. "There was no excitement and but few words," he remembered, "yet even I could see the readiness for action." The inspection ended at the bow with a close look at the great cannon in that location.

Not long after this, Brig. Gen. Wallace observed a couple of sailors "leaning over the bulwark, one on either side of the bow, gazing into the water. They did not look up. The army man also sensed that the timberclad had slowed and inquired the reason from his host. Lt. Phelps told him: "We are in the torpedo zone as reported." "I looked at the two sailors in the bow, and understood why they were fishing with their eyes so intently in the water," Wallace noted. "I, also, mentally approved the going slow."

A total of 12 (some sources say 20 or more) submarine batteries, also known as "torpedoes," or what we now call underwater mines, were anchored in the western channel ("chute") where Panther Island divided Fort Henry from the unfinished Fort Heiman. Each of the sheet-iron cylinders was 5½ feet long with a 1 foot diameter and was loaded with 70 pounds of black powder. Anchored on the bottom and normal river flow level, each was outfitted with a prong or rod which extended upward and sought the bottom of a passing vessel. Any craft hitting a prong would trigger an explosion. A picture of one appears in Admiral Walke's *Battles and Leaders* article on Fort Henry.

When the Tennessee began to flood, a significant number of these broke their moorings and sank; the remainder would prove ineffective. More were sent out and sailors from the *Samuel Orr* attempted to plant them, but they were largely unsuccessful. The *Conestoga*'s sailors did not report finding any on this trip.

Presently, lookouts aboard the timberclads spotted riders on the left bank. Lt. Phelps peered at them through his binoculars: "Soldiers, mounted and going full speed." If the enemy were not already alerted by the smoke from their chimneys, these vedettes, or mounted sentries, would soon announce them.

After a while, the *Conestoga* and *Lexington* entered the western channel of Panther Island. "I could not help admiring the good sense of the maneuver," Wallace observed: "Upon rounding the insular obstruction, the *Conestoga* would be in sight and in easy range of the fort; instead, then, of offering the vessel broadside on to the multiplied chances of a hit, should fire be opened upon her, our bow, built strong for fighting, would be the target; at the same time, we would be in a position to reply immediately."

The colonel inquired of his host whether, if he were fired upon, he would respond. "No, my business is to look," Phelps replied, "and if I should shroud the ship in smoke, my occupation would be gone." Leaving the *Lexington* behind, the *Conestoga* cleared the channel and "moved out boldly into the main stream." It was a dangerous time. "Nobody spoke; everybody strained his eyes seeing what he could of the stronghold at the end of at least two miles of unbroken water."

Brig. Gen. Wallace saw many things he later remembered. First of all was the flagstaff, with an unknown banner lying limp without a breeze. Then there was the "fortification built squat on low ground." Three "bastions offered fronts to us, and in embrasures, I counted three heavy guns commanding all down the river." Of the bastions, one "extended its outward angle into the river."

"What interested me most," the 11th Indiana's colonel recalled, "was the sight of the three great guns manned and trained on us. We had not surprised the enemy!" What were the chances that Fort Henry would fire on them? Uncertain of his naval terminology but certain of results, Wallace noted the "The *Conestoga*, I have said, is a tin-clad. One shell exploded in her hulk might send us all to the bottom." Daring the fates, the timberclad slowed and stopped in midstream, allowing her men an excellent view. While they were checking for new developments, a man, later identified as Fort Henry's commander, Brig. Gen. Lloyd Tilghman, "stepped out on the parapet by the big gun of the lower bastion of the 'fort, and entertained himself returning our bravado like for like."

What the men aboard the timberclad laid their spy glasses upon was known in engineering circles as a "regular bastioned" fort, enclosing a space of about 10 acres. Produced by several engineers, this hybrid lay low on the eastern riverbank. Phelps and Wallace probably noticed that the trees above and behind the citadel bore ringed water marks that indicated the site was usually swept by the river's flood-wash. Close in, felled trees linked up the bogs, forming a secondary line of defense. From a swamp to the north down to a spot behind the fort a line of rifle pits were sited, about three quarters of a mile from the main work. Garrison quarters were situated just east of the fort and were protected by more rifle pits further east.

The fort's commander, Brig. Gen. Tilghman, believed it was built in a very "unfortunate location." Later on, in reporting upon its loss, he commented most forcefully on its configuration, concluding that "The history of military engineering records no parallel to this case."

Phelps was most interested in counting heavy cannon. There were 17 inside the fort, 12 being laid on the river. Most of that dozen pointed at the straight downstream river stretch and had an unobstructed field of fire of about three miles. Fort Henry's river guns included one 10-inch Columbiad, a rifled 62-pounder, two 42-pounders, and eight 32-pounders. Although *Lexington* and *Tyler* had played cat-and-mouse with the Columbus batteries during the Battle of Belmont, these Tennessee River cannon represented more firepower than the Western Flotilla had ever purposefully fought before.

On the other hand, Lt. Phelps noticed, as he doubtless had on earlier scouts, that those laid on the river were all at water level. They did not enjoy the advantage of plunging fire like those on the Iron Banks at Columbus and would be a fairly easy target for Flag Officer Foote's ironclads. "'I am satisfied,'" Phelps said at length. There was one newly-mounted large cannon, "the third one from the water battery." With a wave of his hand to the wheelhouse, the skipper ended the reconnaissance and the *Conestoga* dropped back down, soon going behind the screen of Panther Island.

The *Conestoga* and *Lexington* returned to Paducah, later on the month's last day. After bidding farewell to his guest, Lt. Phelps wrote out his report. In addition to the new cannon, he revealed to Flag Officer Foote that the water had fallen three feet at Panther Island. In its right channel and near its foot, numerous buoys were seen, "evidently marking the location of some kind of explosive machine or obstruction." Phelps was confident the "old boats" could rake them out. Once the channel was clean, the timberclads had to use it while "ascending or be exposed to the ricochet of every shot fired at the casemate boats."

There was a large force at Fort Henry. It was uncertain to the Yankees just how many men were there or how they were armed. It later turned out that the answers were: insufficient and poorly. When the gunboats attacked, there were at Fort Henry roughly 3,400 men in six raw infantry regiments, two light artillery batteries, and some cavalry equipped with all manner of small arms, down to and including personal squirrel guns and shotguns. The best trained regiment, the 10th Tennessee was outfitted with flint-lock "Tower of London" muskets that Gen. Andrew Jackson had used in the Battle of New Orleans 57 years earlier!

Additionally, everyone with whom Phelps spoke to in the area concerning masked batteries, road conditions, or whatever, understood that "an attack is anticipated by the Rebels and that they are prepared to defend the post at all hazards." "Galway" had not written anything home to New York two days earlier that was not commonly believed in country.[7]

At Cairo on February 1, Joseph B. "Mack" McCullagh, the correspondent of the *Cincinnati Daily Gazette*, sent the readership of his paper essentially the same prognostication as Wilkie: "From certain indications, I had concluded that Fort Henry, on the Tennessee River ... was the point aimed at." The newsman "was not surprised to learn on Saturday ... that some 10 regiments of infantry, together with artillery and cavalry, then at Cairo, had received orders to be in readiness to embark next day."

Although their officers did not tell them, many of the enlisted bluecoats were, like the journalists, able to guess their objective. Pvt. Allen Greer of the 20th Illinois noted that "Our destination appears to be Fort Henry on the Tenn. River." Brig. Gen. Lew Wallace, just back from his excursion with Lt. Phelps, remembered: "There was riding in hot haste from camp to camp. Tents went down, and the streets filled with troops in orderly march to the river."

While troop preparation for the Fort Henry advance got underway, the flag officer issued his first operational orders for the campaign. On that date, Foote appointed Cmdr. August H. Kilty, skipper of the *Mound City*, as his Cairo deputy during the time he was away. Kilty was not only to defend the tip of Illinois from any surprise attacks by the "bishop of Columbus," but was to push recruiting and completion of the mortar boats as well as the remaining ironclads. He would, as necessary, cooperate with the U.S. Army, which was leaving eight regiments (plus supporting artillery and cavalry) behind as well.

Pictured with her bow tied to a western riverbank, the Eads-built *Carondelet* was the most famous of all the Union river ironclads. She participated in every major campaign from Fort Henry through the Red River expedition and the Battle of Nashville. Cmdr. Henry Walke, former captain of the timberclad *Tyler*, was the boat's first commander (Naval Historical Center).

Lt. Bryant was instructed to move the *Cairo* down to Fort Holt as guard ship. Sailing orders were also sent Cmdr. Porter. After coaling, he was to start out with the *Essex* for Paducah at 1:00 A.M. on February 2. The captains of the *Carondelet*, *Cincinnati*, and *St. Louis* would depart at 6:00 A.M. Brig. Gen. Grant's troopboats transporting the 1st Division under Brig. Gen. McClernand were also scheduled to leave Cairo that morning. The slow Pook turtles were approaching Mound City when Foote left Cairo aboard Lt. Gwin's *Tyler*. The ironclads anchored inside the mouth of the Tennessee in late afternoon, while the timberclad arrived in the evening.

Both on his voyage up the Ohio and aboard the anchored *Tyler* that evening, Flag Officer Foote had considerable time to write out his battle plan and orders and to send messages. In addition to letters and a telegraph to Cmdr. Kilty largely concerned with recruitment, he also wrote a report to Secretary Welles outlining his activities thus far and immediate hopes for the future once he moved to his new flag boat, the *Cincinnati*. That move would be slightly delayed as the transports were late and did not arrive Sunday night as expected.

Foote's Special Orders to his commanders, published in the Navy *Official Records*, demonstrate much thought and confidence. His seven gunboats were distributed in two divisions: "the four new armored boats and the old gunboats *Tyler*, *Conestoga*, and *Lexington*." Each division received its own set of orders, No. 1 or No. 2. The heavy lifting would be accomplished by the *Essex*, *Carondelet*, *Cincinnati*, and *St. Louis*, directly under his command under terms of SO-1. The timberclads, led by Lt. Phelps, would take a supporting role and were governed by SO-2.

Special Order 2 frankly admitted that the woodenclad gunboats were not as able as the ironclad main division to withstand at close range the expected fire of Fort Henry. Thus Phelps' unit would "take a position astern and, if practicable, inshore on the right of the main division." Then they could throw shells into the fort—as opposed to directly at the water batteries—without too much exposure. It was important, however, that every gun aboard the timberclads be carefully laid. It wouldn't do to waste ammunition or encourage the enemy to greater resistance. What was, of course, left out was the flag officer's concern over "friendly fire."

"So confident was Flag Officer Andrew H. Foote of victory in the coming Union assault on Fort Henry on the Tennessee River," wrote Spencer C. Tucker in 2001, that "four days before the Union attack, he issued bold special orders to Lieutenant Seth Ledyard Phelps." These bold orders, which expanded upon the expectation of Maj. Gen. Halleck, were a separate set from the battle orders. Foote engineered these enhanced directives on his own initiative.

Special Order 3 asked Phelps, in keeping with Halleck's January 30 order to Grant, "as soon as the fort shall have surrendered," to take his three boats 25 miles above to disable the key Memphis, Louisville, and Clarksville Railroad drawbridge at Danville. Once that task was finished, Phelps was free to raid as far up the Tennessee "as the stage of water will admit and capture the enemy's gunboats and other vessels."

Although everyone connected with the Fort Henry invasion embarkation scurried about in semi-coordinated fashion and made every effort to get the troops together from Fort Holt, Cairo, and Bird's Point for departure by 9:00 A.M., it was impossible to get away on schedule. The embarkation of Grant's invasion force "with horses, wagons, baggage, and equipments" was, in fact, "no slight labor." Still, in just three days, according to his biographer, Jean Smith, the brigadier put together the elements of this offensive, the largest so far in the Mississippi Valley. He "organized his command for battle, issued rations and ammunition, provided for resupply, procured river transportation, and coordinated the movement of seven Union gunboats."

In the morning of February 3, Halleck received a slightly optimistic wire from Grant at Paducah: "Will be off up the Tennessee at six o'clock. Command 23 regiments in all." That Cairo district boss, in fact, led 12,000 bluecoats, while Brig. Gen. Smith would bring another 6,000. Men and equipment were loaded aboard boats all during February 2–3.

Those steamers transporting the 11th Illinois, according to diarist Pvt. Greer, were aboard theirs by 5:00 A.M., but did not push out into the Ohio until 9:00 A.M. They would not arrive at Paducah until 8:00 P.M. The 7th Illinois was even further behind schedule and spent "nearly all day loading the camp and garrison equipage." It did not reach the mouth of the Tennessee before midnight. Other regiments also faced long journeys and staggered departures.

It was not until Monday afternoon that *Cincinnati Daily Gazette* journalist McCullagh, who first reported the military call-up on Saturday, was able to report "that the last of the transports left Cairo and steamed up the Ohio in the direction of Paducah. Franc B. Wilkie of *The New York Times* was at Paducah to welcome Cdr. Graham's steamers, "laden with troops and stores," as they began coming in from Cairo. By evening, "the whole landing in front of the town was crowded with the arrivals."

As the boats bringing Brig. Gen. Grant and his staff plus Brig. Gen. McClernand's 1st Division put into shore, "Galway" saw many familiar names: *City of Memphis, Iatan, D.A. January, Chancellor, Alps, W.H. Brown, New Uncle Sam, Rob Roy, Aleck Scott, Minnehaha, Illinois, Keystone, Emerald,* and *Fanny Bullett.* The three timberclads, *Lexington, Tyler,* and *Conestoga,* were anchored nearby. "Inspired by a prescience born of an indisposition to walk when I could ride," the famed newsmen wrote in his memoirs, "I determined to 'assist' at the assault on Fort Henry in company with the fleet rather than the land force."

As the steamers arrived, Brig. Gen. Grant, McClernand, their staffs, plus Lt. Phelps, and possibly Cdr. Graham, held a conference with Brig. Gen. Smith at his residence. Grant did not have sufficient steamer bottoms to take both McClernand's soldiers and Smith's 2nd Division to the vicinity of Fort Henry in one lift. Thus it was decided to move by echelon; the 1st Division would proceed down first and when it was ashore, Graham would bring the boats back for Smith. Phelps, who knew the Tennessee from his many visits, would guide the transport fleet, while Foote's other craft provided escort.

While the U.S. leadership met ashore, Wilkie found himself a spot aboard the *W.H. Brown*, "a gallant little, craft, which would soon lead the upriver parade. Peering out, he thought "everything seemed ominous of evil." Indeed, even "the sky was hung with gloom like a hearse." Other correspondents found other berths. This was going to be a big show and men from the large newspapers in St. Louis, Chicago, and New York wished to be witnesses. One of them, Albert H. Bodman of the *Chicago Daily Tribune*, sent a last minute wire home announcing that the transports were away.

A little before midnight, Brig. Gen. Grant and his staff boarded the *W.H. Brown*. Then, just minutes into February 4, the troop convoy, under the protection of the timberclads, was "ploughing up the muddy, swift waters of the Tennessee." As it breasted a strong wind and heavy rain, "Galway" continued to see evil:

> Not a single kindly star witnessed our departure — not a cheering omen was there.... External indications were all against us — heavy volumes of thick black smoke rushed away like mourning streamers upon a strong South wind, which beat against us as if it would fain deter us from our mission; the machinery clanked dismally below; the steam soughed in harmonious misery from the escape-pepes, or rushed with a hollow roaring from the safety-valves.

Although the *W.H. Brown* was the last boat to back out into the stream, she had, with an hour, distanced the other troopboats into their lead.

The armada continued upstream about 13 miles to Patterson's Ferry, where they found Flag Officer Foote and the four anchored ironclads: *Essex*, *St. Louis*, *Cincinnati*, and *Carondelet*. Here the embarked cavalry regiments (minus one company) were sent ashore from the *Aleck Scott*, *Illinois*, and *New Uncle Sam* to march overland to Pine Bluff Landing, on the Kentucky side of the Tennessee seven miles north of Fort Henry.

While the steamers were unloading the horses and their riders, the *Essex*, *Cincinnati*, and *St. Louis* proceeded ahead to Itra Landing to await the troopboats and Flag Officer Foote. After Graham's transports was reformed, they were escorted by the *Carondelet* and Phelps' timberclads down toward the appointed debarkation point at Itra Landing, across from Pine Bluff. The dark night had successfully cloaked the passage and, luckily, no spies at either Cairo or Paducah had forwarded warning.

Fort Heiman, the unfinished earthworks atop some bluffs across from Fort Henry, was only lightly defended. Its soldiers were largely transferred over the half mile wide Tennessee during the night. That spot, named for Col. Adlophus Heiman, commander of the 10th Tennessee Infantry, would be largely unoccupied when Brig. Gen. Smith's Union forces arrived.

Early in the morning the dispatch tug *Spitfire* delivered debarkation instructions to Brig. Gen. McClernand from Brig. Gen. Grant. He was to come down with his transports as rapidly as possible, making sure to keep them behind the forward gunboats and to land his landing force "where they may anchor." The procession was anything but rapid and, like many later Civil War river convoys, was spaced out over a great distance. Because the convoy was so stretched out, the escorts, particularly the timberclads, had to make their most protective dispositions.

About 4:30 A.M., the *W.H. Brown*. was the first to "run her nose against" Itra Landing on the Kentucky shore. The spot chosen was about five or six miles from Fort Henry. The Confederate picket at nearby Bailey's Landing sent up a rocket, which was immediately acknowledged by Fort Henry. Then three more rockets shot up "announcing the approach of three of the enemy's gunboats." Soon, correspondent Wilkie observed, four other transports, the *City of Memphis*, *Iatan*, *Chancellor*, and *Emerald* arrived and the "work of debarking the troops commenced." Brig. Gen. Grant hoped this location would permit his soldiers to avoid the necessity of crossing swollen Panther Creek in the face of any determined enemy.

Alerted, Col. Heiman, who was temporarily in command of Fort Henry while Brig. Gen. Tilgham was inspecting Fort Donelson, ordered the defenders to their posts, sent a message to his superior, and ordered the *Dunbar* and the *Lynn Boyd* to bring up two regiments stationed at Paris Landing. Just after daylight, reports came in from pickets on both sides of the river of "a large fleet coming up." Smoke from several gunboat was visible over Panther Island.

It was, however, suspected that Itra Landing was within range of Fort Henry's guns. To find out, Grant and Foote elected to make an armorclad reconnaissance. Coming within range of the Rebel citadel, the big naval guns burst shells over Fort Henry. Confederates in the bastion, Peter Franklin Walker later observed, "watched as the solid and spherical shot skipped over the water and dug into the earthen walls of the fort."

The aroused Confederates turned their 24-pounders on the gunboats and cannonballs soon whizzed around them as they withdrew. Having obtained his answer, Brig. Gen. Grant now determined that his men should be removed to a safer location four or five miles below Fort Henry to Fisher's Landing. This point was near a clearing opposite the village of Buffalo. The order was passed and the five troop steamers at Itra Landing halted unloading men and equipment and reembarked that portion of the force already ashore.

Coming abreast of the new landing beaches, Foote's gunboats bombarded the picket quarters "and other buildings in the neighborhood" to chase away any lingering scouts or sharpshooters. Men thus removed reported to Col. Heiman that eight gunboats were in the river and 10 heavy transports were putting their men ashore.

Although not that far away geographically, the town of Clarksville, on the Cumberland River below Nashville, was like many other communities at this time before electronic news, somewhat isolated and starved for war news. Although rumors were heard, it would take four days for the first information on the Yankee advance to appear in that town's *Chronicle*. On February 7, it officially reported this exchange between Foote's ironclads and Fort Henry. "Some thirty shots were exchanged with the gunboats," it was said, "without any serious damage to it [Fort Henry]. It is believed that one of the boats was crippled by our guns.

Heiman had other problems. A large force was necessarily assigned to keep flood waters out of the fort. By this time, its lower magazine had two feet of water, forcing the transfer of ammunition from it to a temporary above-ground magazine.

It took until 2 P.M. to get everyone and everything back aboard Cdr. Graham's steamers, after which they were directed to their new destination. As they eased into the bank about an hour later, they were guarded by the three ironclads plus the *Tyler* and *Conestoga*.

As the first troops of Brig. Gen. McClernand went ashore, some immediately went out on reconnaissance. As fast as others landed, they were disposed in "line of battle" on a range of hills overlooking the river. The 1st Brigade was actually located within three and a half miles of Fort Henry, "nearly in view of the Rebel batteries." The 2nd Brigade joined the first and commanded roads to the bastion. Artillery was unlimbered and the "trains of the whole division" were appropriately disposed and the whole operation was carried out "under cover the Gun-boats."

"The steamer of the enemy was observed frequently during the day," McClernand later wrote, "crossing and recrossing for the purpose of reconnoitering and it may be for passing troops." Which steamer was observed by the brigadier is unknown as both Capt. Fowler's *Dunbar* and Capt. Charles Smedley's *Lynn Boyd* were busily transporting Tennessee troops. For some time, other steamers had also brought in supplies and equipment.

A courier from Col. Heiman at Fort Henry reached the Cumberland River at 4:00 P.M. and informed Brig. Gen. Tilghman of developments. Escorted by cavalry, the citadel commander, with his chief engineer, Maj. Jeremy F. Gilmer, raced back to their post, arriving about 11:30 P.M. Artillery Col. Milton A. Haynes also arrived from Fort Donelson during the night to offer his assistance.

The 2nd and 3rd Federal divisions were not expected until the following morning due to lack of steamer capacity. Once the initial regiments went ashore and their steamers were emptied and reconfigured for maximum use, they returned to Paducah to bring the soldiers of Brig. Gen. Smith. While en route to the mouth of the Tennessee "after the troops from that place," Brig. Gen. Grant admitted in a letter to his wife that "I do not want to boast but I have a confident feeling of success."

The U.S. troops and gunboats up the Tennessee passed a peaceful night. In some of his most artistic prose, "Galway" painted a far more positive picture 24 hours later than he had the night before. The gloom was gone and "the sky was as warm and tender as one that bends over the flowers of May." Looking about, he saw that the wooded hills were "highly silvered by a crescent moon that glittered in the western sky." Adding to the charm of the early evening, a half dozen regimental bands "roused the soul with patriotic strains" or "soothed it with some dreamy waltz."

During the night, the *Dunbar* and the *Lynn Boyd* transferred the 27th Alabama and 15th Arkansas regiments to Fort Henry from Fort Heiman.[8] The troopboats of Brig. Gen. Smith, escorted by the *Carondelet* and *Lexington*, started up the Tennessee before dawn on Wednesday, February 5. By 6:30 A.M., at least part of the convoy was 15 miles above. The *Lexington* landed opposite Aurora at 10:15 A.M. next to the stopped *Chancellor*. A half hour later, the two were passed by the fast *W.H. Brown*.

"The 5th was a day of unwonted animation on the hitherto quiet waters of the Tennessee," Capt. Jesse Taylor observed from Fort Henry's batteries. "All day long the flood-tide of arriving and the ebb of returning transports continued ceaselessly." Further up, near Fisher's Landing, little of interest to the sailors aboard the timberclads was occurring ashore, though the crack of rifle shots could occasionally be heard from pickets or scouts, active on both sides. Despite the protection of the timberclads and Pook turtles, the beaches were vulnerable. Tilghman, like many 19th century generals, chose to rely on the strength of his fort rather than contest Grant's landing. When Maj. Gen. Polk offered some reinforcing cavalry, the defensive-minded commander wired in reply: "I'd rather have disciplined infantry." "Such position warfare ... would," confirms Grant's biographer Smith, "prove to be a mistake."

Out on the Tennessee, lookouts watched a small Rebel steamer busily run from Fort Henry to a point up or across the river. What was it doing? Bringing reinforcements? Perhaps, as Joseph B. "Mack" McCullagh of the Cincinnati *Daily Gazette* suggested, she was taking "observations of our proceedings."

Tyler and *Conestoga* were ordered to proceed up to the area near the center of Panther Island and drop a few shells on the fort, and try — against odds — to hit the steamer. This minor bombardment drew only one shell from Brig. Gen. Tilghman's batteries and it burst at least 400 yards too far off. Lt. Shirk and the men aboard the *Lexington*, resting up the river with several of Brig. Gen. Smith's 2nd Division transports, heard the heavy firing. The timberclad immediately cast loose from shore and stood up the river.

Following their shoot, Lt. Phelps kept his two wooden warriors in their advanced location. During the afternoon, they first sounded the west channel, then reconnoitered the riverbanks, both of the island and of the Tennessee shore. These visits were designed to prevent Rebel troops from throwing up masked batteries or transferring troops. Brig. Gen. Tilghman later admitted that their activities "prevented any communication, except by a light barge, with the western bank."

While the other two timberclads continued their activities, the *Lexington* arrived at Fisher's Landing with the *Aleck Scott*, *D.A. January*, and *Fanny Bullitt*. Other transports would arrive through the remainder of the afternoon and, like the three named, land their bluecoats on the western shore to operate against Fort Heiman and the batteries suspected on that side.

Continuing to reconnoiter in the west channel of Panther Island, the *Tyler* and *Conestoga* "discovered two ugly torpedoes." *New York Tribune* correspondent Albert D. Richardson and his *Boston Morning Journal* colleague Charles Carleton Coffin in their memoirs indicate that the resting place was given away by the "imprudent tongue of an angry Rebel woman." Prophesying earlier in presence of bluecoated scouts visiting her farmhouse that Foote's fleet would soon be blown into atoms, "She was compelled to divulge what she knew, or be confined to the guard house. In mortal terror, she gave the desired information."

Whether, as is probable, the submarine batteries were located by keen-eyed lookouts aboard the timberclads or from Richardson and Coffin's's loose-lipped Tennessee shrew, "Galway" notes, both were carefully swept out and towed out of the way. Rain of the previous few days caused the river stage to stand at 25 feet above low water.

Telling the same story, *Cincinnati Daily Gazette* reporter McCullagh observed that the two gunboats "succeeded in removing six torpedoes ... without injury." At the time, Charles Carleton Coffin assured his Massachusetts audience that "Three were first taken up with grappling hooks, and all but one were found to be so moist that they would not have exploded." Later, toward evening, the *Conestoga* came abreast of the flag boat *Cincinnati* to show one of the monsters to Flag Officer Foote, who was then in conference with the visiting Brig. Gen. Grant. The submarine battery was manhandled over and onto the fantail of the ironclad.

When Grant and his staff officers finished their meeting and were headed toward their yawl, they, together with Flag Officer Foote, spied the mine and expressed a desire to inspect it. This was the first of these "infernal machines" anyone in the U.S. Army high command had ever seen and Grant was particularly interested in its arming mechanism. The *Cincinnati*'s armoror was summoned and proceeded to loosen the iron business end, along with a cap underneath. As he did so, it vented "a quantity of gas inside, probably generated from the wet powder, which rushed out with a loud sizzling noise."

Everyone, including young witness Elliott Callendar, naturally thought that the device was about to explode. The two army staffers hit the deck, while Foote began to rapidly climb the nearby ship's ladder, followed by Grant, who had never ascended a ship's ladder before and "was displaying more energy than grace." As they approached the top, the danger was past. Chuckling, Foote turned and asked, "General, why this haste?" Not missing a beat, the brigadier, already climbing back down, replied, "That the navy may not get ahead of us." The dissection was completed, the pieces carefully removed, and the visitors all departed.

The brass bands resumed their concerts that evening after dinner. Around 8:00 P.M., as many listeners were enjoying the inspiring strains, a tremendous thunderstorm burst over the area. White-blue lightning streaked from the heavens and the thunder sounded like heavy cannon. "Everyone," the soggy journalist Frank Wilkie recorded, was sent "grumbling, wet, and disconsolate to the best shelter he could find."

Out on the river, the current became exceptionally swift and it was difficult to keep the gunboats and the transports securely anchored. Donald Davidson tells us that the "crews had to work constantly to fend off floating trees, driftwood, lumber, and fences." Many vessels, including the *Conestoga*, kept their engine pressure up so that their huge paddle wheels could help keep them properly moored.

Even the ironclads had difficulty maintaining station. "It required all the steam-power of the *Carondelet*, with both anchors down, and the most strenuous exertions of the officers and crew working day and night," Cmdr. Walke later recalled, "to prevent the boat from being dragged downstream." The *Tribune*'s reporter was not too bothered, however. "The night was excessively rainy and severe upon our boys in blue in their forest bivouacs," Albert D. Richardson remembered later, "but in the well-furnished cabin of General Grant's steamer, we found 'going to war' an agreeable novelty."

Before it began to rain in torrents, a number of U.S. troops were put across the river to a point opposite Bailey's Ferry. The growing intensity of the storm prevented horsemen from the Alabama cavalry from intervening. Five more U.S. transports arrived during the night and the amphibious assault on the west bank continued as dawn approached.[9]

February 6 was a day of destiny and it dawned cloudy but without rain. The sun came out about 9:00 A.M. and it began to warm. This was the day designated for the Federal attack. Grant's battle plan, now in the hands of his commanders, incorporated what he had learned from his failed encirclement at Belmont. Among the lessons learned in November was one prominently incorporated here: naval coordination. Tilghman's command held an unknown number of men. There might be more coming to reinforce him, but if he could take the place, he would.

Grant planned to surround Fort Henry. McClernand would make certain that no one got out of the bastion or reinforced it from Fort Donelson. Smith would take possession of the Fort Heiman hill overlooking the fort and then cross to assist McClernand. Foote was to bombard the citadel and, if possible, drive the Rebels away from their cannon. The navy, in the recollection of Charles Coffin, would "shell the Rebels out just as you can pound rats from a barrel or a box." In order to give the soggy countryside time to dry out — at least a little — the advance would not start until almost noon. The *Lexington* and her consorts shifted their anchorage off Fisher's Landing about 8:00 A.M. to make room for the late arriving troopboats, including the *Minnehaha*. By now, even the pokey *Carondelet* was present.

Looking out from Fort Henry, Col. Heiman was able to see "heavy volumes of black smoke" rising over Panther Island. To the officers of the 10th Tennessee and others, these ominous clouds manifested "that the fleet was not to remain idle long." About 10:00 A.M., Brig. Gen. Tilghman and Maj. Gilmer returned to the citadel from the west bank in a small boat belonging to the *Dunbar*, "which was lying during the night at Fort Heiman."

The *Cincinnati* made general signal at the same hour, to which all of the gunboats, anchored with her across from McClernand's camp, made answer. The captains were all rowed to the flag boat, where they received encouragement and handshakes from their commander. Forty minutes, later after the skippers were back aboard their boats, Flag Officer Foote gave the general departure signal and the warships weighed anchor and started to form their line of battle. "No one who witnessed the departure of the fleet," Wilkie later remarked, "had a moment's fear of the result — we were confident that Fort Henry was doomed."

Ashore at 11:00 A.M. McClernand's 1st Division and Smith's 2nd Division set off to complete their parts in the battle plan. Panther Creek, a major reason why the former had been landed where it was, presented no crossing difficulties. Once across, they had only five miles to go to their objective — but it was through thick, gooey, slimy, black Tennessee mud. The soldiers wouldn't make it in time to block any retreating Rebels.

It was warm and pleasant as the four ironclads, all beat to quarters, slowly moved up the shallow eastern channel of the Tennessee River protected by Panther Island, what Charles Coffin called "a long, narrow sand-bank, covered with a thicket of willows." The atoll covered the boats from the long-range cannon the Rebels were believed to possess. When the ironclads came to the foot of the island a mile and a quarter from the fort, they moved abreast of one another, with the *Essex* anchoring the line on the right and the *Cincinnati* on the left.

With all hands at their battle stations, the "old boats" also ranged themselves abreast but followed at least a half mile to the rear. It was noon and it was still warm and pleasant, with a wind from the west. The timberclad captains, Phelps, Gwin, and Shirk, watched both their ironclad colleagues and the menacing Confederate fortress. To many, it appeared, in the words of Franc Wilkie, "simply a rim of new earth that appeared just above the edge of the water."

The men aboard Foote's gunboats did not know that Brig. Gen. Tilghman had supposedly already evacuated most of the soldiers from his untenable location. As the flooding river continued to spill over into Fort Henry, this legend, repeated in Tilghman's after action report, in Capt. Jesse Taylor's *Battles and Leaders* account and elsewhere, has it that 50–75 volunteers from Battery B, 1st Tennessee Heavy Artillery, agreed to stay behind and help him man the cannon. That this was a myth was noted by contemporary Yankee journalists and has recently been argued by Grant biographer Jean Edward Smith:

> Traditional Civil War historiography has accepted the revised Rebel version that Tilghman ordered the men to Fort Donelson before the Union attack began. In reality, the troops were in the trenches when Foote launched his barrage and panicked at the destructive force of the incoming artillery. Discipline collapsed, and the men deserted their posts, desperate to reach the safety of Fort Donelson. The South could scarcely admit that after 10 months of preparation its principal bastion on the Tennessee surrendered after only one hour, or that the garrison ran away; thus the story was concocted that Tilghman ordered the withdrawal and simply maintained a covering fire from the fort to let the garrison escape. Grant was perfectly happy to accept the revised version.... If the troops at Fort Henry had already departed, it freed him of blame for their escape.

Smith's position is supported by any number of Northern newspaper correspondents, some of whom scrambled into the smoking ruins of Fort Henry even before many soldiers. Most remarks were similar to those in the *Philadelphia Enquirer* of February 11: "The infantry fled from their quarters, leaving bag and baggage." In his memoirs, Boston newsman Charles Coffin recorded that the Confederates were "terror-stricken." Both officers and men ran "to escape the fearful storm" and poured "out of the intrenchments into the road leading to Dover, a motley rabble."

After the battle, *New York Tribune* journalist Richardson interviewed an elderly African-American lady who "stood rubbing her hands with glee." Where were all the soldiers, he inquired, expecting to find many more POWs. "Lord A'mighty knows, "she replied. "Dey jus' runned away like turkeys— nebber fired a gun!"

According to the logbook of the *Lexington*, the *Cincinnati* opened the attack on Fort Henry from about 1,700 yards out at precisely 12:27 P.M. The troops of McClernand and Smith were only about half way to their stepping off point when the battle started and the mud made it difficult for them to scramble ahead. Three minutes later, the timberclads also opened their portion of the battle. Accounts of the straight onward march of the ironclads have been told many times in the last 145 years and will not be repeated here, except to say that the fight lasted just one hour and eight minutes. We must, however, review the work of Lt. Phelps' division.

As the ironclads moved into their line, the old gunboats moved to a position on the left bank of the river to participate at longer range. They were successful in throwing their shot without firing over any of the Pook turtles. Lt. Shirk aboard the *Lexington* testified that the "guns were served with much precision, the shells in almost every instance falling and exploding in the fort." Truth be told, their firing was not critical to the outcome of the fight. As George W. Beaman of the St. Louis *Daily Missouri Democrat* later testified, they "remained behind, but within easy hail."

Although the timberclads were not damaged and no one aboard these boats was hurt, they were "at times exposed to the ricochet of the close fire" on the *Cincinnati* and her consorts. During the battle, the *Conestoga* expended seventy-five 32-pounder shells, fourteen 12-pounder rifled shells, and two 32-pounder round shot. The *Lexington* expended thirty-seven 10-second and 15-second shell. Expenditure from the *Tyler* is not recorded.

Very few of the Federal soldiers ashore were able to witness the fight, though almost all heard the heavy booming of the naval guns and some the reply of the fort's defenders. Years later Maj. Gen. Wallace remembered the "almost unintermittent thunder." Albert D. Richardson of the *New York Tribune* and several other correspondents tried to see the action from a riverbank tree located somewhere between the fortifications and the gunboats. "There was little to be seen," he confessed, "but smoke." Over on the western shore, "overs" from the Confederate citadel landed in the woods near the columns of Brig. Gen. Smith. "The effect," remarked Wallace, "was to energize everybody in the march."

At 1:35 P.M., Fort Henry surrendered and five minutes later Foote's vessels, minus the badly damaged *Essex*, moved cautiously toward the enemy citadel, coming to opposite the citadel about 45 minutes later. Brig. Gen. Tilghman later stated that he waved a white flag at 1:50 P.M., but, as he was unseen by the gunboats, the fight continued another five minutes until he lowered the Stars and Bars.

The *Cincinnati*, also severely pummeled during the fight, lost all of her cutters. Flag Officer Foote hailed Lt. Phelps, whose boat had drawn near, and ordered him to take his flagship skipper, Cmdr. Roger Stembel, in one of the *Conestoga*'s longboats to see what Brig. Gen. Tilghman had in mind. Once Stembel and Phelps were rowed directly through Fort Henry's sally port, Tilghman, via Capt. Taylor, wasted no time. At 2:30 P.M., the fort was promptly surrendered to the two officers, along with its surrounding camps, plus some 60 soldiers. The hospital boat *R.M. Patton*, with its crew and 16 patients, was also captured. Taking the brigadier back to the *Cincinnati*, Stembel left Phelps behind to raise the national colors.

Per the *Lexington*'s logbook, the Stars and Stripes were hoisted up the flagpole (the bottom two feet of which were under water in the flooded fort) at 2:43 P.M. Timberclad skipper Phelps was now temporarily in command of the largest Confederate bastion yet occupied by Federal forces in the west. "Mack" McCullagh of the *Cincinnati Daily Gazette* reported that "When the foremost of our cavalry reached the spot, they found Capt. Phelps standing alone, surrounded by his prisoners, waiting for someone to come and occupy the Fort."

In his account of the Fort Henry fight published in *Battles and Leaders*, Cmdr. Walke indicates that, once Brig. Gen. Tilghman arrived aboard the *Cincinnati*, he was introduced to the *Carondelet* skipper by Flag Officer Foote. The flag officer, according to Walke, "then gave me orders to take command of the fort and hold it until the arrival of General Grant." Ashore and seeing the carnage, Walke found his initial view sufficient "to suppress every feeling of exultation and to excite our deepest pity." Capt. Taylor tends to support the idea that Phelps remained in charge — or at least remained: "During the evening, a large number of army officers came into the fort, to whom I was introduced by my old messmates, Lt. Gwin and Shirk."

So which naval officer was temporarily in command of Fort Henry, the ironclad captain Walke or the timberclad skipper Phelps? The answer to this question remains a trivia hunter's

Fort Henry under attack as viewed from the low-lying Tennessee River fortification. The bombardment of the Federal gunboats, including the second division timberclads, was particularly difficult for the Confederates to defend because the river was at full flood stage and the guns were not elevated sufficiently to achieve any kind of plunging fire into the lightly armored top decks of the Yankee ironclads (Leslie, *The Soldier in Our Civil War*, 1893).

dream. As Phelps' division, which included Gwin's *Tyler*, was expected to depart up the Tennessee almost immediately upon the bastion's surrender, it is altogether possible that the newspapermen had it wrong and that the person who greeted Grant upon his arrival was, in fact, Walke and not Phelps. On the other hand, the timberclads did not weigh anchor "for up the river" until 5:00 P.M., which would have been sufficient time for both Phelps and Gwin to have rejoined their boats.

Capt. Gus Fowler and the crew of the *Dunbar* witnessed the battle from an anchorage in a creek a mile above Fort Henry. Some of the escaping soldiers "rushed on board" noted reporter Coffin, while others, in their haste or fear, "plunge[d] into the creek and [sank] to rise no more."

Once the citadel surrendered and her bunting was changed, the longtime fugitive steamer rounded to and made for Danville. The *Dunbar* was joined in escaping by the *Lynn Boyd*, the *Samuel Orr*, and the *Appleton Belle*. The latter, under Capt. William Heffernan, was the regular packet that had connected the fort with Danville.

The U.S. Army took possession of Fort Henry in mid-afternoon. Brig. Gen. Grant was able to wire Maj. Gen. Halleck: "Fort Henry is Ours." On the west bank of the Tennessee, Brig. Gen. Smith, Wallace, and other 2nd Division bluecoats reached deserted Fort Heiman. Looking "across the swelling flood of the Tennessee," Wallace recalled, "the Stars and Stripes flew out lazily from the stump of a flagstaff."

Good men had died and others had fled or been taken prisoner. Years later, however, Capt. Taylor confessed that "If the attack had been delayed 48 hours, there would hardly have been a hostile shot fired; the Tennessee would have accomplished the work by drowning the magazine."

Believing his services indispensable at Cairo and wishing to get his damaged ironclads under repair as quickly as possible, Foote, with the *Cincinnati, Essex,* and *St. Louis,* departed the scene in early evening. Before leaving, the flag officer was able to see off Lt. Phelps and his division, as it departed for "up the river" to fulfill the requirements of Special Order 3. After steaming all night up the Tennessee and down the Ohio, the three Pook turtles dropped anchor off the tip of Illinois on the morning of February 8, the same day that Grant announced Fort Donelson his next target.[10]

CHAPTER 8

To Florence and Fort Donelson, February 1862

FOR THE CONFEDERACY, THE LOSS OF FORT HENRY was nothing short of a disaster. "The Yankees," wrote the editor of the *Atlanta Confederacy*, "have brought their gunboats and forces from Paducah, down the Tennessee River across the entire State of Kentucky, in the most populous and wealthy portion of it, to the Tennessee line." Then, they "captured a fortification which our people considered strong which was intended to keep them out of the State of Tennessee."

Elsewhere, on February 8, the *Nashville Union and American* told its readers that the evacuation of the fort was "inevitable from the high water of the Tennessee rising almost into it." The editors complained that it "was regarded as a weak fort," but had to be sited where it was because, at the time it was started, "Kentucky professed to occupy 'neutral ground.'" The *Memphis Appeal* of the same date informed local citizens that Fort Henry "was purely an earthwork defence, though of considerable magnitude." Its armament "was very inferior" and the efforts to plant submarine batteries "were disturbed before fully perfected."

At Bowling Green, Kentucky, on the day after Foote's victory, Gen. Albert Sidney Johnston met with Gen. Pierre G.T. Beauregard and Maj. Gen. William J. Hardee to decide what next to do. "The plan finally adopted," writes Joseph H. Parks, biographer of Maj. Gen. Leonidas Polk, defender of Columbus, Kentucky, "defies explanation."

Almost immediately, the three men concluded that Fort Donelson was no longer tenable. It was also determined that the two remaining Southern field armies—the one at Bowling Green and the one at Columbus—"must act independently of the other until a concentration could be effected at a later date." Fort Donelson would fight while these retreated. Most reviewing this strategic decision have concluded, with Parks, that "it was poor generalship to send in thousands of men to be crushed or captured by twice their number."

While the shocked South recorded the Union triumph and continued planning to prevent a recurrence, an expedition even more devastating, from a psychological stance, had already begun—the great Tennessee River timberclad raid. The exploits of *Tyler*, *Lexington*, and *Conestoga* had been derisively recorded in sundry Dixie journals over the preceding months. Now many citizens of the Confederacy would have a firsthand opportunity to see the black gunboats.[1]

In keeping with fine points in the battle plan communicated by Maj. Gen. Henry Halleck to Brig. Gen. Ulysses S. Grant on January 30, Flag Officer Andrew Hull Foote on February 1 wrote his own special orders for his commanders. Prepared in three parts, the first two were designed to govern the conduct of the Pook turtles and the timberclads in the anticipated engagement with Fort Henry. The third, however, was handed directly to Lt. S. Ledyard Phelps, skipper of the U.S.S. *Conestoga* and commander of the three-boat provisional timberclad division.

Special Order Three reflected the flag officer's confidence in the outcome of the Fort Henry assault and in his senior timberclad lieutenant. As soon as the fort shall have surrendered," Lt. Phelps was to take his three boats 25 miles above to disable the key 1,200-foot Memphis, Clarksville & Louisville Railroad drawbridge at Danville. Once that task was finished, Phelps was free to raid as far up the Tennessee "as the stage of water will admit and capture the enemy's gunboats and other vessels." He was also to capture or destroy any other reachable property directly aiding the Rebel war effort.

Phelps had been busy at Fort Henry during the early afternoon of February 6, helping to make certain that the citadel, following its surrender to Flag Officer Foote, remained secure until U.S. Army forces could take it over. That duty was completed by 3:30 or 4:00 P.M., permitting the Buckeye sailor to repair aboard the *Cincinnati* for last minute instructions from his superior.

Back aboard the *Conestoga* within an hour, he signaled the also-readied *Tyler* and *Lexington* and, at 5:00 P.M., the trio of gunboats started up the river. A transport steamer, the *Illinois*, was detailed by Brig. Gen. Grant to take several infantry companies and follow Phelps to the Danville railroad bridge. The soldiers, who would complete destruction of the structure, would not get off until hours later. Further upriver, another steamer neared the trans–Tennessee railroad bridge, having made a far more hasty departure.

Capt. Gus Fowler and the crew of the Confederate charter *Dunbar* witnessed the surrender of Fort Henry from an anchorage in a creek a mile above Fort Henry. Seeing activity aboard the timberclads, the steamer's crafty skipper concluded they would weigh anchor and might head upstream. To prevent the capture of other boats and further destruction of Southern property, Fowler pushed his boat upriver toward Danville about 4:00 P.M.

Nearly an hour into their voyage, lookouts aboard the Union gunboats spied the abandoned camp of the 48th and 51st Tennessee at Paris Landing. To make certain that it remained that way, Lt. Phelps sent a landing party ashore from the *Conestoga* to torch the place. The mission resumed after this short delay and continued without incident until 7:00 P.M., when the *Conestoga* stood down the river a short distance to examine an unknown floating object.

Meanwhile, late that afternoon, the Grant-dispatched the *Illinois*, with a small patrol of Missouri infantry embarked, steamed up the river to destroy the railroad bridge at Danville. Along the route, stops were made at the mouth of the Big Sandy River and at Paris Landing, where abandoned Rebel equipage was gathered. By the time they arrived at Danville, the timberclads would be gone and the point reoccupied by the enemy.

About 7:30 P.M. as Lt. Phelps' task group approached the Danville bridge in the dark, musket shots were fired at it from the shore. All three vessels cleared for action and three shells were pumped into the thick brush along the riverbank, dislodging whatever Confederate riflemen were present.

Nearing the bridge in the minutes after the firefight, officers aboard the timberclads were able to see great showers of sparks coming from the river about a mile and a half ahead. These rose from the *Appleton Belle, Lynn Boyd, Samuel Orr,* and *Time.* All had been loaded at Danville with as many supplies as possible before getting away. Out of sight to the Federals, the *Dunbar* was tied to the bank below the drawbridge while Capt. Fowler put sentries on the bridge and tarried to the last moment to gauge Yankee intent. His wait was short.

Although their names may have been suspected, everyone aboard the timberclads realized that a number of Southern steamboats were making rapidly up the river under forced draft. As the *Conestoga* hove into range, she opened fire on the *Dunbar.* Fearful that his favorite craft might be hit, Fowler immediately cast off and followed the four other escapees. Lt. Phelps would deal with those five later; his first objective was the MC & L bridge.

Joined by a few gray-clad soldiers, Fowler's sentries opened fire on the wooden gunboats as they neared the drawbridge. After no more than one or two discharges, they ran to board an escape train waiting for them at the Danville station. Once aboard, along with the local telegraph operator and his equipment, they joined Fowler in exiting the scene. The bridge was now in U.S. hands—but it wouldn't work. Before leaving, men from the *Dunbar* had sabotaged the bridge by jamming into the closed position the mechanism that operated its draw. This prevented Phelps, Gwin, and Shirk from pursuing the five boats now increasing their head start with every minute that passed.

A landing party was dispatched ashore to work on the bridge machinery and it was not long before the draw was repaired. While the sailors and engineers, often employing salty language, worked on the mechanism, Phelps held a mini council-of-war with his colleagues to decide on their next step. As the *Tyler* was not only the largest but the slowest of their number, Phelps asked Lt. Gwin to remain behind.

Second Master Jacob Goudy's men from the big timberclad would destroy the railroad tracks on both sides of the bridge and also secure any military stores. Once these tasks were completed, the *Tyler* was to weigh anchor and join the others. Hopefully, by that time, the soldiers aboard the *Illinois* would have arrived to finish the work of destroying the railroad span. "We passed through the bridge with the *Conestoga* at 9," wrote the officer of the deck in the *Lexington*'s log, "leaving the *Tyler* to watch the bridge."[2]

The *Dunbar* sped into the night. People along the banks heard her frantic whistle and saw the fire and smoke billowing from her chimneys as Capt. Fowler pushed her to the limit. Southern newsmen writing of the incident days later noted how she "flew like a deer before a pack of hounds, giving warning to all boats and all points along the river."

Along the way, the escaping steamers spread tales concerning the depredations the gunboats were bringing: "firebrands, burning, destroying, ravishing and plundering." Entire communities, upon Phelps' approach, were encouraged to flee into the woods. There was time for Fowler to stop and sound the alert. His craft, local papers confessed, was "a fast boat." The other escaping steamers were not.

Having transferred her pilots to Flag Officer Foote a week or so earlier and still fresh off of her Mound City repairs, the U.S.S. *Lexington* was unable to keep pace with the faster *Conestoga.* Sensing something akin to the scent—or soot—of the Rebel boats in the air, the smallest timberclad left her consort behind, speeding on into the night after Fowler and the other captains. If any of them could be caught, there was not only glory but also prize money to be had.

The slowest of the Confederate transports, and consequently the first overtaken, was the *Samuel Orr.* This was the same steamer that a group, led by Wythe Fowler, had seized back on August 23 in retaliation for the *Lexington*'s capture at Paducah of the little *W.B. Terry.*

Operated as a supply and hospital boat at Fort Henry, this fugitive was transporting a cargo of 1,700 pounds of black powder and 27 submarine batteries— some of those not planted near Panther Island — along with a number of sick patients from Fort Henry. Approximately 10 miles from the bridge, she injured her wheel and was compelled to transfer her passengers to the *Dunbar*.

Watching the sparks from the *Conestoga*'s chimneys growing closer, the captain of the *Samuel Orr* determined that he could not outrun the gunboat. Determined to destroy her rather than submit to her capture, the steamer crew lit long fuses to the powder kegs and mines, then abandoned ship. The *Orr* went up in a big explosion off the mouth of Duck River. All of her crew were saved and no damage was done to her pursuer. The *Lexington* passed the hulk of the *Samuel Orr* at 10:25 P.M. It was on fire and so burnt out that Lt. Shirk could make no effort to save her.

The great steamer race continued into the small hours of February 7. It was between the remaining Southern boats and the *Conestoga*. The *Lexington* was now well out of sight and the *Tyler* was just leaving the bridge. The crews of the *Appleton Belle* and the *Lynn Boyd* were next to see Lt. Phelp's boat breathing down their fantails.

By 1:00 A.M., the captains of the *Belle* and the *Boyd* knew they, too, could not escape the *Conestoga*. The Yankee was steadily gaining and, at 1:30 A.M., tried a ranging shot on them from her forward gun. Speaking to one another through trumpets, their captains agreed upon a diabolical plan of self sacrifice that would hopefully work better than the one tried by the *Samuel Orr*. Although the *Boyd* had no explosives aboard, Capt. William Heffernan's *Belle* was transporting a cargo of ammunition and a ton and a half of black powder.

Knowing that a prominent family of Northern sympathizers lived in a large home coming up around one of the next bends, they determined to land their vessels below it successively. Then, as the *Conestoga* came in sight, the steamers were fired by their escaping crews in the hopes that their combined explosion would sink the "Linkum gunboat."

Crafty enough not to be caught by Nathan Bedford Forrest, Phelps was certainly not going to be taken in by civilian steamer captains. Coming to about a thousand yards downstream, the men on the timberclad all instinctively ducked as *Belle* and *Boyd* exploded. The concussion broke the gunboat's skylights, bodily raised the light upper deck, forced open several doors, and broke locks and fastenings everywhere aboard. The Union man's house was flattened and the "whole river bank for half a mile around about was completely beaten up by the falling fragments and the shower of shot, grape, balls, etc."

Realizing that he needed the *Lexington* and the *Tyler*, both without pilots, to catch up, and with his men needing a breather, Lt. Phelps ordered the *Conestoga* to drop anchor just above the wrecks of the two burning Rebel steamers. There she was found by the *Lexington* at 2:45 A.M. The *Tyler* hove into sight in the predawn darkness just prior to daybreak. Before continuing the pursuit, Lt. Phelps met again with Lts. Gwin and Shirk to assess progress. Gwin reported that the Danville bridge was not destroyed prior to his departure. He thought perhaps he might be needed further upstream, so decided to leave it until they returned. His men had, however, cut the telegraph wires that connected Confederate commanders at Columbus and Bowling Green

Further, sailors from the *Tyler* had also broken up the railroad trestles adjoining the Danville bridge and burned a nearby Confederate camp. Before applying the torch, they ransacked the abandoned tents and buildings and, in the process, found some important papers. These belonged to former U.S. Navy Lt. Isaac Newton Brown, who was now in Confederate service. In them, the eventual skipper of the armorclad *Arkansas* detailed Rebel efforts to build gunboats on the Mississippi, Tennessee, and Cumberland rivers. Perhaps loaded with intelligence, the documents would be forwarded on to Flag Officer Foote as soon as the mission was completed.

Gwin did not know that a battalion of the 1st Mississippi Cavalry from Paris, Tennessee, under Lt. Col. John H. Miller, had infiltrated the area of the Danville bridge as soon as the troopers saw the *Tyler* steam on upstream. It was this force which prevented Brig. Gen. Grant's patrol from finishing Gwin's work.

The day was young and the men aboard the Union timberclads, also mostly young, had been at it on this raid with hardly a break for the past 12 hours. Having provided for their breakfast while taking his officer's reports, Lt. Phelps ordered his task group to weigh anchor at 6:00 A.M. for "up the river." Three hours later, the trio came to abreast of Hawesport. A Confederate flag had been sighted waving ashore, but this intolerable insult was promptly removed by a landing party.

The situation was entirely different opposite Perry's Landing (present day Perrysville), a little further upstream. Here strong Union sentiment was found. People along the bank waved handkerchiefs, hats, and occasionally little U.S. flags. Time was taken here to go ashore just before noon and hands were shaken all round by sailors and civilians.

The *Illinois* returned from her trip to Fort Henry during the morning. Brig. Gen. Grant learned that Mississippi cavalry were at Danville bridge and that it was not destroyed. About the same time, both he and Flag Officer Foote received new orders from Maj. Gen. Halleck: "Push the gunboats up the river to cut the railroad bridges. Troops to sustain the gunboats can follow in transports."

Lt. Cmdr. Seth Ledyard Phelps (1824–1885) shown in an 1873 lithograph, was a pivotal figure in the history of the timberclads. He oversaw the completion of their original conversion and guided the boats on their initial voyage down the Ohio River to Cairo in the summer of 1861. He skippered the *Conestoga* in operations through that fall and into the spring of 1862. Phelps' greatest achievement was the Great Tennessee River Raid of February 1862, during which a number of fugitive Confederate steamers were destroyed and the mighty gunboat *Eastport* was captured. Phelps would also captain the *Lexington* briefly at the beginning of 1863. Following years of service, Phelps resigned his commission in 1864 following the failure of the Red River Expedition (Naval Historical Center).

Certain that the timberclads had left the bridge, and armed with Halleck's instructions, Grant turned to Cmdr. Henry Walke to finish the job with the *Carondelet*. Walke, who was in charge of the naval force left at Fort Henry upon the departure of Foote back to Cairo, was instructed to proceed to Danville and put the bridge out of commission.

While the ironclad made ready to depart, two companies of sharpshooters from the 32nd Illinois were ordered aboard. They were joined by Col. Joseph D. Webster and James B. McPherson and Capt. John A. Rawlins of Grant's staff. The *Carondelet* proceeded the 11 miles up to Danville, where the troops were debarked near the bridge. No opposition was met, because Col. Miller was able to see and hear the noisy Pook turtle's approach.

In his rapid departure, Miller abandoned his camp, tents, wagons, some horses, and so forth, leaving it to fall into Union hands. Some of this booty Col. Webster ordered taken back to Fort Henry aboard the gunboat and the accompanying *W.H. Brown*. The soldiers then ripped up trestles and destroyed a major bridge pier, preventing the passage of trains. Such Confederate materiel as was not removed was then burned. When the mission was finished on Saturday morning, the *Carondelet* returned to Fort Henry, where Grant, Foote, and the newspapers were told of her trip. Shortly thereafter, the *W.H. Brown* arrived from the bridge and offloaded captured horses, wagons, and commissary stores. Lt. Gwin would find no functioning bridge when the "old boats" returned.

Further up the river, there were no incidents during the Friday afternoon timberclad cruise until dusk. As the three gunboats approached Cerro Gordo landing, Hardin County, around 6:45 P.M., they were fired upon by Confederate snipers hidden in the bushes along the east bank of the Tennessee. The *Conestoga* returned fire with her 12-pounder while Lt. Gwin sent a cutter ashore from the *Tyler*. To cover the landing party as it was rowed toward the beach, both *Tyler* and *Conestoga* turned their heaviest cannon on the woods and brush behind it. Whatever riflemen had greeted them were gone before the shells fell and the boat nosed into the bank.

Further up the river, the fleeing *Dunbar* landed at the Florence, Alabama, levee at approximately 8:00 P.M. Capt. Fowler rushed ashore to warn of the approaching Yankee gunboats. Alabama soldiers and volunteers began a night's work of loading military stores aboard trains for shipment to Tuscumbia. Also during the night, the fugitive steamers *Sam Kirkman* and *Time* made port.

The 271-ton stern-wheeler *Kirkman* was originally built at Paducah in July 1858. Costing $14,000, she was 157 feet long and had a beam of 36.5 feet. Her machinery was salvaged from another boat, the *Helen Marr*. Before the war, the *Kirkman* served as a packet on the Louisville, Evansville, and Paducah trade. Capt. Smedley was a half owner of the boat with Capt. Joshua V. Throop of Evansville. Now, even though the former had "gone South" without consulting Throop, both were about to lose their investments. We have no information on the *Time*.

Steaming on, the Union timberclads soon reached Cerro Gordo Landing, seven miles below Savannah and 50 miles below Eastport, Mississippi. Small arms fire once more welcomed the Yankee visitors, who retaliated again with cannon. The three gunboats now hove to and launched their cutters, all with heavily armed parties, under the command of Second Master Martin Dun of the *Lexington*. At the levee, they found the large steamer *Eastport*, purchased by Maj. Gen. Polk back in November for conversion into a gunboat. They also learned the truth of the rifle fire they had supposedly just been under.

When the men working on the Rebel gunboat received the news of Fort Henry's demise, they quickly made arrangements to sink her if the Yankees came. A man was stationed on the bluff overlooking the river north of town with orders to fire a shot as a signal if they were seen. At that point, two men would chop a hole in the bottom of the *Eastport* and create whatever other mischief was possible.

Once the watchman fired his gun, the timberclads replied, sending two shells his way, one of which penetrated the ground near the shooter's feet. The axmen aboard the *Eastport* started chopping holes in her bottom but did not linger. In the words of Hardin County historian B.G. Brazelton, "He fled and the men on the *Eastport* fled too, without accomplishing their purpose."

The U.S. boat crews immediately searched the unfinished warship to determine whether she had been rigged to explode. She turned out to be safe. Her conversion already half finished, the fleeing Rebels had further tired to scuttle her by breaking her suction pipes. A Federal damage control party quickly halted the leaks and kept the boat off the bottom. With an armed guard posted, the three Union gunboats anchored for the rest of the night.[3]

The extent of the Union capture was revealed at daylight on February 8. At 260 feet, the steamer was huge. The side-wheeler, partially rebuilt with exposed paddle wheels and an unfinished wooden casemate frame, also had a 43 foot beam and a depth of hold of six foot, three inches. Built at New Albany, Indiana, in 1852, the *Eastport* already had two high pressure engines and five boilers.

Delighted with this prize, Lt. Phelps was also pleased to find large quantities of timber and lumber that the Confederates were employing to finish her, as well as iron plating lying nearby neatly stacked on the river bank. If he could get her home, the *Conestoga*'s commander might yet get command of an ironclad after missing his chance when Lt. Bryant took over the *Cairo*. Also found aboard were a quantity of documents, again from Lt. Brown, among which were several "stating that submarine batteries could not be successfully used in the rapid streams of the West."

Once more, Lt. Gwin was detailed to guard the prize. The *Tyler*'s men were also to load the wood and metal from shore and otherwise make the vessel ready for a trip to Cairo. She would be towed downstream as soon as *Lexington* and *Conestoga* returned from however much further up they were able to go.

After breakfast, the timberclads of Lt. Phelps and Shirk stood up the Tennessee once more. By now, their activities had become a source of Confederate consternation and concern. Rumbling past Savannah, they soon passed Crump's Landing on the western bank. Proceeding, they skirted Diamond Island and reached a high point known as Pittsburg Landing, nine miles above Savannah. Before the war and the advent of the railroads, the tiny settlement was a major link between the river and the Mississippi town of Corinth, 23 miles to the north and known as the "Crossroads of the Confederacy."

Fearful that Phelps would occupy Eastport, Mississippi, Maj. Gen. Polk at Columbus believed that the gunboatmen meant to strike inland from that point and destroy the railroad bridge of the Memphis and Charleston Railroad that crossed Big Bear Creek. To prevent such a calamity, he ordered several small artillery units and six companies from the 38th Tennessee to guard the bridge. He also appealed to the Confederate government for help. Polk also ordered Col. Robert F. Looney to take a section of artillery and his own regiment from Memphis to Tuscumbia to guard bridges in that area. Meanwhile, Brig. Gen. B. Franklin Cheatham at Corinth had also heard that timberclads were headed for Eastport and sent Col. James R. Chalmers and the 9th Mississippi toward Florence as well.

Further up, the great fifteen-pier railroad bridge at Florence, Alabama, became the subject of Southern controversy. The *Dunbar*, *Julius Smith*, *Time*, and *Sam Kirkman* were headed toward it and, unless it was cut, they would be trapped in the face of the oncoming enemy. At 8:30 A.M., a message arrived from Gen. Johnston. It ordered the span connecting the city with the railroad on the south bank cut so the boats could escape. Local leaders and citizens were very unhappy; the bridge, paid for with hometown funds, was the pride and economic joy of their community. They refused to allow its destruction until it was absolutely certain no other course was open to them.

The *Lexington* and *Conestoga* passed peacefully upriver, passing the town of Hamburg and, just over the Mississippi Line, glided by Tyler's Landing, Cook's Landing, and the left bank Tishemingo County community of Eastport soon after daylight. The latter, 270 miles NNE of Jackson, was built on a bluff and was the largest city in the state.

There was no descent to Big Bear Creek as Polk had feared. Moving on another mile, the two swept over another invisible state line and reached Waterloo Landing, near Chickasaw,

Alabama. Here, two more steamers were captured, the *Sallie Wood* and the *Muscle*. The capture of the latter gave Phelps an opportunity to inspect her holds and see just what kind of contraband she might have. After all, hadn't the Florence newspaper just 18 days earlier boasted that she carried illegal goods to Eastport on a regular basis?

Laid up for some months, the Paducah-built *Sallie Wood* was a 256 ton stern-wheeler that was 160 feet long with a beam of 31 feet. The *Muscle*, another stern-wheeler, was much smaller, weighing only 125 tons. She was also sometimes known as the *Cerro Gordo* and had been working the rivers since her construction at Allegheny, Pennsylvania, in 1836. Although the lesser of the two prizes, the *Muscle* was, in fact, transporter of the greater treasure—contraband, to boot. Aboard her the gunboatmen found a cargo of iron under manifest to the Tredgar Iron Works in Richmond, the South's major arms manufacturer. A prize crew was detailed to the *Muscle* from the *Conestoga* with orders to tow the *Sallie Wood* back down to Cerro Gordo.

Meanwhile, the *Dunbar* put into Florence and sent the Fort Henry patients to the Florence hospital. Gus Fowler then got underway again and managed to make it back up to Eastport without being seen or intercepted. Soon he would head for Cypress Creek, a mile and a half away. The stern-wheeler *Alfred Robb* made good her escape up past Five Mile Island and also hid out in Cypress Creek. As the *Dunbar* was eventually sunk to elude the Federals, the *Robb* had the honor of being the only Confederate steamer on the Tennessee to make a clean getaway. Steamboat historian Miller later remarked that "Gus Fowler wept on the occasion of the sinking of these vessels."

Back at Cerro Gordo, work parties from the *Tyler* loaded the *Eastport* with captured materiel. As they labored, Lt. Gwin and other officers were surprised to see many families coming toward them from the surrounding countryside. These were Northern sympathizers, very relieved to witness the arrival of the national fleet. "Old grey-headed men wept like children," Pilot John Sebastian later told the *Cincinnati Daily Commercial*, "and they implored us to stay with them."

During the day, Lt. Gwin took the opportunity to enlist some 25 Union-leaning Tennesseans from among the refugees. From them, he learned that a 700-man Confederate battalion under Lt. Col. James M. Crew was established in a winter camp at Savannah, Tennessee. The newcomers informed the naval officer that a number of the men in the Southern outfit were loyal like themselves but had been "pressed" into Rebel service. Gwin promised to bring the matter to the attention of Lt. Phelps upon his return from Florence.

Although somewhat short-handed, after sending off the prize crews, Lt. Phelps determined to continue his quest. Standing up the Tennessee, the *Conestoga* and *Lexington* approached Florence at 2:45 P.M. The Alabama community, 225 miles into the Confederacy at the foot of the Muscle Shoals, was the head of navigation for large steamers and about as high up as they were going to be able to ascend. The community, never anticipating the appearance of Yankee vessels, was totally unprepared to offer any kind of resistance.

The steamboats *Julian H. Smith*, *Time*, and *Sam Kirkman*, meanwhile, arrived at the Florence levee about a half hour before the gunboats were sighted. Their captains, like those of the vessels lost earlier, knew the game was over and that they had only two choices: surrender or self-destruction. Using what little time was left to them, they and their crews hurriedly set explosives and made their preparations.

The two U.S. timberclads hove in sight of the town at 2:25 P.M. At that point, torches were dropped on powder trails and all three Rebel steamers were fired. As the flames and smoke billowed skyward, riflemen 10 minutes later fired on the *Lexington* and *Conestoga* from the bank, hoping to delay their arrival until the civil craft were destroyed. Phelps' flag boat put an end to that foolishness with a single loud round shot.

While the *Time* and *Kirkman* burned, the crew of the *Smith* set her adrift from the west bank with her engines reversed and running at full throttle. Like the fireships of Sir Francis Drake at the time of the Spanish Armanda, it was hoped that the blazing steamer would somehow collide with one of the gunboats and destroy her. Although this was not to be, five minutes after the rifle shots ceased the *Lexington* was forced to turn about and head downstream to stay out of the way of the floating hulk. At 2:50, the wind blew the *Smith* into the bank and the *Lexington* was able to turn upstream after the *Conestoga*.

The timberclads arrived at the Florence railroad bridge about 3:30 P.M. The *Conestoga* then landed, with the *Lexington* following in under her stern. Lt. Phelps ordered his boarders away onto the enemy steamers. Knowing that time was precious, two landing parties sped onto the burning *Time* and *Kirkman* in an effort to save cargo and maybe even the boats. The former was loaded with Confederate government items valued at $100,000.

Although the conflagration was too large to let either craft be saved, some goods were secured before the task group commander ordered the two smoking steamboats set adrift. The U.S. Navy parties were very efficient. There was actually more war material captured — some of it "marked Fort Henry"— than could be stowed aboard the two gunboats combined. As no barges or flatboats could be found, the surplus, first stacked ashore, had reluctantly to be burned.

While all of this was going on at the Florence waterfront, local citizens were "thrown into a state of excitement." A number loaded up wagons and fled to the country. Although support for the South was, as expected, quite high in the town, there was here, as the gunboatmen learned to their surprise elsewhere during their trip, a number of citizens still loyal to the United States.

It was reported in the *New York Times* on February 13 that these Northern sympathizers even began making preparations to throw a ball in honor of Phelps and his men. An invitation was supposedly made and the celebrants were disappointed when the offer was declined. On the other hand, the *Memphis Avalanche* suggested that, immediately upon landing, the Federals went "straight to the Confederate Government warehouse as if they knew all about it!" Still, the *Tuscumbia Constitution* reported that it had only "heard of one man, who at Florence went down and showed them where to land and took bacon for his services." That, it crowed, was "quite a solus turn out of the Lincolnites of North America."

Lt. Phelps and additional crewmen came ashore to inspect local warehouses and storage facilities for contraband and other Confederate government items. A quantity of iron and plating intended for the *Eastport* was discovered. As his armed party moved about, Phelps was approached by a delegation of citizens concerned about their women, their bridge, and their private goods—in that order. The *Conestoga*'s skipper assured the gentlemen that neither he nor his men were, despite tales told by Gus Fowler and others, "ruffians nor savages." He had come only to enforce the law and protect Union loyalists from violence. As the bridge had no military significance in the sailor's mind, he pledged to leave it intact.

Phelps' decision to respect the bridge came as a surprise not only to local Florence leaders, but also would have startled Northerners as well if they had known of it. Speculating on the raid's outcome downstream at Paducah on February 10, "Tennessean," the correspondent of the *New York Times*, told his readers how important the Memphis and Charleston Railroad was to the Confederacy and how it ran for many miles near the Tennessee "near the Muscle Shoals, and approaches very near it at Tuscumbia, opposite Florence." Thus it was that "it is to be presumed that our gunboats will send ashore men from their crews and destroy such portions of the road as may be necessary to make the interruption of that line of communication sure and complete." It would not be destroyed until Confederate forces did it themselves in 1863.

The businessmen, meanwhile, hastened to their shops or offices to find proof of ownership for many items the gunboatmen were examining for confiscation or destruction. Once affidavits were in hand, Lt. Phelps ordered his men not to disturb the goods or commodities, which included both cotton and whiskey. In a case where some private items were taken aboard the *Conestoga*, he ordered them offloaded and returned to their owner.

This almost-total lack of interest in their town or its private holdings by the sailors from the Yankee gunboats amazed the citizens of Florence. There was no pillaging or plundering, no rape or murder. Once the excitement died down a few days later, the town press reported that the only damage caused to private property was the breaking of a lock on a warehouse door.

This is not to say that the visit occasioned no untrue rumors. For example, the Tuscumbia telegraph operator incorrectly informed Maj. Gen. Polk that the seamen brought their own telegraph operator and equipment and intercepted Confederate military messages as they buzzed along the wires at Florence. Others suggested that the railroad at Tuscumbia was put out of action and one Florence man gave testimony to the local newspaper that he had personally counted 27 Union gunboats on the Tennessee, even though no one else saw more than two or three.

By 4:30 P.M., the gunboatmen had finished with the burnt-out *Time* and *Kirkman*. The two wrecks were cast loose and drifted down the river, clearing the landing. At this point, a vast quantity of Rebel provisions was found in a warehouse near the bridge. Most of this was confiscated or destroyed. Among the welcome booty was 10 tons of salt pork. Many U.S. soldiers and sailors would eat well upon it. According to a later dispatch published in the *Chicago Daily Tribune*, the sailors, who were not permitted to acquire any such souvenirs, learned that calicoes cost $1 per yard at Florence, while good whiskey retailed at $2.50 for a quart.

Approximately three hours after their arrival, as dusk began to mask the scene, the *Conestoga* and *Lexington* cast off from Florence and paddled downstream. Despite the fact that additional bridges beckoned for inspection at places like Tuscumbia, Lt. Phelps, his holds filled to capacity, had to quit. Perhaps once he got the *Eastport* and his other loot home, he or Lt. Gwin could return. A few hours later, the timberclads, their crews doubtless exhausted, dropped anchor next to the *Tyler* off Cerro Gordo.

Way back down at Paris, around 11:00 P.M., Lt. Col. Miller sent a message to Maj. Gen. Polk. The steamers *Orr*, *Appleton Belle*, and *Lynn Boyd* were burned to prevent their capture. Additionally, Federal infantry at the Danville bridge site were burning houses on the western banks near the structure, which itself was on fire.[4]

Just after dawn on February 9, Lt. Phelps ordered additional fatigue parties drafted from the *Conestoga* and *Lexington* and sent ashore to assist those from the *Tyler* in further securing the *Eastport* and the prized materiel. At the same time, he held a council of war with Lt. Gwin and Shirk, hearing of the Savannah camp from the former. After some discussion, Phelps agreed that a trip up to see Lt. Col. Crew was in order.

Together, the three Yankee sailors drafted a bold plan for an amphibious raid on Savannah. Before the sun was much further into the sky, Lt. Shirk, with 30 riflemen, transferred aboard the *Conestoga* which, in company with the *Tyler*, shoved off for "up the river." First Master Jacob S. Hurd and Second Master Martin Dunn, both future gunboat commanders, were left behind with the *Lexington* and orders to speed departure preparations for the *Eastport*.

As Phelps' task group paddled toward Savannah, news of their Southern incursion continued to spread. A delegation from Huntsville, in reply to an apparent urgent telegram, received a response from Jefferson Davis himself. Writing from Richmond, the Confederate chief executive told the civic leaders that parts of two Rebel regiments, with cannon, were headed to their defense. Meanwhile, they were encouraged to get their militia together and "go meet the enemy." The president was appalled. "The number of men who can have been transported by four gunboats," he exclaimed, "should never be allowed to tread upon our soil and return."

When the two gunboats came to off Savannah, a large landing force of 130 men, with a boat howitzer on wheels, was put ashore under Lt. Gwin, with Shirk as his second, to find Lt. Col. Crew's camp back of the town. There was no fight; the Confederates had departed about 1:00 A.M. the night before. Perhaps hoping for a contest, Phelps later wrote that Gwin "had the mortification to find the camp deserted."

While the bluejacket raiders may have escaped a skirmish, they did find a considerable amount of Rebel provisions, implements, clothing, shoes, and camp utensils. All of this was secured or burned, along with the camp's log huts. Among the items prized was a mail sack, the contents of which were later forwarded to Flag Officer Foote.

Departing this location, the *Tyler* and *Conestoga* dropped down to a point where Gwin

The 572-ton timberclad *Conestoga* was the smallest and fastest of the three wooden gunboats acquired in 1861. Her speed made her a favorite for fast reconnaissance missions and dispatch work. She was present at the September 1861 Battle of Lucas Bend, participated in various missions up the Tennessee River, including Fort Henry and the February 1862 raid to Florence, guarded mortar boats at Island No. 10 and participated in the disastrous June 1862 White River expedition. In 1863, she served briefly in the Tennessee River and went up the Red River in Louisiana. At the beginning of March 1864, the gunboat participated in a scout up the Black and Ouachita rivers. The only one of the trio lost during the war, she was accidentally rammed and sunk on the night of March 8 by the *General Price* (Naval Historical Center).

One of the three original timberclads, the 448-ton *Lexington* was perhaps the widest-ranging of the three wooden gunboats. Following her fall 1861 sojourn on the Mississippi in actions against Confederate vessels near Columbus and in support of Brig. Gen. U.S. Grant at Belmont, she participated in the capture of Fort Henry and the great Tennessee River raid of February 1862. She remained in that area and in April joined the *Tyler* in providing naval gunfire support during the Battle of Shiloh. In June 1862, she accompanied two Pook turtles, a land force, and the *Conestoga* up the White River, and in November and December, she operated in the Yazoo. In January 1863, she participated in the capture of Arkansas Post and from February to May guarded convoys, fought guerrillas, and supported Federal army incursions on the Cumberland and Tennessee rivers. During March through May 1864 she participated in the expeditions on the Black, Ouachita, and Red rivers, gaining fame as the first boat to escape low water on the latter stream via Col. Bailey's dam. In June, she helped defeat a Confederate attack on White River Station, Arkansas. During her career, the timberclad hosted as skipper three of the most distinguished officers to command any of the wooden gunboats: Cmdr. Roger N. Stembel, Lieut. Cmdr. James W. Shirk, and Lieut. Cmdr. George M. Bache (*Official Records of the Union and Confederate Navies in the War of the Rebellion*, series I, vol. 25).

had been told a cache of enemy arms might be located. Second Master Jason Goudy was sent ashore with a boat's crew from the *Tyler* and soon thereafter returned with approximately 70 rifles and shotguns.

Having attained all that they could at Savannah, the *Tyler* and *Conestoga* returned to Cerro Gordo. There they found that some 250,000 feet of timber, together with the materiel stockpiled for use in finishing the Confederate armorclad, was loaded. Just before their departure, Lt. Gwin sent a party to burn the local sawmill where the *Eastport*'s lumber was cut. Gwin also took the opportunity to meet with refugee families and to assure them that, if the Rebels "interfered with the Union men, he would, on his return, punish them severely." Certain of the commissary stores captured at Savannah were turned over to the loyalists.

With his mission ashore accomplished by early evening, Lt. Phelps ordered the expedition to return to Fort Henry. To do so required that each of the gunboats now assume another role — that of towboat. The *Eastport* was lashed between *Lexington* and *Tyler* and began down the river first. Those three were followed by the *Conestoga*, towing the *Sallie Wood* and the *Muscle*, the latter at least partially under her own power.

The current was fast and the parade continued slowly and cautiously through the night. One does wonder, however, what might have occurred had any member hit debris or the group was attacked. Early on the morning of February 10, the *Muscle* sprang a leak. Additional hands from the gunboats quickly scrambled aboard and joined her crew in a frantic effort to save her and, more importantly, her cargo of 5,000 feet of prime sawed wood. The struggle was unsuccessful and the stern-wheeler sank.

Lexington's longboat near shore. One of the timberclad's small boats is shown just off the riverbank in this undated photograph. The timberclad is depicted further out in the river. Longboats like this one were used for a variety of purposes, everything from courier receipt, general transport or communications, and refugee rescue, to picket duty and dragging for torpedoes (Naval Historical Center).

As the timberclads, towing the *Sallie Wood* and the *Eastport*, continued down the river, Brig. Gen. Grant at Fort Henry wrote to Flag Officer Foote at Cairo. "I have been waiting very patiently for the return of the gunboats under Cmdr. Phelps," he noted, "to go around on the Cumberland while I march my land forces across to make a simultaneous attack upon Fort Donelson." Not wanting to delay, the brigadier asked whether Foote might immediately send other craft from the tip of Illinois.

Some word on the success of the great raid had by now reached the mouth of the river at Paducah, where the *New York Times*' man "Tennessean" wrote a dispatch for his subscribers. It was known, he told them, that three steamers were already destroyed by the Rebels to keep them away from capture by Phelps' task group and that the others had retreated up the river. Other details were scarce.

"They must be destroyed or captured or else they must destroy a span of the old bridge across the river at Florence," "Tennessean "wrote of the *Dunbar* and her consorts, "and attempt to run above the Muscle Shoals." The scribe did not know "whether the gunboats can follow them over the shoals on the flood tide or not." Like Phelps, the *Times* man also heard stories of Union loyalty along the length of the Tennessee all the way into north Alabama. Pockets were particularly strong, he indicated, in the Volunteer State counties of Wayne, Perry, Hardin, and Decatur.

An hour or so before noon, the remainder of Phelps' convoy reached the railroad bridge at Danville. Two companies of troops from the 14th Missouri, recently ashore from the steamer *Illinois*, were guarding it as the *Sallie Wood* passed under. While attempting to maneuver the *Eastport* with the current through the draw, the giant 260-foot vessel was caught in the pier and swung against the bridge. Once again, jacks from all the gunboats, this time aided by the men of the 14th Missouri, fought to save a prize. In the process, the *Lexington* was somehow damaged and her heavy bottom leakage resumed.

The effort to free the unfinished Rebel ironclad consumed Lt. Phelps, his sailors, and the assisting soldiers during the remainder of that Monday, through the night, and into late morning on February 11. Finally, as the officer of the deck aboard the *Lexington* recorded in her log, "At 10 A.M. pulled the *Eastport* clear of the bridge and dropped her through."

Also around 10:00 a. m., Brig. Gen. Grant, accompanied by Col. Webster, went aboard the *Carondelet* to confer with Cmdr. Walke. The brigadier, anxious to start his Fort Donelson campaign, asked Walke to take his turtle around to the Cumberland next day. He promised to send *Tyler*, *Lexington*, and *Conestoga* after him as soon as they returned.

At 2:15 P.M., Lt. Shirk's *Lexington* was the last of Phelps' task group to pass through the bridge. Forty-five minutes later, the U.S. Timberclad Division dropped anchor off Fort Henry, its spectacular five day odyssey concluded. As the *Cincinnati Daily Gazette* reporter Joseph B. "Mack" McCullagh told his readers, "Commodore Foote has just cause for self-congratulation in devising the expedition."

At Fort Henry, the three timberclads found an armada of transports. Among those lying at the fort were *Minnehaha*, *Hannibal*, *Gladiator*, *Iatan*, *Emerald*, *City of Memphis*, *W.H. Brown*, *G.W. Graham*, *Rob Roy*, *Prairie Rose*, and the former Confederate steamer *R.M. Patton*. On the opposite shore, *Aleck Scott* and *V.F. Wilson* were landing troops, while the *Empress* was seen departing for Cairo with a pair of cannon removed from the all-but-sunken water battery.

Immediately upon reaching the Fort, Lt. Phelps visited Brig. Gen. Grant and his staff to succinctly convey the story of his expedition, the steamers caught or sunk, the goods acquired, and the expressions of loyalty experienced. He also wrote out dispatches for Flag Officer Foote to be sent via the afternoon mail boat to Cairo. These included the bulk of his official report, finished before the *Eastport* hit the Danville bridge.

As Robert Suhr has noted, the results of the timberclad raid to Florence had forcibly demonstrated "the potential of the Union Navy on the western rivers." Their voyage "spearhead[ed] the Union advance into Tennessee" and was instrumental in starting a "chain of events that would culminate in the capture of Vicksburg in 1863 and the complete Union domination of the Mississippi River."

A wire sent later that night from the tip of Illinois would be published in the *St. Louis Daily Missouri Democrat* next morning announcing the timberclad triumph. It would appear in other newspapers all over the North within days.

About the same time Phelps was with Grant, according to Cmdr. Walke's memoirs, Lt. Gwin went aboard the *Carondelet* to pay his respects, on Phelps' behalf, to the senior naval officer present. At that point, the junior officer was informed by Walke that Grant wanted the ironclad and the three timberclads to move over into the Cumberland as soon as possible. According to Walke, Gwin was then ordered to have the "old boats" follow as soon as possible.

Not long after the departure of her visitor, the *Carondelet* steamed down the Tennessee to its mouth at Paducah, where it waited for its three wooden consorts. While halted, Walke communicated to Foote the chain of events leading to his departure around to Fort Donelson on the Cumberland River. He also added the news that "The *Taylor* [Walke never employed the timberclad's other name, *Tyler*] has just returned from up the Tennessee River, as far as navigable. They, with the *Lexington* and *Conestoga*, destroyed or captured all the enemies [sic] boats, broke up their camps, and made a prize of their fine new gun-boat."

Grant, the flag officer was informed, would "send the *Tyler, Lexington,* and *Conestoga* after me."

Returning aboard the *Conestoga*, Lt. Phelps now opened his mail, which included a message from Flag Officer Foote written the previous day. In it, the flotilla chief told his timberclad division leader that all available gunboats, meaning the lieutenant's, should cooperate with Grant in any Donelson assault. Once that was accomplished, they were then to move up the Cumberland to Clarksville in a raid reminiscent of the Florence push.

On the other hand, the letter Phelps received, which is reprinted in the Navy *Official Records* and was undoubtedly read by him after his interview with Brig. Gen. Grant, also states that the flag officer wanted to come to Cairo with the *Conestoga*. Phelps was to show the communication to Walke, but if he were not there, to Grant or Brig. Gen. John A. McClernand. After hearing the details of Gwin's visit aboard the *Carondelet* and reporting ashore, Phelps decided, despite the lateness of the hour, to weigh for Cairo.

When the timberclads failed to show up at Paducah by twilight, Cmdr. Walke ordered a tow line passed from the *Carondelet* to the steamer *Alps*. She then towed the ironclad up and into the Cumberland alone. Walke, believing Phelps a Foote favorite who considered himself above the orders of a mere commander, was livid years later about what he considered to be a deliberate act of defiance on the lieutenant's part. In his memoirs he bluntly stated that "Professional men may understand this conduct on the part of naval officers to be an act of insubordination."

Walke, a "restored officer" perhaps more conscious than most regarding his reputation, most likely made his observations based half on professional frustration and half on ignorance. A member of his own ship's company summed up the frustration felt aboard a number of the ironclads after the Fort Henry fight. "We are scarcely mentioned in the Fort Henry affair," he exclaimed, "while those western bandboxes, the *Conestoga, Lexington,* and *Tyler,* were puffed up by the papers when they were astern during the whole of the fight." And just days ago, hadn't the mighty ironclad steamed up to Danville and put right the destruction of the railroad bridge that Lt. Gwin's old boat boys had failed to complete?

Additionally, Cmdr. Walke probably never knew about the Foote letter to Phelps requiring that the *Conestoga* visit Cairo. He was likely unaware that the *Lexington* required dockyard work and it is also highly probable that he received no word on these matters from the busy Grant or McClernand, who, like Phelps, would also not have been able to reach him on the river.

Still, despite the unhappiness of a gallant colleague, the voyage up and down the Tennessee River proved an apex for the three "old boats" in the timberclad war. For the first and only time, the three wooden gunboats all operated as a single division under one commander. Two of them would, from time to time, ply the rivers together and, at the end of 1862, all three would briefly serve as part of a larger force, coming within eyesight of one another. Never again, however, would all three perform as a single task group.

Phelps' expedition was tactically successful. It cleared the Tennessee of seven valuable enemy transports and captured two others plus the gunboat *Eastport*. In addition to the steamers, significant amounts of lumber and other shipbuilding supplies was acquired, while large caches of other supplies useful to the Confederacy were destroyed. Pro-Union sympathies were displayed briefly, though the people so demonstrating had quickly to submerge their allegiance once Confederate control was reestablished over visited locations. In the words of

Donald Davidson, there would be few future "gratifying proofs of loyalty." Instead, "it would be 'guerrillas.'"

The timberclad adventure demonstrated, as Bruce Catton put it, "the importance of the victory that had been won" at Fort Henry. Many in the South realized, perhaps for the first time, that the entire length of the Tennessee River was unguarded and free of fortifications— or even established batteries. The Union could move up the river as it chose. Gen. Johnston and Maj. Gen. Polk would make a feeble effort at defense, but it would be of little value except to citizen morale.

On February 12, the *Charleston Mercury* conceded that the timberclad visit "up the Tennessee River to Florence and Tuscumbia" was "an audacious and hazardous thing." But it went on to point out that there were many places on that stream where the gunboats could be stopped and that such future excursions would exhibit "more recklessness than judgment and cannot fail to prove disastrous." The South Carolina editor was confident that the "business" of these kinds of daring marauders would cease "so soon as the people of Alabama and Tennessee recover from their astonishment."

By the time Brig. Gen. Daniel Ruggles, commander of the First Corps of the 2nd Division of the Confederate Army of the Mississippi, was given authority to post a two-gun battery at Florence and protect the bridges at Tuscumbia on February 26, the decision to rebuild Rebel defenses on Corinth had already been taken.[5]

Flush with victory at Fort Henry back on February 6, Brig. Gen. Grant wrote out an after-action report for Maj. Gen. Halleck. Coming to Fort Donelson, he noted that he would take and destroy it two days later. "It seems clear," Bruce Catton later suggested, "that both he and Halleck looked upon this step as just part of a mopping-up process."

The next day, *New York Tribune* correspondent Albert D. Richardson stopped by Grant's Fort Henry headquarters to announce his departure for New York and wish the brigadier good luck. "You had better wait a day or two," Grant said, "because I am going over to capture Fort Donelson tomorrow." "How strong is it?" the scribe inquired. "We have not been able to ascertain exactly," Grant replied, "but I think we can take it. At all events, we can try."

"I was very impatient to get to Fort Donelson," Grant revealed in his memoirs, "because I knew the importance of the place to the enemy and supposed he would reinforce it quickly." Far better to send 15,000 up against it now than 50,000 later. Still, as Col. Webster later reported, "Our army approached the place with very little knowledge of its topography."

The evacuees from Fort Henry straggled approximately 12 miles across a series of ridges that serrated the land between the Tennessee and Cumberland rivers and straggled into Fort Donelson on February 6. By dark, the latter's garrison totaled some 3,000 men. Gen. Albert Sidney Johnston now withdrew his right wing from Bowling Green and divided it between Donelson and Nashville. The same day Richardson was invited to remain, 12,000 troops from Kentucky arrived at the Cumberland River fortress.

Also on February 7, Cdr. Foote's ironclads, less the *Carondelet*, reached Cairo from Paducah. Citizens lined up along the Ohio River levee saw the flag boat *Cincinnati*'s arrival with a Confederate flag flying upside down under the Stars and Stripes. Cheering and rejoicing in the great victory was heartfelt, not only among the populace but especially among the bluejackets and officers, like Cmdr. Pennock and Dove, left behind.

Cdr. Foote, on the other hand, knew he had been in a scrape. Repairs would need to be effected soon if he was going to play a role in Grant's proposed Fort Donelson push. The old sea dog had no confidence any ironclad fix would be quickly done and, in a letter written to his wife and quoted by Jay Slagle, promised "I never again will go out and fight half prepared."

Lt. Phelps, as noted in an earlier chapter, was never able to make a full reconnaissance of Fort Donelson as he had Fort Henry. As a result, neither the Federal land nor nautical forces on the scene, let alone at Halleck's St. Louis headquarters, knew very much of anything about the defenses of the bastion east of the just-taken Henry. Indeed, they did not even possess accurate maps of the area.

Fort Donelson sat atop a hill on the west bank of the Cumberland River approximately 1,400 yards southwest of the little Stewart County seat of Dover. Visiting it after the battle, *Chicago Daily Tribune* reporter Irving Carson found it "a straggling place of 20 or 30 houses, with a brick court house, and a church which war has turned to its own use. Everything was dilapidated." "It was," confirmed "Junius," the scribe from the *Cincinnati Times*, "a town of some eight or nine hundred inhabitants in ordinary times."

At this spot chosen for fortification, the narrowing Cumberland makes an abrupt north turn, giving any ridge-mounted cannon a clear mile and a half long field of fire. Irving Carson of the *Chicago Daily Tribune*, who inspected the area after the battle, noticed that the western banks of the river were quite elevated; hills were about a hundred feet high, just like those seen "in Egypt [Southern Illinois] or along the Ohio." It was from these hills that the Rebel guns frowned down on the fast flowing river below.

Two nearby streams, Indian Creek at the elbow end of the curve and Hickman Creek 700 yards further up, were prone to swell with backwater when the river rose, turning the adjacent ground into a quagmire. Great thickets of oak and ash stood in the water further screening the flanks. Unlike Fort Henry, Confederate engineers here well used the topography available to them.

An irregular, bastioned parapet, the main part of Fort Donelson was about 500 feet long at its greatest length and enclosed approximately a hundred acres. Its narrow ridge base slid into a slight neck in the west and the ground sloped away sharply toward the Cumberland and the two creeks. On another ridge about 700 yards west of the parapet and roughly perpendicular to it was a group of earthworks, coupled with abatis.

Fort Donelson — like Fort Henry — existed to mount cannon, hopefully screened from waterborne attack. Two water batteries were constructed on the river side of the fort. The upper battery was 50 feet above the Cumberland and was armed with a 128-pounder rifled gun built at the Tredegar Iron Works. It was rifled to fire a 6.5-inch conical 68-pound shell. Also mounted in this location were two 32-pounder naval carronades, distinguishable by their short iron tubes. The lower battery was 20 feet up and mounted one 10-inch Columbiad that fired a 128-pound shell and eight 32-pounder smoothbores, all on barbette carriages.

The most important feature of Fort Donelson and its greatest advantage over Fort Henry was the ability of both high batteries to deliver plunging fire on targets below. Should the Pook turtles engage, their lightly armored decks and roofs would not be spared as they were at Henry.[6]

Aside from the fact that the Yankee army did not have a clear picture of Fort Donelson or its approaches, the optimistic initial timetable set by Brig. Gen. Grant for the bastion's capture could not be met because of the weather. It rained and there were oceans of mud everywhere. The area between the forts was a morass reminiscent of that experienced by the soldiers on the Kentucky mud marches of late January.

For five days, U.S. Army engineers and cavalry scouted the land, while the gains of Fort Henry were consolidated and, in many cases, carried off. At Cairo, work advanced on the repair of the damaged gunboats, though not as quickly as desired. Cmdr. Porter's *Essex* would be under the hammer for weeks.

At St. Louis on February 8, Maj. Gen. Halleck, who had no personal knowledge of the twin rivers area, was, as he had frequently done since coming west in November, examining

The *Tyler* and *Conestoga*, depicted on the left above, formed a second gunboat division behind the Federal ironclads in the bombardment of the water batteries at Fort Donelson on February 14, 1862. Although the wooden boats were not damaged, many of the Pook turtles were hurt and forced to withdraw at a point somewhat later than that sketched here by Alexander Simplot (*Harper's Weekly*, 1862, via Naval Historical Center).

his maps. Appreciating that the victory at Fort Henry would not stand without the reduction of Fort Donelson, he also cast a strategic eye 30 miles up the Cumberland to the town of Clarksville. The Memphis, Louisville, and Clarksville Railroad crossed a vital bridge at that community and if the span were destroyed Gen. Johnston would lose an important communications link with Bowling Green.

Also on February 8, reinforced on February 10, Halleck ordered Grant to proceed to Clarksville as quickly as possible and get the bridge. He was to "run any risk" to do so. A day later, he told Grant that "some of the gunboats should be sent up the Cumberland with the least possible delay." It was now "of vital importance that Fort Donelson be reduced immediately."

At Cairo, Flag Officer Foote remained uncertain that his ironclads were ready for any such immediate expedition. To help push the sailor along, Halleck dispatched his chief of staff, Brig. Gen. George W. Cullum, to the tip of Illinois to do everything possible to get the flotilla started. Halleck also wrote to Foote imploring him to shove off. "Act quickly," he begged, "even though only half ready." Halleck, Cullum, and Grant would badger the flag officer for several days until he finally agreed on February 10, against his better judgment, to weight anchor with his ironclads. Meanwhile, Cmdr. Henry Walke's *Carondelet* would move up the Cumberland from Paducah and render support until the main fleet could arrive.

Upon his return to Fort Henry from the Tennessee River raid on February 11, Lt. Phelps found a mail sack waiting for the *Conestoga*. Among the letters it contained were fresh orders from Flag Officer Foote penned the previous day. According to these, Phelps was already to have departed for Cairo with his provisional timberclad division, there to rendezvous with the flag officer. At the Illinois town, the western naval chief would come aboard the smallest timberclad and lead the naval contingent of Maj. Gen. Halleck's expedition to the Cumberland.

Phelps had missed Foote's rendezvous by over a day. Leaving the damaged *Essex* and *Cincinnati* behind, the flag officer left Cairo at 10:00 P.M. on February 11 aboard his flagship *St. Louis*, the *Louisville* and the *Pittsburg* in company. Nevertheless, Phelps, the hero of the Tennessee raid, determined to meet the new boats as soon as possible and, despite a misunderstanding with Cmdr. Walke, steamed toward Paducah and the confluence with the Ohio.

It is possible that the three convoyed several steamers, including the *Minnehaha*. That boat had arrived at Fort Henry the night before with Col. E. D. Baldwin's 57th Illinois embarked. To help make up for an earlier near-mutiny over pay by his troops at Springfield, Baldwin was detailed by Grant to ride the steamer back down the river and stop and turn around every troopboat headed toward Fort Henry. He would have for company Franc B. "Galway" Wilkie, correspondent for the *New York Times*.

On the way down the Tennessee, the three timberclads passed the transports *White Cloud*, *Fairchild*, *Baltic*, *Adams* and *Tutt*, all headed upriver. Their captains were ordered to turn around and steam back down to Paduach, as they were headed toward the wrong destination.

The *Conestoga*, *Lexington*, and *Tyler* steamed by Birmingham, Kentucky, at 6:00 P.M. and entered the Ohio River an hour later. When they tied up at the Paducah wharf, Lt. Phelps saw that the *Carondelet* and *Alps* were gone. He would not have to tell Cmdr. Walke in person that he would not be following or that Foote's ironclads were still paddling up the Ohio. "Upon night," Wilkie wrote," the stragglers came slowly creeping up the river."

Through the night, the transport fleet, 12–16 vessels strong (depending upon which source you read), assembled off Paducah. Aboard were two veteran Kentucky regiments and two from Indiana sent down from the Green River area, along with one each from Nebraska and Iowa. Six regiments fresh from camps of instruction were also present, three each from Ohio and Illinois. Altogether, approximately 10,000 soldiers were embarked on the various steamers.

Just after sunrise on Wednesday February 12, the *Lexington* was ordered detached for repair. She would miss the upcoming fight. As Lt. Shirk steamed out into the Ohio sometime later, his colleagues aboard the *Conestoga* and *Tyler* made ready to weigh ship for Smithland. The two old boats would follow the three Pook turtles and the troop steamers, with the *Conestoga* towing a coal barge with fuel for the fleet.

In mid-afternoon of the run, the *Pittsburg* lost a bolt from her boiler, requiring the armada to halt for just over an hour while repairs were made. When she was ready, the fleet continued, gliding slowly up the Ohio. The *St. Louis Daily Missouri Democrat* conjectured next day that the passage would be slow, "in consequence of the high water and the unusually rapid current in al the rivers."

As with the Fort Henry convoy, not all of the troopboats reached their destination together. The premier units dropped anchor off the mouth of the Cumberland at approximately 8:00 P.M., with the remainder of the convoy reaching Smithland during the next two hours. One boat, the *McGill*, with the 2nd Iowa embarked, did not even depart Cairo until dark.

"The scene at Paducah was magnificent beyond description," the *Times*' man Wilkie wrote in his notebook. "The night was as warm as an evening in August in our more northern latitudes," he continued, as "a full moon looked down from an unclouded sky." Every so often, the two forts guarding the town would fire cannon salutes and "the boom of the welcome went reverberating over the hills, till from the long distances in Kentucky, it came back like a whisper." Not to be outdone, "the bands on the boats charmed the ear with most eloquent music."

Probably without a soul obtaining a wink of rest in those last noisy hours, the great nautical caravan was ready to move again by 12:01 A.M. on February 13. Led by the *St. Louis*, followed by the *Louisville*, the fleet got underway. Great dipping paddles soon raised glistening torrents of water as sparks shot into the air from two dozen or more chimneys. From that time on, the extraordinarily swift Cumberland current reduced progress to "the slowest possible description."

As the balmy night bathed the region, a great column of Federal soldiers, Brig. Gen. McClernand's first division, had also started out on a march across the hills between this great river and the Tennessee. According to George W. Beaman of the *St. Louis Daily Missouri Democrat*, it "stretched and coiled" from Fort Henry toward Fort Donelson. The moonlight shown equally on those men, dappling troops under trees with "alternate patches of shadow and light."

According to Wilkie of the *Times*, approximately 20,000 troops, including cavalry and artillery, made the comparatively easy slog across the Dover and telegraph roads by night and day and began to invest Donelson on the twelfth. The weather for this operation was good. Brig. Gen. Lew Wallace, about to assume command of a new 3rd Division, observed that it was like "a day of summer. River, land and sky fairly shimmered with warmth. Overcoats were encumbrances."

While the troops consolidated their positions, the *Carondelet* was the only ironclad — or gunboat, for that matter — available to provide support. It probably did not please Cmdr. Walke or his men when they read, as they surely did, "Junius'" observation that "the sole gunboat taking part [was] the *Conestoga*."

In his memoirs, "Galway" was rather blunt regarding the elapsed time between the fall of Fort Henry and Fort Donelson's investment. "Few such marches are recorded in history; none that I can recall in which less distance was made in more time." The trek, he concluded, "must be regarded as unrivalled."

Having straggled into Paducah well behind the others, the *McGill* headed up the Cumberland in pursuit of Foote's convoy. Aboard her taking notes was Capt. Charles C. Nott of the 5th Iowa Cavalry, who had himself been delayed and had caught the steamer only at the last minute. Awakened as his craft departed the Kentucky port, his impression of the Cumberland was of "a narrow river, winding amid wooded hills and banks covered with noble oaks. The day was soft and beautiful."

It was 9:00 A.M. that Wednesday before the lead transports passed Eddyville, that small town on the east bank only some 45 miles up from Smithland. Women and men waved handkerchiefs and cheered the whistling, smoking steamboats. As the *Minnehaha* passed, the band of the 57th struck up "Yankee Doodle." Everyone appeared loyal, Wilkie later remarked, even the dogs, which "barked and wagged their tails in patriotic joy at the national inundation."

On and on up they steamed, passing numerous farms along the riverbanks. The war had taken a toll on manpower and entire fields of corn and tobacco remained unharvested from the previous fall. Fifteen miles on they came abreast of the Hillman brothers rolling mill, since abandoned. Shrill whistles responded to the waves from several women on the nearby bluff.

In early afternoon, Capt. Nott and the *McGill* caught up with Flag Officer Foote's troop convoy. "We overtook 20 steamboats laden with troops," he remembered, "and led by four black gunboats." This was a singular sight, "to see so imposing a fleet making its way up so small a stream."

Next evening, subscribers to the *Chicago Daily Tribune* would read a dispatch from the war front. "At 4 o'clock in the morning, eleven regiments left Paducah, under convoy of the gunboats, to go up the Cumberland River." They were expected to reach Fort Donelson by 7 o'clock that evening.

Off Canton around 3:00 P.M. on Wednesday, the steamer *Alps* was encountered. She had been sent by Brig. Gen. Grant to find the fleet and to help tow up the ironclads. Her captain reported that skirmishing was already occurring between blue and gray soldiers on the outskirts of Fort Donelson. That Southern post, under the command of ex–President James

Buchanan's secretary of war, Brig. Gen. John B. Floyd, was now defended by upwards of 25,000 gray-coats and there was only one gunboat on the scene. Indeed, the *Carondelet*, in support, threw a number of shells at the bastion during the morning.

The towboat lashed onto Foote's two leading ironclads and the convoy continued to snake upstream. The flag officer, concerned that he was missing the beginning of the action, now had another problem. The balmy weather so eloquently described by reporters now turned more seasonal. It became bitterly cold, and heavy rain, a feature of the last few weeks, now turned to sleet and, worse, snow. Visibility was reduced and the chance for accidents thereby increased. Still, under the guidance of experienced pilots, the fleet pressed onward.

Eleven miles north of Dover at Line Port, Flag Officer Foote made whistle signal for the gunboats and transports to "close up." Another signal was given to "prepare for action," at which point drummers aboard the gunboats "beat to quarters." As darkness overtook the long, sparking line of steamers, the warcraft among them were cleared for action and ready for any eventuality. It now began to snow heavily and, just before midnight, Foote's gunboats reached a landing four miles below Fort Donelson where the *Carondelet* was already tied up.

According to "Try Again," a correspondent for the *St. Louis Daily Missouri Democrat*, the transports came in a little later. The night that followed was cold and noisy, as Rebel cannon fire continued at intervals and an icy wind howled and spent its fury on every person for miles around.[7]

When the sun rose on the morning of February 14, the temperature in Stewart County, Tennessee, was 10 degrees above zero Fahrenheit. There was about 2 inches of snow on the ground and it continued to fall. After a while, however, the sky became clear and bright. The Northern and Southern military participants in and around Fort Donelson, to say nothing of residents in homes around Dover and elsewhere in the twin rivers region, all shivered in the cold.

When Capt. Nott went on the deck of the *McGill*, he was struck by the snow and intense cold, as well as by the high wooded hills on either bank. From his location on the western bank, he could see far down the river the other troop steamers tied to trees along the shore. Smoke trailed upwards from fleet chimneys and the great collective cloud was easily seen from Fort Donelson, tipping off the Confederates that the great convoy had arrived and was about to, if it had not already, begin unloading men and equipment.

"The gunboats lay anchored in the middle of the stream," Nott remembered, "all signs of life hidden beneath their dark decks, save the white steam that slowly issued from their pipes and floated gracefully away." One of them, the flag boat *St. Louis*, later nosed into the bank.

At approximately 9:00 A.M., Brig. Gen. Grant arrived at the *Carondelet*'s landing to confer with Flag Officer Foote. Just after dismounting, and as he prepared to climb aboard the *St. Louis*, he passed word to his aides to have the soldiers disembark from the newly arrived troopboats.

No notes were kept during the Grant-Foote discussion. It is known that the flag officer was very reluctant to engage or run by the water batteries. Grant, who wished the naval magic of Fort Henry reapplied here, believed the ironclads could be successful not only in neutralizing the enemy's heavy ordnance but also in cutting his communication with Nashville. As such an action was deemed a military necessity by generals from Halleck on down, Foote agreed to try.

According to Steven Woodworth, the strategy the two leaders doubtless agreed upon went like this: As at Fort Henry, Foote would, using a favorite civil war phrase, "open the ball" by silencing Donelson's big guns. His boats would then steam up past Dover and assume a position blockading the Cumberland against Confederate reinforcement or retreat. With fleet gunfire support, McClernand's division on the right would drive the Rebels toward the divisions of Brig. Gen. Smith and Wallace and, cornered, they would see the light and surrender.

After the meeting, as the brigadier was jumping down to the bank from the ironclad's deck, he was approached by several Northern newsmen. Stopping to tamp his pipe, he informed the scribes "that, aided by the gunboats, he could capture every man in the fort." The writers had the opinion that the general believed Fort Donelson would be another "easy victory."

It took the remainder of the morning for the bluecoated soldiers to disembark from the steamers and assemble in the center between the units of Brig. Gen. Smith and McClernand. During this time, a series of miscommunications and a foot-dragging decision process prevented the Confederates from opening on the transports with their 10-inch Columbiad.

By noon, the wings of Grant's army arced around the Rebel citadel, with the Confederates occupying trenches and rifle pits from Hickman Creek to Indian Creek to Dover. Looking down from one of the fort's batteries, Confederate soldier Wesley Smith Dorris recorded in his diary that "Today the enemy's drums are within hearing distance.... At noon, the smoke of the enemy's gunboats were seen down the river."

As the troops deployed or stiffened their defenses, the north wind's chilly breath was still felt and the snow made land maneuver difficult. The warmest places for anyone in the Dover area this day was the engine room of a troop or war boat. While only scattered actions occurred ashore, the main event on the day's military calendar would be what Gen. Johnston's son labeled "The Battle of the Gunboats."

Once Brig. Gen. Grant had gone ashore from the *St. Louis*, Flag Officer Foote signaled all of the gunboat captains to repair aboard the flag boat for a conference. Noting that he was not happy with the role they must play, but play it they would, Foote laid out the battle plan, which was essentially the same one employed at Fort Henry. The first division ironclads would move against Fort Donelson in line abreast, with the two timberclads of the 2nd division following behind by a thousand yards. The turtles would get as close to the works as possible, without regard to the elevation of the defending batteries. Writing years later in the *Southern Historical Society Papers*, Rebel Lt. H.L. Bedford observed of Foote that, "flushed with his victory at Fort Henry, his success there paved the way for his defeat at Donelson."

After the war council broke up, the gunboat captains took turns coaling their craft from the barge brought up by the *Conestoga*. While waiting their turn, they employed whatever came to hand (for example, bread bags filled with coal) to strengthen the deck and unarmored protection of their vessels. Coaled and protected with everything not nailed down, the gunboats were as ready as possible by 1:45 P.M. when Flag Officer Foote signaled them to weigh. Within a half hour, all were proceeding up the river. At a point about a quarter mile above the landing, a signal was hoisted to assume battle formation. Slowly, *St. Louis, Louisville, Pittsburg*, and *Carondelet* came into line abreast of one another. Before casting off, the *Conestoga* cut loose her coal barge. Lt. Phelps' boat then joined the *Tyler* about a quarter of a mile behind the ironclads. At approximately 2:35 P.M., the lead gunboats rounded a wooded point and spied the Confederate water batteries ahead. While the gunboats entered their battle echelon and pushed ahead at roughly three miles per hour, soldiers and newsmen on both sides watched, or wanted to, not all of them passively.

Brig. Gen. Grant occupied a shore location from which, as he later put it, "I could see the advancing navy." *Times* correspondent Wilkie "secured a position about half-way between the boats and the fort, a little bit out of the line of fire." George Beaman, the *Daily Missouri*

Democrat reporter, and several others were with the troops ashore and so would see nothing. On the other hand, "Mack" McCullagh of the *Cincinnati Daily Gazette* was with Foote aboard the *St. Louis*, while Frank G. Chapman of the *New York Herald* was on the *Louisville*.

At Fort Donelson, meanwhile, the decision to open fire on the transports had finally been taken and the two largest cannon sent several shells screaming toward the clouds of smoke at about 2:00 P.M. Suddenly, the Rebel gunners saw the combined sooty puff begin to part. A large billow moved downriver while the other approached. The first turned out to be the transports and the second was Flag Officer Foote's gunboats. After a brief pause as the Confederates witnessed the naval formation take shape, the 128-pound. Columbiad opened fire at 2:38 P.M. The range was 1.5 miles and her first ball was a ricochet.

Once again, it is outside our aim to retell the entire story of the fight in the narrow channel between the ironclads and Fort Donelson. As in a modern day Super Bowl, the visiting team headed toward the goal line and was cheered by its supporters while fans of the opponent remained largely silent. In this case, Grant's soldiers were the ones cheering first, "remembering the victory eight days before."

It must have been fascinating to the hundreds of witnesses. In addition to the cannon fire, which was loud enough in and of itself, there was the new and tremendous sound heard only once previously, at Fort Henry — heavy shells and cannonballs hitting the Pook turtle armor. These heavy bolts, many arriving from upon high, were devastating.

The *Louisville*, hit 59 times, was disabled by a shot that cut away her rudder chains. Another ball wounded the flag officer and killed the pilot of the *St. Louis* as it passed through her pilothouse. The flag boat was smashed three dozen more times, while the *Pittsburg*, touched by 20 rounds, was forced to limp to the bank. A rifled cannon burst aboard the *Carondelet*, which, though hit 26 times, was the least hurt of all.

While the ironclads, having closed to 400 yards, were taking a beating and actually firing over their targets, the two timberclads remained well behind. They sent their shot, for the most part, toward the Rebel works from long range. The wooden boats were targeted by several Confederate guns and, though not hit, they may have helped to lessen the number of rounds impacting the units of the ironclad first division. Whether the timberclads actually did any damage to the Rebel position is unknown.

Cmdr. Walke, whose experiences with the timberclads of late now left him no fan, was later very critical of their role at Fort Donelson. "The *Taylor* and *Conestoga* were so far astern that their shell fell short or exploded over our gunboats," he alleged. Their firing did "less damage, evidently, to their enemies than to their friends."

Still bitter over Phelps' perceived slight, the skipper of the *Carondelet* continued his timberclad condemnation in his 1877 reminiscences. "The distressing attempt to help the ironclads by these wooden gunboats," he wrote, "was prompted ... by the hope to share largely in a glorious victory at Fort Donelson." When the battle of the 14th became, instead, a grand disaster, "they soon disappeared and were otherwise engaged on some important business, beyond the sound of battle."

In his *New York Times* account of the battle, "Galway" confirms Walke's point regarding timberclad friendly fire. As the *Louisville* prepared to employ grape shot from a range of 400 miles, a Confederate shot took away the top of her wheelhouse and smashed the steering wheel into a thousand pieces. Unhurt, the boat's pilot raced toward the aft tiller and was just about to regain control of the struggling ironclad when a shot from the *Tyler* took away her rudder. Instantly unmanageable, the *Louisville* swung around and was hit again in the stern before floating, with the smashed *St. Louis*, downstream in the current.

Irving Carson, in his first dispatch to the *Chicago Daily Tribune* on February 15, adds further detail. The wheelhouse ball came in on the starboard side and passed "through the entire length of the boat, killing three men, and breaking her tiller-rope a short distance from the pilothouse." He noted that the rope was being managed by some of the jacktars "when a shell from the *Tyler*, which lay some distance astern, burst over the Louisville, scattering the men at the tiller-rope." This shot "so much disabled her steering-tackle that the boat was compelled to drop astern."

As she too backed off, the *Carondelet* was still badly injured. Her situation was not helped when another of *Tyler*'s 8-inch shells burst astern, showering her casemate with shrapnel fragments. A part of the shell also lodged in the stern casemate and was dug out later by carpenters at Mound City. It was acquired by Cmdr. Walke as a souvenir.

Walke, in his postwar memoirs, includes a letter home from an unnamed member of his crew that provides a lengthy description of the Fort Donelson fight. Coming to the role of the timberclads, he indicates that "The *Conestoga*, *Lexington*, and *Tyler* were on hand on the 14th of February. But what were they doing? One of them gave us three shots in our stern, which fact is suppressed by the newspapers. I suppose they could not see the fort. 'Vive la bandboxes!'"

He also cites the damage report of *Carondelet* carpenter Oliver Donalson, who notes that among the injuries received by his boat was "One piece of shell in after casemate, in the captain's cabin (which was fired from U.S. gunboat *Taylor* by an acting master, against the remonstrances of her gunners)."

After an hour and 10 minutes of Rebel pounding, Flag Officer Foote was forced to order a withdrawal. Aboard the ironclads, there were 54 dead and wounded bluejackets. Covered by the *Carondelet*, *St. Louis*, *Pittsburgh*, and *Louisville* drifted or proceeded under minimal power down around the point from behind which they had earlier emerged. *Tyler* and *Conestoga* joined the retreat. The wooded hills now effectively protected them — at last — from Rebel guns.

Somewhat stunned that they had defeated the vaunted "Linkum" gunboats, the Confederates were at least momentarily jubilant. It was their team and not the Yankees who had scored the big "touchdown." Southern gunners and soldiers in the water batteries, joined by troops in the rifle pits all the way up and down the line, cheered until they were hoarse. "The shouts of triumph," Wesley Smith Dorris jotted in his diary, reverberated "through the hills and valleys, which doubtless went to the ears of the enemy, for they seemed infuriated." Amidst the bastion's celebration, Lt. Col. Alfred Robb of the 49th Tennessee made certain that the day's best Dixie cannoneers received a well-deserved round of good Volunteer State whiskey.

News of the victory over the gunboats was wired all over the South. The *Charleston Mercury*, the following Monday, was able to publish news from a February 15 telegraph which called the "Confederate victory, thus far, complete." It went on to point out that the Cumberland River was falling rapidly. With but 10 feet of water at Harpeth Shoals, it was doubted that the gunboats would be able to pass over if they did not leave soon."

If Brig. Gen. Grant was waiting for Flag Officer Foote to again apply the gunboat touch and make Fort Donelson a pushover, he was not only saddened, as he wrote in his memoirs, but also sorely disappointed. His men, some of whom saw the fight and most of those who did not, heard it end and the huge Rebel cheer that followed.

Newsman Wilkie wrote bluntly in his memoirs what many Yankees must then have felt about the ironclads: "They proved of no value." Indeed, he added, "they did more damage to the Federal right than to the batteries which they engaged."

Still, it has been argued that, while a tactical failure, Flag Officer Foote's attack did have one major operational result. The Confederate leadership was mesmerized by the gunboats before the battle here just as they had been at Fort Henry. This fixation caused them, in the view of Scott W. Stucky, to miss "the opportunity for strategic withdrawal and the saving of the 17,000 who eventually surrendered."

If Union troops were "anything but comforted over the prospects" now before them in the wake of Foote's defeat, their numbers were growing. Newly arrived reinforcements, including Wallace's 11th Indiana just disembarking from the steamboat *Missouri*, finally allowed Grant to have as many or more "boots on the ground" as Floyd. Fresh young faces in blue coats continued to arrive on additional boats, including the *Champion*, which dropped anchor just before the surrender.

Before the day was done, General Order No. 37 came out of the headquarters of the Department of the Missouri in St. Louis: "Brig. Gen. U.S. Grant is assigned to the command of the District of West Tennessee and Brig. Gen. W.T. Sherman to the command of the District of Cairo." The arrangement would be reflected in the new district's first general order, signed by Grant two days later.

With the gunboats out of the picture, the battle became one between blue and gray clothed land forces, a frigid affair over whose participants the northern wind howled equally. From the deck of the *New Uncle Sam*, Grant's headquarters boat later rebuilt into the super tinclad *Blackhawk*, Irving Carson watched the smoke of the fight. "Just ahead of us are the gunboats," he noted, "moving slowly against the stream." His boat came next and "behind us are 20 stately steamers, all rolling out black volumes of smoke and white vapory clouds—their ponderous wheels keeping time to the rol of the drum and crashing of bombs far up the ridges."

We leave it to "Galway" to sum up the next few bloody days with this brief, if slightly inaccurate, outline from his postwar memoir, *Pen and Powder*: "On the fifteenth, the Confederates attacked the right, under McClernand and produced a good deal of confusion. On the sixteenth, General Smith, commanding the Federal left, attacked the works in front of him and held them. The seventeenth, Buckner 'threw up the sponge' and surrendered."[8]

Before sunrise on February 15, a courier arrived at Brig. Gen. Grant's headquarters with a note for the brigadier from Flag Officer Foote. The bewhiskered navy man was too injured to call, but could Grant possibly come down to the *St. Louis* for a conference? Often kindly if taciturn, Grant quickly set off to oblige his loyal webfoot colleague. As he buttoned his tunic to go out the door, his adjutant was told to notify the division commanders that he was off to see Foote and not to start any fights before he returned.

Aboard the *St. Louis* following a grueling five mile ride over icy paths, Grant learned just how badly the gunboats were handled the day before. There could be no question but that at least two of them needed extensive repairs that could only be made at Cairo or Mound City. Foote proposed taking those boats back to the tip of Illinois and, while the army dug in, he would push his carpenters to mend them in time to permit a return within 10 days.

In addition to announcing his departure for Cairo, the flag officer agreed to a request from the general. Suspecting that Maj. Gen. Polk at Columbus would rush reinforcements to Dover by railroad, Grant wanted another timberclad raid up the Tennessee River aimed at destroying rail bridges and halting any possible succor from "The Gibraltar of the West."

The Memphis, Clarksville & Louisville span at Danville was to be revisited, after which an attack was to be made on the Memphis and Charleston's bridge at Big Bear Creek, missed on the first Tennessee foray by the old boats. Foote promised to pass the orders on and the Buckeye soldier made a mental note to order a troop transport readied to accompany the gunboat reaching Fort Henry in a day or so.

While the two military leaders talked, the transport *Minnehaha* started down the river,

This map of Fort Donelson clearly shows the terrain around the citadel faced by Union soldiers after the failure of the gunboats. Once the Cumberland River bastion was secured, the way to Nashville was open to a nautical descent as soon as competing Federal generals could decide who should take the first Southern state capital to be reclaimed to the Union. Fort Donelson was attacked by Confederate cavalrymen Wheeler and Forrest in February 1863 and once more gunboats were present in the defense (*Battles and Leaders*).

transporting military mail and some wounded to Paducah. Among the former were brief reports on the battle and his future plans written by Flag Officer Foote for Maj. Gen. Halleck and Navy Secretary Gideon Welles. When she left, the steamboat's captain later told newsmen at Cairo that it was expected that all of the gunboats were to be "left up the Cumberland, except the *Conestoga*."

As Grant was rowed ashore from the *St. Louis* about noon, he fully expected that he would have to besiege Fort Donelson and bring in still more troops to face a winter campaign. As noted in Wilkie's summary above, that was not to be. While Grant was with Foote, the Confederates had sallied against the Union right and a fight, wanted or not, was on.

Almost as quickly as the ground force commander was gone, Flag Officer Foote transferred his flag to the timberclad *Conestoga*. There he conferred with Lieutenants Phelps and Gwin as well as Cmdr. Dove of the *Louisville*, Cmdr. Walke of the *Carondelet*, and the *Pittsburg*'s skipper, Lt. Egbert Thompson.

Thompson was told to have everything ready for an immediate departure. Dove was instructed to proceed down as soon as his tiller ropes were repaired. Less than an hour and a half after Grant went ashore, the two timberclads were en route down the Cumberland. The *Pittsburg* weighed at 2:15 P.M. to follow. *The Louisville* was unable to cast off as soon as desired because her services were required, with those of the *Carondelet* and *St. Louis*, to make a demonstration in support of the land troops.

Acting in the departed Foote's place, Cmdr. Dove received a message from Brig. Gen. Grant just before 2:00 P.M. on February 15 asking the navy to do something to increase the chances of the men in their increasingly tough battle with Confederate troops. An attack like that made the day before was definitely not wanted; indeed, some long range shelling would serve the purpose. As it turned out, the *St. Louis* and *Louisville* cleared for action and made a brief appearance before the Confederate works that afternoon, lobbing in a few shells from a great distance. These two would remain in the Dover area for some time, while the *Carondelet* started for Cairo on Sunday.

Meanwhile, the *Conestoga* and *Tyler* continued down the Cumberland, passed Smithland and churned the muddy waters of the Ohio on course to Paducah, There Lt. Gwin received his orders to return to the Tennessee and he was left at the Kentucky port to coal as the *Conestoga* took her leave. The *Pittsburg*, delayed with valve and other problems, would not reach Smithland until early Monday morning and Cairo later that day.

The *Conestoga* came to at Cairo just before midnight on Saturday, February 15. The old boat arrived just a few hours after the steamer *Minnehaha*, which boat brought dispatches (including Foote's for Secretary Welles) and the latest news of "the desperate contest." It did not have the wonderful news—nor did Foote—that the fort was about to surrender.

New District of Cairo commander Brig. Gen. William T. Sherman, just arrived at Paducah, was handling Fort Donelson reinforcements for Grant and Halleck. There he met Lt. Gwin, who stopped in to pay his respects. The general praised the timberclad mission to more effectively destroy the Danville bridge.

While the wounded were taken ashore to hospital from the also-arrived *Minnehaha*, her captain noticed a number of mortar boats in port "going up." These scows had been brought to the port earlier but were not employed in the attack on Donelson. Freed to carry messages, the dispatch steamer raced ahead, actually reaching the tip of Illinois before Foote and Phelps.

Fort Donelson, Wilkie's memoirs not withstanding, surrendered early on February 16. In the hours after midnight, approximately 3,000 Confederates escaped. At dawn, the remaining Federal gunboats steamed up to Dover, where, at least on several of them, normal Sabbath religious services were held. Extra editions announcing the surrender appeared in late afternoon papers in the Midwest.

In an effort to insure daily communication was maintained with Cairo, Brig. Gen. Grant, from his Fort Donelson field headquarters, memoed Brig. Gen. Cullum at Cairo asking that a regular mail steamer be dispatched on a round-trip run from Cairo daily at 10:00 A.M. He also indicated his hope to move on Clarksville on Tuesday if Foote's gunboats were ready.

Before dusk, the ironclad *Cairo*, Lt. Bryant, and six mortar boats, under Lt. Joshua Bishop, detached from the laid-up *Lexington*, weighed anchor for the Cumberland. Bryant's fully manned ironclad and the tugboats towing the mortar boats were so slow that this head start was necessary in order that their arrival at Fort Donelson might coincide with the flag officer's later departure aboard the speedy *Conestoga*.

The Confederate line of defense from Columbus to Bowling Green, cracked by the defeat at Fort Henry, was, as Manning Force put it, "now shattered." Gen. Johnston, having ordered the evacuation of Bowling Green on the same day Brig. Gen. Floyd's gunners defeated Foote's ironclads, would, within the next two days, start the transfer of his soldiers from Nashville to Murfreesboro.

Even if Maj. Gen. Polk had planned to send reinforcements to Fort Donelson (which he did not), the capitulation of the bastion did not end the second Tennessee River timberclad raid, this a single-boat adventure by the *Tyler*.

Having arrived at Fort Henry early on surrender morning, Lt. Gwin found that the transport Brig. Gen. Grant had requested was not available. Rather than cancel the trip or wait, the enterprising naval officer recruited 50 idle sharpshooters to come aboard as marines.

Not long after leaving Henry, the *Tyler* came to off the Danville bridge, by now a familiar structure to the boat's tars who had visited it previously. That part of the structure not already burned out was torched once again. The largest timberclad's voyage would continue for another week. During this time, the *Tyler* discovered the bridge at Big Bear Creek was too closely guarded by Brig. Gen. Daniel Ruggles' men to attack. On the other hand, as he cruised up and down the great tributary, Lt. Gwin again found much closet Union loyalty. Seventeen men were enlisted and 14 refugee families given safe passage.

One of these loyalists tipped the gunboat skipper off to a vast deposit of wheat and flour stored at Clifton on behalf of a Memphis firm. Coming to off that town, the gunboatmen turned their craft into a grainboat and loaded its hold and numerous other spaces with 6,000 bushels of wheat, a thousand sacks and a hundred barrels of flour.

The *Tyler* returned to Paducah on February 23, where she offloaded her visitors and grain. Aside from drill, she did not fire her cannon at all during the entire voyage. Gwin sent on a report to Flag Officer Foote, which was passed on to the Navy Department and digested in the *New York Times* on March 2.

Having come away from the Carondelet repair yards two days before and anchored at St. Louis, the *Tyler*'s normal consort, U.S.S. *Lexington*, stood down the Mississippi River that day, making her return to the war zone.

Let us now turn back the clock to the day Fort Donelson surrendered. After divine services on February 16, the *Carondelet* had the honor of weighing for Cairo, where she arrived in a thick pea-soup fog early next day. As the whistle was blown aboard Cmdr. Walke's battered veteran, residents and military personnel, constantly fearing an attack from Columbus, thought the noise signaled a Confederate gunboat ascent. Some civilians actually prepared to leave town. After the ironclad landed and Cmdr. Walke went ashore with the premier firsthand news of the great triumph, fear was changed that Monday "to joy and exultation."[9]

CHAPTER 9

Tennessee River–Columbus–Island No. 10, February–March 1862

A FEBRUARY 17 MESSAGE FROM MAJ. GEN. HENRY HALLECK, commander of the Department of the Missouri, to Maj. Gen. George B. McClellan, detailing the victory announced by the *New York Herald* and other Northern newspapers in their Tuesday issues, revealed the next target on the Federal western list. The gallant Flag Officer Andrew Hull Foote, despite his injuries, would, as Halleck had recommended earlier, immediately follow up the Fort Donelson assault with a move on Clarksville.

That strong point, "distant from Nashville about 50 miles, in a northwesterly direction ... is fortified pretty strongly from the bluffs surrounding it." Employing two ironclads and the mortar boats, the flag officer would attack and occupy it. In a note to Brig. Gen. Ulysses S. Grant, Brig. Gen. William T. Sherman confirmed the movement of mortar boats, two of which were passing Paducah under tow of the *W.H. Brown* even as he wrote.

Flag Officer Foote hoped to make Clarksville quickly, as the Cumberland was falling. During the two day trip up river, he would travel aboard Lt. S. Ledyard Phelps' gunboat and his injured foot could receive much needed rest. Additionally, orders were sent to St. Louis to speed the repair work then underway aboard the *Lexington*. She was needed for the Cumberland River as soon as possible.

On February 18, the *Conestoga* departed Cairo for Fort Donelson. While she rushed up the Ohio to the Cumberland, the *St. Louis* was ascending the latter named stream to visit the Cumberland Iron Works, owned partly by ex–U.S. Senator John Bell. At that point, contracts were found implicating the company in the manufacture and transfer to the Confederacy of guns and iron sheathing. Bell's two partners were taken prisoner and the mills were fired and its machinery broken. The ironclad's men also crushed the nearby Bellwood Furnace.

The *Conestoga* reached Fort Donelson early on February 19. Her passage, as expected, was fast. She had by now earned a reputation, as reported by George Beaman on February 27, for being one of "the racier breed of boats" and for walking "the water like a thing of life." Correspondent Irving Carson of the *Chicago Daily Tribune*, invited onboard for the trip along with Franc Wilkie of the *New York Times*, later assured his readers that he had originated those timberclad accolades, "an entirely original term I beg you to note."

Flag Officer Foote and Lt. Phelps found the *Cairo* and the six mortar boats sent earlier at Fort Donelson, as well as the *St. Louis* and *Louisville*. Indeed, Lt. Nathaniel C. Bryant's ironclad had dropped anchor off the former Rebel bastion only hours before the timberclad.

While meeting with Grant, newly promoted to the rank of major general, and his chief of staff, Col. Joseph D. Webster, the senior naval officer joined them in formulating a last-minute plan for an armed reconnaissance to Clarksville. Even as they spoke, Lt. Bryant, who had already been briefed by Foote, weighed anchor and made steam upstream.

The *Conestoga*, with Foote and Webster embarked, duly raised steam for "up the river" and Clarksville, the first large town to be approached by the Western Flotilla within the Volunteer State. As the timberclad and the *Cairo* steamed up the Cumberland, they passed the smoking ruins of ex–Senator Bell's Cumberland Rolling Mills, as well as the Bellwood Furnace. Both were torched by armed boat parties from the ironclad *St. Louis* on Tuesday and now, as "Galway" put it, "nothing remained but the chimneys and machinery amid the dying embers."

Without interference, the trip continued until the warships passed around the bend opposite Linwood Landing, a few miles from their destination. There atop a high bluff was Fort Defiance, a recently completed Confederate outpost. Beat to quarters, the two gunboats steered closer and saw a white flag floating above the redoubt. As Carson noted, it had a few cannon that "looked almost down into our chimneys from a height 200 feet above our heads."

Foote asked Webster and Phelps to take a boat party from the *Conestoga* and investigate. When the colonel and Yankee tars reached Fort Defiance they found that it had been abandoned the previous day. Taking a folded U.S. flag handed to him by one of the sailors, Lt. Phelps ran it up the parade ground flagpole. Leaving a small group behind, the party's yawl returned and *Conestoga* and *Cairo* raised steam, continuing on their way toward Clarksville.

A few miles on, the task group came to the confluence of the Red and Cumberland rivers and another fort, this one flying no flag. "The Conestogas held their breath an instant, whistled, and watched events." As the *Cairo* and *Conestoga* came to, their guns run out, a soiled white cloth ascended the flagpole of this earthwork, Fort Clark. Once again, Lt. Phelps went ashore to raise the national colors. From locals, it was learned that the white bunting was dirtied in the rain and wind of the previous night after this fort's garrison also fled. Sgt. Charles Wright led the party of marines left in charge.

News of the approach of Foote's gunboats was rushed to the telegraph office at Clarksville. Hurriedly, the key operator, W.H. Allen, wired Brig. Gen. John Floyd, commanding in Nashville: "Gunboats are coming; they are just below the point." Allen reported that the Memphis, Clarksville & Louisville Railroad bridges across the Cumberland and Red rivers had been torched and that he was leaving. At 3:00 P.M., as Allen fled out the door, Foote's reconnaissance vessels reached Clarksville. (Brig. Gen. Floyd wired Gen. Johnston that it was 4:30 P.M. and reporter Carson said 5:00 P.M.) The *Conestoga* put into the landing, while the *Cairo* anchored in midstream with her guns run out. After his craft was tied up, the flag officer summoned the city fathers.

While the sailors waited for the town fathers, many of the citizens who had not run off came down to the landing to see the Yankee craft. According to the *Times*' Wilkie, a man pointed out to the *Cairo* and "asked what the thing was; on being told it was a gunboat, he said 'he be dog-oned if they were the very devil.'" Another inquired as to which craft was the flag boat. On being told it was the *Conestoga*, he replied that he'd "heard of the pirate before, when she carried off their government stores from Florence."

Brought aboard the *Conestoga*, the Hon. Cave Johnson, an antebellum politician and friend of Foote's father, Mayor C. George Smith, and Judge Thomas W. Wisdom in a private meeting respectfully informed Foote that their town was open. All of the Confederate troops within had fled toward Nashville as soon as they learned that the gunboats were approaching. On the way out of town, the butternuts had burned the rail bridges.

The solons went on to tell Foote and Webster that a state of near panic existed in Clarksville. Two-thirds of the citizens had already fled, worried about a bombardment by the black paddle-wheeled monsters, and those remaining feared for their persons and their property. Rumors were rife that all would be made homeless— or worse — by the crusading Northerners. It was further revealed that the same state of chaos existed upriver at Nashville. The capital city could be taken without a fight if a squadron of gunboats would immediately ascend upon it.

Hearing this, both Foote and Webster, speaking for Brig. Gen. Grant, assured the local leaders that the populace should not be concerned. They had not come to destroy "anything but forts, military stores, and army equipment." The two also looked at one another, probably sensing the possibility for another triumph. At the request of his visitors, Foote issued a proclamation assuring the populace of its safety.

While the flag officer and the colonel were engaged with Johnson and Wisdom, Lt. Phelps took another landing party ashore to review any important Confederate messages left at the telegraph office. Here they found a copy of a wire from the town commandant informing Nashville that the gunboats were en route and that the rail bridges were fired, though the one over the Cumberland was burning so slowly that the blaze might be out by the time the Yankees arrived.

As this was occurring, newsman Carson conducted his own interview, with two lads in a dingy off the timberclad's stern. "A good joke on yer dirty old flag," one seemed to taunt. Incensed, the journalist had half a mind to ask the gunner to sink the youngsters when one of them pointed aft. "The *Conestoga*'s coal smoke and the rain had, indeed, turned our ensign into a dusky tint, from which the red, white and blue had disappeared." Pacified, the sometimes military man now acting as a reporter talked with the lads further and elicited information not seen elsewhere in print by this writer.

Since at least the early 18th century, the black flag has been identified with pirates and cutthroats. Thus the Clarksville youth informed Carson that the rumor spread all over town that the *Conestoga*, approaching with a black flag flying, meant great harm and sent people scurrying out of town. The gunboat "nearly scared Clarksville into fits."

Franc Wilkie, still onshore with gawking townspeople, heard another version of the black flag story. They said they believed the Flag Officer's pennant, wet with rain and now very dark in color, was the infamous buccaneer banner. When the talking by the military, politicians, reporter, and youngsters was concluded, the *Conestoga* hauled off into the stream for the night.

Very early in the morning of February 20, *Daily Tribune* correspondent Carson wrote out his impressions of the Clarksville visit. Right at the beginning, he informed his readers that "The *Conestoga* is now lying here and I am writing on her gun deck by the lantern dimly burning." He admitted that his "handwriting is bad. The lantern a little nearer, dear sergeant."

During the morning, an inspection was made of Fort Clark. The *Daily Tribune*'s Carson tagged along and, like the sailors, was surprised by what was found. Before departing, the Confederates had attempted to blow up the outpost but failed. A half consumed trail of powder ash was found, leading to a hundred pounds of powder in cartridges and fixed ammuni-

The Upper Mississippi. Shown are the most prominent towns and cities visited by the timberclads during the first six to eight months of the Civil War (Maclay's *History of the Navy*).

tion next to the magazine. The largest share of ammunition was removed to the *Conestoga*, and the powder from the magazine, of poor quality, was thrown in the river. The two 24-pounders and single 32-pounder were spiked.

Also during the morning, Lt. Phelps, working out of the local telegraph office surrendered by W.H. Allen's departure, received and sent several messages directly to Brig. Gen. George W. Cullum, theater commander Maj. Gen. Henry Halleck's deputy at Cairo. In the first, the *Conestoga*'s captain provided the initial evidence to Union leadership that the "panic in Nashville is very great." Speaking for Foote, he observed that "the city will be surrendered without a fight if a force proceeds at once against it."

At approximately the same time, Cullum received a message from army general in chief George B. McClellan in Washington stating emphatically that it was absolutely necessary that the gunboats and mortar boats be ready for service on Monday, February 24. The brigadier was authorized to use the telegraph to call upon Chicago contractors for the mechanics and material required.

Brig. Gen. Cullum wired McClellan's command on to Phelps at Clarksville, indicating that the reason for the rush was Washington's desire to "move on Columbus with at least four serviceable gunboats and six mortar boats." Only two gunboats and one mortar were then available at Cairo. Phelps promised to relay this information to Foote and get back with a fast response. His own estimation was that the gunboats could not be readied in less than a week.

Even before Phelps returned with Foote's comments, Brig. Gen. Cullum wired Maj. Gen. McClellan that the Navy officers did not believe they could meet the Monday timetable. A copy of the wire went to Maj. Gen. Halleck, who now jumped in to repeat the Monday deadline, ordering Cullum to tell Foote "or ranking naval officer" [i.e., Fleet Captain Alexander Pennock] to wire Cincinnati for mechanics who could come to Cairo and work day and night.

At noon, the *Conestoga* took Foote and Webster back to Dover, while the *Cairo* was left to guard Clarksville. As the timberclad approached the scene of the horrific recent battle, the two senior officers made plans to brief Maj. Gen. Grant and then, assuming his permission, to organize a task force of the available ironclads and mortar boats. They would then employ it to strike and capture Nashville while the citizenry remained in awe of the gunboats.

Before Foote's arrival, Maj. Gen. Grant alerted Brig. Gen. Smith that his division would be needed to occupy Clarksville and that area of Montgomery County immediately adjacent. Neither Grant, Smith, nor Foote knew that back on February 18, Maj. Gen. Halleck had wired the former forbidding Foote's gunboats or the mortars to go higher than Clarksville. Officially, as Brig. Gen. Cullum told Lt. Phelps, the theater commander had other plans: the gunboats would now be used to reduce Columbus and Nashville would be left to Maj. Gen. Don Carlos Buell.

Maj. Gen. Halleck's Nashville order was received by boat at Fort Donelson on the morning of February 21. Tennessee's capital would not be liberated by Grant, Smith and Foote. Indeed, Foote was authorized to go no higher than Clarksville, to take out the railroad bridges there. Afterwards, he was to return to Cairo with the turtles and mortar boats, leaving one ironclad to protect Fort Donelson's water approaches.

While the flag officer and Maj. Gen. Grant were digesting this news from Halleck, adding to it what Phelps had picked up at Clarksville, steamboats, escorted by the *Cairo*, proceeded up to Clarksville. Disembarked Union soldiers occupied the town that Friday afternoon.

The politics of the Union western command in January and February 1862 has consumed whole trees in the printing of its record over the years. Sufficient to say that Maj. Gen. Halleck, Maj. Gen. Buell, and Maj. Gen. McClellan, to say nothing of Secretary of War Edwin Stanton, Maj. Gen. Grant, and even President Abraham Lincoln, were caught up in a web of personal ambition and competition over strategic direction. This confusion impacted not only Foote's operations but the timeliness of the North's entire western campaign.

If the South enjoyed any advantage in the Mississippi Valley at this time at all, it was a single leader—Gen. Albert Sidney Johnston—rather than many. The Federal imbroglio did not allow for fast changes in direction, in this case, the rapid Federal capture of Nashville and the mountain of Confederate supplies sitting in that city.

On the other hand, Tennessee's capital was abandoned as part of a "shameful panic," as the *Charleston Mercury* put it on March 6. Reviewing the collapse of the city, the South Carolina journal concluded that only one lesson was learned: "that gunboats can be resisted with less force than we expected."

Late on February 20, Flag Officer Foote returned to Paducah aboard the *Conestoga*. There, acting through Lt. Phelps, he would employ the post's direct telegraphic link in an effort to determine whether his boats were needed to support a Nashville descent. He would wait in vain. As he waited, Foot was advised that Fleet Captain Pennock would probably be returning to Cairo soon aboard the repaired timberclad *Lexington*. She was to be released from the Carondelet shipyard next morning.

Having received no instruction from Halleck or McClellan as to any possible role he might play in the occupation of Nashville, Flag Officer Foote reluctantly decided on the morning of February 22 that he had best return to Cairo. Before leaving Paducah, he wrote out a message to Maj. Gen. Grant asking the new west Tennessee chief to put matters related to his Cumberland fleet on hold.

Once the message was safely in the Fort Donelson mail sack, the *Conestoga* weighed anchor. She put into the Cairo wharf boat through a thick mist about 10:00 P.M. Following a warm reunion with Cmdr. Pennock, Walke and others on the scene, perhaps including Brig. Gen. Cullum, Foote reviewed earlier plans for a Columbus outing next morning and approved the task force composition. Later, the fleet captain wired Washington that the commander was back and ready to proceed downstream. Returning to the comfort of his room, the hobbling Foote did not know that Union forces, protected by the *Cairo*, would begin to occupy Nashville two days later.[1]

The role of the U.S. timberclads in the coming two months would be one of direct support for the U.S. Army. In light of the increased availability of the ironclads of the City Series, the "old boats," as they were now frequently referred to, would enhance their reputations as convoy escorts, dispatch and command boats, and gunfire support craft. Although the three would be separated by duty and geography, the contribution of *Conestoga*, *Lexington*, and *Tyler* to the success of Federal riverine operations in the Tennessee and upper Mississippi River valleys remained vital.

By the time the ironclad *Cairo* led the Yankee occupation force to Nashville on February 25, making the "Athens of the South" the first Confederate state capital to surrender to the Union, the town was an open community. Gen. Johnston and Pierre G.T. Beauregard had elected weeks earlier to abandon the large city in the face of the Federal attacks down the Tennessee and Cumberland rivers. Indeed, the entire Rebel defensive line from Bowling Green, Kentucky, to Columbus had been cracked, forcing a retreat to new positions.

Columbus, the so-called "Gibraltar of the Mississippi" that had protected the great river for the past six months, was now out-flanked and cut off. With Fort Donelson actually lost, the great works on the Iron Banks were all but surrounded by Yankees in central Kentucky and across in Missouri. The loss of Fort Henry began the North's penetration of the lower Mississippi Valley. The capture of Fort Donelson returned the Union to Nashville and central Tennessee.

An ill Gen. Beauregard, who was to assume command of the new Confederate Army of the Mississippi on March 3, had recommended in mid-February that Columbus be rapidly evacuated, with only a small garrison left behind to mount a rear guard defense. The remainder of the citadel's defenders, under the leadership of Maj. Gen. Leonidas Polk, together with the motley fleet of Cdr. George M. Hollins, C.S.N., would retreat to Island No. 10 and New Madrid or to Jackson, Mississippi. This withdrawal was approved by the Confederate war department and President Jefferson Davis himself.

At 6:00 A.M. on February 23, a thousand soldiers from the 8th Wisconsin and 27th Illinois were loaded aboard the steamers *Continental, Illinois,* and *Chancellor.* Two hours later, the *Cincinnati,* with Flag Officer Foote and Brig. Gen. Cullum embarked, steamed out into the Mississippi and raised a light to her masthead, the signal to proceed. The *Lake Erie No. 2* also came along, towing a pair of mortar boats which might be tested in combat for the first time.

By this time, a thick overnight fog was gone and the weather, according to "G.P.U.," the embedded correspondent George P. Upton from the *Chicago Daily Tribune,* was beautiful: "the air was balmy as on a May day, and the river alive with craft of every description."

Following the flag boat out of harbor was the *St. Louis, Carondelet,* and *Conestoga,* plus the transports. Lt. Phelps' old boat, with the *Times'* correspondent Franc Wilkie again embarked, was specifically charged with convoying the troop and mortar boats.

Watching the great clouds of smoke and the waterfalls of splashing caused by the paddle wheels was a throng of soldiers and civilians on the Cairo levee, attracted by the commotion and rumors of the departure that had spread through the town like wildfire. Adding to the almost festive atmosphere was music from several regimental bands as well as cannon salutes.

Sight of the little armada was soon lost to the civilians as it crept behind Bird's Point. A bit further down, off Fort Holt, the *Cincinnati* signaled the *Mound City* to join the parade. Continuing down the river, an old tradition that held sway with Flag Officer Foote occurred at approximately 10:00 A.M. It being Sunday, the fleet was halted while the gunboats mustered their crews for divine services. Aboard the *Conestoga,* journalist Wilkie, writing as "Galway," jotted down that this Sabbath allowed the men to be absorbed in their devotions "beneath the warm beams of the first sun we had seen for weeks."

A little before noon, the flotilla steamed into Lucas Bend and everyone could see, about two miles below across a promontory, Rebel tents atop the bluffs of Columbus. At this point, about six miles from Columbus, smoke from a single cannon shot curled skyward and many hands witnessed a ball splash into the water 2,000 yards ahead. Stories of a mass evacuation appeared to be untrue.

Proceeding another two miles, the Yankees were saluted once again, yet continued to steam on. This one plunged into the water a short distance from the *Conestoga* and "sent the water splashing skyward like a water spout." On the Yankee boats, heavy gongs sounded, sending the men to general quarters. Coming within about a mile of the Iron Banks about noon, the flotilla was further warned off when another Confederate ball was sent down. This one skipped across the water approximately a half mile ahead of the closest ironclad. The Pook turtles continued on and formed line of battle under the Rebel batteries.

At this point, the troop transports, left behind, started preparations for a landing at Belmont, above which the mortar boats were stationed to provide support. The *Conestoga,* the only timberclad present, was stationed nearby as their protection. Just as it appeared the Union ironclads would engage the Columbus batteries and Wilkie prepared "in another instant to witness a repetition of the Fort Henry and Donelson tragedies," a Rebel transport rounded the promontory point flying a white flag from her jackstaff, her whistles blaring.

The unknown vessel was the Confederate steamer *Red Rover* with gray-clad officials seeking to parlay. Accompanied by a tugboat, the *Cincinnati* went down to meet the stranger, which was granted permission to come alongside. As the Northern flag boat positioned herself between her and the land batteries, both dropped anchor. A number of officers boarded the tug and were taken to board the ironclad. There they held a two to three hour meeting with Foote and Cullum discussing POW issues.

"Wild were the conjectures as to what was going on," Wilkie remembered. The men on the national fleet thought the place might be about to surrender and that they would be having supper that night in Columbus. Eventually, the tug returned the negotiators to the *Red Rover*, which steamed away.

Aboard the *Conestoga* and the other Union craft, three flags were seen gliding up the flagstaff of the *Cincinnati*. First Master John A. Duble remarked to Wilkie, "That's to close up, probably." Opening his signal book to be certain, the veteran was amazed to read the bunting meant: "Fall in line." After the Rebel boat withdrew, the flag boat "bore straight up the river for Cairo, black, grim, and uncommunicative." The other units of the task force took their places and followed.

Foote and Cullum, having achieved their objective to learn the state of Columbus's defenses, elected not to test the mortars, believing the little scows might be targeted by the citadel's big guns. It was decided to return to base and press ahead with repairs to the fleet, the acquisition of additional mortar boats, and the commissioning of the mighty U.S.S. *Benton*.

The transports were the first to arrive at the Cairo levee, about 8:00 P.M.; the *Carondelet* stopped at Fort Holt, and the *Conestoga* was the last to dock, two hours later. By this time, Flag Officer Foote was sequestered; every attempt by the correspondents to elicit information beaten back. "Never was a drum tighter or miser more tenacious than the hero of Henry and Donelson."

In a report to Secretary Welles that evening, the flag officer confessed that Columbus did not show any signs of an evacuation. Great numbers of troops and tents were seen and the batteries appeared to be intact. It should be added that, in this communiqué, Foote noted, for the first time, that he was pairing the newly repaired *Lexington* with the *Tyler* on the Tennessee River. The two, he expected, would "guard our interests effectually on the borders of that river."

Early the next morning, Lt. Phelps drove the *Conestoga* back to Columbus, leaving Wilkie and other members of the press behind and still in the dark. Later on, the smallest timberclad returned, carrying as passengers the wife and children of Fort Donelson's late commander, Brig. Gen. Simon Bolivar Buckner, together with the spouses of several other Confederate officers.

This was also the day that the *Tyler* returned to Cairo from Fort Henry, following her week-long cruise to Alabama and Mississippi. Lt. William Gwin, the timberclad's captain, spoke convincingly of strong Union sentiments in those states. Indeed, so convincing was the skipper's report that Foote told the Navy Secretary that he was planning to ask Brig. Gen. Cullum to provide a regiment to support Gwin on a new cruise up the Tennessee.

Such an amphibious unit, Foote thought, could serve as the nucleus of a large loyalist force to be raised in Tennessee and north Alabama. Although this particular idea never caught on, a year later Indiana Col. Abel D. Streight's provisional ("Mule") brigade would, with initial Navy support, be sent into north Alabama hoping to cut railroads with local aid.

Earlier in the day, as the telegraph wires hummed between Cairo, St. Louis, and Washington, the U.S.S. *Cairo* led seven troop steamers to Nashville. Commanded by Brig. Gen. William Nelson, whose 4th Division of the Buell's army had been seconded to Maj. Gen. Grant at the time of the Donelson battle, the force met no opposition. As February 25 ended, the *Conestoga*, with the *New York Times* correspondent Franc Wilkie embarked again, departed for the Cumberland. She would make a brief run up to Nashville, stopping en route to give Foote's latest orders to the remaining ironclads. At the same time and several hundred miles away, the evacuation of Columbus began.

On February 26, the editors of the *Memphis Avalanche* published a report concerning preparations being made by guerrilla home guardsmen to attack steamers, and especially gunboats, on Tennessee's rivers. Squads of five or six men, the journal told its readers, were going out to live off the land and when the opportunity presented itself to "pick off the Lincoln pilots." Firing from "behind trees, log, and in the narrow bends of the river," they hoped to cause Yankee-employed pilots to "refuse to ascend a steam where death awaits behind any big tree." Amounting almost to an endorsement, the sentiment expressed by the newspaper would increasingly be seen in volunteer actions of the sort over the months and years ahead.

Meanwhile, the *Conestoga* skirted Smithland and paddled up the Cumberland. The puffing black gunboat was known far and wide. Her newsman visitor continued to be amazed that she never passed a single home or hamlet between Cairo and Fort Donelson without "hats, sun-bonnets, pocket-handkerchiefs, hurrahs, and 'How-are-You's' being brought into requisition to show their recognition and joyfulness." On the debit side, Wilkie was frank in noting that the curiosity of onlookers changed once the timberclad passed Clarksville. Instead of waving handkerchiefs and hats, people along the bank stood in "sullen silence," as though "benumbed, stupefied" to see not the Stars and Bars hanging from her flagstaff but the dreaded Federal ensign.

The *Conestoga*, which did not encounter any sharpshooter resistance, reached Nashville late that Thursday. There Lt. Phelps met with Lt. Bryant of the *Cairo*, who undoubtedly filled in his naval colleague as to the military developments in the Tennessee capital. Prior to the old boat's return trip, Wilkie would spend the next day wandering around the city soaking up the story of the Confederate departure and the arrival of U.S. troops.

Confederate Brig. Gen. John McCowan and his command departed Columbus for Island No. 10 and New Madrid on February 27. That Friday, it was recorded in the logbook of the floating battery *New Orleans*, anchored off the town that day: "The army making preparation for the evacuation of Columbus."

On March 1, Brig. Gen. Benjamin Cheatam's men moved to Union City and next day, the last cavalrymen out set fire to all of the abandoned buildings. Just before departing, Maj. Gen. Polk wired War Secretary Judah P. Benjamin: "The work is done. Columbus gone."

The evacuation of Columbus left the Confederacy in the West with a defensive line that ran from Corinth, Mississippi, across western Tennessee to Island No. 10. Included within this line lay such towns or posts as Humboldt, Union City, Paris, Jackson, and Fort Pillow. Also included within this perimeter was a significant railroad network and at least 15,000 reinforcements from Florida and Louisiana.[2]

For the Western commands of Maj. Gen. Henry Halleck and Don Carlos Buell, the question now became what directions their armies should follow. Buell was adamant that he would occupy Nashville and defend it from Gen. Johnston, whom he expected would make a counterattack. Halleck for his part decided that he could employ both the Tennessee and the Mississippi rivers to eliminate Columbus and capture the Confederate railroad center at Corinth. Among the first challenges to be faced in any campaign against Columbus was the seasonal condition of the Mississippi River. As had already been seen, up both the Tennessee and Cumberland rivers this year was one of the worst for flooding since the late 1850s.

As the *Conestoga* was returning down the Cumberland from Nashville, embedded newsman Franc Wilkie took note of this situation. "The water is very high," he wrote in his notebook, "higher, in fact, than it has been in many years." The scribe quickly added that "this has aided the gunboats." At the tip of Illinois, the situation was no different. Both banks of the Mississippi from Cairo to New Madrid and below were under water. Indeed, the entire countryside 30 miles inland was submerged below one to 10 feet of muddy liquid. Fort Holt was nearly under water and Flag Officer Foote would soon be searching for ways to get his ammunition to higher ground.

Cmdr. Henry Walke of the *Carondelet* later remembered the current strength. Even more powerful than that encountered in the twin rivers, the Mississippi flow "carried away every movable thing. Houses, trees, fences, and wrecks of all kinds were being swept rapidly downstream."

The *Conestoga*, nearly back to Cairo from Nashville, broke a piston head. This mechanical casualty could be repaired only at Cincinnati, to which she was now sent with orders to make a rapid turnaround. Prior to her departure, Lt. Phelps was detached and ordered to assume temporary command of the fleet of mortar boats. A man new to the theater was read aboard the timberclad as her next captain.

George M. Blodgett, the second commander of the *Conestoga*, was a native of Huntington, Vermont, but considered himself a resident of Burlington. He was commissioned a midshipman with the U.S. Naval Academy class of 1856, becoming a passed midshipman and master three years later. After serving aboard the sloop of war *John Adams*, he was named gunnery officer of the Portsmouth Navy Yard, where he was stationed at the time of Fort Sumter. Promoted to the rank of lieutenant on February 3, 1861, he would die unexpectedly of an illness at Cairo on November 6, 1862.

Meanwhile, before Flag Officer Foote could ready his flotilla for a return to Columbus, the timberclads *Lexington* and *Tyler*, left on the Tennessee River to support the army, were involved in a spirited action of their own. It has become known as First Shiloh.

Back on February 20, Maj. Gen. Halleck, tired of waiting for assistance or support or even cooperation from Maj. Gen. Buell, elected to begin his movements against Gen. Johnston that would hopefully end with the capture of Memphis and the flanking of all Confederate positions to the north of that city.

Preparations were put in place for an army under Maj. Gen. John Pope to cross over Missouri from Commerce and attack New Madrid from the west while Flag Officer Foote provided naval support. Over on the Tennessee, Brig. Gen. Grant would initially mount a raid-in-force against Corinth.[3]

During his original single-ship visit up the Tennessee in mid–February to destroy the Big Bear Creek railroad bridge, Lt. William Gwin of the *Tyler* had stopped at Hamburg, Tennessee, upstream from Pittsburg Landing. There he told residents that

Maj. Gen. Henry Halleck (1815–1872) was Western Theater commander until July 1862. "Old Brains" was responsible for the direction of military demonstrations in the months leading up to the battles of Fort Henry and Fort Donelson and temporarily shelved Maj. Gen. U.S. Grant for several weeks prior to the Battle of Shiloh. He also pushed Flag Officer Foote to fight even when his fleet was not, in Foote's opinion, prepared. In later years, Halleck served in Washington, D.C., as army chief of staff — working for Lieut. Gen. Grant (***Battles and Leaders***).

troopboats would land soldiers the following day. Needless to say, the Tennesseans were very concerned.

On February 20, the same day Maj. Gen. Halleck reached his strategic deployment decision, the *Tyler* paddled up to Eastport, from whence Gwin hoped to land his marines and swiftly hit the 80-foot long Big Bear Creek span. There, however, locals informed him that the bridges were already guarded by upwards of 4,000 Rebels. The naval officer had only 50 marines and so called off his venture.

As February drew to a close, Lt. Gwin learned that each side had misinformed the other during his recent voyage. There were no troopboats, and only a little over a thousand raw East Tennessee butternuts garrisoned the area around the bridges. With support from his superiors, he vowed to go up again and take out the structures. When the *Tyler* weighed from Fort Henry "for up the river" on February 28, she was accompanied by the *Lexington* and a troop steamer, the *Izetta*. Aboard the latter were two companies of the 32nd Illinois.

Also on the last day of the month, the 18th Louisiana Infantry Regiment broke camp at Corinth, Mississippi. With a company left behind to guard equipment, Col. Alfred Mouton took nine companies 20 miles east toward the Tennessee to guard the northern end of the Corinth road, which came out at Pittsburg Landing on the river. With him on the march was Maj. Silas Grisamore, who recorded the adventure in his diary. When the Rebels arrived at the Hardin County landing, which was never a recognized town, they found two or three buildings. Maj. Grisamore also tells us that the Corinth road was "cut down through the bluffs which are 100 feet above highwater mark." Additionally, a "tract of land about 200 yards wide and a half mile in length along the river was cleared and cultivated; behind which was dense woods."

There are a number of other features of this west bank real estate — soon the site of a great battlefield — about which we learn profitably from Hardin County historian B.G. Brazelton:

> On the east side ... is the river; on the north, Snake Creek; on the west, Owl Creek; and on the south, Lick Creek. The southwest corner ... is without any boundary, and it was through this pass that the whole Confederate force moved into battle. The soil is poor.... The ground is not cut up by any streams of account. Only a few small brooks are to be met with. From the top of the ridge dividing the waters of the Snake and Lick creeks, the ground slopes gradually toward said creeks.

Judge Alexander Walker, reporting for the *New Orleans Daily Delta*, later told his readers that a second main road, besides that to Corinth, ran northwest from Pittsburg Landing to Purdy, "a small town some 5–6 miles from the Mobile and Ohio Railroad." Also, about halfway up the Corinth road was a little village called Monterey where several roads intersected. Just behind the oncoming gray-clad soldiers were 500 horsemen from the 2nd Mississippi Cavalry and the Miles Light Artillery, which had departed New Orleans for Columbus almost a month earlier.

About 10:00 P.M., the slowly chugging Yankee gunboats saw a reflection on the water of a large fire some distance back from the eastern bank "supposed to be caused by the Rebels destroying some property." An hour and a half later, the three boats landed at Savannah, nine miles north of Pittsburg Landing on the right, or eastern, shore. Pickets were posted and preparations were made to lay by for the night.

On the cloudy, windy morning of March 1, a force of 120–150 of the most proficient Illinois riflemen were detailed to go aboard the two Federal gunboats to serve as marines. Of these, 67 were from Company C (Capt. Thaddeus Phillips) and the remainder from Company K (1st Lt. John J. Rider). They would be supplemented during any amphibious strike by armed sailors and, hopefully, wheeled boat howitzers from the timberclads. Just after 9:00 A.M., the two gunboats started upstream.

As the old boats clanked and hooted and churned the swift current, their lookouts keep a sharp eye for debris in the water. Meanwhile, the Confederates up ahead were not idle. Hidden from river sight behind the houses and woods at Pittsburg Landing were the nine companies of the 18th Louisiana, some members of which were already on picket duty as far down the river as Owl Creek, a mile and a half north and just opposite Diamond Island.

During the morning, the Miles Light Artillery hurried onto the scene. Under the command of Capt. Claude Gibson, it was sometimes known as Gibson's Battery. Immediately upon arrival, Gibson ordered Junior 1st Lt. E.D. Terrebonne to plant his four rifled 6-pounders 300 yards upstream from the town on "a high and conspicuous bluff." Second Lt. Charles A. Montaldo posted a pair of 12-pounder howitzers (similar to the U.S. Navy boat howitzers) 100 yards downriver from the landing. The reporter for the *Chicago Daily Post* would later write that the enemy battery "consisted of one 24-pounder rifled gun and three 12-pounder howitzers."

After rounding the large bend at Crump's Landing not far south of Savannah, *Lexington* and *Tyler* enjoyed an uneventful cruise during most of the morning. Sawyers, snags, and other water obstacles were avoided and no one shot at the boats from the riverbank, the entreaties of the *Memphis Avalanche* not withstanding.

Just before noon, the Rebel pickets at Owl Creek spotted the sooty black smoke from the timberclad chimneys reaching skyward above the trees. Shortly thereafter, they could hear "the series of staccato, cracking reports characteristic of almost every steamboat navigating western waters."

Armed with reports from Northern sympathizers, Lt. Gwin and Shirk were quite suspicious of possible Rebel activity as they approached Pittsburg Landing. "Intelligent Unionists," as newspapers like the *Chicago Daily Tribune* called local Union sympathizers along the Tennessee, continued to maintain that "a regiment of men can be raised at short notice to fight the rebels on their own terms, guerrilla for guerrilla."

At noon, the *Lexington* and *Tyler* headed by Diamond Island and their crews were beat to quarters. As they steamed within view of the landing, the Confederates, alerted by their Owl Creek pickets, knew they were coming. One of the men aboard the *Tyler* later remembered that her engines slowed down at this point, leaving her great side wheels "revolving just sufficiently to hold the vessel nearly motionless against the current." On the bridge, Lt. Gwin inspected the southern bluff with his field glasses. The timberclad's skipper, as was usually the case, was dressed "in complete uniform with his sword by his side." Nothing could be seen; the area appeared entirely tranquil. The same precautions and spyglass sweeps were undoubtedly taken aboard the *Lexington*.

It was 1:08 P.M. on Saturday when, from atop the bluff, Lt. Terrebonne's 6-pounders suddenly opened fire as the black gunboats hove into sight in the channel about 1,200 yards away near the head of Diamond Island. The Yankees later reported that these guns were, supposedly, "a portion of those removed from Columbus" that had been secretly mounted.

The premier shells fell short of the gunboats by 200–300 yards, throwing geysers up in the swift river. One passed directly over the *Tyler* and fell into the water astern. Gwin's boat returned fire when 1,000 yards distant and the *Lexington* opened with her No. 1 starboard gun two minutes later.

As Terrebonne, Gwin, and Shirk entertained one another, Col. Mouton, arriving quickly near the landing, sent a company of sharpshooters over the hill into a hastily dug and as yet unfinished rifle pit below the Rebel camp. The butternut soldiers, whose minié balls were uselessly shot into the thick oak armor of the timberclads, were virtually naked in the sights of the Federal gunners. Seeing his error, Moulton signaled his sharpshooters to withdraw, but they could not get away, as one escapee recalled, before "two or three shots passed so close to us that we could feel the wind raising the hair on our heads."

For almost 40 minutes, the gunboats and the Louisianans exchanged fire. From the river, Lt. Gwin thought he was facing a "fortified house," though in fact, his opponents were operating from or near unconnected unfinished rifle pits, a battery, and a log cabin on the river face of the northern hill owned by a local man. On the northern bluff, Lt. Montaldo did not return fire because, he later testified, he did not have sufficient men to man his howitzers. As the fight wore on, the timberclads closed the shore and switched their ammunition to grapeshot.

Without Montaldo's support, and faced with the deadly little balls whirling in from the river, Lt. Terrebonne withdrew, feeling himself "compelled to travel." From his position below the bluff, Lt. Gwin believed that he and Shirk "had the satisfaction of silencing their batteries" with the timberclads' "exceedingly well-directed fire." The *Post*'s man later crowed that "not a single one of their shots from the beginning ... touched either of our boats."

The sailors did not see the butternut lieutenant's exercise of "the better part of valor" for what it was. Onshore, Maj. Grisamore conceded as much when he jotted in his notebook that, "Having never seen but our company and the battery, it is presumed that they imagined the force on land to be small and to have retreated."

The noise from the cannon and musket fire along the riverbank quieted after this withdrawal, even as Col. Moulton secretly formed up his eight other companies in the ravine behind the two bluffs. Not knowing what to expect, the two Union gunboats eased upstream and came to about 50 yards offshore. They then bombarded the banks and woods behind them with grape and canister for the next hour.

With no one shooting back at them, Lt. Gwin decided in early afternoon that the time was ripe to send a landing force ashore to examine the Confederate "works" and to burn or otherwise destroy them. While drawing abreast of Pittsburg Landing, two armed boat parties were told off from each gunboat. Those from the *Tyler* included Lt. Rider's Company K and were under the command of Second Master Jason Goudy, leader of the entire expedition. The second pair, from the *Lexington*, carried Second Master Martin Dunn and Capt. Phillips' Company C. None of the launches made room for wheeled boat howitzers. Once the *Lexington* and *Tyler* lifted fire, the four boats rowed to the bank and their hundred men stormed ashore unopposed about 3:00 P.M. Capt. Phillips immediately led the soldiers up the long slope of the hill toward the top of the northern bluff to cover Goudy's bluejackets, who set off to blow up the "fortified house."

As the Yankee troops came over the top of the hill, they "suddenly found themselves face to face with" several companies from the 18th Louisiana — most of which were lying in wait for this opportunity — "who immediately shot at them." The skirmish that followed was sharp and, like many, was recorded differently by eyewitnesses on both sides. In the end, the two opposing commanders would claim a victory.

Lt. Gwin later reported that Phillips' soldiers and Goudy's sailors were able to hold off the Confederates long enough for them to burn the "fortified house," to determine "the real strength and purpose" of his opponents, and to retreat. As they came over the top of the hill after the Northern troops, the Confederates began to take casualties. Gunners aboard the *Lexington* and *Tyler*, witnessing the charge, discharged additional grape and canister. The Southerners attempted to shield themselves by ducking back under cover while reloading their single-shot weapons. The *Natchitoches Union* later expressed its pride in the men of the

Views of the Columbus fortifications, sketched by the noted artist Alexander Simplot after the citadel was abandoned by the Confederates in late winter 1862. The strategic withdrawal from the town was a masterpiece of deception. Flag Officer Andrew H. Foote and Brig. Gen. William T. Sherman were not actually certain whether they would have to fight to scale the heights or not (*Harper's Weekly*, March 29, 1862).

18th Louisiana during the unit's first skirmish. Among those singled out for praise was a drummer boy named Eugene Rosas.

In the thick of the fight between the gunboat landing party and the Louisiana butternuts, Rosas "climbed up on the trunk of a cut tree." From "this improvised pedestal, from which he overlooked the troops and helped to spoil the aim of the enemy's balls," gloried the newspaper, he "did not cease to beat the charge with an energy which electrified the soldiers." Upon his return to Cairo late next day, the captain of the *Izetta* told reporters from the *Chicago Daily Tribune* that "our men captured a drum upon which was painted 'Captured from the Federal Army at Manassas.'" Whether or not it was Rosas' drum is unknown.

Fenwick Hedley, a 32nd Illinois soldier, states that he and his buddies actually took cover inside the so-called fortified house for a short time. This fact was confirmed in the *Daily Post* report of March 3. Unmounted horsemen from the 2nd Mississippi Cavalry then began working their way along the riverbank to cut off these men from their boats.

It is probable that, as the gunboats quickened their fire on both the gray-clad soldiers and the cavalrymen, Goudy's men fired the cabin and joined Phillips' people in escaping to the boats. As they did so, they received "a most terrific fire of musketry." "The enemy precipitately rushed to their boats," Maj. Grisamore recorded, "our men following them closely." While the Yankees scrambled into their launches and rowed out, "they became good marks for our men." As they boarded or were carried aboard the timberclads, the Northern landing parties found that two of their number were dead and six wounded, with two men from the *Lexington* and one from the *Tyler* missing.

Once the boats were back aboard the timberclads, a few additional cannon rounds were fired toward the beach. Lt. Shirk later noted that a shell from the *Lexington* took "effect upon a field officer, emptying his saddle and dropping three foot soldiers."

At the same time as the Yankee naval artillery was slowing its bark, Col. Moulton's men, having riddled both the landing party and the gunboats, ceased firing and melted back behind the hills. Southern losses, according to the *New Orleans Daily Picayune*, were seven dead and 13 wounded; Col. Moulton reported 21 casualties.

When he could see no further purpose to be gained by expending ammunition, Lt. Gwin disengaged. The *Lexington* and *Tyler*, with sunlight passing through numerous bullet holes in their bulwarks and chimneys, dropped down toward Savannah. As they departed, three Union men hailed the *Lexington* and were allowed to come aboard from a skiff paddled out from the bank.

From atop one of the bluffs ashore, Rebel Maj. Grisamore, who believed the two Federal monsters could have been sunk or forced to surrender" had Terrebonne's "battery been present," watched them go. "They floated off down the river," he wrote, "and did not use their engines until the current had carried them a mile or more below the scene of action."

The first Battle of Shiloh lasted for approximately three hours. Despite a relatively low casualty rate, the engagement was hot. Over 180 minutes, the *Tyler* expended 95 shells, 30 stand of grape and 10 of canister, and 67 rounds of shrapnel. For her part, the *Lexington*, averaging a round every 53 seconds, fired off forty-five 8-inch shells, twenty-five 6-inch shells, and sixteen stand of grapeshot.

In his official report written that evening, Lt. Gwin, naturally, praised his men for having "behaved with the greatest sprit and enthusiasm. Shirk, Goudy, Dunn, and the wounded Capt. Phillips were lauded, as were the *Tyler*'s gunners under First Master Edward Shaw and Third Master James Martin.

Believing he faced a couple of regiments and artillery, Gwin concluded that Col. Moulton and his men were planning to "fortify strongly" the important Pittsburg area. The task group commander reported himself satisfied with the results of his mission and would, in time, receive a message of praise from Flag Officer Foote.

Having gone downstream a short distance, the two Federal gunboats dropped anchor. Conferring among themselves, Gwin and Shirk discovered, to their discomfort, that they did not have sufficient ammunition of the proper type (mainly five-second rather than 15-second fuses) aboard to handle any further engagements with Confederate troops. If they fought the 18th Louisiana again, they would be, according to the *Chicago Daily Post* reporter, "unable to do the execution at short range which they could have done with shorter fire." In short, it would take too long for their shells to burst.

Accordingly, "the *Lexington* was dispatched to Cairo for a supply of the desired ammunition, while the *Tyler* remained behind to look after the new Rebel battery." The *Izetta* and the men of the 32nd having departed downstream almost immediately after the battle, the *Lexington* carried Gwin's dispatches for Flag Officer Foote. After reporting to Maj. Gen. Grant at Fort Henry, the timberclad continued on and arrived off the tip of Illinois early on March 3, many hours behind the *Izetta*. The transport's captain had the honor of providing the newspapers with the first accounts of the Pittsburg fight. He also noted bringing down 20 Union refugees, that his hold was filled with 500 bushels of contraband wheat from Clifton and that "the woods along the river are full of Union men who have been driven from their homes."

Once he heard about the little fight at the river landing, Confederate Brig. Gen. Daniel Ruggles sent a letter of congratulations to Col. Moulton. His thanks were to be shared with all of the troops of the 18th Louisiana "for their brilliant success on their first encounter with the enemy at Pittsburg, Tennessee." The night of the encounter, the commander of the 18th, certain that skirmishing would not be renewed, posted a small observation picket at the landing and withdrew the remainder of his force inland some three miles to the grounds around a Methodist log church called Shiloh.

On March 2, as the *Izetta* and *Lexington* raced toward Cairo, Lt. Gwin steamed back up toward Pittsburg Landing — this time under a flag of truce. Going ashore, the *Tyler*'s skipper was escorted a mile back from shore to discuss a POW exchange with Col. Moulton. When he returned to Cairo on March 6, Gwin reported seeing nine dead bodies and 100 wounded at the enemy camp. He had no word on the three missing sailors.[4]

While *Lexington* and *Tyler* were engaged at Pittsburg Landing and the *Conestoga* steamed slowly up to Cincinnati for repair, fresh rumors about Columbus reached Cairo on the evening of March 1. The "Gibraltar of the Mississippi" was supposedly being evacuated and the Rebels were retreating to make a stand at Island No. 10. Those making the claims suggested the new place was the strongest position on the entire Mississippi. River men and pilots interviewed at Cairo denied the assertion to newsmen from the journalistic fraternity known as the "Bohemian Brigade." The "scuttlebutt," as the gunboatmen called unfounded information, was correct this time. During the day, Lt. Phelps was sent under a flag of true to Columbus by Flag Officer Foote, ostensibly to discuss POW matters. While there, the naval officer observed Maj. Gen. Polk's men burning their winter quarters and removing their heavy cannon. Few infantry were visible, though many cavalrymen were present.

What the Federal naval officer did not see was the actual start of the nautical evacuation. Starting this day and continuing for the next two, 20 steamers would transport Maj. Gen. McCowan's division and Brig. Gen. Alexander P. Stewart's independent brigade down to Island No. 10. Additionally, flatboats took down to Island No. 10 Brig. Gen. James Trudeau and the artillery of his Tennessee Heavy Artillery companies. At Columbus, the floating battery *New Orleans* was readied for departure next day.

Upon his return, Phelps reported to both Flag Officer Foote and Brig. Gen. Cullum that Columbus was definitely being evacuated. Cullum went to the telegraph office and wired the news to Maj. Gen. Halleck, along with the observation that the Western Flotilla would make a demonstration against Columbus on Sunday or Monday.

The theater commander replied almost immediately. Hoping that Maj. Gen. Pope, already in motion, could reach New Madrid from the rear in time to capture it and cut off Rebel reinforcements from Columbus, Halleck also believed that Foote's demonstration could be coordinated with Pope's. The mortar bombardment of Columbus should, he directed, be made from the Belmont side of the river and covered by the gunboats. That way the latter would be out of danger and preserved for "the real attack." Cullum was to work with Foote and Pope to set a day for this coordinated joint effort.

About 9:00 P.M. the sky south of Cairo was "most brilliantly illuminated" by the reflection from a large conflagration. The *Chicago Daily Tribune* reporter thought it "directly in line of Columbus and apparently as far distant." Rumors of the town's evacuation continued to come in and now it became the general opinion that the citadel was being burned.

Sunday, following divine services, Flag Officer Foote laid plans to visit Columbus. Word was received from Polk that he was sending up a team under a flag of truce at noon for further discussions on unspecified subjects. Not knowing what these were, Foote, in a message to Secretary Welles, noted that he would be "governed according to circumstances." Quite possibly the white flag concerned the fate of the women of Columbus, whom Phelps reported remaining in the town.

Over at Fort Henry, Maj. Gen. Grant received a telegraph from Maj. Gen. Halleck, dated the previous day, requiring him to assemble a force to move up to the Eastport area. Once it was on scene, the bluecoats would strike out and disrupt Confederate communications, especially by cutting telegraph wires. The hero of Fort Donelson immediately issued orders for key elements to prepare and assemble for departure on these raids.

By now, the Confederate evacuation of Columbus was nearly finished. When the anticipated flag of truce boat did not arrive off Fort Holt, *Cincinnati* and *Pittsburg* were sent down to reconnoiter. Once the ironclads were reported in the bend of the Mississippi three miles upstream, the Rebel floating battery *New Orleans* "slipped anchor with 30 fathoms of chain and dropped down the river to Island No. 10." Upon their return to Cairo, officers from the Pook turtle informed members of the press, including Joseph B. McCullagh, "Mack" of the *Cincinnati Daily Gazette*, that Columbus was evacuated. The reporters, banned from the ironclad sortie, raced for the telegraph.

Late in the day, Maj. Gen. Polk, in a letter to his wife, wrote that everyone would soon be out and that he was leaving "virtually nothing to the enemy but the works." Just as military necessity had occasioned him to occupy the place, so too did it now, along with orders from the secretary of war, compel its abandonment. That night, the steamer *Izetta* arrived at Cairo from the Tennessee River with early news on the First Battle of Shiloh. Soon after daylight on March 3, Flag Officer Foote made an armed reconnaissance of Columbus. Due to heavy rain and dense fog, he was unable to determine whether or not the water batteries had been removed.

The *Lexington* arrived at Cairo also on Monday morning. Lt. Shirk hand carried reports and communications from Lt. Gwin and himself to Flag Officer Foote, including their afteraction reports on the Pittsburg Landing scrape of March 1. Foote immediately informed Brig. Gen. Cullum of Gwin's adventure and prepared a synopsis for Secretary Welles. Newsmen standing around outside headquarters did not know exactly why she had returned. They bet that she had come down for reinforcements and that several ironclads would be sent back up the Tennessee with her.

Although happy with the outcome of the First Shiloh shootout, Foote in his cover letter told the secretary that he would be issuing a general order to his commanders "not to land from gunboats in my absence, as men must not be risked except in fighting on board." As he undoubtedly confided to Shirk, recruiting officers were still having too much trouble finding men for the flotilla to chance losing any on small boat landings.

Cullum, for his part, telegraphed a brief report to Maj. Gen. Halleck. He was not then thinking of either Gwin's success or Halleck's grand strategy for a coordinated Columbus–New Madrid assault. Having reviewed with Foote the morning's Columbus scout and various other incoming information, it now appeared quite likely that the long-feared fortress was about to drop into his lap like a ripe plumb.

During the afternoon, *St. Louis, Cincinnati, Carondelet, Louisville,* and *Pittsburg* got up steam, preparatory to some move to a new destination. "Mack" of the *Daily Gazette* told his readers it might be Florence, Alabama. That evening, the turtles moved out into the river and anchored. Despite the best efforts of the authorities to hide the true destination of the ironclads, news leaked out around 10:00 P.M. that Columbus would be attacked in the morning. It is possible that word might have slipped out of the telegraph office after Flag Officer Foote wired Secretary Welles: "I go to Columbus at 4 A.M. to-morrow with five gunboats, four mortar boats, and two regiments to take possession." By midnight, Cairo, which many nights did not seem to sleep, was rampant with rumors of Rebel evacuation or reinforcement, conflagration, or forthcoming Yankee occupation.

Unbeknownst to anyone at the tip of Illinois, a 600-man detachment of Lt. Col. H. Hogg's 2nd Illinois Cavalry from Paducah rode into Columbus about 5:00 P.M. and found it unoccupied. In order to alert any Federal forces coming downstream in the morning to this development, Hogg decided to run up a large flag. The only problem was that he didn't have one. At this point, a stash of calico was found in the town and from it an improvised banner was created.[5]

Toward 2:00 A.M. on March 4, three transports began to embark about 4,500 troops from three Illinois and two Ohio infantry regiments, all under the command of Brig. Gen. William T. Sherman from Paducah. Two hours later, after Flag Officer Foote, Brig. Gen. Sherman and Cullum were rowed out to the flagship *Cincinnati*, the order was given for the gunboats and transports, plus several mortar boats, to get underway downriver. Brig. Gen. Cullum rose from his sick bed to go along as he could "not resist landing to examine the works."

A number of Northern correspondents were spread throughout the fleet as witnesses, most aboard the transports, including Junius Henri Browne of the *New York Tribune* onboard the *Illinois*. Joseph B. McCullagh recorded the order of departure: *Cincinnati;* the four other ironclads; the stern-wheelers *Ike Hammet* and *V.F. Wilson*, each towing two mortar boats; the timberclad *Lexington;* and the three troop transports. Proceeding at an estimated speed of 10 mph with a strong current, the fleet reached Lucas Bend in under two hours. At this point, three miles above the feared Confederate citadel, the sun burst from the east, offering a clear morning, bright and cold. In the growing light, the great bluffs of Columbus could be seen, though no one knew for sure whether or not their batteries were manned.

Rounding to, the *Cincinnati*, joined by the other ironclads, idled in the river, their engines providing just enough power to prevent the boats from drifting downstream. The *Lexington*, together with the steamers and mortar boats, remained about two miles behind.

At about 8:00 A.M., the gunboats were beat to quarters and cleared for action. Simultaneously, Lt. Phelps' four mortar boats were towed over to the Missouri shore and tied to some trees near Belmont Point. The troopboats *Illinois, Aleck Scott,* and *T.A. Magill,* meanwhile, drifted as near to the Columbus bluffs as was thought safe and anchored in the middle of the Mississippi about a mile above the gunboats.

Despite these fleet maneuvers, no one aboard any of the Federal vessels yet knew for certain if there were any Confederates in Columbus or anything, really, for them to attack. Spyglasses by the dozen were pointed from decks and pilothouses at the cliffs and the eyes of almost every engaged observer saw something different and nothing conclusive.

Correspondent McCullagh, back with the transports, found it "not a little amusing at this time to notice the varied results of observation made by different persons on board the gunboats." Browne on the *Illinois* noted the cautious approach, as the gunboats "feared the Rebels, as had been often declared, had laid a trap for the 'barbarous Yankees.'"

Flag Officer Foote was by now becoming somewhat anxious. He did not want to open a bombardment if there was no need. Neither did he wish to draw so close as to have his precious gunboats damaged if the Rebels were still there. "Mack" of the *Daily Gazette* provides an interesting account of how this quandary was resolved.

Over on the Missouri shore, a farmer was seen running away from the bank and through his cornfield in an obvious effort to escape danger. Like the 20th century motorist seeking directions, Flag Officer Foote determined to ask the man what he knew. The dispatch boat *Spitfire* was sent over to shore to make the contact. As the auxiliary came abreast of the farmer's location, he was hailed and, being a Union sympathizer, he agreed to tell the sailors what he knew. Taken aboard the *Spitfire*, the local yeoman revealed that the Rebels had, indeed, left Columbus and had burned the greater part of the town.

The agricultural rendezvous had eaten up another half hour, during which time the Union boats all drifted downstream. When the *Spitfire* turned to come abreast the *Cincinnati* and report, the fleet was drawing within range of the Confederate batteries. The farmer's testimony, when added to what was already known before the armada's departure and seen this morning, convinced Foote that Columbus was free of the enemy. Shortly after the flag officer ordered the task force to get underway, lookouts with spyglasses reported a large flag flying on the summit of a hill a short distance south of the main fortifications. A slight breeze, "bathing our faces with early Spring as correspondent Browne put it," lifted it into visibility through the haze of the otherwise pleasant morning weather. The banner they all saw was quite strange in appearance, too large to be a Confederate ensign and with too many stripes to represent the U.S. It was quite unlike any depicted in the few recognition manuals aboard the boats.

Uncertain as to what they were seeing, Foote remained cautious. Brig. Gen. Sherman, accompanied by Lt. Phelps and 30 *Cincinnati* marines, now volunteered to personally check out the fortifications and the mysterious flag. Going aboard the *Spitfire*, the soldier and the sailor still could see no guns or active preparation for resistance as they were brought near shore. The little boat chugged back and forth under the water batteries until Sherman was convinced the place was deserted.

Jumping onto shore, the men scrambled to the location of the flag on the summit, carrying a large U.S. flag with them to display just in case. As they reached the crest, they were greeted by Lt. Col. Hogg and his cheering soldiers. Columbus was indeed a Union prize. After Sherman and Phelps returned and apprised Flag Officer Foote of the situation ashore, hats came off "and three cheers for the Union rang out across the silent bosom of the Mississippi." Browne continued: "The cry was caught up from the gunboats and the distant bluffs echoed the joyous shout." With regimental bands striking up patriotic and other tunes, including *Dixie*, a larger landing force was ordered ashore. Within a few minutes, the three troop transports steamed to the Columbus wharf and the rest of the embarked U.S. troops were landed.

The flag boat *Cincinnati* also came to shore. Flag Officer Foote was able to reach the still operational telegraph office and to send a long wire to Secretary Welles that began, "Columbus is in our possession." Brig. Gen. Cullum was able to have a message Morse-coded off to Maj. Gen. Halleck expressing the same sentiment, which stands as a brief summary of the western war to date: ""Columbus, the Gibraltar of the West, is ours and Kentucky is free, thanks to the brilliant strategy of the campaign, by which the enemy's center was pierced at Forts Henry and Donelson, his wings isolated from each other and turned, compelling thus the evacuation of his strongholds at Bowling Green first and now Columbus."

For five or six hours, Browne, Wilkie, McCullagh and the other embedded journalists were able to inspect the grounds of the place which had given the Union nightmares for months. The estimated 300 to 500 residents of the town had fled, "leaving their houses and stores, where not destroyed, open."

Every manner of destruction consistent with a rapid departure was witnessed at Columbus, including extensive burning. The journalist from the *Philadelphia Inquirer* noticed that the massive chain that had been stretched across the river remained, "although the Missouri end is at the bottom of the river." The shore was "strewn with the greatest quantity of torpedoes and anchors." Browne thought the torpedoes "as harmless as a pretty school-girl who does the tragedy at a literary exhibition." He saw about a hundred of the things piled up on the banks with their accompanying anchors and buoys; all looked "as innocent as unrewarded virtue."

Once the troops were successfully ashore under Brig. Gen. Sherman's temporary command, Flag Officer Foote detailed the *St. Louis* and two motar boats to remain off Columbus to protect it from any attack from the river. Cdr. Hollins' Confederate gunboats were still a threat and it would not do to take unnecessary chances. The flag officer then took the remainder of his fleet back to Cairo.

The *Lexington* did not have a big role to play in the occupation of deserted Columbus. She had been ordered along to guard the troop transports and mortar boats. Still, Lt. Shirk and his men may have been grateful for the invitation and mindful of the irony. Back at the beginning of September, their timberclad, together with the *Tyler*, had been the first United States vessel to engage the Iron Banks batteries. Now, here she was present for their occupation.[6]

Although Maj. Gen. Halleck wished the Western Flotilla to immediately push down on Island No. 10, Flag Officer Foote observed on March 5 that his squadron could not immediately attack those Confederate defenses. Even as Maj. Gen. Pope moved on New Madrid and Maj. Gen. Halleck shoved Cullum and Foote to proceed, the sickly flag officer, stung at both Fort Henry and Fort Donelson, refused to budge until this time his fleet was ready.

"The gunboats have been so much cutup in the late engagements at Forts Henry and Donelson in the pilothouses, hulls, and disabled machinery, that I could not induce the pilots to go in them again in a fight until they are repaired," he told Capt. John A. Dahlgren, chief of the navy's Ordnance Bureau. His boats would be ready for their next outing or he would know the reason why.

On March 11, by Presidential War Order no. 3, Maj. Gen. McClellan was demoted from general in chief to head of the Army of the Potomac, while the Department of the Ohio and the Department of the Missouri were combined into the Department of the Mississippi, under Maj. Gen. Halleck. Maj. Gen. Buell was now a subordinate of the latter rather than a coequal commander.

Once Buell was Halleck's lieutenant, "Old Brains" was free to prosecute the western campaign as he saw fit. To obtain results, Maj. Gen. Grant was ordered to push up the Tennessee River toward Corinth. Buell was now to bring his men down the same watery avenue and effect a rendezvous with Grant. After this mighty force joined together, Halleck would appear from St. Louis and lead the thrust into Mississippi.

Following nearly two weeks of prodding and preparation, the Western Flotilla was finally ready to weigh for Island No. 10 via Columbus. The only timberclad in the large mix of iron-

Island No. 10. This 1862 Currier & Ives lithograph depicts the bombardment and capture of Island No. 10 on the Mississippi River, April 7, 1862. The gunboat, far right, with rear flagstaff, is the *Conestoga*, Lt. George Blodgett commanding. Notice the mortar boats firing from the shore line. It was the duty of the *Conestoga* to protect those rafts, particularly at night, and to run dispatches back up river to Cairo (Naval Historical Center).

clads and mortar boats was the *Conestoga*, repaired and now under the command of Lt. George M. Blodgett. As guardian of the ammunition boats, supply and troop steamers, and mortar boats, her job would be unglamorous but important.

Aboard the *Conestoga* as guest of Lt. Blodgett for the duration of the Island No. 10 campaign was a newsman familiar to Lt. Phelps, his predecessor. Franc B. Wilkie, who wrote under the pen name "Galway" for the *New York Times*, was one of the most famous members of the Civil War press, the "Bohemian Brigade." He was joined by William E. Webb of the *St. Louis Daily Missouri Republican*.

A skilled writer, Wilkie, as we have seen, could often be direct, even though he was paid by the column. Of the advance by the Western Flotilla against its latest target, he was blunt: "Operations about Island No. 10 were not thrilling or exciting in any way." Taking our cue from "Galway," we pay fairly short attention here to the New Madrid and Island No. 10 campaign of March–April 1862. Despite the pyrotechnics that dominated, this was basically a straightforward slugging match that the defenders, whether on land or aboard the remnants of Cdr. Hollins' tiny fleet, could not win.

Our emphasis, thus, will be on a few incidents of interest from the viewpoint of a "Conestogan." In this way, we will conclude the story of that timberclad's first service year before rejoining the saga of her sisters, *Lexington* and *Tyler*, over on the Tennessee.

By Wednesday, March 12, *Daily Missouri Republican* reporter Webb, like Wilkie and other correspondents, knew that movement down the Mississippi was imminent. A day earlier, sailing orders were passed from Western Flotilla headquarters for a state of fleet readiness by the next afternoon. The march to Memphis and below would be hard, his readers were told, but Flag Officer Foote saw this "and although pressed to do so, refused to move until entirely ready, which he now is."

That evening, just minutes before the *Benton* hoisted her departure signals, Flag Officer Foote received orders from Maj. Gen. Halleck requiring that the fleet remain in port until heavy siege cannon were mounted by Maj. Gen. Pope at and near New Madrid. It was not until the following evening that permission to weigh was received. Foote intended to depart at 3:00 A.M. on March 14 but a fierce thunderstorm brought another postponement, albeit a brief one.

Promptly at 7:00 A.M. that Friday, the lead elements of what the *Chicago Daily Tribune* reporter George P. Upton, who wrote as "G.P.U.," called "The Naval Expedition" or "The Great Mississippi River Expedition," departed Cairo for "down the river." At the same time, Maj. Gen. Pope occupied New Madrid.

The Pook turtles *Carondelet*, *Louisville*, and *Cincinnati* were led past Bird's Point by the giant flag boat *Benton*. Following the ironclads were eight mortar boats under Capt. Henry E. Maynadier of the 10th U.S. Infantry. Two each were towed by the *V.F. Wilson*, *Ike Hammitt*, *Pike*, and *Wisconsin No. 2*. The *Ike Hammitt* was host to all of the reporters from the press of Boston, New York, Philadelphia, Cincinnati, and Chicago, not lucky enough to be invited aboard a gunboat. "The *Conestoga* rounded to handsomely and took her position as convoy of the mortar fleet," recorded the *Daily Tribune*'s Upton. The *Cincinnati Daily Commercial* reporter saw that "the gay and gallant United States gunboat *Conestoga* brought up the rear, protecting the transports." In truth, the fastest timberclad guarded all of the support craft.

Three hours later, these vessels made Columbus, passing "under the frowning bluffs which lately bristled with Rebel cannon, and laid up at the landing." At the former Confederate "Gibraltar of the West," Flag Officer Foote was joined by *Mound City*, *Pittsburg*, and *St. Louis*. Of the seven Eads ironclads, only the *Cairo* was missing, on special assignment up the Cumberland River. A few units had yet to arrive.

Several vessels that departed Cairo after the gunboats now caught up. These included two ordnance-provision boats, the *Judge Torrence* and the *Great Western*, the chartered supply boat *Dan Pollard*, and two troop transports, the *Alps* and the *Silver Wave*. From aboard the latter, "S.O.," correspondent of the *Wisconsin State Journal*, recorded the downstream journey for readers in Milwaukee. These steamers were joined by the *Lake Erie No. 2* towing two more mortar boats. Six tugboats were also along.

Enlarged, the parade continued down the river at 2:30 P.M. As the *Lexington* had at Columbus two weeks earlier, the *Conestoga* was now placed to lead and convoy these newcomers Two hours later, the Northern fleet came to off Hickman, Kentucky, having approached cautiously "because the real sentiments of the Hickmanites were ambiguous." Once they were found supportive, the fleet dropped anchor and the men aboard settled down for the night.

The correspondent from the *Philadelphia Inquirer*, quartered with most of his colleagues aboard the *Ike Hammit*, later told his readers that, after dark, several persons came aboard the *Benton* to provide Flag Officer Foote with information on Confederate defenses at Island No. 10. One turned over a complete diagram of the earthworks that was later to be found "exactly as he represented." At this time, the impression prevailed "that Island No. 10 will not offer much resistance."

Despite a low-lying fog, at 7:00 A.M. on March 15, the flag boat *Benton* made signal for the task force to weigh anchor. It was, remembered *Tribune* reporter Upton, "a raw, cold morning." The wind blew furiously from the northwest and the sure sign of a storm could be read on dropping barometers. As the flotilla moved from Hickman, Kentucky, down river, it encountered high rolling waves that forced the boats to plough along very slowly, with much bailing on the mortar scows.

About a half hour later, as lead elements of the squadron passed some two miles below Island No. 8, an old nemesis "poked her nose around a distant point." Providentially, the fog suddenly lifted and she was seen to be Capt. Marsh Miller's Rebel gunboat, the two-gun *Grampus*, bane of the timberclads since the previous fall. Four or five shells were sent in pursuit from the *Benton*, forcing the spyboat, which some regarded as "the sauciest little vessel on the river," to take to her heels, according to Upton. She disappeared back around the point "whether damaged or not it is impossible to say." Aboard the *Ike Hammit*, the *Philadelphia Inquirer* and *Cincinnati Daily Commercial* reporters described the exit of the *Grampus* from the scene: "Suddenly," the Philadelphia man wrote, "she "ran out from behind a small island and ran down the river under a full head of steam, being closely followed by several shells from the flagship *Benton*." Continuing, he concluded that "she succeeded in gaining the cover of the guns on Island No. 10." Agreeing, the Cincinnati scribe noted that Miller's boat "rounded down from the Kentucky shore in a hurry, being some two miles ahead of the flagship *Benton*." Shells from the ironclad fell short and the "*Grampus* scudded off down the river at her best speed, her steam whistle shrieking and screaming incessantly."

Henry Walke, who witnessed the incident from the *Carondelet*, later thought fondly of Upton, the *Inquirer* man, and his fellow scribes. Having "such a tender regard for the fleet and the flag steamer," they collectively refused to tell what really occurred regarding the *Benton* and the *Grampus*. When the fog rose, the *Grampus* was actually, according to Walke, lying motionless in the water across the track of the oncoming fleet and "close aboard." Seeing that she could be run down by the flag boat in the swift current, she actually struck her colors. The men aboard the *Benton* could hardly believe their luck and "thought she was certainly their prize at last."

Alas for the Yankees, it was not to be. The *Benton* could not move quickly and when Capt. Miller perceived this tardiness, he quickly had steam raised (along with his big Rebel flag) and sped away "down the river with such astonishing celerity, like a scared rabbit." The *Grampus* was, Walke remembered, "beyond the reach of the *Benton*'s 9-inch Dahlgren guns before one of them could be fired."

Even as the U.S. gunners began to shoot, the *Grampus* was out of range, "yawing and flirting about, and blowing her alarm-whistle." The shrill noise could be heard all the way to Island No. 10 and New Madrid. Returning alongside the floating battery *New Orleans*, Miller ran aboard, stopping long enough to report "a number of the enemy's gunboats and transports coming down the river." Not for nothing had the skipper won the title "Dare-Devil Jack."

About 8:00 A.M. the head of Island No. 10 loomed into view on the other side of Phillips' Point, together with a number of steamers and the floating battery *New Orleans* lying below. Foote later reported that "The rain and dense fog prevented our getting the vessels in position [to launch a bombardment]." Most of the morning was spent in nautical reconnoitering.

Several gunboats moved up into spyglass range as the mortar boats were tied to trees along the Arkansas shore. Through stands of cottonwoods, shrubs, and dead trees, the men could see tents lining the head of the island. The *Ohio Belle* and other transports could, noted the Cincinnati newsman aboard the *Ike Hammitt*, "be seen occasionally crossing to and from the island to the Kentucky shore." Having fallen back on this location, the Confederates were prepared for an all-out defense of this river bastion.

The bombardment of Island No. 10 began that Saturday afternoon when mortar boats nos. 11–12 lofted the first 220-pound shells toward the Rebel redoubt. From now until the position surrendered, thousands of shot would be hurled high into the sky to fall upon the Confederate defenders. Over the next two days, the Western Flotilla initiated the water-borne

Under her captain, Marsh Miller, the two-gun Confederate steamer *Grampus* was the bane of the Union fleet from the late summer of 1861 through her scuttling off Island No. 10 in April 1862. *Chicago Daily Tribune* newsman Albert H. Bodman, looking upon her wreckage, was moved to write that she was "a little, dingy, inferior-looking tow-boat, but as fast almost as lightning ... known among the Rebels as 'Dare-Devil Jack'.... Her commander was Marsh Miller, a well-known river man, and an inbred, natural, original secessionist. His boat has done the Rebels great service as a courier-post, for which she was admirably adapted" (Naval Historical Center).

softening up of Island No. 10's defenses. The position of mortar boats was extremely unfavorable in that they had to fire at very long range over Phillips Point. Their huge shells flew high into the air and 30 seconds later exploded. Unhappily, the barge gunners could not see their targets and could not independently gauge the fall of their shot. Only when word was received from observers on other craft could corrections be made.

As might be imagined, and widely recorded at the time, the noise of the bombardment was tremendous. Still, even after the expenditure of 733 shells in 48 hours, not a single Confederate casualty attributable to the shooting had occurred on the island. As Capt. Maynadier later reported, "most of the shells were fired with large charges over the bluff, with a view to reach the camps and storehouses in the hollow beyond; in this the success was very limited."

It goes without saying, almost, that confusion reigned on both sides during these initial days of combat. Confederate officers, thinking they saw a Union steamer approaching under a flag of truce on Sunday March 16, sent Capt. Miller and the *Grampus*, under similar bunting, out to investigate. The sighting was a mistake, as Miller encountered the *Benton*'s executive officer, Lt. Joshua Bishop, aboard the ironclad's supporting tugboat, which now raised a like flag in answer to the Rebel's. After a short parlay between Miller and Bishop, during which the matter of the truce signals was sorted out, the tug returned upstream and the little gunboat retired behind the island, her last operational sortie completed.

The Island No. 10 operation from the river now turned into a siege. For the next 20 days, the mortar boats pounded the Rebel defenses with powder and shot supplied via *Judge Torrence* and *Great Western*. "Heavy firing was constantly heard at Island No. 10" by, among others, Col. Graham Newell Fitch and the men of the 46th Indiana Volunteer Infantry, downstream at Riddle's Point.

Throughout this campaign, the ironclad gunboats, together with the *Conestoga* on occasion, would join the mortar boat shelling. At night, the timberclad stood guard over the bomb craft, protecting them from "commando-style" attacks from the water. She was often joined in this duty by the Pook turtles. "For several weeks," Junius Henri Browne of the *New York Tribune*, remembered, "life on the National Flotilla was dull enough." The *Times*' Wilkie, aboard the *Conestoga*, agreed. This was "a siege of intolerable length, and without any variety to break the everlasting monotony."

How dull was it? "There we were, anchored in the midst of the mighty river, or tied to the submerged trees," wrote newsman Browne, "watching the occasional shells from the mortars, the turbid eddying of the swollen stream, or the leaden sky that hung over the dreary scene like a funeral pall.... We could go nowhere.... We had no books to peruse, no papers to read, no letters to expect, no women even to tease or talk to." Indeed, "we were as wretched a set of mortals as ever committed matrimony or contemplated suicide."[7]

Notwithstanding the boredom noted among the Bohemian reporters aboard the mortar boats and steamers tied to or anchored near the Missouri shore above the citadel, soldiers and sailors remained tense. False alarms of Confederate boat attacks or shore raids were constant. There was one such incident involving the *Conestoga* that stood out during these several weeks. For correspondent Franc Wilkie, it was the "one event that increased the pulsation of my blood" during the whole Island No. 10 assault.

At night, the *Conestoga* and the *Judge Torrence* were usually laid up on the western, or Arkansas, shore. Between the boats and the shore was a dense cane-covered swamp from which access to the naval craft by boat was thought to be impossible. During the day on March 19, a number of "suspicious looking" skiffs "laden with butternut natives" were noticed in the vicinity and additional precautions were taken.

Between 9:00 P.M. and 10:00 P.M. that Wednesday, an alarm, false as it turned out, was raised concerning the pending approach of a Rebel force by land. In the only "action" report concerning a flotilla ammunition boat to make it into the ORN during the entire campaign, the mortar fleet abstract log for that date recorded that " The *Judge Torrence* slipped her moorings from the shore, got underway, and stood out into the middle of the stream. Quiet was soon restored and the boat returned to her anchorage."

Franc Wilkie later elaborated and there was much to add. After the discharge of a musket from the *Torrence*, followed by half a dozen shots more, the *Conestoga*'s ready portside cannon roared out into the darkness. By this time, Lt. Blodgett and the scribe were on deck peering into a night as "dark as Erebus." Below, the wardroom officers scrambled up from a game of euchre, in which it was later conceded First Master Duble was about to play the winning hand.

As the *Judge Torrence*, ordered underway by her skipper, Lt. LeRoy Fitch, eased out into the Mississippi, the *Conestoga* prepared to open protective fire with her 32 pounders. As the whistle of the boatswain called her men to action, the timberclad's portside gun fired again, spraying the shoreline with charges of grape and canister. By the light of this cannon fire, Wilkie could see one of the ships' boys—"a suckling tar of about 12 years of age apparently"— blazing into the swamp with a revolver "as fast as he could cock it and pull the trigger."

Downstream, activity was noticeable in the fleet by the twinkling of lights and the flash of signal rockets. After a few minutes, as the timberclad continued to shoot up the swamp, a tug arrived from the *Benton* and Lt. Phelps rushed aboard. He disappeared along the gundeck "and a little later the firing ceased."

As "everybody blazed away into the woods with something," someone, probably Blodgett or Phelps, inquired as to the cause of the alarm. After a general inquiry was made, it was determined that "nobody knew anything." No one had seen or heard an enemy, no one had the remotest idea of what he was firing for or who or what he was firing at." Several boats were lowered away to conduct a search of the surrounding waters, but nothing was seen.

Lt. Blodgett later told Wilkie that, during the uproar after the firing had stopped, the *Torrence*'s sentinel was summoned before himself and Phelps. The man reported something splashing toward his boat in the water. Receiving no answer to his challenge, the sailor fired his musket at the sound. A new search was made at dawn and the body of a cow was found, riddled by grape. "It was she," confessed Wilkie, that "wading through the water had excited the challenge and alarm of the sentinel." The poor animal was solely responsible for "the fierce resistance of the gallant *Conestoga* and a commotion which affected the entire fleet."

In spite of a change in Confederate command on Island No. 10, the digging of an innovative U.S. Army canal, and continued shelling by gunboats and mortars, the situation in this part of the western theater remained largely unchanged. Despite earlier hopes, the thousands of mortar bombs and gunboat shells being dropped in and around the river fortress were not having the intended effect. Indeed, one later analysis bluntly stated that the greatest failure from a Union perspective during the campaign was "the complete ineffectiveness of long-range shelling." The mortar shells forced the defenders to move their camps out of range and dig bombproof shelters for the batteries. Captured prisoners confessed that the fireworks were a "great annoyance to the daily labors of the garrison" but otherwise caused little actual damage.

The *Conestoga* departed the area at dark on March 22 and arrived at the Cairo levee on Sunday morning. While she was gone, newsmen Wilkie and Webb transferred to the *Ike Hammitt*. Lt. Blodgett brought dispatches and requisitions from Flag Officer Foote and news stories from the correspondents. In his of March 23 sent by a later steamer, the *Times*' "Galway" paid another tribute to his friends aboard the timberclad.

Having visited the many Union war craft, Wilkie had heard talk around the flotilla that "the Rebels appear to be very fearful that some attempt will be made to run the blockade. In speaking to Lt. Blodgett, Master Duble, and others of the possibility, he found that "the officers of the *Conestoga*, to a man, have expressed their willingness to make the attempt at any time, if called upon to do so." Was this boasting?

"From what he knew of the men, the writer was "satisfied that they would do it, if ordered or requested, as cheerfully as ever they engaged a Rebel battery or guarded a fleet of transports." Wondering why anyone aboard a timberclad would ever want to rush past all those guns on Island No. 10 save in an act of bravado, Wilkie penned his belief that there was "probably no danger of any boat being called on for any such purpose."

The fleet-wide discussion on breaking the blockade continued over the next several days. "It has been suggested that, by placing flatboats alongside and filling them with bales of pressed hay," Wilkie recorded on March 25, "the thing might be done by the *Conestoga*, which is by all odds the swiftest boat on the river." Her speed guaranteed that the *Conestoga* continue to act not only as a guard ship but as the flotilla's principal dispatch boat. As such, she made another turnaround trip to Cairo on March 27. Among the news items from below was word from a scout that Island No. 10 was being reinforced. This information was not only passed to Maj. Gen. Halleck, but also wired directly to the offices of the *Chicago Daily Tribune*.

Lt. Blodgett and his sailors arrived at the tip of Illinois just as a great storm was pummeling the entire Mississippi Valley. To the north, the Mobile and Ohio Railroad wharf boat was blown across the river from Cairo and entangled in the bushes on the Kentucky shore. The Evansville packet *Courier* barely escaped destruction, while the steamer *Philadelphia* was wrecked a mile north of Columbus. Roofs were torn off and 30 buildings, including the marine hospital, were damaged at Paducah. At least seven people were known dead.

In the area of Island No. 10, the winds howled just as ferociously and, even in this remote area, damage was done. Two Union transports, the *Swallow* and the *Pike*, were among several blown across the river. These two lost most of their upper works, including chimneys, pilothouses, steam-pipes, and so forth. The latter was so severely damaged that, when temporarily repaired, she was sent, with dispatches, back to Cairo. The ironclads and mortar boats were not damaged in what Franc Wilkie called "a hurricane." Fort Pillow and Island No. 10 were rocked. The Confederate steamer *Kanawha Valley* was capsized and wrecked below the island. The men on board got off, many without clothes, and were carried on flotsam toward New Madrid. They were rescued by *DeSoto* and *Grampus*.

The *Conestoga* prepared to return to the river north of Island No. 10 on April 1, there to resume her guardian duties. In order to allow an esteemed member of the Bohemian Brigade to pay a quick visit to the war zone, Lt. Blodgett invited Albert H. Bodman of the *Chicago Daily Tribune* to accompany him as his guest.

Bodman's report of his two-day downstream voyage was published in his newspaper's April 4 edition and should be read by all students of the river war seeking information on the towns and geography of the Mississippi at this point in the war. The weather during the trip was beautiful, "the trees lining either shore just robing

George M. Blodgett, the second commander of the *Conestoga*, was a native of Huntington, Vermont, but considered himself a resident of Burlington. He was commissioned a midshipman with the naval academy class of 1856, becoming a passed midshipman and master three years later. After serving aboard the sloop of war *John Adams*, he was named gunnery officer of the Portsmouth Navy Yard, where he was stationed at the time of Fort Sumter. Promoted to the rank of lieutenant on February 3, 1861, he would die unexpectedly of an illness at Cairo on November 6, 1862 (Library of Congress).

themselves in emerald, the orchards pregnant with white and purple blossoms, and a quite, peaceful air rested over the whole landscape."

For all intents and purposes, the standoff at Island No. 10 ended on the night of April 4-5. Under cover of a thunderstorm, Cmdr. Henry Walke successfully ran the *Carondelet* past the river bastion's cannon and halted off New Madrid. In the words of Capt. Mahan, "the passage of the *Carondelet* was not only one of the most daring and dramatic events of the war; it was also the death-blow to the Confederate defense of this position." Before leaving, Walke was ordered by Foote that, if possible, he was to capture or destroy the illusive Rebel gunboat *Grampus*.

After the *Pittsburgh* followed down next evening, Maj. Gen. Pope had two ironclads with which to cover the crossing of his men from the Missouri shore to Tennessee.

The Confederate stronghold was cut off by lunchtime on April 7. Hoping to blockade the river channel, the Rebels elected to sink the transports now located two miles below the island. Excepting the hospital steamers *Champion* and *Admiral*, the *DeSoto*, the *Red Rover*, the *Mears*, and the *Ohio Belle* were scuttled and partially sunk. Total losses were made of the *Prince*, *John Simonds*, *Mohawk*, *Tazon*, and Marsh Miller's famous *Grampus*.

Island No. 10 was surrendered to Flag Officer Foote on the evening of April 8. Three Confederate generals, 4,500 soldiers, and 109 artillery pieces were now taken off the table. "The circumstances as connected with the surrender of this position, with all its guns, ammunition, &c., are," wrote an editorialist for the *Richmond Press* on April 14, "humiliating in the extreme."

The *Conestoga* would continue her duties with the main fleet on the Mississippi for the next two months. These would be almost routine, even as Flag Officer Foote and his successor, Flag Officer Charles H. Davis, engaged the enemy at Plum Point Bend, Fort Pillow, and Memphis.

Meanwhile, the other two timberclads, *Lexington* and *Tyler*, remained busy on the Tennessee River. At Pittsburg Landing, 110 miles southeast of Island No. 10, they were participants in the largest ever Western theater battle.[8]

CHAPTER 10

Tennessee River: Shiloh, March–April 1862

WHEN THE U.S.S. *LEXINGTON* UNDER LT. JAMES R. SHIRK returned to Cairo following the First Battle of Shiloh on March 1, Lt. William Gwin remained behind with the timberclad *Tyler* to monitor developments in the area of Pittsburg Landing. At St. Louis that Saturday, Maj. Gen. Henry W. Halleck, commander of Department of the Missouri, wrote out orders for Maj. Gen. Ulysses S. Grant, head of the District of West Tennessee. The theater commander, wanting to follow up the success of Fort Donelson, determined to proceed in several directions simultaneously.

In the first thrust, Brig. Gen. John Pope was sent to invest and capture New Madrid, Missouri, on the Mississippi. He would, hopefully soon, be supported by the ironclads of Flag Officer Foote. In the process, Columbus was also to be occupied. Secondly, Halleck envisioned a large-scale raid in the northeastern corner of Mississippi near Eastport. Grant would assemble a fleet of steamers and, once they were loaded, proceed upriver to the far border of Tennessee. From there, he would launch his attacks, emphasizing the destruction of telegraph and rail communications. It was hoped that Corinth, Jackson, Humboldt, and Paris might be captured.

Due to the state of telegraphic communication, Grant, then at Fort Donelson, did not receive Halleck's command until March 2. Once it was in hand, the Buckeye general immediately began assembling his forces at or near his Fort Henry headquarters. Two brigades from the 1st and 4th divisions were ordered to "go into camp at the nearest accessible point for embarking on steamers." There was fine print in Halleck's order, however. Grant was to "avoid any general engagement."

Also on Sunday morning, under a flag of truce, Lt. Gwin went ashore at Pittsburg Landing looking for evidence of the previous day's fight and for a chance to communicate with local Rebel leaders. He was allowed to proceed a mile inland before Confederate pickets stopped him. The U.S. naval officer was taken to the camp of the 18th Louisiana Infantry three miles back from the Tennessee River and engaged in parlay as to the fate of several Union personnel lost in the fight. During his sojourn ashore, Gwinn determined that at least nine and probably as many as 20 Rebels were killed in the contest.

At the time of his visit, the naval officer had a chance to get a better view of the area inland of the west bank landing, information that Brig. Gen. Sherman would confirm later when he chose this location for a huge Federal camp. The landing itself was quite narrow. It had been designed for the docking of no more than five steamboats at one time. From the landing, access could easily be made up a steep hill to a broad plateau covered with various sized fields and growths of timber, many in snarls on choppy hills. Many trails crossed the area and it was flanked by two parallel creeks, Owl and Lick, that flowed into the Tennessee about three to four miles apart. Roads led to Corinth and the neighboring village of Purdy. Over the next two days, the *Tyler* slowly paddled back and forth past the landing "repeatedly firing shell at intervals," remembered Lt. Fenwick Y. Hedley of the 32nd Illinois, "but eliciting no reply."

At Corinth, 15,000 to 20,000 troops were presently believed massing. Another ten to twelve thousand were arriving by rail at Henderson Station, 35 miles from Corinth and 18 miles from Coffee Landing, Tennessee. A heavy battery was being erected at Chickasaw, Alabama, while positions were being fortified at Bear Creek Bridge near Eastport.

Just before his departure from Fort Henry to Fort Donelson on March 4, Maj. Gen. Grant was handed another telegram from Maj. Gen. Halleck. This one turned out to be a bombshell. Halleck now determined to take down the hero of Fort Donelson a peg or two. With approval from Maj. Gen. George B. McClellan, still general-in-chief in Washington, "Old Brains" demanded that Maj. Gen. Charles F. Smith succeed Grant in command of the Tennessee River expedition, claiming, among other concerns, that his famous Tennessee general had not sent in reports on time and was away from his post. Historians and others have written about the cause of this rift for over a century. We will, in generosity, lay it to a mix of bad communication and ego.

Although stung by Halleck's missive, Grant duly returned to Fort Donelson and, as numerous soldiers of his command assembled in the rain, established his headquarters aboard the steamer *Tigress*. She was being joined by over 50 additional steamers summoned up the Tennessee from ports as far away as St. Louis and Cincinnati.

Before returning downriver that day, Lt. Gwin again sent an officer and a party of soldiers ashore under a flag of truce. They found the enemy had withdrawn his guns from the earthworks commanding the river and retired toward Corinth. After reporting these findings, the *Tyler* started for Cairo. Along the way, the big gunboat gathered intelligence concerning Confederate strength inland. In the time frame since the fall of Fort Donelson, Gen. Albert Sidney Johnston had completely fooled the Nationals into believing he was transferring his force to Middle Tennessee, when, in fact, he was headed toward Corinth, Mississippi.

On the evening of March 4, the *Tyler* passed Savannah. Stepping ashore, Lt. Gwin was informed by a "reliable source" that Gen. Johnston was falling back from Murfreesboro to Decatur, Alabama, and was planning to rush another large force up to Bear Creek. Continuing out of the river, the largest timberclad came to off the Cairo levee the following morning.[1]

The same day as the *Tyler* reached the tip of Illinois, the *Lexington*, back from her Columbus excursion, dropped anchor off Savannah, on the right, or eastern, shore of the Tennessee River. As the stream's principal guard ship, she remained alert and on call.

Also on March 5, Maj. Gen. Smith arrived at Fort Henry from Nashville and learned of his new responsibilities. Maj. Gen. Halleck wired Maj. Gen. Grant about the same time warning "that there should be no delay in destroying" the Bear Creek or Corinth bridges. Once that aim was accomplished, Smith's men would return to Savannah, where matters would be prepared for his reinforcement. As with the Kentucky mud march of January, the advance was not to "be communicated to the public."

Early the next morning, 20 armed men signaled their desire to come aboard the *Lexington* seeking protection from Rebel raiders in the vicinity. They were refugees from Wayne County, Tennessee, and several immediately joined the crew. The rest would be sent to Brig. Gen. Smith to enlist in the regiments of his command. Maj. Gen. Halleck's telegram was answered on March 6. The theater commander was notified that Grant was even then loading the transports off Fort Henry. It was possible they could get off before dark, if a "gunboat arrives to convoy them." One of the gunboats (*Lexington*) "has gone to Savannah."

Down the river at Paducah, Brig. Gen. William T. Sherman's new 5th Division boarded its steamers and started toward Fort Henry. Sherman had joined the expedition with Maj. Gen. Halleck's blessing and support and would himself start up two days hence. The gunboats, preparatory to the departure of Union troops further up the Tennessee, began an exploration of "two or three days" of the banks and bends of the stream. These probes were, as Maj. Gen. Lew Wallace remembered in his *An Autobiography*, undertaken to ensure that "there was little danger from the enemy."

In midmorning on March 7, the *Lexington* weighed for Pittsburg Landing, as Lt. Shirk, ever mindful of the need to check any Confederate activity, wished to "take a look at the place." Paddling upstream the nine miles south of Savannah, lookouts spotted several flags of truce at the landing close to the nearby bluff where Southern cannon had spat at them just a week earlier.

A whistle answered the flags and arrangements were made to send in the ship's cutter. Soon thereafter, it returned with a letter for Lt. Gwin concerning POW issues. While awaiting the return of his small boat, Shirk was able to determine that no work had been done to militarily strengthen the site during the past seven days. Just before noon, the gunboat rounded to and returned to Savannah.

Back from Cairo, the *Tyler* came to off Fort Henry that Friday and Lt. Gwin went ashore to report to Maj. Gen. Grant. The local area commander sent him up to wait at the Danville Bridge, 25 miles above, for the fleet of transport steamers then being assembled. During the evening, the *Lexington* puffed up to Craven's Landing, above Savannah, and sent ashore a quantity of provisions. These were for groups of "country people" of Northern sympathy who had fled their homes to the gunboat's protection in order keep their menfolk from being impressed into the Confederate army.

Troops from William H. Robinson's Tennessee Cavalry Company were particularly active in forcibly enlisting people, according to Lt. Shirk. The gunboat lay off Craven's Landing throughout March 8 as more people sought the cover of her big guns. After taking aboard fleeing refugees at Craven's, the *Lexington* headed upstream to Chalk Bluffs on March 9, where she found more loyal Tennesseans. With 120 scared but grateful passengers aboard, the timberclad steamed to Savannah, where they were sent ashore.

As Lt. Shirk was finishing his lunch, a hail was received from Col. Thomas Worthington of the 46th Ohio Volunteer Infantry. Would it be possible to reconnoiter up toward Pittsburg Landing the soldier inquired. Agreeable to the review, the naval officer signaled the officer and his aides to come aboard. Following a leisurely hour and a half cruise, the *Lexington* came in sight of the landing at 2:30 P.M. Unable to determine with spyglasses the extent of any Confederate activity behind the landing, the gunboat's starboard battery dropped nine shells into the area over the next 15 minutes. When there was no reply, Shirk ceased firing, rounded to, and stood back down the river.

During the day, Brig. Gen. Sherman arrived at Fort Henry with his lead divisional steamers. Reporting to Maj. Gen. Smith, he learned that the grand expedition would be launched the next morning.[2] The *Lexington* steamed away from Savannah during the initial hours of March 10, headed for Chalk Bluffs. There she sought information from friendly people along the bank regarding Confederate movements further inland. Before moving on to Craven's Landing, she also rescued additional local men said to be targets for Confederate impressment.

About nine o'clock that morning, the *Tyler*, waiting near Fort Henry at Maj. Gen. Grant's command, began to convoy upriver the main elements of the Tennessee River expedition. The weather had significantly improved over the rain of recent weeks and buds could be seen on much of the riverbank foliage. "The departure of this fleet of 90 boats was a sight seen but once in a life time," wrote a correspondent, from the *St. Louis Daily Missouri Republican*, embedded aboard the steamer *Empress*. According to the historian of the 48th Ohio Volunteer Infantry, a passenger on the same boat, the armada consisted of 82 troop-laden steamers. A number of them were lashed together to give greater power. Not long after its departure, the fleet passed the burnt-out Memphis and Ohio Railroad bridge at Danville.

As the steamers swept upstream, Maj. Gen. Wallace, aboard the *John J. Roe*, also enjoyed the spectacle. "Crowded below and above with their precious humanity," some of the boats were "in dangerous tilt, churning the sparkling flood with their hugh wheels." The sky was pearl blue, he remembered, while the sulphurous smoke whirled up in great clouds. Streaming flags with flower-like colors were displayed aboard each craft. "I can hear the hoarse coughing of the pipes, the cheering, the music," the Hoosier general remembered — also "the boisterous echoes hurtled back upon us from rocky bluff and wooded shore."

Meanwhile, around noon, the steamer *Golden State* landed elements of Col. Worthington's 46th Ohio at Craven's Landing. Borrowing ten of the soldiers, the *Lexington* returned to Chalk Bluffs that afternoon to seize a cache of arms. Her task completed, the gunboat returned to Savannah, where she dropped off the refugees.

During the timberclad's absence, the *Golden State* arrived at Savannah along with the *B.J. Adams*. Their men disembarked and Col. Worthington took possession of the town. Just before dark, Lt. Shirk attempted to borrow additional soldiers, from the *Adams*, to employ as pickets. When he learned of the move, Worthington had the men recalled.

Guarded by the *Tyler*, the great column of Union steamers churned and thrashed their way upstream all that day and into night. Approximately 600 yards wide, with high bluffs and banks, the Tennessee was a sight to behold for those en route. Few of the soldiers or even the embedded reporters knew their destination. "Some say Memphis, via Savannah, Tenn.," wrote the *Cincinnati Daily Commercial* newsman taking passage aboard the transport *Telegraph*. "Others," he added, "think Florence, Ala."

Many of the men aboard the steamboats had never made such a journey before and were awestruck. A few wrote down their impressions as they stared aft on their vessels. Many were surprised to hear or see shouts or gestures of welcome from citizens along the bank, though in several instances they were also guerrilla targets. "It was a sublime spectacle," wrote a 14th Illinois bluecoat, "far exceeding anything we ever saw. Behind us, down the river, the sky was obscured by dense clouds of smoke looking like angry storms." Everywhere else, he concluded, the sky was "pure and stainless ... blue."

Another recalled that "Up and down as far as the eye could see were steamers crowded with blue coats." Further on, masked by the river bends, men "could hear the puffing and snorting and see the smoke curling upward from still other steamers." Even the more-often-than-usual torrential downpours did not detract from the spectacle. The grand procession was of interest to those not only aboard the participating steamers, but also to those watching from the riverbanks. One man kept count as the steamers, belching sparks and smoke, chugged past Reynoldsburg, Humphreys County. After noting 32 transports and a gunboat, he quit scorekeeping when it became too dark to distinguish one boat from another.

Falling out of line as necessary to wood, units of the great steamboat fleet encountered fog later in the evening. It grew so thick that the entire group was forced to lie by. Finally, around 9:00 A.M. on March 11, the fog dissipated and Lt. Gwin was able to get his parade restarted. As it paddled upstream, hooting and puffing, men aboard the individual boats witnessed many demonstrations of loyalty along the shore. The progress was good and, quite the opposite of what might be expected with an assemblage this large, there were no accidents.

The man at Reynoldsburg also returned to the riverbank to take notes and watched as another 14 steamers passed by, "carrying cavalry, wagons, artillery, mules, etc." He then rode west to present his findings to the editor of the *Memphis Daily Appeal*. Just as the lead units were passing Clifton, a man fired on the *Empress* from the bank, but no damage was done. He quickly disappeared.

As the great parade of troopboats plied their way up the Tennessee guarded by the *Tyler* on that Tuesday, Abraham Lincoln issued Presidential War Order no. 3. By its terms, Maj. Gen. George B. McClellan was demoted from general in chief to head of the Army of the Potmac, while the Department of the Ohio and the Department of the Missouri were combined into the Department of the Mississippi, under Maj. Gen. Halleck. Maj. Gen. Don Carlos Buell of the former became a Halleck subordinate instead of a coequal commander. Within a week, the rift between Halleck and Maj. Gen. Grant was also healed. From his Fort Henry base, Maj. Gen. Grant sent a warning to Maj. Gen. Smith to keep a lookout for the Confederate steamer *Dunbar*. It was believed that Capt. Gus Fowler's boat had not disappeared the previous month, but, having run up some creek, could possibly "get below our transports and destroy them."

The initial steamers began to arrive at Savannah on that Tuesday evening, having come up, as Lt. Gwin put it, "without molestation." The remainder of the vessels, transporting elements of the 2nd, 3rd, 4th, and 5th divisions, arrived over the next two days. Fog and wood-gathering stops continued to ensure delays, while driftwood occasionally clogged paddle wheels. There were so many boats that, as they arrived, they had to tie up four or five deep on either side of the Tennessee.

Almost as soon as he had arrived on the scene and assumed command of his force, Maj. Gen. Smith hailed Gwin and was rowed out to the *Tyler* along with members of his staff. The ramrod-straight leader then ordered the gunboat to take them up to Pittsburg Landing on a rapid reconnaissance. No Confederate effort to further fortify the location was detected, "owing to the vigilant watch" made by the *Lexington*.[3]

Late on the evening of March 11, the *Lexington* arrived off Savannah. Reports had reached Lt. Gwin that the Rebels were setting up a battery at Chickasaw, Alabama, a mile and a half above Eastport, Mississippi. Just before midnight, the two gunboats weighed for "up the river" to investigate. The Union naval vessels passed Pittsburg Landing at 1:50 A.M. on March 12 and the *Lexington* threw one 8-inch shell in its general direction, doubtless to awaken any nearby Confederates. By 4:00 A.M., the two steamers reached Boyd's Landing, some 10 miles below Eastport. There, over the next four hours, Lt. Shirk's men joined those of Lt. Gwin in transferring to the *Tyler* 150 of the 5-second shells *Lexington* had brought from Cairo earlier.

Replenished, the two timberclads stood upstream and came in sight of Chickasaw about 7:30 A.M. Their information was correct: the Rebels were establishing a battery along the shore. It was immediately taken under fire at long range by both vessels. Over the next hour,

Memphis, May 1862. The caption on this Currier & Ives print depicts a "brilliant naval victory" by Union forces over the Confederate River Defense Force. Although shown as a virtual participant on the far right side of the lithograph, the *Conestoga* was not directly involved in the fighting. Her role was to guard the Federal mortar boats and transports and seek survivors (Naval Historical Center).

the bombardment was intense. The *Lexington* expended 215 rounds and the *Tyler* 60. Gwin later reported his belief that they had faced at least five guns that were 32-pounders or larger. In truth, there were two 24-pounders atop the bluff, but they were manned by infantry trained on the seacoast cannon at Pensacola, Florida.

Following the *Tyler* back upstream, the *Lexington*, when abreast of Crump's Landing, hurled a shell back of that location, also no doubt to warn Rebels and locals of their presence. At noon, the two gunboats reached Savannah. Going ashore, their captains reported their findings. According to a reporter from the *Cincinnati Daily Commercial*, the naval officers revealed that the Rebels "had some good guns." Thus they "'left them alone in their glory'—but not until we dropped some shell among them." Shoving off, the gunboats cruised the river during the afternoon, encountering numerous troop transports.

Meanwhile, earlier that morning, the soldiers who had arrived at Savannah aboard transport steamers saw another overpowering sight. "As the sun rose over the canebrakes that line the river banks," penned Whitelaw Reid of the Cincinnati *Daily Gazette*, it shown over the fleet lying nearly two miles up and down the Tennessee. "More vessels were constantly arriving," Reid continued. "The channel was filled with them, gliding about in search of landings near their respective brigade headquarters, and the air was heavy with the murky smoke from hundreds of puffing chimneys." Throughout the day, the banks near the town "were covered with the disembarked soldiers, eagerly rushing everywhere and scrutinizing everything."

As dusk descended, it was decided that the *Tyler* would remain off Pittsburg Landing overnight, guarding the troops of Sherman's 5th Division. The *Lexington* dropped anchor off

Crump's Landing to protect Maj. Gen. Lew Wallace's 3rd Division. Indeed, these two locations would become almost "home ports" to these vessels over the next few weeks. Protecting the supply depot at the latter point from Confederate raiders was of particular concern.

Around 10:00 P.M., the first of five of Brig. Gen. Wallace's transports from Savannah dropped anchor at Crump's Landing in yet another rainstorm. To make certain they were not interfered with during their soggy debarkment, the *Lexington* fired another 8-inch shell into the woods above the landing zone. Both Federal gunboat captains retired late that night believing that "everything is working favorably for the cause of the Union." Lt. Shirk's respite was brief, as the last of the five transports did not arrive until 3:00 A.M.

At 7:30 A.M. on March 13, the steamer *Goody Friends* arrived at Crump's Landing from Savannah with news that additional reinforcements were en route. A half hour later, there was a general scare concerning a possible Confederate attack and the steamers nosed into shore all slipped their moorings and transferred to the east side of the river.

Inland, a battalion of the 5th Ohio Cavalry from Crump's, guided by a local Union sympathizer, reached the Beach Creek bridge about 10:00 A.M. and put it out of commission. Capture of the approaching down train from Purdy was narrowly missed when its engineer was tipped off. Having accomplished their task in the rain, the horsemen started back to their embarkation point about 11:00 P.M. Whitelaw Reid told his *Cincinnati Daily Gazette* readers that the weather had cleared "and the boys had a beautiful moonlight march back." By 2:00 A.M. on March 14, Wallace's command was en route back to Savannah. The damaged bridge was repaired in less than a day.

In the days ahead, men from Wallace's command would probe the Confederates on different occasions. Greatly impressed by the power of the gunboats to provide supportive gunfire, the Hoosier was also nervous that "the gunboat may not be here when wanted."

There was at this time still some unfamiliarity with the names of Western Flotilla boats operating on the twin rivers. That Thursday, Capt. William S. Hillyer, on Maj. Gen. Grant's behalf, wrote to Maj. Gen. Smith suggesting that, if he could dispense with her services, the gunboat *Conestoga* should be allowed to "run regularly between your transports and Fort Henry" to provide convoy and to keep the riverbanks free of masked batteries. At this time, the *Conestoga* was at Island No. 10; Hillyer undoubtedly meant the *Lexington*.

Continuing the misidentification, Maj. Gen. Grant wrote to Maj. Gen. Buell on the morning of March 14. With the permission of Flag Officer Foote, he asked that the *Carondelet* be sent around to the Tennessee from Nashville. Next day, he confirmed the request in a wire to Maj. Gen. Halleck, noting that the river was very high and still rising and there was thus no danger that the "turtle" would ground. The *Cairo* was the ironclad at Nashville.

Also that Friday, Brig. Gen. Sherman was summoned to a meeting with Maj. Gen. Smith, who had injured himself two days earlier. The former Paducah post commander was ordered to undertake a raid, similar to that conducted by Wallace's men. Their target was the Memphis & Charleston Railroad, roughly 18–20 miles above. Sherman's division, including another battalion of the 5th Ohio Cavalry, marched down to the landing and were aboard their 19 transports by noon. Escorted by the *Tyler*, called a "saucy-looking Cincinnati gunboat" by the accompanying Whitelaw Reid, the steamers shoved off upstream, passing Pittsburg Landing some time later. To the great enjoyment of the bluecoats stacked aboard their transports, the largest timberclad fired a couple of shells into the woods. There was no return fire "and glasses showed nothing but utter desertion on the shore." A few miles upstream, the *Tyler* came within range of "another dangerous looking bluff." Another shell was lobbed in and again there was no return fire. There would be no more stops before the task group reached its destination.

Meanwhile, when passing Pittsburg Landing at 4:40 P.M., the *Lexington* sent three 8-inch shells into the woods. It is quite possible that this reconnaissance by fire may also have served as gunnery practice. The gunboat rounded to a short distance above the landing and, in passing down, dropped two more rounds onshore before returning to Crump's Landing. No one could see anything for all the rain falling; as the brigadier put it in a letter home a few days later, it came down "in torrents."

Brig. Gen. Sherman's convoy moved all the way up to Eastport, Mississippi, where evidence of Confederate defenses was found. The flotilla next backed down to the mouth of Yellow Creek, 32 miles from Savannah, at about 7:00 P.M., and eased into the bank at Tyler's Landing. Here too it was pouring heavily, but that did not stop Maj. Elbridge Ricker's 5th Ohio Cavalry troops from going ashore with their steeds. The rain let up around 11:00 P.M., allowing the men to trot off toward Burnsville, which they would hopefully reach by sunup or a little before. Two hours after the Buckeye riders set out, the deluge resumed. Time was a concern. Large numbers of Confederate soldiers were known to be at Corinth, only 25 miles away.

Brig. Gen. Sherman had hoped that his infantry could get ashore and set out in staggered waves to support the cavalry. It was 3:00 A.M. on March 15 before the first bluecoats debarked atop a natural levee. About two hours later, the first of two brigades designated for the job slogged forward over a very muddy road. The men could march only four miles over terrible ground intersected by swollen creeks before encountering an impassable bayou a half mile wide. As Sherman pondered what action, if any, to take next, a messenger arrived from Maj. Ricker. His news was also bad: he could not advance further over the treacherous terrain in the cold, driving rain. The 5th Division now chose the better part of valor (or wisdom) and elected to retreat to the landing.

It took the remainder of the day to get all the soldiers and horses, and, most difficult, the field guns, back aboard their transports. Finally, at 6:00 P.M., Sherman's little task group returned downstream, every man aboard cold and with many headed to the sick list. When they had stopped at Tyler's Landing 23 hours earlier, the Federals found it 10 feet above water; it was now five feet below. Indeed, it was "submerged from the bank back to the bluff."

Having meanwhile realized that Lt. Gwin's gunboat offered the easiest way to finish his journey on a positive note, Sherman asked the naval officer to conduct an upstream reconnaissance. With the rain pushing down the smoke from her chimneys, the *Tyler* moved up past the mouth of Indian Creek. There Cook's Landing was found submerged. The big black timberclad cruised on up to Chickasaw, Alabama. There was no activity there either. As they moved back down, picking up the transports in the process, Gwin and Sherman found that the riverbanks from Alabama to Pittsburg Landing were all inundated.

The *Lexington* remained off Crump's Landing on March 15. Earlier on Saturday morning, the *Tyler* convoyed the lead elements of Brig. Gen. Stephen A. Hurlburt's 4th Division to Pittsburg Landing. With that mission accomplished, Lt. Gwin escorted the *Crescent City* up to the location of Brig. Gen. Sherman's advance outpost, 10 miles below Eastport. When Brig. Gen. Sherman returned to Pittsburg Landing, he found Hurlburt's men debarking. After communicating with the expedition leader, he was allowed to put his men ashore there as well.

Over the next several days, five Union divisions, including a new 6th division under Brig. Gen. Benjamin M. Prentiss, clambered off their boats and moved into the area around Pittsburg Landing, the only high ground behind the river for miles. Sherman and his men were charged with providing a defensive ring around the enlarging camp. To be close to his men, he set up his headquarters in a small log cabin known as Shiloh Church.

Brig. Gen. Sherman, like his colleagues, required huge amounts of food, forage, and fuel for his troops. Realizing that it would take some time for his order for "a couple of thousand sacks of corn, as much hay as you can possibly spare, and if possible a barge of coal" to be filled, he decided to "liberate" some corn locally. To do so, he sent "a steamboat under care of the gunboat to collect corn from cribs on the riverbank."

During the next two weeks of Union buildup, the Tennessee River continued to rise rapidly, creating great backwater pools behind the banks. Blossoms popped out everywhere, including those on peach trees the like of which many Yankees had never seen before.

Maj. Gen. Grant arrived at Savannah, Tennessee, from Fort Henry on March 17, St. Patrick's Day. At the same time, Maj. Gen. Buell's Army of the Ohio approached the town of Columbia, on the Duck River, slowly moving away from Nashville toward a link-up with Grant. Muddy roads and bad weather allowed it to move with all the speed of a glacier.

As the Northerners went ashore to set up camps, the Southerners were not idle. Gen. Johnston placed the highest value on defending northern Mississippi, especially the town of Corinth. His Army of the Mississippi, comprised of approximately 44,000 men in units from all over the Deep South, was skillfully assembled there, largely by rail. Johnston had few options. He could dig in and await the charge or he could attack. Kentucky was lost and much of middle and western Tennessee. If Maj. Gen. Buell succeeded in combining his five divisions with Grant's five, the Union could conquer even more of the fledgling Confederate nation.

Throughout late March, each side received intelligence reports on troop dispositions of the other. Not all were accurate, but the overall numbers quoted were reasonably correct. Based on this information, Maj. Gen. Grant believed the Rebels would adopt a defensive position. Johnston, for his part, elected to advance.[4]

While the armies gathered ashore, the timberclads on the river continued to act as guardians, protectors, and nautical scouts. Their work was, for the most part, routine. It was known in Confederate circles that the Yankee buildup was underway. As Judge Alexander Walker told the readers of the *New Orleans Daily Delta* about a month later, the Union was setting up "an immense encampment extending for miles." They were half a mile from the river; Pittsburgh "was the landing place for their boats." From the river side, it was protected "by several gunboats."

On March 18, Maj. Gen. Halleck telegraphed the senior officer at Fort Henry requiring that "Transports in ascending the Tennessee River should in all cases be convoyed by a gunboat." He also wired Maj. Gen. Buell asking that a Cumberland River–based ironclad be sent to support Grant. The same day, Maj. Gen. Smith received a request from Maj. Gen. Grant to have a timberclad ply between the Danville railroad bridge and Savannah on a regular basis. Fearing the "gun-boat *Dunbar* being up Duck Creek and possibly another gun-boat afloat further up," Smith demurred.

Undoubtedly missed in the big picture was a moment of Pittsburg Landing reverence. A number of soldiers from the 48th Ohio visited the area of the March 1 firefight between the Louisiana soldiers and the gunboats. There, according to the regimental historian, "we saw the graves of the Rebel dead." As a result of the hasty burial, the bodies "were but a few inches under ground and many of their faces were exposed to view."

Maj. Gen. Grant concluded a two day visit to Pittsburg Landing and Crumps Landing on March 19. From Savannah, he wired Halleck his view — similar to Sherman's — that, given the stage of water, those were the only two places on the Tennessee all the way down to Eastport where Union forces could go ashore. From Cairo, a dispatch was sent to the *Chicago Daily Tribune* reporting a "collection of 18 transports at Savannah." The boats' presence, readers were told, indicated "the country about the Tennessee River near the Alabama line is to be the theatre of extensive military operations."

The *Lexington* patrolled from Clifton to Reynoldsville on March 19 seeking intelligence. Her reconnaissance was also designed to find and, if possible, to destroy any Rebel masked batteries that might have been thrown up to "annoy our transports." It was also hoped that she could prevent Confederate partisans from shooting up the unprotected transports. At Clifton, a large cache of contraband goods was found. These were hauled by the gunboat-men down to the river and put aboard the transport *Boston*. That afternoon, she made war on flatboats that could be employed to conduct unauthorized transfers across the river. A horse ferryboat was burned at Reynoldsville just before the timberclad anchored for the night.

On March 20, Halleck again cautioned Grant. "Don't let the enemy draw you into an engagement now. Wait till you are properly reinforced [by Buell] and receive orders." Also on Thursday, Lt. Shirk was ordered by Maj. Gen. Grant to convoy troops to the mouth of the Tennessee River. From that point, the *Lexington* traveled down to Cairo to deliver dispatches and to "fill up with provisions, stores, etc." While she was away, the *Tyler* took over the duty of conducting "daily trips as far down the river as Perryville."

The evening edition of the *Chicago Daily Tribune* told its readers that the Tennessee had overflowed its banks and, consequently, "military operations in the vicinity of the river are necessarily restricted." The Confederates, it continued, "avoid the river and keep out of range of the gunboats." Over the next several days, the size of the Federal camp at Pittsburg Landing mushroomed. Over 34,000 men were on hand by the last day of the month.

Brig. Gen. Sherman, writing to his wife Ellen a few weeks later on April 3, remarked that the local people "have mostly fled, abandoning their houses, and such as remain are of a neutral tint, not knowing which side will turn up victors." The brigadier privately contradicted the public statements of Lt. Gwin and others that had appeared in Northern newspapers for a month as simply "not true." The poor citizenry, mostly farmers, "certainly do want peace and protection, but all the wealthier classes hate us Yankees with a pure unadulterated hate." Sherman did agree with Gwin, Foote, and Halleck on one major point, as he told Ellen: "They fear the gunboats which throw heavy shells and are invulnerable to their rifles and shotguns, and await our coming back from the River."

The *Lexington* arrived at Cairo on the morning of March 22. Lt. Shirk reported that Union forces were "scattering into the country round about Savannah, accomplishing nothing of importance." Also, on March 22, weeks of wet and chilly weather came to an end, as temperatures rose and the sun was often seen. Indeed, it would soon be downright hot. Still, few soldiers complained. Many were caught up in the enjoyment of the new foliage; blossoms on dogwoods, redbuds, and peach trees were everywhere. Earlier than they were used to, men saw buds on familiar Northern trees such as maple, oak, ash, poplar, and beech.

In this time, according to the *Memphis Daily Appeal* of March 23, Rebel "cavalry skirmishers" harassed Yankee shipping between Fort Henry and Savannah. Three troopboats, *Iowa*, *War Eagle*, and *Bay City*, were fired into and three bluecoats were killed.

The *Lexington* returned to Pittsburg Landing early on March 24. Shortly thereafter, she joined the *Tyler* in weighing anchor and steaming upriver toward Eastport. Lt. Gwin knew that a recently established battery commanded the Tennessee below the town, but believed it of no importance, "our base of operations being so much below them." Still, the senior local naval officer believed it was his responsibility "to annoy them, where I could with little or no risk to our gunboats." In that way, the Rebels would think twice, he hoped, before mounting cannon lower down the river. As the pair of old gunboats paddled up the Tennessee, Maj. Gen. Buell, via his chief of staff, passed new orders to Lt. Nathaniel C. Bryant, commander of the *Cairo*. In accordance with instructions from Maj. Gen. Halleck, the ironclad was to be moved from Nashville to either Savannah or Pittsburg Landing.

About 3:00 P.M. the two timberclads discovered the Confederates planting a new battery in an earthwork on a hill about two miles below Eastport. Two cannon were present, one ready for action. Several shells were thrown at the emplacement, which did not reply. Puffing on, the two were engaged at a range of about 200 yards by the two-gun battery about which Gwin already knew. Lt. Gwin claimed its shot fell short. The *Chicago Daily Tribune* informed its subscribers on March 29 that, in fact, the masked battery was able to hit one of the *Tyler*'s chimneys.

Moving up just outside the battery's range, the *Tyler* threw three or four 20-second shells at the Rebels, but none exploded. It was determined that these fuses, obtained from a U.S. Army supply, were defective. The *Lexington* dropped 24 rounds on or near her target. This engagement, reported the Chicago newspaper, "was extremely spirited while it lasted." The Confederate batteries made no reply once the gunboats ceased firing.

The shoot completed, the two timberclads returned to Pittsburg Landing. Meeting aboard the *Tyler*, Gwin and Shirk decided to divide their daily patrol areas. The *Lexington* would cruise downriver below the landing, while the *Tyler* could move above. In his written report to Cmdr. Alexander M. Pennock at Cairo sent out that night, Lt. Gwin confirmed that he, too, had heard that the *Dunbar* had been raised. In four trips upstream of late, he had not discovered any signs of her and doubted the accuracy of the report.

As March drew to a close, the great freshet subsided. Within a few days, the land back of Eastport, for example, would become hard and dry where, for a distance of 300 to 500 yards inland, it had earlier been under water. At Island No. 10, Flag Officer Foote was worried about a possible disaster should his flotilla be attacked by the many Rebel gunboats reported abuilding at New Orleans. On March 26, he wrote to Fleet Captain Pennock at Cairo on the matter.

The commanders of *Cairo*, *Tyler*, and *Lexington* were warned not to be caught with too little water under their bottoms to permit a rapid return to the tip of Illinois. In a worst case scenario, they, together with the *Louisville*, were "to meet at Cairo, or as far down as Columbus and even Hickman, to prevent the rebel gunboats from ascending the river above Cairo." Of course, before leaving the Tennessee to meet any such threat, the timberclads and *Cairo* were to notify Maj. Gen. Grant.

On March 27, *Tyler* and *Lexington* received high praise from Warren P. Isham, the *Chicago Daily Times* reporter covering the expedition. "There have been numerous, ineffectual attempts to oppose our free passage along the river," he wrote, "but the two wooden gunboats, the *Lexington* and the *A.O. Tyler*, have served an admirable purpose as a roving police, preventing the erection of batteries."

After going their separate ways for most of a week, *Lexington* and *Tyler* made rendezvous at Pittsburg Landing before dawn on March 30. From the now immensely busy port, the two chugged upriver to once again visit the Eastport batteries. At a few minutes after 8:00 A.M., the men on both timberclads were beat to quarters as the Rebel earthworks came into sight. The boats lingered in the stream out of range for the next two hours, with the *Tyler* occasionally tossing in an explosive shell. Tiring of the exchange, the two gunboats broke off the one-sided engagement and returned downstream. As they were passing Wynn's Landing, several rifle or musket shots were fired at them from the shore. Both Lt. Gwin and Lt. Shirk immediately responded, returning the fire with charges of grape and several shells.[5]

On the last day of March, the *Lexington* destroyed a ferryboat near Horse Creek. Late that afternoon, Maj. Gen. Grant sent fresh orders to Brig. Gen. Sherman. As soon as the

Cairo, momentarily expected to pass Savannah, arrived at Pittsburg Landing, the 5th Division commander was to push upon the Rebel batteries near Chickasaw. His landing force was to go ashore and destroy the cannon, but only if they were protected by unsupported artillerists. They were not to engage any larger Confederate infantry or cavalry units.

Sherman received Grant's request at 6:00 P.M. and within about an hour had all but completed preparations for his expedition. Two battalions from the 57th and 77th Ohio Volunteer Infantry and 150 horsemen from the 5th Ohio Cavalry were loaded, along with two wheeled 12-pounder howitzers, aboard the transports *Empress* and *Tecumseh*. Believing "we should move at night," Sherman also sent word to *Lexington* and *Tyler*, which also came on scene. All that remained was for the *Cairo* to arrive, which she did sometime after midnight.

At 6:00 A.M. on April 1, Lt. Bryant signaled Sherman, Gwin, and Shirk that he was ready to immediately move up the river. Three and a half hours later, the task group departed, with the timberclads following the *Cairo*, and the transports about 300 yards behind them. It did not take long to learn that the *Cairo*, which had a reputation as one of the fastest Pook turtles, could not proceed rapidly against the current of the Tennessee River. She would not reach Chickasaw anytime soon unless she had help. The *Lexington* was signaled to receive a tow line and she pulled the ironclad to her objective. At approximately 1:00 P.M., the *Cairo* dropped her tow and all of the gunboats were beat to quarters. Soon, they were hurling shells at the battery located just above Indian Creek. There was no return fire.

Rear Admiral Charles H. Davis (1807–1877) commanded the Western Flotilla between the departure of Rear Adm. Andrew H. Foote and the appointment of Rear Adm. David Dixon Porter. During his watch, a Federal victory was achieved at the Battle of Memphis, followed by disaster to the *Mound City* up the White River in June. In July, as his fleet and that of Rear Adm. David G. Farragut lay at Vicksburg, the Rebel ram *Arkansas* appeared. It is little known that Davis was one of the fathers of the small tinclads, successor boats to the timberclads (National Archives).

The three gunboats proceeded cautiously upstream and shot up the locations engaged by the timberclads on their previous visits. After about an hour, the trio came to abreast of the Chickasaw battery. Shells from the gunboats pounded its breastworks and great holes were torn. When no reply was elicited, the area was deemed deserted. At that point, Bryant ordered "cease fire." During this time, the *Lexington* alone expended 45 shells.

At this point, the 77th Ohio was dropped off at Eastport, while Sherman took the 57th Ohio directly to Chickasaw and landed. All of the emplacements were abandoned and people who had fled the area during the bombardment returned, telling the brigadier that the Tennessee artillerists manning the place had gone some time before.

Some hours after landing, Sherman, upon consultation with Bryant and Gwin, determined to drop downstream a mile to Eastport Landing. The 5th Division commander found the landing "at the present stage of water" to be the best he had seen on the entire Tennessee. Having accomplished their objective and determined that Chickasaw was not a threat, the soldiers were loaded back aboard their transports and, at 6:40 P.M., the five vessels started back to Pittsburg Landing, where they arrived some hours after dark.

In his report to Grant, Sherman noted that the river was "all clear of batteries between us and Chickasaw. Not a hostile shot was fired at any of the boats during the trip." In an April 4 letter to his father-in-law, former U.S. Senator Thomas Ewing, Sr., the brigadier boasted that "We now hold complete control of the River from Eastport to its mouth—just above Eastport are shoals that the gunboats will not venture to pass, less the rapid falling of the River should leave them above." Just after Sherman's expedition returned to Pittsburg Landing, orders arrived from Flag Officer Foote rotating the *Cairo* back to Illinois.

Also on the afternoon April 2, Maj. Gen. Grant ordered his chief of staff, Col. Joseph D. Webster, to revisit the Eastport-Chickasaw area, this time with a view to learning how difficult it would be to destroy the railroad east of Corinth. Grant, who still believed his opponent to be "hunkered down" at Corinth awaiting him and had no spies or scouts out testing that theory, might well have been shocked to learn that, earlier in the evening, Gen. Johnston ordered an advance on Pittsburg Landing.

During the morning of April 3, Col. Webster accompanied Lt. Gwin and the *Tyler* on their usual daily trip upstream, though the naval officer paid special attention to his guest's requirements. When the largest timberclad reached the Eastport-Chickasaw area, Webster was able to confirm that the Rebel abandonment of batteries there "seems to be permanent."

The distance inland to the Memphis and Charleston Railroad at its closest point to the river was short. Webster saw that the ground over which men would have to march to get at it was broken and filled with easily defended ravines. Besides, if the river continued to drop at its current rate, Hamburg, not Eastport, would be the head of navigation for the gunboats within a few days.

While the *Tyler* was upriver during the day, the *Lexington* cruised below Pittsburg Landing. During the morning, she destroyed two small ferryboats at Carrollville. Steaming on past Clifton, she later came to off Eagle Nest Island and sent her launch ashore to burn another one.

While the timberclads undertook their patrols, the *Cairo* weighed anchor from Pittsburg Landing and steamed down the river. *Lexington* and *Tyler* were left to face coming events without her. Increasingly during the day, Union pickets and patrols encountered Confederates on the outskirts of their camp perimeter.

Despite their repulse at Fort Donelson, the gunboats still occasioned nightmares among Confederate planners. It has since become apparent to several writers that "the Confederates were deathly afraid of the gunboats, even issuing orders to the troops to stay out of their range." Robert C. Suhr has gone so far as to state that "Johnston must have been afraid of the Union gunboats, since he developed a plan of attack at Shiloh with them foremost in his mind."

It is probably going too far to suggest that Johnston was actually "afraid" of the power of the gunboats, but no one in that day and age recommended glibly maneuvering within range of naval shell or canister. Having given considerable thought to the operation he had sanctioned, Gen. Johnston, via his assistant adjutant general, bade his senior generals to be extremely wary of the boats. "In the approaching battle," Col. Jacob Thompson wrote from Corinth on April 3, "every effort should be made to turn the left flank of the enemy so as to cut off his line of retreat to the Tennessee River." If that escape route could be blocked, the Federals would be thrown back on Owl Creek and compelled to surrender. In the process of bringing off this plan, however, he said, "Every precaution must also be taken on our part to prevent unnecessary exposure of our men to the enemy's gunboats."

The same bad or muddy roads that Col. Webster noticed behind Chickasaw-Eastport, coupled with almost 40,000 inexperienced soldiers (officers and enlisted), and missed or misunderstood orders conspired to slow the descent of the Confederate Army of the Mississippi. On top of this, the Rebel line of march was exceptionally noisy, giving every possible notice of approach. Errors in conspiracy included the beating of drums, loud shouts and other noises, and even musket tests. Still, the Confederates slogged on. Without baggage and but five days' rations, they moved forward by the various roads that converged beyond Monterey. Only ambulances and a few forage wagons accompanied, streams were swollen, and the nights were cold and damp.

All through the latter part of April's first week, Federal officers held rigidly to Grant's orders from Halleck not to spark a fight. This directive was repeatedly reinforced all the way down the chain of command. When Union pickets or skirmishers ran into Rebel parties, they retreated and reported. Their reports were ignored.

Great thunderstorms blasted the Tennessee Valley over the next 24 hours and the night of April 4 and there was some hail. There was also additional contact between Confederate cavalry and Union outposts. The mounted vedettes were probing the defenses most Union officers believed.

April 5 was dry and quite warm. The soldiers at Pittsburg Landing drilled. Some swam in the Tennessee. Rebel horsemen continued to prowl around the perimeter of the camp while their main body drew closer.

Neither Grant or Sherman expected a large scale attack, but both hoped to be ready if one came. As he later told a reporter, the former believed that the continuing sparring between his men and the Confederates was part of a reconnaissance in force rather than preliminaries to a "determined attack."

Also during the morning, the first unit of the Army of the Ohio, Brig. Gen. William Nelson's 4th Division, walked into Savannah. During those hours and later, the *Tyler* and *Lexington* maintained their patrols. After dark, the former tied up across from Pittsburg Landing while the latter did likewise at Crump's Landing to the north.

All the while, as the remainder of Maj. Gen. Buell soldiers slowly approached from the northeast, Gen. Johnston, two days behind schedule, reached his attack position that night. Judge Alexander Walker, with the Rebel troops that night, later informed the citizens of New Orleans that the Army of the Mississippi "bivouacked near the enemy's outposts. It was the only pleasant night since we had left Corinth."[6]

In the lyrical phrase of Maj. Gen. Lew Wallace, "the gray light was still in the eastern sky, trembling between vanishing night and opening day" when the Battle of Shiloh (or Pittsburg Landing) began on April 6, 1862. It started, as might be expected, with a clash between pickets and small units in the near darkness. They found one another just to the southwest of the Federal positions.

In the minutes around 5:30 A.M., Gen. Johnston and his officers rode to the front. The Confederate line was advancing; Basil W. Duke, brother in law of Brig. Gen. John Hunt Morgan, later testified that "the wild cheers that arose made the woods stir as if with the rush of a mighty wind." Federal troops had time to form only the most rudimentary lines of defense. Writing for the *Savannah Republican*, Peter Wellington Alexander observed that the Northerners recovered "and met our onslaught with firmness and resolution."

The fighting on April 6–7 was the most intense of the war to date and almost all of it occurred on land. The battleground upon which Northern and Southern blood was spilled occupied, as Frank Moore portrayed it, "a semi-circle of about three and a half miles out from Pittsburg Landing." The right rested at a point north of Crump's Landing, the center was almost directly in front of the Corinth road, and the left rank to the river toward Harrisburg, a village north of Pittsburg Landing.

The steadily escalating din of battle inaugurated by the initial Rebel charges was soon heard by Maj. Gen. Grant at Savannah and by bluecoated soldiers and sailors throughout the area. It would not recede for 12 long hours.

Some miles away, the Rev. John H. Aughey and his four-year-old daughter started out for a stroll on "a truly lovely Sabbath, even for a southern clime." They had proceeded only a few hundred yards when the child remarked that they should return home: "Pa, don't you hear the thunder?" Aughey and his daughter soon recognized the sharp, stunning reports as the sound of cannon. The firing "continued incessantly during the day. The whole country became intensely excited." Many locals, the reverend remembered, "hastened to the battlefield, the majority bent on plunder."

We defer to others to capture infantry, horse artillery, and cavalry details of that desperate military struggle within that semi-circle. Our purpose here is to review the role of the two timberclads, *Lexington* and *Tyler*, adding only enough situational information from ashore as to provide context.[7]

Within a few minutes of the initial cannon shots, the jack-tars aboard both the U.S.S. *Tyler* and the U.S.S. *Lexington*, even though separated by six miles, heard the larger sounds of escalating battle. Lt. Gwin and Shirk both believed immediately that the guns of their timberclads would be required. Throughout the day, the question was not only how best they could be employed, but also whether they could be employed at all. As the fighting was inland of the river and the riverbank was too high to see over, Gwin, at Pittsburg Landing, could do little, initially. Still, the *Tyler* was cleared for action. The clatter of fighting intensified and soon convinced Gwin that an overwhelming force had fallen upon their soldier colleagues. For now, they could make certain that the transports were protected.

Gen. Johnston's initial battle plan was disrupted because of fanatical Federal resistance put up after the shock and, in some places, rout of the initial attack. In addition to stiff opposition on the river flank, a new Union line was formed through a heavily wooded area along an old sunken road. Confederate troops would assault this "Hornet's Nest," unsuccessfully, eleven times.

At approximately 10:15 A.M., the *Lexington* arrived off Crump's Landing. Lt. Shirk received his initial confirmation of the Rebel attack and its success from the transport *John Ramm* as she passed down. Believing he, too, could provide needed gunfire support, Shirk hurried upstream. Her arrival permitted Lt. Gwin to leave his subordinate as transport guard and to explore intervention possibilities further.

As the Union troops on the left continued to "fall back in some confusion," the *Tyler* stood up about a mile above her normal anchorage at 10:30 A.M. ready to provide covering fire for any bluecoats forced down toward the riverbank. At one point, she was signaled by a number of retreating infantrymen from the 71st Ohio. The same bluffs and hills that so well hid the enemy's Louisiana troops from her guns on March 1 now prevented their aiding these Buckeyes.

Frustrated, Lt. Gwin returned abreast the *Lexington*. By this time, many soldiers were coming down to the riverbank or to nosed in transports, reporting heavy losses ashore. Firing continued without cessation all morning and, as the sun rose higher, great numbers of wounded appeared, along with additional disheartening stories.

Given an inability to see what was transpiring on the other side of the riverbank and with no communications from the U.S. military, the captains of the two timberclads remained without orders or direction. Remembering that Maj. Gen. Wallace was encamped at Crump's,

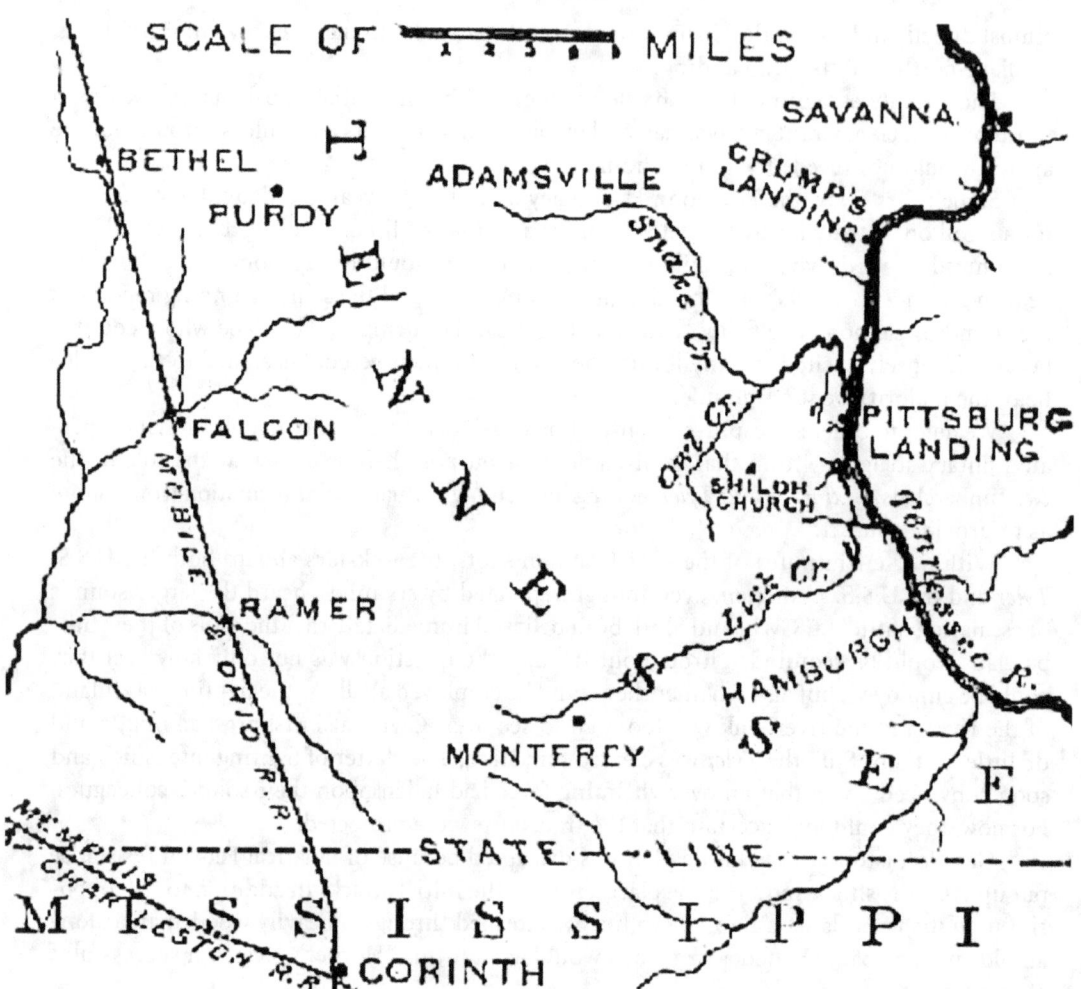

The Tennessee River area near Pittsburg Landing, March–April 1862. Various tributaries and little landings are clearly visible up and down the large stream, but what cannot be discerned is the natural wonder of the untouched area inland and along the banks (*Battles and Leaders*).

Lt. Shirk received permission to return and offer support. The *Lexington* rounded to and departed Pittsburg Landing at 12:15 P.M. When she came to a half hour later, a signal quickly clarified that Wallace and his men had departed. There was nothing to do but drop anchor and await developments or instructions.

Having no way to actively participate in the huge fight, the gunboatmen at both landings were, as Shirk put it, "forced to remain inactive hearers." With the battle still raging much closer to where he had been than where he was, Lt. Shirk came about and returned to Pittsburg Landing at 4:00 P.M.

While the *Lexington* was downriver, the *Tyler* continued to impatiently wait for orders from a Union general, preferably Grant. During this period of inactivity, as Lt. Gwin later reported, "for an hour or more shot and shell were falling all around us." Realizing that the National general closest to him was probably too distracted to think of seeking nautical support, Lt. Gwin elected not to repeat the error of Belmont. If the army wouldn't—or didn't think to—come to him, the navy would offer its services to the army.

Pittsburg Landing. A contemporary sketch of the Tennessee River from not far from little Shiloh Church. This scene is considerably more stripped of vegetation than was the case in April 1862 (*Harper's Weekly*, April 1862).

Were it possible to establish some system of communication between the military leadership ashore and the *Tyler*, the gunboat, Gwin believed, could be of "great advantage to our left wing." At 1:25 P.M., Gunner Herman Peters was sent ashore from the timberclad with a note to the headquarters of Brig. Gen. Stephen A. Hurlburt. Would it be helpful if the *Tyler*, Lt. Gwin's note read, opened fire on the woods in the direction of the batteries and advancing Rebel forces? Delighted, the beleaguered 4th Division commander promptly granted permission and provided detailed instructions on how best to shoot without hitting his men. Expressing himself grateful, the brigadier noted that, without help, he could not hold on for more than an hour.

When Peters arrived with the army approval, Lt. Gwin ordered the great guns of the *Tyler* brought to bear and opened fire at 2:50 P.M. The 60-minute shoot was conducted along a line indicated to Peters by Hurlburt, being directed primarily upon Rebel artillery positions, and, according to Manning Force, upon the Reserve Corps of Brig. Gen. John C. Breckenridge.

Cincinnati Daily Times reporter E.M. "Ned" Spencer was a witness. Passing slowly up the river to a viable point, the gunboat "poured in a broadside from her immense guns." The shells, according to the scribe, "went tearing and crashing through the woods, felling trees in their course, and spreading terror wherever they fell." Spencer, like others, recalled later that the "explosions were tremendous, and the shells falling far inland most probably from their direction in the very heart of the secessionist force must have told with a startling effect."

A deliberate delivery was maintained for an hour, after which the gunboat ceased firing and dropped down opposite Pittsburg Landing where the *Lexington* now waited. Gwin was pleased, Hurlburt was pleased, and so was at least one 55th Illinois soldier who used the falling naval shells as cover to make his escape. Newsman Spencer later attributed "the failure of the foe to carry the left wing in a great measure to the well-directed shots of the *Tyler*."

As the great wheels of the gunboats held them in the current ready for additional action, further instruction was needed. Mr. Peters was again dispatched, this time to the temporary headquarters of the commanding general. Grant was wearing a rumpled uniform, as was his custom, and Peters, according to Charles Carleton Coffin, had "gold-lace upon his coat-sleeve, and a gold band on his cap." The sailor briefly explained that "shot and shell from the Rebel batteries" were "falling in the river." Lt. Gwin, he continued, "would like to toss some into the woods." Peters returned aboard the *Tyler* shortly thereafter with Grant's curt answer to use his "own judgment in the matter." The navy now had authority to fire wherever Gwin and Shirk thought best.

The Confederate onslaught on Union positions ashore had continued without letup all afternoon. Names like the Sunken Road, the Peach Orchard, Jones Field, and the Hornet's Nest entered the history books. Even after the death of Gen. Johnston about 2:30 P.M., the gray surge continued. As the zenith of the afternoon approached, it seem likely that the Federal flanks might collapse. If that happened, Grant and his men would be forced into the river and suffer a stunning defeat.

At 3:30 P.M., Col. Joseph D. Webster, chief of staff and a noted artilleryman, was ordered by Grant to take over command of all Yankee cannon and form a last ditch line of defense on the ridge south of the landing. Using time purchased dearly by the troops at Jones Field and Sunken Road, Webster began to assemble a formidable bulwark of cannon that became the rallying point for all Federal troops returning from the front. Placed on a ridge overlooking Dill's Branch, it was the only place remaining to make a stand short of Pittsburg Landing on the riverbank itself.

The largest unit in the line was a battery of five 24-pounder siege guns from Battery B, 2nd Illinois Artillery. These had remained aboard ship for later use, but were now hurriedly gotten ashore. As retreating Northern cannon became available, they were placed on the line, including four 20-pounder Parrotts from Battery H, First Illinois Light Artillery and six more from Batteries H and D, First Missouri Light Artillery.

At almost the exact time as Webster was straining to get his big guns mounted, Confederate Brig. Gen. Daniel Ruggles and Brig. Gen. James Trudeau massed 53 fieldpieces opposite the right of the Sunken Road position. An objective of Rebel attack since morning, it was believed that the largest concentration of field artillery employed on the North American continent to that date might break its Yankee resistance. Large numbers of panicked Federal soldiers raced for shelter at the river during this time and, in many units, it was feared that the Confederates might succeed in driving even more that way. This activity could, at times, be seen by those on the main landing below.

Despite assistance from the *Tyler* earlier, Brig. Gen. Hurlburt was, meanwhile, forced to withdraw from the Peach Orchard positions his men had occupied and move toward new defenses to the north of the Dill Branch ravine. Many of his troops were, in fact, also fleeing. The sight of Webster's cannon on the ridge inspired many to find their courage and come to grips for the final fight many believed remained.

On the other hand, several thousand bluecoats lost all hope in the smoke and carnage and fled the battlefield, seeking refuge along the riverbank. These men were witnessed by the arriving Maj. Gen. Buell and *New York Herald* correspondent Henry Villard, who cried to Army of the Ohio chief of staff Capt. James B. Fry, "Oh heavens! Captain, here is Bull Run all over again!"

At approximately 4:15 P.M., the *Tyler* and *Lexington* took a position about three quarters of a mile above Pittsburg Landing. Their men, per Coffin, "sprang to the guns" and opened a heavy fire on the Confederate batteries on their right. The massed Southern guns opened fire on Union Sunken Road positions at approximately 4:30 P.M.

The artillery duel between the Rebel cannoneers and their counterparts afloat and ashore was fierce. Not only did Ruggle's people shoot at Union field artillery, but at the timberclads as well. Fortunately for the sailors, the counterbattery fire from the Rebels, who dropped their "missiles all around us," was not concentrated upon them and did no damage.

While Col. Webster feverishly built up his massed battery, he may have been comforted to hear the 8-inch guns of the *Tyler* and *Lexington*. Both he and the naval lieutenants, along with many others, would be pleased to know that Brig. Gen. Nelson's lead brigade would also soon be joining them from the riverbank across from Pittsburg Landing.

Frank Moore later wrote that the shells from the gunboats "struck terror to the Rebel force." The projectiles "went tearing and crashing through the woods, felling trees in their course and spreading havoc wherever they fell." The explosions "were fearful, the shells falling far inland." Large numbers of the gunboat shells going inland missed their intended Southern targets and burst in or over the woods behind Pittsburg Landing. Many trees were hit and knocked over or their limbs blown off; more than a few of these landed near or on the troops of Col. James Geddes 8th Iowa and several other 6th Division units. The *Lexington* expended 12 rounds before she stood down the river at 4:37 P.M. to pick up one of her returning masters. She would not rejoin the *Tyler* for an hour.

The massed Southern cannon fire was preliminary to a renewed effort to defeat, by flanking, the Northern hold on the Hornet's Nest. This time, the push by 14 of the 16 Rebel brigades on the field succeeded. Federal troops on either side withdrew toward Pittsburg Landing, leaving those of Brig. Gen. Prentiss and W.H.L. Wallace trapped. Though the 2nd Division commander was killed, part of Wallace's command escaped in confusion through "Hell's Hollow." Between 5:00 P.M. and 5:30 P.M., however, the encircled Brig. Gen. Benjamin Prentiss surrendered the survivors of his division.

Watching all of this, Brig. Gen. Benjamin F. Cheatman, commander of the 2nd Division of the Confederate I Corps, noted that his enemy "never rallied again until he reached the shelter of his gunboats on the river bank." Now all that remained between Southern victory and U.S. defeat was Col. Webster's guns, tired and reformed survivors—and two timberclads.[8]

It took time, perhaps half an hour, for the Confederates to consolidate their achievement. The many units involved in the final reduction of the Hornet's Nest needed to be reformed and given more ammunition. Additionally, the prisoners, over 2,000 bluecoats, had to be sent to the rear and guarded. As Brig. Gen. Cheatham put it, "A halt was made for the purpose of some concentration of our forces of all commands for a concerted attack upon the enemy." He and other Rebel generals understood that Grant's men had "concentrated on the river bank under the shelter of his gunboats."

Following the surrender of Brig. Gen. Prentiss, approximately 18,000 soldiers were available for "Grant's Last Line" (GLL). Originally built around the siege cannon and fieldpieces from a few unengaged outfits, it soon came to include all retreating horse artillery—reformed, resupplied, and manned by the least demoralized available gunners regardless of unit. GLL covered a distance of about one mile west from Pittsburg Landing to a point where it curved north to cover the Snake Creek Bridge. Maj. Gen. Lew Wallace, who had departed Crump's Landing on foot earlier, was still expected to appear here even as the Confederates, just about a mile before them, continued sorting out their units.

Fifty plus guns were ready in the second largest concentration of field artillery employed on the North American continent to that date. Most faced to the south along the Pittsburg–Corinth Road and all were placed to enfilade any attempt to get over Dill Branch. Added to that firepower were the guns of the *Lexington* and *Tyler*, which now anchored directly in the mouth of flooded Dill's Branch, "sitting gracefully upon the placid river." Because the creek's brushy ravine twisted about, there was still only a limited line of sight from the gunboats, but if any enemy ventured too close, they could be taken under fire. As Charles Coffin, enthusiastically if somewhat erroneously, wrote it two years later, "All day long the men of the gunboats have heard the roar of the conflict coming nearer and nearer, and have had no opportunity to take a part. Now [however] their time had come."

There was about a half hour to one hour of daylight remaining when, about 5:30 P.M., the victorious Confederates began their "inevitable charge," as Woodworth puts it, on Pittsburg Landing. Five minutes later, Lt. Gwin, looking through his glasses, saw the Rebels "on the left of our line, an eighth of a mile above the landing and the transports at Pittsburg and a half a mile from the river." They were right where the sailors wanted them, caught on or near the river with no riverbank to obstruct direct sight targeting.

Four brigades under direction of Maj. Gen. Braxton Bragg, in a half-mile-long line, began its assault toward the Dill Branch ravine. As these 4,000 men ascended the northern slope, they became targets for Col. Webster's guns, muskets and rifles of the infantry survivors, and the gunboats. Charles Hubert of the 50th Illinois later wrote that "the smoke was so great, however, that I could not see the enemy in our front." Hubert was not alone. The *Lexington* and *Tyler* had opened a "heavy and well-directed" fire on the advancing Rebels "with shot and shell." "They cover themselves with white clouds," Coffin pictured, "and the deep-mouthed cannon bellow their loudest thunders, which roll miles away along the winding stream."

Lt. Shirk's timberclad dropped in 32 rounds, while the *Tyler* employed an unknown number of "5-second and 10-second shell." Georgia writer J.P. Austin later said that "The heavens were ablaze with bursting shells and the air was thick with sulphurous smoke." The naval craft actually fired up the length of Dill's Branch only about 10 minutes, but their "shots were thick and fast," as Frank Moore said later, "and told with telling effect." Thereafter, they shot only at what they considered to be targets of opportunity.

The roar of the gunboats, whether effective or ineffective as later debated, was "sweet music to those disheartened men" manning Grant's line against the Confederate advance, now, as Coffin put it, "almost within reached of the coveted prize." Leading the 10th Brigade of Maj. Gen. Buell's army toward the river, Col. Jacob Ammen could hear the timberclads. "Even our unpracticed ears could easily distinguish the heavy booms of their great 32-pdrs.," he testified later, "in the midst of all that storm of artillery explosions."

"The citizens living miles away, who had listened attentively to the roar of cannon from early morn," wrote historian Brazelton two decades later, "could tell when this critical moment came by the different sound produced by the shell guns on the *Tyler* and *Lexington*, which up to this time had not been used. Now the shells from these boats came whizzing through the timber, exploding in the air and on the ground, greatly terrifying the advancing enemy."

The withering fire ashore was so concentrated and the Union line so densely manned that the Confederate counterattack lasted only about 20 minutes. The brigades of Brig. Gen. James Chalmers and John Jackson vainly attempted to ascend the hill. "In attempting to mount the last ridge, we were met by a fire from a whole line of batteries," Chalmers later reported. These were "protected by infantry and assisted by shells from the gunboats." Gage's Alabama Battery, attached to the 2nd Battalion of the 2nd Division of Confederate II Corps, was roughly handled by the gunboats. A single shell killed three horses, with seven in all disabled in the blasts. One man was wounded and a piece was abandoned on the Dill Creek slope before the unit could retire.

On the other hand, riflemen from the 10th Mississippi, also from the 2nd Battalion, 2nd Division, II Corps, were able to creep along a lightly defended road under a hill near the river. Sniping at one of the timberclads, they forced it to briefly steam across the river. Brig. Gen. Jackson noted that his men were out of ammunition and advancing "only with bayonets." They, too, came under "a heavy fire from light batteries, siege-pieces, and gunboats." The Rebels had no choice but to retire or be blown into atoms. As Lt. Gwin put it, "the enemy was forced to retreat in haste."

Writing for the *Savannah Republican,* Peter Wellington Alexander reviewed the turnabout scene:

> At half past five o'clock, the enemy was in full retreat and hotly pursued by the victorious Confederates. He fled back to the Tennessee, and took shelter under his gunboats and river works, the fire from which was too heavy for our light field batteries. Night too had come on, and our army returned to the enemy's camp.

E.M. "Ned" Spencer of the *Cincinnati Daily Times* saw that, as the Confederates retreated, "the gunboats continued to send their shell after them until they had entirely got beyond their reach." As shells from the gunboats "fly up the ravine," their skippers had no idea they might be targeted by horse artillery. Unbeknownst to any of the Federals, Capt. Thomas Stanford, commander of Stanford's Mississippi Battery, had planned a daring attack.

Just before sunset, as troops withdrew from Dill's Branch, Stanford's battery, attached to Brig. Gen. Alexander P. Steward's 2nd Brigade, 1st Division, was lowered down a hill near the river and made ready to fire from the creek's south bank. Watching the increasingly bright muzzle flashes from the big guns aboard the timberclads, the Southern officer realized that, if he could see them in the growing darkness, any firing of his could also be spotted — and ranged. Unwilling to go up against naval artillery, Stanford quietly withdrew. Thereafter, a second attack was considered by several Confederate regimental commanders, but it was abandoned when Gen. Beauregard, Johnston's second in command and successor, ordered attacks halted for the night. An aide had informed him that Southern arms were carrying all before them to the "Tennessee River." The famous Creole general, believing he had won a great victory, calmly ended the day's combat with the words "Then do not unnecessarily expose your command to the fire of the gunboats."

Unhappy with Gen. Beauregard's order, II Corps commander Brig. Gen. Braxton Bragg, nevertheless, issued instructions for his men to "fall back out of the range of the gunboats and encamp for the night." Maj. Gen. Leonidas Polk, formerly in charge at Columbus and now leading I Corps, did likewise. Neither Bragg nor Polk knew that Beauregard, still threatened by the gunboats, sent stand down orders directly to eight different brigade commanders as well as their superiors. For example, Col. Robert M. Russell, leading the 1st Brigade of I Corps, remembered that "orders were received from Gen. Bragg to fall back out of range of the gunboats and encamp for the night."[9]

Once the firing by the land forces had ceased and darkness fell, the *Lexington* rounded to and returned to Crump's Landing. Arriving about 8:00 P.M. to find all quiet at her previous night's anchorage, Lt. Shirk returned to Pittsburg Landing, tying up across the river at 10:00 P.M. Both she and the *Tyler* would make notations in their logbooks through the night concerning the arrival of transports with Maj. Gen. Buell's troops.

In response to a request from Brig. Gen. William "Bull" Nelson, himself a former naval officer, the *Tyler* opened night harassment fire against the Confederates at 9:00 P.M. At 10 minute intervals, the timberclad lofted a shell toward perceived enemy locations, hoping to prevent the exhausted soldiers from sleeping. Each shell on every occasion employed a different fuse length: 5-second, 10-second, or 15-second. Once in a while, the gunboat's howitzer would also send of a charge of shrapnel. Writing as "Agate," *Cincinnati Daily Gazette* reporter Whitelaw Reid told his readers three days later that no one knew then "the effect of this gunboat cannonading." On the other hand, it was impressive:

> But presently there came a flash that spread like sheet-lightning over the ripples of the river current, and the roar of a heavy naval gun went echoing up and down the bluffs, through the unnatural stillness of the night. Others speedily followed. By the flash you could just discern the black outline of the piratical-looking hull, and see how the gunboat gracefully settled into the water at the recoil; the smoke soon cast up a thin veil that seemed only to soften and sweeten the scene; from the woods away inland you caught faintly the muffled explosion of the shell, like the knell of the spirit that was taking its flight.

By 10:00 P.M., Southern correspondent Alexander noted that "it is now raining very hard." The day had been lovely up until sunset. "The change," he observed, "is the result, doubtless, of the heavy cannonading kept up since early morning." Later, as he tried to get some rest by a campfire, the *Republican* man wrote in his journal that the Yankees were "still throwing shells from his gunboats and some of them fall uncomfortably near our tent." Alexander pondered on the shelling, unable to ascertain if it was undertaken "because he fears a night attack, or is seeking to cover the transfer of his army to the other bank of the river." During the night, Buell's army crossed three divisions over the Tennessee.

To help determine Confederate positions in the darkness, Lt. Col. Nicholas Anderson of the 6th Ohio, one of the first of Buell's regiments to cross the Tennessee, was instructed to send out two companies on reconnaissance. Advancing cautiously, they reached a point where the *Tyler*'s 8-inch shells were falling directly in front of them. This, they decided, was the edge of the Rebel lines.

At 1:00 A.M., the *Lexington* moved up to relieve the *Tyler* and continue the 15-minute interdiction for the remainder of the evening. "It rained and rained almost the entire night," remembered William J. McMurray of the 20th Tennessee, "and the Yankee gunboats were shelling the woods all around with their big guns, and we were there in the mud and rain waiting for another day that the machines of death might make their work." One shell dropped right atop four Southerners playing cards in a Sibley tent in the rain and exploded. When the bodies were found, four cards lay in the center of an oilcloth between them and each man had three cards in his left hand.

There did not seem at the time to be any precision behind the fire of the gunboats. Years later, fragments of naval shells and fuses were found not only in the Dill Branch ravine, but as much as two-plus miles beyond at Shiloh churchyard and in Fraley Field. This was far in excess of their normal range.

The Southerners were not the only ones annoyed. The guns also kept Northern soldiers awake as well. Thomas W. Connelly, a soldier of the 70th Ohio Volunteer Infantry, remembered the craft tossing "a hissing shell over to the enemy every quarter of an hour until daylight." These gigantic shrieking rounds must have been having not only a sleep-privation effect upon the Confederates, but may also have caused several units to change locations. In any event, they were "soul-stirring music to [the Northerner's] ears."

Brig. Gen. Patrick R. Cleburne, leading the 2nd Brigade, Confederate III Corps, was particularly incensed by the timberclad harassing fire. He bitterly recalled that "Every fifteen minutes the enemy threw two shells from his gunboats, some of which burst close around my men, banishing sleep from the eyes of a few, but falling chiefly among their own wounded, who were strewn thickly between my camp and the river. History records few instances of more reckless inhumanity than this."

Lieutenants Gwin and Shirk were asked to not only harass the enemy as they dropped shells on different parts of the battle field, but, also, if possible, to do him injury. How they could do that shooting up over the high riverbank is not immediately clear.

To borrow a thought from Gary D. Joiner's latest book, *Mr. Lincoln's Brown Water Navy*, just how exactly did the *Lexington* and *Tyler* execute their night-long assignment? Joiner undertook a close study of the matter and found, when he was finished, that the method "adds to an appreciation of Gwin's genius." He also made a case that the action "was the most famous naval incident at the Battle of Shiloh and also the most misunderstood, not from controversy but from how it was accomplished."

Basing his observations upon conversations with Shiloh National Military Park personnel and U.S. Geological Survey maps, Joiner, the noted historian of the 1864 Red River campaign, concluded that, in April 1862, the Tennessee River was 10 feet above flood stage and that the 80-foot deep ravine was partially filled with water. As both he and the author later noticed, there is, at the northern side of the western end of the ravine, a deflection toward the south. With that geography in mind, it became rather easy to imagine that Lts. Gwin and Shirk maneuvered their timberclads into the swollen ravine area and conducted their bombardments by shooting up over the ravine's deflection. Their shots were made blind. Here the timberclads demonstrated a tactic that would be employed nearly 100 years later when, during the island-hopping campaigns of World War II, giant U.S. battleships, with aerial spotting, "walked" their shells inland on Pacific islands toward perceived Japanese targets such as pillboxes or masked batteries, seeding their lead over large areas.

Turning to Gunner Peters, Lt. Gwin ordered that the *Tyler*'s guns be elevated a half degree after every shot. When maximum elevation was achieved and shells were arching out along their greatest angle trajectory, the process was reversed. Occasionally, shells went great distances; at other times, they ploughed into the side of the ravine. Historian Joiner has also conjectured that a number of shells were "skipped" and that the great distances achieved were obtained by ramming extra heavy powder charges into the smoothbore cannon. Lt. Shirk, when it was his turn, executed the shoot in the same manner as Gwin. It is easy to understand how few ashore got any sleep just from the noise and uncertain course of the naval shells.

For Federal arms, the second day at Shiloh was much different from the first. It opened about 5:30 A.M. with bluecoated soldiers pushing south away from Pittsburg Landing. Immediately, the two gunboats ceased their overnight harassment. Neither timberclad was engaged against the enemy on April 7, but both continued to actively patrol. Much of their time was taken up with what Lt. Shirk called "acts of mercy" in "picking up the wounded who had found their way to the river and conveying them to the hospital boats." *Cincinnati Daily Times* journalist E.M. "Ned" Spencer speculated on their noninvolvement. Within half an hour of the opening shots, the contest had again spread in various directions. "The Rebels were not so anxious to fight their way to the river's bank as on the previous day," the reporter observed, "having had a slight experience of what they might again expect if brought again under the powerful guns of the *Tyler* and *Lexington*." Their "black hulls steamed slowly about the stream, keeping a careful wariness." With luck, they might be able to catch signs of "the exact location of the enemy in the dense forest, which stretched away to their right."

Despite numerous charges against the refreshed Northern lines, the Confederates were unable to prevail. When it was finally conceded that forward progress could not be made, that any hope of reinforcement was nonexistent, and that victory could not be achieved, Gen. Beauregard ordered his troops to withdraw. By 4:00 P.M. the Rebel flood of the previous morning was receding slowly and without interference back toward Corinth.

In two days of fighting, the Union lost 1,754 men killed, the Confederacy, 1,728. Despite these "appalling casualties on both sides," the ultimate irony of the battle was that "not an inch of ground had exchanged hands" permanently. "Probably no battle fought during the Civil War excited a greater amount of controversy," wrote media historian J. Cutler Andrews, "than did the Battle of Shiloh." The Northern press, by and large, "exaggerated the extent of both the Union defeat on Sunday and the Union victory on the following day." This was the first big fight of the conflict in which there was large scale "faking of eyewitness accounts." The effect, perceived and real, of cannon fire from the gunboats during the Battle of Shiloh later elicited various opinions as to what its role was in influencing the Confederates to leave the field. Views varied among those who were on either the throwing or receiving end of the timberclad shells. Likewise, the roles of the *Lexington* and *Tyler* during the campaign became one of the topics discussed in several of the print controversies that swirled around the battle in the years after it was fought.[10]

The controversy over the effectiveness of the timberclads at Shiloh was also part of a larger, but not yet full-blown, debate over the effectiveness of river gunboats against land forces. "There has been a time when the prowess of iron-clads [or any river gunboats] was claimed by the Federals and acknowledged by us," wrote ex–Confederate soldier W.A. Wash in 1870. After the triumph of Fort Henry, the gunboats had suffered defeat at Fort Donelson and delay at Island No. 10. As noted in the famous March 26, 1862, *Memphis Daily Appeal* editorial, partisans would now assail convoys and convoy escorts.

The First Battle of Shiloh, fought on March 1, demonstrated that Confederate gunners could engage the "Linkum" craft. In the months ahead, at St. Charles, Arkansas, and again at Fort Donelson, as well as in engagements against cavalrymen like John Hunt Morgan, Nathan Bedford Forrest, and Joseph O. ("Jo") Shelby, the question of effectiveness by lightly armored warships against Confederate horse artillery would be raised. Much of the new-found courage of Confederate forces to take on the Yankee gunboats was born of battle-won wisdom that the boats could, in fact, be fought on equal or better terms and defeated. "But, before the year 1862 had died out," veteran Wash continued, "gunboats had dwindled down from elephantine proportions to almost pigmies in the estimation of the Southern soldiery." Some of that Dixie courage can be laid directly to lessons learned or observed about timberclad effectiveness at Shiloh.

Given the importance of growing Southern resistance to Federal gunboats in the months ahead, it is useful to review here the opinions of various Shiloh participants, witnesses, and writers, contemporary and later. As might be expected, a number of these found the services of the *Lexington* and *Tyler* to be extremely valuable. In his after action report, Lt. Gwin told Flag Officer Foote that "Your old wooden boats rendered invaluable service on the 6th instant to the land forces." Lt. Shirk added his belief that the gunboat fire "silenced the enemy, and as I hear from many army officers on the field, totally demoralized his forces, driving them from their positions in a perfect route in the space of 10 minutes." The complete Shiloh reports of the two officers were printed in full in the April 18, 1862, issue of the *New York Times*.

Foote immediately passed the statements of the timberclad captains on to Secretary Welles, who shortly thereafter offered praise of yet "another evidence of the gallant and invaluable service rendered by the Navy on the Western waters." In particular, he summarized, "although the force was small and auxiliary to the army, the successful efforts of the gunboats in checking the enemy and repelling their advance are felt and acknowledged by the country."

Although memories "improve" with the passage of time, Ensign William H. Michael could still vividly recall the *Tyler*'s role in 1886, lying as she did "with her broadside at the mouth of the ravine upon which the extreme left of our army rested." Spinning his yarn, the sailor continued:

> And when the enemy hurled their dense ranks into the depression to reach our sadly weakened line, she rained shell and canister and shrapnel upon him so thick and fast that he withdrew precipitately, leaving his dead and dying piled one upon the other in the ravine. Those who saw that windrow of mangled human forms after the battle needed no other proof of the awful havoc wrought by the fire of the gunboats at that critical moment.

While it might be expected that the U.S. Navy might smile upon the perceived accomplishments of Gwin and Shirk, no less a figure than Maj. Gen. Grant also waxed eloquent regarding their help. He wrote in his April 9 report to Maj. Gen. Halleck that, "In this repulse, much is due to the presence of the Gun boats *Tyler* and *Lexington* and their able Commanders Capt. Gwinn and Shirk." In his *Century* magazine article on "The Battle of Shiloh," later reprinted in the four-volume *Battles and Leaders*, Grant maintained that the two gunboats "aided the army and effectually checked [the Confederates] further progress."

Historian Timothy Smith reviewed the after action reports of Union military officers published in the army *Official Records*. From Grant down to regimental commanders, the gunboats were "mentioned eleven times." Although most simply mentioned the safety the craft provided, many paid high praise. One, Col. Geddes, whom we have already mentioned, was not impressed. A number of Southern commanders also found the gunboats intimidating late in the afternoon. It will be recalled that, after the surrender of Brig. Gen. Prentiss, a final charge was made against Pittsburg Landing.

Gen. Pierre G.T. Beauregard had taken over from Gen. Johnston upon the latter's death but obviously did not have a complete picture of the fighting due to the confusion rampant within his lines. Some years later, he observed for the "Battles and Leaders" series that the "ground in front of this position [Webster's massed artillery] was swept by the guns of the steamers *Lexington* and *Tyler*, properly posted for that purpose." Continuing, he added that "several most gallant uncombined efforts (notably Chalmers) were made to reach and carry the Federal battery [Webster]." Italicizing, he concluded that "*in every instance the effort failed.*" Aware of this, the commander ordered his men withdrawn "from under fire of the Federal gun-boats."

Brig. Gen. Alexander P Stewart, commander of the 2nd Brigade, I Corps, recalled how, after his unit had taken position to aid in pursuit of the enemy, it was "checked by a fire from the gunboats." Brig. Gen. Patrick R. Cleburne, leading the 2nd Brigade, III Corps, remembered how his men had tried to move forward, "until checked by a heavy fire of artillery from the enemy's field artillery and gunboats." Col. Thomas Jordan, Beauregard's chief of staff, later wrote in his biography of Maj. Gen. Nathan Bedford Forrest that "the gunboats threw their ponderous shells in the thick of the up-coming mass of Confederates with such profusion that General Polk ordered the cavalry to take shelter in the wooded ravine," were, he continued, "they were exposed to a raking fire from the gunboats." In his *Century* magazine commentary penned a few years after this, Jordan would change his observation.

Having halted briefly at the crest of a hill overlooking Pittsburg Landing, Col. Robert Trabue's 1st Kentucky Brigade, of the Reserve Corps, "endured a most terrific cannonade and shelling from the enemy's gunboats." Some of his men fell back through the lines of the 4th Kentucky "in confusion." Col. Marshall J. Smith, of the 3rd (Pond's) Brigade, III Corps, also had a hard time withstanding timberclad shelling. Their cannonade was "a most destructive fire, which we endured for some time, not being able to reply; and under orders, we retreated from the front ground." Ordered with the 9th Texas Infantry from the Confederate left toward heavy firing on the right, Col. W.A. Stanley's butternuts of the 2nd Brigade (Anderson's), III Corps, also "fell within range of shot and shell from the gunboats in that vicinity, and there night put a close to the action of the day."

Col. C.D. Venable of the 5th Tennessee, part of the 2nd Brigade of I Corps, was badly snared by the timberclads. He remembered that "I then flanked to the left about 300 yards and halted to rest, but in a very few minutes, the shelling from the gunboats was so as to be unbearable, killing and wounding several of my men. I thereupon retired to a ravine and remained until dusk, and then moved back and encamped for the night."

A number of local Hardin County citizens also heard the battle. One of them, Rev. John Aughey, was absolutely convinced that Grant was surprised "and would have lost his whole army but for the gunboats in the river." These timberclads, he wrote a year later, "shelled the pursuing rebels, checking their advance and saving the discomfited Federals."

Among the Northern press, the impression was that the gunboats were of vital importance in holding and repulsing the Sunday Confederate victory march. E.M. "Ned" Spencer of the *Cincinnati Daily Times*, who praised the *Tyler*'s afternoon shoot in support of Brig. Gen. Hurlburt, also believed the timberclads were instrumental in defeating the last Confederate push of Sunday. "Their shots," he told readers of the Queen City, "were thick and fast and told with a thrilling effect."

On April 12, the *Cincinnati Daily Gazette*'s Whitelaw Reid, writing under the penname "Agate," summarized the first day at Shiloh for his editors. The Federals, he explained, "were driven within half a mile of the Landing, when the approach of night, the timely arrival and aid of the gunboats, the tremendous efforts of our artillerists, and General Buell's approach saved us." Three days earlier, in a 19,000-word report subsequently both praised and scoffed, Reid had detailed the Tennessee River fight in realistic terms that contributed to his reputation as one of the war's finest reporters. He too reported the devastating work of "our Cincinnati wooden gunboats."

After waiting all of Sunday "impatiently chafing for the time to come," the opportunity to act arrived. This was made possible because the Rebels had "incautiously ventured within reach of their most dreaded antagonists, as broadside after broadside of seven-inch [i.e., eight-inch] shells and 64-pound shot soon taught them." The boats "fired admirably and with a rapidity that was astonishing." This was an opponent the Confederates were not ready for and "the unexpected fire in flank and rear sadly disconcerted their well-laid plans."

At Cairo, also on April 9, Albert H. Bodman of the *Chicago Daily Tribune* wrote his impressions, picked up from others, that "The Federal gunboats *Lexington* and *Tyler* opened a tremendous fire of shell upon the enemy." They also "kept it up every half hour during the night, saving the army from utter ruin." Henry Bentley of the *Philadelphia Inquirer*, who was briefly captured during the fight, initially praised both Webster and the gunboats. Of the latter, he noted that "the gun-boats *Tyler* and *Lexington* poured in their shells with tremendous effect." In a further elaboration on points missed in earlier reports, the editors of the *Philadelphia Inquirer* also wrote of Webster's guns on April 12, but laid the gunboat praise on even more thickly: "For in the waning afternoon when Beauregard, with his multitudes, was by sheer weight pressing our army back towards the river ... the *Lexington* and *Tyler*, from his left, poured continuous death into his ranks, and checked his advance by mowing down its front."

Several Southern newsmen also believed the gunboats were effective. Peter Wellington Alexander, writing for the *Savannah Republican*, praised the *Lexington* and *Tyler* during the last charge at sunset. "The enemy received the most important aid from his gunboats." Indeed, the Union was "indebted to these gunboats for his escape from certain destruction." The noted *New Orleans Daily Crescent* reporter and historian George W. Stoddard was also impressed. He believed Lt. Gwin and Shirk knew every inch of the countryside they were shelling. The "tremendous fire" of their gunboats "swept every contiguous portion of the battlefield."

On April 26, Flag Officer Foote received a message from Navy Secretary Welles extremely commendatory of the part taken by the *Tyler* and *Lexington* in the Shiloh battle. The Western Flotilla commander forwarded the communication to Lt. Gwin with instructions that it be read to the assembled crews of the two timberclads. When the message was presented on May 7, all "were much gratified with its contents."

On July 30, President Lincoln received a letter from Leonard Swett, an old Illinois friend and practicing government lawyer. It contained, in essence, a view held in Northern circles for most of a century. For three days after the Shiloh battle, Swett visited the field talking to generals and soldiers. In his view, "the gunboats *Lexington* and *Tyler* ... saved our army from defeat. At least it is within bounds to say they rendered us invaluable services." Swett recommended that both Gwin and Swett be promoted for their gallantry.[11]

There was a different perspective on the evening April 6 gunboat bombardment among certain Southern participants and writers. It has already been stated that Confederate military authorities had developed an unusual fear of Northern gunboats. The boats were big, fearsomely black, noisy, and the Rebels had none to equal them. However, at Shiloh, as at Fort Donelson, it was learned by a significant number of commanders that the bark of such a Yankee craft was worse than its actual bite.

Maj. Gen. Leonidas Polk, commander of the Confederate I Corps, who had watched Union timberclads ever since the days before the Battle of Belmont, was quite unimpressed with their contribution at Shiloh. He later testified that, in late afternoon on April 6, they "dropped down the river, near the Landing, where his troopers were collected, and opened a tremendous cannonade of shot and shell over the bank in the direction from where our forces were approaching." The terrain was a big factor in what next occurred. "The height of the plain on which we were, above the level of the water, was about 100 feet, so that it was necessary to give great elevation to his guns to enable him to fire over the bank." Such extreme shooting meant, in consequence, "that shot could take effect only at points removed from the river's edge." In summary, Maj. Gen. Polk believed that the timberclads "were comparatively harmless to our troops nearest the bank, and became increasingly so as we drew near the enemy and placed him between us and his boats."

Maj. Gen. Braxton Bragg, II Corps commander, also believed that nature reduced the effect of the *Lexington* and *Tyler*. In addition to Col. Webster's "well-served" siege guns, he remembered that the Federals were also covered by "their two gunboats, which now poured a heavy fire upon our supposed positions, for we were entirely hid by the Forest." The timberclad bombardment, "though terrific in sound and producing some consternation at first, did us no damage, as the shells passed over and exploded far beyond our positions." Some years later, Bragg also advised William Preston Johnston, then writing a biography of his father, that the gunboat fire was not harmful to the Confederate late afternoon advance: "The enemy's gunboats, his last hope, took position opposite us in the river and commenced a furious cannonade at our supposed position." Bragg echoed the argument made by Maj. Gen. Polk, in that, "from the elevation necessary to reach the high bluff, on which we were operating, " their fire "proved 'all sound and fury signifying nothing,' and did not in the slightest degree mar our prospects or our progress." On the other hand, he did concede to Johnston that the heavy gunboat shells "fell among the reserves and stragglers."

Changing his opinion from one earlier expressed, Col. Thomas Jordan opined for the "Battles and Leaders" series that the gunboats were not a serious problem after all. Remembering that he had reached a wooded point close to the Tennessee River, he observed that "the large ordnance of the gun-boats was raking this position, creating more noise in some quarters than harm to the Confederates, as the heavy projectiles tore and crashed in all directions through the heavy forest." Col. John C. Moore, leading the 2nd Texas, part of the 3rd Brigade of II Corps, reported that the gunboat shells flew high and caused little hurt among his men.

From the lower ranks, Arkansas soldier Henry Morton Stanley, a future journalistic superstar, recalled that "the huge bombs from the gun-boats" had little effect on the soldiers closest to the bluecoats." Indeed, they "discomfited only those in the rear." Judge Alexander P. Walker of the *New Orleans Daily Delta* conceded that the gunboat shelling alarmed the Confederate troops. It did not, he believed, do any appreciable damage.[12]

Later historians have also rendered a split verdict on the effectiveness of the gunboat bombardment, but most, of late, have tended to dismiss its value. The first Civil War naval historian to lavish grand praise upon the role of the gunboats at Shiloh was Charles B. Boynton. In his 1867–1868 review, the Union-oriented author colorfully pictured the timberclad bombardment. His conclusion was that the ravine, "by the rapid fire from the gunboats, became a valley of death that the living could not pass."

Writing in 1874, Benson J. Lossing revealed that the *Tyler* and *Lexington* had not by late afternoon on April 6 seen action. They were then "placed in position and commenced work." They fired their huge shells "up that hollow in the bluff, in curves that dropped them in the midst of the Confederates." Manning Force, who was a battle participant, was very specific as to what he believed was accomplished late in the afternoon of April 6. "This fire," he wrote in 1882, "drove a battery from its position." It also threw one brigade and part of another into disorder and killed 10 and wounded many in two others.

In his still-cited and measured review authored a year later than Force, Alfred T. Mahan was disappointed that Maj. Gen. Grant's report did "not make clear how much was due to the gunboats before Buell and Nelson arrived." On the other hand, the famous naval writer received the "impression among Confederates there present" that the "gunboats saved the army by saving the landing and transports, while during the night, the shrieking of 8-inch shells through the woods, tearing down branches and trees in their flight and then sharply exploding, was demoralizing to a degree."

David Dixon Porter, himself commander of the Mississippi Squadron from October 1862, wondered in his Civil War naval history of 1886 "why Gen. Grant did not have a large number of gun-boats at Pittsburg Landing ... as it was a most favorable position for their use."

On the other hand, Porter came down firmly on the service side of the gunboats. "There is a tradition in the Navy which will go down to posterity, that the *Taylor* [sic] and *Lexington* prevented part of our Army on that day from being driven into the river and turned the enemy back when he considered that victory was in his hands."

In 1899, Southern writer J.P. Austin prepared a series of sketches on what he called "a portion of the unwritten history" of the Civil War. Coming to the late afternoon of April 6 at Shiloh, he opined that Maj. Gen. Grant "tried to rally his shattered forces, under cover of his gunboats, which by this time had opened a terrific fire on our advancing columns, with but very little effect." Darkness, he claimed, "closed the bloody drama."

Bruce Catton tells us that "Out in the river, *Lexington* and *Tyler* continued to slam in their 8-inch shells, firing down the length of the supposed location of the Confederate battle line." But, "since this line was withdrawn, they did little actual damage."

Mississippi River war authority John D. Milligan was generous in his praise of Webster and the gunboats, who made the Confederate advance "melt away under a massive army and navy barrage." Writing in 1965, the historian argued as forcefully as anyone that the "woodclads contributed importantly in this repulse," and noted that reports from all level of Confederate command on the right indicated that "the fire of the gunboats" combined with Webster's "to break their advance." Grant, Buell, and Union commanders on the left all "agreed that the presence of the gunboats greatly strengthened their defense."

In 1977, James Lee McDonough shattered the long-held position that the gunboats were effective fire retardant to the Confederate late afternoon April 6 advance at Shiloh. The Rebels did not suffer heavy casualties from the timberclad shells. "The worst damage that was done was psychological." So far in the war, Confederate troops and their commanders had "an inordinate dread of the gunboats." Yes, they were noisy when their great guns spoke and the bursting shells could cause harm and terror if they landed close by. Most soldiers, however, "realized in time that the shelling was not really hurting them." McDonough's conclusion, widely supported presently, is "that rather than being decisive in turning back the Confederate attack on the Union left, the gunboats were simply another element in the Federal armor."

One of the most important lessons regarding the role of the gunboats at Shiloh was taken by Maj. Gen. Henry Halleck, the western theater commander. Reviewing his correspondence after Shiloh, Rowena Reed was convinced that Halleck quickly came to believe "that only the Union gunboats *Tyler* and *Lexington* had kept Grant's army from being destroyed before Buell arrived." Rather than seek a decisive battle at Corinth, Halleck now changed his tactical plan in favor of a slow and methodical approach.

In 1983, Grady McWhiney offered "General Beauregard's 'Complete Victory' at Shiloh: An Interpretation." He, too, found fault with the Beauregard's belief that gunboat fire was effective. It did, he contended, "far less damage than he supposed." This was, as Maj. Gen. Polk noted, because the elevated timberclad guns were firing over the high riverbank and hitting targets far beyond.

Ivan Musicant, in his 1995 Civil War naval history, gave wholehearted subscription to the vital role of the timberclads. "But into the chaos that was Grant's collapsed left flank," he wrote, "came the stinkpots *Tyler* and *Lexington*." Their heavy shells "provided just enough of a check to give Grant's reeling regiments time to consolidate and make a stand." On the other hand, Jack D. Coombe in his under-recognized 1996 *Thunder Along the Mississippi*, takes the opposite tack, supporting McDonough and suggesting that the influence of the gunboats "on this quintessential Civil War battle has sometimes been exaggerated." "The truth is," Coombe boldly states, "with a shifting front of 40,000 Confederates spread out through wooded and undulating terrain for seven miles, the effect of the two gunboats' fire could not have been a decisive factor. It would be remarkable to find that the ships even knew what they were aiming at."

Everyone engaged in the fight remembered the timberclads, however, "if only because, all night long, they kept on firing every fifteen minutes." In 2000, Robert C. Suhr summed up his noted article on the gunboats at Shiloh with the conclusion that their true impact came not from their 8-inch shells. Rather, the *Tyler* and *Lexington* made their greatest contribution through "the psychological effect their presence had on the Confederate generals, both in how they made their plans and how they executed them."

"In addition to the tactical support provided by the gunboats," concluded Timothy B. Smith in 2004, "the major naval contributions at the Battle of Shiloh were psychological and logistical." He added that "once the damage to the Confederate psyche was done ... the Southerners recovered too late to make a difference."

In his February 2005 profile of the U.S.S. *Tyler*, Steven R. Davis briefly examined her role and that of the *Lexington* at Shiloh and returned to the traditional view. "The fire of the gunboats," he concluded, "kept the Confederates from advancing along the river and contributed greatly to Grant's ability to hold his final line at dusk, with his back to the landing." As Suhr notes, the Union infantry won the Battle of Shiloh on the ground. The gunboats "watched and waited in the river, helpful bystanders at best."

In 2006, Spencer C. Tucker provided helpful perspective in the latest all-purpose Civil

Left: Major General William Tecumseh Sherman (1829–1891) was a key figure in the Union Western Theater throughout the Civil War. Taking command of the Military District of Cairo in January 1862, he had the opportunity over the next couple of months to make a number of reconnaissance trips aboard the timberclads as they scouted Confederate positions along the banks of the Tennessee River. After his participation in the Battle of Shiloh in April, he later commanded the failed Federal attempt to reach Vicksburg via the Chickasaw Bluffs. His contact with the gunboats was refreshed in October 1863 when their aid was required to expedite the passage of his troops over the Tennessee River en route to Chattanooga (Library of Congress). *Below:* Shiloh. The timberclads *Tyler* and *Lexington* provide gunfire support to Federal troops at Pittsburg Landing, April 6, 1862 (Library of Congress).

War naval history, while echoing Davis that the two craft "played an important role in the battle." Although suggesting, like the 19th century fife-and-drum scribes, that the gunboat bombardment of late afternoon April 6 was tactically beneficial, Tucker provides significant enhancement. Falling far behind the front lines, the timberclad shells actually "helped bring about" Beauregard's "decision at dusk to call off the attack." Tucker backs up Timothy Smith's analysis of the logistical importance. Buell's army crossed the Tennessee on the night of April 6-7. "That these troops could cross the river, bring in supplies, and evacuate wounded was, according to the Virginia Military Institute historian, "owing to the U.S. Navy, an important fact often overlooked in accounts of the battle."[13]

In the days following April 7, there was no serious follow-up pursuit of Gen. Beauregard's forces by the Union armies of Maj. Gen. Grant or Buell. Daniel suggests four reasons for this: the division between the Northern generals; exhaustion of the bluecoats— a theme echoed by Bruce Catton; the unknown possibility of a Confederate counterattack; and an order from Maj. Gen. Halleck instructing Grant "to avoid another battle, if you can." The Southerners were virtually unmolested as they returned to Corinth.

Halleck's order was sent from St. Louis on April 9, just a few hours before he boarded a steamer for Pittsburgh Landing, where he arrived aboard the transport *Continental* two days later. Stepping ashore, he immediately took over command of Federal armies in the field and officially thanked all of the soldiers for their participation in the great Shiloh fight.

While the armies on both sides were busily attempting to re-form, the timberclads *Tyler* and *Lexington* maintained their active patrols of the Tennessee River. The pair scouted for Southern stragglers, cavalry riders, and partisans, while offering protection to and observation over Northern steamers. On April 11, the same day Maj. Gen. Halleck arrived at Pittsburg Landing, the *Lexington* visited Hamburg. There she put a number of men ashore to look around. These were soon attacked by Confederate horsemen, who also fired on the gunboat. Unaware of the size of the party confronting him, Lt. Shirk put out into the middle of the stream and opened fire on the cavalry with grape and canister. After dropping three rounds and receiving no response, the ship's boats were landed and the shore party was re-embarked.[14]

Having learned of the arrival of the *Continental* from St. Louis the previous evening, Brig. Gen. Sherman repaired aboard Maj. Gen. Halleck's flag boat on the morning of April 12. There he received orders for a new river reconnaissance. Ascending to Florence, he and his men would destroy the bridge at that town as well as the Memphis and Charleston Railroad spans over Bear Creek. Taking his leave of the theater commander, the brigadier paid a courtesy call to Maj. Gen. Grant, then aboard the *Tigress*, where his instructions received verbal confirmation pending the delivery of written orders. At the same time, Sherman learned that Grant was now "second in command" and that overall strategic orders would now come directly from Halleck.

That afternoon, 100 men of the 4th Illinois Cavalry, together with about 1,900 men from the 2nd Brigade, 6th Division, under Brig. Gen. James B. Fry, Maj. Gen. Buell's chief of staff, were detailed aboard the transports *Tecumseh* ad *White Cloud*. Once the *Lexington* and *Tyler* returned to Pittsburg Landing from patrol that evening and their commanders were acquainted with the mission, the little task group departed "for up the river." The four Union craft covered the 32 miles to Chickasaw Landing, "on the corner of Alabama," by 7:00 A.M. on Sunday. The soldiers, together with Maj. S.M. Bowman's horsemen, were landed, with the latter starting out immediately toward Iuca and the Bear Creek Bridge. The superstructures of the two 110-foot spans and 500 feet of trestles were destroyed by the cavalry and infantry units, all of which were safely returned to their boats by 9:00 P.M. Only minimal Confederate opposition was encountered. Sherman next determined to visit Tuscumbia Landing and

Florence, about 20 miles further upstream. The Florence bridge was spared by Lt. Phelps back in February but remained a prime Union target. But it was not destroyed this time either.

The river was now falling and it was impossible to reach the objective. All of the pilots, those onboard the transports as well as those aboard the gunboats, supported by Gwin and Shirk, advised Sherman that only one of the transports would be able to make it over Beetree Shoals and Colbert Shoals without serious risk of destroying the underside of her hull on the rock bottom. Without personal knowledge of the river, the brigadier felt himself "bound to defer to the opinion of pilots who have navigated the Tennessee for 30 years." Consequently, the descent upon Florence Bridge was abandoned. His mission a partial success, Sherman returned to Pittsburg Landing on April 14 and reported his results to Maj. Gen. Halleck, who "was delighted."[15]

While the Battle of Shiloh and its horrific casualties gripped the attention of the Northern public, the nearly bloodless victory at Island No. 10, universally hailed, was largely overshadowed. Following Gen. Beauregard's retreat from the Tennessee River on April 7, Union theater commander Maj. Gen. Halleck reassessed his approach toward Corinth, in Mississippi. Thus it was decided on April 15 to, among other things, bring General Pope's Army of the Mississippi inland to the Tennessee River, there to assist Halleck's own advance. The twin Confederate reversals at Shiloh and Island No. 10 meant, in fact, that the large scale battle for the upper Mississippi Valley was over; Fort Pillow and nearby Fort Randolph could be outflanked from the east and Memphis could not really be protected. Pope's army arrived at Hamburg, Tennessee, on April 21 and Halleck's grand advance toward Corinth kicked off eight days later.

Born in Pennsylvania, Lieut. Cmdr. James W. Shirk (1832–1873) was a midshipman aboard Commodore Matthew C. Perry's *Mississippi* during the 1850s opening of Japan. Constantly at sea prior to his Western Rivers assignment, he skippered both the timberclad *Lexington* and the ironclad *Chillicothe*. He would later serve as commander of the Tennessee River district, eventually becoming the longest-serving junior officer in the Mississippi Squadron (Naval Historical Center).

Sensing this probable consequence in events and that his Union army was now in control of Middle Tennessee and almost all of West Tennessee, Halleck chose to leave only one small U.S. Army brigade of 1,200 men attached to the Western Flotilla on the Mississippi River for garrison duty — Col. Graham Newell Fitch's 46th Indiana Volunteers.[16]

Meanwhile, even as the stream continued to fall, the *Tyler* and *Lexington* maintained their Tennessee River patrols, running between the mouth of the stream and the head of navigation. On April 21, the same day Pope's army arrived at Hamburg, the former made one of the most important captures of her career. While inspecting riverbanks and adjoining creeks near Florence, Alabama, Lt. Gwin came across the sunken hull of Gus Fowler's steamer, the *Dunbar*. Not destroyed as believed back in February, the transport lay on the bottom of Cypress Creek, some two miles below Florence, with water covering her up above her wheel guards. It being impossible to raise her with the resources available to the timberclad, sailors went aboard and put her to the torch. A second Rebel transport, also believed lost two months earlier, was taken at the mouth of Crane Creek. The 86 ton *Alfred Robb*, a stern-wheeler, was captured in good running order.

After administering the Federal oath to the boat's pilot Joseph N. Smith, Gwin placed an 11-man prize crew, under Second Master Jason Goudy, on the vessel and renamed her *Lady Foote* in honor of his superior. Flag Officer Foote himself would find the latter action embarrassing and, as soon as he learned of the well-intentioned honor, he had the *Robb*'s name restored. That evening, Smith and Goudy departed Florence for Cairo with dispatches. There the *Robb* would face disposition, though Lt. Gwin hoped she could return with provisions for his boat and the *Lexington* and then stay on as a tender.

The *Tyler* was in very bad shape and needed major restoration, Gwin reported. Her engines and boilers were fouled and she was hogged "to the extent of 14 inches." A hogged vessel, according to Gershom Bradford, is one whose bow and stern have drooped. It was hoped that she could go on the ways, leaving the *Lexington* and *Robb* to protect the Tennessee. In his covering communications sent with the *Robb*, the captain of the *Tyler* revealed that the railroad bridge at Florence, which Brig. Gen. Sherman was unable to destroy a week earlier, was gone, burned by order of Gen. Beauregard. While visiting the town and inspecting the wrecked span, the *Tyler*'s bluejackets came across the last Confederate cannon remaining in the community. As the sailors hustled it aboard the timberclad, Gwin commiserated with town leaders about the bridge in which they had held so much civic pride. They were all "very indignant at such a wanton destruction," he later reported. Although there was no speculation in his report, the naval officer was probably grateful that the local populace was angry with Beauregard rather than with Sherman or himself.

Next day, the *Robb* arrived at Pittsburg Landing. In reporting her seizure, *Philadelphia Inquirer* newsman Henry Bentley also remembered to add a note that the "weather is rather more pleasant." By order of Flag Officer Foote and at the urging of General Halleck, who had been deeply impressed by the sterling roles played by the *Tyler* and *Lexington* in the April 6 Battle of Shiloh, the two timberclads remained on the Tennessee River into May. On May 3, sailors aboard the gunboats were able to hear "heavy firing in the direction of Corinth."

With the heavy units of the Western Flotilla engaged in the campaign against Fort Pillow, Capt. Charles H. Davis (1807–1877) temporarily assumed squadron command on May 9 from the injured Flag Officer Foote. Foote's choice to act as his deputy and successor if need be was his friend and a year younger than he and, in the Antebellum period, developed an enviable reputation, like Cmdr. John Rodgers, as a scientific officer. Born in Boston, Davis earned a degree from Harvard University, becoming superintendent of the Nautical Almanac Office located there. With sea service during the expedition to capture filibuster Walker in Nicaragua and with the South Atlantic Blockading Squadron, Davis would succeed Foote in June 1862, only to be himself succeeded in command of the Mississippi Squadron by David Dixon Porter in October (effective July). Constantly on duty ashore and afloat, he would die at his desk as superintendent of the Naval Observatory.

Meanwhile, as he continued his approach to Corinth, Maj. Gen. Halleck was informed by Lt. Gwin on May 17 that his warships would have to depart the Tennessee due to rapidly falling water. Though "Old Brains" was not pleased by this development and, in fact, asked that Gwin remain as long as it was deemed safe, he recognized that a boat with a draft much lighter than the six feet of the 420 ton side-wheeler *Tyler* or her compatriot, the 362-ton *Lexington*, was required. Writing to Lt. Gwin from his camp on the Corinth road the same day, the top Federal general in the west stated his view simply: "I think the *Robb* should be fitted up to render us all the assistance possible on the [Tennessee] River." Halleck's message to Gwin was forwarded to Capt. Davis three days later.[17] During the next week, that portion of

Davis' fleet on the Mississippi invested Fort Pillow and fought an engagement with the Confederate River Defense Force at Plum Point Bend. During the remainder of the month, the ironclads and mortar boats continued to smash at Confederate defenses.

While operational activities occupied Davis, Gwin, and their sailors, Captain Alexander M. Pennock, in his capacity of fleet captain and Cairo naval base commander, was daily attending to the myriad administrative matters behind the lines, while attempting to keep an eye on Rebel activities in the areas of the Ohio, Tennessee, and Cumberland rivers. On May 20, Lt. Gwin wrote to Capt. Davis, via Cmdr. Pennock, advising that the timberclads would have to depart the Tennessee River within a day or two. In forwarding the communication to Davis next day, the Cairo station chief asked that they might be permitted to remain at the tip of Illinois in order to protect public property and serve as a mobile strike force that could "go up the Ohio, Mississippi, and Tennessee rivers whenever it may be required."

Among Pennock's responsibilities was supervision of the construction, outfitting, and supply of new or captured warships and the repair, outfitting, and supply of others. Thus it was that the *Alfred Robb* came into his care when she arrived at the Cairo river base from up the Tennessee.

In the same May 21 letter to Davis in which he asked to retain the *Tyler* and *Lexington*, the fleet captain advised "in accordance with the suggestion of General Halleck in his letter of May 17, I shall prepare the *Robb* so as to protect her pilothouse, etc., against rifle shots from the shore." The next day, the interim Western Flotilla chief, who had received Pennock's report by a swift dispatch boat, replied that the "fitting up" of the *Robb*, as she was sometimes known, was all right." On the other hand, as soon as the *Tyler* and *Lexington* arrived at Cairo, they were to proceed down to rendezvous with the main battle fleet off Fort Pillow. In order to have a gunboat available in case of emergency, the *Conestoga* was ordered stationed at Columbus, to ply between that city and Hickman and on to Cairo as needed.

When the *Tyler* arrived at Cairo on June 2, Cmdr. Pennock saw that Lt. Gwin was correct; the largest timberclad was in very sad shape after months of hard use. A board of survey was conducted on the vessel's hull, machinery, and boilers next day by the flotilla's ordnance officer, Lt. J.P. Sanford, Chief Engineer William D. Faulkner, and master carpenter J.K. McGee. The *Lexington*, which arrived a day after her sister, was found to be "in comparatively good condition." She was ordered coaled and made ready to steam downstream.

The Sanford board reported to Pennock on Tuesday afternoon. Its findings were so dire as to prohibit the vessel's immediate return to duty. The hull of the *Tyler*, it was pointed out, was "much hogged, the forward and after ends drooping several inches." There was only one remedy, the installation of a fore-and-aft hog chain and cross hog chains to support wheel timbers. The hull also needed caulking throughout and the forward part of her hurricane deck required sheathing and strengthening in order to support the oft-employed 12-pdr. howitzer. Additionally, the deck should be recanvased as the great awning covering it was worn out and leaked badly.

Down below, Engineer Faulkner found that the boilers were in such terrible condition that it would be necessary to install "some four or five new sheets." The engines required general overhaul and repair. The "doctor" engine was broken and, he pointed out, it would actu-

Opposite, top: The *Lexington* on the Mississippi. The date of this photograph is unknown but it is perhaps the best available. Note the two towering chimneys forward and the small boat alongside. The men in the bow give the size of the vessel perspective. **Bottom:** Pittsburg Landing, Tennessee River. A number of steamers are shown tied up to the bank shortly after the April 1862 Battle of Shiloh. The timberclad *Tyler* is seen lying on the opposite shore (both photographs: Naval Historical Center).

10. *Tennessee River: Shiloh, March–April 1862* 315

ally be less expensive to replace it with a new one than to attempt its repair. Being unable to haul the timberclad out of the water to work on her without seriously disrupting ongoing work on the ironclad *Eastport*, Cmdr. Pennock decided to send her up to the Carondelet yards at St. Louis.

That night, Pennock again communicated with his distant chief in one of a series of detail-laden reports he would compose on what was often called "general matters." In addition to a variety of miscellaneous flotilla detail, the fleet captain explained that the renovation of the *Robb* was well underway. "She will carry four howitzers," Pennock wrote, "and be well supplied with small arms, etc." For protection, the Cairo man revealed that he had ordered a "bullet-proof bulkhead around her forecastle and also iron-plated the pilothouse." Lt. Gwin, who had originally captured her, thought that the new little light draft gunboat would be "equal to any emergency that may occur." A total of 30 officers and men would be detailed to the boat, under the command of First Master Goudy.

That Tuesday evening, acting under Pennock's orders, the *Alfred Robb* departed Cairo for Pittsburg Landing on the Tennessee River. Master Goudy would be expected to employ his rebuilt craft, in actuality the first "tinclad," to protect Union interests in a stream considerably more shallow than when the timberclads left it days earlier. On the afternoon of June 4, with Chief Engineer Faulkner and carpenter McGee embarked, the *Tyler* departed Cairo for St. Louis. There, Pennock's top men would superintend work on Lt. Gwin's vessel; it was hoped she would be ready for action shortly.

Bright and early (6:00) on June 5, Lt. Shirk's sailors "commenced to work on the guns" of the *Lexington*. One six-inch Columbiad was sent ashore and two 30-pdr. Parrott guns and their carriages were received aboard. The *Lexington* cleared Bird's Point and headed down the Mississippi on Thursday evening, reaching Hickman by dawn on June 6. Her availability and that of the *Conestoga* would result in the two being assigned to participate in what would prove the last significant operation of the year dependant upon more than one timberclad.[18]

CHAPTER 11

White River and the C.S.S. *Arkansas,* June–July 1862

AT DAWN ON FRIDAY, JUNE 6, C.S.S. *Earl Van Dorn, General Beauregard, General M. Jeff Thompson, General Bragg, General Sumter, General Sterling Price,* and *Little Rebel* of Com James E. Montgomery's Confederate River Defense Fleet cast off, dropped below Railroad Point, and were drawn up in a double line in front of Memphis. There they were seen through Federal spyglasses. At 4:20 A.M., the Western Flotilla flagship *Benton* and the Pook turtles *Louisville, Carondelet, St. Louis,* and *Cairo* headed down stream toward the Rebel warships, that had, meanwhile, opened fire.

As the two squadrons approached, Col. Charles Ellet, Jr., who was charging to the sound of the guns, suddenly appeared with the rams *Monarch* and *Queen of the West* from his independent Mississippi Marine Brigade and attacked at full steam. The close action which followed the appearance of the U.S. Army rams was dramatic, with fast-paced give-and-take fighting between the ships of Ellet and Montgomery ensuing before the heavier ironclads could come up. After smashing into the *Lovell,* the *Queen of the West* was rammed by the *Beauregard* and disabled; Colonel Ellet received a mortal wound. The *Beauregard* and *General Sterling Price* then aimed at the *Monarch,* missed, and collided, with the *General Sterling Price* the worst for the assault. The *Beauregard* was rammed by the *Monarch* and sunk by a shot from the *Benton* as Davis' boats came closer.

The surviving Rebels fled and an hour-long running duel ensued that carried the opposing units 10 miles downstream past President's Island. In the end, only the *Van Dorn* escaped, with all the others captured, sunk, or grounded on the riverbank to avoid sinking. Cdr. Montgomery and Brig. Gen. M. Jeff Thompson, who had both promised better results, "were hurried," as the latter subsequently reported to Gen. Beauregard, in their "retirement from Memphis." By lunchtime, Union soldiers were being landed at the Memphis docks.[1]

When the *Lexington* arrived above Island No. 10 on the morning of June 6, she met the steamer *De Soto,* en route to Cairo with dispatches from Capt. Davis. Coming to, Lt. Shirk hailed the transport, which reported that the Mississippi was open all the way to Memphis. Continuing on, the timberclad reached Fort Pillow, where she rounded to next to the Pook turtle *Pittsburg.* Feared at one time, the Rebel fortifications were now abandoned. Capt. Davis' flotilla was downriver and the only activity to be seen from the deck of the *Lexington* was deckhands taking captured ammunition aboard the steamer *Jacob Musselman.*

The *Lexington* continued on to Memphis, where she joined in the naval occupation. On June 8, Lt. Shirk — accompanied by a number of officers from the *Mound City*, including new Master's Mate Symmes E. Browne — went ashore "with the intention of going to church." Walking up from the landing, they were able to get a close-up view of the "good, large brick houses" that had presented "a very fine appearance from the river." As the men searched for an appropriate house of worship, it became quite late. They grew fearful that, if they entered after congregations were seated, " the secesh preachers might take a notion to insult us." Rather than run the risk of an incident, Shirk and his companions decided "to see what there was to see and then return" to their boats. A call was paid to the office of the *Memphis Daily Avalanche* to obtain souvenir newspapers. The city square was also seen: "beautiful, being nicely laid out and full of fine foliage."

Later in the day, the timberclad received a gun taken from one of the damaged Rebel boats, along with 23 bales of Confederate oakum. These were taken to the naval shipyard, a one-time U.S. Navy facility located seven miles downriver. That morning, Capt. Davis had received a single sentence telegram from Navy Secretary Gideon Welles requiring that an immediate inspection of and report on the captured navy yard be undertaken. Davis assigned the duty to Shirk and most of the day was taken up by the *Lexington*'s sailors in a fruitless search for old iron and a rough inventory inspection.

Lt. Shirk's boat remained off Memphis for the next five days, generally providing a guard for the captured Southern vessels or those being salvaged. A new man aboard, Able Seaman Frederic E. Davis, formerly of the 4th Rhode Island Infantry Regiment who had joined the navy at New Bedford, Massachusetts, on April 3, wrote home on June 10. His letter explained that the local citizens were "proud and it is galling [for them] to come down." Memphis, on the other hand, was "a large and pretty place."

On June 11, the timberclad transferred her 12-pdr. howitzer, together with its ammunition and appurtenances, to the tugboat *Restless.* Additionally, her men continued to examine the Memphis navy yard. Shirk turned his findings over to Cmdr. Benjamin Dove and Lt. S. Ledyard Phelps.

As Federal soldiers took possession of Memphis and Southern forces scurried south after having evacuated Corinth, Mississippi, Maj. Gen. Ulysses S. Grant, who had played almost no major role in the fall of either, assessed the Union's strategic situation in the area:

> The railroad from Columbus to Corinth was at once put in good condition and held by us. We had garrisons at Donelson, Clarksville and Nashville, on the Cumberland River and held the Tennessee River from its mouth to Eastport. New Orleans and Baton Rouge had fallen into the possession of the National forces so that now the Confederates at the west were narrowed down for all communications with Richmond to the single line of road running east from Vicksburg.

Grant and other Northerners, notably Maj. Gen. William T. Sherman and Western Flotilla commodore U.S. Navy Capt. Charles H. Davis, believed that the capture of that road, together with possession of the Mississippi River from Memphis down to Baton Rouge, was a matter of war-winning significance." It would," Grant later wrote, "be equal to the amputation of a limb in its weakening effects upon the enemy."

It was argued then, and later much more frequently, that a well-led combined operation might have achieved those aims. President Lincoln himself observed that Vicksburg was the key to controlling the Mississippi and that "the war could never be brought to a close until the key was in our pocket." The chief executive, a midwesterner, understood that Vicksburg, like Nashville, was a logistical center of vast importance. Produce from the Red and Arkansas rivers was run across the Mississippi and from Vicksburg, by rail to Jackson and the east. Taking that one town would not only reopen north-south commerce for the northwest, it would also badly damage the South's ability to feed itself.

But it was Maj. Gen. Henry Halleck who was in tactical charge at Corinth, not Grant or Lincoln, and he now elected to disperse his force, "the largest army ever assembled west of the Alleghenies." Exact figures are disputed, but, in general, it is believed that the Union armies in the west totaled about 137,000 effectives (those not sick, wounded, or otherwise unfit for service) against 105,000 Confederates. On June 3, Maj. Gen. John A. McClernand and Maj. Gen. Lew Wallace of the Army of the Tennessee were sent to the Mississippi Central Railroad center at Bolivar. Maj. Gen. John Pope, who was chasing Rebel Gen. Beauregard south of Corinth, was ordered next day to break off his pursuit. On June 9, the divisions of Maj. Gen. Sherman and Brig. Gen. Stephen A. Hurlbut were sent to Memphis, while Maj. Gen. Don Carlos Buell was ordered to take his men to Chattanooga, repairing railroads en route. Halleck, who had broken up his overall command into a series of "wings" back on April 30, cancelled that formation on June 10 and their previous names, Armies of the Tennessee (Grant), Ohio (Buell), and Mississippi (Pope) respectively, were restored. Halleck wrote letters from his Corinth headquarters for the next five weeks and otherwise did little other than demand that local railroads be improved.

This inactivity left the forces under Gen. Braxton Bragg, the new Confederate theater commander appointed in June, to refresh and reequip, to undertake the difficult mission of halting the advance of Union troops into the heartland, and to plan and execute a counterattack into Kentucky. What was immediately available to accomplish these goals was a combination of guerrilla attacks, cavalry raids, and relatively small Rebel army counter initiatives all of which had one overriding goal: sever Northern lines of communications and prevent Maj. Gen. Buell from reaching Chattanooga. Irregulars and partisans raided throughout the region attacking their favorite targets: railroads, overland wagon trains, and river supply steamers.

As he pushed toward Chattanooga, Buell was unable to repair his first railway, the Memphis & Charleston, as quickly as Confederate raiders could destroy key links. A switch to the Nashville & Chattanooga Railroad was just as fruitless.

Gen. Bragg's Army of Tennessee occupied Chattanooga on July 24; his army had arrived in the mountainous city on the Tennessee River by riding the rails from Tupelo, Mississippi, via Mobile. It would now be his aim to march up into Kentucky across the Cumberland plateau. During this period, Bragg was aided substantially both by his cavalry and by the great obstruction of the Tennessee River, Muscle Shoals. The shoals were, wrote historian Donald Davidson in 1948, "in effect a flank guard, as good as a mountain range, or better." This was because the Confederate leader knew that, east of the rapids, any army coming against him had to move overland by road and railroad; Muscle Shoals prevented interference with him by steamer or gunboat.

Meanwhile, on July 16, Maj. Gen. Halleck departed east to become general-in-chief of all Union armies. Fifteen days later, he telegraphed Maj. Gen. Grant, whom he had placed in charge of troops in the Corinth-Memphis-Columbus area, leaving it up to him to figure out what to do next: "You must judge for yourself the best use to be made of your troops. Be careful not to scatter them too much."[2]

In the first weeks after the fall of Memphis on June 6, the sailors and soldiers reporting to Capt. Davis and Col. Graham Newell Fitch were occupied with matters in and around the Tennessee city. Ashore, the Hoosier bluecoats provided support to the civilian government. On the banks of the Mississippi, workers from the Western Flotilla attempted to salvage as many of the former Confederate warships as possible, while their commander pondered what moves he could make next.

Gunboatmen and soldiers at Memphis, "and everyone who listened," heard stories of Confederate activities further below on the White, Arkansas, and Yazoo rivers. Rebel ravages on those streams were committed daily and included, in the words of *Chicago Daily Tribune* reporter "W" (probably Horace White), "burning cotton, destroying sugar, molasses, and other property" of loyal residents.

Although steamboat traffic northward up the Mississippi was quickly reestablished, the first period of occupation would not be easy for a people "more or less in sympathy" with the Confederate cause. In fact, upon his arrival, Maj. Gen. Sherman would find "the place dead; no business doing, the stores closed, churches, schools, and every thing shut up."

Without significantly more troops than the 1,200 or so of the 46th Indiana, it was useless to head downriver toward Vicksburg, the obvious next big target in the brown water war. That fortress city, with its many batteries, was located atop a high bluff on the left side of the river adjacent to a sharp river bend. In some ways, it was very reminiscent of Columbus, Kentucky. It would be better, Davis reasoned, to continue raising and repairing the sunk or damaged Confederate vessels. The captured steamers could then be made serviceable for future use. Additionally, as news of the Halleck force realignment trickled in, the scholar-seaman determined to run small sweeps up the White and Arkansas rivers until more soldiers actually reached Memphis and a firmer plan for their use was available.[3]

While Union troops fanned out over parts of Tennessee, Alabama, Mississippi, and Kentucky under Maj. Gen. Halleck's June dispersal orders and Confederate troops regrouped under their new leader, Gen. Braxton Bragg, major campaigning in the west slowed almost to a standstill. This is not to say that the fighting ceased. On the contrary, in the words of historian Benjamin Franklin Cooling, "The conflict became a 'war in the shadows' in which rebel horsemen garnered most of the honors." Southern units both official and unofficial, military raider, partisan, and guerrilla, struck back at the Yankee invaders, hitting Union outposts, small or isolated contingents, supply dumps, loyalist leaders and, homesteads, and most especially, rail and water transport and telegraph communications.

There was at least one high level systematic and organized Rebel effort to create and harness guerrilla bands, "in the proper sense of the term," to a state's defense. This measure would be, in effect, to quote irregular warfare historian Robert Mackey, an effort "to give the Yankee army a taste of what Napoleon's army experienced in Spain." In late May, Maj. Gen. Thomas C. Hindman, a one-time U.S. congressman known as "The Lion of the South," was sent by Richmond to reorganize the defense of Confederate Arkansas, then in turmoil, with most of her soldiers east of the Mississippi.

When Hindman and his entourage arrived at Little Rock on May 30 (after stopping en route to liberate a quantity of arms and $1 million from Memphis banks "by the authority of the sword," as one eastern newsman put it), they found Arkansas virtually defenseless and facing an invasion by Yankee troops from Missouri. As commander of the new Trans-Mississippi District, Hindman immediately set to work building up as much resistance as possible to halt an expected Northern influx. Martial law was declared, all supplies and munitions were taken in hand, rationing was introduced, and men were conscripted to re-form a conventional army. Building a new regular military force would take time and, to help buy that time, Hindman authorized the raising of independent guerrilla companies to fight behind enemy lines.

Hindman's decree, General Order No. 17, later known as the "Bands of Ten" order, was published in regional newspapers; the *Nashville Daily Union* carried it on July 18. It specifically called upon the populace (meaning primarily Caucasian males) to organize into independent 10-man companies, each under the leadership of an elected captain. "Without waiting for special instructions," the little non-uniformed outfits were ordered to undertake guerrilla activities "for the more effective annoyance of the enemy upon our rivers and in our mountains and woods." When the general order took effect on June 17, Arkansas found that it had mobilized a guerrilla army "but without providing for the command and control needed to oversee the independent companies."

In addition to this rudimentary land defense, the protection of Arkansas rivers in the wake of the loss of Memphis was also problematic. After the fall of Island No. 10 on April 7, two of the surviving Confederate warships from Cdr. George Hollins' fleet, the *Pontchartrain* and the *Maurepas*, were sent up the White River to do what they could to aid the Rebel cause. Lt. Joseph Fry's 399-ton *Maurepas* was originally constructed as the *Grosse Tete* at New Albany, Indiana, during 1858. The side-wheeler was 180 feet long, with a 34 foot beam and a seven foot draft. Caught at New Orleans at the outbreak of the Civil War, she was purchased by the Confederate States of America in 1861, outfitted with five guns, and assigned to Cdr. Hollins. The *Maurepas* arrived at New Madrid, Missouri, on March 12, 1862. Writing about her after the White River battle of June 17, *New York World* correspondent Richard T. Colburn stated she was "partially placed [protected] with flat railroad iron." He also believed she "was formerly the towboat *Ivy* of New Orleans."

Major General Thomas Hindman (1828–1868) left the Shiloh battlefield to take over command of the Confederate Trans-Mississippi Department. Hindman, a believer in unconventional and irregular warfare, attempted to cut off Federal resupply via the White River to the army of Major General Samuel Curtis. This defense led to the June Battle of St. Charles in which the ironclad *Mound City* was nearly destroyed (*Battles and Leaders*).

Also arriving at New Madrid in March was Lt. John W. Dunnington's *Pontchartrain*. Her lineage is uncertain; in the prewar period she was known as the *Lizzie Simmons* or the *Eliza Simmons*. In any event, the 454-ton merchantman also was purchased at New Orleans, on October 12, 1861, and converted to a warship with seven guns. Dunnington's side-wheeler was 204 feet long, with a 36.6 foot beam and a 10 foot draft. Her depth of hold made it very difficult for her to operate on the White or Arkansas rivers and largely accounts for her inactivity prior to her deliberate destruction on October 9, 1863.

The *Pontchartrain* was held at Little Rock; however, Maj. Gen. Hindman personally ordered the *Maurepas* into the White. There she was to "capture or destroy the supplies collected at Grand Glaise and Jacksonport and to alarm the enemy by threatening his communication with Batesville." Her adventures between May 22 and June 6 were recorded in messages from Fry to Hindman, quoted by newsman Colburn in the June 30 issue of the *New*

York World. Her logbook, seized by U.S. forces, allowed the journalist to reveal the Rebel gunboat's movements from May 29 to June 12.

Additionally, Confederate engineers planned blocking points. Having learned about Northern gunboat vulnerabilities at Fort Donelson, locations were sought where heavy cannon could be mounted to deliver a plunging fire on targets below them. The choke point chosen for the Arkansas River was 50 miles above its mouth. There, at a place called the Post of Arkansas, work was immediately launched on an earthenwork bastion to be known as Fort Hindman. The little hamlet of St. Charles, on the White River, offered the greatest possibilities for the protection of that stream and plans were immediately made to plant batteries on the high bluffs behind the village. The community itself was at a rough S-shaped bend in the river reminiscent of the one near New Madrid on the Mississippi.[4]

While Hindman was occupied with attempting to salvage the defense of Arkansas, Capt. Davis received a message that would send the two serviceable timberclads, and several other warships, directly into the face of the ex-congressman's guerrilla army. Maj. Gen. Samuel R. Curtis, who had earlier won the victory at Pea Ridge, was frustrated in his effort to march his Army of the Southwest from Missouri to northeastern Arkansas. Out of supplies and forage and harassed by Rebel guerrillas, Curtis fell back behind the White River near Batesville and petitioned Maj. Gen. Halleck for help. Later, he would transfer to Jacksonport at the confluence of the White and Black rivers.

When the Curtis message, sent via wire from St. Louis, reached Corinth on June 8, the western commander, who appeared to some to have been erratic of late, sprang into action. The telegraph sang again with pleas for support, this time to both Secretary of War Stanton and Capt. Davis. Due to technical problems and outages caused by irregulars, both Stanton and Davis received their messages two days later. Like Halleck, both moved. The secretary forwarded his to Navy Secretary Welles asking the former Connecticut newspaperman to order Davis' support, while Davis was already acting on Halleck's request, planning an expedition to open army communications on the White River.[5]

In response to the Army entreaty, Capt. Davis revised an earlier scheme he had devised to chase Confederate steamers and the few gunboats reported to be in the White and Arkansas rivers. His plan was, instead, scaled back to an ascent up the White River to Jacksonport. Knowing that the Arkansas stream was falling and short of lighter-draught gunboats, Davis sought Charles Ellet's cooperation in a joint enterprise. Ellet, who was dying, responded by saying the request was made on very short notice and, if it were to be granted, Davis would have to surrender command of the expedition to Ellet's associate, U.S. Army Lt. George E. Currie.

Although Davis would gain use of the three available Ellet rams and one of the soldier's tugs, he could not bring himself to agree to a force "acting under divided authority." Consequently, Davis called upon his senior captain, Augustus H. Kilty of the U.S.S. *Mound City*, to put together a small task group and lead it on an expedition to White River. Upon his arrival, according to Davis' orders quoted by *New York Tribune* reporter Junius Henri Browne, he would ascend 350 miles upstream to Jacksonport and supply Curtis with provisions. Additionally, he was to capture the transports "the Rebels were supposed to have stolen and concealed there."[6]

Cmdr. Kilty's group included the *Mound City* as flagship, plus the Pook turtle *St. Louis*, the timberclad *Lexington*, towing a coal barge, and the tugboat *Spitfire*. Delays in assembling the force pushed back the expedition's departure date until June 13. Early that Friday morning, the four boats got underway for the White River, 181 miles below. News then came in that the Confederates had sunk a heavy timber raft in the lower reaches of that target stream and were planning to defend it with sharpshooters and artillery.

Early in the afternoon, Task Group Kilty passed the mouth of the St. Francis River. At this point, the *Mound City* signaled the others to "round to" and steam back up the Mississippi. While the warships anchored at the bar off the entrance to the St. Francis, the *Spitfire* was directed to steam up that stream on a brief reconnaissance. The tug returned an hour later to report that large stacks of cotton bales awaited shipment from the steamboat landing. Making a mental note to possibly return and seize the valuable commodity, Kilty, pressed for time, ordered his vessels to stand down the river again.

The Union warships rounded the point above Helena, Arkansas, at 3:00 P.M., according to the *Lexington*'s logbook. Glasses, sweeping the "beautiful little town," situated as it was on a sparse plain, spied a steamer at the wharf. Kilty immediately ordered speed increased; under a full head of steam, the task group went down as fast as possible in order to prevent the transport from getting away or her captain from ordering her torched. Cmdr. Kilty's suspicions were correct. Hardly was the smoke from the warships seen upriver than the large transport, soon identified as the *Clara Dolson*, backed out, rounded to, and started down the Mississippi.

Later appraised by the government as what Capt. Davis called "one of the largest, handsomest, and in every respect, finest steamers on the river," the 852-ton Confederate merchantman was 268 feet long, with a beam of 42 feet and an 8 foot, 9 inch depth of hold. Built at Cincinnati the previous year, her great speed came from the five boilers employed to power her two 9-foot by 28-inch paddle wheels. As the steamer sped away, the *Mound City*, half a mile closer to her than any of the other warboats, fired one of its big Dahlgren guns ahead of her, but the resulting geyser only increased the fugitive's speed. As the Pook turtle aimed another 8-inch shot, the *Spitfire* was sent in pursuit. Soon both the fleeing transport, great clouds of smoke puffing up from her twin chimneys, and the Yankee tug were pulling far ahead of the task group.

Kilty, uncertain whether or not a small auxiliary like the *Spitfire* could take the big Rebel steamer, next ordered Mr. Browne to take six hands and row his private gig back to the tailing *Lexington*. The fastest warship of the three would be enlisted in the chase. When Browne reached the side of the timberclad about five minutes later, the gig was tied off to the barge and the master's mate clamored aboard and relayed Kilty's order to Lt. Shirk. Hardly had Browne jumped back into his little craft than the barge was cut adrift and the *Lexington* surged ahead, her great wheels throwing up sheets of river water. Already her hands were beat to quarters as the black gang in the boiler room stoked her fires. The coal barge was quickly captured and made fast by the *St. Louis*. Browne and his men, who all drifted momentarily with the barge, were invited aboard the ironclad to watch what they could of the great steamboat race.

From the upper deck of the *St. Louis*, the *Spitfire* was seen to be gaining upon the *Clara Dolson*. Soon, the *Lexington* was almost abreast of the *Mound City* and the two warships appeared almost as in a race. Within a few minutes, however, the flagship signaled the wooden gunboat to move ahead. As the timberclad passed, she was cheered by sailors aboard the turtle. Thereafter, the tugboat, ironclad, and timberclad ran out of sight of the *St. Louis*. Mate Browne, the ironclad's new skipper, Lt. Wilson McGunnegle, and the rest of the crew could thereafter "once in a while ... see them six or eight miles off."

As the chase continued, the water pump for the *Spitfire*'s boilers broke down and she was forced to stop and round to. The *Lexington* continued on, passing her within an hour of first taking up the pursuit. The *Mound City* fell way behind, with the *St. Louis* bringing up the rear with the coal barge. As twilight turned into night, the ironclads anchored at Island No. 66. In the darkness, a bright light appeared ahead and many on the Union craft thought

In a joint expedition up the White River in June 1862, Col. Graham Newell Fitch and Captain Augustus Kilty attempted to reach with relief supplies a force under Brig. Gen. Samuel Curtis believed trapped in Arkansas. Led by the *Mound City* and *St. Louis*, with the *Conestoga* and *Lexington*, the task group was engaged near St. Charles and a Confederate shot into the steam drum of the *Mound City* resulted in significant casualties. The gunboat depicted in the left center of this drawing is one of the timberclads (*Harper's Weekly*, 1862, via the Naval Historical Center).

it was the *Clara Dolson* being burned. It turned out to be cotton, set alight by its Southern owners to prevent it falling into Northern hands. This practice became endemic as the task group approached. Up the White, seaman from the C.S.S. *Maurepas* participated in the destruction under direct orders from Maj. Gen. Hindman; indeed, the Confederate sailors had orders "should the citizens interfere, to fire upon them."

The *Lexington*, meanwhile, pursued her quarry to within 15 miles of the mouth of White River. Darkness and her superior speed enabled the *Dolson* to escape. The timberclad, unwilling

Capt. Augustus H. Kilty (1807–1879) was skipper of the Pook turtle *Mound City* at the battles of Plum Point Bend and Memphis (April–June 1862) and led the naval component of the first White River expedition in June. When the *Mound City* was hit and exploded during the action at St. Charles, Kilty was badly wounded, losing his left arm. Billeted ashore for most of the remainder of his career, he was named a rear admiral on the Retired List in 1870 (Naval Historical Center).

to proceed alone in the dark so far in advance of her companions, dropped anchor about 9:00 P.M. off the abandoned Confederate earthworks on Island No. 69. By 4:30 A.M. on June 14, the other boats of Cmdr. Kilty's task group, including the repaired *Spitfire*, had come up with the *Lexington*. After the coal barge was transferred back to the timberclad from the *St. Louis*, all four craft were once again en route down the river. Three and a half hours later, the Union flotilla arrived off Montgomery's Point at the mouth of the White River. Responding to a signal from the *Mound City*, the vessels entered that stream and came to.

Fortuitously, a small skiff was crossing the stream just as the Northern boats were dropping their hooks and it was hailed. The little boat's occupant, undoubtedly frightened by the huge naval cannon protruding from a number of Yankee gunports, freely answered inquiries. Cmdr. Kilty was informed by the boatman that several steamers were, indeed, up the White River and that a big recently arrived one named the *Clara Dolson* was hiding above in a small creek. After learning that their potential prize was near, all four Federal craft departed the confluence and steamed the six miles up the White to the Arkansas River Cut-off, where they came to anchor. Taking 50 tars aboard the *Spitfire*, First Master Cyrenius Dominy, executive officer of the *Mound City*, led a reconnaissance mission upstream.

Coming up with the secreted *Clara Dolson* in Bayou Lareux, about 15 miles above the task group anchorage, Dominy sent a boarding party from the *Spitfire* over the big steamer's side. There her officers were informed that they were POWs and their vessel and its cargo of 100 cotton bales was a prize of the Western Flotilla. With Federal gunboatmen at the controls and in the engine room, the *Clara Dolson* made steam back down the White River. In mid-afternoon, as she and the tug approached Kilty's vessels, the gunboat captains, seeing the approaching chimney smoke, were initially concerned. Fearing a possible Confederate attack, they sent their crews to their battle stations.

When the *Spitfire* rounded a bend, followed by the *Dolson*, and both became visible, spontaneous cheers erupted from the men aboard the *Lexington* and the ironclads. The former Rebel transport anchored near the *Mound City*, permitting Cmdr. Kilty to easily inspect the vessel, a potential source of prize money for all hands. After his visit, Kilty determined to send the big side-wheeler to Memphis next morning, along with dispatches. That night, the Union warships lay to, "tortured dreadfully," according to *Lexington* sailor Fred Wise, "by musquitoes [sic]."

Col. Graham Newell Fitch commanded the land force component of the June 1862 White River expedition. It was his soldiers who charged the Confederate St. Charles defenses and ended Rebel gunfire against sailors escaping from the badly damaged Pook turtle *Mound City*. The physician and former Indiana U.S. senator was the older half brother of Lieut. Cmdr. LeRoy Fitch, who commanded the *Lexington* on the Cumberland River in the spring of 1863 (John T. Fitch).

Also during the day, the chartered steamer *White Cloud*, loaded with supplies for the Army of the Southwest, arrived at Memphis from St. Louis. Her captain immediately called upon Capt. Davis asking for escort. Davis, who was expecting the request, had already sent up to Columbus for the timberclad *Conestoga* and tasked Lt. George Blodgett for the duty. What he did not have was marines to clear away the rumored Rebel raft.

Meeting with Col. Fitch, the navy chief provided a verbal briefing of the White River enterprise and asked for his help (which request was so important as to also be put into writing), even going so far as to remind him of Maj. Gen. John Pope's original orders that the Hoosier soldiers cooperate with his flotilla. Graham Newell Fitch, a former U.S. senator, quickly appreciated the gravity of the situation as Capt. Davis outlined it. If his men did not help the bluejackets, they would be unable to run supplies up to Curtis, who would be trapped and maybe lost. By evening, Col. Fitch had the men of the 46th Indiana embarked upon the steamer *New National*.[7]

At 5:00 A.M. on June 15, the Hoosier expedition pushed off. With the *Conestoga*, accompanied by the tug *Spiteful*, in the van, the steamers *Jacob Musselman*, *New National*, and *White Cloud* steamed downstream, attempting to catch up with Cmdr. Kilty's *Mound City* group. Having learned of the Fitch mission, those warships remained anchored at the Arkansas River Cut-off awaiting the soldiers' arrival. The downriver passage, though made at all deliberate speed, was still rather leisurely for the soldiers and crewmen aboard the *Musselman*, *New National*, and *White Cloud*. Those not familiar with the vessels had ample opportunity to become acquainted with them.

Built at Paducah in 1860, the 144-ton stern-wheeler *Jacob Musselman* was one of the many civilian steamers employed to transport Union soldiers to Fort Donelson back in February, and to Pittsburg Landing in March. Home-ported at Paducah before the war, she was the smallest and most maneuverable of the three merchantmen sent to White River. The *New National*, on the other hand, was prized at Memphis on June 6. Constructed at Cincinnati in 1851, the 317-ton side-wheeler was 178 feet long, with a beam of 29 feet and a 6 foot, 5 inch depth of hold. Although the number is not recorded, it would have required at least four to six boilers to provide her power. She would remain with the Western Flotilla, and its successor, the Mississippi Squadron, throughout the war. The *White Cloud* was also part of the Fort Donelson and Shiloh invasion fleets. Built at McKeesport, Pennsylvania, in 1857, the 345-ton side-wheeler was originally home-ported at St. Louis. Her dimensions are unknown.

At some point in the afternoon, the *Conestoga*'s convoy met the *Clara Dolson* passing up, escorted by the tugboat *Spitfire*. Making rendezvous in midstream, the two groups briefly came to as Lt. Blodgett hailed the *Dolson*, seeking information from her acting captain, Third Master James Fitzpatrick of the *Lexington*. After briefly detailing the capture of the huge transport, Fitzpatrick told Blodgett that Cmdr. Kilty was awaiting him at the Arkansas River Cut-off. The two groups now took their leave of one another, continuing on to their destinations. For the *Conestoga* and her flock, that was the mouth of the White River, where all anchored for the night.

The *Conestoga* task group entered the White River at 5:25 A.M. on June 16. At the Cut-off, lookouts reported a huge cloud of smoke downriver. Expecting Blodgett, Cmdr. Kilty signaled his fellow captains to beat to quarters, build heads of steam, and make ready to raise anchor. As soon as the *Conestoga* hove into sight, anchors were raised and the *Mound City* waved for the newcomers to fall in line and, without a pause, follow his warships up the White. Given the shape of the river, a smaller tributary than the Cumberland or the Tennessee, the boats proceeded in single file. Cmdr. Kilty's flag boat led the parade, the *St. Louis* followed in her wake, and the wooden boats were about a half mile behind. If no obstructions were found, it was expected that the little flotilla could steam right up the White all the way to DeVall's Bluff, 75 miles above St. Charles. A railroad met the river at that point, linking it with Little Rock 45 miles to the west.

At this time, the White River could be navigated by steamboats in all stages of water for about 350 miles, up to the mouth of the Black River, which was, of course, higher than Kilty planned to go. During high water, boats could ascend 50 miles further to Batesville, below which point the channel was about four-feet deep all year. This is not to say it was an easy ride. Churning up the White all day Monday, the trip was rather boring; nothing of consequence was met nor, in the words of Junius Henri Browne, was there "the least exciting occurrence."

In his review of the week's action, newsman Browne noted that, while the stream was very deep, it was very narrow, "being in some places no more than two hundred yards from bank to bank." As on the Cumberland and the Mississippi above Memphis, there were tall bluffs, or ridges. These often rose to heights of 30–50 feet. "Almost anywhere on the White," Browne told his readers, "a skilled marksman could shoot an enemy in the middle of the river, and in many places, on the opposite bank." A key, as always, was to locate snipers' nests and hidden batteries before they could fire.

The Union gunboats and transports paddled about fifty miles up the river, dropping anchor at 4:30 in the afternoon at a point some 77 miles above the river's mouth, although the spot chosen was, as E. M. "Ned" Spencer of the *Cincinnati Daily Times* had it, "quite deep, but ... very narrow." As the expedition's land and nautical commanders both had intelligence that the river was blocked at St. Charles, some eight miles above, it seemed prudent to stop and scout.

Col. Fitch and Cmdr. Kilty, acting in consultation, decided to send a reconnaissance toward St. Charles. Lt. Charles A. Brownlee of the 46th was detailed to take a detachment along the shore, while Lt. Franklin Swigart and his men would board the *Spiteful* and proceed upstream, keeping abreast of Brownlee, who had the more difficult assignment of hiking through the underbrush. According to Rebel sources, the tug sent in advance had "a Confederate flag and a flag of truce, both flying." The white bunting was in the bow and the ensign aft. Several hours were required to slowly and cautiously conduct the survey and the two scouting groups became separated. By and by, back at the fleet anchorage, a report was heard from the *Spiteful*'s howitzer, as well as several other smaller guns, probably muskets, fired quickly in succession.

The tugboat returned to report having been fired on from both sides of the river. Lt. Swigart reported "rebels and boats ahead," though he had opened fire on Rebel pickets before rounding to. Eventually, Brownlee's sweaty men came back and their report was somewhat more detailed. The Confederates, he said, had placed two infantry-protected batteries at St. Charles, both zeroed in on the river. Neither lieutenant could guess at the number of supporting Southern soldiers deployed near the city. Maj. Gen. Hindman later said there were 79.[8]

In fact, the Confederate defenders of the White River had been busily preparing the St. Charles area to withstand just such a Federal advance as now confronted them. Two gun emplacements were thrown up on a high bluff back from the left bank of the river. The upper battery was outfitted with a pair of rifled 32-pdrs. unshipped from the C.S.S. *Pontchartrain*, then at Little Rock, by her captain, 1st Lt. John W. Dunnington, and sent down to St. Charles by rail and water. These two pieces were joined by a pair of 3-inch fieldpieces the navy man found in the capital city arsenal.

On June 14, the C.S.S. *Maurepas*, under Lt. Joseph Fry, arrived at St. Charles. At a key location just above the main battery, the small gunboat was anchored athwart the river. Fry announced that he would soon be unshipping the guns of his command and having them transported ashore. First, however, the stores would be removed.

In the days before the Yankees arrived, Capt. A.M. Williams, Hindman's chief engineer, was sent down from Little Rock to establish the St. Charles defenses and block the river. A 100-man detail, including 35 armed soldiers from the 29th Arkansas, cut down trees in the woods behind the town. The cleared logs were floated downstream in great rafts where a pair of steam pile drivers, also forwarded, were employed to drive them into the river bottom.

Word was received by Maj. Gen. Hindman at his Little Rock headquarters on June 16 concerning the advance of Cmdr. Kilty's task group. The general knew that the St. Charles defenses were not yet finished and, even if they were, there were insufficient soldiers to man them. Unable to find any soldiers, Hindman turned to Lt. Duningham and the men of the *Pontchartrain*. The gunboat's captain, who had accompanied the cannon to St. Charles from Little Rock a few days before, four officers, and 30 enlisted tars volunteered to join in the St. Charles defense. Taking the train to DeVall's Bluff, the sailors boarded a waiting steamer and arrived at the river obstructions about 6:00 P.M.

Stepping ashore, Dunnington was immediately met by Capt. Williams. Together, the two ascended the bluff and even without their glasses were able to spy the dense cloud of steamer smoke puffing up into the sky. Hardly had the officers descended than scouts arrived on sweaty horses to announce that the Yankees were coming. Lt. Duningham and the *Pontchartrain* crewmen now manned the upper battery while Lt. Fry hastily set to sending ashore the *Maurepas* battery, which was placed under the command of Midshipman Francis M. Roby. A 12-pdr. brass howitzer from the *Maurepas* was provided to Capt. Williams 35 infantrymen, who dragged it down and placed it where they thought they could best guard the land approaches to the batteries. When the Federals were upon them, overall command of the St. Charles fort was entrusted to Fry, a prewar U.S. Navy lieutenant, well known by several local Union officers, including Lt. John A. Winslow of the *Cincinnati* and Lt. McGunnegle of the *St. Louis*. He was the senior officer of either Rebel service on the field.

Darkness descended upon St. Charles without an attack. This was communicated to Maj. Gen. Hindman, along with confirmation that the obstructions in the river were not finished.

There was at this time three vessels tied up above the St. Charles obstructions. Two were transports, the *Eliza G.* and *Mary Patterson*, and the third was Capt. Fry's gunboat C.S.S. *Maurepas*. Aboard the latter, Fry and his men were working hastily to unship their craft's two rifled 3-inch guns and two 12-pdrs. brass howitzers. All would be hauled ashore and mounted in a lower battery 400 yards below the *Pontchartrain* guns. The *Eliza G.* had ventured to Augusta from Memphis on June 8 with provisions for the *Maurepas*. Previously known as *Dr. Buffington*, the 262-ton side-wheeler was constructed at Cincinnati and home-ported there before the war. The *Mary Patterson*, on the other hand, was a 105-ton stern-wheeler, built locally at Grand Glaize, Arkansas, in 1859 and home-ported at Memphis.

By the evening of June 16, Hindman, Fry and the others at the St. Charles choke point knew that Cmdr. Kity's gunboats were coming and would probably attack in the morning. In an effort to further augment the defense, a tough decision was taken by Hindman. The three boats were ordered sunk as a line of obstructions. It was expected that this blockade would, as a participant told the *Mobile Tribune*, "make him [Kilty] fight our rifled guns." All night the Confederates worked to scuttle their boats. Lt. Fry and his men placed the *Maurepas* in what was determined to be a key location and then chopped holes in her bottom. Fry was the last man off as the water submerged the vessel's gun deck.

No ballast was available to place aboard the transports and their hasty scuttling was not altogether successful. In sinking, the *Eliza G.* was dragged out of position by the current, leaving a 60-foot gap big enough for a large gunboat to get through. The first rays of dawn appeared in the east as the sailors returned ashore. The time had arrived for Fry to join Roby's battery and assume command.[9]

When sunlight first lightened the Union anchorage around 5:30 A.M., sailors aboard the gunboats were horrified to see murky shapes descending upon them from above. Upon closer inspection, the unknown beasts, believed to be rafts or some other infernal contraptions, were found to be lost cotton bales. In the confusion and the noise of alarms and whistles, the transports *New National* and *White Cloud*, moving to avoid the danger, collided. Fortunately for the Northern expedition, neither was badly damaged and no one was hurt. A half hour later, the *White Cloud* took over towing the *Lexington*'s coal barge.

The Kilty-Fitch strategy for an assault on St. Charles was relatively simple: the gunboats would attack the Rebel emplacements from the river while the Indiana soldiers, having been landed, came against them from behind. This is the same plan that Graham Fitch's brother, Lt. Col. Le Roy Fitch, and Brig. Gen. Richard Johnson would employ against the Confederate batteries at Bell's Mill, near Nashville, in December 1864. The gunboats moved out at 6 A.M. on June 17, steaming slowly upstream in single file. Every man was at his station and all of the big guns were manned. As the Yankees passed a point some two and a half miles below St. Charles, lookouts aboard the *Mound City* and other boats spotted Confederate outriders. These scouts were keeping tabs on their progress of the Federals from the woods on the right bank of the White. Several spurred their steeds back to St. Charles and informed Capt. Fry that the Federals were approaching.

Appraised of the butternut observers, Cmdr. Kilty called to his gun captains to open fire. At 7:36 A.M., the great guns of the flag boat opened fire, spraying the shore with grape and canister. They were quickly followed into action by those aboard the *St. Louis*. There is no indication that this deadly burst caused casualties among the Rebel pickets. In accordance with their amphibious plan, Cmdr. Kilty dispatched the *Spiteful* back to the *New National* to inform Col. Fitch that the time was ripe to land the landing force. Sliding over into the bank, the *National* and the *Jacob Musselman* disembarked Companies A, B, and G of the 46th Indiana. The unit's historian remembered going ashore "about two miles below the town and just below where a little bayou put out."

Once Fitch's units were formed up, they began marching through the woods and foliage toward St. Charles, climbing up to within 300 yards of the top of the bluff where the 32-pounders were mounted. As they waited, Signal Corps Lt. George Gray and two soldiers were sent to scout the enemy "fort."[10] The ironclad Yankee gunboats began a close-in protective bombardment along the shores while the Hoosier troops climbed. *New York Tribune* reporter Junius Henri Browne later observed that Kilty's fire was designed to not only obtain early indication of Rebel locations, but also to cleanse "various localities [that] offered fine opportunities for ambuscade."

Just before 8:00 A.M., the *Spiteful* sped back past the transports to their shepherd, the *Lexington*, with orders for her to move ahead. Within minutes, the timberclad was beat to quarters, had steamed up ahead of the troopboats, and added the fire from her No. 1 thirty-pdr. Parrott gun to that from the other warships. The Kilty-Fitch plan called for land-sea (a later term, admittedly) movement coordination. As the Hoosiers slogged along, the gunboats were to keep pace, shelling the woods in front of the Indiana troops. Slowly paddling along, the two ironclads and two timberclads blasted targets, seen and unseen, on both sides of the river.

There was a slight pause around 8:45 A.M. when the Hoosier soldiers signaled that the gunboats were proceeding too quickly. The *Spiteful* went up to take a message from Fitch and the watery parade resumed 10 minutes later. Within five minutes of this exchange, the Yankee gunboat column rounded a White River bend and its tars sighted the sunken superstructures of the *Maurepas*, *Eliza G.* and *Mary Patterson* rising from the waters swirling around them. It was estimated that the trio was about a mile ahead near a second bend in the stream. A bluff rose from the west bank abreast of the steamer barricade. Heavily wooded, the hill kept its secrets, and the bluejackets, despite the use of their spyglasses, could make out no masked batteries.

Before 7:00 A.M., the hidden Confederates manned their cannon and sent a howitzer and a line of sharpshooters under Capt. Williams along the river below the lower battery.[11] As Cmdr. Kilty prepared to move ahead around the bend, he signaled the commanders of the *Lexington* and *Conestoga*. They were not to engage any masked batteries that were found. The task group leader, believing his cannonade was effective, pushed the gunboats "boldly on" around the bend below the bluff. Everywhere on both sides of the river explosions from their shells continued to knock down trees, clear the underbrush, and excavate great sections of shoreline. Still, none of the gunboatmen knew for certain where the foe was lurking.

As soon as the timberclads rounded the point trailing the ironclads, they stopped, becoming as they had at Forts Henry and Donelson, something of a second division. The two anchored abreast of one another, with the *Lexington* on the right, prepared to offer covering fire to the Pook turtles. Like the lookouts aboard the *Mound City* and *St. Louis*, the men aboard the old gunboats also failed to sight any hostile gun emplacements. When the *Mound City* was just about abreast of the lower Confederate battery, Capt. Fry gave the order to open fire. Midshipman Roby's *Maurepas* gunners launched three projectiles directly at Cmdr. Kilty's vessel — but all three bounced off.

The battery was so well hidden among the trees that the Federal sailors still could not see its exact location. Instead, the smoke from Roby's guns gave away the Southern position and brought an immediate response from gunners aboard the *Mound City* and *St. Louis*. In the next 15 minutes, neither side seemed to gain an advantage. Fighting bows on, the two ironclads, their wheels turning just fast enough to keep them stationary in the current, pounded away at Fry and Roby. At least two shells, E.M. "Ned" Spencer reported, hit the *St. Louis*, but the rest "passed over the deck."

The Rebel gunners, protected by their earthwork, were unhurt. "The entire vicinity was enveloped in a vail of smoke," wrote "W," "through which the flames glared red from the mouths of the cannon, as through the darkness of night." The smoke billowing above the trees ahead gave the captains of the *Lexington* and *Conestoga* some idea of the Confederate location. Lt. Shirk and Blodgett, after cautioning them to aim carefully, permitted their bow gunners to shoot toward the target area.

The tars aboard the "old boats" could not see the enemy gunners concealed behind the river bend, but certainly tasted their wrath. "Their balls whistled freely over and around us," remembered Seaman Wise aboard the *Lexington*. The shots struck "the water some 20 yards in front of us, and ricocheting some 10 feet over our heads, with that peculiar whistling sound by which a rifled ball can always be distinguished."

During the ship-shore exchange, Lt. Dunnington waited, keeping his powder dry and his location secret. From the gunboats, correspondent Spencer wrote later, it appeared as though the Southern enemy was "fatigued with his efforts and fired only at intervals."

Around 10:00 A.M., Cmdr. Kilty, believing his boats were gaining the upper hand, ordered the *Mound City* to ease ahead, leaving the first battery to the *St. Louis*. When the flag boat was within point-blank range (approximately half a mile) Dunnington's lower rifled 32-pdr. spat out a 68-pdr. Read projectile, which narrowly missed. This cylindrical shot with iron flanges on each side was known by the Confederates, according to reporters Browne and Spencer, as a "pigeon-shot." The first one flew on to cut the branches off a tree 200 yards behind the ironclad before burying itself deep in the opposite bank.

The *Mound City*, faced with a second battery, immediately came to. Her bow gunners opened fire on the new menace. As her shells harassed the lower Confederate cannon, Lt. Dunnington waved permission for the upper piece to fire. It scored a hit on its first discharge, though the Read noisily ricocheted off the gunboat's casemate. Cmdr. Kilty now ordered the *Mound City* to move still closer, coming within 600 yards. Both his boat, struck 15 times already, and the *St. Louis* behind poured 8-inch shells from their bow guns at Dunnington, and lesser projectiles from their other cannon at Fry and Roby. At this point, Capt. Fry was advised that Col. Fitch was advancing upon Capt. Williams and signaling Kilty to cease fire that he might charge the Rebel defenses without fear of "friendly fire." A few unneeded hands were sent by Fry to assist Williams' soldiers.

It was only about three minutes from the time Lt. Dunnington's upper cannon engaged the *Mound City* to the time the boat suffered catastrophe. At 10:03 A.M., according to the *Lexington*'s logbook, the timberclad's men "suddenly observed steam coming out of all the port holes of the *Mound City*, soon enveloping the ship." As the *Mound City* engaged from her inshore position, there was a great explosion. A 68-pound Read projectile from Dunnington's upper battery smashed into the portside casemate near the first gun at about a 90 degree angle. It passed through the casemate and its heavy timber backing, in the words of the *Chicago Daily Tribune* reporter "W," "as if it was an inch board." Flying on, it killed a gunner on the starboard side and alighted in the steward's pantry.

If that were not bad enough, worse still was the fact that, as it entered, the Read severed the turtle's steam drum — a large cylinder or "pipe" connecting the boilers. The shrill hissing sound was ghastly as the boat quickly filled with scalding steam. As the ironclad was closed up, there was no way for the hot vapors— or most of their victims— to escape except through the gunports or skylights. The ironclad's crewmen in that disastrous minute were largely driven overboard into the river, many horribly burned. "The water was full of men struggling with the swift current," Seaman Wise remembered, one which swept the lucky "away to a speedy death."

The stricken vessel drifted to the right bank of the river, where Capt. Fry called upon the few survivors aboard to lower their flag. When this didn't occur, Fry reportedly ordered his men "to shoot all in the water that attempted to escape." Wrote correspondent Browne, "The devilish enemy needed no second bidding." A number of men in the water were hit several times and at least a dozen sank out of sight. Lt. Gray and his men, secreted upon a knoll, saw the tragedy and also witnessed that "the enemy then came out of the fort and rushed the river bank, firing at the men in the water and on the boats ... they shot and killed all they could." Some of the Confederate bushwhackers, as related by a Southern source, even ran up to the stranded *Mound City* and "put their hands on her anchor stock in a token of triumph."

Some years later, when Jeanie Mort Walker published her biography of Fry, by then known as the "Cuban Martyr," she included a number of interviews (most anonymous) with eyewitnesses, all of whom denied the charges that Fry ordered his men to fire. "I know them [the assertions] to be false," commented U.S.S. *St. Louis* executive officer John V. Johnston, a former packet captain. "They never had any foundation whatever." Fry himself reportedly admitted, "in after times when 'fighting his battles o'er again,'" stationing riflemen to open fire on Yankee small boats reportedly moving to cut off his retreat.

Reacting swiftly to the disaster aboard the flag boat, Lt. Shirk and Lt. Blodgett immediately ordered their gigs lowered and sent to save survivors. Ignoring the fire from Fry's men, the gunboatmen pulled many of their horribly burned fellows from the brown water. According to the *Tribune*'s "W," a shot passed through the *Conestoga*'s launch, but killed no one." His impression was contradicted by Seaman Wise on the *Lexington*, who noted that a shot went "through the launch of the *Conestoga*, which was filled with scaled men, killing and wounding several."

E.M. "Ned" Spencer of the *Cincinnati Daily Times* added that, in fact, each of the gigs was hit, one in the bow and one in the stern, "but "strange to say, they were not swamped, nor were they prevented from rescuing from the river some of the ill-fated crew." "J.B.W.," a battle participant and *Jackson Mississippian* correspondent, believed (so he stated in print) that the Union navy men were attempting "to land forces in small boats." These, the *Conestoga*'s gigs, "were fired upon by our howitzer and two of them cut to pieces and sunk." Spencer, the veteran of Shiloh, also tells us that a third boat, from the *St. Louis*, was "shattered to pieces, but none of the inmates were hurt or drowned." One of these may have been among those seen by "J.W.B."

In a few minutes, numbers of scalded men were aboard the *Lexington* and *Conestoga*, taken to spots around the decks and even to the wardrooms. The stricken were gently handled by the many helpful men — "In such a case, everybody is a doctor," said Wise — and once their clothes were off, were "deluged with oil and flour" and covered with raw cotton. Besides screaming in pain, the dying constantly cried for water and more cooling water.

As the fight continued, the *St. Louis* moved to take up the firing. Dunnington and Lt. McGunnegle fought a tough duel, with neither side taking advantage. Meanwhile, Lt. Gray and his party, briefly detained by, but escaping from, Rebel pickets, made it back to report to Col. Fitch. "Do you suppose I can take the works from the rear?" asked the Hoosier; Gray replied "yes," so, 10 minutes after the *Mound City* disaster, Fitch ordered the gunboats to cease firing.

Led by Gray and Fitch, the 46th Indiana then carried the Rebel position "in the most dashing and gallant manner, and with no loss of [bluecoat] life." Eight Southern defenders were killed in the attack and 29 were captured, including a wounded Capt. Fry. "A portion of insurgents," including Dunnington and Williams, wrote Spencer, made their way to a number of small boats moored by the obstructions, "crossed the stream and disappeared in the woods."

With no further fortifications upriver and only the *Ponchartrain* upstream to offer nautical resistance, the costly St. Charles victory in effect gave the North at least temporary control of the White River. As the action ended, the *Lexington* and *Conestoga*, accompanied by the *Spiteful*, proceeded up to the *Mound City*. The latter two lashed onto the ironclad and towed her downstream a mile. The effort was complicated by the pilot of the New National, who, not once but thrice, so poorly maneuvered his vessel as to hinder the extraction.

While the flag boat was being withdrawn downstream, the *St. Louis*, accompanied by the *Lexington*, steamed up to the mid-river obstruction. Boarding parties examined the steamer wrecks, finding official papers and a logbook in the cabin of the sunken *Maurepas*. Once Lt. McGunnegle was convinced that the St. Charles emplacements were truly won, he ordered the surviving units of the task group to congregate in the area of the tied up *Mound City*. Here every effort was made to ameliorate the suffering of the scalded men yet alive.

The Confederate shot into her steam drum left 125 of the *Mound City*'s 175-man crew dead or mortally wounded, one of the greatest single ship losses for the Union navy in the entire war. The deadly effects of pressurized steam, long known to steamboatmen, were made plain to landsmen and soldiers alike.

Screams from the wounded and dying broke morale among many of the surviving soldiers and sailors. Even Flag Officer David G. Farragut was repulsed; in an interview with Junius Henry Browne of the *New York Tribune*, the hero of New Orleans indicated that he "would rather be cut to pieces than touched with hot water." Initially, the gunboat commanders became reluctant to proceed and falling water only heightened their unease.[12]

Lt. McGunegle, now the senior naval officer, directed Doctors William H. Wilson of the *Conestoga* and George W. Garner of the *Lexington* to organize the care of the *Mound City* survivors. Both timberclads tied on to the stricken ironclad to help take care of the scalded men. Five *Lexington* tars were detailed aboard the *Conestoga* to assist the physicians. The injured were gently transferred aboard the *Conestoga* and the *Jacob Musselman*.

During this process, about 11:30 A.M., a badly burned gunner, "crazed with pain," grabbed the lanyard of the portside 8-inch *Mound City* bow gun and pulled. The giant piece went off, sending a charge of grape into the *New National*, passing through her engine forward of the wheel, cutting her port steam pipe. This time the steam, which was not trapped, quickly dissipated and there were few wounded beyond the engineer, who was badly scalded.

Amidst the horror and screams "of those whose skins had been stripped from them by the rush of the steam," McGunegle's inspection of the ironclad revealed not only a damaged warship, but one virtually without officers and men. The "butcher's bill" from the *Mound City* disaster was later determined to be 82 men killed by gunshot wounds or scalded to death, with 43 others drowned or shot while struggling in the water. Only three officers (not including Cmdr. Kilty, who survived but lost an arm) and 22 men escaped uninjured.

Col. Fitch and others were appalled by the "inhumanity" of Confederate attacks against the *Mound City* men who had jumped overboard. In his June 19 report of the action, Fitch recorded that scarcely had the sailors abandoned their ship before "A party of the enemy's sharpshooters descended the bluff from batteries and, under cover of fallen timber on the river bank, commenced murdering those who were struggling in the water, and also firing upon those in our boats sent to pick them up. At the same time, another party of the enemy, concealed in the timber on the opposite of the river, pursued the same barbarous course." Fitch went on to further express his outrage and that of his men: "So strongly marked was the contrast between this conduct on their part and that of our sailors and soldiers at Memphis, who risked their lives to save those of the enemy who had been driven into the river by steam or flames, as to excite an intense desire upon the part of the land forces to end the scene and punish the barbarity."

Although it appears likely that the Confederates were, as Donald Barnhart, Jr., has opined, "shooting at Union sailors trying to avoid capture and not the wounded who jumped overboard," Capt. Fry was, until such time as he convinced Northern authorities of his innocence, made the scapegoat. E.M. "Ned" Spencer told his subscribers that "The world is bad enough, God knows, but such villains as Fry, thank Heaven, are few."

If there was an officer who ordered his men to fire, it was Williams, not Fry. The engineer later stated that after the explosion he saw a number of men jump "into the water and into boats to escape the scalding steam that was pouring out of every hole and crevice." Damning himself, he confessed in his official report that "I immediately ordered all the sharpshooters, about 20 in number, to the river bank to shoot them." Williams controlled the sharpshooters and not Fry, as Fitch noted in his report.

Capt. Davis, upon hearing accounts of the tragedy, wrote home that the "scene of horror was rendered more frightful by the enemy's shooting our wounded and scalded men in the water and by firing into the boats of the other vessels of the squadron which came to the assistance of the poor, helpless, drowning, and scalded victims. This barbarous conduct on the part of the enemy "will lead to terrible retaliation. The men of the squadron are now very much excited and vow vengeance." David Dixon Porter, who would succeed Flag Officer Davis as squadron commander in October, later directly suggested that the ship's death toll was so high because Rebel sharpshooters purposely shot Union sailors struggling in the White River.

The commander of the *St. Louis*, far from Memphis support, was now faced with several simultaneous problems. First of all, he needed to determine what to do with the dead and injured, as well as the *Mound City* herself. Then, he would need to speak with Col. Fitch concerning the future of their joint expedition. Finding a temporary captain for the *Mound City* was McGunnegle's initial personnel problem. Gunnery officer Thomas McElroy had no navigational or other line experience, while her first master, Cyrenius Dominy, had panicked in the wake of the explosion and would have to be sent back to Memphis, to face either court-martial or hospitalization. Indeed, as his boat drifted into the right bank and the *St. Louis* came up, Dominy, standing in the stern, had called to McGunnegle at the top of his lungs, "Come and tow me down; we are all lost; we are all lost." The ironclad officer shouted back, telling Dominy to pipe down as the tug was en route to tow him and he was frightening the men. Historian Boynton later laid the uninjured Dominy's unsettlement to "the terror of the scene." The man's "bravery was never disputed" and he would eventually progress back up the command structure.

Quite possibly at Lt. Blodgett's suggestion, the veteran first master of the *Conestoga*, John A. Duble, was tapped to become the ironclad's acting captain. The latter extended his hand to Mr. Dominy and asked for his help. The ironclad's executive officer refused. Meanwhile, Col. Fitch was requested by Lt. McGunnegle to order a number of his soldiers to form burial details. Others would probably be needed to go aboard next day to help operate the stricken warship and perform other tasks. By late afternoon, most of the critically injured were transferred off the *Mound City*. Seamen from the Lexington put some 65 scalded men on the *Jacob Musselman*, but within a quarter of an hour of finishing the transfer, seven were carried out dead.

At 5:00 P.M., the *Conestoga*, accompanied by the *Musselman*, weighed for Memphis. The badly hurt Cmdr. Kilty was aboard the timberclad. After another inspection of the wreck site in early evening, McGunnegle and Fitch determined to push on the next day.

The captain of the *St. Louis* was told by his pilots that it would take several days to tow the powerless *Mound City* back down the narrow, twisting White River. At 8:00 P.M., the *Lexington* made fast to the ironclad and towed her up the White to the task group anchorage abreast the Confederate batteries. Once she was tied up to the trees on the west bank, Col. Fitch's soldiers filed aboard.

In addition to succoring the living, the soldiers had to bury the many dead. Wrapped in blankets, the bodies of 58 men were taken ashore from the *Mound City* by burial parties from the 46th Indiana. A mass grave had been prepared for them in the lower batteries. It was, according to the *Lexington*'s logbook, 2:00 next morning before all of the dead were removed ashore. After the war, all would be disinterred and moved elsewhere. To the great relief of many, the heat of the day was now cut, briefly, by a rainstorm.

Steaming down the White and up the Mississippi at forced draft, the *Conestoga* and *Musselman* could not make Memphis before four scalded hands died aboard the former and 21 on the latter. These men were taken ashore at Islands 67 and 68 in the Mississippi River and, after the customary prayer service read by Lt. Blodgett, interred "in a single grave, or square well." When the two steamers dropped anchor off the naval base at Memphis on June 19, the 41 survivors were immediately transferred aboard the *Red Rover*, the U.S. Navy's first hospital boat. Once he had seen them into the hands of the military doctors, Blodgett hastened to the *Benton* and reported to Flag Officer Davis.

In addition to a verbal recitation, the captain of the *Conestoga* also handed over Lt. McGunnegle's official report. Blodgett also noted that Capt. Fry was aboard the floating hospital, but that several other Confederate prisoners, transported to Memphis in irons, had been turned over to the provost marshal. While Blodgett was aboard the *Benton*, the other timberclad officers and sailors were immediately questioned by the many Northern "specials" in town. Initial brief accounts of the disaster soon hummed out across the telegraph to newspapers large and small. After filing his account, "W" of the *Chicago Daily Tribune* spent the day conversing with his colleagues and others on the subject. "This news," he revealed in a longer story penned that night, "is at present the all-absorbing topic in Memphis."[13]

On June 18, Col. Fitch, in response to Lt. McGunnegle's earlier request, sent a 46th Indiana lieutenant and 48 enlisted men to help clean up and operate the *Mound City*. The ship would be left at St. Charles, while the *St. Louis*, *Lexington*, *Spiteful* and the two transports pushed on upriver. A stringer from the *Cincinnati Daily Commercial* was now aboard the timberclad.

While the other gunboats were gone, First Master Duble was to organize his tars into "half watches and guns' crews," to keep all 20 of the Rebel prisoners not en route to Memphis in double irons, and to keep a sharp lookout for marauding Confederates. Led by the *St. Louis*, the relief expedition cast off at 2:15 P.M., "proceeded through the sunk boats," and headed up the White. With neither opposition nor difficulty, the ironclad, timberclad, tug and two transports made 10 miles before anchoring for the night near a sawmill.

Curious, Lt. McGunnegle sent a landing party ashore to gather intelligence from local citizens. A friendly man on the riverbank told the Federal sailors that a big force of Confederates from a nearby camp was en route toward St. Charles to recapture the place and, possibly, the damaged *Mound City*. To prevent surprise, the ironclad commander hastily sent the *Spiteful* back downsteam to warn Duble. Although the little tug quickly returned, putting the *Mound City* on alert, no attack developed. That night, "a copious rain, with hail and wind" cooled the atmosphere, the *Cincinnati Daily Commercial* man noted.

After passing Adams Bluff early on June 19, the gunboats and troopships were engaged in a running series of off-and-on firefights with Rebel soldiers and guerrillas firing at them from the woods and underbrush along the riverbank. The Hoosier soldiers on the *White Cloud* and *New National* were favorite targets and four Union men died in the attacks.

The task group passed Aberdeen just after lunch but no activity could be seen in the town. Paddling on, it came to abreast of Clarendon, a town about 53 miles east of Little Rock, at mid-afternoon. Under the intense sun, the shores were seen to be "lined with burned cotton." The *Commercial* special aboard the *Lexington* revealed that "there is considerable hidden back from the river." Col. Fitch went ashore to speak with persons gathered at the wharf who, although professing neutrality, were sternly warned that "firing on the boats from the banks of the river would not be permitted, and if it was connived at by the citizens, they would be held accountable and their property destroyed."

That evening, with the river stage still dropping, the *St. Louis* and her consorts reached Crooked Point Cut-off in Monroe County, 63 miles above St. Charles and approximately 15 miles distant from Devall's Bluff. Due to "a scarcity of White River pilots" aboard the gunboats, noted the *Lexington* newsman, as well as the river stage, "we are unable to run nights."

The commanders of the *St Louis* and *Lexington*, alarmed by the fall of the river, sought mission prognostication from the only knowledgeable White River pilot available, the veteran aboard the *White Cloud*. He warned the officers of the dangers and they, in turn, informed an unhappy Fitch that the expedition must turn back. Although the soldier met personally with the transport pilot and argued strenuously against retreat, the advance was abandoned. Next morning the boats dropped back down toward St. Charles. En route, the *St. Louis* touched bottom twice in places where, a few days earlier, there was two feet of water to spare.

When first sighted, the smoke and sparks from the *St. Louis*, *Lexington*, and the army transports caused First Master Duble to send all *Mound City* hands to battle stations. There was great relief aboard the stricken ironclad that June 20 when McGunnegle rounded the bend above. In the cool of the evening, mechanics from the *St. Louis* and *Lexington* reported aboard the turtle and worked through the night on her machinery. It would require skilled boilermakers to finish the repairs.

Flag Officer Davis, upon receiving word of the St. Charles tragedy, called in Cmdr. John A Winslow and ordered him to go down and take command of the White River naval task group. Winslow, the future commander of the U.S.S. *Kearsarge* in her victory over the Rebel raider *Alabama*, had been in Memphis for several weeks, his vessel, the *Cincinnati*, largely unemployed. In the hours after the *Conestoga* delivered the *Mound City* injured to the *Red Rover*, Winslow paid a visit, offering his respects to, among others, Cmdr. Kilty. During his visit, he encountered *Chicago Daily Tribune* newsman "W" (most likely Horace White). During the course of their interview, the "Old War Horse," as "W" called him, invited the journalist to join him. As the men were preparing to leave, they encountered Lt. Fry, with whom Winslow had served as a midshipman on the U.S.S. *Missouri* in prewar days.

Winslow told Fry that he would be sent on to Fort Warren. Admitting that he had commanded at St. Charles, Fry knew that he was charged with ordering his men to fire on the hapless *Mound City* survivors and denied the charge. The ironclad captain, in a letter home, remarked that "I knew him too well to believe that such an order could emanate from him and I fully believed him." "W" also wanted to accept the Rebel captain's account, but he also told his readers that "we have the dying statements of several of his men, who unite in asserting that Fry gave the order." If the charge were true, "hanging is a far too easy death." On a less emotional matter, Winslow told Fry that the *Cincinnati* was being sent to the White River and inquired as to what he might expect up that stream. "He said he was sorry it was nothing but jungle," the Commander related, "and I must keep close or the guerrillas would shoot me."

Her coaling completed and with provisions newly sent aboard, the *Cincinnati* weighed "for down the river" at 2:00 A.M. on June 21. She did not steam far, however, before stopping at the navy yard. There through the remainder of the night and past dawn, her crew, using one-time Confederate lumber newly "liberated," built a solid timber bulkhead on each side, four feet thick abreast the boiler.

Accompanied by the transport *Catahoula*, the *Conestoga* joined Lt. McGunnegle's task group in White River later in the morning of June 21. A number of boilermakers from Memphis quickly boarded the *Mound City* and set to work repairing her machinery. Additionally, First Master Dominy, having regained his nerves, was ordered back aboard the *Mound City* by Flag Officer Davis. Consequently, acting captain Duble reported back aboard his timberclad. Also joining Dominy were two other *Mound City* crewmen, James O. Canida and Dan Clements, who had ridden to Memphis tending to their scalded shipmates. While Lt. Blodgett delivered dispatches to Lt. McGunnegle and told his superior that Cmdr. Winslow was en route, Canida and Clements called Duble aside.

According to the two men, Dominy was attempting to make serious trouble for Duble because McGunnegle had trusted him and not the ironclad's first master in the hours after the disaster. The two went with Duble to confront Dominy, who was suggesting that the *Conestoga*'s first master had stolen Cmdr. Kilty's money out of his cabin on June 17. Dominy initially denied making the charge, but then he told Duble that Kilty had asked him to look for the cash, which Dominy claimed he could not find. Duble watched Dominy search the cabin without success. Very displeased by this time, Duble interrupted the search to remind Dominy that he himself had taken it on June 17 and had it counted in front of the second master of the *St. Louis*. Duble went on to remind his acting captain replacement that he had been honor bound to take the money to Kilty at Memphis "instead of pretending to return here to look for what he had on his person." Dominy now admitted he was mistaken. Duble, one of the longest serving timberclad officers, who would leave the gunboat service within a few weeks, later opined that Dominy "wanted to steal this money, from all the circumstances, and lay the blame on me."

In a very fast and uneventful passage of less than 36 hours, Winslow and the *Cincinnati* arrived off St. Charles that Saturday evening. Winslow immediately met with the navy men and Col. Fitch, and determined to lay to at St. Charles two days awaiting orders. The falling water was of greater concern to the navy than to the colonel of the 46th Indiana. Early on June 22, the speedy *Conestoga* paddled up toward Memphis carrying after-action reports and requests for orders. It was Sunday and, after reading prayers aboard the *Cincinnati*, Cmdr. Winslow prepared to go ashore and inspect the St. Charles gun emplacements.

About this time, Arkansas guerrillas hiding in the dense nearby foliage on the right bank began a day of sniping, with a volley of 50 shots. Before it was over, one man each on the *Mound City* and *New National* were killed, while a *Lexington* sailor, rowing in the boat's gig, was hit in the face and died later. The *Cincinnati*'s gunner, John R. Hall, and two of the timberclad's officers, also in the little boat, escaped with flesh wounds.[14]

In an effort to push the insurgents back from the river bank, Col. Fitch caused three companies of Hoosier soldiers to be landed. The troops scoured the woods in every direction, but found nothing and no one. News having come in from informants that the Rebels firing at them were from Monroe County, Col. Fitch and Cmdr. Winslow decided that a punitive expedition would be dispatched to that region.

After breakfast on the 23rd, four companies from the 46th Indiana, led by Maj. Thomas Bringhurst, were sent aboard the *Cincinnati* and *Lexington*. The two, ahead of the *Catahoula* and *Spiteful*, then proceeded ten miles down twisting and turning water to the mouth of Indian Bay, a small bayou that emptied into the White River some eight miles below St. Charles. The task group then entered the bayou, "whose waters were as clear as crystal and whose banks were studded with cypress trees of the largest and most luxuriant growth."

Frequently the warships halted and heavily armed landing parties were put ashore. Eventually, the Winslow-Fitch group reached shoal water at Lawrenceville Landing, about six miles from the mouth of Indian Bay. Here the troops were headquartered for movements into the bush. In their travels, the soldiers posted notices signed by Col. Fitch addressed "To the Inhabitants of Monroe County, Arkansas." In short declarative sentences, the locals were informed that guerrilla bands raised in their vicinity had fired from the woods upon the United States gunboats and transports on the river in a mode of warfare Fitch labeled as "that of savages." The local inhabitants were warned not to aid the guerrillas because, if they did, the Federal government would hold them responsible, revisit them, and confiscate or burn their homes. Fitch's broadside was "the first open declaration by Federal authorities that guerrilla attacks would be followed by Federal punitive measures against the civilian populace."

When the troops returned to St. Charles, they learned that the Confederate irregulars had been shooting at the ships in their absence, though no casualties resulted. Although Fitch did not order any Monroe County habitat burnings, he may have wished he had. Before the Indiana colonel could organize any more raids or poster placements, Cmdr. Winslow pulled the plug on the Hoosier's activities. The task group commander had been specifically warned that he "must at once leave the river" to avoid being trapped by low water. During the evening of the return from Indian Bay, observations proved that the water stage was falling unusually fast. A conference with the White River pilot brought about the unified opinion that an exit was required.

Early on Tuesday, Winslow signaled the task group, ordering that it be readied for departure. As men and supplies were embarked, demolition parties were sent to the three river wrecks to destroy them. Leading the little parade, the *Cincinnati* weighed around 9:00 A.M. and promptly swung onto a sandbar and "stuck there hard and fast." All day long, the *Lexington* and the *Catahoula*, fastened on to the heavy ironclad, struggled to pull her off. Finally, in late afternoon, they succeeded.

The Union vessels resumed their voyage downstream on June 25, their passage "marked by several lucky escapes from bars. At almost every turn, refugees hailed the boats seeking passage. Most were natives of Northern states caught in Arkansas by the war. By 5:00 P.M. Wednesday, all of Cmdr. Winslow's vessels were back at the mouth of the White. The *St. Louis* and *Mound City*, now of little use in the low river stage, were ordered back to Memphis with dispatches. Winslow remained behind with Shirk and the *Lexington* "to protect the soldiers who are in transports."

In a letter home two days earlier, Flag Officer Davis had summed up the failed White River situation, assigning the reversal "to the low stage of the river." On June 25, he pointed out another detail not commented upon in official reports: "We are having now one of the hot terms and it is worse, I think, than Central America."[15]

Up the Mississippi at Memphis, wheels were turning to send Col. Fitch and his Hoosiers back up the White River in a second attempt to reach Maj. Gen. Curtis. Responding to a June 25 request by Maj. Gen. Halleck for another logistical effort, Maj. Gen. U.S. Grant, who had arrived in the West Tennessee city two days earlier, took charge of the effort, agreeing to dispatch additional transports.

While matters were resolved at the West Tennessee river city, Cmdr. Winslow sanctioned another sortie on June 26. That morning, according to the *Chicago Daily Tribune* scribe "W," two Arkansans were permitted to board the *Cincinnati* with information that a floatboat loaded with 200 bales of cotton was trapped in a bayou six miles above.

A fact alluded to earlier, cotton was a Civil War source of sailor prize money. To earn it in this case, a cutting out party was organized under the *Cincinnati*'s master's mate, Elliott Callender. It was then sent with the ironclad's launch and the tug *Spiteful*, carrying a howitzer crew from the *Lexington*, to seize the goods. The little party went up about three miles and found they were too late, as a large but unidentified party had beat them to the cotton raft's location. Returning by an unknown bayou, Callender and his men found a stranded and unnamed stern-wheeler. It was inspected and liberally ransacked.

While the cutting out party was away, refugees continued to come in. From these, Winslow learned that the great ram *Arkansas*, about which much had been heard over the past several months, was aground up the Yazoo. Five steamboat loads of Confederate troops were busily engaged in digging her out.

At Memphis, also on June 26, Flag Officer Davis promised to provide escorting warships for Grant's expedition, which allowed this expedition to sail that very day. Late on June 27, five additional steamers bearing supplies and elements of the 34th and 43rd Indiana Volunteer Infantry, all covered by the *Conestoga*, made rendezvous with the *Cincinnati*, *Lexington* and their flock off Montgomery's Point at the mouth of the White River. Following the linkup, Col. Fitch received Maj. Gen. Grant's instructions, handed to him by Col. William E. McLean of the 43rd Indiana. The Hoosier brigade was to make another attempt to reach Curtis, but it was not to be suicidal. If it were determined that the obstacles before him were too great, Fitch was authorized to turn back.

Cmdr. Winslow likewise was handed his superior's orders to escort the transports as far up the White as practicable. Winslow was not very optimistic about the chances for success. Not only was low water going to be a problem, but "well-grounded" rumors had reached the fleet that Lt. Dunnington and other Confederates had set up batteries at DeVall's Bluff using five more guns unshipped from the *Pontchartrain*.

When the *Cincinnati* departed for Memphis the next morning, Lt. Shirk, the senior timberclad officer, was left in charge of the naval portion of the second Fitch excursion. Upon his arrival, Cmdr. Winslow reported that chances of getting supplies to Curtis up the White were poor. Hearing the commander's assessment, Maj. Gen. Grant called in Col. William T. Spicely of the 24th Indiana. This fourth Hoosier regiment was to board a pair of transports at the docks on the morn and set out to reinforce the Curtis relief operation. With the *Lexington* in the lead and the *Conestoga* and *Spiteful* appropriately spaced, the Curtis relief convoy began single file up the White at dawn on June 28. Once again, as the three warboats and eight steamers—several towing barges—paddled away from Montgomery's Point, a vast and easily recognizable cloud of smoke gave their course away.

Lt. John W. Dunnington, CSN, was commander of the Confederate gunboat *Pontchartrain* at Island No. 10, later retreating up the White River. As Federal troops and naval craft, including the *Lexington* and *Conestoga*, approached St. Charles in June, Dunnington had already removed two 32-pdr. cannon from his craft and mounted them as part of the land defenses at that location. Dunnington escaped after the June 17 battle and later resurfaced as a colonel in the Confederate army, defending Fort Hindman at Arkansas Post in January 1863. After surrendering that position, he was later paroled and went east to the James River, where he captained the armorclad *Virginia II* from December 1864 through the end of the war (Naval Historical Center).

That afternoon, Lt. Shirk halted the procession a little below St. Charles. Col. Fitch had information that Confederate troops were, again, supposedly moving on the place. Three companies from the 46th were landed and entered the town. Residents who were interviewed reported that some 200 butternut horsemen had evacuated less than two hours before. At 5:00 P.M., the timberclads, tug and transports came to anchor off St. Charles for the night.[16]

The Yankee convoy, bearing almost 1,500 Indiana troops, began back up the White River with the first rays of sunlight on June 29. Unhappily, only 21 miles would be made before a barge, being towed by the *Catahoula*, was snagged. Damage control parties from the timberclads were quickly sent aboard but much time was taken in sealing the hole in its bottom.

At least Sunday had otherwise been peaceful. Intensive small-arms attacks on the boats began on June 30. The men of the *New National*, for example, could by noon point to 30 places where bullets had passed through their boat. One man was killed and seven wounded aboard the *Ella*, troopboat of the 43rd Indiana. The expedition, continuously plagued by Hindman's fighters, came to within about a mile of Clarendon by lunchtime. Here, several of the vessels touched bottom and Lt. Shirk decided to call a halt. There was only 6½ feet over the bar and the river stage was declining at a rate of five inches per day. At this rate, many of the snags and dead trees secreted on the bottom would soon pose serious problems.

Fortunately for the Federals, the countryside bordering the White opened out and Col. Fitch was able to send his men ashore. When they were formed up, the bluecoats marched on the town, again, as at St. Charles, arriving as Confederate horsemen departed.

While the Indiana Brigade occupied Clarendon, Lt. Shirk sent his best pilot aboard the *Spiteful* to reconnoiter the White above the town. The tug returned within a couple of hours with very bad news. Above Clarendon, the river narrowed. As it did so, it became more crooked and seemed to exhibit even more exposed sandbars. Armed with this news, the timberclad veteran decided it would not be possible to "venture any farther up the river with any certainty of getting the gunboats out with safety." A note was sent to Col. Fitch advising him of the situation and indicating that Shirk would not remain at Clarendon after July 1.

Fitch had several patrols out on both sides of the river seeking enemy contact and intelligence. One company seized a number of horses at neighboring plantations, while another fought a mounted group on the DeVall's Bluff road. Meanwhile, the colonel himself visited with Clarendon citizens, who gave him an inflated picture of Maj. Gen. Hindman's DeVall fortifications.

In his cabin aboard the *New National*, Fitch replied to Lt. Shirk's afternoon message. The Hoosier implored the sailor to remain on station, at least until he could communicate with Grant or Curtis. Shirk received the soldier's message early next morning as he was departing for his own personal scout up the White. Taking the *Lexington* upstream about five miles, the naval officer personally confirmed everything the *Spiteful* pilot had reported. Because of the "narrowness of the stream," the task group commander believed it would be impossible for the transports to tow their barges beyond their present anchorage.

When the *Lexington* returned to Clarendon on the afternoon of July 1, Col. Fitch was all excited. A number of scouts had recently returned from a sweep near DeVall's Bluff and reported artillery fire in the distance. Was this Curtis moving down on that point from the north? No one knew with any certainty whether, for the past two weeks, Curtis had, in fact, been moving down the east bank of the White toward Clarendon. Lt. Shirk, encouraged past his natural caution, agreed to postpone his withdrawal for 24 hours. The gunboatman promised Fitch that he would not be abandoned and that, indeed, the *Lexington* would run up the White on a more extended reconnaissance.

Bright and early on July 2, Col. Fitch sent a detachment of sharpshooters aboard the timberclad. Moving cautiously upstream, looking for both snags and guerrillas, the *Lexington* made frequent stops. Landing parties were sent ashore to quiz local citizens. All of them, as if reading from the same script, told the same story: DeVall's Bluff was heavily defended and Curtis was bogged down somewhere to the north of it. Writing home, Seaman Frederic Davis noted that they were trying, without much luck so far, to reach Curtis' "half-famished Army with provisions." Having bumped and chugged along for some 15 miles, receiving identical intelligence wherever he stopped, Lt. Shirk decided the game was up. Rounding to, the *Lexington* returned to Clarendon. En route, she "grounded once, and scraped over logs and stumps in the bottom several times."

Clarendon was evacuated on July 3. After the soldiers were reembarked, the gunboats and transports rounded to in the narrow stream, a process that took some time. Eventually,

Mississippi Squadron vessels off Memphis. This photograph depicts a number of Union warships. Francis Miller's *Photographic History* (vol. 7) suggests that it was taken after the June 6, 1862, battle. Other sources identify the ironclad (third from left, center) as the *St. Louis* and the timberclad off her stern (fourth from left) as the *Tyler*. Such timing for these vessels would not have been possible, as the largest of the wooden gunboats was undergoing repairs at St. Louis following the Battle of Shiloh. More than likely, the photograph was snapped in early July when, en route to the Vicksburg area, the *Tyler* halted at Memphis (Naval Historical Center).

as the heat hit awning and deck, the fleet was underway back down the river. When the leading *Lexington* rounded the bend above Crockett's Bluff, lookouts saw a pair of transports tied to the west bank loaded with troops, one of them being the *Golden Era*. Under the command of Capt. Osborne, the decade-old *Era* was a 275-ton side-wheeler originally built and homeported at Wheeling, Virginia. A coal barge lay by the former. Moving closer, a hail disclosed that this force was Col. Spicely and the 24th Indiana. The fuel was for the transports.

While Fitch discussed the situation with his regimental commanders, all of the soldiers disembarked. Lt. Shirk also learned from dispatches that Flag Officer Davis was now at Vicksburg. Once Shirk and Fitch had their dispatch pouches ready, Lt. Blodgett and the *Conestoga* once more sped off to Memphis. Fitch remained adamant that he try, without undue risk, to "pass the supplies to General Curtis or to communicate with him." He would take his steamers back up the White whether the one remaining gunboat supported him or not.

By the morning of July 4, Lt. Shirk, with a change of heart in the face of the colonel's insistence, informed Fitch that he was willing to reverse course. As the soldiers reembarked aboard their transports, some may have been startled by a 21 gun salute fired by the *Lexington* in honor of the day. Others were probably soothed by the brief program of patriot tunes rendered by the band of the 34th Indiana.

With the timberclad in the lead, the single-file of boats pulled away. Chugging along, all was peaceful that Friday until the *Lexington* passed Adams Bluff. Hidden above, a Rebel sniper fired at the gunboat, doing no damage and bringing a noisy and equally ineffective response in grape and canister. Angered, Lt. Shirk sent a cutter ashore to torch the Adams Bluff ferryboat. As it was now evening, the convoy dropped anchor.

That evening, the *Conestoga* arrived off Vicksburg. Newspapermen, such as the correspondent for the *Philadelphia Inquirer*, learned from her officers that there has been "no great change in the condition of affairs since the victory at St. Charles." Col. Fitch has made no important movements "lately," and guerrillas were reported quiet on both the White and Mississippi rivers.

On the morning of July 5, the White River parade restarted, going only a short distance before halting at Aberdeen at 8:30 A.M. Scouts were sent ashore and returned a couple of hours later to report the Arkansas community deserted. They did, however, have a prisoner.

It was the man who had fired at the *Lexington* the day before. On his person, according to a later article in the *Memphis Bulletin*, were orders from Maj. Gen. Hindman directing him to shadow the boats and "pick off the officers whenever he could." The rifleman was taken aboard the *White Cloud* for confinement.

That evening, as the convoy lay to off Aberdeen, Rebel troops avoided Fitch's pickets and surprised a recreating swim party of sailors. Firing into the sailors, they wounded several and killed the gunboat's chief engineer, Joseph Huber, a "well known steamboat engineer" prewar, according to news reports. The Southern infiltrators did not wait around to be subjected to the timberclad's reaction, an hour-long shelling of the nearby woods.

On July 6, an overland sweep by 800 men from the four Hoosier regiments, accompanied by a pair of boat howitzers, resulted in an inconclusive skirmish near the little Confederate outpost at Grand Prairie, approximately "four miles back of Clarendon." The intense July heat prevented the Yankees, who had a man killed in the skirmish, from pursuing the Rebel troops who escaped the field.

While the soldiers were away, the *Lexington* maintained her guard over the troopboats. Early that morning, Lt. Shirk had the confessed sniper brought aboard the timberclad and dressed in a sailor's jumper. He was then "posted" with ropes in a prominent position near the wheelhouse. Plainly seen from shore, the tied man was fired at from shore but not hit. A fireman aboard was wounded. This episode reveals something of the hatred now boiling over between the gunboatmen and those who would fire upon them from hiding. In the wake of the *Mound City* disaster and Engineer Huber's death, glasses-wearing Shirk, the veteran task group commander, later confessed his hope that Confederate riflemen "would pick [the sniper] off, but he remained there all day, with only the injury that he received from the sun." At dusk, the hostage was taken down and thrown into irons "to await the examination of his case by the military authorities."

The *Conestoga* departed St. Charles in late afternoon. After stopping at Vicksburg with the latest news for Flag Officer Davis, she steamed up to Memphis, arriving there late on July 11. Her accounts of the travels of Col. Fitch would appear in the Chicago *Daily Tribune* on July 15. In the interim, a second sweep of the White River region on July 7 engaged several Confederate parties, but was equally nonproductive. As Col. Fitch operated inland, the *Lexington* and transports ascended slowly toward Clarendon. That evening, they reached the bar below the town. Men were sent ashore to look into the possibility of cutting a path to link up with the Little Rock–Clarendon road. The scouts returned to say that the underbrush was too thick for any roadwork, and thus Lt. Shirk elected to haul himself and the steamers over the bar. Even as the river continued to fall, this daunting task was accomplished and the vessels once more anchored off Clarendon.

On July 8, the troops returned aboard their transports while intelligence was studied which indicated that Maj. Gen. Curtis was about 30 miles away to the north near the Cache River. Before this data could be acted upon, July 6 dispatches arrived, via the transport *Robert Allen*, from Maj. Gen. Grant. Because no more men could be spared and the rivers were still falling, it was recommended that Fitch return. Ironically, Curtis and his army reached Clarendon on July 9, where they learned that Fitch had withdrawn. Without supplies, any advance upon Little Rock was out of the question. It now became necessary to march east toward Helena.

This second wilderness trek, every bit as arduous as the first, turned out to be equally fruitless, with the only benefit, if such it be counted, that the casualty list was confined to men shot by snipers. The number of Hoosiers killed by guerrilla attacks during the two incursions was at least seven. Several gunboatmen were also lost. On July 15, a month after he had departed Memphis, Col. Fitch led his men out of the White River to Helena. There he and they were greeted by soldiers of Maj. Gen. Curtis' army, who had safely reached the river town by another route a day or so before. "A more ill-conceived and fruitless affair could not have been contrived than this combined foray into the Arkansas wilds," wrote historian Rowena Reed.

During his excursions up the Arkansas stream, Lt. Shirk, as he later reported, was not able "to discover a particle of Union sentiment." By now, as Robert Mackey points out, Rebel guerrillas infested the entire White River valley. The White River campaign was not, however, without instruction and some value for both sides. For the Confederates, the most important lesson was that their Fort Donelson strategy of high-level river blocking points covered by plunging fire from heavy guns was reconfirmed. The number of these obstructions would be intensified on western rivers in the months ahead, often accompanied by torpedoes. Like the *Mound City*, the *Cincinnati* at Vicksburg would be sunk by shells dropped down on her, though with nowhere near as many casualties. Seen as a plus by the Union was the opening of the White River — at least temporarily. It would remain a scene of masked battery versus gunboat combat for several more years. Additionally, Col. Fitch and Cmdr. Kilty proved that coordinated amphibious assaults on Rebel earthworks could succeed.

The surge in irregular activities, together with the hindrances caused by the low state of water not only in the White, but in the Ohio, Tennessee, and Cumberland, would prove a major annoyance to Northern forces pushing into Dixie. To combat both nature and the hit-and-run raiders, the Federal navy worked smartly to develop an important technological asset. Spurred by Flag Officer Davis, Rear Adm. Porter and others, efforts were redoubled to provide a fleet of relatively inexpensive, light-draught, howitzer-armed gunboats. These highly maneuverable and fairly speedy craft were so thinly armored that they were collectively known as "tinclads."[17]

While two of the timberclads were engaged in the White River expeditions, the third, *Tyler*, remained under repair at St. Louis. For almost a month, workmen labored to correct the hull and machinery problems plaguing her after the Battle of Shiloh. Flag Officer Davis, anxious for the return of the largest of the old gunboats, pointedly wrote Fleet Captain Alexander M. Pennock on June 16 asking what progress Lt. Gwin was making with her repairs. Two more weeks would be required by carpenters and mechanics, many of whom were also toiling aboard the *Essex*, laid up since Fort Henry.

Meanwhile, the Confederacy was also struggling to prepare a special river warship. On May 26 Lt. Isaac N. Brown, CSN, who lost a similar project, the *Eastport*, to the timberclads earlier in the year, was ordered to take command of C.S.S. *Arkansas* and "finish the vessel without regard to expenditure of men or money." Progress on completing the vessel was spotty after her removal from Memphis to the Yazoo River.

Lt. Brown's superior, Flag Officer William F. Lynch, after inspecting the unfinished ram reported to Secretary of the Navy Mallory that "the *Arkansas* is very inferior to the *Merrimac[k]* in every particular. The iron with which she is covered is worn and indifferent, taken from a railroad track, and is poorly secured to the vessel; boiler iron on stern and counter; her smokestack is sheet iron." Nevertheless, exhibiting great energy that he used to overcome shortages and difficulties of every nature, Lt. Brown completed *Arkansas*. Not only did he secure a workforce under the most difficult circumstances, he was also able to complete her in a backwater only a few miles from the Federal fleet. The armorclad, according to her commander, "appeared as if a small seagoing vessel had been cut down to the water's edge at both ends, leaving a box for guns amidships."

Ready just five weeks after Brown's arrival, the *Arkansas* mounted a formidable armament of 10 guns on locally constructed carriages. Such was the force of her captain that a number of Southern army artillerists volunteered to act as her gunners and part of a 200-man ship's company. In addition to Brown's impressions of the ship, future lucky readers would learn of the vessel from several other officers, including Executive Officer Henry Kennedy Stevens; Tennessean George W. Gift, commander of the portside Columbiads; and Charles W. Read from Mississippi, who oversaw the two stern chasers.

Although our purpose here has not been to tell the valiant story of the *Arkansas*'s construction, which we leave to those cited in the footnotes, we do pay tribute to the men with little means who built the single most powerful warship any of the timberclads would ever face. In justice, we provide minimal detail.

Laid down with the aborted *Tennessee* at Memphis by John T. Shirley in October 1861, the *Arkansas* was launched there on April 25, 1862. Just a day or so before the arrival of the Federal fleet at Memphis, she was taken, under order of Navy Secretary Stephen R. Mallory, for completion first to Greenwood, Mississippi, and then to Yazoo City, where she was commissioned on May 26. The Yazoo River was then home to upwards of 30 steamboats that escaped the doomed Tennessee city.

A 1,200-ton casemate armorclad with a ram bow built on a flat hull, the warship was seen as a "sea-going steamer ... built upon the most approved model." Henry Bentley, in a lengthy *Philadelphia Inquirer* article on July 25, told Northern readers that her design was "a combination of the flat-bottomed boats of the West and the keel-built steamers designed for navigation in the ocean or deep inland waters."

She was propelled by two independently-acting screws, seven feet in diameter. Each four-bladed propeller was, said Bentley, powered by a shaft from an inefficient low-pressure engine. The cylinders were 24 inches in diameter and of seven-foot stroke. Although the screws, protected by a "network of iron rods" from logs and other debris, allowed great maneuverability, the 99-hp units themselves were unreliable. Salvaged as they were from the steamer *Natchez*, these would, in the end, prove to be the vessel's Achilles' heel.

Sufficiently overhauled, the power plants initially allowed the *Arkansas* to be rated at 8 knots (4 knots against the current). A large single chimney protruded from the hurricane deck behind her small raised pilothouse. Protected by 18-inch dovetailed T-railroad plating bolted atop thick wood bulwarks and compressed cotton and timber casemating, the *Arkansas* was 165 feet long. She had a 35 foot beam and an 11.6 foot depth of hold. Bentley's report was off a bit, calling her 180 × 60. Unlike the sloping protection of most of the other Confederate armorclads, her casemate sides were not slanted but stood perpendicular to the water. Her fore and aft shields, were, however, slanted. Iron also covered the stern and hurricane deck. Her cast-iron bow was shaped, bolted, and riveted into a nine-ton running beak that projected underwater as a battering ram four feet forward of the hull.

There has been some discussion over the years as to the paint scheme of the *Arkansas*. After all, the timberclads were painted black, as were many other Union vessels. In fact, she was, as Donald Barnhart, Jr., tells us, a "dull brown" hue. One crewman confirmed that it was sort of a camouflage that "could not been seen at a distance." Flag Officer Farragut later called it "chocolate."

The *Arkansas* was armed with two 9-inch smoothbores, two 8-inch smoothbores, two 6-inch rifles, and two 32-pdrs. These protruded through small portholes with heavy iron shutters. Her complement was 200 and she was, admitted Cmdr. Henry Walke, "commanded by one of the best of the Confederate officers." Not having been to sea in some time, Brown was confused by newsman Bentley for "an old steamboat man, resident of Memphis."[18]

The weather was hot throughout the Mississippi Valley and sickness (primarily malaria) plagued Northern and Southern forces, afloat and ashore, in the Vicksburg vicinity. A variety of measures were adopted to combat prickly heat, another bothersome irritation, including, according to the *Cincinnati Daily Commercial,* vinegar baths. The summer sun beat down unmercifully from Cairo to New Orleans and, as happened every year, the rivers fell. The 4th of July at St. Louis "passed tamely" due largely to the fact that the "day was intensely hot," causing a "want of spirit." On the rivers, canvas awnings were erected over the decks of the warships and gunboats, but the heated iron plates on the latter turned their inboard decks almost into ovens. Deckhands aboard civilian steamers suffered equally.

On the morning of July 6 at 11:00 A.M. the *Tyler* and rebuilt *Essex* both departed St. Louis "for the South." Viewing their departure with a good deal more enthusiasm than citizens mustered for Independence Day celebrations, the *Chicago Daily Tribune* specially praised both boats. Of Lt. Gwin's *Tyler*, it was added that "in keeping the river clear," she could "perform inestimable services."

Another reporter from the same Chicago newspaper was on hand when the big timberclad arrived at Cairo. After taking on stores and coal, he reported, she departed for Vicksburg on the evening of July 7, via Memphis. Both the *Tyler* and the *Essex* would join Flag Officer Davis during the next week and, as noted by the *New York Times,* "The crews of the vessels have been put on a war footing and expect warm work soon."

Master's Mate Symmes E. Browne, who would muster aboard the *Tyler*, noted the superiority of the timberclads to the Pook turtles in at least one regard. "There is one very important advantage this boat has over our old one," he wrote home, "which is being much cooler, and in this climate, *temperature* is quite an item."

On the Mississippi before Vicksburg, Flag Officer Farragut and Davis grew concerned that the former would be forced to come about and run back down past the Rebel batteries to New Orleans. Soundings revealed the channel was becoming worrisomely shallow for his oceangoing vessels, many of which had drafts around 16 feet. In less than a fortnight, the "Father of Waters" was down to 18 feet. How much longer he could remain on station was unknown.

As July deepened, the weather became hotter, the disease rate higher, and the fuel situation for the two flotillas questionable. To preserve the precious amounts of coal received by barge all the way from Memphis, many vessels banked their fires and some even took advantage of this opportunity to clean their boilers.

In these days, refugees and Rebel deserters brought Flag Officer Davis a steady stream of details concerning the building of "this devil, the *Arkansas,*" up the Yazoo, the mouth of which was only six miles from his anchorage. Many of their details differed. Even as Farragut sought Secretary Welles' permission to leave and continued to discuss the possibility of a downriver departure with Davis, the commander of the Western Flotilla knew that some sort of Confederate naval threat loomed. Flag Officer Davis and his colleagues believed that the ram "was unfinished and aground." "Delta," the imbedded correspondent of the *New Orleans Daily Delta,* a reborn Southern newspaper, told his readers that "The great terror of modern times, 'the Ram,' was discussed in all its ramifications." He went on to agree with others that "there was a good deal of bugaboo in Ram fears."

At the beginning of the month, Lt. Col. Alfred W. Ellet, commander of the experimental War Department unit known as the Mississippi Ram Brigade, scouted the Yazoo River for Flag Officer Farragut,. Two fast rams, the *Monarch* and the *Lancaster,* traveled the winding, twisting tributary for a distance of 65 miles. The stream was found to be shallow in places and too narrow for any of the seagoing warships to turn. The Confederate ram was reported at Liverpool, not yet ready to sortie. Additionally, a giant raft was reported blocking the

The *Arkansas*, one of the most successful of all the Confederate armorclads, fought a running battle with the Pook turtle *Carondelet*, the Ellet ram *Queen of the West*, and the timberclad *Tyler* on July 15, 1862, before coming out of the Yazoo River to engage the combined fleets of Flag Officers David G. Farragut and Charles H. Davis. The manner in which the *Tyler* was maneuvered by Lt. William Gwin kept her from sharing the fate of the *Carondelet* and made her commander a legend among western river naval officers. This is a 1904 rendering by noted naval artist Robert Skerrett (Naval Historical Center).

stream. Upon his return, Ellet recommended to Farragut that Flag Officer Davis be approached. His vessels drew less water than Farragut's and might be able to ascend further.

On July 7, a Vicksburg correspondent of the *Philadelphia Inquirer* wrote for subscribers that "The ram and gun-boat *Arkansas* is finished and ready for active service." He went on to opine: "If the *Arkansas* is anything like what those who have seen her represent her to be, she will give our flotilla a good deal of trouble." Until he knew for certain what blue-water sailor Farragut intended, however, the Western Flotilla commander had to be prepared to cover his departure as well as defend against any nautical surprises. Plans were made to send a gunboat or two "up the Yazoo to reconnoiter and prepare the way for an expedition, which will go up in considerable force if necessary."

The same heat, sickness, and water level issues which faced Farragut and Davis on the Mississippi and, as earlier noted, Lt. Shirk and Col. Fitch on the White, also concerned Lt. Brown up the Yazoo. By the second week of July, as his sailors and work crews placed the finishing touches on the *Arkansas*, the determined sailor noted that "the now rapid fall of the river rendered it necessary for us to assume the offensive."

"Confederate military authorities," noted Michael B. Ballard a century later, "counted on Brown to break up the enemy naval presence in front of Vicksburg." If the ram did not leave soon, it would be stranded. In that event, she would be of no use and would probably, like the *Merrimack-Virginia*, have to be destroyed. Fully loaded, the *Arkansas* drew nearly 13 feet and could be trapped behind the Satartia Bar if it did not leave soon. Two days earlier, Maj. Gen. Earl Van Dorn, Vicksburg's new commander as of June 20 (arrived June 23), sent a note to Brown telling him that the combined Union fleet off his city numbered at least 37 men-of-war.

On July 12, the ram sortied Yazoo City on her desperate mission and dropped below Satartia Bar to within five hours' steaming time of the Mississippi. Lt. Steven was given the next day to whip the new crew into shape and test the big guns.

The "breakout" of the *Arkansas* began after breakfast on Monday morning, July 14. It ground to a halt at the mouth of the Sunflower River 15 miles below when it was discovered that leaky boilers had dampened all of the powder in the forward magazine. The armorclad came to off an old Yazoo River sawmill and made fast to the bank. The crew then painstakingly hauled all of the powder ashore and dried it in the sun on tarpaulins. By dusk, it was stored aboard once more, this time in the aft magazine. The vessel anchored near Hayne's Bluff at midnight.

All hands turned to aboard the *Arkansas* about 3:00 on Tuesday morning. True to deserter tales, the ram now weighed anchor, hoping to surprise the Federal fleet at sunrise. Unhappily, just as she gathered way, the big warship ran aground in the darkness. An hour was lost getting free. As the first rays of another hot day glowed in the east, the pride of the Confederacy entered Old River, a lake or "old channel" 12 miles north of Vicksburg formed at the north curve of the Yazoo. It flows into the main river three miles below the mouth of the Yazoo. There was a light mist, but nothing that really interfered with visibility.

Steaming along Old River's expanse, *Arkansas* lookouts peering to the left at about 7:00 A.M. suddenly saw "a few miles ahead, under full steam, three Federal vessels in line approaching." Peering out his porthole, Lt. Gift saw them "round a point in full view, steaming towards us gallantly and saucily, with colors streaming in the wind." Standing just behind the pilothouse, Lt. Brown also saw the three Yankees. Summoning his officers, he offered a quick pep talk: "Gentlemen, in seeking the combat as we now do, we must win or perish. Should I fall, whoever succeeds to the command will do so with the resolution to go through the enemy's fleet, or go to the bottom." If there was a close action, the armorclad was to be blown up rather than surrendered. His comments finished, the peppery leader barked, "Go to your guns!"[19]

On the evening of July 13, two men were allowed to go onboard the ram *Lancaster* from a skiff and reported that the *Arkansas* would depart her anchorage the next evening. The pair, deserters from Gen. Pierre G.T. Beauregard's army, were sent to Lt. Col. Ellet as POWs. Scharf and Cmdr. William D. "Dirty Bill" Porter reported that, on the following night, two other deserters from Vicksburg went aboard the *Essex* and reported that the *Arkansas* would assault the Union anchorage within hours, or just after dawn on July 15. Porter immediately had the men transferred to the *Benton*, where they repeated their story for Flag Officer Davis and later for Flag Officer Farragut. The two squadron leaders, who may not have heard about or from the men taken aboard the *Lancaster*, were reportedly skeptical of the tale told by the Vicksburg men, preferring to believe in "Ram bugaboo."

As noted, stories had been circulating for some time that a powerful warship was abuilding up the Yazoo "equal to the 'cleaning out' of the Mississippi River, the recapture of New Orleans, and perhaps an excursion to New York and the destruction of that city." Thus, historian John D. Milligan reminds us, they were "perfectly aware that the enemy was finishing the *Arkansas* up the Yazoo, but refused to believe that he would dare to bring her out." However, the two commanders were, according to Scharf, "moved by the persistency of the two deserters." They agreed, as New Orleans correspondent "Delta" put it, to "floating Rams ought to be tied up" by shortly sending an exploring expedition. Davis, the more concerned of the Union flag officers, undoubtedly took the testimony of the Rebel sailors as confirmation of the necessity for a reconnaissance.

Final preparations for Davis' examination of the Yazoo began in earnest on the morning of July 14. Just before 9:00, Lt. Gwin was summoned aboard the flag boat *Benton* for a strategy session with Flag Officer Davis and Farragut, plus Brig. Gen. Thomas Williams, who had come up the Mississippi with Farragut. The general's men were presently attempting to build a canal nearby at De Soto Point on the peninsula of that name (also known as "Swampy Toe") across from the city. When completed, it would link Tuscumbia Bend with the Mississippi south of the citadel.

The latest intelligence available to the Federals indicated that there was, indeed, a raft obstructing passage of the Yazoo about 80 miles from its mouth, with a battery below as additional protection. The *Arkansas* was above the raft and was said to be very well protected, with a heavy battery of her own.

When the planning team broke for lunch at noon, Lt. Gwin return to the *Tyler*. There he informed his lieutenants, First Master Edward Shaw, Second Master Jefferson French, Third Master James Martin, and Fourth Master Ferdinand T. Coleman that the timberclad would soon weigh on a new and special mission. Each was given specific associated duties, including coaling and the acquisition, later in the afternoon, of 15 barrels of pork. Master Martin was detailed to shepherd onboard a group of sharpshooters that Brig. Gen. Williams had offered to provide.

Kentuckian Lt. Isaac N. Brown (1817–1889), a 28-year prewar veteran of the U.S. Navy, was the driving force behind the completion and operation of the Confederate ram *Arkansas*. On July 15, 1862, Brown took his armorclad from its lair up the Yazoo River and headed for Vicksburg on the Mississippi. During the early morning run, he fought the Federal ironclad *Carondelet* into the weeds and engaged Lt. William Gwin and the timberclad *Tyler* in one of the great ship-to-ship duels of the entire conflict (*Battles and Leaders* 3).

Davis and Farragut, with some officers from the morning team and additional personnel, including Davis' assistant Lt. S. Ledyard Phelps and Lt. Edward T. Nicholas from the U.S.S. *Winona*, resumed their meeting in early afternoon. It was now agreed that the *Tyler*, strengthened by U.S. Army riflemen, would carry out the reconnaissance. Backup would be provided by one of the Ellet rams as well as an Eads ironclad that would assume a station at the mouth of Old River about seven miles from the Mississippi.

Gwin's instruction, as he later told his aide and the boat's signal officer, Paymaster Silas B. Coleman, was to take the *Tyler* and *Queen* up the Yazoo looking for the *Arkansas*. If she were underway, as the deserters had warned, he was to bring her to action and destroy her with the assistance of the two other vessels. At this point, it was discovered that no one at the conference had a copy of the latest issue of the signal book. Gwin, just down from Cairo, had a copy in his cabin and a tug was quickly sent to retrieve it. Once the meeting concluded, practical and logistical matters continued to occupy the planners. Davis got off a dispatch outlining his scheme to Navy Secretary Welles. In it, he announced that he was sending the *Tyler* on a reconnaissance up the Yazoo River "preparatory to an expedition in that direction."[1]

Sometime after writing his superior, the flag officer also wrote out orders for Cmdr. Henry Walke, commander of the *Carondelet* then anchored four miles upstream from the *Benton*. It is uncertain why the hero of Island No. 10 was not involved in the Farragut-Williams-Gwin discussions. It is probable that someone, after the meeting broke up, suggested that the timberclad might require support. Walke, the flotilla's senior operational captain, was not then expecting movement because his ship was "so reduced and debilitated by sickness that she could not fight more than one division of guns." This situation notwithstanding, Lt. S. Ledyard Phelps "suddenly delivered" Davis' "formal, brief, and verbal" orders via steam tug late in the evening. Phelps, the acting fleet captain, and Walke, the "restored officer" and *Tyler*'s former commander, were not the best of friends.

Phelps may or may not have elaborated on the Davis instructions. Walke, according to his memoirs, "was induced to think" his ship would cruise alone up the Yazoo next morning. Nothing was intimated "that any other gunboats were to join him." In short, even though Walke would be the ranking officer, he was either not given or did not fully understand the full plan Davis and Farragut had worked out with Lt. Gwin. For his part, Flag Officer Farragut contacted Lt. Col. Ellet, with whom he got on better than Davis, and asked that he contribute one of his rams to the expedition. Davis and the Ellets had quarreled over possession of salvageable Confederate vessels after the Battle of Memphis, as well as ram fleet participation in the White River expeditions. Responding to Farragut's request, Ellet agreed to sent his fastest vessel, the *Queen of the West*, skippered by Lt. James M. Hunter of the 63rd Illinois.

A hero of the Memphis engagement a month earlier, Hunter had commanded the *Queen*'s marines during the big fight; the late Col. Ellet was the ram's commanding officer. After the victory was secured, Hunter took the steamer to Cairo for repairs and, upon her return to the waters off Vicksburg, remained in charge. Ellet told Hunter to follow Lt. Gwin of the *Tyler* next morning "as far as the officer of that boat deems it necessary to proceed for the purposes he has in view." Hunter was to take care that his guns were loaded and his men ready. If Gwin were attacked by the *Arkansas*, the *Queen* was to "dash to her rescue" and sink the armorclad "by running full speed right head on into her." It appears that Hunter did not know that the *Carondelet* would be in the vicinity.

Brig. Gen. Williams, meanwhile, sent orders for the 4th Wisconsin to provide a detail of 20 sharpshooters for the *Tyler*. The men were initially sent aboard the *Benton*, but this was unknown to Master Martin, who returned aboard the timberclad in early evening empty handed. Ten minutes later after conferring with Lt. Gwin, Martin returned to the flag boat. The men, led by Capt. John W. Lynn, arrived alongside the old gunboat aboard a tug at 10:15 P.M. At the same time, another 20-man detail from the 13th Massachusetts, under Lt. E.A. Fiske, went aboard the ram *Queen of the West*.

It was still dark and as cool as the day would get when the gunboatmen assigned to the reconnaissance prepared to cast off on July 15. Lookouts aboard the craft had to keep a close eye for other units of the combined fleet, anchored as they were in a mixed order. Steam was down on every vessel except those of Gwin, Hunter, and Walke. At 3:55 A.M. that Tuesday, observed the officer of the deck of the U.S.S. *Hartford*, the *Tyler* got underway a short distance up the river. Going alongside the *Lancaster*, she requested the services of an experienced Yazoo River pilot.

Finally, after an hour's delay, the ram's U.S. Army captain, Sgt. E.W. Sutherland, detailed

Dick Smith for the task. In the interim, *New York Herald Tribune* correspondent Junius Henri Browne and a colleague made arrangements to accompany Gwin. Unfortunately, the *Tyler* cast off early, leaving the newsmen behind. It being the middle of the night when the reconnaissance kicked off, it is perhaps understandable that several of the embedded correspondents, sleeping on civilian steamers, thought the advance units had departed earlier. Frank Knox from the *New York Herald* actually told his readers that the *Tyler* and *Carondelet* had arrived at the mouth of the Yazoo "about 7 P.M. on the 14th and lay to until morning."

While Lt. Gwin sought a guide, the pokey *Carondelet* actually tripped her anchor at 4:00 A.M. and began slowly steaming up the Mississippi. A half hour later, the ironclad entered the Yazoo. Cmdr. Walke, an artist ever alert to color and aura, recorded that "All was calm, bright and beautiful. The majestic forest echoed with the sweet warbling of its wild birds, and its dewy leaves sparkled in the sunbeams." Finally, at 5:00 A.M., the *Tyler* was also able to depart the fleet anchorage, trailed by the *Queen of the West*. The two arrived at the mouth of the Yazoo 45 minutes later and stood on up, soon catching up with Cmdr. Walke's famous boat.[20]

As reported by newsman Knox, the initial miles covered by the three Union vessels were peaceful, with nothing out of the ordinary sighted, even though there was at this time a number of Rebel-employed civilian steamboats up the Yazoo River in addition to the *Arkansas*. The occasional local youth or old man "gazed wonderingly at the 'Linkum gunboats' until they disappeared from sight." A number of African Americans, having first made certain that they could not be seen by their Caucasian masters, came to the bank and "waved hats and branches of trees in token of their delight at our appearance." Knox also reported that one "butternut hero" shouted to the three boats as they passed near him in the river that "the *Arkansas* was coming and would meet them soon." He then retired from sight into "a neighboring canebrake." Whether true or not, the bluejackets dismissed the Southerner's message as a Rebel canard.

Between 6:00 A.M. (Brown) and 7:00 A.M. (Gwin), the *Tyler* and *Queen of the West*, paralleling the sides of the river right and left respectively, came within three miles of the mouth of the stream. The *Carondelet*, plodding along roughly in the middle between the two, was a mile and a half further back. Despite Cmdr. Walke's joyful observation on the morning's wonder, there was a slight haze that prevented full forward visibility.

At this point, the officer of the deck aboard the *Tyler* saw what he thought was smoke from one of those fugitive transports—or what Knox called a "foraging tug"—coming down the river. Most of the officers and men were at breakfast, but Lt. Gwin, attired as usual in his full uniform, was summoned on deck. The same puffs across a point of land were seen aboard the *Carondelet*. Captain Walke and, later, correspondent Knox learned from Pilot John Deming that the billowing "was caused by wood smoke and not by the bituminous coal used exclusively by the boats of our fleet." As it could be from any of the civilian boats known to be operating in the area that could have exhausted their normal fuel, no special attention was paid.

As soon as the interloper was seen rounding a bend above about half a mile away, the timberclad commander ordered Gunner Herman Peters to fire a shot across her bow with the 12-pound howitzer. The unusual tout ensemble of the mysterious craft was very suspicious. "Surely," wrote Browne, "there never was such a queer tug before." If this were a civilian vessel, its captain would know to heave to and await boarding or would round to and make a run for it. In the worst case, it would fight.

The little shell made absolutely no difference to the oncoming stranger. With the haze lifting, the officers assembled on the old gunboat's deck were able to clearly see her shape, her rust brown color, and smoke at her bow, all accompanied by a loud roar. Within seconds, a giant projectile passed overhead. This was not a complimentary missile across her bow, but a cannon ball that whizzed between the *Tyler*'s chimneys, just above the pilothouse, and splashed into the water far astern.

Neither the veterans Lt. Brown and Cmdr. Walke nor Lieutenants Gwin and Hunter had ever fought an ironclad before. Indeed, "Delta" tells us that the Union boats were as surprised to find the *Arkansas* as she was to find them. "There was common astonishment." Undeterred, the Confederate commander, also garbed "in full-dress uniform," according to Carter, "his tawny beard parted by the wind," ordered the *Arkansas* to stand for the *Carondelet*. "I had determined," Brown later revealed, "to try the ram on our iron prow upon the foe, who was so gallantly approaching."

To avoid any loss of speed, the *Arkansas*' forward gunners were ordered to hold their fire. The armorclad would yaw back and forth from side to side as she came on, firing her broadside guns as they bore. Brown knew that the ensuing concussion from the guns when fired in this manner would not arrest her progress as significantly as would otherwise have been the case. This zigzag tactic would permit the *Arkansas* to gain on the Eads boat. All of them were slow, although Lt. Brown, exercising command from an exposed position outside of the pilothouse, did not immediately know that he was facing his old friend Walke in the *Carondelet*, the pokiest of all seven. The maneuver would also permit her to keep the *Tyler* and the ram *Queen of the West* occupied and away from her own quarter.

Lookouts aboard the Union vessels could not immediately discern a flag flying aboard the oncoming enemy. Still, everyone from commander to cabin boy quickly figured out that this was, indeed, the "celebrated ram *Arkansas*." Many Northern sailors doubtless reflected that the refugees and deserters were correct after all. Paymaster Coleman later remembered that, onboard the *Tyler*, "The men sprang to the guns without waiting for the boatswain's whistle; the breakfast things were hastily brushed aside." There would be ship-to-ship action this day.

Once the armorclad opened fire, Lt. Gwin immediately returned fire with his bow guns. The *Tyler*, too, had to yaw to accomplish this maneuver. This was not a matter of choice, however, as his most forward guns still had to be angled out of broadside ports. Gwin's courage (and his forward location in the river) brought the initial Southern armorclad wrath down upon the *Tyler*. As soon as the Confederate pilot knew he was safe from grounding, the *Arkansas* steered directly for the one-time Ohio River packet. Upwards of the maximum 120 pounds of steam pressure powered her engines and screws as she launched her pursuit. Almost immediately, two of the *Tyler*'s 8-inch shells struck the armorclad's bow shield. "The gunnery of the enemy was excellent," remembered Lt. Gift, captain of the *Arkansas*' port side bow and broadside Columbiads. "His rifle bolts soon began to ring on our iron front, digging into and warping up the bars, but not penetrating."

Coming to a stop, the *Tyler* reversed engines and began to slowly drop back down, maintaining a continuous fire. "'Stinkpot' against ironclad ram was suicide," Ivan Musicant put it in 1995. Every effort was made to maintain enough speed to remain ahead of the enemy, now only 150 yards behind. Gwin hoped to reach the "protection" of the *Carondelet* before Mr. Brown punched in his square stern and smashed his boat into kindling.

Lt. Gift, however, soon got in an opportune and telling shot at Gwin's boat from his huge, black bow gun. An 8-inch shell with a five-second fuse smashed through the *Tyler*'s wooden bulwark, sending up showers of splinters over the decks, and struck in her engine room "fair and square." Rebel gunner Gift later wrote that, when it exploded, the Confederate projectile killed a pilot in its flight, burst in the engine room, and killed 17, while wounding 14 others. "I think this shell did the better part of the day's work on him," he later opined.

In fact, the men killed were Capt. Lynn and six men from the 4th Wisconsin, along with Third Assistant Engineer Oscar S. Davis and Seaman Thomas Jefferson Hood. All of the men were killed instantly, but also "horribly mutilated." Six other privates were wounded, along with six seamen, a fireman, and a coal heaver. Additionally, Pilot David Hiner was hit twice by shrapnel and Second Assistant Engineer James M. Walker was slightly hurt.

While the *Arkansas* and *Tyler* were paying their mutual respects to one another, the *Carondelet* also opened fire on the Confederate steamer with her three bow guns, but her shot went wide. The *Queen of the West*, according to Lt. Gift, now appeared to "summon courage," as Lt. Hunter "shot up as though he would poke us gently in our starboard ribs." To dissuade the Illinois soldier from any thoughts of ramming their ram, Lt. Brown's gunners quickly put three shots into the water near his unprotected steamer. The *Queen* quickly turned away and headed toward the *Carondelet*. Correspondent Browne excused Hunter's initial retreat. Seeing that his consort was avoiding action with the ram, the soldier "thought it proper to imitate her example."

The revolutions of the *Arkansas'* twin screws in the fast current soon made it evident to the *Tyler*'s captain that his initial evasion plan was not working. The armorclad, steaming slowly but with determination, was nearly on top of him. Now just 300 yards from the Rebel, Lt. Gwin ordered the *Tyler* to round to and follow Lt. Hunter's *Queen of the West*. As the timberclad yawed, Gunner Peters' men replied with a broadside, but all of their shot seemed to bounce off. The timberclad would remain within 200–300 yards of the *Arkansas* for the next six miles. The *Tyler* then chugged downstream at flank speed attempting to reach the *Carondelet*. Under the personal direction of Gunner Peters, the timberclad's defense was maintained with her aft 30-pdr. Parrott rifle, newly received while under repair at St. Louis. Fire from this lone stern chaser, plus occasional rounds from her broadside guns, would not be enough if the *Arkansas* got any closer.

As the fireworks continued, the *Tyler* came within "about 100 yards distant on the port bow of the *Carondelet*." When his consort achieved hailing distance, Cmdr. Walke shouted through his speaking trumpet to Lt. Gwin, ordering him to speed on down and warn the fleet. The Eads gunboat would meanwhile attempt to keep up the running fight. As if awaiting orders, the *Queen of the West* maintained station on the *Tyler* with her borrowed Massachusetts riflemen firing at the *Arkansas* only occasionally.

Often criticized in the weeks and years after for the decision he took next, Cmdr. Walke, sensing that he was a potential ramming target for the *Arkansas*, also swung about. Taking increasingly serious punishment, the *Carondelet* stood down the Yazoo, trying to stay ahead of the Confederate's dangerous ram. She returned fire from her unarmored stern with two aft-mounted 32-pdrs. Even though he knew, in the words of historian Chester Hearn, that he "had no business fighting an ironclad with his flimsy wooden gunboat," Lt. Gwin refused to leave Cmdr. Walke to his fate. Even as the *Arkansas* relentlessly bore down on the *Carondelet*, the *Tyler* stood by her, firing as her guns bore. This did not go unnoticed aboard the *Arkansas*, where Lt. Brown acknowledged that "the stern guns of the *Carondelet* and the *Tyler* were briskly served on us."

For the better part of an hour, the Confederate vessel pursued her Northern enemies in a zigzag fashion designed, wrote Brown, to keep the *Tyler*, primarily, "from inspecting my boiler plate armor." At one point, the armorclad captain, who continued to fight his ship from an exposed position on the hurricane deck, received a severe head contusion, but, upon examining the clotted blood, he was most relieved not to see any "brains mixed with" it.

The Pook turtle, the principal target of the Southern vessel, was hit repeatedly. While the armorclad's bullets repeatedly ploughed into the *Carondelet*'s stern, her missiles and those of the timberclad struck the inclined shield of the *Arkansas* and disappeared. Watching the fall of shot through his glasses, Lt. Gwin could not see that those from either vessels were doing much good, "though one of them raised the iron on her bow." As Cmdr. Walke's boat lost headway, Lt. Brown doubtless rubbed his hands together, believing that his original plan was coming together. "There was a near prospect of carrying out my first intention of using the ram." The stern of the Eads boat was the "objective point" for the prow of the *Arkansas* as the distance between the major combatants steadily shrank from 500 to 50 yards.

The single-minded approach of the *Arkansas* was not made without cost. Aboard the *Tyler*, Gunner Peters and his men were able to blast away at the armorclad, the guns of which remained focused on the *Carondelet*. A moment or so after Lt. Brown escaped the loss of his gray matter, a shell from the timberclad hit the hurricane deck at his feet. The *Tyler*'s shell penetrated into the pilothouse, cut away the forward rim of the steering wheel, and mortally wounded Chief Pilot John G. Hodges, the one guide aboard familiar with Old River. The Mississippi pilot J.R. Shacklett was also hurt, leaving only Missouri volunteer James Brady to take over. As they were taken below, the wounded screamed for Brown to remain in the middle of the channel. Lt. Brown, still wanting to smash Walke's boat, told Brady to "keep the ironclad ahead."

Within approximately half an hour of the mutual sighting, the *Arkansas* overtook the *Carondelet*. The *Tyler*, keeping pace with the turtle, was now able to intervene again. By this time, the Confederate armorclad was within easy range of the surviving riflemen from Capt. John W. Lynn's 4th Wisconsin detachment. The Yankee sharpshooters began rapid volley fire at the *Arkansas*, aiming at her gunports, portholes—and Lt. Brown, the only human target outside the casemate. Although Lt. Gwin was unable to see a single man "on her upper deck during the entire engagement," a Wisconsin minié-ball found his opposite number. Brown's left temple was grazed and he was knocked down the hatchway to the gundeck below.

Lts. Stevens and Gift thought their valiant commander a casualty and ordered several sailors to carry him to the sick bay. En route, Brown awoke and, brushing aside worried hands, climbed back up the ladder to his topside post. At this point, the flagstaff of the *Arkansas* was shot away and no effort was made to rehoist the colors. "I ought to have told Stevens to hold off" the gunners "from the iron-clad," the Rebel captain later confessed, "till they could finish the *Tyler*, but neither in nor out of battle does one always do the right thing." If Brown had done "the right thing," there is little doubt that the timberclad's story would have ended in the Yazoo right then.

Meanwhile, the *Carondelet* was badly hurt, taking 13 Confederate rounds in her unprotected stern. Cmdr. Walke, after her steering ropes were cut, rode the crippled vessel toward shallow water where Brown could not safely follow and ram. "The crippled duck," crowed the refugee *Granada Appeal* (which had formerly been published in Memphis) a few days later on July 23, "commenced his favorite dodge of hunting for shallow water, and for this purpose sheered to the left bank of the river." Still, the Confederate commander ordered his craft as close as possible, even as he watched the *Tyler* and the *Queen*, out in deeper water, looking as though they were "awaiting our entanglement."

As the armorclad passed the Eads turtle, she loosed a terrible broadside from a 30-foot distance, causing Walke's command to heel to port before violently righting herself. "The rascal," boasted the *Granada Appeal* editor, was seen to "haul down his colors, set a white flag, and desert his vessel." The *Carondelet* was badly damaged, silent, and left "hanging in the willows," as Isaac Brown reported to Confederate Flag Officer William Lynch later that day. Indeed, after the armorclad reached Vicksburg, the story was magnified. Walke's vessel became the Western Flotilla flag boat *Benton* and she, in the hurried prose of *Jackson Mississippian*

***Arkansas* vs. *Carondelet*.** The Pook turtle *Carondelet*, originally dispatched as heavy support for a Yazoo River reconnaissance made by the *Tyler* and the *Queen of the West* on July 15, 1862, fared worse at the hands of the Confederate armorclad than either the Ellet ram or Lt. Gwin's timberclad (*Battles & Leaders*).

correspondent "Subaltern, "was on the bottom of the river near the shore, careened to one side, and her career ended forever!"

When the armorclad captain announced to the sweating crew the victory the *Arkansas* had achieved, there was, according to Lt. Gift, considerable "yelling and cheering" all over the boat. In 15 minutes, the Confederate seamen had "thrashed three of the enemy's vessels— one carrying arms as good as ours."

Although Cmdr. Walke vehemently protested that he did return fire and that his flag was not down as all of the *Arkansas'* officers later testified, two facts stood out. The heaviest of the three reconnoitering Northern craft was out of action, steam escaping from her as she lay on the bank a mile and a half from the mouth of the Yazoo. Four men aboard were killed, 16 wounded, and 10 missing. On the other hand, although effectively hit 13 times, *Carondelet* could be repaired. There would be no need, as Walke frankly feared during the heat of battle, that she might need to be salvaged from the bottom of the channel.[21]

The entire close quarters engagement between the *Arkansas* and *Carondelet* was witnessed with uncertainty and alarm from the *Tyler* and *Queen*. It was difficult for their officers and men to tell exactly what was happening, though the Pook boat did suddenly seem to run into the bank. At that point, the *Arkansas* moved toward Walke, coming almost abreast, and fired every gun brought to bear.

"Until it was evident that the ram was intent upon continuing her journey down the river," Paymaster Coleman remembered, "we considered the capture of *Carondelet* certain." Once the Yankee ironclad was disabled in the weeds of a riverbank sandbar, the *Arkansas* "turned toward the spiteful *Tyler* and the wary ram." Lt. Brown now determined "to do the right thing" and get the timberclad.

The boats of Gwin and Hunter were never a match for the armorclad and now both "very properly" took advantage of a speed double Brown's to seek the safety of the combined fleet. "Our last view of *Carondelet*," Coleman confessed as *Tyler* and *Queen* left the scene, "was through a cloud of enveloping smoke with steam escaping from her ports and of her men jumping overboard."

The commander of the largest of the old wooden gunboats, watching the rust-colored enemy plough back into the channel, knew that he dare not linger or he would die. As Lt. Gwin unashamedly later confessed, "I stood down the river with all speed." Everyone aboard the *Tyler* knew that their only salvation lay in speed and perhaps some gallantry. Having deliberately held down speed and lingered off the battle scene to offer any support, the officer knew that the engines of the idling timberclad were not yet churning fully. The *Arkansas*, on the other hand, was charging down on her like a fire-breathing rhinoceros.

Hailing the *Queen of the West*, now trailing close behind, Lt. Gwin, under the terms of Lt. Col. Ellet's orders, requested that Lt. Hunter circle around and, in words more or less similar to Ellet's, run "full speed right head on into" the *Arkansas*. Such a maneuver would allow the *Tyler* to come back up to full speed, while she enjoyed something of a respite from the armorclad's assault. Unhappily, no one from the gallant Ellet family was aboard the *Queen* that day to enforce discipline. The "badly scared" Hunter, stressed earlier by *Arkansas* cannonballs, did exactly the opposite of what Lt. Gwin requested. "He pointed his vessel for the fleet," the timberclad sailors dumbfoundedly observed, "and the last we saw of him, he was making off at the top of his speed."

Gwin was absolutely livid at Hunter's defection and boiled over with rage at the imminent possibility that the perfidy might cause him to lose the *Tyler*. As the *Queen* made off, she was followed, according to Coleman, who was standing near his captain, "by a storm of what the darkey called the 'luwustest' kind of language." The salty language was later cleaned up when Gwin bluntly informed Flag Officer Davis that Hunter "behaved in a most cowardly and dastardly manner, having deserted us without making an attempt to bring his vessel into action." The *Queen* would shortly attempt to redeem herself against the *Arkansas* under the personal command of Lt. Col. Ellet.

As Hunter ran away, the *Arkansas* closed and began to fire grapeshot at the timber bulwarks of the *Tyler*. Her pistons pushing as fast as possible, the old gunboat zigzagged. Her gunners fired every time a cannon was brought to bear, while musketry from the 4th Wisconsin crashed out in almost continuous volleys. Running like an energized paddle-wheel bunny, though nowhere near as fast, the *Tyler* took a pounding. Paymaster Coleman confessed that "things looked squally." The occasional crash of timbers, heard throughout the boat, "seemed to indicate that some vital part would be soon struck."

One of the big missiles from the *Arkansas* smashed the *Tyler*'s steering apparatus. Pilot John Sebastian, with the boat since the beginning, was badly wounded and eventually lost his arm. He refused to leave the wheel until Pilot Hiner, hurt and relieved earlier, was able to return and, with assistance from *Lancaster* pilot Smith, take over.

All *Tyler* hands knew they were fighting for their very existence, no one more so than Lt. Gwin. The Shiloh veteran "was ablaze with the spirit of battle." About this time, First Master Shaw suggested the possibility was fast approaching when the timberclad would be so battered she might be forced to surrender. Gwin would have none of it. The vessel might go down, everyone aboard might be killed, but he would sanction no surrender.

After the *Carondelet* went *hors d'combat*, the running pursuit of the *Tyler* by the *Arkansas* consumed about an hour. Aboard the timberclad, most of the men had, according to Paymaster Coleman, "practically nothing to do." Their time was occupied watching "the gunners of *Arkansas* as they handled their battery" or rendering "such assistance as was practicable to the wounded encumbering our decks." Occasionally, the pumps were sounded "to see if we had been struck below the belt." Sometimes a few men were able to help out "the crew of our one stern gun working it for all it was worth."

The impact of Confederate shells continued. During the last half hour of the engagement with the armorclad, the *Tyler* ran with her entire after part full of steam. Until repairs could be made, Gunner Peters and his men fought their stern chaser, despite being almost suffocated by steam escaping from the timberclad's damaged port safe pipe.

As demonstrated earlier, the battle with the Confederate monster was not all one sided. Throughout the steamer race, the *Tyler* peppered the armorclad, shooting away her boats and destroying a hawse-pipe. Those were incidental targets, as gun captains and sharpshooters alike focused on her one most vulnerable target — the huge chimney atop the hurricane deck and its breechings (the connections between the chimney and the engine furnaces). As the *Arkansas* neared the Mississippi, the effectiveness of the *Tyler*'s shot began to tell. With her chimney "shot through and through" and smoke pouring out the shrapnel and minié-ball perforations, the draft for her fires was lessened. Destruction of the breechings added to the problem.

The steam pressure so necessary to propulsion now dropped steadily from 120 pounds to about 20 pounds, which was barely enough to keep the engines turning. Using the ram fell completely out of the question as the speed of the *Arkansas* approached just 3 mph. The armorclad's reduced pace permitted the timberclad "to gain a little on her." Even as the Yankee tars caught a breath, the editor of the *Granada Appeal* later reported an onboard *Arkansas* admission. The *Tyler*'s spurt "gave us breathing time before the final struggle, which was soon to come."

The chimney and breechings damage had other consequences. As the *Tyler* chased the *Queen* still seeking the safety of the Union fleet, temperatures aboard the pursuing armorclad skyrocketed. On the gundeck they hit 120 degrees, while an incredible 130 degrees was registered in the fire room as raw flame shot out. Firemen had to be relieved every 10 minutes.

At long last, at 8:30 A.M. according to the timberclad's logbook, the *Tyler* was able to turn out of Tuscumbia Bend into the broad Mississippi around De Soto Point, with the *Arkansas* snapping at her heels. Aided by the current, the two boats rapidly approached the Farragut-Davis fleet. Scharf says the timberclad was actually a half hour ahead of the armorclad, which gave the Federal fleet "sufficient time to prepare for the reception of the unwelcome visitor."

Peering ahead, Lt. Brown, still dodging bullets atop the earth-colored armorclad, was able to see "a forest of masts and smokestacks — ships, rams, iron-clads, and other gun-boats on the left side, and ordinary river steamers and bomb-vessels along the right." If he had had the time to reflect, Scharf later opined, the gallant officer might have been somewhat awed by the odds facing him: "3,000 men, 300 heavy guns, and a vast squadron ... against a solitary Confederate vessel of 10 guns and 200 men."

As the *Tyler* came down the wide river, Coleman oversaw the hoisting of bright colored signal flags as a warning "of the company" she kept. A newsman reported that lookouts, supposedly posted by Flag Officer Davis near De Soto Point, now "came down like a streak of lightning, screaming, 'The *Arkansas* is coming! The *Arkansas* is coming!'"

"Not one of the lower fleet," a Northern officer later recalled, "had fires kindled." Many bluejackets just stared at the oncoming vessels with their mouths open. After all the cannon fire of the last hour and a half, the men aboard the *Tyler* thought the fleet would be prepared to give the *Arkansas* a warm reception. Aboard the units of the Federal fleet, the thunder back up the Yazoo had been heard for some time. The officer of the deck aboard Flag Officer Farragut's flagship, U.S.S. *Hartford*, wrote in her log at 7:00 A.M.: "Heavy firing heard up the river, supposed to be artillery onshore."

In a letter to Flag Officer Foote written on August 29, Lt. Phelps spoke for many when he said that the firing was thought to be upon "guerrillas, bushwhackers, or the like." On the other hand, the Federals could just be shelling the woods. Since the first days of the war, gunboatmen, said Coleman, "let off our surplus loyalty by shelling the woods where we thought the enemy might be," even when there was no enemy in sight. Maybe that strange vessel behind the timberclad was nothing to worry about. Perhaps Gwin had captured one of the steamers lurking up the Yazoo. Incredibly, Coleman reports, one naval officer remarked, when she first came in sight, "There comes *Tyler* with a prize." Henry Bentley of the *Philadelphia Inquirer*, and several other spectators, initially believed her to be "one of the gunboats expected daily from St. Louis."

The blue-water officer and the others were disabused of their earlier ideas as the timberclad and the armorclad drew closer, continuing to exchange shots. As Lt. Gwin's scrappy vessel passed the U.S.S. *Hartford*, a seaman aboard the *Tyler* suffered the boat's final casualty when a cannonball from the *Arkansas* took his head off.

The noisy commotion was noticed in Vicksburg. Hundreds of civilians hurried to rooftops, the bluffs, and the levee to watch and cheer. A century later, the town newspaper opined that "Probably no vessel in history had the hopes of so many people riding with her."

At 8:30 A.M. (7:30 A.M., *Hartford* logbook), the *Tyler* rounded to under the stern of the *Essex*, delivering a broadside at her nemesis as the *Arkansas* continued past. Lt. Brown had warned his pilot to steer as close to Farragut's wooden ships as possible in order that Ellet's rams could not strike. Thus it was that the Confederate armorclad fought her way "within pistol shot" right through an intense bombardment by the vessels of the stationary Union fleet. Easily visible throughout the fight was "the smoke from the heavy guns in the still air" as it "began to settle on the water."

Surviving this fiery gauntlet, she reached the protection of Vicksburg's batteries and received a rousing Rebel reception. Years later, Lt. Gift reflected that their day's work represented "the first and *only* square, fair, *equal* stand-up and knock-down fight between the two navies in which the Confederates came out first best." Flag Officer Davis himself observed that Brown's passage "was certainly a very exciting and pleasing sight so far as the gallantry of the thing was concerned."

"Much of Brown's spectacular success against the Federal Fleet was due to the fact," Jack D. Coombe opines, "that his enemy was asleep on the watch, with its steam down to conserve fuel." Writing immediately after the war, Northern naval historian Charles Boynton was straightforward in his review. "Her appearance was so sudden, our officers were so conscious of having been caught unprepared, and the success of the bold maneuver was so complete that, for a time," he revealed, "the prevailing feeling was simply astonishment."

Flag Officer Farragut in particular has been roundly criticized over the years for not being more fully prepared, knowing as he did that a sortie by the *Arkansas* was a distinct possibility. In all honesty, as Musicant reminds us, "For both Davis and Farragut, it was an inexcusable lapse." "Delta" told readers in the Crescent City that they could surely believe that "our folks were chagrined and chopfallen for a moment." To paraphrase and continue Coombe's thought, both flag officers, however, "should have been more prepared for the much anticipated sortie by the Confederate ram down the Yazoo." They "should have alerted the entire fleet, instead of just several vessels—even if one of them was the legendary *Carondelet*."

When Washington heard details of the fiasco, Navy Secretary Welles was, to say the least, embarrassed. Northern newspapers, unlike those in the South, downplayed the success of the armorclad and, as reported in a headline of the *Philadelphia Inquirer* on July 22, dwelt on the "desperate encounter" fought against her. On July 25, Welles wrote to both Farragut and Davis, stating the Department's "regret" that the *Arkansas* had slipped through the fleet "owing to the unprepared condition of the naval vessels." That vessel, he ordered, "must be destroyed at all hazards."[22]

Even as the *Arkansas* was receiving broadsides from the line of Northern warships, the *Tyler* dropped anchor. The *Hartford* was hailed and quickly sent a doctor. Small boats from other craft hurriedly pulled over with physicians and surgeons, offering assistance. A number of curious officers not otherwise engaged also arrived "to note the results of the encounter." Looking around at the shambles that was the timberclad, they must have been amazed at her survival.

Still, Lt. Gwin was pleased. The *Tyler*, although struck and penetrated by eleven solid shot and shell—plus grapeshot—was not seriously damaged. Her machinery, including her extremely vulnerable and thinly protected side-wheels, were only superficially hurt. "It is astonishing that we sustained so little injury," the boat commander told Flag Officer Davis, "considering the length of time we were engaged and the number of heavy shot and shell that struck us." The officer of the deck, in taking stock, also noted that "the gig was knocked to pieces and the dingey [sic] shot away."

A total of 13 men were killed, 34 wounded, and 10 missing aboard the timberclad. The *Arkansas*, from the combined Federal return fire, lost 10 dead and 15 wounded. Also, upon his arrival, Lt. Gwin dispatched Lt. Joshua Bishop, commander of the newly arrived *General Bragg*, to assist Cmdr. Walke. The assistance of the one-time timberclad officer was not required, as the *Carondelet*, her immediate injuries addressed, was able to rejoin the fleet before noon.[23]

Later on July 15, even as the *Arkansas* was under attack from the combined Union fleet, Lt. Gwin received fresh orders from Flag Officer Davis to move the battered *Tyler* to Memphis. The fire-eating Gwin and his men were badly needed by Davis so, for the first time since the days of the Fort Henry advance, a compete crew-swap was initiated. Upon reaching the Tennessee river town, the captain of the *Tyler* was instructed to transfer his able-bodied officers and men, less "the wardroom and steerage boys," to the newly repaired *Mound City*. Lt. Gwin was also to take aboard most of the ironclad's officers and to assume her command.

First Master Dominy, executive officer of the Pook turtle, would take command of the timberclad. The *Tyler*, guided by a few *Mound City* petty officers, plus the most capable of the sick and injured from both ships, would then continue on to Cairo for refitting.

The *Lexington*, "broken down" in supporting the White River expeditions of Col. Graham Newell Fitch, had been dispatched to Memphis for restoration earlier. Unhappily, it was found that the vessel had to go on the ways in order for corrections to be completed and the Tennessee navy yard was not so equipped. The *Lexington* continued on to Cairo, where she arrived on July 17. Unwilling to drop other projects in progress that required use of the ways at Cairo, Fleet Captain Cmdr. Alexander M. Pennock dispatched her to St. Louis the following afternoon.

Upon his return from White River, Lt. George Blodgett requested that a survey be conducted on the state of the *Conestoga*. Reports were taken from the surgeon, engineer, and carpenter and forwarded to Flag Officer Davis. Acting upon these technical reports, Davis, on July 19, also ordered the *Conestoga* north for repairs and relief. Before his departure, Blodgett was warned not to tarry or undertake any major refit, as the services of his little timberclad were "much wanted." On the way up, however, he was to look in on the river crossing at Gaines Landing and make certain to destroy any barges, scows, flatboats, or ferryboats that might be employed by Southerners to get across.

The officers and men aboard the *Mound City* learned of their impending transfer to the *Tyler* on July 23. The news caused a pall of gloom to settle over the crew. It was, Master's Mate Symmes E. Browne wrote home, like "parting with a family group for the old officers and old sailors who have been together for six months to be separated without prospects of a reunion."

Due to illness and the falling river level, the blue-water fleet of Flag Officer David G. Farragut, in Vicksburg waters since the end of June, departed its station below the Southern citadel on July 24 and headed back down to Baton Rouge and New Orleans. The troops of Brig. Gen. Thomas Williams who had arrived with Farragut returned with him.

The *Tyler* arrived off Memphis a day or so later, anchoring near the *Mound City*. Here the personnel transfer was accomplished and a bit more. Still in need of items following the White River combat and subsequent repairs, Lt. Gwin ordered his men to remove from the timberclad, as Mate Browne told his family, almost everything "they could, hardly leaving us utensils enough to work the boat."

Before the largest timberclad could proceed, Master Dominy had first to run ashore and procure some 10 contrabands, the Civil War term for escaped African-American slaves. These men would help provide the manpower necessary to operate the craft on her upstream trip. Additionally, hours were consumed in taking aboard about 500 boxes—1,000 bushels—of coal, which would be sufficient to power the boat to Cairo.

Acting Captain Dominy appointed Mate Browne as his personal assistant and the latter hoped for promotion if the *Mound City*'s ex–Executive Officer became the timberclad's new commander. In writing home, he spoke to the additional space and more comfortable staterooms found on the big old gunboat as compared to the *Mound City*. Browne, and possibly some of the other newcomers, were, however, appalled at one condition. "Of all the houses, barns, cellars, or pantries, ships, steamboats, or crafts of any kind I ever was in, this beats them all," the petty officer confided. After a year of war, the *Tyler* was "actually alive with roaches and rats, mosquitoes and flies, gnats and bugs, of every description." It was also "awful dirty." It was impossible to understand "how respectable men could live in it in such a condition."

The *Tyler* departed Memphis about 8:45 P.M. on Sunday, July 27, but was only able to steam 10 miles before lack of a second pilot forced her to anchor. With first light at 4:00, the gunboat got underway and by 8:30 P.M. that night had steamed some 85 miles. The second night of the journey was spent anchored in Plum Point Bend, about 5 miles above Fort Pillow. Two days later, she tied up to the naval wharf boat at Cairo.

On the morning of July 30, Fleet Captain Pennock wired Navy Secretary Gideon Welles with information on the status of repair and construction work along the western rivers. He took the opportunity to inform the department's civilian head that all three timberclads were repairing. Unhappily, the *Tyler* required 115 new crewmen and the *Lexington* and *Conestoga* 60 between them. Local rivermen could not be convinced to sign on, as their wages were "$40 to $50 per month," far more than jack's pay.

Farragut's withdrawal from Vicksburg forced Flag Officer Davis to abandon the month long close-in nautical presence off Vicksburg and, initially, move upstream to the mouth of the Yazoo River. On July 30, that anchorage was shifted to Helena, from which Davis and Maj. Gen. Samuel R. Curtis two days later began attempts to prevent the Rebels from obtaining some supplies for the eastern armies from Texas, Arkansas, and Louisiana. As July came to a close, workmen swarmed over the three "old gunboats," attempting to repair the damages of the recent campaigns. They may even have fumigated them.

Master's mate Browne was very optimistic about the *Tyler*. In a July 31 letter home, he noted that his "whole boat is in confusion and looks more like a carpenter shop than a man-of-war." Still, the frantic pace portended a swift return to duty. "If things go on as they now do," he opined, "I think our detention will not last more than a week."[24]

CHAPTER 12

An Anniversary, POW Convoys, and the Death of a Timberclad Hero, July–December 1862

THE ORDEAL FACED BY THE *LEXINGTON* AND *CONESTOGA* in the White River during June and by the *Tyler* against the *Arkansas* in mid–July took their toll. All three required substantial repair before they could return to service. These took approximately two weeks for the *Tyler* and the *Lexington* and three for the *Conestoga*.

While the old boats were out of action, the Western Flotilla strained to meet its commitments up and down the Mississippi, as well as on the Ohio, Tennessee, and Cumberland. Confederate forces held Vicksburg and were on the move inland of the rivers. Rebel partisans and guerrillas were intensifying their war on Union logistics, not only in Arkansas but throughout the west. Able Seaman Frederic E. Davis wrote home on August 27 that "Guerrilla bands are getting bold on the Ohio, Missouri, Mississippi, Arkansas & Yazoo rivers."

As Master's mate Symmes E. Browne had predicted in a letter home on July 31, the *Tyler* was the first of the timberclads to be refurbished. Upgraded, she now, according to official records, completed her improved armament. The largest timberclad shipped one 32-pdr. and six 8 inch guns back on June 16. At least one 30-pdr. Parrott was known to be aboard during the *Tyler*'s encounter with the *Arkansas*. By August, that number was increased from one to three. These heavy caliber cannon far surpassed the little howitzers carried aboard the tinclads soon coming on line and continued to make the timberclads useful assets, particularly in anti-partisan operations.

Mate Browne had hoped that his friend, First Master Cyrenius Dominy, executive officer of the *Mound City*, would be named the *Tyler*'s skipper. Such was not the case, as on

August 11 Flag Officer Charles H. Davis tapped Lt. James M. Pritchett to the post, leaving Dominy executive officer. Hoosier Pritchett (1836–1871) graduated from the naval academy in 1857 and, after service afloat and ashore, was commissioned a Lt. in April 1861. Sent out to join the Western Flotilla early on, he remained largely out of sight, serving first ashore, then holding temporary command of the ironclad *Cairo* (January 1862) and, since April, of the receiving ships *Maria Denning* and *Clara Dolson*.

Pritchett won command of the *Tyler* by impressing Flag Officer Davis and Fleet Captain Alexander M. Pennock with his handling of the *Dolson* during that Cairo naval base chieftain's pick-me-up expedition to save Henderson, Kentucky, from a July 19 Rebel attack. With Pennock embarked, the *Dolson*, armed with four howitzers and perhaps the least likely gunboat of the Civil War, and the single howitzer armed tug *Restless*, joined in the Indiana Legion's defense of the town. All involved were warmly praised by Hoosier officials. Promoted to the rank of Lt. Cmdr. in January 1864, Pritchett was soon thereafter transferred to the South Atlantic Blockading Squadron to finish the war. The one-time timberclad skipper commanded steamers at sea from 1866 until his death at the age of just 35.

The *Tyler* departed Cairo to serve as the flotilla's picket at the mouth of the White River during the second week of August. It was just one year earlier that she, together with the *Lexington* and *Conestoga*, first arrived at the tip of Illinois and inaugurated their Civil War careers. There was probably not now a single sailor still serving on the big timberclad who was aboard when she dropped anchor off the mushy little town those 12 long months ago.[1]

For a variety of reasons and with the Civil War now over a year old, the decision was taken to organize a formal exchange of prisoners. In July, Union Maj. Gen. John A. Dix and Confederate Gen. Daniel Hill drafted the first formal agreement specifying terms for the exchange of prisoners. The Dix-Hill Cartel, as this agreement was called, provided for an orderly swap of prisoners of war (POWs) at two major points, one in the east and the other, Vicksburg, in the west. Rebel prisoners held in the north, primarily in Illinois, would be forwarded down the Mississippi in steamers flying white flags under escort of the Western Flotilla. At Vicksburg, Federal POWs would be freed, placed aboard the same steamers, and returned north.

Each government appointed a pair of exchange agents to handle the stipulations in the cartel. The initial western exchanges were supervised by Union Capt. Henry M. Lazelle and Confederate Maj. N.G. Watts. Lazelle was later superseded by Col. Charles C. Dwight. The Western Flotilla was among the first Federal units to profit from the Dix-Hill Cartel. On July 18, the brothers James and Patrick Sullivan, seamen from the *Lexington* who were captured during the First Battle of Shiloh in March, were returned under parole. Flag Officer Davis, acting in accordance with the terms of the new POW program, ordered Lt. Shirk to send the men to the Cairo receiving ship, where they were to perform shipboard duties until they were officially exchanged in about a month.

During the last week of August, the initial western POW exchange got underway. A total of 3,900 Rebel POWs held at Camp Morton, Indiana, were transported by rail to Cairo. Flag Officer Davis received a letter and documents from Capt. Lazelle detailing the first exchange on August 27. Immediately, the flag officer wrote back promising his assistance and, "with the greatest readiness," detailed the new flag boat *Eastport* and the Ellet ram *Queen of the West* to provide the inaugural escort. Indeed, Davis was so enthusiastic that he pledged to accompany Lazelle on the first leg of the voyage, to Helena.

That evening, the two men met aboard the *Eastport*, where they hammered out the details of convoy that would be employed during the entire exchange program. In general, the instructions, handed out to gunboat and steamer captains alike, called for the convoy to remain

12. Anniversary, POW Convoys, and Death of a Timberclad Hero, July–December 1862

closed-up, with the *Eastport* in the van and the *Queen of the West* in the rear. The steamers were not to pass the *Eastport* nor drop astern of the *Queen*. Whistles would be employed for communications and signals, while lights, flags, and ensigns would also denote certain commands or directions.

The POW convoy departed Cairo on August 28. The *Eastport* proved a poor escort, as she grounded in low water several times on the way down to Helena and developed boiler problems. Reaching the Arkansas town on September 5 after an August 29 stop at Memphis, Davis decided to take the flag boat back to Illinois. Cmdr. Benjamin Dove was ordered to take over the convoy, shepherding it behind his Pook turtle, the *Louisville*. The vessels were by now all prominently flying large white flags of truce. Dove was authorized to impress the services of the timberclad *Tyler* should he meet the White River picket while en route.

The *Lexington* completed her repairs on September 1 and the *Conestoga* about a week later. Learning of these happy developments, Flag Officer Davis sent Lieutenant Commanders Shirk and Blodgett orders requiring that they make their way to Cairo as quickly as possible and be prepared to escort the next POW convoy.

During the first week or so of September, upwards of 6,000 Confederate POWs arrived at Cairo from three Illinois camps. These were shuffled aboard six chartered steamers and made ready for departure. The inaugural *Dove* convoy reached Young's Point, near Vicksburg, on September 10, coming to at the place designated for exchange. The same day, Navy Secretary Gideon Welles sent Flag Officer Davis plans for the reorganization of the Western Flotilla into the Mississippi Squadron on October 1.

When, under command of Lt. Cmdr. Shirk, the second convoy departed Cairo on September 16, its vessels also prominently displayed large white flags. The *Lexington* and *Conestoga* were to guard the POWs to Helena, where the detachment would come under the authority of Cmdr. Dove. The *Louisville* remained off Helena, leaving it to Lt. Cmdr. Shirk to complete the Vicksburg leg of the operation with assistance from the Pook turtle *Cairo* (Lt. Cmdr. Thomas O. Selfridge, Jr.) and the Ellet ram *Monarch*. The *Conestoga* would take the premier return convoy of freed Northern soldiers back to Memphis. As the second exchange convoy steamed south, it encountered that Federal fleet; cheers and jeers were exchanged between the liberated Johnnys and Yanks on both sides. Without further excitement save the *Lexington*'s continued difficulty with a mud valve that refused to close, the Shirk convoy reached Young's Point on September 21. A few days later, the six chartered steamers, with about a thousand bluecoats embarked, returned upriver toward Cairo.[2]

The Western Gunboat Flotilla, brought into being by Cmdr. John Rodgers and Flag Officer Andrew Hull Foote, under jurisdiction of the War Department, for operations on the inland waters of the Mississippi Valley, finished a little over 13 months of service on October 1. On that day, in accordance with a law enacted by the U.S. Congress and signed by President Lincoln in July, the War Department unit was transferred to the Navy Department and renamed the Mississippi Squadron.

Energetic 49-year-old Cmdr. David Dixon Porter was appointed Acting Rear Admiral and ordered to relieve Acting Rear Admiral Davis, who had commanded naval forces on the western waters since June 17. Following an inspection tour of building facilities along the Ohio River, Porter reached Cairo on October 15 and assumed command. Davis returned to Washington, D.C., to take over the Bureau of Navigation. Porter launched an organizational overhaul of his new command, reviewing the disposition and caliber of both men and equipment. Almost immediately, tinclad acquisition was pushed, while newly promoted Capt. Henry Walke was placed in charge of the lower division headquartered on Helena.

The POW convoys meanwhile continued. They would not last much longer with the same spirit in which they began. While they did, however, the timberclads continued their escort services. In general, the *Tyler* handled convoys between Cairo and Memphis or Helena and the *Lexington* guarded vessels plying between Memphis or Helena and the Vicksburg area. Life aboard the escorts settled down to a routine. On October 7, Seaman Davis learned from Lt. Cmdr. Shirk that he would soon receive "a first class 'Petty Officer's Billet'" and also become a Yeoman "at $24 per month." The little *Conestoga* not only joined in the escort service, but also served as a dispatch boat on occasion. Lt. Blodgett was too ill to continue. It is unknown exactly which disease he contracted, but it may have been malaria. His place was taken on a temporary basis by the boat's first master, George Hentig, John A. Duble's successor following the June–July White River campaign.

The prisoner exchange convoys were no longer news in the weeks surrounding the arrival in the west of Rear Adm. Porter. For example, on October 14, Maj. Gen. William T. Sherman, Memphis area commander, asked Fleet Captain pro tem Lt. Cmdr. S. Ledyard Phelps to provide special escort for a lone steamer, the *Dacotah*. Separated from the larger convoy, the

Rear Admiral David Dixon Porter (1813–1891) led the Mississippi Squadron from October 1862 to October 1864, during which time he oversaw the nautical portions of the Vicksburg and Red River campaigns. Porter was fond of the "old boats" but did not hesitate to employ them for their heavy guns (Library of Congress).

transport was permitted to continue to Vicksburg, being met at Helena by the *Tyler*. Once the largest timberclad completed her mission, she returned to Cairo, arriving on October 27. There both she and the *Conestoga* were appointed exchange and general convoy escorts by ARAM Porter "to go up and down the river constantly between this place and Memphis." The *Lexington* would share the duty, while also handling special missions that might arise. While the *Tyler* and *Conestoga* shepherded their charges, Lt. Shirk of the *Lexington* found himself called upon almost immediately to make an inquiry. In some respects, the timberclad mission was a case of déjà vu, as the location for the visit was Commerce, Missouri, the site of the boat's first wartime operations just over a year earlier.

On Sunday morning, October 19, Col. William J. Preston led a party of 200–300 Confederate irregulars into the town. During the raid, the riders made off with some $2,000 worth of goods from local stores and captured about 30 young members of the local guard, the Missouri State Militia. Word of the strike reached the *Lexington*. Lt. Shirk was immediately dispatched upriver to investigate. Upon reaching Commerce, he learned that most of the Rebel riders were residents of surrounding counties and made their headquarters near the Bernard ferry crossing. Unhappily, none of the "guerrillas" lived on the river or near enough to it for the timberclad to send a boat party. Capture of the band would have to be left to the 29th

Missouri Volunteers, from which nine infantry companies were on the march toward Commerce from Cape Girardeau.

Having departed Cairo on the afternoon of October 23, the mail steamer *Sovereign*, guarded by the *Conestoga*, anchored off Columbus for the night. On the following morning, the pair departed downstream, proceeding without incident until reaching a point near the foot of Island No. 25 where the *Eastport* was caught on a bar. The *Sovereign* was ordered to anchor while the *Conestoga* assisted the *Eastport* across the bar, an operation that consumed several hours. As the smallest timberclad labored to haul the ironclad into deeper water, the largest old gunboat, the *Tyler*, passed up, protecting the dispatch boat *Brown* and a tug.

The *Conestoga* and *Sovereign* resumed their trip down the river about 9:00 P.M., with the gunboat in the lead. The two had proceeded only about half a mile below the shoal when the *Conestoga* struck an obstruction. She immediately attempted to back away, but failed to make a signal. Attempting to take last-second evasive action, the *Sovereign* ran bows-on into the timberclad's stern, damaging her tiller. Both boats anchored until the *Conestoga*'s damage repair parties could restore her steering. When the two got underway on Saturday morning, the *Sovereign* led the way until both boats anchored opposite Ashport, Tennessee, in a snowstorm. As the blizzard whistled around him, the transport's captain, First Master Thomas Baldwin, wrote a scathing letter to Acting Rear Adm. Porter correctly blaming the damages on his escort.

The POW exchange began to fall apart in late fall when the South found out that the North was actively recruiting black regiments. Then, in the weeks after Antietam, it was also learned that President Lincoln was planning to issue an emancipation proclamation freeing the slaves in all rebelling states. The first part of the cartel to collapse was the exchange of officers. Although the release of enlisted personnel continued, Union and Confederate positions could not be reconciled regarding the parole of black soldiers. By spring 1863, the cartel was dead and both governments were forced to house and feed large numbers of POWs.[3]

On November 2, Maj. Gen. Ulysses S. Grant led the Army of the Tennessee south from Bolivar, Tennessee, on a campaign into central Mississippi designed to not only capture a huge portion of that state, but also to reopen the Mississippi River. Hoping to reach Granada and attract all regional Confederate defenders, the Buckeye general hoped that Maj. Gen. William Tecumseh Sherman, with navy support, could move out of Memphis and capture Vicksburg. Although Acting Rear Adm. Porter declared himself ready to participate, Grant's month-long military campaign was fought out of sight of the vessels of his Mississippi Squadron. In a speedy advance, Northern troops acquired Holly Springs, where a supply base was established, and reached Oxford.

Administratively, this time was a busy one for Porter and his officers; operationally, there was little action. There were only a few non-ordinary incidents involving any of the timberclads, though the death rate aboard them spiked from the many diseases afflicting all the gunboatmen. The exchange convoys continued, despite the death from sickness of a sailor aboard the *Tyler* on November 2 and of Lt. Blodgett on November 6. In each case, the men received proper burials attended by their comrades.

While en route down the Mississippi in a dense fog on the evening of November 8, the Pook turtle *Pittsburgh* and the *Conestoga*, each with a coal barge in tow, elected to stop rather than run aground. As they prepared to anchor, both were fired into by bushwhackers on nearby Island No. 34. That four-mile-long atoll was located in midstream about three miles below the Second Chickasaw Bluff. Fortunately, no one was injured, save Acting Master Hentig of the *Conestoga*, who was cut by a spent musket ball.

The river stage was dangerously low and both the ironclad and the timberclad, upon pro-

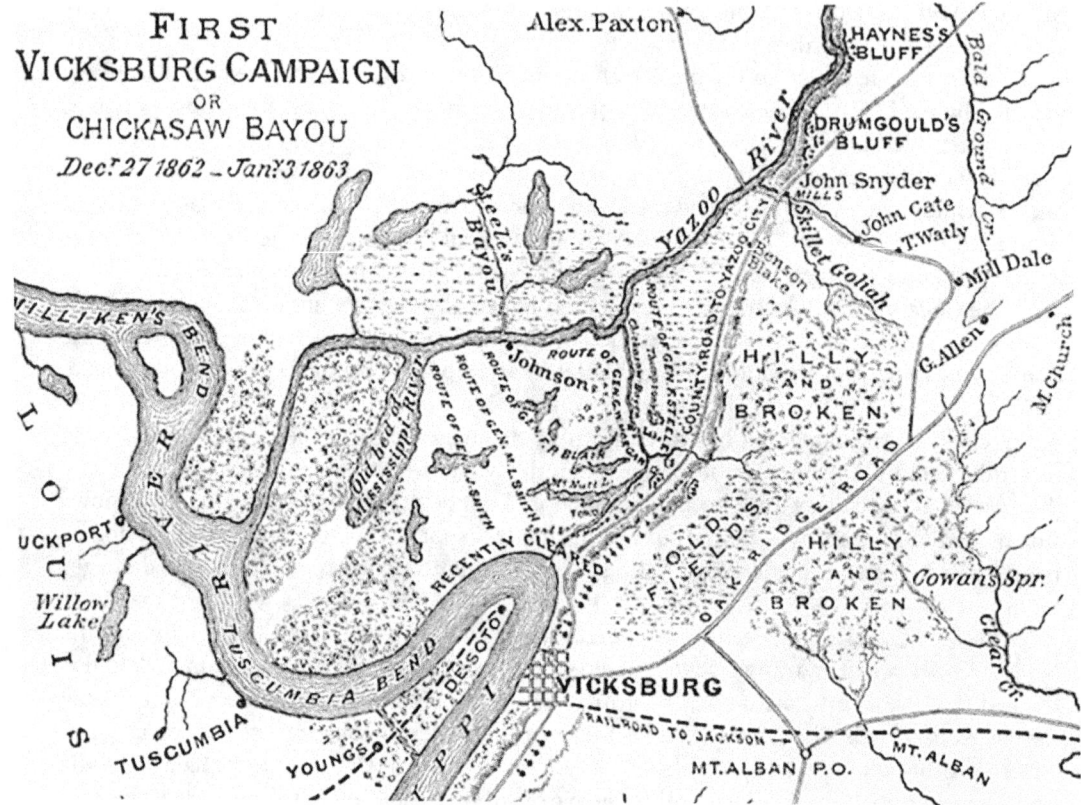

Vicksburg Area, December 1862–January 1863. The Timberclads, particularly the *Lexington*, were involved in the failed Federal attempt to get at Vicksburg from above during the holiday season of 1862. Notice the location of Drumgould's Bluff, near which Lt. William Gwin was mortally wounded (*Battles and Leaders* 3).

ceeding, were caught below the bar at Island No. 25. Pilots from the two craft were unable to find a deeper channel and so Lt. William R. Hoel and Acting Master Hentig found it necessary to lighten the warships. This was done, though the coal was largely lost. When Acting Rear Adm. Porter heard of the plight of the *Pittsburg* and *Conestoga* on November 11, he immediately wired orders to them, relayed via the first southbound mail boat from Memphis. Hoel and Hentig were directed to revisit Island No. 34 and shell it out. Once the boats had completed their bombardment, landing parties were to be sent ashore to conduct a thorough search and to destroy all non–U.S. property. All prisoners were to be sent to Cairo in irons, though anyone caught with arms was to be punished "on the spot; they should receive no terms." The mission was accomplished within a few days, but no lurking irregulars were found.

Ever since the return of Col. Fitch's White River expedition in July, cotton expeditions had become almost daily events along the Mississippi. Eliminating the South's most valuable commodity was official policy and often private speculators, accompanied by soldiers, were allowed to "collect" bales just inland of the rivers. It was during one of these missions, on September 14, that soldiers of the 33rd Illinois had destroyed the town of Prentiss, Mississippi, in response to "guerrilla" attacks.

On November 14, Acting Rear Adm. Porter ordered Lt. Shirk to provide protection to a civilian boat, owned by a Mr. Tucker and with soldiers embarked, about to engage in the confiscation of cotton along the riverbanks south of Helena. With Hunter delayed, the *Lexington*, accompanied by the tinclad *Signal*, steamed to Helena, where a message was found from Capt. Walke ordering any available light-draughts sent below to join him. The *Signal* was duly dispatched.

In the middle of November, Maj. Gen. Grant and Sherman, in collaboration with Acting Rear Adm. Porter, initiated plans for a second effort to overwhelm Vicksburg and "liberate" the last 250 miles of the Mississippi held by the Confederacy. While Grant came in from the east, Sherman and Porter would undertake an amphibious operation up the Yazoo River. If the strategy worked, the Southern citadel would be squeezed between the Federal forces and the wide river.

For some time, such an expedition was the talk of the river — and of newspapermen reporting from its local towns. On November 11, Junius Henri Browne of the *New York Tribune* told his readers that there was considerable doubt in his mind — and Acting Rear Adm. Porter's, he presumed — that a water-borne campaign could get "fairly under way before a rise occurs in the river."

Before any ascent could be made up the Yazoo, the Northern commanders had to be certain that no masked batteries would attempt to block their progress. To handle that possibility, Acting Rear Adm. Porter, on November 21, ordered Capt. Walke to take his ironclads and several lighter vessels from Helena down to the mouth of that river. In addition to ironclads and the tinclads *Signal* and *Marmora*, the *Carondelet*'s commander was also directed to take "the *Lexington* and *Tyler*, which you will pick up as you go along." If Walke missed sighting the timberclads and they arrived at Helena, Porter promised to "see that they are with you in time." Although Porter cut orders next day for both the *Tyler* and *Lexington* to join Walke, they were not with him when the *Carondelet* arrived off Milliken's Bend, Louisiana, on November 28. The *Tyler* was near the tip of Illinois, although the *Lexington* was en route.

Lt. Shirk's speedy timberclad departed Helena on November 22 for "down the river," with three civilian passengers bound for Choctaw Bend with passes from the military governor of Kentucky. Toward noon, the *Lexington* overhauled the *Carondelet* and Shirk reported to Capt. Walke. Wishing further information on developments below, the squadron's forward commander dispatched the timberclad on reconnaissance toward Ashton, Louisiana. The *Lexington* rounded to off Ashton on Sunday, November 23, and headed back upstream, destroying ferryboats and taking aboard refugees and contrabands en route. Shirk was particularly pleased to have been able to "put a stop to quite a large transportation of salt from Lake Bistineau, Louisiana, into Mississippi." The African Americans from Ashton hailed the boat from shore and universally explained that they had run away because their owners were "getting ready to move them back from the river as soon as possible." If that happened, their chances of escape or rescue would be significantly diminished.

Along the way back, the *Lexington* put in at several riverfront plantations and her commander spoke with their owners. Lt. Shirk endeavored to convince these citizens that neither they nor their property would be harmed by the gunboats ("of which they are in mortal terror") if no armed resistance was made. Several plantation proprietors asked Lt. Shirk about their slaves, many of whom were escaping to the rivers so they could be taken aboard U.S. steamers. The sailor replied that the owners were responsible for their African Americans. Demonstrating just how quickly word spread even in remote areas, Shirk was told in response that the "slaves had heard of the President's [emancipation] proclamation and that in spite of all the owners could do, they would get to the river."

The shallow Mississippi considerably delayed Capt. Walke's progress toward the Yazoo.

Consequently, the *Lexington* was able to once more rendezvous with the *Carondelet*, meeting her off Bolivar on November 26. Permission was received for the timberclad to make a fast trip to Helena to drop off her refugees and contrabands. She was then to head directly to the Yazoo.

Rebel resistance from the area near Prentiss, Mississippi, was not dead, at least not in spirit. Several miles from that town, just after dark, about 25 Southern partisans (Albert H. Bodman in a *Chicago Daily Tribune* story reported 100) drew beads on the *Lexington* as she headed upstream in the moonlight close to the Arkansas shore. Employing rifles, muskets, and possibly light cannon, the well-hidden bushwhackers opened fire. No one aboard the wooden gunboat was injured in the ambush, though she "suffered in her hull and upper works … pierced in 100 places." Fortunately, as Bodman told his Illinois readers, none of the Southern missiles impacted the timberclad's steam boilers and pipes. A bit of time was lost from the trip as Lt. Shirk "caused the woods in the vicinity to be well scoured with shell and canister." Unable to determine whether any of his shot had any effect, the *Lexington*'s commander vowed that "I will pay my respects to the vicinity on my way to join the squadron."

Together with the ironclad *Pittsburg*, the *Lexington* departed Helena on November 27. As it turned out, they could not sail directly, but were the escort for the 313-ton side-wheeler *Metropolitan*. Originally constructed at McKeesport, Pennsylvania, in 1856, she was homeported at St. Louis, where she had taken aboard 900 Southern POWs for the latest exchange trip. As the convoy steamed by a few shells were thrown by the *Lexington* in the area of Prentiss, Mississippi, as promised.

The *Carondelet* dropped anchor near the mouth of the Yazoo River on November 28. Walke, still suffering from the malaria he contracted when last above Vicksburg in July, was well familiar with the area's physical features, though he was professionally quite interested in the defensive improvements made by the Rebels during the intervening months. *New York Times* correspondent Franc B. Wilkie, known as "Galway" to his readers, later took the time to describe the local geography. He noted that a line of hills ran from Vicksburg and struck the Yazoo about 20 miles above its mouth. The country between the river and the bluffs was alluvial, with swamps and lakes. It was known as the "Bottoms" of Mississippi. At the northern intersecting point of hills and waterway on the Yazoo, there was a fort of eight or nine guns called Haynes' Bluff. All the way back down to Vicksburg, "the slope of the hills toward the river is fortified to command every accessible avenue of approach." The rich land up to the riverbank was home to "a half dozen plantations scattered here and there, while along the river and around the lakes are built broad, high levees."

The *Lexington* became the first timberclad to join the squadron's advance unit off the Yazoo, having moved ahead of the slower *Metropolitan* and *Pittsburg*. It was Sunday and the Federal vessels lay easy, the *Signal* and *Marmora* having completed a lengthy review of the river the day before all the way up to Drumgould's Bluff. In company with the timberclad was the store boat *David Tatum*, loaded with fresh provisions requested earlier.

Also on November 30, First Master George Hentig and the *Conestoga* once more drew escort duty for the mail steamer *Sovereign*. In advising the transport's captain of the assignment, Acting Rear Adm. Porter advised First Master Baldwin to be "particularly careful … for the *Conestoga*." Hentig was admonished that, on the Memphis trip, he was to be "careful to keep astern of the *Sovereign* and see that the same accidents do not occur as did the last time." Just to be safe, the timberclad was to follow "at last half a mile astern." There were no problems this time and the *Conestoga* and *Sovereign* duly arrived off Memphis a day or so later. At that point, First Master Baldwin's boat offloaded provisions to the *General Bragg* and weighed for Helena on December 3 under escort from Lt. Joshua Bishop's former Confederate gunboat.

The POW steamer *Metropolitan*, with 900 Confederate POWs embarked, arrived off Milliken's Bend on December 1, following a five-day voyage from Helena. The ironclad *Pittsburg* was her primary escort after the *Lexington* went on ahead. As the Pook turtle dropped anchor, the *Lexington* got up steam and guided the large steamer on down to the exchange landing at Young's Point. The *Chicago Daily Tribune* that day noted that the water in the Yazoo River was rising and was higher than that in the Mississippi. Indeed, any boat drawing more than eight feet could not cross the bar off Helena.

Far up the river at Cairo that Monday, Lt. Cmdr. Pritchett received an urgent order from Acting Rear Adm. Porter. Rebel riflemen were shooting up Federal steamers in the vicinity of Hickman, Kentucky, and the outrage had to be stopped. Despite the low river stage, the *Tyler* was to immediately get up steam and proceed. The *V.F. Wilson* would accompany the big timberclad to provide a tow if necessary. Porter was particularly adamant about the justice to be meeted out if Pritchett determined local inhabitants "had a hand in the business." The *Tyler* was to "shell them out" and "make an example by destroying their property."[4]

The exchange of the *Metropolitan*'s prisoners was completed early on December 4. With hundreds of released Union soldiers aboard, she returned to Milliken's Bend with the *Lexington*. Dropping anchor, the big transport, hoping for an early upstream departure, was required to wait while the timberclad escorted three newly arrived POW steamers to Young's Point. The old gunboat returned from Young's Point later in the day. The *Metropolitan* was able to weigh for Helena under her convoy several hours before dark. In his cabin, Lt. Shirk had orders to make arrangements for provisions and coal before his return, as well as a box of Coston night signals.

Having received Washington authority and avoided a number of political pitfalls outside the scope of this account, Maj. Gen. Grant launched the Union's latest Vicksburg expedition on December 8. In a telegram to Maj. Gen. Sherman at Memphis, Grant authorized his subordinate to so organize his troops that they could be loaded on steamers and, with cooperation from Acting Rear Adm. Porter, moved to the Vicksburg vicinity as soon as possible. Once down the river, Sherman and Porter were to "proceed to the reduction of that place" the best way possible. Sherman immediately sought the aid of his naval counterpart, who was only too happy to join in the adventure.

Around noon on December 8, the *Lexington* picked up three more prisoner exchange transports at Young's Point. With them under her wing, she returned to Milliken's Bend after dark. At daybreak the next day, the four weighed for Helena not long before the *Champion* appeared towing the coal barges Lt. Shirk had ordered during his pervious up river visit.

The *Tyler* departed Cairo for Hickman on December 9, stopping an hour en route before arriving late in the evening. The difficulties that had caught the attention of Acting Rear Adm. Porter several days earlier had abated and there was no need for Lt. Cmdr. Pritchett to take any action. Leaving Hickman at daybreak on Wednesday, the *Tyler* steamed carefully in low water past Island No. 10 and New Madrid. Just before lunch, she ran aground on Point Pleasant Bar and could not get off. The civilian steamer *Fort Wayne* came to her rescue about noon, but it required three hours of desperate work before she could free the big gunboat. Continuing to "tug away," Pritchett's timberclad safely reached Island No. 16 at nightfall. Water levels in the Mississippi had dropped so low that progress by the larger gunboats of the Mississippi Squadron was severely hampered. As the *Tyler* struggled to perform her duties, it was not uncommon for the second cutter to be sent out ahead to sound the water on the various bars that were now quite common.

The largest timberclad lay over at Memphis on December 12 and several of her officers received liberty. Talk of an impending flanking movement against Vicksburg was rampant about the town and security was so lax that the *Tyler*'s Ensign Symmes Browne heard of the pending expedition in casual conversation with a lieutenant on the staff of Brig. Gen. Morgan L. Smith.

Neither the *Tyler* nor the *Lexington* were in the forward area when the *Cairo*, supporting tinclads on an anti-torpedo sweep up the Yazoo at a point about three miles below Drumgould's Bluff, was herself sunk that Friday by one of the "infernal machines." She was the first warship ever successfully sunk by an underwater mine. Acting Rear Adm. Porter regarded the *Cairo* sinking as an accidental fortune of war and did not hold it against her skipper, Lt. Cmdr. Selfridge. The next day that officer and the ironclad's crew took passage aboard the tinclad *Marmora* to the vessel's namesake town.

Departing in company with the *Sovereign* and a POW steamer at daylight on November 13, the *Tyler* made good time down the river, for once encountering no unusual bars or obstructions. About noon, a wagon and ferry barge, operating without authorization, was caught plying across the river. The local craft was halted and boarded by Union sailors, who took off its crew and sent it to the bottom by cutting holes in its bottom.

The *Tyler*'s good sailing fortune did not last. Trying for the town levee toward Saturday dusk, the gunboat steamed onto the Helena bar and remained hard aground throughout the rainy night and Sunday. Early on Monday morning, a pair of steamers were sent out to pull her off and one of them got stuck off the warship's starboard bow. The remaining viable assistant, the *Champion*, hauled away, but although the *Tyler* moved forward and backward slightly, it appeared she was "only making a bed in the sand from which it will be impossible to get out until the river rises."

The *Marmora*, meanwhile, also reached Helena on December 15, relaying word of the *Cairo*'s loss before continuing upstream. The *Tyler* was finally pulled off the Helena bar about midafternoon on Tuesday, December 16. As she reached the wharf, Ensign Browne, seeing the town for the first time, was appalled at its appearance. "Such a mud hole I never saw the equal," he wrote home, "not even that noted and world renowned mud hole, Cairo."

Delayed by low water while en route to Memphis, Acting Rear Adm. Porter's new flag boat *Black Hawk* (formerly the civilian *New Uncle Sam*) encountered the *Marmora* on December 17. After reporting the *Cairo*'s sinking, Selfridge was named by the naval chief as the *Conestoga*'s latest commander. The *Marmora*, with Lt. Cmdr. Selfridge embarked, sped on to Cairo. There the former *Cairo* commander handed Fleet Captain Pennock orders from Porter allowing him to take over the *Conestoga*. The smallest and fastest timberclad was completing preparations for departure down the river and the timing could not have been more fortunate. After reading himself aboard, the new captain ordered his men to cast off. Shortly thereafter, the *Conestoga*, in company with the *Marmora*, overtook the *Black Hawk* and together the three dropped anchor off Memphis on December 20.[5]

While Porter and Selfridge made their way to Memphis, Col. Lewis B. Parsons and Robert Allen, quartermasters, were, after some difficulty, able to send sufficient charter steamers to lift Maj. Gen. Sherman's soldiers. The river stage was just as difficult for civilian operators as for the U.S. Navy and assembling the vessels took time. The *Tyler* departed Helena on December 17, but as she steamed downstream, she was rudely greeted by local riflemen at various spots along the shore. Mindful of Rear Adm. Porter's antiguerrilla General Order No. 4 of October 18, Lt. Cmdr. Pritchett ordered his gunners to answer every Rebel "salute." After shots rang out from Ashley's Landing, Arkansas, the big timberclad not only rounded to and shelled the place, but also sent a boatload of sailors ashore to burn cotton gin barns and several dwellings.

Pritchett's boat arrived off the mouth of the Yazoo River on December 19, just in time to watch the *Lexington* depart for Young's Point with another flag of truce exchange transport. Everything was quiet aboard the *Tyler* on Sunday, save for an unusual number of visitors come to salute her return to those waters for the first time since July.

Also, by December 20, some 15 transport vessels were available at Memphis, with another 10 at Helena. These chartered boats from St. Louis and Cairo, Maj. Gen. Sherman later opined, were admirably fitted for every logistical consideration necessary, particularly in loading and offloading, "except fuel." As the riverbank wood supply from Cairo south toward Vicksburg was largely used up, the expedition commander made certain that "plenty of axes" were supplied so that his men could run ashore and acquire or confiscate "fence rails, old dead timber, the logs of houses, etc."

While the Army completed its preparations for departure, Acting Rear Adm. Porter dispatched fresh orders to Capt. Walke and 31-year-old Lt. Cmdr. William Gwin. The latter, newly married former commander of the *Tyler* just back from the New York City nuptials and a three-week honeymoon, was the latest skipper of the great ironclad *Benton*, now anchored at Helena. Knowing that his wife was about to travel west to take up residence at Cairo where he could hopefully soon join her, Gwin had orders to hold himself ready to depart Arkansas waters immediately after Porter's arrival and report to Walke off the Yazoo.

Walke was advised that the fighting Gwin would take charge of an expedition to ascend the Yazoo at least as high as Drumgould's Bluff. En route, he would clear out any torpedoes and hold landing beaches until the admiral, with Sherman and his transports, came down. The *Benton*'s captain, one of the navy's rising officers, was to be given anything he required and his task group would include the timberclads *Tyler* and *Lexington* and two army rams. "I expect to find the landing in possession of our vessels when I arrive," Porter concluded.

Over the next two days, the three Union divisions at Memphis were loaded and set off down the river. Each was lifted in about 12–15 steamboats and headed toward an intermediate rendezvous at Friar's Point, some 12 miles below Helena on the eastern shore. Maj. Gen. Sherman remembered long afterward that, "in proceeding down the river, one or more of Admiral Porter's gunboats took the lead; others were distributed throughout the column, and some brought up the rear." The *Conestoga* was always the rear guard, with the *Black Hawk* having the van and the *Marmora* patrolling the center. The steamer caravan itself was extremely spread out, covering many miles of the river. This Memphis to Vicksburg convoy, what Sherman called a "magnificent sight," was among the last large scale troop deployments for which any of the timberclads would serve as escorts. Only the *Lexington*'s participation in the Arkansas Post and Red River campaigns remained.

Unaware that Maj. Gen. Grant had been in trouble in northern Mississippi, Sherman's flotilla floated onward. "What few inhabitants remained at the plantations on the river bank were unfriendly," the amphibious commander recalled, "except for slaves." A number of the boats steamed downstream, 77th Illinois veteran William Wiley later reminisced, "with flags flying, bands playing and men cheering." William Winters from the 76th Indiana believed the grand procession worthy of a portrait. "One of the grandest spectacles [sic] to be seen," Winters cheerfully recorded in his diary. There were "fifteen boats all with colors flying & covered with men all dressed in uniforms & cheering each other as they pass, a fitting sight for an artist's pencil." Henry Walke, already the navy's best known painter, would soon see the picture, but not draw it.

As the lead elements of Sherman's fleet approached Friar's Point that Sunday afternoon, Rebel sharpshooters fired upon them. The escorts quickly moved in and shelled the town and surrounding woods, though to what effect was unknown. Troops were landed and the remaining structures were torched. Once danger was perceived to be past, the boats tied up along the shore to spend the night waiting for those behind.

The grand procession, which never really stopped thereafter except as individual boats fell out to gather wood, continued south on December 22. At night, an unofficially embedded correspondent from the *New York World* remembered that the transport fleet presented a beautiful sight. The boats, running in close order, displayed "signal lights of red, white and green." Their cabins were all "lighted up, making a scene surpassing any panorama that was ever painted." Along the way, individual steamers were bushwhacked and the landings or woods from which their assailants shot were shelled. As the men moved deeper into Dixie and closer to their destination, the intermingled dry and swampy geography of the Delta became increasingly evident.[6]

As Gwin's *Benton* and the Porter-Sherman convoy, separated by some miles, headed south, the Mississippi River continued to rise. Not yet having received the admiral's orders concerning Gwin, Capt. Walke elected to take advantage of the growing river stage to execute a Yazoo reconnaissance of his own, perhaps as high as 15 miles from the mouth of the river.

On December 21, arrangements were concluded for the *Carondelet* to go up the river next morning with the tinclad *Signal* and the Ellet boat *Queen of the West*. The latter, like the other War Department rams, had a pair of 12-pdr. brass pieces mounted on her upper deck. These could fire over the higher banks, something the elevated guns on the navy boats could not do. During the night, Walke suffered a relapse of "the intermittent [malarial] fever" he had suffered for several months and the Monday cruise was scrubbed. He remained too ill to leave his cabin for several more days. Finding himself too feeble to personally launch his mission, Walke had Lt. Cmdr. John G. Walker summoned from the Pook turtle *Baron de Kalb* (formerly the *St. Louis*) on December 22 and asked that he take over the mission. Porter's message was, meanwhile, received. With the *Lexington* reserved for Lt. Gwin, her forthcoming passage as POW convoy escort to Helena was cancelled. During the night, the *Benton* anchored at the mouth of the Yazoo River where, just after breakfast, Lt. Cmdr. Gwin planned to meet with Capt. Walke and the commanders of the vessels detailed to support him.

Before dawn on December 23, the Walker group steamed up the Yazoo hunting the same sort of subsurface mines that had earlier sunk the *Cairo*. The little parade was led by the *Laurel* and *Signal*, followed by Capt. Edwin W. Sutherland's *Queen of the West* and the *Baron de Kalb*. Sutherland had taken over his boat in the wake of the *Arkansas* fiasco and had firsthand experience with the dangers of torpedo disarmament, having been along on the *Cairo* expedition back on December 12.

As Task Group Walker disappeared upstream, Lt. Cmdr. Gwin was able to confer with Capt. Walke, his old colleague Lt. Cmdr. Shirk, and his fellow gunboat skippers. The *Carondelet*'s commander doubtless provided a review of the dangers of Yazoo River torpedo removal and the loss of the *Cairo*. He may even have suggested that the fresh army troops would have to land farther downstream from the Rebel river bluff defenses. Lt. Cmdr. Gwin informed the captains that the Porter-Sherman expeditionary force was en route behind him and showed them a lengthy letter from Acting Rear Adm. Porter advising on the best methods for minesweeping. Mr. A. Strausz of the Coast Survey was introduced to the captains by Gwin. He had personally been assigned to the *Tyler* by Porter to draw a "good map of the river and the topography of the country."

Promptly at noon, the *Benton*, followed by the *Lexington* and *Tyler*, the tinclads *Romeo* and *Juliet*, and the Army ram *Lioness*, stood up the river. Their mission was to ensure the river's safety for the army and, as everyone said he had done at Shiloh, the energetic Gwin was determined to do just that.

Some hours ahead, the *Baron de Kalb* and her consorts were able to ascend the Yazoo between 12 and 14 miles from the river's mouth before encountering difficulty abreast of Capt. and honorary Col. W.H. Johnson's plantation. The place was opposite the mouth of Steele's Bayou and down from the entrance into Chickasaw Bayou, as well as from Drumgould's Bluff and the spot where the *Cairo* was mined. Maj. Gen. Sherman, years later in his memoirs, noted that his landing site right in this area was, in fact, an island, separated by a broad shallow bayou from the Walnut Hills bluff upon which Vicksburg stood. "On our right," he wrote, "was another wide bayou, known as Old River"— scene of the descent of the *Arkansas* months earlier. There was yet another bayou on the left. It was "much narrower, but too deep to be forded, known as Chickasaw Bayou." The whole island was heavily wooded, save in the area of Johnson's farm, right up to the Yazoo "and a series of old cotton-fields along Chickasaw Bayou." Much of the ground along a road from Johnson's toward Vicksburg was crisscrossed by swamps and smaller bayous. Heavy artillery protruded from bluffs with names like Drumgould's, Snyder's, and Haynes'.

Ownership of the well-cultivated farm, officially known as Belle Isle, has sometimes been attributed, despite the surname spelling difference, to the deceased Gen. Albert Sidney Johnston. Capt. Johnson, his son, had recently been appointed "special agent for the accumulation of Government supplies." He also served as a volunteer aide-de-camp for Rebel Maj. Gen. Stephen D. Lee. Sometime earlier, all but three of Johnson's slave force of 56 fieldhands had been transported to Vicksburg to help dig entrenchments. When the gunboats appeared, the portion of his family remaining fled the five miles overland to Vicksburg to join the patriarch.

The *Laurel* steamed cautiously a half mile beyond the plantation, covered by the *Queen of the West*, *Signal*, and *De Kalb*, which busied themselves firing a cannonball reconnaissance of the woods. Suddenly, secreted Confederate riflemen on both sides of the stream opened up on the tug. The volleys riddled her with dozens of rife balls, some of which passed straight through the boiler plate covering her vitals. The cook was killed and her engineer wounded. The *Queen of the West* and *Signal* immediately dashed to the *Laurel*'s aid, pumping canister at the Southern perpetrators, who were believed to be a group of 70 pickets stationed at a camp a mile from the Yazoo up Cypress Bayou.

Task Group Walker now continued on upstream exercising extreme caution, occasionally taking fire and returning it. As the boats steamed slowly along toward Drumgould's Bluff, the planned scouting terminus ordered by Capt. Walke, Lt. Cmdr. Walker's men found suspicious buoys with wires attached. As they climbed into cutters to row over and haul them out, the bluejackets were fired upon by musketry from both banks. The danger of the retrieval work was obvious, as additional torpedoes were found and the sailors had to work "under a galling fire of musketry" from the bank. With no letup in Confederate resistance, Lt. Cmdr. Walker ordered a retreat, firing at the unseen riflemen en route downstream. It was believed at the time that the outbuildings on Johnson's plantation were used for shelter by men shooting into the boats.

While Walker's boats were returning, Lt. Cmdr. Gwin's group was moving ahead. Early on, its trip was uneventful. Ensign Browne later wrote home that "we did not see a man, woman, or child, nor hear a sound save that made by the boat." Upon nearing Walker's force, "we heard heavy firing ... musketry, and then we knew that the guerrillas were firing on the boats and the boats were shelling the banks."

Gwin's craft continued their advance until they were within approximately a mile of the spot where the *Cairo* was sunk. There they halted and small boats were sent out torpedo hunting. At about 3:00 P.M., the *Baron de Kalb*, *Laurel*, *Signal*, and *Queen of the West* met the later group at the Union anchorage a mile above Johnson's plantation. Coming to, Walker and his subordinate captains all reported aboard the *Benton*. Lt. Cmdr. Shirk and the other skippers from Gwin's task group were also summoned. As the *Lexington*'s gig headed for the *Benton*, Southern fighters poured a hailstorm of lead at her. Miraculously, neither Shirk nor his boat crew were hurt.

A conference aboard the *Benton* reviewed Walker's findings that numerous torpedoes were seeded in the waters ahead. The captain of the *Baron de Kalb* offered to once more tackle the explosive devices while Gwin located appropriate landing sites for Sherman's troops. His men, Walker explained, were not afraid to undertake the work, but would require gunfire support to suppress Rebel soldiers. Lt. Cmdr. Gwin, who wished to retain Walker's services and said so, had another mission for him to complete first. He was to take his ironclad and, together with the *Lexington*, return down the Yazoo to destroy the Belle Isle farm in retaliation for the day's casualties. While that business was addressed, cutters and yawls from the *Benton* and the other boats, including the *Tyler*, would continue to seek torpedoes, as well as landing sites. Although the former task was not easy, identifying good beachheads from which to slog to the foot of the Walnut Hills would also be difficult.

"The terrain of the Delta was a nightmare landscape in which to conduct military operations," wrote Steven Woodworth years later. Adding to Maj. Gen. Sherman's earlier description, the historian noted that local watercourses "writhed like twisting serpents across the flat alluvial ground," changing course into different ones every few years. "The abandoned riverbeds became sloughs, bayous, backwaters, and when silt deposits severed them from the main stream, oxbow lakes."

Turning to Capt. Sutherland, the commander of the suddenly enlarged task force asked him to assume the van position, a deviation from Acting Rear Adm. Porter's instructions requiring "that the rams should remain in the rear." The *Queen*'s captain was overwhelmed by Gwin's vote of confidence and ever after spoke of "the courtesy of that gallant officer."

The *Lexington* and *Baron de Kalb*, with *New York World* scribe Richard T. Colburn and the *Chicago Daily Tribune* correspondent F.C. Foster embedded on the former, duly steamed back to Johnson's plantation, coming to at a point where the river was only about 150 yards wide. Some considerable time was spent scouting the farm before Shirk and Walker sent several cutters ashore, with their armed sailors carrying torches. Rushing inland, the Union tars fired every house, outbuilding, and anything else deemed of value to Johnson or the Confederates, save one small house left as a shelter for the slaves. Even the ornamental trees and flower garden were not spared. A considerable amount of cotton, corn, fodder, and farm equipment was located and destroyed. Indeed, the quantity was so large that the *Lexington* remained off the farm for another day in order for her men to complete their efforts. During a flag of truce meeting on December 31, Capt. Johnson would inform his Union counterparts that damages from these fires alone cost him $60,000.

As men from the *Lexington* and *Baron de Kalb* applied the torch, Lt. Cmdr. Gwin's group moved back upstream. Coming to anchor about two miles above Johnson's plantation, a pair of cutters were sent out from the *Tyler*, along with one from the *Benton*. As the Union men attempted to pick up torpedoes with their grappling hooks and drags, they were once again subjected to "a fearful volley of musketry from the bank." Responding to the gunfire from shore, the flag boat, together with the timberclad and the tinclad *Juliet*, loosed their broadsides. The many riflemen contesting Federal naval progress fired from behind levees and the high overhanging banks, in Porter's words, "almost with impunity." Fortunately, they could not hurt the light draughts, though they made their upper works look like Swiss cheese.

Ensign Browne optimistically believed the bushwhackers suffered horribly, claiming later

Torpedoes in the Yazoo. Sweeping for these "infernal machines" cost the Federal navy the ironclad *Cairo* and the lives of a number of sailors on other vessels tasked to remove them using small boats. Both the *Lexington* and *Tyler* provided gunfire support for the "sweepers" as they attempted to remove the dangerous mines with ropes and grappling hooks (*Harper's Weekly*, February 7, 1863).

that he could see "shells bursting directly where they were standing." His hopeful view was not correct. Although the chances were slim that many Southerners were hurt in the exchange, their rifle fire was so annoying that Lt. Cmdr. Gwin ordered the boats called in. Having recovered only one torpedo, the combined unit dropped downstream a mile and came to anchor for the night.

Correspondent Foster observed that, for the rest of the evening, Gwin's gunners "occasionally shelled the banks and were now and then fired upon without serious results."

Meanwhile, as the early December darkness stole visibility, the *Baron de Kalb* and the *Laurel* returned to the mouth of the Yazoo, where Lt. Cmdr. Walker reported on the day's adventure to Capt. Walke.

As all of this action was unfolding in the Yazoo, far up the Mississippi near the mouth of the Arkansas River the Sherman-Porter armada was spied from the Wilbourn plantation by a squad of scouting Texas cavalry from the W.P. Lane Rangers. One of the men dispatched as a vedette from the relatively new Fort Hindman, built 50 miles upstream on the first bluff of the Arkansas River at Arkansas Post, William W. Heartsill, noted in his diary that, about three minutes after their arrival, "A gunboat hove in sight coming down and then another, then several transports. Our squad fell back behind some corn pens. By 8 o'clk ONE HUNDRED AND THREE transports and gunboats passed, 13 of which anchored in front of Wilbourn's house." Heartsill thought it a grand sight to see the bluecoats "on board these Mississippi Palaces, with their colors flying and bands playing their national airs." He was even pleased to note that "occasionally they [struck] off on 'Dixie' or 'The Bonnie Blue Flag.'"

Fearing that pro–Union slaves would give their position away to the gunboats (of which there were actually only three) and knowing they "would not stand much showing against SIXTY THOUSAND," the Confederates moved to the rear. After dark, "we retrograde" and, Heartsill boasted, "I think it would take the oldest mosquito in Louisiana to have found us."

After a fitful night, the Texas Rangers observed the Union invasion fleet move down the river at daylight on December 14. "So we get very brave," remembered Trooper Heartsill, "and march boldly back to Wilbourn's house." There they captured a deserter from the 54th Illinois who told them the boats were headed toward Vicksburg, their troops confident of victory and as merry as "if they had been on a Picnic excursion."

Further south, the *Tyler* and the other vessels with Lt. Cmdr. Gwin got underway up the Yazoo at 6:40 A.M. The banks along the river averaged between 20 and 30 feet high and the stream was still quite narrow, perhaps 150 to 170 yards. The *Queen of the West* moved ahead about three miles toward the wreck of the *Cairo*, finding the river clear. Within a few minutes, however, large numbers of "infernal machines" were located, initially when the ram was entangled in a torpedo line her lookouts had failed to discover.

Capt. Sutherland immediately reported his uncomfortable situation to Lt. Cmdr. Gwin and boats were sent out from the flagship to remove it. As the sailors in their gigs approached the dangerous lines, they were greeted with, as the army skipper put it, "such a volley as to plainly indicate the impracticability of ever destroying the torpedoes by that [men in open boats] means." Nevertheless, the *Queen* was safely freed.

After firing upon the rowing bluejackets, snipers along the shore opened up on all the gunboats, immediately killing a *Benton* lookout. The flag boat replied with her 4, 5, and 11 guns and a boat howitzer, and was joined by gunners and sharpshooters aboard all the other vessels. Hiding behind the natural breastworks provided by the levees, none of the butternut soldiers were hit. These men were not a part of any small picket force, but, rather, among an estimated 2,000 Confederate soldiers dug into rifle pits along the shore.

At approximately 11:00 A.M., an anti-torpedo party under Master's Mate Edward Brennan of the *Benton* took the boat's first cutter and started dragging the river. Cover was provided by the big guns of the *Tyler*, *Juliet*, and the top-mounted guns of the *Queen of the West*. At the same hour, a large body of troops were seen arriving in an area behind Johnson's plantation. These were taken under fire by the *Lexington*. At noon, Mate Brennan returned aboard the *Benton* and informed Lt. Cmdr. Gwin that he had found lines stretched across the river, lines he believed led to a torpedo. Heavy fire from the bank kept him from reaching it.

After lunch, Brennan and his men returned to their work. Again, despite big gun support from the *Tyler* and the smaller pieces of the *Juliet* and *Queen*, the probing sailors were driven away by Confederate gunfire. Several additional attempts were made during the afternoon, without a fatality. Each time Federal rowers set out, Southern gunmen in the thickets and rifle pits did their best to create havoc. This always brought a thunderous big gun U.S. Navy response that failed to hurt the nimble Rebel foe.

Still, as Acting Rear Adm. Porter informed Navy Secretary Gideon Welles later, the rise in the river stage, as at Fort Henry 10 months earlier, made the removal effort somewhat easier. Additionally, when enemy sharpshooters appeared in small numbers, they were driven off. This pattern would continue for several more days. The Federal tars did achieve some measure of success; however, the gunboats withdrew down the river a short distance. It was 9:30 P.M. and even with torches it was just too dark to continue. From midnight to daylight, the *Queen of the West* patrolled the river. Confederates seeding the river with additional torpedoes were easily able to avoid her.

Earlier on Christmas Eve, the first steamers in the grand Sherman-Porter convoy reached the 10-mile-long Mississippi River curve known as Milliken's Bend. A settlement of the same name on the Louisiana shore was about 30 miles above Vicksburg. Richard T. Colburn of the *New York World* told his readers that it was an important trading and shipping center for a large territory. It had half a dozen stores, several large warehouses, two or three dozen houses, churches, and a school house.

Still at Granada, Maj. Gen. Pemberton received what he considered to be "definite and reliable" information that the Sherman-Porter flotilla "had arrived at the mouth of the Yazoo River, six miles above Vicksburg." In light of the Rebel triumph at Holly Springs, he immediately ordered the fortress city reinforced and set out to assume personal charge of the upcoming campaign. The reinforcements would be vital; Maj. Gen. Martin L. Smith, in charge at the fortress town in Pemberton's absence, had only 6,500 men.

Despite orders from the commanding general for members of the press to stay away, a number of reporters were along on Sherman's campaign, secreted aboard steamers in the grand convoy. In addition to Colburn and Foster, these included Thomas W. Knox of the *New York Herald* and the already mentioned Franc B. "Galway" Wilkie of the *New York Times*. Both gentlemen had missed the timberclads' Shiloh and *Arkansas* adventures, but their reporting of the Chickasaw Bayou battle would receive nationwide attention. It also landed Knox in hot water with Maj. Gen. Sherman in a famously interesting campaign sidelight beyond the scope of this work.

At daybreak on December 25, the gunboats under Lt. Cmdr. Gwin again steamed cautiously up the Yazoo, the great clouds of smoke rising from their stacks a sure sign of their activity. To their horror, even more torpedoes were discovered in the waters leading to Drumgould's Bluff than were seen the day before. Grimly, the gunboat men set to work dragging the Yazoo, immediately coming under "a terrific fire from both banks of the river." Eventually, the small-boat sailors were able to reach the stream below the Rebel fortifications at Mill Dale. Throughout the day, the big guns of Task Force Gwin fired a few shots into the woods behind the banks, attempting to chase off Southern harassers.

Newsman Wilkie, when he heard about the contest between cannon and squirrel rifles, called the firepower exchange "a modern rendering of the fable of the lion and the gnat." Writing as "Galway," he provided some idea of the contest in a column published in January 1863: "It was in vain that rifled-shot cut down huge trees and tore great furrows in the bank, or went howling like a tempest over the country; none of this was half as efficient as the whip-like crack of a rifle, whose small pellet of lead searched every point of the armor of the huge leviathan." A few more Yankee sailors were wounded (none on the *Tyler*) and, wrote Symmes Browne, "these were men who carelessly exposed themselves."

At 6:30 P.M., Lt. Cmdr. Gwin's boats anchored about a half mile below Chickasaw Bayou. By this time, artist Strausz, with support from Lt. Cmdr. Pritchett, had completed his drawings for the admiral. They were placed into a folder and delivered next day. Porter would later acknowledge Strausz's work in a letter to the Coast Survey superintendent.

Although Union soldiers on the transports out on the Mississippi were ordered not to go ashore or vent their patriotic fervor upon local residents, the buildings at Milliken's Bend were set ablaze sometime between Christmas Eve and morning. When Wilkie reached the place in the morning with Knox aboard Maj. Gen. Frederick Steele's flag steamer *Continental*, everything of importance was in flames.

Numerous steamers hove to off the Bend during the day, including those transporting Sherman, Porter and their staffs. Almost as soon as the *Black Hawk* dropped anchor, the Mississippi Squadron commander penned a general order to all of his fighting captains, dividing up the larger units of the fleet into two divisions. Despite their age and armor, the timberclads were numbered among Porter's larger and heavier units. The *Lexington* was assigned to Capt. Walke's First Division, while the *Conestoga* and *Tyler* were with Lt. Cmdr. Gwin in the Second Division. Acting Rear Adm. Porter's order went on to explain not only the formations in which the divisions should anchor, but also the procedures by which commanders should communicate to the admiral through their divisional commanders. Walke and Gwin were also cautioned to learn the distinguishing pennants of their vessels in order that signals could be exchanged in case of necessity. (For benefit of this work's reader, the front half of the *Lexington*'s pennant was blue and the rear half red, while the scheme for the *Tyler* was exactly the reverse. The *Conestoga* wore a tricolor pennant, equally divided, front to back, between white, blue, and red.)

Later in the morning, the majority of the Federal invasion fleet steamed down the 11 miles from Milliken's Bend to Young's Point, below the Yazoo's mouth and around a sharp bend from Vicksburg proper. Christmas for the men aboard these craft was not very nice, even if the weather was quite pleasant. An Ohio soldier on one of the transports observed in his diary that "It was a very dull Christmas and very unlike those I had spent at home."

That afternoon, Porter welcomed Maj. Gen. Sherman aboard the *Black Hawk* for a final planning session. Having before them all of the latest intelligence of the area (but unhappily, no firm word on the Holly Springs disaster and retreat), the two determined to move up the Yazoo about 12 miles next morning and debark the troops "on an island formed by the Yazoo and Mississippi rivers and a system of bayous or old channels." About 5:00 P.M., while the red-headed general and bearded admiral were yet in discussion, the steamer *Sampson*, in rounding to, struck the anchored *Baron de Kalb* with one of the two coal barges she was towing. Neither the ironclad nor the transport was injured, but the fatally damaged barge sank almost immediately, taking her precious cargo to the bottom. The entire fleet had now to rely on but one barge carrying a scant 7,000 bushels of anthracite.

At 12:15 A.M. on December 26, Lt. Cmdr. Gwin, knowing Porter's approximate timetable, dispatched a dinghy with five men ahead to serve as lookouts. Meanwhile, his two attached army rams operated river patrols.[7] Bright and early on Boxing Day, the *Black Hawk* led most of the Federal fleet into the Yazoo River. A number of steamers and auxiliary vessels were, however, left behind at Milliken's Bend, guarded by the *Conestoga*. Their mission was to provide for the soldiers not yet arrived and to guard the Yazoo entrance.

The troop convoy was kept closed up by Sherman's general orders and the escorting gunboats interspersed among the steamers "to cover them against sharpshooters from the jungle and canebrake that cover the low banks" of the river. As silently as was possible for such a gigantic procession, the invasion fleet steered for the landing beaches upstream at Johnson's plantation (also called Johnson's Landing). Many of the midwesterners in blue continued to marvel at the South's diverse scenery passing before them — there was nothing like it in Illinois, Minnesota, Indiana, or Ohio.

Jake Ritner of the 25th Iowa was sufficiently impressed to note in a letter home that the riverbanks were "covered with a very thick growth of timber and underbrush of all kinds — swamp and cane break." Even more impressive, and perhaps foreboding, was an unknown kind of moss that seemed to be everywhere. It grew "all over the trees and hangs down almost to the ground," the Hawkeye recorded. "It is of a kind of gray color, and looks very curious and makes it impossible to see any distance although there are no leaves on the trees." Ritner was describing Spanish moss, which, although familiar to many gunboatmen by now, was strange to the Yankee troops.

As the Porter-Sherman fleet paddled along, Lt. Cmdr. Gwin's daring bluejackets resumed their anti-torpedo campaign. Once more, Southern soldiers, protected by high levees on the south bank, peppered them every time they set out in their yawls to look for the deadly mines and their tripwires. Gwin's men spent most of their morning belowdecks, trying to keep from being shot. "The armored portion of the light draught gunboats" largely resisted these bullets, Admiral Mahan later recorded, "but their upper works were badly cut up." No progress would be recorded this day.

At 10:00 A.M., the officer of the deck aboard the *Benton* recorded in the ship's log that "The *Black Hawk*, bearing the broad pennant of Rear Admiral D.D. Porter, hove in sight and made a landing a short distance above Johnson's Landing." Throughout the remainder of the morning and into the afternoon, troop-

The 207-ton tinclad *Marmora* was active on the Western Rivers from October 1862 through the end of the war. She was often employed in company with one or more of the timberclads, including operations in the Yazoo River in December 1862, the campaign against Arkansas Post in January 1863, and expeditions up the White and Little Red rivers in 1864. Note the side-wheel river steamer in the background behind the gunboat's pilothouse. Its identity has yet to be established (Naval Historical Center).

boats and naval vessels, including the returning *Baron de Kalb*, put into the bank above and below the farm. The 3rd Division of Brig. Gen. George W. Morgan was on the left, Brig. Gen. Frederick Steele's 4th Division was in the center, and Brig. Gen. Morgan L. Smith's 2nd Division came ashore on the right. The 1st Division of Brig. Gen. Andrew J. Smith would arrive next day.

Brig. Gen. Stephen D. Lee, commander of the forward Provisional Division being assembled to guard the Yazoo and its bluffs and bayous, alerted Vicksburg that bluecoats were going ashore not only at Johnson's but also "at a point a mile below Chickasaw Bayou." These 30,000 Yankees were about three miles below the string of bluffs and the dry ground behind them that led to Vicksburg. If they could make it across the morass to the foot of the hills and then scale those heights, the way to the town was, at the moment at least, open to them.

As quickly as the staging planks were lowered, soldiers debarked. The landing beaches on the south side of the river covered a three-mile stretch — in the words of reporter Richard T. Colburn, "from the junction of the Yazoo with the Old River up to Johnson's Ferry." Upwards of three regiments pushed inland to establish a protective perimeter with occasional big gun help from the gunboats. There was uncertainty and confusion in the landing. As a result, most Union troops bivouacked near their transports.

Nearby Southern forces were driven back some distance, a number of houses a half mile inland were burned, and a "good line of pickets" was established. Ensign Browne on the *Tyler* noted that "we shelled the woods beyond our troops, thus making it hot for them (Confederates) for over a mile back from the river bank." Correspondent F.C. Foster of the *Chicago Daily Tribune* complimented the *Lexington* and *Tyler* for their Boxing Day fire support activities. "After materially assisting the reconnaissance by shelling the enemy," the scribe applauded, "(with as great precision as their ability to see them would permit) in obedience to the directions given them from time to time by messengers from the scene" the timberclads, then about two miles above Cypress Bayou, "retained the position to which they had been assigned."

At 2:00 P.M., the *Tyler* weighed anchor to return to the mouth of the Yazoo for coal. As her hook was being drawn out of the mud, Seaman Daniel C. Bice slipped and fell overboard, hitting his head on the anchor toe, and disappeared. His body was not recovered and the tragedy cast a gloom over the boat. A survivor of the *Mound City* disaster up the White River in June, Bice was popular with his messmates and his loss was, according to Ensign Browne, the first unnatural death aboard the timberclad.

By Porter's command, Lt. Cmdr. Gwin took the *Benton* and *Lexington* upstream to Antony's Ferry about 3:00 P.M. There, at a point just short of two miles from Drumgould's Bluff, they opened diversionary fire on the heavy batteries and an adjoining Confederate camp. There was some return fire from the big Rebel guns which, at that point and at Snyder's Bluff, capped the eastern end of Vicksburg's defenses. Local Confederate commanders hoped that their huge cannon in these places could stop any Yankee attack on Yazoo City, where a number of Confederate gunboats were under construction. Maj. Gen. Pemberton arrived on the scene during Gwin's attack. He later reported that his enemy's gunboats were engaged in shelling the banks of the Yazoo River all the way up "to the vicinity of the first bluffs at Snyders Mill" (13 miles north of Vicksburg). This deliberate cannonade "covered the disembarkation of his troops."

The first night ashore, the Union troops slept, without benefit of tents, on the ground or leaning against tree trunks. Many made use of their oilcloths to protect themselves against a cold rain. The miserably damp and rainy winter weather of the South was now upon them.[8] In the soggy predawn cold of December 27, Acting Rear Adm. Porter, who was probably not asleep, was handed a note written at 4:00 A.M. by Maj. Gen. Sherman. Rain, plus the nonarrival of Maj. Gen. Smith, the communication read, required a modification in the day's schedule.

The original plan to move three columns inland would proceed. Additionally, Maj. Gen. Steele would take two brigades to Blake's Plantation. Benson Blake, like W.H. Johnson, was a wealthy local farmer whom Capt. Sutherland of the *Queen of the West* labeled "an officer of some note in the Rebel army." From Blake's, Steele could cover the levee, making it impossible for Confederates to operate their torpedoes. He could also follow it back along Chickasaw Bayou and, with luck, secure a lodgment back on the bluffs. Once the army was on the scene, Porter's gunboats "could then threaten Haynes' Bluff battery."

Porter, comfortable from the weather in the great cabin of the *Black Hawk*, now rapidly engaged his clerks in copying a huge cargo of orders for delivery to his various captains. The first one was to Lt. Cmdr. Gwin and spoke of a possible demonstration against the Rebel batteries in conjunction with his anti-torpedo sweep. Such a shoot would provide the diversionary support requested by the army by drawing "off a large portion of the troops from Vicksburg."

The daring newlywed and former *Tyler* skipper was informed that Brig. Gen. Steele would land two brigades at Blake's Landing, at the mouth of Chickasaw Creek, sometime during the morning. In the process, the general's men would take possession of the plantation home as well as enfilade and threaten the Yazoo levee, "behind which the enemy works his torpedoes." Steele would then follow the levee back to the hills where he would hopefully "secure a lodgment."

Lt. Cmdr. Gwin was to take his boats and sweep up the Yazoo as before, being careful when firing inland so as not to hit any Union soldiers. At some point, Porter would "order up the *Cincinnati* and *Louisville* as if going to attack Haynes' Bluff." The two words in the last sentence would be a key later: "as if." This diversion would be made in support of Steele's troops and was not directly a part of Gwin's anti-torpedo operation.

Another set of orders was sent along to Lt. Cmdr. Walker requiring that the *Baron de Kalb* get underway when Gwin did, keeping 100 yards behind him and following his lead. He too was cautioned regarding gunfire, as Federal troops would be on the right bank of the river going up. Lt. George M. Bache, commander of the *Cincinnati*, received the next order envelope. Anchored near the landing fleet, the veteran Eads ironclad was to steam up the Yazoo until she found the *Benton* and was to anchor 400 yards astern of her. If the giant ironclad moved, she was to follow her at the same interval.

Bache, like Gwin and Walker, was cautioned against friendly fire. Unlike his more senior colleagues, the lieutenant had not yet been under fire on this expedition. He was cautioned not to waste shot and to make certain that his crew was kept "completely under cover from riflemen." In any event, he was to be in position no later than 9:30 A.M.

Having received a request from Brig. Gen. Willis A. Gorman for assistance in a forthcoming campaign in Arkansas. Porter ordered the *Conestoga* to shortly begin the requested patrolling action "between the White and Arkansas rivers as occasion may require. But," he added in his instructions to Lt. Cmdr. Selfridge, "Arkansas is the main point to look after. We will occupy it soon with troops."

Between 8:00 A.M. and noon, as Maj. Gen. Sherman later reported, "the whole army was distributed and moved out" in columns. Brig. Gen. Steele's 4th Division, one of the units, set off above the mouth of Chickasaw Bayou. Part of the command was tasked to move up to enfilade the levees, aiding the ram *Queen of the West* as she and her consorts provided gunfire support for the men being sent back into torpedo alley. Under the protection of the *Queen* and other boats, the *Benton*'s first and second cutters were again dispatched to drag for torpedoes. Rowboats with brave and exposed sailors from other vessels were also employed.

Fire was brisk from 400 Confederates concealed in rifle pits, particularly on the left side of the river. At one point, the *Queen of the West* advanced too far, necessitating a recall signal from Lt. Cmdr. Gwin. Capt. Sutherland did not have a spyglass so, instead of withdrawing, he moved ahead, firing upon a Rebel masked battery. When Sutherland found himself unsupported by the U.S. Navy vessels behind, he rounded to only to drift ashore. It required half an hour for the ram to refloat herself. At noon, the *Queen* advanced again as before but withdrew out of range of the Confederate field guns as soon as they fired.

As the minesweeping continued, Acting Rear Adm. Porter came up to observe and was both pleased and worried over what he saw. The work of the crewmen was valiant, but unless soldiers could be found to clear the Rebels from the banks, there would be many more casualties than the three already killed, despite the heavy gunfire from the gunboats and rams. As he prepared to return to his flag steamer, the admiral took Lt. Cmdr. Gwin aside and gave him permission to "make feint only at the fort to see what they had," while at the same time avoiding their heavy shot. Porter actually hoped "they would burst their guns."

Reconnaissance by fire is what the squadron commander had in mind. This was the same sort of game that Capt. Walke and Lt. Cmdr. Phelps had played with the timberclads against the defenses of Columbus, Kentucky, the previous year. As then, it was never Porter's intention, as he later told Lt. Cmdr. Elias K. Owen, "to engage the batteries, but to draw their fire and see what guns they had."

Back aboard the *Black Hawk*, Porter wrote to Sherman asking that, in accordance with a conversation he had on the way back with Brig. Gen. Charles E. Hovey, commander of Brig. Gen. Steele's 1st Brigade, troops be sent to drive away the defenders. The bluecoats would be taken across the river to disperse the Confederate sharpshooters on the west side, keeping them from further impeding the progress of the mine warfare sailors. It was also suggested that, by working through the night with soldiers about 200 yards ahead of the cutters on each side of the river, the gunboats would come within range of the fortifications at Drumgould's

Bluff next day. Neither Sherman nor his subordinates were keen on leaving their troops so exposed and this recommendation would not be followed.

During the morning, the minesweeping was advanced approximately three miles. At that point, the boats approached a bend that bowed toward the west. Before them toward its northern end and on the Vicksburg side of the river about a mile upstream was 90-foot high Drumgould's Bluff, just down from Snyder's Bluff. Maj. Gen. Pemberton boasted that "a strong battery had been planted on the heights to cover the stream below and the river blockaded by a raft" covered with railroad iron. The Drumgould-Snyder's salient was protected by nine large guns. Acting Rear Adm. Porter later indicated that the guns within the different forts were 50-pounder rifles and 64-pounder smoothbores. F.C. Foster told his Chicago *Daily Tribune* readers that these "well mounted" pieces were in "three batteries about equal distance above each other." In addition to the gunners, 1,300 men of the 22nd Louisiana and 3rd Mississippi, commanded by Col. Edward Higgins, were also on hand.[9]

There has been some confusion among writers as to exactly where the following events occurred. Pemberton's "Snyder's Mill" was at Drumgould's Bluff, where the *Benton*'s executive officer, George Lord, Capt. Walke, Acting Rear Adm. Porter, Admiral Mahan, and John D. Milligan all placed the action. Haynes' Bluff (also written as Haines' Bluff), a few miles above Drumgould's and also around a bend in the Yazoo, was chosen as their location by Prof. James R. Soley, Jack D. Combe, and Chester G Hearn among others. Remarking that the cliffs that protected Vicksburg's vulnerable right flank were Haynes' Bluff, Snyder's Bluff, and Drumgould's Bluff, Jim Miles, in his part history, part tour guide referred to them collectively, "for the sake of simplicity," as Haynes' Bluff.

Dr. Christopher R. Gabel and the Staff Ride Team of the Combat Studies Institute, U.S. Army Command and General Staff College, have given us the clearest description of this Confederate defensive position, labeled by the Confederates as Snyder's Bluff or Snyder's Mill:

> The U.S. Navy referred to it as "Drumgould's Bluff," which is the next hill to the south, where the left wing of the position rested. The U.S. Army usually called the position "Haynes' Bluff," which is actually the name for the next hill to the north and which was not part of the main defensive works. Nevertheless, the name "Haynes' Bluff" is the term used by most historians to designate this fortified position, which actually occupied Drumgould's and Snyder's bluffs. By any name, this piece of ground and the defensive works located here constituted some of the most important terrain in the campaign for Vicksburg.

Given the slow work involved in the torpedo removal — or attempted removal — as well as Confederate resistance and the U.S. Navy designation preference, we will center our story at Drumgould's Bluff.[10]

As 4th Division men cut roads through the timber between their position and the levee, Brig. Gen. Steele received Acting Rear Adm. Porter's request of Maj. Gen. Sherman. Steele, in his official report of the day's activities, noted simply that "I sent the 17th Missouri Infantry." Clamoring ashore from a pair of transports, Col. Francis Hassendenbel's Missourians quickly chased away the Rebels shooting up the boats below them. "After having accomplished the work," Brig. Gen. Steele later summed up, "they returned."

Also during the morning, the *Louisville* and *Cincinnati* felt their way up to the vicinity of the *Benton*. Conserving ammunition and making every effort to avoid any rogue torpedoes, the two Pook turtles dropped anchor off her stern as Acting Rear Adm. Porter had directed. Once the army troops near her position were tasked, the *Lexington* was also permitted to steam up and join Lt. Cmdr. Gwin. By lunchtime, according to the Porter map reproduced on page 575 of ORN, vol. 23, the vessels lay in this order north to south: *Benton, Baron de Kalb, Cincinnati, Louisville, Queen of the West, Marmora,* and *Lexington.* Although he was, to borrow a later term, the "Tail-end Charlie," Lt. Cmdr. Shirk's big guns could easily fire on Drumgould's Bluff over the point of land separating the two. Accuracy, of course, was another matter.

The Union tars continued their arduous task of torpedo removal, even as Col. Higgins, using a spyglass from atop Drumgould's Bluff, was able to keep track of their progress. By now, the Yankee tars had succeeded in removing five torpedoes on the day without any accidents or explosions. At approximately 2:00 P.M., Higgins saw a launch and several boats row around the point immediately below the big cannon of the Confederate fortifications. They were no more than about 1,200 yards away. A half hour later, Rebel gunners fired twice at the minesweepers. Higgins claimed the cannoneers caused them to retire, a fact disputed by Porter.

In any event, you can almost feel the awe among the Confederate Drumgould's Bluff defenders when Col. Higgins reported what happened next. In an effort to protect the sweepers, the *Benton* weighed anchor and advanced. As the Rebel leader put it, "In a few minutes, a steamer (an immense iron-clad, between 300 and 400 feet in length) rounded the point." The *Benton*'s length was actually 202 feet. Lt. Cmdr. Gwin was not making a feint just to draw fire and count puffs of muzzle smoke to determine battery location. He was determined to aggressively protect his small-boat torpedo hunters and believed he had to duel the enemy to accomplish that end.

The former *Tyler* captain wanted to mass fire on the shore batteries from boats idling in the river. This proved impossible. In the first place, the Yazoo here was very narrow and would not permit the *Benton* and the Pook turtles to steam and shoot abreast as they had at Fort Henry. The gunboatmen did not know for certain how many guns faced them

Lt. Cmdr. William Gwin (1832–1863) succeeded Cmdr. Henry Walke as captain of the *Tyler* in January 1862 and commanded her during the battles of Forts Henry and Donelson, on the great Tennessee River raid, at Shiloh, on the June 1862 White River expedition, and during her battle with the Confederate armorclad *Arkansas* in July. During the fall, he was married and, upon his return from his honeymoon, assumed command of the giant ironclad *Benton.* Within weeks, he was killed aboard her during an attack on Drumgould's Bluff on the Yazoo River. Always impeccably dressed and gallant in every assignment, he was one of the U.S. Navy's rising stars when he was cut down. Had he lived, he would undoubtedly have retired an admiral (Naval Historical Center).

or exactly where they were located. In that respect, Drumgould's elevated gun emplacements were more like those at Fort Donelson or at St. Charles, Arkansas, than Fort Henry anyway. Additionally, an unknown number of torpedoes and other obstructions remained, making it impossible to move farther up the river or engage from closer quarters. Finally, the weather and water were bad. There was a stiff breeze blowing after lunch that checked the current. Porter later reported that "the *Benton*, at all times an unmanageable ship, had a tendency to turn head or broadside to wind. The only way to keep her from being thrown across the river while firing was to have her tied to the bank."

In view of all the uncertainties, Lt. Cmdr. Gwin ordered his ship to the left bank. His executive officer, Acting Master George P. Lord, testified later that this was "the only position in which he could place his vessel in range of the batteries." As Higgins and his men watched, the *Benton* "made fast to the other shore and engaged our batteries." At the bank, the *Benton*'s gunners had found that it would be possible to work her bow or starboard batteries by slacking or tautening the lines holding her to shore. Reassured, Lt. Cmdr. Gwin gave the order to start shooting with the bow guns at 3:35 P.M. A few minutes later, a number of other gunboats stationed behind the point, including the *Lexington*, opened their portion of the ball with, in Higgins' words, "shell upon our batteries."

It was, however, the *Benton*, exposed as she was in the van position, that was the plumpest target. Cannonballs and shells hit her 24 times, while splinters and shrapnel were frequent unwanted visitors. Shot caused no harm to the giant's armored pilothouse or sides other than some denting. Those that struck her deck were the culprits, plunging "straight through everything."

The battle between the exposed and unexposed Federal gunboats and the Confederate batteries continued for the next hour. The small craft involved in torpedo removal naturally could not work during the battle so they all rowed back around the point out of the line of fire. As they were departing, according to Col. Higgins, a Rebel cannonball found one of them and turned it over. The wind was blowing so hard during the shoot that the *Cincinnati*, *Baron de Kalb*, and *Louisville* were also unmanageable. Although they, together with the *Lexington*, brought their batteries to bear "as well as the very narrow stream would permit, they could not fire effectively."

By half past four, it had become fairly certain that the Rebels had, in Lord's words, "succeeded in obtaining a dead range upon our vessel." The *Benton* would have to be moved somewhere else or the fight given up. Lt. Cmdr. Gwin, anxious to see if his guns were causing any damage, left the *Benton*'s armored pilothouse and went out onto deck armed only with a spyglass. Impeccably uniformed as usual, the *Tyler*'s former skipper exposed himself to enemy fire, aptly demonstrating his motto that "the quarterdeck was the place for a commander to be in time of action."

While "braving fearlessly their balls," as he had during the heated battle with the *Arkansas* back in July, Gwin was mortally wounded by a rifled Confederate shell that took off most of his right breast. As he fell, according to F.C. Foster of the *Chicago Daily Tribune*, he knew his wound was fatal and supposedly screamed his final words: "My love to my wife — my wishes to my country." As her captain lay on deck in a pool of blood, the *Benton* continued across the stream. With shells whizzing all about them, several seamen rushed to their captain's aid. Acting Master Lord, injured himself, signaled Lt. Cmdr. Walker and Owen that Gwin was down. Plunging fire also killed Master-at-Arms Robert Royal and wounded nine others aboard. Besides Gwin, one seaman was mortally wounded. A boat was sent back to the *Baron de Kalb* for a surgeon and Owen from the *Louisville* ordered Lord to take the *Benton* back down the river and report her to Porter. In the primitive conditions of the day, the doctor amputated the shattered arm of the ironclad captain and bandages were applied to the stump and his other terrible wounds.

The Federals closed their hour and 35 minute engagement with the guns of Drumgould's Bluff at 5:10 P.M. and withdrew. Col. Higgins was overjoyed to report that his batteries and works were not injured. One man from the 22nd Louisiana was killed and two from that regiment were wounded. Maj. Gen. Pemberton was delighted to pass on word to his superiors that "our guns were handled with spirit and precision and the officers and men deserve the highest praise for their gallant conduct during the engagement."

The *Benton*, herself unhurt during the fight save for incapacitating damages to a pair of bow guns, dropped anchor off Johnson's Landing about 9:00 P.M. An hour later, Acting Rear Adm. Porter was piped aboard to see his gallant subordinate. Porter immediately rushed to the side of Lt. Cmdr. Gwin, who would linger until January 2 in great pain. Paying tribute to his gallantry, Admiral Mahan and others later said Gwin had exhibited "noble rashness."

As the navy's terrible day ticked toward midnight, Porter was once more writing messages and orders. Lt. Cmdr. Owen of the *Louisville*, the senior officer with the gunboats below Drumgould's Bluff, received the first. In it, he was told to withdraw out of range of the Confederate batteries and to make certain that none of the other craft, large or small, with him came within reach of the Southern gunners. General Sherman received the next message, one which began "We have been unfortunate today." The Drumgould's fort was, the admiral conveyed, "a strong one in front, but open from the rear." It cut up the *Benton* badly and the popular Gwin was, alas, "I fear, mortally wounded."

Having written to Owen and Sherman, Porter next penned orders to Lt. Cmdr. Shirk for the timberclads. The *Lexington*, he wrote, was to move down around the next turn from her position at daybreak to drive off any Rebels who might descend upon the transports via Johnson's Road. The *Tyler* was to be stationed halfway between the *Lexington* and Old River.

All day on Sunday and Monday, Sherman's soldiers gallantly attempted to fight their way inland toward the bluffs. Chickasaw Bayou, the swamps, natural and manmade defenses, and the dug-in Confederates blocked their progress. A perfect storm of canister and bullets fired by the increasingly reinforced foe met every Federal attempt — and the damp wet weather did not cooperate. During those two days of heavy rain, the gunboats, including *Lexington* and *Tyler*, attempted to provide gunfire support, but they had to be extremely careful in order to prevent friendly fire incidents. Feints were made, firing was conducted across the Mill Dale road, and even a pair of mortar boats were engaged.

Firing was often conducted by compass based on information brought by orderlies and contrabands. The gunboats covered the army in an eight-mile semicircle. Little of this was seen by the Northern reporters; scribes like Wilkie and Knox were too busy keeping themselves from being shot, run over, or sinking in the ooze.

At one point, Acting Rear Adm. Sherman was informed that Confederates were advancing on Brig. Gen. Steele's left, near the Benson Blake place. As the navy chief wrote Maj. Gen. Sherman, the gunboats would attempt to provide assistance but could only promise accuracy "from the supposition that General Steele is where the orderly says he is." Late on December 29, with his men making no further headway and running low on ammunition, Sherman confided to Porter that "Chickasaw Bayou is our line of attack and we can do or attempt nothing till we make a lodgment on the hills at its head."

Far upstream at Cypress Bend, eight miles below Napoleon, Arkansas, Confederate cavalry with mobile "horse artillery" captured the chartered merchant steamer *Blue Wing*, with her cargo of ammunition and towing two vital coal barges. The riders were from Arkansas

Post and, as they guided their prize back up the risen Arkansas River to Fort Hindman, they were very excited by their success.[11]

Making little headway, Sherman was forced to call off his Chickasaw Bayou thrust and rethink his Vicksburg approach. Not willing to quit just yet, he and Porter came up with a plan to assault Drumgould's Bluff "after a dark and rainy night" when the sky was clear. If they could take the heights, hopefully they would be able to open a path for reinforcements from Maj. Gen. Grant, who was still believed to be en route. Col. Ellet won approval to send a ram ahead of the troopboats with a crude minesweeping rake attached to her bow. It was hoped that this would neutralize the infernal machines more effectively than the small boats. Sherman cut orders for Brig. Gen. Steele to proceed upstream under naval protection on the evening of December 30-31 and launch an attack at daybreak on the last day of the year. The rest of the army would restart its efforts to get over Chickasaw Bayou.

Hardly anyone below the rank of rear admiral or major general believed this plan would work any better than those tried the past several days. Capt. Strew Emmons of the 76th Ohio Infantry later told his wife that this latest idea was "a most reckless fool hardy undertaking & could possibly have succeeded."

Well into the night of December 30, the designated midwestern troops escaped their inundated camps and boarded steamers at Johnson's Landing. Simultaneously, five ironclads, two rams, several tinclads and the *Lexington* moved upstream towards Drumgould's Bluff. Fortunately for the Federals, particularly the amphibious troops embarked on the 12 transports that started upstream at 3:00 A.M., a thick fog arose around 4:30 A.M. December 31. The gunboats that had ascended first were two hours late in reaching their stations and when they, together with Steele's vessels, were recalled, it was still too soupy to see much. As Porter later lamented, "Man proposes, God disposes." This effort to capture Vicksburg was over and an unhappy Sherman pulled the plug on it.

New Year's Eve and New Year's Day were quiet for Union troops, though Confederates on the hills above them celebrated and even provided a band concert of patriotic Rebel tunes, "Dixie" often among them. Earlier in the day, the *Tyler* hove up her anchor and moved closer to Johnson's Landing. Late on 1863's first night, in secret, the Federals quietly began to retreat, marching as silently as possible back aboard their boats. Upon his inquiry, Ensign Browne on the *Tyler* was informed by Lt. Cmdr. Pritchett that a strategic move was being made "to flank the enemy."

Most of the Northerners were embarked by mid-morning, when Rebel scouts discovered what was going on. As fast as the vessels were loaded, they slipped out into the Yazoo. Simultaneously, the gunboats *Lexington* and *Marmora* and the ram *Queen of the West* weighed anchor and dropped down from their anchorage to cover the embarkation.

In an effort to break up the retreat, Confederate troops, led by the 2nd Texas, charged the landing beaches just after noon, killing two bluecoats. Watching their oncoming rush, 114th Ohio soldier Michael Sweetman aboard the steamer *Pembina* remembered that "the Rebs came close enough to fire on us when we cut loose and started." The sound of the famous Rebel yell could hardly be heard as the troopboats left their opponents "to the tender mercies of the gunboats." The deafening roar of naval cannon fire from the *Lexington*, *Marmora*, and *Queen of the West* beat back the attempt to smash the embarkation.

Until approximately 2:30 P.M., gunboat fire continued to be aimed at the Confederate soldiers who harassed the flotilla as it withdrew to the mouth of the Yazoo and Milliken's Bend beyond. Following the *Mound City*, *Pittsburg*, *Benton*, and *Rattler*, the *Tyler* reached the river's mouth about 5:15 P.M. The *Lexington* group arrived later. Maj. Gen. Pemberton believed that his men were "under the incessant fire of twelve gunboats."

12. Anniversary, POW Convoys, and Death of a Timberclad Hero, July–December 1862

This visit to the Yazoo was unprofitable, what the correspondent from the *St. Louis Daily Missouri Democrat* called "a stupid blunder." Sherman's casualties reached 1,776 for the campaign, while Confederate losses were far fewer. When paired with the dismal failure by Maj. Gen. Burnside at Fredericksburg in Virginia, it is understandable that there was significant Union gloom. What was needed was a quick victory by the Union navy and Northern soldiers to erase public memory of the western failure.

The *Conestoga* hove to opposite Napoleon, Arkansas, on January 2 and sent word to its citizens that if another transport were fired into near the town "the place shall be destroyed." Word of the Selfridge decree reached Fort Hindman next day.

Further south, as recorded in the journal of Pvt. Sweetman of the 114th Ohio, "The boats moved up the river about thirty miles and stopped. It rained heavily all day and the weather was cold and disagreeable."

Lt. Cmdr. Gwin died at 6:00 P.M. on January 3 and it is fitting that we here pause to remember the gallant gentleman who faced his death squarely. Mrs. Mary L. Gwin and her father, Hiram Hutchinson, had just arrived at Cairo for a visit. So it was with shock and horror that they learned the death news from Lt. Cmdr. S. Ledyard Phelps. Acting for the ill Capt. Alexander M. Pennock, Phelps provided such comfort as he could. Promised that Lt. Cmdr. Gwin would receive a martial salute and immediate return to New York City, the grieving relatives departed for home to make final arrangements.

Late on the evening of January 19, the gunboat *New Era* arrived at Cairo with Confederate POWs from Arkansas Post and the body of Lt. Cmdr. Gwin. It is not known to be the case, but it is probable that the corpse was dressed in the full uniform worn so regularly and proudly in life. Early on Tuesday, the flags on all Federal vessels in port were lowered to half staff. Also during the morning, arrangements were completed for the shipment of the casket via the Illinois Central Railroad.

Promptly at noon, Lt. Cmdr. Phelps, acting on behalf of Capt. Pennock, received Gwin's

Benton. Originally the Eads snagboat *Submarine No. 7*, rejected for government service by Cmdr. John Rodgers in 1861, this vessel became the most powerful vessel in the Mississippi Squadron. Lt. Cmdr. William Gwin was mortally wounded while in command (Naval Historical Center).

remains, covered in an American flag. After appropriate comments and a prayer, the coffin, born upon the shoulders of his six-man boat crew, was taken to the railroad station under a U.S Marine Corps escort. Led by Capt. Walke, all of the available naval officers at the station from ship and shore, in full uniform, walked in procession behind the leathernecks to the depot. There they mingled a while. "De Soto," the *New York Times* resident Cairo correspondent, who was probably Franc B. Wilkie's associate William George, later wrote that "Unfeigned respect and even admiration is entertained among all naval men in the West for this gallant officer."

Lt. Cmdr. Gwin's boat crew, led by a petty officer, accompanied his body home. The noncom also bore a paper with the deceased's last requests. It would be delivered to his wife, in care of his father-in-law. Despite a winter storm which abated to drizzling rain, a large crowd assembled on January 27 at the Zion Church, at the corner of Madison Ave. and 38th St. in Manhattan. The mourners were nearly identical to the people assembled in the same church for Gwin's wedding two months earlier.

The flag-covered casket, borne by the western boat crew and escorted by marines, was met at the church door and escorted to the alter by clergy, including a bishop, and a number of naval officers from the receiving ship *North Carolina*. Following the funeral mass, the body was borne from the church outside into the rain by six commissioned U.S. Navy officers. Lt. Cmdr. Gwin's funeral cortege was destined for the Jersey Ferry, the final leg of a journey that would end at a cemetery in Newark, New Jersey. It was preceded by a band, marines, and clergy. The procession included not only family members, but also his boat's crew, the *North Carolina*'s entire company, a company of volunteer soldiers, the other attending naval officers, friends and citizens. As the day ended, salutes were fired over the hero's grave.

Earlier, on January 4, the Lincoln favorite and Illinois Maj. Gen. John McClernand, slated earlier to take over Sherman's part of the Army of Tennessee, arrived at Milliken's Bend and assumed command, renaming his new unit the Army of Mississippi. Sherman was demoted to corps commander; however, he and ARAM Porter worked with the newcomer on planning for a new expedition.

In order to secure their marine supply line and prevent any more episodes such as the capture of the *Blue Wing*, a Federal armada would immediately steam to and reduce Fort Hindman at Arkansas Post. As McClernand later told it in his official report, Arkansas Post was the county seat of Arkansas County and was located 117 miles below Little Rock. At its location, the stream made a sharp northward bend that formed a complete U, with the town striking the outside of the bend. The village was built above the reach of floods on elevated grounds about 80 feet high and overlooked the left bank of the river for some miles. Built within town limits, diamond-shaped Fort Hindman was located at the head of the horseshoe shaped bend. It was an earthen, full-bastioned citadel protected with railroad iron. Westward from the fort for almost a mile to a stream called Post Bayou ran a line of rifle pits.

Garrisoned by about 5,000 men, Fort Hindman offered a view that looked about three miles down the sweep below the bend and over a mile in the other direction. Back of the town was a cleared half-mile wide sloping strip of land that extended to forest on the edge of the bottom land reaching to the river. The bottom land was covered mostly with cypress. Otherwise, there were only a few farms and clearings.

No one on the Federal side knew that the fort's commander, acting under recently assigned Brig. Gen. Thomas J. Churchill, was Col. John W. Dunnington. In June, Dunnington, then a CSN lieutenant, had aided Capt. Fry in the defense of St. Charles against Col. Graham N. Fitch and the *Mound City*.[12]

CHAPTER 13

1863: Arkansas Post to Helena

IT WOULD HAVE BEEN FOOLISH TO PREDICT during the busy start to 1863 that in the years ahead the timberclads would continue as vital squadron mainstays. Yet, despite wooden armor in a river navy increasingly made up of a large number of heavier, better gunned ironclads or swift light-draught tinclads, the "old gunboats" still had service to offer. The *Conestoga*, *Lexington*, and *Tyler* would each have a few more moments in the sun. In the space ahead, we will profile a number of incidents and activities that kept the timberclad war active in the first half of 1863.

The reader will recall that the *Conestoga* was dispatched back upstream at the end of December to guard the army's supply line and to patrol against attacks upon it by Confederate guerrillas. She was also to conduct reconnaissances up the White and Arkansas rivers in order to keep abreast of both regular and irregular Rebel forces. Stationed near Montgomery Point, Mississippi, opposite the mouth of the White River, the smallest timberclad's primary mission during the early months of 1863 would be, in the words of her captain, Lt. Cmdr. Thomas O. Selfridge, Jr., "to insure the safe passage of supply steamers and transports between that point and the mouth of the Arkansas River, a distance of about 25 miles."

During the first quarter, the *Tyler* served primarily in and off the mouth of the Yazoo. Lt. Cmdr. James M. Pritchett's boat was tasked with essentially the same duties as the *Conestoga*, with the added responsibility of keeping an eye on Vicksburg.[1]

Just after retiring from the Yazoo River, the *Lexington* was tapped for more work, becoming the busiest timberclad in the next quarter or so. On January 3, Lt. Cmdr. James W. Shirk received orders from Acting Rear Adm. David Dixon Porter to take his fast vessel up to the mouth of the Arkansas River and join the *Conestoga*. Upon his arrival, he was to briefly relieve Lt. Cmdr. Selfridge, who had orders to Memphis. With the aid of the light draft *New Era* and the army ram *Lancaster*, the *Lexington* was to ensure the closure of the mouth of the Arkansas, as well as the White.

Just after noon on January 4, the squadron command steamer *Black Hawk* weighed anchor and led all of the U.S. Navy gunboats, save the *Tyler*, *Benton*, and *Pittsburg* up the Mississippi from Milliken's Bend, together with the troop transports of Maj. Gen. John

McClernand. The Arkansas Post campaign was beginning. As a part of his battle strategy, Maj. Gen. McClernand planned to keep his destination secret as long as possible. To do so, it was determined that the armada would bypass the mouth of the Arkansas River. It would continue on up to Montgomery Point, Mississippi, and, across from it, the White River entrance. Steaming up that stream, the vessels could then take the cut-off and proceed back into the Arkansas and hence to its goal. With insufficient coal, the ironclads were often towed by the lighter gunboats or by troop transports. Boats were constantly required to put landing parties ashore to cut wood for fuel.

Pvt. Michael Sweetman of the 114th Ohio Volunteers recorded the armada's progress in his diary:

> M. January 5 — Moved a short distance up the river. Nothing new, strange or startling occurred during the day.
>
> T. January 6 — We moved a short distance up the river and stopped all day and night....
>
> W. January 7 — Remained at the same place until night and then moved up the Mississippi to the mouth of the White river.

The fleet was met off Montgomery Point, Mississippi, by the *Lexington*. Earlier in the day, Lt. Cmdr. Shirk picked up a starving local refugee (originally from Illinois) in a small boat; the man provided additional intelligence on Fort Hindman's layout. Between seven and nine major caliber guns were mounted on the bastion's river side and Hindman was manned by 11 regiments. This information, spotty in some regards, was quickly passed to the top commanders.

Later that evening, Porter's General Order No. 30 informed all of the captains of the sailing order for the advance up the White and Arkansas rivers that would commence on Thursday morning. A number of tinclads would precede the main fleet, keeping watch for Rebels, checking water depth, and guarding against torpedoes. These would be followed by the *Marmora*, *Black Hawk*, and the *Juliet*, the latter towing a coal barge. Those three were to be succeeded by the ironclads and troopboats. "The *Lexington*," it was commanded, "will bring up the rear."

As the fleet assembled on Wednesday, the *Conestoga* moved up the Arkansas River. Early on the afternoon of rainy January 8, she took the cut-off and proceeded down the light gray-colored White River, finding an abundance of fuel-quality wood all along the riverbank. Only several riders were seen. One of these returned to Fort Hindman at dark to report Selfridge's achievement to Brig. Gen. Churchill.

Additional scouts were sent out from the Confederate camp early on the morning of January 9. Within a matter of hours, one of these returned to report that the entire Yankee fleet, 70 or 80 transports convoyed by gunboats, had gone through the cut-off and was now in the Arkansas River "steaming their way with all possible dispatch for this place." The startled Brig. Gen. Churchill ordered all of the Rebel troops outside of Fort Hindman brought in except for those at Napoleon. As Porter had originally passed that town as if en route to Helena, they were blissfully unaware that the Arkansas River "was alive with Yankees."

The three Confederate brigades defending around Arkansas Post were then ordered to ready themselves for instant action. Col. Dunnington's Marine Battery was in Fort Hindman manning three heavy cannon and four 10-pounder Parrott rifles. Among the 500 men numbered within his ranks were soldiers from the 19th Arkansas and the veteran naval gunners brought down from the inactive Little Rock–moored ram *Pontchartrain*. Additionally, final preparations were made to have men move to rifle pits inland of the river, while log chains were checked on opposite the bastion. Throughout the day, the Rebels busied themselves making as many last minute preparations as possible.

The ironclads attack Fort Hindman at Arkansas Post in January 1863. The overwhelming Federal victory came after the disaster at Chickasaw Bayou in December and, temporarily at least, diverted Northern attention away from the Yazoo River (Library of Congress).

It was about 30 miles, Pvt. Sweetman remembered, from the cut-off to the landing beaches near Arkansas Post. The first of the transports bringing in Maj. Gen. Sherman's XV Corps nosed into the Notrebe Farm, three miles below Fort Hindman, at about 5:00 P.M. It was decided not to disembark the men until next morning, as all of the boats would not all be tied up at the bank until well after dark. The same conditions faced Brig. Gen. George W. Morgan's XIII Corps. Its transports put in on the opposite shore at Fletcher's Landing, about nine miles downstream. Belleville, a small town on the south bank of the river, was the only other community of note in the area.

A number of difficulties frustrated the advance by the Federal corps upon Fort Hindman and much time was wasted on the morning and afternoon of January 10. As McClernand personally worked to sort them out, he sent a message to ARAM Porter. A ground assault should be ready for launch about 2:00 P.M., the former Illinois congressman promised, and the navy consequently made ready to cooperate at that hour.[2] About 5:30 P.M., McClernand finally informed Porter that his corps were ready and four ironclads subsequently advanced to within 400 yards of the Confederate fort and, in the words of Findley Anderson of the *New York Herald*, "opened the ball."

Once the engagement warmed, Porter ordered Lt. Cmdr. Shirk to have the *Lexington* throw in shrapnel, while the flag boat *Black Hawk* entertained the Rebels with her rifled guns. "The cannonading was," Anderson told his readers, "at one time grand and terrible, fairly causing the earth to tremble with the vast volume of sound." According to Porter, the shot thrown by these two light draughts "was very destructive, killing nearly all the artillery horses in and about the fort." Lt. Cmdr. Shirk later reported that his gunners had expended 14 Parrott shells and two 8-inch shells during the evening shoot.

After some time, the combined weight of Yankee shells forced the Confederates, whose powder was contaminated, to stop shooting. Having suffered little damage in the spirited engagement, the gunboats also ceased firing. It was now too dark to see, so no ground assault was mounted. The warboats, meanwhile, dropped down the Arkansas and tied up to the bank.

During the night, Confederate troops feverishly struggled to complete or add to their defenses. Those trying to sleep on both sides were disturbed as the gunboats maintained a desultory firing. As the *Lexington* and *Tyler* did at Shiloh, the *Lexington* and her consorts here now got off a single round into the Confederate perimeter every half hour.

After midnight, Brig. Gen. Churchill received an order that would be bitterly resented by his men. Confederate Trans-Mississippi Department head Maj. Gen. Theophilus H. Holmes wrote from Pine Bluff that everyone in Fort Hindman should "hold out till help arrived or until all dead."

Sunday, January 11, was the climactic day. During the morning hours, Maj. Gen. McClernand made certain that his 32,000 soldiers were prepared to assault the 4,900 Rebel stalwarts at Fort Hindman. When he was ready, the general sent a note to Acting Rear Adm. Porter briefly saying that as soon as the navy attacked his men would advance on the enemy works.

It was originally planned that Porter's boats would resume their bombardment at daylight. However, the morning dawned with an intense fog that kept the ironclads and others from moving up. As they waited, divine services were held aboard several of the boats. At 1:00 P.M. just after lunch, the navy once more took the lead and attacked, now under a "clear sky and the gladsome sun." As soon as the *Louisville*, *Cincinnati*, and *Baron de Kalb* were hotly engaged, the *Lexington* again joined in, just as she had the night before. Those few with long memories recalled her long-range shooting at the Tennessee River forts almost a year earlier.

The citadel's defenders were further endangered when, from the head of Stillwell Peninsula opposite them, a terrific enfilading fire started. This terrible rain came from two 20-pounder Parrotts and two 3-inch rifles of the Chicago Mercantile Battery.

Texas Ranger William W. Heartsill penciled his thoughts on the fort's defenders in his hastily written diary: "The air is filled with the missels [sic] of death.... The two batteries on our left and nine gunboats are sending inside our lines a perfect storm of shot and shell, the woods are torn to splinters, fences scattered broad cast, while the constant whiz of the minie is convincing evidence of the mighty work of death that is now going on."

Pounded for the better part of three hours, the defenders of Fort Hindman were worn down. The *Lexington* alone threw 40 Parrott shells and forty-nine 8-inch shells toward the Confederates. Just before 4:00 P.M., Ranger Heartsill noticed, "a lone nine pounder is defiantly speaking his rebellious sentiments from our Fort, as all the balance of our guns are disabled." It was hoped that the remaining piece could hold out to the last. In particular, the huge 100-pounder Parrott in which Col. Dunnington had placed so much faith was gone. "Our large pivot gun on the upper corner of the Fort is broken square off at the middle," Heartsill despaired.

A few minutes after the ranger jotted down his observations, Fort Hindman ceased firing. Every gun within was either dismounted or destroyed and the railroad iron protecting the batteries was smashed. "Finally the last came," noted newsman Anderson. Although several of the ironclads were hit and 31 sailors killed, none of the vessels were put out of action. The *Lexington* suffered damages to her upper works and two of her boats.

A half hour later, a white flag was seen waving over Fort Hindman. Shortly thereafter, Col. Dunnington and 36 of his nautical gunners personally surrendered to ARAM Porter. Once Dunnington's command was out of the picture, the remainder of the local Confederate defense

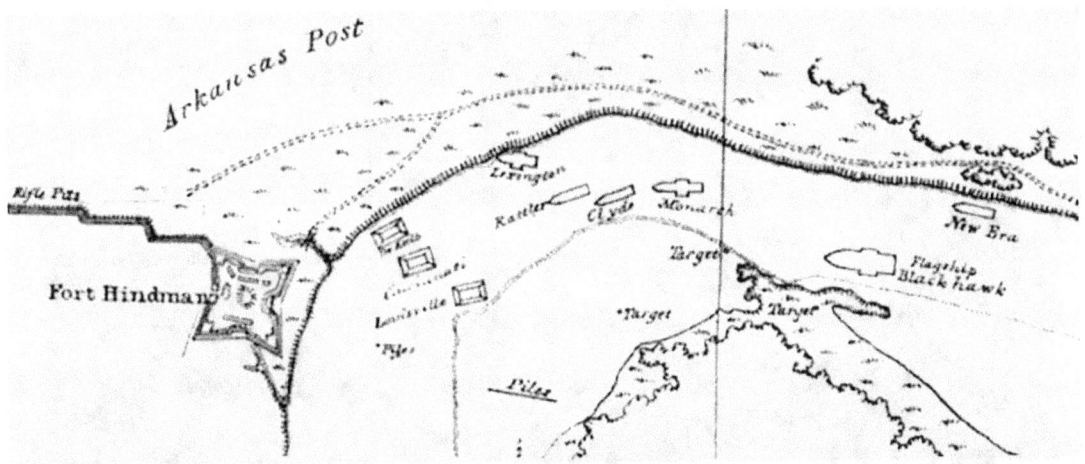

Action at Arkansas Post, January 1863. The timberclad *Lexington*, under the command of Lt. James W. Shirk, played a supporting role in the relatively easy Union victory, one which deflected Northern press coverage away from the disaster at Chickasaw Bayou the month before. In this map she is shown during the Federal descent upon Fort Hindman (*Battle and Leaders*).

collapsed like a house of cards. Well before dark, Fort Hindman and 4,791 Confederates (give or take a couple) were completely within Federal hands. About 134 Union and 60 Confederate soldiers were killed. As McClernand wrote to Porter after dark, "We have disposed of this tough little nut, the capture of which is alike creditable to the Army and Navy."

Throughout the next day, the magnitude of the victory was sorted out, along with the booty and debris of the battle. The Rebel prisoners were sent aboard transports and, as muster lists were made out, orders were prepared for their removal to St. Louis.

Early on January 13, Acting Rear Adm. Porter placed the finishing touches on his official report for Navy Secretary Gideon Welles in Washington. Speaking of Lt. Cmdr. Shirk, he noted that the *Lexington* was brought up "in good time" and opened her "broadside on the fort." One of her first shots supposedly "destroyed a rifled piece" that was "boring" her "pretty effectively."

An initial review of the battle appeared in the January 18 issue of the *New York Times*. Had any family member from the timberclad read it — which is unlikely — they might have been concerned. Based on testimony from officers aboard the steamer *Storm*, recently arrived at Cairo, was the *Times* report that "three balls entered the portholes of the *Lexington*, killing four men." Happily, this news was wrong.

The ink on Porter's document was not dry before new orders were en route to the timberclad. Opening them, Shirk learned that he would convoy the POWs north. Once that duty was finished, he was "to proceed to New Albany and take command of the *Tuscumbia*," a brand new ironclad.

At daylight on January 14, the steamers *John J. Roe*, *Nebraska*, and *Gatey*, escorted by the *Lexington*, departed Arkansas Post for "up the river." Fleet Captain Alexander M. Pennock would wire Navy Secretary Welles when the timberclad arrived on January 21, noting that she had convoyed up 4,793 POWs. A bit later that Wednesday, Maj. Gen. McClernand received orders from Maj. Gen. Grant demanding that the Army of the Mississippi return to Milliken's Bend. Following so soon upon the Chickasaw Bayou disaster, many, like newsman Finley Anderson, sincerely hoped that the Arkansas Post achievement would be warmly received in the North and serve as a "partial atonement for our recent defeat."[3]

An artist's depiction of the Battle of Arkansas Post as published in *Harper's Weekly*, February 7, 1863.

The situation inland on the Cumberland and Tennessee rivers was not quiet during the winter months of 1863. As the old year turned into the new, Maj. Gen. William S. Rosecrans' Army of the Cumberland engaged Gen. Braxton Bragg's Confederate Army of Tennessee in a titanic fight at Stone's River, near Murfreesboro, Tennessee. For weeks prior to the battle, Rosecrans' quartermasters assembled supplies in Nashville to gird the soldiers in their campaign; for weeks afterward, additional succor was deemed necessary.

In the fall of 1862, Capt. Alexander M. Pennock, the Mississippi Squadron fleet captain based at Cairo, was deputized by Acting Rear Adm. Porter to operate an upper river division in support of Rosecrans. His executive officer for the actual provision of gunboat services on the Ohio, Tennessee, and Cumberland rivers was 28-year-old Logansport, Indiana, native Lt. Cmdr. Le Roy Fitch.

The younger half brother of Col. Graham Newell Fitch of White River memory and an 1856 U.S. Naval Academy graduate, Le Roy Fitch (1835–1875) spent most of the war in command of the tinclads operating on the Upper Rivers, particularly the Ohio and Cumberland. He is remembered for blocking Maj. Gen. John Hunt Morgan's return south from his great Indiana-Ohio Raid (1863), his aggressive duels with Maj. Gen. Nathan Bedford Forrest and his several combats with Rebel gunners during the Battle of Nashville (1864). He would die of a mysterious illness at home just before his 40th birthday.)[4]

Fitch operated his command with only a handful of howitzer-armed tinclads. Arrayed against him were powerful Confederate regular and irregular forces determined to halt his usually successful convoys of Federal troop and supply steamers up the Cumberland from Smithland, Kentucky, to Nashville.

In addition to Rebel opposition and the usual hazards of shepherding and coast-guarding river transportation on the windy, twisty Cumberland, Fitch had also to contend with constant complaints from Rosecrans and the Union quartermasters. These gentlemen constantly complained to Capt. Pennock and the Washington establishment about the methods of escort, the timing of convoys, and the successes too often, in their opinion, enjoyed by the enemy in his hit and run strikes. Navy Secretary Welles referred the comments to his western commanders.

Often ill, Capt. Pennock, though maintaining supreme confidence in his subordinate, required an independent survey of the Cumberland River situation. To that end, Lt. Cmdr. Seth Ledyard Phelps, whom the fleet commander had known since he had brought the Confederate *Eastport* to Cairo as a prize the previous February, was dispatched on January 25 to conduct a survey and provide an unbiased assessment. Phelps was also to find a Fitch convoy and confer with its escort commander. As Lt. Cmdr. Shirk had been posted to command of the new ironclad *Tuscumbia*, the heavily armed *Lexington* was between captains and available for this duty.

While the latest Federal supply armada ascended towards Clarksville, great billows of smoke pouring from its collective chimneys, Lt. Cmdr. Phelps' *Lexington* was in the Cumberland on January 26 where she met a steamer sailing independently. The vessel had been fired upon by Confederate artillery at Betsy Town Landing, a point some 20 miles above Clarksville. Phelps, perhaps remembering his time up this stream early the previous year, determined to extract satisfaction and so pushed on up. Passing Clarksville in the dark, the timberclad reached the riverbank location described by the civilian craft's pilot early the following morning; there a landing party went ashore and burned a storehouse supposedly used by Rebels as a "resort and cover."

With his armed reconnaissance completed, Phelps was returning to Clarksville when Rebel cannoneers, firing a couple of Parrot rifles from shore, hit the *Lexington* three times "without injury." She quickly returned fire with her big 8-inch guns and, as Nashville post commander Brig. Gen. Robert Mitchell put it in his telegram on the event to Maj. Gen. Rosecrans, "We succeeded in driving the rebels out." The offending Confederate artillerymen were among those handling the six field guns of Maj. Gen. Joseph Wheeler's combined regular army division. Made up of an 800-man brigade led by Brig. Gen. Nathan Bedford Forest and another with 2,000 soldiers under Brig. Gen. John Wharton, Wheeler's force had been tasked with the interruption of Union navigation of the Cumberland.

Observed from the *Lexington* as well as from shore, the Fitch group reached Clarksville toward dusk on January 27and anchored for the night. There the Indiana commander met with his escort skippers, as well as many of the steamer captains, explaining that the rest of the trip was potentially dangerous. To lessen the chance of Confederate attack, the convoy would leave at midnight and proceed under cover of darkness. It would be closely maintained and the three tinclads would always be available, with one in the van, one in the center, and one in the rear. Lt. Cmdr. Phelps, joining in the discussions, not only learned the tactical situation from Fitch and his lieutenants, but also agreed to lead the convoy into Nashville.

Colonel Sanders D. Bruce of the 20th Kentucky Infantry, post commander at Clarksville, reported the fleet's arrival to Maj. Gen. Rosecrans. He also noted that Confederate raiders were on the south side of the Cumberland, near Harpeth Shoals; their force was reckoned at 5,000, with eight pieces of artillery. The butternut cavalry had been "collecting such supplies as the country affords." Rebel horsemen could be seen on the south side of the shoals, though Bruce kept a strong picket force on his side of the shoals. Brig. Gen. Mitchell informed Rosecrans' headquarters a few hours later that the fleet, with four gunboats, was on its way up that night.

Mitchell reported to Rosecrans later on January 28 that the "Fleet [was] passing Shoals at 1 P.M. without interruption." The convoy made Nashville that evening without, as Phelps put it in his report to Capt. Pennock, "so much as a musket shot having been fired upon a single vessel of the fleet." The *Lexington* remained at Nashville only long enough to coal before returning to Cairo, where she arrived after dark on January 29.

Acting Rear Adm. Porter had also anticipated, given the flurry of communications between Washington, Murfreesboro, and Cairo, the need for additional gunboats on the upper rivers. On January 28, he wrote Pennock from the Yazoo River authorizing his retention of the *Lexington* and two light-draught gunboats then at Cairo. "If the army officers would only notify us when they want a convoy, there would be no trouble," he lamented.

After conferring with Capt. Pennock early on January 30, Lt. Cmdr. Phelps wrote out what he told his superior verbally. The main points of his report were exactly those Pennock, Fitch, Porter, and others had known for some time, but which the army and the civilian contractors had been unwilling to recognize or appreciate. Rebel forces were thick on both the Cumberland and Tennessee rivers; they had a number of guns "with considerable covering force" along the eight to 10 miles of Harpeth Shoals, as well as near Savannah on the Tennessee River.

The remedy, Phelps saw, was not exactly in keeping with Fitch's request of Pennock for more boats and heavier guns for those he had, but it was held to be a happy substitute. The captain-designate of the *Eastport* believed the Confederates would not stay away from attacking howitzer-equipped tinclads but would back off from assaulting any fleet guarded by the big guns of a heavier ship. He recommended that the *Lexington* be sent to Fitch and, further reinforcing Porter's order, reiterated just how important it was that no steamer be permitted to run on either of the twin rivers without a naval escort. In conclusion, Phelps had no doubt that, "with the aid of the *Lexington*, Captain Fitch will be able effectually to protect all the government vessels in those rivers."

Even as the month ended, the Army remained concerned over the safety of its supply convoys, as well as a new and large troop convoy setting out from Cincinnati under the command of Maj. Gen. Gordon Granger. Department of the Ohio Commander Horatio G. Wright wrote Capt. Pennock from the *Queen City* and noted once more "the importance to the army service of keeping the line of the Cumberland River between its mouth and Nashville constantly open to the use of our steam transports." To make certain that the Rebels would not interfere, Wright requested the navy "assign to that portion of the river an ironclad gunboat, plated with sufficiently heavy iron to resist field artillery, to assist in the above object."

Recognizing the Army's dependence on the gunboats, the squadron fleet captain was prepared to comply with the request almost before it was made. Though no true ironclad was available, the *Lexington*, with her giant cannon, was seen as the next best thing. Pennock was relatively certain that her presence would secure what the Ohio general desperately wanted: "the safe passage thereon of the many transports engaged in furnishing any supplies."[5]

As February began, Brig. Gen. Forrest's contingent, coming over from Columbia, reached Palmyra, Tennessee, where his men were concealed and his guns masked. There a rendezvous was effected with Maj. Gen. Wheeler, who had been seeking the most favorable position from which he, Wharton, and Forrest could challenge Yankee shipping.

There did not appear to be a good attack location for the Rebels. Besides, Wheeler was now convinced that his enemies had divined his intentions and had also stopped dispatching transports up or down the Cumberland. In this, he was only partially correct. The bluecoats did by this time know he was loose in the area, but their reactions did not extend to the river. Steamers were still plying the waterway, but now most were under naval protection and convoys sailed far more infrequently than independent steamers. On top of this, gunboats and army patrols had eliminated all of the miscellaneous ferryboats above Dover, making a Rebel river crossing impossible.

Additional problems for the Confederate raiders at this point were the weather, forage, and intelligence on local defenses. The former was bad and the latter two absent. The most difficult challenges facing Wheeler were a lack of rations and ammunition. Forrest's cavalry had only about 15 small arms rounds per man, with a total of 45 cannon rounds; Wharton's brigade fared only slightly better: 20 shots per man and 50 artillery rounds. Cumulatively, these adversities were seen by Wheeler as necessitating a fast decision, either action in or retreat from the area.

Despite a strong protest from Forrest, Gen. Bragg's cavalry chief elected to launch an assault on Fort Donelson, or, more correctly, the fortified nearby hamlet of Dover. If he could capture and hold the place, he postulated, his people might better interdict Federal shipping.[6]

Fort Donelson, the scene of the great battle of February 1862, was a year later still covered by leavings from that miserable fight, and for that reason, the fortifications had been abandoned. Easier and more attractive for Union forces to maintain was the town of Dover which, since the fall, had been garrisoned by the 83rd Illinois Infantry, under Col. Abner C. Harding, along with elements of the 5th Iowa Cavalry.

Four 12-pounder cannon were also available, courtesy of Battery C, 2nd Illinois Artillery, along with an ex–Confederate 32-pounder brought over from the fort's unused water batteries. All the big guns and most of the 750 soldiers were assigned to prepared rifle pits or battery emplacements dug south and east of the town. Dover itself was 600 feet south of the Cumberland and was surrounded by deep natural ravines on its north side. Despite a series of false alarms, It was suspected that Confederate forces known to be in the area might attempt something.

By 1:30 P.M. on February 3, Confederate forces were surrounding Dover and Col. Harding had been sent an ultimatum from Maj. Gen. Wheeling demanding unconditional surrender. Harding, who had been able to wire Lowe seeking aid, replied that he wouldn't surrender the post without a fight. He was also able to send away the town's noncombatants aboard two steamers. Simultaneously, the colonel dispatched the *Wild Cat* with orders to seek out gunboats and bring them to the town's relief and he sent messengers to Col. Lowe seeking reinforcements.

Once it started, the combat, which is described by Cooling and other historians and is captured in the pages of the army and navy *Official Records*, continued throughout the afternoon. Although Yankee infantry was pushed back and the Confederates, at one point, occupied the entire western half of Dover, the Rebel assaults were, in the end, repulsed by the determined Northern defenders.

As dusk fell that cold, snowy winter evening, the Confederate leadership met to consider options. Given his lack of ammunition and the fact that Col. Harding would not surrender (a second ultimatum was sent and refused — Harding did not reveal that he was nearly out of ammunition as well) and realizing that Federal relief was en route, Maj. Gen. Wheeler decided "that it would be better to retire." In darkness, his men undertook an orderly withdrawal to a bivouac area some four miles south of Dover.[7]

"We could faintly hear the cannonading away up the river at a great distance," diarist King recalled. He and the 92nd Illinois men aboard the transport *Tempest*, as well as soldiers on other boats being convoyed by Lt. Cmdr. Fitch's six gunboats, were aware of the Dover fight early in the afternoon of February 3. Entirely by dint of Yankee luck, the Granger fleet was only 24 miles downstream from Dover when it was located by the *Wild Cat*.

As the procession continued, Harding's steamer and the flag boat *Fairplay* made rendezvous and Fitch received the colonel's message sent some hours earlier at the beginning of the battle. Harding's note was brief: his pickets had been driven in, he was being assaulted in force, and he needed immediate assistance. Lt. Cmdr. Fitch instantly made signal to the other gunboats, ordering that they all push on up toward Dover "with all possible speed." The transports were left to follow "as fast as possible."

The trip to Dover took Fitch's flotilla about five hours. A short distance below the town, the *Fairplay* spoke to another steamer, the captain of which cried that the place had been entirely surrounded and could not hold out much longer. Pushing on up, the gunboats arrived off Dover about 8:00 P.M. The encircled Col. Harding and his men were found, Fitch later remembered, holding off overwhelming numbers from small breastworks back about 300 yards from the riverbank. With no intelligence at all as to Confederate dispositions, Lt. Cmdr. Fitch decided he could at least "let off a gun up the ravine" to give Union forces "encouragement by letting them know that assistance was at hand."

Two other pieces of luck now fell the Federal way. "Just then the moon shone out bright," the Indiana sailor recalled. At the same time, an officer from the 83rd Illinois arrived at the riverbank, having secreted himself through Rebel lines at the sound of the naval gun. The man was taken aboard and pointed out the enemy positions. The main body of Confederates had been formed in line of battle through the graveyard at the west end of the town, about 700 to 800 yards from Col. Harding's positions, with its left wing resting in a ravine leading down to the river and possibly extending almost to the riverbank. It was perfectly obvious to the men aboard the gunboats that Rebel forces were not expecting them. While moving close inshore to make it easier to rake nearly the entire length of the enemy line, the sailors could hear Confederate soldiers talking in the darkness.

In position, all six Federal gunboats, including the *Lexington* with her 8-inch guns, opened fire up the exposed ravine, into the graveyard, and into the valley beyond — almost every location known or suspected of holding Southern troops, active or reserve, and horses. "The rebels were so much taken by surprise," Fitch reported, "that they did not even fire a shot, but immediately commenced retreating." So well directed was the naval bombardment that they departed precipitately and "could not even carry off a caisson that they had captured from our forces, but were compelled to abandon it, after two fruitless attempts to destroy it by fire."

"I was enabled to throw shell right in their midst," Fitch rejoiced. Once the main body was dispersed, the *Alfred Robb* and *Silver Lake* were stationed abreast of Dover to throw random shells and to prevent Confederates from returning to carry off their wounded. The *Fairplay* led the *Lexington*, *St. Clair*, and *Brilliant* above to shell the roads leading out toward the east. Believing that other retreating Rebel units would follow the river for some distance, the *Lexington* and *St. Clair* were sent on up to shell the woods along the riverbank, primarily to harass and annoy any Southerners choosing that exit. The *Fairplay* and *Brilliant*, meanwhile, lay opposite the upper ravine and tossed howitzer shells up the various roads.

Except for harassment fire, the gunboats ceased fire at 10:00 P.M. An hour later, Col. Harding sent word that the Confederates were completely gone from around the town. The gunboats were then positioned to provide night guard over the roads approaching Dover.

Fitch honestly believed that, in the words of Admiral Mahan, his arrival had occurred with the Union garrison *in extremis* and that his intervention turned the tide in favor of Dover's defenders. Thereafter the naval officer — and the U.S. Navy — always maintained that his men were right to "claim the honor of dispersing" Maj. Gen. Wheeler's forces "and saving Fort Donelson." Indeed, Fitch's officers and men "were very glad to have a shot at these river infesters, having been somewhat annoyed by them on previous occasions." While the task group leader also acknowledged that much of his late evening firing "after the enemy broke" was random, he and his men had "the gratification of knowing that scarcely a projectile went amiss, and out of the four hundred and odd reported killed and wounded," the gunboats "could claim their share."

The decisiveness of the action by the *Lexington* and the tinclads that February night was later challenged by a number of writers and historians. In his review of the battle in 1994, Terry Wilson admits the considerable disagreement as to the effect of Fitch's 28 cannon. His assessment is probably the most balanced: "If the naval gunfire did not force the Confederates off the field, it did solidify Harding's somewhat tenuous position."

Wheeler, Forrest, and Wharton may have failed to take Dover, "but the Rebels still effectively controlled the southerly banks of the lower Cumberland River and thereby remained a potent threat to Union supply lines." Rosecrans was not wrong to be concerned, but with Dover in Federal hands, Fitch and his gunboats could continue to move his supplies almost "at will during the balance of the navigable season."[8]

With the second battle at Fort Donelson history, the supply convoys to and from Nashville continued without losing a beat. The smokey, often noisy parades were magnificent. As the U.S. government-chartered steamers and their naval escorts churned up the Cumberland on February 14, for example, civilians—or others—watching from the riverbanks must have found the sight awe-inspiring. Acting Assistant Surgeon William W. Howard on the *Brilliant* tried to describe the majesty of a similar passage in a letter home to his wife: "*Lexington* in advance, 64s [gun caliber]—then five transports, *Fairplay*, 24s and 12s—then five transports, *St. Clair*, 24s and 12s—five transports, *Brilliant*, 24s and 12s—5 transports, *Silver Lake*, 24s and 12s—five transports, and *Robb*, 12s."

About this same time, a small Union force mounted a daring little raid, gaining one of the North's few successful military surprises that month in the Federal anti-insurgency conflict. On February 19, intelligence was received by a scouting party from the 3rd Michigan Cavalry, headquartered at Lexington, Tennessee, that noted guerrilla leader Col. John F. Newsom and his men were staying across the Tennessee at Clifton. Having found and refloated a sunken flatboat and mounted a small deception designed to convince local spies that they had returned to base, Capt. Cicero Newell took 60 of his fellow Grand Rapids horsemen across after midnight and surrounded Clifton before dawn, February 20, doing in the weary gray-clad pickets.

Downstream, five Union gunboats up on patrol were tied up to the shore for the night. At 3:00 A.M., the task group commander, Lt. Cmdr. Fitch, ordered them to get underway. In a furious dawn attack upon the sleeping but fast-responding Rebels at Clifton, 3rd Michigan Cavalry Capt. Newell was wounded in the left leg and was succeeded in command by Capt. Frederick C. Adamson. After a short time, 54 Confederates were captured, including Col. Newsom, who was wounded. Horses and small arms were also taken and the rest of the "guerrillas" fled. When the battle was done, the town was set ablaze.

As smoke rose from several burning structures, the U.S. Navy came around the bend from Fort Heiman, the *Lexington* leading. Looking through his telescope, Lt. Cmdr. Fitch observed Capt. Adamson signaling him to land. Once ashore, the navy leader and the army officer conferred on the Michigander's raid. Adamson feared a Rebel counterattack and asked the sailor to take his troopers, the Confederate prisoners, and the captured property, including the horses, back across the river. Fitch agreed to all the soldier's requests before inspecting what was left of the community. He then took the time to interview a number of prisoners. Meanwhile, as the *Chicago Daily Tribune* later reported, tars aboard the *Lexington* made certain that "our boys were given a capital dinner, which they needed."

Later that afternoon the prisoners, whom Surgeon Howard described in a letter home as "the most ragamuffin collection that can be found," were distributed around the gunboats. After dark, the task group landed Adamson and his men on the west bank of the Tennessee, from whence they proceeded back to Lexington. The gunboats steamed on to complete their patrol upstream before returning to Fort Heiman.

March 1863 saw the *Lexington* engaged in a number of Tennessee River patrols with the *Alfred Robb* and *Silver Lake*. These were designed to catch or disperse irregulars along the banks and to stop illicit trade and traffic. The expeditions were usually undertaken from Fort Heiman, the post opposite Fort Henry. To assist in a March 27 enterprise, 150 soldiers, under the command of Lt. Col. Chauncey Griggs, were taken aboard the timberclad as part of an amphibious landing force, the second component of which would comprise tinclad sailors led by the *Lexington*'s executive officer and Second Master, Acting Volunteer Lieutenant Martin Dunn. At several spots, Fitch ordered men put ashore where intelligence indicated guerrilla infestations might be present. Nothing was found and the little task group continued steaming up the Tennessee toward Savannah.

With information provided by friendly locals, quite possibly African-Americans, the *Lexington*'s captain learned that an active cotton factory was, at the very least, indirectly doing Confederate business from a place about four miles inland of Boyd's Landing. The place would have to be approached cautiously, as troops from Col. Nathaniel N. Cox's 10th Tennessee Regiment (C.S.A.) were believed stationed only two to three miles away.

The entire complement of bluecoated soldiers led by Griggs and 50 Yankee tars under Dunn went ashore and made it to the mill without incident. Upon arrival, cordwood breastworks were thrown up across the road and several people were questioned about what went on in the facility. The mill was apparently run on shares with surrounding country people and the material produced was said to be sent from friends among them to aid Rebel soldiers in the field. The company books were clear and contained no entries sufficient on their own merit to warrant the factory's destruction. Consequently, Fitch, who did not regularly fire Southern property for the sake of destruction, decided to "effectively prevent its doing more work."

Acting Volunteer Lieutenant Dunn's men, guarded by the army troops, disassembled the factory, removing the plant's running gear, pistons, cylinder heads, brasses, and "all like portable portions." A pair of mules and wagons were pressed and hauled the machinery down to the riverbank, from whence it was loaded aboard the *Lexington*. The mules, wagon, and a pair of horses caught nearby were retained as lawful prizes.[9]

Palmyra, Tennessee, is located on the Cumberland River 27.2 miles upstream from Dover and 10 miles below Clarksville. Elements of Maj. Gen. Wheeler's force had congregated there before the February attack on Dover, as the place, one of the highest to overlook a straight portion of the river, offered such a wonderful position to shoot down from its bluff into approaching Union shipping. At the beginning of April, Col.. Thomas Woodward's 2nd Kentucky Cavalry (C.S.A.), plus local irregulars, took up positions on the bluff. Several cannon, including a depressed 6-pounder Parrott rifle and a 12-pounder smoothbore, were prepared to interdict Yankee transports.

By this time, Northern logistics officials, military and civil, were somewhat complacent with the operation of their Louisville–Nashville–Louisville supply train. After all, some 180 steamers and 30 barges had been safely escorted up the river from Smithland or Fort Donelson in convoys to Nashville on January 24 and 28, February 7, 15, and 20, and March 6 and 15. Rations sufficient for an advance had, by now, reached Murfreesboro. The major sticking point, at least officially, to a new Federal move south was the provision of adequate numbers of efficient Union cavalry.

On April 2, another convoy departed Fort Donelson to complete a trip up to Nashville. It was comprised of the steamers *Eclipse* and *Lizzie Martin* lashed together, the tinclad *St. Clair*, the transport *Luminary*, the towboats *C. Miller* and *J.W. Kellogg*, each with a barge drawing 7.5 feet of water, and the tinclad *Fairplay*. This fleet approached Palmyra in mid-morning. When off the bluff immediately above that town, it was fired into by Woodward's battery. Paired as they were, the *Eclipse* and *Lizzie Martin* were an easy target for the Confederate gunners, who missed badly damaging either largely because the two were already too far upstream to be easily targeted.

Unhappily, the *St. Clair* and the *Luminary* were only about 400 feet from their attackers, who now gave them their full attention with cannon and small arms. The *Luminary* was struck by numerous minie balls; however, it was the *St. Clair* which took the brunt of the assault. Her guns run out, the tinclad's gunners were unable to elevate their howitzers sufficiently to hit the guns up on the bluff. Still, they fired away and "the contest was spirited for a short time." It was also all one-sided, with the *St. Clair* struck by small arms, canister, and at least six shells, one of which went through her deck and struck her supply pipe, letting all the water out of her boilers and making the boat unmanageable. *St. Clair* went dead in the water, but fortunately the undamaged *Luminary* heeded her captain's hail, came alongside, and took the warship under tow.[10]

When Lt. Cmdr. Fitch at Smithland received word of the attack late on April 3, he immediately ordered all of his captains to prepare for departure. They were already coaled and making last minute preparations for another patrol up the Tennessee. Rushing to the telegraph office, Fitch wired Capt. Pennock news on the assault and also noted that "I leave in 10 minutes for Palmyra with all the boats. Will whip them out." The Cairo station chief quickly messaged back: "Go ahead and whip them out on both rivers."

Over night, the USS *Lexington, Brilliant, Alfred Robb, Silver Lake,* and *Springfield* steamed up the Cumberland intent upon retaliation for the convoy attack by Confederate irregulars. Downriver from Dover, the warships encountered the *Fairplay* and the crippled *St. Clair*, under tow of the *J.W. Kellogg*. During the ensuing mid-river rendezvous, the unlucky convoy commodore made a preliminary report aboard the *Lexington* while other officers and men not on watch or asleep learned what they could of the Rebel assault.

The *Fairplay* joined the avenging fleet, which continued up to Fort Donelson, where it arrived during the morning of April 4. There the latest intelligence was sought and final preparations for a visit to Palmyra were completed, including the placement of hay bales around the boilers of the five tinclads. When ready, the fleet proceeded on up, arriving at Palmyra (Surgeon Howard called it "the cursed spot") late that Saturday afternoon. Although the men on the warships were "beat to quarters" and every cannon was ready, no enemy battery or forces were found as the Federals approached the town.

Lt. Cmdr. Fitch was one of the few Union naval officers still somewhat opposed to the more draconian aspects of Northern antiguerrilla policy then being employed, including "the wanton destruction of property." Many of the men of his command had no such qualms. Surgeon Howard on the *Brilliant* seemed to speak for most of the bluejackets now off Palmyra: "every town harboring Rebel sympathizers should be burned" because the irregulars did not believe in a fair fight — "they hide in the bush, shoot and run." If it were left to Howard and his fellow tars to set Federal counterinsurgency policy, they would "make this accursed Reb country a howling wilderness, and trust in the goodness of the Lord that it might be peopled by a better race in the future."

As it was, Fitch agreed that in this instance the destruction of Palmyra was justifiable. As he had been telling his superiors for some time, "It was one of the worst secession places on the river." Every Yankee believed that "unarmed transports had been fired into from doors and windows of the houses in the town." The inhabitants, as passengers aboard the returning steamer told the *Chicago Daily Tribune* reporter at Cairo, "had encouraged, if not assisted in the outrage." So it was that the *Lexington* landed opposite the town and a detachment was sent onshore, in charge of Acting Volunteer Master James Fitzpatrick. Lt. Cmdr. Fitch informed citizens that they had a certain amount of time to get out with their valuables before his men obeyed orders to burn every building in the town. Fitzpatrick was to make certain that his men did not "remove or pillage a single article," because everything was to be torched as an object lesson.

Once the work of retribution was completed, the gunboats "left the town of Palmyra by its own light" at moonrise. There was real satisfaction among the sailors; as Howard put it, "It was clean work — every building was in flames and falling." The task group commander, in a mission-ending telegram to Capt. Pennock, was matter of fact: "Burned the town; not a house left; a very bad hole; best to get rid of it and teach the rebels a lesson." Palmyra was a small town, the *Daily Tribune* told its readers a few days later, "but it is now numbered among the things that were and are not." Writing more than 130 years later, Nashville judge Brandt reaffirmed what many Middle Tennesseans had long been taught: Fitch's raid "ruined" Palmyra.[11]

Anticipating Union navy retribution, the Confederates, according to several captured at Palmyra, had hitched up their guns and retreated toward Harpeth Shoals shortly after the *St. Clair* attack. The exact destination, as the bluejackets learned, was Betsey Town Landing, another notorious guerrilla hangout, some 32–33 miles upstream beyond Clarksville and Hinton. Determined to catch the bushwhackers, Fitch took his fleet up the Cumberland toward it, but was unable to catch up with the faster Rebels.

The Cumberland River was now rapidly falling and it was simply too risky to take the huge *Lexington* over the shoals. Believing he had accomplished all that was possible in pursuit of the Palmyra ambushers and needing to ready his next foray up the Tennessee, the Indiana sailor sent the accompanying transports on up to Nashville and started the long run back to Smithland, arriving late on April 6. Nothing but smoldering ruins were seen by the warships as they passed the rubble of Palmyra.[12]

While the Cumberland River flotilla was engaged in the pacification of Palmyra, another larger enterprise, with a far less happy ending for the Federals, was beginning to unfold: the Streight Raid. Lt. Cmdr. Fitch, employing the *Lexington* and his tinclads, would attempt to support the first incursion into Confederate territory by a large force of mounted bluecoat infantry.

The 51st Indiana Volunteer Infantry commander, Col. Abel D. Streight, was an energetic, original thinker. Like others in the Federal army, he was disappointed that the Union had, thus far, been unable to match in effectiveness — or glory — the disruptive behind-the-lines raids of such Confederate saddle wizards as John Hunt Morgan and Nathan Bedford Forrest. At the same time, Maj. Gen. Rosecrans was under continuous pressure from Washington, D.C., to move south. "It occurred to his fertile mind," John Wyeth later wrote, "that if he could secure the destruction of the two important railroads leading from Chattanooga — one to Atlanta and the other to Knoxville — about the time he could force Bragg" south out of Tullahoma, Chattanooga would be cut off.

Streight, like Rosecrans and others familiar with the region, knew that Dalton was a key Confederate rail hub where tracks met connecting Chattanooga and Atlanta. That Georgia junction was vulnerable, so the colonel believed, to a large mounted party riding east through the local mountains from towns accessible via the Tennessee River at Eastport. If the railroad center was taken, easy Rebel transportation into Tennessee would be terminated. Gen. Bragg would have to retreat and Chattanooga could be swiftly taken.

It was true that the north Alabama country had few roads and little forage, but that in turn could be spun into an advantage. Known pockets of local Union sympathizers, the proper mounts, and timely coordination with other Northern units offered feasibility. Naturally, Streight would make the thrust to Dalton, leading a newly formed "Independent Provisional Brigade." Aside from its audacious concept, the Streight project is primarily remembered for the mounts the men were supposed to ride: mules. These animals, it was believed, would be more adept in the hilly country of north Alabama and hence led to the unit's sometime derisive label: "the Mule Brigade."

Streight sold his idea to future U.S. president Brig. Gen. James A. Garfield, Department of the Cumberland chief of staff, who persuaded Rosecrans that the Indianian's concept had significant merit. On April 7, Streight received orders to travel up to Nashville and there to speedily assemble his 2,000-man command "for an expedition to the interior of Alabama and Georgia for the purpose of destroying the railroads in that country."[13]

Despite unpredictable levels in the Tennessee River, both the navy under Fitch and the Mississippi Marine Brigade under Brig. Gen. Alfred Ellett were tasked to assist the forthcoming enterprise. As his contribution, the "mosquito fleet" commander employed the *Lexington* and the new *Argosy*, *Covington*, and *Queen City*, "four of my best boats." The *Covington* and *Argosy* were left at Fort Henry to convoy Ellet and Streight's transports to Eastport, while the *Lexington* and the *Queen City* pushed up.

Fitch took his two boats up toward Eastport on the morning of April 17, planning to patrol between Duck River and Chickasaw before rounding to off Eastport on the following evening. When the *Lexington* and *Queen City* arrived at Eastport, they found Rebel cavalry exchanging fire with a small squad of Union troops. "Shelled; drove them off," the sailor wired Cairo just after dawn on Saturday.

Streight and Ellet arrived at Eastport after dark on Sunday, April 20. The next day, Lt. Cmdr. Fitch was forced to inform the army and Capt. Pennock that his gunboats could not get over the Colbert shoals. Indeed, the deep draft amphibious boats of Brig. Gen. Ellet were forced to steam back downstream that very morning, departing after a significant portion of Eastport had mysteriously burned to the ground. His mission of army support had thus far largely failed.[14]

On April 22 and 23, the *Lexington* cruised down the river ahead of Brig. Gen. Ellet's fleet. Ellet, for his part, had been asked to make a demonstration at Savannah. Rather than honoring the request, the amphibious leader elected to steam slowly down toward Clifton, putting men ashore on both sides of the river to destroy Confederate mills, stores and other property and to "liberate" any reachable cotton bales, horses, or mules.

All of the noise along the Tennessee from Streight, Ellet, Fitch, and others did not go unnoticed at Gen. Bragg's headquarters. On April 23, the Confederate leader wired Brig. Gen. Nathan Bedford Forrest at Spring Hill, Tennessee, and directed him to put an end to the Streight incursion. To finish the Mule Brigade story before returning to the navy requires but a paragraph. On Sunday April 26, Streight and his men slipped away from Tuscumbia into north Alabama, headed toward Russellville, Georgia. In one of his most celebrated exploits, Forrest, meanwhile, launched a relentless pursuit of the Hoosier colonel that did not end until the 1,446 surviving officers and men of the Independent Provisional Brigade were all cornered and taken on the Alabama-Georgia line on May 3.[15]

Ellet and Fitch were themselves drawn into a fight on April 24 with Confederates secreted on the banks of the Tennessee River. Among the enemy units now unleashed against the

Union river invaders was a battery of four fieldpieces belonging to Maj. Robert M. White's 6th Texas Cavalry (C.S.A.). White, a native of the area, had placed his guns at Green Bottom Bar, on the Duck River Shoals just above Waverly Landing. White hoped to catch Union steamers coming his way and maybe even shoot up a gunboat or Mississippi Marine Brigade ram. River pilots had long considered this stretch "one of the worst in the river navigation," making it an ideal spot for an ambush.

White's first target was Acting Volunteer Master William N. Griswold's brand new light draught *Emma Duncan*, later known as the *Hastings*, or Tinclad No. 15. The *Emma Duncan*, which had once had a fieldpiece aboard and served briefly as a quasi-army gunboat, was built at Monongahela, Pennsylvania, in 1860 and was purchased from J. Batchelor and others at Cairo on March 24 for $39,000. The 293-ton side-wheeler was 173 feet long, with a beam of 34.2 feet and a hold depth of 5.4 feet. She possessed two engines, three boilers, and was armed with two 30-pdr. Parrott rifles forward, two 32-pdrs. aft, and four 24-pdr. brass howitzers in broadside. On April 7, Acting Rear Adm. Porter ordered the warship's name changed to *Hastings*, but that moniker did not initially stick.

Hiram H. Martin was one of the new crewmen aboard, recruited with his friend Robert Wheeler at Chicago at the beginning of the month. The first warship for both men was the *Emma Duncan*, which Martin later recalled was a "mosquito boat, only protected against bullets." Within a fortnight, the boat was altered and ready to go to war. Actually, "ready" is not the correct word; "available" might better suit. The *Emma Duncan*, like most of the new tinclads, was, in the words of First Class Fireman Martin, "hardly in condition for service and the crew consisted mostly of green men unaccustomed to service of that kind." It would be the responsibility of her captain, with assistance from men like the chief engineer, "Mr. Watson, an old River Engineer and a very fine man," to turn his crew into fighting bluejackets.[16]

The *Emma Duncan* was at general quarters, engaged in its first-ever general exercise in "enemy country," as it approached Green Bottom Bar about 2:00 A.M. on Friday, April 24, her second night out. As the boat slowed in anticipation of the obstruction, she was fired into by the four guns of the Texas battery. The enemy, as Fireman Martin recalled, "was peppering it into us hot and heavy." The *Emma Duncan* "commenced turning around so that the guns first on one side and then the other could be used." The *Emma Duncan* engaged by the light of gun flashes in the dark for a short time. That was the only way the men aboard the gunboat could guess where their enemy was. "But we were a good target for them," Fireman Martin remembered, "as they could see the lights from our furnaces and on the boat." The cannonading continued for about 45 minutes, until the riverbank force ceased firing. The tinclad went to full steam and shelled the woods at every nearby suspicious point, but there was no return fire because the Confederates had withdrawn. During the sharp exchange, the *Emma Duncan* was hulled seven times and three men were badly wounded.

Late on the 24th, the *Emma Duncan* met the *Lexington*, coming down ahead of Ellet's fleet, and her captain reported his shot-up craft for duty. Taking a boat over to the timberclad, the master reported his encounter with the unknown Rebel force. Fitch immediately ordered the newcomer to take station astern as the two ran down toward Green Bottom Bar "in hopes of catching the rebels at or near the same place." The Yankee warships reached the bar toward dusk, but there was no enemy.

After coaling at Fort Henry on April 25, the *Lexington* and *Emma Duncan* returned to the foot of Green Bottom Bar about midnight. Guards were posted and a sharp lookout was maintained until dawn. At first light on April 26, a search for the enemy was made but again nothing was found. The two boats next proceeded upriver to meet and communicate with

Brig. Gen. Ellet. The cruise continued without incident until the two gunboats came about a mile from Duck River Shoals, where they met the ram *Monarch*.

The same gunners who had fired into the *Emma Duncan* were now taking aim on the other Ellet rams *Autocrat*, *Diana*, and *Adams* as they maneuvered their way into and through the swift current of the shoal's narrow channel. Fieldpieces and rifles raked the wooden boats with canister and minie balls, sending splinters flying into the air but doing remarkably little damage to the boats' heavy oak planking. The rams, unable to round to or back out of the channel, pushed on over the bar taking punishment. Coming upon this fiery duel, Lt. Cmdr. Fitch pushed over the Green Bottom Bar and met Ellet's fleet at the head of the shoals, where it was engaging the Texan battery, firing back at it with its onboard fieldpieces and small arms.

The *Lexington* moved into good range and opened fire with her 8-inch guns. Fitch took the battery side of the river to cover Ellet's craft while raking the bank. "The brush was so thick I could not see the enemy's guns, yet the smoke enabled me to fire directly at them," he later recorded. As soon as the big timberclad rounded the point, the Confederate gunners went into something of a panic. After sending a parting shot toward a brigade boat, Maj. White ordered his gunners to limber up and make off. A few sharpshooters were left behind to take potshots at the boats and attempt to impede any Yankee response.

Fitch took his leave of Ellet about 11:00 P.M. With the *Emma Duncan* and the *Monarch* in company, the *Lexington* steamed on up to Eastport, The two navy gunboats returned to their principal base at Smithland, Kentucky, on May 1. The *Lexington* remained in the Cumberland through May, her usefulness steadily declining with the river stage. By May 28, six days after Maj. Gen. Ulysses S. Grant launched the climactic siege of Vicksburg, the water level had fallen to such a low point that Lt. Cmdr. Fitch could no longer employ her. Keenly aware of ARAM Porter's constant need of reinforcements, Capt. Pennock ordered her returned to Cairo for basic repairs prior to her rotation below.[17]

While the *Lexington* was engaged on the Cumberland and Tennessee Rivers, the *Conestoga*, under Lt. Cmdr. Selfridge, remained active in the Mississippi. Her duty during the first third of the year remained protection of commerce and guerrilla control in the areas near the Arkansas and White Rivers. "In the main," remembered the timberclad's captain years later, "the patrol duty was monotonous and to me rather irksome." A few incidents, as recorded in the vessel's logbook, reveal the *Conestoga*'s service highlights into May.

As she was moving up the Mississippi on February 14, the gunboat happened to speak to the steamers *Empress* and *Ed. Walsh*, also northbound. Their captains reported being fired into by a Rebel band with five fieldpieces at Bolivar Landing. The *Conestoga* rounded to and moved to the waters off the landings. There she threw seven shells into the woods and set fire to a nearby building. In mid-afternoon, "some straggling mounted cavalry" were seen and they too were targets for a few shells. The following afternoon, the transport *Warsaw* also reported having been fired into by guerrillas, this time at Cypress Bend. Lt. Cmdr. Selfridge ordered his boat to that location, where she pounded the woods in the vicinity. A landing party then went ashore and "burned the buildings." Despite prompt response and the expenditure of a significant amount of ammunition on the two days, there is no indication that any Confederates were hurt — or dissuaded.

Early on March 12, the *Conestoga* started a reconnaissance up the twisty Arkansas River, looking for flatboats and Southern riders. At mid-morning, a party of cavalry was seen and fired upon. Reaching the vicinity of the cut-off to the White River, the gunboat came to and opened fire. Confederate concentrations had been reported in the area and Selfridge's gunners chewed up the ground with sixteen 8-inch shells and six from her 32-pounder. Again, no proof of damages or casualties.

Late in the day on May 3, the *Conestoga* saw the wreck of the towboat *Minnesota* and two barges on fire in the waters off Greeneville, Mississippi. The damages were the obvious work of irregulars that had fired from woods along the shore. Moving toward the bank, the gunboat dropped four 32-pounder and one 12-pounder howitzer shells into suspected ambush locations.[18]

During the first half of 1863, the *Tyler* was stationed closer to Vicksburg, the main western campaign site, than either of her sisters. Consequently, she was, in the end, a party to the sharpest fighting. Prior to the shooting, however, the largest timberclad was the scene of the most festive social occasion yet staged on a Mississippi gunboat.

In January, after the Chickasaw Bayou defeat, the Ellet ram *Queen of the West* remained in the Yazoo River. At some point shortly after the new year, as she was anchored off the plantation of widow Mrs. J.R. Harris, the vessel ran short of provisions. Capt. Edwin Sutherland, known to Lt. Cmdr. Pritchett, the *Tyler*'s skipper, since they worked together attempting to pull torpedoes out of the stream just before Christmas, took a party of men to the widow's farm to obtain food.

Sutherland and Mrs. Harris struck up a conversation, which, over the next two weeks and following numerous visits by the ram captain ashore, developed into an intense attraction. On or about January 20, it was announced that the two wanted to be married and she wanted to "accompany him down the river on the ram." Before supper on January 24, Lt. Cmdr. Pritchett accompanied black-haired Mrs. Harris and her chambermaid aboard the *Tyler*, giving the ladies his own cabin. There they stashed a number of bandboxes and parcels. The skipper temporarily moved next door with one of the vessel's masters.

Before the bride readied herself, the captain's cabin was prepared for a festive wedding. Acting Rear Adm. Porter, followed by captains and officers from the other gunboats lying in and about the mouth of the Yazoo, arrived about 6:30 P.M. The last to board was the bridegroom, Capt. Sutherland. An hour after the squadron commander's arrival, CAP Pritchett was notified that all was in readiness and the assembled officers were invited to his cabin. Forty-five minutes later, the bride entered, followed by the groom. Mrs. Harris wore a "rich satin dress," while Capt. Sutherland was outfitted in a dress infantry officer's uniform complete with sword and sash. Regarded by all as a brave patriot, he was not, remarked witness Symmes Brown, "a handsome man nor at all prepossessing in appearance."

The short ceremony was conducted by a Rev. Snow. Afterwards, Porter was the first to congratulate the bride, bowing and kissing her hand in a moment somewhat embarrassing to himself and others. She immediately and briefly excused herself. A lavish wedding banquet — as lavish as wartime in the middle of the Yazoo River permitted — followed the ceremony. As there was insufficient room for all of the invited guests to take supper, many of the junior officers departed. By midnight, the visitors were gone and the happy couple had retired.[19]

Both the *Tyler* and *Conestoga* spent much of the next four months patrolling the Mississippi. Their principal missions were to ensure a steady supply for extra food (what the army called "forage") to the fleet, the provision of coast guard services to Union steamers, antiguerrilla watch, and the interruption of the Southern economy. This latter, entailing primarily the capture of baled cotton, was most happily conducted by all of the gunboats. Their officers and men were entitled to a percentage of the value of whatever the crops could be sold for — prize money. Soldiers were not so lucky, they could not earn extra cash no matter what they liberated.

As the timberclads were engaged in Mississippi or Cumberland pursuits, elements of the main fleet, in support of Maj. Gen. Grant, attempted to secure flanking routes around Vicksburg. These schemes involved gunboats weaving their way through vine-covered, narrow streams that would hopefully connect them to a strategic point that would allow the Confederates to be turned. Names like Yazoo Pass and Steele's Bayou entered the Civil War lexicon in February and March and, like Chickasaw Bayou, also came to serve as synonyms for frustration.

"De Soto," the *New York Times* resident Cairo correspondent, who may have been Franc B. ("Galway") Wilkie's associate William George, tells us that the latter expedition actually began on March 12. On that Thursday, the *Carondelet* and *Tyler* proceeded up the Yazoo and dropped anchor off Johnson's Landing. That farm, as the reader will recall, was directly across from the entrance to Steele's Bayou.

The following morning, Acting Rear Adm. Porter arrived and, following a series of reconnaissances a short distance up, a number of ironclads and transports started up the stream, leaving the *Tyler* to act as picket at its mouth. It was hoped that this advance could join with that in Yazoo Pass and together flank the Rebel citadel. Indeed, the timberclad's captain offered to bet $300 that Vicksburg would be evacuated in under a fortnight. We do not know if Lt. Cmdr. Pritchett's bet was taken; if it were, he lost a lot of money for those days because both the Yazoo Pass and Steele's Bayou gambits failed. "Galway" himself advised Northern readers that the "experience of the two late expeditions in these backwoods bayous are anything but encouraging."

It had become clear that another way was required in order for the Army of Tennessee to get at Vicksburg. At one point, Maj. Gen. Grant believed he had no choice but to return to the bluffs up the Yazoo and attempt to carry them by storm. If that were necessary, he expected huge losses. As April and spring arrived, it was determined that the army would make an assault crossing of the Mississippi below the Confederate fortress. To that end, Maj. Gen. Grant marched his army about 50 miles down the west side of the river, stopping first at New Carthage before continuing down to Hard Times Landing.

For his part, Acting Rear Adm. Porter agreed to take the ironclads and transports necessary to ferry the troops directly downstream past the Vicksburg batteries. Most of the Pook turtles, the *Lafayette*, *General Price*, *Tuscumbia*, and the *Benton*, would make the trip. Under the temporary command of his downriver fleet captain, Lt. Cmdr. K. Randolph Breese, the Eads ironclad *Baron de Kalb*, the new *Choctaw*, and all of the light draughts and the *Tyler* remained behind to guard the mouth of the Yazoo. The April 17 Vicksburg passage was a grand success. Only one transport was sunk. A few nights later, additional transports ran the gauntlet. Pritchett and Brown from the *Tyler* were both able to get away to witness both exploits from the deck of a tugboat.

For the next couple of weeks, the *Tyler* remained almost at the same station she had occupied since the beginning of the year. "A perfect monotony prevails with us," wrote Browne, the boat's new executive officer, on April 23. A week later, he confided that there were only three vessels available at the mouth of the Yazoo that could protect the local portion of the fleet—"and the *Tyler* is one of the three."[20]

With the gunboat task group below Vicksburg and Grant's army at Hard Times Landing, the practicalities of undertaking an assault landing across the Mississippi at Grand Gulf were now worked out between the local Union army and navy leadership. During the spring, the dual roles of the staging and garrison areas at Young's Point and Milliken's Bend were enhanced. Not only were supplies brought in, particularly to the latter location, transshipped by wagon over rough, corduroy roads down the west side of the Mississippi, but new African-American legions were trained at these locations.

The first step in the successful completion of any trans–Mississippi amphibious operation was naval gunfire suppression of the defender's batteries. While bluecoat transport was arranged and the battle plans for the ironclads were worked out, Maj. Gen. Grant on April 27 sent a suggestion to Maj. Gen. Sherman, upriver off the Yazoo River. When the attack on Grand Gulf began, would it be possible for XV Corps and the remaining units of the Mississippi Squadron to stage a demonstration against Drumgould's Bluff? Such a feint would prove helpful and allow the push to begin next day.

Delays prevented by a day the implementation of the Grand Gulf scheme. Admiral Porter's gunboats duly attacked the Confederate defenses, which proved stronger than expected. It would be another day or so before a landing could be undertaken, and that at Bruinsburg, Mississippi. Below the original beaches planned, the crossing, when it came, was mysteriously unopposed.

While the Federal amphibious forces resolved their impasse below, Maj. Gen. Sherman launched his April 30 diversion above Vicksburg. Once again, gunboats and transports entered the Yazoo as if on the attack and the men aboard the craft continued to marvel at the beauties of spring along the banks. As the water level in the Mississippi fell, that in the Yazoo demonstrated a greater rush as it drained into the main stream. Every manner of debris hurried down in the swift current.

Followed by four transports, three tinclads, several ironclads, and the flag boat *Black Hawk*, the *Tyler* entered the Yazoo River just after lunchtime on April 29. The task group steamed on for nearly four hours, during which time, in mid-afternoon, the timberclad fired a Parrott shell at several Confederate pickets observed on the bank. The gunboats made fast on the right side of the river for the night abreast of Chickasaw Bayou.

Precisely at 9:00 A.M. on Thursday, Lt. Cmdr. Breese took his gunboat task group upstream until it was within easy range of Drumgould's Bluff. The parade was lead by the mighty thousand ton *Choctaw*, followed by the *Baron de Kalb*, *Tyler*, *Black Hawk*, and several tinclads. Just over an hour later and from a range of a thousand yards, Lt. Cmdr. Francis M. ("Frank") Ramsay, commander of the *Choctaw*, "opened the ball." The vessel's huge 100-pounder Parrott rifle and 9-inch Dahlgren smoothbore shots aimed at the main Confederate battery were immediately answered. About 100 yards astern of her, the *Baron de Kalb* took aim from a sheltered point.

While the ironclads tackled the higher guns on the Bluff, the *Tyler* and *Black Hawk* shot at the enemy fieldworks and lesser lower batteries. From a distance of a mile to a mile and a half, the former employed primarily her 30-pounder Parrotts. From their entrenchments and all batteries, the Southern soldiers led by Brig. Gen. Louis Hebert returned fire with 16 heavy cannon and countless small arms. Covered by the guns of three tinclads anchored abaft the *Tyler*, XV Corps soldiers, in plain sight of Confederate defenders, stormed ashore on the left bank, giving every appearance of mounting a determined effort to get up the cliffs. Rebel soldiers were rushed to the Yazoo front and any decision to rush reinforcements to the Grand Gulf area were, at least temporarily, shelved.

About 10:30 A.M., the water being too swift for her to anchor or be held steady, the timberclad tied up to the left bank, from which she maintained her fire. It proved to be her misfortune that, as Ensign Browne noted, she "stirred up a field battery of Whitworth guns which paid their especial compliments to the Tyler." During the next half hour, the Confederate artillerymen "walked off" the range of the wooden warrior. Their first shot struck the river near, but short, of the *Tyler*. The second passed across her bow about 100 feet ahead. The next fell short and struck the bank on the opposite side of the river. The fourth Rebel blast, however, was right on. "I was standing on the forecastle watching the gun when it fired," Browne later wrote home, "and I assure you, it did not create the most pleasant feelings, for I could distinctly hear the ball whistling thro' the air as it approached."

At 11:00 A.M., the *Tyler* was hit at the waterline ("between wind and water," Pritchett later said) under no. 3 port on the starboard side. The Whitworth rifle shell passed through several bulkheads, the coal bunker and barricade in front of the fire room — smashing three iron ash buckets and two shovels in flight — and lodged in the port coal bunker. Lt. Cmdr. Pritchett's command was immediately forced to drop out of the contest. She steamed back across the Yazoo and made fast to the bank behind an outgrowth of trees located below the *Black Hawk*. Thereafter, she was heeled over and damage control parties quickly made repairs.

While the *Tyler* was mended, the battle raged for most of another three hours. By the time the Federals retired around 1:40 P.M., the mighty *Choctaw* had been struck by over 50 Confederate shells or cannonballs. Once her repairs were completed in mid-afternoon, the *Tyler* was ordered to steam down opposite Chickasaw Bayou. There she tied to the bank and guarded the troop transports, her lookouts making certain that the enemy did not plant a battery that could reach the soldiers. During her morning shoot, she had expended 16 Parrott and seven 8-inch 10-second shells.

The Drumgould's Bluff feint continued on May 1, beginning at approximately 3:00 P.M. From a range of about 3,000 yards, the Tyler resumed her shooting so prematurely interrupted the previous day. A large Confederate cannon — Browne thought it an 8-inch piece — now took the old gunboat under fire. The initial shot just cleared the *Tyler*'s wheelhouse and the next three all fell short. The fifth, however, exploded high over the forecastle. A piece of shrapnel from it passed through the starboard wheelhouse and narrowly missed hitting the boat's paymaster and several other sailors. These five shots were the only ones directly aimed at the *Tyler* this day, so far as any of its crew could tell. The timberclad continued to fire upon her unseen foe until 8:00 pm., at which point Lt. Cmdr. Breese signaled cease-fire. Next day, the *Tyler* led the vessels, gunboats and transports alike, back to the mouth of the Yazoo.

The Drumgould's Bluff confrontation was, in the words of Rowena Reed, "an impressive display that accomplished nothing." This movement "further revealed the Navy's powerlessness against well-constructed shore batteries." In fact, as Dave Page points out, the Drumgould's Bluff feint was successful as a ploy. When the Federal sailors watched Confederate ox teams hauling big guns to reinforce Southern positions along the bluffs, they knew their gambit had worked. Damage to the *Choctaw* and *Tyler* was "a small price to pay to confuse the enemy," leading as it did to inaction on the part of Maj. Gen. Pemberton.[21]

The campaign to reduce the Confederate's prime Mississippi River choke point continued through the remainder of May and into June. "After the crossing to Bruinsburg," wrote Ronald Scott Mangum in 1991, "the Vicksburg campaign turned into a land battle." Still, the navy continued to assist, with bombardment and logistical support.

After the Drumgould's Bluff feint, the *Tyler* remained briefly at the mouth of Yazoo River. Fortunately for him, but unfortunately for us as his historically useful letters would now be penned from another vessel her executive officer, Acting Ensign Symmes E. Browne, assumed the same position aboard the tinclad *Signal* on May 13. On May 15, the *Tyler* was ordered back to the mouth of White River where, together with the *Conestoga* and several tinclads, she could once more interdict Confederate commerce (read "cotton") and patrol against Rebel crossings and guerrilla attacks.

Within a few days of the Federal victory at Jackson on May 14, Maj. Gen. Grant was driving behind Vicksburg, upon which the troops of Lt. Gen. John C. Pemberton were now falling back. Four days later, a junction was completed between Sherman and Porter up the Yazoo. The campaign for the final reduction of the fortress now began. Reacting to these events, Pemberton begged Richmond for reinforcements and orders to somebody that a campaign be launched to relieve the pressures on the Louisiana side of the river. These pressures to avoid catastrophe prompted President Jefferson Davis into action.

Meanwhile, the mighty defenses at Drumgould's, Snyder's, and Haynes' bluffs were neutralized and captured. The possibility of providing logistics up this stream rather than past the riverfront guns of the citadel must have been very appealing to Union military and river transportation officers alike. Milliken's Bend "lost its military significance," wrote Martha Bigelow a hundred years later.

As Maj. Gen. Grant's operations shoved around the Confederate fortress via the Big Black River, the supply, garrison and staging locations on the northwest side of the river above Vicksburg were largely transformed into training and assembly points for a large number of former slaves the North was turning into bluecoated combatants. A number of depots and hospitals remained at and between Milliken's Bend and Young's Point, manned or guarded by black soldiers. Although they knew that black soldiers were being recruited in the area, Confederate leaders did not realize just how dramatic was the shift in Grant's line of logistical support. They continued to believe that his supply route remained vulnerable the same as it had for weeks on the west bank of the Mississippi, on the Louisiana side across from Vicksburg.

As a result of this misperception, President Davis passed orders for Lt. Gen. Edmund Kirby Smith, commander of the Confederate Trans-Mississippi Department, to dispatch troops to break up what was now a nonexistent supply line. Smith, in turn, ordered Maj. Gen. Richard "Dick" Taylor to mount this attack, to provide succor to Vicksburg, and to cooperate in every way with Lt. Gen. Pemberton. To help carry off the assignment, Maj. Gen. John George Walker's Texas Division ("Walker's Greyhounds") was assigned to Taylor's command. Taylor initially objected to his orders, citing the sloppy nature of the terrain and the uncertainty that the supply line even continued to exist. He was overruled by Lt. Gen. Smith, so reluctantly took his men from Alexandria to Richmond, Louisiana, on steamers via the Red and Ouachita rivers.

In a further effort to assist the defenders of Vicksburg, Confederate Secretary of War James A. Seddon recommended on May 23 that forces from the Trans-Mississippi Department mount a diversion. Perhaps, he suggested, Lt. Gen. Smith's people could capture Helena, thereby removing a Union choke point on the Mississippi while also requiring that Grant dispatch vital troops, steamers, and gunboats back to Arkansas. The executive's communication was delayed in delivery and, besides, Smith had another objective: the Mississippi River supply chain upstream from Young's Point.

While the Confederates were making one of their last big movements by steamboat of the entire war, the *Lexington* was approaching the Yazoo River from Cairo. Returned by Lt. Cmdr. Fitch because the river stage of the Cumberland was too low for her to operate, the fast timberclad was returned to the lower portion of the Mississippi Squadron under the command of her executive officer second master, Acting Volunteer Lieutenant Martin Dunn.

When Taylor and Walker arrived at Richmond late on June 5, they confirmed that the Yankee supply line from Milliken's Bend, 10 miles to the east, was largely history. Still, if a portion of the Mississippi's west bank could be captured and held, it might somehow be possible to herd cattle and send other supplies across to Vicksburg's beleaguered garrison.

The medical/supply areas at Milliken's Bend, Young's Point and Lake Providence were under the command of Brig. Gen. Elias S. Dennis at Young's Point. Operational control of the Milliken's Bend facilities was held by Col. Hermann Lieb, with a new black unit, the African Brigade. The physical layout of the camp was strong, with its river side protected by a 15-foot bank and a six-foot levee. The surrounding fields were intersected by thick hedges (*bois d'arc*) and the perimeter was anchored by heavy timber and drainage ditches.

Having learned that Confederates were approaching from the west, Brig. Gen. Dennis, on June 6, ordered Col. Lieb to make a reconnaissance. Two companies from the 10th Illinois Cavalry were sent to join a detachment of African-American infantry. The graycoats were duly engaged and, after hard fighting, Lieb returned to Milliken's Bend, seeking assistance from Dennis. The steamer *St. Cloud*, on her way up from below, happened, meanwhile, to drop anchor offshore. When her captain heard of the Rebel advance, he immediately volunteered to return downstream to Young's Point and seek help from the navy.

Handed Lieb's plea by the steamboat skipper, Acting Rear Adm. Porter dispatched the giant *Choctaw* to lay off Milliken's Bend. Aboard were a number of men from the 23rd Iowa Infantry, who were disembarked when the gunboat reached the camp. The Illinois cavalrymen, meanwhile, returned to their camp some distance away. Later that night, the Mississippi Squadron commander also sent up the *Lexington*.

Rebel Maj. Gen. Walker proceeded east from Richmond at dusk, reaching Oaklawn Plantation at midnight. This farm was approximately seven miles from Milliken's Bend to the north and an equal distance from Young's Point to the south. In the dark, Walker split his command. One brigade was left in reserve at Oaklawn. One, under Brig. Gen. James M. Hawes was ordered to Young's Point, while Brig. Gen. Henry E. McCulloch tackled Milliken's Bend. Hopefully, they could reach their destinations, surprise their opponents, and avoid the gunboats. They would strike at night and carry the Federal "works at the point of the bayonet."

Around 3:00 A.M. on June 7, Confederates appeared on the Richmond road in force. There was some delay and Brig. Gen. McCulloch did not reach his objective until dawn. At that point, his Texans drove in the Milliken's Bend pickets and continued their movement toward the Union left flank.

Lt. Cmdr. Ramsay, captain of the *Choctaw*, first learned of the Confederate assault at 3:15 A.M. when an army officer came aboard and reported an attack upon Col. Lieb's pickets. Twenty minutes later, the flashes from many rifles and muskets indicated sharp fighting close to the Union camp. The big ironclad immediately opened fire on perceived Southern locations with her 100-pounder rifle.

The Federal African Brigade and 23rd Iowa (1,061 men) resisted sharply and, with explosions caused by the *Choctaw*'s huge shells, caused the Rebel line to pause momentarily. Soon, however, the Southerners resumed their push and shoved the defenders on to the levees. Despite additional Union volleys, the Rebels came on, and intense hand-to-hand combat ensued. During this action, the Confederates succeeded in flanking the Northern force and caused tremendous casualties with enfilade fire. The Yankees, black and white alike, fell back to the river's bank. As Porter later put it, "The fight was desperate and our men, overpowered, had to retreat behind the bank."

During the savage fighting ashore, it was impossible for Lt. Cmdr. Ramsay to learn the exact position of the enemy. A few soldiers, serving as amateur forward controllers, attempted to signal the Rebel positions out to the *Choctaw*, but it was impossible for the men aboard the gunboat to obtain visual sightings due to the high banks. During this segment of the predawn fighting, according to the *Cincinnati Gazette*, an "unfortunate shot" from the gunboat accidentally landed in the midst of a black regiment, killing several soldiers.

After sunrise, the Confederates continued firing and began extending to their right to in an effort to envelop the Federals but failed in their objective. As the Rebels moved through the Union camp, they, like Maj. Gen. Grant's men at Belmont in November 1861, stopped to plunder tents. At the same time, with the Northern soldiers gone, more inviting targets were offered to the navy. The *Choctaw*, joined by the newly arrived *Lexington*, pounded the Texans milling about. The heavy shells frightened many.

On the Confederate southern, or right, flank later in the morning, Brig. Gen. McCulloch decided to pull his men back behind the levee and call for reinforcements. What came was not expected — the *Lexington* paddled into range and her gunners sent a storm of 8-inch shells into the butternut ranks.

Fighting at Milliken's Bend continued until noon when Walker and McCulloch, who in all fairness had the battle won — except for the stubbornness of the African-American defenders and the gunboats— decided to withdraw and retreat toward Walnut Bayou. The Union soldiers pursued for a short distance. The gunboats maintained a sporadic fire as long as possible, or, as Lt. Cmdr. Ramsay said of the *Lexington*'s action-ending shots, "she threw a few shells into the woods."

The contest would not be remembered today but for the distinguished involvement of the Federal African-American troops. For the first time in the west, the defenders of this little bend in the Mississippi answered a question on the minds of many whites: "Will they fight?" Despite little serious military training and equipped with inferior weaponry, the former slaves fought bravely and, with help from the *Lexington* and *Choctaw*, drove the Confederates from the field. Maj. Gen. Taylor wrote after the war that, as foretold, his entire "movement resulted, and could result, in nothing."

Riding away from the scene, Maj. Gen. Walker thought of what he would later tell his superiors. In short, he understood and cautioned remembrance "that the enemy behind a Mississippi levee, protected on the flanks by gunboats, is as securely posted as it is possible to be outside a regular fortification." Analyzing the event years later, Michael Ballard agreed with Walker and opined that the reason the campaign failed was "because Confederates could not combat the Federal navy, which provided firepower and mobility for the shifting infantry and field artillery." Thereafter, Maj. Gen. Grant gave closer attention to the protection of his supply bases. Confederates attacking Helena a few weeks later did not have benefit of Walker's council.

The death throes of Vicksburg continued through what remained of June and into the first days of July. However, on the fittingly symbolic date of July 4, after a 45-day siege, the fortress city was surrendered. The event, coming with the equally vital retreat of Gen. Lee from Gettysburg in Pennsylvania, marked for all to see the receding of the political tide that was the Confederacy.[22]

In the hot, dry month after the Milliken's Bend scrape, Helena, the Union enclave on the western bank of the Mississippi River, was manned by a very small force of Iowa, Wisconsin, and Indiana troops, as most of its garrison was engaged near Vicksburg. Few of them were very happy to be there and, if given the opportunity, many would probably have echoed the thoughts of Pvt. Charles O. Musser of the 29th Iowa Infantry when he wrote that "It is one of the dirtiest holes on the river." A reporter from the *St. Louis Daily Missouri Democrat* was in the Arkansas town at this time and offered his readers a description of its layout and defenses in a column dated July 12. "About a quarter of a mile from the river and running parallel to it," he wrote, "high ridges command the city and approaches." Ravines ran between the ridges.

Earlier, it was decided to make use of the local topography by placing batteries atop four prominent hills that overlooked the major roads into town. A redoubt on the western edge of Helena was also constructed; upon its completion, it was named Fort Curtis. Breastworks and a series of rifle pits were dug between the ridges and in front of the four batteries. Abatis were planted before these. These defenses formed a rough semicircle about the town. The batteries, running right to left, were numbered A, B, C, and D. The hills upon which they were placed were named Rightor, Carvill, Graveyard, and Hindman. Three 30-pounder Parrott rifles were mounted in Fort Curtiss, with a pair of fieldpieces in each of the linking batteries. Ten to twelve other field guns were also available, while gunboats in the river were on call.

Even before War Secretary Seddon's May 23 message arrived across the Mississippi, high ranking officers in the Confederate Trans-Mississippi Department were reviewing the possibilities of eliminating the Helena thorn. Indeed, the Federal supply and staging point had vexed them since it first fell to the North almost a year earlier. This point was driven home by Lt. Gen. Smith when he wrote to Rebel Missouri war governor Thomas C. Reynolds on June 4 from his Shreveport headquarters. "Helena is the point looked to," he observed. "It is the strategic point in that section, and, if a favorable opportunity offers for securing its possession, it should be improved."

On June 8, two days before Smith received Seddon's communication, Little Rock–based District of Arkansas commander Lt. Gen. Theophilus H. Holmes also suggested such an attack might be undertaken. Next day, Maj. Gen. Sterling Price at Jacksonport, Arkansas, was advised by Brig. Gen. John S. Marmaduke that his scouts placed the number of Federal soldiers at Helena at somewhere between four thousand and five thousand. The actual number was 4,129, drawn from the 29th, 33rd, and 36th Iowa, the 28th Wisconsin, the 33rd and 35th Missouri (U.S.A.), the 43rd Indiana, along with a new black regiment (2nd Arkansas) and cavalry from Indiana and Kansas. If the assault were "conducted with celerity and secrecy," Price thought it might succeed.

Lt. Gen. Smith, meanwhile, had received the war secretary's May 23 message and endorsed it on to Holmes, instructing him "to act as circumstances may justify." When the latter received his superior's communication, he immediately replied, stating, "I believe we can take Helena. Please let me attack." Knowing that Smith would allow such a gambit, Holmes traveled to Jacksonport on June 18. There, in a meeting with Price and Marmaduke, the wheels were placed into motion for an assault upon Helena. Four days later, the attacking infantry and cavalry set out over dry roads bordered by treeless plains.

Celerity, one of the criteria for Rebel success in the campaign, was lost when several days of heavy rain prevented the columns from reaching the town's outskirts until July 3. Brig. Gen. Joseph O. "Jo" Shelby's friend John N. Edwards later recalled how, as a result of the unceasing deluge, the entire area between Jacksonport and the Mississippi "became one vast lagoon streaked innumerably by now swimming streams and bottomless bayous." Secrecy was another ingredient required for Confederate success and it, too, was lacking. Even before Price departed Jacksonport, Shiloh veteran Brig. Gen. Benjamin M. Prentiss, District of Eastern Arkansas and thus the Helena commander, began receiving reports that Lt. Gen. Holmes was contemplating a visit to his town.

In addition, Maj. Gen. Stephen A. Hurlbut, XVI Corps commander at Memphis, was given information that Price was en route to hit either Helena or New Madrid. On June 21, Acting Rear Adm. Porter, near Vicksburg, began picking up reports from spies, deserters, etc., that Price was headed toward the Mississippi with a large force and heavy cannon. Believing that his target was Union shipping in the area between the White River and Island No. 10, he divined that Helena would be the most likely west bank target. Acting upon his intuition, Porter immediately wrote Lt. Cmdr. Phelps, in command of naval forces in the area, advising him of developments. Phelps, in turn, detailed the *Tyler, General Bragg,* and the tinclad *Hastings* to support Prentiss. Phelps also stopped into the office of Maj. Gen. Hurlbut to learn what he could of the objectives of Lt. Gen. Price, then thought to be the moving force behind any Helena adventure. Hurlbut insisted that the Confederate's "movements were known." No advance on Helena was expected; rather, if one were coming, it would be directed once more at Milliken's Bend.

The *Tyler*, long plagued with boiler and engine problems, was at Memphis undergoing repairs, as was the *General Bragg*. Only the light draught gunboat *Hastings* was immediately available to support Helena. Phelps detailed the other two to resume patrolling downstream just as soon as possible. Before departing Memphis, Lt. Cmdr. Pritchett of the *Tyler* was briefed by Maj. Gen. Hurlbut, who believed the Confederate target was Island No. 35. With her power plant still questionable, the old gunboat returned to her duties on June 25. The *General Bragg*, in even worse propulsion difficulty, was taken in hand at Memphis on June 28 for a three-week engine upgrade.

While cruising between Memphis and the mouth of White River during June 26–30, Pritchett stopped several times at Helena and interviewed Brig. Gen. Prentiss. That officer, paroled after his capture at Shiloh, maintained for some days that Price was moving to join Lt. Col. Smith at Alexandria, Louisiana, on the Red River. As Porter later put it, he had "no apprehension of an attack." On the last day of the month, Pritchett warned Porter that the *Tyler* just had to go back to Memphis. He did not expect to be gone long, maybe "a few hours." Some rivets needed to be placed into the boilers or there was "great danger of one of the bottom sheets blowing out." When the *Tyler* returned to the Memphis Navy Yard, engineers found her "boiler in a dangerous condition." A work gang was immediately assigned to her in an effort to provide sufficient temporary repairs to allow her to return quickly to duty.

As June faded, events in the vicinity of Helena changed and Brig. Gen. Prentiss became more suspicious that something bad was heading his way. His scouts were unable to penetrate very far out while daily, small squad classes occurred on the town's perimeter. As a result of these developments, the entire Federal garrison was put under arms until further notice and remedial work was undertaken on any weaknesses perceived in the town's defenses. Until further notice, the men would be awakened every morning at 2:30 A.M. and, after breakfasting, sent to their labors. Caught by surprise at Pittsburg Landing, Prentiss was determined not to be taken unawares ever again.

On July 1, as the laborers pounded away inside Pritchett's gunboat, Brig. Gen. Prentiss received definite intelligence that a powerful Rebel force was coming toward him down the Spring Creek road. A big Independence Day celebration planned for three days hence was cancelled.[23] At Memphis, Lt. Cmdr. Phelps was able to get the *Tyler*'s temporary repairs expedited and completed by midnight on July 1. The remainder of the night her crew coaled ship. Early in the morning of July 2, the wooden warrior steamed to Helena. Upon her arrival, the tinclad *Hastings* was sent up to review reports of Confederate activities at Island No. 40. Much of the rest of the day was spent drilling the Second Division at the broadside guns.

In view of his boat's "good battery," Lt. Cmdr. Pritchett was given orders to remain off the town until something definite was known concerning Maj. Gen. Price's intentions. Thus she was the only boat stationed at Helena as events unfolded. At the same time, the timberclad was to watch the vicinity of Walnut Bend. Refugees had reported that the Rebels would mount a raid upon it.

Despite a variety of hardships, most of the Confederate assault force reached the vicinity of Helena about sunup on July 3. With cavalry guarding the approaches, infantry started to push down the lower Little Rock and Spring Creek roads. Lt. Gen. Holmes, upon his arrival, was alarmed. "[T]he place was very much more difficult to access," he later confessed, "and the fortifications very much stronger than I had supposed before undertaking the expedition." At noon, the top Rebel field commanders met in a farmhouse five miles west of town to plot their final strategy. It was decided that, at dawn the following morning of the great Federal anniversary, coordinated attacks would be launched against Batteries A, C and D. Once the battle plan was ready, Lt. Gen. Price, according to historian Bearss, predicted that "As sure as the sun rises, the fort ... will be ours."

There were 7,646 Confederate soldiers available to Lt. Gen. Holmes for the attempt to capture Helena. Among them, 1,700 dismounted cavalry would assault fortified Rightor Hill northwest of the town and take its artillery battery (A). Another 1,300 men were tasked with the capture of Hindman's (Crowley's) Hill and guns (Battery D), southwest of the city. The main attack however, would take place near the center of the Yankee perimeter, with Maj. Gen. Price's 3,100 men seizing Graveyard Hill and its battery (C). If the Confederates were able to achieve success in their coordinated attack — an ever elusive goal in wartime — they might be able to not only take Fort Curtis, but, as the *St. Louis Daily Missouri Democrat* reporter on the scene initially feared, "the whole wharf, entirely cutting off our retreat by means of the transports."

Through the remainder of the afternoon and evening, the Rebel field commanders readied their forces. The St. Louis newsman believed their entire plan and preparations "entirely ignored the presence of the gunboat, which they were not expecting to find at our landing." Just as Maj. Gen. Prentiss and his men knew by July 3 that they were to be the object of a Rebel strike, so too did the men aboard the *Tyler* know that they most likely would be called to action soon. Just after breakfast that Friday, all hands were turned to exercising at various duties in preparation for the expected action. At 9:00 A.M., the men were beat to quarters and exercised at the great guns; the marines practiced with their small arms and rifles.

At dark, Maj. Gen. Prentiss' officers informed their men that a large force "of from 18,000 to 22,000 men" were within three miles of Helena prepared to attack during the night or at dawn. Capt. Edward Redington of the 20th Wisconsin Infantry told his wife in a July 7 letter home that the men of the garrison "had received so many false alarms that nobody believed there was any cause for alarm." With extra gunners sent to all of his batteries, Maj. Gen. Prentiss bid his camp retire at an early hour. Arrangements were made for a signal gun to sound in the event of attack. With foreboding, Redington and the other men of his company finally lay down around midnight to "snatch" some sleep. Meanwhile, Confederate soldiers were marched to staging areas to await the order for advance.[24]

In the predawn darkness of July 4, whispers stalked about the Union camp. Were those men over yonder shaping up into formations? At 3:00 A.M., a half hour after the now-regular muster according to Capt. Redington, drums beat assembly. A courier had come in from outside the lines to warn Maj. Gen. Prentiss that his outpost on the Upper Little Rock road was taken. The bluecoats gave up ideas of rest and milled about, many still not believing that battle was imminent. The hazy night largely concealed the staging of the Confederate assembly. "In plain view," wrote Jo Shelby's chronicler, "the Mississippi River lay wrapped in an impenetrable vail [sic] of fog, that whirled and twisted in vast formless clouds upon the sleeping town and on the giant trees upon its banks."

Sunrise was predicted to be about 4:00 A.M. and as the orange sphere climbed and "the river tied its bonnet of sunbeams on and lay very quiet," the haze dissipated, quickly revealing all and everything in the area. It was just a few minutes after 4:00 A.M. when skirmishing Confederates saw the breastworks atop Hindman Hill, 150 yards away. All along the line Rebel soldiers started to drive in the Union pickets. Simultaneously, the butternut soldiers were seen from the Helena defense line and the alarm gun at Fort Curtis went off. Out on the Mississippi, crewmen aboard the *Tyler* were beat to quarters.

Capt. Redington and his buddies initially thought the Fort Curtis cannon fire a salute to the National holiday, but it wasn't. The Wisconsin soldier described what happened next:

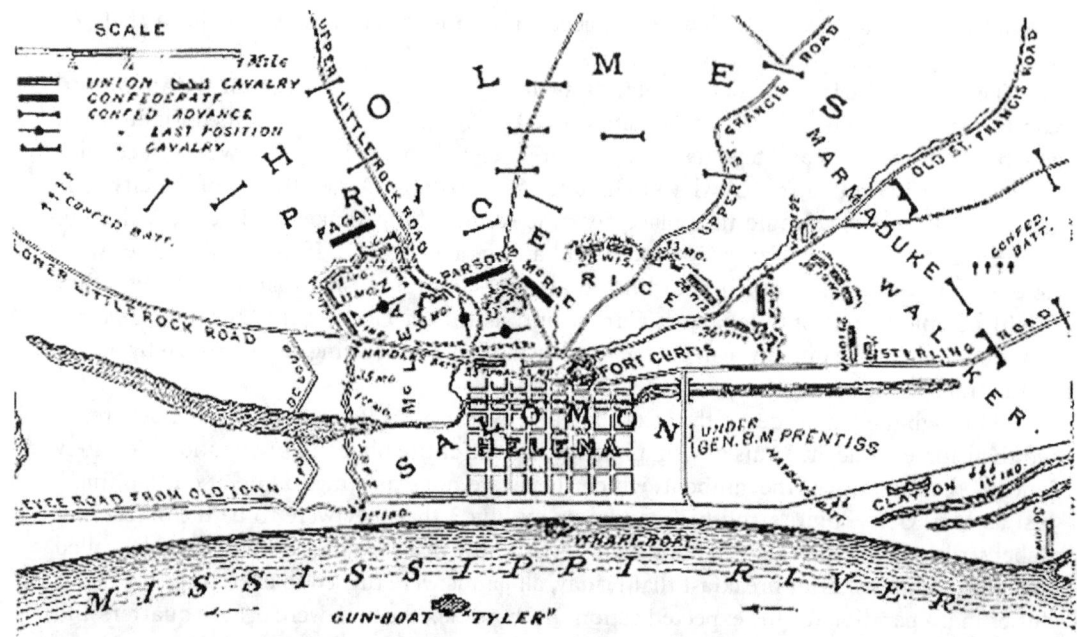

The little town of Helena, Arkansas, was the site of a major Confederate attack by Lieutenant General T.H. Holmes on July 4, 1863, the same day Vicksburg surrendered. With assistance from the timberclad *Tyler*, the Federal defenders, under Major General B.M. Prentiss, were able to beat off assaults upon their hilltop fortifications (***Battles and Leaders***).

In about 20 minutes all such notions [of an Independence Day salute] were scattered by our pickets beginning to dance, first by pop, pop, our right, then pop, on our left, then a dozen pops, and a volley in front, a bang, bang, bang, from two batteries of four guns each, one on our right, and one on our left, then an awful roar from the gunboat *Tyler*, a 60-lb. shell howling and screaming through the air over our heads, and plunging into the timber a mile or more beyond us and exploding with a roar almost as loud as the gun that sent it, and that came back as evidence that its mission was accomplished. Thus the ball was fairly opened.

Maj. Gen. Price, meanwhile, made a crucial mistake. Despite evidence that dawn was near, he misinterpreted Lt. Gen. Holmes' orders to attack "at daylight" as meaning after the sun was actually up. The other Confederate brigade commanders believed the kick off would come at "first light" and so began their assaults upwards of an hour before him. Redington and his companions watched the Southerners come "swarming out of the woods, first one regiment, then a brigade, then a whole division."

Masked by shadows and protected in the early mist, five Confederate columns converged on Helena. Those Arkansas troops headed toward Fort Hindman, as the *Little Rock True Democrat* later said, passed "over and around the spurs of the steep hills, running into the bottom." The confusion of Maj. Gen. Price resulted in the attacking Rebels suffering a severe enfilade fire from the defenders of Graveyard Hill, particularly from Battery D at Fort Hindman. The largely Arkansas contingent continued to attack up the hill "amid the leaden rain and iron hail."

Coming up with Maj. Gen. Price, Lt. Gen. Holmes corrected the former's error and his brigades charged up the tree-strewn slopes of Graveyard Hill, through the mist toward Union Battery C. The Southerners gave a "good shout" as they moved.

About 5:00 A.M., the tars aboard the *Tyler* became concerned as the noise of gunfire back of Helena intensified. Lt. Cmdr. Pritchett now received a signal from shore that enemy troops were coming down the Old Little Rock Road. These were men from Col. W. H. Brooks' 34th Arkansas Infantry and they dispersed themselves astride Clements Hill (actually the rise where a house belonging to people named Clements stood) below the town.

The *Tyler* weighed anchor at 5:50 A.M. and dropped downstream about three quarters of a mile where she rounded to. Her portside gun ports were opened and then, perhaps a bit later than Capt. Redington notes, the timberclad opened fire. Within seconds, gigantic 8-inch shells began to explode among Brooks' soldiers and, for that matter, at other locations where Confederates were suspected of gathering. With a huge roar, one fell among a knot of Southern cavalry, several of whom simply disappeared.

In desperate need of help, Col. Brooks sent a runner to headquarters seeking artillery support. In response, Lt. John C. Arnett rushed forward with a pair of 10-pounder Parrotts from Etter's Arkansas Battery. The terrain at Clements Hill was so difficult that he was only able to get one gun correctly positioned, but, even though it was located in an exposed position, it started spitting at the black gunboat in the river. Arnett's horse artillerymen were able to splash a pair of 10-pounder shells into the water astern of the *Tyler* before the gunboatmen knew they were there. Before the artillerymen could improve their shooting, they were themselves taken under fire by the timberclad's "stinger," her 32-pounder rifled stern gun. The blasts from the naval Parrot soon persuaded Arnett to relimber his cannon and depart the area.

At Clements Hill, Col. Brooks was left to reorganize his men when, about 7:30 A.M., Lt. Cmdr. Pritchett received an urgent message from Maj. Gen. Prentiss. Price had taken the summit of Graveyard Hill and the *Tyler* was needed to help contain the Southerners or drive them out. Should the enemy find a way to get artillery atop the ridge, disaster would surely follow. With great billows of black smoke rising from her chimneys, the old gunboat steamed back up the Mississippi approximately half a mile, toward the center of Helena. Col. Brooks and his men watched her start up the river.

Gallant Southern attempts to take Battery D were, in the meantime, unsuccessful. The Arkansas troops tasked with its capture were blocked from bringing up artillery by the Union expedient of cutting down trees across the approach roads. Still, the Rebels almost reached the top of the hill and managed to seize the outer fortifications but were pinned down just short of the summit by Union batteries. Fort Hindman remained momentarily safe.

As the fighting continued, Battery D was able to fire in support of other Union locations. Later in the battle, Rebel troops would try again to take it, but these were also beaten back, largely by the 43rd Indiana, with help from several other Federal units. While Price's men battled for the Graveyard heights, Col. Brooks decided it was now safe to reintroduce horse artillery to Clements Hill. A messenger was sent back and one of Etter's 6-pounder field guns was brought up, unlimbered, and opened fire on Federal rifle pits south of town.

The second Brooks attempt to provide cannon support to his fellows was no more successful than the first. His little gun was within range of the *Tyler*'s 32-pounder stern gun, which speedily took the butternut artillerists under fire. The Etter gun got off just eight rounds before it, too, left the scene. As Brooks retreated, he ordered the destruction of the slave quarters near the Clements' mansion, plus that of 2½ tons of bacon and 1,500 bushels of corn.

Twice more Price's Confederates made desperate charges before successfully capturing Battery C. "Yelling like demons," the Missourians, observed by Capt. Redington at Battery B, drove to and over the breastworks; the fighting was often a matter of "crossed bayonets."

On both occasions of their advance, the Southerners displayed, as an admiring Brig. Gen. Prentiss put it, "a courage and desperation rarely equaled."

As they were about to be overrun, the Union gunners from the 33rd Missouri Infantry (U.S.A.) disabled their pieces and fled. In their retreat, they had the presence of mind to remove all of the friction-primers, "so rendering," in the words of the *St. Louis Daily Missouri Democrat*'s man on the scene, "the battery entirely useless to the enemy." The coolness of the departing Federal gunners prevented Lt. Gen. Price from turning the guns of Battery C on the Federals in other hilltop positions or upon the town. Pausing to catch his breath, the tall officer may have noted that his men were the only Confederate troops on the field so far this day to achieve their objective. Price's soldiers actually held that achievement for the duration of the whole battle — and, in the process, became targets for every available enemy cannon, rifle, musket, and pistol. Graveyard Hill was aptly named, commented the *Chicago Daily Tribune* reporter Albert H. Bodman a few days later, because it "really was to the Rebel division which sought to possess it."

When the Southern generals, Holmes and Price, entered the captured works atop Graveyard Hill and realized that the Federal guns were useless to them, confusion reigned again. Lt. Gen. Holmes, as Albert Castel tells us, now began to act like "a man in a state of panic." A staff officer was dispatched to the rear with orders to bring up field batteries. Orders were also passed for some men to go to the aid of those tied down below Battery D.

All this while, the *Tyler* puffed steadily upstream, eventually reaching a position abreast of Helena and about a thousand yards from Battery C. Coming to, she opened her portside battery and prepared to open upon Confederate targets of opportunity. Her "gun elevations were set at five degrees," wrote historian Steven Jones years later, "and the range was between 1,600 and 2,350 yards." The largest timberclad was ready, just as she had been 16 months earlier at Shiloh.

Simultaneously, the guns of Batteries A, B, and D were also trained on the fallen Battery C. As the Union military and naval gunners began to pound it, the decimal level reached intense, thundering heights. "Our Hill Batterys," Pvt. Newton Robert Scott of the 36th Iowa afterwards wrote his parents, "and the Gun Boat *Tyler* with 8 or ten guns were throwing shells amongst them thick as hail."

There now occurred another amazing Southern maneuver. Lt. Gen. Holmes directed a colonel in Brig. Gen. Mosby M. Parson's brigade to attack Fort Curtis. Seeing his advance, Parson's other regimental commanders, believing a general assault was unfolding, eagerly joined the push. The scribe from the St. Louis newspaper in town this Saturday tells us that the crest of Graveyard Hill was 600 yards from Fort Curtis and that the base was 500 yards. On top of that, the Confederates found themselves without supporting artillery.

Still, within minutes of the gunboat's arrival off the wharf, elements of the 7th, 8th, 9th, and 10th Missouri Infantry (C.S.A.) rushed down the hill toward Fort Curtis. Wildly cheering and shouting the "Rebel yell," the men were immediately caught in a cross fire from Prentiss' gunners and riflemen. The editor of the *Little Rock True Democrat* later acknowledged that this fire "was terrific."

Over at Battery B, Capt. Redington joined others in watching in awe. "As they charged down the hill (and a braver charge was never made)," he remembered, "how grand they looked." The *Daily Missouri Democrat* special was less generous. To him, the Missourians were seen bolting, "not in line or in column, not with fixed bayonet showing a glittering line of polished steel, not as the 'Old Guard' charged at Waterloo." Rather, the butternuts "charged *en masse*, or worse yet, *en mobbe*, every man being himself a small host with a leader of its own." Looking grand or not, they "were met by a storm of shot and shell, and by a murderous flank fire," said Redington. "Steadily," the St. Louis newsman wrote, "the shell, case, grape, and canister flew, with the swiftness of lightning and the precision of fate, straight into the faces of the infuriated mob."

When Lt. Cmdr. Phelps reached the scene a few days later and reviewed the battle with Northern military and naval personnel, he wrote to ARAM Porter concerning the events occurring after "Captain Pritchett discovered the enemy pressing down the hillside after the capture of the battery in the center."

If the Yankee onshore volleys were not enough, the Confederates running down from the crest of the ridge were now targeted by the *Tyler*. Lookouts aboard pointed out gray-clad soldiers endeavoring "to break through in force into our lines through a ravine about 200 feet deep." The skipper of the *Tyler* "took up such a position that his broadside guns poured a destructive fire upon the slopes and enfiladed the ravines." Additionally, Phelps reported, "his stern guns effectually silenced the rebel battery below, and his bow guns played simultaneously upon the upper one."

Eight-inch shells rained down upon Missouri soldiers in an area "now bounded by Columbia, Arkansas, Don/College, and Rightor streets in Helena." As they exploded in great thunderclaps, some tore huge holes in the Rebel ranks, to say nothing of literally shredding the bodies of some Missourians into little pieces. Faced with the combined fire, a number of survivors threw down their arms and hightailed it back to the rear. Others were terrified and huddled along the lower slopes of Graveyard Hill. Still others just lay down their arms; at one point, more than a hundred terrified by the gunboat shells surrendered en masse.

A few more determined Missouri heroes rushed onward but were cut down by dismounted Union cavalry and defending riflemen. It was not long before the remaining, dazed Southerners retreated in complete disorder, many exhausted and others suffering from heatstroke. "Not one in three ever got away," Capt. Redington later told his wife. Lt. Gen. Holmes was now a victim of his own confusing orders, as well as those of his subordinates. All of these had led to partial measures that failed to turn the tide at any of the three contested ridge positions. Especially at Battery C and on the various corners of Hindman and Graveyard hills, the exposed Confederates were continuously targeted by every Federal gun on the battlefield as well as the heavy cannon of the *Tyler*. "Grape-shot and canister, round-shot and shell, followed them mercilessly, bore them down and battered them to pieces."

By 10:30 A.M., Lt. Gen. Holmes realized that his position had so deteriorated that no further headway could or would be made. A general retreat was ordered and the attack on Helena was over, though rear guard actions continued past 2:00 P.M. The 36th Iowa's Newton Scott summed up the opinion of many in a letter to neighborhood friend Hanna Cone: "We gave them one of the most Signal Thrashings that they Ever got from the Yankees."

The *Tyler* had bombarded targets of opportunity from her location abreast of town for the better part of five hours. When she ceased firing at 12:30 P.M., it was noted in her log that 264 rounds of 8-inch and 169 Parrott shells had been expended. The Confederate assault on the Union base left 206 Union casualties and 1,636 Confederate. Of the latter, 1,078 were from Price's command. Pritchett's superior, Phelps, was convinced that the "*Tyler* contributed greatly to the defeat of the enemy and the terrible slaughter in his ranks is largely hers." Pritchett "used his battery in a manner alike creditable to himself and to his officers and men."

The tinclad *Covington* reached Helena on the evening of Independence Day along with the steamer *Silver Moon*, bringing a quantity of shells to replenish the *Tyler*'s magazine. The *Hastings* returned next morning. Many of the Confederate dead still lay on the battlefield, though most of the wounded were being cared for along with Union injured. Acting Ensign Smith was sent ashore to inspect the carnage. When he returned, he told Lt. Cmdr. Pritchett that the *Tyler*'s shells had "a very destructive effect among the enemy. The killed and wounded by our shells on this place were about 600."

Lieut. Cmdr. James M. Pritchett (1836–1871) took over command of the *Tyler* in early 1863. The Hoosier officer's greatest claim to fame while with the Western Flotilla was the defense of Helena, Arkansas, made on Independence Day 1863, the same day Vicksburg surrendered. Pritchett transferred to the South Atlantic Blockading Squadron in the fall of 1864 (*Battles and Leaders*).

All day the garrison remained in position anticipating another attack. At 4:30 P.M., a signal gun was fired from Fort Curtis and Lt. Cmdr. Pritchett believed action was imminent. The men aboard the *Tyler* were beat to quarters and she got underway. Steaming downstream about half a mile, she rounded to expecting a request for bombardment, but it did not come. The timberclad retired upriver from her advance station at 6:00 P.M., and went alongside the wharf boat.

The old gunboat remained at her post off Helena for the remainder of July. On July 6, Lt. Cmdr. Pritchett sent a brief report to Rear Adm. Porter reviewing his boat's success. "I am informed by the officers of the Army," he wrote, "that had it not been for the assistance rendered by this vessel, the town would have been captured." Maj. Gen. Prentiss also praised Pritchett for his "unusual" efficiency "in procuring timely reinforcements."

Lt. Gen. Smith at Shreveport learned on July 7 that Lt. Gen. Holmes "attacked Helena at daylight on the 4th instant and was repulsed with a heavy loss." At noon the next day, the *Tyler* fired a 21-gun victory salute in honor of the fall of Vicksburg. When Port Hudson surrendered on July 9, all of the Mississippi River was once more in Federal hands. The same day, Maj. Gen. Prentiss wrote to ARAM Porter, without Pritchett's knowledge, seeking a promotion for the *Tyler*'s skipper. Bubbling over with praise for the timberclad officer, Helena's commander informed the Mississippi Squadron that "not a little of our success in the late battle" was attributable to Pritchett's skill.

On July 11, ARAM Porter sent to the navy secretary "a full report of the late affair at Helena, where the gunboat *Tyler* saved the day [for] our little band of soldiers." On July 27, the grateful cabinet officer sent a letter of commendation to Lt. Cmdr. Pritchett acknowledging that Prentiss' command was "saved, in all probability, from serious disaster by the valuable assistance rendered by the *Tyler*."

Although there was almost immediately much controversy concerning Rebel strategy and actions in this campaign, it was generally believed across the land that the Union forces fought well and that the Mississippi Squadron garnered additional laurels. Lt. Cmdr. Phelps paid special tribute to the old gunboat: "First at Belmont, then at Pittsburg Landing, and now here, the *Tyler* has been of inestimable value and has saved the fortunes of the day."

It would be many years before critics began to nitpick the Federal defense. As at Pittsburg Landing, much of the concern would center upon the activities and effectiveness of the *Tyler*'s fire support. The claim, as made by Bearss and many others, that "the Union navy's domination of the "Western Waters," characterized by the intervention of *Tyler*, helped turned

The *Tyler*. This wash drawing by Muller, which was commissioned by the U.S. Navy about 1906, depicts the largest timberclad anchored off the Mississippi River at some point during the Civil War. Two mortar rafts are tied up to the riverbank. Note the large awning over the foredeck. Such stretches of canvas were extremely important during the periods from April through September to ward off the direct sun as it beat down on the open decks (Naval Historical Center).

the tide at a critical moment" has been disputed.[25] The Confederate attack on Helena was, wrote Albert Castel a century afterwards, "a blunder in its very conception." Even if by some miracle it could have been carried off, former Southern Col. Thomas L. Snead was of the opinion that, because it was virtually under the protection of the Mississippi Squadron, the town "could not have been held 24 hours."

Horace Greeley, in his contemporary Civil War history, bluntly stated that the only way Maj. Gen. Prentiss could have lost the battle was if he were "a coward, a traitor, or an idiot." Although they did not know it at the time, Holmes and his followers were simply too late to have any impact on Vicksburg's fortunes. The whole effort was a failure from beginning to end.[26]

The transports *New Bon Accord* and *Niagara* arrived at Memphis late on July 5 and brought news of the previous day's Helena encounter. In addition to dispatches, their captains and passengers relayed to the editor of the *Memphis Bulletin* what they knew of the fight. As is usual with initial reports in wartime — then or now — there were some difficulties with accuracy.

According to the people aboard the two transports, the Rebels had actually made it to the suburbs of Helena before the guns at Fort Curtis opened upon them around 4:00 A.M. on July 4. Meanwhile, Maj. Gen. Prentiss had formed up his men in order of battle and, according to the passengers, "advanced to the charge, while the gunboat *Tyler*, which completely commanded the ravine from the river, began to pour shot and shell among them with the most destructive effect." After sketching out the battle's results, the *Bulletin* paid tribute to the gallant manner in which the troops behaved, noting that "the negro regiments fought well."

"The gunboat *Tyler*," he concluded, "rendered very essential service, having thrown upward of 500 shells among the enemy's troops."

In a message to Maj. Gen. Hurlbut carried aboard the transport, Maj. Gen. Prentiss noted his victory, the number of casualties, and that the "*Tyler* has been today a valuable auxiliary." He called upon the XVI Corps commander for reinforcements, as he expected that the enemy was "massing their troops for a renewal at an early moment."

When the transport *Silver Moon* arrived at Cairo on the morning of July 7 with 726 Confederate prisoners, personnel aboard gave particulars to the battle to the local correspondent of the *Chicago Daily Tribune*. They, like the scribe from the *St. Louis Daily Missouri Democrat*, described the battle in great detail. Unlike the *Memphis Bulletin*, both barely mentioned the role of the *Tyler*. Where the St. Louis man mentioned that the Helena garrison had received some assistance from "a gunboat" not named, the Chicago newsman was told that Maj. Gen. Prentiss "was also assisted by the gunboat *Tyler* and three other gunboats, which arrived about the time the battle was over." He was also given a number of dispatches from Prentiss that had been cleared for publication. One of these had originally been sent to Maj. Gen. Hurlbut at Memphis three days earlier. "Send another gunboat if possible," it read. "The *Tyler* has done good service to-day."

Albert H. Bodman, the ace reporter of the *Chicago Daily Tribune* who had covered much of the campaign as well as the surrender of Vicksburg, traveled to Helena on July 8 to interview Maj. Gen. Prentiss and get a firsthand report on the battle. After providing several paragraphs of battle description, the Chicago writer offered several other observations. According to Prentiss, the "colored regiment here—the 2nd Arkansas—did nobly during the engagement, standing like veterans in the thickest of the fight." The noted journalist also wrote at length about naval assistance. "Our troops were materially assisted by the gunboat *Tyler*," he revealed, "which did effective service. Capt. Pritchard managed his boat admirably, throwing 500 shells during the engagement." In summary, Bodman noted, "Gen. Prentiss expresses unqualified admiration and gratitude at the assistance rendered him by the *Tyler*."

Not everyone agreed with the rosy picture presented in official reports and the newspapers. In a letter home to his wife on July 7, Wisconsin Capt. Edward S. Redington, reacting to the stories published in the *Memphis Bulletin* and *Chicago Daily Tribune*, was extremely critical of the help offered by both the Black troops and the *Tyler*. "As to the niggers, they were not in the fight at all," he proclaimed; indeed, "they did not fire a gun." In the tone of the times, his dismissal of the black contribution is understandable. Redington was also one of the first to deny the gunboat's contribution. His observation is worth noting in full:

> The gunboat *Tyler* lay in front of the town and threw shells away over our heads, not knowing where they were going any more than a boy knows where a stone will fall that he has thrown into the Air. All the damage we can hear of being done by them was by a shell that went full a mile beyond us and happened to fall in the woods where a Rebel surgeon was dressing their wounded and killed twenty already more than half dead.

The most vocal modern critic of the *Tyler*'s supporting role is Arkansas historian Steven W. Jones. His thesis was originally published in the March 1977 issue of the *Phillips County Historical Quarterly*. Jones dismissed out of hand the praise heaped upon the timberclad and her captain by Maj. Gen. Prentiss and the U.S. Army, indicating that the general recognized the ship only "as a valuable support unit." Her fire did not "physically devastate" the Confederates, he claimed, nor did she "save the day."

As proof of his allegation, Jones indicates that the rolling of the *Tyler* in the river caused by the discharge of her cannon would force her rounds to either carry over or fall short of their target. His estimate is that upwards of 40 percent of her shells went astray. Her guns may gone off rapidly, Jones contends, but because of the spillage, the timberclad in effect "only fired about a shell a minute into the Confederate charge down the slopes of Graveyard Hill." At that rate, if there was no supporting bombardment from other redoubts, Fort Curtis could have been "easily carried" by the attacking columns under this fire. But there was other Union resistance, from guns of Battery C and D and many riflemen. As at Shiloh, the *Tyler* had some influence upon this battle. Like her role in the Tennessee River contest, however, "she probably dealt a greater psychological blow to the Confederate troops at Helena than she did a physical one."

Admiral Porter's most recent biographer, Chester G. Hearn, notes that the Tyler's 8-inch shells "stopped the attack [on Fort Curtis] before it could gather steam. Marksmanship from the timberclad was extraordinary." During the battle, the *Tyler* expended 413 rounds, mostly 8-inch shells, cut to explode at 10 or 15 seconds. This was, one of the ship's historians, computer specialist Stephen R. Davis, later revealed "a sustained rate of roughly one full broadside every 60 seconds."

The Helena garrison remained in its position for two days before venturing out and its commander "failed to follow up on the advantage given him by the navy." For this tardiness, Prentiss, like Maj. Gen. George G. Meade at Gettysburg, was criticized for lack of initiative. Consequently, as historian Davis reveals "much of the credit" for the victory at Helena went to the *Tyler*." Even today, from the steep slopes and towering heights of Hindman's (Crowley's) Hill, the visitor gets "a startling image of what the Confederates faced as they attacked." One can imagine himself facing the bluecoat volleys and the naval gunfire "that broke up the Confederate advance" and, as Dave Page puts it, "the all-important Mississippi River can still be seen through the trees."[27]

CHAPTER 14

Peripheral Streams and Red River, 1863–1864

THE UNION MERCHANT STEAMER *IMPERIAL* operated the first St. Louis–New Orleans voyage, July 8–16, to be completed since the early spring of 1861. This did not, however, mean that Confederate forces would forego attempts to molest Federal shipping on the Mississippi. To the contrary, its disruption remained a high priority.

To disturb or counter regular and irregular Rebel ambitions and commercial intercourse in the interior portions of those Southern states adjacent to the great natural waterways continued as a cornerstone of Federal naval policy in the west. Immediately after the fall of Vicksburg, RAM David Dixon Porter ordered a series of raids up the Yazoo, Red, White, Black, and Tennessee rivers. Specifically, these were designed, in the words of Lt. Cmdr. Thomas O. Selfridge, Jr., "to make such captures of cotton and other stores as might prove practicable and to drive Confederate forces away from the vicinity of" river mouths. Two of these 1863 cruises, one up the Red, Black and Tensas rivers and the other on the White River, are of interest here.

The first, led by Lt. Cmdr. Selfridge in the *Conestoga*, in company with the tinclads *Forest Rose*, *Petrel*, *Manitou*, and *Rattler*, departed Vicksburg for the mouth of the Red River on July 10, the day after the fall of Port Hudson. Two days later, the little task group weighed for Trinity, Louisiana, reaching it by evening. Interestingly, the *Conestoga* towed a flat with a 100-pounder Parrott gun mounted. The path chosen for ascent was, in fact, a waterline that ran parallel with the Mississippi and featured at its furthest extent a large region of navigable waters, Tensas Lake and Bayou Macon. This head of navigation for the Tensas River was at a point but 30 miles from Vicksburg and only five miles from the Mississippi.

The group's specific mission was to capture cotton and fugitive steamers and to interrupt irregular Rebel attacks on Mississippi River transports by men firing from the shores of the intervening narrow strip of land. Moving from the Red into the Black, Selfridge's gunboats steamed with some care up the narrow channels of that stream and the connecting Tensas. Navigating the difficulties of the water approaches without incident, the timberclad and tinclads suddenly emerged that afternoon on the lake and bayou.

As the Federals arrived it was dusk, but lookouts aboard the gunboats spied a pair of transports in the distance, the *Dr. Beatty* and *Nelson*. The keen-eyed Confederates, momentarily taken by surprise, succeeded in escaping up a maze of uncharted channels. Still, a large quantity of ammunition recently arrived from Natchez was seized on the lake shore.

The little task group anchored about 8:00 P.M. and Lt. Cmdr. Selfridge called his captains together to plot the next day's activities. July 12–13 was dark and rainy, but before sunrise on Monday the gunboats were further divided into task units, with two tinclads sent up the Tensas and two up the Little Red River, a tributary of the Black River. The *Manitou* and *Rattler*, after groping their way carefully up the twisty Little Red River, returned at noon with a prize, the *Louisville*. She was one of the largest vessels remaining in Confederate service anywhere. Indeed, the noted 572-ton, 227.6 foot long side-wheel Mississippi packet would be converted into the largest tinclad of all, the 40-gun *Ouachita*. About the same time, the *Petrel* and *Forest Rose* exited from the Tensas with the stern-wheeler *Elmira* in custody. She was caught with a cargo of Confederate sugar, rum, and military stores.

A further tinclad reconnaissance was conducted up the Tensas that afternoon, but no captures were made. Great quantities of burning cotton were observed, along with a few miscellaneous Rebel troops that were surprised to see the Federal craft.

The *Conestoga* led the *Rattler*, *Forest Rose*, and *Manitou* up the Ouachita River on July 14 on a reconnaissance towards a fort reportedly being built near Harrisonburg, a town of about 800. Meanwhile, the *Petrel* convoyed the prizes to the mouth of the Red River. The task group anchored slightly below the wooden Confederate bastion for the night, its gun crews at their stations. At 5:00 A.M. on Wednesday, the *Conestoga* and *Manitou* cruised up to within two miles of the fort. Lt. Cmdr. Selfridge elected to test its strength by firing three shells toward it from the 100-pounder Parrot mounted on the raft the timberclad was towing. There was no response. A thick fog came on about an hour later that required the gunboats to withdraw. The scout, Selfridge later wrote, did, however, reveal that the enclave "contained guns too heavy to be trifled with by wooden gunboats."

The Selfridge group returned to Trinity later that evening, its mission completed to the great satisfaction of Rear Adm. Porter. The capture of the ammunition from Natchez left the army of Maj. Gen. Walker without the bullets and powder it needed, the squadron commander later wrote, and so "he moved his forces into the interior and troubled the Mississippi no more."

Thereafter, the *Conestoga* was detailed to continue its Mississippi River picket duty in the vicinity of the Red River's mouth. It was recorded that, on January 30, 1864, her battery consisted of three 32-pounder smoothbores, two 30-pounder Dahlgren rifles, a 30-pounder Parrott rifle, and a 12-pounder smoothbore boat howitzer.[1]

The next expedition, in August, involved the reliable old *Lexington*. It would be more than just a pinprick. The capture of Vicksburg freed thousands of Union troops for other duty and one of the places they would now attempt to visit was Little Rock. Before the end of July, Maj. Gen. Frederick Steele, a West Point classmate of Maj. Gen. Ulysses S. Grant, arrived at Helena to take command of all Federal troops in Arkansas and to mount an assault on its capital. At the same time, Confederate Lt. Gen. Theophilus Holmes, who had failed so miserably at Helena, turned over command of the District of Arkansas to Lt. Gen. Sterling Price. The latter did not believe he would be able to hold the town.

On July 15, Maj. Gen. Henry W. Halleck, Union army general-in-chief at Washington, wired Brig. Gen. Benjamin Prentiss at Helena reporting on Price's elevation and possible prospects. He recommended that the Shiloh veteran contact ARAM Porter for gunboat support on the White River. The request was made and Porter announced to both the western generals and Navy Secretary Gideon Welles that a task group was ready to offer assistance.

Lt. Cmdr. George M. Bache was at this time with the *Lexington* and four tinclads operating interdiction missions off the mouth of the White River. Alerted that elements of the Federal army would soon be headed his way, the little naval force congregated near Montgomery Point, Mississippi, across from the White's entrance. In the meantime, plans were being finished for a ground attack on Little Rock. The first Federals underway were a large contingent of cavalry from St. Louis under the command of Brig. Gen. John Davidson.

On July 28, the timberclad commander wrote Porter that his boats had been "lying here some days waiting for the army, who have not yet made their appearance." Meanwhile, the river stage of the White was falling.

Brig. Gen. Davidson, with 6,000 "sabers," reached the L'Anguille River at Crowley's Ridge, Arkansas, from St. Louis on August 1. In a letter to Maj. Gen. Grant, he indicated that he was headed for Clarendon and needed the protection of a pair of gunboats while a bridge was thrown across for his horsemen. The tinclads *Romeo* and *Juliet* were eventually dispatched.

Responding to Bache's letter, Porter, who was visiting New Orleans at the moment, indicated on August 3 that the *Lexington* and her consorts just had to remain off the White River entrance until Maj. Gen. Steele arrived. The navy had

George M. Bache (1840–1896), a Washingtonian and 1861 Naval Academy graduate named for his naval hero father, was commissioned a lieutenant in July of 1862, the same month he was posted to the ironclad *Cincinnati*. He would command her until she was sunk off Vicksburg in May 1863. Porter next gave Bache the *Lexington*, which he skippered into the summer of 1864. His tenure aboard the timberclad was spent in the waters below Memphis. Bache participated in the Red River campaign and his vessel was the first to push over Colonel Bailey's improvised dam at Alexandria. Afterwards, he led the larger *Tyler* and a number of tinclads in the White and Arkansas river regions battling irregulars, including Confederate general Jo Shelby. He was commissioned a lieutenant commander in 1866 and a commander on April 5, 1875, the same day he retired.

given its word and, wrote the admiral, "I never let the soldiers say I am not ready for them." In his absence, Lt. Cmdr. Phelps was called upon to oversee naval operations in this region. Phelps, aware that Porter was not totally in the loop concerning Steele's forthcoming trip, took it upon himself "with the air, though not so intended, of interference," to inform Lt. Cmdr. Bache from Memphis on August 3 of what would be required, including an interview by the *Lexington*'s skipper with Maj. Gen. Steele. He also sent copies of his instructions down to Porter, along with advice that Steele, then in Memphis, had told him he would depart Helena within the week.

The XVI Corps commander, Maj. Gen. Stephen A. Hurlbut, upon orders from Maj. Gen. Grant, was orchestrating an expedition against Little Rock. Marching overland from Helena, the assigned VII Corps infantry would halt at Clarendon or Des Arc to join the cavalry from Missouri. At whichever place turned out to be the rendezvous point, naval cooperation was desired. While supply depots were established, Bache's gunboats were to scout as far up the White as possible, hopefully to Jacksonport. Speaking for Porter, Phelps indicated in the cover letter explaining these matters that the timberclads should just "go ahead and do your duty."

On August 6, Lt. Cmdr. Bache received a communiqué from Brig. Gen. Davidson indicating that he planned to throw a bridge across the White River at Clarendon. Gunboat protection during the construction and subsequent crossing was needed. Upon receipt of Phelps' messages a day later, Bache, who had already anticipated their contents, also forwarded copies to Porter. In his letter to New Orleans, the *Lexington*'s skipper noted that he had spoken with Maj. Gen. Steele a few days before and was up to speed on the goals of the military movement. The task group, its commander explained, would depart for Clarendon on August 8, from which location the tinclads would patrol the river. The White was now "bank full." For that reason, Bache felt comfortable in taking up the big *Lexington* ("in case we should meet with any formidable batteries"), but planned to send her back down once the expedition was safely along.

The timberclad *Lexington* is at the left background in this January 18, 1864, photograph of the gunboat *Sterling Price*, taken off Baton Rouge. Within a couple of weeks, Lt. George M. Bache's gunboat would join a naval reconnaissance expedition in an ascent of Louisiana's Black and Ouachita rivers (Naval Historical Center).

Steele had but two available transports, but Bache informed him later in the day he would make certain they were escorted. As the naval officer was visiting the general's headquarters, Brig. Gen. Davidson's troopers arrived up the White at Clarendon following their 350 mile trek. The *Lexington* task group weighed for Clarendon on the morning of August 8. Embedded aboard the *Cricket* was an unnamed correspondent from the *St. Louis Daily Missouri Democrat*. When only a few miles upstream, Lt. Cmdr. Bache took Acting Ensign Charles C. Briggs and the gig's crew and transferred to the *Cricket*, leaving his timberclad under the command of her brand new executive officer, Acting Ensign Henry Booby.

Booby's craft rounded to and steamed down past Napoleon, Arkansas, coming to anchor off Cypress Bayou. The rebels were reported as having a small steamer hiding at that location ready to cross to Mississippi. The tinclads continued on, meeting neither natural nor human obstruction. St. Charles, where the *Mound City* had been so badly damaged the previous year, was found deserted, and "but little signs of life" were seen on the river.[2]

Lt. Cmdr. Bache's four tinclads came to at Clarendon, 130 miles up the White River from Helena, on the morning of August 9. There the naval officer shook hands with Brig. Gen. Davidson, who was tremendously frustrated. Although the entire area was clear of guerrillas, it was impossible to bridge the river anywhere near the village, "the country being overflowed on the opposite bank." As Davidson reported, the water was "higher than it has been at this season of the year since '44."

Considering the alternatives, Lt. Cmdr. Bache offered a nautical idea. If Davidson would send down for a pair of coal barges that could be employed as ferries, he would send two of his light draughts back to Helena. One would convoy up Steele's VII Corps troops while the other towed up the barges to be employed in crossing the legions. The *Marmora* and *Linden* were dispatched before dusk. Not long after the two tinclads departed, Bache decided it would be a good idea to have the *Lexington*. The *Prairie Bird* was sent down with orders for the timberclad to steam up to Clarendon and for Acting Volunteer Lieutenant Edward E Brennand to guard Cypress Bayou with his *Marmora*. In the end, it was determined that no threat existed at that spot and the entire task force was free to support Steele.

While Bache and his tinclads were assembling at Clarendon, Acting Ensign Booby was off Cypress Bayou. That afternoon he led a 25-man reconnaissance team ashore to reconnoiter. No sign was found of any Confederate steamer; indeed, nothing was found at all. Unable to justify remaining at the scene, the *Lexington* stood up the river during the afternoon.

On August 10 and 11, Steele's 6,000-man Army of Arkansas, with 39 cannon, quit Helena and headed for Clarendon. There it was to rendezvous with the cavalry under Brig. Gen. John Davidson that were moving his way from Missouri. Steele's transports were convoyed by the *Linden* while the *Marmora* towed barges. Also on August 10, the tinclad *Cricket* pushed on up the river on reconnaissance hoping to catch the Confederate mail at Devall's Bluff. A detachment of Brig. Gen. Davidson's cavalry was also taken along.

A Rebel 12-man picket was surprised at Devall's. Although the men escaped, a horse and much gear was captured. A mail was also taken, but it was learned that the Little Rock train had ceased running, thereby negating the need for the cavalry to disembark. The White River remained high, but it started to fall as the tinclad returned. Back at Clarendon next day, Lt. Cmdr. Bache found the *Lexington*. She had arrived at 9:00 A.M. following an overnight stay at St. Charles and the officer was glad to transfer back aboard. The St. Louis newspaperman returned as well.

Rear Adm. Porter wrote to the timberclad commander on August 11 noting that, upon his return from the White River, he was to take charge of the new naval district being created between the mouth of the White River and Milliken's Bend. As there was little necessity for convoy at the moment, the *Lexington* was to patrol up and down the Mississippi making certain that every point was guarded as well as possible.

In a report to Rear Adm. Porter next day, Bache indicated that he would be pushing on up toward Jacksonport on the morrow, together with the *Cricket* and *Marmora*, each with two companies embarked from Lt. Col. G.A. Eberhart's 32nd Iowa Infantry. The *Linden* would be left behind to guard Steele and Davidson's crossing. The boats would seek information on the location of the Confederate army under Lt. Gen. Price and hopefully come up with the Rebel side-wheel steamers *Kaskaskia* and *Thomas Sugg*. The soldiers were to land at Des Arc and destroy the telegraph.

The *Lexington* task group departed at 3:00 on the morning of August 13 and, with great clouds of invisible black smoke escaping their chimneys, thrashed their way upriver toward Des Arc. The timberclad was preceded by the *Cricket* and followed by the *Marmora*. As the trio approached Devall's Bluff, enemy pickets were seen in the woods about 100 yards from the river. They allowed the *Cricket* to steam by until, passing the bend of the river, her stern was presented toward them. At that point, they loosed a volley into her. At that very moment, the *Lexington* appeared and flaming messages from her broadside forced the horsemen to rapidly disappear.

Following the fleet's passage of Devall's, one of the *Cricket*'s chimneys, riddled by rifle balls, carried away. Following brief repairs, the push upstream was continued. The remainder of the morning was spent aboard all three vessels in the productive work of covering boilers with crewmens' hammocks and placing cotton bales alongside pilothouses. The Federal gunboats landed at Des Arc at 2:30 in the afternoon. The soldiers, under the command of Eberhart, were sent ashore from the tinclads, while Lt. Cmdr. Bache personally led the *Lexington*'s second division, "40 or 50 marines," the newsman called them. As planned and over the next several hours, the bluecoats and bluejackets destroyed the telegraph and its wires out of town for half a mile. About 5:30 P.M., the Hawkeye troops also burned a warehouse filled with Southern cornmeal and detained three men for questioning later by Brig. Gen. Davidson. One of them was Confederate Army Col. C. H. Matlock, in town on a recruiting mission.

As the soldiers and sailors went about their work ashore, mounted Confederate pickets were spied about 300 or 400 yards behind the town on a road leading west. A runner was sent back to the *Lexington* and, shortly thereafter, at Acting Ensign Booby's direction, one of the 8-inch guns spat out a shell. It was speedily followed by a second which, like the first, rambled over the heads of the Yankees on the ground and landed in a puff on smoke on the road beyond. Great clouds of dust arose and the Southern horsemen "were seen no more."

When the Federal soldiers returned to the boats, their commander, Lt. Col. Eberhart, was invited to transfer from the *Marmora* aboard the *Lexington* for the remainder of the cruise. The expedition continued on up the river for a short while and then anchored about 7:00 P.M. some two miles below Peach Orchard Bluffs. It was relatively cool when the gunboats got underway at 4:10 the following morning and stood up the river. The three vessels reached the mouth of the Little Red River, the same narrow, twisting waterway traversed by Lt. Cmdr. Selfridge the month before, at approximately 8:00 A.M. Believing the two fugitive steamers Bache sought were up this stream, Acting Volunteer Lieutenant A.R. Langthorne was sent to fetch them with the *Cricket*.

As the tinclad disappeared up the tree-lined Black River tributary, the *Lexington* and *Marmora* continued on toward Augusta, 30 miles further up the White and 75 miles below Jacksonport. Upon landing at that town an hour before noon, the gunboat captains sent skirmishers ashore to surround it, but no Rebel soldiers were found. When the St. Louis newspaperman stepped ashore, he found that the surprised citizens were "much alarmed." Happily for all, within a half an hour, Lt. Cmdr. Bache accomplished one of his principal objectives. The location of Brig. Gen. John S. Marmaduke's command was revealed and information received earlier was confirmed, namely that the bulk of the Arkansas rebels were concentrating at Bayou Meto, 12 miles northeast of Little Rock. Meanwhile, during the time Bache was absent up the river, Brig. Gen. Davidson started the transfer of his cavalrymen across the White on the coal barges towed up earlier by the *Marmora*.

After stopping to burn some corncribs at Georgie's Landing about 2:00 P.M. while on the way back down, the *Lexington* and *Marmora* came to the mouth of the Little Red about 3:00 P.M. Bache did not find the *Cricket* and had no knowledge of her fate. Leaving the *Marmora* to guard the entrance after waiting for her consort an hour and a half, Lt. Cmdr. Bache took the big black timberclad into the crooked little river to conduct a search. "There was plenty of water," the reporter noted, "but the channel is narrow and very crooked, making it very difficult for a boat the size of the *Lexington*." Pushing up about 25 miles, "nearly as high as we could go," Bache met the *Cricket* at about 6:15 P.M. Behind her, wearing Union flags, were the *Kaskaskia* and *Thomas Sugg* that she had taken at Searcy, 15 miles farther on.

While en route back down the Little Red, the *Cricket* and her prizes were attacked by several companies of Rebel soldiers belonging to Brig. Gen. Marmaduke. The encounter was quite ferocious and two of the seven sailors wounded eventually died. Following the rendezvous, the *Cricket* passed with her charges, leaving the *Lexington* to bring up the rear. As the procession meandered back down the river, the newsman aboard the timberclad heard a volley of musketry up ahead. No more than five miles downstream after the naval rendezvous, all four boats were attacked once more, beginning with the tinclad. The ambush, executed from a distance of between 70 and 100 yards, was mounted by over 60 Southerners hidden in weeds along the bank and behind a levee.

Lt. Col. Eberhart remembered what happened next: "The *Cricket* opened with her howitzers; the old *Lexington* with her 8-inch guns." The latter, he continued, "must have given them such a scare as they never had before, for they left very suddenly." The soldier's testimony was later contradicted in print by the St. Louis special. As he recalled, the fire was returned by the "infantry, marines and guns of both boats, but they [the Confederates] held their position and fired on us until we were out of their range." In fact, the newspaperman concluded, three or four shots entered "the stern port of the timberclad, as she was leaving, but as luck would have it, no one was injured during the encounter." The *Lexington*, while expending 18 rounds of 5-second shell, was hit a number of other times, but no one aboard was wounded from those bullets either. No further damage was really done to the Federal boats before they returned to the White River about 9:00 P.M.

Throughout the remainder of the group's voyage, the vessels were "fired on with small arms at almost every available spot, though by no very large number of men." Wherever enemy pickets could be spotted, they were subjected to howitzer fire. At Taylor's Bluff, a Rebel party of 40 to 50 men appeared, but they were chased off "in haste" by several shells. Later, at Arkapola, a few stray shots were fired at the vessels, but these did no damage. During the exit voyage, the timberclad expended 13 additional 8-inch shells.

When the *Lexington* task group returned to Clarendon on the evening of August 15, it recorded that the White was falling at the rate of 12 inches per day. During the day, under protection from the *Linden*, Brig. Gen. Davidson started the transfer of his men. Climbing the bank, Bache and Eberhart waited upon Davidson to give him a firsthand account of their voyage and the intelligence gathered at Augusta. Additionally, the three prisoners captured at Des Arc were sent ashore under charge of Acting Master's Mate Howard Hale. When Davidson saw and heard the details of the cruise, he was, in the words of his Iowa military subordinate, "tickled wonderfully at the unexpected success of the expedition."

The *Lexington* returned to the mouth of the White River on August 17. The aged Amazon was in need of repairs "very much. Her water-wheel beams are very shaky." In addition, while running into the bank during her exit trip, she broke a wheel arm. Fortunately, it could be repaired on the scene.

By August 19, all of Brig. Gen. Davidson's cavalry division was across the river on the coal barge ferries. Writing to Porter from Clarendon during the day, Lt. Cmdr. Bache predicted that Steele's men would be over three days hence.

Little Rock was evacuated by Price on September 9 and occupied by the U.S. VII Corps within a day or so. Lt. Cmdr. Bache was able to pay a brief visit to the Arkansas capital, but he took ill. Five days later, the *Tyler*, with Bache embarked, arrived at Cairo from the mouth of the White River. The *Lexington*'s sick commander would recover at home, while she returned down river and the *Tyler* underwent a period of repair.

Writing from newly liberated Little Rock on September 22, Maj. Gen. Steele praised his naval support, indicating to Maj. Gen. Grant that Phelps and Bache did "everything in their power to further the object of the expedition."[3]

On October 10, Secretary Welles transmitted to Rear Adm. Porter at Mound City a War Department request for gunboat assistance for the operations of Maj. Gen. William T. Sherman on the Tennessee River. Sherman was marching to the relief of Chattanooga and naval craft were required not only to help transfer troops across the river but also to convoy the additional supplies required. Porter replied that the shallowness of the water prevented his immediate action but promised that "The gunboats will be ready to go up the moment a rise takes place."

Ten days later, General Grant urged that "The sooner a gunboat can be got to him [Sherman] the better." Porter answered that gunboats were on their way up the Tennessee and Cumberland rivers. "My intention," he wrote, "is to send every gunboat I can spare up the Tennessee. I have also sent below for light-drafts to come up. Am sorry to say the river is at a stand." While Grant, Porter, and Sherman waited for a Tennessee freshet, the *Conestoga*, under Acting Master Gilbert Morton commanding *pro tempore*, seized the steamer *Lillie Martin* and tug *Sweden*, suspected of trading with the Confederates, near Napoleon, Mississippi, on October 24. She then continued her patrols in the Cypress Bend area.

With a sizable naval force already supporting army operations along the Tennessee River, Rear Adm. Porter on October 29 ordered the officers of his Mississippi Squad run "to give all the aid and assistance in their power" to the Chattanooga relief force. The same day, Sherman was appointed commander of the Federal Department of the Tennessee as Grant, elevated to lieutenant general was transferred to the east. Next day, Porter advised Secretary Welles that "The *Lexington, Hastings, Key West, Cricket, Robb, Romeo,* and *Peosta* are detached for duty in the Tennessee River; and the *Paw Paw, Tawah, Tyler,* and one or two others will soon join them, which will give a good force for that river."

The *Tyler* arrived at Perryville, Tennessee, 105 miles below Eastport on the Tennessee River, on October 31. In reporting his position to Rear Adm. Porter, Lt. Cmdr. Pritchett also warned of her dire situation. "The chief engineer has just reported," he wrote, "that the crank of the starboard wheel is so badly cracked that it will be dangerous to run with it." Indeed, if it broke while running, "it would knock out the cylinder heads and probably scald many persons." The only remedy was for a new crank to be cast. As a result of this situation, the operational activities of the largest timberclad were curtailed. By mid-month, she was detailed to Paducah as station ship. There, Lt. Cmdr. Pritchett found himself not only organizing escorts but also working closely with the local army contingent in the defense of the town.

The *Lexington*, also in need of machinery repair, nevertheless transferred into the Tennessee River at the beginning of November. A week later, she undertook to shepherd the transport *Sunny South* from Eastport to Paducah, but she was encountered en route 20 miles below that town by the tinclad *Hastings*, Lt. Cmdr. Phelps, district commander, embarked. Phelps stopped her and ordered the tinclad *Cricket* to take over the convoy, sending the timberclad back to Eastport the *Lexington* remained idle at Eastport for another week as the Tennessee River started to fall once more. At mid-month, she was ordered to Paducah and hence to Cairo and on to Memphis for repairs.

When the *Tyler* started back down to the tip of Illinois on November 20, Col. Stephen G. Hicks, Paducah's garrison commander, wired Porter, noting that his small force would be left without naval protection. The admiral immediately sent a swift boat to catch Lt. Cmdr. Pritchett at the Head of Grand Chain and order him back to Paducah, indicating that the town "was never to be left without a gunboat." Two days later, Hicks informed Pritchett that a large force of Rebels under Maj. Gen. Nathan Bedford Forrest was concentrating behind Mayfield in preparation for a descent upon Paducah. Over the next few days, as additional gunboats arrived, they were pressed into the town's defense. On November 24, Porter was informed that, in the event of an attack on Paducah, the *Peosta* would go up the Tennessee and cover the Mayfield Road, the *Cricket* would cover the lower part of the town, and the *Tyler* would be positioned "to rake the streets and support the fort."

Meanwhile, the motively challenged *Lexington* arrived at Memphis, ostensibly to serve as station ship. A night or two after her arrival, the station commander, Lt. Col. Thomas Pattison, was awakened by two citizens who informed him that steamers were fired into 40 miles above the city that afternoon. Further, they provided information that a group of Rebels planned to capture transports near Island No. 37 and use them to take other vessels plying the Mississippi. Pattison immediately ordered Booby to steam up with the *Lexington* and investigate.

On November 28, Rear Adm. Porter wrote to Pattison requiring the *Lexington*'s services on another matter — and she was not in port. In his defense of her delay, as the station chief replied two days later, Acting Ensign Booby had neglected to inform him that the timberclad had very bad engines and that she had orders not to leave the city until Rear Adm. Porter instructed otherwise. After several days, the Paducah emergency evaporated and the *Tyler* was finally released to return to Cairo on November 30. With the navy's help, Sherman's "formidable corps" was able to get into action during the Battle of Chattanooga.

In a lengthy report sent to Secretary Welles on December 2, Rear Adm. Porter claimed that "In the operations lately carried on up the Tennessee and Cumberland rivers, the gunboats have been extremely active and have achieved with perfect success all that was desired or required of them."

As 1863 closed, the three timberclads were back on the Mississippi, operating between the White and Red rivers. Despite their age and hard service, the old gunboats would still be required in 1864, even as a new campaign was being planned for the Trans-Mississippi.[4] Lt. Cmdr. Bache resumed command of the *Lexington* at the beginning of 1864. A new man joining the boat was Acting Assistant Surgeon Henry M. Mixer, one of whose letters home in March would be of great aid to later historians.

Estimating the situation west of the Mississippi on January 4, Confederate Lt. Gen. E. Kirby Smith, C.S.A., wrote to Maj. Gen. Richard Taylor: "I still think the Red and Washita [Ouachita] rivers, especially the former, are the true lines of operation for an invading column, and that we may expect an attempt to be made by the enemy in force before the rivers fall." Little did he know at that time that, within eight weeks, Rear Adm. Porter would be leading just such a joint expedition.

For some months now, Federal forces from Washington to the west had been involved in planning an incursion into the Trans-Mississippi theater. By the beginning of the new year, generals as diverse as Maj. Gen. Grant, Sherman, and Nathaniel Banks, the eventual leader, were on board with a plan to move up the Red River through Louisiana toward Texas. The forthcoming operation would, in actuality, be a "rather grand undertaking," in the words of historian William Riley Brookshire. Although championed by, among others, President Lincoln and Maj. Gen. Halleck, the undertaking was initially opposed by Grant and Banks.

Although, in the end, it would really consist of a "loosely connected joint land and naval exercise," it did have as its ultimate military objective "completion of the subjugation of Louisiana and Arkansas." If this thrust was successful, it "would effectively remove the Confederate Trans-Mississippi Department from an active role in the conflict." In addition to the purely military benefits of such a gambit, a big Red River offensive could disrupt Confederate commerce and have some hope of dissuading a northward view by French forces then trying to subdue Mexico. Naturally, the Mississippi Squadron was invited along to provide support and guard the many necessary transports.

While the political, military, and logistical difficulties of a Red River campaign were reviewed and resolved (details far outside the scope of our story), the work of the gunboats on the Lower Mississippi continued apace. Guerrilla and irregular force suppression remained a constant concern, as did terrible winter weather so bad that horses were covered with snow and tents were frozen so stiff they could not be struck.

Without a steady supply of coal, the gunboats maintaining station off the entrances to the White and Red rivers were often forced to stop and gather wood. This was not often easy or safe along the shores. In some places, woodpiles were available but mostly they were not. As a result, and even though they had to be cut shorter to fit the boilers, a favorite fuel for the boats was fence rails. Lt. Cmdr. Selfridge and the *Conestoga* was at the head of Morgan

Bend, off Tunica, Mississippi, on Monday of the last week of January. A small party was sent ashore to gather rails, but it was attacked by Confederate cavalry and the men were driven back to the boat. The cutter was able to safely put out even as the great guns dispersed the horsemen. Firing upon fuel parties was not always wise. The timberclad landed a larger force and destroyed 14 houses and huts "that they [the riders] had been in the habit of using for quarters" and a thousand bushels of corn.

On January 27, a landing party went ashore in search of several 7th Texas Cavalry troopers who were seen crossing the river the night before Two men were taken about a mile inland near the village of Tunica, carrying mail that described the garrisoning by the 14th Texas of Fort De Russy, on the Red River. That stream was reported as being so low that only small transports could run from Alexandria down.

While heading into Morgan Bend with the steamer *Continental* under convoy on February 3, the smallest timberclad was shot at by irregulars from shore. Lt. Cmdr. Selfridge later reported: "Drove them off without any trouble. No casualties. Several bullets in the hull and chimneys."

On February 19, Lt. Cmdr. Selfridge reported to his superiors on a large contraband trade being maintained with the Confederate army through the agency of Federal cotton buyers. The perpetrators of this economic crime obtained their trade goods at Baton Rouge or New Orleans and then hauled them to Waterloo on civil steamers. There the items were unloaded and taken by wagon behind Rebel lines. The merchants then received cotton bales at 25 cents a pound which they hauled back to the river and shipped back to New Orleans. During the preceding few weeks, the *Conestoga* had captured two men engaged in the trafficking and 55 bales of cotton. Selfridge estimated that he interrupted less than 20 percent of the trade. Contraband trade had been a significant problem for the Union along the rivers since the earliest days of the Civil War. It would continue to manifest itself until the fighting stopped.

On February 21, Lt. Cmdr. Frank M. Ramsay, commander of the Third District, reported that the water level of the Red River was falling again. Three Confederate gunboats reportedly at Shreveport at the end of January could not get over the falls there due to the low river stage.[5]

While the ironclads and troop transports assembled for the upcoming Trans-Mississippi campaign, Rear Adm. Porter arrived off the mouth of the Red River during the last week of February. Calling Lt. Cmdr. Ramsay aboard the flag boat *Black Hawk*, the squadron commander ordered that a naval reconnaissance expedition ascend Louisiana's Black and Ouachita (pronounced Washitaw) rivers. Consulting their maps, the two officers noted that the Ouachita rose in Arkansas and emptied into the Red, about 45 miles from the mouth of the latter. The last 60 miles or so of the course of the Ouachita was sometimes called the Black River. Porter wished to test Confederate defenses in this river system, geographically located next in line above the Red. Specifically, he was to destroy bridges and break up Confederate posts being formed along those rivers, destroying provisions in the process.

Ramsay would lead the Ouachita scout in the river monitor *Osage* Together with the *Neosho*, one of two stern-wheel light draught river monitors completed by James B. Eads the year before, the 523-ton craft featured a single turret forward. Like that aboard the famous type namesake *Monitor*, it protected a pair of 11-inch Dahlgren smoothbores. Unlike the Ericcson vessel, the profile of Ramsay's boat was broken aft by her covered wheel-box. The Third District commander would also be permitted to take three tinclads, the giant *Ouachita*, the *Fort Hindman*, and the *Cricket*. Also along would be the *Lexington* and *Conestoga*, the latter on her final campaign (a fact not known at the time).

The *Ouachita*. The former Confederate cargo steamer *Louisville* was captured on the Little Red River in July 1863 during an expedition led from the timberclad *Conestoga*. Converted into the largest tinclad, complete with upper and lower deck gunports and circular pillboxes fore and aft, the craft joined the *Lexington* and *Conestoga* on an armed reconnaissance up the Black and Ouachita rivers in March 1864 (Naval Historical Center).

Ramsay's task group departed the mouth of the Red River at 1:30 P.M. on February 29, in this leap year. With the *Osage* leading, the six proceeded without incident, anchoring at dark about 15 miles from the mouth of the Black. The men were awakened from their rest well before dawn and by 4:10 A.M., the fleet was again underway up the Red. Two hours later it passed Beard's Point and entered the Black River. Although it continued on still unmolested, the group was seen by the lower river pickets of one of the war's most romantic Southern officers, the six-foot-four Brig. Gen. Count Camile Armand Jules Marie de Polignac, the only foreigner to achieve high rank in the Confederate army. When intelligence of the gunboat approach reached his Harrisonburg headquarters, Brig. Gen. Polignac immediately

The *Fort Hindman* (formerly the *James Thompson* and the *Manitou*). Purchased into Federal service as the *James Thompson*, the *Manitou* was rechristened *Fort Hindman* in November 1863. As the *Manitou*, she participated in an expedition up the Little Red River in July led by Lt. Cmdr. Thomas O. Selfridge aboard the *Conestoga*. The trip resulted in the capture of the giant packet *Louisville*, subsequently rebuilt into the largest tinclad, the *Ouachita*. In March 1864, she joined the *Lexington* and *Tyler* in operations on Louisiana's Black and Ouachita rivers during which she was badly damaged in an attack on river defenses at Harrisonburg. During the next two months she was part of the ill-fated Red River campaign, at one point joining the *Lexington* in an unsuccessful effort to keep the damaged ironclad *Eastport* afloat (Naval Historical Center).

ordered his few men downstream to take defensive precautions. Three 32-pounders at Trinity were of particular concern, as was a pontoon bridge over the Little River.

Two of the cannon were rolled into the water at the mouth of the Little River and the third was hastily buried nearby. Unfortunately, as the water was falling rapidly, those submerged soon became partly visible above the surface. A number of men from the 15th Texas Infantry were posted on the north bank of Little River to protect the bridge, while a warning message was sent to the captain of the steamboat *Ruby*, then hauling wood on that stream for the Confederate engineer corps.

Downstream, the Federals began to encounter tough going, as the river was narrow and twisty, permitting only one vessel to paddle ahead at a time. Consequently, the order of battle and steaming was *Osage, Fort Hindman* (with Ramsay embarked), *Ouachita, Cricket, Lexington,* and *Conestoga*. Acting Surgeon Mixer, aboard the *Lexington* near the rear, believed the countryside was about the "finest in the South I have yet seen." The climate was delightful, the snows of January having long since been relegated to memory. The boats had arrived during "the first blush of spring. Flowers of many varied hues beautify the turf of richest green." The forest trees were "brightening into verdure hourly" while the "peach and plum are in full bloom." Except that it was malarious like so much of the South, Mixer came to believe "there is no finer country in the world."

The first inhabited place on the stream was Trinity, a small town of about 300 inhabitants on the west bank of the river. Having reached a point about 15 miles below it by 4:00 P.M., the Ramsay fleet encountered its first resistance. Sharpshooters concealed behind the left bank levee opened fire. There were about 50, under the command of Capt. W.H. Gillespie, who had orders to contest the navy passage as long as possible. All of the boats immediately opened up with shrapnel, grape, and canister, quickly driving the Rebels away. Moving on, the regrouped Rebels unloaded a volley of musketry onto the *Osage* about 5:15 P.M., but she quickly chased them off with a pair of 11-inch shells. The men aboard Ramsay's boats thought of the snipers as "guerrillas." As the boats paddled upstream, they intermittently shelled the woods along the banks every time they were shot at.

The six Federal warships reached Trinity, at 5:30 P.M., where a pair of "excellent earthworks" had been thrown up, one of which commanded the river for more than two miles. White flags were shown on the lower side of the town. Even so, a reporter from the *Chicago Daily Tribune* later indicated that "everything about the town showed the inhabitants to be intensely sesech and actuated by the deepest hostility to our Government." As the National craft rounded the point, however, they were fired upon by small arms and a pair of cannon that, according to Surgeon Mixer, were "planted in the center of the town." Making a shield of the town was interpreted as "the most atrocious piece of folly ever committed."

The cannon were a pair of 12-pounder field howitzers of Lt. O. Gaudet's section of Capt. T.A. Faries' Louisiana Battery. The small guns, about the size of those aboard the Federal tinclads, were located about 100 yards from the river on "the road or street leading into the town on the open bank." They were not, testified the Confederates, within the town itself. Before the Yankees could reply, Gaudet's gunners pummeled the *Osage* with "five shell without fuse as solid shot." These hit her iron casing "without effecting any injury or retarding her progress."

If the Confederate gunners counted on the gunboats not shooting at them for fear of hitting homes in the nearby community, they were quite in error. The entire task group immediately opened fire and, of the 70 cannon available to the Nationals, fully 40 of them returned fire and these, per the doctor, "almost simultaneously." Although the shock might be imagined, it could not be described. Rear Adm. Porter later commented on the first fire in anger from the new *Ouachita*, calling it withering. He tried to imagine Gaudet's astonishment when a vessel previously well known as a packet "opened on him with 40 guns, firing two shells from each gun a minute, the shells and shrapnel bursting in all directions and tearing the village almost to pieces."

The cannonade continued for approximately 40 minutes, during which time great clouds of gunsmoke mushroomed and hid everything from view. According to Capt. Fairies, the vessels following the monitor all remained below the town out of range until the *Osage* passed in front of the village and, closing in, took the Rebel guns under fire from a range of about 50 yards. Once the ironclad was by Trinity, the *Fort Hindman* entered the mouth of the Little River on her right flank and opened on the right and rear of the howitzer section. No one aboard the gunboats knew if they hit anything, including those closest to the action.

The outgunned Confederates, fighting from "a very exposed position, pulled back. Luckily for them, they suffered no casualties. Under forced march, Lt. Gaudet retired up the Harrisonburg road. In the process, he was forced to leave two of his caissons behind. When Lt. Cmdr. Ramsay determined, about 6:15 P.M. that there was no return shooting, a cease-fire was signaled.

Although crewmen did not go ashore to inspect, it was soon apparent that the damage to the town was extensive. Nearly every house and building was riddled with shrapnel or evidenced other holes. Additionally, there was great fear. "Huddled down close to the water under the bank," remembered Surgeon Mixer, "were scores of women, in an agony of terror, beseeching us, for God's sake, not to kill them." The ordinary horrors of war were bad enough, thought Mixer, and undoubtedly many of his fellow tars, "but the atrocity of making it necessary to open fire upon a village filled with women I have never seen equaled."

Following the shootout, the monitor, tinclads, and old gunboats steamed up two miles above the town into the Ouachita River. They did not, as Brig. Gen. Polignac thought they might, enter the Little River after either the *Ruby* or the pontoon bridge. The Northern vessels all anchored for the night at 6:50 P.M. Lt. Cmdr. Ramsay passed orders that no lights were to be shown and that all men remain fully clothed. Officers were told that tomorrow they would attack a fort at Harrisonburg, 15 miles further upstream. A thick fog covered the Trinity area on the morning of March 2 and so delayed the resumption of the Federal reconnaissance. This allowed Brig. Gen. Polignac to complete his defensive assignments.

At sunrise, Capt. Faries took position with the section of his battery directly under his command, a pair of 3-inch rifled guns. He also had two companies of Texas infantry that had reported to him at 2:00 A.M. The spot chosen by Faries for his emplacement was a large circular Indian mound about 10 feet high where Confederate engineers were beginning work on a small fort. It was located in an old field about midway between Harrisonburg and Bayou Bushly, which entered the Ouachita River on its right bank some 800 yards below the mound. A curved ditch was cut through the level surface near the river face and below the mound. It was occupied by the newly arrived one-time horse soldiers. The Bayou Bushly ferry permitted the transfer of men between Trinity and Harrisonburg.

The Bushly Ferry Road, a soggy dirt highway, led away from the mound. Knowing that his location was not a safe place for his caissons and horses, Capt. Faries ordered them placed at the rear on the road near a woods. Lt. Gaudet's howitzer section was unable to participate in the anticipated fight. It had insufficient caissons and its horses, double-teamed, were badly used up traveling back in the dark on poor roads. Elsewhere, Brig. Gen. Polignac placed a pair of infantry regiments on the bank of the Ouachita River, spreading them out from the vicinity of Harrisonburg back to the mouth of the Bushly Bayou. As the mists began to thin over the water, the visiting Frenchman could see it replaced by huge clouds of smoke from the chimneys of his floating enemy.

The Ramsay group weighed anchor at 6:14 A.M., but paddled only a short distance without incident. At 8:00 A.M., the *Osage*, no more than five miles from where she began the morning, suffered an equipment casualty. Her turret, while being tested, was disabled. The fleet immediately halted while Lt. Cmdr. Ramsay went aboard the monitor to inspect. Reviewing the situation with the ironclad's captain, Acting Master Thomas Wright, the expedition commander was distressed but thankful. The main wheel of the turret was broken into three pieces, making it impossible for the 72-ton circular casemate to revolve. Fortunately, however, the two big guns were pointed directly ahead at the time of the accident. Until repairs were effected, there would be nothing the *Osage* could do except fight bows-on in the manner of the *Carondelet* and the other Pook turtles. Ramsay returned to the *Fort Hindman* and signaled the other vessels to proceed. Having spent a half hour with Wright, the commander may not have been cheered when he ordered another halt at 9:15 A.M. Still, the tinclad was eased to the bank and a landing party quickly brought aboard a pair of horses left wandering on the bank by Confederate pickets.

Between 9:45 and 10:00 A.M., the Federal task group arrived within two miles of Harrisonburg and halted about 400 yards offshore. Peering through their spyglasses, the vessel captains were able to see even more clearly than their men that the Confederates occupied a relatively high position. Capt. Faries' mound was believed to be the first of four earthworks, with many connecting rifle pits, situated on hills commanding the river from where the boats halted to more than a mile above. Ramsay's visual inspection concluded, the *Osage* moved ahead, turning the point at the junction of the Ouachita and Bayou Bushly. She was followed by the tinclads and timberclads.

Watching from shore, Capt. Faries and his men saw the ironclad monster approach. They also believed that they saw infantry aboard the tinclads preparing to fire from loopholes in their cabins. What Lt. Cmdr. Ramsay believed to be a full brigade of Confederate riflemen then attacked his boats from behind the levee and below the mound, while the 3-inch cannon also opened fire. Brig. Gen. Polignac believed that both his soldiers and gunners started shooting at the same time. Over the next minutes, Faries blasted the four Federal supporting craft with 47 time-fused shells and 16 solid shot. Nearly all of those from his two guns, the battery commander believed, "took effect in the pilot-houses and upper works for the four tinclads, all of which lay together in a mass."

Once the Union captains were certain there were no guns directly on their front, Lt. Cmdr. Ramsay ordered the *Osage* and her consorts to move slowly upstream. The boats fired as they came, aiming at both the military emplacements and trenches as well as targets of opportunity in the town. The Frenchman leading the Confederates later reported that "several houses were riddled with shot." About 10:30, Ramsay ordered the *Fort Hindman* to pass the battery, even as musketry and cannon fire from the shore continued unabated. A shot hit the tinclad's starboard engine, disabling it. Indeed, during a half hour ordeal, the vessel was struck 27 times by shot and shell. Eight men were wounded, one seaman mortally. The damaged *Fort Hindman* dropped down below the mouth of the Bushly Bayou and behind the *Conestoga* even as the expedition leader transferred his flag to the *Ouachita*. The ex–flag boat tied up to the bank to address her injuries, employing her stern guns as opportunity offered.

While all of this was going on, the *Osage* passed up past the Southern guns. The tinclads made no such effort due to the crookedness of the waterway and in light of the *Fort Hindman* situation. The monitor was so low in the water as she ran by Faries' mound that the Rebel captain could not see any part of her hull, her "funnel alone indicating her movements," as he later recalled.

The battle continued, though, as Ramsay later said, complementing Capt. Faries' observation, it was "impossible for the vessels abreast of the sharpshooters to do them any damage" because the river shoreline was so high. The lower gunboats, including the timberclads, were, however, able to enfilade the banks. Most of the navy shells actually passed over the two guns on the Indian mound and exploded at or near the rear near their caissons. Capt. Faries' offending battery ceased firing around 11:45 A.M., clearing the way for the gunboats to steam on up the river. All of the vessels were hit, "more or less," remembered Surgeon Mixer, "except the *Conestoga* and *Lexington*." Capt. Faries reported no casualties to his command, save the death of a horse.

Mixer, and possibly others aboard the task group, were impressed by the fighting spirit of their Rebel opponents, outgunned (and "entirely without cover," as Maj. Gen. Taylor said). Faries' little band was assaulted by a fleet that many believed had as much artillery as a 75,000-man army. "In a good cause, they would have been heroes," the healer opined, but under present circumstances, "they are desperadoes." It can be taken as a certainty that the butternut defenders believed the worst of the Yankees.

Leaving the *Hindman* in what he considered to be a safe location, Lt. Cmdr. Ramsay ordered his remaining five boats to round to at 1:30 P.M. and continue up the river. They steamed gingerly along the narrow, turning stream to Bayou Louis, which entered at Sicily Island. The water was so shallow, however, that the *Cricket*, his lightest craft, would not enter. Rebuffed at this turn, the gunboats paddled on to Catahoula Shoals, where sufficient water was found to take them to Monroe. Unhappily, the river stage was declining rapidly, and Lt. Cmdr. Ramsay determined that the better part of valor was to return the five miles or so back downstream to his starting point below Harrisonburg.

As the boats filed past Harrisonburg the better part of an hour later, the *Ouachita* landed at the town. Ramsay personally led a party ashore and "set fire to some of the largest houses in the town." Porter called his action "a warning to the inhabitants not to assist in attacking river-boats, which often had women and children on board." As the bluejackets were torching the structures, a picket observed a body of infantry and some cavalry rushing down a ravine in their direction. The expedition leader quickly ordered a recall and the Federals raced back aboard the *Ouachita*.

About 2:30 P.M. the *Conestoga* and *Lexington* were the first to return, rounding to below the *Fort Hindman*. Alerted to the commotion above, they immediately returned upstream, handing over their newly ordered guardian positions to the *Cricket*. A little while later, the *Osage* came down and tied up to the bank. When the timberclads came to, their broadsides were joined with those from the *Ouachita* in opposition to the defending Confederates. The racket was every bit as intense as that of the morning and, after a while, even the *Osage* arrived on the scene to join in, followed within minutes by the *Cricket*. The firefight with the Southern protectors of Harrisonburg was concluded by 3:30 P.M. In bright sunshine, the fleet stood back down the river to the bank where the *Fort Hindman* was tied.

Happily for the citizens of Harrisonburg, Brig. Gen. Polignac now ordered his men to turn their attention to firefighting. With considerable exertion, they were able to stop a growing conflagration. Several houses were ashes, but had the soldiers not stepped in, the fires "liked to have swept over the whole place." The *Chicago Daily Tribune*, basing its story of the day's fight on reports from the departed Federal gunboatmen, actually informed its readers on March 15 that the "town was burned to the ground."

The *Conestoga*, meanwhile, rounded to directly behind the damaged tinclad. Lt. Cmdr. Bache dispatched Acting Third Assistant Engineer James O'Neil to look into the repair of the *Hindman*'s disabled engine. The mechanic's mission had been interrupted earlier by the timberclad's charge back up to the *Ouachita*'s assistance. O'Neil could not immediately effect a remedy for the tinclad and, within the hour, the decision was taken to return to Trinity. At 4:30 P.M., the *Fort Hindman* cast off from the bank and proceeded downstream on one engine, closely following the *Conestoga*. This arrangement did not last for long and the *Cricket* soon thereafter took the tinclad under tow. The *Fort Hindman* was essentially unmanageable with just one paddle wheel and thus it was decided that the *Cricket* would be lashed to her side. Thereafter, the task group pushed on down in this slightly modified version of its original battle order, the *Conestoga* by now having returned to the end of the column. At 7 P.M., the vessels came to five miles above Trinity and anchored for the night. As they halted, *Hindman* sailor McNeil Rayburn died from the wounds he had received that morning.

After dark a Rebel deserter was permitted aboard the *Lexington*. Lt. Cmdr. Bache was informed that the Confederates were assembling a force at Trinity for another fight in the morning. The intelligence was passed to Lt. Cmdr. Ramsay. The men of the Federal task force did not know what might occur when they approached Trinity shortly after 8:00 A.M. on March 3. Many bluejackets expected a fight. Lt. Cmdr. Ramsay had it in mind to burn the town if serious resistance was encountered.

When the gunboats arrived off Trinity no active opposition was encountered. Just to make certain, the *Lexington* shelled the woods below and in back of the town for a few minutes. No response was forthcoming. As he passed among the timberclad's sick, Surgeon Mixer continued to marvel that he and his shipmates "went through the battle of yesterday and came off without a mark."

Upstream at Harrisonburg, Brig. Gen. Polignac sent a report to Maj. Gen. Taylor. After praising his men, the tall debonair "Polecat" expressed his belief that, in the previous day's battle, the enemy had expended no less than 1,000 rounds from guns of many calibers. Total Confederate losses were three dead and three wounded, all mortally. Years later, Taylor reminisced briefly on the little Trinity-Harrisonburg campaign. In his eyes, perhaps the greatest achievement earned in the scrape was Polignac's. "By his coolness under fire," the theater commander wrote, "he gained the confidence of his men, as he soon gained their affections." Not initially impressed, Taylor came to believe that this son of France came to show "great gallantry and talent for war while serving with me."

Lt. Cmdr. Ramsay took a sizeable party ashore to torch the community. "But finding so many women and children in it," he later reported, "I spared it." While ashore, the task group commander learned that Confederate forces had a pontoon bridge about a mile from the mouth of the Little River. The *Cricket* was sent up about 9:00 A.M. to find and burn it. Also while ashore, the Union men sought the location of the 32-pounders the Rebels had supposedly secreted in the vicinity. Three were duly found by noon, two of them poking out of the falling river. The tubes were removed and carried aboard the *Fort Hindman*. A few nearby buildings were burned.

The *New York Times*, *Philadelphia Inquirer*, and the *Chicago Daily Tribune* would all report in their March 15 coverage of the Ouachita expedition that the cannon used to oppose the task group at Trinity were these 32-pounds. In fact, they were Lt. Gaudet's 12-pounder howitzers. It only took an hour to secure the cannon, and everyone expected that, as soon as the *Cricket* returned, the little flotilla would be freed to engage in "picking up a little stray cotton, thus combining business with pleasure." Such was not immediately to be.

Shortly after 1 P.M. the *Conestoga* got stuck at the mouth of the Little River. Brig. Gen. Polignac later informed Maj. Gen. Taylor that she was caught by the current and, "in swirling to she ran aground." As work began on freeing Lt. Cmdr. Selfridge's small timberclad, everyone aboard her consorts knew that they would eventually get her off, even in the falling river. She would not be forsaken and abandoned. In the meantime, small boats from the other five vessels lying just below the mouth of the Little hauled with great energy the many lines attached to her. Still, the accident was "extremely vexatious," as Surgeon Mixer put it.

The task group lay to off Trinity for the remainder of the afternoon awaiting the return of the *Cricket* and attempting to pull off the *Conestoga*. The time was also spent repairing the damaged turret aboard the *Osage*, a project underway now for some time. Although broken teeth remained in some of the gearing, it was eventually possible to train the turret for a few degrees on either side of dead ahead. When the *Cricket* hove to, the task group commander learned that she had successfully dispatched the pontoon bridge and thereby interrupted communication between both banks of the Little River. The Northerners, not aware of her presence, made no effort to come up with the lumber steamer *Ruby*.

Lt. Cmdr. Ramsay passed orders that the vessels would remain one more night below the town. At approximately 7:55 P.M., a fire raft was seen coming down the Little River toward the anchorage. The *Osage* fired two shots at it and it disappeared. A few minutes later, the *Conestoga* got afloat. The task group weighed at 6:30 A.M. on March 4 and stood downstream.

The *Osage*. A single-turreted river monitor built by James B. Eads, the *Osage* was skippered by Lt. Cmdr. Thomas O. Selfridge, Jr., last captain of the *Conestoga*. The unique paddle-wheel warship accompanied that timberclad and her sister, the *Lexington*, up the Black and Ouachita rivers in March 1864, and stood with the *Lexington* in defense of the transports at Blair's Landing on the Red River in April (Naval Historical Center).

About 45 minutes later, Confederate soldiers were spied on the west bank of the river and the leading *Osage* shelled the woods near where they were seen.

The remainder of the day was taken up with the Federal sailors "picking up all the cotton near the bank." On several occasions, suspicious horsemen were observed. These were occasionally taken under fire, beginning with a 9:00 A.M. bombardment of nearby woods by the *Lexington* and the monitor. The *Osage* repeated the west bank scouring exercise just before noon. Fireman Hiram Walker from the *Ouachita* was a firsthand observer of the day's cotton gathering. "We stopped at a large plantation," he later remembered, "where we heard they had a quantity of Cotton stored back in the woods about a half mile in great piles." The sailors "pressed into service all of the darkies and old mules and carts we could get and had them haul the cotton to the banks of the river." There the crews loaded their booty onto "two or three empty coal barges we had with us besides filling in between the decks."

Having secured as much of the baled fluffy produce as was transportable, the units of Ramsay's group proceeded downstream about 6:00 P.M. They dropped anchor an hour later about 12 miles from the mouth of Black River. Bright and early at 5:20 A.M. on March 5, the timberclads and their consorts resumed their voyage to the mouth of the Red River. All safely entered the Mississippi at 11:40 P.M., where they found the *Black Hawk*, *Little Rebel*, *Bragg*, and *Chillicothe*. Lt. Cmdr. Ramsay hastened aboard the flag boat to review the success of the venture with Rear Adm. Porter. Particular emphasis was placed upon the silencing of the forts and the capture of the 32-pounders. Ramsay was able to comment not only upon the reception given him by Brig. Gen. Polignac but also on the conditions of the rivers and their banks.[6]

With the launch date for the Red River expedition drawing near, the *Conestoga*, the fastest timberclad, was dispatched to New Orleans to bring back additional ammunition for the Mississippi Squadron. It was her last mission. While on her return and near Bondurant Point at the mouth of Bayou Pierre, about 20 miles below Grand Gulf and not far from Bruinsburg, Mississippi, on March 8, she met the *General Price* coming down. As the two ships made to pass one another at 4:20 on that dark morning, there was a sudden mix-up in signals, with the result that the ram accidentally smashed into the old timberclad, hitting into her engine area. The force of the unintended attack by the *General Price* was so great that that *Conestoga* sank to the top of her hurricane deck in 30 feet of water in less than four minutes.

All of the men aboard both craft were immediately ordered to abandon ship and escaped in the small boats quickly launched from the two vessels. Lt. Cmdr. Selfridge was the last man off the *Conestoga*, having organized and executed the evacuation. The survivors clamored aboard the *General Price*, where a muster was held and it was determined that two men were missing (drowned). Selfridge, who was otherwise very successful in the war, had singularly bad luck in having his ships sunk under him. He commented later in his memoirs: "Thus for the third time in the war, I had my ship suddenly sunk under me. It is a strange coincidence that the names of these three ships all begin with the letter 'C,' and that two of these disasters occurred on the 8th day of March; the other on the 12th of December."

When the *General Price* reached the mouth of the Red River, the *Conestoga*'s now ex-commander was forced to inform ARAMD Porter that the little fleet greyhound was a total loss. Only the tops of her wheelhouses were visible, even in the current low water stage of the Mississippi. "Well, Selfridge," the bearded admiral replied, "you do not seem to have much luck with the top of the alphabet. I think that for your next ship, I will try the bottom." The bottom of the list was not then available, so, within a few days, Lt. Cmdr. Selfridge found himself in command of the *Osage*.

Before moving off up the Red River, Rear Adm. Porter wrote to Navy Secretary Welles asking that the timberclad's officers and crew be reimbursed for the loss of their personal effects. They were now without anything save the clothes on their backs and would need to renew their wardrobes at the earliest moment. Upon hearing of the loss of his first western command, Lt. Cmdr. Phelps was moved to write home: "Poor old *Conestoga*! A vessel whose good fortune has been a marvel for years has at length met a tragic end. It is a great pity, for there are few vessels whose history is so full of adventure in this war."

Of the three original timberclads, two were left, *Lexington* and *Tyler*. Each has at least one more adventure to relate and we begin with the former.[7]

By the beginning of March, Maj. Gen. Richard "Dick" Taylor knew that a large Federal force would soon be headed his way. To meet it, he had just 25,000 men. Maj. Gen. Nathaniel Banks and Acting Rear Adm. Porter enjoyed a force superiority of 42,000 men, including 10,000 on loan from Maj. Gen. Sherman and 15,000 more from Maj. Gen. Steele, though his VII Corps would, in the end, not fully participate, leaving the land force total at 32,500. Maj. Gen. A.J. "Whiskey" Smith and his men arrived at the mouth of the Red River on March 11 aboard 21 transports. They were borrowed; Sherman wanted his men back by April 15. These soldiers, their munitions and supplies, would be guarded by the Mississippi Squadron of the U.S. Navy.

In addition to the civil steamers chartered by the U.S. Quartermaster Department to transport the Union army, Rear Adm. Porter, over the previous few days, gathered what Lt. Cmdr. Selfridge later called "the most formidable force that had ever been collected in the western waters." It drew from every flotilla in the squadron. The admiral was "determined there should be no want of floating batteries for the troops to fall back on in case of disaster."

The Red River campaign begins. A depiction of the entrance into the Red River of units of the fleet under Rear Admiral David Dixon Porter. The timberclad *Lexington*, chosen because of her speed and great guns, accompanied this armada (***Battles and Leaders***).

The task force featured 13 ironclads (*Lafayette, Essex, Benton, Choctaw, Chillicothe, Ozark, Louisville, Carondelet, Eastport, Pittsburg, Mound City, Osage,* and *Neosho*), six tinclads (*Ouachita, Black Hawk, Juliet, Fort Hindman, Cricket,* and *Gazelle*), and a number of auxiliaries. It also included one timberclad, *Lexington*, added for her heavy guns and her speed. The naval and quartermaster transport force assigned to the operation was thus 104 vessels, mounting 300 guns (210 naval).

In reviewing this naval strength, the embedded *Philadelphia Inquirer* reporter was moved to observe that "a more formidable fleet was never under single command than that now on the Western rivers under Admiral Porter." On the other hand, "it might be said, also, never to less purpose. At the time of departure, the strength of the Rebellion in the inland waters had been crushed."

As reported earlier, the river stage of the Red was not good. The gung-ho Porter knew from recent surveys that this was "the most treacherous of all rivers; there is no counting on it, according to the rules which govern other streams." Writing for "Battles and Leaders" after the war, Lt. Cmdr. Selfridge explained that the whole expedition hinged upon "the usual spring rise; but this year, the rise did not come." Indeed in looking back, it was his opinion that, "Had the river been bank full, no force that the Confederates could have controlled could have stood for a moment against the fleet."

Just before Smith's arrival, Porter received the news that heavy rains were delaying Maj. Gen. Banks. He could not possibly reach Alexandria, one of the principal targets, before March 21. Additionally, the sailor found that work on the completion of the unfinished Fort De Russy, 30 miles south of Alexandria, was being pushed hard by the Rebels. While the naval and military men bobbed on their vessels observing the overgrown marshlands ashore, Rear Adm. Porter and Maj. Gen. Smith held a meeting to decide what to do next in light of Banks' delay. The two men decided to capture Alexandria, taking Fort De Russy while en route.

Porter's invasion armada started up the Red River at 8:30 A.M. on March 12. Several of the larger ironclads had difficulty making it over the big sandbar that guarded the entrance. The *Lexington*, as fell to her lot during this and other adventures, was specifically tasked with protecting the troop transports and thus led them from her position last in the line of battle.[8] Once the armada sailed, the Porter-Smith plan began to unfold. At the junction of the Old Red River and the Atchafalaya River, Lt. Cmdr. Phelps was ordered to take a force and push ahead up the former to remove a series of obstructions in the river eight miles below Fort De Russy. Porter took the remainder of his fleet, including the transports convoyed by the *Lexington*, into the Atchafalaya to cover the army landing at Simmesport.

On the morning of March 13, the soldiers disembarked at Simmesport and pursued the Confederates falling back on Fort De Russy. At 9:00 A.M., the *Lexington* and the *Gazelle* stood down the Atchafalaya. Meanwhile, Phelps' gunboats, having continued up the Red River, reached the obstructions that the Southerners spent five months building. It would take hours to remove them.

Early in the afternoon, the *Lexington* landed at a plantation and sent out a party to gather fuel (fence rails). The bluejackets were fired upon by a squad of butternut soldiers. Watching this exchange through his spyglass, Lt. Cmdr. Bache immediately ordered his gunners to open fire. Eleven times the 8-inch guns spat shells toward the offending Confederates, most of whom escaped unharmed.

Before sundown on March 14, the Federal naval and military forces had converged upon Fort De Russy and compelled its surrender. Upon taking possession, they learned that most of the defenders had already withdrawn, leaving but a gallant 300 to offer what turned out to be token resistance.

An order from Porter for pursuit of a known Confederate steamboat fleet toward Alexandria was delayed five hours in transmission. Upon its receipt, Lt. Cmdr. Phelps dispatched his two fastest vessels, *Lexington* and *Ouachita*, on the chase. Chugging off in the dark at 1:00 A.M. on March 15, they were soon followed by the *Eastport*. The *Fort Hindman* and *Cricket* also joined in the pursuit. The *Lexington* and *Ouachita* passed Fort de Russy at 8:30 A.M. As they sped by, Lt. Cmdr. Bache hailed the *Cricket* and *Fort Hindman*, ordering them to follow upstream. The quartet came in sight of Alexandria about 5:00 P.M.

The initial Porter-Phelps communications failure caused the Federal vessels to miss coming up with the Rebel steamers before they succeeded in getting over the Alexandria falls. One tail-end vessel, the *Countess*, grounded in her panic and, together with a barge left behind, was burned to prevent capture. The hulk of the blazing *Countess* was passed by the U.S. gunboats about 6:30 P.M. A half hour later, the four anchored off the town. Maj. Gen. Taylor, who had decided not to contest the Federal occupation, passed orders for his units to rendezvous at Natchitoches.

Several volleys of musketry were fired at the gunboats in the semidarkness two hours later. Lt. Cmdr. Bache sent a boat ashore and removed the town mayor, sending him aboard the *Ouachita*. He was undoubtedly lectured on the fiery fate awaiting Alexandria if the sniping continued. Late that night, the *Fort Hindman* returned downstream.

Nine Union vessels arrived at Alexandria by the morning of March 16 and a landing party under Lt. Cmdr. Selfridge from the *Osage* occupied the town. An additional shore party was sent from the *Lexington* shortly thereafter. Happily for the gunboatmen, the troop transports arrived at 1:30 P.M. and Maj. Gen. Smith's men occupied the town.

Rear Adm. Porter was not at all pleased that Maj. Gen. Banks, plagued as he was by heavy rains, remained absent. The campaign seemed to be at a stand-still. Shreveport, the principal objective, was still 350 miles up the Red. So far, the arriving soldiers, many of them from places like Wisconsin, New York, and Rhode Island, were not impressed with the Red River. "It is a dirty, sluggish stream, about an eighth of a mile wide," wrote Harris Beecher of the 114th New York, "flowing in an extremely crooked channel. Its ends and curves are so exaggerated that they seem almost unnatural."

Until Banks arrived, Porter elected to use his men to make a little money. The law which gave sailors a third of the value of captured items applied to cotton as well as ships. Even though the Confederates had an active policy of burning cotton to prevent its capture by the Northerners, there was just too much for all of it to be fired. The bluejackets on this big outing were naturally excited to be turned loose to gather as much undestroyed cotton as possible. Before Maj. Gen. Banks finally turned up, Federal sailors seized in excess of 3,000 bales. It goes without saying that Union soldiers, who could not participate in the rewards of these spoils, were displeased. Maj. David C. Houston later told the War Conduct Committee that it "was rather demoralizing to the soldiers to see the navy seizing the cotton for prize on land, while they did not get any."

Maj. Gen. Banks' troops started reaching Alexandria on March 19. When, eight days late, the last of them trekked into the city on March 26, the Federals finally were able to assemble what Ludwell Johnson called "an impressive display of military might—the greatest in the history of the Southwest." But could it be effectively employed? Also on March 26, Lt. Gen. Grant issued a call for the return of Maj. Gen. Smith's command. By this time, the spring rise that the Yankees were counting upon simply failed to materialize—for the first time in nine years. Earlier, Porter was informed by Sherman, who once lived near Alexandria, that this annual increase in the water level offered the only opportunity during a year that the deep-draft gunboats could reach Shreveport.

But instead of rising the Red was actually falling at an alarming rate, sometimes as much as an inch an hour. As the water stage dropped, channel bottom irregularities increased the number of dangerous rapids and exposed countless rocks, sandbars, snags, and other obstructions. At this point, Maj. Gen. Smith's corps undertook a march to Bayou Rapides, 21 miles above Alexandria. Despite the slow rise in the water, elements of the Mississippi Squadron were needed to provide support.[9] Having elected not to turn back in the face of falling water, Rear Adm. Porter was faced with the problem of getting his fleet over the double set of rapids just north of Alexandria. At the time of the Civil War, these obstructions caused the same difficulties for river traffic as Harpeth Shoals on the Cumberland River or Muscle Shoals on the Tennessee.

"The rapids of Alexandria," wrote Steven D. Smith and George J. Castille III in 1986, "were composed of rocky outcroppings or boulders of sandstone and siltstone forming shoals along a mile stretch of the Red River, even at times of high water. At low water, the upper and lower ends of the rapids were exposed." Gary D. Joiner noted that, in normal springtimes, careful navigation around the exposed obstructions, with their eddies and swirls, was possible. Indeed, the "swift twisting course through the boulders was called 'the chute' and lent its French name to Alexandria parish: Rapides."

A great secret of the campaign not realized until this decade was the effectiveness of Confederate countermeasures against Porter's fleet. True, placement of the *New Falls City* as a blocking agent was acknowledged at the time. But unknown to Banks, Porter, and the Generals Smith was the direct Rebel intervention that caused the water level to fall. By direct order of the Confederate War Department, an obstruction was built the previous year between

Tones Bayou and Bayou Coushatta on the Red River near the village of Coushatta. Accordingly, Southern engineer Capt. Thomas P. Hotchkiss built a raft-like dam located near the southern bend of Scopini Island near the river cut-off bearing its name.

Sometime between March 18 and April 5, as the Union invasion started, the dam was blown, draining most of the water (about 75 percent) from Red River above Grand Ecore "like pulling the plug out of a bathtub." As soon as the Confederate black powder barrels exploded, mountains of water flowed into an old channel known as Bayou Pierre, located about 30 miles south of Shreveport. As it cascaded in, a 19-mile wide floodplain was created.

As the water level fell over several days, as observed by the Union navy, a small amount of water exited Bayou Pierre into the Red, giving the false appearance of a rise. Most of the water remained trapped for some days before backing up into the Red River as planned, a few miles above Grand Ecore. This Confederate river manipulation was the reason, and not an accident of nature, that the Union navy later in the campaign found the water level so low. The little freshet occasioned by the backup gave Porter the encouragement needed to advance from Alexandria toward Grand Ecore. In the end, it nearly cost him his fleet.

Electing to keep below a number of vessels obviously too deeply laden, the Mississippi Squadron leader sent others ahead into the danger zone. The

Lt. Gen. Richard ("Dick") Taylor, C.S.A., commanded the Confederate District of Western Louisiana from July 1862. Taylor was the Southern field general most directly responsible for the defense of the Red River against the combined Federal army and navy expedition in the spring of 1864. Following his victory over the Union army at Mansfield in May, he directed every effort to hinder the Northern escape, particularly that of the gunboats and transports on the river (U.S. Army Military History Institute).

river stage looked passable for some of the lighter vessels, though questionable for others. Almost as soon as this effort began, the giant *Eastport*, taken along due to a continuing fear of possible Shreveport-based Rebel gunboats, grounded. It would take days to get her free.

On March 29, Porter sent a letter to Navy Secretary Welles announcing that he was about to depart for Shreveport "or as high up the river as I can get." The low level of the Red River continued to hinder efforts to get his gunboats above the rapids at Alexandria for the mission. The admiral continued: "After a great deal of labor and two and a half days' hard work, we succeeded in getting the *Eastport* over the rocks on the falls, hauling her over by main force." All the Army transports maneuvered safely above the rapids, but the hospital ship *Woodford* was battered against the rocks and sank. Porter added that "I shall only be able to take up part of the force I brought with me, and leave the river guarded all the way through."

With the *Eastport* finally available, the Porter-Smith expedition resumed its trek up the Red River on April 2. In addition to Lt. Cmdr. Phelps' pride, a number of other ironclads, plus the *Lexington*, *Cricket*, and *Fort Hindman*, all successfully passed over the rapids. Maj. Gen. Banks, meanwhile, marched overland. The last of 26 civilian charter steamers with Maj. Gen. Smith's men and supplies passed the obstructions early the next day. By noon, the task force reached Grand Ecore, a little west bank town four miles north of Natchitoches, where Maj. Gen. Banks' soldiers started to walk in overland almost simultaneously. Here the bluffs were 120 feet high and contained fortifications dating back to the Mexican War. Banks was expected to join Porter and Maj. Gen. Smith at the little river community later in the day. While they waited for the expedition commander, naval tugs pulled a pair of grounded troopboats free. Additionally, Maj. Gen. "Whiskey" Smith's soldiers disembarked, save for the XVII Corps Provisional Division, under Brig. Gen. T. Kilby Smith, which was detailed to remain with the transports. Maj. Gen. Banks arrived during the evening.

Just before 5:00 P.M., Lt. Cmdr. Bache's *Lexington* led a small task unit up the river to search for Rebel torpedoes that may have been laid in the Red. The river narrowed above Grand Ecore as the speed of its current grew more swift. The banks were elevated at a number of points from the surrounding countryside, but not so high as most major Rebel fortifications. Bache's command was also to examine reports that Confederates were burning large quantities of cotton near the riverbank. The rumors were true and as the timberclad, followed by the *Fort Hindman*, *Chillicothe*, and *Osage*, arrived on the scene about five miles above Grand Ecore, Rebel horsemen were seen "lurking about."

The *Lexington* fired two howitzer rounds at the butternut riders, who returned fire immediately. Indeed, the men on the bank opened fire at all four vessels as they passed the blazing cotton, the *Chillicothe* now at the end of the line. As the ironclad's captain, Acting Volunteer Lieutenant Joseph P. Couthony, stepped on deck to see what the shooting was about, a minie ball passed through the starboard chimney and entered his body. The wound was mortal.

As the gunboats above Grand Ecore fought the Rebel horsemen, the Union army and navy commanders congregated at the town. There the generals agreed to a new plan for the rapid capture of Shreveport. The National expeditionary corps, comprising Banks' corps and most of A.J. Smith's, both of which thus far had moved mainly along the Red River, would strike inland away from water along the Shreveport road on April 6 headed toward Mansfield, and Porter would move upstream on April 7.

Under escort of navy gunboats, Brig. Gen. Smith's 2,000 provisionals, aboard 20 transports also carrying "many hundred thousand rations," would steam up to the northern DeSoto Parish village of Springfield Landing, located four miles from the Red on Bayou Pierre and situated on a narrow channel that linked Bayou Pierre Lake with Lake Cannisnia. The river dot was some 60 road miles and 110 river miles from Grand Ecore. Looking at it another way, it was about six miles northeast of Mansfield and about 30 miles south of Shreveport, but 110 miles from that town by water. It was expected that Banks and Porter would communicate at Springfield Landing in three days as the soldiers and sailors linked up. Meanwhile, up the Red, the *Fort Hindman* ran onto a sandbar. In backing off, the wind blew her stern into the bank, unshipping her starboard rudder and breaking her tiller. Putting the damages right consumed most of the night, so Lt. Cmdr. Bache ordered the undamaged gunboats to anchor or tie up nearby.

The naval portion of the Banks grand scheme did not unfold immediately. As preparations for departure continued, the *Lexington* and her consorts, especially the repaired *Fort Hindman*, undertook a torpedo sweep on April 4. Armed cutters from all four vessels were called away near Madame De Roe's plantation, not far from Campti, and dragged for the nefarious mines. During the process, they sounded the channel's depth. Bache's men drug just over an hour when cavalry from the 5th Brigade of the Cavalry Division of the Army of the Gulf attempted to make a reconnaissance into the town. Riding in, they were met by a hail of gunfire from approximately 125 Confederate defenders, who were hidden in houses. The butternuts were led by Brig. Gen. St. John R. Liddell, commander of the Sub-District of North Louisiana.

At the start of this skirmish, the boat crews returned to their respective vessels, while those jacks remaining aboard were beat to quarters. The gunboats got underway and headed upstream toward the sound of the guns. Meanwhile, the 3rd Rhode Island Cavalry was ordered to push into Campti from the flank and fire the defenders' houses. Out on the river, the first gunboat on the scene was the *Fort Hindman*, which fired five rounds toward suspected Confederate positions in the town. The *Lexington* passed her a few minutes later and also threw in a number of shells, as did the *Chillicothe*. The navy shoot made it impossible for the Rhode Islanders to get to the homes, which were spared — for now.

As the cavalry pressed in from the front, Liddell's men retreated through some woods and over a bridge across a bayou, which structure they burned behind them. Toward 9:00 A.M., soldiers from the 5th Minnesota Infantry arrived and joined the troopers, charging on the butternut positions. Continuous musketry could be heard from all four gunboats, which continued firing on targets of opportunity for an hour. Once the dust settled ashore and the Confederates were driven off, the Union commander on the ground, Col. Oliver P. Gooding, burned Campti. When the bluecoats withdrew back to Grand Ecore, Liddel simply moved back into the void, planning to harass the Northern fleet whenever possible.

The Federal gunboats, meanwhile, had tied up to the riverbank. Signal flags ran up the *Lexington*'s halyards sending the anti-torpedo men back to work. The river was dragged and sounded until just after 11:00 A.M. Once the hands had returned aboard and consumed lunch, Lt. Cmdr. Bache ordered his craft to get underway and stand upstream. Meeting no further obstacles, the four tied up to the right bank at 6:40 P.M. and threw out pickets. Next morning, the *Lexington* and her consorts rejoined the main fleet.

By the morning of April 7, the bluecoat soldiers of Major Generals Banks and Smith, save for those of the latter detailed to remain with the transports, were disappearing into the distance ashore. It was now time for at least a portion of the nautical force to shove off from Grand Ecore as well. As the waterborne portion of the Shreveport expedition was governed largely by the depth of water in the Red, Rear Adm. Porter was forced to order his chief subordinate, Lt. Cmdr. Phelps, to remain behind off the town in command of the heavier gunboats. The squadron commander personally led the advance up the Red River toward Shreveport in those available vessels of the lightest draft. He flew his blue flag aboard the sternwheel tinclad *Cricket*.

Porter's task group comprised the light draught monitors *Osage* and *Neosho*, the ironclad *Chillicothe*, the tinclads *Fort Hindman* and *Cricket*, and the *Lexington*. If the water level would only begin to rise, the remaining gunboats could be brought up. Those with the admiral were deemed sufficient, for the moment, to protect the U.S. Army convoy. As the task group prepared to depart the Grand Ecore hills, no one aboard knew that the water, now visibly falling, was going down because Rebel engineers had blown the Bayou Tones dam up ahead.

The parade departed Grand Ecore on the four hour trip to Campti at 1:00 P.M. Steaming behind the monitors, the *Lexington* led the *Hastings*, with Brig. Gen. Smith embarked, plus the *Clara Bell*, *Emerald*, *W.L. Ewing*, *Liberty*, *Hamilton*, *J.H. Lacy*, *Thomas E. Tutt*, *Sioux City*, *Mars*, *Des Moines*, *Adriatic*, *Southwestern*, and *Diadem*. The *Hastings*, *Emerald*, *W.L. Ewing*, *Thomas E. Tutt*, and *Sioux City* were troop transports, while the others carried supplies. The *Fort Hindman* and *Chillicothe* paddled toward the rear. The naval contingent was supported by the tug *Dahlia* and the towboats *Benefit* and *William H. Brown*.

The naval commander later reported that Maj. Gen. Banks' quartermasters inserted an additional 10 supply transports to the convoy even after squadron leadership had expressly stipulated that they not be added. When Porter and Smith came upon these waiting at Campti, they were immediately ordered to the rear of the fleet. Included among the new arrivals was the ammunition-ordnance steamer *Rob Roy* as well as the *Iberville, John Warner, Universe, Colonel Cowles,* and *Meteor.* The monitor *Osage* was tasked to follow them.

In addition to the extra supply vessels, the headquarters boat of Maj. Gen. Banks and the XIX Corps, the *Black Hawk,* was also present. She was not the same boat as the navy flag tinclad now at the mouth of the river. Aboard was the commanding general's personal staff representative, Col. William S. Abert. In deference to him, Brig. Gen. Smith ordered that she fall in behind the *Hastings* and serve as her consort.

Even though the ironclads with the deepest drafts were left behind, those with Porter, along with some of the larger transports, experienced very rough navigation. The muddy water often made it almost impossible to spot obstructions such as stumps or snags under the surface. Many bottoms scraped or struck hidden bars and rocks. Damage to paddle wheels and unshipped or broken rudders was common. Steaming around the numerous sharp bends against the current was laborious, to put it gently, and the maximum speed of the entire fleet was just one or two miles per hour.

In addition to navigational problems, Porter's gunboats continued to suffer fuel shortages. The fleet supply of coal having long since been exhausted, the vessels depended upon wood for their motive power. The problem was that there were not many suitable trees available and even with those that were, mostly cottonwood, the work of cutting and trimming them would take much time. So it was, as Lt. Cmdr. Selfridge learned in January, that fence rails, basically small trees already shaped by farmers and ranchers, became a happy substitute. From the start of the expedition, with some exceptions, Porter's gunboats and the quartermaster steamers tied up ever night two hours before sunset for the express purpose of hunting rails. Whole crews, including those from the *Lexington,* as well as soldiers from the transports, scoured the countryside. Every man was expected to return with at least two rails. After they were handed over, the poles were then sawed up by the "black gangs" of engineroom personnel into the lengths necessary to fit into the various furnaces. Lt. Cmdr. Selfridge later confirmed that a lament came to be heard among the Confederates concerning the dependence of the gunboatmen on the rail forage. The Banks-Porter campaign might have been defeated more easily, they realized, if soldiers had "destroyed the fences and not the cotton."

Rear Adm. Porter's gunboats and the army transports of Brig. Gen. Smith slowly steamed up the so-called Narrows towards Shreveport for three days. Rebel riflemen treated them to regular lead greetings. A favorite tactic was to lie in wait for the craft as they entered the upriver side a bend below a high bluff. Having volleyed, the butternuts would disappear before the return shells could explode and race across the hill to the downriver side and fire down on the continuing vessels as they passed below. Very few men on either side were actually badly hurt during the trip, but many Northern nerves were undoubtedly frayed. By and by, the boats arrived as scheduled at what was believed to be the mouth of Loggy Bayou about 2:00 P.M. on April 10. Perhaps stroking his beard, the admiral wondered why the stream was not the same one marked on his map.

Gary Joiner has recently looked into the question of just where Porter had halted. The admiral's own writings are contradictory and it is possible that he just did not know. Springfield Landing, where he thought he might be, was four miles west of Red River. On the other hand, he might have been at the mouth of Loggy Bayou or even the nonexistent Shreveport River. "It is possible," Joiner wrote in 2006, that the task group "was as close as two miles south from Tones Bayou or as much as four to five miles below the bayou."

Here, nearly 100 miles in the rear of Banks' army, they were stopped cold by Confederate ingenuity. The large steamer *New Falls City* was scuttled and her hull, stretched end to beached end, was sunk directly across the river. An invitation writ large to a Shreveport ball, Porter later told Maj. Gen. Sherman, "was kindly left stuck up by the rebels, which invitation we were never able to accept." Before the bluejackets could manhandle the broken packet out of the way of the fleet, units of which stretched at various intervals back downstream, Capt. William H.C. Andres of Banks' staff, escorted by 50 men from the 14th New York Cavalry, streaked to a halt on the riverbank with terrible news. The courier revealed the Federal defeat at the Battle of Sabine Cross-Roads, near Grand Ecore, and indicated that the Army of the Gulf, and the attached corps from the Army of the Tennessee, was retreating toward Pleasant Mill.

Though not fully realized by all at that moment, the Union's Red River campaign had reached its zenith. Porter later told Maj. Gen. Smith that his disappointment was great upon learning "that all our perseverance and energy had been thrown away." As that thought took hold with others, the horseman offered a verbal command for Brig. Gen. Smith from Maj. Gen. Banks, indicating that it would soon be followed up in writing. The amphibious XVII Corps Provisional Division, just disembarked, was to return aboard its steamers and find Banks' main force near Grand Ecore as fast as possible. Porter and Brig. Gen. Smith elected to quickly retreat south in order to avoid entrapment. "The confusion which immediately followed" the revelation of Banks' defeat "was frightful," remembered Nicholas Smith, an officer aboard the steamer *John Warner*. Interviewed by the *Columbus (Wisconsin) Democrat* in 1895, Smith recalled that the quartermaster transport "captains became frantic and disorder seemed to control every movement."

The commanders of the gunboats were signaled to meet aboard the *Cricket*, where Rear Adm. Porter informed them of the army's defeat and retreat. He also revealed his decision that the boats would be returning to Grand Ecore. A plan was worked out in conjunction with Brig. Gen. Smith to provide a maximum of defense against the Confederate troops, regular and irregular, that were anticipated on the southern exodus. During the trip downstream, the gunboats were to be distributed among the transports, with the *Osage* at the rear. Soldiers from the various regiments constructed rude breastworks of hay and cracker boxes on the hurricane decks of their steamboats. Sharpshooters would man these barricades if the vessels came under attack.

Because there were only six gunboats to defend the long line of quartermaster steamers, three Army transports were turned into ersatz gunboats by the addition of military cannon. A section of Battery M of the First Missouri Light Artillery was detailed aboard the *Emerald* and another went aboard the *Thomas E. Tutt*. The steamer *Rob Roy*, already loaded with cannon and ammunition, became the most formidable of these auxiliaries. Four 30-pounder Parrott guns from the First Indiana Heavy Artillery were placed in her bow. A number of other boats were protected by 12-pounder howitzers mounted atop their hurricane decks.

Guerrillas and others were not the only obstacles to cause concern. The river going back down would be just as hazardous, or worse, as it had been coming up. Although the speed of the convoy might be a fraction faster because it was not paddling against the current, a significant negative was the fact that the larger craft, particularly the monitors, would be almost unmanageable. "The river was exceedingly narrow and torturous," remembered Brig. Gen. Smith, "the bottom covered with logs and snags and the banks full of drift, rendering the navigation most difficult and dangerous." On top of that, the banks in some stretches were even taller than the pilothouses of the boats, a situation which greatly favored the Rebel defenders.

Within a couple of hours of encountering the *New Falls City*, the Federal convoy was ready to return. Smith and Porter knew that they did not have the width of river required for the boats to round to, so orders were given that "the fleet back down the river in the order the boats then lay." Once the procession began, the rearmost boat took the lead downstream and, though it would take the whole night, they would turn as the bayous and pockets of the stream afforded facility." Steamers of the day were not built for such backward motion over an extended distance and it was known that the physical strain on propulsion and steerage functions would be significant.

The number of miles the vessels had to travel in reverse was directly related to their size, with the smaller ones able to turn sooner. By 6:00 A.M. on April 11, all had rounded to or otherwise come about. From this point on, Porter, his gunboats and the military transports, faced a desperate battle against falling water and Confederate riflemen to avoid entrapment above the Alexandria rapids.[10] Maj. Gen. Banks' corps reached Grand Ecore on April 11 and went into camp behind rapidly constructed entrenchments. It would remain at this location for the next 10 days.

During the day, the boats of Brig. Gen. Smith and Rear Adm. Porter worked their way down the frustrating Red River. The men aboard did not know that at dawn Maj. Gen. Taylor had dispatched Brig. Gen. Arthur P. Bagby from Mansfield, with a brigade of cavalry and a battery, to cut off the boats at the docks of Bayou Pierre. Luckily for the Federals, they passed Grand Bayou Landing several hours before the Rebel horsemen arrived. On several occasions, Brig. Gen. Liddel's Confederate riflemen atop the riverbank bluffs peppered the vessels with musketry just as they had on the way up. Such bee stings continued to elicit massive cannon fire in response.

"In the first years of the war," Richard Taylor wrote later, it "was popularly believed that the destructive power of these monsters ... could "not be resisted." Many of the Confederate soldiers pursuing Porter's task group still believed this, though, notably, at least one did not. Advised of the movements of the Federal fleet, Confederate Brig. Gen. Thomas Green determined to catch it at Blair's Landing. About 45 miles north of Grand Ecore and due west of Pleasant Hill, that point would most likely be passed by Porter next day. Green was specifically instructed to find an attack point before Porter passed it.

At 6:00 P.M., Green departed Pleasant Hill with 1,200 men, including the brigade of Col. William H. Parsons (12th, 19th, and 21st Texas Cavalry), the new Texas 23rd and 36th Cavalry, and two artillery units, the 6th Louisiana Battery (known as the Grosse Tete Flying Artillery) and a section of 12-pdr. howitzers under Capt. John A.A. West. The latter were particularly important, but hard recent usage severely limited the number and abilities of their tired horses.

Out on the river toward dusk, the *Emerald* ran briefly aground. All of the boats nevertheless arrived at Coushatta Chute about 8:00 P.M. A detachment of 40 cavalry from the headquarters of Maj. Gen. Banks met the fleet to give Brig. Gen. Smith Banks' written order to return to Grand Ecore immediately. The lead rider signaled his intention from the bank and, once the *Lexington* drew near, indicated that it would be difficult to return to camp through the superior Confederate force blocking the way. Lt. Cmdr. Bache caused one of the transports astern to take the horsemen aboard.

Maj. Gen. Green and his men marched through the night and reached John Jordan's Bayou Pierre ferry not long before sunrise. Here the men were allowed to bivouac, but were prohibited from building campfires lest they give their presence away to any curious Northern eyes. At daybreak, Rebel scouts were dispatched to locate the retreating convoy. About the same time, Capt. West arrived at Jordan's Ferry with his five howitzers.

April 12 did not begin well for the men of the return convoy. Underway at 7:00 A.M., the vessels encountered what Brig. Gen. Smith called "exceedingly difficult" navigation. In an effort to avoid collisions while turning the narrow bends, the fleet was ordered to separate as much as possible. Most of the wooden transports, guarded by the tinclads and the *Chillicothe*, were up ahead and passed Blair's Landing before noon. Those few army transports at the rear were covered by the *Lexington* and *Osage*.

Moving slowly down, the *Osage* proved to be almost unsteerable in the current. Lt. Cmdr. Selfridge hailed the nearby XIX Corps flag boat *Black Hawk* and, in response, the latter was lashed to the monitor's starboard quarter. This practice, not uncommon on western rivers, greatly aided the naval craft's descent. The huge billowing clouds of wood smoke puffed out by the Northern vessels were visible for miles. Thus, the progress of the Yankee craft was easily and continuously monitored by Brig. Gen. Liddel.

Like Brig. Gen. Bagby, Texan Green was also delayed at Bayou Pierre. His scouts returned, to camp, however, with word that the convoy was devoid of infantry accompanying it onshore. Indeed, they reported seeing several transports and a grounded gunboat near Blair's Landing, a point located at a fairly narrow levee-lined spot in the river. The shoreline location provided access to the Red for the Blair family farm, which comprised a large house, various outbuildings, and slave quarters. In describing the scene, the scouts informed Green that between the 20-foot high levee and a forest at the rear of the property was a fence-lined road located about 500 feet from the landing.

The *Lexington*, meanwhile, was not immune to the hazards of the tricky stream. Around 9:00 A.M. she collided with the *Rob Roy*, staving in the transport's wheelhouse and launch and damaging her chimneys. The accident forced her to lay to and make repairs, which took her out of the picture for five hours. As her carpenters worked feverishly to restore her to service, they and other members of the timberclad crew became aware toward noon that their enemy had begun to appear in strength. When her repairs were finished at about 2:00 P.M., the *Lexington* stood down the river.

While the boats were engaged out on the river, the cavalry of Brig. Gen. Green struggled across Bayou Pierre in its quest to catch Porter's fleet before it got away. Working all morning and into the afternoon, the pride of Rebel Texas was able to cross about half of his men and Capt. West's battery. At about the same time the *Lexington* returned to duty, Green arrived in the crest of the promontories that followed the Red River. Moving down through woods and into the fields of Blair's Plantation, his Rebels sought the cover of the brush and sycamores that lined the bluffs overlooking the banks of the considerably fallen stream.

As they approached the bluffs later in the afternoon, the Texas horsemen could see the rear portion of the Porter convoy near Blair's Landing, though exactly what was going on with the various halted boats was not immediately clear. The good news was that the Yankee vessels were all bunched together in a comparatively short space, making any attack on them that much easier. Looking at their maps, the Southern leaders saw that they were due west of Pleasant Hill some 45 miles north of Grand Ecore.

It was about this time that the *Osage* and *Black Hawk* came into view, bringing up the rear of the convoy as it headed into the tight bend above the landing. Suddenly, the monitor, unable to negotiate the bend, ran hard aground, bows downstream with her turret guns pointed toward the right bank.

Wanting to be sure that he was not seen assembling for attack, Brig. Gen. Green made certain that his men exited the plains of Blair's Plantation and took cover in ravines running parallel to the Red. Additionally, a small scouting force was dispatched to examine the shoreline and it soon reported back that no Federal pickets were ashore. A brief council of war was called between the commanders of the assault force: Green, Col. Parsons, Peter C. Woods,

Blair's Landing, 1864. Attempting to retreat toward Alexandria on the Red River on April 12, several transports, as well as the monitor *Osage* and the timberclad *Lexington*, were attacked by Confederate troops under Brig. Gen. Tom Green. The attack proved futile and Green was killed, but this was among the stiffest of assaults suffered by the Union navy during the Red River campaign (*Battles and Leaders* 4).

and Nicholas C. Gould plus artilleryman West. Taking stock, the men knew that there was at least two hours of daylight left and a chance that they could be discovered or the stuck Federal boats might get free. Additionally, West's howitzers were not "ship busters" and heavier guns were not available. Parsons counseled a night attack, but Green elected to attack immediately. Because his brigade made up most of the available force, it was decided that Col. Parsons would lead the charge while a small reserve force remained behind to cover contingencies and the withdrawal. West's guns would get as close to the fleet as possible before opening fire.

About an hour later, as she made the limited speed possible in the dangerous waters, the *Lexington* was taken under fire from the bank. No one aboard was hurt and her howitzer spit out a noninjurious reply. The ship's officers thought the perpetrators were the usual lurking snipers. As the old boat engaged her assailants, the rear element of the transport fleet, about three miles further on near Blair's Plantation, was now in trouble. At 3:15 P.M., five whistles could be heard sounding from the boats further back. Yelling through his speaking trumpet, Lt. Cmdr. Bache ordered the nearby dispatch steamer/towboat *William H. Brown* go and offer assistance.

Brig. Gen. Smith in his official report laid out the situation leading to the day's climactic encounter. At approximately 4:00 P.M., his command steamer, the *Hastings*, went under the riverbank on the south side of the stream near Blair's or Pleasant Hill Landing, as it had become necessary to repair one of her unserviceable paddle wheels. This action was taken not far from the stranded *Alice Vivian*, which had gone hard aground in midstream with 400 cavalry mounts onboard. Despite her best exertions, she was not yet afloat. The quartermaster steamer and XIX Corps flag boat *Black Hawk* remained on the scene lashed to the grounded monitor *Osage*. Hoping to resolve the situation, Brig. Gen. Smith personally ordered the transports *Clara Bell* and *Emerald* to assist the *Vivian*.

The *Lexington*, meanwhile, overhauled the transports tied up at the bank. As she approached, it was easy for her lookouts to see the *Alice Vivian* aground and the *Osage* and *Black Hawk* lying below her on the opposite bank half a mile up. Lt. Cmdr. Bache ordered his vessel halted near the monitor in order that he might go aboard and offer assistance. Just as the *Lexington* headed toward the bank, the Parrott-equipped *Rob Roy*, unable to pass, pulled in astern of the *Black Hawk*.

With the attack plan communicated to his officers, Col. Parsons during this time moved his dismounted Rebel horsemen forward "in columns of regiments" out of the ravine where they had been hiding and into the trees lining the south side of the riverbank. It was hoped that this gathering atop the 20-foot high mud dike would not be seen by the enemy — a dream unrealized. From his elevated upper deck pilothouse, the pilot of Col. Abert's tethered *Black Hawk*, working with others to free the *Osage*, saw and reported a large force deploying in the woods along the western riverbank. Because the *Osage* was lying so close, he was able to get the attention of Lt. Cmdr. Selfridge, who quickly determined that the men were Confederate soldiers getting ready to attack.

Noticing the *Lexington* steaming around the bend, Selfridge quickly signaled Lt. Cmdr. Bache to take a position from which he could open an enfilading fire on the gathering threat along the riverbank. Brig. Gen. Smith also organized a defense, warning the gunners and sharpshooters on the *Emerald*, *Rob Roy*, and *Black Hawk*. In addition to the butternut soldiers, the vessels had also to content with Capt. West's artillery. While Parsons and his men slipped forward, the 12-pdr. howitzers were unlimbered at the lower river bend and took the *Hastings* under fire. Lt. Cmdr. Bache's big black timberclad loomed over past the transports toward the bank firing her 8-inch guns at West's five-gun battery. The caisson of one of the newly unlimbered field guns was disabled.

Coming within 600 yards of the Confederate guns, the *Lexington* was now subjected to heavy musket fire from a force reckoned by her captain to be about 1,500 men. The vessel slowed, gliding by at a distance from shore of about 20 feet. "The enemy came boldly up to the edge of the bank," Lt. Cmdr. Bache later testified, "yelling and waving their side arms, so close that as a portion of the bank caved in from our fire, one of the rebels tumbled down within a few feet of the vessel."

The timberclad's attack forced the unmasked Confederate battery to shift location to another spot. Hoping to achieve total surprise, Green and Parsons were probably disappointed. As Brooksher has quoted, honors for the first round were won "by the ... ambushee rather than the ... ambusher." As the *Lexington* continued to move toward a position from which she could rake the enemy, the Texas riders along the bank opened "a very heavy fire of musketry" on the *Osage* and the transports. This small arms fire from about 100 yards' range was designed not only to provide cover to West's relocation, but also to pin down the sharpshooters on the decks of the Federal transports. Hopefully, the boats would be damaged as badly as possible.

It was 5:40 P.M., according to the *Lexington*'s logbook, when Capt. West's two remaining fieldpieces opened on the transports from the right bank. And now all hell broke loose as Blair's Landing became the hottest place in Louisiana.

Capt. West's guns were mounted on the bank within point-blank range of the *Hastings*. Seeing this, the XIX Corps headquarters boat *Black Hawk*, having cast off from the *Osage*, signaled the *Hastings* to also cast off. As she did so, West opened anew on Smith's steamer, his first shot falling short and others passing over. The Federal general aboard later dryly observed that "their practice was defective." West moved his howitzers closer to the levee to better their success. Simultaneously, Brig. Gen. Smith signaled his gunners on the other Union army transports to fire upon West. Lt. John H. Tiemeyer opened from the hurricane deck of the *Emerald*, while the Hoosier Parrots roared from the forecastle of the *Rob Roy*. Col. Abert, visiting aboard from the staff of Maj. Gen. Banks, personally took charge of the howitzer mounted on the hurricane deck of the *Black Hawk*.

The gunfire contribution of the quartermaster transports, and *Rob Roy* in particular, was significantly downplayed in later years. In a letter written to Admiral Porter on June 2, 1880, and republished in his *Memoirs*, Lt. Cmdr. Selfridge testified regarding the siege guns on the exposed forecastle of the ordnance boat. "If fired," he concluded, they were "at too long range to have been of any service."

While the Confederate troopers ashore blazed away at the boats afloat, Union soldiers lay behind their makeshift emplacements aboard the transports firing back. The bulwarks of cotton and hay bales, plus cracker boxes and even sacks of oats, provided excellent protection for the marksmen as they sent a cloud of minie balls ashore. The gunfire exchange between ship and shore soon shrouded this portion of the Red River valley with a blanket of smoke reminiscent of the one first encountered by Federal soldiers and sailors at the Battle of Belmont over two years earlier. The lead from the riverbank caused splashes in the water of all sizes while also sweeping into all of the vessels. Chimneys took a particularly hard pounding, many being perforated to the appearance of colanders.

Given their proximity to one another, the *Black Hawk* and *Osage* were especially hard hit. "Everything that was made of wood," Lt. Cmdr. Selfridge later wrote, "was pierced by bullets" on the two boats. At one point, 40 exposed crewmen aboard the former had to flee to the latter's ironclad protection. It was not long before the iron shield placed in the *Black Hawk* pilothouse was dented by over sixty balls. As the fight wore on, Col. Abert's transport was hit repeatedly, forcing the remainder of the *Black Hawk*'s crew to also seek refuge aboard the monitor. When Rear Adm. Porter met the brigadier and colonel aboard the XIX Corps command steamer several days later, the bearded seaman observed that "there was not a place six inches square not perforated by a bullet."

Upstream, the *William H. Brown*, the *Fort Hindman*, and the grounded monitor *Neosho* were also attacked by Green's unmounted cavalry. The warships responded, smashing the woods along the shore at a point some two miles from the *Lexington*. Sometime after 6:00 P.M., the *Hindman* and the *Neosho*, the latter having freed herself, dropped down and made fast to the bank astern of the *Rob Roy*. The new arrivals then opened fire, employing, as did the *Lexington* and *Osage*, a mix of canister, grape, and short-fused shrapnel shells. This barrage, along with the musketry and cannon fire from the transports, sliced into the riverbank with a deafening noise. Mounds of dirt and grass flew into the air while trees were cut in half and bushes were shredded.

As smoke, spray and dirt combined with flying wood chips and the sound of clanking and pinging as bullets hit iron, the *Osage* wiggled off her sandbar. After dropping the hawsers holding her to the *Black Hawk*, the monitor puffed over toward the western bank, her giant 11-inch cannon now firing virtually at point-blank range. It was during this engagement that a unique mirrored instrument, developed by the monitor's chief engineer, Thomas Doughty, and mounted behind the turret, was employed in combat for the first time. In his *Memoirs*, Lt. Cmdr. Selfridge described it as "a method of sighting the turret from the outside, by means of what would now be called a periscope."

As the ironclad moved closer to Green's men, those inside the turret of the *Osage* found that the restricted vision available from its peepholes when it was in the loading position made calculation of the aiming points for the 11-inch guns quite difficult. Hitting the flitting targets atop the high banks was largely a matter of guesswork. "In this extremity," the vessel's commander later reminisced, "I thought of the periscope, and hastily took up station there, well protected by the turret, yet able to survey the whole scene and to direct an accurate fire." As the *Osage* moved to the attack, the *Lexington* continued to target West's gunners, chasing them hither and yon with 8-inch and 30-pounder Parrott shells, grape and canister. Eventually, after a running exchange clocked as lasting over an hour, the remaining fieldpieces were disabled.

The noise level was now so high that it could be heard miles away at Pleasant Hill. Confederate soldier H.C. Wetmore recorded in his diary that "Heavy cannonading in the direction of Red River, which is eighteen miles distant. All of our division of cavalry is there." Despite the tremendous and continuing burst of bullets from both sides, casualties were not heavy. The bluecoats and tars aboard the flotilla were protected by wooden or iron walls, cotton bales or oat sacks. Although Maj. Gen. Green knew that the *Lexington*'s gunners were vulnerable when her gun ports were opened to run out the great guns, his men were not shooting low enough to hit those targets.

On the other hand, the Confederates ashore were partially safeguarded by the high river levees that made it difficult for the Federal timberclad's gunners to elevate their guns sufficiently. Only the *Osage* benefited from her periscope. Additionally, the butternuts hunkered down close to the ground for the most part, presenting targets only when firing. Commenting on this years later in his B & L piece, Lt. Cmdr. Selfridge observed that the fire of his vessel "was reserved till the heads of the enemy were seen just above the bank when both guns were fired."

It was the exceptions to the "for the most part" of their tactics that got Southern soldiers killed. On several occasions, small groups of Texans charged the boats, screaming the famous Rebel yell or a Lone Star variation of it. Occasionally they pressed their rush so close to the edge of a bluff that some of the men fell into the river when the gunboats fired into the overhang causing its collapse. "The rebels fought with unusual pertinacity for over an hour," Lt. Cmdr. Selfridge later observed, "delivering the heaviest and most concentrated fire of musketry that I have ever witnessed." On the other hand, Rear Adm. Porter, known for sweeping, sometimes embarrassing, statements, believed that Green and his men fought so hard only because they must have been drunk.

With West's artillery dispersed by continuing attention from the *Lexington*, and knowing that his men were not going to sink any boats with rifle shot, Brig. Gen. Green now boldly—some would say impetuously—chose to attempt to capture one or more of the Yankee steamers. The river depth was horse shoulder high in spots and several boats were very close to the bank. If he could get enough men aboard one to take it over, it could be sunk it in the channel and thereby block the escape of any remaining upstream craft.

Tom Green, atop his white horse near the edge of the bank, attempted to rally his men for a charge into the river. As he was waving his hat and shouting, his animation was seen aboard the *Osage*. Slowly the great turret was rotated until one of the huge cannon was pointed in his direction. Upon command, it belched out an 11-inch shell and, according to Lt. Cmdr. Selfridge, when the smoke cleared, "saw him no more." It was getting dark when a piece of shrapnel from the monitor's shell killed the Confederate leader. The confusion in Rebel ranks brought an end to the hard fighting within a half hour of Green's death. Seeming to take this almost as a cue, the *Vivian* was freed at approximately the same time.

About 7:00 P.M., a few minutes after the firing ceased, Rear Adm. Porter's dispatch boat *Gazelle* approached the *Lexington*, bearing orders for her to drop down a mile and protect the transports halted in that area. Two hours later, the remainder of the fleet came down. Before their departure, several officers, including Selfridge and probably Bache, went ashore on a hasty inspection. The captain of the *Osage* asked a wounded cavalryman why they "had been so persistent and headlong in attacking a gunboat." The trooper replied that most of the men were new recruits who were assured by their officers that the vessels would surrender if faced with a determined assault. The old timberclad played a big part in the Battle of Blair's Landing. During the fight she expended no less than 97 shells. Although Porter credited the *Osage* with eliminating "the best officer the Confederates had in this quarter," he did not forget to praise Lt. Cmdr. Bache, who "managed the *Lexington* beautifully and did great execution with his guns."

No one is certain exactly how many were killed in what the Federal admiral called a "curious affair of a fight between infantry and gunboats." Porter estimated that, in addition to Green, 20 officers and 400–500 Confederate soldiers died. The number was more likely to have been just over a dozen. Although Confederate returns were not made, the U.S. Navy figures for them are severely inflated. Brig. Gen. Smith, in a list provided with but not printed as part of his OR report, indicates that two Northern soldiers were killed and 17 wounded aboard the quartermaster steamers. Aboard the *Lexington*, African-American Landsman Philip Dudley was wounded in the arm so severely that it had to be amputated.[11]

Brig. Gen. Smith was uncertain whether or not the Confederates would resume their attack that evening. Taking no chances, either with his crews or the supplies aboard his transports, he and Porter ordered the fleet to make the best speed away from Blair's Landing as river conditions permitted. Actually, the progress of the Union task group was not very fast considering the many sandbars encountered. In pitch dark, the boats had only torches by which to navigate the risky stream. Several struck rocks or were temporarily grounded. About 1:00 A.M. on April 13 the fleet finally tied up for the night.

The withdrawal to Grand Ecore resumed about 6:00 A.M. when it was light enough to check for obstructions ahead. A half hour later, the *Lexington* passed the *Cricket* and took Rear Adm. Porter's signal to return to the rear and follow the transports. Not long after this the quartermaster steamer *John Warner*, while moving through a dense patch of fog, hit a snag and grounded so firmly that she could not be immediately worked off. Finding himself in a situation not unlike that faced the day before, Brig. Gen. Smith immediately sent a courier to Grand Ecore and hoped that his superior, Maj. Gen. Smith, would come up soon.

Word of the running ship-shore battle had actually reached Grand Ecore hours earlier. Maj. Gen. Smith immediately set about organizing a relief force. When it was ready that morning, he set out toward Campti leading two brigades, two batteries of field artillery, and cavalry.

Confederate Brig. Gen. Liddell, who continued to follow the fleet on the east side of the river, now determined to take advantage of the *Warner* situation to harass the Federals again. The two sections of field artillery available to him (two 6-pounders and two 12-pounder howitzers) were unlimbered atop the hill overlooking Bouledeau's Point where the grounded steamboat lay. Between noon and 4:00 P.M., Liddell's gunners attempted to hit her or any of the vessels strung out across the river under a bluff, realizing that a lucky shot might blow up an ammunition steamer or penetrate a boiler. Their efforts were supported by riflemen whose balls were dangerous from that distance to Union crewmen but not, if they came no closer, to their vessels.

To make certain that Liddell did not score a lucky hit, Brig. Gen. Smith ordered those few steamers not required to assist the *Warner* to continue on downstream. The inexact blockade by the Rebel cannoneers, firing from so far away, was deemed passable. Following the lead boat *Sioux City*, the *Clara Bell* towed the ersatz gunboat/ammunition boat *Rob Roy* around the point, all of them taking small arms hits that caused neither damage nor casualties. Once the merchantmen were away, the *Osage* and *Lexington* steamed up to take on the batteries, while the *Fort Hindman* and two other steamers unsuccessfully hauled away on big hawsers run over from the *Warner*.

A few Parrott shells were fired by the *Lexington* at the supposed location of one of the

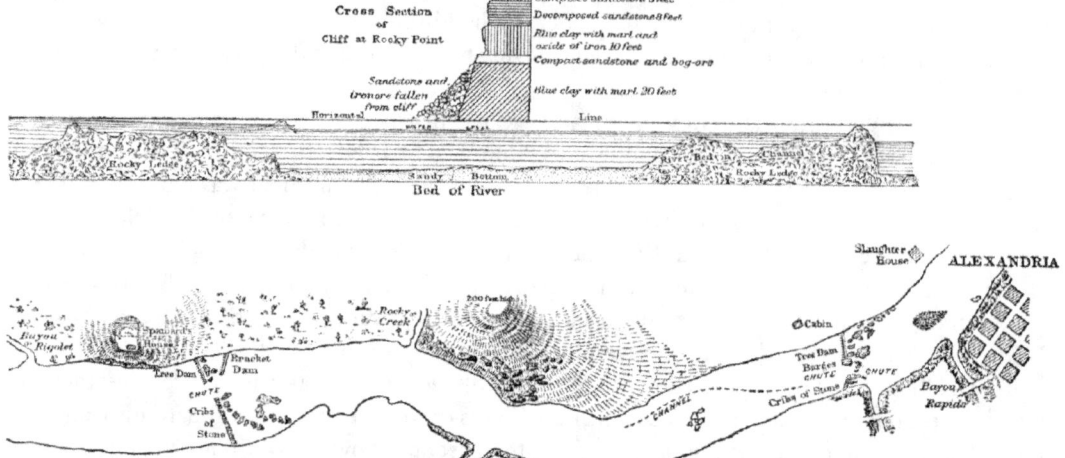

MAP AND SECTIONS OF THE RED RIVER DAMS ABOVE ALEXANDRIA.

Red River dams above Alexandria, Louisiana, in May 1864. The top drawing shows the construction of the dams, while that on the bottom depicts their placement (*Battles and Leaders* 4).

Confederate batteries shooting at the transports. Along about 5:30 P.M., Rebel cavalry appeared on the hill overlooking the gunboat's location but stayed out of range of her 8-inch guns. Once the *Sioux City* and the other transports were past Bouledeau Point, the *Lexington* followed, bringing up the rear. While the *Hindman* remained behind with the *Warner* for the next couple of hours until she was freed, the timberclad convoyed the others to Campti.

As the quartermaster steamers reached the village. "much confusion was caused," wrote Selfridge later, "by many vessels grounding." Despite this difficulty, most of the soldiers and sailors aboard the fleet were excited when Maj. Gen. Smith and his men arrived at the village about 4:00 P.M. The man nicknamed "Whiskey" was overjoyed that Kilby Smith's craft had arrived. He had "by energy, good judgment, and rare good fortune, succeeded in running the batteries and land forces of the enemy without the loss of a boat." Though to be accurate, it had to be admitted that "some were completely riddled with shot."

The *Lexington*, *Fort Hindman*, and *John Warner* arrived at Campti around 7:00 A.M. on April 14. After reporting to the generals ashore, Lt. Cmdr. Bache returned aboard his timberclad and ordered her to cast off for "down the river." She, the other steamers, and the gunboats were en route to Grand Ecore. As the soldiers withdrew, any building not completely destroyed earlier in the month was set ablaze. The old gunboat was underway for only a short while when, around 10:00 A.M., she was involved in a collision with the *Thomas E. Tutt*. The civilian steamer was damaged somewhat, while the *Lexington* was shoved aground and her cutter was destroyed.

As the spring sun shone high above, the gunboatmen were able to repair and free the *Lexington*. Just before she got afloat, heavy musketry was heard up the river. This was attention paid to the Federal transports by Brig. Gen. Liddell's butternuts. In an effort to dissuade this practice, Bache ordered his gunners to spray the woods with shells as they passed suspicious locations. At 7:30 P.M., the *Lexington* tied up to her previous berth at Grand Ecore.

Although many of the vessels that escaped Springfield Landing bore the marks of Rebel sharpshooters, the transports reassembling at Grand Ecore were, in fact, little the worse for their ordeal. Still, the *St. Louis Daily Missouri Democrat* newsman embedded with Smith's transports called the fleet's escape to Grand Ecore "one of the most daring, as well as one of the most successful ... feats of the whole war."

When Rear Adm. Porter was called down to Alexandria on April 15 to discuss with Maj. Gen. Banks the possibility of resuming an advance, the *Lexington* and *Osage* were left off Grand Ecore to provide protection.

The reader will recall that while Porter was away upstream he left his largest vessels behind under Lt. Cmdr. Selfridge, commander of the *Eastport*. Determined that these units should now retire from the river regardless of whether or not the Army of the Gulf returned to the offensive, he ordered them to cross the bar below the town and steam for Alexandria. Following the *Ozark*, the giant *Eastport* was about eight miles below Grand Ecore at 4:00 P.M. that Friday when her bow struck a torpedo. It was one of six positioned by the Confederates below the Grand Ecore ferry in mid–March. The explosion of the subsurface mine caused the ironclad to tremble, not unlike the times already when, while steaming ahead, she had hit sandbars or snags. Rushing on deck, her captain quickly ordered her steered toward the riverbank.

The damage to the *Eastport* was more serious than a mere glancing blow. Water rushed into her forward holds even as damage control parties were told to man a steam siphon pump and the ship's three hand pumps. Idle sailors were set to work bailing by hand. A half hour into this melee, Phelps ordered the whistle blown five times in the prearranged distress signal. The sound was heard at Grand Ecore.

With his boilers already lit, Lt. Cmdr. Bache ordered the *Lexington* to cast off and steam to the scene. The ironclad captain, meanwhile, dispatched a tug down to Alexandria to get word to Porter and to return with the two pump boats stationed there with other fleet auxiliaries. When the big black timberclad arrived about 5:00 P.M., she immediately maneuvered alongside the sinking *Eastport*. A hose was run over from her steam siphon pump and hand pumps were quickly engaged in the effort to keep Phelps' pride afloat.

The *Lexington*'s effort to help save the *Eastport* failed. At 11:00 P.M., the giant's bow struck bottom and water covered the forward end of her gun deck. As soon as Rear Adm. Porter arrived aboard the *Cricket*, he met with Phelps and Bache and ordered that the *Eastport*'s battery and ammunition be removed next morning while he sought additional aid at Alexandria. Damage control parties worked through the night to try to find and isolate the damage; the vessel's heavy wooden bulkheads frustrated their efforts.

As the sun rose on April 16, the *Lexington*'s steam pump was fired up again, along with that of the *Eastport*. Those two were joined by another provided by the newly arrived tinclad *Juliet*. The two undamaged vessels alternated this bailing service as the day wore on. Crews from the *Eastport* and the *Lexington* were also set to work passing ammunition to the nearby monitor *Ozark*. When that task was completed, parties from the timberclad dismounted the aft 9-inch guns, which were manhandled through the gunports to the waiting *Ozark*.

Although all of the big guns were transferred by dark, the men of the *Lexington* and the *Juliet* stood to their pumps off and on throughout the night and into the morning of April 17. Just after 9:00 A.M., the specialized steam pump boat *Champion No. 5* arrived and tied up alongside the sunken ironclad. Once the salvage boat had her giant 10-inch and 20-inch steam pumps in action, the *Lexington* was able to disengage and return to Grand Ecore. She would have no further role to play in the tragic *Eastport* story. Although she had a great role in her original capture on the Tennessee River in February 1862, the timberclad would not be present when, all efforts to save and move the Federalized prize having failed, the *Eastport* was blown up near the town of Montgomery on April 26 to prevent her capture.

On April 19, Maj. Gen. Banks authorized Maj. Gen. Smith to cover the retreat of the army, and the fleet and the visiting troops from the Army of the Tennessee next day moved to Natchitoches, a town "as old as Philadelphia." Banks, having thrown in the towel on any further Red River exploits, began his withdrawal at 5:00 P.M. on April 21.[12]

Rear Adm. Porter, finding it impossible to remain upstream longer, ordered his transports and lighter gunboats to initiate their withdrawal from Grand Ecore on April 19. At 11:00 A.M. that Tuesday, the *Lexington* cast off and stood down the river. Four hours later, as was now customary, she landed on the opposite bank a short distance below Montgomery. There her hands were set to wooding ship, a euphemism for stealing fence rails.

About 4:30 P.M., the steamer *J.H. Lacey* came down and rounded to. Her captain came aboard to inform Lt. Cmdr. Bache that his transport was fired into by a Rebel squad on a bend a little above Montgomery. Calling in the men ashore, the naval officer ordered his timberclad to get underway and stand upstream. When the *Lexington* reached the location mentioned by the *Lacey*'s captain, her gunners fired a single 8-inch shell into the woods. The boom of the great cannon could be heard for miles, which was the intent. Coming about, the old gunboat eased into the bank at Montgomery, where Lt. Cmdr. Bache went ashore to see the townspeople, many of whom had gathered upon his approach.

Under the menacing guns of the timberclad, Bache informed the citizens that, if they allowed anymore firing on nearby passing vessels, the U.S. Navy would burn their town to the ground. Federal commanders, against evidence to the contrary, continued to cling to the notion that civilians, in fact, had influence on military actions. This policy may have had some impact against citizens hiding guerrillas, but not upon regular troops.

Like other units of the Northern armada, the *Lexington* continued her withdrawal toward Alexandria, a voyage which consumed several days. On at least two occasions, she put into Cotile's Landing, while several times she convoyed individual steamers that reported incidents of being fired into by Confederate outriders.

Late in the afternoon of April 25, the timberclad landed about a mile below Rocky Point, in the shadow of Deloach's Bluff on the opposite shore, at the mouth of the Cane River. There, across from the craggy shoreline known as Deloach's Rocks, her sailors were put to work sounding and buoying the channel in anticipation of the arrival of the *Eastport*. None of them knew that the hill across the river was actually named for the Deloges family, whose cemetery lay just inland from the top of the hill. The family name for the spot would be recognized by geographers on maps in the next century and so we use it here.

Early the following morning, as the *Lexington*'s men continued their work in what their skipper called "the intricacy of the channel," a squad of Rebel soldiers approached but were quickly driven off by a pair of howitzer shells. Just after 9:00 A.M., the *Osage* stopped to procure wood near Deloges Rocks. As Lt. Cmdr. Bache, aboard the timberclad across the river, drilled hands with small arms, the monitor landed a party of pickets to guard the working party.

Elsewhere during this time, other Union gunboats, especially those working to save the *Eastport*, were subjected to merciless Confederate attacks. According to Maj. Gen. Taylor, these were carried off by Brig. Gen. Liddell and a number of reinforcing mounted riflemen. To intercept these gunboats and transports as they worked their way downstream as well as to blockade the river against other Federal craft, Taylor deployed one of the largest forces to yet assail Porter's retreating Yankee bluejackets. Dispatched early in the morning were at least 200 additional soldiers and a number of cannon. Historian Chuck Viet, in his internet article, admits that the number of guns rushed to the scene to fight the Northerners could have ranged between four and eleven cannon.

The tinclads and pumpboats of the *Eastport* rescue group were assaulted throughout the day, particularly later in the afternoon as they attempted to depart after the mighty ironclad was destroyed. Porter daringly ran past the batteries, attempting to reach the *Lexington* and *Osage* known to be below.

Confederate artillery units represented in the fray included Capt. Florian O. Cornay's St. Mary's Cannoneers (1st Louisiana Battery) with two 12-pounders and two 24-pounder howitzers, the 3rd Louisiana Light Artillery ("Bell's Battery"), with two rifled cannon, and the Val Verde Battery under Capt. Thomas O. Benton, armed with three 6-pounder Napoleons and two recently-prized 12-pound rifled cannon. It is the latter unit that elicits our attention here.

When Capt. Benton arrived at Deloges Bluff around 8:00 A.M., he could clearly see the *Lexington* lying in the Red River about 450 yards away. The *Osage* lay even closer to him, but was shielded by her position under the bank. During the next three hours, the butternut artillerymen struggled their guns into a protected position by hand. Meanwhile, when the *Osage* cast off to continue her voyage, her pilot ran her aground. A small boat took a line over to the *Lexington* on the opposite shore, and the timberclad pushed off into midstream to assist her ironclad consort. The eddy currents of the Red at this rocky spot made it exceptionally difficult to get the *Osage* afloat. Lt. Cmdr. Selfridge feared that, once she was free, she would become unmanageable. Consequently as soon as her head swung off, she was anchored.

At 10:30 A.M., a section of Confederate riflemen drove in the monitor's pickets, severely wounding her quarter gunner. Two officers and 12 volunteers gallantly and safely charged up Deloges Hill and safely retrieved the stricken sailor. Shortly thereafter, Benton's guns opened on the *Lexington*. Where she lay, the timberclad could not bring her battery to bear. As she attempted to drop down to a more favorable position, she was hit by a 6-pound ball. After the *Lexington* shifted, Lt. Cmdr. Bache ordered his gunners to open up on Benton with the broadside and stern guns. A heavy cannonade shook the river for the next half hour as the wooden boat slugged it out with the Rebels.

Meanwhile, the *Osage* from her position under the riverbank unleashed a constant barrage of grape, shrapnel and canister. Benton fired back and although a number of shots hit her turret none penetrated. No sailors were hurt and no gentlemen of Dixie were harmed by this exchange, although one horse was killed and two wounded. On the other hand, plunging fire from Benton's fieldpieces smashed into and through the *Lexington* 18 times. One shot hit her steam pipe but without sufficient force to penetrate it and blow up the boat. Two men were wounded and one, Hold Captain Henry Orth, was killed.

This punishment was far more than the wooden gunboat was designed to absorb. Lt. Cmdr. Bache now elected to retire downriver about a mile. Maneuvering just enough to avoid presentation of a stationary target, the *Lexington* continued to engage with her stern guns from a safe distance. As the timberclad moved off, Capt. Benton shifted two of his rifled cannon in order to obtain a more direct field of fire against the *Osage*. In so doing, according to the monitor's captain, the Rebels were exposed to two or three 11-inch Dahlgren shells that quickly "made them limber up and clear out."

The two Federal gunboats and the six Confederate cannon continued to exchange fire until some point between 1:00 P.M. and 2:00 P.M., when the breech of one of Benton's rifled guns was fouled by a piece of primer. At this point, the Southerners withdrew to the rear, having expended 48 rounds from their 6-pounders and 18 from the rifled cannon. When the shooting stopped, the *Lexington* dropped anchor to check the roster and make repairs. A quick magazine inventory found that forty-nine 8-inch and Parrott shells were fired. For her part, the *Osage* returned fire with but nine 11-inch shrapnel, a 5-second shell, two stands of grape and one of canister, suffering no casualties.

Units of the Mississippi Squadron grouped together above Alexandria, Louisiana, at the end of April 1864. Many of the naval vessels were, in actuality, tied to the bank and not spread out as depicted. Nevertheless, the drawing conveys the sense of urgency that faced every Federal sailor in the days before the success of Lt. Col. Bailey's dam (*Harper's Weekly*, April 30, 1864).

While the *Lexington* and *Osage* engaged Benton, other Confederate batteries not far upstream assailed the withdrawal of the *Eastport* rescue group. Two Northern tinclads were disabled in the process, but Porter, aboard the *Cricket*, was able to pass Taylor's gunners. The feisty Mississippi Squadron commander now headed for the location of a pair of pre-positioned ironclads. Before getting far, however, the damaged *Cricket* ran ashore. It took three hours for Porter to get his command tinclad afloat and during this time a rather constant noise of cannon fire could be heard from above.

It was well after dark when the admiral reached the place appointed for the heavy reinforcements. There he found the *Osage* lying opposite Benton's battery, which had returned at 2:00 P.M. to block the river. He also observed that the *Lexington*, which "had been hard at work on them," was badly splintered. Selfridge—who had been ill during most of the day's contest—and Bache met with Porter to determine if anything more could be done yet that night. The noise of gunfire from above had ceased. Unbeknownst to the three Federals, Capt. Benton would be recalled two hours before midnight.

There really was not much Porter could do. The *Lexington* was for all intents and purposes out of action. Darkness and the tricky channel prevented the dispatch of the *Osage;* had she attempted, she might very well have run aground and become another victim.

On the morning of April 27, the *Lexington* and *Cricket* steamed toward Alexandria, where their most serious damages could be repaired, while the *Osage* steamed back upstream. The survivors of the *Eastport* rescue group battled past the chain of Confederate guns on the bluffs during the morning, finally reaching the safety of the anchored *Osage* shortly after 1:00 P.M. By 7:45 the next morning, these vessels, together with the Selfridge monitor, had joined the other vessels anchored above Alexandria's upper falls.

The ordeal of Deloges Bluff was over, but the challenge of getting past the Alexandria rapids remained. Indeed, Porter later confided that he not only had the rapids to deal with, but also the rocks below them, which were "for a mile quite bare, with the exception of a channel 20 feet wide and 3 feet deep."[13] On April 28, Rear Adm. Porter, stranded above the rapids at Alexandria, advised Navy Secretary Welles of his precarious position due to the falling water level of the Red River as well as Banks' withdrawal. "I find myself blockaded," he wrote, "by a fall of 3 feet of water, 3 feet 4 inches being the amount now on the falls; 7 feet being required to get over." Facing the distinct possibility that he would need to destroy his entire $3 million squadron, as he had the *Eastport*, to keep it out of Confederate hands, he lamented to his superior that "You may judge of my feelings at having to perform so painful a duty."

Porter initially had some success in getting at least a portion of the transports and his flotilla through the available little 20 foot-wide channel. Led by the admiral aboard the Cricket, a number of quartermaster boats and tinclads thumped their bottoms along to safety in the deeper waters south of Alexandria caused by a growing back-swell from the Mississippi. Still, the heaviest vessels, including the *Lexington*, remained stranded above behind the falls. Working with Maj. Gen. Banks and his officers, the Mississippi Squadron chief fortunately came up with the correct solution and the right man to carry it out, XIX Corps staff engineer Lt. Col. Joseph Bailey, whom Nicholas Smith years later called "the Moses of Porter's fleet." For years, the story of Bailey's dam was the most celebrated single event of the entire Federal Red River fiasco.

The presence of the one-time 4th Wisconsin Cavalry officer with Banks' expedition was, wrote Smith and Castille in 1986, "one of those coincidences of history that sometimes result in turning the course of events." So it was that, on April 29, Bailey was tasked by Banks and Porter with constructing a dam that would raise the water sufficiently to allow the fleet to escape. Straightaway, Maj. Gen. Banks set over 3,000 men to work chopping down trees or dismantling whole buildings, finding stone and rock, and hauling the materials to the sites on either bank where the dam would be constructed. Interestingly, Black troops worked the Alexandria side, while soldiers from Wisconsin, Maine, and New York labored on the Pineville shore.

Around the clock for eight days the men strained without cessation, beginning the initial dam not far above the lower, downstream rapids where the river was about 758 feet wide. It was hoped that, when the project was finished, the water behind the structure would have risen enough to float the gunboats over the upper rapids. Then when the time was just right, the dam could be broken and the gunboats could rush free over the lower rapids, carried by the force of the released water. Despite a 9 mph current, the work continued and gradually the water level began to rise. On May 8, the stage on the upper falls was up sufficiently to allow the lighter gunboats and monitors *Osage*, *Neosho*, and *Fort Hindman* to move down and make ready to pass the main dam the instant it was ready.

Early the next morning, great crashing sounds were heard in the vicinity of the dam. The tremendous water pressure against the dam forced two of the barges employed in its construction to burst loose, swinging in below the dam on one side. The admiral quickly understood the situation and, skilled equestrian that he was, jumped on a steed and galloped up to the upper falls where the ironclads were anchored. Screaming from horseback at 6:00 A.M., Porter ordered Lt. Cmdr. Bache, the only one of the captains with steam up fully ready to go, to immediately pass the upper falls, run down over the rocky stretch before the level fell, and exit to safety through the dam. Also a gifted yarn-spinner, the squadron commander later essentially reprinted in his *Incidents and Anecdotes* the same account of the *Lexington*'s exodus as he sent Secretary Welles in his official report. Colorful, it is worth quoting here:

The *Lexington* going over Col. Bailey's dam. When the Union's Red River flotilla was stranded in low water above Alexandria, Louisiana, at the beginning of May 1864 an ingenious dam was constructed to raise the water level sufficiently to allow the trapped boats to pass. Unhappily, part of the dam began to give way on the morning of May 8, at which point Lt. George M. Bache, with steam up and a wave from Rear Admiral Porter, took the *Lexington* through the gap (*Battle and*

> The *Lexington* succeeded in getting over the upper falls just in time, the water rapidly falling as she was passing over. She then steered directly for the opening in the dam, through which the water was rushing so furiously that it seemed as if nothing but destruction awaited her. Thousands of beating hearts looked on anxious for the result; the silence was so great as the *Lexington* approached the dam that a pin might almost be heard to fall. She entered the gap with a full head of steam on, pitched down the roaring torrent, made two or three spasmodic rolls, hung for a moment on the rocks below, was then swept into deep water by the current and rounded to, safely into the bank. Thirty thousand voices rose in one deafening cheer, and universal joy seemed to pervade the face of every man present.

It only took 20 minutes for the timberclad to speed from the upper falls through the dam to the safety of the waters below the town. There she anchored and observed the monitors and *Fort Hindman* come down a short time later. Still, it was more of a near run thing than Porter admitted.

Watching the proceedings from the shore with the admiral, Lt. Cmdr. Selfridge suggested the ending might not have been as happy if one of the two barges had not bilged and sunk, blocking a prominent rock close below: "As the *Lexington* approached the gap, the current prevented any further control and she was thrown against the barge, bounced off, and shot safely below without damage. But for the fender action of the barge, she would undoubtedly have been wrecked on the rock, and had she stuck there, would have blocked the further passage of the fleet."

The *Lexington* proved Lt. Col. Bailey's dam would work and he resumed his work on it with spirit. By May 13, all of the gunboats were safely below the rapids and Union forces were now able to exit Alexandria, reaching the mouth of the river eight days later. "And thus ended the 69-day Red River expedition," Lt. Cmdr. Selfridge wrote in his B & L contribution, "one of the most humiliating and disastrous that had been recorded during the war."

The Federal Red River expedition of 1864 has been the subject of debate from the day it first entered that stream. It is far outside the scope of this work to enter into such a review. We can report that, during the adventure, the U.S. Navy lost about 320 men, two tinclads, one ironclad, two pump boats, and four transports. The *Lexington* survived and, like the *Tyler*, would continue to serve.[14]

Chapter 15

Cavalry Versus Timberclads, June 1864

"After the Red River campaign," wrote Lt. Col. Richard Irwin, "no important operation was undertaken by either side in Louisiana." For the timberclads, the scene of action now reverted to their familiar territory in and off the mouth of the White and Arkansas rivers. Events within the interior of Arkansas now largely controlled their activities.

In the 11 months between the Red River trek and the end of the war, the elderly *Tyler* and *Lexington* remained popular in those circumstances, front-line and otherwise, where heavy firepower was required. Opportunities for the timberclads to provide fire support in major amphibious operations largely dried up, though one or the other might be hastily added to an armed reconnaissance or upriver surge of anticipated short duration. Often the sisters served as flag boats or station-keeping vessels, lying off the mouths of rivers or towns, or, like the covering cruisers with World War II Atlantic convoys, supplied extra artillery strength in escort situations.

As a flood of tinclads continued to join the squadron, the role of the timberclads became more frequently mundane. Still, strong lookouts were maintained and gunners kept the big guns ready. During 1864–1865, the lower deck crews of the old boats, like those of the other vessels in the Mississippi Squadron, had a heavy multiracial nature as lower deck manpower became increasingly African American. Regardless of their personnel mix, the vessels remained ready to combat marauding Confederate irregulars or interrupt insurgent attempts to run contraband or interfere with local Union garrisons, sympathizers and loyalists.

Maj. Gen. Frederick Steele's VII Corps' participation in the Red River campaign is often called the Camden expedition because that is as far as his Federal army was able to get from Little Rock before turning about and returning to the capital city on May 3. The details of the various actions and operations involved in the Camden enterprise are not important to this story except to say that the general's failure emboldened Confederates within Arkansas to resume the offensive. As May progressed, Maj. Gen. Sterling Price, commander of the Confederate District of Arkansas, turned the cavalry division of Brig. Gen. John S. Marmaduke loose upon Federal logistics.

Before we tell the story of gunboat involvement with Marmaduke's brigades, we must

The *Lexington* tied up to a Louisiana bank. This picture, long noted simply as depicting a damaged timberclad, was most likely taken following the return of the gunboat from her sojourn up the Red River in the spring of 1864 (Miller's *Photographic History*).

digress to note one last instance in which the *Lexington* had a big prize day. Having earned considerable coin "liberating" cotton on the Ouachita and Red River expeditions, Lt. Cmdr. George M. Bache was doubtless pleased when three transports fell into his lap. After her excursion up the Red River, the *Lexington* was minimally refreshed and returned to her old post off the mouth of the White River on June 14. In fact, the old boat, after three years of war, was about used up. The bumping received running to, from, and above Alexandria, coupled with the jarring caused by the firing of her great guns on the Grand Ecore retreat and the rushed escape through Bailey's dam caused her significant structural deficiency. Indeed, when Lt. Cmdr. S. Ledyard Phelps, who had known the vessel since her 1861 conversion, initially saw her some weeks after her Red River ordeal, he exclaimed, "The *Lexington* is the hardest looking old wreck I ever saw!"

Upon his arrival at the Montgomery Point anchorage, Lt. Cmdr. Bache found the *Tyler* with a temporary commander, Acting Ensign George L. Smith. Lt. Cmdr. James M. Pritchett, having been promoted into the South Atlantic Blockading Squadron, had turned her over to her executive officer on May 21. The *Lexington*'s lone remaining wooden sister was also entering her third year of service, but, not having been so roughly treated of late, was in somewhat better physical shape.

Once more the black boats' job entailed interdictive control of the Mississippi, White, and Arkansas rivers, making certain that no unauthorized crossings were made or trade conducted. Preventative patrols would be undertaken and any suspicious craft would be required to show cause as to why they should not be seized or destroyed. Unhappily for Bache, like other Western naval officers, the Treasury Department granted permits for many traders to deal in and ship cotton. This made it very difficult for the gunboats to restrict commerce. Occasionally, a steamer would be seized and it was left to the courts to decide whether the prize was legitimate.

Having heard while en route to his station that three vessels were involved in illegal cotton trading in the Old River between Napoleon and the mouth of the White, Bache's first action was to dispatch the *Tyler* down to investigate. Later that evening, the largest timberclad returned, bearing a witness who had actually been aboard the boats in question. Brought before Lt. Cmdr. Bach, the man swore the officers of the offending craft were "in communication with rebel soldiers, openly receiving them on the boats, and trading with them. "They were also trafficking in liquor.

Taking onboard a detachment of men from the *Tyler*, the weary *Lexington* paddled down into the Old River early on the morning of June 15. As she approached Beulah Landing, Mississippi, the steamers *Mattie*, *M. Walt*, and *Hill* were found anchored about 100 yards offshore. After the gunboat came to, small boats, with the men from the *Tyler*, were dispatched to seize the vessels. During their absence, Lt. Bache saw 25 to 30 Caucasian males at the landing. Before he could give an order for their interception, they disappeared into the nearby woods.

Telling off prize crews under direction of Acting Ensign Joseph G. Megler, Bache ordered the three captives to proceed the gunboat back to the small U.S. Army post on a small island at the mouth of White River known as White River Station. Capt. John R. C. Hunter of the 12th Iowa Infantry, with 50 men and a number of African-American workers, had recently arrived and were nearly finished with the erection of a small stockade. All four vessels anchored in the stream at dark, for their mutual protection and that of the unfinished post ashore. That evening, Lt. Cmdr. Phelps, commander of the 7th District of the Mississippi Squadron, arrived from Helena aboard the tinclad *Hastings*.

Early on Sunday morning, 8-man prize crews from the timberclads, under the direction of Acting Ensign Megler, returned aboard the anchored steamers and relieved their sentries. The *Mattie*, *M. Walt*, and *Hill* then stood up the Mississippi for Cairo and a rendezvous with a Federal district judge of the Southern District of Illinois. As smoke from the *Lexington*'s prize steamers disappeared upriver on June 16, Lt. Cmdr. Bache assumed temporary command of the *Tyler*. Some months later, the *Lexington* and *Tyler* would both be credited with the captures and prize monies would be distributed.

The old wooden gunboats not only specialized in economic regulation, but were called upon to undertake more familiar duties: station keeping and convoy escort. Although much of this responsibility was shared with smaller tinclads, the wooden veterans of '61 continued to make their presence felt.

In the wake of the VII Corps' retreat to Little Rock after the Camden adventure, Confederate horsemen rode roughshod over the state, "plundering and overawing the Unionists," as Benson J. Lossing put it right after the war. Lt. Cmdr. Phelps and Bache now found themselves facing the same dilemma as their colleague, Lt. Cmdr. Le Roy Fitch, on the Cumberland River. Their opponent was not Nathan Bedford Forrest, but another legendary butternut cavalryman, Brig. Gen. Joseph O. "Jo" Shelby, the most famous horse soldier in the Trans-Mississippi theater and commander of one of Brig. Gen. Marmaduke's two brigades.

During May and June, Shelby and his mounted force of between 2,000 and 3,000 men with the Missouri battery of Capt. Richard Collins, moved across the Arkansas River east of Little Rock and headed toward the White River country, marching down the east bank of that stream toward Devall's Bluff. His purpose was threefold: to recruit soldiers to the Southern cause, to end the depredations of guerrillas turned terrorists, and to block Maj. Gen. Steele's logistical flow by attacking his supply lines between Little Rock and the Bluff.

While Shelby undertook a difficult march toward Clarendon that led him through the overflowing bottoms of Cache River and Bayou DeVue, Col. Colton Greene of the Third Missouri Cavalry (C.S.A.), leading Marmaduke's other brigade, led his horsemen in a series of raids along the west bank of the Mississippi. His battery of Missouri horse artillery frequently engaged Northern gunboats and transports, though not the timberclads. The activities of the

Confederate horsemen did not occur without some rumor or intelligence concerning them reaching Federal ears. This was particularly true of those mounted by the well-known Jo Shelby. While on a reconnaissance up to DeVall's Bluff, Lt. Cmdr. Phelps learned that the Rebel cavalry was loose, but that all was quiet so far as Shelby was engaged in a recruitment campaign.

Despite a modicum of momentary confidence, Phelps still took precautions to protect river shipping and local bases or communities. The *Queen City*, *Naumkeag*, and *Fawn* were spaced out between Clarendon and St. Charles, while the *Tyler* was tasked to directly protect the former town. And then these preparations were knocked into a cocked hat.

Supplies for Maj. Gen. Steele's Little Rock garrison were usually taken up the White River to DeVall's Bluff, 30 miles below the state capital, and then transferred for shipment by the Little Rock and DeVall's Bluff Railroad. Soldiers often came in overland, but occasionally by steamboat. The U.S. Quartermaster Department was always quite insistent about running supply convoys up the chalk-colored White or its sister stream, the Arkansas, and required naval protection. Sometimes local area commanders suddenly demanded escort for waterborne troop movements.

When the sailors protested the danger, there was always a gnashing of teeth and barrages of complaint from the logisticians or thoughtless generals. Added to the Federal navy difficulty was the fact that the local Mississippi Squadron district commanders, whether on the White or Arkansas or Tennessee or Cumberland, were not always informed of steamer movements. Just such an occurrence took place at the mouth of the White on the evening of June 18. Both Lt. Cmdr. Phelps and Lt. Cmdr. Bache were dumbfounded when, toward dusk, a convoy of nine troop transports emerged from the White River to go up the rising Arkansas. Maj. Gen. Steele wished to move some of his men around to Little Rock from DeVall's Bluff and believed the trips would not be overly difficult to make.

Brig. Gen. Joseph O. "Jo" Shelby, C.S.A. (1830–1897), was a cavalry leader of the Trans-Mississippi region who, like Maj. Gen. Nathan Bedford Forrest, believed Federal forces in 1864 Arkansas could be significantly hampered if their White River supply chain was blockaded. In late June, he personally led a force to Clarendon and sank the tinclad *Queen City*. Within hours, he fought and withdrew from an intense combat with several other Union vessels led by Lt. George M. Bache aboard the timberclad *Tyler* (U.S. Army Military History Institute).

Welcomed aboard the *Hastings*, Col. William P. Fenn informed the two naval officers that he was charged with getting his men and supplies upstream to Little Rock and beyond to Fort Smith while the river was in good stage and rising. He then handed over dispatches from Maj. Gen. William Rosecrans, the St. Louis commander and Maj. Gen. Steele indicating that large risks should be mounted to get the personnel through. On top of these, he produced an order from Rear Adm. Porter authorizing the provision of convoy if the water stage made it prudent.

Lt. Cmdr. Phelps found himself in a box. Wanting to make certain that the rivers were covered against Shelby and Greene, he had nevertheless to provide escort. After conferring with Bache, Phelps informed Fenn that he would send along an escort from the mouth of the Arkansas up the most dangerous 25 miles to South Bend, but that only one small gunboat would ascend beyond that point. And, of course, if Bache learned that the enemy was blockading the river, he was authorized to turn the combined fleet back immediately.[1]

The *Tyler*, in company with the tinclads *Fawn* and *Naumkeag*, steamed up the Arkansas next morning with Col. Fenn's nine transports, leaving the *Lexington*, under Acting Ensign Booby, to literally hold the little fort at White River Station. The *Queen City* was shifted up to guard Clarendon. After ferrying the Cache River and wading the mires of Bayou DeVue, Brig. Gen. Shelby paused on June 20 to review his options. DeVall's Bluff, he knew, was the closest point to Little Rock on the White River and its railroad to the capital was the only train system then working in Arkansas. The Federal logistical hub at the Bluff was fortified, contained a good-sized garrison, and was constantly watched by gunboats. Attacking it directly would be difficult.

On the other hand, this heart in the Union supply chain could be killed if the vital water artery to it could be cut below. It was obvious from the map that the *point d'appui* should be the town of Clarendon, 14 miles downstream. Easy to reach or escape from, the largely deserted community offered a good position at which to plant cannon and blockade movement up or down the river. Shelby led his regiments toward Clarendon next day. The trek was hard. It rained incessantly, resulting in swift streams without bridges, roads without bottoms, and endless swamps and muck.

Also on the afternoon of June 21, Col. Robert R. Lawther, leading the 10th Missouri Cavalry (C.S.A.) of Brig. Gen. Marmaduke's division, prepared to pay a visit to White River Station. The just completed stockade was manned by a small 50-man garrison from the 12th Iowa Infantry, under the command of Capt. Joseph R. C. Hunter, armed only with muskets. Leaving their horses on the opposite side of the Arkansas River, Lawther's 300 men crossed the stream in small boats or skiffs and marched all night to the outskirts of the National camp. Arriving at approximately 4:00 A.M. on June 22, the men made their final preparations to charge from the nearby woods.

Capt. Hunter's pickets failed to pick up the movement of Lawther's men as they assembled. When the butternuts burst forward from the tree line with the first rays of sun at about 4:30, the Yankees were surprised. Advancing steadily, Lawther's dismounted horsemen were nearly upon the garrison before they were discovered. Acting Ensign Booby had steamed up on the *Lexington* and, as the Confederates charged, the creaky timberclad moved out into the stream and opened fire upon them with her port battery. After the battle was joined, the skirmish at White River Station that Wednesday lasted about 20 or 30 minutes.

Beaten back, Col. Lawther's men retired into the woods and back toward the Arkansas River. Not knowing if they would return, Booby shelled the woods and the road by which it was supposed they were leaving for another 15 minutes. When the *Lexington* ceased firing, a check of the magazine by Acting Gunner L. Frederic revealed the expenditure of 71 rounds of shell and shrapnel. Once it was determined that the enemy would not be back, the timberclad moved back to her anchorage abreast of the stockade.

In his report, Capt. Hunter claimed that 30 Rebels were killed or wounded, while admitting to five casualties (one dead). This figure was confirmed by Acting Ensign Booby, who reported to Lt. Cmdr. Bache that most gray-clad wounded were carried off. The four wounded Northern soldiers were taken aboard the *Lexington* and cared for under terms of an arrangement worked out with Lt. Cmdr. Phelps some days earlier. Next day, they were sent aboard the steamer *May Duke* for transfer to Helena.

A few days later, the Memphis newspapers, in a report republished by the *New York*

Times, briefly noted that 600 of Marmaduke's marauders attacked the two Iowa companies and were repulsed after severe fighting. Not knowing that the assault was part of a larger Confederate antilogistics operation, the newspapers opined that "the removal of the gunboat *Tyler* from that station probably emboldened the rebels." Continuing, they noted that, "but for the fortunate arrival of the gunboat *Lexington*, the result might have been unfavorable to us."[2]

While Brig. Gen. Shelby was en route toward Clarendon and the *Lexington* was safeguarding White River Station, Lt. Cmdr. Bache ascended the Arkansas with his convoy. At Red Fork Landing, he found batteries blocking the river and, in accordance with his orders, turned back. The nine troop steamers were then escorted to DeVall's Bluff, where the men could be unloaded and sent to Little Rock by train.

Maj. Gen. Steele happened to be at the Bluff when Bache's vessels arrived on June 23 and angrily confronted the sailor as to why they had not gone up the Arkansas River as he wanted. When the *Tyler*'s commander explained that it was blocked by Rebel cannon, Steele refused to believe him and indicated his desire that the boats be turned around and sent back down the White and up the Arkansas to Little Rock. Of course, Steele added, the matter at that point was left to Bache's judgment.

In reporting this interview, Lt. Bache, perhaps having heard of similar charges of nonsupport leveled earlier by the army against Lt. Cmdr. Fitch over on the Cumberland, noted he would fulfill the general's wish and return as suggested. "Not wishing that the army should think us backward in cooperation," he indicated, "I determined to shove them there as far as the gunboats could go and let them trust to luck afterwards!"

As the cavalry and horse artillery of Brig. Gen. Shelby rested near Clarendon on that sultry Thursday afternoon, an advance party of scouts went forward to reconnoiter. Carefully, the men examined the town and the nearby woods, finding them nearly devoid of activity. The river was a different matter; about 170 feet (10 rods) from the wharf lay the wooden paddle-wheeler *Queen City*, "dark sentinel of the place." Advised of the situation ahead, Brig. Gen. Shelby ordered his advance riders to throw a cordon around the town. To maintain secrecy, anyone entering or attempting to leave was to be arrested. By dark, the remainder of the command was quietly stationed within the community and in the trees along the riverbank within 100 yards of the gunboat.

Just before his craft buttoned up for the night, Acting Volunteer Lieutenant Hickey sent a reconnaissance through the streets of Clarendon. The check was thorough and just missed Shelby's advanced skirmishers, who were able to duck out of the way while maintaining their vigil.

Plans made earlier to surprise the *Queen City* at dawn and capture or destroy her progressed to the next stage. Just after midnight, while the unmounted horsemen rested beneath the gigantic cottonwoods, the four-gun Missouri Battery of Capt. Collins drew up to Clarendon's outskirts on its main road. At a point out of earshot of the water, the guns were unlimbered and their horses led away. Then, aided by the sweat of a hundred soldiers, the cannon were stealthily and noiselessly dragged by hand to within 50 feet of the river's edge. Once the guns were in position, the troopers also advanced to the shore of the White, "crouching and clinging to the shadows of the houses." "Silence, like a tired queen, brooded in the whisperings of the leaves." The "thug-like" warriors watched ahead, some with "suppressed breathings." Personally curious, Brig. Gen. Shelby went up close to the tinclad to check its state of preparedness. It seemed ready, with steam up and its guns loaded.

Right after the war, Shelby's friend John Edwards painted the picture:

> A low, large moon, lifting a real of romance out of the waves, lit up the scene with a weird light, and crested the "stars and stripes" that flapped in melancholy motion against the painted

Once a ferry, the tinclad ***Queen City*** was disabled during a night attack by troops of Brig. Gen. Joseph O. "Jo" Shelby at Clarendon, Arkansas, on June 24, 1864, and captured. She was blown up before Lt. Cmdr. George M. Bache could rescue her with the timberclad ***Tyler*** and two other small gunboats (Naval Historical Center).

gaff.... The drowsy sentinel paced his narrow beat.... Somber as an iron island, with all her red lights in gloom, and the deep peal of her time-bell sounding solumn and chill, the doomed craft sat upon the water unconscious of the coming daylight.

The nights were shorter now as the earth approached its summer equinox, but still the hours after midnight passed slowly for the sleep-deprived Southerners. There were no clouds and the only sounds that could be heard were the waves in the river as they "sobbed on the beach, and curled and sparkled in sheer wantonness around the iron beak of the river falcon." At approximately 4:00 A.M., "little shreds of daylight" poking up in the east, Brig. Gen. Shelby ordered his men to open fire on the *Queen City*, while, at the same time in his words, he "notified her commander of my approach and intentions." Caught in as complete a surprise as any in U.S. naval history, the tinclad was immediately subjected to a heavy barrage of musketry from two regiments and shells from 10-pounder Parrott rifles and 12-pounder smoothbores.

The first or second round from Capt. Collins' guns smashed into the *Queen City*'s starboard engine. A piece of it flew on into the steam pipe of the starboard power plant, which fortunately did not burst. The one-sided contest continued for about 15 minutes, during which, a Memphis newspaper later stated, the gunboat was struck 45 times by artillery shots "and her pilothouse was completely torn away." The St. Louis *Daily Missouri Democrat* July 2 coverage indicates that the *Queen City* attempted to drop down with the current to get a range for his cannon. This was a goal she was unable to accomplish. It was not long into the fight before Acting Volunteer Lieutenant Hickey knew that he would have to surrender. Writing about the white flag years later, Adm. Porter was contemptuous of Hickey for "not having the bravery to fight it out as many of his contemporaries would have done."

As the ship was riddled with cannon shell and rifle bullets, the able men in his crew (Shelby's count was 65, but it was far less) were advised by their captain that they could also give up or dive overboard and swim to the freedom of the opposite bank. The ethnic makeup of the crew is not certain, but it was not the band of "devil-may-care Irishmen" John Edwards later reported. There were many African Americans and the fate of any of those tars who gave up was very uncertain. Rumor had it that Shelby routinely ordered such prisoners shot.

With one seaman dead in the fight and nine wounded, Hickey signaled his surrender and Shelby's men stopped shooting. The wreck of the heavily perforated tinclad was pulled to shore, where Hickey was taken prisoner, along with four officers, 20 seamen (four wounded), and eight African-American contrabands. The latter, reported the *Chicago Daily Tribune* on Independence Day, "were immediately put to death." The remainder of the crew had escaped to the opposite shore, though one white crewman and one African American were drowned. As late as July 12, the *Memphis Argus* would report that 23 men got away and 11 were killed or remained missing.

While the crewmen were interrogated and the officers paroled preparatory to their release to Helena authorities, Confederate horsemen ran aboard and ransacked the gunboat. Immediate prizes included in excess of $10,000 just drawn by the paymaster a few days earlier, the paymaster's stores, wearing apparel, small arms, most of the ammunition, and a brass 12-pounder wheeled boat howitzer. Fearing that there were other gunboats in the vicinity that could arrive before he was finished, Shelby cancelled plans to unship the 24-pounders and a 32-pounder and use them in a formidable blockading battery ashore.

Within a half an hour of the time Shelby's gunners opened fire on the *Queen City*, the nine-boat troop convoy of Federal supply steamers departed DeVall's Bluff for Clarendon under escort of Lt. Cmdr. Bache's gunboats. Puffing slowly ahead in standard escort formation with the *Fawn* in the lead, the *Naumkeag* in the center, and the *Tyler* at the rear, the fleet paddled along peacefully for almost 30 miles.

As daylight intensified, the leading steamer *Pike* was hailed from the western shore by two officers, a powder monkey, and five African American "contrabands" who had escaped the *Queen City*. Putting in, the transport picked up the men and took them out to the *Fawn*, where they told their story to its captain, Acting Master John R. Grace. Signaling the following vessels to pause, Grace came to and awaited the arrival of *Naumkeag* and *Tyler*, which sped ahead to learn what was holding up the procession. Following the 9:00 A.M. rendezvous of the three guardians, now less than 10 miles from Clarendon, Grace gave Bache and Acting Master John Rogers the news that the *Queen City* was captured and that Shelby occupied the town with 2,700 men.

Decisive as always, the intrepid Bache immediately ordered the eight other merchantmen to follow the *Pike* back to DeVall's Bluff and for her captain to let their U.S. Army colleagues know what was happening. Realizing that it was only five hours since the *Queen City* was seized, the officer knew that Shelby did not have time to get much out of her, particularly her cannon. On the other hand, it was possible that she could be manned by butternut artillerymen and employed, in conjunction with the Rebel guns on the bank, against him or any force Lt. Cmdr. Phelps might send from the mouth of the river.

Lt. Cmdr. Bache, fresh from combat with blocking cannon on the Red River just over a month earlier, was determined that Shelby and his cavalrymen would face the wrath of his big guns just as the Texas riders had earlier. Thus it was that he ordered his fellow officers to form their gunboats into line of battle, *Tyler*, *Naumkeag*, and *Fawn*. There would be action this day as Confederate horsemen, like those at Blair's Landing, were engaged by the aggressive gunboatman.

While the Federals assessed the situation upstream, Brig. Gen. Shelby made his own preparations for the fight all in his command knew to be coming. The pieces of Collins' battery were dispersed to prevent them from taking massed naval fire, while the remainder of the brigade deployed as skirmishers, lining the bank in front of the town and down around a bend and on both sides of its wharf.

It was understood from their whistles that the Union boats were being kept close up and in good order. How many there were was unknown. Was there a transport fleet or just warships? In addition, Shelby did not know if his enemy would attempt to run by or whether they would actually engage him as the pesky *Lexington* did with Brig. Gen. Green down above Grand Ecore.

John Edwards, in his colorful account of the Clarendon skirmish, makes it perfectly clear that the Confederates knew that Bache was coming long before he arrived. For over an hour, they could hear the whistles of the leading vessel. As the morning grew warmer, "louder and louder sounded the dull puffing of the advancing boats." Knowing that he could get no more out of the captured tinclad before the Yankee rivercraft arrived, Brig. Gen. Shelby ordered her destroyed. When within a few miles of Clarendon, Lt. Cmdr. Bache and his crews heard two successive reports, which they later learned were the sounds of the *Queen City* blowing up.

Great clouds of smoke, heavy and dark in the light blue of the morning sky, could be seen up the river by the Confederates just before and certainly after their enemy advanced to a spot a little over a mile away. Soon the first pitch black object, not quite distinguishable to those without field glasses, loomed into sight followed by several more. Banners streamed out in the wind from their tall vertical staffs that looked for all the world like flagpoles.

"The leading boat, gigantic and desperate, forged slowly ahead," wrote Edwards, "every port closed, and a stern defiance on her iron crest." This was the *Tyler*, "scarred and rent in previous fights, but wary and defiant still." As the timberclad and her tinclad consorts ("a noble trio," according to the *Daily Missouri Democrat*) came abreast of the Cache River at 9:45 A.M., Brig. Gen. Shelby gave the order to his artillery chief to open fire on the leading gunboat. Collins' men were good; Bache later reported that one of their "first shots went through the pilothouse."

"A white puff of smoke burst suddenly from the bow of the *Tyler*," Edwards relates, and curled gracefully in thin wreaths far astern." A large shell then "passed overhead with a noise like an express train and burst in the river half a mile away." Even though the approaching timberclad could initially reply to Shelby's overtures only with a bow Parrott, the ball was truly opened as the *Fawn* and *Naumkeag* also joined in with their forward guns. The three Federal gunboats paddled defiantly toward the Confederate guns, coming within an easier range. "With a bravery worthy of a better cause," said a St. Louis scribe, "the rebel general with his men worked their batteries."

Early in the engagement, shrapnel from a 12-pounder flew through the port shutter of the *Fawn*'s pilothouse, mortally wounding her pilot and carrying away the bell system. This rang the bells and the engineers thought they were to stop the boat, which they did—directly under the Rebel guns. At least 10 shells or heavy pieces of shrapnel found the little tinclad, to say nothing of musket balls. She was fortunate to escape, but could offer little more immediate aid to her consorts.

In the meantime, the *Tyler*, followed by the *Naumkeag*, steamed slowly past the batteries, pumping out broadside after broadside of one-half second shrapnel and canister. When she came abreast of the town wharf, Brig. Gen. Shelby, who was riding between pieces encouraging his gunners, was heard to shout: "Concentrate fire of every gun on the *Tyler*." To some it appeared that the big dark craft now, indeed, "staggered over the water like a drunken man." The defiant old timberclad and the *Naumkeag* continued through the fiery gauntlet and, after they passed by it, a number of Confederates thought that the two would continue on down the river toward its mouth. Thus it was they were amazed when both craft rounded to and steamed up at them again. Bache was later told that "the rebels now exclaimed in despair, 'There comes that black devil again!'"

The ship vs. shore contest had now eaten a half hour, with, according to Brig. Gen. Shelby, his men on open ground "and not 60 yards from the boats." The masked batteries ashore dished out considerable punishment, but the gunboats scored as well. The *Queen City*'s captured howitzer, for example, manned by Rebel crew near the bank, was only able to get off a couple of shots before the timberclad's shooting drove everyone from it. Moving ahead, the *Naumkeag* and *Tyler* were joined by the *Fawn*, now restored and steaming above the wharf. Together, the three boats now had Shelby in a crossfire. The *Tyler*, of course, being the larger vessel with the biggest guns, remained the center of butternut concern, even as the tinclad poured in her own enfilading fire of grape and canister.

"Full broadside to the wharf she [*Tyler*] stood sullenly at bay, giving shot for shot and taking her punishment like a glutton." Edwards suggests that one two-gun battery was destroyed in a cloud of dust and smoke by one of her broadsides that sounded "like the rush of 500 steeds in motion." As 10:30 A.M. approached, Lt. Cmdr. Bache, from his position aboard the *Tyler*, her head pointed upstream and her guns continuing to blaze, thought he discerned some of the briskness pass out of the Rebel fire. ("The result was the usual one between field batteries and gunboats," opined Duane Huddleston and his colleagues over a century later.) Bache was probably not surprised at this situation. The Red River veteran found that the pace of shooting by his own command had thus far been "terrific; the trees onshore for the space of a mile" were marked by the timberclad's projectiles "and that low down."

Caught in a gunboat trap, Brig. Gen. Shelby threw in the towel and ordered his men to withdraw to their "former camp, some two miles from town." Watching from his pilothouse, Lt. Cmdr. Bache "had the pleasure of seeing them skedaddling from the field." Clarendon was back in Union hands. Under protection of the *Tyler*'s big guns, a landing party from the *Naumkeag*, led by Acting Master Rogers, went ashore to assess. During their exit from the scene, the butternut troopers abandoned nearly everything they took within 300 yards of the riverbank. The *Queen City*'s wheeled boat howitzer, somewhat the worse for battle, was recovered, along with a significant quantity of ammunition, her cutter and four oars, and an anchor. Five crewmen (two badly wounded) from the sunken tinclad, including Acting Assistant Surgeon Lewis Westfall, were rescued, while several wounded Confederates, left behind, were also saved.

Parts of the wreck of the *Queen City* herself could be seen in the water about a mile below the town. She was completely burned out and her casemates had tumbled in. A portion of the afternoon was spent by men from the Union vessels in attempting to salvage some of her guns. The *Tyler* would locate and raise three on a subsequent visit.

Once these men were transferred to the *Tyler* to join seven officers and 24 other ratings recovered earlier, Lt. Cmdr. Bache ordered a large gristmill and a sawmill destroyed, along with "a pair of timber trucks, which might have been useful in transporting heavy pieces of artillery." Brig. Gen. Shelby called this an act of vandalism and later reported to District of Arkansas headquarters that the sailors "took revenge for their boat by burning all the private and public buildings in Clarendon."

During the afternoon, the *Fawn* and the *Naumkeag* patrolled up and down the river for a mile or two, occasionally being subjected to musketry. Every time they were shot at, they replied "with one-half second shrapnel." Meanwhile, aboard the *Tyler*, the task group commander wrote out a report on damages and casualties. Although the Confederates liked to believe that she was hard hit and "bled fearfully with half her crew dead," the fact of the matter is that the old gunboat stood up fairly well. It is true that she was hulled 11 times, but she was not really damaged. The casemates erected around the *Tyler*'s boiler after her battle with the ram *Arkansas* did stop a 12-pounder shot that could have been climactic. The worst loss was six men wounded, none seriously.

The tinclads, on the other hand, lived up to their own reputations as death traps, an unenviable status earned by their class over the previous year. Not meant to stand against land batteries, they were hurt. It was fortunate for them, as well as the *Lexington*, that Brig. Gen. Shelby located his guns on nearly level banks. The three vessels were not faced with the effects of plunging shot, as, for example, the *Cricket* was on Red River. Still, the *Naumkeag* was hit at least twice but suffered more serious damage from the concussion of her guns, which caused her to leak and the eyebolts of the casemates to break. Acting Master's Mate John Dunlap, who took himself off the sick list to lead his division, was mortally wounded. The *Fawn* suffered 10 hits during the battle. In addition to the loss of Pilot Thomas Barnett, 10 other crewmen were casualties, including her acting surgeon.

On the other side of the community, Brig. Gen. Shelby plotted his return next day after the gunboats were gone. If he could throw up somewhat better temporary earthworks and hold the spot for 10 days, he could seriously disrupt Union river navigation.

Unfortunately for the Rebel brigadier, the gunboats did not all leave. The *Naumkeag* and *Fawn*, under command of Acting Master Rogers, remained off Clarendon to prevent any further mischief, while the *Tyler*, with the wounded and shipless aboard, steamed back up to DeVall's Bluff. Bache hoped to personally persuade Maj. Gen. Steele to send a force to "capture the guerrillas." Later, Shelby told his superiors that the *Tyler* was forced to return to the Bluff for repairs. It did not take much effort for the *Tyler*'s commander to convince Steele that an expedition should return to Clarendon right away. The next morning, June 25, a body of cavalry under Brig. Gen. E.A. Carr boarded two transports and prepared to depart downstream under escort of the timberclad.

While Carr's force was assembled at the Bluff, Brig. Gen. Shelby made an effort to return to Clarendon and throw up some earthworks or rifle pits. Patrolling the river, the *Naumkeag* and *Fawn* rounded a point and discovered the Confederates at work digging. Puffing into easy range, they fired over 50 shells at the butternuts, who retired into some woods.

The little DeVall's Bluff armada pushed off at 2:00 P.M. but was unable to proceed more than 10 or 15 miles when, toward evening and in the modest words of her captain, "an accident happened to the *Tyler*." The force lay to as repairs were made and finally reached Clarendon at 9:00 on Sunday morning. Carr was landed and persuaded Shelby to move further back toward Bayou DeVue. With the Southern cavalryman gone for the moment, Carr and Bache returned to DeVall's Bluff on the evening of June 28.

The story of the *Tyler*'s sudden need to halt Carr's convoy was rather more involved than Bache revealed. He "had quite an accident happen to him," his superior, Lt. Cmdr. Phelps, revealed in a July 5 letter to Rear Adm. Porter. Bache was watching the shoreline from the quarter gallery of the *Tyler*'s roundhouse when she suddenly lurched. One of the most common and yet fearful navigational dangers facing western steamboats had just occurred. Her port side paddle wheel picked up a big log that badly damaged it. The tree trunk also tore off the outside of its wheelhouse and the whole after angle "and with it, of course, the quarter gallery."

Lt. Cmdr. Bache, one of those sailors who for some reason never learned to swim, was

Top: Tyler. An excellent full-length profile of the largest gunboat as she lay at anchor in one of the western rivers. Note the cutter in the foreground and the unidentified Pook turtle astern. The exact location and time of this shot is unknown; however, the photograph was found in the Naval Historical Center's collection of the papers of Lt. Cmdr. George M. Bache. As he commanded the vessel after returning from the Red River campaign, it is likely that the photograph was made in June 1864 or later. *Bottom:* While leading a White River troop convoy on June 25, 1864, the *Tyler* became a victim of one of the most common and yet fearful navigational dangers facing western steamboats. Her port side paddle wheel picked up a big log that badly damaged the wheel. The tree trunk also tore off the outside of the *Tyler*'s wheelhouse and the whole after angle "and with it, of course, the quarter gallery." Lt. Cmdr. George M. Bache, one of those sailors who for some reason never learned to swim, was thrown into the river. He was saved through a lucky combination of slow current, a large piece of floating wheelhouse wreckage, and quick-thinking crewmen. The gunboat was repaired at the riverbank within 12 hours, employing planking from a barge, and was able to resume her escort (both photographs, Naval Historical Center).

thrown into the river and found himself floundering about trying to tread water. Fortunately, the current was not very swift and he was able to grab hold of a piece of wheelhouse wreckage. With the same determination displayed in facing the guns of Green and Shelby, he hung on until a boat lowered to hunt for him came alongside and "fished" him out.

No worse for wear and brushing off the very real possibility that his gallant career might have ended in the river as surely as Lt. Cmdr. William Gwin's did aboard the *Benton*, Bache immediately set to work directing the *Tyler*'s repairs. The wheel was fixed and boards from the roofing of an old barge were employed to plank the wheelhouse. "Although it will not bear inspection at close quarters," Phelps told Porter tongue in cheek, "it looks tolerably well at a distance."[3]

Epilogue

Winding Down, July 1864–August 1865

The battle between the *Tyler* and Shelby at Clarendon was the last big gunfight in which the timberclads participated. Hereafter, they would, as the war wore down, continue their patrol and escort activities without incident. Their stations were normally in that stretch between Helena and the mouth of the Red River, with continuing attention to the White and Arkansas.

Lt. Cmdr. Bache remained in command of the more active *Tyler* during the summer, though occasionally he transferred back aboard the nearly stationary *Lexington*. In early September, Bache went on leave while the *Tyler* was under repair at Memphis, getting her chimneys replaced and her wheelhouses repaired. For a brief period after Lt. Cmdr. Phelps September 12 detachment and before taking his own final leave from the Mississippi Squadron, Bache served as acting commander of the 7th District.

Active at the Mound City naval station, Acting Volunteer Lieutenant Frederic S. Hill also served aboard the *Benton* and was assigned by Lt. Cmdr. Phelps to command the tinclad *Forest Rose*. That order was countermanded by Fleet Captain Alexander M. Pennock who, instead, named Hill to the *Tyler* on September 9. Hill was originally appointed an Acting Master on July 12, 1861, and was promoted to Acting Volunteer Lieutenant on December 11, 1862. Active on the rivers of North Carolina prior to his transfer west in late 1863, he would remain aboard until the following spring when he was ordered to return to Mound City and assume charge of the vessels being decommissioned. Honorably discharged on May 12, 1865, he was succeeded in command of the largest timberclad by her executive officer, Acting Master Charles Ackley.

Originally brought into the Mississippi Squadron as a mate in November 1862, the capable Ackley was named an acting ensign on October 31, 1863, and an acting master on July 16, 1864. Most of his experience was aboard the *Tyler*, where he served under both Lt. Cmdr. Pritchett and Bache. He remained employed at the Mound City naval station until honorably discharged on June 27, 1868.

Acting Master William Neil, who began 1864 eight months into his initial appointment as an acting ensign aboard the *Conestoga*, was executive officer of the tinclad *Juliet* during her

By the end of the Civil War, Mound City, Illinois, on the Ohio River eight miles from Cairo, had become the major Mississippi Squadron base. It was here that the *Lexington* and *Tyler*, together with the other surviving vessels of the organization, were sold off in a gigantic auction in August 1865. Fortunately, the sale was conducted in much drier conditions than those depicted here during an earlier period in the facility's history (Miller's ***Photographic History of the Civil War***).

days of great trial up the Red River in April and May. In early November he briefly served as commander of the *Lexington*, stationed at the mouth of White River. At the end of that month, he was charged with misconduct by Brig. Gen. Napoleon Buford in a complaint to Rear Adm. Porter and lost his billet. He was eventually cleared of any wrongdoing and was honorably discharged on December 4, 1865.

The *Lexington*'s final commander was Acting Volunteer Lieutenant William Flye, appointed on December 1. Transferred west from an oceangoing squadron in April, Flye previously commanded the river monitor *Osage*, succeeding Lt. Cmdr. Selfridge. He would hold his post aboard until the timberclad was decommissioned the following summer. On July 18, 1865, he was one of the few men appointed to the rank of acting volunteer lieutenant commander. He would be honorably discharged on December 24.

The *Lexington*'s long-time executive officer and sometime commander, Acting Ensign Henry Booby, remained aboard until his detachment on July 19, 1865, the day his ship was formally decommissioned.[1]

As the Civil War in the West wound down in the weeks after Appomattox, the *Lexington* and *Tyler* remained at their posts. On May 1, the former, fresh from repairs at Mound City, was reported in the Fifth District, which ran for 125 miles between Natchez and Vicksburg. The *Tyler*, newly refreshed at Memphis, was posted in the Sixth District. That 210 mile stretch between Vicksburg and the mouth of the Arkansas River included her old White River stomping grounds.

When 1865 began, the U.S. Navy Department, believing that the Rebellion would soon be over, began seeking significant economy in its operations. As winter turned into spring, this movement intensified and by May, with the war over, the Mississippi Squadron in particular was downsized at a rapid pace. On May 28, both the *Lexington* and *Tyler* were ordered to report to the commandant of the Mound City naval station for disposition.

Removal of the guns from the timberclads, as well as other units of the fleet, took some time, as did the dismantlement of their military bulwarks, casemates or other protection. By the first days of July, the remaining pair of the flotilla's first gunboats were well on their way to resuming something of a civilian appearance. Both the *Lexington* (Acting Ensign Booby) and the *Tyler* (Acting Master John R. Grace) were formally decommissioned on July 19, the day those officers were ordered ashore.

Even as the timberclads were being retired, the Navy Department, appreciating the fact that it would soon need to unload a large number of surplus river naval vessels, came up with a traditional American plan for liquidation. The boats would be auctioned. Beginning in late June, advertisements were placed by department officials in all of the leading newspapers from the East Coast through the Midwest and down to New Orleans for a "Large Sale of Gunboats." Noting that over 50 craft were available, officials placing the notices anticipated that all of them would be sold in a giant one-day sale at Mound City on August 17.

From its practice of covering large absolute sales, the editors of the *Chicago Daily Tribune* knew the impact that such a large auction could have on people. Consequently, they sent one of their better known war correspondents, J.A. Austen, to Mound City about a fortnight ahead of the sale. Austen was asked to review the atmosphere of the community, examine the mechanics of the sale, and take the pulse of potential buyers.

As it turned out, according to Austen, the navy's sale was probably one of the largest meetings of steamboat men in a generation. It was even possible, he suggested, that "so great a meeting of boatmen was never before held in the West." Austen found a total of 63 boats and tugs anchored in the Ohio River between Mound City and Cairo "nearly filing the bend between the two places." At night, they hung lights and lanterns aboard. Sparkling on the water, all who saw this illuminated parade perceived it a most beautiful and striking sight, reminiscent of the myriad lights of a large town or city.

In the week before the August 17 sale, earnest buyers and the idly curious took passage aboard every small craft available to examine the merchandise, both from the water and by inspections aboard. Potential purchasers were encouraged to seek every nugget of information available on those boats of interest and to ply their sometimes immense knowledge in gauging their value. So thorough was this process, Austen believed, that "if any buyer paid more than his boat was worth, he did so with full knowledge of what he was doing."

The arrangements for the sale were familiar to all then and to anyone today who has ever attended the auction of a house, automobile, or farm animals. A large stand was placed in the center of the naval station ordnance building, "handsomely decorated with national ensigns." Here space and every convenience was afforded to clerks, reporters, and purchasers. At exactly noon on that sweltering Thursday, Solomon A. Silver of Cairo took the stand and began the alphabetical disposal with the tinclad *Argosy*. The sale proceeded rapidly.

When it came their turn, the tired old timberclads actually fetched a larger price than some of their famous contemporaries. Daniel Jacobs purchased the *Carondelet* for $3,600 and the *Benton* for $600 less. Thinking there might be life left in the *Lexington*, Thomas Scott & Woodburn bought her for $6,000. David White of St. Louis gave the same amount for the *Tyler*. "Thus ended the great Government sale," reporter Austen wrote as the auction concluded around dusk, "and with it vanished the Mississippi Squadron."

The post–Civil War fate of the timberclads *Lexington* and *Tyler* is unknown. The ball they opened in 1861 was now truly closed as they faded into the mists of time and the recollections of the unhappy national trauma.[2]

Conestoga II. The second U.S. Navy vessel named *Conestoga* (AT-54) was commissioned in 1917 and undertook general escort and towing duties on the U.S. East Coast through 1919. In early 1921, she was assigned to serve as the station ship at Tutuila, American Samoa, but she disappeared before reaching her post. No trace of her was ever found (Naval Archives).

A second *Conestoga*, a 170-foot, 420-ton gunboat (AT-54) was commissioned at the Sparrows Point, Maryland, naval shipyard on November 10, 1917. Following World War I service, she was transferred to the West Coast at the end of 1920. Repaired at Mare Island, she set sail for Tutila, American Samoa, on March 21, 1921—and disappeared. A lifeboat was found but no other trace and, after a three-month search, she was declared lost with all hands. No ship since has borne the name.[3]

The fourth and fifth *Lexingtons* were both aircraft carriers. The former (CV-2), built on the hull of an unfinished battle cruiser, displaced 41,000 tons and was 888 feet long. Commissioned at Quincy, Massachusetts, on December 14, 1927, she served in both peace and war until sunk during the Battle of the Coral Sea on May 8, 1942. The next *Lexington* (and last to date) joined the fleet at Quincy as CV-16 on February 17, 1943. The 27,100-ton floating airfield was an 872-foot-long member of the *Essex* class of fast carriers. This *Lexington* served with the fast carrier task forces throughout the Central Pacific campaign during 1943–1945, winning a Presidential Unit Citation and 11 battle stars for her World War II service. Although she saw no service during the Korean conflict, she returned to duty in 1958. Though not again

U.S.S. *Lexington* (CV-2) photographed in 1936 with members of her crew spelling out the word "NAVY" on her flight deck. The second U.S. aircraft carrier was armed with modern 8-inch naval guns fore and aft of her island (right side of her superstructure), perhaps reminiscent of the 8-inch shell gun which protected her timberclad forebearer. The vessel was sunk during the Battle of the Coral Sea in 1942 (Naval Historical Center).

involved in actual combat, she kept an offshore vigil during tensions in Formosa, Laos, and Cuba.

At the end of 1962, the *Lexington* sailed into Pensacola Bay to assume her new duties as the U.S. Navy's Training Carrier (CVT-16). New aviators were trained to fly and land on her decks, while countless visitors (including the author) were awed by her historic stature. The final *Lexington* was decommissioned on November 26, 1991, and became a museum ship at Corpus Christi, Texas.[4]

The *Tyler* was unique in American naval history. No other ship has since borne her name.

Three wooden gunboats, conceived as stopgaps in a period of uncertainty, performed far more effectively than might have been expected. The vessels, due to be replaced by stronger boats, soldiered on because they were needed as the conflict intensified. Despite known limitations, they became, as ADM Porter put it, "famous in the annals of the navy." The bearded seadog was even moved to immortalize them in a line of shaky verse:

> See the old warriors out in the stream,
> Open in many a wood-end and seam![5]

Their guns, their flexibility, and the grit of truly gifted commanders and dedicated, well-trained crews made the timberclads a force to be reckoned with on the western waters. Even after the loss of the *Conestoga*, the *Lexington* and *Tyler* steamed on, winning additional accolades. Truly, this trio of Union warships ever deserve in our memory the terse words the Navy awards as its highest praise: "Well done!"

Chapter Notes

Foreword

1. Benjamin Franklin Cooling, "War on Inland Waters," in *The American Civil War: A Handbook of Literature and Research*, ed. Steven E. Woodworth (Westport, CT: Greenwood Press, 1996), chapter 23.

2. Start with Steven E. Woodworth, *The American Civil War: A Handbook of Literature and Research*, chapters 23 and 24, and James M. McPherson and William J. Cooper, Jr., eds., *Writing the Civil War: The Quest to Understand* (Columbia: University of South Carolina Press, 1998), 32–35 especially.

3. The classic study of the naval Civil War remains that of William M. Fowler, Jr., *Under Two Flags: The American Navy in the Civil War* (New York: W.W. Norton, 1990); there is also a dated H. Allen Gosnell, *Guns on the Western Waters: The Story of River Gunboats in the Civil War* (Baton Rouge: Louisiana State University Press, 1949). These two are ably supplemented by Rowena Reed, *Combined Operations in the Civil War* (Annapolis, MD: Naval Institute Press, 1978).

4. Two solid reference works on ships of the Civil War navies are Paul R. Silverstone, *Warships of the Civil War Navies* (Annapolis, MD: Naval Institute Press, 1989), 147–184 (especially 158–160), and Donald L. Canney, *The Old Steam Navy*, vol. 2, *The Ironclads, 1842–1885* (Annapolis, MD: Naval Institute Press, 1993), chapter 4 (especially p. 37), and William H. Roberts, *Civil War Ironclads: The U.S. Navy and Industrial Mobilization* (Baltimore, MD: Johns Hopkins University Press, 2002), chapter 4.

5. Canney, *The Ironclads*, ch. 4.

Preface

1. Throughout this account, we refer to the various military and naval vessels noted by their name only, occasionally with type designation but always without prefix. Into the early years of the 20th century there was no fixed form for navy ship prefixes, including "USS" for "United States Ship." Although the designation was occasionally employed (and does appear from time to time in the Navy Official Records), it was not until 1907 that an executive order of the president was issued officially establishing the present usage (The U.S. Navy Department, Naval Historical Center, *Frequently Asked Questions*, no. 63, Ship Naming in the United States Navy: A Note on Navy Ship Name Prefixes, http://www.history.navy.mil/faqs/faq63–1.htm

2. Gary Joiner, *Mr. Lincoln's Brown Water Navy: The Mississippi Squadron* (Lanham, MD: Rowman & Littlefield, 2007).

3. David D. Porter, *Incidents and Anecdotes of the Civil War* (New York: D. Appleton and Co, 1885; repr., Harrisburg, PA: The Archive Society, 1997), 124.

Chapter 1

1. According to the Valley of the Shadows Resource Center's 1861 timeline, the river blockade was officially launched on May 13, the day after Rodgers received orders to go west and almost a month after President Lincoln had ordered establishment of a coastal blockade. (*Valley of the Shadow Homepage*, http://valley.vcdh.virginia.edu/reference/timelines/timeline1861.html); William B. Cogar, *Dictionary of Admirals of the U.S. Navy* (Annapolis, MD: Naval Institute Press, 1989), 1:150–152; Edward W. Callahan, *List of Officers of the Navy of the United States and of the Marine Corps from 1775 to 1900, Comprising a Complete Register of All Present and Former Commissioned, Warranted, and Appointed Officers of the United States Navy, and of the Marine Corps, Regular and Volunteer (Compiled from the Official Records of the Navy Department)* (New York: L.R. Hamersly & Co., 1901; repr., New York: Haskell House, 1969), 469; Lewis R. Hamersly, *The Records of Living Officers of the U.S. Navy and Marine Corps, Compiled from Official Sources*, rev. ed. (Philadelphia: J.B. Lippincott, 1870), 21–22; John D. Milligan, *Gunboats Down the Mississippi* (Annapolis, MD: Naval Institute Press, 1965), 5; Spencer C. Tucker, *Blue & Gray Navies: The Civil War Afloat* (Annapolis, MD: U.S. Naval Institute, 2006), 114; Ivan Musicant, "The Fires of Norfolk," *American Heritage* 41 (March 1990): 63; Nelson D. Lankford, "Fire and Water: Disaster at the Gosport Navy Yard, April 1861," *North and South* 9 (February 2007): 22–29; Fletcher Pratt, *The Navy, a History: The Story of a Service in Action* (Garden City, NY: Garden City Publishing Co., 1941), 282. Following

his midwestern posting, Rodgers (1812–1882) served on the Atlantic coast, beginning in the experimental ironclad gunboat *Galena.* He was promoted to the rank of Capt. in June 1862. Twelve months later, while in command of the monitor *Weehawken,* he defeated and captured the Confederate armorclad *Atlanta,* for which he received the "Thanks of Congress" and a promotion to commodore. Following his 1869 promotion to the rank of Rear Adm., he commanded the Asiatic Squadron, served as president of the U.S. Naval Institute from 1879 until his death, and was first president of the Naval Advisory Board, 1881. Rodgers was the subject of a flattering profile in *Harper's Weekly,* August 15, 1863 (Cogar, 150–152; James R. Soley, "Rear Admiral John Rodgers, President of the Naval Institute, 1870–1882," *U.S. Naval Institute Proceedings* 20 (1882), 251–265). The efficient and politically adroit Meigs (1816–1892) was named QMG on May 15, 1861, and held that post through the war, winning appointment as a brevet Maj. Gen. in July 1864. His name would appear often in support of the western river war. He was also brother-in-law to the new postmaster general, Montgomery Blair of MO (Mark M. Boatner III, *The Civil War Dictionary* (New York: David McKay, 1959), 542).

2. Charles B. Boynton, *History of the Navy During the Rebellion* (New York: D. Appleton and Company, 1867–1868), I:497, 500; Adam I. Kane, *The Western River Steamboat* (College Station: Texas A & M University Press, 2004), 6. It was Boyton who first reported that Rodgers and Eads went west together. The west and western rivers in Civil War literature refers generally to the western theatre of operations, which encompassed the area beyond the Allegheny Mountains. See Bruce Catton, "Glory Road Began in the West," *Civil War History* 6 (June 1960): 229–237. Indeed, at this time, southern Illinois and the area south of St. Louis were known as the "Southwest."

3. Louis C. Hunter, *Steamboats on the Western Rivers: An Economic and Technological History* (Cambridge, MA: Harvard University Press, 1949), 484–485; Kane, 16; James Mak and Gary M. Walton, "Steamboats and the Great Productivity Surge in River Transportation," *Journal of Economic History* 3 (September 1972): 623; Erick F. Haites and James Mak, "The Decline of Steamboating on the Antebellum Western Rivers: Some New Evidence and an Alternative Hypothesis," *Explorations in Economic History* 11 (Fall 1973): 25–36; Haites, Mak, and Gary M. Walton, *Western River Transportation: The Era of Early Internal Development, 1810–1860* (Baltimore, MD: The Johns Hopkins University Press, 1975), 120. The Rodgers-Eads probable route from Washington to Cincinnati is shown in a map in John F. Stover's *History of the Baltimore and Ohio Railroad* (West Lafayette, IN: Purdue University Press, 1987), 82.

4. Kane, 7.

5. Charles Dana Gibson, with E. Kay Gibson, *Assault and Logistics: Union Army Coastal and River Operations, 1861–1866* (Camden, ME: Ensign Press, 1995), 2:615–616.

6. Ron Powers, *Mark Twain: A Life* (New York: Free Press, 2005), 76–77; U.S. War Department, *The War of the Rebellion: A Compilation of the Official Records of the Union and Confederate Armies,* 128 vols. (Washington, DC: Government Printing Office, 1880–1901), series I, vol. 52, 707–708 (cited hereafter as OR, followed by a comma, the series number in Roman numerals, a comma, the volume number in Arabic, any part number in Arabic, a colon, and the page in Arabic, e.g., OR, I, 52: 707–708); U.S. Navy Department, *Official Records of the Union and Confederate Navies in the War of the Rebellion,* 31 vols. (Washington, DC: Government Printing Office, 1894–1922), series I, vol. 25, 474 (cited hereafter as ORN, followed by a comma, the series number in Roman numerals, a comma, the volume number in Arabic, a colon, and the page in Arabic); Alan Aronson, "Strategic Supply of Civil War Armies," *General Histories of the American Civil War,* http://members.cox.net/rb2307/content/STRATEGIC_SUPPLY_OF_CIVIL_WAR_ARMIES.htm>, (accessed March 30, 2000); Lawrence M. Smith, "Rise and Fall of the Strategy of Exhaustion," *Army Logistician* (November-December 2004): 35; Hunter, 547–556; Benjamin W. Bacon, *Sinews of War: How Technology, Industry and Transportation Won the Civil War* (Novato, CA: Presidio Press, 1997), 75–97.

7. James G. Wiener et al., "Mississippi River," U.S. Geological Survey, Biological Resources Division home page, http://biology.usgs.gov/s+t/SNT/noframe/ms137.htm (accessed August 26, 2006); "Mississippi River," Wikipedia, http://en.wikipedia.org/wiki/Ohio_River (accessed August 25, 2006); Kane, 22–26; *The Navigator, Containing Directions for Navigating the Monongahela, Allegheny, Ohio and Mississippi Rivers,* 8th ed. (Pittsburgh: Cramer, Speark and Eichbau, 1814; Repr. University of Michigan Press, 1966), 149–152, 174; *Webster's Geographical Dictionary,* rev. ed. (Springfield, MA: G. & C. Merriam Co., 1966), 712; Alfred T. Mahan, *The Navy in the Civil War,* vol. 3, *The Gulf and Inland Waters* (New York: Scribner's, 1883), 9. Dickens is quoted at the head of Thomas E. Rice's "Managing the Mississippi," The Nature of Illinois home page, http://www.natureillinois.org/news/mississippi.html (accessed August 26, 2006).

8. Gibson, 56; OR, I, 52, 165. Scott (1786–1866) was a hero of both the War of 1812 and the Mexican War, while Totten (1788–1864) was Scott's chief engineer during the latter conflict. Scott retired from his post in November 1861, but Totten died in office. Boatner, 728, 843–844. J.S. Neal and his brother R.S. Neal, together with William Johnson, owned the Jefferson Foundry and Machine Works behind Vine Street in Madison. Brig. Gen. Totten described their operation as "a large building establishment" (INGenWeb, "Madison City Directory, 1859–1860," Madison and Jefferson County Directories, http://myindianahome.net/gen/jeff/records/direct/maddir.html [accessed September 30, 2006]); OR, I, 52, 1:165. Russell was far from impressed with the Mississippi during a mid–June 1861 steamboat passage from New Orleans to Cairo, calling it "assuredly the most uninteresting river in the world.... Not a particle of romance," he observed, "in spite of oratorical patriots and prophets, can ever shine from its depths, sacred to cat and buffalo fish, or vivify its turbid waters" (William H. Russell, *My Diary North and South* (Boston: T.O.H.P Burnham, 1863), 295).

9. *The Navigator,* 150, 195–197, 206, 222; Russell, 306–308. 330; Wiener et al., "Mississippi River"; Mahan, 10–11; OR, I, 52, 165; *Goodspeed's General History of Tennessee* (Chicago: Goodspeed Publishers, 1887; Repr., Nashville, C. and R. Elder, 1973), 797; Harold Fisk, *Geological Investigations of the Alluvial Valley of the Lower Mississippi River* (Washington, DC: U.S. Army Corps of Engineers, 1944), 27; Uriah Pierson James, *James' River Guide* (Cincinnati: U.P. James, 1866), 92–97; Marion Bragg, *Historic Names and Places on the Lower Mississippi River* (Vicksburg, MS: Mississippi River Commission, 1977), 1–267; S. Chamberlain, "Opening of the Upper Mississippi and the Siege of Vicksburg," *Magazine of Western History* 5 (March 1887): 619; Robert D. Whitesell, "Military and Naval Activities Between Cairo and Columbus," *The Register of the Kentucky Historical Society* 61 (April 1963): 111; David E. Roth, "The Civil War at the Confluence: Where the Ohio Meets the Mississippi," *Blue & Gray* 2 (July 1985): 6–8, 13–14, 16; Francis Vinton Greene, *The Mississippi,* Great

Campaigns of the Civil War (New York: C. Scribner's Sons, 1885), 8:7; Henry Walke, *Naval Scenes and Reminiscences of the Civil War in the United States on the Southern and Western Waters During the Years 1861, 1862 and 1863, with the History of That Period Compared and Corrected from Authentic Sources* (New York: F.R. Reed and Company, 1877), 27; Edward J. Huling, *Reminiscences of Gunboat Life in the Mississippi Squadron* (Saratoga Springs, NY: Sentinel Print, 1881), 11–27, 29; *New York Herald*, October 2, 1863; Mark Twain, *Life on the Mississippi* (Modern Classics; New York: Harper & Brothers, 1950), 215, 335–336; Steven E. Woodworth, *Nothing But Victory: The Army of the Tennessee, 1861–1865* (New York: Alfred A. Knopf, 2005), 30, 35; "Commerce Missouri," Wikipedia, http://en.wikipedia.org/wiki/Commerce,_Missouri (accessed August 29, 2006).

10. *The Navigator*, 195–197; James P. Henry, *Resources of the State of Arkansas, with Description of Counties, Railroads, Mines, and the City of Little Rock* (Little Rock: Price & McClure, 1872), 54; "White River," Wikipedia, http://en.wikipedia.org/wiki/White_River_%28Arkansas%29 (accessed September 2, 2006); Gibson, 617; *Chicago Daily Tribune*, January 20, 1863; *New York Herald*, January 21, 1863.

11. Henry, 54; *The Navigator*, 197; Hunter, 51; Grant Foreman, "River Navigation in the Early Southwest," *The Mississippi Valley Historical Review* 15 (June 1928): 39 ff; "Arkansas River," Wikipedia, http://en.wikipedia.org/wiki/Arkansas_River (accessed September 2, 2006); *Chicago Daily Tribune*, January 20, 1863.

12. *The Navigator*, 206; "Yazoo River," Wikipedia, http://en.wikipedia.org/wiki/Yazoo_River (accessed September 2, 2006).

13. "Red River," LoveToKnow 1911, http://www.1911encyclopedia.org/Red_River (accessed September 3, 2006); *The Navigator*, 222; "Red River (Mississippi Watershed)" Wikipedia, http://en.wikipedia.org/wiki/Red_River_%28Mississippi_watershed%29 (accessed September 3, 2006); Tucker, 300; Mahan, 194–195.

14. "Ohio River," in *Wikipedia: The Free Encyclopedia*, <http://en.wikipedia.org/wiki/Ohio_River>, (August 25, 2006); David M. Smith, "The Defense of Cincinnati— The Battle That Never Was: Past Presentations of the Cincinnati Civil War Roundtable, January 15, 1998," Cincinnati Civil War Roundtable Homepage, <http://www.cincinnaticwrt.org/data/ccwrt_history/talks_text/smith_defense_cin.html>, (September 4, 2006); ORN, I, 25: 610–61; OR, I, 52: 166. In an 1863 Ohio River survey undertaken for Rear Adm. David Dixon Porter, Lt. Cmdr. Le Roy Fitch offered some thoughts on certain Ohio River communities. In this manner, his wartime observations, albeit from a Yankee perspective, will serve to enlighten us much as those of Paymaster Huling did for the Lower Mississippi. Cairo, IL, Fitch observed, had a "population floating"; Caledonia, IL was a "small town"; Paducah, KY had "very few loyal citizens"; Caseyville, KY suffered from "guerrillas live in vicinity"; Uniontown, KY was "very disloyal"; Evansville, IN "requires watching"; and Owensboro, KY was "very disloyal and smuggles goods." Myron J. Smith, Jr., *Le Roy Fitch: The Civil War Career of a Union River Gunboat Commander* (Jefferson, NC: McFarland & Co., Inc., 2007), 87–88.

15. "Tennessee River," Wikipedia, http://en.wikipedia.org/wiki/Tennessee_River (accessed August 5, 2005); Ann Toplovich, "Tennessee River System," in Carroll Van West, ed., *The Tennessee Encyclopedia of History and Culture* (Nashville: Rutledge Hill Press for the Tennessee Historical Society, 1998), 943–945; Stanley J. Folmsbee, Robert E. Corlew, and Enoch L. Mitchell, *Tennessee: A Short History* (Knoxville: University of Tennessee Press, 1969), 12–13; Donald Davidson, *The Tennessee*, vol. 2, *The New River, Civil War to TVA* (New York: Rinehart & Co., 1948), 1–118; ORN, I, 24: 59–60; *Wisconsin State Journal*, May 12, 1862. In his 1863 Ohio River survey undertaken for Rear Adm. Porter, Lt. Cmdr. Fitch offered some thoughts on certain communities: Paducah, KY, "very few loyal citizens"; Callowaytown, KY, "two houses"; Paris Landing, TN, "one house and mill"; New Portland, TN, "three houses, Union"; Reynoldsburg, TN, "three families, rebel"; Fowler's Landing, TN, "very bad rebels"; Perryville and East Perryville, TN, "rebels"; Marvin's Bluffs, TN, "two houses, Union"; Brownsport, TN, "iron foundry, Union"; Cedar Creek, TN, "iron furnace"; Decatur, TN, "iron furnace, Union, yet rebel"; Carrollville, TN, "four houses, Union"; Clifton, TN, "rebels town burned February 1863"; Point Pleasant, TN, "three houses"; Cerro Gordo, TN, "deserted"; Coffee's Landing, TN, "hot secesh"; Savannah, TN, "mixed, Union and rebels"; Pittsburgh Landing, TN, "deserted"; Big Bend Landing, TN, "deserted and destroyed"; Chickasaw, AL, " eight families, four Union, rest doubtful; Waterloo, AL, "all rebels"; Tuscumbia, AL, "all rebels back"; Florence, AL, "rebels" (Smith, Ibid.).

16. "Cumberland River," Wikipedia, http://en.wikipedia.org/wiki/Cumberland_River, (accessed August 6, 2005); Ann Toplovich, "Cumberland River," in *The Tennessee Encyclopedia of History and Culture*, ed. Carroll Van West (Nashville: Rutledge Hill Press for the Tennessee Historical Society, 1998), 227–228; Stanley J. Folmsbee, Robert E. Corlew, and Enoch L. Mitchell, *Tennessee: A Short History* (Knoxville: University of Tennessee Press, 1969), 13–14; "Towns of the Cumberland," Save the Cumberland, http://www.savethecumberland.org/towns.htm (accessed July 21, 2005); Byrd Douglas, *Steamboatin' on the Cumberland* (Nashville: Tennessee Book Company, 1961), 28–31; ORN, I, 24: 58–59; ORN, I, 25: 160.

17. Hunter, 219–222, 225, 231, 233–236; OR, I, 52, 1: 158, 164; ORN, I, 23: 360; Twain, 83; *New York Times*, May 2, 1861. Totten's cousin Mansfield (1801–1880) was editor of the *Cincinnati Chronicle* for 13 years and once employed Harriet Beecher Stow. Dallas Bogan, "Edward Deering Mansfield was a True Jack-of-All-Trades," Warren County Ohio GenWeb Project, August 30, 2004, http://www.rootsweb.com/~ohwarren/Bogan/bogan235.htm (accessed October 1, 2006).

18. Our chronology of 1860–1861 is based on Richard B. Morris, *The Encyclopedia of American History*, rev. ed. (New York: Harper & Bros., 1961), 228–229, with additional details from Kenneth M. Stamp, *And the War Came: The North and the Secession Crisis, 1860–1861* (Baton Rouge: Louisiana State University Press, 1970), 63, 110, 123, 128–140, 215, 217; Stephen D. Engle, *Struggle for the Heartland: The Campaigns from Fort Henry to Corinth* (Lincoln: University of Nebraska Press, 2001), 2; Henry Clyde Hubbart, *The Older Middle West, 1840–1880: Its Social, Economic and Political Life, and Sectional Tendencies Before, During, and After the Civil War* (New York: Russell and Russell, 1936), 74–89, 155–157; E. Merton Coulter, "Effects of Secession Upon the Commerce of the Mississippi Valley," *Mississippi Valley Historical Review* 3 (December 1915): 276–278; David Herbert Donald, *Lincoln* (New York: Simon and Schuster, 1995), 284; *Cincinnati Daily Gazette*, December 11, 24, 1860; *Cincinnati Enquirer*, January 4, 10, 12, 22 and March 8, 1861.

19. Byrd Douglas, *Steamboatin' on the Cumberland* (Nashville: Tennessee Book Company, 1961), 112.

20. Hubbart, 155–158; *Cincinnati Enquirer*, February 3, 5, 13, 22, 24, 26, 1861; *St. Louis Daily Republican*, quoted in *Cincinnati Enquirer*, March 6, 1861.

21. Hubbart, 158–160; Stamp, 216; *Cincinnati Enquirer,* January 15, 22, 23 and March 3, 1861; *Cincinnati Daily Commercial,* January 25, 28, 1861; *Evansville Daily Journal,* January 14, 1861; *New Albany Ledger,* January 17, 1861; *Chicago Tribune,* January 22, 1861; *Memphis Evening Argus,* January 17, 1861; S. Chamberlain, "Opening of the Upper Mississippi and the Siege of Vicksburg," *Magazine of Western History* 4 (March 1887): 610; Charles Henry Ambler, *A History of Transportation in the Ohio Valley* (Glendale, CA: The Arthur H. Clark Company, 1932), 242; "First Shots of the War Between the States," *Vicksburg Sunday Post,* January 7, 1996; Gary Matthews, "First Shots of the ACW?" Civil War Navy Messageboard, http://history-sites.com/mb/cw/cwnavy/index.cgi?noframes;read=1005 (accessed August 4, 2006); Henry Lowe, "Reminiscences of Cincinnati in War Time," in *Historical Collections of Ohio,* 3 vols. (Cincinnati: C.J. Krikbiel & Co., 1888), I: 765.

22. *Indianapolis Daily Journal,* November 17, 1860; Morris, 230; Lowe, 1, 765; Chamberlain, 611; Milford M. Miller, "Evansville Steamboats During the Civil War," *Indiana Magazine of History* 37 (December 1941): 359. For the record, Virginia (April 17), Arkansas (May 6), Tennessee (May 7), and North Carolina (May 20) seceded, while Kentucky declared its neutrality (May 20) and Missouri was divided between the followers of Unionist general Nathaniel Lyon and Gov. Claiborne F. Jackson (Morris, 230–231).

23. Milford, 360–361; Coulter, 289–291; *Evansville Daily Journal,* April 22 and 30, May 7 and 10, 1861; *New York Times,* April 30, 1861; Julius A. Lemcke, *Reminiscences of an Indianian: From the Sassafras Log Behind the Barn in Posey County to Broader Fields* (Indianapolis: Hollenbeck Press, 1905), 148; T.K. Kionka, *Key Command: Ulysses S. Grant's District of Cairo* (Shades of Blue and Gray Series; Columbia: University of Missouri Press, 2006), 37. Two steamers, the *Grampus* and *Mohawk,* which belonged to a Capt. Chester, who also owned the *Alps,* were also taken over at Memphis around this time for conversion into gunboat-dispatch boats. Under her captain, Marsh Miller, the *Grampus,* "a towboat," would win a measure of notoriety in Rebel service, though Chicago reporter George P. Upton, writing as "GPU," would label her a "wretched concern" (*Chicago Daily Tribune,* March 19, 1862).

24. Ambler, 246–247; Coulter, 287–288, 292–293; *Louisville Courier,* April 18, 1861; *Cincinnati Daily Commercial,* April 19, 1861; Whitelaw Reid, *Ohio in the War: Her Statesmen, Her Generals, and Soldiers,* 2 vols. (Cincinnati: Moore, Wilstach & Baldwin, 1868), I: 37–38, 41–42.

25. Milford, 360–361; Coulter, 288–289.

26. Drew E. VandeCreek, "And the War Came, 1861–1862," Illinois During the Civil War, http://dig.lib.niu.edu/civilwar/narrative2.html (accessed August 30, 2006); Augustus H. Burley, *The Cairo Expedition: Illinois' First Response in the Late Civil War* (Chicago: Fergus Printing, 1892), 1–4; Richard Kellogg Swift, "Final Report of the Military Expedition from Chicago to Cairo, April 26, 1861," Illinois During the Civil War, http://www.illinoiscivilwar.org/orders2.html (accessed August 30, 2006); Kionka, 27–28, 38–41; Benson J. Lossing, *Pictorial Field Book of the Civil War: Journeys through the Battlefields in the Wake of Conflict,* 3 vols. (Hartford, CT: T. Belknap, 1874, repr. Johns Hopkins University Press, 1997), I: 472; Roth, 14, 17–18; Coulter, 292; Woodworth, 22–23; Alexander Davidson and Bernard Stuve, *A Complete History of Illinois from 1673 to 1873* (Springfield, IL: Illinois Journal Company, 1874), 731–732, 743; T. M. Eddy, *The Patriotism of Illinois: A Record of the Civil and Military History of the State in the War for the Union,* 2 vols. (Chicago: Clarke & Co., Publishers, 1865), I: 98–102; Robert P. Howard, *Illinois: A History of the Prairie State* (Grand Rapids: William B. Eerdmans Publishing Co., 1973), 122–123, 269, 299; Victor Hicken, *Illinois in the Civil War* (Urbana: University of Illinois Press, 1991), 12; Theodore Watson to John Watson, April 27, 1861, Theodore Watson Letters, the Newberry Library (Chicago); ORN, I, 22: 786; *Chicago Daily Tribune,* April 23, 25, 1861; *New York Times,* May 5, 1861; *Illinois Weekly State Journal,* May 1 and 5, 1861.

27. *Evansville Daily Journal,* April 25, May 1, 1861; *New Orleans Picayune,* April 30, 1861; *New York Times,* May 3, 5, 1861; *Chicago Daily Tribune,* May 15, 1861; *National Intelligencer,* May 7, 1861; Coulter, 292; Davidson and Stuve, 731–732, 743; Eddy, I: 98–102; Gustave Koerner, *Memoirs of Gustave Koerner: Written at the Suggestion of His Children,* ed. Thomas J. McCormick, 2 vols. (Grand Rapids, IA: The Torch Press, 1909), II: 129–130; "Correspondence of Governor Isham Green Harris, 1861," TNGenWeb Project: The Biographies of Our Ancestors, http://www.tngenweb.org/bios/h/18610429.html (accessed September 11, 2006). A few days later, Lincoln started a reply stating that he had no official information on the incident and reminding Harris of his recent "malicious and disrespectful" refusal to supply the U.S. with volunteer troops. The note was not sent, probably because, by about the time it could be mailed, the boat had been returned and Tennessee was out of the Union.

28. Coulter, 289–291, 299–300; Milford, 362; *Evansville Daily Journal,* May 10, 1861; Benjamin Franklin Cooling, *Forts Henry and Donelson: The Key to the Confederate Heartland* (Knoxville: University of Tennessee Press, 1987), 5; OR, I, 52, 1: 137, 140–141. The April 19 blockade proclamation can be found in Frank Moore, ed., *The Rebellion Record: A Diary of American Events,* 12 vols. (New York: G.P. Putnam, 1861–1866; repr., New York: Arno Press, 1977), I: 78. The rather extensive contraband list was published in the *Columbus (Ohio) Crisis* on May 16, 1861. Although maintaining such a prior stance, Governor Beriah Magoffin did not issue his state's official neutrality proclamation until May 20 (*Columbus Crisis,* May 23, 1861).

Chapter 2

1. Charles B. Boynton, *History of the Navy During the Rebellion,* 2 vols. (New York: D. Appleton and Company, 1867–1868), I: 500; S. Chamberlain, "Opening of the Upper Mississippi and the Siege of Vicksburg," *Magazine of Western History* 5 (March 1887), 612–613; Benjamin Franklin Cooling, *Forts Henry and Donelson: The Key to the Confederate Heartland* (Knoxville: University of Tennessee Press, 1987), 9; Arthur L. Conger, *The Rise of U.S. Grant* (New York: Century, 1931), 48. Seeking every advantage, the editors of the *New York Times* even advised its readers on May 2, 1861, that the Mississippi River was "one of the most dangerous agencies that may be employed against the welfare and wealth of the South" and urged them to note the damages to the insurrection that might be caused when the stream, in its annual flood, went over the banks at points below Cairo.

2. Charles Dana Gibson, with E. Kay Gibson, *Assault and Logistics: Union Army Coastal and River Operations, 1861–1866* (Camden, ME: Ensign Press, 1995), 2:54; Fletcher Pratt, *The Navy, a History: The Story of a Service in Action* (Garden City, NY: Garden City Publishing Co., 1941), 282; "Edward Bates, 1793–1869," *Bi-*

ographical Directory of the United States Congress, 1774-Present, http://bioguide.congress.gov/scripts/biodisplay.pl?index=B000231, (accessed October 1, 2006); John D. Milligan, *Gunboats Down the Mississippi* (Annapolis, MD: Naval Institute Press, 1965), 3; Richard Webber and John C. Roberts, "James B. Eads: Master Builder," *The Navy* 8 (March 1965): 23–25; Boynton, I: 498–500; James B. Eads, "Recollections of Foote and the Gunboats," in *Battles and Leaders of the Civil War,* ed. Robert V. Johnson and Clarence C. Buel, 4 vols. (New York: The Century Company, 1884–1887; repr. Thomas Yoseloff, 1956), I: 338 (cited hereafter as *B&L,* followed by a comma, the volume number in Arabic numerals, a colon, and the page numbers); U.S. Navy Department, Naval History Division, *Riverine Warfare* (Washington, DC: GPO, 1968), 21; U.S. Navy Department, *Official Records of the Union and Confederate Navies in the War of the Rebellion,* 31 vols. (Washington, DC: Government Printing Office, 1894–1922), series I, vol. 22, 278, 280 (cited hereafter as ORN, followed by a comma, the series number in Roman numerals, a comma, the volume number in Arabic, a colon, and the page in Arabic).

3. Boynton, I: 498–500. Lawrenceburg, IN, native Eads (1820–1887), whose mother was a cousin of ex-president James Buchanan, demonstrated an early mechanical aptitude. After the death of his father in 1833, the youth found his way to St. Louis, where he sold apples while barefoot in the street to sustain his mother and sisters. Gaining employment in a mercantile house, he was granted permission by its senior partner to employ the company library, from which he taught himself mechanics, machinery and civil engineering. He then gained a knowledge of the shipping business as a steamboat purser. In 1842, he devised a successful diving bell that was widely employed for cargo recovery from wrecked Mississippi River steamers. After selling his bell interest in 1845, he turned to another interest and established at St. Louis the first glassworks west of the Ohio River. The glassworks and he were financially ruined by the Mexican War. With his last $1,500 Eads bought his way back into the salvage business in 1847, improved his earlier innovations, and earned a second fortune. Ill health forced him to retire in 1857, though he remained interested in all things having to do with his beloved river. Following his work building ironclads during the Civil War, he constructed the steel Mississippi River arch bridge (1867–1874) and oversaw river jetty improvement projects at New Orleans. At the time of his death, he was planning a ship-railway across Mexico's Isthmus of Tehuantepec (Boynton, I: 499; "James Buchanan Eads," in *Appleton's Cyclopedia of American Biography,* ed. James Grant Wilson and John Fisk, 5 vols. (New York: D. Appleton Co., 1888), II: 287; "James Buchanan Eads," University of Illinois at Urbana-Champagne, http://www.riverweb.uiuc.edu/TECH/TECH20.htm (accessed September 18, 2006). Welles and Eads struck up a friendship which continued over the years. When the navy secretary left office in 1869, he contacted the engineer, then constructing his famous bridge, for advice on western railroad investments. See John Niven, *Gideon Welles: Lincoln's Secretary of the Navy* (New York: Oxford University Press, 1973), 569.

4. George B. McClellan, *The Civil War Papers of George B. McClellan: Selected Correspondence, 1860–1865,* ed. Stephen W. Sears (New York: Ticknor and Fields, 1989), 6–7; Ethan S. Rafuse, *McClellan's War: The Failure of Moderation in the Struggle for the Union* (Bloomington: Indiana University Press, 2005), 93. George Brinton McClellan (1826–1885) became a central military figure of the Civil War. Better known as an organizer than a field commander, his 1862 Peninsula campaign was a failure and he was relieved after failing to follow up after the Battle of Antietam. He was the Democratic presidential candidate in 1864 (Mark M. Boatner III, *The Civil War Dictionary* (New York: David McKay, 1959), 524).

5. Rafuse, *McClellan's War,* 94–99; Rafuse, "Impractical? Unforgivable?: Another Look at George B. McClellan's First Strategic Plan," *Ohio History* 110 (Summer-Autumn 2001), 153–164; Stephen W. Sears, *George B. McClellan: The Young Napoleon* (New York: Ticknor and Fields, 1988), 73–77. McClellan's plan was offered at a time when Kentucky was still neutral. On the other hand, it also favored overland marches rather than water transport via the Ohio or Mississippi (Rafuse, *McClellan's War,* 96).

6. Edward Townsend, *Anecdotes of the Civil War in the United States* (New York: D. Appleton, 1884), 47, 56; U.S. War Department, *The War of the Rebellion: A Compilation of the Official Records of the Union and Confederate Armies,* 128 vols. (Washington, DC: Government Printing Office, 1880–1901), series I, vol. 51, 369–370 (cited hereafter as OR, followed by a comma, the series number in Roman numerals, a comma, the volume number in Arabic, any part number in Arabic, a colon, and the page in Arabic); Timothy D. Johnson, *Winfield Scott: The Quest for Military Glory* (Lawrence: University Press of Kansas, 1998), 226–228; T. Harry Williams, *Lincoln and His Generals* (New York: Alfred A. Knopf, 1952; Repr. Vintage Books, 1962), 16; Bern Anderson, "The Naval Strategy of the Civil War," *Military Affairs* 26 (Spring 1962): 15; Anderson, *By Sea and By River,* 33–34; Ivan Musicant, *Divided Waters: The Naval History of the Civil War* (New York: HarperCollins, 1995), 180; Milligan, 3–4; Gideon Welles, *The Diary of Gideon Welles, Secretary of the Navy Under Lincoln and Johnson,* ed. John T. Morse, Jr., 3 vols. (Boston: Houghton, Mifflin and Company, 1911), I: 242; *St. Louis Daily Democrat,* May 10, 1861. A recent review of the Anaconda and later Union plans is Brian Holden Reid's "Rationality and Irrationality in Union Strategy, April 1861-March 1862," *War in History* 1 (March 1994): 25–29. A totally revisionist new review states bluntly that "there is no evidence that Scott ever offered a plan for a huge, slowly constricting cordon to Lincoln." Geoffrey Perret, "Anaconda: The Plan That Never Was," *North and South* 6 (May 2003): 36.

7. *New York Times,* May 11, 1861.

8. Pratt, 282; Charles Henry Ambler, *A History of Transportation in the Ohio Valley* (Glendale, CA: The Arthur H. Clark Company, 1932), 248; James Monaghan, *Civil War on the Western Border, 1854–1865* (Boston: Little, Brown & Co., 1955), 130–132; John W. Allen, *Legends and Lore of Southern Illinois* (Carbondale, IL: University Graphics, 1978), 288–289; T.K. Kionka, *Key Command: Ulysses S. Grant's District of Cairo* (Shades of Blue and Gray Series; Columbia: University of Missouri Press, 2006), 49; *Chicago Daily Tribune,* May 21, 1861; U.S. Navy Department, Naval History Division, *Civil War Naval Chronology, 1861–1865* (Washington, DC: Government Printing Office, 1966), 12–13; Chamberlain, 611; Milford M. Miller, "Evansville Steamboats During the Civil War," *Indiana Magazine of History* 37 (December 1941): 363; *Cincinnati Daily Commercial,* May 8, 1861; *New York Evening Post,* May 11, 1861; *Evansville Daily Journal,* May 14, 1861; Niven, 378.

9. OR, I, 53: 490–491; ORN, I, 22, 277–279; Gibson, 160; Milligan, 5; Paul W. Gates, *The Illinois Central Rail-*

road and Its Colonization Work (Cambridge, MA: Harvard University Press, 1934), 275; Rafuse, *McClellan's War*, 100; McClellan, *The Civil War Papers of George B. McClellan*, 37; Dave Dawley, "William J. Kountz," *Steamboat,* http://members.tripod.com/~Write4801/captains/k.html (accessed September 15, 2006); Theodore R. Parker, "William J. Kountz, Superintendent of River Transportation Under McClellan, 1861–62," *Western Pennsylvania Historical Magazine* 21 (December 1938): 237–238.

10. Boynton, I: 499; ORN, I, 22: 280; Milligan, 5; Robert E. Johnson, *Rear Admiral John Rodgers, 1812–1882* (Annapolis, MD: Naval Institute Press, 1967), 156–157; Milligan, 5.

11. William B. Cogar, *Dictionary of Admirals of the U.S. Navy*, 2 vols. (Annapolis, MD: Naval Institute Press, 1989), I: 146, 150; Johnson, *Rear Admiral John Rodgers, 1812–1882*, 156–157; Musicant, *Divided Waters*, 181; ORN, I, 22, 319–320. In addition to coverage in the pre–Civil War chapters of Johnson's biography, edited records of the exploring expedition were published by Allan B. Cole in his *Yankee Surveyors in the Shoguns Sea: Records of the United States Expedition to the North Pacific Ocean, 1853–1856* (Princeton, NJ: Princeton University Press, 1947). The Rodgers family papers are in the Library of Congress.

12. Johnson, *Rear Admiral John Rodgers, 1812–1882*, 157; *Chicago Daily Tribune*, May 21, 1861; Milligan, 5–6; McClellan, *The Civil War Papers of George B. McClellan*, 22; ORN, I, 22: 281; Louis C. Hunter, *Steamboats on the Western Rivers: An Economic and Technological History* (Cambridge, MA: Harvard University Press, 1949), 485; Robert C. Suhr, "Converted River Steamers Dubbed 'Timberclads' Gave the Union Navy an Important Presence on Southern Wates," *America's Civil War* 11 (July 1998): 20. The sailor's route from Cincinnati to St. Louis is shown in a map in John F. Stover's *History of the Baltimore and Ohio Railroad* (West Lafayette, IN: Purdue University Press, 1987), 82.

13. ORN, I, 22: 278–279; William H. Roberts, *Civil War Ironclads: The U.S. Navy and Industrial Mobilization* (Baltimore, MD: The Johns Hopkins University Press, 2002), 121; *Chicago Daily Tribune*, May 19, 24, 1861; William H. Russell, *My Diary North and South* (Boston: T.O.H.P Burnham, 1863), 331; Donald L. Canney, *The Old Steam Navy*, vol. 2, *The Ironclads, 1842–1885* (Annapolis, MD: Naval Institute Press, 1993), 41; James B. Eads to Gideon Welles, May 8, 1861, Gideon Welles Papers, Library of Congress. The Stevens concept lingered on into 1862 even as the navy sought to kill it. Further south, the Confederates had a floating battery at Charleston and several under powered or un-engined ironclads; the *Georgia* at Savannah and the *Louisiana* at New Orleans served the purpose. A purpose-built floating battery, the *New Orleans*, would be towed to Columbus, KY, in December 1861. It would later form part of the defense of Island No. 10 and be scuttled there to avoid capture in April 1862 (Robert C. Suhr, "Military Technology: The Confederate Floating Battery Revival During the American Civil War," TheHistoryNet, http://www.historynet.com/wars_conflicts/military_technology/3035991.html?featured=y&c=y [accessed October 1, 2006]).

14. Pratt, 282 ; Boynton, 500–501; ORN, I, 22: 279; Milligan, 5; Canney, 41; Edwin C. Bearss, *Hardluck Ironclad: The Sinking and Salvage of the Cairo* (Baton Rouge: Louisiana State University Press, 1966), 13; Robert J. Rombauer, *The Union Cause in St. Louis in 1862* (St. Louis, MO: Press of Nixon-Jones Printing Co., 1909),

222. In August, the government purchased the *Submarine No. 7* and Eads, who sold it at a price much reduced from that quoted to Cmdr. Rodgers, converted her into the powerful flotilla flagship U.S.S. *Benton*. Costing about one and a half times that of a Pook turtle, the underpowered vessel usually had to be towed into action. In a blot on his otherwise brilliant and patriotic record (conveniently forgotten), Eads, as a part owner of the Missouri Wrecking Company, was later accused of conflict of interest in the *Benton* conversion matter, while Rodgers' original evaluation of the snag boat was shown to be accurate (Canney, 44; Johnson, *Rear Admiral John Rodgers, 1812–1882*, 166).

15. Ron Powers, *Mark Twain: A Life* (New York: Free Press, 2005), 76–77; ORN, I, 22: 281; *Chicago Daily Tribune*, May 23, 1861; Russell, 348; Henry Lowe, "Reminiscences of Cincinnati in War Time," in *Historical Collections of Ohio*, 3 vols. (Cincinnati: C.J. Krikbiel & Co., 1888), I: 770. While in the Queen City, Cmdr. Rodgers, like other notable visitors, stayed at the Burnett House, the Midwest's largest and most elegant hotel. Bostonian Samuel Moore Pook (1804–1878) had been a naval constructor since 1841 and had built, among others, "sloops-of-war *Preble* and *Saratoga*, the frigates *Congress* and *Franklin*, and the steamers *Merrimack* and *Princeton* ("Samuel Moore Pook," in Wilson and Fisk, *Appleton's Cyclopedia of American Biography,* 5: 64).

16. OR, I, 51, 1:157–160, 164–168; David D. Porter, *Naval History of the Civil War* (New York: Sherman Publishing Company, 1886; Repr., Secaucus, N.J.: Castle Books, 1984), 268; Hunter, 548; John D. Milligan, "From Theory to Application: The Emergence of the American Ironclad War Vessel," *Military Affairs* 48 (July 1984): 126; Ambler, *A History of Transportation*, 245–246; *St. Louis Daily Democrat*, June 5, 1861. Well-known naval architect John Lenthall (1807–1882) was chief of his bureau from 1853 to1871. During this time, he compiled a large collection of ship plans. In 1991, the Library of the Philadelphia Maritime Museum released the 52-page booklet *John Lenthall, Naval Architect: A Guide to Plans and Drawings of American Naval and Merchant Vessels, 1790–1874, with a Bibliography of Works on Shipbuilding ... Collected by John Lenthall (b. 1807–d.1882)*.

17. Jay Slagle, *Ironclad Captain: Seth Ledyard Phelps and the U.S. Navy* (Kent, OH: Kent State University Press, 1996), 115; *Biographical Directory of the United States Congress, 1774-Present*, "James Kennedy Moorhead," http://bioguide.congress.gov/scripts/biodisplay.pl?index=M000929 (accessed October 1, 2006); *Biographical Directory of the United States Congress, 1774-Present*, "Cyrus Aldrich," http://bioguide.congress.gov/scripts/biodisplay.pl?index=A000081 (accessed October 12, 2006); ORN, I, 22: 281–282, 286; Parker, 238–239; Suhr, "Converted River Steamers," 20. One wonders how much time Maj. Gen. McClellan actually had at the end of May to even think about riverboats. Although he may have considered them earlier in connection with the Anaconda Plan, within a week of becoming Department of the Ohio CO on May 13, "Little Mac" had his hands filled with a Rebel thrust into Virginia north of the Kanawha River that might have been aimed at western Pennsylvania (Rafuse, *McClellan's War*, 101). Cdr. Kountz continued to oversee waterborne transport for Maj. Gen. McClellan from his own headquarters at Marietta, OH. On June 13, "the experienced Western river navigator" led an unescorted convoy of ten U.S. chartered light draught steamers from Pittsburgh to Bellair, where they embarked 2,000 troops for a "secret" destination thought to be up the Kanawha River (*New York*

Times, June 23, 1861). Following McClellan's departure for Washington, DC, Kountz was posted west. On November 16, he was commissioned an assistant quartermaster of volunteers with the rank of Capt. and sent to St. Louis; in mid–December, he was sent down to Cairo to "examine into All River Transportation," its efficiency and expense by the U.S. government groups reviewing the supposed malfeasance of Maj. Gen. Frémont. He would later serve as Brig. Gen. Robert Allen's St. Louis river transportation deputy (Parker, 250–254; Ulysses S. Grant, *The Papers of Ulysses S. Grant, October 1, 1861–January 7, 1862*, ed. John Y. Simon, 24 vols. (Edwardsville: Southern Illinois University Press, 1967), 3:321–322; OR, I, 2: 197, 213).

18. Johnson, *Rear Admiral John Rodgers, 1812–1882*, 157; ORN, I, 22: 318; Mark Twain, *Life on the Mississippi* (New York: Harper & Brothers, 1950), 33–34; George Ward Nichols, "Down the Mississippi," *Harper's New Monthly Magazine* 41 (November 1870): 839; "Alex," "Our Western Letter," *Philadelphia Inquirer*, August 30, 1861; E.J. Huling, *Reminiscences of Gunboat Life in the Mississippi Squadron* (Saratoga Springs, NY: Sentinel Print, 1881), 31–32; Adam Kane, *The Western River Steamboat* (College Station: Texas A & M University Press, 2004), 91–93; Hunter, 160; Paul H. Silverstone, *Warships of the Civil War Navies* (Annapolis, MD: Naval Institute Press, 1989), 151, 155; William C. Lytle, comp., *Merchant Steam Vessels of the United States, 1807–1868*, "The Lytle List," publication no. 6 (Mystic, CT: The Steamship Historical Society of America, 1952), 180; Carl D. Lane, *American Paddle Steamboats* (New York: Coward-McCann, 1943), 33. Interestingly, "Alex" claimed in his newspaper piece to have sought the derivation of his host vessel's name, *Sucker State*. No one knew for certain, but most believed it referred to Illinois and her fiscal condition, allegedly formed by the many wildcat bankers who had moved there.

19. Kane, 67–80; Slagle, 118; Hunter, 133–142; Silverstone, 172–173; Huling, 29; Fred Brown, "*Sultana* Burning," *Appalachian Life*, no. 41 (March 2000), 3–4, 8; Canney, 36; "Alex," "Our Western Letter," *Philadelphia Inquirer*, August 30, 1861; William H. King, *Lessons and Practical Notes on Steam*, revised by James W. King (New York: D. Van Nostrand, 1864), 159–170; John D. Milligan, ed., *From the Fresh Water Navy, 1861–1864: The Letters of Acting Master's Mate Henry R. Browne and Acting Ensign Symmes E. Brown*, Naval Letters Series (Annapolis, MD: Naval Institute Press, 1970), 3:111. Coal was the preferred fuel of the Union gunboats, though the timberclads and later the tinclads could use wood if necessary. Brig. Gen. Totten pointed out in his memorandum to Lt. Gen. Scott that "Pittsburgh coal is the best. Pomeroy coal nearly if not quite as good (Pomeroy is half way between Pittsburgh and Cincinnati)." He also noted that there were about 200 coal barges available on the Ohio River, each able to carry an average load of 10,000 bushels. The naval base at Cairo did not have a significant coal depot and the "nearest considerable coal supply above Cairo," was at Caseyville, about 120 miles up the Ohio River (OR, I, 52, 1: 164).

20. Kane, 81–82; Hunter, 72, 167–172, 219; Huling, 30–31; ORN, I, 25: 681; Gary Matthews, "'Tinclad'— In Response to: Re: Tinclad (Terry Foenander),'" Civil War Navies Message Board, http://history-sites.com/mb/cw/cwnavy/index.cgi?noframes;read=1314 (accessed December 7, 2005).

21. OR, I, 52, 1: 157, 164; Canney, 37; Milligan, 6; Parker, 250–254; *Rear Admiral John Rodgers, 1812–1882*, 157; Musicant, 182; William H. Roberts, *Civil War Ironclads*, 51–52; ORN, I, 22: 283, 319; Suhr, "Converted River Steamers," 20; Milligan, ed., *From the Fresh Water Navy, 1861–1864*, 110; Steven R. Davis, "Workhorse of the Western Waters: The Timberclad *Tyler*," *Civil War Times Illustrated* 44 (February 2005): 34–36. There were no formal plans drawn up for the conversion of the three boats. The *A.O. Tyler* was, indeed, the same vessel that had been fired upon by Vicksburg batteries back in January. The penalty clause approach set a precedent followed later in the building of the City Series ironclads. Donald Canney states, and I am inclined to agree with him, that there was, briefly, a fourth timberclad. The ferryboat *New Era*, purchased by Maj. Gen. John C. Frémont, became, Canney notes, "a timberclad by the simple expedient of constructing wooden bulwarks high on the perimeter of the cargo deck." After one cruise, the boat, armed with three 9-inch Dahlgren smoothbores, would be taken in hand and converted into the ironclad U.S.S. *Essex*. Canney, 38; Dana Wegner, "S.X.: The Federal Gunboat *Essex*," *Nautical Research Journal* 19 (Spring 1972): 49–51.

22. ORN, II, 1: 65; Suhr, "Converted River Steamers," 20–21; Lytle, 39; Charles Dana Gibson, with E. Kay Gibson. *Assault and Logistics: Dictionary of Transports and Combat Vessels Steam and Sail Employed by the Union Army, 1861–1868* (Camden, ME: Ensign Press, 1995), 1:69; Silverstone, 158. Slagle (118) indicates that Conestoga possessed only one engine.

23. ORN, II, 1: 126–127; Suhr, "Converted River Steamers," 20–21; Lytle, 112; Gibson, 199; Silverstone, 158.

24. ORN, I, 22: 282; ORN, II, 1: 227–228; Suhr, "Converted River Steamers," 20–21; Lytle, 1; Gibson, *Transports and Combat Vessels*, 4; Silverstone, *Warships*, 159–160; Milligan, ed., *From the Fresh Water Navy, 1861–1864*, 110; Davis, "Workhorse," 34–36. Per Rodgers' plan, a combined total of 131 men would crew *Conestoga* and *Lexington*. When the *Tyler* returned to Cairo for repairs at the end of July 1862, it was revealed that she would require an entirely new crew of 115 sailors (ORN, I, 23: 270).

25. ORN, I, 22: 283–286; Bern Anderson, *By Sea and By River: The Naval History of the Civil War* (New York: Knopf, 1962), 42–86; Milligan, 7. Charles Henry Ambler wrongly asserts that Rodgers "was authorized by Secretary of War Stanton to purchase three strong towboats and to convert them into war vessels, without iron plating." Stanton was not yet war secretary and Rodgers did not receive Cabinet-level authority (Ambler, 248). Rodgers' efforts to have the *A.O. Tyler* renamed *Taylor* fizzled for the most part. True, a few die-hard Unionists, namely Cmdr. Henry Walke, and a number of newspapers did use the new designation, but the boat's name, albeit shortened to just *Tyler*, remained the same throughout the war (Johnson, *Rear Admiral John Rodgers, 1812–1882*, 158).

26. Bearss, 15; ORN, I, 22: 285–286. On May 24 the Confederate marshal at New Orleans seized all ships from Northern states which had arrived after May 6; two days later, the U.S.S. *Brooklyn* arrived to set up the Union blockade of New Orleans and the mouth of the Mississippi River. By June 10, batteries had been erected on the Mississippi north of Memphis and a complete blockade against upriver traffic was in place. No steamers were allowed to pass without a permit from the local "blockade committee." The Confederacy knew that it did not need to control the entire river; holding it at one or more key locations would prevent Northern commerce from reaching the Gulf of Mexico (U.S. Navy De-

partment, Naval History Division, *Civil War Naval Chronology, 1861–1865*, 6 vols., rev. ed.; Washington, DC: Government Printing Office, 1966), 1: 15; Musicant, 179; *Cincinnati Daily Gazette*, June 10, 24, 1861).

27. *New York Times*, April 29, June 2, 12–13, 1861; *National Intelligencer*, June 13, 1861; *Evansville Daily Journal*, June 8, 12, 1861; *Philadelphia Inquirer*, June 29, 1861; *Cairo City Weekly Gazette*, May 16, 30, 1861; Russell, 335–337; Miller, 364; Milligan, 7–8; George W. Driggs, *Opening the Mississippi, Or Two Years Campaigning in the Southwest* (Madison, WI: William J. Park Co., 1864), 64–65; Charles Wright Wills, *Army Life of an Illinois Soldier*, comp. Mary E. Kellogg (Washington, DC: Globe Printing Co., 1906), 17; Johnson, *Rear Admiral John Rodgers, 1812–1882*, 158–159; ORN, I, 22: 287, 291, 354, 367; Slagle, 120; *Cincinnati Commercial*, June 25, 1861. Of the three civilian boat captains, only Duble was retained as a gunboatman, becoming the *Conestoga's* first master and briefly, after the White River disaster in June 1862, acting commander of the ironclad U.S.S. *Mound City*.

28. ORN, I, 22: 319; Slagle, 116; Musicant, *Divided Waters*, 179. McClellan's order of authority is found in the collection of papers assembled by the Naval Historical Society, McClellan to Rodgers, June 26, 1861, John Rodgers Collection, Manuscript Division, Library of Congress (hereafter cited as JRC).

Chapter 3

1. William H. Russell, *My Diary North and South* (Boston: T.O.H.P Burnham, 1863), 334; Charles Wright Wills, *Army Life of an Illinois Soldier*, compiled by Mary E. Kellogg (Washington, DC: Globe Printing Co., 1906), 20; Jay Slagle, *Ironclad Captain: Seth Ledyard Phelps and the U.S. Navy* (Kent, OH: Kent State University Press, 1996), 116–117; John D. Milligan, *Gunboats Down the Mississippi* (Annapolis, MD: Naval Institute Press, 1965), 8; *Cincinnati Daily Commercial*, June 25, 1861; *St. Louis Daily Republican*, June 28, 1861; *New York Times*, July 3, 1861; U.S. War Department, *The War of the Rebellion: A Compilation of the Official Records of the Union and Confederate Armies*, 128 vols. (Washington, DC: Government Printing Office, 1880–1901), series I, vol. 52, part 1, 164 (cited hereafter as OR, followed by a comma, the series number in Roman numerals, a comma, the volume number in Arabic, any part number in Arabic, a colon, and the page in Arabic);. U.S. Navy Department, *Official Records of the Union and Confederate Navies in the War of the Rebellion*, 31 vols. (Washington, DC: GPO, 1894–1922), series I, vol. 22, 319, 791–792 (cited hereafter as ORN, followed by a comma, the series number in Roman numerals, a comma, the volume number in Arabic, a colon, and the page in Arabic); Robert E. Johnson, *Rear Admiral John Rodgers, 1812–1882* (Annapolis, MD: Naval Institute Press, 1967), 159. Neither the *McRae* nor *Jackson* survived a year in service (U.S. Navy Department, Naval History Division, *Civil War Naval Chronology, 1861–1865*, 6 vols., rev. ed. (Washington, DC: GPO, 1966), I: 253–254, 269; R. Thomas Campbell, *Confederate Naval Forces on Western Waters* (Jefferson, NC: McFarland & Co., 2005), 15–16; J. Thomas Scharf, *History of the Confederate Navy from Its Organization to the Surrender of Its Last Vessel* (New York: Rodgers and Sherwood, 1887, Repr., New York: Fairfax Press, 1977), 242–244, 263. Scharf reports that the *McRae*, along with the *General Polk* and the *Ivy*, also joined the *Jackson* near Columbus. Information on the armor plating aboard the *Jackson* comes from a *St. Louis Daily Democrat* story of September 5, 1861, published several days later.

2. Slagle, 8–395; "Sketches of the Officers of the Fort Donelson Fleet," *Philadelphia Inquirer*, February 18, 1862; William B. Cogar, *Dictionary of Admirals of the U.S. Navy*, 2 vols. (Annapolis, MD: Naval Institute Press, 1989), I, 179; Edward W. Callahan, *List of Officers of the Navy of the United States and of the Marine Corps, from 1775 to 1900, Comprising a Complete Register of All Present and Former Commissioned, Warranted, and Appointed Officers of the United States Navy, and of the Marine Corps, Regular and Volunteer (Compiled from the Official Records of the Navy Department)* (New York: L.R. Hamersly & Co., 1901; Repr., New York: Haskell House, 1969), 58, 519; Lewis R. Hamersly, *The Records of Living Officers of the U.S. Navy and Marine Corps, Compiled from Official Sources*, rev. ed. (Philadelphia: J.B. Lippincott, 1870), 90. Bishop's legal case, *Bishop v. U.S., 197 U.S. 334 (1905)*, was decided on April 3, 1905, and is printed on the Internet's *Find Law* site, <http://caselaw.lp.findlaw.com/scripts/getcase.pl?nav by=case&court=us&vol=197&invol=334> (accessed October 1, 2006), while his Lt. appointment is noted in the July 26, 1861, issue of the U.S. Senate's *Executive Journal, American Memory*, <http://memory.loc.gov/cgi-bin/query/r?ammem/hlaw:@field(DOCID+@lit(ej011131))> (accessed October 1, 2006).

3. Slagle, 117–119; ORN, I, 22: 291–292; Edwin C. Bearss, *Hardluck Ironclad: The Sinking and Salvage of the Cairo* (Baton Rouge: Louisiana State University Press, 1966), 16–17; *Philadelphia Inquirer*, June 29, 1861; Rodgers to Phelps, June 29, July 2, July 5, 1861, *Seth Ledyard Phelps Papers*, Missouri Historical Society, St. Louis (hereafter cited as SLPC); Phelps to Rodgers, June 30, 1861; John Rodgers Papers, Manuscript Division, Library of Congress (hereafter cited as JRC). Lockhart's first name is unknown, but we believe it may have been William. A number of sources cover the construction story of the Eads gunboats; indeed, it is what first drew me to an interest in the river war. My take was published as *U.S.S. Carondelet, 1861–1865* (Manhattan, KA: MA/AH Publishing, 1982).

4. ORN, I, 22: 289, 298, 319; Slagle, 121; Johnson, *Rear Admiral John Rodgers, 1812–1882*, 159–162; Louis C. Hunter, *Steamboats on the Western Rivers: An Economic and Technological History* (Cambridge, MA: Harvard University Press, 1949), 470; Mark Twain, *Life on the Mississippi* (New York: Harper & Brothers, 1950), 127–142. Phelps did not believe all of the pilots were attempting to use the low water as a way to extort high fees from the government for their expertise in getting down. John Sebastian, another *Lexington* pilot, "ranks high as a pilot and is quite as honest as anyone among them." His brother, Benjamin, would be the *Conestoga's* third master (ORN, I, 22: 550–551).

5. ORN, I, 22: 290–293; Gershom Bradford, *The Mariner's Dictionary* (New York: Weathervane Books, 1970), 42; Slagle, 121.

6. OR, I, 3: 390, 406; Johnson, *Rear Admiral John Rodgers, 1812–1882*, 165; Bearss, 17; Milligan, 15–16; Ethan S. Rafuse, *McClellan's War: The Failure of Moderation in the Struggle for the Union* (Bloomington: Indiana University Press, 2005), 116–117; William E. Smith, *The Francis Preston Blair Family in Politics*, 2 vols. (New York: Macmillan, 1933), II: 52; Allen Nevins, *Frémont: Pathmarker of the West* (New York: D. Appleton-Century Company, 1939), 473–477; Tom Chaffin, *Pathfinder: John Charles Frémont and the Course of American Empire* (New York: Hill & Wang, 2002), 461; John C. Frémont, "In Command in Missouri," in *Battles and Leaders of the Civil War*, ed.

Robert V. Johnson and Clarence C. Buel, 4 vols. (New York: The Century Company, 1884–1887, Repr. Thomas Yoseloff, 1956), I: 283–284. Fox and Meigs, according to Frémont, left the question of what additional craft, ironclads, mortar craft, or whatever to acquire to him because he was "in charge of military operations on the Mississippi."

7. ORN, I, 22: 290, 292–293, 319, 550–551; Johnson, *Rear Admiral John Rodgers, 1812–1882*, 163; Milligan, 8–9; Phelps to Rodgers, July 13, July 15 1861; John Rodgers Collection, Manuscript Division, Library of Congress (hereafter cited as JRC); Seth Ledyard Phelps to John Rodgers, July 24, 1861, SLPC; Phelps to Colonel Cook, August 13, 1863, SLPC; Milligan, 9; *Chicago Daily Tribune,* August 22, 1861; David A. Pfeiffer, "Bridging the Mississippi: The Railroads and Steamboats Clash at the Rock Island Bridge," *Prologue* 36 (Summer 2004), 40–47. Though relaxed somewhat in the west where the manpower need was great, the standard process of enlistment and joining ship is described by Dennis J. Ringle in his *Life in Mr. Lincoln's Navy* (Annapolis, MD: U.S. Naval Institute Press, 1998), 26–27; Michael J. Bennett examines how men came into the gunboat service in *Union Jacks: Yankee Sailors in the Civil War* (Chapel Hill: University of North Carolina Press, 2004), 79–82. Jacob Hurd and Edward Shaw both rose to the rank of Acting Volunteer Lieutenant. The latter, after becoming commander of the tinclad *Juliet,* resigned on August 4, 1863, while the former, skipper of the light draughts *St. Clair,* and *Covington,* quit on April 13, 1864 (Callahan, 286, 492).

8. ORN, I, 22: 290; Slagle, 118, 121; Jacob D. Cox, *Military Reminiscences of the Civil War,* 2 vols. (New York: Scribner's, 1900), I, 10.

Hoosier Lovel Rousseau (1818–1869) enjoyed an active Civil War career, becoming a Maj. Gen. of volunteers; he remained a Brig. Gen. in the army after the war and accepted Alaska from the Russians in 1867 (Mark M. Boatner III, *The Civil War Dictionary* (New York: David McKay, 1959), 710–711). On July 25, Cmdr. Rodgers was able to obtain eight boxes of muskets from Camp Dennison. He immediately put Master Bishop in charge of their distribution. Three boxes were to be retained at the local rendezvous while five boxes were sent to Lt. Phelps' next port, New Albany, via Mitchell, IN, on the Ohio and Mississippi Railroad and the New Albany and Salem Railroad (ORN, I, 22: 294).

9. ORN, I, 22: 291; Slagle, 121–122; Phelps to Rodgers, July 13, 1861, JRC.

10. ORN, I, 22: 295; Nevins, 492; Charles B. Boynton, *History of the Navy During the Rebellion,* 2 vols. (New York: D. Appleton and Company, 1867–1868), I: 503.

11. ORN, II, 1: 65, 127, 227; ORN, I, 22: 296, 302, 319; OR, III, 2: 816–817; Eugene B. Canfield, *Civil War Naval Ordnance* (Washington, DC: Naval History Division, U.S. Navy Department, 1969), 5, 20–21; Chaffin, 463; Jay Carlton Mullen, "The Turning of Columbus," *The Register of the Kentucky Historical Society* 64 (July 1966): 211, 214; Scharf, 242; Boynton, 501; Phelps to Hon. George A. Bicknell, August 6, 1861, SLPC; *Cincinnati Daily Commercial,* August 7, 1861; William C. Lytle, comp., *Merchant Steam Vessels of the United States, 1807–1868, "The Lytle List,"* publication no. 6 (Mystic, CT: The Steamship Historical Society of America, 1952), 155. Information on the transfer of the gunboats from Portland to New Albany is found in the "From Louisville" column published in the *Philadelphia Inquirer,* July 31, 1861; the edition next day noted the arrival of the 30 additional crewmen. Our story of the Confederate arrival at New Madrid comes from the *Memphis Avalanche,* July 28, 1861. Reports on Frémont's fleet at Cairo and the seizure of the *B.F. Cheney* comes from the *Cincinnati Daily Gazette,* August 5, 1861; *St. Louis Daily Democrat,* August 5, 1861; Benson J. Lossing, *Pictorial Field Book of the Civil War: Journeys through the Battlefields in the Wake of Conflict,* 3 vols. (Hartford, CT: T. Belknap, 1874, Repr. Johns Hopkins University Press, 1997), II: 60–61, and Dave Dawley, "Barton Able," *Steamboat,* <http://members.tripod.com/~Write4801/captains/a.html> (accessed September 15, 2006).

12. Bearss, 18–20; Slagle, 122; Boynton, I: 501–503; Johnson, *Rear Admiral John Rodgers, 1812–1882,* 161–163; *Louisville Daily Journal,* August 8, 1861; *Evansville Daily Journal,* August 9, 1861; ORN, I, 22: 297–298. Interestingly, the Blairs and Meigs would become major opponents of Maj. Gen. Frémont, though for reasons having nothing to do with the navy man, shortly after the Rodgers recall request was sent. Johnson, *Rear Admiral John Rodgers, 1812–1882,* 165–166; Nevins, *Frémont,* 512–514. Robert Johnson also quotes an undated note from Frémont to Blair that is far less diplomatic. "I don't like Commander Rodgers who is in charge of the Gun boat operations," he complained. "Will you ask to have him removed and some younger officer put in his place" (Johnson, *Rear Admiral John Rodgers, 1812–1882,* 391).

13. ORN, I, 22: 298–299, 305, 307; Milligan, 10–11; *Evansville Daily Journal,* August 12, 1861; *Cincinnati Daily Gazette,* August 14, 1861; Robert C. Suhr, "Converted River Steamers Dubbed 'Timberclads' Gave the Union Navy an Important Presence on Southern Waters," *America's Civil War* 11 (July 1998): 21; Slagle, 122–123. For details that led to the Wilson's Creek disaster, as well as those about the incident itself, see Albert Castel's *General Sterling Price and the Civil War in the West* (Baton Rouge: Louisiana State University Press, 1968), 25–47, William Riley Brooksher, *Bloody Hill: The Civil War Battle of Wilson's Creek* (Washington, DC: Brassey's, Inc., 1995), and William Garret Piston and Richard W. Hatcher III, *Wilson's Creek: The Second Battle of the Civil War and the Men Who Fought It* (Chapel Hill: University of North Carolina Press, 2000). "The Confederate victory at Bull Run," wrote Jay Carlton Mullen in 1966, "put Southern thought in an offensive tenor" (Mullen, "The Turning of Columbus," *Register of the Kentucky Historical Society* 64 (July 1966): 214). Oglesby (1824–1899) was no stranger to unusual looking innovations, though his were human in the form of politicians. A Mexican War veteran and Illinois Republican legislator successfully introduced the rail-splitter image into Abraham Lincoln's 1860 presidential campaign. Promoted to Maj. Gen. after the Battle of Corinth in which he was wounded, Oglesby later served as Illinois governor and U.S. Senator Mark A. Plummer, *Lincoln's Rail-Splitter: Governor Richard J. Oglesby* (Champaign: University of Illinois Press, 2001), 1–272).

14. Slagle, 122–123; *St. Louis Daily Missouri Democrat,* August 16, 1861; ORN, I, 22: 299; Phelps to Col. John Cook, August 13, 1861, SLPC.

15. ORN, I, 22: 299–300, 777–778; *Cincinnati Daily Commercial,* August 19, 1861; *Memphis Appeal,* August 24, 1861; *Memphis Avalanche,* August 16, 1861; *Chicago Daily Tribune,* August 22, 1861; *New York Times,* October 19–20, 1861; Lytle, 58, 78; George Wright, "Re: Confederate River Gunboats," Civil War Navies Messageboard,<http://history-sites.com/mb/cw/cwnavy/index.cgi?read=1948> (accessed November 10, 2006). From August 16 on, we have the advantage of drawing from the logbooks of the three timberclads. Although some of these records are not available at the National Archives, key portions of the missing journals were abstracted and printed in ORN, usually in the final hundred pages or so of vols. 22 onward. Phelps'

ORN account of his first wartime cruise is also supplemented by information in the column "Western Military Movements" in the *Philadelphia Inquirer,* August 22, 1861.

16. ORN, I, 22: 301–303; *Evansville Daily Journal,* August 22, 1861. The gunboat flotilla was about to receive a large shipment of ordnance from the Washington Navy Yard. On August 19, fifty cases of 8-inch grapeshot, 48 boxes of 32-pdr. canister, 420 boxes of 32-pdr. shells, 500 boxes of 8-inch shells, 40 boxes of 32-pdr. grapeshot, and 350 boxes of munitions of war were received in Cincinnati to be forwarded to Cairo. This was the largest quantity of munitions yet to arrive in the Queen City (*Philadelphia Inquirer,* August 20, 1861).

17. ORN, I, 22: 300–305, 778; *Chicago Daily Tribune,* August 20, 22, 1861.

18. Julius A. Lemcke, *Reminiscences of an Indianian: From the Sassafras Log Behind the Barn in Posey County to Broader Fields* (Indianapolis: Hollenbeck Press, 1905), 191–193; Milford M. Miller, "Evansville Steamboats During the Civil War," *Indiana Magazine of History* 37 (December 1941): 366–368; E.B. Long, "The Paducah Affair: Bloodless Action That Altered the Civil War in the Mississippi Valley," *The Register of the Kentucky Historical Society* 60 (July 1972): 256; *Philadelphia Inquirer,* August 23, 1861; *Cincinnati Daily Enquirer,* August 24–25, 1861; *Evansville Daily Journal,* August 27–28, 1861; OR, I, IV: 176–178; ORN, I, 22: 304, 778; Scharf, 242; Lytle, comp., *Merchant Steam Vessels of the United States, 1807–1868, "The Lytle List,"* 17. Built near McKeesport, PA, in 1855, the *Charley Bowen* was 138 feet long, with a 25-foot beam and a 4.8-foot depth of hold. She entered service on November 12, 1858. The 213-ton *Dunbar* was built at Brownsville, PA, in 1859 and originally home-ported at Pittsburgh. Try as they might, the Yankees could not capture the slippery side-wheeler and she continued to plague them into September 1863. The 271-ton *Sam Kirkman* was constructed at Paducah in 1857 for $14,000, using the engines from the wrecked Helen Marr. Named for an Evansville citizen, the *Samuel Orr,* sometimes called the *Sam Orr,* was built at New Albany and finished at Evansville in February 1861. The stern-wheeler was 150 feet long, with a 29-foot beam and a five-foot depth of hold. The 175-ton *W.B. Terry* was constructed at Belle Vernon, PA, in 1856 and home-ported at Paducah. Col. Oglesby did not know exactly what to do with her, legally, after her capture, so Federal forces held onto her, using her as a supply boat until she ran aground in the Tennessee River and was lost on September 1 (Miller, 362, 364, 369; Lytle, comp., *Merchant Steam Vessels of the United States, 1807–1868, "The Lytle List,"* 50–51, 170–171, 196; Charles Dana Gibson, with E. Kay Gibson, "Assault and Logistics," *Dictionary of Transports and Combat Vessels Steam and Sail Employed by the Union Army, 1861–1868* (Camden, ME: Ensign Press, 1995), 1: 56, 89, 285, 328; OR, I, IV:179).

19. ORN, I, 22: 304–305, 307–308, 321, 778–779; Milligan, 16–17, 19; Suhr, 21; *St. Louis Missouri Democrat,* August 25, 27 1861; *Evansville Daily Journal,* September 3, 1861; Johnson, *Rear Admiral John Rodgers, 1812–1882,* 165; Nevins, *Frémont,* 492, 497; Mullen, 215; Spencer C. Tucker, *Andrew Foote: Civil War Admiral on Western Waters* (Annapolis, MD: Naval Institute Press, 2000), 114. In his *Century* magazine memoir, Capt. Eads does not tell us how Frémont came to purchase his salvage boat, but says only that before the seven Pook gunboats were finished that "I engaged to convert the snag boat *Benton* into an armored vessel of still larger dimensions" (James B. Eads, "Recollections of Foote and the Gunboats," *B&L,* 1:339; Frémont, "In Command in Missouri," *B&L,* 1:288). Our information on Frémont's late August push, Grant's appointment, failed Confederate Missouri activities, and the Columbus target comes from OR, I, 3: 141–142; Ulysses S. Grant, *Personal Memoirs of U.S. Grant,* 2 vols. (New York: C.L. Webster & Co., 1885–1886; Repr. [2 vols. in 1], New York: Penguin Books, 1999), I: 154–155); Grant, *The Papers of Ulysses S. Grant, April-September 1861,* ed. John Y. Simon, 24 vols. (Edwardsville: Southern Illinois University Press, 1969), 2:140–155; Jean Edward Smith, *Grant* (New York: Simon and Schuster, 2001), 116–118; Brooks D. Simpson, *Ulysses S. Grant: Triumph Over Adversity, 1822–1885* (New York: Houghton, Mifflin, 2000), 87–92; Steven E. Woodworth, *Nothing But Victory: The Army of the Tennessee, 1861–1865* (New York: Alfred A. Knopf, 2005), 33–35; Frémont, "In Command in Missouri," *B&L,* 1:284–285;. Nevins, *Frémont,* 521; Mullen, 214–215. Our profiles of Foote are from Cogar, 63–65; Tucker, "Sketches of the Officers of the Fort Donelson Fleet," *Philadelphia Inquirer,* February 18, 1862; and James Mason Hoppin, *Life of Andrew Hull Foote, Rear Admiral United States Navy* (New York: Harper & Brothers, 1874).

Chapter 4

1. U.S. Navy Department, *Official Records of the Union and Confederate Navies in the War of the Rebellion,* 31 vols. (Washington, DC: GPO, 1894–1922), series I, vol. 22, 319 (cited hereafter as ORN, followed by a comma, the series number in Roman numerals, a comma, the volume number in Arabic, a colon, and the page in Arabic); Robert E. Johnson, *Rear Admiral John Rodgers, 1812–1882* (Annapolis, MD: Naval Institute Press, 1967), 164. From a humble and inauspicious beginning, U.S. Grant (1822–1885) rose to become the North's generalissimo and later served two terms as president (1869–1877). Gideon J. Pillow (1806–1878) was Tennessee's senior militia general and became a Confederate Brig. Gen. Fighting at both Belmont and Fort Donelson, he was dismissed after the latter battle. Friend of Jefferson Davis and the Episcopal bishop who helped found the University of the South, Leonidas Polk (1806–1864) was charged with defending the Mississippi River during the summer of 1861. Rising to the rank of Lt. Gen., he was killed during the Atlanta campaign (Mark M. Boatner III, *The Civil War Dictionary* (New York: David McKay, 1959), 352–353, 653–654, 657–658.

2. ORN, I, 22: 310–311, 779; U.S. War Department, *The War of the Rebellion: A Compilation of the Official Records of the Union and Confederate Armies,* 128 vols. (Washington, DC: GPO, 1880–1901), series I, vol. 3, 142, 151–152 (cited hereafter as OR, followed by a comma, the series number in Roman numerals, a comma, the volume number in Arabic, any part number in Arabic, a colon, and the page in Arabic); John C. Frémont, "In Command in Missouri," in *Battles and Leaders of the Civil War,* ed. Robert V. Johnson and Clarence C. Buel, 4 vols. (New York: The Century Company, 1884–1887; Repr. Thomas Yoseloff, 1956), I: 284; Jesse Taylor, "The Defense of Fort Henry," *B&L,* 1:368–369; Thomas L. Snead, "The First Year of the War in Missouri," *B&L,* 1:273–274; Jay Monaghan, *Swamp Fox of the Confederacy: The Life and Military Services of M. Jeff Thompson* (Tuscaloosa, AL: Confederate Publishing, 1956), 30–40; William P. Johnston, *The Life of Gen. Albert Sidney Johnston* (New York: D. Appleton and Company, 1878), 368; William B. Feis, *Grant's Secret Service: The Intelligence War from Belmont to Appomattox* (Lincoln: University of Nebraska Press, 2002), 19–20, 31–32; Nathaniel Cheairs Hughes, Jr., *The Battle of Belmont: Grant Strikes South* (Chapel Hill: University of North Carolina Press,

1991), 3–5; *Evansville Daily Journal*, September 3, 1861; *Chicago Daily Tribune*, September 5, 1861.

3. Joseph H. Parks, *General Leonidas Polk, C.S.A.: The Fighting Bishop* (Baton Rouge: Louisiana State University Press, 1962), 179–182; Jefferson Davis, *Rise and Fall of the Confederate Government*, 2 vols. (New York: D. Appleton and Company, 1881), I: 385, 391; Thomas L. Connelly, *Army of the Heartland: The Army of Tennessee, 1861–1862* (Baton Rouge: Louisiana State University Press, 1967), 51–52; E Merton Coulter, *The Civil War and Readjustment in Kentucky* (Chapel Hill: University of North Carolina Press, 1926), 54–56; ORN, I, 22: 301; OR, I, 3: 151–152, 683; Stanley F. Horn, *The Army of Tennessee* (Indianapolis: Bobbs-Merrill, 1941), 44; OR, I, 4: 179–192; *Philadelphia Inquirer*, October 3, 1861; Hughes, 3–5; Steven E. Woodworth, *Nothing But Victory: The Army of the Tennessee, 1861–1865* (New York: Alfred A. Knopf, 2005), 36; Jean Edward Smith, *Grant* (New York: Simon and Schuster, 2001), 118; Edward Conrad Smith, *The Borderland in the Civil War* (New York: Macmillan, 1927), 301; E.B. Long, "The Paducah Affair: Bloodless Action That Altered the Civil War in the Mississippi Valley," *The Register of the Kentucky Historical Society* 60 (July 1972): 255, 257–260, 262; Bruce Catton, *This Hallowed Ground: The Story of the Union Side of the Civil War* (Garden City, NY: Doubleday, 1956) , 70; *Chicago Daily Tribune*, September 7, 12, 1861. Nothing is known of the armament of the *Equality*. What else we know of the steamers *Jeff Davis* and *Grampus* appears in U.S. Navy Department, Naval History Division, *Civil War Naval Chronology, 1861–1865*, 6 vols., rev. ed. (Washington, DC: GPO, 1966), 1: 242, 255.

4. ORN, I, 22: 309–311; OR, I, 2: 148; Ulysses S. Grant, *The Papers of Ulysses S. Grant, April–September1861*, ed. John Y. Simon, 24 vols. (Edwardsville: Southern Illinois University Press, 1969), 2:186; Arthur L. Conger, *The Rise of U.S. Grant* (New York: Century, 1931), 54; Robert D. Whitesell, "Military and Naval Activities Between Cairo and Columbus," *The Register of the Kentucky Historical Society* 61 (April 1963): 10; *Cincinnati Daily Enquirer*, September 10, 1861; Frank A. Montgomery, *Reminiscences of a Mississippian in Peace and War* (Cincinnati: The Robert Clarke Company Press, 1901), 60–61.

5. Frémont, "In Command in Missouri," *B&L*, 1:281–285; OR, I, 3: 141, 147, 150, 166, 471; OR, I, 4: 196; ORN, I, 22: 301, 313; *St. Louis Daily Democrat*, September 7, 1861; Feis, 21–24; E.B. Long, 263–268; Ulysses S. Grant, *Personal Memoirs of U.S. Grant*, 2 vols. (New York: C.L. Webster & Co., 1885–1886, Repr. [2 vols. in 1], New York: Penguin Books, 1999], I: 264–267; Grant, *The Papers of Ulysses S. Grant*, 2:189–193, 196–197; Joseph Parks, *General Leonidas Polk, C.S.A.: The Fighting Bishop* (Baton Rouge: Louisiana State University Press, 1962), 181; William M. Polk, *Leonidas Polk, Bishop and General*, 2 vols. (New York: Longmans, Green & Co., 1915), II: 17–29; William P. Johnston, *The Life of Gen. Albert Sidney Johnston* (New York: D. Appleton and Company, 1878), 292; Bruce Catton, *Grant Moves South* (Boston: Little, Brown, 1960), 48–49; Woodworth, 36–37; Smith, 118–119. Frémont was displeased with Grant's telegram to the Kentucky legislature and next day ordered him not to again send wires on "public service" matters (OR, I, 52, 1: 189). Gen. Johnston (1803–1862) had been offered a commission as second in command to Lt. Gen. Scott but did not receive it before casting his lot with the South. He would be mortally wounded at Shiloh in April 1862. Boatner, 440.

6. *St. Louis Daily Democrat*, September 7, 1861; "Sketches of the Officers of the Fort Donelson Fleet," *Philadelphia Inquirer*, February 18, 1862; *Chicago Daily Tribune*, September 11, 1861; Grant, *The Papers of Ulysses S. Grant*, 2:198; OR, I, 4: 196; ORN, I, 22: 319, 321, 328; Robert E. Johnson, *Rear Admiral John Rodgers, 1812–1882* (Annapolis, MD: Naval Institute Press, 1967), 165–167; Boatner, 522, 525, 615–616; Edward W. Callahan, *List of Officers of the Navy of the United States and of the Marine Corps, from 1775 to 1900, Comprising a Complete Register of All Present and Former Commissioned, Warranted, and Appointed Officers of the United States Navy, and of the Marine Corps, Regular and Volunteer. Compiled from the Official Records of the Navy Department* (New York: L.R. Hamersly & Co., 1901; Repr., New York: Haskell House, 1969), 236, 496, 541, 564, 594; Lewis R. Hamersly, *The Records of Living Officers of the U.S. Navy and Marine Corps, Compiled from Official Sources*, rev. ed. (Philadelphia: J.B. Lippincott, 1870), 45, 111, 178–179; 201; William B. Cogar, *Dictionary of Admirals of the U.S. Navy*, 2 vols. (Annapolis, MD: Naval Institute Press, 1989), I: 200–201. Having learned that Cmdr. Walke and other officers of his rank with more seniority would soon arrive and that he would be third or fourth down on the command ladder, Rodgers determined to seek sea duty. As a professional courtesy, he agreed to remain on Frémont's staff and to work with Foote until orders to a new billet arrived. There are only a few recent studies on the naval efficiency board process. We have relied upon Kenneth J. Blume, "'Concessions Where Concessions Could Be Made': The Naval Efficiency Boards of 1855–1857," in *New Interpretations in Naval History: Selected Papers form the 14th Naval History Symposium*, ed. Randy Carol Balano and Craig L. Symonds (Annapolis, MD: Naval Institute Press, 2001), 147–159. Here are capsule biographies for the three brigadiers mentioned since our last note: Paine (1815–1882) was a veteran of the Second Seminole War who had served as Brig. Gen. of Ohio militia from 1845 to1848. He would resign in April 1862 and take up business interests. McArthur (1826–?), a Scottish immigrant, owned a foundry before the war. After conspicuous service at Fort Donelson and Shiloh, he was promoted to command several divisions, obtaining the rank of bvt. major general of volunteers. An Illinois politician and Black Hawk War veteran, John McClernand (1812–1900) would develop a reputation for dubious military leadership, while demonstrating his disdain for West Pointers. Raised to the rank of Maj. Gen., he resigned for ill health in November 1864.

7. ORN, I, 22: 317, 321; OR, I, 4: 196–198; Long, 268–270; Woodworth, 36–40; Grant, *Personal Memoirs of U.S. Grant*, 265–266; *St. Louis Daily Democrat*, September 7, 1861; *Chicago Daily Tribune*, September 11, 1861; William C. Lytle, comp., *Merchant Steam Vessels of the United States, 1807–1868*, "The Lytle List," publication no. 6 (Mystic, CT: The Steamship Historical Society of America, 1952), 58.

8. OR, I, 3: 141–142, 167–168, 478–479, 481; OR, II, 1: 130; OR, I, 4: 198; ORN, I, 22: 319–323, 326–328; *St. Louis Daily Democrat*, September 7, 1861; *Chicago Daily Tribune*, September 10–11, 1861; Lytle, 100, 293; Nathaniel Cheairs Hughes, Jr., *The Battle of Belmont: Grant Strikes South* (Chapel Hill: University of North Carolina Press, 1991), 5; Catton, 39–40; Long, 271; Grant, *The Papers of Ulysses S. Grant*, 2:209–210, 217–218, 224–225, 276–277. Brig. Gen. Charles Ferguson Smith (1807–1862), a Mexican war hero, commanded the Military District of Western Kentucky from this date through January 1862. A hero of Fort Donelson, the bvt. major general died of wounds at the end of April. Boatner, 769. On September 14, Brig. Gen. McClernand stated that the *John Gault* was needed for Cairo post duties and three days later Maj. Gen. Frémont concurred in her takeover. She would be returned to her

captain on September 23 (Grant, *The Papers of Ulysses S. Grant*, 2:259, 276–277, 308).

9. ORN, I, 22: 322–330; ORN, I, 24: 132; OR, I, 3: 481; *Chicago Daily Tribune*, September 11, 1861; Grant, *The Papers of Ulysses S. Grant*, 2:217–218, 222; Jay Slagle, *Ironclad Captain: Seth Ledyard Phelps and the U.S. Navy* (Kent, OH: Kent State University Press, 1996), 124–125; Gershom Bradford, *The Mariner's Dictionary* (New York: Weathervane Books, 1970), 205; Charles Wright Wills, *Army Life of an Illinois Soldier*, comp. Mary E. Kellogg (Washington, DC: Globe Printing Co., 1906), 28–29. Stembel said later that the greatest lesson for the timberclads from the Lucas Bend affair was that each should have a stern gun. Thereafter, Capt. Foote would authorize alterations to make certain that at least a 32-pdr. was pointed aft in each of the three wooden gunboats (ORN, I, 22: 327, 336).

10. Catton, 59; Feis, 32–33; Albert Castel, *General Sterling Price and the Civil War in the West* (Baton Rouge: Louisiana State University Press, 1968), 48–50; Frémont, "In Command in Missouri," *B&L*, 1:286–287; James A. Mulligan, "The Siege of Lexington, MO," *B&L*, 1:307–313; Allen Nevins, *Frémont: Pathmarker of the West* (New York: D. Appleton-Century Company, 1939), 521–526; Tom Chaffin, *Pathfinder: John Charles Frémont and the Course of American Empire* (New York: Hill & Wang, 2002), 463–470; Grant, *The Papers of Ulysses S. Grant*, 2:224–226, 233–236, 252–253; ORN, I, 22: 322, 328–336, 338–339, 772; OR, I, 3: 168–169, 484, 487; Henry Walke, "The Gun-Boats at Belmont and Fort Henry," *B&L*, 1:359–360; Walke, *Naval Scenes and Reminiscences of the Civil War in the United States on the Southern and Western Waters During the Years 1861, 1862 and 1863, with the History of That Period Compared and Corrected from Authentic Sources* (New York: F.R. Reed and Company, 1877), 26–27; Wills, 30; R. Thomas Campbell, *Confederate Naval Forces on Western Waters* (Jefferson, NC: McFarland & Co., Inc., 2005), 26–28; J. Thomas Scharf, *History of the Confederate Navy from Its Organization to the Surrender of Its Last Vessel* (New York: Rodgers and Sherwood, 1887; Repr., New York: Fairfax Press, 1977), 275–299; Chester G. Hearn, *The Capture of New Orleans, 1862* (Baton Rouge: Louisiana State University Press, 1995), 81–95, 195, 270; Lytle, 193; *Nashville Daily Gazette*, September 18, 1861; *St. Louis Daily Republican*, quoted in *Macon Daily Telegraph*, October 3, 1861. Vernon Stevenson abandoned Nashville for Atlanta in February 1862, where he reputedly became a war profiteer. He moved to New York City after Appomattox. Eliza B. Woodall, *The Stevenson Story* (Stevenson, AL: Stevenson Depot Museum, 1982), 178–179; Walter T. Durham, *Nashville—the Occupied City: The First Seventeen Months, February 16, 1862 to June 30, 1863* (Nashville: The Tennessee Historical Society, 1985), 15.

11. ORN, I, 22: 341, 772, 779; OR, I, 3: 501–502; Grant, *The Papers of Ulysses S. Grant*, 2:288–289, 292–295, 301; *Philadelphia Inquirer*, September 23, 1861; Wills, 33. Cmdr. Walke mistakenly dates his report of the Lucas Bend shelling and his Mound City departure as September 22–23 (ORN, I, 22: 349).

12. Catton, 70; ORN, I, 22: 344–352, 356, 358, 772, 779–780; OR, I, 3: 504–505, 507; OR, I, 4, 266, 273–274, 275, 279; Grant, *The Papers of Ulysses S. Grant*, 2:294, 300–304; Grant, *Personal Memoirs of U.S. Grant*, I: 269–270; Frémont, "In Command in Missouri," *B&L*, 1:286–287; Castel, 48–56; John Y. Simon, "Grant at Belmont," *Military Affairs* 45 (December 1981): 162–163; Donald L. Canney, *The Old Steam Navy*, vol. 2, *The Ironclads, 1842–1885* (Annapolis, MD: Naval Institute Press, 1993), 38; Dana Wegner, "S.X.: The Federal Gunboat *Essex*," *Nautical Research Journal* 19 (Spring 1972): 49–51;

Robert E. Johnson, *Rear Admiral John Rodgers, 1812–1882* (Annapolis, MD: Naval Institute Press, 1967), 167–168; *Chicago Times*, September 27, 1861. William Porter (1809–1864) first joined the U.S. Navy in 1823. Scalded at Fort Henry in 1862, he recovered to serve in the Natchez, Vicksburg, and Port Hudson campaigns (Mark M. Boatner III, *The Civil War Dictionary* (New York: David McKay, 1959), 662).

13. ORN, I, 22: 354–357, 355, 780; OR, I, 3: 510; Feis, 35–38; Slagle, 133–134; *Nashville Banner*, October 1, 1861; Grant, *The Papers of Ulysses S. Grant*, 2:321, 329–330, 507–508; Grant, *The Papers of Ulysses S. Grant, October 1, 1861-January 7, 1862*, ed. John Y. Simon, 24 vols. (Edwardsville: Southern Illinois University Press, 1970), 3:4–5, 8–9, 14, 17. The 145-ton paddle-wheeler *Champion No. 2* was built at Newport, KY, in 1853 and was homeported at Cincinnati (Lytle, 28).

14. Conger, 79; Frémont, "In Command in Missouri," *B&L*, 1:286–287; Feis, 38–39; Chaffin, 470; Walke, *Naval Scenes*, 28–29; Allan Nevins, *The War for the Union: War The Improvised War* (New York: Charles Scribner's Sons, 1959), 378; Louis S. Gerteis, *Civil War St. Louis* (Lawrence: University Press of Kansas, 2001), 126–161; T.K. Kionka, *Key Command: Ulysses S. Grant's District of Cairo*, Shades of Blue and Gray Series (Columbia: University of Missouri Press, 2006), 117–118; Grant, *The Papers of Ulysses S. Grant*, 3:16, 18–19, 23, 33; ORN, I, 22: 360–364, 793; OR, I, 3: 712–714, 748; *Chicago Daily Tribune*, October 8, 1861; *St. Louis Daily Republican*, October 10, 1861; *Atlantic Democrat*, October 12, 1861; *Charleston Mercury*, October 14, 1861; *Philadelphia Inquirer*, October 9, 1861; the *St. Louis Daily Democrat* story was reprinted around the country, including within the pages of *The Philadelphia Inquirer* on October 10.

Chapter 5

1. U.S. Navy Department, *Official Records of the Union and Confederate Navies in the War of the Rebellion*, 31 vols. (Washington, DC: GPO, 1894–1922), series I, vol. 22, 361–374 (cited hereafter as ORN, followed by a comma, the series number in Roman numerals, a comma, the volume number in Arabic, a colon, and the page in Arabic); Alan Westcott, "Alexander Mosely Pennock," in *Dictionary of American Biography*, 10 vols. (New York: C. Scribner's, 1937), 14: 444; William B. Cogar, *Dictionary of Admirals of the U.S. Navy*, 2 vols. (Annapolis, MD: Naval Institute Press, 1989), 1: 126–127; Lewis B. Hamersly, *The Records of Living Officers of the U.S. Navy and Marine Corps* (Philadelphia: J.B. Lippincott & Co., 1870), 54. Pennock, again like Walke, deserves a full-scale biography. Cmdr. Perry (?–1880) was yet another "restored" officer. Having joined the U.S. Navy from Maryland in 1828, after years of sea service he held shore billets during the Civil War, retired in 1865, was promoted to Captain in 1867, and died in November 1880. A close friend of Capt. Foote, Joseph Sanford was appointed a midshipman in 1832. Lt. Sanford resigned in 1853 to run a foundry but came back to join his colleague as ordnance officer when Foote was named to replace Rodgers. Promoted to the rank of commander, he would remain with the squadron through the war. Reaching the rank of captain in 1866, he resigned again in 1869 (ORN, I, 22: 391–392; Edward W. Callahan, *List of Officers of the Navy of the United States and of the Marine Corps, from 1775 to 1900, Comprising a Complete Register of All Present and Former Commissioned, Warranted, and Appointed Officers of the United States Navy, and of the Marine Corps, Regular and Volunteer. Compiled*

from the Official Records of the Navy Department (New York: L.R. Hamersly & Co., 1901; Repr., New York: Haskell House, 1969), 432, 482; Lewis R. Hamersly, *The Records of Living Officers of the U.S. Navy and Marine Corps, Compiled from Official Sources,* rev. ed. (Philadelphia: J.B. Lippincott, 1870), 133–134; Jay Slagle, *Ironclad Captain: Seth Ledyard Phelps and the U.S. Navy* (Kent, OH: Kent State University Press, 1996), 215–216).

2. ORN, I, 22: 371; U.S. War Department, *The War of the Rebellion: A Compilation of the Official Records of the Union and Confederate Armies,* 128 vols. (Washington, DC: GPO, 1880–1901), series I, vol. 4: 362–363, 372–373 (cited hereafter as OR, followed by a comma, the series number in Roman numerals, a comma, the volume number in Arabic, any part number in Arabic, a colon, and the page in Arabic); Lew Wallace, *An Autobiography,* 2 vols. (New York: Harper and Brothers, 1906), 1: 338–339; R.M. McMurry, *Two Great Rebel Armies* (Chapel Hill: University of North Carolina Press, 1989), 142; George Edgar Turner, *Victory Rode the Rails: The Strategic Place of Railroads in the Civil War* (Indianapolis: Bobbs-Merrill, 1953), 118; Anne J. Bailey, *The Chessboard of War: Sherman and Hood in the Autumn Campaigns of 1864,* Great Campaigns of the Civil War (Lincoln: University of Nebraska Press, 2000), 135; T.L. Connelly, *Civil War Tennessee* (Knoxville: University of Tennessee Press, 1979), 13–18; Byrd Douglas, *Steamboatin' on the Cumberland* (Nashville: Tennessee Book Company, 1961), 112; Benjamin F. Cooling, *Forts Henry and Donelson: The Key to the Confederate Heartland* (Knoxville: University of Tennessee Press, 1987), 13–14; *Harper's Weekly,* VI (March 15, 1862), 162.

3. Cooling, 29, 42; Thomas L. Connelly, *Army of the Heartland: The Army of Tennessee, 1861–1862* (Baton Rouge: Louisiana State University Press, 1967), 18–19, 20, 79–80; Ulysses S. Grant, *Personal Memoirs of U.S. Grant, A Modern Abridgment.* New York: Premier Books, 1962), 80; Peter Franklin Walker, "Building a Tennessee Army: Autumn, 1861," *The Tennessee Historical Quarterly* 16 (June 1957): 113; Joseph H. Parks, *General Leonidas Polk, C.S.A.: The Fighting Bishop* (Baton Rouge: Louisiana State University Press, 1962), 188; Stanley F. Horn, comp., *Tennessee's War, 1861–1865, Described by Participants* (Nashville: Tennessee Civil War Centennial Commission, 1965), 29; Kenneth R. Johnson, "Confederate Defense and Union Gunboats on the Tennessee River," *The Alabama Historical Quarterly* 64 (Summer 1968): 40–41; Surveys to establish Forts Henry and Donelson were actually started in April 1861 and it was soon determined that the bastions were not located in prime locations. Labor and equipment shortages followed and the works were never made as powerful as possible (OR, I, 4: 506, 544–545; James L. Nichols, *Confederate Engineers* (Tuscaloosa, AL: Confederate Publishing Company, 1957), 42–44).

4. ORN, I, 22: 365–366, 371–372, 430, 794; OR, I, 3: 531; Ulysses S. Grant, *The Papers of Ulysses S. Grant, October 1, 1861-January 7, 1862,* ed. John Y. Simon, 24 vols. (Edwardsville: Southern Illinois University Press, 1970), 3:31–33; Slagle, 135–136; *New York Times,* October 19–20, 1861. The steamer Polk eventually reported being purchased with Mallory's approval was the *Eastport* (Johnson, 42).

5. Grant, *The Papers of Ulysses S. Grant,* 3:54–56; ORN, I, 22: 372–373; OR, I, 3: 248; William M. Polk, "General Polk and the Battle of Belmont," in *Battles and Leaders of the Civil War,* ed. Robert V. Johnson and Clarence C. Buel, 4 vols. (New York: The Century Company, 1884–1887; Repr., Thomas Yoseloff, 1956), 1: 356; Frank A. Montgomery, *Reminiscences of a Mississippian in Peace and War* (Cincinnati: The Robert Clarke Company Press, 1901), 63.

A great mile-long chain was being stretched across the Mississippi River to restrict the passage of Union gunboats. It was held in place by a gigantic six-ton, 16-foot long anchor, each fluke of which measured nine feet. Each of the links in the huge chain weighed between 15 and 20 pounds and most people believe it was the combined weight that caused the guardian to snap shortly after its installation. The anchor itself can still be seen at the Columbus-Belmont Battlefield State Park in Kentucky (David E. Roth, "The Civil War at the Confluence: Where the Ohio Meets the Mississippi," *Blue & Gray* 2 (July 1985): 11.

6. ORN, I, 22: 375–378; OR, I, 3: 22, 225–226; Grant, *The Papers of Ulysses S. Grant,* 3:54, 56–57, 116; M. Jeff Thompson, *The Civil War Reminiscences of General M. Jeff Thompson,* ed. Donal J. Stanton, Goodwin F. Berquist, and Paul C. Bowers (Dayton, OH: Morningside Bookshop, 1988), 106–117; William B. Feis, *Grant's Secret Service: The Intelligence War from Belmont to Appomattox* (Lincoln: University of Nebraska Press, 2002), 38–39; Jennifer L. Weber, *Copperheads: The Rise and Fall of Lincoln's Opponents in the North* (New York: Oxford University Press, 2006), 25, 49, 54, 80; Henry Walke, *Naval Scenes and Reminiscences of the Civil War in the United States on the Southern and Western Waters During the Years 1861, 1862 and 1863, with the History of That Period Compared and Corrected from Authentic Sources* (New York: F.R. Reed and Company, 1877), 30.

7. ORN, I, 22:379–384; Slagle, 136–137; William P. Johnston, *The Life of Gen. Albert Sidney Johnston* (New York: D. Appleton and Company, 1878), 358; *Chicago Daily Tribune,* October 27, 1861; *Louisville Courier,* October 28, 1861; MJR Jesse J. Phillips (1837–1901) was later wounded at Shiloh. At the end of the war he was named a bvt. brigadier general He went on to serve as a circuit court judge in the 5th District of Illinois from June 16, 1879, until he joined the Illinois Supreme Court on June 5, 1893. He remained on the high court until his death on February 2, 1901, during which time he served once as chief justice, in 1897 ("Jesse J. Phillips," Illinois Courts, <http://www.state.il.us/Court/SupremeCourt/Previous/Bio_JPhillips.asp> (accessed October 6, 2006); Mark M. Boatner III, *The Civil War Dictionary* (New York: David McKay, 1959), 651. The Lake Erie No. 2 was a 150-ton stern-wheeler built at West Brownsville, PA, in 1851 and originally home-ported at Pittsburgh (William C. Lytle, comp., *Merchant Steam Vessels of the United States, 1807–1868,* "The Lytle List," publication no. 6 (Mystic, CT: The Steamship Historical Society of America, 1952), 109).

8. ORN, I, 22: 383, 389–390, 395–397, 430, 798–801; OR, I, 3: 343; OR, I, 52, 2: 213; OR, I, 53: 725, 730; *New York Times,* December 11, 1861; Slagle, 138; Nichols, 51; Grant, *The Papers of Ulysses S. Grant,* 3:55, 84–85, 99–100; Nathaniel Cheairs Hughes, Jr., *The Battle of Belmont: Grant Strikes South* (Chapel Hill: University of North Carolina Press, 1991), 36–38; John Bell Battle, "The Battle of Belmont: Pvt. John Bell Battle's Eyewitness Account," in *Confederate Chronicles of Tennessee,* ed. R.W. Rosser 2(1987), 2: 33; Polk, "General Polk and the Battle of Belmont," *B&L,* 1:286–287; William G. Stevenson, *Thirteen Months in the Rebel Army, Being a Narrative of Personal Adventures* (New York: A.S. Barnes & Burr, 1862), 65–66; Charles Wright Wills, *Army Life of an Illinois Soldier,* comp. Mary E. Kellogg (Washington, DC: Globe Printing Co., 1906), 39; *St. Louis Daily Republican,* September 29, 1861. Once again we rely, in addition to ORN, I, 22, on two major sources for the final story of the Pook turtle construction: Edwin C. Bearss, *Hardluck Ironclad: The Sinking and Salvage of the Cairo* (Baton Rouge: Louisiana State

University Press, 1966), 10–39, and Donald L. Canney, *The Old Steam Navy*, vol. 2, *The Ironclads, 1842–1885* (Annapolis, MD: Naval Institute Press, 1993), 47–55. The *St. Louis* was the first of the "turtles" launched (October 12, 1861) and the last commissioned (January 31, 1862); the first commissioned was Henry Walke's famous *Carondelet* (January 15, 1862) (Canney, 54). As the name of the C.S.S. *Howard* never appeared again and no such contemporary civilian riverboat is listed in the standard steamboat directories, it is safe to say she did not enter service.

9. ORN, I, 22: 267, 390; OR, I, 3: 540–554, 560–565, 727–728, 731–732; Allan Nevins, *The War for the Union: War The Improvised War* (New York: Charles Scribner's Sons, 1959), 379–383; Nevins, *Frémont: Pathmarker of the West* (New York: D. Appleton-Century Company, 1939), 538–547; Tom Chaffin, *Pathfinder: John Charles Frémont and the Course of American Empire* (New York: Hill & Wang, 2002), 470–473; John C. Frémont, "In Command in Missouri," *B&L*, 1:287–288; Albert Castel, *General Sterling Price and the Civil War in the West* (Baton Rouge: Louisiana State University Press, 1968), 58–60; T. Harry Williams, *Lincoln and His Generals* (New York: Alfred A. Knopf, 1952; Repr. Vintage Books, 1962), 39–40; Bruce Catton, *Grant Moves South* (Boston: Little, Brown, 1960), 72. Halleck officially succeeded Hunter on November 20.

10. OR, I, 3, 256, 259, 267–269, 273, 296, 300–301; OR, I, 4: 491, 513–517, 554; OR, I, 52: 18–19, 25, 30, 53: 507; Grant, *The Papers of Ulysses S. Grant*, 3:42–43, 47, 63–64, 72, 78, 105, 108–109, 111–113, 115, 121–122, 143–144, 152; Hughes, 4, 45–47; Polk, "General Polk and the Battle of Belmont," *B&L*, 1:287–288.; Feis, 42–43; Catton, 60, 71–74; Johnston, 359; *Louisville Daily Journal*, November 15, 1861; John Y. Simon, "Grant at Belmont," *Military Affairs* 45 (December 1981): 163; *St. Louis Daily Republican*, January 16, 1886.

11. OR, I, 3: 269, 275, 278, 285, 296; OR, I, 4: 522; ORN, I, 22: 397, 399–402, 404, 427–428, 430, 780; Ulysses S. Grant, *Personal Memoirs of U.S. Grant*, 2 vols. (New York: C.L. Webster & Co., 1885–1886; repr. [2 vols. in 1], New York: Penguin Books, 1999), 1: 271–272; Grant, *The Papers of Ulysses S. Grant*, 3:127, 150–151; Hughes, 48–55; Jean Edward Smith, *Grant* (New York: Simon and Schuster, 2001), 126–127; Simon, "Grant at Belmont," 164–165; Walke, *Naval Scenes*, 32–33; Walke, "The Gun-Boats at Belmont and Fort Henry," *B&L*, 1:360–361; James H. Wilson, *The Life of John A. Rawlins* (New York: Neale, 1916), 425; Mrs. John A. Logan, *Reminiscences of a Soldier's Wife* (New York: Scribner's Sons, 1913), 121–122; W.H.L. Wallace, *Life and Letters of W.H.L. Wallace*, ed. Isabel Wallace (Chicago: R.R. Donnelly, 1909), 141; John S.C. Abbott, *The History of the Civil War in America* (New York: H. Bill, 1863), 1: 437; Steven E. Woodworth, *Nothing But Victory: The Army of the Tennessee, 1861–1865* (New York: Alfred A. Knopf, 2005), 43–47; William S. McFeely, *Grant, A Biography* (New York: W.W. Norton, 1981), 92; John Seaton, "The Battle of Belmont," in *War Talks in Kansas: A Series of Papers Read Before the Kansas Commandery, Military Order of the Loyal Legion of the United States* (Kansas City, KS: Franklin Hudson, 1906), 305–308; James E. McGhee, "The Neophyte General: U.S. Grant and the Belmont Campaign," *Missouri Historical Review* 47 (July 1975): 480; John D. Milligan, *Gunboats Down the Mississippi* (Annapolis, MD: Naval Institute Press, 1965), 34; *St. Louis Daily Republican*, November 9–10, 1861; *Chicago Daily Tribune*, November 9, 11, 1861; *Chicago Evening Journal*, November 9, 1861; *New York Times*, November 12, 1861; *St. Louis Missouri Democrat*, November 19, 1861; *Memphis Avalanche*, November 10, 1861; Lytle, 5, 29, 96, 107, 126, 164; Paul H. Silverstone, *Warships of the Civil War Navies* (Annapolis, MD: Naval Institute Press, 1989), 158; Catton, 81; Arthur L. Conger, *The Rise of U.S. Grant* (New York: Century, 1931), 99–101. The *Aleck Scott* was a 709-ton side-wheeler built at St. Louis in 1848 and home-ported at that city. Brig. Gen. McClernand's headquarters boat would be purchased by the Quartermaster Department at the end of the year and converted by Eads, from a design by Cdr. William D. Porter, into the ironclad *Lafayette*. Ironically, Capt. Henry Walke, commander of the Belmont naval escort, would be her first skipper. The 392-ton *Chancellor* was another side-wheeler, built at New Albany, IN, in 1856. She would be destroyed by Confederate agents in 1863. The 536-ton *James Montgomery*, often called just the *Montgomery*, was the third largest boat in Grant's Belmont fleet. Built at New Albany, IN, in 1856 and home-ported there before the war, she would remain in government employ through the year. The 306-ton side-wheeler *Keystone* was constructed at Brownsville, PA, in 1852 and originally home-ported at Pittsburgh. The 645-ton *Belle Memphis* was also known as the *Belle of Memphis* or the *Memphis*. The second largest boat in the Belmont invasion group was built at Jeffersonville, IN, in 1860 and home-ported at St. Louis. The smallest boat in the flotilla was the 148-ton *Rob Roy*, a brand new sternwheeler constructed at Madison, IN, earlier in the year.

12. OR, I, 3: 270, 275–276, 278, 291, 294, 306, 352–353, 355, 359–362; ORN, I, 22: 395, 400–402, 425, 780; Hughes, 56–64, 173; Grant, *The Papers of Ulysses S. Grant*, 3:136–138; Milligan, 34–35; Smith, 127–129; Seaton, "The Battle of Belmont," 309; *Nashville Daily Patriot*, November 15, 1861; *Chicago Daily Tribune*, November 9, 11, 15, 16, 1861; *Chicago Evening Journal*, November 9, 1861; *New York Times*, November 12, 1861; *New York Herald*, November 12, 1861; *St. Louis Daily Democrat*, November 19, 1861; *St. Louis Daily Republican*, November 10, 14, 1861, January 16, 1886; *Memphis Daily Appeal*, November 12, 19, 1861; *Memphis Avalanche*, November 12, 1861; *New Orleans Daily Picayune*, November 14, 1861; *New Orleans Daily Crescent*, November 15, 1861; Walke, "Naval Scenes, 38–39, 41–42; Walke, "The Gun-Boats at Belmont and Fort Henry," *B&L*, 1:358–361; Walke, *Naval Scenes*, 34–40; John H. Brinton, *Personal Memoirs of John H. Brinton, Major and Surgeon, U.S.V., 1861–1865* (New York: Neale, 1914), 71, 73, 76–77, 84–85, 88; William M. Polk, *Leonidas Polk, Bishop and General*, 2 vols. (New York: Longmans, Green & Co., 1915), 1: 306, 2: 39; Henry M. Stanley, *The Autobiography of Sir Henry Morton Stanley*, ed. Dorothy Stanley (Boston: Houghton, Mifflin, 1909), 175; Marcus J. Wright, "The Battle of Belmont," *Southern Historical Society Papers* 15 (January-December 1888): 69–71; Catton, 75–77; Woodworth, 48–51; Feis, 42–43; J. Thomas Scharf, *History of the Confederate Navy from Its Organization to the Surrender of Its Last Vessel* (New York: Rodgers and Sherwood, 1887; Repr., New York: Fairfax Press, 1977), 241–242; H. Allen Gosnell, *Guns on the Western Waters: The Story of the River Gunboats in the Civil War* (Baton Rouge: Louisiana State University Press, 1949), 15–16; Charles B. Boynton, *History of the Navy During the Rebellion*, 2 vols. (New York: D. Appleton and Company, 1867–1868), 1: 501.

13. OR, I, 3: 267–272, 276, 280–281, 284–285, 290, 305–310, 346, 348; ORN, I, 22: 398–427, 772, 780; Hughes, 91–163, 170–177, 236n; Brinton, 77–78, 89; Smith, 129–131; Boynton, 1: 513; Grant, *Personal Memoirs of U.S. Grant*, 274–281; Grant, *The Papers of Ulysses S. Grant*, 3:128, 138; Simon, "Grant at Belmont," 161; Woodworth, 49–56; *St. Louis Daily Republican*, November 10, 1861, January 16, 1886; *St. Louis Missouri Democrat*, November 19, 1861; *New Orleans Daily Crescent*, November 13, 1861; *Memphis Daily*

Appeal, November 9–10, 12–13, 15, 21, 1861; *Chicago Daily Tribune,* November 9, 11, 15, 1861; *Chicago Evening Journal,* November 9, 1861; *New York Times,* November 12, 1861; *New York Herald,* November 12, 1861; *Harper's Weekly,* December 7, 1861; Lytle, 30, 80, 90, 106, 157; Polk, "General Polk and the Battle of Belmont," *B&L,* 1:349–350; H.C. Bradsby, "History of Cairo, Illinois," in *History of Alexander, Union and Pulaski Counties, Illinois,* ed. William Henry Perrin, (Chicago: O.L. Baskin & Co., 1883), 64; Seaton, "The Battle of Belmont," 315–316; Abbott, 438–440; Simon, "Grant at Belmont," 164; Robert D. Whitesell, "Military and Naval Activities Between Cairo and Columbus," *The Register of the Kentucky Historical Society* 61 (April 1963): 116–117; Parks, 190–192; Catton, 76–79; ORN, I, 22: 780; Walke, *Naval Scenes,* 36–41; Mark Twain, *Life on the Mississippi* (New York: Harper & Brothers, 1950), 217. "The Lytle List" tells us that the *Charm* was a tiny, 33-ton, three year old side-wheeler built at Louisville. The *Hill,* on the other hand, was a 602-ton side-wheeler built in 1852 at New Albany, IN. The side-wheeler *Ingomar,* at 730 tons, was even larger; she was constructed at Louisville in 1854. With a 21-ton advantage over the *Aleck Scott,* she was the largest transport employed by either side this day. Another side-wheeler, the 118-ton *Kentucky,* was built at Newport, KY, in 1852, while the 223-ton *Prince,* also a side-wheeler, was constructed at Cincinnati in 1859.

14. OR, I, 3: 257, 267–272, 304, 310, 312, 553–554, 740–749.; ORN, I, 54: 399, 405, 506; Hughes, 194, 204, 274n; Simon, "Grant at Belmont," 161; *New York Herald,* November 19, 1861; *Cincinnati Gazette,* November 9, 1861; *St. Louis Missouri Democrat,* November 8, 1861; *St. Louis Missouri Republican,* November 10, 1861; *Chicago Daily Tribune,* November 9, 16 1861; *Chicago Evening Journal,* November 9, 1861; *New York Times,* November 9, 12, 1861; *Ohio State Journal,* November 12, 1861; *Memphis Appeal,* November 9–11, 1861; *Nashville Banner,* November 10, 1861; *Macon Daily Telegraph,* November 9, 1861; Castel, 60; T.K. Kionka, *Key Command: Ulysses S. Grant's District of Cairo,* Shades of Blue and Gray Series (Columbia: University of Missouri Press, 2006), 132; Woodworth, 55; Grant, *The Papers of Ulysses S. Grant,* 3:128–129, 148; Bern Anderson, *By Sea and By River: The Naval History of the Civil War* (New York: Knopf, 1962), 90; Walke, *Naval Scenes,* 43, 47; Smith, 131; Milligan, 35–36; Paul Calore, *Naval Campaigns of the Civil War* (Jefferson, NC: McFarland & Co., 2002), 106–109. The second fire support mission was at Shiloh in April 1862 and the third at Helena, AK, in July 1863. Cmdr. Benjamin Dove (?-1868) became a U.S. Navy midshipman in 1826 and a Lt. in 1839. He enjoyed the dubious prewar record of having been twice court-martialed, having been dismissed from the service in 1841 only to be returned to duty by direct order of President John Tyler, and then later being subjected to a court of inquiry. Although given command of the Pook turtle *Louisville,* he would be passed over for promotion and retired in October 1864. Promoted to Capt. on the retired list in 1867, he died on November 19, 1868 (Callahan, 168; Slagle, 133).

Chapter 6

1. John Milton Hubbard, *Notes of a Private* (Memphis, TN: E.H. Clarke and Brother, 1909), 11–13; U.S. Navy Department, *Official Records of the Union and Confederate Navies in the War of the Rebellion,* 31 vols. (Washington, DC: GPO, 1894–1922), series I, vol. 22, 428, 435 (cited hereafter as ORN, followed by a comma, the series number in Roman numerals, a comma, the volume number in Arabic, a colon, and the page in Arabic); U.S. War Department, *The War of the Rebellion: A Compilation of the Official Records of the Union and Confederate Armies,* 128 vols. (Washington, DC: GPO, 1880–1901), series I, vol. 3: 567 (cited hereafter as OR, followed by a comma, the series number in Roman numerals, a comma, the volume number in Arabic, any part number in Arabic, a colon, and the page in Arabic); OR, I, 4: 349; Ethan S. Rafuse, *McClellan's War: The Failure of Moderation in the Struggle for the Union* (Bloomington: Indiana University Press, 2005), 148; Jay Slagle, *Ironclad Captain: Seth Ledyard Phelps and the U.S. Navy* (Kent, OH: Kent State University Press, 1996), 143–144; Ulysses S. Grant, *The Papers of Ulysses S. Grant, October 1, 1861-January 7, 1862,* ed. John Y. Simon, 24 vols. (Edwardsville: Southern Illinois University Press, 1970), 3:163, 173; William P. Johnston, *The Life of Gen. Albert Sidney Johnston* (New York: D. Appleton and Company, 1878), 378; Jay C. Mullen, "The Turning of Columbus," *Register of the Kentucky Historical Society* 64 (July 1966): 220.

2. Donald L. Canney, *The Old Steam Navy,* vol. 2, *The Ironclads, 1842–1885* (Annapolis, MD: Naval Institute Press, 1993), 54; *St. Louis Daily Democrat,* October 14, 1861; ORN, I, 22: 431; Edwin C. Bearss, *Hardluck Ironclad: The Sinking and Salvage of the Cairo* (Baton Rouge: Louisiana State University Press, 1966), 26–27.

3. Mark Twain, *Life on the Mississippi* (New York: Harper & Brothers, 1950), 54–62, 208–214; Paul H. Silverstone, *Warships of the Civil War Navies* (Annapolis, MD: Naval Institute Press, 1989), 181; *St. Louis Daily Democrat,* November 11, 1861; ORN, I, 22: 432–433; ORN, II, 1: 135; William C. Lytle, comp., *Merchant Steam Vessels of the United States, 1807–1868,* "The Lytle List," publication no. 6 (Mystic, CT: The Steamship Historical Society of America, 1952), 121; Bearss, 28. Though not remembered as success during his western waters tour, Cmdr. Winslow (1811–1873) would become one of the most famous U.S. Navy officers of the Civil War. A North Carolinian, Winslow became a U.S. Navy midshipman in 1827, the same year as Cmdr. Henry Walke. A Mexican War hero, Winslow would obtain his great fame on June 10, 1864, when, in command of the U.S.S. *Kearsarge,* he sank the C.S.S. *Alabama* off the coast of France. He commanded several warships postwar and was named a Rear Adm. in 1870 (William B. Cogar, *Dictionary of Admirals of the U.S. Navy,* 2 vols. (Annapolis, MD: Naval Institute Press, 1989), I, 211–212).

4. ORN, I, 22: 434–436, 440; John Allan Wyeth, *Life of General Nathan Bedford Forrest* (New York: Harper & Bros., 1904; repr., New York: Harper, 1959), 27–28; Thomas Jordan and J.P. Pryor. *The Campaigns of Lieut. Gen. N. B. Forrest and of Forrest's Cavalry* (New Orleans and New York: Blelock & Co., 1868; repr., New York: DaCapo Press, 1996), 44–46; Slagle, 143, 145–146; Johnston, 385; *Cincinnati Daily Commercial,* November 25, 1861. According to "The Lytle List," the *Pink Marble* was actually the *Pink Varble No. 2,* a three-year-old steamer out of Louisville (Lytle, 153).

5. OR, I, 8: 45; ORN, I, 22: 436–437, 439–442; "Jeff Thompson's Exploit at Price's Landing, Mo., November 18, 1861," in *The Rebellion Record: A Diary of American Events,* ed. Frank Frank, 12 vols. (New York: G.P. Putnam, 1861–1863; *Chicago Daily Tribune,* November 21, 26–27, 1861; D. Van Nostrand, 1864–1868; repr., New York: New York: Arno, 1977), 3: 402–403; Charles W. Wills, *Army Life of an Illinois Soldier* (Washington, DC: The Globe, 1906), 44; *Chicago Post,* November 29, 1861, quoted in *New York Times,* December 4, 1861; *New York Times,* No-

vember 25, 1861. The western naval force received full access to the wharf boat *Graham* on December 6 (Grant, *The Papers of Ulysses S. Grant*, 3:247–248n; Bearss, 28–29). Owned by her captain, a man named Carroll, the *Maria Denning* was an 870-ton side-wheel steamboat constructed at Cincinnati in 1858. This latest War Department auxiliary was 275 feet long, with a beam of 41 feet and an eight-foot depth of hold. She was powered by five boilers and at least two engines. Each of her paddle wheels measured nine feet by 26 inches. She would serve the army's naval flotilla until it was transferred to the Navy Department 11 months hence.

    6. OR, I, 7: 442; ORN, I, 22: 439–443, 452, 800, 803, 805; ORN, II, 1: 261; Grant, *The Papers of Ulysses S. Grant*, 3:213, 230–231; James M. Hoppin, *Life of Andrew Hull Foote, Rear-Admiral United States Navy* (New York: Harper & Brothers, Publishers, 1874), 162; Henry Walke, *Naval Scenes and Reminiscences of the Civil War in the United States on the Southern and Western Waters During the Years 1861, 1862 and 1863, with the History of That Period Compared and Corrected from Authentic Sources* (New York: F.R. Reed and Company, 1877), 31; Bearss, 29; *St. Louis Daily Democrat*, November 23, 1861; *New York Times*, December 11, 1861; "Egypt Mills, Missouri," in *Midwest Gazetteer*, <http://gazetteer.midwestplaces.com/mo/cape/egypt-mills> (accessed November 30, 2006); *Chicago Post*, November 29, 1861, quoted in *New York Times*, December 4, 1861. The Quartermaster Department acquired the year-old stern-wheeler *W.H. Brown* (also known as *Brown*) on June 13. Built at Monongalela, PA, the 200-ton craft was 230 feet long with a 26-foot beam. She would be transferred to the navy in October 1862 and was employed in military service as a dispatch and towboat auxiliary (Silverstone, 183).

    7. ORN, I, 22: 447; Grant, *The Papers of Ulysses S. Grant*, 3:230, 240–241; *Columbus Daily Enquirer*, December 5, 1861; *New York Times*, December 4, 12 1861.

    8. OR, I, 3, 739; OR, I, 4: 532, 550–551, 553, 557, 560–561; OR, I, 7: 703–704, 708; OR, I, 52, 2: 221–222; *Chicago Daily Tribune*, December 3, 1861; *Savannah Republican*, n.d., quoted in *New York Times*, December 11, 1861; Nathaniel Cheairs Hughes, Jr., *The Battle of Belmont: Grant Strikes South* (Chapel Hill: University of North Carolina Press, 1991), 191–192; Thomas Lawrence Connelly, *Army of the Heartland: The Army of Tennessee, 1861–1862* (Baton Rouge: Louisiana State University Press, 1967), 104–105; Joseph H. Parks, *General Leonidas Polk, C.S.A.: The Fighting Bishop* (Baton Rouge: Louisiana State University Press, 1962), 194, 200–201; William M. Polk, *Leonidas Polk, Bishop and General*, 2 vols. (New York: Longmans, Green & Co., 1915), 2: 44–46; ORN, II, 1: 478, 464, 253, 256; Charles W. Read, "Reminiscences of the Confederate States Navy," *Southern Historical Society Papers* 1 (1876): 336; J. Thomas Scharf, *History of the Confederate Navy from Its Organization to the Surrender of Its Last Vessel* (New York: Rodgers and Sherwood, 1887; repr., New York: Fairfax Press, 1977), 243–244; Silverstone, 244, 229.

    9. Daniel L. Ambrose, *History of the Seventh Regiment Illinois Volunteer Infantry* (Springfield, IL: Illinois Journal Company, 1868), 21; ORN, I, 22: 448, 451, 772; OR, I, 7: 6–7, 462–463; *Chicago Daily Tribune*, December 3, 1861; *Memphis Avalanche*, December 5, 1861; *New York Times*, December 12, 1861; Grant, *The Papers of Ulysses S. Grant*, 3:245–248.

    10. ORN, I, 22: 451–453, 807; OR, I, 4: 550; OR, I, 7: 736, 741–742, 773–774, 7976, 803, 828–829; OR, I, 52, 2: 223–226, 236; *Chicago Daily Tribune*, December 3, 1861; Connelly, 105; Parks, 200–201. Like Lt. Shirk, Lt. Paulding (1826–1867) was born in Erie County, PA. Entering the U.S. Navy in 1840, he was promoted to the rank of lieutenant in 1855, lieutenant-commander in 1862, and commander in 1865. He died on April 29, 1867 (Edward W. Callahan, *List of Officers of the Navy of the United States and of the Marine Corps, from 1775 to 1900, Comprising a Complete Register of All Present and Former Commissioned, Warranted, and Appointed Officers of the United States Navy, and of the Marine Corps, Regular and Volunteer, Compiled from the Official Records of the Navy Department* (New York: L.R. Hamersly & Co., 1901; repr., New York: Haskell House, 1969), 425.

    11. OR, I, 7: 430–433; ORN, I, 22: 457–458, 461–462, 513, 781, 799–800, 804–805; Bruce Catton, *Grant Moves South* (Boston: Little, Brown, 1960), 104; *Memphis Avalanche*, November 26, 1861; *Cincinnati Daily Commercial*, December 8, 1861, quoted in *New York Times*, December 14, 1861; *New York Times*, December 21, 28, 31, 1861; *Chicago Daily Tribune*, December 13, 1861; Slagle, 147–148; J. Haden Alldredge, et al., *A History of Navigation on the Tennessee River* (Washington, DC: GPO, 1937), 84–85. Nashville, TN, iron magnate John Bell (1797–1869) was a Tennessee congressman (1827–1841), secretary of war, 1841, U.S. senator (1847–1860), and Constitutional Union Party presidential candidate in 1860 ("John Bell," *The Learning Curve*, <http://www.spartacus.schoolnet.co.uk/USAbellJ.htm> (accessed December 24, 2006).

    12. Grant, *The Papers of Ulysses S. Grant*, 3:252–253, 304; *New York Times*, December 28, 31, 1861, and January 6, 1862; ORN, I, 22: 469–470, 476, 479–480; Gustavus Vasa Fox, *Confidential Correspondence of Gustavus Vasa Fox, Assistant Secretary of the Navy, 1861–1865*, ed. Robert Means Thompson and Richard Wainwright, 2 vols. (New York: De Vinne Press, 1918–1919), 2: 23–24; Slagle, 148; Catton, 110; *Philadelphia Inquirer*, April 17, 1862. The log of the floating battery *New Orleans* was captured after the fall of Island No. 10; extracts were published in the *Inquirer* on the date cited.

Chapter 7

    1. U.S. Navy Department, *Official Records of the Union and Confederate Navies in the War of the Rebellion*, 31 vols. (Washington, DC: GPO, 1894–1922), series I, vol. 22, 480–486, 773, 781, 813 (cited hereafter as ORN, followed by a comma, the series number in Roman numerals, a comma, the volume number in Arabic, a colon, and the page in Arabic); U.S. War Department, *The War of the Rebellion: A Compilation of the Official Records of the Union and Confederate Armies* (128 vols.), Washington, DC: GPO, 1880–1901), series I, vol. 7: 527–529, 532–534, 850–851 (cited hereafter as OR, followed by a comma, the series number in Roman numerals, a comma, the volume number in Arabic, any part number in Arabic, a colon, and the page in Arabic); OR, I, 52, 2: 248, 257–259; *New York Times*, January 6, 8, 12, 1862; *Memphis Appeal*, January 9, 1862; *Chicago Daily Tribune*, January 31, 1862; *Philadelphia Inquirer*, April 17, 1862; R.M. Kelly, "Holding Kentucky for the Union," in *Battles and Leaders of the Civil War*, ed. Robert V. Johnson and Clarence C. Buel, 4 vols. (New York: The Century Company, 1884–1887; Repr. Thomas Yoseloff, 1956), 1: 386–387; Thomas Lawrence Connelly, *Army of the Heartland: The Army of Tennessee, 1861–1862* (Baton Rouge: Louisiana State University Press, 1967), 106; Bruce Catton, *Grant Moves South* (Boston: Little, Brown, 1960), 118–119; Ethan S. Rafuse, *McClellan's War: The Failure of Moderation in the Struggle for the Union* (Bloomington: Indiana University Press, 2005), 168–169; Ulysses S. Grant, *Personal Memoirs of U.S. Grant*,

2 vols. (New York: C.L. Webster & Co., 1885–1886; repr. [2 vols. in 1], New York: Penguin Books, 1999), 1: 286–287; Ulysses S. Grant, *The Papers of Ulysses S. Grant, October 1, 1861-January 7, 1862*, ed. John Y. Simon, 24 vols. (Edwardsville: Southern Illinois University Press, 1970), 3:375–377; Jean Edward Smith, *Grant* (New York: Simon and Schuster, 2001), 137; Benjamin F. Cooling, *Forts Henry and Donelson: The Key to the Confederate Heartland* (Knoxville: University of Tennessee Press, 1987), 91; William B. Feis, *Grant's Secret Service: The Intelligence War from Belmont to Appomattox* (Lincoln: University of Nebraska Press, 2002), 60–61; Steven E. Woodworth, *Nothing But Victory: The Army of the Tennessee, 1861–1865* (New York: Alfred A. Knopf, 2005), 65–66; Milton F. Perry, *Infernal Machines: The Story of Confederate Submarine and Mine Warfare* (Baton Rouge: Louisiana State University Press, 1965), 10–11.

2. OR, I, 7: 541–543; ORN, I, 22: 487–491, 497–500; *Cincinnati Enquirer*, January 11, 1862, quoted in the *Philadelphia Enquirer*, January 15, 1862; *New York Times*, January 11, 18, 25, 27, 1862; Woodworth, 66; Ulysses S. Grant, *The Papers of Ulysses S. Grant, January 8-March 31, 1862*, ed. John Y. Simon, 24 vols. (Edwardsville: Southern Illinois University Press, 1972), 4:30–31, 36–37, 40.

3. OR, I, 7: 551–552; ORN, I, 22: 500, 773; *St. Louis Missouri Democrat*, January 10, 13, 16, 1862; *Chicago Daily Tribune*, January 14, 1862; *New York Times*, January 15, 23, 27, 1862; *New Orleans Crescent*, n.d., quoted in *Macon Daily Telegraph*, January 25, 1862; Grant, *The Papers of Ulysses S. Grant*, 4:41, 53–55; Rafuse, 171; Smith, 137; Woodworth, 67; Theodore R. Parker, "William J. Kountz, Superintendent of River Transportation Under McClellan, 1861–62," *Western Pennsylvania Historical Magazine* 21 (December 1938): 250–254. The 1862 difficulties between Grant and Kountz subsequently are dealt with at length in volume 4 of the Grant papers, 108–119. Kountz, who pressed charges against Grant all the way up to new War Secretary Stanton, later served as Brig. Gen. Robert Allen's St. Louis river transportation deputy. We note his difficulties here largely to finish the story of a man whose connection with the birth of the timberclads has not received wide circulation. Parker, 250–254; Catton, 500–501n.

4. OR, I, 7: 68–74. 107–108, 114, 561, 847; ORN, I, 22: 404, 501, 507–508, 551, 773; *New York Times*, January 23–24, 27, 1862; *New York Herald*, January 25, 1862; *Chicago Evening Journal*, January 24, 1862; *Chicago Daily Tribune*, January 31, 1862; William P. Johnston, *The Life of Gen. Albert Sidney Johnston* (New York: D. Appleton and Company, 1878), 400–401, 422; Lew Wallace, *An Autobiography*, 2 vols. (New York: Harper & Brothers, 1906), 356; Catton, 120–122; Woodworth, 67–68; Cooling, 70–72; Feis, 60–63; James W. Jessee, *Civil War Diaries of James W. Jessee, 1861–1865, Company K, 8th Regiment of Illinois Volunteer Infantry*, ed. William P. LaBounty (Normal, IL: McLean County Genealogical Society, 1997), 4; Grant, *Personal Memoirs of U.S. Grant*, 74–75, 90–91n, 286–287; Smith, 137–138; Jesse Taylor, "The Defense of Fort Henry," *B&L*, 1:369; Donald Davidson, *The Tennessee*, vol. 2, *The New River, Civil War to TVA*, Rivers of America (New York: Rinehart & Co., 1948), 14; C. Peter Ripley, "Prelude to Donelson: Grant's January 1862 March into Kentucky," *Register of the Kentucky Historical Society* 68 (October 1970): 311–318; Grant, *The Papers of Ulysses S. Grant*, 4:74–75, 90–91n; Kelly, "Holding Kentucky for the Union," *B&L*, 1:387–392; Jay Slagle, *Ironclad Captain: Seth Ledyard Phelps and the U.S. Navy* (Kent, OH: Kent State University Press, 1996), 149. Grant's biographer, Smith, suggests that the timing of his request to visit Halleck was good. It offered "Old Brains" an opportunity to possibly avoid political difficulties because, "Unless Thomas victory could be offset, Buell could easily emerge as the overall Union commander west of the Appalachians" (Smith, 138).

5. ORN, I, 22: 501, 508–515, 520–521, 773; OR, I, 7: 72–74; Connelly, 106; *New York Times*, January 28, 31 1862; *Florence (AL) Gazette*, January 22, 1862; *Clarksville (TN) Chronicle*, January 31, 1862; *Memphis Appeal*, n.d., quoted in *Macon Weekly Telegraph*, January 31, 1862; *New York Herald*, February 2, 1862; *Chicago Daily Tribune*, January 29, 1861; Slagle, 149–150; Donaldson, 25; Slagle, 149–150; Clarence Edward Macartney, *Mr. Lincoln's Admirals* (New York: Funk and Wagnalls, 1956), 91.

6. Feis, 62–66; ORN, I, 22: 512–513, 524–526; OR, I, 7: 120–122, 440, 561, 571; OR, I, 8: 509; *New York Times*, February 5, 1862; *Chicago Daily Tribune*, January 29, 1862; Cooling, 44–46, 66; Grant, *The Papers of Ulysses S. Grant*, 4:90–91, 99, 103–104, 121–122; Grant, *Personal Memoirs of U.S. Grant*, 287–288; Gustavus Vasa Fox, *Confidential Correspondence of Gustavus Vasa Fox, Assistant Secretary of the Navy, 1861–1865*, ed. Robert Means Thompson and Richard Wainwright, 2 vols. (New York: De Vinne Press, 1918–1919), 2: 32; Smith, 138; Woodworth, 68–69; Johnston, 420; Peter Franklin Walker, "Command Failure: The Fall of Forts Henry and Donelson," *Tennessee Historical Quarterly* 16 (December 1957): 335; Manning F. Force, *From Fort Henry to Corinth*, Great Campaigns of the Civil War, vol. 2 (New York: C. Scribner's Sons, 1881; repr., New York: T.Y. Yoseloff, 1963), 25–28; Gen. Beauregard did come west. He arrived at Bowling Green, KY, on February 5 accompanied by two staff officers (Smith, 148).

7. ORN, I, 22: 528, 556; OR, I, 7: 149; Donaldson, 16–19; Cooling, 88; Smith, 143–144; Wallace, 1: 356–364; Slagle, 152–155; Henry Walke, "The Gunboats at Belmont and Fort Henry," *B&L*, 1:364; Taylor, "The Defense of Fort Henry," *B&L*, 1:369–370; John L. Holcombe and Walter J. Buttgenbachli, "Coast Defense in the Civil War: Fort Henry, Tennessee," *Journal of the United States Artillery* 39 (January 1913): 84–86, 89; Kenneth R. Johnson, "Confederate Defense and Union Gunboats on the Tennessee River," *The Alabama Historical Quarterly* 64 (Summer 1968): 41. The African American rescued by the *Conestoga* may have escaped from a group sent from northern Alabama at the beginning of the month to help strengthen Fort Henry's defenses (Johnson, 47).

8. ORN, I, 22: 529, 531–537, 552–554, 565–567; OR, I, 7: 121–122, 136–140, 149, 151, 579, 581, 858; Woodworth, 71–74; *Clarksville (TN) Chronicle*, February 7, 1862; *New York Times*, February 9, 12, 1862; Grant, *The Papers of Ulysses S. Grant*, 4:141, 145–146, 148–149; Grant, *Personal Memoirs of U.S. Grant*, 290; Allen Morgan Geer, *The Civil War Diary of Allen Morgan Geer, 20th Regiment, Illinois Volunteers*, ed. Mary Ann Anderson (Denver, CO: Robert C. Appleman, 1977), 5, 15; Walker, 339–340; Lew Wallace, *Smoke, Sound & Fury: The Civil War Memoirs of Major General Lew Wallace, U.S. Volunteers*, ed. Jim Leeke (Portland, OR: Strawberry Hill Press, 1998), 60; Daniel L. Ambrose, *History of the Seventh Regiment Illinois Volunteer Infantry* (Springfield, IL: Illinois Journal Company, 1868), 25; Franc B. Wilkie, *Pen and Powder* (Boston: Ticknor and Company, 1888), 99; Cooling, 89, 92–93; Slagle, 158; Walke, "The Gunboats at Belmont and Fort Henry," *B&L*, 1:362; Spencer C. Tucker, "Timberclads Attack Up the Tennessee," *Naval History* 16 (February 2001): 27; Tucker, *Andrew Foote: Civil War Admiral on Western Waters* (Annapolis, MD: Naval Institute Press, 2000), 136–140; *Cincinnati Daily Gazette*, February 10, 1862. The *Gazette* story is reprinted in Frank Moore, ed., *The Rebellion Record: A Diary of American Events*, 12 vols. (New York:

G. P. Putnam, 1861–1863; D. Van Nostrand, 1864–1868; repr., New York: Arno, 1977), 4: 69–73.

9. ORN, I, 22: 555–556, 567, 781–782; OR, I, 7: 580–587; *New York Times*, February 12, 1862; *Cincinnati Daily Gazette*, February 10, 1862; *Boston Morning Journal*, February 12, 1862; Davidson, 19; Woodworth, 74–76; Albert D. Richardson, *The Secret Service: The Field, the Dungeon and The Escape* (Hartford, CT: American Publishing Company, 1866), 214; Charles Carleton Coffin, *My Days and Nights on the Battlefield: A Book for Boys*, by "Carlton," pseud., 2nd ed. (Boston: Ticknor and Fields, 1864), 76–77; Taylor, "The Defense of Fort Henry," *B&L*, 1:369; Elliot Callendar, "What a Boy Saw on the Mississippi," in *Military Essays and Recollections: Papers Read Before the Commandry of the State of Illinois, Military Order of the Loyal Legion of the United States* (Chicago: A.C. McClurg and Company, 1891), 1:53–55; Smith, 144–145; Slagle, 158; Walke, "The Gunboats at Belmont and Fort Henry," *B&L*, 1:362; The *Morning Journal* story is reprinted in Frank Moore, ed., *The Rebellion Record* 4: 69–73.

10. OR, I, 7: 124, 140–153, 861; ORN, I, 22: 539, 541–542, 557–561, 567–569, 782; Smith, 144, 147; Richardson, 215–216; Woodworth, 75–78; Force, 30–31; Cooling, 101–113; Walker, 340–344; Johnston, 429–436; Coffin, 77–87; *Chicago Daily Tribune*, February 8, 1862; *New York Herald*, February 14, 1862; *Philadelphia Enquirer*, February 11, 1862; *New York Times*, February 12, 1862; *Boston Morning Journal*, February 12, 1862; *Cincinnati Daily Gazette*, February 10, 1862; *St. Louis Missouri Democrat*, February 9, 1862; Taylor, "The Defense of Fort Henry," *B&L*, 1:370–372; Wallace, *Smoke, Sound & Fury*, 62, 70; Slagle, 160–162; Wilkie, 99–100; Walke, "The Gunboats at Belmont and Fort Henry," *B&L*, 1:363–367; Kenneth R. Johnson, "Confederate Defenses and Union Gunboats on the Tennessee River," *The Alabama Historical Quarterly* 64 (Summer 1968): 49–50. The "G.W.B." *Democrat* story is reprinted in Frank Moore, ed., *The Rebellion Record* 4: 69–73, though Moore's printer mistakenly changed the final letter of the reporter's initials from "B" to "F." In addition to the accounts contained in the resources, newspaper, monograph, and article already cited in the notes to this chapter, we recommend, for the role of the ironclads at Fort Henry, these reviews, among others: Henry Walke, *Naval Scenes and Reminiscences of the Civil War in the United States on the Southern and Western Waters During the Years 1861, 1862 and 1863, with the History of That Period Compared and Corrected from Authentic Sources* (New York: F.R. Reed and Company, 1877), 54–68; Spencer C. Tucker, *Unconditional Surrender: The Capture of Forts Henry and Donelson* (Abilene, TX: McWhiney Foundation Press, 2001), 47–60; Tucker, *Andrew Foote*, 140–145; Edwin C. Bearss, "The Fall of Fort Henry," *West Tennessee Historical Society Publications* 17 (1963): 85–107; John D. Milligan, *Gunboats Down the Mississippi* (Annapolis, MD: Naval Institute Press, 1965), 37–42; Alfred T. Mahan, *The Navy in the Civil War*, vol. 3, *The Gulf and Inland Waters* (New York: Scribner's, 1883), 20–24; Jack D. Coombe, *Thunder Along the Mississippi: The River Battles That Split the Confederacy* (New York: Sarpedon Publishers, 1996), 43–52.

Chapter 8

1. *Atlanta Confederacy*, n.d., quoted in the *Macon Daily Telegraph*, February 10, 1862; Joseph H. Parks, *General Leonidas Polk, C.S.A.: The Fighting Bishop* (Baton Rouge: Louisiana State University Press, 1962), 209–210; William P. Johnston, *The Life of Gen. Albert Sidney Johnston* (New York: D. Appleton and Company, 1878), 435–439; Jean Edward Smith, *Grant* (New York: Simon and Schuster, 2001), 148–150; Benjamin F. Cooling, *Forts Henry and Donelson: The Key to the Confederate Heartland* (Knoxville: University of Tennessee Press, 1987), 123–125; T. Harry Williams, *P.G.T. Beauregard* (Baton Rouge: Louisiana State University Press, 1954), 151–154; Charles P. Roland, *Albert Sidney Johnston: Soldier of Three Republics* (Austin: University of Texas Press, 1964), 289–291.

2. U.S. Navy Department, *Official Records of the Union and Confederate Navies in the War of the Rebellion*, 31 vols. (Washington, DC: GPO, 1894–1922), series I, vol. 22, 537, 782 (cited hereafter as ORN, followed by a comma, the series number in Roman numerals, a comma, the volume number in Arabic, a colon, and the page in Arabic); U.S. War Department, *The War of the Rebellion: A Compilation of the Official Records of the Union and Confederate Armies*. 128 vols. (Washington, DC: GPO, 1880–1901), series I, vol. 7: 153 (cited hereafter as OR, followed by a comma, the series number in Roman numerals, a comma, the volume number in Arabic, any part number in Arabic, a colon, and the page in Arabic) OR, I, 2, 154–156; Ulysses S. Grant, *The Papers of Ulysses S. Grant, January 8-March 31, 1862*, ed. John Y. Simon, 24 vols. (Edwardsville: Southern Illinois University Press, 1972), 4:168–169, 171–172; *Cincinnati Daily Gazette*, February 17, 1862; J. Haden Alldredge et al., *A History of Navigation on the Tennessee River* (Washington, DC: GPO, 1937), 84–85; Jay Slagle, *Ironclad Captain: Seth Ledyard Phelps and the U.S. Navy* (Kent, OH: Kent State University Press, 1996), 162–163; Henry Walke, "The Western Flotilla at Fort Donelson, Island Number Ten, Fort Pillow and Memphis," in *Battles and Leaders of the Civil War*, ed. Robert V. Johnson and Clarence C. Buel, 4 vols. (New York: The Century Company, 1884–1887; repr., Thomas Yoseloff, 1956), 1: 430; Spencer C. Tucker, "Timberclads Attack Up the Tennessee," *Naval History* 16 (February 2001): 27; Edwin C. Bearss, "A Federal Raid Up the Tennessee River," *The Alabama Review* 17 (October 1964), 261–262, 268. The most complete newspaper account of the raid was turned in by Joseph B. "Mac" McCullagh of the *Cincinnati Daily Gazette* on February 12; it reached print five days later. "Mack's" account was based on information contained in Lt. Phelps' official report and interviews conducted at Paducah.

3. *Philadelphia Inquirer*, February 10, 1862; *St. Louis Daily Missouri Republican*, February 10, 1862; *St. Louis Daily Missouri Democrat*, February 10, 1862; *Memphis Avalanche*, February 12, 1862; *Memphis Daily Appeal*, February 12, 1862; *Chicago Daily Tribune*, February 10, 1862; *Cincinnati Daily Gazette*, February 17, 1862; ORN, I, 22: 572, 574–575; 782; OR, I, 7: 153–154, 591; Grant, *The Papers of Ulysses S. Grant*, 4:172–173; Bearss, 262–263; Slagle, 163–167; Tucker, 28–29; Paul H. Silverstone, *Warships of the Civil War Navies* (Annapolis, MD: Naval Institute Press, 1989), 249; Donald Davidson, *The Tennessee*, vol. 2, *The New River, Civil War to TVA*, Rivers of America (New York: Rinehart & Co., 1948), 23; B.G. Brazelton, *A History of Hardin County, Tennessee* (Nashville: Cumberland Presbyterian Publishing House, 1885), 63–64; Kenneth R. Johnson, "Confederate Defenses and Union Gunboats on the Tennessee River," *The Alabama Historical Quarterly* 64 (Summer 1968): 50–52; Milford M. Miller, "Evansville Steamboats During the Civil War," *Indiana Magazine of History* 37 (December 1941): 368–369. Kentuckian I.N. Brown (1817–1889), a messmate of Cmdr. Henry Walke, is best known as the commander of the *Arkansas*. After his adventure with that armorclad, he

went on to skipper another ironclad, the C.S.S. *Charleston,* at her namesake South Carolina city. After the war, he farmed in Mississippi before relocating to Texas (U.S. Navy Department, Naval Historical Center, "Commander Isaac Newton Brown, CSN (1817–1889)," OnLine Library of Selected Images— People — United States, http://www.history.navy.mil/photos/pers-us/uspers-b/in-brwn.htm (accessed March 30, 2007).

4. Silverman, 156, 182, 248; Paul H. Silverstone, *Warships of the Civil War Navies* (Annapolis, MD: Naval Institute Press, 1989), 156; ORN, I, 22: 572–573, 643, 782–783; OR, I, 7: 153–155, 858, 864–867; *Cincinnati Daily Commercial,* February 15, 1862; *Cincinnati Daily Gazette,* February 13, 17, 1862; *Florence (AL) Gazette,* January 22 and February 12, 1862; *Memphis Avalanche,* February 12, 1862; *Richmond Dispatch,* February 12, 1862; *New York Times,* February 13, 1862; *Tuscumbia Constitution,* n.d., quoted in *Memphis Appeal,* February 13, 1862; *Chicago Daily Tribune,* February 12, 1862; *Harper's Weekly,* March 1, 1862; Bearss, 264–265; Alldredge, 86; Slagle, 165–169; Tucker, 28–30; Johnson, 53–56; Miller, 369; Timothy B. Smith, "'Gallant and Invaluable Service': The United States Navy at the Battle of Shiloh," *West Tennessee Historical Society Papers* 58 (2004): 36–37.

5. ORN, I, 22: 578, 583–585, 783; OR, 1, 7: 156, 600; 894; Davidson, 23–24; Grant, *The Papers of Ulysses S. Grant,* 4:182–183; Henry Walke, *Naval Scenes and Reminiscences of the Civil War in the United States on the Southern and Western Waters During the Years 1861, 1862 and 1863, with the History of That Period Compared and Corrected from Authentic Sources* (New York: F.R. Reed and Company, 1877), 68, 82; Robert C. Suhr, "Converted River Steamers Dubbed 'Timberclads' Gave the Union Navy an Important Presence on Southern Waters," *America's Civil War* 11 (July 1998): 25; Steven R. Davis, "Workhorse of the Western Waters: The Timberclad *Tyler,*" *Civil War Times Illustrated* 44 (February 2005): 38; Slagle, 170–176; Johnson, 57–60; Bearss, 265; OR, I, 7: 865–867; Tucker, 29; *Cincinnati Daily Commercial,* February 17, 1862; *Cincinnati Daily Gazette,* February 17, 1862; *St. Louis Daily Missouri Democrat,* February 11, 1862; *New York Times,* February 12, 19, 1862; the *Charleston Mercury,* February 12, 1862; Bruce Catton, *Grant Moves South* (Boston: Little, Brown, 1960), 148.

6. Catton, 146, 150; OR, I, 7: 124, 165, 388–389, 409–410; *St. Louis Daily Missouri Democrat,* February 14, 1862; *Cincinnati Times,* February 13, 1862, quoted in *New York Times,* February 20, 1862; *Chicago Daily Tribune,* February 14, 19–20, 1862; Spencer C. Tucker, *Andrew Foote: Civil War Admiral on Western Waters* (Annapolis, MD: Naval Institute Press, 2000), 146–150; Albert D. Richardson, *The Secret Service: The Field, the Dungeon and The Escape* (Hartford, CT: American Publishing Company, 1866), 213; Smith, 149–152; Jay Carlton Mullen, "The Turning of Columbus," *The Register of the Kentucky Historical Society* 64 (July 1966): 223; Slagle, 176; Walter J. Buttgenbach, "Coast Defense in the Civil War: Fort Donelson," *Journal of the U.S. Artillery* 39 (March 1913): 211; William B. Feis, *Grant's Secret Service: The Intelligence War from Belmont to Appomattox* (Lincoln: University of Nebraska Press, 2002), 68–70; Ulysses S. Grant, *Personal Memoirs of U.S. Grant,* 2 vols. (New York: C.L. Webster & Co., 1885–1886; repr. [2 vols. in 1], New York: Penguin Books, 1999), 1: 291, 297–298; Cooling, 116, 140.

7. Catton, 150–151; Grant, *Personal Memoirs of U.S. Grant,* 241, 298; Grant, *The Papers of Ulysses S. Grant,* 4:183, 201–207; Johnston, 448–449; OR, I, 7: 162, 170–171, 183–184, 594–596, 600–601, 603–604, 613–614; ORN, I, 22: 583–584, 587–588, 592, 594; *Cincinnati Times,* February 13, 1862, quoted in *New York Times,* February 20, 1862; *St. Louis Daily Missouri Democrat,* February 13, 18, 1862; Lew Wallace, *Smoke, Sound & Fury: The Civil War Memoirs of Major General Lew Wallace, U.S. Volunteers,* ed. Jim Leeke (Portland, OR: Strawberry Hill Press, 1998), 67; Steven E. Woodworth, *Nothing But Victory: The Army of the Tennessee, 1861–1865* (New York: Alfred A. Knopf, 2005), 79–88; Franc B. Wilkie, *Pen and Powder* (Boston: Ticknor and Company, 1888), 99–100; Edwin C. Bearss, "The Ironclads at Fort Donelson," *Register of the Kentucky Historical Society* 74 (January 1976): 1–9; Cooling, 121; *New York Times,* February 18, 1862; *St. Louis Daily Missouri Democrat,* February 19, 1862; Slagle, 176–177; Walke, "The Western Flotilla at Fort Donelson, Island Number Ten, Fort Pillow and Memphis," 433; Tucker, *Andrew Foote,* 150–154; Charles C. Nott, *Sketches of the War: A Series of Letters to the North Moore Street School of New York,* cited in E. McCleod Johnson, *A History of Henry County, Tennessee* (Paris, TN: Priv. Print., 1958), 90.

8. ORN, I, 22: 584–585, 591–592; OR, I, 7: 163, 166 172–174, 262–263, 399, 629; Grant, *Personal Memoirs of U.S. Grant,* 242–248, 301–309; Grant, *The Papers of Ulysses S. Grant,* 4:230–231; *New York Herald,* February 17, 1862; *New York Times,* February 17, 22, 1862; *St. Louis Daily Missouri Democrat,* February 16–17, 1862; *Chicago Daily Tribune,* February 16–17, 19–20, 1862; *Philadelphia Inquirer,* February 17, March 3, 1862; *Charleston Mercury,* February 17, 1862; Walke, "The Western Flotilla at Fort Donelson, Island Number Ten, Fort Pillow and Memphis," 433–436; Walke, *Naval Scenes,* 79, 84–86; Bearss, 167–181; Wallace, 75; Johnston, 449–452; Woodworth, 88–120; H.L. Bedford, "Fight Between the Batteries and Gunboats at Fort Donelson," *Southern Historical Society Papers* 13 (1885): 171–172; Nott, 90; Cooling, 155–160; Smith, 153–155; Peter Franklin Walker, "Command Failure: The Fall of Forts Henry and Donelson," *Tennessee Historical Quarterly* 16 (December 1957): 348–349; Thomas Lawrence Connelly, *Army of the Heartland: The Army of Tennessee, 1861–1862* (Baton Rouge: Louisiana State University Press, 1967), 120; Scott W. Stucky, "Joint Operations in the Civil War," *Joint Forces Quarterly* 6 (Autumn-Winter 1994–1995): 98; Wesley Smith Dorris quoted in David C. Allen, *Winds of Change: Robertson County, Tennessee in the Civil War* (Nashville: Land Yacht Press, 2000), 25–26; Wilkie, 100–101, 104, 110–112; James M. Hoppin, *The Life of Andrew Hull Foote, Rear Admiral, United States Navy* (New York: Harper and Brothers, 1874), 223; Spencer C. Tucker, *Unconditional Surrender: The Capture of Forts Henry and Donelson* (Abilene, TX: McWhiney Foundation Press, 2001), 61–104; Tucker, *Andrew Foote: Civil War Admiral on Western Waters* (Annapolis, MD: Naval Institute Press, 2000), 154–158; Buttgenbach, 213; Sometime later, when he heard of the defeat, Cmdr. John Rodgers II, replaced by Foote in command of the timberclad flotilla back in September, suggested his successor's tactics were faulty. Ironclads, he noted, were to fight wooden vessels and forts from a distance great enough to insure the ironclads remained unscathed. They were not to close and, as in the old school of sailing ships, exchange smashing broadsides (Robert E. Johnson, *Rear Admiral John Rodgers, 1812–1882* (Annapolis, MD: Naval Institute Press, 1967), 167–168).

9. Bearss, 182–186; ORN, I, 22: 585–590, 592–614, 634–635, 783; OR, I, 7: 166–167, 212, 275, 288, 295, 364, 386–387, 396, 401, 421, 618–619, 889–891, 894–895; Grant, *Personal Memoirs of U.S. Grant,* 249–250; Grant, *The Papers of Ulysses S. Grant,* 4:214–217, 227, 230n-231; *St. Louis Daily Missouri Democrat,* February 17, 1862; *New York Herald,* February 17, 1862; *New York Times,* March 2, 1862; Johnson, 59; Walke, "The Western Flotilla at Fort Donel-

son, Island Number Ten, Fort Pillow and Memphis," 436–437; Walke, *Naval Scenes*, 92; Catton, 164–169. Brooks D. Simpson, *Ulysses S. Grant: Triumph Over Adversity, 1822–1885* (New York: Houghton, Mifflin, 2000), 115; Tucker, *Andrew Foote*, 158–164; Connelly, 121–125; Smith, 155–165; Cooling, 229; Manning F. Force, *From Fort Henry to Corinth*, Great Campaigns of the Civil War, vol. 2 (New York: C. Scribner's Sons, 1881; repr., New York: T.Y. Yoseloff, 1963), 64; Larry J. Daniel, *Shiloh: The Battle That Changed the Civil War* (New York: Simon & Schuster, 1997), 69.

Chapter 9

1. *New York Herald*, February 18, 24, 1862; *Chicago Daily Tribune*, February 21, 25, 1862; *St. Louis Daily Missouri Democrat*, February 26–27, 1862; *New York Times*, March 4, 1862; *Nashville Times*, March 5, 1862; *Charleston Mercury*, March 6, 1862; U.S. Navy Department, *Official Records of the Union and Confederate Navies in the War of the Rebellion*, 31 vols. (Washington, DC: GPO, 1894–1922), series I, vol. 22, 587, 614–627, 637–638, 640–641, 676 (cited hereafter as ORN, followed by a comma, the series number in Roman numerals, a comma, the volume number in Arabic, a colon, and the page in Arabic); U.S. War Department, *The War of the Rebellion: A Compilation of the Official Records of the Union and Confederate Armies*, 128 vols. (Washington, DC: GPO, 1880–1901), series I, vol. 7: 422–423, 620–645, 648, 655–668, 682 (cited hereafter as OR, followed by a comma, the series number in Roman numerals, a comma, the volume number in Arabic, any part number in Arabic, a colon, and the page in Arabic); Benjamin F. Cooling, *Forts Henry and Donelson: The Key to the Confederate Heartland* (Knoxville: University of Tennessee Press, 1987), 225–231; 246–248; Steven E. Woodworth, *Nothing But Victory: The Army of the Tennessee, 1861–1865* (New York: Alfred A. Knopf, 2005), 122–127; Ulysses S. Grant, *Personal Memoirs of U.S. Grant*, 2 vols. (New York: C.L. Webster & Co., 1885–1886; repr., [2 vols. in 1], New York: Penguin Books, 1999), 1: 317–321; Ulysses S. Grant, *The Papers of Ulysses S. Grant, January 8–March 31, 1862*, ed. John Y. Simon, 24 vols. (Edwardsville: Southern Illinois University Press, 1972), 4:231, 245–246, 252–254, 257–262, 272–273, 278–279, 282–284, 299; Curt Anders, *Henry Halleck's War: A Fresh Look at Lincoln's Controversial General-in-Chief* (Indianapolis: Guild Press of Indiana, 1999), 76–88; Stephen E. Ambrose, *Halleck: Lincoln's Chief of Staff* (Baton Rouge: Louisiana State University Press, 1962), 33; Arthur L. Conger, *The Rise of U.S. Grant* (New York: Century, 1931), 201; Edwin C. Bearss, *Hardluck Ironclad: The Sinking and Salvage of the Cairo* (Baton Rouge: Louisiana State University Press, 1966), 38–42; Thomas Lawrence Connelly, *Army of the Heartland: The Army of Tennessee, 1861–1862* (Baton Rouge: Louisiana State University Press, 1967), 126–135; Ursula Smith Beach, *Along the Warioto, or A History of Montgomery County, Tennessee* (Clarksville, TN: Clarksville Kiwanis Club and the Tennessee Historical Commission, 1964), 201–206. The Buell-Halleck feud is covered by Larry J. Daniel in his *Days of Glory: The Army of the Cumberland, 1861–1865* (Baton Rouge: Louisiana State University Press, 2004), 57–73.

2. ORN, I, 22: 624–640, 654, 783; OR, I, 7: 153–156, 424, 436–438, 677, 683, 860–861, 890–892, 896–897, 944–945; *Memphis Avalanche*, February 26, 1862; *New York Times*, March 1, 5, 1862; *Chicago Daily Tribune*, February 25, 1862; *Cincinnati Daily Commercial*, March 1, 1862; Connelly, 136–142; Grant, *Personal Memoirs of U.S. Grant*, 1: 215–217; Grant, *The Papers of Ulysses S. Grant*, 4:278–280, 282–283; Jean Edward Smith, *Grant* (New York: Simon and Schuster, 2001), 168–174; Henry Walke, *Naval Scenes and Reminiscences of the Civil War in the United States on the Southern and Western Waters During the Years 1861, 1862 and 1863, with the History of That Period Compared and Corrected from Authentic Sources* (New York: F.R. Reed and Company, 1877), 94–95; Joseph H. Parks, *General Leonidas Polk, C.S.A.: The Fighting Bishop* (Baton Rouge: Louisiana State University Press, 1962), 208–219; Robert D. Whitsell, "Military and Naval Activities Between Cairo and Columbus," *The Register of the Kentucky Historical Society* 61 (April 1963): 120–121; Spencer C. Tucker, *Andrew Foote: Civil War Admiral on Western Waters* (Annapolis, MD: Naval Institute Press, 2000), 165–167; Walter T. Durham, *Nashville: The Occupied City—the First Seventeen Months—February 16, 1862–June 30, 1863* (Nashville: Tennessee Historical Society, 1985), 1–54; Jay C. Mullen, "The Turning of Columbus," *Register of the Kentucky Historical Society* 64 (July 1966): 223–225; Daniel, 67–71; Cooling, 226–239; Henry R. Browne and Symmes E. Browne, *From the Fresh Water Navy, 1861–1864: Letters of Acting Master's Mate Henry R. Browne and Acting Ensign Symmes E. Browne*, ed. John D. Milligan, Naval Letters Series, vol. 3 (Annapolis, MD: Naval Institute Press, 1970), 31–32. The logbook of the Confederate floating battery *New Orleans* was captured upon the fall of Island No. 10 and an extract was published in the *Philadelphia Inquirer* on April 4, 1862.

3. Larry J. Daniel, *Shiloh: The Battle That Changed the Civil War* (New York: Simon & Schuster, 1997), 73–74; Daniel and Lynn N. Bock, *Island No. 10: Struggle in the Mississippi Valley* (Tuscaloosa: University of Alabama Press, 1996), 41, 70; *St. Louis Daily Missouri Democrat*, March 4, 1862; *New York Times*, March 5, 1862; Henry Walke, "The Western Flotilla at Fort Donelson, Island Number Ten, Fort Pillow and Memphis," in *Battles and Leaders of the Civil War*, ed. Robert V. Johnson and Clarence C. Buel, 4 vols. (New York: The Century Company, 1884–1887; repr., Thomas Yoseloff, 1956), 1: 439; Edward W. Callahan, *List of Officers of the Navy of the United States and of the Marine Corps, from 1775 to 1900, Comprising a Complete Register of All Present and Former Commissioned, Warranted, and Appointed Officers of the United States Navy, and of the Marine Corps, Regular and Volunteer, Compiled from the Official Records of the Navy Department* (New York: L.R. Hamersly & Co., 1901; repr., New York: Haskell House, 1969), 62; Tom Ledoux, "United States Navy Biographies: George M. Blodgett," VermontCivilWar.Org, <http://vermontcivilwar.org/units/navy/bios.php?input=33437> (accessed January 27, 2007). The Island No. 10 campaign is concisely reviewed by Howard P. Nash in his "Island No. 10," *Civil War Times Illustrated* 5 (December 1966): 42–50, and by Peter Cozzens in his "Roadblock on the Mississippi," *Civil War Times Illustrated* 41 (March 2002): 40–49.

4. ORN, I, 22: 643–648; OR, I, 7: 421, 619, 887–888, 890, 894–895, 909; OR, I, 10, 1: 646; OR, I, 10, 2: 8; Timothy B. Smith, "'Gallant and Invaluable Service': The United States Navy at the Battle of Shiloh," *West Tennessee Historical Society Papers* 58 (2004): 32, 36–38; Daniel, *Shiloh*, 68–70; F. Van Wyck Mason, *Blue Hurricane* (Philadelphia: J. B. Lippincott Co., 1954), 161; B.G. Brazelton, *A History of Hardin County, Tennessee* (Nashville: Cumberland Presbyterian Publishing House, 1885), 67–68; E.Y. Hedley, *Marching Through Georgia: Pen-Pictures of Every-Day Life in General Sherman's Army from the Beginning of the Atlanta Campaign Until the Closing of the War* (Chicago: Donohue, Henneberry & Co., 1890), 34–41;

Silas T. Grisamore, *The Civil War Reminiscences of Major Silas T. Grisamore, C.S.A.*, ed. Arthur W. Bergeron, Jr. (Baton Rouge: Louisiana State University Press, 1993), 19–22; Chuck Velt, "The First Battle of Shiloh," *Naval History* 18 (October 2004): 43–45; Velt, "First Shiloh," *Navy and Marine*, http://www.navyandmarine.org/ondeck/1862firstshiloh.htm (accessed January 25, 2007); Joseph Richard, *The 18th Louisiana Infantry Regiment: A Brief History and Roster*, <http://members.tripod.com/j_richard/> (accessed February 1, 2007); *New Orleans Daily Delta*, April 16, 1862; *New Orleans Daily Picayune*, February 8, March 9, 11, 1862; *Mobile Advertiser & Register*, March 14, 1862; *Chicago Daily Tribune*, March 3–4, 7–8, 1862; *Chicago Daily Post*, March 3, 1862; *Cincinnati Daily Commercial*, March 4–5, 1862; *Natchitoches Union*, April 3, 1862; *Nashville Times*, March 11, April 9, 1862; *New York Times*, March 8, 1862; *St. Louis Daily Missouri Democrat*, March 7, 1862.

5. ORN, I, 22: 643, 646, 649–655; OR, I, 7: 437–438; OR, I, 8: 149–151, 179, 186, 726, 760, 762; *New York Times*, March 10, 1862; *Chicago Daily Tribune*, March 4, 1862; Woodworth, 128; Grant, *The Papers of Ulysses S. Grant*, 4:310–312; Daniel and Bock, *Island No. 10*, 28–30; *Philadelphia Inquirer*, April 17, 1862; Parks, 214–215; William M. Polk, *Leonidas Polk, Bishop and General*, 2 vols. (New York: Longmans, Green & Co., 1915), 2:75–81; *Cincinnati Daily Gazette*, March 5, 8, 1862.

6. ORN, I, 22: 651–654; *Cincinnati Daily Gazette*, March 8, 1862; *Philadelphia Inquirer*, March 9, 1862; *New York Times*, March 10, 1862; Daniel and Bock, *Island No. 10*, 153; Jay Slagle, *Ironclad Captain: Seth Ledyard Phelps and the U.S. Navy* (Kent, OH: Kent State University Press, 1996), 194–195; Junius Henri Browne, *Four Years in Secessia: Adventures Within and Without the Union Lines* (Hartford, CT: O.D. Case and Company, 1865), 87–90; William T. Sherman, *Sherman's Civil War: Selected Correspondence of William T. Sherman, 1860–1865*, ed. Brooks D. Simpson and Jean V. Berlin (Chapel Hill: University of North Carolina Press, 1999), 195; Tucker, 168.

7. ORN, I, 655–666, 693, 770; ORN, I, 23: 279; Allen C. Guelzo, *The Crisis of the American Republic: A History of the Civil War and Reconstruction* (New York: St. Martin's Press, 1995), 153–154; Daniel and Bock, *Island No. 10*, 68–78; Franc B. Wilkie, *Pen and Powder* (Boston: Ticknor and Company, 1888), 148–153; Browne, *Four Years in Secessia*, 117–118; *St. Louis Daily Missouri Democrat*, March 19, 1862; *St. Louis Daily Missouri Republican*, March 17, 1862; *Cincinnati Daily Commercial*, March 18, 1862; *New York Tribune*, March 24, 1862; *Chicago Daily Tribune*, March 17, 19, 21, 1862; *New York Times*, March 17, 1862; *Wisconsin State Journal*, March 19, 1862; *Philadelphia Inquirer*, March 20, 1862; Walke, *Naval Scenes*, 98; Walke, "The Western Flotilla at Fort Donelson, Island Number Ten, Fort Pillow and Memphis," 439; James M. Hoppin, *The Life of Andrew Hull Foote, Rear Admiral, United States Navy* (New York: Harper and Brothers, 1874), 266; Regimental Association, *History of the 46th Regiment, Indiana Volunteer Infantry, September 1861-September 1865* (Logansport, IN: Press of Wilson, Humphries & Co., 1888), 25.

8. Daniel and Bock, 87–141, 148; Spencer C. Tucker, *Andrew Foote: Civil War Admiral on Western Waters* (Annapolis, MD: Naval Institute Press, 2000), 180–188; C.B. Boynton, *History of the Navy During the Rebellion*, 2 vols. (New York: D. Appleton and Company, 1867), 1:549–553; Wilkie, 151–153; ORN, I, 22: 696–718, 721, 757; ORN, I, 23: 279; Slagle, 189–209; Walke, *Naval Scenes*, 99–199; Myron J. Smith, Jr., *Le Roy Fitch: The Civil War Career of a Union River Gunboat Commander* (Jefferson, NC: McFarland & Co., Inc., 2007); Alfred T. Mahan, *The Navy in the Civil War*, vol. 3, *The Gulf and Inland Waters* (New York: Scribner's, 1883), 34; Ivan Musicant, *Divided Waters: The Naval History of the Civil War* (New York: HarperCollins, 1995), 206–210; Charles Dana Gibson, with E. Kay Gibson, *Assault and Logistics: Union Army Coastal and River Operations, 1861–1866* (Camden, ME: Ensign Press, 1995), 2:80–87; *Cincinnati Daily Commercial*, April 11, 1862; *Chicago Daily Tribune*, March 26, March 28, April 3–4, April 11, 1862; *New York Times*, March 25, April 9–10, 1862; *Philadelphia Inquirer*, April 16, 1862; *St. Louis Daily Missouri Democrat*, April 7, 1862; *Macon Daily Telegraph*, April 7, 1862; *St. Louis Daily Missouri Republican*, April 11, 1862. On April 8, after the surrender, Albert H. Bodman was among the reporters aboard the Union vessels examining the wreckage of the Confederate fleet below Island No. 10. Among those seen was the *Grampus* and we enter his remarks here to put final payment to an account that, despite the news writer's natural Yankee disdain, is worthy of fuller telling: "Next [in line] lay the *Grampus*, a little, dingy, inferior-looking tow-boat, but as fast almost as lightning. Her armament, consisting of two six-pounders, had been carried off or thrown into the river. The *Grampus* was known among the Rebels as 'Dare-Devil Jack.' Her days in the Rebel service, however, are ended, and she will probably be for some time in her present position, sunken nearly to her hurricane deck, as she is hardly worth the raising. The Rebel flag was flying defiantly from her stern at daylight, but is now a trophy onboard the *St. Louis*. Her commander was Marsh Miller, a well-known river man, and an inbred, natural, original secessionist. His boat has done the Rebels great service as a courier-post, for which she was admirably adapted by her great speed. The exaggerated accounts of the Rebel papers, and the magnified stories consequent thereupon in vogue amongst our own people, have clothed the *Grampus* with a mystery and fame sounding very like romance. She has been ubiquitous. Now at Memphis, now at New Madrid; one day at the island watching for our gunboats, the next day at the mouth of the bayou watching for our transports to emerge from the woods, and the next running Pope's blockade. Her commander has been magnified into a bold, shrewd, magnanimous Dick Turpin kind of a man. But the reality strips off the romance. The *Grampus* is a dirty little tow-boat, which one 32-pound shot would tear to pieces; her commander a poor devil, fleeing for his life through swamps and marshes" (*Chicago Daily Tribune*, April 11, 1862).

Chapter 10

1. U.S. Navy Department, *Official Records of the Union and Confederate Navies in the War of the Rebellion*, 31 vols. (Washington, DC: GPO, 1894–1922), series I, vol. 22, 647–648, (cited hereafter as ORN, followed by a comma, the series number in Roman numerals, a comma, the volume number in Arabic, a colon, and the page in Arabic); U.S. War Department, *The War of the Rebellion: A Compilation of the Official Records of the Union and Confederate Armies*, 128 vols. (Washington, DC: GPO, 1880–1901), series I, vol. 7: 674, 678–680 (cited hereafter as OR, followed by a comma, the series number in Roman numerals, a comma, the volume number in Arabic, any part number in Arabic, a colon, and the page in Arabic); OR, I, 10, 2: 13, 15, 24–25, 38; *Chicago Tribune*, August 10, 1885; Steven E. Woodworth, *Nothing But Victory: The Army of the Tennessee, 1861–1865* (New York: Alfred A. Knopf, 2005), 128–130; William B. Feis, *Grant's Secret Service: The*

Intelligence War from Belmont to Appomattox (Lincoln: University of Nebraska Press, 2002), 80–81; Jean Edward Smith, *Grant* (New York: Simon and Schuster, 2001), 173–176, 180; Bruce Catton, *Grant Moves South* (Boston: Little, Brown, 1960), 191–193; Ulysses S. Grant, *The Papers of Ulysses S. Grant, January 8–March 31, 1862*, ed. John Y. Simon, 24 vols. (Edwardsville: Southern Illinois University Press, 1972), 4:305–306, 310–312, 319–320; Ulysses S. Grant, *Personal Memoirs of U.S. Grant,* 2 vols. (New York: C.L. Webster & Co., 1885–1886; repr. [2 vols. in 1], New York: Penguin Books, 1999), 1:326; Fenwick Y. Hedley, *Marching Through Georgia: Pen-Pictures of Everyday Life in General Sherman's Army, from the Beginning of the Atlanta Campaign Until the Close of the War* (Chicago: M.A. Donohue & Co., 1884), 40; Thomas Lawrence Connelly, *Army of the Heartland: The Army of Tennessee, 1861–1862* (Baton Rouge: Louisiana State University Press, 1967), 138–139; Charles P. Roland, *Albert Sidney Johnston: Soldier of Three Republics* (Austin: University of Texas Press, 1964), 301–305; Wiley Sword, *Shiloh: Bloody April* (New York: Morrow, 1974; repr., Morningside Bookshop Press, 1983), 6–11. As almost 200 transport steamers were eventually involved in the Shiloh campaign, space does not permit us to profile each. A full list, based upon exhaustive research, of 174 vessels is provided in Charles Dana Gibson, with E. Kay Gibson, *Assault and Logistics: Union Army Coastal and River Operations, 1861–1866* (Camden, ME: Ensign Press, 1995), 2:78–79. Other lists include J. Haden Alldredge et al., *A History of Navigation on the Tennessee River* (Washington, DC: GPO, 1937), 150–151; Tim Hurst, "The Battle of Shiloh," *Tennessee Historical Quarterly* 5 (July 1919): 87–88; and *Cincinnati Daily Commercial,* March 19, 1862.

2. ORN, I, 22: 667–668, 783–784; OR, I, 10, 1: 28; OR, I, 10, 2: 9–10, 12, 20; Grant, *The Papers of Ulysses S. Grant,* 4:327; Grant, *Personal Memoirs of U.S. Grant,* 1:328; Woodworth, 132–133; William T. Sherman, *Sherman's Civil War: Selected Correspondence of William T. Sherman, 1860–1865;* ed. Brooks D. Simpson and Jean V. Berlin (Chapel Hill: University of North Carolina Press, 1999), 192–193, 195; William T. Sherman, *Memoirs,* 2 vols. (New York: Appleton, 1875; repr., Penguin Classics. New York: Penguin Books, 2000), 208–209; Lew Wallace, *An Autobiography,* 2 vols. (New York: Harper & Brothers, 1906), 1:443. During March 6–8, Brig. Gen. Samuel R. Curtis was attacked at Pea Ridge (Elkhorn Tavern), AK, by a larger force under Confederate Maj. Gen. Earl Van Dorn, but Curtis turned the assault, despite heavy casualties, into a Union victory (Thomas A. DeBlack, *With Fire and Sword: Arkansas, 1861–1874* (Fayetteville: University of Arkansas Press, 2003), 45–49).

3. ORN, I, 22: 666, 784; OR, I, 10, 2: 316–317; Wallace, *An Autobiography,* 1:442–443; Grant, *The Papers of Ulysses S. Grant,* 4:344; *St. Louis Daily Missouri Republican,* March 25, 1862; *Memphis Daily Appeal,* March 14, 1862; James Dugan, *History of Hurlbut's Fighting Fourth Division* (Cincinnati: Morgan & Co., 1863), 98; Larry J. Daniel, *Shiloh: The Battle That Changed the Civil War* (New York: Simon & Schuster, 1997), 71–77; John A. Bering and Thomas Montgomery, *History of the Forty-Eighth Ohio Vet. Vol. Inf.,* in Don Worth, 48th OVVI, http://www.riovvi.org/oh48hist.html (accessed January 25, 2007); George Mason, "Shiloh," in *Papers of the Military Order of the Loyal Legion of the United States,* 56 vols. (Repr., Wilmington, NC: Broadfoot Publishing Co., 1994), 10:93; Charles Wright, *A Corporal's Story: Experiences in the Ranks of Company C, 81st Ohio Vol. Infantry,* ed. W.H. Chamberlain (Philadelphia: James Beal, Printer, 1887), 27–28; *Cincinnati Daily Commercial,* March 9, 1862, quoted in the *Chicago Daily Tribune,* March 20, 1862; Allen Morgan Geer, *The Civil War Diary of Allen Morgan Geer, 20th Regiment, Illinois Volunteers,* ed. Mary Ann Anderson (Denver, CO: Robert Appleman, 1977), 21; Woodworth, 134–135. When Sherman arrived at Savannah, he was very displeased to see that Col. Worthington had assumed command of the town without orders. The ofttimes fiery red-headed general "made him get back to his boat and gave him to understand that he must thereafter keep his place" (Sherman, *Memoirs,* 209).

4. ORN, I, 22: 666–668, 784; OR, I, 10, 1: 8–13, 15, 22–23, 25, 28, 30–31; OR, I, 10, 2, 41, 44, 46, 50–51, 53, 59, 64–66, 302–303, 317–319, 327–328; Daniel, *Shiloh,* 108–111; Sherman, *Memoirs,* 209–211; Feis, 86–87; Sword, 33–34, 44–47, 64–65, 74; Sherman, *Sherman's Civil War,* 197, 207; Mason, 94; *St. Louis Daily Missouri Democrat,* March 17, 24, 1862; *New York Times,* March 30, 1862; *Cincinnati Daily Commercial,* March 14, 17, 21, 1862; *Cincinnati Daily Commercial,* March 13, 1862, quoted in the *Chicago Daily Tribune,* March 20, 1862; *Cincinnati Daily Gazette,* March 21, 1862; *Memphis Daily Appeal,* March 16, 1862; Wallace, *An Autobiography,* 1:447; Wallace, *Smoke, Sound & Fury: The Civil War Memoirs of Major General Lew Wallace, U.S. Volunteers,* ed. Jim Leeke (Portland, OR: Strawberry Hill Press, 1998), 103–104; Smith, "Gallant and Invaluable," 38–40; Lucien B. Crooker, Henry S. Nourse, and John G. Brown, *The 55th Illinois, 1861–1865* (Huntington, WV: Blue Acorn Press, 1993), 64–67; John H. Rerick, *The 44th Indiana Volunteer Infantry: History of Its Services in the War of the Rebellion* (Lagrange, IN: Priv. Print., 1880), 43.

5. ORN, I, 22: 668–670, 674, 677, 700, 784–785; OR, I, 10, 2: 48–51, 73–74, 84; Sherman, *Sherman's Civil War,* 198; *Chicago Daily Tribune,* March 20, 29, 1862; *Memphis Daily Appeal,* March 23, 1862; *Chicago Daily Times,* March 27, 1862; *Cincinnati Daily Gazette,* April 5, 1862; *New Orleans Daily Delta,* April 16, 1862; Daniel, *Shiloh,* 110–111; Bering and Montgomery, *History of the 48th* ; Edwin C. Bearss, *Hardluck Ironclad: The Sinking and Salvage of the Cairo* (Baton Rouge: Louisiana State University Press, 1966), 45–46, 48.

6. ORN, I, 22: 785; OR, I, 8: 121–122; OR, I, 10, 1: 83–86, 379; OR, I, 10, 2: 83–84, 89–94; *New Orleans Daily Delta,* April 16, 1862; Sherman, *Memoirs,* 215–216; Sherman, *Sherman's Civil War,* 200; Bearss, 47–48; Grant, *The Papers of Ulysses S. Grant, April 1–August 31, 1862,* ed. John Y. Simon, 24 vols. (Edwardsville: Southern Illinois University Press, 1973), 5:3–5; *New York Herald,* May 3, 1862; R.R. Hancock, *Hancock's Diary, or A History of the Second Tennessee Cavalry, with Sketches of the First and Seventh Battalions* (Nashville: Brandon Printing Co., 1887), 138; Woodworth, 146–151; Daniel, *Shiloh,* 94–95, 139–141; Sword, 97–117; Feis, 87–94; Roland, 317–325; Timothy B. Smith, "Myths of Shiloh," *America's Civil War* 19 (May 2006): 33; Smith, "Gallant and Invaluable," 46; Robert C. Suhr, "Saving the Day at Shiloh," *America's Civil War* 13 (January 2000): 36.

7. Wallace, *An Autobiography,* 1:459; *Savannah Republican,* April 14, 1862; Basil W. Duke, "Life of Morgan," quoted in William Preston Johnston, *The Life of Gen. Albert Sidney Johnston* (New York: D. Appleton and Company, 1878), 585; Frank Moore, "The Great Battle of Shiloh," in *Reminiscences of Pioneer Days in St. Paul: A Collection of Articles Written for and Published in the Daily Pioneer Press* (St. Paul, MN: Daily Pioneer Press, 1908), 110; John H. Aughey, *The Iron Furnace, or Slavery and Secession* (Philadelphia: William S. and Alfred Martien, 1863), 285. The literature on the battle of Shiloh is enormous; the bibliography in Larry J. Daniel's recent *Shiloh: The Battle That Changed the Civil War* runs 23 single-

spaced pages and is an excellent starting place. For a quick overview of a complex subject, one is directed to Albert Dillahunty's *Shiloh National Military Park, Tennessee* (National Park Service Historical Handbook Series, no. 10; Washington, DC: GPO, 1951).

8. ORN, I, 22: 762–764, 786; OR, I, 10, 1: 166, 204–205, 259–261, 337, 397; *Cincinnati Daily Times,* April 10, 1862; *Philadelphia Inquirer,* April 14, 1862; *The Story of the 55th Regiment Illinois Volunteer Infantry in the Civil War* (Clinton, MA: W.J. Coulter, 1887), 102; Manning F. Force, *From Fort Henry to Corinth*, Great Campaigns of the Civil War, vol. 2 (New York: Scribner's, 1882; repr., T.Y. Yoseloff, 1963), 155; O. Edward Cunningham, *Shiloh and the Western Campaign of 1862,* ed. Gary D. Joiner and Timothy B. Smith (New York: Savas Beatie, 2007), 306–307; Moore, 112; Smith, *Grant,* 197–198; Suhr, 38–39; Dillahanty, 10–13; Larry J. Daniel, *Cannoneers in Gray: The Field Artillery of the Army of Tennessee, 1861–1865* (Birmingham: University of Alabama Press, 1984), 36–40; Woodworth, 186–187; Smith, "Gallant and Invaluable," 42–44; Charles C. Coffin, *My Days and Nights on the Battlefield: A Book for Boys* (Boston: Ticknor and Fields, 1864), 206; Henry Villard, *Memoirs of Henry Villard, Journalist and Financier, 1835–1900,* 2 vols. (Boston: Houghton, Mifflin, 1904), 1:243. Newsman Villard later completed the Northern Pacific, the first northwestern transcontinental railroad, and was in the 1880s the best-known spokesman for the rail industry. The *Boston Journal's* Coffin was not actually present at Shiloh, but he wrote the depictions in his book from other accounts, both written and oral.

9. ORN, I, 22: 765, 766, 786; OR, I, 10, 1: 418, 423, 425, 432, 439–440, 467, 480, 499, 533–534, 550–551, 555, 582, 601; *Indianapolis Daily Journal,* April 19, 1862; *Louisville Daily Journal,* April 18, 1862; *Cincinnati Daily Commercial,* April 15, 1862; Coffin, 207, 211; Connelly, 167; Cunningham, 313–314; Smith, *Grant,* 199; Grant, *Memoirs,* 1:347–348; Force, 155; Alexander Robert Chisolm, "The Shiloh Battle Order and the Withdrawal Sunday Evening," in *Battles and Leaders of the Civil War,* ed. Robert V. Johnson and Clarence C. Buel, 4 vols. (New York: The Century Company, 1884–1887; repr., Thomas Yoseloff, 1956), 1:606; Cunningham, 325; *Mobile Evening News,* April 14, 1862; *Charleston Daily Courier,* April 20, 1862; *Savannah Republican,* April 14, 1862; Woodworth, 184–188; Daniel, *Shiloh,* 245–246, 253–256; F.A. Shoup, "The Art of War in '62 — Shiloh," *The United Service: A Monthly Review of Military and Naval Affairs* 11 (July 1884): 10; Daniel, *Cannoneers in Gray,* 44; Smith, "Gallant and Invaluable," 44; Gudmens, 113–114; Suhr, 39–40; Moore, 113; Brazelton, 72; Charles F. Hubert, *History of the 50th Regiment, Illinois Volunteer Infantry in the War of the Union* (Kansas City, MO: Western Veteran Publishing Co., 1894), 93; J.P. Austin, *The Blue and the Gray: Sketches of a Portion of the Unwritten History of the Great American Civil War* (Atlanta: Franklin Printing and Publishing Co., 1899), 31.

10. ORN, I, 22: 763–764, 786; OR, I, 10, 1: 293–296, 325, 387–388, 582–583; *Cincinnati Daily Times,* April 10, 1862; *Philadelphia Inquirer,* April 14, 1862; *Savannah Republican,* April 14, 1862; Smith, "Gallant and Invaluable," 45–48; Suhr, 40; William J. McMurray, *History of the Twentieth Tennessee Regiment Volunteer Infantry, C.S.A.* (Nashville: The Publication Committee, 1904), 210; Daniel, *Shiloh,* 263, 265, 294; Thomas W. Connelly, *History of the 70th Ohio Regiment: From Its Organization to Its Mustering Out* (Cincinnati: Peak Bros., 1902), 24; Gudmens, 117; Dillahunty, 19–20; J. Cutler Andrews, *The North Reports the Civil War* (Pittsburgh: University of Pittsburgh Press, 1985), 179. James Lee McDonough, *Shiloh — in Hell Before Night* (Knoxville: University of Tennessee Press, 1977), 173, 208–209.

11. W.A. Wash, *Camp Field and Prison Life, Containing Sketches of Service in the South* (St. Louis, MO: Southwestern Book and Pub. Co., 1870), 114–115; ORN, I, 22: 763–766; ORN, I, 23: 90; OR, I, 10, 1: 109, 428, 434, 509, 524, 582, 616; Grant, "The Battle of Shiloh," *B&L,* 1:475; Grant, *The Papers of Ulysses S. Grant,* 5:35–36; William H. Michael, "The Mississippi Squadron in the Civil War," in *Sketches and Incidents: Paper Read By Companions of the Commandery of the State of Nebraska, Military Order of the Loyal Legion of the United States* (Omaha: The Commandery, 1902), 40; Aughey, 285–286; *Chicago Daily Tribune,* April 11, 1862; *Philadelphia Inquirer,* April 10, 12, 1862; *Cincinnati Daily Gazette,* April 9, 12, 1862; *Savannah Republican,* April 19, 1862; *New Orleans Daily Crescent,* April 15, 1862; *Mobile Daily Advertiser and Register,* April 11, 1862; *Charleston Mercury,* April 21, 1862; Pierre G.T. Beauregard, "The Campaign of Shiloh," *B&L,* 1:590–591; Thomas Jordan and J.P. Pryor, *The Campaigns of Lieut. Gen. N.B. Forrest and of Forrest's Cavalry* (New Orleans and New York: Blelock & Co., 1868; repr., New York: Da-Capo Press, 1996), 134–135.

12. OR, I, 10, 1: 410, 466; Gudmens, 114; *New Orleans Daily Delta,* April 12, 16, 1862; Johnston, 633; Daniel, *Shiloh,* 253; Thomas Jordan, "Notes of a Confederate Staff-Officer at Shiloh," *B&L,* 1:602; Henry M. Stanley, *Sir Henry Morton Stanley, Confederate,* ed. Nathaniel C. Hughes, Jr. (Baton Rouge: Louisiana State University Press, 2000), 132.

13. Charles B. Boynton, *History of the Navy During the Rebellion,* 2 vols. (New York: D. Appleton and Company, 1867–1868), 1:562; Benson J. Lossing, *Pictorial Field Book of the Civil War: Journeys through the Battlefields in the Wake of Conflict,* 3 vols. (Hartford, CT: T. Belknap, 1874; repr., Johns Hopkins University Press, 1997), 2:277; Force, 155; Catton, 240; Alfred T. Mahan, *The Navy in the Civil War,* vol. 3, *The Gulf and Inland Waters* (New York: Scribner's, 1883), 38–39; David Dixon Porter, *Naval History of the Civil War* (New York: Sherman Publishing Co., 1886; repr., Secaucus, NJ: Castle Books, 1984), 154; Austin, 31; John D. Milligan, *Gunboats Down the Mississippi* (Annapolis, MD: Naval Institute Press, 1965), 61; McDonough, 172–175; Rowena Reed, *Combined Operations in the Civil War* (Annapolis, MD: Naval Institute Press, 1978), 206; Grady McWhiney, "General Beauregard's 'Complete Victory' at Shiloh: An Interpretation," *Journal of Southern History* 49 (August 1983): 426; Ivan Musicant, *Divided Waters: The Naval History of the Civil War* (New York: HarperCollins, 1995), 210; Jack D. Coombe, *Thunder Along the Mississippi: The River Battles That Split the Confederacy* (New York: Sarpadon Publishers, 1996), 96; Suhr, 41; Smith, "Gallant and Invaluable," 50–51; Steven R. Davis, "Workhorse of the Western Waters: The Timberclad *Tyler*," *Civil War Times Illustrated,* 44 (February 2005): 39; Spencer C. Tucker, *Blue & Gray Navies: The Civil War Afloat* (Annapolis, MD: Naval Institute Press, 2006), 132–133. Gary D. Joiner, one of the editors of O. Edward Cunningham's *Shiloh and the Western Campaign 1862,* revealed in the 2006 History Channel television production *Battlefield Detectives: Shiloh* his theory that the gunboats were able "to shell the interior of the battlefield by ricocheting shells off the ridges surrounding Dill Branch ravine." This is the theory that he amplified in his recent account of the Mississippi River war (Cunningham, 314; Gary D. Joiner, *Mr. Lincoln's Brown Water Navy: The Mississippi Squadron* (Lanham, MD: Rowman & Littlefield, 2007), 52–54). For a look at how one U.S. battle-

ship "walked" her shells at Kavieng, New Ireland, on March 15, 1944, see my *Volunteer State Battlewagon: U.S.S. Tennessee (BB-43)* (Missoula, MT: Pictorial Histories Publishing Company, 1992), 43.

14. Daniel, Shiloh, 293–294; ORN, I, 22: 786; OR, I, 10, 1: 295, 398–400; Grant, *The Papers of Ulysses S. Grant*, 5:19–21; Catton, 245–247, 250.

15. Daniel, *Shiloh*, 309; ORN, I, 23: 59–61; OR, I, 10, 1: 644–646; OR, I, 10, 2: 102, 398–400; Grant, *The Papers of Ulysses S. Grant*, 5:42–43; Sherman, *Sherman's Civil War*, 203, 205; Catton, 267. In firing a salute to mark Maj. Gen. Halleck's assumption of local command on April 12, one of the guns aboard the *Tyler* discharged prematurely. The explosion mortally wounded Boatswain's Mate John D. Seymore, who died a day later (ORN, I, 23: 59).

16. Mahan, 36–39; General Halleck's strategy is discussed in Reed, *Combined Operations in the Civil War*, 203–208; Stephen E. Ambrose, *Halleck: Lincoln's Chief of Staff* (Baton Rouge: Louisiana State University Press, 1962), 45–48; Spencer C. Tucker, *Andrew Foote: Civil War Admiral on Western Waters* (Annapolis, MD: Naval Institute Press, 1998), 189–194; Robert D. Whitesell, "Military and Naval Activity Between Cairo and Columbus," *Register of the Kentucky Historical Society* 61 (1963): 110–111; Woodworth, 206–207; Force, 183–186. When Maj. Gen.. Halleck's soldiers finally showed up at Corinth on May 29, Beauregard simply moved down the road to Tupelo, first making certain that Southern journalists were prohibited from reporting the evacuation (Tucker, 189; J. Cutler Andrews, *The South Reports the Civil War* (Pittsburgh: University of Pittsburgh Press, 1985), 156–157).

17. Mahan, 51; Paul H. Silverstone, *Warships of the Civil War Navies* (Annapolis, MD: Naval Institute Press, 1989), 159; ORN, I, 23: 76–77, 91, 93, 98; *Philadelphia Inquirer*, April 24, 1862; Gershom Bradford, *The Mariner's Dictionary* (New York: Weathervane Books, 1970), 126; Tucker, *Andrew Foote: Civil War Admiral on Western Waters*, 194–196; Junius Henri Browne, *Four Years in Secessia: Adventures Within and Without the Union Lines* (Hartford, CT: O.D. Case and Company, 1865), 147–149, 165–168; "Alfred Robb," in *Dictionary of American Naval Fighting Ships*, rev. ed. (Washington, DC: GPO, 1991), 1:179. Our profile of Rear Adm. Davis is taken from William B. Cogar, *Dictionary of Admirals of the U.S. Navy*, 2 vols. (Annapolis, MD: Naval Institute Press, 1989), 1:41–43, and Charles Henry Davis, *Life of Charles Henry Davis, Rear Admiral, 1807–1877* (Boston and New York: Houghton, Mifflin and Company, 1899).

18. ORN, I, 23: 98–99, 102–103, 115–116. One of Pennock's communications to Capt. Davis reporting the *Tyler*'s problems is wrongly dated and out of sequence in the Navy *Official Records*; it should read June 2 instead of June 20 (ORN, I, 23: 217). When the Mississippi Squadron adopted its now famous tinclad numbering system on June 19, 1863, the number 21 was painted in large black letters on the pilothouse of the *Alfred Robb* (Silverstone, 165). Named an acting volunteer lieutenant on October 1, 1862, Goudy would rise to command the ironclad U.S.S. *Cincinnati*. He died at Paducah, KY, on March 28, 1865, and was buried with full honors (ORN, I, 24, 74; ORN, I, 27: 125; Edward W. Callahan, *List of Officers of the Navy of the United States and of the Marine Corps, from 1775 to 1900, Comprising a Complete Register of All Present and Former Commissioned, Warranted, and Appointed Officers of the United States Navy, and of the Marine Corps, Regular and Volunteer, Compiled from the Official Records of the Navy Department* (New York: L.R. Hamersly & Co., 1901; repr., New York: Haskell House, 1969), 225).

Chapter 11

1. U.S. Navy Department, *Official Records of the Union and Confederate Navies in the War of the Rebellion*, 31 vols. (Washington, DC: GPO, 1894–1922), series I, vol. 23: 114–141 (cited hereafter as ORN, followed by a comma, the series number in Roman numerals, a comma, the volume number in Arabic, a colon, and the page in Arabic); ORN, I, 23: 114–141; *Memphis Daily Argus*, June 6, 1862; *Chicago Daily Tribune*, June 10, 1862; *Cincinnati Daily Commercial*, June 11, 1862; *New York Tribune*, June 11, 1862; *St. Louis Daily Missouri Democrat*, June 10–11, 1862; *Charleston Daily Courier*, June 17, 1862; Alfred T. Mahan, *The Navy in the Civil War*, vol. 3, *The Gulf and Inland Waters* (New York: Scribner's, 1883), 48–49; John D. Milligan, *Gunboats Down the Mississippi* (Annapolis, MD: Naval Institute Press, 1965), 73–77; Charles B. Boynton, *History of the Navy During the Rebellion*, 2 vols. (New York: D. Appleton and Company, 1867–1868), 1:573–574; Henry Walke, *Naval Scenes and Reminiscences of the Civil War in the United States on the Southern and Western Waters During the Years 1861, 1862 and 1863 with the History of That Period Compared and Corrected from Authentic Sources* (New York: F.R. Reed and Company, 1877), 277–297; Jay Slagle, *Ironclad Captain: Seth Ledyard Phelps and the U.S. Navy* (Kent, OH: Kent State University Press, 1996), 233–241; Warren D. Crandall and Isaac D. Newell, *History of the Ram Fleet and Mississippi Marine Brigade* (St. Louis, MO: Buschart Brothers, 1907), 60–80; Chester G. Hearn, *Ellet's Brigade: The Strangest Outfit of All* (Baton Rouge: Louisiana State University Press, 2000), 30–38; Alfred W. Ellet, "Ellet and His Steam Rams at Memphis," in *Battles and Leaders of the Civil War*, ed. Robert V. Johnson and Clarence C. Buel, 4 vols. (New York: The Century Company, 1884–1887; repr., Thomas Yoseloff, 1956), 1:456–459, cited hereafter as B&L, followed by a comma, the volume number in Arabic numerals, a colon, and the page numbers; Charles C. Coffin, *My Days and Nights on the Battlefield: A Book for Boys* (Boston: Ticknor and Fields, 1864), 291–311; Charles Dana Gibson, with E. Kay Gibson, *Assault and Logistics: Union Army Coastal and River Operations, 1861–1866* (Camden, ME: Ensign Press, 1995), 2:111–115.

2. Ulysses S. Grant, *Personal Memoirs of U.S. Grant*, abridged ed. (New York: Premier Books, 1962), 128–129; Frederic E. Davis to Family, June 10, 1862, Frederic E. Davis Papers, Emory University; Francis Vinton Green, *The Mississippi*, Great Campaigns of the Civil War (New York: Charles Scribner's Sons, 1885; repr., n.p.: The Blue & The Gray Press, n.d.), 8:29–30, ORN, I, 23: 144, 156, 692; 34; David D. Porter, *Incidents and Anecdotes of the Civil War* (New York: D. Appleton and Co, 1885; repr., Harrisburg PA: The Archive Society, 1997), 95–96; Donald Davidson, *The Tennessee*, vol. 2, *The New River, Civil War to TVA* (New York: Rinehart & Co., 1948), 41–43; John D. Milligan, ed., *From the Fresh Water Navy, 1861–1864: The Letters of Acting Master's Mate Henry R. Browne and Acting Ensign Symmes E. Brown*, Naval Letters Series, vol. 3 (Annapolis, MD: Naval Institute Press, 1970), 88–89. Navy Secretary Welles was appalled at Gen. Halleck's lack of action at this time and later reflected that "Halleck was good for nothing then, nor is he now!" Charles Lee Lewis, *David Glasgow Farragut* (Annapolis, MD: Naval Institute Press, 1943), 107. Symmes E. Browne (1837–1927) later served aboard the *Tyler*, as well as the tinclads *Signal* and *Forest Rose*, eventually rising to the rank of acting ensign before his resignation on May 31, 1864 (Milligan, ed., *From the Fresh Water Navy, 1861–1864*, xvi; Edward W. Callahan, *List of Officers of the Navy of the*

United States and of the Marine Corps, from 1775 to 1900, Comprising a Complete Register of All Present and Former Commissioned, Warranted, and Appointed Officers of the United States Navy, and of the Marine Corps, Regular and Volunteer, Compiled from the Official Records of the Navy Department (New York: L.R. Hamersly & Co., 1901; repr., New York: Haskell House, 1969), 84.

3. William Tecumseh Sherman, *Memoirs* (New York: Penguin Books, 2000), 243; *Chicago Daily Tribune*, June 25, 1862; Edwin C. Bearss, "The White River Expedition, June 10-July 15, 1862," *Arkansas Historical Quarterly* 21 (Winter 1962): 305–207.

4. ORN, I, 23: 198; Benjamin Franklin Cooling, *Fort Donelson's Legacy: War and Society in Kentucky and Tennessee, 1862–1863* (Knoxville: University of Tennessee Press, 1997), 70–73, 219–222; Robert M. Mackey, *The Uncivil War: Irregular Warfare in the Upper South, 1861–1865* (Norman: University of Oklahoma Press, 2004), 28–31; U.S. War Department, *The War of the Rebellion: A Compilation of the Official Records of the Union and Confederate Armies*, 128 vols. (Washington, DC: GPO, 1880–1901), series I, vol. 8: 28, 814–815 (cited hereafter as OR, followed by a comma, the series number in Roman numerals, a comma, the volume number in Arabic, any part number in Arabic, a colon, and the page in Arabic); OR, I, 13: 103, 831–832; OR, I, 16, 1: 300; *Chicago Daily Tribune*, June 25, 1862; *New York World*, June 30, 1862; *Philadelphia Inquirer*, July 1, 16, 1862; *Nashville Daily Union*, July 18, 1862; Diane Neal and Thomas W. Kremm, *Lion of the South: General Thomas C. Hindman* (Macon, GA: Mercer University Press, 1993), 116–119; Bearss, 315–316; Thomas A. DeBlack, *With Fire and Sword: Arkansas, 1861–1874* (Fayetteville: University of Arkansas Press, 2003), 53–55; Daniel E Sutherland, "Guerrillas: The Real War in Arkansas," *Arkansas Historical Quarterly* 52 (Autumn 1993): 257–285; R. Thomas Campbell, *Confederate Naval Forces on Western Waters: The Defense of the Mississippi River and Its Tributaries* (Jefferson, NC: McFarland & Co., 2005), 98. General Order No. 17 is cited in OR, I, 13: 835 and Mackey, 207–208; U.S. Navy Department, Naval History Division, *Civil War Naval Chronology*, 6 vols. in 1 (Washington, DC: GPO, 1966), 6:268, 288. Hindman's martial law activities, more than his guerrilla warfare policy, led to his replacement on August 12, 1862. After the war, he became involved in Arkansas reconstruction politics and was shot and killed on Sept. 28, 1868, "while sitting in his house, near Helena, by an assassin, who shot him through the window" (Mark M. Boatner III, "Thomas Carmichael Hindman," *The Civil War Dictionary* (New York: David McKay, 1959), 402; Regimental Association, *History of the 46th Regiment, Indiana Volunteer Infantry, September 1861-September 1865* (Logansport, IN: Press of Wilson, Humphries & Co., 1888), 34).

5. OR, I, 13: 421; ORN, I, 23:161–162 ; Bearss, 305–307. W. Danny Honnoll, "Engagement at St. Charles," *The Encyclopedia of Arkansas History and Culture*, <http://encyclopedia of arkansas.net/encyclopedia/entry-detail.aspx?entryID=532> (accessed, March 26, 2007).

6. ORN, I, 23: 162–163; Bearss, 308–309; Rowena Reed, *Combined Operations in the Civil War* (Annapolis, MD: Naval Institute Press, 1978), 214; Junius Henri Browne, *Four Years in Secessia: Adventures Within and Without the Union Lines* (Hartford, CT: O.D. Case and Company, 1865), 192. Charles Ellet, Jr., died on June 21, 1862, from the wound he received during the Battle of Memphis (Hearn, 42).

7. ORN, I, 23: 158–159, 164–165. 692; *New York Times*, June 20, 1862; *New York World*, June 30, 1862; *Cincinnati Daily Times*, June 20, 1862; Bearss, 312–313; Regimental Association, 34; John D. Milligan, ed., *From the Fresh Water Navy, 1861–1864*, 90–91; Paul H. Silverstone, *Warships of the Civil War Navies* (Annapolis, MD: Naval Institute Press, 1989), 180; William C. Lytle, comp., *Merchant Steam Vessels of the United States, 1807–1868, "The Lytle List,"* publication no. 6 (Mystic, CT: The Steamship Historical Society of America, 1952): 34. The *Clara Dolson* served as a receiving ship and was transferred to the Mississippi Squadron on September 30, 1862; she was not actually purchased from the Illinois prize court until May 25, 1863. In May 1864, she was returned to her original owners. Rerated, she plied the Mississippi until February 4, 1868, when she was destroyed by fire at St. Louis (ORN, II, 1: 59; Silverstone, 180). Wilson McGunnegle (1829–1863), eldest son of a Pennsylvanian turned St. Louis businessman, George Kennedy McGunnegle, joined the U.S. Navy as a midshipman in December 1845, becoming a Lt. in September 1855. Promoted to the rank of Lt. Cmdr. in July 1862, he died of natural causes on April 2, 1863 (Callahan, 368; "George Kennedy McGunnegle," in *History of Crawford County, Pennsylvania: Containing a History of the County, Its Townships, Towns, Villages, Schools, Churches, Industries, etc., Portraits of Early Settlers and Prominent Men, Biographies, History of Pennsylvania, Statistical and Miscellaneous Matter* (Chicago: Warner, Beers & Co., 1885), 751). Peoria, Illinois-born steamboatman and Western Flotilla volunteer Cyrenius Dominy (1829–1907) was the only *Mound City* officer to escape the June 17 disaster unhurt, though he was shaken. He would later command the tinclad *Signal* (Callahan, 166; the Wise letter, cited hereafter as Wise Letter, was originally published in volume 5 of Frank Moore, ed., *The Rebellion Record: A Diary of American Events* (New York: G.P. Putnam, 1863; repr., New York: Arno Press, 1977), 224–225.

8. ORN, I, 23, 165–166, 198, 200–205; OR, I, 13, 34–35, 103; Bearss, 313–323; Browne, 192–193; Regimental Association, 34; *Cincinnati Daily Times*, June 26, 1862; *Chicago Daily Tribune*, June 23, 1862; *Philadelphia Inquirer*, June 26, 1862; *Mobile Daily Tribune*, July 2, 1862; *Jackson Mississippian*, July 3, 1862, cited in the *Houston Tri-Weekly Telegraph*, July 25, 1862; Wise Letter; Silverstone, 181; Lyle, 95, 201; Honnoll, "Engagement at St. Charles."

9. Bearss, 315–318; OR, I, 13: 34–35, 103; ORN, I, 23: 165–166, 200–202, 205; *Chicago Daily Tribune*, June 23, July 3, 1862; *New York World*, June 30, 1862; *Mobile Daily Tribune*, July 2, 1862; Honnoll, "Engagement at St. Charles"; Campbell, 99–100; DeBlack, 55; Lytle, 49, 123. Fry, an unknown at this time, would gain international notoriety in 1873 when, as "Captain Fry of the *Virginius*," he and several crewmen were executed by Spanish authorities in Cuba after having been captured during an unsuccessful filibustering gunrunning operation (Robert L. Scheina, *Latin America's Wars: The Age of the Caudillo, 1791–1898* (Washington, DC: Brassy's, Inc., 2003), 356; Jeanie Mort Walker, *Life of Capt. Joseph Fry, the Cuban Martyr* (Hartford, CT: J.B. Burr Publishing Co., 1875), 156–157).

10. ORN, I, 23: 166, 692; OR, I, 13: 104; Regimental Association, 34–35; George N. Gray, "Narrow Escapes: Just a Little Bit of History," *Ironton (OH) Register*, December 23, 1886, submitted by Donald E. Darby to *Sons of Union Veterans of the Civil War Patriotic Recollections*, http://suvcw.org/pr/art008.htm (accessed July 12, 2005); Honnoll, "Engagement at St. Charles."

11. OR, I, 13: 104; ORN, I, 23: 166, 168, 692; Regimental Association, 34–35; Bearss, 320–322; Browne, 194; Wise Letter; Honnoll, "Engagement at St. Charles." The *Grand Prairie Historical Society Bulletin* ran a number of

interesting pieces on the St. Charles battle 40 years ago and these are noted in our bibliog-raphy.

12. ORN, I, 23: 166–158, 178, 200–204, 240, 692–693; OR, I, 13: 104–105; *Cincinnati Daily Commercial*, June 20, 1862; *Harper's Weekly*, July 5, 1862; *Chicago Daily Tribune*, June 20, 23, 1862; *New York Tribune*, July 23, 1862; *Cincinnati Daily Times*, June 26, 1862; *Philadelphia Inquirer*, June 23, 26 1862; *Mobile Daily Tribune*, July 2, 1862; *Jackson Mississippian*, July 3, 1862, cited in the *Houston Tri-Weekly Telegraph*, July 25, 1862; Gray, "Narrow Escapes; Regimental Association, 34–35; Browne, 194–200; Wise Letter, 225; Bearss, 323–330; Boynton, 1:260; Honnoll, "Engagement at St. Charles"; William M. Fowler, Jr., *Under Two Flags: The American Navy in the Civil War* (New York: W.W. Norton, 1990), 184–185; Jay Slagle, *Ironclad Captain: Seth Ledyard Phelps and the U.S. Navy* (Kent, OH: Kent State University Press, 1996), 245–248; Alfred T. Mahan, *The Gulf and Inland Waters*, Great Campaigns of the Civil War (New York: Scribner's, 1883), 50. It was later recorded that Col. Fitch recovered and retained after the battle the logbook and rebel flag of the C.S.S. *Mauripus*. Acting Master's Mate Henry Browne was one of those killed on the *Mound City*; the entire episode was reported home by his brother. Upon his return to Memphis, Symmes Browne also told the St. Charles story to St. Louis newsman William A. Fayel, who acknowledged the noncom in print as the source for his next day's story (Milligan, ed., *From the Fresh Water Navy, 1861–1864*, 92–99; *St. Louis Daily Missouri Republican*, June 20, 1862).

13. Mahan, 50; Brian Hogan, Conrad Bush and Mike Brown, "The 76th New York and the Navy," 76th New York Infantry Regiment, http://www.bpmlegal.com/76NY/76navy.html (accessed July 12, 2005); ORN, I, 23: 167–171, 178, 180–181, 201–203, 205, 240; OR, I, 13: 105; *Cincinnati Daily Times*, June 26, 1862; *Chicago Daily Tribune*, June 23, 25, 1862; *Philadelphia Inquirer*, June 26, 1862; Regimental Association, 35; Wise Letter; Boynton, 1:260; Honnoll, "Engagement at St. Charles"; Bearss, 331-335; Donald Barnhart, Jr., "The Deadliest Shot," *Civil War Times Illustrated* 30 (March-April 2006): 36; Charles H. Davis, *Life of Charles Henry Davis, Rear Admiral, 1808–1877* (Boston: Houghton, Mifflin and Company, 1899), 245–246; David Dixon Porter, *The Naval History of the Civil War* (New York: Sherman, 1886; repr., Secaucus, NJ: Castle Books, 1984), 173–174. Davis was appointed flag officer and commander of the Western Flotilla on June 17, formally relieving Flag Officer Foote. Telegraphic news of the St. Charles disaster was printed in the *New York Times* on June 22. In a slightly enlarged report next day, the unidentified reporter opined that the *Mound City* "can easily be repaired. The flag officer has sent to Cairo for another crew" *(New York Times*, June 29, 1862).

14. ORN, I, 23: 169–171, 174–177, 181, 693 ; OR, I, 13: 106; Regimental Association, 35–36; *New York World*, June 30, 1862; *Philadelphia Inquirer*, July 1, 1862; *Cincinnati Daily Commercial*, June 20, 1862, quoted in *New Orleans Daily Delta*, July 10, 1862; *Chicago Daily Tribune*, July 3, 1862; Bearss, 335–339; John M. Ellicott, *The Life of John Ancrum Winslow, Rear-Admiral, United States Navy, Who Commanded the U.S. Steamer Kearsarge in Her Action with the Confederate Cruiser Alabama* (New York: G.P. Putnam's Sons, 1905), 83–85. The 227-ton side-wheeler *Catahoula* was constructed at Murraysville, VA, in 1858 (Lytle, 27).

15. ORN, I, 23: 175–177, 181–182, 184, 693 ; OR, I, 13: 106–107; Mackey, 32; *Chicago Daily Tribune*, July 3, 1862; Bearss, 341; Regimental Association, 41; Davis, 248; Ellicott, 85; Charles Dana Gibson, with E. Kay Gibson, *Assault and Logistics: Union Army Coastal and River Operations, 1861–1866* (Camden, ME: Ensign Press, 1995), 2:123–125.

16. OR, I, 13: 107, 117–119; ORN, I, 23: 182–184, 188; Ellicott, 83–85; Regimental Association, 36; Ulysses S. Grant, *The Papers of Ulysses S. Grant, April 1–August 31, 1862*, ed. John Y. Simon, 24 vols. (Edwardsville: Southern Illinois University Press, 1973), 5:149–150, 161–162; Bearss, 342–350. On June 29, Flag Officer Davis took the ironclads *Benton, Cincinnati, Louisville,* and *Carondelet* and a few miscellaneous boats downriver from Memphis to a point above Vicksburg for a planned rendezvous with the fleet of Flag Officer David G. Farragut. Men from the two groups met on July 1 and lingered near the Mississippi bastion for about a month (ORN, I, 23: 235; OR, I, 17, 2: 43).

17. OR, I, 13: 37, 107–113, 118–119; ORN, I, 23:183–184, 188–194, 197–198; Regimental Association, 36–40; Bearss, 343–362; *Memphis Bulletin*, July 12, 1862; *Chicago Daily Tribune*, July 15–17, 1862; *Philadelphia Inquirer*, July 16, 1862; Frederic E. Davis to Family, July 2, 1862; Jack D. Coombe, *Thunder Along the Mississippi: The River Battles That Split the Confederacy* (New York: Sarpadon Publishers, 1996), 146–147 , Frederic E. Davis Papers, Emory University; Robert L. Kerby, *Kirby Smith's Confederacy: The Trans-Mississippi South, 1863–1865* (New York: Columbia University Press, 1972), 32–33; Lytle, 77; DeBlack, 57–61; Reed, 215; Mahan, 50–51; Mackey, 32. Another casualty of the White River expeditions, largely unnoticed at the time and definitely in the years since, was interim task group commander Lt. Wilson McGunnegle. On July 12, he requested relief from duty due to ill health. "His rough experiences," wrote "W" of the *Chicago Daily Tribune* on July 12, "have had their effect of rendering his disease — that of the lungs — somewhat more severe." The Navy would thus "lose the aid of one of its most able, most daring, chivalric and gentlemanly officers."

18. ORN, I, 18: 647–652; ORN, I, 23: 210; ORN, II, 1: 782–783; Isaac Newton Brown, "The Confederate Gun-Boat *Arkansas*," B&L, 3:572; Cynthia E. Moseley, "The Naval Career of Henry Kennedy Stevens as Revealed in His Letters, 1839–1863," (Unpublished master's thesis, University of North Carolina, 1951), 303–306; George W. Gift, "The Story of the *Arkansas*," *Southern Historical Society Papers* 8 (1884): 48–49; Milligan, *Gunboats Down the Mississippi*, 82; Harriet Castlen, *Hope Bids Me Onward* (Savannah, GA: Chatham Printing Co., 1945), 63–64; Charles W. Read, "Reminiscences of the Confederate States Navy," *Southern Historical Society Papers* 1 (1876): 349–353; *Philadelphia Inquirer*, July 25, 1862; Kevin Carson, "21 Days to Glory: The Saga of the Confederate Ram *Arkansas*," *Sea Classics* 39 (July 2006): 38–40; Spencer C. Tucker, *Blue & Gray Navies: The Civil War Afloat* (Annapolis, MD: Naval Institute Press, 2006), 210; Ivan Musicant, *Divided Waters: The Naval History of the Civil War* (New York: HarperCollins, 1995), 248; William N. Still, *Iron Afloat: The Story of the Confederate Armorclads* (Nashville: Vanderbilt University Press, 1971; repr., University of South Carolina Press, 1985), 62–66; John Johnson, "Story of the Confederate Armored Ram *Arkansas*," *Southern Historical Society Papers* 33 (1905): 1–4; Mary Emerson Branch, "The Story Behind the Story of the *Arkansas* and the *Carondelet*," *Missouri Historical Review* 74 (1985): 322; Daniel Barnhart, Jr., "Junkyard Ironclad," *Civil War Times Illustrated* 40 (May 2001): 31–35, 37; J. Thomas Scharf, *History of the Confederate Navy from Its Organization to the Surrender of Its Last Vessel* (New York: Rodgers and Sherwood, 1887; repr., New York: Fairfax Press, 1977), 306–309; Henry Walke, *Naval Scenes and Reminiscences of the Civil War in the United States on the*

Southern and Western Waters During the Years 1861, 1862 and 1863 with the History of That Period Compared and Corrected from Authentic Sources (New York: F.R. Reed and Company, 1877), 302–303; Silverstone, 202; Campbell, 103–111.

19. ORN, I, 18: 584–585, 675; ORN, I, 19: 4; ORN, I, 23: 130–131, 233, 243; OR, I, 15: 515; *Chicago Daily Tribune,* July 9, 1862; *New York Times,* July 13, 1862; *Granada Appeal,* July 16, 23, 1862; *Philadelphia Inquirer,* July 16, 1862; *New Orleans Daily Delta,* July 22, 1862; *Cincinnati Daily Commercial,* July 17, 1862; *Vicksburg Daily Citizen,* June 20, 1862; Milligan, ed., *From the Fresh Water Navy, 1861–1864,* 110; Brown, 572–574; Gift, 51; Coombe, 234; Milligan, *Gunboats Down the Mississippi,* 82; Michael B. Ballard, *Vicksburg: The Campaign that Opened the Mississippi* (Chapel Hill: University of North Carolina Press, 2004), 57; Scharf, 310–311; Charles H. Davis, 262–263; Hearn, 46–47; Steven R. Davis, "Workhorse of the Western Waters: The Timberclad *Tyler,*" *Civil War Times Illustrated* 44 (February 2005): 39. The *Monarch* and *Lancaster,* together with the *Queen of the West,* which would actually meet the *Arkansas,* were three of six converted steamers that comprised the unique marine unit established by Charles Ellet, Jr., under War Secretary Edwin Stanton's direct patronage. Built at Cincinnati in 1854, the 406-ton side-wheel *Queen* was 181 feet long, with a beam of 36 feet and a six-foot depth of hold. Her two engines were powered by three boilers and her complement of nautical soldiers totaled 120. Relying upon speed and a reinforced bow filled with lumber, neither she nor her sisters were originally armed. With the guerrilla menace growing, she had by this time received three 12-pdr. howitzers (Silverstone, 161).

20. ORN, I, 19: 4, 6, 37–39, 44, 56, 60, 705; ORN, I, 23: 131, 244, 258, 636, 671, 685; OR, I, 15: 32; *New Orleans Daily Delta,* July 22, 1862; *New York Herald,* July 25, 1862; Browne, 214; Thomas Williams, "Letters of General Thomas Williams, 1862," *American Historical Review* 14 (January 1909): 322–323; Logbooks of the U.S.S. *Carondelet,* May 1862–June 1865, Records of the Bureau of Navigation, Record Group 19, U.S. National Archives, Washington, DC, July 14–15, 1862 (cited hereafter as Logbook of the U.S.S. *Carondelet,* with date); Milligan, *Gunboats Down the Mississippi,* 82; Silas B. Coleman and Paul Stevens, "A July Morning with the Rebel Ram *Arkansas,*" *U.S. Naval Institute Proceedings* 88 (July 1962): 86; Davis, "Workhorse of the Western Waters," 39; Scharf, 309–310; Musicant, 249; Hearn, 49–50; Walke, 304–305. Supplementing formal reports, an unusually high number of participants wrote or offered for transcription accounts of the Yazoo River encounter between the *Arkansas* and the three Union steamers. In addition to those already noted aboard the Rebel armorclad, we are fortunate that Cmdr. Walke left his impressions. In addition, and more to our point, Paymaster Coleman, also known in the ORN as William, was an eyewitness aboard the *Tyler.* In 1890, the Michigander revealed his unique view of the only major engagement between a timberclad and a Confederate armorclad for the Detroit chapter of the Loyal Legion of the United States. We have noted that version in the bibliography and quote here from a reprint. Incidentally, Coleman was promoted to the rank of acting ensign on October 1, 1862, when the Western Flotilla became the Mississippi Squadron. He was named an acting volunteer lieutenant on June 15, 1864, and was honorably discharged on December 12, 1865. Coleman was one of three officers (Fourth Master F.T., Paymaster Silas, and Master's Mate Gilbert L.) by that name aboard the *Tyler* on July 15; it is not known if they were related (Edward W. Callahan, *List of Officers of the Navy of the United States and of the Marine Corps, from 1775 to 1900, Comprising a Complete Register of All Present and Former Commissioned, Warranted, and Appointed Officers of the United States Navy, and of the Marine Corps, Regular and Volunteer, Compiled from the Official Records of the Navy Department* (New York: L.R. Hamersly & Co., 1901; repr., New York: Haskell House, 1969), 123.

21. ORN, I, 19: 37–39, 41, 68, 132; ORN, I, 23: 685–686; *Granada Appeal,* July 16, 23, 1862; *New York Herald,* July 25, 1862; *Philadelphia Inquirer,* July 22, 1862; *New Orleans Daily Delta,* July 22, 1862; *Jackson Mississippian,* July 15, 1862, quoted in *Columbus (GA) Daily Enquirer,* July 23, 1862; Logbook of the U.S.S. *Carondelet,* July 15, 1862; Coleman and Stevens, 86, 88; Gift, 51–54; Brown, 574–575; Walke, 309–324; Branch, 324–325; Carson, 40; Hearn, 51; Tucker, 211; Samuel Carter III, *The Final Fortress: The Campaign for Vicksburg 1862–1863* (New York: St. Martin's Press, 1980), 69–70; Davis, "Workhorse of the Western Waters," 39; Musicant, 249–250; Milligan, *Gunboats Down the Mississippi,* 83–84; Browne, 214–217; Still, 68. Even the acerbic Walke originally admitted that Lt. Gwin sustained him "through the fight in a very gallant and effective manner" (ORN, I, 19: 41). The debate over Cmdr. Walke's handling of the *Carondelet,* which we have no intention of entering, began to rage within days of its occurrence and has continued ever since. Despite a ferocious defense of his actions in his memoirs, the hero of Island No. 10 lived long enough to read perhaps the most unfavorable review of an impartial critic. In 1882, Alfred T. Mahan, who Walke knew, bluntly stated that the loyal Virginian's tactics were "not judicious" because they exposed the weakest part of his craft. "Besides," he continued, "when two vessels are approaching on parallel courses, the one that wishes to avoid the ram, may perhaps do so by a maneuver of her helm." But when the slowest ship, in this case the *Carondelet,* "has presented her stern to the enemy, she has thrown up the game, barring some fortunate accident" (Alfred T. Mahan, *The Navy in the Civil War,* vol. 3, *The Gulf and Inland Waters* (New York: Scribner's, 1883), 99–100).

22. ORN, I, 19: 39–40, 44, 56, 71, 705; Brown, 575–576; *Granada Appeal,* July 16, 23, 1862; *Philadelphia Inquirer,* July 22, 25, 1862; *New York Herald,* July 25, 1862; *New Orleans Daily Delta,* July 22, 1862; *Vicksburg Evening Post,* July 1, 1961; Gift, 51–54; Browne, 217–219; Coleman and Stevens, 86–88; Coombe, 234; Carter, 70–71; Barnhart, 31–35, 37; Davis, 263; Milligan, *Gunboats Down the Mississippi,* 84–85; Charles B. Boynton, *History of the Navy During the Rebellion,* 2 vols. (New York: D. Appleton and Company, 1867–1868), 2:246; Branch, 324–325; Still, 68–69; Musicant, 250–252; Davis, "Workhorse of the Western Waters," 40; Scharf, 312–315. Paymaster Coleman of the *Tyler,* along with many others in the years since, paid high tribute to the *Arkansas,* frankly stating that there was "no pluckier exploit in the war. In the process, she disabled the *Carondelet* and "badly injured and all but sunk *Tyler*" before passing through the fleet "without material injury." The armorclad was eventually lost during the August 1862 campaign for Baton Rouge. Her weak engines failed and, rather than surrender, her crew blew her up (Coleman and Stevens, 88–89; Still, 76–78).

23. ORN, I, 19: 37–40, 69, 686, 705; *Philadelphia Inquirer,* July 22, 1862; Logbook of the U.S.S. *Carondelet,* July 15, 1862; Davis, "Workhorse of the Western Waters," 40; Coleman and Stevens, 88–89. Although there was no "Thanks of Congress" for the Federal officers involved in this particular episode, the highest legislative accolade

available to naval men on both sides was awarded to Lt. Brown. A joint resolution of appreciation was sent to the daring commander by the Confederate Congress on October 2. Brown had earlier been promoted to the rank of commander (ORN, I, 19: 36).

24. ORN, I, 23: 260–263, 270–271; Milligan, ed., *From the Fresh Water Navy, 1861–1864,* 110–112, 114. On July 22, Cmdr. Walke was also ordered to take the *Carondelet* to Cairo; he made stops en route at Carlton Landing and Memphis to review matters and communicate with local commanders (ORN, I, 23: 268).

Chapter 12

1. U.S. Navy Department, *Official Records of the Union and Confederate Navies in the War of the Rebellion,* 31 vols. (Washington, DC: GPO, 1894–1922), series I, vol. 23: 216, 262–265, 289, 324, 346 (cited hereafter as ORN, followed by a comma, the series number in Roman numerals, a comma, the volume number in Arabic, a colon, and the page in Arabic); ORN, I, 22: 500, 759; Frederic E. Davis to Family, August 27, 1862, Frederic E. Davis Papers, Emory University; John D. Milligan, ed., *From the Fresh Water Navy, 1861–1864: The Letters of Acting Master's Mate Henry R. Browne and Acting Ensign Symmes E. Brown,* Naval Letters Series (Annapolis, MD: Naval Institute Press, 1970), 3:111, 116; Edward W. Callahan, *List of Officers of the Navy of the United States and of the Marine Corps, from 1775 to 1900, Comprising a Complete Register of All Present and Former Commissioned, Warranted, and Appointed Officers of the United States Navy, and of the Marine Corps, Regular and Volunteer, compiled from the Official Records of the Navy Department* (New York: L.R. Hamersly & Co., 1901; repr., New York: Haskell House, 1969), 447; Lewis R. Hamersly, *The Records of Living Officers of the U.S. Navy and Marine Corps, Compiled from Official Sources,* rev. ed. (Philadelphia: J.B. Lippincott, 1870), 200.

2. *New York Times,* July 24, September 20, 1862; *Cairo City Weekly Gazette,* August 28, September 25, 1862; U.S. War Department, *The War of the Rebellion: A Compilation of the Official Records of the Union and Confederate Armies,* 128 vols. (Washington, DC: GPO, 1880–1901), series II, vol. 4: 261, 266–268, 454 (cited hereafter as OR, followed by a comma, the series number in Roman numerals, a comma, the volume number in Arabic, any part number in Arabic, a colon, and the page in Arabic); ORN, I, 23: 325–326; 330–332, 334–335, 338–341, 346, 348, 357–358; Frederic E. Davis to Family, September 13, 1862, Frederic E. Davis Papers, Emory University; Lonnie R. Speer, *Portals to Hell: Military Prisons of the Civil War* (Mechanicsburg, PA: Stackpole Books, 1997), 102–103. The son of a Union naval officer and the only commissioned Civil War seaman aboard three sunken ships (*Cumberland, Cairo, Conestoga*), Lt. Cmdr. Selfridge (1836–1924) was an 1854 naval academy graduate. A Porter favorite, Selfridge followed his mentor to the North Atlantic Blockading Squadron in 1864 and the naval academy in 1865. In addition to various sea and shore posts, he was the American naval delegate to the coronation of Czar Nicholas II in 1896. Rear Adm. Selfridge did not retire until 1898 (William B. Cogar, *Dictionary of Admirals of the U.S. Navy,* 2 vols., Annapolis, MD: Naval Institute Press, 1989), 2:163–164).

3. Chester G. Hearn, *Admiral David Dixon Porter: The Civil War Years* (Annapolis, MD: Naval Institute Press, 1996), 143–144; ORN, I, 23: 278, 394, 422–423, 427, 440–441, 454, 482; Frederic E. Davis to Family, October 7, 1862, Frederic E. Davis Papers, Emory University; Speer, 103–105; U.S. Department of the Interior, National Park Service, "Social Impacts of the Civil War: Seven Prisoners Make a Shadow,'" Experience Your America, <http://www.itd.nps.gov/cwss/manassas/social/andersonville.htm> (accessed April 22, 2007). Although First Master Hentig was rated an Acting Master on October 1, he would be dismissed from the service on June 1, 1863 (Callahan, 262). Seaman Davis was promoted to the rank of acting master's mate and transferred from the *Lexington* to the Pook turtle *Baron de Kalb* (Frederic E. Davis to Family, November 12, 1862, Frederic E. Davis Papers, Emory University).

4. ORN, I, 23: 474–476, 478–479, 481, 495, 498, 508–511, 515–518, 524, 536, 618; OR, II, 5: 774; *Cincinnati Times,* November 11, 1862, reprinted in the *Philadelphia Inquirer,* November 17, 1862; *Chicago Daily Tribune,* December 2, 1862; *New York Times,* January 19, 1863; Logbooks of the U.S.S. *Carondelet,* May 1862–June 1865, Records of the Bureau of Navigation, Record Group 19, U.S. National Archives, Washington, DC, November 30–December 1, 1862 (cited hereafter as Logbook of the U.S.S. *Carondelet,* with date); Charles E. Wilcox, "Diary of Captain Charles E. Wilcox," *The Journal of Southern History* 4 (November 1938): 513; Chris Wehner, "The Burning of Prentiss, Mississippi, 1862: A Case Study in Total War," Blog4 History: American History & Civil War History, http://www.blog4history.com/?m=200607, (May 3, 2007); Ronald S. Mangum, "The Vicksburg Campaign: A Study in Joint Operations," *Parameters* 21 (Autumn 1991): 75; William C. Lytle, comp., *Merchant Steam Vessels of the United States, 1807–1868,* "The Lytle List," publication no. 6 (Mystic, CT: The Steamship Historical Society of America, 1952), 127; Milligan, ed., *From the Fresh Water Navy, 1861–1864,* 117. Illinois politician and Maj. Gen. John C. McClernand, with President Lincoln's blessing, was assigned to take command of this Vicksburg expedition but was outmaneuvered by Grant, who wished Sherman to handle it. Steven E. Woodworth, *Nothing But Victory: The Army of the Tennessee, 1861–1865* (New York: Alfred A. Knopf, 2005), 264–265. Hentig was ordered to return to Cairo forthwith to assume command of the new tinclad *Curlew;* Lt. Selim E. Woodworth was named to take over the *Conestoga,* but ARAM Porter, needing a warship for Lt. Thomas O. Selfridge, Jr., after the loss of the *Cairo,* gave Woodworth the tinclad *Glide* instead (ORN, I, 23: 635).

5. ORN, I, 23: 530, 539, 546–556, 558, 693; Logbook of the U.S.S. *Carondelet,* December 4, 8–9, 12, 17, 1862; *St. Louis Daily Missouri Democrat,* December 19, 1862; *Cairo City Weekly Gazette,* December 23, 1862; Milligan, ed., *From the Fresh Water Navy, 1861–1864,* 119–123; H.D. Brown, "The First Successful Torpedo and What It Did," *Confederate Veteran* 18 (1910): 169; Edwin C. Bearss, *Hardluck Ironclad: The Sinking and Salvage of the Cairo* (Baton Rouge: Louisiana State University Press, 1966), 95–103; Thomas O. Selfridge, *Memoirs of Thomas O. Selfridge, Jr., Rear Admiral, U.S.N.* (New York: Knickerbocker Press, 1924; repr. Columbia: University of South Carolina Press, 1987), 76; Elizabeth Hoxie Joyner, *The U.S.S. "Cairo": History and Artifacts of a Civil War Gunboat* (Jefferson, NC: McFarland & Co., 2006), 7–9; John C. Wideman, *The Sinking of the U.S.S. Cairo* (Jackson: University Press of Mississippi, 1993), 30–46.

6. ORN, I, 23: 421, 556–558, 566–568; *New York World,* January 8, 1863; William Tecumseh Sherman, *Memoirs* (New York: Penguin Books, 2000), 265–269; William Wiley, *The Civil War Diary of a Common Soldier,* ed. Terrence J. Winschel (Baton Rouge: Louisiana University

Press, 2001), 26; William Winters, *The Musick of the Mocking Birds, the Roar of the Cannon: The Diary and Letters of William Winters*, ed. Steven E. Woodworth (Lincoln: University of Nebraska Press, 1998), 13; Woodworth, *Nothing But Victory*: 261–263; "The Civil War Diary of Michael Sweetman, Co. K, 114th O.V.I.," ed. Johnda T. Davis, Fortunecity http://www.fortunecity.com/westwood/makeover/347/id229.htm (accessed May 5, 2007); James E. Northup and Samuel W. Northup, *"Drifting to an Unknown Future": The Civil War Letters of James E. Northup and Samuel W. Northup*, ed. Robert C. Steensma (Sioux Falls, SD: Center for Western Studies, 2000), 54; Milligan, ed., *From the Fresh Water Navy, 1861–1864*, 123–124; *New York World*, January 8, 1863. On December 20, the same day Sherman was loading his steamers at Memphis, Confederate Maj. Gen. Earl Van Dorn led a cavalry raid upon the key Union supply depot at Holly Springs and destroyed it. This disaster forced Grant to retreat and cancel his own Vicksburg advance, something Sherman did not know. The very next day at Granada, MS, Maj. Gen. John C. Pemberton, commander of the Confederate Department of Mississippi and Eastern Louisiana, learned that "a large fleet of gunboats and transports was moving down the Mississippi River for the supposed purpose of attacking Vicksburg" (Woodworth, 263–264; Sherman, 272; OR, I, 17, 1: 665–666). An informative tribute to Lt. Cmdr. Gwin is to be found in the *Chicago Daily Tribune*, February 19, 1863.

7. ORN, I, 23: 554–555, 567–571, 674–675, 591; ORN, I, 24: 132; OR, I, 17, 1, 605, 620, 666, 695, 778 ; OR, I, 17, 2: 683–684, 885; Milligan, ed., *From the Fresh Water Navy, 1861–1864*, 125–126, 257; *Chicago Daily Tribune*, January 6, 1863; *New York World*, January 8, 1863; *New York Times*, January 18–19, 1863; Sherman, 269; Arthur Marvin Shaw, ed., "A Texas Ranger Company at the Battle of Arkansas Post," *Arkansas Historical Quarterly* 9 (Winter 1950): 280; "The Civil War Diary of Michael Sweetman, Co. K 114th O.V.I.," ed. Johnda T. Davis, Fortunecity, http://www.fortunecity.com/westwood/makeover/347/id229.htm (accessed May 5, 2007); Chester G. Hearn, *Ellet's Brigade: The Strangest Outfit of All* (Baton Rouge: Louisiana State University Press, 2000), 84–85; Edwin C. Bearss, *The Vicksburg Campaign*, 3 vols. (Dayton, OH: Morningside Book Shop, 1985–1986), 1:139–142; J. Cutler Andrews, *The North Reports the Civil War* (Pittsburgh, PA: University of Pittsburgh Press, 1985), 376–382; Bruce Catton, *The American Heritage Picture History of the Civil War* (New York: American Heritage Publishing Co., 1960), 184; Woodworth, 266–267. Sherman censored the mail going out of the Yazoo and so it was mid-month before the major eastern newspapers ran the battle stories of their ace Western reporters.

8. ORN, I, 23: 675; OR, I, 17, 1: 606, 666, 681; OR, I, 17, 2: 884–885; *New York World*, January 8, 1863; *New York Times*, January 19, 1863; *Chicago Daily Tribune*, January 6, 1863; John D. Milligan, *Gunboats Down the Mississippi* (Annapolis, MD: Naval Institute Press, 1965), 108; Milligan, ed., *From the Fresh Water Navy, 1861–1864*, 126–127; Woodworth, 266–268; Bearss, *The Vicksburg Campaign*, 1:157–159, 164–165; Jacob Ritner and Emeline Ritner, *Love and Valor: The Intimate Civil War Letters Between Captain Jacob and Emeline Ritner*, ed. Charles F. Larimer (Western Springs, IL: Sigourney Press, 2000), 86; Alfred T. Mahan, *The Navy in the Civil War* , vol. 3, *The Gulf and Inland Waters* (New York: Scribner's, 1883), 118.

9. ORN, I, 23: 571–574, 576–577, 579, 591, 675; OR, I, 17, 1: 604, 651, 666; OR, I, 17, 2: 878, 885; *Chicago Daily Tribune*, January 5, 1863. Washingtonian and 1860 Naval Academy graduate Bache (1840–1896) was commissioned a lieutenant in July 1862, the same month he was posted to the *Cincinnati*. He would command her until she was sunk off Vicksburg in May 1863. Just as he had with Selfridge, who lost a Pook turtle, Porter next gave Bache a timberclad, the *Lexington*, which he would skipper until summer 1864. Bache finished the war in the North Atlantic Blockading Squadron. Serving afloat and ashore after the war, he was commissioned a lieutenant commander in 1866 and a commander on April 5, 1875, the same day he retired (Edward W. Callahan, *List of Officers of the Navy of the United States and of the Marine Corps, from 1775 to 1900, Comprising a Complete Register of All Present and Former Commissioned, Warranted, and Appointed Officers of the United States Navy, and of the Marine Corps, Regular and Volunteer, Compiled from the Official Records of the Navy Department* (New York: L.R. Hamersly & Co., 1901; repr., New York: Haskell House, 1969), 33; Lewis R. Hamersly, *The Records of Living Officers of the U.S. Navy and Marine Corps, Compiled from Official Sources*, rev. ed. (Philadelphia: J.B. Lippincott, 1870), 214.

10. Henry Walke, *Naval Scenes and Reminiscences of the Civil War in the United States on the Southern and Western Waters During the Years 1861, 1862 and 1863, with the History of That Period Compared and Corrected from Authentic Sources* (New York: F.R. Reed and Company, 1877), 337–338; Ibid.; Milligan, *Gunboats Down the Mississippi*, 108; James R. Soley, "Naval Operations in the Vicksburg Campaign," in *Battles and Leaders of the Civil War*, ed. Robert V. Johnson and Clarence C. Buel, 4 vols. (New York: The Century Company, 1884–1887; repr. Thomas Yoseloff, 1956), 3:560; Jack D. Coombe, *Thunder Along the Mississippi: The River Battles That Split the Confederacy* (New York: Sarpedon Publishers, 1996), 184; Hearn, *Admiral David Dixon Porter*, 161–162; Jim Miles, *A River Unvexed: A History and Tour Guide to the Campaign for the Mississippi River*, Civil War Campaign Series (Nashville: Rutledge Hill Press, 1994), 267; Christopher R. Gabel and the Staff Ride Team, *Staff Ride Handbook for the Vicksburg Campaign, December 1862–July 1863* (Fort Leavenworth, KS: Combat Studies Institute, U.S. Army Command and General Staff College, 2001), 24–25.

11. OR, I, 17, 1: 604, 651, 675, 694, 885; OR, I, 22, 1: 886; OR, I, 22, 2: 11; ORN, I, 23: 576–577, 579, 581, 585–592, 675; ORN, I, 24: 93; *Chicago Daily Tribune*, January 5–6, 11, 1863; *New York World*, January 8, 1863; Shaw, ed., "A Texas Ranger Company at the Battle of Arkansas Post," 281; Mahan, 118–119; Franc B. Wilkie, *Pen and Powder* (Boston: Ticknor and Company, 1888), 238–239; Bearss, *The Vicksburg Campaign*, 1:143–229; Paul H. Silverstone, *Warships of the Civil War Navies* (Annapolis, MD: Naval Institute Press, 1989), 155. On December 29, Porter sent a message to Fleet Captain Alexander Pennock at Cairo asking him to wire Mrs. Mary L. Gwin in care of her father, Hiram Hutchinson, Esq., at 35 East 37th Street in New York City to tell her the bad news. She took the next train to the tip of Illinois (ORN, I, 23, 586).

12. ORN, I, 23: 387, 593–597, 604–605, 614; ORN, I, 24: 124, 700, 708; OR, I, 17, 1: 625, 701; OR, I, 17, 2: 534; OR, I, 18: 884–885; OR, I, 22, 1: 887, 902; Sherman, *Memoirs*, 315–316; *St. Louis Daily Missouri Democrat*, January 15, 1863; *Chicago Daily Tribune*, January 12, 14, 1863; *New York Herald*, January 18, 21, 1863; *New York World*, January 16, 1863; *New York Times*, January 19, 24–25, 28, 1863; *Cincinnati Daily Commercial*, February 18, 1863; Woodworth, 281–283; Milligan, ed., *From the Fresh Water Navy, 1861–1864*, 130–131; Shaw, ed., "A Texas Ranger Company at the Battle of Arkansas Post," 282; Emmons' letter is quoted in Charles A. Willison, *Reminiscences of a Boy's*

Service with the 76th Ohio in the 15th Army Corps, Under General Sherman, During the Civil War, by That "Boy" at Three Score (Menasha, WI: Press of The George Banta Publishing Co., 1908; repr., Huntington, WV: Blue Acorn Press, 1995), 131; "The Civil War Diary of Michael Sweetman, Co. K, 114th O.V.I.," ed. Johnda T. Davis, Fortunecity, http://www.fortunecity.com/westwood/makeover/347/id229.htm (May 5, 2007); Thomas A. DeBlack, "'We Must Stand of Fall Alone,'" in Mark K. Christ, ed., *Rugged and Sublime: The Civil War in Arkansas* (Fayetteville: University of Arkansas Press, 1994), 60; DeBlack, *With Fire and Sword: Arkansas, 1861–1874* (Histories of Arkansas; Fayetteville: University of Arkansas Press, 2003), 78–79; Winters, *The Musick of the Mocking Birds*, 16–17; Hearn, *Admiral David Dixon Porter*, 166; David Dixon Porter, *Naval History of the Civil War* (New York: Sherman Publishing Company, 1886; repr., Secaucus, NJ: Castle Books, 1984), 287; Porter, *Incidents and Anecdotes of the Civil War* (New York: D. Appleton and Co, 1885; repr., Harrisburg, PA: The Archive Society, 1997), 130–131. While the campaign flared and fizzled, Lt. Cmdr. Gwin lay dying in the *Black Hawk's* sick bay. Maj. Gen. Sherman, who considered the former *Tyler* commander his "favorite in the fleet," vainly attempted to find a Catholic priest to offer the last rites, but could locate none within his entire army (ORN, I, 23: 603; ORN, I, 24: 137, 191, 700; William T. Sherman, *Sherman's Civil War: Selected Correspondence of William T. Sherman, 1860–1865*, ed. Brooks D. Simpson and Jean V. Berlin (Chapel Hill: University of North Carolina Press, 1999), 350; Jay Slagle, *Ironclad Captain: Seth Ledyard Phelps and the U.S. Navy* (Kent, OH: Kent State University Press, 1996), 319–321.

Chapter 13

1. U.S. Navy Department, *Official Records of the Union and Confederate Navies in the War of the Rebellion*, 31 vols. (Washington, DC: GPO, 1894–1922), series I, vol. 24: 95, 696–697, 708–709 (cited hereafter as ORN, followed by a comma, the series number in Roman numerals, a comma, the volume number in Arabic, a colon, and the page in Arabic); Thomas O. Selfridge, *Memoirs of Thomas O. Selfridge, Jr., Rear Admiral, U.S.N.* (New York: Knickerbocker Press, 1924; repr. Columbia: University of South Carolina Press, 1987), 76; John D. Milligan, ed., *From the Fresh Water Navy, 1861–1864: The Letters of Acting Master's Mate Henry R. Browne and Acting Ensign Symmes E. Brown*, Naval Letters Series (Annapolis, MD: Naval Institute Press, 1970), 3:131–159.

2. U.S. War Department, *The War of the Rebellion: A Compilation of the Official Records of the Union and Confederate Armies*, 128 vols. (Washington, DC: GPO, 1880–1901), series I, vol. 17, part 1: 711–713, 722, 730, 780, 783, 790–791 (cited hereafter as OR, followed by a comma, the series number in Roman numerals, a comma, the volume number in Arabic, any part number in Arabic, a colon, and the page in Arabic); ORN, I, 24: 94, 100–102, 107, 708; *New York Herald*, January 8, 1863; Alfred T. Mahan, *The Navy in the Civil War*, vol. 3, *The Gulf and Inland Waters* (New York: Scribner's, 1883), 120; Chester G. Hearn, *Admiral David Dixon Porter: The Civil War Years* (Annapolis, MD: Naval Institute Press, 1996), 168–169; Edwin C. Bearss, "The Battle of the Post of Arkansas," *Arkansas Historical Quarterly* 18 (Autumn 1959): 247–255; Arthur Marvin Shaw, ed., "A Texas Ranger Company at the Battle of Arkansas Post," *Arkansas Historical Quarterly* 9 (Winter 1950): 283; "The Civil War Diary of Michael Sweetman, Co. K, 114th O.V.I.," ed. Johnda T. Davis, Fortunecity, http://www.fortunecity.com/westwood/makeover/347/id229.htm (accessed May 5, 2007).

3. ORN, I, 24: 107–108, 110, 113, 119, 126; OR, I, 17, 1: 706–708, 721, 752, 781–782, 792; OR, I, 17, 2: 553, 559, 757; *New York Herald*, January 8, 1863; *New York Times*, January 18, 24, 29, 1863; Bearss, "The Battle of the Post of Arkansas," 255–264, 274–276, 279, Mahan, 122; Hearn, *Admiral David Dixon Porter*, 170–175; Shaw, ed., "A Texas Ranger Company at the Battle of Arkansas Post," 285, 288–289, 292–293, 297; Arthur F. Surovic, "Union Assault on Arkansas Post, " *Military History* 12 (March 1996): 34–40; Thomas A. DeBlack, *With Fire and Sword: Arkansas, 1861–1874*, Histories of Arkansas (Fayetteville: University of Arkansas Press, 2003), 79–81.

4. For an overview of the Murfreesboro campaign, see James Lee McDonough's *Stones River: Bloody Winter in Tennessee* (Knoxville: University of Tennessee Press, 1980), 81–216; Fitch is profiled in my *Le Roy Fitch: The Civil War Career of a Union Gunboat Commander* (Jefferson, NC: McFarland & Co., 2007).

5. ORN, I, 24: 12–19, 21–22 192, 472; OR, I, 20, 2: 342; OR, I, 23, 2: 38–39; Jay Slagle, *Ironclad Captain: Seth Ledyard Phelps and the U.S. Navy* (Kent, OH: Kent State University Press, 1996), 322; Smith, *Le Roy Fitch*, 126–129; Thomas Jordan and J.P. Pryor, *The Campaigns of Lieut. Gen. N. B. Forrest and of Forrest's Cavalry* (New Orleans and New York: Blelock & Co., 1868), 224. In a January 24 letter, Secretary Welles let Capt. Pennock know in no uncertain terms that "the Department" was not pleased with the way in which the station chief had recently handled relations with the prickly Murfreesboro-based army leadership. "It is expected," Pennock was reminded, that every service possible be extended to military colleagues and, "in an emergency such as that now on the Cumberland and Tennessee rivers, that every exertion will be made to meet it." The hard-pressed Pennock, who was disappointed with the reprimand but nevertheless carbonded his immediate superior with that and all correspondence, would be buoyed a week later by a letter from David Porter. The rear admiral, more knowledgeable of the local scene than the Washington establishment, expressed his complete confidence in his subordinate's ability to "always do what is right." Besides, Porter added, he hoped that Pennock would "take every opportunity to write these army officials and inform them" that the Cairo office did not have information to disseminate concerning squadron activities, that "General Halleck has no control here," and that he [Porter] and nobody else in country, disposed of western navy assets (ORN, I, 24: 13–14, 18).

6. OR, I, 23, 1: 40; Smith, *Le Roy Fitch*, 130–131; Jordan and Pryor, 225–227; Thomas B. Van Horne, *History of the Army of the Cumberland*, 2 vols. (Wilmington, NC: Broadfoot, 1988), 1:289; John Allan Wyeth, *Life of General Nathan Bedford Forrest* (New York: Harper & Bros., 1904), 146; Benjamin Franklin Cooling, "The Battle of Dover, February 3, 1863, "*Tennessee Historical Quarterly* 22 (June 1963): 143–144; Cooling, *Fort Donelson's Legacy: War and Society in Kentucky and Tennessee, 1862–1863* (Knoxville: University of Tennessee Press, 1997), 192–196; Terry Wilson, "'Against Such Powerful Odds': The 83rd Illinois Infantry at the Battle of Dover, Tennessee, February 1863," *Tennessee Historical Quarterly* 53 (December 1994): 261–264; John E. Fisher, *They Rode with Forrest and Wheeler: A Chronicle of Five Tennessee Brothers' Service in the Confederate Western Cavalry* (Jefferson, NC: McFarland & CO., 1995), 29.

7. OR, I, 23, 1: 32–41; OR, I, 23, 2: 41–42; ORN, I, 24: 15; Robert Selph Henry, "*First with the Most*" *Forrest* (Indianapolis: Bobbs-Merrill, 1944), 123; Claire E. Swedberg,

ed., *Three Years with the 92nd Illinois: The Civil War Diary of John M. King* (Mechanicsburg, PA: Stackpole Books, 1999), 46–47; Smith, *Le Roy Fitch,* 131–132; Cooling, "Battle of Dover," 147; Cooling, *Fort Donelson's Legacy,* 196–199; Jordan and Pryor, 228–229; Wyeth, 147–150; Van Horne, 1:289–290; Wilson, 266–268; *Nashville Daily Union,* February 4, 1863.

8. OR, I, 23, 1: 146–147; OR, I, 23, 2: 31–45; ORN, I, 23: 313–314; ORN, I, 24: 25–27, 30; *Nashville Daily Union,* February 4–6, 1863; *Chicago Daily Tribune,* February 11, 1863; Smith, *Le Roy Fitch,* 132–136; Cooling, "Battle of Dover," 150; Cooling, *Fort Donelson's Legacy,* 202–204; Richard P. Gildrie, "Guerrilla Warfare in the Lower Cumberland River Valley, 1862–1865," *Tennessee Historical Quarterly* 54 (Fall 1990): 168; Wyeth, 154, 161; Jordan and Pryor, 229–230; Swedberg, 47–52; Mahan, 181; Henry M. Cist, *Army of the Cumberland,* Great Campaigns of the Civil War (New York: Charles Scribner's Sons, 1892), 141; Mary Bess McCain Henderson, Evelyn Janet McCain Young, and Anna Irene McCain Naheloffer, *"Dear Eliza": The Letters of Michel Andrew Thompson* (Ames, IA: Carter Press, 1976), 23; Byrd Douglas, *Steamboatin' on the Cumberland* (Nashville: Tennessee Book Company, 1961), 139–140; Robert R. Mackey, *The Uncivil War: Irregular Warfare in the Upper South, 1861–1865* (Norman: University of Oklahoma Press, 2004), 171. The most complete newspaper account of the gunboat participation in the Second Battle of Fort Donelson was written by *New York Herald* correspondent T. Herbert Whipple; we have used the special reprinted in the *Chicago Daily Tribune,* February 13, 1863.

9. ORN, I, 24: 30–46, 57–58, 60–65, 71, 472–473; OR, I, 23, 2: 200; *Chicago Daily Tribune,* February 26, 1863; Smith, *Le Roy Fitch,* 140–141, 149–151; Cooling, *Fort Donelson's Legacy,* 226–227; William H. Howard to wife, February 18, 20, 24, 1863, William H. Howard Papers, University of Tennessee Library, Knoxville (cited hereafter as Howard Papers, with date). Howard would be honorably discharged on December 9, 1865; William R. Morris, "The Burning of Clifton," *Wayne County Historian* 2 (June 1989), reprinted on the Civil War Page, http://www.netease.net/wayne/burningclifton.htm (accessed March 3, 2004); Edward W. Callahan, *List of Officers of the Navy of the United States and of the Marine Corps, from 1775 to 1900, Comprising a Complete Register of All Present and Former Commissioned, Warranted, and Appointed Officers of the United States Navy, and of the Marine Corps, Regular and Volunteer, Compiled from the Official Records of the Navy Department* (New York: L.R. Hamersly & Co., 1901; repr., New York: Haskell House, 1969), 278. As we have noted earlier, most of the territory bordering the Cumberland and Tennessee rivers was not friendly to the Union; consequently, it would have been possible to uncover many farmers and others aiding the Southern cause. At the end of May, Acting Volunteer Lieutenant Dunn would succeed Lt. Cmdr. Fitch as skipper of the *Lexington,* but he resigned from the service on August 3, perhaps because his command was given to Lt. Cmdr. Bache on June 15 and he was not offered a new one (Callahan, 174).

10. William M. Lamers, *The Edge of Glory: A Biography of General William S. Rosecrans, USA* (New York: Harcourt, Brace, 1961), 257; Walter T. Durham, *Nashville—the Occupied City: The First Seventeen Months, February 16, 1862–June 30, 1863* (Nashville: The Tennessee Historical Society, 1985), 221–222; ORN, I, 24: 66–71; Robert Brandt, *Touring the Middle Tennessee Backroads* (Winston-Salem, NC: John F. Blair, 1995), 82; Howard Papers, April 4–6, 1863; Smith, *Le Roy Fitch,* 151–152; Cooling, *Fort Donelson's Legacy,* 196–199.

11. ORN, I, 23: 317; *Chicago Daily Tribune,* April 8, 1863; Smith, *Le Roy Fitch,* 152–156; Cooling, *Fort Donelson's Legacy,* 227–228; Howard Papers, April 4–5, 1863; Brandt, 82. Fitzpatrick would go on to command the U.S.S. *Chickasaw* and *Signal* and would be honorably discharged on December 30, 1865 (Callahan, 196).

12. ORN, I, 23: 317; ORN, I, 24: 71–72, 75, 78; OR, I, 23, 1, 333, 346–347; OR, I, 23, 2: 212, 219, 240, 253; Cooling, *Fort Donelson's Legacy,* 196–199; Smith, *Le Roy Fitch,* 152–156; Howard Papers, April 5–6, 1863. On April 8, Captain Pennock bundled up all of *Cairo*'s telegrams relative to the Palmyra episode and forwarded them, along with Fitch's report, down to Admiral Porter; four days later, Porter reshipped them to Secretary Welles in Washington (ORN, I, 24: 72–73, 78).

13. OR, I, 23, 1: 281–294; Wyeth, 185–187; Charles Dana Gibson and E. Kay Gibson, comps., *Dictionary of Transports and Combat Vessels, Steam and Sail, Employed by the Union Army, 1861–1868* (Camden, ME: Ensign Press, 1995), 304; Cooling, *Fort Donelson's Legacy,* 251; Smith, *Le Roy Fitch,* 157–158; Lamers, 257. Also at this time, a highly successful Union cavalry raid through Mississippi was planned and undertaken by the Michigan schoolmaster Col. Benjamin H. Grierson; the strike was as celebrated as Streight's would be ridiculed.

14. ORN, I, 24: 76–77, 79–80, 522–523; OR, I, 23, 2: 232, 251, 254–255, 264; Wyeth, 188–190; Chester G. Hearn, *Ellet's Brigade: The Strangest Outfit of All* (Baton Rouge: Louisiana State University Press, 2000), 154–156; Cooling, *Fort Donelson's Legacy,* 252; Smith, Le Roy Fitch, 158–160. Upon the army commanders' departure inland, Fitch, in his role in the plan, would be left in charge of the transport fleet off Eastport. It would be his decision as to when the water level might compel its transfer downstream (ORN, I, 23: 286).

15. OR, I, 24, 3, 246–261; Weyeth, 190–222; Cooling, *Fort Donelson's Legacy,* 253; Smith, *Le Roy Fitch,* 161–162; ORN, I, 24: 87; Stanley, 132; Jordan and Pryor, 278–279. Streight's report is found in OR, I, 23, 1: 281–294, while Forrest's account is in the same volume, pages 120–121.

16. ORN, II, 1: 100; Paul H. Silverstone, *Warships of the Civil War Navies* (Annapolis, MD: Naval Institute Press, 1989), 107; "Hastings," in *Dictionary of American Naval Fighting Ships* (Washington, DC: GPO, 1968), 3:269; Gibson, 231; Hiram H. Martin, "Service Afield and Afloat: A Reminiscence of the Civil War Ed. Guy R. Everson," *Indiana Magazine of History* 89 (March 1993): 44; Smith, *Le Roy Fitch,* 162–163.

17. OR, 23, 1, 1: 278–280; ORN, I, 24: 85–88, 90–91; ORN, I, 25: 132, 139, 141, 145, 160; Hearn, *Ellet's Brigade,* 156–159; Smith, *Le Roy Fitch,* 163–166; Martin, 45–47; Warren D. Crandall and Isaac D. Newell, *History of the Ram Fleet and Mississippi Marine Brigade* (St. Louis, MO: Buschart Brothers, 1907), 277–281.

18. ORN, I, 24: 696–697; Selfridge, 79.

19. ORN, I, 24: 708; Milligan, ed., *From the Fresh Water Navy, 1861–1864,* 135–136.

20. OR, I, 24, 3: 152, 168; Milligan, ed., *From the Fresh Water Navy, 1861–1864,* 138, 155–159, 163–167; *New York Times,* April 16, 1863; Hearn, *Admiral David Dixon Porter,* 177–219; Steven E. Woodworth, *Nothing But Victory: The Army of the Tennessee, 1861–1865* (New York: Alfred A. Knopf, 2005), 298–331; Michael B. Ballard, *Vicksburg: The Campaign That Opened the Mississippi* (Chapel Hill: University of North Carolina Press, 2004), 168–203. The literature on the bayou expeditions and the task group passing of Vicksburg (all of which is outside the scope of this title) is quite large; the *Official Records,* memoirs, and periodical literature record them in great detail. The pas-

sages noted in the following general works are recommended: Mahan, 123–158; John D. Milligan, *Gunboats Down the Mississippi* (Annapolis, MD: Naval Institute Press, 1965), 121–161; Jack D. Coombe, *Thunder Along the Mississippi: The River Battles That Split the Confederacy* (New York: Sarpedon Publishers, 1996), 193–214; Spencer C. Tucker, *Blue & Gray Navies: The Civil War Afloat* (Annapolis, MD: Naval Institute Press, 2006), 222–230; Bern Anderson, *By Sea and By River: The Naval History of the Civil War* (New York: Knopf, 1962), 141–143, 148.

21. OR, I, 24, 1: 25, 49, 79–83, 574–578; OR, I, 24, 3: 151–152, 168, 221, 225–226, 228, 231, 246, 294–205, 211, 246, 260–261, 325, 792–793, 797, 800, 804; ORN, I, 24: 590–593, 595, 607–609, 610–628, 613, 615–623, 625–626, 659, 682–683, 704, 708; Ulysses S. Grant, *The Papers of Ulysses S. Grant, October 1, 1861-January 7, 1862*, ed. John Y. Simon, 24 vols. (Edwardsville: Southern Illinois University Press, 1976), 8:130–131; William Tecumseh Sherman, *Memoirs* (New York: Penguin Books, 2000), 295; Milligan, ed., *From the Fresh Water Navy, 1861–1864*, 168–171; Woodworth, 332–335; Edwin C. Bearss, *The Vicksburg Campaign*, 3 vols. (Dayton, OH: Morningside Book Shop, 1985–1986), 2:269–319; Ballard, 212, 214–221; Hearn, *Admiral David Dixon Porter*, 220–227, 229–230; Mahan, 161–162; Dave Page, *Ships versus Shore* (Nashville TN: Rutledge Hill Press, 1994), 241; Martha M Bigelow, "The Significance of Milliken's Bend in the Civil War," *Journal of Negro History* 45 (Fall 1960): 156–157; Rowena Reed, *Combined Operations in the Civil War* (Annapolis, MD: Naval Institute Press, 1978), 254. U.S. Naval Academy graduate (1856) Lt. Cmdr. Francis M. ("Frank") Ramsay (1835–1914) served afloat and ashore in the east, including the Africa Squadron, until 1862. Upon his promotion, he was given the new ironclad *Choctaw*, which he had skippered up the Yazoo and at Milliken's Bend the previous May and June. He received his district after the fall of Vicksburg but would depart to the North Atlantic Blockading Squadron in the fall. He participated in the capture of Fort Fisher and, after the war, continued a long career, leading to his promotion to the rank of rear admiral in 1894. Lewis B. Hamersly, *The Records of Living Officers of the U.S. Navy and Marine Corps* (Philadelphia: J.B. Lippincott & Co., 1870), 171; Callahan, 451; William B. Cogar, *Dictionary of Admirals of the U.S. Navy*, 2 vols. (Annapolis, MD: Naval Institute Press, 1989), 1:139–140.

22. OR, I, 24, 1: 45, 95–96, 219; OR, I, 24, 2: 446–448, 453–454, 457–458, 462–470; OR, 26, 2: 15; ORN, I, 25: 162–166; Milligan, ed., *From the Fresh Water Navy, 1861–1864*, 175–176; *Cincinnati Gazette*, June 12, 1863, quoted in the *New York Times*, June 15, 1863; *New York Times*, June 11, 1863; Richard Taylor, *Destruction and Reconstruction: Personal Experiences of the Late War* (New York: D. Appleton and Company, 1879), 137–139; James M. McPherson, *The Negro's Civil War* (New York: Ballantine Books, 1991), 187–191; Joseph P. Blessington, *The Campaigns of Walker's Texas Division* (Austin, TX: The Pemberton Press, 1968), 79–93; Ronald Scott Mangum, "The Vicksburg Campaign: A Study in Joint Operations," *Parameters: US Army War College Quarterly* 21 (Autumn 1991), 77; Reed, 257; Ballard, 391; Noah Andre Trudeau, *Like Men of War: Black Troops in the Civil War, 1862–1865* (Boston: Little, Brown, 1998), 46–59; John D. Winters, *The Civil War in Louisiana* (Baton Rouge: Louisiana State University Press, 1963), 198–203; Joseph H. Parks, *General Edmund Kirby Smith, C.S.A.* (Baton Rouge: Louisiana State University Press, 1954), 277–278; Vinton Green, *The Mississippi*, Great Campaigns of the Civil War (New York: Charles Scribner's Sons, 1885; repr., The Blue & The Gray Press, n.d.), 8:234; Page, 243; David Dixon Porter, *Naval History of the Civil War* (New York: Sherman Publishing Company, 1886; repr., Secaucus, NJ: Castle Books, 1984), 335. Brig. Gen. Hawes' advance toward Young's Point was stillborn; mistaking several transports for gunboats, he did not attack. Not long after the Milliken's Bend fight, the base was abandoned, its men and supplies being removed to Young's Point. On a happier note, the "acting" was removed from Porter's title and he would be known for the remainder of the war as Rear Admiral Porter.

23. OR, I, 22, 1: 338, 387–388, 407, 413; OR, I, 22, 2: 335, 339, 863–856, 866–868; OR, I, 26, 2: 43; ORN, I, 25: 209, 211, 220, 227, 234, 261; *Chicago Daily Tribune*, July 12, 1863; *St. Louis Daily Missouri Democrat*, July 14, 1863; Parks, *General Kirby Smith*, 279; DeBlack, 88–89; Slagle, 335; Hearn, *Admiral David Dixon Porter*, 238–239; Charles O. Musser, *Soldier Boy: The Civil War Letters of Charles M. Musser, 29th Iowa*, ed. Larry Popchock (Iowa City: Iowa State University Press, 1995), 24; Albert G. Castel, *General Sterling Price and the Civil War in the West* (Baton Rouge: Louisiana State University Press, 1968), 143–144; John N. Edwards, *Shelby and His Men, or The War in the West* (Cincinnati: Miami Printing and Publishing Co., 1867; repr., Waverly, MO: General J.O. Shelby Memorial, 1993), 164–165; Castel, "Fiasco at Helena," *Civil War Times Illustrated* 7 (August 1968): 12–14; Edwin C. Bearss, "The Battle of Helena, July 4, 1863," *Arkansas Historical Quarterly* 20 (Autumn 1961): 257–258; Gregory J.W. Urwin, "'A Very Disastrous Defeat': The Battle of Helena, Arkansas," *North & South* 6 (December 2002): 26–29; Steven W. Jones, "The Logs of the U.S.S. *Tyler*," *Phillips County Historical Quarterly* 15 (March 1977): 25–27.

24. OR, I, 22, 1: 388, 395, 400, 409–410, 413, 427, 426; OR, I, 22, 2: 897–903; ORN, I, 25: 219, 225, 227–228; *Little Rock True Democrat*, July 8, 1863; *Chicago Daily Tribune*, July 12, 1863; *St. Louis Daily Missouri Democrat*, July 14, 1863; Edwin C. Bearss, *The Vicksburg Campaign*, 3 vols. (Dayton, OH: Morningside Book Shop, 1985–1986), 3:1217; Urwin, 29–31; Bearss, "The Battle of Helena," 268; DeBlack, 89–90; Porter, 336; Castel, "Fiasco at Helena," 14–15; Jones, 27–28; Edward S. Redington to Mary Redington, July 7, 1863, unpublished transcribed letter, Redington Papers, University of Wisconsin Digital Collections, <http://digital.library.wisc.edu/1711.dl/WI.EdRed 01> (accessed August 30, 2006).

25. OR, I, 22, 1: 388–389, 391, 395, 398–400, 403–414, 417–418, 421–432, 435–437; ORN, I, 25: 228–234, 261; *Little Rock True Democrat*, July 8, 1863; *Chicago Daily Tribune*, July 12, 1863; *St. Louis Daily Missouri Democrat*, July 14, 1863; DeBlack, 90–91; Slagle, 336; Castel, *General Sterling Price*, 147–150; Castel, "Fiasco at Helena," 15–17; Bearss, "The Battle of Helena," 273–274, 281–284, 286–288, 293; Edwards, 165–166; Porter, 336–337; Urwin, 31–37; Jones, 27–37; Robert Newton Scott to Hullum and Mary Scott, July 6, 1863, *Letters Home from an Iowa Soldier in the American Civil War*, http://www.civilwarletters.com/scott_7_6_1863.html (accessed July 2, 2007); Scott to Hannah M. Cone, July 23, 1863, *Letters Home*; Redington Papers, Edward Redington to Mary Redington. The role of Lt. Gen. Price and his men in the battle is summarized in Robert E. Shalhope, *Sterling Price: Portrait of a Southerner* (Columbia: University of Missouri Press, 1971), 238–242. Acting Ensign Smith had a spotty naval war. Appointed to that rank in December 1862, he resigned on January 29, 1863. Thinking better of his action, he returned as a mate at the end of March and was rerated an acting ensign on April 10. He would resign for good on July 15, 1864 (Callahan, 504).

26. Castel, *General Sterling Price*, 150–152; Horace

Greeley, *The American Conflict: A History of the Great Rebellion in the United States of America, 1860–1865*, 2 vols. (Hartford, CT: O.D. Case & Company, 1879), 2:320; Thomas L. Snead, "The Conquest of Arkansas," in *Battles and Leaders of the Civil War*, ed. Robert V. Johnson and Clarence C. Buel, 4 vols. (New York: The Century Company, 1884–1887; repr. Thomas Yoseloff, 1956), 3:456.

27. ORN, I, 25: 233; *Memphis Bulletin*, July 6, 1863; *St. Louis Daily Missouri Democrat*, July 14, 1863; *Chicago Daily Tribune*, July 8, 12, 1863; *New York Times*, July 15, 1863; Redington Papers, Edward Redington to Mary Redington; Hearn, *Admiral David Dixon Porter*, 238–239; Steven R. Davis, "Death Takes No Holiday," *America's Civil War* 5 (May 1993): 74; Davis, "Workhorse of the Western Waters: The Timberclad *Tyler*," *Civil War Times Illustrated* 44 (February 2005): 80; Page, 340–341, 343; Jones, 36–37.

Chapter 14

1. U.S. Navy Department, *Official Records of the Union and Confederate Navies in the War of the Rebellion*, 31 vols. (Washington, DC: GPO, 1894–1922), series I, vol. 25: 264–271 (cited hereafter as ORN, followed by a comma, the series number in Roman numerals, a comma, the volume number in Arabic, a colon, and the page in Arabic); ORN, II, 1, 65; Thomas O. Selfridge, *Memoirs of Thomas O. Selfridge, Jr., Rear Admiral, U.S.N.* (New York: Knickerbocker Press, 1924; repr., Columbia: University of South Carolina Press, 1987), 84–86; David Dixon Porter, *Naval History of the Civil War* (New York: Sherman Publishing Company, 1886; repr., Secaucus, NJ: Castle Books, 1984), 332–333; Alfred T. Mahan, *The Navy in the Civil War*, vol. 3, *The Gulf and Inland Waters* (New York: Scribner's, 1883), 177–178; Paul H. Silverstone, *Warships of the Civil War Navies* (Annapolis, MD: Naval Institute Press, 1989), 164. The *Manitou* was renamed *Fort Hindman* on November 5, 1863 (ORN, I, 25: 533).

2. U.S. War Department, *The War of the Rebellion: A Compilation of the Official Records of the Union and Confederate Armies*, 128 vols. (Washington, DC: GPO, 1880–1901), series I, vol. 22, part 1: 472–476, 511 (cited hereafter as OR, followed by a comma, the series number in Roman numerals, a comma, the volume number in Arabic, any part number in Arabic, a colon, and the page in Arabic); OR, I, 22, 2: 942; ORN, I, 25: 347–353, 357, 362; *St. Louis Daily Missouri Democrat*, quoted in the *Chicago Daily Tribune*, August 27, 1863; Thomas A. DeBlack, *With Fire and Sword: Arkansas, 1861–1874* (Histories of Arkansas; Fayetteville: University of Arkansas Press, 2003), 93; Albert G. Castel, *General Sterling Price and the Civil War in the West* (Baton Rouge: Louisiana State University Press, 1968), 152–155. Originally rated a mate in October 1862, Booby was made an acting ensign on February 16, taking up his duties on the *Lexington* on August 8. He would continue to serve at that rank and achieve an honorable discharge on November 24, 1865. He was the last man off the timberclad when she was deactivated at the end of the war. Edward W. Callahan, *List of Officers of the Navy of the United States and of the Marine Corps, from 1775 to 1900, Comprising a Complete Register of All Present and Former Commissioned, Warranted, and Appointed Officers of the United States Navy, and of the Marine Corps, Regular and Volunteer, Compiled from the Official Records of the Navy Department* (New York: L.R. Hamersly & Co., 1901; repr., New York: Haskell House, 1969), 66.

3. OR, I, 22, 1: 511–512; ORN, I, 25: 352–363, 367; *St. Louis Daily Missouri Democrat*, quoted in the *Chicago Daily Tribune*, August 27, 1863; *Chicago Daily Tribune*, September 19, 1863; Castel, 154, 158; DeBlack, 92–98. The entire Little Rock campaign is covered in Leo E. Huff, "The Union Expedition Against Little Rock, August-September 1863," *Arkansas Historical Quarterly* 22 (Fall 1963): 223–237.

4. ORN, I, 25: 466–471, 480–481, 484–486, 488–496, 507, 513–516, 526–529, 609, 612, 614–615, 621, 638, 642–643, 664.

5. OR, I, 26, 1: 384, 559, 653, 673; ORN, I, 25: 734–736, 770–773; U.S. Congress, Joint Committee on the Conduct of the War, *Report: Red River* (38th Cong., 2nd sess.; Washington, DC: GPO, 1864; repr., Greenwood Press, 1971), 5 (cited hereafter as Joint Committee, with page number in Arabic); Selfridge, 87–88; William Riley Brooksher, *War Along the Bayous: The 1864 Red River Campaign in Louisiana* (Washington, DC: Brassey's, 1998), xi–xii, 1–24; *A Brief and Condensed History of Parsons' Texas Cavalry Brigade* (Waxhachie, TX: J.M. Flemister, 1893), 268; Elias P. Pellet, *History of the 114th Regiment, New York State Volunteers* (Norwich, NY: Telegraph & Chronicle Power Press, 1866), 166–167. Acting Assistant Surgeon Mixer joined the squadron on October 1, 1862, and the *Lexington* on January 1. He would remain aboard another year, resigning from the service on February 28, 1865. Edward W. Callahan, *List of Officers of the Navy of the United States and of the Marine Corps, from 1775 to 1900, Comprising a Complete Register of All Present and Former Commissioned, Warranted, and Appointed Officers of the United States Navy, and of the Marine Corps, Regular and Volunteer, Compiled from the Official Records of the Navy Department* (New York: L.R. Hamersly & Co., 1901; repr., New York: Haskell House, 1969), 386. Gary D Joiner reports that a crucial piece of evidence received by Rear Adm. Porter on February 14 was a chart of Shreveport and vicinity drawn on the back of the death certificate of *Black Hawk* seaman James O'Leary. The detail on this map was "perhaps the greatest influence of Admiral Porter's decision of which vessels should be included in the expedition" (Gary D. Joiner, *Through the Howling Wilderness: The 1864 Red River Campaign and Union Failure in the West* (Knoxville: University of Tennessee Press, 2006), 24–26).

6. ORN, I, 25: 787–788; ORN, I, 26: 783, 788; OR, I, 34, 1: 155–160; *New York Times*, March 15, 1864; *Philadelphia Inquirer*, March 15, 1864; *Chicago Daily Tribune*, March 15, 1864; Silverstone, 149; "Surgeon Mixer's Account, March 2, 1864," in Frank Moore, ed. *The Rebellion Record: A Diary of American Events*, 12 vols. (New York: G.P. Putnam, 1861–1863); D. Van Nostrand, 1864–1868; repr., New York: Arno Press, 1977), 8:445–446; Hiram H. Martin, "Service Afield and Afloat: A Reminiscence of the Civil War, Ed. Guy R. Everson," *Indiana Magazine of History* 89 (March 1993): 52–53; Selfridge, 92; Porter, *Naval History*, 556. Forgetting about leap year, Surgeon Mixer's account is off by one day. Count Polignac (1832–1913), who wore a beard in the fashion of Napoleon III and spoke with a heavy accent, was a descendant of a favorite of Queen Marie Antoinette. A veteran of the Crimean War, he volunteered his services to the Confederacy and was named colonel and chief of staff to Gen. Beauregard in early 1861. Coming west, he participated in the Battle of Corinth, after which he was made a brigadier and assigned to command a brigade of unhappy unmounted Texas cavalry under Maj. Gen. Dick Taylor. At this point, he was still regarded with some hostility and disapproval by the disgruntled horsemen, who nicknamed him "Polecat." He would later be given a division and, returning to Europe in 1865, enjoyed a successful postwar career

(Richard Taylor, *Destruction and Reconstruction: Personal Experiences of the Late War* (New York: D. Appleton and Company, 1879), 153–154; Alwyn Barr, *Polignac's Texas Brigade*, 2nd. ed. (College Station: Texas A & M University Press, 1998), 1–30; Mark M. Boatner III, *The Civil War Dictionary* (New York: David McKay, 1959), 657). Acting Third Assistant Engineer O'Neil joined the squadron on April 22, 1863; he would be promoted to acting second assistant engineer on April 30, 1864. Among the last of the volunteer U.S. Navy officers employed in the west, he was honorably discharged on February 26, 1868. Acting Master Wright had served in various squadron vessels since joining up on December 7, 1861. He was placed in command of the *Osage* on January 1 but surrendered his post to Lt. Cmdr. Selfridge on March 15. Wright resigned from the service on April 7 (Callahan, 415, 605).

7. ORN, I, 26: 18–20; *New York Times,* March 15, 1864; *Chicago Daily Tribune,* March 15, 1864; *Philadelphia Inquirer,* March 15, 1864; Mahan, 189; Selfridge, 89–91; Jay Slagle, *Ironclad Captain: Seth Ledyard Phelps and the U.S. Navy* (Kent, OH: Kent State University Press, 1996), 352. The cause of the collision was laid to a confusion in whistle signals onboard *General Price.* Selfridge was later made captain of the ram *Vindicator.* There was no immediate effort to salvage the wreck of the timberclad. As late as 1923, the editor of the Navy *Official Records* wrote in her profile that she remained where sunk, "with all her armament, machinery, and stores yet on board" (ORN, II, 1: 65).

8. OR, I, 34, 1: 168, 304, 476; OR, I, 34, 2: 448–449, 494–496, 554, 616; ORN, I, 26: 23–26, 789; *New York Daily Tribune,* March 28, 1864; *St. Louis Daily Missouri Republican,* March 28, 1864; *Philadelphia Inquirer,* March 30, 1864; Joint Committee, 21; Mahan, 189–190; Porter, *Naval History,* 494–496; Porter, *Incidents and Anecdotes of the Civil War* (New York: D. Appleton and Co, 1885; repr., Harrisburg, PA: The Archive Society, 1997), 213; Richard Taylor, *Destruction and Reconstruction: Personal Experiences of the Late War* (New York: D. Appleton and Company, 1879), 180–181; Richard B. Irwin, "The Red River Campaign," in *Battles and Leaders of the Civil War,* ed. Robert V. Johnson and Clarence C. Buel, 4 vols. (New York: The Century Company, 1884–1887, repr. Thomas Yoseloff, 1956), 4:349–351; Thomas O. Selfridge, Jr., "The Navy in the Red River," *B&L,* 4:362; David Dixon Porter, "The Mississippi Flotilla in the Red River Expedition," *B&L,* 4:367; Walter G. Smith, ed., *Life and Letters of Thomas Kilby Smith* (New York: G.P. Putnam, 1898), 356; Joiner, *Through the Howling Wilderness,* 54–57; Joiner and Charles E. Vetter, "The Union Naval Expedition on the Red River, March 12-May 22, 1864," *Civil War Regiments: A Journal of the American Civil War* 4 (1994): 26–41; Curtis Milbourn and Gary D. Joiner, "The Battle of Blair's Landing," *North and South* 9 (February 2007): 12; Chester G. Hearn, *Admiral David Dixon Porter: The Civil War Years* (Annapolis, MD: Naval Institute Press, 1996), 245–246; Mahan, 190–191.

9. OR, 34, 1: 305, 313, 338–339, 500, 506, 561; OR, I, 34, 2: 494, 610–611; ORN, I, 26: 29–31, 35, 41, 50, 781, 784–785, 789; Mahan, 190–191; *New York Daily Tribune,* April 4, 1864; *St. Louis Daily Missouri Republican,* March 26, 1864; *Columbus (WI) Democrat,* May 29, 1895; Porter, *Naval History,* 499–500; Taylor, 156, 181–183; Joint Committee, 8–9, 18, 71, 74, 224–225; Joiner, *Through the Howling Wilderness,* 59–69; Joiner and Vetter, 1–49; Selfridge, "The Navy in the Red River," *B&L,* 4:367; Selfridge, *Memoirs,* 96–98; Mahan, 193–194; Harris H. Beecher, *Record of the 114th Regiment, New York State Volunteer Infantry* (Norwich, NY: J. F. Hubbard, Jr., 1866), 299–300; John D. Winters, *The Civil War in Louisiana* (Baton Rouge: Louisiana State University Press, 1963), 330–331; Ludwell H. Johnson, *Red River Campaign: Politics & Cotton in the Civil War* (Kent, OH: Kent State University Press, 1993), 99–105; Ivan Musicant, *Divided Waters: The Naval History of the Civil War* (New York: HarperCollins, 1995), 295–296; Irwin, "The Red River Campaign," *B&L,* 4:349–350; Robert L. Kerby, *Kirby Smith's Confederacy: The Trans-Mississippi South, 1863–1865* (New York: Columbia University Press, 1972), 297; Hearn, *Admiral David Dixon Porter,* 246–248

10. OR, I, 26, 2: 54–55, 323; OR, I, 34, 1: 168, 179–180; 282–284, 308–309, 322, 324, 331, 341, 380–381, 384, 388–393, 407, 428, 445, 452, 468, 471–472, 633–634; OR, I, 34, 2: 610–611; OR, I, 34, 3: 98–99, 172; *New York World,* April 16, 1864; *Columbus (WI) Democrat,* May 29, 1895; Joint Committee, 35, 210, 275–276, 282, 286–287, 323; ORN, I, 26: 38–39, 42–44, 46, 50–51, 54, 60–61, 777–778, 781, 785, 789; Musciant, 296–297; Thomas O. Selfridge, Jr., "The Navy in the Red River," *B&L,* 4:363; Selfridge, *Memoirs,* 99–101; Mahan, 195–196; Brooksher, 69–78; Irwin, "The Red River Campaign," *B&L,* 4:351–356; Porter *Naval History,* 502, 511–512; Porter, *Incidents and Anecdotes,* 232; Gary D. Joiner, *One Damn Blunder from Beginning to End: The Red River Campaign of 1864* (Wilmington, DE: Scholarly Resources, 2003), 140–141; Joiner, *Through the Howling Wilderness,* 21, 33–34, 41–42, 69–77, 131–136; Curtis Milbourn and Gary D. Joiner, "The Battle of Blair's Landing," *North and South* 9 (February 2007): 12–14; Joiner and Vetter, 49–51; Mahan, 193–196; Hearn, *Admiral David Dixon Porter,* 248–250; Steven D. Smith and George J. Castille III, "Bailey's Dam," Louisiana Department of Culture, Recreation and Tourism Anthropological Study No. 8, March 1986, http://www.crt.state.la.us/archaeology/BAILEYS/baileys.htm (accessed August 7, 2006). Acting Volunteer Lieutenant Couthouy joined the Western Flotilla on August 26, 1861; he was given command of the *Chillicothe* on February 20. When Lt. Cmdr. Bache learned of the death, he immediately caused an airtight coffin to be made, hoping to preserve the body until it could reach his family (Callahan, 133; ORN, I, 26: 42).

11. ORN, I, 26: 49–52, 55, 777–778, 781, 789; OR, I, 34, 1: 168, 172–204, 381–383, 384–385, 388, 570–571, 633; OR, I, 34, 3: 174; *Houston Daily Telegraph,* April 22, 1864; *Columbus (WI) Democrat,* May 29, 1895; Kerby, 309; Thomas O. Selfridge, Jr., "The Navy in the Red River," *B&L,* 4:363–364; Selfridge, *Memoirs,* 102–106; Porter, *Naval History,* 512–513; Smith, ed., *Life and Letters of Thomas Kilby Smith,* 102–103, 117; Musciant, 298–300; Taylor, *Destruction and Reconstruction* 118, 177–178, 181–182, 212; Joiner, *Through the Howling Wilderness,* 135–137; Joiner and Vetter, 55–59; Milbourn and Joiner, "The Battle of Blair's Landing," 15–20; Brooksher, 153–157; Mahan, 197–198; Irwin, "The Red River Campaign," *B&L,* 4:357–358; Anne J. Bailey, "Chasing Banks Out of Louisiana: Parsons' Texas Cavalry in the Red River Campaign," *Civil War Regiments: A Journal of the American Civil War* 2 (1992): 219–221; Bailey, *Between the Enemy and Texas: Parson's Texas Cavalry in the Civil War* (Fort Worth: Texas Christian University Press, 1989), 170–176; Rebecca W. Smith and Marion Mullins, eds., "The Diary of H.C. Medford, Confederate Soldier, 1864," vol. 34, no. 2, *Southwestern Historical Quarterly,* <http://www.tsha.utexas.edu/publications/journals/shq/online/v034/n2/contrib_DIVL1540.html> (accessed July 22, 2007); H.P. Gallaway, *Ragged Rebel: A Common Soldier in W.H. Parsons' Texas Cavalry, 1861–1865* (Austin: University of Texas Press, 1988), 86–87, 93–94, 97–100; Odie Faulk, *General Tom Green, Fightin' Texan* (Waco, TX: Texian Press,

1963), 62; Carl L. Duaine, *The Dead Men Wore Boots: An Account of the 32nd Texas Volunteer Cavalry, CSA, 1862–1865* (Austin, TX: San Felipe Press, 1966), 63, 90–91, 118; Alwyn Barr, "Confederate Artillery in the Trans-Mississippi" (master's thesis, University of Texas, 1961), 150–151; Barr, "The Battle of Blair's Landing," *Louisiana Studies* 2 (Winter 1963): 204–212; Bruce S. Allardice, "Curious Clash at Blair's Landing," *America's Civil War* 9 (July 1997), 60–64; Boatner, 349. The loss of Brig. Gen. Green (1814–1864), a Virginian by birth and a veteran of the 1836 Battle of San Jacinto, was acknowledged at the time to be a great loss to Southern arms. Maj. Gen. Taylor, a relative, believed it "an irreparable one." Common soldier Medford told his diary on April 13 that "This is sad indeed. There is no estimate as to his worth to our country. Our Country has certainly lost the best cavalry field officer on this side the river. This dreadful casualty has thrown a sad gloom over our otherwise elated army." Porter's charge of drunkenness on the part of Green and his men was bitterly disputed at the time and since then. Confederate Surgeon David Frentress, as quoted in Anne Bailey's article, denied it in a *Galveston Tri-Weekly News* letter on June 3, 1864, saying in part that there was insufficient medicinal liquor in the Trans-Mississippi theater, let alone any left over for healthy soldiers.

12. OR, I, 34, 1: 190, 310, 382–383, 505; ORN, I, 26: 62, 66, 69, 72–78; 790; *Philadelphia Press*, April 29, 1864; *St. Louis Daily Missouri Democrat*, May 10, 1864; *Columbus (WI) Democrat*, May 29, 1895; Musicant, 300–301; Mahan, 198; Brooksher, 158–159; Joiner, *Through the Howling Wilderness*, 137–140; Joiner and Vetter, 58–59; Selfridge, Jr., "The Navy in the Red River," *B&L*, 4:364; Selfridge, *Memoirs*, 102–106; Slagle, 365–367; Hearn, *Admiral David Dixon Porter*, 253–254; Porter, *Naval History*, 515–519; Porter, *Incidents and Anecdotes*, 235–239; Pellet, 222; Joint Committee, 247–248. The unique *Ozark* was an unsuccessful 578-ton river monitor that featured a single turret with two 11-inch guns forward and a casemate with four cannon aft (Silverstone, 147–148).

13. ORN, I, 26: 73–75, 79–81, 166–169, 176, 787–787, 790–791; OR, I, 34, 1, 583–584, 632, 634. 782, 790–791; *Columbus (WI) Democrat*, May 29, 1895; Chuck Veit, "Engagement at Deloges Bluff," Navy and Marine, <http://www.navyandmarine.org/ondeck/1862delogesbluff.htm> (accessed July 24, 2007); Taylor, 183–185; Hearn, *Admiral David Dixon Porter*, 255–257; Slagle, 367–378; Joiner, *Through the Howling Wilderness*, 138–140; Joiner and Vetter, 60–62; Mahan, 198–203; Selfridge, Jr., "The Navy in the Red River," *B&L*, 4: 364–365; Selfridge, *Memoirs*, 102–106; Taylor, *Destruction and Reconstruction*, 218; Brooksher, 190–193; Joint Committee, 245–248; Porter, *Naval History*, 520–524; Porter, *Incidents and Anecdotes*, 239–243; Musicant, 301–302. Like Viet, Brooksher also disputes the number of cannon involved in the Deloges Bluff battle, suggesting the 18 Porter claimed was a stretch (Brooksher, 253n). Surprisingly, *Osage* captain Selfridge does not mention steaming to meet the *Eastport* rescue group in his Deloges Bluff report, his *B&L* article, or his *Memoirs*.

14. ORN, I, 26: 92–95, 130–132; OR, I, 34, 1: 209, 310, 209, 254, 402–406, 491, 585–586; OR, I, 34, 3: 316; *New Orleans Era*, May 17, 1864; *New Orleans Times*, May 18, 1864; *Columbus (WI) Democrat*, May 29, 1895; Mahan, 203–207; Steven D. Smith and George J. Castille III, "Bailey's Dam," Louisiana Department of Culture, Recreation and Tourism Anthropological Study No. 8, March 1986, http://www.crt.state.la.us/archaeology/BAILEYS/baileys.htm (accessed August 7, 2006); Porter, *Incidents and Anecdotes*, 248–249; Porter, *Naval History*, 525–534; Johnson, 256–262; Musicant, 303–304; Kerby, 318; Taylor, 186–189; Irwin, "The Red River Campaign," *B&L*, 4:358–362; Hearn, *Admiral David Dixon Porter*, 258–265; Slagle, 378–381; Joiner, *Through the Howling Wilderness*, 151–154; Joiner and Vetter, 64–67; Selfridge, Jr., "The Navy in the Red River," *B&L*, 4:365–366; Selfridge, *Memoirs*, 109–111; Brooksher, 209–215. Lt. Col. Bailey received the "Thanks of Congress" for saving the fleet (OR, I, 34: 586).

Chapter 15

1. U.S. Navy Department, *Official Records of the Union and Confederate Navies in the War of the Rebellion*, 31 vols. (Washington, DC: GPO, 1894–1922), series I, vol. 26, 392–393, 414, 464, 562, 791 (cited hereafter as ORN, followed by a comma, the series number in Roman numerals, a comma, the volume number in Arabic, a colon, and the page in Arabic); U.S. War Department, *The War of the Rebellion: A Compilation of the Official Records of the Union and Confederate Armies*, 128 vols. (Washington, DC: GPO, 1880–1901), series I, vol. 34, part 1: 783, 946–953 (cited hereafter as OR, followed by a comma, the series number in Roman numerals, a comma, the volume number in Arabic, any part number in Arabic, a colon, and the page in Arabic); OR, I, 41, 1: 191–192; "Where We've Been: U.S.S. *Queen City* Sinking," Clarendon, Arkansas, http://www.clarendon-ar.com/been/uss_queen_city/index.html (accessed July 6, 2007); Richard B. Irwin, "The Red River Campaign," in *Battles and Leaders of the Civil War*, ed. Robert V. Johnson and Clarence C. Buel, 4 vols. (New York: The Century Company, 1884–1887; repr., Thomas Yoseloff, 1956), 4:362; Thomas A. DeBlack, *With Fire and Sword: Arkansas, 1861–1874* (Fayetteville: University of Arkansas Press, 2003), 66–67, 118; David Dixon Porter, *Naval History of the Civil War* (New York: Sherman Publishing Company, 1886; repr., Secaucus, NJ: Castle Books, 1984), 562; Jay Slagle, *Ironclad Captain: Seth Ledyard Phelps and the U.S. Navy* (Kent, OH: Kent State University Press, 1996), 383–384; Benson J. Lossing, *Pictorial Field Book of the Civil War: Journeys through the Battlefields in the Wake of Conflict*, 3 vols. (Hartford, CT: T. Belknap, 1874; repr., Johns Hopkins University Press, 1997), 3:274; Alfred T. Mahan, *The Navy in the Civil War*, vol. 3, *The Gulf and Inland Waters* (New York: Scribner's, 1883), 212; John N. Edwards, *Shelby and His Men, or The War in the West* (Cincinnati: Miami Printing and Publishing Co., 1867; repr., Waverly, MO: General J.O. Shelby Memorial, 1993), 317–318. Acting Ensign Smith was originally given that rank on December 5, 1862, but resigned on January 29, 1863. He was reinstated as a mate on March 31 and promoted to his original rank on April 10, becoming the *Tyler's* executive officer. After Lt. Cmdr. Bache permanently took over her command during the Clarendon battle on June 24, Smith resigned for a final time on July 15. Edward W. Callahan, *List of Officers of the Navy of the United States and of the Marine Corps, from 1775 to 1900, Comprising a Complete Register of All Present and Former Commissioned, Warranted, and Appointed Officers of the United States Navy, and of the Marine Corps, Regular and Volunteer, Compiled from the Official Records of the Navy Department* (New York: L.R. Hamersly & Co., 1901; repr., New York: Haskell House, 1969), 504.

2. OR, I, 34, 1: 1044–1045; ORN, I, 26: 402–403, 415–417, 791; Slagle, 385; *New York Times*, June 29, 1864. The 174 ton civil *Fanny Barker* was acquired in May 1863. Commissioned *Fawn*, the 158.8 foot stern-wheeler was 30.5 feet wide with a depth of hold of 3.6 feet. Her arma-

ment consisted of six 24-pounder howitzers and a single 12-pounder Parrott rifle. Famous for her role in the Ohio River pursuit of Brig. Gen. John Hunt Morgan, the newly built 148 ton *Naumkeag* entered service in April 1863. With a 5.6 foot depth and a beam of 30.5 feet, the same as that of the *Fawn*, this stern-wheeler was 154.4 feet long. She was outfitted with four 24-pounder howitzers and two 30-pounder Parrott rifles. Acting Volunteer Lieutenant Michael Hickey's *Queen City*, a 210 ton side-wheeler, was also commissioned in April 1863. Her armament comprised two 30-pounder Parrott rifles, two 32-pounder smoothbores, and four 24-pounder howitzers (Paul H. Silverstone, *Warships of the Civil War Navies* (Annapolis, MD: Naval Institute Press, 1989), 168, 171, 175).

3. ORN, I, 26: 417–433, 464; OR, I, 34, 1: 1051–1052; Edwards, 321–326; *St. Louis Daily Missouri Democrat*, July 2, 1864; *Chicago Daily Tribune*, July 3–4, 1864; *Memphis Argus*, July 12, 1864; "Where We've Been: U.S.S. *Queen City* Sinking," Clarendon, Arkansas, http://www.clarendon-ar.com/been/uss_queen_city/index.html (accessed July 6, 2007); DeBlack, 118; Mahan, 212–213; Porter, 562–563; Duane Huddleston, Sammie Cantrell Rose, and Pat Taylor Wood, *Steamboats and Ferries on the White River: A Heritage Revisited* (Conway: University of Central Arkansas Press, 1995; repr., Fayetteville: University of Arkansas Press, 1998), 63; Despite support from Rear Adm. Porter, Fitch, one of the most innovative convoy commanders of the Civil War, was regularly pilloried by army commanders for his tactics. His most famous dustup with the soldiers involved no less a figure than Maj. Gen. Grant. Myron J. Smith, Jr., *Le Roy Fitch: The Civil War Career of a Union Gunboat Commander* (Jefferson, NC: McFarland & Co., 2007), 221–226. A Kentuckian like John Hunt Morgan and a wealthy slave-holder like Nathan Bedford Forrest, Joe Shelby (1830–1897) joined the CSA cavalry under Sterling Price in 1861. Rising to the rank of colonel, he raised his own cavalry brigade, sometimes called the "Iron Brigade," and led it throughout the Trans-Mississippi theater for the remainder of the war. Refusing to surrender, he led his brigade into Mexico to support Maximilian, returning to Missouri after the end of the French adventure. He was appointed a U.S. marshal in 1893 (Mark M. Boatner III, *The Civil War Dictionary* (New York: David McKay, 1959), 737). There is a difference in the estimated length of the Clarendon battle. Bache claimed 45 minutes, Shelby in his OR report said an hour and a half, and Edwards reported that it took two hours (ORN, I, 26: 424; OR, I, 34, 1: 1050; Edwards, 325).

Epilogue

1. U.S. Navy Department, *Official Records of the Union and Confederate Navies in the War of the Rebellion,* 31 vols. (Washington, DC: GPO, 1894–1922), series I, vol. 26, 84, 273, 517, 553, 555, 558, 731 (cited hereafter as ORN, followed by a comma, the series number in Roman numerals, a comma, the volume number in Arabic, a colon, and the page in Arabic); ORN, I, 27: 301; Edward W. Callahan, *List of Officers of the Navy of the United States and of the Marine Corps, from 1775 to 1900, Comprising a Complete Register of All Present and Former Commissioned, Warranted, and Appointed Officers of the United States Navy, and of the Marine Corps, Regular and Volunteer, Compiled from the Official Records of the Navy Department* (New York: L.R. Hamersly & Co., 1901; repr., New York: Haskell House, 1969), 16, 198, 266, 402; David Dixon Porter, *Naval History of the Civil War* (New York: Sherman Publishing Company, 1886; repr., Secaucus, NJ: Castle Books, 1984), 808.

2. ORN, I, 27: 146, 173, 249, 300–301; ORN, II, 1: 127, 228; Paul H. Silverstone, *Warships of the Civil War Navies* (Annapolis, MD: Naval Institute Press, 1989), 159; Steven R. Davis, "Workhorse of the Western Waters: The Timberclad *Tyler*," *Civil War Times Illustrated* 44 (February 2005): 80; *Philadelphia Inquirer*, June 24, 1865; *Chicago Daily Tribune*, August 18, 21, 1865 .

3. "Conestoga," in *Dictionary of American Naval Fighting Ships* (Washington, DC: GPO, 1963), 2:161.

4. "Lexington," in *Dictionary of American Naval Fighting Ships* (Washington, DC: GPO, 1969), 4: 104–106; "U.S.S. *Lexington*: Museum on the Bay," <http://www.usslexington.com/index.php?option=com_content&task=view&id=38&Itemid=49 (accessed July 30, 2007).

5. David D. Porter, *Incidents and Anecdotes of the Civil War* (New York: D. Appleton and Co, 1885; repr., Harrisburg PA: The Archive Society, 1997), 124.

Bibliography

This bibliography is divided into sections: Primary Sources, Newspapers, Internet Sources, Books, Articles and Essays in Books or Journals, and Unpublished Sources.

Primary Sources

Bache, George M. Collection. Navy Department Library, Naval Historical Center, Washington, DC.
Bock, William N. Papers. Illinois State Historical Society, Springfield.
Browne, Symmes. Papers. Ohio Historical Society, Columbus.
Carondelet, U.S.S., Logbook: May 1862–June 1865. Record Group 24: U.S. Navy Department, Records of the Bureau of Naval Personnel. National Archives, Washington, DC.
Civil War, Confederate and Federal. Collection. Tennessee State Library and Archives, Nashville.
Civil War Times Illustrated. Collection. U.S. Army Military History Institute, Carlisle Barracks, PA.
Confederate States of America. War Department. *Official Reports of Battles*. Richmond, VA, Enquirer Book & Job Press, 1862.
Davis, Frederic E. Papers. Emory University, Atlanta.
Eads, James B. Papers. Missouri Historical Society, St. Louis.
Johnson, Robert V., and Clarence C. Buell, eds. *Battles and Leaders of the Civil War*. 4 vols. New York: The Century Company, 1884–1887; reprint Thomas Yoseloff, 1956.
Meigs, Montgomery C. Papers. Manuscript Division, Library of Congress, Washington, DC.
Pennock, Alexander Mosley. Papers. Illinois State Historical Society, Springfield.
Phelps, Seth Ledyard. Papers. Missouri Historical Society, St. Louis (SLPC).
Porter, David Dixon. Papers. Manuscript Division, Library of Congress, Washington, DC.
_____. Papers. Missouri Historical Society, St. Louis.
Rodgers, John. Collection. Library of Congress (JRC).
Rodgers Family. Papers, Library of Congress.
United States Congress. Joint Committee on the Conduct of the War. Report: *Red River*. 38th Cong., 2nd sess. Washington, DC: GPO, 1864; reprint, Greenwood Press, 1971.
_____. Navy Department. *Official Records of the Union and Confederate Navies in the War of the Rebellion (ORN)*. 31 vols. Washington, DC: GPO, 1894–1922.
_____. Navy Department. Records of the Bureau of Naval Personnel: Record Group 24. National Archives, Washington, DC.
_____. Navy Department. Records of the Office of Naval Records and Library, Naval Records Collection: Record Group 45. National Archives, Washington, DC.
_____. Navy Department. Timberclad Logbooks. Records of the Bureau of Naval Personnel: Record Group 24. National Archives, Washington, DC.
Watson, Theodore. Letters. Newberry Library (Chicago).
Welles, Gideon. Papers, Library of Congress.

Not all of the logbooks kept on the timberclads have survived. Those available by ship and date include: *Conestoga* (December 23, 1862–May 21, 1863; July 8–December 31, 1863). *Lexington* (January 23, 1863–July 2, 1865). *Tyler* (April 24, 1862–June 26, 1865).

Before they went missing, abstracts were taken from the deck logs of the three ships; these appear in the Navy Official Records and include information for dates of deck logs no longer available.

U.S. War Department. *Atlas to Accompany the Official Records of the War of the Rebellion*. Compiled by Calvin D. Cowles. 3 vols. Washington, DC: GPO, 1891–1895.
_____. *The War of the Rebellion: A Compilation of the Official Records of the Union and Confederate Armies* [OR]. 128 vols. Washington, DC: GPO, 1880–1901.
Watson, Theodore. Letters. Newberry Library (Chicago).
Welles, Gideon. Papers. Manuscript Division, Library of Congress, Washington, DC.

Newspapers

Atlantic Democrat
Boston Morning Journal

Cairo City Weekly Gazette
Charleston Daily Courier
Charleston Mercury
Chicago Daily Post
Chicago Daily Times
Chicago Daily Tribune
Chicago Evening Journal
Cincinnati Daily Commercial
Cincinnati Daily Enquirer
Cincinnati Daily Gazette
Cincinnati Times
Clarksville Chronicle
Cleveland Daily Plain Dealer
Columbus (Ohio) Crisis
Columbus (GA) Daily Enquirer
Evansville Daily Journal
Florence (AL) Gazette
Frank Leslie's Illustrated Newspaper
Granada (MS) Appeal
Harper's Weekly
Houston Daily Telegraph
Houston Tri-Weekly Telegraph
Illinois Weekly State Journal
Indiana Herald
Indianapolis Daily Journal
Indianapolis News
Jackson Mississippian
Little Rock True Democrat
Louisville Courier
Louisville Daily Journal
Macon Daily Telegraph
Macon Weekly Telegraph
Memphis Argus
Memphis Daily Appeal
Memphis Daily Avalanche
Memphis Bulletin
Mobile Daily Advertiser & Register
Mobile Daily Tribune
Mobile Evening News
Nashville Banner
Nashville Daily Patriot
Nashville Daily Union
Nashville Dispatch
Nashville Times
Nashville Union and American
Natchitoches (LA) Union
National Intelligencer
New Albany Ledger
New Orleans Daily Crescent
New Orleans Daily Delta
New Orleans Daily Picayune
New Orleans Era
New Orleans Times
New York Herald
New York Times
New York Tribune
New York World
Richmond Dispatch
St. Louis Daily Missouri Democrat
St. Louis Daily Missouri Republican
Savannah Republican
Vicksburg Evening Post
Vicksburg Sunday Post
Wisconsin State Journal

Internet Sources

Aronson, Alan. "Strategic Supply of Civil War Armies." *General Histories of the American Civil War.* http://members.cox.net/rb2307/content/STRATEGIC_SUPPLY_OF_CIVIL_WAR_ARMIES.htm (accessed March 30, 2000).

"Arkansas River." In *Wikipedia*. http://en.wikipedia.org/wiki/Arkansas_River> (accessed September 2, 2006).

Bailey, Anne J. "Parson's Texas Cavalry." *Handbook of Texas.* http://www.tsha.utexas.edu/handbook/online/articles/PP/qkp1.html (accessed July 22, 2007).

"Battle of Shiloh Timeline." *Civil War Gazette.* http://www.civilwargazette.com/csacw/tours/shiloh/shiloh_timeline.htm (accessed January 25, 2007).

Bering, John A., and Thomas Montgomery, *History of the Forty-Eighth Ohio Vet. Vol. Inf.* In Don Worth, *48th OVVI.* http://www.riovvi.org/oh48hist.html (accessed January 25, 2007).

Biographical Directory of the United States Congress 1774–Present. http://bioguide.congress.gov/scripts/biodisplay.pl?index=B000231 (accessed October 1, 2006).

Bishop v. U.S., 197 U.S. 334 (1905). *Find Law.* <http://caselaw.lp.findlaw.com/scripts/getcase.pl?navby=case&court=us&vol=197&invol=334> (accessed October 1, 2006).

Bogan, Dallas. "Edward Deering Mansfield Was a True Jack-of-All-Trades." *Warren County Ohio GenWeb Project*, August 30, 2004. http://www.rootsweb.com/~ohwarren/Bogan/bogan235.htm (accessed October 1, 2006).

"The Civil War Diary of Michael Sweetman, Co. K, 114th O.V.I." Edited by Johnda T. Davis. Fortunecity. http://www.fortunecity.com/westwood/makeover/347/id229.htm (accessed May 5, 2007).

"Commerce Missouri." In *Wikipedia*. http://en.wikipedia.org/wiki/Commerce,_Missouri (accessed August 29, 2006).

"Cumberland River." In *Wikipedia.* http://en.wikipedia.org/wiki/Cumberland_River (accessed August 6, 2005).

Dawley, Dave. "William J. Kountz." *Steamboat.* <http://members.tripod.com/~Write4801/captains/k.html> (accessed September 15, 2006).

Donn, John W. "War Record of J.W. Donn, Including Reminiscences of Frederick W. Dorr, July 1861 to June 1865." *NOAA History.* http://www.history.noaa.gov/stories_tales/donn.html (accessed April 4, 2005).

"Egypt Mills, Missouri." In *Midwest Gazetteer.* <http://gazetteer.midwestplaces.com/mo/cape/egypt-mills> (accessed November 30, 2006).

Epperson, James F. "Shiloh Chronology." *Epperson Home Page.* http://members.aol.com/jfepperson/shiloh.html (accessed January 25, 2007).

Harris, Isham G. "Correspondence of Governor Isham Green Harris, 1861." TNGenWeb Project: The Biographies of Our Ancestors. http://www.tngenweb.org/bios/h/18610429.html (accessed September 11, 2006).

History of the Val Verde Battery. http://www.geocities.com/valverde_battery (accessed July 24, 2007).

Hogan, Brian, Conrad Bush and Mike Brown. "The 76th New York and the Navy." *76th New York Infantry Regiment.* http://www.bpmlegal.com/76NY/76navy.html (accessed July 12, 2005).

Honnoll, W. Danny. "Engagement at St. Charles." *Encyclopedia of Arkansas History and Culture.* <http://encyclopedia of arkansas.net/encyclopedia/entry-detail.aspx?entryID=532> (accessed March 26, 2007).

INGenWeb. "Madison City Directory, 1859–1860." *Madison and Jefferson County Directories.* http://myindiana

home.net/gen/jeff/records/direct/maddir.html (accessed September 30, 2006).

"James Buchanan Eads." *University of Illinois at Urbana-Champagne River.* http://www.riverweb.uiuc.edu/TECH/TECH20.htm (accessed September 18, 2006).

Jenkins, Mark F. "Timberclads." *Ironclads and Blockade Runners of the Civil War.* http://www.wideopenwest.com/~jenkins/ironclads/tinclads.htm (accessed July 29, 2005).

"Jesse J. Phillips." *Illinois Courts.* <http://www.state.il.us/Court/SupremeCourt/Previous/Bio_JPhillips.as> (accessed October 6, 2006).

"John Bell." *The Learning Curve.* <http://www.spartacus.schoolnet.co.uk/USAbellJ.htm> (accessed December 24, 2006).

Ledoux, Tom. "United States Navy Biographies: George M. Blodgett." VermontCivilWar.Org. <http://vermontcivilwar.org/units/navy/bios.php?input=33437> (accessed January 27, 2007).

Letters Home from an Iowa Soldier in the American Civil War. http://www.civilwarletters.com/scott_7_6_1863.html (accessed July 2, 2007).

Matthews, Gary. "First Shots of the ACW?" Civil War Navy Messageboard. http://history-sites.com/mb/cw/cwnavy/index.cgi?noframes;read=1005 (accessed August 4, 2006).

_____. "'Tinclad'—In Response to: Re: Tinclad (Terry Foenander)." Civil War Navies Message Board. http://history-sites.com/mb/cw/cwnavy/index.cgi?noframes;read=1314 (accessed December 7, 2005).

"Mississippi River." In *Wikipedia.* <http://en.wikipedia.org/wiki/Ohio_River> (accessed August 25, 2006).

Morris, William R. "The Burning of Clifton." *Wayne County Historian.* Vol. 2 (reprinted June 1989): reprinted on the Civil War Page. http://www.netease.net/wayne/burningclifton.htm (March 3, 2004).

"My Pollard Family: Chapter 2 & Chapter 3, Daniel, the War Years." *My American Family* http://freepages.family.rootsweb.com/~ricksgenealogy/e_book.htm (accessed July 13, 2005).

Noomen, Eric-Jan. "The Transfer of Napoleon's Corpse." *The Second Page of the Dead.* http://www.xs4all.nl/~ejnoomen/story101.html (accessed June 23, 2005).

"Ohio River." In *Wikipedia.* http://en.wikipedia.org/wiki/Ohio_River (accessed August 5, 2005).

"The Origin of the Ranks and Rank Insignia Now Used by the United States Armed Forces, Officers: Lieutenants." *Traditions of the Naval Service.* http://www.history.navy.mil/trivia/triv4-5d.htm (accessed July 7, 2005).

Paxson, Frederic L. "The Railroads of the 'Old Northwest' Before the Civil War." In *Transactions of the Wisconsin Academy of Sciences, Arts, and Letters.* Vol. 18. (accessed October 1912): reprinted in Thomas Ehrenreich, *Railroad Extra, 2001.* http://www.catskillarchive.com/rrextra/abonw.html (accessed July 3, 2005).

"Red River." In *LoveToKnow 1911.* http://www.1911encyclopedia.org/Red_River (accessed September 3, 2006).

"Red River (Mississippi Watershed)." In *Wikipedia.* http://en.wikipedia.org/wiki/Red_River_%28Mississippi_watershed%29 (accessed September 3, 2006).

Redington Papers. University of Wisconsin Digital Collections. <http://digital.library.wisc.edu/1711.dl/WI.EdRed01> (accessed August 30, 2006).

Rice, Thomas E. "Managing the Mississippi." The Nature of Illinois. <http://www.natureillinois.org/news/missississippi.html> (accessed August 26, 2006).

Richard, Joseph. *The 18th Louisiana Infantry Regiment: A Brief History and Roster.* <http://members.tripod.com/j_richard/> (accessed February 1, 2007).

Smith, David M. "The Defense of Cincinnati — The Battle That Never Was: Past Presentations of the Cincinnati Civil War Roundtable, January 15, 1998." Cincinnati Civil War Roundtable. <http://www.cincinnaticwrt.org/data/ccwrt_history/talks_text/smith_defense_cin.html> (accessed September 4, 2006).

Smith, Rebecca W., and Marion Mullins, eds. "The Diary of H.C. Medford, Confederate Soldier, 1864." Vol. 34, No. 2. *Southwestern Historical Quarterly Online.* <http://www.tsha.utexas.edu/publications/journals/shq/online/v034/n2/contrib_DIVL1540.html> (accessed July 22, 2007).

Smith, Steven D., and George J. Castille III. "Bailey's Dam." Louisiana Department of Culture, Recreation and Tourism Anthropological. Study No. 8, March 1986. http://www.crt.state.la.us/archaeology/BAILEYS/baileys.htm (accessed August 7, 2006).

Suhr, Robert C. "Military Technology: The Confederate Floating Battery Revival During the American Civil War." TheHistoryNet. <http://www.historynet.com/wars_conflicts/military_technology/3035991.html?featured=y&c=y> (accessed October 1, 2006).

Swift, R.K. "Final Report of the Military Expedition from Chicago to Cairo, April 26, 1861." Illinois During the Civil War. <http://www.illinoiscivilwar.org/orders2.html> (accessed August 30, 2006).

"Tennessee River." Wikipedia. <http://en.wikipedia.org/wiki/Tennessee_River> (accessed August 5, 2005).

"Timeline 1861." *Valley of the Shadow.* http://valley.vcdh.virginia.edu/reference/timelines/timeline1861.html (accessed September 1, 2006).

"Towns of the Cumberland." *Save the Cumberland.* http://www.savethecumberland.org/towns.htm (accessed July 21, 2005).

U.S. Department of the Interior. National Park Service. "Social Impacts of the Civil War: Seven Prisoners Make a Shadow.'" Experience Your America. <http://www.itd.nps.gov/cwss/manassas/social/andersonville.htm> (accessed April 22, 2007).

_____. Navy Department. Naval Historical Center. "Commander Isaac Newton Brown, CSN (1817–1889)." *OnLine Library of Selected Images — People — United States.* http://www.history.navy.mil/photos/pers-us/uspers-b/in-brwn.htm (accessed March 30, 2007).

_____. Navy Department. Naval Historical Center. *Frequently Asked Questions No. 63: Ship Naming in the United States Navy, A Note on Navy Ship Name Prefixes.* http://www.history.navy.mil/faqs/faq63-1.htm (accessed April 16, 2007).

"U.S.S. *Lexington*: Museum on the Bay." <http://www.usslexington.com/index.php?option=com_content&task=view&id=38&Itemid=49> (accessed July 30, 2007).

"The Valverde Battery." *The Road to Glorieta Readers Companion.* http://darkwing.uoregon.edu/~donh/page78.html (accessed July 24, 2007).

VandeCreek, Drew E. "And the War Came, 1861–1862." Illinois during the Civil War. http://dig.lib.niu.edu/civilwar/narrative2.html. (accessed August 30, 2006).

Veit, Chuck. "Engagement at Deloges Bluff." Navy and Marine. <http://www.navyandmarine.org/ondeck/1862delogesbluff.htm> (accessed July 24, 2007).

_____. "First Shiloh." Navy and Marine. http://www.navyandmarine.org/ondeck/1862firstshiloh.htm (accessed January 25, 2007).

Wehner, Chris. "The Burning of Prentiss, Mississippi, 1862: A Case Study in Total War." *Blog4 History: American History & Civil War History.* http://www.blog4history.com/?m=200607 (accessed May 3, 2007).

"Where We've Been: U.S.S. *Queen City* Sinking." *Clarendon, Arkansas*. http://www.clarendon-ar.com/been/uss_queen_city/index.html. (accessed July 6, 2007).

"White River." In *Wikipedia*. http://en.wikipedia.org/wiki/White_River_%28Arkansas%29 (accessed September 2, 2006).

Wiener, James G., et al. "Mississippi River." U.S. Geological Survey, Biological Resources Division. <http://biology.usgs.gov/s+t/SNT/noframe/ms137.htm> (accessed August 26, 2006).

Williams, Scott K. "St Louis' Ships of Iron: The Ironclads and Monitors of Carondelet (St. Louis): Missouri." Missouri Civil War Museum. http://www.moissouricivilwarmuseum.org/lironclads.htm (accessed July 12, 2005).

Wright, George. "Re: Confederate River Gunboats." Civil War Navies Messageboard. <http://history-sites.com/mb/cw/cwnavy/index.cgi?read=1948> (accessed November 10, 2006).

"Yazoo River." In *Wikipedia*. <en.wikipedia.org/wiki/Yazoo_River> (accessed September 2, 2006).

Books

Abbott, John S.C. *The History of the Civil War in America*. Vol. 1. New York: H. Bill, 1863.

Abdill, George R. *Civil War Railroads: Pictorial Story of the Iron Horse, 1861–1865*. Seattle: Superior Publishing Co., 1961.

Ackerman, William K. *Historical Sketch of the Illinois Central Railroad*. Chicago: Fergus, 1890.

Alden, Carroll Storrs, and Ralph Earle. *Makers of Naval Tradition*. Boston: Ginn and Company, 1925.

Alldredge, J. Haden et al. *A History of Navigation on the Tennessee River*. Washington, DC: GPO, 1937.

Allen, David C. *Winds of Change: Robertson County, Tennessee, in the Civil War*. Nashville: Land Yacht Press, 2000.

Allen, John W. *Legends and Lore of Southern Illinois*. Carbondale, IL: University Graphics, 1978.

Ambrose, Daniel L. *History of the Seventh Regiment Illinois Volunteer Infantry*. Springfield, IL: Illinois Journal Company, 1868.

Ambrose, Stephen E. *Halleck: Lincoln's Chief of Staff*. Baton Rouge: Louisiana State University Press, 1962.

Anders, Curt. *Disaster in Damp Sand: The Red River Expedition*. Carmel, IN: Guild Press of Indiana, 1997.

_____. *Henry Halleck's War: A Fresh Look at Lincoln's Controversial General-in-Chief*. Indianapolis: Guild Press of Indiana, 1999.

Anderson, Bern. *By Sea and By River: The Naval History of the Civil War*. New York: Knopf, 1962.

Andrews, J. Cutler. *The North Reports the Civil War*. Pittsburgh, PA: University of Pittsburgh Press, 1985.

_____. *The South Reports the Civil War*. Pittsburgh, PA: University of Pittsburgh Press, 1985.

Angle, Paul M., ed. *Illinois Guide and Gazetter: Prepared Under the Supervision of the Illinois Sesquicentennial Commission*. Chicago: Rand McNally & Company, 1969.

Ash, Stephen V. *Middle Tennessee Society Transformed, 1860–1870: War and Peace in the Upper South*. Baton Rouge: Louisiana State University Press, 1988.

_____. *When the Yankees Came: Conflict and Chaos in the Occupied South, 1861–1865*. Chapel Hill: University of North Carolina Press, 1995.

Asprey, Robert B. *The War in the Shadows: The Guerrilla in History, Two Thousand Years of the Guerrilla at War from Ancient Persia to the Present*. 2 vols. New York: William Morrow, 1975.

Aughey, John H. *The Iron Furnace, or Slavery and Secession*. Philadelphia: William S. and Alfred Martien, 1863.

Austin, J.P. *The Blue and the Gray: Sketches of a Portion of the Unwritten History of the Great American Civil War*. Atlanta: Franklin Printing and Publishing Co., 1899.

Bacon, Benjamin W. *Sinews of War: How Technology, Industry and Transportation Won the Civil War*. Novato, CA: Presidio Press, 1997.

Badeau, Adam. *Military History of Ulysses S. Grant*. 3 vols. New York: D. Appleton and Co., 1868–1881.

Bailey, Anne J. *Between the Enemy and Texas: Parsons's Texas Cavalry in the Civil War*. Fort Worth: Texas Christian University Press, 1989.

_____. *The Chessboard of War: Sherman and Hood in the Autumn Campaigns of 1864*, Great Campaigns of the Civil War. Lincoln: University of Nebraska Press, 2000.

Ballard, Michael B. *Vicksburg: The Campaign that Opened the Mississippi*. Chapel Hill: University of North Carolina Press, 2004.

Banta, Richard E. *The Ohio*. Rivers of America. New York: Rinehard, 1949.

Barr, Alwyn. *Polignac's Texas Brigade*. 2nd ed. College Station: Texas A & M University Press, 1998.

Barrett, Edward. *Gunnery Instruction Simplified for the Volunteer Officers of the U.S. Navy, with Hints for Executive and Other Officers*. New York: D. Van Nostrand, 1863.

Barron, Samuel B. *The Lone Star Defenders: A Chronicle of the Third Texas Cavalry, Ross' Brigade*. New York and Washington, DC: The Neale Publishing Co., 1908.

Bartols, Barnabas H. *A Treatise on the Marine Boilers of the United States*. Philadelphia: R.W. Barnard, 1851.

Bates, Edward. *The Diary of Edward Bates, 1859–1866*. Edited by Howard Kennedy Beale. Washington, DC: GPO, 1933; reprinted, Da Capo Press, 1971.

Beach, Ursula Smith. *Along the Warioto, or a History of Montgomery County, Tennessee*. Clarksville, TN: Clarksville Kiwanis Club and Tennessee Historical Commission, 1964.

Beale, Howard K., ed. *Diary of Gideon Welles: Secretary of the Navy Under Lincoln and Johnson*. 2 vols. New York: W.W. Norton, 1960.

Bearss, Edwin C. *The Fall of Fort Henry*. Dover, TN: Eastern National Park and Monument Association, 1989.

_____. *Hardluck Ironclad: The Sinking and Salvage of the Cairo*. Baton Rouge: Louisiana State University, 1966.

_____. *Unconditional Surrender: The Fall of Fort Donelson*. Dover, TN: Eastern National Park and Monument Association, 1991.

_____. *The Vicksburg Campaign*. 3 vols. Dayton, OH: Morningside Book Shop, 1985–1986.

Beecher, Harris H. *Record of the 114th Regiment, New York State Volunteer Infantry*. Norwich, NY: J.F. Hubbard, Jr., 1866.

Bennett, Frank M. *Steam Navy of the United States: A History of the Growth of the Steam Vessel of War in the U.S. Navy and of the Naval Engineer Corps*. Pittsburgh: Warren, 1896; reprinted, New York: Greenwood, 1970.

Bennett, Michael J. *Union Jacks: Yankee Sailors in the Civil War*. Chapel Hill: University of North Carolina Press, 2004.

Beringer, Richard E., Herman Hattaway, Archer Jones, and William N. Still, Jr. *Why the South Lost the Civil War*. Athens: University of Georgia Press, 1986.

Birtle, Andrew J. *U.S. Army Counterinsurgency and Contingency Operations Doctrine, 1860–1941*. Washington, DC: GPO, 1998.

Blessington, Joseph P. *The Campaigns of Walker's Texas Division*. Austin, TX: The Pemberton Press, 1968.

Boatner, Mark M. III. *The Civil War Dictionary*. New York: David McKay, 1959.

Boynton, Charles B. *History of the Navy During the Rebellion*. 2 vols. New York: D. Appleton and Company, 1867–1868.

Bragg, Marion. *Historic Names and Places on the Lower Mississippi River*. Vicksburg, MS: Mississippi River Commission, 1977.

Brandt, J.D., *Gunnery Catechism as Applied to the Service of Naval Ordnance*, New York: D. Van Nostrand, 1864.

Brandt, Robert. *Touring the Middle Tennessee Backroads*. Winston-Salem, NC: John F. Blair, Publisher, 1995.

Brazelton, B.G. *A History of Hardin County, Tennessee*. Nashville: Cumberland Presbyterian Publishing House, 1885.

A Brief and Condensed History of Parsons' Texas Cavalry Brigade. Waxhachie, TX: J.M. Flemister, Printer, 1893.

Brinton, John H. *Personal Memoirs of John H. Brinton, Major and Surgeon, U.S.V., 1861–1865*. New York: Neale, 1914.

Brock, Eric, and Gary D. Joiner. *Red River Steamboats*. Charleston, SC: Arcadia Publishing, 1999.

Brookshire, William Riley. *Bloody Hill: The Civil War Battle of Wilson's Creek*. Washington, DC: Brassey's, Inc., 1995.

_____. *War Along the Bayous: The 1864 Red River Campaign in Louisiana*. Washington DC: Brassey's, 1998.

Browne, Henry R., and Symmes E. *From the Fresh Water Navy, 1861–1864: Letters of Acting Master's Mate Henry R. Browne and Acting Ensign Symmes E. Browne*. Edited by John D. Milligan. Naval Letters Series. Vol. 3. Annapolis, MD: Naval Institute Press, 1970.

Browne, Junius Henri. *Four Years in Secessia: Adventures Within and Without the Union Lines*. Hartford, CT: O.D. Case and Company, 1865.

Brownlee, Richard S. III. *Gray Ghosts of the Confederacy: Guerrilla Warfare in the West, 1861–1865*. Baton Rouge: Louisiana State University Press, 1958.

Bucy, Carole. *A Path Divided: Tennessee's Civil War Years*. Nashville: Tennessee 200, 1996.

Burley, Augustus H. *The Cairo Expedition: Illinois' First Response in the Late Civil War*. Chicago: Fergus Printing, 1892.

Callahan, Edward W. *List of Officers of the Navy of the United States and of the Marine Corps, from 1775 to 1900, Comprising a Complete Register of All Present and Former Commissioned, Warranted, and Appointed Officers of the United States Navy, and of the Marine Corps, Regular and Volunteer, Compiled from the Official Records of the Navy Department*. New York: L.R. Hamersly & Co., 1901; reprint, New York: Haskell House, 1969.

Calore, Paul. *Naval Campaigns of the Civil War*. Jefferson, NC: McFarland & Co., Inc., 2002.

Campbell, R. Thomas. *Confederate Naval Forces on Western Waters: The Defense of the Mississippi River and Its Tributaries*. Jefferson, NC: McFarland & Co., Inc., 2005.

_____. *Gray Thunder*. Exploits of the Confederate Navy. New Orleans: Burd Street Press, 1996.

_____. *Southern Thunder*. Exploits of the Confederate Navy. New Orleans: Burd Street Press, 1996.

Canfield, Eugene B. *Civil War Naval Ordnance*. Washington, DC: Naval History Division, U.S. Navy Department, 1969.

Canney, Donald L. *Lincoln's Navy: The Ships, Men and Organization, 1861–65*. London and New York: Conway Maritime Press, 1998.

_____. *The Old Steam Navy*. Vol. 2, *The Ironclads, 1842–1885*. Annapolis, MD: Naval Institute Press, 1993.

Capers, Gerald M. *The Biography of a River Town: Memphis — Its Heroic Age*. Chapel Hill: University of North Carolina Press, 1939.

Carter, Samuel III. *The Final Fortress: The Campaign for Vicksburg 1862–1863*. New York: St. Martin's Press, 1980.

Castel, Albert. *General Sterling Price and the Civil War in the West*. Baton Rouge: Louisiana State University Press, 1968.

Castlen, Harriet (Gift). *Hope Bids Me Onward*. Savannah, GA: Chatham Printing Co., 1945.

Catton, Bruce. *The American Heritage Picture History of the Civil War*. New York: American Heritage Publishing Co., 1960.

_____. *The Centennial History of the Civil War*. 3 vols. Garden City, NY: Doubleday, 1961–1965.

_____. *Grant Moves South*. Boston: Little, Brown, 1960.

_____. *Never Call Retreat*. New York: Pocket Books, 1973.

_____. *This Hallowed Ground: The Story of the Union Side of the Civil War* .Garden City, NY: Doubleday, 1956.

Cayton, Andrew R.L. *Ohio: The History of a People*. Columbus: Ohio State University Press, 2002.

Chaffin, Tom. *Pathfinder: John Charles Frémont and the Course of American Empire*. New York: Hill & Wang, 2002.

Chamberlain, William H., ed. *Sketches of War History, 1861–1865: Papers Prepared for the Ohio Commandery of the Military Order of the Loyal Legion of the United States*. 6 vols. Cincinnati: R Clarke & Co., 1890–1908.

Chappelle, Howard I. *History of the American Sailing Navy*. New York: W.W. Norton, 1935.

Christ, Mark K., ed. *Rugged and Sublime: The Civil War in Arkansas*. Fayetteville: University of Arkansas Press, 1994.

Cist, Henry M. *Army of the Cumberland*. Campaigns of the Civil War. New York: Charles Scribner's Sons, 1892.

Clark, Orton. *The One Hundred and Sixteenth Regiment of New York Volunteers*. Buffalo, NY: Matthews & Warren, 1868.

Cleaves, Freeman. *Rock of Chickamauga: The Life of General George H. Thomas*. Norman: University of Oklahoma Press, 1948.

Coffin, Charles C. *My Days and Nights on the Battlefield: A Book for Boys*. By "Carlton," pseud. 2nd ed. Boston: Ticknor and Fields, 1864.

Cogar, William B. *Dictionary of Admirals of the U.S. Navy*. 2 vols. Annapolis, MD: Naval Institute Press, 1989.

Cole, Allan B. *Yankee Surveyors in the Shoguns Sea: Records of the United States Expedition to the North Pacific Ocean, 1853–1856*. Princeton, NJ: Princeton University Press, 1947.

Coleman, Silas B. *A July Morning with the Rebel Ram "Arkansas."* War Papers Read Before the Commandery of the State of Michigan, Military Order of the Loyal Legion of the United States, No. 1. Detroit: Winn & Hammond, 1890; reprint, *Papers of the Military Order of the Loyal Legion of the United States*. reprint ed., 56 vols. Wilmington, NC: Broadfoot Publishing Co., 1994.

Confederate States of America. Congress. House of Representatives. Special Committee on the Recent Military Disasters. *Report of the Special Committee on the Recent Military Disasters at Forts Henry & Donelson & the Evacuation of Nashville*. Richmond: Enquirer, 1862.

Conger, Arthur L. *The Rise of U.S. Grant*. New York: Century, 1931.

Connelly, Thomas Lawrence. *Army of the Heartland: The Army of Tennessee, 1861–1862*. Baton Rouge: Louisiana State University Press, 1967.

_____. *Autumn of Glory: The Army of Tennessee, 1862–1865*. Baton Rouge: Louisiana State University Press, 1971.

_____. *Civil War Tennessee: Battles and Leaders*. Knoxville: University of Tennessee Press, 1979.

Connelly, Thomas W. *History of the 70th Ohio Regiment from Its Organization to Its Mustering Out*. Cincinnati: Peak Bros., 1902.

Cooling, Benjamin F. *Fort Donelson's Legacy: War and Society in Kentucky and Tennessee, 1862–1863*. Knoxville: University of Tennessee Press, 1997.

_____. *Forts Henry and Donelson: The Key to the Confederate Heartland*. Knoxville: University of Tennessee Press, 1987.

Coombe, Jack D. *Thunder Along the Mississippi: The River Battles That Split the Confederacy*. New York: Sarpedon Publishers, 1996.

Coulter, E. Merton. *The Civil War and Readjustment in Kentucky*. Chapel Hill: University of North Carolina Press, 1926.

Cox, Douglas E. *Joint Operations During the Campaign of 1862 on the TN & Cumberland River*. Carlisle Barracks, PA: US Army War College, 1989.

Cox, Jacob D. *Military Reminiscences of the Civil War*. 2 vols. New York: Scribner's, 1900.

Crandall, Warren D., and Isaac D. Newell. *History of the Ram Fleet and Mississippi Marine Brigade*. St. Louis: Buschart Brothers, 1907.

Crocker, Helen B. *The Green River of Kentucky*. Lexington: University Press of Kentucky, 1976.

Crook, George. *General George Crook: His Autobiography*. Edited by Martin F. Schmitt. Norman: University of Oklahoma Press, 1946.

Crooker, Lucien B., Henry S. Nourse, and John G. Brown. *The 55th Illinois, 1861–1865*. Huntington, WV: Blue Acorn Press, 1993.

Cunningham, O. Edward. *Shiloh and the Western Campaign of 1862*. Edited by Gary D. Joiner and Timothy B. Smith. New York: Savas Beatie, 2007.

Currie, George E. *Warfare Along the Mississippi: The Letters of Lt. George E. Currie*. Edited by Norman E. Clark. Mount Pleasant: Central Michigan University, 1861.

Daniel, Larry J. *Cannoneers in Gray: The Field Artillery of the Army of Tennessee, 1861–1865*. Birmingham: University of Alabama Press, 1984.

_____. *Days of Glory: The Army of the Cumberland, 1861–1865*. Baton Rouge: Louisiana State University Press, 2004.

_____. *Shiloh: The Battle That Changed the Civil War*. New York: Simon & Schuster, 1997.

Daniel, Larry J., and Lynn N. Bock. *Island No. 10: Struggle in the Mississippi Valley*. Tuscaloosa: University of Alabama Press, 1996.

Davidson, Alexander, and Bernard Stuve. *A Complete History of Illinois from 1673 to 1873*. Springfield, IL: Illinois Journal Company, 1874.

Davidson, Donald. *The Tennessee*. Vol. 2, *The New River, Civil War to TVA*. Rivers of America. New York: Rinehart & Co., 1948.

Davis, Charles H. *Charles H. Davis: Life of Charles Henry Davis, Rear Admiral, 1807–1877*. Boston and New York: Houghton, Mifflin and Company, 1899.

Davis, Jefferson. *Rise and Fall of the Confederate Government*. 2 vols. New York: D. Appleton and Company, 1881.

DeBlack, Thomas A. *With Fire and Sword: Arkansas, 1861–1874*. Fayetteville: University of Arkansas Press, 2003.

Dewey, George. *Autobiography of George Dewey: Admiral of the Navy*. New York: Charles Scribner's Sons, 1913.

Dickey, Thomas S., and Peter C. George. *Field Artillery Projectiles of the American Civil War, Revised and Supplemented 1993 Edition*(tm). Mechanicsville, VA: Arsenal Publications II, 1993.

Dictionary of American Naval Fighting Ships. 8 vols. Washington, DC: GPO, 1916–1981.

Dillahunty, Albert. *Shiloh National Military Park, Tennessee*. National Park Service Historical Handbook Series, no. 10. Washington, DC: GPO, 1951.

Dodge, Grenville M. *The Battle of Atlanta and Other Campaigns, Addresses, Etc*. Council Bluffs, IA: The Monarch Printing Company, 1911; reprint, Denver, CO: Sage Books, 1965.

Dodson, W.C. *Campaigns of Wheeler and His Cavalry*. Atlanta: Hudgins, 1897.

Donald, David Herbert. *Lincoln*. New York: Simon and Schuster, 1995.

Douglas, Byrd. *Steamboatin' on the Cumberland*. Nashville: The Tennessee Book Company, 1961.

Driggs, George W. *Opening the Mississippi, or Two Years Campaigning in the Southwest*. Madison, WI: William J. Park Co., 1864.

Duaine, Carl L. *The Dead Men Wore Boots: An Account of the 32nd Texas Volunteer Cavalry, CSA, 1862–1865*. Austin, TX: San Felipe Press, 1966.

Du Bose, John W. *General Joseph Wheeler and the Army of Tennessee*. New York: Neale Publishing Co., 1912.

Duffy, James P. *Lincoln's Admiral: The Civil War Campaigns of David Farragut*. New York: Wiley, 1997.

Dugan, James. *History of Hurlbut's Fighting Fourth Division*. Cincinnati: Morgan & Co., 1863.

Dunnavent, R. Blake. *Brown Water Warfare: The U.S. Navy in Riverine Warfare and the Emergence of a Tactical Doctrine, 1775–1970*. New Perspectives on Maritime History and Nautical Archaeology. Gainesville: University of Florida Press, 2003.

Durham, Walter T. *Nashville: The Occupied City — the First Seventeen Months — February 16, 1862–June 30, 1863*. Nashville: The Tennessee Historical Society, 1985.

_____. *Reluctant Partners: Nashville and the Union — July 1, 1863 to June 30, 1865*. Nashville: The Tennessee Historical Society, 1987.

Dyer, Frederick H. *A Compendium of the War of the Rebellion*. 3 vols. Des Moines: Dyer Publishing Co., 1908; reprint, New York: Thomas Yoseloff, 1959.

Dyer, Joseph P. *"Fightin' Joe" Wheeler*. Southern Biography Series. Baton Rouge: Louisiana State University Press, 1941.

_____. *From Shiloh to San Juan: The Life of "Fighting Joe" Wheeler*. Baton Rouge: Louisiana State University Press, 1961.

Eddy, T.M. *The Patriotism of Illinois: A Record of the Civil and Military History of the State in the War for the Union*. 2 vols. Chicago: Clarke & Co., Publishers, 1865.

Edwards, John N. *Shelby and His Men, or The War in the West*. Cincinnati: Miami Printing and Publishing Co., 1867; reprinted, Waverly, MO: General J.O. Shelby Memorial, 1993.

Ellicott, John M. *The Life of John Ancrum Winslow, Rear-Admiral, United States Navy, Who Commanded the U.S. Steamer "Kearsarge" in Her Action with the Confederate Cruiser "Alabama."* New York: G. P Putnam's Sons, 1905.

Engle, Stephen D. *Don Carlos Buell: Most Promising of All*. Chapel Hill: University of North Carolina Press, 1999.

_____. *Struggle for the Heartland: The Campaigns from Fort Henry to Corinth*. Lincoln: University of Nebraska Press, 2001.

Evans, Robley D. *A Sailor's Log: Recollections of a Naval Life*. New York: D. Appleton, 1901.

Faulk, Odie. *General Tom Green, Fightin' Texan*. Waco, TX: Texian Press, 1963.

Faust, Patricia L. *Historical Times Illustrated Encyclopedia of the Civil War*. New York: Harper Collins Publishers, 1986.

Feis, William B. *Grant's Secret Service: The Intelligence War from Belmont to Appomattox*. Lincoln: University of Nebraska Press, 2002.

Ferguson, John L., ed. *Arkansas and the Civil War*. Little Rock: Arkansas Historical Commission, 1962.

Fisher, John E. *They Rode with Forrest and Wheeler: A Chronicle of Five Tennessee Brothers' Service in the Confederate Western Cavalry*. Jefferson, NC: McFarland & Co., Inc., 1995.

Fisk, Harold. *Geological Investigations of the Alluvial Valley of the Lower Mississippi River*. Washington, DC: U.S. Army Corps of Engineers, 1944.

Folmsbee, Stanley J., Robert E. Corlew, and Enoch L. Mitchell, *Tennessee: A Short History*. Knoxville: University of Tennessee Press, 1969.

Foote, Shelby. *The Civil War: A Narrative*. 3 vols. New York: Random House, 1958–1974; reprint, New York: Vintage Books, 1986.

Force, Manning F. *From Fort Henry to Corinth*. Campaigns of the Civil War, No. 2. New York: Scribner's, 1882; reprint, T.Y. Yoseloff, 1963.

Forsyth, Michael J. *The Red River Campaign of 1864 and the Loss by the Confederacy of the Civil War*. Jefferson, NC: McFarland & Co., Inc., 2001.

Fort Henry & Fort Donelson Campaigns, February, 1862: Source Book. Fort Levenworth, KS: The General Service Schools Press, 1923.

Fowler, William H. *Under Two Flags: The American Navy in the Civil War*. New York: W.W. Norton, 1990.

Fox, Gustavus Vasa. *Confidential Correspondence of Gustavus Vasa Fox, Assistant Secretary of the Navy, 1861–1865*. Edited by Robert Means Thompson and Richard Wainwright. 2 vols. New York: De Vinne Press, 1918–1919.

Frankignoul, Daniel. *Prince Camille de Polignac, Major General, C.S.A., "The Lafayette of the South."* Brussels, Belgium: Confederate Historical Association of Belgium, 1999.

Franklin, Samuel R. *Memories of a Rear Admiral Who Has Served for More Than Half a Century in the Navy of the United States*. New York: Harper and Brothers, 1898.

Freemon, Frank R. *Gangrene and Glory: Medical Care During the American Civil War*. Urbana: University of Illinois Press, 2001.

Gabel, Christopher R., and the Staff Ride Team. *Staff Ride Handbook for the Vicksburg Campaign, December 1862–July 1863*. Fort Levenworth, KS: Combat Studies Institute, U.S. Army Command and General Staff College, 2001.

Gallaway, H.P. *Ragged Rebel: A Common Soldier in W.H. Parsons' Texas Cavalry, 1861–1865*. Austin: University of Texas Press, 1988.

Gates, Paul W. *The Illinois Central Railroad and Its Colonization Work*. Cambridge, MA: Harvard University Press, 1934.

Geer, Allen Morgan. *The Civil War Diary of Allen Morgan Geer, 20th Regiment, Illinois Volunteers*. Edited by Mary Ann Anderson. Denver, CO: Robert C. Appleman, 1977.

Gerteis, Louis S. *Civil War St. Louis*. Lawrence: University Press of Kansas, 2001.

Gibbons, Tony. *Warships and Naval Battles of the Civil War*. New York: Gallery Books, 1989.

Gibson, Charles Dana, with E. Kay Gibson. *Assault and Logistics*. Vol. 1, *Dictionary of Transports and Combat Vessels Steam and Sail Employed by the Union Army, 1861–1868*. Camden, ME: Ensign Press, 1995.

_____. *Assault and Logistics*. Vol. 2, *Union Army Coastal and River Operations, 1861–1866*. Camden, ME: Ensign Press, 1995.

Gildrie, Richard, Philip Kemmerly, and Thomas H. Winn. *Clarksville, Tennessee, in the Civil War, a Chronology*. Clarksville, TN: Montgomery County Historical Society, 1984.

Glazier, Willard. *Battles for the Union*. Hartford, CT: Dustin, Gilman & Co., 1875.

Goodspeed's General History of Tennessee. Chicago: Goodspeed Publishers, 1887; reprint, Nashville, C. and R. Elder, 1973.

Gosnell, H. Allen. *Guns on the Western Waters: The Story of the River Gunboats in the Civil War*. Baton Rouge: Louisiana State University Press, 1949; reprint, Louisiana State University Press, 1993.

Gott, Kendall D. *Where the South Lost the War: An Analysis of the Fort Henry-Fort Donelson Campaign, February 1862*. Mechanicsburg, PA: Stackpole Books, 2003.

Grant, Ulysses S. *The Papers of Ulysses S. Grant*. Edited by John Y. Simon. 24 vols. Edwardsville, Southern Illinois University Press, 1967.

_____. *Personal Memoirs of U.S. Grant*. 2 vols. New York: C.L. Webster & Co., 1885–1886; reprint (2 vols. in 1): New York: Penguin Books, 1999.

_____. *Personal Memoirs of U.S. Grant*. A Modern Abridgment. New York: Premier Books, 1962.

Greeley, Horace. *The American Conflict: A History of the Great Rebellion in the United States of America, 1860–1865*. 2 vols. Hartford, CT: O.D. Case & Company, 1879.

Green, Francis Vinton. *The Mississippi*. Campaigns of the Civil War, vol. 8. New York: Charles Scribner's Sons, 1885; reprint, The Blue & The Gray Press, n.d.

Griess, Thomas E., ed. *Atlas for the American Civil War*. The West Point Military History Series. Wayne, NJ: Avery Publishing Group, 1986.

Grimsley, Mark. *The Hard Hand of War: Union Military Policy Toward Southern Civilians*. New York: Cambridge University Press, 1995.

Grisamore, Silas T. *The Civil War Reminiscences of Major Silas T. Grisamore, C.S.A*. Edited by Arthur W. Bergeron, Jr. Baton Rouge: Louisiana State University Press, 1993.

Gudmens, Jeffrey J. *Staff Ride Handbook for the Battle of Shiloh, 6–7 April 1862*. Fort Leavenworth, KS: Combat Studies Institute Press, 2004.

Guelzo, Allen C. *The Crisis of the American Republic: A History of the Civil War and Reconstruction*. New York: St. Martin's Press, 1995.

Hackemer, Kurt. *The U.S. Navy and the Origins of the Military-Industrial Complex, 1847–1883*. Annapolis MD: Naval Institute Press, 2001.

Haites, Erik F., James Mak, and Gary M. Walton, *Western River Transportation: The Era of Early Internal Developments, 1810–1860*. Baltimore, MD: The Johns Hopkins University Press, 1975.

Hallock, Judith Lee. *Braxton Bragg and Confederate Defeat*. Tuscaloosa: University of Alabama Press, 1991.

Hamersly, Lewis B. *The Records of Living Officers of the U.S. Navy and Marine Corps*. Philadelphia: J.B. Lippincott & Co., 1870.

Hamilton, James J. *The Battle of Fort Donelson*. South Brunswick, NJ: Joseloff, 1968.

Hancock, R.R. *Hancock's Diary; or, A History of the Second Tennessee Cavalry, with Sketches of the First and*

Seventh Battalions. Nashville: Brandon Printing Co., 1887.

Hannaford, Ebenezer. *The Story of a Regiment: A History of the Campaigns and Associations in the Field of the Sixth Regiment Ohio Volunteer Infa*ntry. Cincinnati: Priv. Print., 1868.

Harrington, Fred Harvey. *Fighting Politician: Major General N.P. Banks.* Westport, CT: Greenwood Press, 1948.

Harris, NiNi. *History of Carondelet.* St. Louis: Southern Commercial Bank, 1991.

Harrison, Lowell H. *The Civil War in Kentucky.* Lexington: University Press of Kentucky, 1975.

Hartigen, Richard S. *Lieber's Code and the Law of War.* South Holland, IL: Precedent Publishing, 1983.

Hartjie, Robert C. *Van Dorn: Life and Times of a Confederate General.* Nashville: Vanderbilt University Press, 1967.

Hearn, Chester G. *Admiral David Dixon Porter: The Civil War Years.* Annapolis, MD: Naval Institute Press, 1996.

_____. *The Capture of New Orleans, 1862.* Baton Rouge: Louisiana State University Press, 1995.

_____. *Ellet's Brigade: The Strangest Outfit of All.* Baton Rouge: Louisiana State University Press, 2000.

_____. *Rebels and Yankees: Naval Battles of the Civil War.* San Diego: Thunder Bay Press, 2000.

Hedley, F.Y. *Marching Through Georgia: Pen-Pictures of Every-Day Life in General Sherman's Army from the Beginning of the Atlanta Campaign Until the Closing of the War.* Chicago: Donohue, Henneberry & Co., 1890.

Henderson, Mary Bess McCain, Evelyn Janet McCain Young, and Anna Irene McCain Naheloffer. *"Dear Eliza": The Letters of Michel Andrew Thompson.* Ames, IA: Carter Press, 1976.

Henry, James P. *Resources of the State of Arkansas, with Description of Counties, Railroads, Mines, and the City of Little Rock.* Little Rock: Price & McClure, 1872.

Henry, Robert Selph. *"First with the Most" Forrest.* Indianapolis: Bobbs-Merrill, 1944.

Herr, Kincaid. *The Louisville and Nashville Railroad, 1850–1963.* Louisville, KY: Public Relations Department, L & N, 1964; reprint, University of Kentucky Press, 2000.

Hicken, Victor. *Illinois in the Civil War.* Urbana: University of Illinois Press, 1991.

Hill, Jim Dan. *Sea Dogs of the Sixties.* Minneapolis: University of Minnesota, 1935; reprint, New York: A.S. Barnes & Company, 1961.

History of Crawford County, Pennsylvania: Containing a History of the County, Its Townships, Towns, Villages, Schools, Churches, Industries, etc., Portraits of Early Settlers and Prominent Men, Biographies, History of Pennsylvania, Statistical and Miscellaneous Matter. Chicago: Warner, Beers & Co., 1885.

Holbrook, Stewart H. *The Story of American Railroads.* New York: Crown Publishers, 1947.

Hollandsworth, James G., Jr. *Pretense of Glory: The Life of General Nathaniel P. Banks.* Baton Rouge: Louisiana State University Press, 1998.

Hoobler, James A. *Cities Under the Gun: Images of Occupied Nashville and Chattanooga.* Nashville: Rutledge Hill Press, 1986.

Hood, John Bell. *Advance and Retreat: Personal Experiences in the United States and Confederate States Armies.* New Orleans: Pub. For the Hood Orphan Memorial Fund, 1880.

Hoppin, James M. *The Life of Andrew Hull Foote, Rear Admiral, United States Navy.* New York: Harper and Brothers, 1874.

Horn, Stanley F. *The Army of Tennessee.* Indianapolis: Bobbs-Merrill, 1941.

_____, comp. *Tennessee's War, 1861–1865: Described by Participants.* Nashville: Tennessee Civil War Centennial Commission, 1965.

Hosmer, James K. *A Short History of the Mississippi Valley.* New York: Houghton, Mifflin and Co., 1902.

Howard, Robert P. *Illinois: A History of the Prairie State.* Grand Rapids, MI: William B. Eerdmans Publishing Co., 1973.

Hubbard, John Milton. *Notes of a Private.* Memphis, TN: E.H. Clarke and Brother, 1909.

Hubbart, Henry Clyde. *The Older Middle West, 1840–1880: Its Social, Economic and Political Life and Sectional Tendencies Before, During and After the Civil War.* New York: Russell & Russell, 1963.

Hubbell, John T., and James W. Geary, eds. *Biographical Dictionary of the Union: Northern Leaders of the Civil War.* Westport, CT: Greenwood Press, 1995.

Hubert, Charles F. *History of the 50th Regiment, Illinois Volunteer Infantry in the War of the Union.* Kansas City, MO: Western Veteran Publishing Co., 1894.

Huddleston, Duane, Sammie Rose, and Pat Wood. *Steamboats and Ferries on White River: A Heritage Revisited.* Conway: University of Central Arkansas Press, 1995; reprinted, Fayetteville: University of Arkansas Press, 1998.

Hughes, Nathaniel Cheairs, Jr. *The Battle of Belmont: Grant Strikes South.* Chapel Hill: University of North Carolina Press, 1991.

Hughes, Nathaniel Cheairs, Jr., and Roy P. Stonesifer, Jr. *The Life and Wars of Gideon J. Pillow.* Chapel Hill: University of North Carolina Press, 1993.

Huling, Edmund J. *Reminiscences of Gunboat Life in the Mississippi Squadron.* Saratoga Springs, NY: Sentinel Print, 1881.

Hunter, Louis C. *Steamboats on the Western Waters: An Economic and Technological History.* Cambridge, MA: Harvard University Press, 1949; reprint, New York: Dover Publications, 1993.

Huston, James A. *The Sinews of War: Army Logistics, 1775–1953.* Army Historical Series. Washington, DC: Office of the Chief of Military History, United States Army, 1966.

James, Uriah Pierson. *James' River Guide.* Cincinnati: U.P. James, 1866.

Jessee, James W. *Civil War Diaries of James W. Jessee, 1861–1865, Company K, 8th Regiment of Illinois Volunteer Infantry.* Edited by William P. LaBounty. Normal, IL: McLean County Genealogical Society, 1997.

Johnson, Adam R. *"Stovepipe." The Partisan Rangers of the Confederate Army.* Edited by William J. Davis. Louisville, KY: George G Fetter, 1904; reprint, Austin, TX: State House Press, 1995.

Johnson, E. McCleod. *A History of Henry County, Tennessee.* Paris, TN: Priv. Print., 1958.

Johnson, Ludwell H. *Red River Campaign: Politics and Cotton in the Civil War.* Baltimore: Johns Hopkins Press, 1958.

Johnson, Robert E. *Rear Admiral John Rodgers, 1812–1882.* Annapolis, MD: Naval Institute Press, 1967.

_____. *Thence Round Cape Horn: The Story of United States Naval Forces on Pacific Station, 1812–1923.* Annapolis, MD: Naval Institute Press, 1963.

Johnson, Timothy D. *Winfield Scott: The Quest for Military Glory.* Lawrence: University Press of Kansas, 1998.

Johnston, William Preston. *The Life of Gen. Albert Sidney Johnston.* New York: D. Appleton and Company, 1878.

Joiner, Gary. *Mr. Lincoln's Brown Water Navy: The Mississippi Squadron.* Lanham, MD: Rowman & Littlefield, 2007.

_____. *Through the Howling Wilderness: The 1864 Red River Campaign and Union Failure in the West.* Knoxville: University of Tennessee Press, 2006.

Joiner, Gary, ed. *Little to Eat and Thin Mud to Drink: Letters, Diaries, and Memoirs from the Red River Campaigns, 1863–1864.* Knoxville: University of Tennessee Press, 2007.

Jones, Archer. *Confederate Strategy: From Shiloh to Vicksburg.* Baton Rouge: Louisiana State University Press, 1961.

Jones, James P., and Edward F. Keuchel, eds. *Civil War Marine: A Diary of the Red River Expedition, 1864.* Washington, DC: Naval History Division, Navy Department, 1975.

Jones, Virgil C. *Gray Ghosts and Rebel Raiders.* New York: Holt, 1956.

Jordan, Thomas, and J.P. Pryor. *The Campaigns of Lieut. Gen. N.B. Forrest and of Forrest's Cavalry.* New Orleans and New York: Blelock & Co., 1868; reprint, New York: DaCapo Press, 1996.

Joyner, Elizabeth Hoxie. *The U.S.S. "Cairo": History and Artifacts of a Civil War Gunboat.* Jefferson, NC: McFarland & Co., Inc., 2006.

Kane, Adam. *The Western River Steamboat.* College Station: Texas A & M University Press, 2004.

Kerby, Robert L. *Kirby Smith's Confederacy: The Trans-Mississippi South, 1863–1865.* Tuscaloosa: University of Alabama Press, 1972.

Killebrew, J.B. *Introduction to the Resources of Tennessee.* 2 vols. Nashville: Tavel, Eastman, and Howell, 1874.

King, Lester L. *Transformations in American Medicine from Benjamin Rush to William Osler.* Baltimore: Johns Hopkins University Press, 1991.

King, William H. *Lessons and Practical Notes on Steam.* Revised by James W. King. New York: D. Van Nostrand, 1864.

Kionka, T.K. *Key Command: Ulysses S. Grant's District of Cairo.* Shades of Blue and Gray Series. Columbia: University of Missouri Press, 2006.

Kitchens, Ben Earl. *Gunboats and Cavalry: A History of Eastport, Mississippi, with Special Emphasis on Events of the War Between the States.* Florence, AL: Thornwood Book Publishers, 1985.

Klein, Benjamin F. *The Ohio River Atlas: A Collection of the Best Known Maps of the Ohio River, from 1713 to 1854.* Cincinnati: Picture Marine, 1954.

Knapp, David. *The Confederate Horsemen.* New York: Vantage, 1966.

Koerner, Gustave. *Memoirs of Gustave Koerner, Written at the Suggestion of His Children.* Edited by Thomas J. McCormick. 2 vols.; Grand Rapids, IA: The Torch Press, 1909.

Konstam, Angus. *Confederate Ironclad, 1861–65.* Illustrated by Tony Bryan. New Vanguard 41. Oxford, UK: Osprey Publishing, 2001.

_____. *Mississippi River Gunboats of the American Civil War, 1861–65.* Illustrated by Tony Bryan. New Vanguard 49. Oxford, UK: Osprey Publishing, 2002.

_____. *Union River Ironclad, 1861–65.* Illustrated by Tony Bryan. New Vanguard 56. Oxford, UK: Osprey Publishing, 2002.

Lamers, William M. *The Edge of Glory: A Biography of General William S. Rosecrans, USA.* New York: Harcourt, Brace, 1961.

Lane, Carl D, *American Paddle Steamboats.* New York: Coward-McCann, 1943.

Lansden, John M. *History of the City of Cairo, Illinois.* Chicago: R.R. Donnelley, 1910.

Lemcke, Julius A. *Reminiscences of an Indianian: From the Sassafras Log Behind the Barn in Posey County to Broader Fields.* Indianapolis: Hollenbeck Press, 1905.

Lewis, Berkeley R. *Notes on Ammunition of the American Civil War, 1861–1865.* Washington, DC: American Ordnance Association, 1959.

Lewis, Charles Lee. *David Glasgow Farragut.* Annapolis, MD: Naval Institute Press, 1943.

Lewis, Lloyd. *Sherman: Fighting Prophet.* New York: Harcourt, Brace and World, 1960.

Lieber, Francis. *Guerrilla Parties Considered with Reference to the Laws and Usages of War.* New York: D. Van Nostrand, 1862.

Logan, Mrs. John A. *Reminiscences of a Soldier's Wife.* New York: Scribner's Sons, 1913.

Longacre, Edward G. *Mounted Raids of the Civil War.* New York: A.S. Barnes & Co., 1975.

Lonn, Ella. *Foreigners in the Union Army and Navy.* Baton Rouge: Louisiana State University Press, 1951.

Lossing Benson J. *Pictorial Field Book of the Civil War: Journeys Through the Battlefields in the Wake of Conflict.* 3 vols. Hartford, CT: T. Belknap, 1874; reprint, Johns Hopkins University Press, 1997.

Lowe, Richard. *Walker's Texas Division, C.S.A.: Greyhounds of the Trans-Mississippi.* Baton Rouge: Louisiana State University Press, 2004.

Luraghi, Raimondo. *A History of the Confederate Navy.* Translated by Paolo E. Coletta. Annapolis MD: Naval Institute Press, 1996.

Lytle, William C., comp. *Merchant Steam Vessels of the United States, 1807–1868, "The Lytle List."* Publication No. 6. Mystic, CT: The Steamship Historical Society of America, 1952.

Macartney, Clarence Edward. *Mr. Lincoln's Admirals.* New York: Funk and Wagnalls, 1956.

Mackey, Robert M. *The Uncivil War: Irregular Warfare in the Upper South, 1861–1865.* Norman: University of Oklahoma Press, 2004.

Mahan, Alfred T. *The Navy in the Civil War.* Vol. 3, *The Gulf and Inland Waters.* New York: Scribner's, 1883.

Marshall, Edward Chauncey. *History of the Naval Academy.* New York: D. Van Nostrand, 1862.

Marshall-Cornwall, James. *Grant as Military Commander.* New York: Van Nostrand Reinhold, 1970.

Marszalek, John F. *Commander of All Lincoln's Armies: A Life of General Henry W. Halleck.* Cambridge, MA: Belknap Press, 2004.

_____. *Sherman: A Soldier's Passion for Order.* New York: Free Press, 1993.

Martin, David G. *The Shiloh Campaign: March-April, 1862.* Bryn Mawr, PA: Wieser & Wieser, Inc., 1987.

Marvel, William. *Burnside.* Chapel Hill: University of North Carolina Press, 1991.

Maslowski, Peter. *"Treason Must Be Made Odious": Military Occupation and Wartime Reconstruction in Nashville, Tennessee, 1862–1865.* New York: K.T.O. Press, 1978.

Mason, F. Van Wyck. *Blue Hurricane.* Philadelphia: J.B. Lippincott Co., 1954.

Mayeux, Steven M. *Earthen Walls, Iron Men: Fort DeRussy, Louisiana, and the Defense of Red River.* Knoxville: University of Tennessee Press, 2006.

McClellan, George B. *The Civil War Papers of George B. McClellan: Selected Correspondence, 1860–1865.* Edited by Stephen W. Sears. New York: Ticknor and Fields, 1989.

McCutchan, Kenneth P., ed. *"Dearest Lizzie": The Civil War as Seen Through the Eyes of Lieutenant Colonel James Maynard Shanklin, of Southwest Indiana's Own 42nd Regiment, Indiana Volunteer Infantry, and Re-*

counted in *Letters to His Wife*. Evansville, IN: Friends of Willard Library Press, 1988.

McDonough, James L. *Shiloh: In Hell Before Night*. Knoxville: University of Tennessee Press, 1977.

——. *Stones River: Bloody Winter in Tennessee*. Knoxville: University of Tennessee Press, 1980.

McDowell, Robert Emmett. *City of Conflict: Louisville in the Civil War, 1861–1865*. Louisville, KY: Civil War Roundtable, 1962.

McFeely, William S. *Grant: A Biography*. New York: W.W. Norton, 1981.

McMurray, William J. *History of the Twentieth Tennessee Regiment Volunteer Infantry, C.S.A.* Nashville: The Publication Committee, 1904.

McPherson, James M. *Battle Cry of Freedom: The Civil War Era*. New York: Oxford University Press, 1988.

——. *The Negro's Civil War*. New York: Ballantine Books, 1991.

McWhitney, Grady. *Braxton Bragg and Confederate Defeat*. New York: Columbia University Press, 1969.

Melton, Maurice. *The Confederate Ironclads*. New York: Thomas Yoseloff, 1968.

Merrill, James M. *Battle Flags South: The Story of the Civil War Navies on Western Waters*. Rutherford, NJ: Fairleigh Dickinson University Press, 1970.

——. *The Rebel Shore: The Story of Union Sea Power in the Civil War*. Boston: Little, Brown, 1957.

Miller, David W. *Second Only to Grant: Quartermaster General Montgomery C. Meigs*. Shippensburg, PA: White Mane Books, 2000.

Miller, Francis Trevelyan, ed. *The Photographic History of the Civil War*. Vol. 4, *The Navies*. New York: Castle Books, 1911; reprint, New York: Thomas Yoseloff, 1957.

Milligan, John D. *Gunboats Down the Mississippi*. Annapolis, MD: Naval Institute Press, 1965.

Mitchell, Joseph B., ed. *The Badge of Gallantry: Recollections of Civil War Congressional Medal of Honor Winners*. New York: Macmillan, 1968.

Monaghan, James. *Civil War on the Western Border, 1854–1865*. Boston: Little, Brown & Co., 1955.

Monaghan, Jay. *Swamp Fox of the Confederacy: The Life and Military Services of M. Jeff Thompson*. Tuscaloosa, AL: Confederate Publishing, 1956.

Montgomery, Frank A. *Reminiscences of a Mississippian in Peace and War*. Cincinnati: Robert Clarke Company Press, 1901.

Moore, Frank, ed. *The Rebellion Record: A Diary of American Events*. 12 vols. New York: G.P. Putnam, 1861–1863; D. Van Nostrand, 1864–1868; reprint, Arno, 1977.

Morgan, James Morris. *Recollections of a Rebel Reefer*. Boston: Houghton, Mifflin, 1917.

Morison, Samuel Eliot. *The Oxford History of the American People*. New York: Oxford University Press, 1965.

Morris, Richard B. *The Encyclopedia of American History*. Rev. ed. New York: Harper & Bros., 1961.

Morton, John Watson. *The Artillery of Nathan Bedford Forrest's Cavalry*. Paris, TN: The Guild Bindery Press, 1988.

Mulesky, Raymond. *Thunder from a Clear Sky: Stovepipe Johnson's Confederate Raid on Newburgh, Indiana*. New York: iUniverse, Inc., 2005.

Musgrove, George D. *Kentucky Cavaliers in Dixie: Reminiscences of a Confederate Cavalryman*. Edited by Bell I Wiley. Jackson, TN: McCowat-Mercer Press, 1957; reprint, Lincoln: University of Nebraska Press, 1999.

Musicant, Ivan. *Divided Waters: The Naval History of the Civil War*. New York: HarperCollins, 1995.

Musser, Charles O. *Soldier Boy: The Civil War Letters of Charles O. Musser, 29th Iowa*. Edited by Larry Popchock. Iowa City: Iowa State University Press, 1995.

The Navigator, Containing Directions for Navigating the Monongahela, Allegheny, Ohio and Mississippi Rivers. 8th ed. Pittsburgh, PA: Cramer, Speark and Eichbau, 1814; reprint, University of Michigan Press, 1966.

Neal, Diane, and Thomas W. Kremm, *Lion of the South: General Thomas C. Hindman*. Macon, GA: Mercer University Press, 1993.

Neuman, Frederick G. *The Story of Paducah, Kentucky*. Paducah: Young Printing, 1927.

Nevin, David. *The Road to Shiloh: Early Battles in the West*. Alexandria, VA: Time-Life Books, 1983.

Nevins, Allan. *Frémont: Pathmarker of the West*. New York: D. Appleton-Century Company, 1939.

——. *The War for the Union: The Improvised War*. New York: Charles Scribner's Sons, 1959.

Nichols, James L. *Confederate Engineers*. Tuscaloosa, AL: Confederate Publishing Company, 1957.

Nicolay, John G. *The Outbreak of Rebellion*. Campaigns of the Civil War, no. 1. New York: Scribner's, 1881; reprint Castle Books, 2002.

Niven, John. *Gideon Welles: Lincoln's Secretary of the Navy*. New York: Oxford University Press, 1973.

Noe, Kenneth W., ed. *A Southern Boy in Blue: The Memoir of Marcus Woodcock, 9th Kentucky Infantry* (U.S.A.). Knoxville: University of Tennessee Press, 1996.

Northup, James E., and Samuel W. *"Drifting to an Unknown Future": The Civil War Letters of James E. Northup and Samuel W. Northup*. Edited by Robert C. Steensma. Sioux Falls, SD: Center for Western Studies, 2000.

Nott, Charles C. *Sketches of the War: A Series of Letters to the North Moore Street School of New York*. New York: C.T. Evans, 1863.

Oates, Stephen B. *Confederate Cavalry West of the River*. Austin: University of Texas Press, 1961.

O'Flaherty, Daniel. *General Jo Shelby: Undefeated Rebel*. Chapel Hill: University of North Carolina Press, 1954.

Olmstead, Edwin, Wayne E. Stark, and Spencer E. Tucker. *The Big Guns: Civil War Siege, Seacoast and Naval Cannon*. Ontario, Bloomfield, New York: Alexandria Bay Museum Restoration Service, 1997.

Page, Dave. *Ships versus Shore*. Nashville: Rutledge Hill Press, 1994.

Palmer, Patricia J. *Frederick Steele: Forgotten General*. Stanford, CA: Stanford University Press, 1971.

Paludan, Philip Shaw. *A People's Contest: The Union and Civil War, 1861–1865*. New York: Harper & Row, 1988.

——. *Victims: A True Story of the Civil War*. Knoxville: University of Tennessee Press, 1981.

Parker, Foxhall A. *The Naval Howitzer Afloat*. New York: D. Van Nostrand, 1866.

——. *The Naval Howitzer Ashore*. New York: D. Van Nostrand, 1865.

Parks, Joseph H. *General Edmund Kirby Smith, C.S.A.* Baton Rouge: Louisiana State University Press, 1954.

——. *General Leonidas Polk, C.S.A.: The Fighting Bishop*. Baton Rouge: Louisiana State University Press, 1962.

Parrish, T. Michael. *Richard Taylor: Soldier Prince of Dixie*. Chapel Hill: University of North Carolina Press, 1992.

Parrish, Tom Z. *The Saga of the Confederate Ram "Arkansas."* The Mississippi Valley Campaign, 1862. Hillsboro TX: Hill College Press, 1987.

Paullin, Charles Oscar. *Paullin's History of Naval Administration, 1775–1911*. Annapolis, MD: Naval Institute Press, 1968.

Pellet, Elias P. *History of the 114th Regiment, New York State Volunteers*. Norwich, NY: Telegraph & Chronicle Power Press Print, 1866.

Perrin, William Henry, ed. *History of Alexander, Union and Pulaski Counties, Illinois.* Chicago: O.L. Baskin & Co., 1883.

Perry, James M. *A Bohemian Brigade: The Civil War Correspondents, Mostly Rough, Sometimes Ready.* New York: John Wiley, 2000.

Perry, Milton F. *Infernal Machines: The Story of Confederate Submarine and Mine Warfare.* Baton Rouge: Louisiana State University Press, 1965.

Peterson, Harold L. *Notes on Ordnance of the American Civil War, 1861–1865.* Washington, DC: American Ordnance Association, 1959.

Petrie, Donald A. *The Prize Game: Lawful Looting on the High Seas in the Days of Fighting Sail.* Annapolis, MD: Naval Institute Press, 1999.

Philadelphia Maritime Museum, Library. *John Lenthall, Naval Architect: A Guide to Plans and Drawings of American Naval and Merchant Vessels, 1790–1874, With a Bibliography of Works on Shipbuilding Collected by John Lenthall (b. 1807–d.1882).* Philadelphia: Philadelphia Maritime Museum, 1991.

Piston, William Garret, and Richard W. Hatcher III. *Wilson's Creek: The Second Battle of the Civil War and the Men Who Fought It.* Chapel Hill: University of North Carolina Press, 2000.

Plum, William R. *The Military Telegraph During the Civil War in the United States.* 2 vols. Chicago: Jansen, McClurg, 1882.

Plummer, Mark A. *Lincoln's Rail-Splitter: Governor Richard J. Oglesby.* Champaign: University of Illinois Press, 2001.

Polk, William M. *Leonidas Polk, Bishop and General.* 2 vols. New York: Longmans, Green & Co., 1915.

Pollard, E.B. *The Lost Cause: A New Southern History of the War of the Confederates.* New York: E.B. Treat & Co., 1867.

Porter, David D. *Incidents and Anecdotes of the Civil War.* New York: D. Appleton and Co, 1885; reprint, Harrisburg, PA: The Archive Society, 1997.

———. *Naval History of the Civil War.* New York: Sherman Publishing Company, 1886; reprint, Secaucus, NJ: Castle Books, 1984.

Powers, Ron. *Mark Twain, a Life.* New York: Free Press, 2005.

Pratt, Fletcher. *The Civil War on Western Waters.* New York: Holt, 1958.

———. *The Navy, a History: The Story of a Service in Action.* Garden City, NY: Garden City Publishing Co., 1941.

Prokopowicz, Gerald K. *All for the Regiment: The Army of the Ohio, 1861–1862.* Chapel Hill: University of North Carolina Press, 2001.

Prushankin, Jeffrey S. *A Crisis in Confederate Command: Edmund Kirby Smith, Richard Taylor, and the Army of the Trans-Mississippi.* Baton Rouge: Louisiana State University Press, 2005.

Puleston, William D. *Annapolis: Gangway to the Quarterdeck.* New York: D. Appleton-Century Co., 1942.

Putnam, A.W. *History of Middle Tennessee.* Knoxville: University of Tennessee Press, 1971.

Rafuse, Ethan S. *McClellan's War: The Failure of Moderation in the Struggle for the Union.* Bloomington: Indiana University Press, 2005.

Ramage, James A. *Rebel Raider: The Life of General John Hunt Morgan.* Lexington: University Press of Kentucky, 1986.

Ramold, Steven J. *Slaves, Sailors, Citizens: African Americans in the Union Navy.* DeKalb: Northern Illinois University Press, 2002.

Reed, Rowena. *Combined Operations in the Civil War.* Annapolis, MD: Naval Institute Press, 1978.

Regimental Association. *History of the 46th Regiment, Indiana Volunteer Infantry, September 1861–September 1865.* Logansport, IN: Press of Wilson, Humphries & Co., 1888.

Reid, Whitelaw. *Ohio in the War: Her Statesmen, Her Generals, and Soldiers.* 2 vols. Cincinnati: Moore, Wilstach & Baldwin, 1868.

Rerick, John H. *The 44th Indiana Volunteer Infantry: History of Its Services in the War of the Rebellion.* Lagrange, IN: Priv. Print., 1880.

Rice, Ralsa C. *Yankee Tigers: Through the Civil War with the One Hundred and Twenty-Fifth Ohio.* Edited by Richard A. Baumgartner and Larry M. Strayer. Huntington, WV: Blue Acorn Press, 1992.

Richardson, Albert D. *A Personal History of Ulysses S. Grant.* Hartford, CT: Winter and Hatch, 1885.

———. *The Secret Service: The Field, the Dungeon and the Escape.* Hartford, CT: American Publishing Company, 1866.

Ringle, Dennis J. *Life in Mr. Lincoln's Navy.* Annapolis, MD: Naval Institute Press, 1998.

Ritner, Jacob and Emeline. *Love and Valor: The Intimate Civil War Letters Between Captain Jacob and Emeline Ritner.* Edited by Charles F. Larimer. Western Springs, IL: Sigourney Press, 2000.

Roberts, William H. *Civil U.S. Navy and Industrial Mobilization.* Baltimore: Johns Hopkins University Press, 2002.

Roe, Francis Asbury. *Naval Duties and Discipline, with the Policy and Principles of Naval Organization.* New York: D. Van Nostrand, 1865.

Roland, Charles P. *Albert Sidney Johnston: Soldier of Three Republics.* Austin: University of Texas Press, 1964.

Roman, Alfred. *Military Operations of General Beauregard.* 2 vols. New York: Harper and Brothers, 1884.

Rombauer, Robert J. *The Union Cause in St. Louis in 1862.* St. Louis: Press of Nixon-Jones Printing Co., 1909.

Russell, William H. *My Diary North and South.* Boston: T.O.H.P. Burnham, 1863.

Safford, James M. *Geology of Tennessee.* Nashville: S.C. Mercer, 1869.

Sayers, Brian. *On Valor's Side: Tom Green and the Battles for Early Texas.* Hemphill, TX: Dogwood Press, 1999.

Scharf, J. Thomas. *History of the Confederate Navy from Its Organization to the Surrender of Its Last Vessel.* New York: Rodgers and Sherwood, 1887; reprint, New York: Fairfax Press, 1977.

Schlay, Cora R. *Alexandria in the Civil War. Four Louisiana Civil War Stories.* Baton Rouge: Louisiana Civil War Centennial Commission, 1961.

Sears, Stephen W. *George B. McClellan: The Young Napoleon.* New York: Ticknor and Fields, 1988.

Seitz, Don C. *Braxton Bragg: General of the Confederacy.* Columbia, SC: The State Co., 1924.

Selfridge, Thomas O., Jr. *Memoirs of Thomas O. Selfridge, Jr., Rear Admiral, U.S.N.* New York: Knickerbocker Press, 1924; reprint, Columbia: University of South Carolina Press, 1987.

Shalhope, Robert E. *Sterling Price: Portrait of a Southerner.* Columbia: University of Missouri Press, 1971.

Sherman, William Tecumseh. *Memoirs.* 2 vols. New York: Appleton, 1875; reprint, New York: Penguin Books, 2000.

———. *Sherman's Civil War: Selected Correspondence of William T. Sherman, 1860–1865.* Edited by Brooks D. Simpson and Jean V. Berlin. Chapel Hill: University of North Carolina Press, 1999.

Silverstone, Paul H. *The Sailing Navy, 1775–1854*. Annapolis, MD: Naval Institute Press, 2001.

———. *Warships of the Civil War Navies*. Annapolis, MD: Naval Institute Press, 1989.

Simpson, Brooks D. *Ulysses S. Grant: Triumph Over Adversity, 1822–1885*. New York: Houghton, Mifflin, 2000.

Simson, Jay W. *Naval Strategies of the Civil War: Confederate Innovations and Federal Opportunism*. Nashville: Cumberland House, 2001.

Slagle, Jay. *Ironclad Captain: Seth Ledyard Phelps and the U.S. Navy*. Kent, OH: Kent State University Press, 1996.

Smart, James G., ed. *A Radical View: The "Agate" Dispatches of Whitelaw Reid, 1861–1865*. 2 vols. Memphis, TN: Memphis State University Press, 1976.

Smith, Edward Conrad. *The Borderland in the Civil War*. New York: Macmillan, 1927.

Smith, Jean Edward. *Grant*. New York: Simon and Schuster, 2001.

Smith, Myron J., Jr. *Le Roy Fitch: The Civil War Career of a Union River Gunboat Commander*. Jefferson, NC: McFarland & Co., Inc., 2007.

———. *U.S.S. "Carondelet," 1861–1865*. Manhattan, KA: MA/AH Publishing, 1982.

———. *Volunteer State Battlewagon: U.S.S. "Tennessee" (BB-43)*. Missoula, MT: Pictorial Histories Publishing Company, 1992.

Smith, Timothy B. *The Great Battlefield of Shiloh: History, Memory and the Establishment of a Civil War National Military Park*. Knoxville: University of Tennessee Press, 2004.

Smith, Walter G., ed. *Life and Letters of Thomas Kilby Smith, Brevet Major General United States Volunteers*. New York: G.P. Putnam, 1898.

Smith, William E. *The Francis Preston Blair Family in Politics*. 2 vols. New York: Macmillan, 1933.

Speer, Lonnie R. *Portals to Hell: Military Prisons of the Civil War*. Mechanicsburg, PA: Stackpole Books, 1997.

Stamp, Kenneth M. *America in 1857*. New York: Oxford University Press, 1990.

———. *And the War Came: The North and the Secession Crisis, 1860–1861*. Baton Rouge, Louisiana State University Press, 1970.

Stanley, Henry M. *The Autobiography of Sir Henry Morton Stanley*. Edited by Dorothy Stanley. Boston: Houghton, Mifflin, 1909.

———. *Sir Henry Morton Stanley, Confederate*. Edited by Nathaniel C. Hughes, Jr. Baton Rouge: Louisiana State University Press, 2000.

Starr, Stephen. *The Union Cavalry in the Civil War*. Vol. 3, *The War in the West, 1861–1865*. Baton Rouge: Louisiana State University Press, 1985.

Stevenson, William G. *Thirteen Months in the Rebel Army, Being a Narrative of Personal Adventures*. New York: A.S. Barnes & Burr, 1862.

Still, William N., Jr. *Confederate Shipbuilding*. Athens: University of Georgia Press, 1969; reprint, Columbia: University of South Carolina Press, 1987.

———. *Iron Afloat, The Story of Confederate Armorclads*. Nashville: Vanderbilt University Press, 1971; reprint, Columbia: University of South Carolina Press, 1985.

Still, William N., ed. *The Confederate Navy: The Ships, Men, and Organization, 1861–1865*. Annapolis, MD: Naval Institute Press, 1997.

The Story of the 55th Regiment Illinois Volunteer Infantry in the Civil War. Clinton, MA: W.J. Coulter, 1887.

Stotherd, R.H. *Notes on Torpedoes, Offensive and Defensive*. Washington, DC: Government Printing Office, 1872.

Stover, John F. *History of the Baltimore and Ohio Railroad*. West Lafayette, IN: Purdue University Press, 1987.

Stutler, Boyd B. *West Virginia in the Civil War*. Charleston, WV: Education Foundation, Inc., 1963.

Surdam, David G. *Northern Naval Superiority and the Economics of the American Civil War*. Columbia: University of South Carolina, 2001.

Swedberg, Clair E., ed. *Three Years with the 92nd Illinois: The Civil War Diary of John M. King*. Mechanicsburg, PA: Stackpole Books, 1999.

Sweetman, Jack. *The U.S. Naval Academy: An Illustrated History*. Annapolis, MD: Naval Institute Press, 1979.

Sword, Wiley. *The Battle of Shiloh*. Philadelphia: Eastern Acorn Press, 1982.

———. *Shiloh: Bloody April*. New York: Morrow, 1974; reprint, Morningside Bookshop Press, 1983; rev. ed., Morningside Bookshop Press, 2001.

Taylor, Lenette S. *"The Supply for Tomorrow Must Not Fail": The Civil War of Captain Simon Perkins, Jr., a Union Quartermaster*. Kent, OH: Kent State University Press, 2004.

Taylor, Richard. *Destruction and Reconstruction: Personal Experiences of the Late War*. New York: D. Appleton and Company, 1879.

Thomas, David Y. *Arkansas in War and Reconstruction, 1861–1874*. Little Rock: Central Printing Co., 1926.

Thomas, Dean S. *Cannons: Introduction to Civil War Artillery*. Arendtsville, PA: Thomas Publications, 1985.

Thompson, M. Jeff. *The Civil War Reminiscences of General M. Jeff Thompson*. Edited by Donal J. Stanton, Goodwin F. Berquist, and Paul C. Bowers. Dayton, OH: Morningside Bookshop, 1988.

Thompson, M.S., ed. *General Orders and Circulars Issued by the Navy Department from 1863 to 1887*. Washington DC: Government Printing Office, 1887.

Todorich, Charles. *The Spirited Years: A History of the Antebellum Naval Academy*. Annapolis, MD: Naval Institute Press, 1984.

Troutman, Richard, ed., *The Heavens Are Weeping: The Diaries of George R. Browder, 1852–1886*. Grand Rapids, MI: Zondervan Publishing House, 1987.

Townsend, Edward. *Anecdotes of the Civil War in the United States*. New York: D. Appleton, 1884.

Trudeau, Noah Andre. *Like Men of War: Black Troops in the Civil War, 1862–1865*. Boston: Little, Brown, 1998.

Tucker, Louis L. *Cincinnati During the Civil War*. Publications of the Ohio Civil War Centennial Commission, no. 9. Columbus: The Ohio State University Press, 1962.

Tucker, Spencer C. *Andrew Foote: Civil War Admiral on Western Waters*. Annapolis, MD: Naval Institute Press, 2000.

———. *Arming the Fleet: U.S. Navy Ordnance in the Muzzle-Loading Era*. Annapolis, MD: Naval Institute Press, 1988.

———. *Blue & Gray Navies: The Civil War Afloat*. Annapolis, MD: U.S. Naval Institute, 2006.

———. *Unconditional Surrender: The Capture of Forts Henry and Donelson*. Abilene, TX: McWhiney Foundation Press, 2001.

Turner, George Edgar. *Victory Rode the Rails: The Strategic Place of Railroads in the Civil War*. Indianapolis: Bobbs-Merrill, 1953.

Twain, Mark. *Life on the Mississippi*. New York: Harper & Brothers, 1950.

U.S. Navy Department. *Laws of the United States Relating to the Navy*. Washington, DC: GPO, 1866.

———. Navy Department. *Regulations for the Government of the United States Navy*. Washington, DC: GPO, 1865.

———. Navy Department. Mississippi Squadron. *General*

Orders, Rear Adm. D.D. Porter, Commanding, from Oct. 16th 1862 to Oct. 26th 1864. St. Louis: R.P. Studley, 1864.

———. Navy Department. Mississippi Squadron. *General Orders, Rear Adm. S.P. Lee Commanding, from Nov. 1st 1864 to April 24th, 1865.* St. Louis: R.P. Studley, 1865.

———. Navy Department. Naval History Division. *Civil War Naval Chronology, 1861–1865.* 6 vols. in 1. Rev. ed. Washington, DC: GPO, 1966.

———. Navy Department. *Riverine Warfare: The United States Navy's Operations on Inland Waters.* Rev. ed. Washington, DC: GPO, 1968.

———. Office of the Secretary of the Navy. *Report of the Secretary of the Navy.* 6 vols. Washington, DC: GPO, 1861–1866.

———. Shiloh National Military Park Commission. *The Battle of Shiloh & the Organizations Involved, Compiled from the Official Records of Maj. D.W. Reed Under the Authority of the Commission, 1902 (Rev. 1909).* Washington, DC: GPO, 1913.

Van Doren Stern, Philip. *The Confederate Navy, a Pictorial History.* New York: Bonanza Books, 1961.

———, ed. *Soldier Life in the Union and Confederate Armies.* New York: Premier Books, 1961.

Van Horne, Thomas B. *History of the Army of the Cumberland.* 2 vols. Wilmington, NC: Broadfoot, 1988.

Villard, Henry. *Memoirs of Henry Villard, Journalist and Financier, 1835–1900.* 2 vols. Boston: Houghton, Mifflin, 1904.

Walke, Henry. *Naval Scenes and Reminiscences of the Civil War in the United States on the Southern and Western Waters During the Years 1861, 1862 and 1863 with the History of That Period Compared and Corrected from Authentic Sources.* New York: F.R. Reed and Company, 1877.

Walker, Jennie M. *Life of Capt Joseph Fry, the Cuban Martyr.* Hartford, CT: J.B. Burr Publishing Co., 1875.

Wallace, Edward. *Destiny and Glory.* New York: Coward-McCann, 1957.

Wallace, Lew. *An Autobiography.* 2 vols. New York: Harper & Brothers, 1906.

———. *Smoke, Sound & Fury: The Civil War Memoirs of Major General Lew Wallace, U.S. Volunteers.* Edited by Jim Leeke. Portland, OR: Strawberry Hill Press, 1998.

Wallace, W.H.L. *Life and Letters of W. H.L. Wallace* Edited by Isabel Wallace. Chicago: R.R. Donnelly, 1909.

Warner, Ezra. *Generals in Blue: Lives of Union Commanders.* Baton Rouge: Louisiana State University Press, 1964.

———. *Generals in Gray: Lives of Confederate Commanders.* Baton Rouge: Louisiana State University Press, 1959.

Wash, W.A. *Camp, Field and Prison Life, Containing Sketches of Service in the South.* St. Louis, MO: Southwestern Book and Pub. Co., 1870.

Waters, Charles M. *Historic Clarksville: The Bicentennial Story, 1784–1984.* Clarksville, TN: Historic Clarksville Publishing Co., 1983.

Way, Frederick, Jr. *Way's Packet Directory, 1848–1994: Passenger Steamboats of the Mississippi River System Since the Advent of Photography in Mid-Continent America.* Athens, OH: Ohio University Press, 1983; rev. ed., Athens: Ohio University, 1994.

Weber, Jennifer L. *Copperheads: The Rise and Fall of Lincoln's Opponents in the North.* New York: Oxford University Press, 2006.

Webster, William G. *The Army and Navy Pocket Dictionary.* Philadelphia: J.B. Lippincott & Company, 1865.

Webster's Geographical Dictionary. Rev. ed. Springfield, MA: G. & C. Merriam Co., Publishers, 1966.

Weigley, Russell F. *Quartermaster General of the Union Army: A Biography of M.C. Meigs.* New York: Columbia University Press, 1959.

Welcher, Frank J. *The Union Army, 1861–1865: Organization and Operations.* Vol. 3, *The Western Theater.* Bloomington: Indiana University Press, 1993.

Welles, Gideon. *The Diary of Gideon Welles, Secretary of the Navy Under Lincoln and Johnson.* Edited by John T. Morse, Jr. 3 vols. Boston: Houghton, Mifflin and Company, 1911; Reprint, New York: W.W. Norton, 1960.

Wells, Tom H. *The Confederate Navy: A Study in Organization.* Birmingham: The University of Alabama Press, 1971.

West, Richard S. *Gideon Welles, Lincoln's Navy Department.* Indianapolis: Bobbs-Merrill, 1943.

———. *Mr. Lincoln's Navy.* New York: Longman's, Green, 1957.

———. *The Second Admiral: A Life of David Dixon Porter, 1813–1891.* New York: Coward-McCann, 1937.

Wideman, John C. *The Sinking of the U.S.S. "Cairo."* Jackson: University Press of Mississippi, 1993.

Wiley, Bell I. *The Life of Billy Yank, the Common Soldier of the Union.* New York: Bobbs-Merrill, 1952. Reprint. Baton Rouge: Louisiana State University Press, 1991.

———. *The Life of Johnny Reb, the Common Soldier of the Confederacy.* New York: Bobbs-Merrill, 1943. Reprint. Baton Rouge: Louisiana State University Press, 1990.

Wiley, William. *The Civil War Diary of a Common Soldier.* Edited by Terrence J. Winschel. Baton Rouge: Louisiana University Press, 2001.

Wilkie, Franc B. *Pen and Powder.* Boston: Ticknor and Company, 1888.

Williams, T. Harry. *Lincoln and His Generals.* New York: Alfred Knopf, 1952. Reprint, New York: Vintage Books, 1962.

———. *P.G.T. Beauregard.* Baton Rouge: Louisiana State University Press, 1954.

Willison, Charles A. *Reminiscences of a Boy's Service with the 76th Ohio in the 15th Army Corps, Under General Sherman, During the Civil War, by That "Boy" at Three Score.* Menasha, WI: Press of The George Banta Publishing Co., 1908; reprint, Huntington, WV: Blue Acorn Press, 1995.

Wills, Charles Wright. *Army Life of an Illinois Soldier.* Compiled by Mary E. Kellogg. Washington, DC: Globe Printing Co., 1906.

Wilson, James Grant, and John Fiske, eds. *Appleton's Cyclopaedia of American Biography.* 5 vols. New York: D. Appleton & Co., 1888.

Wilson, James H. *The Life of John A. Rawlins.* New York: Neale, 1916.

Winters, John D. *The Civil War in Louisiana.* Baton Rouge: Louisiana State University Press, 1963.

Winters, William. *The Musick of the Mocking Birds, the Roar of the Cannon: The Diary and Letters of William Winters.* Edited by Steven E. Woodworth. Lincoln: University of Nebraska Press, 1998.

Witham, George F. *Shiloh, Shells, & Artillery Units.* Memphis, TN: Riverside Press, 1980.

Woodall, Eliza B. *The Stevenson Story.* Stevenson, AL: Stevenson Depot Museum, 1982.

Woodworth, Steven E. *Nothing but Victory: The Army of the Tennessee, 1861–1865.* New York: Alfred A. Knopf, 2005.

Woodworth, Steven E., ed. *Grant's Lieutenants: From Cairo to Vicksburg.* Lawrence: University Press of Kansas, 2001.

Worthington, Thomas. *Shiloh, or the TN Campaign of 1862, Written Especially for the Army of the TN in 1862.* Washington, DC: M'Gill & Witherow, 1872.

Wright, Charles. *A Corporal's Story: Experiences in the Ranks of Company C, 81st Ohio Vol. Infantry.* Edited by W. H. Chamberlain. Philadelphia: James Beal, Printer, 1887.

Wyeth, John Allan. *Life of General Nathan Bedford Forrest.* New York: Harper & Bros., 1904; Reprint, New York: Harper, 1959.

Zimmerman, Mark. *Battle of Nashville Preservation Society Guide to Civil War Nashville.* Nashville: Lithographics, Inc., 2004.

Articles and Essays in Books or Journals

Allardice, Bruce S. "Curious Clash at Blair's Landing." *America's Civil War* 9 (July 1997): 60–64.

Ambrose, Stephen E. "The Union Command System and the Donelson Campaign." *Military Affairs* 24 (Summer 1960): 78–86.

Anderson, Bern. "The Naval Strategy of the Civil War." *Military Affairs* 24 (Spring 1962): 11–21.

Aptheker, Herbert. "The Negro in the Union Navy." *Journal of Negro History* 32 (April 1947): 169–200.

Ash, Stephen V. "A Community at War: Montgomery County, 1861–65." *Tennessee Historical Quarterly* 34 (Spring 1977): 30–43.

_____. "Sharks in an Angry Sea: Civilian Resistance and Guerrilla Warfare in Occupied Middle Tennessee, 1862–1865." *Tennessee Historical Quarterly* 45 (Fall 1986): 217–320.

Atack, Jeremy, et al. "The Profitability of Steamboating on Western Rivers, 1850." *Business History Review* 49 (Autumn 1975): 346–354.

Bailey, Anne J. "Chasing Banks Out of Louisiana: Parson's Texas Cavalry in the Red River Campaign." *Civil War Regiments: A Journal of the American Civil War* 2 (1992): 212–233.

_____. "The Mississippi Marine Brigade: Fighting Rebel Guerrillas on Western Waters." *Military History of the Southwest* 22 (Spring 1992): 34–41.

Barnhart, Donald, Jr. "The Deadliest Shot." *Civil War Times Illustrated* 30 (March-April 2006): 31–36.

_____. "Junkyard Ironclad." *Civil War Times Illustrated* 40 (May 2001): 31–37, 67–68.

Barr, Alwyn. "The Battle of Blair's Landing." *Louisiana Studies* 2 (Winter 1963): 204–212.

_____. "Confederate Artillery in Arkansas." *Arkansas Historical Quarterly* 22 (Fall 1963): 238–272.

_____. "Confederate Artillery in Western Louisiana, 1864." *Louisiana History* 5 (Winter 1964): 53–73.

_____. "Polignac's Texas Brigade." *Texas Gulf Coast Historical Association Publications* 8 (November 1964): 1–72.

Bastian, David F. "Opening of the Mississippi During the Civil War." In U.S. Navy Academy, Department of History, ed. *New Aspects of Naval History: Selected Papers from the Fifth Naval History Symposium.* Baltimore, MD: Nautical & Aviation Pub. Co., 1985.

Battle, John Bell. "The Battle of Belmont: Pvt. John Bell Battle's Eyewitness Account." Edited by R.W. Rosser. *Confederate Chronicles of Tennessee* 2 (1987): 21–54.

Bearss, Edwin C. "The Battle of Helena, July 4, 1863." *Arkansas Historical Quarterly* 20 (Autumn 1961): 256–297.

_____. "The Battle of the Post of Arkansas." *Arkansas Historical Quarterly* 18 (Autumn 1959): 237–279.

_____. "Civil War Operations In and Around Pensacola." *Florida Historical Quarterly* 36 (October 1957): 125–165.

_____. "The Construction of Forts Henry and Donelson." *West Tennessee Historical Society Publications* 21 (1967): 24–47.

_____. "The Fall of Fort Henry, Tennessee." *West Tennessee Historical Society Publications* 17 (1963): 85–107.

_____. "A Federal Raid Up the Tennessee River." *The Alabama Review* 17 (October 1964): 261–270.

_____. "The Ironclads at Fort Donelson." *The Register of the Kentucky Historical Society* 74 (January, April, July 1976): 1–9, 73–84, 167–191.

_____. "Unconditional Surrender: The Fall of Fort Donelson." *Tennessee Historical Quarterly* 21 (June 1962): 47–62.

_____. "The Union Raid Down the Mississippi and Up the Yazoo—August 16–27, 1862." In Editors of *Military Affairs, Military Analysis of the Civil War: An Anthology.* Millwood, NY: KTO, 1977.

_____. "The White River Expedition, June 10–July 15, 1862." *Arkansas Historical Quarterly* 21 (Winter 1962): 305–207.

Bedford, H.L. "Fight Between the Batteries and Gunboats at Fort Donelson." *Southern Historical Society Papers* 13 (1885): 165–173.

Bergeron, Arthur W., Jr. "General Richard Taylor as a Military Commander." *Louisiana History,* 23 (Winter 1982): 35–47.

Bigelow, Martha M. "The Significance of Milliken's Bend in the Civil War." *Journal of Negro History* 45 (Fall 1960): 156–163.

Billias, George A. "Maine Lumbermen Rescue the Red River Fleet." *New England Social Studies Bulletin* 16 (January 1958): 5–8.

Blake, W.H. "Coal Barging in Wartime, 1861–1865." *Gulf States Historical Magazine* 1 (May 1903): 409–412.

Blume, Kenneth J. "'Concessions Where Concessions Could Be Made': The Naval Efficiency Boards of 1855–1857." In *New Interpretations in Naval History: Selected Papers form the 14th Naval History Symposium.* Edited by Randy Carol Balano and Craig L. Symonds. Annapolis, MD: Naval Institute Press, 2001.

Bogle, Robert V. "Defeat Through Default: Confederate Naval Strategy for the Upper Tennessee and Its Tributaries, 1861–1862." *Tennessee Historical Quarterly* 18 (Spring 1968): 62–71.

Branch, Mary Emerson. "The Story Behind the Story of the *Arkansas* and the *Carondelet.*" *Missouri Historical Review* 79 (1985): 313–331.

Brewer, Charles C. "African-American Sailors and the Unvexing of the Mississippi River." *Prologue* 30 (Winter 1996): 279–286.

Brown, Fred. "*Sultana* Burning." *Appalachian Life* 41 (March 2000): 3–4, 8.

Brown, H.D. "The First Successful Torpedo and What It Did." *Confederate Veteran* 18 (1910): 169.

Brown, Henry. "The Dark and the Light Side of the River War." Edited by John D. Milligan. *Civil War Times Illustrated* 9 (December 1970): 12–18.

Burt, Jesse C., Jr. "Sherman's Logistics and Andrew Johnson." *Tennessee Historical Quarterly* 15 (1956): 195–215.

Buttgenbach, Walter J. "Coast Defense in the Civil War: Fort Donelson," *Journal of the U.S. Artillery* 39 (March 1913): 210–216.

Campbell, James Edwin. "Recent Addresses of James Edwin Campbell: The Mississippi Squadron." *Ohio Archaeological and Historical Quarterly* 34 (January 1925): 29–64.

Carson, Kevin. "21 Days to Glory: The Saga of the Confederate Ram *Arkansas.*" *Sea Classics* 34 (July 2006): 38–41, 58–59.

Castel, Albert. "Fiasco at Helena." *Civil War Times Illustrated* 7 (August 1968): 12–17.

———. "The Guerrilla War." *Civil War Times Illustrated* 34 (October 1974): 1–50.

Catton, Bruce. "Glory Road Began in the West." *Civil War History* 4 (June 1960): 229–237.

Chamberlain, S. "Opening of the Upper Mississippi and the Siege of Vicksburg." *Magazine of Western History* 5 (March 1887): 609–624.

Coggins, Jack. "Civil War Naval Ordnance: Weapons and Equipment." *Civil War Times Illustrated* 4 (November 1964): 16–20.

Coleman, Silas B., and Paul Stevens. "A July Morning with the Rebel Ram Arkansas." *U. S. Naval Institute Proceedings* 88 (July 1962): 84–97.

Conger, A.L. "Fort Donelson." *The Military Historical and Economist* 1 (January 1916): 33–62.

Cooling, Benjamin Franklin. "The Attack on Dover, Tenn." *Civil War Times Illustrated* 2 (August 1963): 10–13.

———. "The Battle of Dover, February 3, 1863, "*Tennessee Historical Quarterly* 22 (June 1963): 143–151.

Coulter, E. Merton. "Commercial Intercourse with the Confederacy in the Mississippi Valley, 1861–1865." *Mississippi Valley Historical Review* 5 (March 1919): 377–395.

———. "Effects of Secession upon the Commerce of the Mississippi Valley." *Mississippi Valley Historical Review* 3 (December 1916): 275–300.

Cozzens, Peter. "Roadblock on the Mississippi." *Civil War Times Illustrated* 41 (March 2002): 40–49.

Davis, Steven R. "Death Takes No Holiday." *America's Civil War* 5 (May 1993): 22–28, 74.

———. "Workhorse of the Western Waters: The Timberclad *Tyler*." *Civil War Times Illustrated* 44 (February 2005): 34–40, 80.

DeBlack, Thomas A. "'We Must Stand of Fall Alone.'" In *Rugged and Sublime: The Civil War in Arkansas.* Edited by Mark K. Christ. Fayetteville: University of Arkansas Press, 1994): 59–104.

East, Sherrod E. "Montgomery C. Meigs and the Quartermaster Department." *Military Affairs* 25 (Winter 1961-1962): 183–196.

Eisterhold, John A. "Fort Heiman: Forgotten Fortress." *West Tennessee Historical Society Papers* 28 (1974): 43–54.

Ferguson, John L. "The Engagement at St. Charles in Its Historical Context." *Grand Prairie Historical Society Bulletin* 5 (July 1962): 52–53.

Fisher, Noel C. "'Prepare Them for My Coming': General William T. Sherman, Total War, and Pacification in West Tennessee." *Tennessee Historical Quarterly* 51 (Summer 1992): 75–86.

Fitzhugh, Lester N. "Texas Forces in the Red River Campaign." *Texas Military History,* 3 (Spring 1963): 15–22.

Foreman, Grant. "River Navigation in the Early Southwest." *The Mississippi Valley Historical Review* 15 (June 1928): 34–55.

Freidel, Frank. "General Orders 100 and Military Government." *Mississippi Valley Historical Review* 32 (March 1946): 541–546.

Gaden, Elmer L., Jr. "Eads and the Navy of the Mississippi." *American Heritage of Invention & Technology* 9 (Spring 1994): 24–31.

Gift, George W. "The Story of the *Arkansas.*" *Southern Historical Society Papers* 8 (1884): 48–54.

Gildrie, Richard P. "Guerrilla Warfare in the Lower Cumberland River Valley, 1862–1865." *Tennessee Historical Quarterly* 49 (Fall 1990): 161–176.

Glen, H.V. "The Battle of St. Charles." *Grand Prairie Historical Society Bulletin* 4 (October 1961): 1–14, and 5 (January 1962): 1–11.

Goodwin, Martha. "The Ram *Arkansas.*" *Confederate Veteran* 28 (January–December 1920): 263–264.

Hagerman, Edward. "Field Transportation and Strategic Mobility in the Union Armies." *Civil War History* 34 (June 1988): 143–171.

Haites, Erick F., and James Mak. "The Decline of Steamboating on the Antebellum Western Rivers: Some New Evidence and an Alternative Hypothesis." *Explorations in Economic History* 11 (Fall 1973): 25–36;.

Hess, Earl J. "The Mississippi River and Secession, 1861: The Northwestern Response." *The Old Northwest* 10 (Summer 1984): 187–207.

Hirsch, Charles B. "Gunboat Personnel on the Western Waters." *Mid-America* 34 (April 1952): 73–86.

Hogan, George M. "Parson's Brigade of Texas Cavalry." *Confederate Veteran* 33 (January 1925): 17–19.

Holcombe, John L., and Walter J. Buttgenbachli. "Coast Defense in the Civil War: Fort Henry, Tennessee." *Journal of the United States Artillery* 39 (January 1913): 83–90.

Horn, Stanley F. "Nashville During the Civil War." *Tennessee Historical Quarterly* 4 (March 1945): 3–22.

Huff, Leo E. "The Union Expedition Against Little Rock, August-September 1863." *Arkansas Historical Quarterly* 22 (Fall 1963): 223–237.

Huffshot, Robert S. "The Story of the C.S.S. *Arkansas.*" *Civil War Times Illustrated* 7 (July 1968): 20–27.

Hurst, T.M. "The Battle of Shiloh." *The American Historical Magazine and Tennessee Historical Society Quarterly* 7 (January 1902): 22–37.

———. "The Battle of Shiloh." *Tennessee Historical Quarterly* 5 (July 1919): 81–96.

Huston, James A. "Logistical Support of Federal Armies in the Field." *Civil War History* 7 (March 1961): 36–47.

Johnson, Boyd W. "The Battle of St. Charles." *Grand Prairie Historical Society Bulletin* 1 (July 1958): 8–12.

Johnson, John. "Story of the Confederate Armored Ram *Arkansas.*" *Southern Historical Society Papers* 33 (1905): 1–15.

Johnson, Kenneth R. "Confederate Defense and Union Gunboats on the Tennessee River." *The Alabama Historical Quarterly* 64 (Summer 1968): 39–60.

Johnson, Ludwell H. *Red River Campaign: Politics & Cotton in the Civil War.* Kent, OH: Kent State University Press, 1993.

Joiner, Gary D. "The Congressional Investigation Following the Red River Campaign." *North Louisiana History* 35 (Fall 2004): 147–167.

———. "The Red River Campaign." *Louisiana Cultural Vistas* (Fall 2006): 58–69.

———. "Up the Red River and Down to Defeat." *America's Civil War* (March 2004): 22–29.

Joiner, Gary D., and Charles E. Vetter. "The Union Naval Expedition on the Red River, March 12–May 22, 1864." *Civil War Regiments: A Journal of the American Civil War* 4, no. 2 (1994): 26–67.

Jones, Archer. "Tennessee and Mississippi: Joe Johnston's Strategic Problem." *Tennessee Historical Quarterly* 18 (June 1959): 134–147.

Jones, Steven W. "The Logs of the U.S.S. *Tyler.*" *Phillips County Historical Quarterly* 15 (March 1977): 23–39.

Jordan, Thomas. "The Battle of Shiloh." *Southern Historical Society Papers* 35 (1907): 204–230.

———. "The Campaign and Battle of Shiloh." *The United*

Service: A Monthly Review of Military and Naval Affairs 12 (March-April 1885): 262–280, 393–403.

Landers, H.L. "Wet Sand and Cotton: Banks' Red River Campaign." *Louisiana Historical Quarterly* 19 (January 1936): 150–195.

Lankford, Nelson D. "Fire and Water: Disaster at the Gosport Navy Yard, April 1861." *North and South* 9 (February 2007): 22–29.

Long, E.B. "The Paducah Affair: Bloodless Action That Altered the Civil War in the Mississippi Valley." *The Register of the Kentucky Historical Society* 60 (July 1972): 253–276.

Mak, James, and Gary M. Walton, "Steamboats and the Great Productivity Surge in River Transportation," *Journal of Economic History* 3 (September 1972): 619–640.

Mangum, Ronald S. "The Vicksburg Campaign: A Study in Joint Operations." *Parameters* 21 (Autumn 1991): 74–86.

Martin, David. "The Red River Campaign." *Strategy and Tactics* 106 (1986): 11–20.

Martin, Hiram H. "Service Afield and Afloat: A Reminiscence of the Civil War." Edited by Guy R. Everson. *Indiana Magazine of History* 89 (March 1993): 35–56.

Mason, George. "Shiloh." In *Papers of the Military Order of the Loyal Legion of the United States*. Vol. 10. Reprint ed., 56 vols. Wilmington, NC: Broadfoot Publishing Co., 1994.

Maury, D.H. "Sketch of General Richard Taylor." *Southern Historical Society Papers* 7 (1879): 343–345.

McCammack, Brian. "Competence, Power, and the Nostaligic Romance of Piloting in Mark Twain's *Life on the Mississippi*." *The Southern Literary Journal* 38, no. 2 (March 2006): 1–18.

McClinton, Oliver W. "The Career of the Confederate States Ram *Arkansas*." *Arkansas Historical Quarterly* 7 (Winter 1948): 329–333.

McCreary, James Bennett. "Journal of My Soldier Life." *Register of the Kentucky State Historical Society* 33 (April–July 1935): 97–117, 191–211.

McGhee, James E. "The Neophyte General: U.S. Grant and the Belmont Campaign." *Missouri Historical Review* 47 (July 1975): 465–483.

McWhiney, Grady. "General Beauregard's 'Complete Victory' at Shiloh: An Interpretation." *Journal of Southern History* 49 (August 1983): 421–434.

Merrill, James M. "Cairo, Illinois: Strategic Civil War River Port." *Journal of the Illinois State Historical Society* 76 (Winter 1983): 242–257.

_____. "Capt. Andrew Hull Foote and the Civil War on Tennessee Waters." *Tennessee Historical Quarterly* 30 (1971): 83–93.

_____. "Union Shipbuilding on Western Waters During the Civil War." *Smithsonian Journal of History* 3 (Winter 1968-1969): 17–44.

Michael, William H. "The Mississippi Squadron in the Civil War." In *Sketches and Incidents: Paper Read by Companions of the Commandery of the State of Nebraska, Military Order of the Loyal Legion of the United States*. Omaha, NE: The Commandery, 1902.

Milbourn, Curtis, and Gary D. Joiner. "The Battle of Blair's Landing." *North and South* 9 (February 2007): 12–21.

Miller, Milford M. "Evansville Steamboats During the Civil War." *Indiana Magazine of History* 37 (December 1941): 359–381.

Milligan, John D. "From Theory to Application: The Emergence of the American Ironclad War Vessel." *Military Affairs* 48 (July 1984): 126–132.

_____. "Navy Life on the Mississippi River." *Civil War Times Illustrated* 33 (May-June 1994): 16, 66–73.

_____, ed. "The Dark and the Light Side of the River War." *Civil War Times Illustrated* 9 (December 1970): 12–19.

Moore, Frank. "The Great Battle of Shiloh." In *Reminiscences of Pioneer Days in St. Paul: A Collection of Articles Written for and Published in the "Daily Pioneer Press."* St. Paul, MN: Daily Pioneer Press, 1908, pp. 107–121.

Mullen, Jay C. "Pope's New Madrid and Island No. 10 Campaign." *Missouri Historical Review* 49 (April 1965): 325–343.

_____. "The Turning of Columbus." *Register of the Kentucky Historical Society* 64 (July 1966): 209–225.

Musicant, Ivan. "The Fires of Norfolk." *American Heritage* 41 (March 1990): 63ff.

Nash, Howard P. "Island No. 10." *Civil War Times Illustrated* 5 (December 1966): 42–50.

Newcomer, Lee N. "The Battle of Memphis, 1862." *West Tennessee Historical Society Papers* 12 (1958): 41–57.

Nichols, George Ward. "Down the Mississippi." *Harper's New Monthly Magazine* 41 (November 1870): 836–845.

Parker, Theodore R. "William J. Kountz, Superintendent of River Transportation Under McClellan, 1861–62." *Western Pennsylvania Historical Magazine* 21 (December 1938): 237–254.

Paschall, Rod. "Tactical Exercises—Mission: Protection," *MHQ: The Quarterly Journal of Military History* 4 (Spring 1992): 56–58.

Patrick, Jeffrey L., ed. "A Fighting Sailor on the Western Waters: The Civil War Letters of [De Witt C. Morse] 'Gunboat.'" *Journal of Mississippi History* 58 (September 1996): 255–283.

Perret, Geoffrey. "Anaconda: The Plan That Never Was." *North and South* 6 (May 2003): 36–43.

Pfeiffer, David A. "Bridging the Mississippi: The Railroads and Steamboats Clash at the Rock Island Bridge." *Prologue* 36 (Summer 2004): 40–47.

Rafuse, Ethan S. "Impractical? Unforgivable?: Another Look at George B. McClellan's First Strategic Plan." *Ohio History* 110 (Summer-Autumn 2001): 153–164.

_____. "McClellan and Halleck at War: The Struggle for Control of the Union War Effort in the West, November 1861–March 1862." *Civil War History* 49 (January 2003): 32–51.

Read, Charles W. "Reminiscences of the Confederate States Navy." *Southern Historical Society Papers* 1 (1876): 333–362.

Reid, Brian Holden. "Rationality and Irrationality in Union Strategy, April 1861–March 1862." *War in History* 1 (March 1994): 25–29.

Ripley, C. Peter. "Prelude to Donelson: Grant's January 1862 March into Kentucky." *Register of the Kentucky Historical Society* 68 (October 1970): 311–318.

Roberts, Bobby L. "General T.C. Hindman and the Trans-Mississippi District." *Arkansas Historical Quarterly* 32 (Winter 1973): 297–311.

Roberts, John C. "Gunboats in the River War, 1861–1865." *U.S. Naval Institute Proceedings* 91 (March 1965): 83–99.

Rose, F.P. "The Confederate Ram *Arkansas*." *Arkansas Historical Quarterly* 12 (Winter 1953): 333–339.

Roth, David E. "The Civil War at the Confluence: Where the Ohio Meets the Mississippi." *Blue & Gray Magazine* 2 (July 1985): 6–20.

Sanger, D.B. "Red River: A Mercantile Expedition." *Tyler's Quarterly Historical and Genealogical Magazine* 17 (October 1935): 70–81.

Saunders, Herbert. "The Civil War Letters of Herbert

Saunders." Edited by Ronald K. Hutch. *Register of the Kentucky Historical Society* 69 (March 1971): 17–29.

Sawyer, William D. "The Western River Engine." *Steamboat Bill* 35 (1978): 71–80.

Seaton, John. "The Battle of Belmont." In *War Talks in Kansas: A Series of Papers Read Before the Kansas Commandery, Military Order of the Loyal Legion of the United States*. Kansas City, KS: Franklin Hudson, 1906, pp. 305–320.

Shaw, Arthur Marvin, ed. "A Texas Ranger Company at the Battle of Arkansas Post." *Arkansas Historical Quarterly* 9 (Winter 1950): 270–297.

Shoup, F.A. "The Art of War in '62 — Shiloh." *The United Service: A Monthly Review of Military and Naval Affairs* 11 (July 1884): 1–13.

Siddali, Silvana R. "'The Sport of Folly and the Prize of Treason': Confederate Property Seizures and the Northern Home Front in the Secession Crisis." *Civil War History* 4 (Fall 2001): 310–333.

Simon, John Y. "Grant at Belmont." *Military Affairs*, 45 (December 1981): 161–166.

Smith, Lawrence M. "Rise and Fall of the Strategy of Exhaustion." *Army Logistician* (November-December 2004): 33–37.

Smith, Timothy B. "'Gallant and Invaluable Service': The United States Navy at the Battle of Shiloh." *West Tennessee Historical Society Papers* 58 (2004): 32–54.

_____. "The Myths of Shiloh." *America's Civil War* 9 (May 2006): 30–36, 71.

Soley, James R. "Rear Admiral John Rodgers, President of the Naval Institute, 1870–1882." *U.S. Naval Institute Proceedings* 20 (1882): 251–265.

Spenser, Kay Terry. "History of St. Charles During the Civil War." *Grand Prairie Historical Society Bulletin* 2 (January 1960): 29–32.

Still, William N., Jr. "The Common Sailor — The Civil War's Uncommon Man: Part I, Yankee Blue Jackets." *Civil War Times Illustrated* 2 (February 1985): 25–39.

Stucky. Scott W. "Joint Operations in the Civil War." *Joint Forces Quarterly* 6 (Autumn-Winter 1994-1995): 92–105.

Suhr, Robert C. "Converted River Steamers Dubbed 'Timberclads' Gave the Union Navy an Important Presence on Southern Waters." *America's Civil War* 11 (July 1998): 20–25.

_____. "Personality: Charles Henry Davis' Brilliant U.S. Navy Career was Interrupted, Not Enhanced, by the Civil War." *Military History* 21 (January-February 2005): 74–75.

_____. "Saving the Day at Shiloh." *America's Civil War* 13 (January 2000): 34–41.

Surovic, Arthur F. "Union Assault on Arkansas Post." *Military History* 12 (March 1996): 34–40.

Sutherland, Daniel E. "Guerrillas: The Real War in Arkansas." *Arkansas Historical Quarterly* 52 (Autumn 1993): 257–285.

_____. "Sideshow No Longer: A Historiographical Review of the Guerrilla War." *Civil War History* 46 (March 2000): 5–23.

Swift, John. "Letters from a Sailor on a Tinclad." Edited by Lester L. Swift. *Civil War History* 10 (March 1961): 48–62.

Toplovich, Ann. "Cumberland River." In *The Tennessee Encyclopedia of History and Culture*. Edited by Carroll Van West. Nashville: Rutledge Hill Press for the Tennessee Historical Society, 1998.

_____. "Tennessee River System." In *The Tennessee Encyclopedia of History and Culture*. Edited by Carroll Van West. Nashville: Rutledge Hill Press for the Tennessee Historical Society, 1998.

True, Rowland Stafford. "Life Aboard a Gunboat [U.S.S. *Silver Lake*, No. 23]: A First-Person Account." *Civil War Times Illustrated* 9 (February 1971): 36–43.

Tucker, Spencer C. "Capturing the Confederacy's Western Waters." *Naval History* 20 (June 2006): 16–23.

_____. "Timberclads Attack Up the Tennessee." *Naval History* 16 (February 2001): 27–29.

United States. Naval Historical Foundation. "River Navies in the Civil War." *Military Affairs* 18 (Spring 1954): 29–32.

Urwin, Gregory J. W. "'A Very Disastrous Defeat': The Battle of Helena, Arkansas." *North & South* 6 (December 2002): 26–39.

Velt, Chuck. "The First Battle of Shiloh," *Naval History* 18 (October 2004): 42–45.

Vitz, Carl. "Cincinnati: Civil War Port." *Museum Echoes* 34 (July 1961): 51–54.

Walker, Peter F. "Building a Tennessee Army: Autumn, 1861." *Tennessee Historical Quarterly* 16 (June 1957): 99–116.

_____. "Command Failure: The Fall of Forts Henry and Donelson." *Tennessee Historical Quarterly* 16 (December 1957): 335–360.

_____. "Holding the Tennessee Line: Winter 1861-1862." *Tennessee Historical Quarterly* 16 (September 1957): 228–249.

Walton, Gary M. "River Transportation and the Old Northwest Territory." In David C. Klingaman and Richard K. Vedder, eds. *Essays on the Economy of the Old Northwest*. Athens: Ohio University Press, 1987.

Webber, Richard, and John C. Roberts, "James B. Eads: Master Builder," *The Navy* 8 (March 1965): 23–25.

Wegner, Dana. "S.X.: The Federal Gunboat *Essex*." *Nautical Research Journal* 19 (Spring 1972): 49–51.

Weigley, Russel F. "Montgomery C. Meigs: A Personality Profile." *Civil War Times Illustrated* 3 (November 1964): 42–48.

West, Richard, Jr. "Lincoln's Hand in Naval Matters." *Civil War History* 4 (June 1958): 175–181.

White, Lonnie J. "Federal Operations at New Madrid and Island No. 10." *West Tennessee Historical Society Papers* 17 (1963): 47–67.

Whitesell, Robert D. "Military and Naval Activity Between Cairo and Columbus." *Register of the Kentucky Historical Society* 61 (April 1963): 107–121.

Wilcox, Charles E. "Hunting for Cotton in Dixie: From the Diary of Captain Charles E. Wilcox." Edited by Edgar L. Erickson. *The Journal of Southern History* 4 (November 1938): 493–513.

Williams, Thomas. "Letters of General Thomas Williams, 1862." *American Historical Review* 14 (January 1909): 304–328.

Wilson, Terry. "'Against Such Powerful Odds': The 83rd Illinois Infantry at the Battle of Dover, Tennessee, February 1863." *Tennessee Historical Quarterly* 53 (December 1994): 260–271.

Wright, Marcus J. "The Battle of Belmont." *Southern Historical Society Papers* 15 (January–December 1888): 69–82.

Unpublished Sources

Barksdale, Ethelbert. "Semi-Regular and Irregular Warfare in the Civil War." Ph.D. diss., University of Texas at Austin, 1941.

Barr, Alwyn. "Confederate Artillery in the Trans-Mississippi." Master's thesis, University of Texas, 1961.

Bogle, Victor M. "A 19th Century River Town: A Social-Economic Study of New Albany, Indiana." Ph.D. diss., Boston University, 1951.

Chapman, Jesse L. "The Ellet Family and Riverine Warfare in the West, 1861–1865." Master's thesis, Old Dominion University, 1985.

Chunney, James Robert. "Don Carlos Buell: Gentleman General." Ph.D. diss., Rice University, 1964.

Cunningham, O. Edward. "Shiloh and the Western Campaign of 1862." Ph.D. diss., Louisiana State University, 1966.

Daniel, John S., Jr. "Special Warfare in Middle Tennessee and Surrounding Areas, 1861–1862." Master's thesis, University of Tennessee, 1971.

Gentsch, James F. "A Geographic Analysis of the Battle of Shiloh." Master's thesis, University of Memphis, 1994.

Goodman, Michael Harris. "The Black Tar: Negro Seamen in the Union Navy." Ph.D. diss., University of Nottingham, 1975.

Grimsley, Mark. "A Directed Severity: The Evolution of Federal Policy Toward Southern Civilians and Property, 1861–1865." Ph.D. diss., Ohio State University, 1992.

King, George L. "Campaign of Fort Henry & Fort Donelson, 1862." Master's thesis, U.S. Army Infantry School, Fourth Section, Committee "H," 1989.

Moseley, Cynthia E. "The Naval Career of Henry Kennedy Stevens as Revealed in His Letters, 1839–1863." Master's thesis, University of North Carolina, 1951.

Parker, Theodore R. "The Federal Gunboat Flotilla on the Western Waters During Its Administration by the War Department to October 1, 1862." Ph.D. diss., University of Pittsburgh, 1939.

Polser, Aubrey Henry. "The Administration of the United States Navy, 1861–1865." Ph.D. diss., University of Nebraska, 1975.

Sharpe, Hal F. "A Door Left Open: The Failure of the Confederate Government to Adequately Defend the Inland Rivers of Tennessee." Master's thesis, Austin Peay State University, 1981.

Smith, Myron J., Jr. "A Construction and Recruiting History of the U.S. Steam Gunboat *Carondelet*, 1861–1862." Master's thesis, Shippensburg State University, 1969.

Stonesifer, Roy P., Jr. "The Forts Henry-Heiman & Fort Donelson Campaigns: A Study of Confederate Command." Ph.D. diss., Pennsylvania State University, 1965.

Wright, Aubrey Gardner. "Henry Walke, 1809–1896: Romantic Painter and Naval Hero." Master's thesis, The George Washington University, 1971.

Index

Number in **bold *italics*** indicate pages with photographs.

Able, Capt. Barton 80; *see also* Atlantic and Mississippi Steamship Company
Ackley, U.S. Acting Master Charles 478; *see also Tyler* (U.S. timberclad)
Adams (steamer) 243
Adams, U.S. Seaman Michael 154
Adams, Theodore (contractor) 93
Adamson, U.S. Capt. Frederick C. 399–400; *see also* Clifton, TN, Battle of (1863); Michigan (U.S.) regiments, cavalry, 3rd
Admiral (steamer) 280
Adriatic (steamer) 448
"Agate," pseud. *see* Reid, Whitelaw ("Agate") (Cincinnati *Daily Gazette* correspondent)
Alabama (C.S.) regiments: infantry: 27th 218
Aldrich, U.S. Congress Cyrus 54, 61; *see also* Timberclads (U.S. wooden gunboats), purchase of (1861)
Aleck Scott (steamer) 134–135, 148, 151, 153, 160, 174, 201, 215–216, 219, 238, 270; *see also* Clemens, Samuel ("Mark Twain")
"Alex," pseud. *see* Bentley, Henry (*Philadelphia Inquirer* correspondent).
Alexander, Peter Wellington (*Savannah Republican* correspondent) 294, 301–302, 306
Alexandria, LA *see* Red River campaign (1864)
Alfred Robb (steamer/U.S. tinclad) 232, 313–314, 316, 398–401, 431; *see also* Dover, TN, Battle of (1863); Palmyra, TN, convoy battle at and destruction of (1863)
Alice Vivian (steamer) 453
Allen, U.S. Brig. Gen. 370; *see also* Logistics, River
Alonzo Child (steamer) 43, 80
Alps (steamer) 215, 243–244, 274
"Anaconda Plan" (1861) 42–44, 52, ***66***, 68, 133; *see also* Scott, U.S. Lt. Gen. Winfield
Anderson, Finley (*New York Herald* correspondent) 19–20, 391
Anderson, U.S. Lt. Col. Nicholas 302; *see also* Ohio (U.S.) regiments, infantry, 6th
Anderson, U.S. Brig. Gen. Robert 31, 122; *see also* Fort Sumter, SC
A.O. Tyler (steamer) 30, 59, 61, 69; *see also Tyler* (U.S. timberclad)
Appleton Belle (steamer) 223, 227–228, 234
Archer, Capt. J.B. 33; *see also Commercial* (steamer)
Argosy (U.S. tinclad) 403, 480; *see also* Streight Raid (1863)
Arkansas (C.S. armorclad) 338, 343–***346***, 347–353, ***354***–358, 361; *see also Carondelet* (U.S. ironclad); *Queen of the West* (U.S. ram); *Tyler* (U.S. timberclad)
Arkansas (C.S.) regiments: infantry: 6th ("Dixie Greys") 153–154, 199, 308; 15th 218; 19th 390; 29th 328; 34th 417
Arkansas (U.S.) regiments: infantry: 2nd 413, 422
Arkansas Post, AK 19, 375; Battle of (1863) 387–***391***, 392–392, ***393–394***
Arkansas River, AK 18–19; *see also* White River Cut-off, AK
Arnett, C.S. Capt. John C. 417; *see also* Etter's Arkansas Battery (C.S.)
Arter, Charles D., U.S. port surveyor Cairo, IL 125
Asboth, Brig Gen. Alexander S. 75, 78
Atlantic and Mississippi Steamship Company 80; *see also* Able, Capt. Barton; Frémont, U.S. Maj. Gen. John C.
Aughey, Rev. John H. 295; *see also* Pittsburg Landing, TN, Battle of (April 1862)
Austen, J.A. (*Chicago Daily Tribune* correspondent) 480
Autocrat (steamer/U.S. ram) 34, 405

Bache, U.S. Lt. Cmdr. George M., 381, 425–***426***, 427–430, 432–464, 466–475, 477, 478; *see also Cincinnati* (U.S. ironclad); Clarendon, AK, Battle of (June 1864); *Lexington* (U.S. timberclad); Little Rock, AK/White River Federal campaign (August 1863); Red, Black and Ouachita Federal expedition (February 1864); Red River campaign (1864); *Tyler* (U.S. timberclad)
Bailey, U.S. Lt. Col. Joseph 463–464; *see also* Colonel Bailey's Dam
Bailey's Dam *see* Colonel Bailey's Dam

Baldwin, U.S. Col. E.D. 243; *see also* Illinois (U.S.) regiments, infantry, 57th
Baldwin, Master Thomas 365, 368; *see also Sovereign* (steamer)
Baltic (steamer) 37, 243
Baltimore and Ohio Railroad 12
Baltimore, MD 12; *see also* Naval Academy, U.S.
Banks, U.S. Maj. Gen. Nathaniel P. 432, 442–464; *see also* Red River campaign (1864)
Barnett, Pilot Thomas 475; *see also Fawn* (U.S. tinclad)
Baron de Kalb (U.S. ironclad) 372–375, 378, 380–381, 383, 392, 407–408; *see also St. Louis* (U.S. ironclad)
Bates, U.S. Attorney Gen. Edward 40–41, 49–51, 145, 208
Bay City (steamer) 290
Beaman, George W. "G.W.B." (*St. Louis Daily Missouri Democrat* correspondent) 199, 222, 244, 246, 253
Beauregard, C.S. Gen. Pierre G.T. 225, 258, 301, 305–306, 309, 312, 347; *see also* Pittsburg Landing, TN, Battle of (April 1862)
Bedford, C.S. Lt. H.L. 245; *see also* Fort Donelson, TN
Bee (steamer) 121–123, 125
Beecher, U.S. Pvt. Harris 445; *see also* New York (U.S.) regiments, infantry, 114th
Bell, ex-U.S. Senator John 253–254
Belle Creole (steamer) 91
Belle Memphis (steamer) 100, 108, 138, 147, 149, 150–151, 157–159, 163
Bell's Battery (C.S.) *see* Louisiana (C.S.) regiments, artillery, 3rd Light
Belmont, MO 17, **98**, 99, 102; Battle of (November 1861) **131–132**, **145**, 146–161, **162**, 163–165, 213; occupation (C.S.) of (August 1861) 97, 100
Benjamin, C.S. War Secretary Judah P. 261
Bentley, Henry (*Philadelphia Inquirer* correspondent) 56, 306, 313
Benton (U.S. ironclad) 105, 168, 173, 176, 184, 202, 210, 274–276, 317, 335, 347, 353, 371–**387**, 407, 443, 478
Benton, C.S. Capt. Thomas O. 461–462; *see also* Val Verde Battery (C.S.)
Betsytown, TN 24, 402
B.F. Cheney (steamer) 80, 85
Bice, U.S. Seaman Daniel C. 379–380; *see also Tyler* (U.S. timberclad)

Bird, Confederate Col. John 64
Bird's Point, MO 17, 64
Bishop, U.S. Lt. Joshua 70, 76, 80, 87, 100, 251, 276, 358
Bixby, Pilot Harold 169
B.J. Adams (steamer) 284
Black Hawk (steamer) 449, 452–455
Black Hawk (U.S. tinclad) 370, 377–379, 390, 392, 408–410, 433, 441–443, 449; *see also* Lee, U.S. RAdm. Samuel P.; Porter, U.S. RAdm. David Dixon
Blair, Francis P., Jr. 44, 75, 145, 199
Blair, U.S. Postmaster Gen. Montgomery 40, 75, 82, 92, 145
Blair's Landing, LA, Battle of 1864) **451**–**453**, 454–457
Blake, Benson, 380; *see also* Chickasaw Bayou–Vicksburg campaign (December 1863)
Blake's Plantation *see* Blake, Benson; Chickasaw Bayou–Vicksburg campaign (December 1863)
Blodgett, U.S. Lt. George M., 262, 273, 277–**279**, 318–343, 358, 363–364; *see also Conestoga* (U.S. timberclad)
Blue Wing (steamer) 385–386, 388; *see also* Arkansas Post, AK, Battle of (1863)
Bodman, Albert H. (*Chicago Daily Tribune* correspondent) 216, 278–279, 306, 368, 418, 422
Booby, U.S. Acting Ensign Henry 427–429, 431–432, 469–470, 479; *see also Lexington* (U.S. timberclad)
Boston (steamer) 289
Brady, Volunteer Pilot James 353; *see also Arkansas* (C.S. armorclad)
Bragg, C.S. Maj. Gen. Braxton 300, 307, 319–320, 394, 403; *see also* Chattanooga, TN; Pittsburg Landing, TN, Battle of (April 1862)
Breckenridge, C.S. Brig. Gen. John C. 297
Breese, U.S. Lt. Commander K. Randolph 407–410; *see also Benton* (U.S. ironclad); Yazoo River, site of Federal diversion (April–May 1863)
Brennan, U.S. Master's Mate Edward 376; *see also Benton* (U.S. ironclad); Chickasaw Bayou–Vicksburg campaign (December 1862)
Brennand, U.S. Acting Volunteer Lt. Edward E. 427; *see also Marmora* (U.S. tinclad)
Briggs, U.S. Acting Ensign Charles C. 427; *see also Lexington* (U.S. timberclad)

Brilliant (U.S. tinclad) 398–399, 401; *see also* Dover, TN, Battle of (1863); Palmyra, TN, Convoy battle at and destruction of (1863)
Bringhurst, U.S. Maj. Thomas 337; *see also* Indiana (U.S.) regiments, infantry, 46th
Brinton, U.S. Surgeon John 150–151, 155; *see also* Belmont, MO, Battle of (November 1861)
Brooks, C.S. Col. W.H. 417; *see also* Arkansas (C.S.) regiments, infantry, 34th
Brown, C.S. Cmdr. Isaac N. 228, 343–**348**, 349–358; *see also* Arkansas (C.S. armorclad); Eastport (C.S. gunboat)
Browne, Junius Henri (*New York Tribune* correspondent) 270–272, 277, 322–323, 327, 330, 333, 350, 352, 367
Browne, U.S. Master's Mate Symmes 57, 59, 61, 345, 359–361, 370, 373, 377, 379–380, 406, 410; *see also Tyler* (U.S. timberclad)
Brownlee, U.S. Lt. Charles A. 327; *see also* Indiana (U.S.) regiments, infantry, 46th
Bruce, U.S. Col. Sanders D. 395; *see also* Kentucky (U.S.) regiments, infantry, 20th
Bryant, U.S. Lt. Commander Nathaniel C. 203, 214, 251, 254, 261, 290–291; *see also Cairo* (U.S. ironclad)
Buchanan, U.S. President James 26
Buckner, C.S. Brig Gen. Simon Bolivar 260; *see also* Fort Donelson, TN
Buell, U.S. Maj. Gen. Don Carlos 167, 189, 192, 197, 208, 257–258, 260–261, 272, 285, 287, 289–290, 294, 298, 300–302, 308, 311, 319; *see also* Nashville, TN; Pittsburg Landing, TN, Battle of (April 1862)
Buford, U.S. Brig. Gen. Napoleon 148, 154, 157, 161, 163, 199, 479

C. Miller (steamer) 401; *see also* Palmyra, TN, convoy battle at and destruction of (1863)
C.E. Hillman (steamer) 37
Cairo, IL 11, 16–17, 21–22, 48, **89**, 186; attempted bombardment by Confederate fleet (November 1861) 180–182; blockade of Mississippi River (April–July 1861) 36–39, 43–44, 47, 51–52, 64–**65**, 68; fortification of (1861) 35–37, 180; visit by U.S. Maj. Gen. Frémont (August 1861) 80
Cairo (U.S. ironclad) 202–203,

214, 251, 254–257, 260–261, 287, 291–293, 317, 370, 373, 376
Calhoun (C.S. gunboat) 179
Callender, U.S. Master's Mate Elliott 338; *see also Cincinnati* (U.S. ironclad)
Calloway County, KY *see Lexington* (U.S. timberclad), Tennessee River reconnaissance (January 1862)
Cameron, U.S. War Secretary Simon 35, 38, 41, 43–44, 53, 63, 66–67, 117
Camp Johnston, MO *see* Belmont, MO
Canby, U.S. Col. Edward R.S. 167
Canida, U.S. Seaman James O. 336; *see also Mound City* (U.S. ironclad)
Cape Girardeau, MO 16, 86, 95, 126
Carondelet (U.S. ironclad) 177, **214**, 216, 218, 220, 222, 229–230, 238, 243–252, 259–260, 262, 270, 274–275, 280, 287, 317, 349–353, **354**–355, 358, 367, 407, 443, 480; *see also Arkansas* (C.S. armorclad); Island No. 10 (Mississippi River); Walke, U.S. Capt. Henry
Carroll, Anna Ella 208; *see also* Fort Henry, TN
Carson, Irving (Chicago *Daily Tribune* correspondent) 99, 139, 148, 152, 154, 156, 159–161, 181, 201, 241, 247, 254–255
Carthage, TN 23–24
Castle, Union Quartermaster Nelson 112
Catahoula (steamer) 336–338
Chalk Bluffs, KY 17; *see also* Columbus, KY
Chalmers, C.S. Brig. Gen. James R. 231, 300
Champion (tugboat) 69
Champion No. 2 (steamer) 125, 249, 280, 369–370
Champion No. 5 (steamer) 459
Chancellor (steamer) 148, 150, 158, 160–161, 163, 215, 217, 219, 259
Chapman, Frank G. (*New York Herald* correspondent) 247
Charleston, MO 17, 97, 99
Charley Bowen (steamer) 37–38, 65, 90
Charm (steamer) 155–157
Charmer (steamboat) 100
Chase, U.S. Treasury Secretary Salmon P. 38
Chattanooga, TN 22, 319, 431
Cheatham, C.S. Brig. Gen. Benjamin F. 155, 157–158, 231, 261, 299
Chester, Capt. Thomas, 85; *see also Grampus* (steamer/ersatz C.S. gunboat)

Chicago Light Artillery *see* Illinois (U.S.) regiments, artillery, 1st Light
Chicago Zouaves 36
Chickasaw, AL 23, 285–286, 292
Chickasaw Bayou–Vicksburg campaign (December 1862) 365–**366**, 367–388
Chickasaw Bluffs 18; *see also* Memphis, TN
Chillicothe (U.S. ironclad) 441, 443, 447–448, 452
Chocktaw (U.S. ironclad) 407–409, 411–412, 443; *see also* Milliken's Bend, LA, C.S. attack upon (June 1863); Red River campaign (1864); Yazoo River, site of Federal diversion (April–May 1863);
Churchill, C.S. Brig. Gen. Thomas J. 388–393; *see also* Arkansas Post, AK, Battle of (1863)
Cincinnati (U.S. ironclad) 214, 216, 220–222, 224, 226, 240, 242, 245–251, 259–260, 269–271, 274, 328, 336–339, 343, 380–384, 392
Cincinnati, OH 11–12, 21, **55**; *see also* Timberclads (U.S. wooden gunboats), outfitting of
Cincinnati Pilots Association 72
City of Alton (steamer) 80
City of Memphis (steamer) 45, 215, 217, 238; *see also* Kountz, U.S. Steamboat Commodore William J.
Clara Bell (steamer) 448, 453, 457
Clara Dolson (steamer) 323–324, 362
Clarendon, AK, Battle of (June 1864) 467, 470–475
Clarksville, TN 24, 253–258; *see also* Memphis, Louisville, and Clarksville Railroad bridge (Danville, TN)
Cleburne, C.S. Brig. Gen. Patrick R. 302, 305; *see also* Pittsburg Landing, TN, Battle of (April 1862)
Clemens, Samuel ("Mark Twain") 16, 19, 55–57, 134, 157; *see also Aleck Scott* (steamer); *H.W.R. Hill* (steamer)
Clements, U.S. Seaman Dan 336; *see also Mound City* (U.S. ironclad)
Clifton, TN 23; Battle of (1863) 399–400
Coffin, Charles Carleton (*Boston Morning Journal* correspondent) 219–221, 298–299
Colburn, Richard T. (*New York World* correspondent) 321, 374, 377, 379
Coleman, U.S. Master Ferdinand T. 348; *see also Tyler* (U.S. timberclad)

Coleman, U.S. Paymaster Silas 203, 348, 351, 354–356; *see also Tyler* (U.S. timberclad)
Collier, Capt. Daniel 65
Collier, Capt. John 30; *see also A.O. Tyler* (steamer)
Collins, C.S. Capt. Richard *see* Collin's Missouri Battery (C.S.)
Collins Missouri Battery (C.S.) 467, 470–473; *see also* Clarendon, AK, Battle of (June 1864)
Colonel Bailey's Dam **458**, **462**, 463–464; *see also* Red River campaign (1864)
Colonel Cowles (steamer) 449
Columbus, KY 17, 69, 81, 97, 101–102, **109**, 116; actions during Battle of Belmont (November 1861) 148–149, **150**–165; C.S. evacuation of (February–March 1862) 260–262, 268–269; C.S. occupation (September 1861) 100–101; defenses (C.S.) 144, 176, 178–179, **266**; Federal feint against (January 1862) 196–199; Federal feint against and reconnaissance (February 1862) 259–260; Federal naval bombardment upon (October 1861) 126–127; Federal naval "torpedo" sweep (January 1862) 192–193, 196–197; U.S. occupation (March 1862) 270–271; *see also* Belmont, MO, Battle of (November 1861)
Commerce *see* Logistics; Mississippi River, pre-war commerce
Commerce, MO 16, 86–89, 93, 98, 364–365
Commercial (steamer) 33
Conestoga (U.S. gunboat AT-54) **481**–482
Conestoga (U.S. timberclad) 24, 59–60, 64, 85, **94**, 95–96, 98–99, 102–106, 108, 110–112, 114, 117–119, 121, 123–125, 129–130, 133–135, 138–141, 143, 148, 170–171, 182, 186–187, 190, 193–195, **235**, 261–262, 314, 316, 368, 370–371, 378, 381, 387, 389–390, 405–407, 432–433, 478, 482; at battle of Fort Henry, TN 214–224; at battle of Fort Donelson, TN **242**–252; in collision with steamer *Sovereign* (October 1862) 365; in Cumberland River advance to Clarksville, TN (February 1862) 253–258; in Cumberland River reconnaissance (November 1861) 166–167, 171; in Cumberland River reconnaissance (December 1861) 182–184; in Eddyville, KY, raid (October 1861) 138–140; in engagement with C.S. *Jackson* (September 1861) 111–114; in Federal feint against Columbus, KY and reconnaissance (Febru-

ary 1862) 259–260; in Federal Red, Black and Ouachita expedition (February 1864) 433–441; in Federal Red, Black and Tensas Rivers Raid (July 1863) 424–425; in Federal White River relief expedition (June–July 1862) 317–323, *324*–343, 358–359; in Island No. 10 (Mississippi River) campaign (March–April 1862) 273–280; prisoner of war (POW) exchange convoy escort (1862) 363–365; rammed and sunk by *General Sterling Price* (C.S./U.S. gunboat) 442; in Tennessee River raid (February 1862) 215, 223, 225–238; in Tennessee River reconnaissance (November 1861) 178; in Tennessee River reconnaissance (January 1862) 190, 192, 199–202, 205–207, 210–213; *see also* Timberclads (U.S. wooden gunboats)

Confederate River Defense Fleet 69, 317; *see also* Hollins, C.S. Commodore George N.; Memphis, TN, Battle of (May 1862)

Connelly, Pvt. Thomas W. 302; *see also* Ohio (U.S.) regiments, infantry, 70th

Continental (steamer) 259, 311, 377, 433

Cook, U.S. Brig. Gen. John 199

Cornay, C.S. Capt. Florian O. 461–462; *see also* Louisiana (C.S.) regiments, artillery, 1st

Courier (steamer) 279

Couthony, U.S. Acting Volunteer Lt. Joseph P. 447; *see also Chillicothe* (U.S. ironclad)

Covington (U.S. tinclad) 403, 419; *see also* Streight Raid (1863)

Cox, C.S. Nathaniel N. 400; *see also* Tennessee (C.S.) regiments, infantry, 10th

Crawford, ____ (*Wisconsin State Journal* correspondent) 22–23

Crescent City (steamer) 288

Cricket (U.S. tinclad) 427–429, 431, 433–441, 443, 459–464

Crimean War 48

Crittenden, C.S. Maj. Gen. George B. 202; *see also* Logan Cross Road, KY, Battle of

Crittenden, Sen John J. 26

Crittenden Compromise 26–27

Crystal Palace (steamer) 45; *see also* Kountz, U.S. Steamboat Commodore William J.

Cullum, U.S. Brig. Gen. George W. 242, 251, 256–257, 259–260, 268–272; *see also* Halleck, U.S. Maj. Gen. Henry

Cumberland River 23–24, *191*–192

Cumberland Rolling Mills *see* Bell, ex–U.S. Senator John

Currie, U.S. Lt. George E. 322; *see also* Mississippi Marine Brigade (U.S.)

Curtis, U.S. Maj. Gen. Samuel R. 145–146, 170, 322, 339, 341–343, 360; *see also* White River, AK, Federal Relief Expedition (June–July 1862)

D.A. January (steamer) 80, 120, 215, 219

Dacotah (steamer) 364

Dahlgren, U.S. Capt. John A., 272

Danville, TN *see* Memphis, Louisville, and Clarksville Railroad bridge (Danville, TN)

D'Arnaud, U.S. spy Charles, 208

David Tatum (steamer) 368

Davidson, U.S. Brig. Gen. John, 426–427, 429–430; *see also* Little Rock, AK/White River Federal campaign (August 1863); Federal White and Little Red River expedition (August 1863)

Davis, U.S. RAdm. Charles H. 25, 70, *292*, 313–314, 316–320, 322, 333, 336, 338, 343, 345–349, 356–360, 362–363; relieved by RAdm David Dixon Porter 363; succeeds RAdm. Andrew H. Foote 313

Davis, U.S. Seaman Frederic E. 318, 340, 361, 364; *see also Lexington* (U.S. timberclad); Rhode Island (U.S.) regiments, infantry, 4th

Davis, C.S. President Jefferson 28, 68, 147, 163, 235, 258

Davis, U.S. Brig. Gen. Jefferson C. 115

Davis, U.S. Seaman Oscar S. 352; *see also Tyler* (U.S. timberclad)

Deloach's Bluff, LA *see* Deloges Bluff, LA, Battle of (1864)

Deloges Bluff, LA, Battle of (1864) 460–463; *see also* Red River campaign (1864)

"Delta," pseud. (*New Orleans Daily Delta* correspondent) 345, 347, 357

Deming, Pilot John 350; *see also Carondelet* (U.S. ironclad)

Dennison, Ohio Gov. William 32–33, 41–42, 45

Des Moines (steamer) 88, 448

DeSoto (steamer) 279–280, 317

"DeSoto," pseud. (*New York Times* correspondent) *see* George, William (*New York Times* correspondent)

DeVall's Bluff, AK 327–328, 339–340, 468–470, 472, 475

Dexter, Capt. Henry T. 37–38, 90; *see also Charley Bowen* (steamer)

Diadem (steamer) 94, 448

Diana (U.S. ram) 405

Dickinson, U.S. Capt. J.H. 54–55, 62; *see also* Timberclads (U.S. wooden gunboats), Purchase of (1861)

Dill Branch Ravine *see* Pittsburg Landing, TN, Battle of (April 1862)

Dix, U.S. Maj. Gen. John A. *see* prisoner of war (POW) exchange (1862)

Dr. Beatty (steamer) 425

Dominy, U.S. Acting Volunteer Lt. Cyrenius 325, 334, 336–337, 358, 361; *see also Mound City* (U.S. ironclad); St. Charles, AK, Federal Relief Expedition (June–July 1862)

Donelson, Tennessee Attorney General Daniel S. 133; *see also* Fort Donelson

Dougherty, U.S. Col. Henry 148

Dove, U.S. Cmdr. Benjamin 165, 169, 174, 176, 181, 240, 251, 318, 363

Dover, TN 23–24; Battle of (1863) 396–400

"D.R.K.," pseud. *see* Keim, DeBenneville Randolph ("D.R.K.") (*New York Herald* correspondent)

Drumgould's Bluff (Yazoo River) *see* Chickasaw Bayou–Vicksburg campaign (December 1862); Yazoo River, site of Federal diversion (April–May 1863)

Duble, U.S. Master John A. 65, 77, 81–82, 260, 277, 334–337, 364; *see also Conestoga* (U.S. timberclad)

Duke, C.S. Col. Basil W. 294; *see also* Morgan, C.S. Brig. Gen. John Hunt

Dunbar (steamer/ersatz C.S. gunboat) 65, 90–91, 97, 201, 205–206, 217–218, 220, 223, 226–227, 230, 232–233, 285, 288, 291, 312

Dunlap, U.S. Acting Master's Mate John 475; *see also Naumkeag* (U.S. tinclad)

Dunn, U.S. Master Martin 234, 264–268, 400; *see also Conestoga* (U.S. timberclad); *Lexington* (U.S. timberclad)

Dunnington, C.S. Lt. later Col. John W. 321, 327–334, *339*, 388–393; *see also* Arkansas Post, Battle of (1863); White River, AK, Federal Relief Expedition (June–July 1862)

Dwight, U.S. Capt. Charles C. *see* Prisoner of War (POW) exchange (1862)

E. Howard (steamer) 80

Eads, James B. (contractor) 11–12, *36*, 40–41, 43–53, 72, 75, 80–82,

Index

106, 112, 133, 141, 167–168, 170, 173, 175–178, 433
Earl Van Dorn (C.S. gunboat) 317; *see also* Memphis, TN, Battle of (May 1862)
Eastport (C.S./ U.S. gunboat) 183, 230–231, 234, 236–239, 343, 362–363, 395–396, 443–444, 446, 459–460 ; *see also* Red River campaign (1864)
Eberhart, U.S. Lt. Col. G.A. 428–430; *see also* Iowa (U.S.) regiments, infantry, 32nd
Eclipse (steamer) 401; *see also* Palmyra, TN, Convoy battle at and destruction of (1863)
Ed Walsh (steamer) 405
Eddyville, KY 24, 117, 135; raid (October 1861) 138–140
"Egypt" (*New York Times* correspondent) 177, 184–186, 193
Eliza G (steamer) 328–330; *see also* St. Charles, AK, Battle of (1862)
Ella (steamer) 340
Ellet, U.S. Brig. Gen. Alfred W. 345, 347, 349, 355, 386, 403–405; *see also* Mississippi Marine Brigade (U.S.); Streight Raid (1863)
Ellet, U.S. Col. Charles, Jr. 317, 322; *see also* Memphis, TN, Battle of (May 1862); Mississippi Marine Brigade (U.S.)
Elston, U.S. Maj. I.C. 200, 203; *see also* Lexington (U.S. timberclad), Tennessee River reconnaissance (January 1862)
Emerald (steamer/U.S. receiving ship) 65, 170, 177, 215, 217, 238, 448, 451, 453–454
Emma Duncan (steamer) 92; *see also* Hastings (U.S. tinclad)
Emmons, U.S. Capt. Stew 386; *see also* Ohio (U.S.) regiments, infantry, 76th
Empress (steamer) 80, 88–89, 108, 238, 284, 292, 405
Equality (steamer/ersatz C.S. gunboat) 85, 100
Essex (U.S. ironclad) 177, 184, 186, 190, 192–198, 201–202, 214, 216, 222, 224, 241–242, 343, 345, 443; *see also* Fort Henry, TN; *New Era* (U.S. timberclad); Porter, U.S. Cmdr. William D. ("Dirty Bill")
Etter's Arkansas Battery (C.S.) 417; *see also* Helena, AK, Battle of (1863)
Eugene (steamer) 65
Ewing, ex-U.S. Senator Thomas, Sr. 293; *see also* Sherman, U.S. Maj. Gen. William T.

Fairchild (steamer) 243
Fairplay (U.S. tinclad) 397–399, 401; *see also* Dover, TN, Battle of (1863); Palmyra, TN, Convoy battle at and destruction of (1863)
Falls of the Ohio (River) 21, 26, 70–**71**
Fanny Bullitt (steamer) 33, 215, 219
Faries, C.S. Capt. T.A. *see* Faries Louisiana Battery (C.S.)
Faries Louisiana Battery (C.S.) 436–438; *see also* Red, Black and Ouachita Federal expedition (February 1864)
Farragut, RAdm. David G. 118, 345–349, 356–359
Faulkner, U.S. Chief Engineer William D. 314, 316
Fawn (U.S. tinclad) 467, 469, 472–475
Fitch, U.S. Col. Graham Newell 277, 312, 320–324, **325**–343, 358, 394–396; *see also* Indiana (U.S.) regiments, infantry, 46th; White River, AK, Federal relief expedition (June–July 1862)
Fitch, U.S. Lt. Commander Le Roy 22–24, 277–278, 329, 394–405, 467; *see also* Lexington (U.S. timberclad)
Fitzgerald, C.S. Lt. William B. 70
Fitzpatrick, U.S. Master James 326, 402; *see also* Lexington (U.S. timberclad); Palmyra, TN, convoy battle at and destruction of (1863)
Florence, AL 22–23, 232–234, 311–312
Floyd, C.S. Brig. Gen. John B. 245–252, 254; *see also* Fort Donelson, TN
Flye, U.S. Acting Volunteer Lt. Cmdr. William 479; *see also* Lexington (U.S. timberclad); Osage (U.S. monitor)
Foote, RAdm. Andrew H. 16, 70, 82–83, 92, 95, 104–108, 110, 112–**113**, 114–120, 122–123, 125–127, 129–130, 137–138, 140–142, 145, 150, 163, 165–169, 173–178, 181–182, 184, 186, 188–189, 192–198, 201–203, 206, 209, 253–260, 287, 290, 293, 307, 363; in Battles of Fort Henry and Fort Donelson, TN 210–252; in Island No. 10 (Mississippi River) campaign (March-April 1862) 261–262, 268–280; promoted to rank of flag officer 167; relieved by RAdm. Charles H. Davis 313; succeeds Cmdr. Rodgers 105, 107
For, Pilot William 200
Forest Rose (U.S. tinclad) 424–425, 478
Forrest, C.S. Maj. Gen. Nathan Bedford 24, 171–172, 303, 394–400, 431, 467; *see also* Streight Raid (1863)
Forsyth, Robert (St. Louis entrepreneur) 199
Fort Clark, TN 255–256
Fort De Russy, LA 443–444; *see also* Red River campaign (1864)
Fort Donelson, TN 24, 26, 133, 142, 167, 183, 185, 192, 208–209, 224, 239–**242**, 243–249, **250**–252; *see also* Dover, TN, Battle of (1863)
Fort Heiman, TN 218–219, 223; *see also* Dover, TN, Battle of (1863)
Fort Henry, TN 23, 26, 97, 133–134, 148, 185, 190–192, **195**, 199, 201, **204**–222, **223**–226
Fort Hindman (U.S. tinclad) 424–425, 433–**435**, 436–441, 443–444, 446–448, 455, 457–458, 463–464; *see also* Federal Red, Black and Tensas Rivers Raid (July 1863); Red River campaign (1864)
Fort Hindman, AK *see* Arkansas Post, AK
Fort Holt, IL *see* Cairo, IL
Fort Jefferson, KY 17, 196–199
Fort Pillow, TN 18, 80, 93, 261
Fort Randolph, TN 80, 93
Fort Sumter, SC 28, 30–31, 40
Foster, F.C. (Chicago *Daily Tribune* correspondent) 374, 377, 382, 384
Fouke, U.S. Col. Philip B. 148
Fowler, Dick 65
Fowler, Capt. Gus 65, 90–92, 178, 205–206, 218, 223, 226–227, 233, 285, 312; *see also* Dunbar (steamboat/ersatz C.S. gunboat)
Fowler, Joe 65
Fowler, Whyte 65, 91
Fowler, Willie 65
Fox, U.S. Assistant Navy Secretary Gustavus V. 25, 75, 82, 92, 105, 188
Fred Lorenz (steamer) 47
Frederic, U.S. Acting Gunner L. 469; *see also* Lexington (U.S. timberclad)
Frémont, U.S. Maj. Gen. John C. 75, 78, 81–83, 89, 91–**92**, 93, 95–97, 100, 102–104, 106–108, 110, 112–115, 117, 119–126, 129, 136, 144, 198; requests replacement of Cmdr. John Rodgers, II 82–83, 146; succeeded by Maj. Gen. David Hunter 145–146
French, U.S Master Jefferson 348; *see also* Tyler (U.S. timberclad)
Fry, C.S. Lt. Joseph 321, 327–336; *see also* St. Charles, AK; White River, AK, Federal relief expedition (June–July 1862)

Gage's Alabama Battery (C.S.) 300
Galloway, C.S. Col. M.C. 35
"Galway," pseud. *see* Wilkie, Franc B. ("Galway") (New York Times correspondent)
Garfield, U.S. Brig. Gen. James A. 403; *see also* Streight Raid (1863)
Garner, U.S. Acting Assistant Surgeon George W. 333; *see also* Mound City (U.S. ironclad)
Gatey (steamer) 393
Gaudet, C.S. Lt. O. 436–437; *see also* Faries' Louisiana Battery (C.S.)
Gazelle (steamer) 117–118
Gazelle (U.S. tinclad) 443
Geddes, U.S. Col. James 299; *see also* Iowa (U.S.) regiments, infantry, 8th
General Beauregard (C.S. gunboat) 317; *see also* Memphis, TN, Battle of (May 1862)
General Bragg (C.S./ U.S. gunboat) 317, 358, 413–414, 441; *see also* Memphis, TN, Battle of (May 1862)
General Lovell (C.S. gunboat) 317; *see also* Memphis, TN, Battle of (May 1862)
General M. Jeff Thompson (C.S. gunboat) 317; *see also* Memphis, TN, Battle of (May 1862)
General Polk (C.S. gunboat) 175, 179–180, 196
General Price (U.S. gunboat) *see* *General Sterling Price* (C.S./U.S. gunboat)
General Sterling Price (C.S./U.S. gunboat) 317, 407, **427**, **442**; *see also* Conestoga (U.S. timberclad); Memphis, TN, Battle of (May 1862)
General Sumter (C.S. gunboat) 317; *see also* Memphis, TN, Battle of (May 1862)
George, William ("DeSoto") (*New York Times* correspondent) 388, 407
Gibson, C.S. Capt. Claude *see* Miles Light Artillery (C.S.)
Gibson's Battery *see* Miles Light Artilery (C.S.)
Gift, C.S. Lt. George W. 344, 351–354, 357; *see also* Arkansas (C.S. armorclad)
Gilmer, Confederate Maj. Jeremy F. 142, 218, 220; *see also* Fort Donelson, TN; Fort Henry, TN
Gladiator (steamer) 238
Golden Era (steamer) 340
Golden State (steamer) 284
Gooding, U.S. Col. Oliver P. 448; *see also* Minnesota (U.S.) regiments, infantry, 5th
Goody Friends (steamer) 287

Gorman, U.S. Brig. Gen. Willis A. 381
Gosport Navy Yard, VA 11, 43
Goudy, Acting Volunteer Lt. Jason 227, 236, 264–268, 313, 316; *see also* Tyler (U.S. timberclad)
Gould, C.S. Col. Nicholas C. 453; *see also* Blair's Landing, Battle of (1864)
"G.P.U.," pseud. *see* Upton, George P. (Chicago *Daily Tribune* correspondent)
Grace, U.S. Acting Master John R. 480; *see also* Tyler (U.S. timberclad)
Graham, George Washington ("Wash") (contractor/steamboat commodore) 127, 135, 198–199, 215–217
Grampus (steamer/ersatz C.S. gunboat) 80, 85, 99–103, 108–111, 116, 128, 135–136, 177–178, 182, 185, 193, 197–198, 201, 205, 275–**276**, 279–280; *see also* Miller, Capt. Marshall J. ("Marsh")
Granger, U.S. Maj. Gen. Gordon, 396–400; *see also* Dover, TN, Battle of (1863)
Grant, U.S. Maj. Gen. Ulysses S., 95–97, 100, 102–107, 109–116, 119–122, 124–127, 129, 133–**136**, 138, 141–143, 146–147, 167, 170, 174–178, 180–181, 184–187, 189, 192, 194, 196–199, 206–208, 253–261, 268–269, 318–319, 342, 425–426, 430, 432, 445; at Battle of Belmont (November 1861) 148–165; at Battle of Pittsburgh Landing, TN (April 1862) 281–311; at battles of Fort Henry and Fort Donelson (February 1862) 209–252; in Chattanooga, TN campaign (October–November 1863) 430–431; in Vicksburg campaigns (November 1862–July 1863) 365, 368, 406–408, 410–412
Gray, U.S. Signal Corps Lt. George 329, 331–333; *see also* White River, AK, Battle of (1862)
Great Western (U.S. ordnance steamer) 274, 277
Green, C.S. Brig. Gen. Thomas 451–457, 473; *see also* Blair's Landing, Battle of (1864)
Greene, C.S. Colton 467–468; *see also* Missouri (C.S.) regiments, cavalry, 3rd
Greer, U.S. Pvt. Allen 213, 215; *see also* Illinois (U.S.) regiments, infantry, 20th
Grey Eagle (steamer) 65
Griggs, U.S. Lt. Col. Chauncey 400; *see also* Illinois (U.S.) regiments, infantry, 83rd
Grisamore, C.S. Maj. Silas 263–

268; *see also* Louisiana (C.S.) regiments, infantry, 18th
Grosse Tete Flying Artillery *see* Louisiana (C.S.) regiments, artillery, 6th Battery
Guthrie, C.S. Lt. John Julius 175, 184–185, 193; *see also* New Orleans (C.S. floating battery)
G.W. Graham (steamer) 80, 98, 100, 104, 238
Gwathmey, Confederate Lt. Washington 69; *see also* Jackson (C.S. gunboat)
"G.W.B.," pseud. *see* Beaman, George W. "G. W. B." (*St. Louis Daily Missouri Democrat* correspondent)
Gwin, Mrs. Mary L. 387; *see also* Gwin, U.S. Lt. Cmdr. William
Gwin, U.S. Lt. Cmdr. William 105, 202–203, 214, 224, 226–239, 251–252, 260, 262–268, 281–314, 316, 343–358, 370–**382**, 384–385, 387–388; *see also* Arkansas (C.S. armorclad); Benton (U.S. ironclad); Chickasaw Bayou–Vicksburg campaign (December 1862); Tyler (U.S. timberclad)

Hale, U.S. Acting Master's Mate Howard 430; *see also* Lexington (U.S. timberclad)
Hall, U.S. Gunner John R. 337; *see also* Cincinnati (U.S. ironclad)
Halleck, U.S. Maj. Gen. Henry ("Old Brains") 146, 167, 176–177, 180, 182, 184–185, 189–190, 192, 194–195, 198–199, 208–210, 215, 223, 226, 229, 240–242, 250–251, 256–257, 261–**262**, 263, 268–272, 274, 278, 281–283, 285, 290–291, 305, 309, 311–314, 319–320, 322, 425, 432
Hambleton Collier & Company (Mound City, IL) 83, 124, 141, 202
Hamilton (steamer) 448
Hancock House (Henderson, KY) 34
Hannibal (steamer) 238
Hardee, C.S. Maj. Gen. William J. 225
Harding, U.S. Col. Abner C. 397–400; *see also* Dover, TN, Battle of (1863); Illinois (U.S.) regiments, infantry, 83rd
Harper, U.S. Capt. James 119
Harpeth Shoals (Cumberland River) 24, 402
Harris, Mrs. J.R. 406; *see also* Sutherland, U.S. Capt. Edwin
Harris, Tennessee (C.S.) Gov. Isham G. 38, 97, 101, 133, 179–180, 201
Harrison, Capt. H.H. 142; *see also* Fort Donelson

Hartford (U.S. sloop-of-war) 357–358
Harwood, U.S. Capt John A. 82
Hassendenbel, U.S. Col. Francis 382; *see also* Missouri (U.S.) regiments, infantry, 17th
Hastings (steamer) 448, 453–454
Hastings (U.S. tinclad) 404–405, 413–414, 419, 431, 467–468; *see also Emma Duncan* (steamer); Helena, AK, Battle of (1863); Streight Raid (1863)
Hat Island, IL 169
Hawes, C.S. Brig. James M. 411–412; *see also* Milliken's Bend, LA, C.S. attack upon (June 1863)
Haynes, Confederate Lt. Col. Milton A. 97, 142, 218; *see also* Fort Donelson, TN; Fort Henry, TN
Haynes' Bluff (Yazoo River) *see* Chickasaw Bayou–Vicksburg campaign (December 1862)
Heartsill, Pvt. William W. 375–376, 392; *see also* Texas (C.S.) regiments, cavalry, W.P. Lane Rangers
Hebert, C.S. Brig. Gen. Louis 409; *see also* Yazoo River, Site of Federal diversion (April–May 1863)
Hedley, U.S. Lt. Fenwick 267; *see also* Illinois (U.S.) regiments, infantry, 32nd
Heffernan, Capt. William 228; *see also Lynn Boyd* (steamer) 228
Heiman, Confederate Col. Adolphus 142, 216–220; *see also* Fort Heiman, TN; Fort Henry, TN
Helena, AK 18, 323, 360; Battle of (1863) 412–*416*, 417–423
Henderson, KY 21
Henry (steamer) 135
Henry, Tennessee C.S. Senator Gustavus A. 133; *see also* Fort Henry
Hentig, U.S. Master George 364, 366, 368; *see also Conestoga* (U.S. timberclad)
Hickey, U.S. Acting Volunteer Lt. Michael 470–472; *see also Queen City* (U.S. tinclad)
Hickman, KY 17–18, 100–102; guerrilla attack upon (December 1862) 369–370; naval battle off (September 4, 1861) 101–102
Hicks, U.S. Col. Stephen G. 431; *see also* Tennessee River Chattanooga relief force (October–November 1863)
Higgins, C.S. Col. Edward 382–385; *see also* Mississippi (C.S.) regiments, infantry, 3rd
Hill (steamer) 467
Hill, C.S. Maj. Gen. Daniel *see* Prisoner of War (POW) exchange (1862)
Hill, U.S. Acting Volunteer Lt. Frederic S. 478; *see also Tyler* (U.S. timberclad)
Hillyer, U.S. Capt. William S. 287; *see also* Grant, U.S. Maj. Gen. Ulysses S.
Hindman, C.S. Maj. Gen. Thomas C. 320–*321*, 327, 340, 342; *see also* White River, AK, Federal relief expedition (June–July 1862)
Hiner, Pilot David A. 73, 352, 355; *see also Tyler* (U.S. timberclad)
Hodges, Pilot John G. 353; *see also Arkansas* (C.S. armorclad)
Hoel, Acting Volunteer Lt. William R. 366; *see also Pittsburg* (U.S. ironclad)
Hogg, U.S. Lt. Col. H. 270–271; *see also* Illinois (U.S.) regiments, cavalry, 2nd
Hollins, Confederate Commodore George N. 69, 118, 127, 174, 179–183, 185, 196–197, 258, 272, 321
Holmes, C.S. Maj. Gen. Theophilus H. 392, 412–423, 425; *see also* Arkansas Post, AK, Battle of (1863); Helena, AK, Battle of (1863)
Hood, U.S. Seaman Thomas Jefferson 352; *see also Tyler* (U.S. timberclad)
"Hornet's Nest," *see* Pittsburg Landing, Battle of (April 1862)
Hotchkiss, C.S. Capt Thomas P. 446; *see also* Red River campaign (1864)
Hovey, U.S. Brig. Gen. Charles E. 381
Howard, U.S. Acting Assistant Surgeon William W. 399–401; *see also Brilliant* (U.S. tinclad); Dover, TN, Battle of (1863); *see also* Palmyra, TN, convoy battle at and destruction of (1863)
Hubert, U.S. Col. Charles 300; *see also* Illinois (U.S.) regiments, infantry, 50th
Huger, Confederate Lt. Thomas B. 69; *see also McRae* (C.S. gunboat)
Huling, Paymaster Edward J. 16, 18
Hunter, U.S. Maj. Gen. David 146, 163, 167
Hunter, U.S. Lt. James M. 349–355; *see also Arkansas* (C.S. Armorclad); Illinois (U.S.) regiments, infantry, 63rd; *Queen of the West* (U.S. ram)
Hunter, U.S. Capt. John R.C. 467–468; *see also* White River Station, AK, Battle of (1864)
Hurd, U.S. Acting Volunteer Lt. Jacob S. 77, 81–82, 88, 234; *see also Lexington* (U.S. timberclad)
Hurlbut, U.S. Maj. Gen. Stephen A. 288, 296–298, 306, 319, 413–414, 422, 426; *see also* Pittsburg Landing, TN, Battle of (April 1862)
H.W.R. Hill (steamer) 155–157

Iatan (steamer) 51, 215, 217, 238
Iberville (steamer) 449
Ike Hammet (steamer) 270, 274–275
Illinois (steamer) 215–216, 226–227, 229, 238, 259, 270–271
Illinois Central Railroad 35, 45, 48–49, 104
Illinois (U.S.) regiments: artillery: 1st Light (Chicago Light Artillery) 36, 148, 160, 206, 298; 2nd 298, 397–400; cavalry: 2nd 270; 4th 311; infantry: 7th 64, 180, 215; 8th 64, 83, 111, 116, 120; 9th 116, 138–140; 12th 98, 104, 106; 20th 213, 215; 22nd 148, 150; 23rd 115; 27th 148, 157, 259; 30th 148; 31st 148, 160; 32nd 263–268, 282; 33rd 366; 40th 108; 41st 108; 50th 300; 57th 243–244; 63rd 349; 77th 371; 83rd 397–400
Imperial (steamer) 424
Indiana (U.S.) regiments: artillery: 1st Heavy 450; infantry: 11th 249; 24th 339, 341; 34th 338, 341; 43rd 338–340, 413; 46th 277, 312, 320–343; 51st 402–403; 76th 371
Ingomar (steamer) 100, 155
Iowa (steamer) 290
Iowa (U.S.) regiments: cavalry: 5th 244, 397–400; infantry: 2nd 243; 7th 119–120, 148; 8th 299; 12th 467; 23rd 411–412; 25th 378; 29th 412–413; 32nd 428–430; 33rd 413; 36th 413, 418–419
Iron Bluff, KY 17; *see also* Columbus, KY
Irwin, Capt. James M. 85; *see also Equality* (steamer); *New Uncle Sam* (steamer)
Isham, Warren P. (Chicago *Daily Times* correspondent) 291
Island No. 5 (Mississippi River) *see* Wolf Island, KY
Island No. 10 (Mississippi River) 16, 99; Federal siege of (March–April 1862) 258–272, *273*–280
Island No. 34 (Mississippi River), bombardment of (November 1862) 365–366
Ivy (C.S. gunboat) 179–180, 196; *see also Maurepas* (C.S. gunboat)
Izetta (steamer) 263, 267–269

Jackson (C.S. gunboat) 69, 100–101, 103, 108, 110–115, 118, 128, 144, 179–181, 196; *see also Yankee* (tugboat)

Jackson, Missouri Gov. Claiborne F. 44
Jackson, C.S. Brig. John 300; see also Pittsburg Landing, TN, Battle of (April 1862)
Jacob Musselman (steamer) 318, 326, 329, 333–334
James Montgomery (steamer) 148, 152, 157
J.B. Howard (C.S. gunboat) 144, 182
J.C. Swon (steamer) 51
Jeff Davis (steamer/ersatz C.S. gunboat) 108, 110, 123–124, 134
Jefferson (steamer) 106
Jeffersonville and Indianapolis Railroad 21
Jennie Deans (steamer) 80
J.H. Lacy (steamer) 448, 460
John D. Perry (steamer) 37
John Gault (steamer) 108, 120
John J. Roe (steamer) 393
John R. Roe (steamer) 284
John Ramm (steamer) 295
John Simons (steamer) 80, 280
John Walsh (steamer) 100
John Warner (steamer) 449–450, 457–458
Johnson, Hon. Cave (Tennessee politician) 255
Johnson, Capt. Jacob 90–91; see also *W.B. Terry* (steamer)
Johnston, C.S. Gen. Albert Sidney 104, 125, 127, 133, 142, 147, 159, 179–180, 189, 202, 225, 231, 245, 252, 254, 257–258, 262, 288, 293–295, 298; see also Fort Donelson, TN; Fort Henry, TN; Pittsburg Landing, TN, Battle of (April 1862)
Johnston, U.S. Master John V. 331; see also *St. Louis* (U.S. ironclad)
Johnston, C.S. Col. William H. 373–374; see also Chickasaw Bayou–Vicksburg campaign (December 1862); Johnston, C.S. Gen. Albert Sidney
Johnston's Landing see Johnston's Plantation
Johnston's Plantation see Chickasaw Bayou–Vicksburg campaign (December 1862); Johnston, C.S. Col. William H.
Judge Torrence (U.S. ordnance steamer) 274, 277–278
Juliet (U.S. tinclad) 372, 374, 376, 390, 426, 443, 459, 478
Julius H. Smith (steamer) 38, 232–233
J.W. Kellogg (steamer) 401; see also Palmyra, TN, convoy battle at and destruction of (1863)
"J.W.B.," pseud. (*Jackson Mississippian* correspondent) 332

Kanawha Valley (steamer) 279
Kaskaskia (steamer) 428–429

Keim, DeBenneville Randolph ("D.R.K.") (*New York Herald* correspondent) 153, 160
Kellogg, Fourth Master S. 175; see also *Tigress* (steamer)
Kentucky (barge) 141
Kentucky (steamer) 155, 157
Kentucky (C.S.) regiments: cavalry: 2nd 400–401
Kentucky (U.S.) regiments: infantry: 3rd 77; 20th 395
Key West (U.S. tinclad) 431
Keystone (steamer) 148, 161, 215
Kilty, U.S. Cmdr. August H. 213, 322–323, *324*–337; see also *Mound City* (U.S. ironclad)
Knights of the Golden Circle 138
Knox, Frank (*New York Herald* correspondent) 20, 350, 377, 385
Kountz, U.S. Quartermaster/Steamboat Commodore William J. 45, 48, 51, 53–55, 59–60, 62, 78, 198–199; see also McClellan, Maj. Gen. George B.; Rodgers, U.S. Cmdr. John, II; Timberclads (U.S. wooden gunboats), purchase of (1861)

Lady Polk (cannon) see Columbus, MO, Defenses of
Lafayette (U.S. ironclad) 407, 443
Lake Erie No. 2 (steamer) 138–140, 178, 274
Lancaster (U.S. ram) 345, 347, 349, 389
Langthorne, U.S. Acting Volunteer Lt. A.R. 429; see also *Cricket* (U.S. timberclad)
Lauman, U.S. Col. Jacob G. 120, 148
Laurel (tugboat) 373, 375; see also Chickasaw Bayou–Vicksburg campaign (December 1862)
Lawther, C.S. Col. Robert R. 469–470; see also Missouri (C.S.) regiments, cavalry, 10th
Lazelle, U.S. Capt. Henry M. see prisoner of war (POW) exchange (1862)
Lee, C.S. Maj. Gen. Stephen D. 373, 379; see also Chickasaw Bayou–Vicksburg campaign (December 1863)
Lemcke, Capt. Julius A. ("Gus") 33; see also *Fanny Bullitt* (steamer)
Lenthall, U.S. Naval Constructor John, 53, 63, 67, 72
Lexington (U.S. aircraft carrier CV-2) 481–*482*
Lexington (U.S. aircraft carrier CV-16/CVT-16) 481–482
Lexington (U.S. timberclad) 56, 59, 61, 64, 85–88, 93–*94*, 95–104, 109–112, 118–121, 125–126, 128–129, 137–138, 141, 166–167, 171–176, 178, 180–184, 188–190, 192–197, *236*–*237*, 238, 243, 251, 260, 272, 314–*315*, 316, 366–367, 465, *466*, 478–482; in Battle of Arkansas Post, AK (January 1863) 388–393; in Battle of Blair's Landing, LA (1864) 451–457; in Battle of Deloges Bluff, LA (1864) 460–463; at Battle of Fort Henry, TN 214–223; in Battle of White River Station, AK (June 1864) 467, 469–470; at Belmont (November 1861) *145*, 148–150, *151*–165; captures steamer *W.B. Terry* (1861) 89–91; in Chickasaw Bayou–Vicksburg campaign (December 1862) 367–388; on Cumberland and Tennessee Rivers (spring 1863) 394–405; in defense of Milliken's Bend, LA (June 1863) 410–412; in engagements with C.S. *Jackson* (September 1861) 101–102, 111–114; in Federal Little Rock, AK/White River campaign (August 1863) 425–*427*, 428; in Federal Red, Black and Ouachita expedition (February 1864) 433–441; in Federal White and Little Red River expedition (August 1863) 428–430; in Federal White River relief expedition (June–July 1862) 317–323, *324*–343, 358; passes over Colonel Bailey's Dam (1864) 463–*464*; at Pittsburg Landing, TN, first Battle of (March 1862) 262–268, 362; at Pittsburg Landing, TN, Battle of (April 1862) *12*, 281–309, *310*–311; prisoner of war (POW) exchange convoy escort (1862) 362–365, 368–370; in Red River campaign (1864) 20, 442–464; sale to Thomas Scott & Woodburn (August 1865) 480; in Streight Raid (May 1863) 402–403; in Tennessee River Chattanooga relief force (October–November 1863) 431; in Tennessee River raid (February 1862) 215, 223–224, 226–238; in Tennessee River reconnaissance (January 1862) 199–203, 204–207, 210–213; see also Timberclads (U.S. wooden gunboats)
Lexington, MO, Battle of (1861) 114–115, 122
Liberty (steamer) 448
Liddell, C.S. Brig. Gen. St. John R. 447–448, 451–452, 457–458, 460; see also Red River campaign (1864)
Lincoln, U.S. President Abraham 26, 28, 31–32, 38, 41, 75, 92, 110, 120, 145–146, 190, 192, 209, 257, 285, 307, 319

Linden (steamer) 82
Linden (U.S. tinclad) 427, 430
Lioness (U.S. ram) 372
Litherbury, John (construction supervisor) 82
"Little Egypt" *see* Cairo, IL
Little Rebel (C.S./U.S. gunboat) 317, 441; *see also* Memphis, TN, Battle of (May 1862)
Little Rock, AK Federal campaign (1863) *see* Little Rock, AK/White River campaign (August 1863)
Little Rock, AK/White River Federal campaign (August 1863) 425–428
Livingston (C.S. gunboat) 179
Lizzie Martin (steamer) 401; *see also* Palmyra, TN, convoy battle at and destruction of (1863)
Logan, U.S. Maj. Gen. John A. 148
Logan Cross Roads, KY, Battle of 201–202
Logistics 12–14; pre-war commerce 26–33; rail 13; river 13–14, 370–371, 395–398, 400–401, 468–469; road 13
Lonergan, Acting Mate William, 157; *see also James Montgomery* (steamer)
Lord, U.S. Acting Volunteer Lt. George, 382, 384; *see also Benton* (U.S. ironclad); Chickasaw Bayou–Vicksburg Campaign (December 1862)
Lou Eaves (steamer) 65
Louisiana (steamer) 64, 80, 108, 143
Louisiana (C.S.) regiments: artillery: 1st 461–462; 3rd Light 461–462; 6th Battery 451–457; infantry: 11th 155; 18th 263–268, 281; 22nd 382, 385
Louisville (steamer) 425; *see also Ouachita* (U.S. tinclad)
Louisville (U.S. ironclad) 177, 242–243, 245–251, 270, 274, 317, 362–363, 380, 382–383, 392, 443
Louisville and Cincinnati Mail Boat Line 69–70; *see also* Shirley, Capt. S.W.
Louisville and Portland Canal 21, 70–71, 76
Lucas, Missouri Gov. J.B.C. 17
Lucas Bend, MO 17, 108; naval battle of (September 1861) 111–114; naval battle of (January 1862) 196
Luminary (steamer) 401; *see also* Palmyra, TN, convoy battle at and destruction of (1863)
Lynch, C.S. Flag Officer William F. 343, 353; *see also Arkansas* (C.S. armorclad)
Lynn, U.S. Capt. John W. 352–353

Lynn Boyd (steamer) 217–218, 227, 234
Lyon, U.S. Brig. Gen. Nathaniel 44, 75, 83

M. Walt (steamer) 467
Madison, IN 16, 21, 25
Madison and Indianapolis Railroad 21
Magoffin, Kentucky Gov. Beriah 100
Major Anderson (steamer) 80
Mallory, C.S. Navy Secretary Stephen R. 134, 344
Manassas (C.S. armorclad) 179, 182, 185
Manassas Creek, VA (Bull Run), Battle of (1861) 83
Manitou (U.S tinclad) *see Fort Hindman* (U.S. tinclad)
Mansfield, Edward D. (writer) 25, 52; *see also* Totten, U.S. Brig. Gen. Joseph B.
Marengo (steamer) 30
Maria Denning (U.S. receiving ship) 165, 169–**170**, 362; delivery voyage, St. Louis–Cairo (November 1861) 169–174; target of C.S. naval attack toward Cairo, IL (November 1861) 179–181
Marietta, OH 12, 21
Marietta and Cincinnati Railroad 12
Marine Railway and Drydock Company (Cincinnati) *see* Morton, Daniel
Marmaduke, C.S. Brig. Gen. John S. 412–423, 429–430, 465, 467; *see also* Federal White and Little Red River expedition (August 1863); Helena, AK, Battle of (1863)
Marmora (U.S. tinclad) 367–368, 370–371, **379**, 383, 386, 390, 427–429
Marquis de la Habana see McRae (C.S. gunboat)
Mars (steamer) 32, 448
Martin, U.S. Fireman Hiram H. 404; *see also Hastings* (U.S. tinclad)
Martin, U.S. Master James 267, 348; *see also Tyler* (U.S. timberclad)
Mary Patterson (steamer) 328–330; *see also* St. Charles, AK, Battle of (1862)
Mason Gem (steamer) 32, 44
Matlock, C.S. Col. C.H. 429; *see also* Federal White and Little Red River expedition (August 1863)
Mattie (steamer) 467
Maurepas (C.S. gunboat) 179, 321, 324, 327, 328, 330, 332
Maxwell, Capt. Thomas 78; *see also* Frémont, U.S. Maj. Gen. John C.
May Duke (steamer) 469
Maynadier, U.S. Capt. Henry E., 274, 276; *see also* Island No. 10 (Mississippi River)
McArthur, U.S. Brig. Gen. John 98, 104, 106, 199
McCammant, Pilot Joseph 200
McClellan, U.S. Maj. Gen. George B. 32, 38, 41–48, 50–55, 60, 62, 64–65, 67, 69, 75–76, 78, 144, 167, 182, 190, 199, 208, 253, 257, 272, 283, 285
McClernand, U.S. Maj. Gen. John A. 103, 105, 114, 148, 155, 158, 161, 163, 194–195, 197, 214–217, 220–221, 239, 245, 249, 319, 388; *see also* Arkansas Post, AK, Battle of (1863)
McClurg, Capt. W H. 90–91; *see also Sam Orr* (steamer)
McCowan, Confederate Brig. Gen. John P. 144, 152–153, 155, 261, 268; *see also* Belmont, MO, Battle of (November 1861)
McCullagh, Joseph B. ("Mack") (Cincinnati *Daily Gazette* correspondent) 83, 213, 218–219, 222, 238, 247, 269–272
McCulloch, C.S. Brig. Gen. Henry E. 411–412; *see also* Milliken's Bend, LA, C.S. attack upon (June 1863)
McCullouch, C.S. Brig. Gen. Ben 83
McGee, U.S. Master Carpenter J.K. 314, 316
McGill (steamer) 243–245
McGunnegle, U.S. Lt. Wilson 323, 328, 332–337; *see also St. Louis* (U.S. ironclad)
McKenney, U.S. Capt. J.C. 146; *see also* Frémont, U.S. Maj. Gen. John C.
McLean, U.S. Col. William E. 339; *see also* Indiana (U.S.) regiments, infantry, 43rd
McMurray, Pvt. William J. 302; *see also* Tennessee (C.S.) regiments, infantry, 20th
McRae (C.S. gunboat) 68, 179
Mead (steamer) 280
Megler, U.S. Acting Ensign Joseph G. 467; *see also Lexington* (U.S. timberclad)
Meigs, U.S. Quartermaster General Montgomery C. 65–67, 72, 75, 80–81, 119, 145–146; relationship to Cmdr. John Rodgers 11, 66, 82, 105; sends U.S. Brig. Gen. Totten to review rivers 15
Memphis (steamer) 86
Memphis and Charleston Railroad 133, 319
Memphis, Louisville, and Clarks-

ville Railroad bridge (Clarksville, TN) 242, 254
Memphis, Louisville, and Clarksville Railroad bridge (Danville, TN) 215, 226–227, 229, 249
Memphis, TN 18, *29*, 133, 320
Memphis, TN, Battle of (May 1862) **286**, 317
Meteor (steamer) 449
Metropolitan (steamer) 368–369; see also prisoner of war (POW) exchange (1862)
Michigan (U.S.) regiments: cavalry 399–400
Miles Light Artillery (C.S.) 263–268; see also Pittsburg Landing, TN, first Battle of (March 1862)
Miller, Pilot George 85; see also *Grampus* (steamer/ersatz C.S. gunboat)
Miller, C.S. Lt. Col. John H. 229; see also Mississippi (C.S.) regiments, cavalry, 1st
Miller, Capt. Marshall J. ("Marsh") 80, 85, 101–102, 116, 135–136, 178, 193, 197–198, 201, 276; challenge from *Essex* (U.S. ironclad) Capt. Porter 197–198; engagement with *Benton* (U.S. ironclad) 275; scuttles *Grampus* at Island No. 10 (Mississippi River) 280; see also *Grampus* (steamer/ersatz C.S. gunboat)
Milliken's Bend, LA 377; burning of (December 1862) 377; C.S. attack upon (June 1863) 410–412
Mills Point, KY see Hickman, KY
Minnehaha (steamer) 215, 220, 238, 243–244, 249, 251
Minnesota (U.S.) regiments: infantry: 5th 448
Mississippi (C.S.) regiments: cavalry: 1st 101, 136, 229; 2nd 263, 267; infantry: 3rd 382; 9th 231; 10th 301
Mississippi Central Railroad 319
Mississippi Marine Brigade (U.S.) 317, 403–405; see also Streight Raid (1863)
Mississippi River 14–19; blockade at Cairo (April–July 1861) 36–39; pre-war commerce 26–31
Missouri (C.S.) regiments: cavalry: 3rd 467; 10th 469–470; infantry: 7th 418; 8th 418; 9th 418; 10th 418
Missouri (U.S.) regiments: artillery: 1st Light 298, 450, 454; infantry: 6th 108; 14th 238; 17th 382; 29th 364; 33rd 413; 35th 413
Missouri State Guard-Militia 96, 364; see also Preston, C.S. Col. William J.; Thompson, C.S. Brig. Gen. M. Jeff
Missouri Wrecking Company 48; see also Eads, James B. (contractor)
Mitchell, C.S. Capt. John K. 179; see also Hollins, C.S. Commodore George N.
Mitchell, U.S. Brig. Gen. Robert 395; see also Nashville, TN
Mixer, U.S. Acting Assistant Surgeon Henry M. 432, 435–437; see also *Lexington* (U.S. timberclad)
Mobile, AL 17; see also Mobile & Ohio Railroad
Mobile & Ohio Railroad 17; see also Columbus, KY
Mohawk (steamer) 280
Monarch (U.S. ram) 317, 345, 363; see also Memphis, TN, Battle of (May 1862)
Monongahela Navigation Canal 53
Monongahela River, PA 20
Montaldo, C.S. 2nd Lt. Charles A. 264–268; see also Miles Light Artillery (C.S.)
Montgomery, C.S. Lt. Col. Frank A. 101, 136
Montgomery, C.S. Commodore James E. 317; see also Memphis, TN, Battle of (May 1862)
Moore, C.S. Col. John C. 308; see also Texas (C.S.) regiments, infantry, 2nd
Moorhead, U.S. Congressman James K. 53–54, 61; see also Timberclads (U.S. wooden gunboats), purchase of (1861)
Moose (U.S. tinclad) 73
Morgan, U.S. Brig. Gen. George W. 379, 391; see also Arkansas Post, AK, Battle of (1863); Chickasaw Bayou–Vicksburg campaign (December 1863)
Morgan, C.S. Brig. Gen. John Hunt 294, 304, 394, 402
Morton, Daniel (contractor) 60, 63, 65, 68, 73; see also Timberclads (U.S. wooden gunboats), conversion of (1861)
Morton, Indiana Gov. Oliver 32, 34, 78, 122, 138
Moulton, C.S. Col. Alfred 263–268; see also Louisiana (C.S.) regiments, infantry, 18th
Mound City (U.S. ironclad) 213, 259–260, 274, 318, 322–323, **324**–338, 358–359, 361, 386, 443; see also White River, AK, Federal relief expedition (June–July 1862)
Mound City, IL 21–22, 51, **479**; Mississippi Squadron sale (August 1865) 480; see also *Lexington* (U.S. timberclad); *Tyler* (U.S. timberclad)
Mulligan, U.S. Col. James A. 115; see also *Lexington*, MO, Battle of (1861)
Muscle (steamer) 207, 232, 237–238
Muscle Shoals (Tennessee River) 22, 26, 319
Musser, U.S. Pvt. Charles O. 412; see also Iowa (U.S.) regiments, infantry, 29th

Napoleon, AK 18–19
Nashville and Chattanooga Railroad 118, 319
Nashville, TN 23–24, 131–133, 395–396; Battle of (1864) 394; Federal occupation (February 1862) 257–258, 260
Naumkeag (U.S. tinclad) 468–469, 472–475
Naval Academy, U.S. 44
Navigation, seasons/difficulties of and on the Western rivers 24–26, 169
Neal, Capt. J.S. 16, 24
Nebraska (steamer) 393
Neil, U.S. Acting Master William 478–479; see also *Conestoga* (U.S. timberclad); *Juliet* (U.S. tinclad); *Tyler* (U.S. timberclad)
Nelson (steamer) 425
Nelson, U.S. Brig. Gen. William ("Bull") 260, 294, 299, 301–302, 308; see also Nashville, TN; Pittsburg Landing, TN, Battle of (April 1862)
Neosho (U.S. monitor) 433, 443, 455, 463; see also Red River campaign (1864)
New Bon Accord (steamer) 421
New Era (US timberclad) 93, 123–124, 127–129, 134, 137–138, 141–142, **168**, 176; conversion into *Essex* (U.S. ironclad) 143–144; Tennessee River reconnaissance (October 1861) 142–143
New Era (U.S. tinclad) 387, 389
New Falls City (steamer) 80, 445, 449–450; see also Red River campaign (1864)
New Golden Gate (steamer) 178
New Madrid, MO 16, 80, 88, 93, 99, 262, 268, 272–274, 280, 282; see also Island No. 10 (Mississippi River)
New National (steamer) 326, 329, 333, 336, 339–340
New Orleans (C.S. floating battery) 175, 179, 184–185, 193, 261, 269, 275
New Uncle Sam (steamer) 85, 215–216, 249, 370; see also *Black Hawk* (U.S. command steamer)
New York (U.S.) regiments: cavalry: 14th 45; infantry: 114th 445
Newell, U.S. Capt. Cicero 399–400; see also Clifton, TN, Battle

of (1863); Michigan (U.S.) regiments, cavalry, 3rd
Newsom, C.S. Col. John F. 399–400; *see also* Clifton, TN, Battle of (1863)
Niagara (steamer) 421
Nicholas, U.S. Lt. Edward T. 348; *see also Winona* (U.S. gunboat)
Norfolk Landing, MO 17, 88, 98, 111–112, 114, 116, 119, 138
North Carolina (U.S. receiving ship) 388; *see also* Gwin, U.S. Lt. Cmdr. William
North Pacific Exploring Expedition (1854–1856) 11, 46; *see also* Ringgold, U.S. Cmdr. Cadwalader; Rodgers, U.S. Cmdr. John, II
Nott, U.S. Capt. Charles C. 244–245; *see also* Iowa (U.S.) regiments, cavalry, 5th
N.W. Thomas (steamer) 121

Oglesby, U.S. Maj. Gen. Richard 83–**84**, 86, 90–91, 102, 111–112, 114, 116, 118–120, 122, 146–147, 149, 163, 199
Ohio and New Orleans Railroad 106
Ohio Belle (steamer) 275, 280
Ohio (U.S.) regiments: cavalry: 5th 287–288, 292; infantry: 6th 302; 46th 283–284; 48th 284, 288; 57th 292; 70th 302; 71st 295; 76th 386; 77th 292; 114th 386–387, 389
Ohio River 20–22, 68; contraband trade (April–July 1861) 32–36
O'Neil, U.S. Acting Third Assistant Engineer James 439; *see also Conestoga* (U.S. timberclad)
Osage (U.S. monitor) 433–**441**, 442–463 ; *see also* Blair's Landing, LA, Battle of (1864); Deloges Bluff, LA, Battle of (1864); Red, Black and Ouachita Federal expedition (February 1864); Red River campaign (1864)
Ouachita (U.S. tinclad) 425, 433–**434**, 435–441, 443–444; *see also Louisville* (steamer)
Owensboro, KY 21; occupation by Federal forces (September 1861) 120–122
Ozark (U.S. monitor) 443, 459; *see also* Red River campaign (1864)
Ozburn, U.S. Pvt. Lindorf 160; *see also* Illinois (U.S.) regiments, infantry, 31st

Paducah, KY 17, 21–22, 24, 90–92, 119; occupation by Federal forces (September 1861) 103–108, 110, 133
Paine, U.S. Brig. Gen. Eleazer A. 192
Palmyra, TN 24; convoy battle at and destruction of (1863) 400–402
Panther Island (Tennessee River) *see* Fort Henry, TN
Paris Landing, TN 22; Battle of (1862) **12**, 22–23
Parsons, U.S. Col. Charles 14, 370; *see also* Logistics, River
Parsons, C.S. Brig. Gen. Mosby M. 418; *see also* Helena, AK, Battle of (1863)
Parsons, C.S. Col. William H. 451–452, 454; *see also* Blair's Landing, Battle of (1864)
Paulding, U.S. Commodore Hiram 41
Paulding, U.S. Lt. Leonard 182, 198
Paw Paw (U.S. tinclad) 431
Peach Orchard *see* Pittsburg Landing, TN, Battle of (April 1862)
Pemberton, C.S. Maj. Gen. John 377, 380, 382, 385, 410; *see also* Vicksburg, MS
Pennock, U.S. Capt. Alexander 130, 177, 240, 258, 291, 314, 316, 343, 387, 393–396, 401–403, 405, 478
Peosta (U.S. tinclad) 431
Perry, U.S. Commodore Matthew Calbraith 46; *see also* North Pacific Exploring Expedition (1854–1856)
Perry, U.S. Commodore Oliver Hazard 177
Perry, U.S. Cmdr. Roger 129, 163, 174, 176, 188
Peters, U.S. Gunner Herman 297–298, 303, 350, 352–353, 356; *see also Arkansas* (C.S. armorclad); Pittsburg Landing, TN, Battle of (April 1862); *Tyler* (U.S. timberclad)
Petrel (U.S. tinclad) 424–425; *see also* Federal Red, Black and Tensas Rivers Raid (July 1863)
Pettis, Mississippi Gov. John J. 30
Peytona (steamer) 34
Phelps, U.S. Paymaster Alfred 77
Phelps, U.S. Lt. Cmdr. Seth Ledyard 53, 69–74, 76–77, 80–81, 83–87, 97, 99, 104, 108, 110–112, 114–115, 117–119, 121, 123–125, 130, 134–135, 138–139, 141, 148, 166–167, 170–171, 178, 183–184, 186–190, 193–194, 197, 199–203, 205–207, 210–215, 224, 226–**229**, 230–240, 242, 246–247, 251, 253–259, 262, 268, 271–273, 318, 348, 357, 364, 387–388, 395–396, 412–423, 426, 430–431, 442, 444, 446, 448, 459–460, 466–469, 475, 478; *see also Conestoga* (U.S. timberclad); *Eastport* (U.S. ironclad); *Hastings* (U.S. tinclad)
Phillips, U.S. Maj. Jesse J. 138–140; *see also* Illinois (U.S.) regiments, infantry, 9th
Phillips, U.S. Capt. Thaddeus 263–268; *see also* Illinois (U.S.) regiments, infantry, 32nd
Pike (steamer) 279, 472
Pillow, Confederate Maj. Gen. Gideon J. 64, 68–69, 80–81, 88, 93, 96–97, 106, 127, 133, 179–180, 182–183; at Battle of Belmont, MO (November 1861) 148–165
Pink Marble (steamer) 172
Pittsburg (U.S. ironclad) 175–176, 242, 246–248, 251, 269–270, 274, 280, 318, 365–366, 368–369, 386, 443; *see also* Island No. 10 (Mississippi River); Island No. 34 (Mississippi River); prisoner of war (POW) exchange (1862); Red River campaign (1864)
Pittsburg Landing, TN, Battle of (April 1862) 281–**297**, 298–311, 315
Pittsburg Landing, TN, First Battle of (March 1862) 262–268, 281
Pittsburgh, PA 12, 21
Platte Valley (steamer) 104, 173–174
Pocahontas (steamer) 44, 81
Polignac, C.S. Brig. Gen. Count Camile Armand Jules Marie de 434–440; *see also* Red, Black and Ouachita Federal expedition (February 1864)
Polk, Confederate Maj. Gen Leonidas 80–81, 91, 93, 96–97, 99, 103–**104**, 127, 133–134, 144, 174, 176–177, 179, 182–184, 189–190, 201, 208, 219, 230–231, 249, 252, 258, 261, 268–269, 301, 305; at Battle of Belmont, MO (November 1861) 147–165; at Pittsburg Landing, TN, Battle of (April 1862) 301, 305, 307; *see also* Columbus, MO
Pontchartrain (C.S. gunboat) 179, 321, 327, 332, 339, 390
Pook, U.S. Naval Constructor Samuel M. 48, 53–55, 59–60, 63, 67, 69, 72, 82
Pope, U.S. Maj. Gen. John 35, 115, 262, 268, 272, 274, 280, 282, 312, 319, 326; *see also* Island No. 10 (Mississippi River); New Madrid, MO
Port Royal, SC, capture of by Union forces (November 1861) 164
Porter, RAdm. David Dixon, 70, 123, 308, 343, **364**–365, 396, 406, 420, 424–428, 430–432, 468, 475, 477, 482; in Battle of Arkansas Post, AK (January

1863) 388–393; in Chickasaw Bayou–Vicksburg campaign (December 1862) 367–388; opinion of steamboat machinery 58; passes Vicksburg batteries (April 1863) 407; in Red River campaign (1864) 432, 442–464; rules for cutting fuzes 112; in sieges of Vicksburg and Grand Gulf, MS (February–July 1863) 365, 368, 406–408, 410–412; succeeds RAdm. Charles H. Davis, 363

Porter, U.S. Cmdr. William D. ("Dirty Bill") 123–124, 127, 134, 137–138, 141–142, 150, 175, 177, 184, 194–198, 347; challenge to *Grampus* (C.S. gunboat) Capt. Miller 197–198; see also *Essex* (U.S. ironclad); *New Era* (U.S. timberclad)

Post of Arkansas see Arkansas Post, AK

Postal, Capt William C. 174; see also *Platte Valley* (steamer)

Prairie Bird (U.S. tinclad) 427

Prairie Rose (steamer) 238

Prentiss, U.S. Brig. Gen. Benjamin M. 37, 47, 81, 288, 299, 412–423, 425; see also Pittsburg Landing, TN, Battle of (April 1862); Helena, AK, Battle of (July 1863)

Prentiss, MS, destruction of 366, 368

Preston, C.S. Col. William J. 364; see also Commerce, MO

Price, C.S. Maj. Gen Sterling 83, 96, 114, 122, 124, 146–147, 163, 176, 412–423, 425, 428, 465; see also Helena, AK, Battle of (1863); Little Rock, AK/White River Federal campaign (August 1863)

Prince (steamer) 100, 155–156, 280

Prince of Wales (steamer) 100

Prisoner of war (POW) exchange (1862) 362–365, 368–370

Pritchett, U.S. Lt. Cmdr. James M. 362, 369–370, 377, 386, 389, 406–410, 412–*420*, 421–423, 431, 466, 478; see also Helena, AK, Battle of (1863); Tennessee River Chattanooga relief force (October–November 1863)*Tyler* (U.S. timberclad); Yazoo River, site of Federal diversion (April–May 1863)

Queen City (U.S. tinclad) 396, 403, 469–475; see also Streight Raid (1863); Clarendon, AK, Battle of (June 1864)

Queen of the West (U.S. ram) 317, 349–355, 362, 372–374, 376, 380–381, 383, 386, 405; see also *Arkansas* (C.S. armorclad);

Memphis, TN, Battle of (May 1862)

Ramsay, U.S. Lt. Cmdr. Frank 408, 411–412; see also *Chocktaw* (U.S. ironclad); Red, Black and Ouachita Federal expedition (February 1864); Red River campaign (1864)

Rattler (U.S. tinclad) 386, 424–425; see also Federal Red, Black and Tensas Rivers Raid (July 1863)

Rawlings, U.S. Brig. Gen. John A. 150, 207, 229

Ray, Dr. Charles H. (Chicago *Daily Tribune* co-owner) 35; see also Cairo, IL, Fortification of (1861)

Raymond, Henry J. (editor, *New York Times*) 184

Read, C.S. Lt. Charles W. 344; see also *Arkansas* (C.S. armorclad)

Red, Black and Ouachita Expedition (February 1864) 433–441

Red, Black and Tensas Rivers Raid (July 1863) 424–425

Red River Campaign (1864) 432, 442–*443*, 444–464

Red River, LA 19–20, 445, 450; campaign (1864) 432, 442–*443*, 444–464; dam see Colonel Bailey's Dam

Red Rover (steamer/U.S. hospital boat) 193, 259–260, 280, 335–336

Reid, Whitelaw ("Agate") (Cincinnati *Daily Gazette* correspondent) 286–287, 302, 306

Reilly, Capt. Robert A. 153; see also *Aleck Scott* (steamer)

Restless (tugboat) 318

Reynolds, Missouri (C.S.) Gov. Thomas C. 413

Rhode Island (U.S.) regiments: cavalry: 3rd 448; infantry: 4th 318

Richardson, Albert D. (*New York Tribune* correspondent) 219–222, 240

Ricker, U.S. Maj. Elbridge 288; see also Ohio (U.S.) regiments, cavalry, 5th

Rider, U.S. 1st Lt. John J. 263–268; see also Illinois (U.S.) regiments, infantry, 32nd

Ringgold, U.S. Cmdr. Cadwalader 46; see also North Pacific Exploring Expedition (1854–1856)

Ritner, U.S. Pvt. Jake 378; see also Iowa (U.S.) regiments, infantry, 25th

R.M. Patton (steamer) 222, 238

Rob Roy (steamer) 120, 148, 163, 238, 449–450, 452, 454–455

Robb, C.S. Lt. Col. Alfred 248; see also Fort Donelson, TN

Robert Allen (steamer) 342

Robinson, A.A., U.S. port surveyor Evansville, IN 125

Roby, C.S. Midshipman Francis M. 328, 330–331; see also *Maurepas* (C.S. gunboat); St. Charles, AK, Battle of (1862)

Rodgers, U.S. Commodore John 11

Rodgers, U.S. Cmdr. John, II 11–12, 24, *34*, 40, 45–55, 58–67, 69–70, 72, 76–78, 81–84, 86–89, 92, 94–97, 100–108, 114–115, 119, 123–124, 129, 146, 164, 167, 175, 177, 188, 363; see also North Pacific Exploring Expedition (1854–1856); Timberclads (U.S. wooden gunboats); *Tyler* (U.S. timberclad)

Rogers, U.S. Acting Master John 470–475; see also *Fawn* (U.S. tinclad)

Rogers, Capt. Thomas 94

Romeo (U.S. tinclad) 372, 426, 431

Rosecrans, U.S. Maj. Gen. William S. 394–395, 402–403, 468; see also Chattanooga, TN; Stone's River, TN, Battle of (1863); Streight Raid (1863)

Rousseau, U.S. Brig. Gen. Lovell H. 77

Royal, U.S. Master-at-Arms Robert 384; see also *Benton* (U.S. ironclad)

Ruby (steamer) 435, 437, 440

Ruggles, C.S. Brig. Gen. Daniel 240, 252, 268, 298–298; see also Pittsburg Landing, TN, Battle of (April 1862)

Russell, William H. (London *Times* correspondent) 16–18, 64

Rziha, U.S. Capt. John 200

St. Charles, AK 19, 322; Battle of (1862) 321, *324*, 327–334; see also Mound City (U.S. ironclad)

St. Clair (U.S. tinclad) 398–399, 401–402; see also Dover, TN, Battle of (1863); Palmyra, TN, convoy battle at and destruction of (1863)

St. Cloud (steamer) 411

St. Louis (U.S. ironclad) 167, 170, 175–176, 182, 186, 194–195, 197, 201, 214, 216, 224, 242–243, 245–251, 259, 272, 274, 317, 322–338; see also *Baron de Kalb* (U.S. ironclad)

St. Louis and New Orleans Packet Company, 45; see also Kountz, U.S. Steamboat Commodore William J., McClellan, U.S. Maj. Gen. George B.

St. Louis, MO 16; riots (1861) 44

St. Mary's Cannoneers (C.S.) see Louisiana (C.S.) regiments, artillery, 1st

Sallie Wood (steamer) 232, 237–238

Sam Kirkman (steamer) 92, 230–234

Samuel ("Sam") Orr (steamer) 65, 90–92, 97, 212, 223, 227–228, 234

Sampson (tugboat/steamer) 175–176, 378

Sanford, U.S. Lt. Joseph P. 129, 314

Saunders, A.L. ("torpedo" inventor) 182, 193

Scott, Pilot Charles M. 147, 149, 199, 208; *see also Memphis Belle* (steamer)

Scott, U.S. Pvt. Newton Robert 418–419; *see also* Iowa (U.S.) regiments, infantry, 36th

Scott, U.S. Lt. Gen. Winfield 15, 38, 42–45, 51–52, 63, 68, 75, 144; *see also* "Anaconda Plan" (1861)

Seaton, U.S. Capt. John 150

Sebastian, U.S. Master Benjamin 117–118; *see also Conestoga* (U.S. timberclad)

Sebastian, Pilot John 355; *see also Tyler* (U.S. timberclad)

Seddon, C.S. War Secretary James A. 410, 413

Selfridge, U.S. Lt. Cmdr. Thomas O., Jr. 363, 370, 381, 387, 389, 405, 424–425, 432–444; *see also Cairo* (U.S. ironclad); *Conestoga* (U.S. timberclad); *Osage* (U.S. monitor); Red, Black and Ouachita Federal expedition (February 1864)

Shacklett, Pilot J.R. 353; *see also Arkansas* (C.S. armorclad)

Shaw, U.S. Acting Volunteer Lt. Edward 77, 81–82, 267, 348, 355; *see also Tyler* (U.S. timberclad)

Shelby, C.S. Brig. Gen. Joseph O. ("Jo") 303, 412–423, 467–**468**, 469–475; *see also* Clarendon, AK, Battle of (June 1864); Helena, AK, Battle of (1863)

Sheridan, C.S. Maj. Thomas B. 172

Sherman, U.S. Maj. Gen. William T. 170, 208, 249, 251, 253, **310**, 312–314, 318, 320, 364–365, 408, 432, 442, 445; in Battle of Arkansas Post, AK (January 1863) 388–393; in Battle of Pittsburg Landing, TN, Battle of (1862) 282–311; in Chickasaw Bayou–Vicksburg campaign (December 1862) 365–388; in Chattanooga, TN campaign (October–November 1863) 430–432; at occupation of Columbus, KY (March 1862) 270–272; on value of river transport 14; in Yazoo River diversion (April 1863) 408–410

Shiloh, Battle of *see* Pittsburg Landing, TN, Battle of (April 1862)

Shiloh, First Battle of *see* Pittsburg Landing, TN, First Battle of (March 1862)

Shirk, U.S. Lt. Cmdr. James 105, 112, 123, 129, 175–176, 188–190, 193, 197, 199–203, 205–207, 210–213, 224, 226–238, 262–268, 272, 281–**312**, 385 314, 317–343, 362–364, 366–367, 369, 372, 374, 383, 389–393; *see also Lexington* (U.S. timberclad); *Tuscumbia* (U.S. ironclad)

Shirley, John T. (contractor) 344; *see also Arkansas* (C.S. armorclad)

Shirley, Capt. S.W. 69–70; *see also* Louisville and Cincinnati Mail Boat Line

"Signal" (*New York Times* correspondent) 195–196

Signal (U.S. tinclad) 367–368, 372–373

Silver, Auctioneer Solomon A. 480; *see also* Mound City, IL, Mississippi Squadron sale (August 1865)

Silver Lake (U.S. tinclad) 398–401; *see also* Dover, TN, Battle of (1863); Palmyra, TN, Convoy battle at and destruction of (1863)

Silver Moon (steamer) 419, 422

Silver Wave (steamer) 30, 274

Sims, Capt. Wiley 118

Sioux City (steamer) 448, 457, 458

Sir William Wallace (steamer) 43

Smedley, Capt. Charles 218; *see also Lynn Boyd* (steamer)

Smedley & Co. (Paducah, KY) 90

Smith, U.S. Maj. Gen. Andrew Jackson ("A.J." or "Whiskey") Smith 379–380, 442–464; *see also* Chickasaw Bayou–Vicksburg campaign (December 1863); Red River campaign (1864)

Smith, U.S. Maj. Gen. Charles F. 108, 110, 114–115, 119, 121–122, 125, 129–130, 138, 140–142, 147–148, 163, 170, **173**, 177–178, 183, 186, 190, 193, 199–203, 204–207, 209, 216, 218, 220–223, 245, 249, 257, 282–283, 285, 288; *see also Conestoga* (U.S. timberclad), Pittsburg Landing, TN, Battle of (April 1862); Fort Henry, TN; Fort Donelson, TN; Tennessee River reconnaissance (January 1862)

Smith, Pilot Dick 349, 355; *see also Lancaster* (U.S. ram); *Tyler* (U.S. timberclad)

Smith, C.S. Lt. Gen. Edmund Kirby 410, 413, 420, 432; *see also* Milliken's Bend, LA, C.S. attack upon (June 1863)

Smith, Nashville Mayor C. George 255

Smith, U.S. Acting Ensign George L. 466; *see also Tyler* (U.S. timberclad)

Smith, Pilot Joseph N. 313; *see also Alfred Robb* (steamer/U.S. tinclad)

Smith, C.S. Maj. Gen. Martin L. 377; *see also* Chickasaw Bayou–Vicksburg campaign (December 1862)

Smith, C.S. Capt. Melancthon 153; *see also* Belmont, MO, Battle of (November 1861)

Smith, U.S. Brig Gen. Morgan L. 370, 379; *see also* Chickasaw Bayou–Vicksburg campaign (December 1863)

Smith, C.S. Col. Preston 157; *see also* Belmont, MO, Battle of (November 1861)

Smith, U.S. Brig. Gen. Thomas Kilby 447–458; *see also* Red River campaign (1864)

Smithland, KY 21, 24, 109–110

Snyder's Bluff *see* Chickasaw Bayou–Vicksburg campaign (December 1863)

"S.O.," pseud. (*Wisconsin State Journal* correspondent) 274

Southwestern (steamer) 448

Sovereign (steamer) 365, 368; *see also Conestoga* (U.S. timberclad)

Spencer, E.M. ("Ned") (Cincinnati *Daily Times* correspondent) 297–298, 301, 303, 305, 327, 330–333

Spicely, U.S. Col. William T. 339, 341; *see also* Indiana (U.S.) regiments, infantry, 24th

Spiteful (tugboat/dispatch boat) 326–327, 329–330, 335–337, 339–340

Spitfire (tugboat/dispatch boat) 216, 271, 323, 325–326

Springfield (U.S. tinclad) 401; *see also* Palmyra, TN, convoy battle at and destruction of (1863)

Stanford's Battery (C.S.) 301

Stanley, Confederate Pvt. Henry Morton 153–154, 199, 308; *see also* Arkansas (C.S.) regiments, infantry, 6th ("Dixie Greys"); Belmont, MO, Battle of (November 1861)

Stanton, U.S. War Secretary Edwin 257

Star of the West (steamer) 28, 30; *see also* Fort Sumter, SC

Steamboats 55–59; sidewheel **15**, 57–58; sternwheel **14**, 58

Steele, U.S. Maj. Gen. Frederick

377, 379–383, 385–386, 425–428, 430, 465, 467, 470; *see also* Arkansas Post, AK, Battle of (1863); Chickasaw Bayou–Vicksburg campaign (December 1862); White River, Federal Little Rock, AK/White River campaign (August–September 1863)

Stembel, U.S. Cmdr. Roger N. 70, 76, 86–87, 89–91, 95, 104, 108, 110–112, 114, 118, 120–121, 125–126, 167, 171–172, 174–175, 180–184, 186, 189, 202, 222; in Battle of Belmont, MO (November 1861) 148–165; *see also Cincinnati* (U.S. ironclad); *Lexington* (U.S. timberclad)

Stephen Decatur (steamer) 121

Stephens, William J. (released *Conestoga* recruit) 80

Stevens, C.S. Lt. Henry Kennedy Stevens 344, 347, 353; *see also Arkansas* (C.S. armorclad)

Stevens Battery 48

Stevenson, Vernon K. 118; *see also* Nashville and Chattanooga Railroad

Stewart, C.S. Brig Gen. Alexander P. 268, 301, 305; *see also* Pittsburg Landing, TN, Battle of (April 1862)

Stewart, U.S. Capt. Richard A. 152; *see also* Belmont, MO, Battle of (November 1861)

Stoddard, George W. (*New Orleans Daily Crescent* correspondent) 307

Stone's River, TN, Battle of (1863) 394

Storm (steamer) 393

Strausz, U.S. Coast Survey Artist A. 372, 377; *see also* Chickasaw Bayou–Vicksburg campaign (December 1862)

Streight, U.S. Col. Abel D. 260, 402–403; *see also* Indiana (U.S.) regiments, infantry, 51st; Streight Raid (1863)

Streight Raid (1863) 402–403

Sturgis, U.S. Brig. Gen. Samuel D. 115

"Subaltern," pseud. (*Jackson Mississippian* correspondent) 353–354

Submarine No. 7 (snagboat) 49–50, 52, 93, 129, 168, 177; *see also Benton* (U.S. ironclad); Eads, James B. (contractor); Rodgers, U.S. Cmdr. John II

Sucker State (steamer) 56

Sullivan, U.S. Seaman James 362; *see also Lexington* (U.S. timberclad), at Pittsburg Landing, TN, First Battle of (March 1862)

Sullivan, U.S. Seaman Patrick 362; *see also Lexington* (U.S. timberclad), at Pittsburg Landing, TN, First Battle of (March 1862)

Sutherland, U.S. Sgt. E.W. 349; *see also Lancaster* (U.S. ram)

Sutherland, U.S. Capt. Edwin W. 372, 374, 376, 380–381, 406; *see also Queen of the West* (U.S. ram)

Swallow (U.S. armed tugboat) 36–37, 68, 279

Sweetman, U.S. Pvt Michael 386–387, 391; *see also* Ohio (U.S.) regiments, infantry, 114th 386, 389

Swett, Leonard (attorney) 307

Swift, U.S. Gen. Richard Kellogg 35

Swigart, U.S. Lt. Franklin 327; *see also* Indiana (U.S.) regiments, infantry, 46th

T.A. Thomas (steamer) 270

Tappan, Confederate Col. James C. 151; *see also* Belmont, MO, Battle of (November 1861)

Tate, Samuel (contractor) 144, 182; *see also J.B. Howard* (C.S. gunboat)

Tawah (U.S. tinclad) 431

Taylor, U.S. Capt. Ezra 148, 160; *see also* Illinois (U.S.) regiments, artillery, 1st Light

Taylor, C.S. Capt. Jesse 97, 201, 219, 221–222, 224; *see also* Fort Henry, TN

Taylor, C.S. Maj. Gen. Richard ("Dick") 410, 412, 432, 438–439, 442–*446*, 447–464; *see also* Milliken's Bend, LA, C.S. attack upon (June 1863)

Tazon (steamer) 280

Tecumseh (steamer) 292, 311

Telegraph (steamer) 284

Tennessee (C.S.) regiments: artillery: 1st 97, 201, 219, 221; infantry: 5th 305; 10th 216, 400; 15th 155; 20th 302; 38th 231; 48th 226; 49th 248; 51st 226; 154th 154, 157–158

Tennessee River 22–23, *191*, *195*, *296*

Tennessee River Federal Chattanooga relief force (October–November 1863) 432

"Tennesseean" (*New York Times* correspondent) 185, 201–202, 206, 233, 237

Terrebonne, C.S. Junior 1st Lt. E.D. 264–268; *see also* Miles Light Artillery (C.S.)

Texas (C.S.) regiments: cavalry: 6th 404–405; 12th 451–457; 19th 451–457; 21st 451–457; 23rd 451–457; 36th 451–457; W.P. Lane Rangers 375–376, 392; infantry: 2nd 308, 386; 9th 306

Thomas, U.S. Maj. Gen. George H. 190, 201–202

Thomas E. Tutt (steamer) *see Tutt* (steamer)

Thomas Scott & Woodburn 480; *see also Lexington* (U.S. timberclad)

Thomas Sugg (steamer) 428–429

Thompson, U.S. Lt. Cmdr. Egbert 105, 251; *see also Pittsburg* (U.S. ironclad)

Thompson, Henry (*New York Herald* correspondent) 16

Thompson, C.S. Brig. Gen. M. Jeff 96–97, 110, 125–126, 136, 146–147, 172–174, 317

Throop, Capt. Joshua V. 230; *see also Sam Kirkman* (steamer)

Tiemeyer, U.S. Lt. John H. 454; *see also* Missouri (U.S.) regiments, artillery, 1st Light

Tigress (steamer) 175, 311

Tilghman, C.S. Brig. Gen. Lloyd 106, 201, 207–208, 212, 217–222; *see also* Fort Henry, TN

Timberclads (U.S. wooden gunboats): acting civilian captains 65, 69, 77; armament of (1861) 61, 65–67, 77, 80, 87; conversion (1861) 59–76, 87; crewing (July–August 1861) 76–77, 80, 82, 87; Ohio River delivery trip (July–August 1861) 69–*74*, 75–83; outfitting of (1861) *50*, 61–62, 68–76; purchase (1861), 53–55, 59–62, 119 (*see also* Kountz, U.S. Steamboat Commodore William J.; McClellan, U.S. Maj. Gen. George B.; Rodgers, U.S. Cmdr. John II; Welles, U.S. Navy Secretary Gideon); St. Louis *Daily Missouri Democrat* description (August 1861) 84, 88; sale out of service (1865) 480; *see also Conestoga* (U.S. timberclad); *Lexington* (U.S. timberclad); *Tyler* (U.S. timberclad)

Time (steamer) 227, 230–234

Tobacco Port, TN 166–167

Totten, U.S. Brig. Gen. Joseph G. 15–16, 25, 44–45, 51–53, 63, 68

Trade Water Belle (steamer) 110

Trask, Capt. William L. 156; *see also Charm* (steamer)

Trudeau, C.S. Brig. Gen. James 268, 298; *see also* Island No. 10 (Mississippi River); Pittsburg Landing, TN, Battle of (April 1862)

"Try Again," pseud. (St. Louis Daily Missouri Democrat correspondent) 245

Tuscarora (C.S. gunboat) 182

Tuscumbia (U.S. ironclad) 73, 393, 395

Tutt (steamer) 243, 448, 450, 458

Twain, Mark *see* Clemens, Samuel ("Mark Twain")
Tyler (U.S. timberclad) 59, 61, 64, 83–88, 93–**94**, 95–98, 100, 103–106, 108, 112–116, 118–120, **122**–125, 129, 137–138, 142–143, 166–167, 174, 178, 180–184, 186–**187**, 189–190, 192–199, 202, 209, 260, 314–**315**, 316, **341**, 359–360, 362–365, 367, 369–370, 406–408, **421**, 465–467, **476**, 478–480, 482; at Battle of Belmont, MO (November 1861) **145**, 148–150, **151**–165; in Battle of Clarendon, AK (June 1864) 467, 470–475; at Battle of Fort Henry, TN (February 1862) 214–223; at Battle of Fort Donelson, TN (February 1862) **242**–252; in Chickasaw Bayou–Vicksburg campaign (December 1862) 374–380, 385–386; in defense of Helena, AK (July 1863) 412–423; in engagement with C.S. *Arkansas* (July 1862) 343–358, 361; in engagement with C.S. *Jackson* (September 1861) 101–102; in Federal Yazoo River diversion (April–May 1863) 408–410; fires first Western waters shots of Civil War 30; at Pittsburg Landing, TN, Battle of (April 1862) **12**, 281–309, **310**–311; at Pittsburg Landing, TN, First Battle of (March 1862) 262–268; prisoner of war (POW) exchange convoy escort (1862) 362–365, 370; proposed name change (1861) 62; sale to David White (August 1865) 480; in Tennessee River Chattanooga relief force (October–November 1863) 431; in Tennessee River raid (February 1862) 215, 223–238; *see also* *A.O. Tyler* (steamer); *Arkansas* (C.S. armorclad); Gwin, U.S. Lt. Cmdr. William; Timberclads (U.S. wooden gunboats); Walke, U.S. Capt. Henry
Tyler, U.S. President John 27

Union City, TN 93, 99, 261
United States regiments: infantry: 10th 274
Universe (steamer) 449
Upton, George P. ("G.P.U.") (Chicago *Daily Tribune* correspondent) 259, 274

Val Verde Battery (C.S.) 461–462; *see also* Deloges Bluff, LA, Battle of (1864)
Van Dorn, C.S. Maj. Gen. Earl 347; *see also* Vicksburg
V.F. Wilson (steamer) 200–203, 205, 238, 270, 274

Vicksburg, MS 18, 20, 345–347, 355–359; first (Sherman) campaign (December 1862) *see* Chickasaw Bayou–Vicksburg campaign (December 1862); second (Grant) campaign (February–July 1863) 365, 368, 406–408, 410–412
Villard, Henry (*New York Herald* correspondent) 298
Vincennes (U.S. sloop of war) 46; *see also* Rodgers, U.S. Cmdr. John II
V.K. Stevenson (steamer) 118

"W," pseud. *see* White, Horace ("W") (Chicago *Daily Tribune* correspondent) 320
Waagner, U.S. Col. Gustave 86–87, 97–101, 108–109, 111, 113, 116
Walke, U.S. Capt. Henry 105, 112–**113**, 114–116, 118–122, 125–126, 130, 135–137, 142–143, 167, 171, 174, 180–182, 185–186, 197–198, 202, 220, 222, 229–230, 238–239, 242–244, 247–248, 252, 262, 275, 279, 378, 388; in Battle of Belmont, MO (November 1861) 148–165, 192; engagement with C.S. armorclad *Arkansas* (July 1862) 344, 349–353, **354**–355, 358; in Chickasaw Bayou–Vicksburg campaign (December 1862) 363–376, 378, 382; commands lower division of U.S. Mississippi Squadron (October–December 1862) 363–376; runs past batteries at Island No. 10 (Mississippi River) 280; *see also* *Carondelet* (U.S. ironclad); Fort Donelson, TN; Fort Henry, TN; *Tyler* (U.S. timberclad)
Walker, Judge Alexander (*New Orleans Daily Delta* correspondent) 263, 288, 294, 308
Walker, U.S. Fireman Hiram 441; *see also* *Ouachita* (U.S. tinclad)
Walker, U.S. Engineer James M. 352; *see also* *Tyler* (U.S. timberclad)
Walker, U.S. Lt. Cmdr. John G. 372–375, 380–381, 384; *see also* *Baron de Kalb* (U.S. ironclad)
Walker, C.S. Maj. Gen. John George 410–413, 425; *see also* Federal Red, Black and Tensas Rivers Raid (July 1863); Milliken's Bend, LA, C.S. attack upon (June 1863)
Walker, C.S. War Secretary Leroy P. 35, 38, 68, 101
Wallace, U.S. Maj. Gen. Lew 130, **183**, 199, 210–213, 222–223, 245, 249, 283–284, 287. 294–296,

299, 319; *see also* *Conestoga* (U.S. timberclad), Tennessee River reconnaissance (January 1862)
Wallace, U.S. Brig. Gen. W.H.L. 149–150, 199, 299
Walnut Hills *see* Vicksburg, MS
War Eagle (steamer) 290
Warsaw (steamer) 80
Watts, C.S. Maj. N.G. *see* prisoner of war (POW) exchange (1862)
W.B. Terry (steamer) 89–90, 97, 99, 104–105, 227
Webb, William E. (St. Louis *Daily Missouri Republican* correspondent) 273, 278
Webster, U.S. Col. Joseph D. **128**, 192–193, 229–230, 238, 254–255, 293–294, 298–300, 306–307; *see also* Pittsburg Landing, TN, Battle of (April 1862)
Welles, U.S. Navy Secretary Gideon 11, 43–47, 54–55, 61–63, 65–67, 69, 78, 82, 87, 92, 95, 102, 105, 115, 117, 140, 164, 194, 250, 260, 307, 318, 322, 345, 358, 363, 376, 393, 425, 430, 442, 463
West, C.S. Capt. John A.A. 451–457; *see also* Blair's Landing, Battle of (1864)
Westmoreland (steamer) 32
W.H. Brown (steamer also known as *Brown* or *W. H. B.*) 100, 104, 120, 175–176, 181, 215–216, 219, 230, 238, 253, 453, 455
Wharton, C.S. Brig. Gen. John 395–400; *see also* Dover, TN, Battle of (1863)
Wheeler, C.S. Maj. Gen. Joseph 395–400; *see also see also* Dover, TN, Battle of (1863)
Wheeler, U.S. Fireman Robert 404; *see also* *Hastings* (U.S. tinclad)
White, David 480; *see also* *Tyler* (U.S. timberclad)
White, Horace ("W") (Chicago *Daily Tribune* correspondent) 320, 330–332, 335–336, 338
White, C.S. Maj. Robert M. 404; *see also* Streight Raid (1863); Texas (C.S.) regiments, cavalry, 6th
White Cloud (steamer) 311, 326, 329, 336
White River, AK 18–19, 327; Federal relief expedition (June–July 1862) 317–323, **324**–343; Federal White and Little Red River expedition (August 1863) 428–430; Little Rock, AK/White River campaign (August 1863) 425–428
White River Cut-off, AK 19–20; *see also* Arkansas Post, AK, Battle of (1863)
White River Station, AK, Battle of (June 1864) 467, 469–470

Wiggins Ferry Company 93; *see also New Era* (U.S. timberclad)

Wilcox, C.S. Capt. M.D. 135, 138–140; *see also* Eddyville, KY, Rain on (October 1861)

Wild Cat (steamer) 397–398; *see also* Dover, TN, Battle of (1863)

Wiley, U.S. Pvt. William 371; *see also* Illinois (U.S.) regiments, infantry, 77th

Wilkie, Franc B. ("Galway") (New York Times correspondent) 172, 177–178, 181, 184–185, 194, 198–202, 207, 209, 215–216, 218–219, 221, 243–244, 246–249, 251, 254–255, 259–261, 272–274, 277–279, 368, 377, 385, 407

William H. Brown (steamer) *see W.H. Brown* (steamer also known as *Brown* or *W.H.B.*)

William M. Harrison (steamer) 100

Williams, C.S. Capt. A.A. 328, 331, 333; *see also* St. Charles, AK, Battle of (1862)

Williams, U.S. Brig. Gen. Thomas 348–349, 359; *see also* Farragut, U.S. RAdm. David G.

Wills, Illinois Private Charles Wright 64, 111, 116, 120

Wilson, U.S. Lt. Byron 105

Wilson, U.S. Acting Assistant Surgeon William H. 333; *see also Mound City* (U.S. ironclad)

Wilson's Creek, MO, Battle of (1861) 83

Winona (U.S. gunboat) 348

Winslow, U.S. Cmdr. John 170, 188, 328, 336–339; *see also Cincinnati* (U.S. ironclad)

Winters, U.S. Pvt. William 371; *see also* Indiana (U.S.) regiments, infantry, 76th

Wisconsin No. 2 (steamer) 274

Wisconsin (U.S.) regiments: cavalry: 4th 463; infantry: 4th 352–353; 8th 259

Wisdom, Judge Thomas W. 255

Wise, U.S. Seaman Fred 325, 330, 332; *see also Lexington* (U.S. timberclad)

Wise, U.S. Quartermaster George D. 130

W.L. Ewing (steamer) 448

Wolf Island, KY 17; *see also* Columbus, KY

Woodford (U.S. hospital boat) 446

Woods, C.S. Col. Peter C. 452; *see also* Blair's Landing, Battle of (1864)

Woodward, C.S. Col. Thomas 400–401; *see also* Kentucky (C.S.) regiments, cavalry, 2nd; Palmyra, TN, convoy battle at and destruction of (1863)

Worthington, U.S. Col. Thomas 283–284; *see also* Ohio (U.S.) regiments, infantry, 46th

Wright, U.S. Brig. Gen. Horatio G. 396

Wright, C.S. Lt. Col. Marcus J. 154, 158; *see also* Belmont, MO, Battle of (November 1861)

Wright, U.S. Acting Master Thomas 437; *see also Osage* (U.S. monitor)

W.V. Gillum (steamer) 44

Yankee (tugboat) 69; *see also Jackson* (C.S. gunboat)

Yates, Illinois Gov. Richard 32, 35, 187

Yazoo River, MS 18, 20, 368–369, 373–374, 382; descent of C.S. armorclad *Arkansas* (July 1862) 338, 343–**346**, 347–353, **354**–358; site of Chickasaw Bayou–Vicksburg campaign (December 1862) 367–388; site of Federal diversion (April–May 1863) 408–410

"Zouave" (*New York Times* correspondent) 43

www.ingramcontent.com/pod-product-compliance
Lightning Source LLC
Chambersburg PA
CBHW080934020526
44116CB00034B/2594